FOR REFERENCE

Do Not Take From This Room

Nineteenth-Century Literature Criticism

Topics Volume

Guide to Gale Literary Criticism Series

For criticism on	Consult these Gale series
Authors now living or who died after December 31, 1959	***CONTEMPORARY LITERARY CRITICISM (CLC)***
Authors who died between 1900 and 1959	***TWENTIETH-CENTURY LITERARY CRITICISM (TCLC)***
Authors who died between 1800 and 1899	***NINETEENTH-CENTURY LITERATURE CRITICISM (NCLC)***
Authors who died between 1400 and 1799	***LITERATURE CRITICISM FROM 1400 TO 1800 (LC)*** ***SHAKESPEAREAN CRITICISM (SC)***
Authors who died before 1400	***CLASSICAL AND MEDIEVAL LITERATURE CRITICISM (CMLC)***
Black writers of the past two hundred years	***BLACK LITERATURE CRITICISM (BLC)***
Authors of books for children and young adults	***CHILDREN'S LITERATURE REVIEW (CLR)***
Dramatists	***DRAMA CRITICISM (DC)***
Hispanic writers of the late nineteenth and twentieth centuries	***HISPANIC LITERATURE CRITICISM (HLC)***
Native North American writers and orators of the eighteenth, nineteenth, and twentieth centuries	***NATIVE NORTH AMERICAN LITERATURE (NNAL)***
Poets	***POETRY CRITICISM (PC)***
Short story writers	***SHORT STORY CRITICISM (SSC)***
Major authors from the Renaissance to the present	***WORLD LITERATURE CRITICISM, 1500 TO THE PRESENT (WLC)***

ISSN 0732-1864

Volume 68

Nineteenth-Century Literature Criticism

Topics Volume

Excerpts from Criticism of Various Topics in Nineteenth-Century Literature, including Literary and Critical Movements, Prominent Themes and Genres, Anniversary Celebrations, and Surveys of National Literatures

Daniel G. Marowski
Denise Evans
Editors

DETROIT • LONDON

Riverside Community College
Library
4800 Magnolia Avenue
Riverside, California 92506

REFERENCE
PN761 .N5
Nineteenth-century
literature criticism

STAFF

Denise Evans, Daniel G. Marowski, *Editors*
Amy K. Crook, Jelena Krstovic, Marie Lazzari, James E. Person, Jr., *Contributing Editors*
Ira Mark Milne, *Assistant Editor*
Aarti D. Stephens, *Managing Editor*

Susan M. Trosky, *Permissions Manager*
Kimberly F. Smilay, *Permissions Specialist*
Steve Cusack, Kelly A. Quin, *Permissions Assistants*

Victoria B. Cariappa, *Research Manager*
Tamara C. Nott, Tracie A. Richardson, Cheryl L. Warnock, *Research Associates*
Phyllis Blackman, Jeffrey Daniels, *Research Assistants*

Mary Beth Trimper, *Production Director*
Deborah L. Milliken, *Production Assistant*

Christine O'Bryan, *Desktop Publisher*
Randy Bassett, *Image Database Supervisor*
Robert Duncan, Michael Logusz, *Imaging Specialists*
Pamela A. Reed, *Imaging Coordinator*

Since this page cannot legibly accommodate all copyright notices, the acknowledgments constitute an extension of the copyright notice.

While every effort has been made to secure permission to reprint material and to ensure the reliability of the information presented in this publication, Gale Research neither guarantees the accuracy of the data contained herein nor assumes any responsibility for errors, omissions or discrepancies. Gale accepts no payment for listing; and inclusion in the publication of any organization, agency, institution, publication, service, or individual does not imply endorsement of the editors or publisher. Errors brought to the attention of the publisher and verified to the satisfaction of the publisher will be corrected in future editions.

This publication is a creative work fully protected by all applicable copyright laws, as well as by misappropriation, trade secret, unfair competition, and other applicable laws. The authors and editors of this work have added value to the underlying factual material herein through one or more of the following: unique and original selection, coordination, expression, arrangement, and classification of the information.

All rights to this publication will be vigorously defended.

Copyright © 1998
Gale Research
835 Penobscot Building
Detroit, MI 48226-4094

All rights reserved including the right of reproduction in whole or in part in any form.

This book is printed on acid-free paper that meets the minimum requirements of American National Standard for Information Sciences—Permanence Paper for Printed Library Materials, ANSI Z39.48-1984.

Library of Congress Catalog Card Number 84-643008
ISBN 0-7876-1908-6
ISSN 0732-1864
Printed in the United States of America

10 9 8 7 6 5 4 3 2 1

Contents

Preface

Since its inception in 1981, *Nineteenth-Century Literature Criticism* has been a valuable resource for students and librarians seeking critical commentary on writers of this transitional period in world history. Designated an "Outstanding Reference Source" by the American Library Association with the publication of its first volume, *NCLC* has since been purchased by over 6,000 school, public, and university libraries. The series has covered more than 300 authors representing 29 nationalities and over 17,000 titles. No other reference source has surveyed the critical reaction to nineteenth-century authors and literature as thoroughly as *NCLC.*

Scope of the Series

NCLC is designed to introduce students and advanced readers to the authors of the nineteenth century, and to the most significant interpretations of these authors' works. The great poets, novelists, short story writers, playwrights, and philosophers of this period are frequently studied in high school and college literature courses. By organizing and reprinting commentary written on these authors, *NCLC* helps students develop valuable insight into literary history, promotes a better understanding of the texts, and sparks ideas for papers and assignments. Each entry in *NCLC* presents a comprehensive survey of an author's career or an individual work of literature and provides the user with a multiplicity of interpretations and assessments. Such variety allows students to pursue their own interests; furthermore, it fosters an awareness that literature is dynamic and responsive to many different opinions.

Every fourth volume of *NCLC* is devoted to literary topics that cannot be covered under the author approach used in the rest of the series. Such topics include literary movements, prominent themes in nineteenth-century literature, literary reaction to political and historical events, significant eras in literary history, prominent literary anniversaries, and the literatures of cultures that are often overlooked by English-speaking readers.

NCLC continues the survey of criticism of world literature begun by Gale's *Contemporary Literary Criticism (CLC)* and *Twentieth-Century Literary Criticism (TCLC),* both of which excerpt and reprint commentary on authors of the twentieth century. For additional information about *TCLC, CLC,* and Gale's other criticism series, users should consult the Guide to Gale Literary Criticism Series preceding the title page in this volume.

Coverage

Each volume of *NCLC* is carefully compiled to present:

- criticism of authors, or literary topics, representing a variety of genres and nationalities
- both major and lesser-known writers and literary works of the period
- 4-8 authors or 4-6 topics per volume
- individual entries that survey critical response to an author's work or a topic in literary history, including early criticism to reflect initial reactions, later criticism to represent any rise or decline in reputation, and current retrospective analyses.

Organization

An author entry consists of the following elements: author heading, biographical and critical introduction, list of principal works, excerpts of criticism (each preceded by a bibliographic citation and an annotation), and a bibliography of further reading.

- The **Author Heading** consists of the name under which the author most commonly wrote, followed by birth and death dates. If an author wrote consistently under a pseudonym, the pseudonym will be listed in the author heading and the real name given in parentheses on the first line of the biographical and critical introduction. Also located at the beginning of the introduction to the author entry are any name variations under which an author wrote, including transliterated forms for an author whose language uses a nonroman alphabet.

- The **Biographical and Critical Introduction** outlines the author's life and career, as well as the critical issues surrounding his or her work. References are provided to past volumes of *NCLC* in which further information about the author may be found.

- Most *NCLC* entries include a **Portrait** of the author. Many entries also contain reproductions of materials pertinent to an author's career, including manuscript pages, title pages, dust jackets, letters, and drawings, as well as photographs of important people, places, and events in an author's life.

- The list of **Principal Works** is chronological by date of first publication and identifies the genre of each work. In the case of foreign authors with both foreign-language publications and English translations, the English-language version is given in brackets. Unless otherwise indicated, dramas are dated by first performance, not first publication.

- **Criticism** in each author entry is arranged chronologically to provide a perspective on changes in critical evaluation over the years. All titles of works by the author featured in the entry are printed in boldface type to enable the user to easily locate discussion of particular works. Also for purposes of easier identification, the critic's name and the publication date of the essay are given at the beginning of each piece of criticism. Unsigned criticism is preceded by the title of the journal in which it appeared. Publication information (such as publisher names and book prices) and some parenthetical numerical references (such as page and line references to specific editions of works) have been deleted at the editors' discretion to provide smoother reading of the text. Footnotes that appear with previously published pieces of criticism are reprinted at the end of each essay or excerpt. In the case of excerpted criticism, only those footnotes that pertain to the excerpted text are included.

- A complete **Bibliographic Citation** provides original publication information for each piece of criticism.

- Critical excerpts are prefaced by **Annotations** providing the reader with a summary of the critical intent of the piece. Also included, when appropriate, is information about the critic's reputation, individual approach to literary criticism, and particular expertise in an author's works, as well as information about the relative importance of the critical excerpt. In some cases, the annotations cross-reference excerpts by critics who discuss each other's commentary.

- An annotated list of **Further Reading** appearing at the end of each entry suggests secondary sources on the author. In some cases it includes essays for which the editors could not obtain reprint rights.

Cumulative Indexes

- Each volume of *NCLC* contains a cumulative **Author Index** listing all authors who have appeared in Gale's Literary Criticism Series, along with cross-references to such biographical series as *Contemporary Authors* and *Dictionary of Literary Biography.* Useful for locating authors within the various series, this index is particularly valuable for those authors who are identified with a certain period but who, because of their death dates, are placed in another, or for those authors whose careers span two periods. For example, Fyodor Dostoevsky is found in *NCLC,* yet Leo Tolstoy, another major nineteenth-century Russian novelist, is found in *TCLC* because he died after 1899.

- Each *NCLC* volume includes a cumulative **Nationality Index** which lists all authors who have appeared in *NCLC*, arranged alphabetically under their respective nationalities.

- Each new volume in Gale's Literary Criticism Series includes a cumulative **Topic Index**, which lists all literary topics treated in *NCLC, TCLC, LC 1400-1800*, and the *CLC* Yearbook.

- Each new volume of *NCLC*, with the exception of the Topics volumes, contains a **Title Index** listing the titles of all literary works discussed in the volume. In response to numerous suggestions from librarians, Gale has also produced a **Special Paperbound Edition** of the *NCLC* title index. This annual cumulation lists all titles discussed in the series since its inception. Additional copies of the index are available on request. Librarians and patrons have welcomed this separate index: it saves shelf space, is easy to use, and is recyclable upon receipt of the following year's cumulation. Titles discussed in the Topics volume entries are not included in the *NCLC* cumulative index.

Citing *Nineteenth-Century Literature Criticism*

When writing papers, students who quote directly from any volume in Gale's Literary Criticism Series may use the following general forms to footnote reprinted criticism. The first example pertains to material drawn from periodicals, the second to material reprinted from books:

[1]T.S. Eliot, "John Donne," *The Nation and Athenaeum*, 33 (9 June 1923), 321-32; excerpted and reprinted in *Literature Criticism from 1400-1800,* Vol. 10, ed. James E. Person, Jr. (Detroit: Gale Research, 1989), pp. 28-9.

[2]Clara G. Stillman, *Samuel Butler: A Mid-Victorian Modern* (Viking Press, 1932); excerpted and reprinted in *Twentieth-Century Literary Criticism,* Vol. 33, ed. Paula Kepos (Detroit: Gale Research, 1989), pp. 43-5.

Suggestions Are Welcome

In response to suggestions, several features have been added to *NCLC* since the series began, including annotations to excerpted criticism, a cumulative index to authors in all Gale literary criticism series, entries devoted to criticism on a single work by a major author, more illustrations, and a title index listing all literary works discussed in the series.

Readers who wish to suggest authors, single works, or topics to appear in future volumes, or who have other suggestions, are cordially invited to write: The Editors, *Nineteenth-Century Literature Criticism,* 835 Penobscot Bldg., 645 Griswold St., Detroit, MI 48226-4094; call toll-free at 1-800-347-GALE; or fax to 1-313-961-6599.

Acknowledgments

The editors wish to thank the copyright holders of the excerpted criticism included in this volume and the permissions managers of many book and magazine publishing companies for assisting us in securing reproduction rights. We are also grateful to the staffs of the Detroit Public Library, the Library of Congress, the University of Detroit Mercy Library, Wayne State University Purdy/Kresge Library Complex, and the University of Michigan Libraries for making their resources available to us. Following is a list of the copyright holders who have granted us permission to reproduce material in this volume of CLC. Every effort has been made to trace copyright, but if omissions have been made, please let us know.

COPYRIGHTED EXCERPTS IN *NCLC,* VOLUME 68, WERE REPRODUCED FROM THE FOLLOWING PERIODICALS:

Bulletin of the New York Public Library, v. 67, May, 1963. Reproduced by permission.–***Comparative Literature***, v. 94, December, 1979 for "Keats and the Historical Method in Literary Criticism" by Jerome McGann. Reproduced by permission of the author.–***Keats-Shelley Journal***, v. XXIX, 1980. Reproduced by permission.–***Nineteenth-Century Fiction***, v. 24, September, 1969. Reprinted by permission.–***PMLA***, v. LXXIX, September, 1964. Copyright © 1964 by the Modern Language Association of America. Reproduced by permission of the Modern Language Association of America.–***Studies in English Literature: 1500-1900***, v. 36, No. 4, Autumn, 1996. Copyright © 1996 William Marsh Rice University. Reproduced by permission of *SEL Studies in English Literature 1500-1900.* –***Studies in Romanticism***, v. 25, Summer, 1986. Copyright © 1986 by the Trustees of Boston University. Reproduced by permission.

COPYRIGHTED EXCERPTS IN *NCLC,* VOLUME 68, WERE REPRODUCED FROM THE FOLLOWING BOOKS:

Bronfen, Elizabeth. From ***Over Her Dead Body: Death, Femininity and the Aesthetic***. Manchester University Press, 1992. Copyright © 1992 Elizabeth Bronfen. Reproduced by permission.–Bush, Douglas. From ***Mythology and the Romantic Tradition in English Poetry***. Cambridge, Mass.: Harvard University Press, 1969. Copyright 1937, © 1969 by the President and Fellows of Harvard College. Renewed 1965 by Douglas Bush. All rights reserved. Excerpted by permission of the publishers.–Dowling, Linda. From ***Hellenism and Homosexuality in Victorian Oxford***. Cornell University Press, 1994. Copyright © 1994 by Cornell University. Used by permission of the publisher, Cornell University Press. All additional uses of this material–including, but not limited to, photocopying and reprinting–are prohibited without the prior written approval of Cornell University Press.–Grafton, Anthony. From ***Perceptions of the Ancient Greek***. Edited by K. J. Dover. Blackwell Publishers, 1992. Copyright © 1992 Basil Blackwell, Ltd. All rights reserved. Reproduced by permission of Blackwell Publishers.–Hayden, John O. From ***The Romantic Reviewers: 1802-1824***. University of Chicago Press, 1969. Routledge & Kegan Paul, 1969. Copyright © 1969 by University of Chicago Press. Reproduced by permission of The University of Chicago Press. In the United Kingdom by Routledge, and the author.–Jenkyns, Richard. From ***The Victorians and Ancient Greece***. Cambridge, Mass.: Harvard University Press, 1980. Blackwell Publishers, 1980. Copyright © 1980 by the President and Fellows of Harvard College. All rights reserved. Reproduced by permission of the Harvard University Press. In the United Kingdom by Blackwell Publishers.–Kaplan, Fred. From ***Sacred Tears: Sentimentality in Victorian Literature***. Princeton University Press, 1987. Copyright © 1987 by Princeton University Press. All rights reserved. Reprinted by permission of Georges Borchardt, Inc. for the author.–Levin, Harry. From ***The Broken Column: A Study in Romantic Hellenism***. Cambridge, Mass.: Harvard University Press, 1931. Copyright, 1931 by the President and Fellows of Harvard College. Renewed 1959 by Harry Levin. All rights reserved. Excerpted by permission of the publishers.–MacKay, Carol Hanbery. From ***Sex and Death in Victorian Literature***. Edited by Regina Barreca. The Macmillan Press, Ltd., 1990. Indiana University Press, 1990. Copyright © 1990 by Regina Barreca. All rights reserved. Reproduced by permission of Macmillan Press, Ltd. In North America by Indiana University Press.–Ogilvie, R. M. From ***Latin and Greek: A History of the Influence of the Classics on English Life from 1600 to 1918.*** Routledge and Kegan Paul, 1964. Copyright © 1964 by R. M. Ogilvie. Reproduced by permission of the publisher.–Reed, John R. From ***Victorian Conventions***. Ohio University Press, 1975. Copyright © 1975 by John R. Reed. All rights reserved. Reproduced by permission.–Sanders, Andrew. From ***Charles Dickens Resurrectionist***. St. Martin's Press, 1982, Macmillan Administration (Basingstoke) Ltd., 1982. Copyright © 1982 by St. Martin's Press and Macmillan Administration (Basingstoke) Ltd. All Rights reserved. Reproduced by permission of St. Martin's Press, Inc. In the United Kingdom by permission of Macmillan, London and Basingstoke.–Shelley, Percy Bysshe. From "Letters from Naples" in ***English Romantic Hellenism 1700-1824*** by Timothy Webb. Manchester University Press, 1982, Barnes and Noble Books, 1982. © Manchester University Press 1982. All rights reserved. Reproduced by permission in North America by Barnes & Noble Books. In the United Kingdom by Timothy Webb.–Spencer, Terence. From ***Fair Greece, Sad Relic: Literary Philhellenism from Shakespeare to Byron***. Weidenfeld & Nicholson, 1954. Reproduced by permission.–Turner, Frank M. From ***The Greek Heritage in Victorian Britain***. Yale University Press, 1981. Copyright © 1981 by Yale University Press. All rights reserved. Reproduced by permission.–Turner, Frank M. From "Why the Greeks and Not the Romans in Victorian Britain," in ***Rediscovering Hellenism***. Edited by G. W. Clarke. Cambridge University Press, 1989. Copyright © 1989 Cambridge University Press. Reproduced by permission of the publisher and the author.–Wardle, Ralph M. From ***Hazlitt***. University of Nebraska Press, 1971. Copyright © The University of Nebraska Press 1971. All rights reserved. Reproduced by permission.–Webb, Timothy. From the introduction to ***English Romantic Hellenism***. Manchester University Press, 1982, Rowman and Littlefield, 1982. © Manchester University Press 1982. All rights Reserved. Reproduced by permission of Barnes & Noble Books. In the United Kingdom by the author.

PHOTOGRAPHS AND ILLUSTRATIONS APPEARING IN *NCLC,* VOLUME 68, WERE RECEIVED FROM THE FOLLOWING SOURCES:

Ajax defending the Greek ships against the Trojans, illustration. Archive Photos, Inc. Reproduced by permission.–Arnold, Matthew, engraving. AP/Wide World Photos. Reproduced by permission.–Bronte, Emily (profile), painting by Bramwell Bronte.–Byron, George Gordon (6th Baron Byron, 1788-1824), painting by Thomas Phillips, photograph. Corbis-Bettmann. Reproduced by permission.–Colman, Ronald, in the film *A Tale of Two Cities*, 1935, photograph. Springer/Corbis-Bettmann. Reproduced by permission.–Coleridge, Samuel Taylor, drawing by J. Kayser.–Dickens, Charles, photograph. Viking Press.–Elgin, James B. (turned right, seated, sash across right shoulder), painting. The Library of Congress.–Funeral of Hector , illustration. Archive Photos, Inc. Reproduced by permission.–Gladstone, William E. (seated, right leg crossed over left), photograph. The Library of Congress.–Gravestone of John Keats, photograph. AP/Wide World Photos. Reproduced by permission.–Howarth Parsonage, home of the Bronte family, photograph.–Hunt, Leigh, painting. International Portrait Gallery.–Keats, John (seated, book open, left hand under chin), painting. The Library of Congress.–Pater, Walter Horatio, (wearing a tie with a thick Windsor knot, and wing-tipped collar), drawing. The Library of Congress.–Peacock, Thomas Love (holding book), photograph. The Library of Congress.–Shelley, Percy B. (facing front, shirt open at neck), engraving. The Library of Congress.–The Acropolis, Athens, photograph by Brian Escamilla. Reproduced by permission.–Wordsworth, William, photograph.

The Cockney School

INTRODUCTION

Consisting of a group of literary figures who generally shared political and literary views, the Cockney School of poetry included such writers as Leigh Hunt (1784-1859), William Hazlitt (1778-1830), John Keats (1795-1821), and Percy Bysshe Shelley (1792-1822). Condemned and despised by conservative Tory critics who claimed that the low birth of the Cockneys engendered their liberal politics and colloquial verse, the Cockney School centered around the Whig poet and editor Hunt, who with his brother John established in 1808 the *Examiner*, a weekly liberal newspaper whose attacks on the Prince Regent earned them each jail sentences. During his imprisonment Leigh Hunt was visited by several important figures, including Lord Byron (1788-1824), Thomas Moore (1779-1852), Jeremy Bentham (1748-1832), and Charles Lamb (1775-1834), and upon his release Hunt became more eagerly engaged in poetry. His *The Story of Rimini* (1816)—an adaptation of the Paolo and Francesca story from Dante's *Divine Comedy*—was well received, and the preface, which calls for "a freer spirit of versification," inspired a number of other writers, most notably Shelley and Keats.

Although Hunt's political views attracted like-minded liberals, and his thoughts on a freer and more colloquial style strongly influenced Hazlitt's familiar essays and Keats' early poetry, critics who endorsed the traditional Augustan couplet and political conservativism resisted what they took to be a denigration of poetry. John Gibson Lockhart, editor and contributor to the Tory periodical *Blackwood's Edinburgh Magazine*, labeled the group "The Cockney School" in 1817 and, in a series of articles published over the next eight years, assailed Keats and Hunt in particular for their political beliefs and, indirectly, for their inferior education and upbringing. Along with other critics such as John Wilson Croker (known as the "slashing critic") of the *Quarterly Review,* Lockhart—writing under the pseudonym "Z"—criticized the unaccomplished work of the Cockney poets, which they claimed revealed the "low birth and low habits" of its authors and whose couplets they claimed only rhymed in a Cockney accent.

The literary careers of the Cockney writers, especially Hazlitt and Keats, were dominated at one point or another by public feuds with their Tory critics. Hazlitt was successful in a libel lawsuit against *Blackwood's*, and Keats' early reputation was dominated by two hostile, unsigned reviews of his allegorical poem *Endymion: A Poetic Romance* (1818), one by Lockhart and the other by Croker. Lockhart attacked not only Keats' poem, which he abhorred on artistic and moral grounds, but also the poet's lack of taste, education, and upbringing. Furthermore, although Croker was neither as vitriolic nor as personally cutting as Lockhart, his essay was singled out as damaging and unjust by Keats' supporters. While Keats was apparently disturbed only temporarily by these attacks, the story circulated after his death that his demise had been caused, or at least hastened, by Lockhart's and especially Croker's reviews. A chief perpetrator of this notion was Percy Bysshe Shelley, whose famous work *Adonais: An Elegy on the Death of John Keats* (1821) was published with a bitter preface implicating Croker as the murderer of Keats.

The political views and radical poetics expressed by Hunt's literary circle were thus largely defined by their most adamant detractors, but the Cockney School nonetheless was highly influential beyond its liberal sympathizers. Hunt pioneered the evolution of the contemporary journal; Hazlitt's familiar essay, characterized by conversational diction and personal opinion, recast the character of the personal essay; and Keats and Shelley, whose impassioned tone and sensual imagery appeared shockingly effusive to critics schooled in the poetics of the eighteenth century, helped to liberate English poetry from the constraints of neoclassicism. Along with the Lake poets, the Cockney School marks a major Romantic shift in British letters and has indelibly changed the course of modern literature.

REPRESENTATIVE WORKS

William Hazlitt
Characters of Shakespeare's Plays (criticism) 1817
The Round Table: A Collection of Essays on Literature, Men, and Manners. 2 vols. [with Leigh Hunt] (essays) 1817
Table-Talk. 2 vols. (essays) 1821-22

Leigh Hunt
The Feast of the Poets, with Notes, and Other Pieces in Verse (poetry) 1814
The Story of Rimini (poetry) 1816
Foliage: or, Poems Original and Translated (poetry) 1818

John Keats
Poems (poetry) 1817
Endymion: A Poetic Romance (poetry) 1818

Percy Bysshe Shelley
Queen Mab (poetry) 1813
The Cenci [first publication] (verse drama) 1819
Prometheus Unbound, with Other Poems (verse drama and poetry) 1820
Adonais: An Elegy on the Death of John Keats (poetry) 1821

OVERVIEW

T. Hall Caine (essay date 1883)

SOURCE: "Leigh Hunt," in *Cobwebs of Criticism: A Review of the First Reviewers of the 'Lake,' 'Satanic,' and 'Cockney' Schools,* Elliot Stock, 1883, pp. 123-57.

[*In the excerpt that follows, Caine recounts how the Cockney School writers came to be grouped together, chronicling the contemporary critical appraisal of the writers and their works in such periodicals as the* Examiner *and* Blackwood's Magazine.]

Leigh Hunt, English poet and essayist, 1784-1859

It will be remembered that Southey attempted, late in life, to repudiate the allegation that he had ever been concerned with Wordsworth in the formation of a new school of poetry; and that Coleridge said the only thing he claimed to possess in common with either of these poets was good sense, confirmed by long study of the best models of Greece, Italy, and England. It is nevertheless not too much to say that all three were influenced by exactly the same forces of rational conviction, and that, notwithstanding their personal opposition to such classification, they may properly be named together as leaders of a single poetic school. Urged doubtless by kindred motives to those which operated in the cases of Southey and Coleridge in their attitude towards Wordsworth, Keats and Shelley endeavoured to repudiate the charge of having been concerned with Leigh Hunt in the formation of a school of poetry. It will be easy to show that in the latter case, unlike the former one, there was ample justification for such repudiation, and that, therefore, it is to some extent injudicious and injurious to class together these three poets under the name by which they were known to the great body of their contemporaries. Accident, not special poetic affinity, brought them together; and they never had much more in common than is usually the case between any three poets who are the creatures of any single age. Certainly their several theories of poetry were dissimilar, if not in absolute antagonism; and there cannot be shown to exist in "Rimini," "Endymion," and "The Revolt of Islam" any such kinship of purpose and contrast of means as gave unity of aim to the associated pieces in the first "Lyrical Ballads." Indeed, so much were these men at variance as to the true mission of poetry, that Keats went the rather audacious length of advising Shelley to put aside a little of his exuberant magnanimity, and trouble himself more to load every rift of his work with ore; and Shelley's last warm tribute to the genius of his friend did not go forth without a side-reference to the author's known repugnance to the principles of art on which Keats's best work had been constructed. With so many and such emphatic points of difference, it may be asked with proper surprise how, at any time, the three poets came to be classed together; and the answer is one that must be sought for where poetry plays no part. The story that requires to be told is short, and is full of interest and suggestion.

In 1816, Leigh Hunt was editor of the *Examiner,* then a sixteen-page Sunday paper, devoted chiefly to politics and plays. Towards the close of that year the journal developed a literary character, and began to review poetry with peculiar animation. One of the last issues of 1816 contained an article entitled "Three Young Poets," treating of inedited poetry by three unknown writers—Cornelius Webb, Percy B. Shelley, and John

Keats. Internal evidence pointed to the editor as author; and certainly the little paper was characterized by the confidential personal tone out of which Leigh Hunt's enemies made so much. Subsequent issues of the *Examiner* contained sonnets and lyrical pieces by all three authors dealt with in the article in question; and so the inference remained an obvious one that a little coterie had been formed, of which the office in London of the Sunday journal formed the rallying-point.

A few months later (April, 1817), *Blackwood's Magazine* was founded in Edinburgh. The new periodical venture was established primarily to break the supremacy of the *Edinburgh Review* in politics; but this was not mooted in the prospectus that preceded it. One of the new features of the magazine was announced to be 'Notices of the most celebrated publications, and the contents of minor journals.'

Blackwood's first issues contained little or no political matter; but it was not the less easy on that account to see that party bias lay at the root of all its criticisms of men and books. Sweltering as it was under the full rigour of united northern Toryism and northern Puritanism, the *Examiner* speedily fell in its way; and the number of *Blackwood* (October, 1817) which contained the justly celebrated *jeu d'esprit* entitled "Chaldee Manuscript" (an allegorical account, in Scriptural language, of the quarrels of the founders of the magazine), contained also the first of a series of audacious attacks on the little band of London poets, of whom Leigh Hunt was at the time the only notable public figure. No two articles could be more dissimilar in spirit than the two in question. The one has been said to be worthy of a permanent place in literature by reason of its felicitous humour; the other has, not unjustly, been stigmatized as one of the most cowardly and malignant assaults that ever disgraced the annals of literature.

The first article of the series began playfully enough:

> While the whole critical world is occupied with balancing the merits, whether in theory or in execution, of what is commonly called the Lake School, it is strange that no one seems to think it necessary to say a single word about another new school of poetry which has of late sprung up amongst us. The school has not, I believe, received any name; but if I may be permitted to have the honour of christening it, it may henceforth be referred to by the designation of the Cockney School. Its chief doctor and professor is Mr. Leigh Hunt, a man certainly of some talent, of extraordinary pretensions both in wit, poetry, and politics, and withal of exquisitely bad taste, and extremely vulgar modes of thinking, and manners in all respects.

One of the characteristics of these childish persons was, according to *Blackwood,* the restless interest which they summoned the public to take in everything belonging to their own triviality. The critic says:

> If Mrs. Robinson's dog had a bad night's repose, it was duly announced to the world; Mr. Merry's accident in paring his nails solicited a similar sympathy; the falling off of Mrs. R.'s patch at the last ball, or the stains on Mr. M.'s full-dress coat, from the dropping of a chandelier, came before the earth with praiseworthy promptitude.

Keats's volume of poems had appeared, containing an address to Leigh Hunt, as well as the well-known sonnet, beginning,

> Great spirits now on earth are sojourning,

and ending,

> Listen awhile, ye nations, and be dumb.

On the latter line, *Blackwood* says:

> The nations are to listen and be dumb! And why, good Johnny Keats? because Leigh Hunt is editor of the *Examiner,* and Haydon has painted the "Judgment of Solomon," and you and Cornelius Webb, and a few more city sparks are pleased to look upon yourselves as so many future Shakspeares and Miltons?

This may, so far, be harmless banter enough, calculated rather to make the victims laugh than cry, and capable of giving serious offence only to the thickest of skulls and the thinnest of skins. Not to blink the facts, it is quite true that the young poets did render themselves liable to much good-humoured chaff. There was a deal of effeminacy in their social relations; they presented each other with wreaths of bay, bouquets of roses, locks of hair, shells and sea-weed; and wrote laudatory verses each to each, anticipatory of the renown they were soon to win:

> We'll talk of . . . Keats
> The muse's son of promise, and what feats
> He yet may do.

Naturally, such behaviour called down the wrath of robust Scotch masculinity. *Blackwood* said:

> None of them are men of genius—none of them are men of solitary habits . . . Why then do they perpetually chatter about themselves? Why is it they seem to think the world has no right to hear one single word about any other persons than Hunt, the cockney Homer; Hazlitt, the cockney Aristotle; and Haydon, the cockney Raphael. These are all very eminent men in their own eyes. . . . Mr. Hazlitt cannot look round him at the Surrey, without resting his smart eye on the idiot admiring grin of several dozens of aspiring apprentices and critical clerks.

> Mr. Hunt cannot be *at home* at Hampstead, without having his Johnny Keatses and his Corny Webbs to cram sonnets into his waistcoat-pockets, and crown his majestic brows with
>
> 'The wreath that DANTE wore!!!'

Good-humoured raillery was not prominent among the accomplishments of the Edinburgh writer who made it his business to 'wither and blast' the young London poets; so playful chaff had speedily to make way for scalding invective:

> It is quite ridiculous to see how the vanity of these Cockneys makes them over-rate their own importance, even in the eyes of us that have always expressed such plain unvarnished contempt for them, and who do feel for them all a contempt too calm and profound to admit of any admixture of anything like anger or personal spleen. We should just as soon think of being wroth with vermin, independently of their coming into our apartment, as we should about having any feelings at all about any of these people, other than what are excited by seeing them in the shape of authors.

And again, four years later:

> There is but one word—of many melancholy and miserable meanings—and which we should not dare to apply to any of our brethren; but it may be applied, not only innocently but rightfully, to a Cockney; that one word is—*Fool!*

After saying that between thirty or forty years ago the *Della Crusca* school was in great force, pouring out monthly, weekly and daily the whole fulness of its sorrows in verse, revelling in moonlight, sighing with evening gales, lamenting over plucked roses, and bidding melodious farewells to the last butterfly of the season; after announcing the death and burial of the obscure morning paper in which this 'reign of sympathy' was first promulgated, and in which milliner's maids and city apprentices pined over the mutual melancholies of *Arley* and *Matilda, Blackwood* pathetically remarks that in this world folly is immortal, and that no sooner has one mass of tuneful nonsense been swept away than another succeeds to its glories and its fate.

> The *Della Crusca* School has visited us again. . . . Its verses now transpire at one time from the retreats of Cockney dalliance in the London suburbs; sometimes they visit us by fragments from Venice, and sometimes invade us by wainloads from Pisa. In point of subject and execution there is but slight difference; both schools are "smitten with nature and nature's love," run riot in the intrigues of anemones, daisies, and buttercups, and rave to the "rivulets *proud,* and the deep-*blushing* stars."

The critic goes on to show that the defunct school had at least the merit of moral innocence; they might talk nonsense without measure; be simple down to the very lowest degree of silliness, and 'babble of green fields' enough to make men sick of summer; but they kept their private irregularities to themselves, and sought for no reprobate popularity by avowing a pestilent hatred of everything generous, true and honourable, by desperate personal licentiousness, and a fiend-like desire to insult every moral tie and Christian principle. It was reserved for the foolish and profligate Cockney School to raise the banner of an insensate and black ambition 'whose only aim was to ruin society.' Of course, much capital was made from time to time of the known facts of Shelley's private life, and of the circumstance that the "Revolt of Islam" had first appeared as "Laon and Cythna"—a poem portraying the love of a brother and sister. In like manner much was made of the few questionable lines which found their way into the otherwise pure poetry of 'the amiable but infatuated bardling' known to the critics as 'Master Johnny Keats.' Now Keats's private life was on the whole so chaste, and his conception of the natural dignity of woman was so exalted, that the mere presence of the other sex in the drawing-room is stated to have either thrilled him with a spiritual rapture 'such as might be induced by a symphony of Mozart,' or tortured him with a sense (in which sensuality had no share) of the measure in which the real woman fell short of his ideal. It will be agreed that, however far this attitude of the sexes may have been removed from a rational and enduring relation, it was least of all liable to the charge of raising the banner of a profligate ambition 'whose only aim was to ruin society.' Yet the public were not merely informed that from some of Keats's verses addressed to various amiable females it appeared, 'notwithstanding all his gossamer work, that Johnny's affections' were not 'entirely confined to objects purely ethereal,' but that sheer *indecency* of theme and treatment had been throughout the foul moral blot which had caused good men and virtuous women to turn from "Endymion," "Lamia," "Eve of St. Agnes," and "Hyperion" with loathing or contempt. Leigh Hunt fared yet worse than Shelley and Keats. He was styled 'the meanest, the filthiest, the most vulgar of Cockney poetasters;' 'the most worthless and affected versifier of the time;' one who had 'dared to write in the solitude of a cell—whose walls ought to have heard only the sighs of contrition and repentance—a lewd tale of incest, adultery and murder, in which the violation of Nature herself was wept over, palliated, justified, and held up to imitation, and the violators themselves worshipped as holy martyrs.' One cannot forbear remarking upon the marvellous skill displayed by these critics in scenting out indecency of whatever kind in quarters whence people of healthier organs would scarcely hope to extract it; or upon the yet more extraordinary puritanism with which they reproduced at full length the poetry which they said ought never to have been written. Surely, impartial judges would think the reviewers increased the mischief in the measure in which they helped to disseminate it, notwithstanding that they attempted to fence it with withering denunciations. It must be said that some Scotch critics enjoy the questionable distinction of having ferreted out more filthiness than any other men whatever, and most of us will be content and happy to leave them in full possession of the inglorious boast which one of the keenest of the brotherhood advanced in his own favour, namely, that he had 'torn off the gaudy veil, and transparent drapery, and exhibited the painted cheeks and writhing limbs, and branded with a burning iron the false face and brazen brow of many a literary harlot.'

In a review (1822) of a romance by Hunt, *Blackwood,* once again in a playful vein, says:

> It is a gross impertinence in any Cockney to write about—love. Love, correctly speaking, is a tender affair between a lady and a gentleman; whereas King Leigh and his subjects imagine it to be merely a congress between a male and a female. There is the mistake, and it is a very gross one. . . . We have no doubt that Leigh supposes he can *make love;*—not he—any more than he can *write grammar*. No lady in this land could even comprehend what he wished to have, with his eternal sidling and sliding about, and perking up his mouth, and swaling with his coat-tails. The lady would suspect that he wished to throw her off her guard, and that he was watching an opportunity to pick her pocket. But Leigh forgets that ladies do not nowadays wear pockets. However, be that as it may, any Cockney who writes about love deserves to be kicked—that is the short and long of the matter, and there is no occasion to say a single word more on the subject.

The Edinburgh critics believed that of all the manias of the mad age in which it was their misfortune to live, the most incurable, as well as the most common, seemed to be no other than the 'Metromanie.' Of course the poetry of the London School was then a shut book to their northern intellects, just as the poetry of the Lake School had, ten years earlier, been a volume to whose cipher they had possessed no key. A good idea of the notion they entertained of the general characteristics of the poetry of such men as Hunt, Shelley, and Keats, may be gathered from the following parody, which appeared in *Blackwood* as late as 1821. Any apology that may be considered necessary for quoting such doggerel must be grounded in the belief which obtains credit in some quarters, that men as frequently put their deepest feeling into their nonsense as their philosophy:

LOVE SONG
BY A JUNIOR MEMBER OF THE COCKNEY SCHOOL.

Oh! lovely Polly Savage,
  Oh! charming Polly Savage,
Your eyes beat Day and Martin,
  Your neck is like red cabbage.

Oh! once I loved another girl,
  Her name it was Maria;
But, Polly dear, my love for you,
  Is forty-five times high*er*.

. . . . .

Oh, then our little son shall be
  As wanton as a spaniel,
Him that we mean to christen'd be
  Jacques Timothy Nathaniel.

And if we have a little girl,
  I'm sure you won't be sorry
To hear me call the little elf,
  Euphemiar Helen Laur*ar*.

This rare effusion appeared in a journal to which Christopher North and our friend 'Z' (is the conjunction necessary?) contributed! That such sorry stuff could be put forth by a reputable magazine as a legitimate parody of anything written by Shelley, Keats or even Hunt in his flightiest mood is truly inexplicable. The parody is not, however, without a certain interest as a satire on an article published in the *Examiner* some time previously in which the editor endeavoured to enforce the propriety of calling children by fine-sounding names.

Putting aside the petty envy, which alone might have incited the Edinburgh censors to reprobate the work of their London rivals, there can, as we have said, be little doubt that political animosity lay at the root of their antagonism. Indeed *Blackwood* says:

> The Cockney School of Politics is so intimately connected with the Cockney School of Poetry that it is almost impossible to describe the one without using many expressions equally applicable to the other. They are twin establishments created about the same time, supported by the same dupes and enlightened by the same quacks.

The *Examiner* was the extreme Liberal organ of its day; yet but little can be seen in its pages that would excite attention in these times from the vehemence of its utterance or the disloyalty of its purpose. The journal contains much that must have been in serious opposition to ministerial measures; and what it says is put forth in uncompromising language; but it is hard to find anything more extravagant than a passionate resistance of the policy which, in the person of a certain Rev. Mr. Wilson, preacher at St. John's Chapel, Bedford Row, recommended the revival of implicit obedience and non-resistance 'even towards a Nero.' So much for Leigh Hunt's political partisanship: that of his brother poets was even less emphatic. Shelley was at this time too much concerned with hatching in his unpractical brain entirely new universes, year after year, to care a rush what direction was taken by the political sympathies of the Prince Regent; and Keats (had *Black-*

wood but known it!) was at first inclining towards Toryism, and was certainly refusing to join Hunt in his abuse of the Liverpool-Castlereagh administration.

On Leigh Hunt, as the head and front of the political offending of the London School, the whole rigour of rancorous diatribe was brought to bear. A serious and honest impeachment of Hunt might easily be forged out of the material which the *Examiner* alone affords. It could be shown that he spared no man whose political convictions were opposed to his own, and that he was so far from confining his criticisms to the direct political utterances of those who differed from him that he availed himself, in his early years, of nearly every unlawful weapon of personal abuse to draw down upon his adversaries the full measure of ridicule and contempt. He charged Gifford with being a servile Court tool, whose championship in the *Quarterly* was paid for in advance out of the purse of the Government. Now, Gifford was a stern, hard-natured man, who gave way but rarely to the promptings of the more generous side of his nature; but he was a scholar, a patriot, and, so far as we can see, a gentleman: one who desired sincerely to make public the best that he knew and thought on politics and literature, and who blundered oftenest in argumentative deduction from his self-chosen code of laws. The worst of Hunt's accusations were not confined to the impeachment of Gifford. He called Southey 'a canting hypocrite,' 'an apostate,' and 'a shallow idiot.' He said, or permitted another to say, that Coleridge was the 'Wandering Jew of Letters,' and 'the dog in the manger of literature.' Nay, it was he who, at the very time when he sat with others at the feet of the 'Seer of Highgate,' and gathered there more scraps perhaps than he found in all the world beside, said anonymously (or was responsible for its being said), that 'no man would give Mr. Coleridge a penny for his thoughts,' and that the author of such nonsense as "Kubla Khan" had never in his life been caught in 'the fact of a single intelligible sentence.'

It would be a serious conviction indeed, and such as would shatter for ever all faith in Hunt's character, if it were proved that the many and signal benefits conferred upon him by Shelley had been taken without ungrudging and lifelong gratitude; but it could be shown that he rarely manifested the same marked and even obtrusive eagerness to rebut grave charges when made wrongfully against his friend, as was evinced when the libels were directed against himself. The silence of friends has been well said to serve too frequently as the confirmation of enemies; and the present writer has elsewhere confessed to some feeling of astonishment at the silence of Hunt when Keats was being assailed, and to some feeling of contempt for the explanation which came later, when in full view of the pain that silence inflicted and of the suspicion (on Keats's part) which it engendered.[1] Be this as it may, the editor of the *Examiner,* who had so often run *a-muck* with others, should surely have been prepared for many thrusts and lunges, and ought to have borne the pains of them, when they came, with equal fortitude and composure. In justice to him, however, let it be said that no man was ever more mendaciously attacked or more dogged by the feet of malice in disguise. We all think he was an able man, and, as Byron said, we are sure he was a poor one; and he bore the full brunt of hatred and assault which always falls to the share of him who, fenced by no other armour than united poverty and power, dares to hate all rank, and the contumely of all rank, and to ask no quarter from the votaries of toadyism and the slaves of trimming and time-serving. . . .

Notes

[1] What I said on this point in the 'Recollections of Rossetti' (p. 177) called forth more than one protest. The following extract from the letter of an eminent poet explains very fully the grounds of objection to my so-called impeachment of Hunt: 'The cruel injustice you have—of course unwittingly—done to the memory of Leigh Hunt is no matter of opinion; it is one of fact and evidence. So far from attempting no defence of Keats in 1820, he published, on the appearance of the "Lamia and other Poems" in that year, perhaps the most cordial, generous and enthusiastic tribute of affectionate and ardent praise that had ever been offered by a poet to a poet, in the shape of a review almost overflowing the limits of the magazine in which it appeared (the *Indicator*). A more "loud and earnest defence of Keats" could not be imagined or desired. And if Keats ever forgot this, or ever expressed doubts of Hunt's loyal and devoted regard, it simply shows that Keats was himself a disloyal and thankless son of genius, as utterly unworthy as he was utterly incapable of grateful, and unselfish, and manly friendship.' My reply to this, and to such objections as this, is as follows. First, I have nowhere mentioned 1820 as the year in which Hunt attempted no defence of Keats. I have pointed distinctly to 1818, the year of the publication of "Endymion" and of the *Quarterly* attack upon it. Next, the Advertisement to the "Lamia" volume bears date June, 1820, the volume was probably published in July, 1820, and at the middle of September, 1820, Keats left England for Italy. Third, the *Indicator* article appeared in the numbers for August 2nd and 9th (being written by Hunt while Keats was residing with him at Kentish Town), and the laudatory *Edinburgh* article had appeared before it. Fourth, Keats's letter touching Hunt's neglect was written before he left England. Fifth, Hunt gave a shabby notice of "Lamia" in his introduction to the last edition of "The Story of Rimini." I shall be rejoiced if the facts I state can be explained away.

BLACKWOOD'S MAGAZINE AND THE CONTEMPORARY CRITICAL RESPONSE

John Gibson Lockhart (review date 1817)

SOURCE: "On the Cockney School of Poetry," in *Blackwood's Edinburgh Magazine,* Vol. II, No. 7, October, 1817, pp. 38-41.

[*In the following review, Lockhart criticizes Leigh Hunt, founder of what Lockhart dubs the "Cockney School," for his obviously low class and improper poetry. He also compares Hunt unfavorably with the Lake poets, especially William Wordsworth, and laments his literary influence.*]

Our talk shall be (a theme we never tire on)
Of Chaucer, Spenser, Shakspeare, Milton,
Byron,
(Our England's Dante)—Wordsworth—Hunt,
and Keats,
The Muses' son of promise; and of what feats
He yet may do.

Cornelius Webb.

While the whole critical world is occupied with balancing the merits, whether in theory or in execution, of what is commonly called The Lake School, it is strange that no one seems to think it at all necessary to say a single word about another new school of poetry which has of late sprung up among us. This school has not, I believe, as yet received any name; but if I may be permitted to have the honour of christening it, it may henceforth be referred to by the designation of The Cockney School. Its chief Doctor and Professor is Mr Leigh Hunt, a man certainly of some talents, of extravagant pretensions both in wit, poetry, and politics, and withal of exquisitely bad taste, and extremely vulgar modes of thinking and manners in all respects. He is a man of little education. He knows absolutely nothing of Greek, almost nothing of Latin, and his knowledge of Italian literature is confined to a few of the most popular of Petrarch's sonnets, and an imperfect acquaintance with Ariosto, through the medium of Mr Hoole. As to the French poets, he dismisses them in the mass as a set of prim, precise, unnatural pretenders. The truth is, he is in a state of happy ignorance about them and all that they have done. He has never read Zaïre nor Phèdre. To those great German poets who have illuminated the last fifty years with a splendour to which this country has, for a long time, seen nothing comparable, Mr Hunt is an absolute stranger. Of Spanish books he has read Don Quixote (in the translation of Motteux), and some poems of Lope de Vega in the imitations of my Lord Holland. Of all the great critical writers, either of ancient or of modern times, he is utterly ignorant, excepting only Mr Jeffrey among ourselves.

With this stock of knowledge, Mr Hunt presumes to become the founder of a new school of poetry, and throws away entirely the chance which he might have had of gaining some true poetical fame, had he been less lofty in his pretensions. The story of Rimini is not wholly undeserving of praise. It possesses some tolerable passages, which are all quoted in the *Edinburgh Reviewer*'s account of the poem, and not one of which is quoted in the very illiberal attack upon it in the *Quarterly.* But such is the wretched task in which the greater part of the world is executed, that most certainly no man who reads it once will ever be able to prevail upon himself to read it again. One feels the same disgust at the idea of opening Rimini, that impresses itself on the mind of a man of fashion, when he is invited to enter, for a second time, the gilded drawing-room of a little mincing boarding-school mistress, who would fain have an *At Home* in her house. Every thing is pretence, affectation, finery, and gaudiness. The beaux are attorneys' apprentices, with chapeau bras and Limerick gloves—fiddlers, harp-teachers, and clerks of genius: the belles are faded fan-twinkling spinsters, prurient vulgar misses from school, and enormous citizens' wives. The company are entertained with lukewarm negus, and the sounds of a paltry piano-forte.

All the great poets of our country have been men of some rank in society, and there is no vulgarity in any of their writings; but Mr Hunt cannot utter a dedication, or even a note, without betraying the *Shibboleth* of low birth and low habits. He is the ideal of a Cockney Poet. He raves perpetually about "green fields," "jaunty streams," and "o'er-arching leafiness," exactly as a Cheapside shop-keeper does about the beauties of his box on the Camberwell road. Mr Hunt is altogether unacquainted with the face of nature in her magnificent scenes; he has never seen any mountain higher than Highgate-hill, nor reclined by any stream more pastoral than the Serpentine River. But he is determined to be a poet eminently rural, and he rings the changes—till one is sick of him, on the beauties of the different "high views" which he has taken of God and nature, in the course of some Sunday dinner parties, at which he has assisted in the neighbourhood of London. His books are indeed not known in the country; his fame as a poet (and I might almost say, as a politician too,) is entirely confined to the young attorneys and embryo-barristers about town. In the opinion of these competent judges, London is the world—and Hunt is a Homer.

Mr Hunt is not disqualified by his ignorance and vulgarity alone, for being the founder of a respectable sect in poetry. He labours under the burden of a sin more deadly than either of these. The two great elements of all dignified poetry, religious feeling, and patriotic feeling, have no place in his writings. His religion is a poor tame dilution of the blasphemies of the *Encyclopædie*—his patriotism a crude, vague, ineffectual, and sour Jacobinism. His works exhibit no reverence either for God or man; neither altar nor throne have any dignity in his eyes. He speaks well of nobody but two or three great dead poets, and in so speaking of them he does well; but, alas! Mr Hunt is no conjurer. . . . He pretends, indeed, to be an admirer of Spenser and Chaucer, but what he praises in them is never what is most deserving of praise—it is only that which he humbly conceives bears some resemblance to the more perfect productions of Mr Leigh Hunt; and we can always discover, in the midst of his most violent ravings about the Court of Elizabeth, and the days of Sir Philip Sidney, and the Fairy Queen—that the real objects of his admiration are the Coterie of Hamp-stead and the Editor of the Examiner. When he talks about chivalry and King Arthur, he is always thinking of himself, and *"a small party of friends, who meet once a-week at a Round Table, to discuss the merits of a leg of mutton, and of the subjects upon which we are to write."*—Mr Leigh Hunt's ideas concerning the sublime, and concerning his own powers, bear a considerable resemblance to those of his friend Bottom, the weaver, on the same subjects; "I will roar, that it shall do any man's heart good to hear me."—"I will roar you an 'twere any nightingale."

The poetry of Mr Hunt is such as might be expected from the personal character and habits of its author. As a vulgar man is perpetually labouring to be genteel—in like manner, the poetry of this man is always on the stretch to be grand. He has been allowed to look for a moment from the antichamber into the saloon, and mistaken the waving of feathers and the painted floor for the *sine qua non's* of elegant society. He would fain be always tripping and waltzing, and is sorry that he cannot be allowed to walk about in the morning with yellow breeches and flesh-coloured silk-stockings. He sticks an artificial rosebud into his button hole in the midst of winter. He wears no neckcloth, and cuts his hair in imitation of the Prints of Petrarch. In his verses he is always desirous of being airy, graceful, easy, courtly, and ITALIAN. If he had the smallest acquaintance with the great demi-gods of Italian poetry, he could never fancy that the style in which he writes, bears any, even the most remote, resemblance to the severe and simple manner of Dante—the tender stillness of the lover of Laura—or the sprightly and good-natured unconscious elegance of the inimitable Ariosto. He has gone into a strange delusion about himself, and is just as absurd in supposing that he resembles the Italian Poets, as a greater Quack still (Mr Coleridge) is, in imagining that he is a Philosopher after the manner of Kant or Mendelshon—and that "the eye of Lessing bears a remarkable likeness to MINE," i.e. the eye of Mr Samuel Coleridge.[1]

The extreme moral depravity of the Cockney School is another thing which is for ever thrusting itself upon the public attention, and convincing every man of sense who looks into their productions, that they who sport such sentiments can never be great poets. How could any man of high original genius ever stoop publicly, at the present day, to dip his fingers in the least of those glittering and rancid obscentities which float on the surface of Mr Hunt's Hippocrene? His poetry resembles that of a man who has kept company with kept-mistresses. His muse talks indelicately like a tea-sipping milliner girl. Some excuse for her there might have been, had she been hurried away by imagination or passion; but with her, indecency seems a disease, she appears to speak unclean things from perfect inanition. Surely they who are connected with Mr Hunt by the tender relations of society, have good reason to complain that his muse should have been so prostituted. In Rimini a deadly wound is aimed at the dearest confidences of domestic bliss. The author has voluntarily chosen—a subject not of simple seduction alone—one in which his mind seems absolutely to gloat over all the details of adultery and incest.

The unhealthy and jaundiced medium through which the Founder of the Cockney School views every thing like moral truth, is apparent, not only from his obscenity, but also from his want of respect for all that numerous class of plain upright men, and unpretending women, in which the real worth and excellence of human society consists. Every man is, according to Mr Hunt, a dull potato-eating blockhead—of no greater value to God or man than any ox or drayhorse—who is not an admirer of Voltaire's *romans,* a worshipper of Lord Holland and Mr Haydon, and a quoter of John Buncle and Chaucer's Flower and Leaf. Every woman is useful only as a breeding machine, unless she is fond of reading Launcelot of the Lake, in an antique summer-house.

How such an indelicate writer as Mr Hunt can pretend to be an admirer of Mr Wordsworth, is to us a thing altogether inexplicable. One great charm of Wordsworth's noble compositions consists in the dignified purity of thought, and the patriarchal simplicity of feeling, with which they are throughout penetrated and imbued. We can conceive a vicious man admiring with distant awe the spectacle of virtue and purity; but if he does so sincerely, he must also do so with the profoundest feeling of the error of his own ways, and the resolution to amend them. His admiration must be humble and silent, not pert and loquacious. Mr Hunt praises the purity of Wordsworth as if he himself were pure, his dignity as if he also were dignified. He is always like the ball of Dung in the fable, pleasing himself, and amusing bye-standers with his "nos poma natamus." For the person who writes *Rimini,* to admire the Excursion, is just as impossible as it would be for a Chinese polisher of cherry-stones, or a gilder of tea-cups, to burst into tears at the sight of the Theseus or the Torso.

The Founder of the Cockney School would fain claim poetical kindred with Lord Byron and Thomas Moore. Such a connexion would be as unsuitable for them as for William Wordsworth. The days of Mr Moore's follies are long since over; and, as he is a thorough gentleman, he must necessarily entertain the greatest contempt for such an under-bred person as Mr Leigh Hunt. But Lord Byron! How must the haughty spirit of Lara and Harold contemn the subaltern sneaking of our modern tufthunter. The insult which he offered to Lord Byron in the dedication of Rimini,—in which he, a paltry cockney newspaper scribbler, had the assurance to address one of the most nobly-born of English Patricians, and one of the first geniuses whom the world ever produced, as "My dear Byron," although it may have been forgotton and despised by the illustrious person whom it most nearly concerned,—excited a feeling of utter loathing and disgust in the public mind, which will always be remembered whenever the name of Leigh Hunt is mentioned. We dare say Mr Hunt has some fine dreams about the true nobility being the nobility of talent, and flatters himself, that with those who acknowledge only that sort of rank, he himself passes for being the *peer* of Byron. He is sadly mistaken. He is as completely a Plebeian in his mind as he is in his rank and station in society. To that highest and unalienable nobility which the great Roman satirist styles "sola atque unica," we fear his pretensions would be equally unavailing.

The shallow and impotent pretensions, tenets, and attempts, of this man,—and the success with which his influence seems to be extending itself among a pretty numerous, though certainly a very paltry and pitiful, set of readers,—have for the last two or three years been considered by us with the most sickening aversion. The very culpable manner in which his chief poem was reviewed in the Edinburgh Review (we believe it is no secret, at his own impatient and feverish request, by his partner in the Round Table), was matter of concern to more readers than ourselves. The masterly pen which inflicted such signal chastisement on the early licentiousness of Moore, should not have been idle on that occeasion. Mr Jeffrey does ill, when he delegates his important functions into such hands as those of Mr Hazlitt. It was chiefly in consequence of that gentleman's allowing Leigh Hunt to pass unpunished through a scene of slaughter, which his execution might so highly have graced, that we came to the resolution of laying before our readers a series of essays on *the Cockney School*—of which here terminates the first.

Note

[1] Mr Wordsworth (meaning, we presume, to pay Mr Coleridge a compliment,) makes him look very absurdly, "A noticeable man, with *large grey eyes*."

John Wilson Croker (review date 1818)

SOURCE: Review of *Endymion,* in *Quarterly Review* (London), Vol. XIX, No. 37, April, 1818, pp. 204-08.

[*In the following review of* Endymion, *Croker excoriates Keats for his preoccupation with rhyme, claiming that he focuses too little on subject matter and palely imitates Leigh Hunt, his Cockney model.*]

Reviewers have been sometimes accused of not reading the works which they affected to criticise. On the present occasion we shall anticipate the author's complaint, and honestly confess that we have not read his work. Not that we have been wanting in our duty—far from it—indeed, we have made efforts almost as superhuman as the story itself appears to be, to get through it; but with the fullest stretch of our perseverance, we are forced to confess that we have not been able to struggle beyond the first of the four books of which this Poetic Romance consists. We should extremely lament this want of energy, or whatever it may be, on our parts, were it not for one consolation—namely, that we are no better acquainted with the meaning of the book through which we have so painfully toiled, than we are with that of the three which we have not looked into.

It is not that Mr. Keats, (if that be his real name, for we almost doubt that any man in his senses would put his real name to such a rhapsody,) it is not, we say, that the author has not powers of language, rays of fancy, and gleams of genius—he has all these; but he is unhappily a disciple of the new school of what has been somewhere called Cockney poetry; which may be defined to consist of the most incongruous ideas in the most uncouth language.

Of this school, Mr. Leigh Hunt, as we observed in a former Number, aspires to be the hierophant. Our readers will recollect the pleasant recipes for harmonious and sublime poetry which he gave us in his preface to 'Rimini,' and the still more facetious instances of his harmony and sublimity in the verses themselves; and they will recollect above all the contempt of Pope, Johnson, and such like poetasters and pseudo-critics, which so forcibly contrasted itself with Mr. Leigh Hunt's self-complacent approbation of

> ———'all the things itself had wrote,
> Of special merit though of little note.'

This author is a copyist of Mr. Hunt; but he is more unintelligible, almost as rugged, twice as diffuse, and ten times more tiresome and absurd than his prototype, who, though he impudently presumed to seat himself in the chair of criticism, and to measure his own poetry by his own standard, yet generally had a meaning. But Mr. Keats had advanced no dogmas which he was bound to support by examples; his nonsense therefore is quite gratuitous; he writes it for its own sake, and, being bitten by Mr. Leigh Hunt's insane criticism, more than rivals the insanity of his poetry.

Mr. Keats's preface hints that his poem was produced under peculiar circumstances.

> 'Knowing within myself (he says) the manner in which this Poem has been produced, it is not without a feeling of regret that I make it public,—What manner I mean, will be *quite clear* to the reader, who must soon perceive great inexperience, immaturity, and every error denoting a feverish attempt, rather than a deed accomplished.'—*Preface,* p. vii.

We humbly beg his pardon, but this does not appear to us to be *quite so clear*—we really do not know what he means—but the next passage is more intelligible.

> 'The two first books, and indeed the two last, I feel sensible are not of such completion as to warrant their passing the press.'—*Preface,* p. vii.

Thus 'the two first books' are, even in his own judgment, unfit to appear, and 'the two last' are, it seems, in the same condition—and as two and two make four, and as that is the whole number of books, we have a clear and, we believe, a very just estimate of the entire work.

Mr. Keats, however, deprecates criticism on this 'immature and feverish work' in terms which are themselves sufficiently feverish; and we confess that we should have abstained from inflicting upon him any of the tortures of the *'fierce hell'* of criticism, which terrify his imagination, if he had not begged to be spared in order that he might write more; if we had not observed in him a certain degree of talent which deserves to be put in the right way, or which, at least, ought to be warned of the wrong; and if, finally, he had not told us that he is of an age and temper which imperiously require mental discipline.

Of the story we have been able to make out but little; it seems to be mythological, and probably relates to the loves of Diana and Endymion; but of this, as the scope of the work has altogether escaped us, we cannot speak with any degree of certainty; and must therefore content ourselves with giving some instances of its diction and versification:—and here again we are perplexed and puzzled.—At first it appeared to us, that Mr. Keats had been amusing himself and wearying his readers with an immeasurable game at *bouts-rimés;* but, if we recollect rightly, it is an indispensable condition at this play, that the rhymes when filled up shall have a meaning; and our author, as we have already hinted, has no meaning. He seems to us to write a line at random, and then he follows not the thought excited

John Keats, English poet, 1795-1821

by this line, but that suggested by the *rhyme* with which it concludes. There is hardly a complete couplet inclosing a complete idea in the whole book. He wanders from one subject to another, from the association, not of ideas but of sounds, and the work is composed of hemistichs which, it is quite evident, have forced themselves upon the author by the mere force of the catchwords on which they turn.

We shall select, not as the most striking instance, but as that least liable to suspicion, a passage from the opening of the poem.

> ———'Such the sun, the moon,
> Trees old and young, sprouting a shady boon
> For simple sheep; and such are daffodils
> With the green world they live in; and clear rills
> That for themselves a cooling covert make
> 'Gainst the hot season; the mid forest brake,
> Rich with a sprinkling of fair musk-rose blooms:
> And such too is the grandeur of the dooms
> We have imagined for the mighty dead; &c.
> &c.'—pp. 3, 4.

Here it is clear that the word, and not the idea, *moon* produces the simple sheep and their shady *boon,* and that 'the *dooms* of the mighty dead' would never have intruded themselves but for the '*fair musk-rose blooms*.'

'For 'twas the morn: Apollo's upward fire
Made every eastern cloud a silvery pyre
Of brightness so unsullied, that therein
A melancholy spirit well might win
Oblivion, and melt out his essence fine
Into the winds: rain-scented eglantine
Gave temperate sweets to that well-wooing sun;
The lark was lost in him; cold springs had run
To warm their chilliest bubbles in the grass;
Man's voice was on the mountains; and the mass
Of nature's lives and wonders puls'd tenfold,
To feel this sun-rise and its glories old.'—p. 8.

Here Apollo's *fire* produces a *pyre*, a silvery pyre of clouds, *wherein* a spirit might *win* oblivion and melt his essence *fine*, and scented *eglantine* gives sweets to the *sun*, and cold springs had *run* into the *grass*, and then the pulse of the *mass* pulsed *tenfold* to feel the glories *old* of the new-born day, &c.

One example more.

'Be still the unimaginable lodge
For solitary thinkings; such as dodge
Conception to the very bourne of heaven,
Then leave the naked brain: be still the leaven,
That spreading in this dull and clodded earth
Gives it a touch ethereal—a new birth.'—p. 17.

Lodge, dodge—heaven, leaven—earth, birth; such, in six words, is the sum and substance of six lines.

We come now to the author's taste in versification. He cannot indeed write a sentence, but perhaps he may be able to spin a line. Let us see. The following are specimens of his prosodial notions of our English heroic metre.

'Dear as the temple's self, so does the moon,
The passion poesy, glories infinite.'—p. 4.
'So plenteously all weed-hidden roots.'—p. 6.
'Of some strange history, potent to send.'—p. 18.
'Before the deep intoxication.'—p. 27.
'Her scarf into a fluttering pavilion.'—p. 33.
'The stubborn canvass for my voyage
  prepared———.'—p. 39.
'"Endymion! the cave is secreter
Than the isle of Delos. Echo hence shall stir
No sighs but sigh-warm kisses, or light noise
Of thy combing hand, the while it travelling cloys
And trembles through my labyrinthine
  hair."'—p. 48.

By this time our readers must be pretty well satisfied as to the meaning of his sentences and the structure of his lines: we now present them with some of the new words with which, in imitation of Mr. Leigh Hunt, he adorns our language.

We are told that 'turtles *passion* their voices,' (p. 15); that 'an arbour was *nested*,' (p. 23); and a lady's locks '*gordian'd* up,' (p. 32); and to supply the place of the nouns thus verbalized Mr. Keats, with great fecundity, spawns new ones; such as 'men-slugs and human *serpentry*,' (p. 41); the '*honey-feel* of bliss,' (p. 45); 'wives prepare *needments*,' (p. 13)—and so forth.

Then he has formed new verbs by the process of cutting off their natural tails, the adverbs, and affixing them to their foreheads; thus, 'the wine out-sparkled,' (p. 10); the 'multitude up-followed,' (p. 11); and 'night up-took,' (p. 29). 'The wind up-blows,' (p. 32); and the 'hours are down-sunken,' (p. 36.)

But if he sinks some adverbs in the verbs he compensates the language with adverbs and adjectives which he separates from the parent stock. Thus, a lady 'whispers *pantingly* and close,' makes '*hushing* signs,' and steers her skiff into a '*ripply* cove,' (p. 23); a shower falls '*refreshfully*,' (45); and a vulture has a '*spreaded* tail,' (p. 44.)

But enough of Mr. Leigh Hunt and his simple neophyte.—If any one should be bold enough to purchase this 'Poetic Romance,' and so much more patient, than ourselves, as to get beyond the first book, and so much more fortunate as to find a meaning, we entreat him to make us acquainted with his success; we shall then return to the task which we now abandon in despair, and endeavour to make all due amends to Mr. Keats and to our readers.

Thomas Babington Macaulay on John Wilson Croker:

Macaulay said of John Wilson Croker, the "talking potato" who, as one of [*Quarterly Review* editor William] Gifford's favorite contributors, had been assigned to deal with Keats, that he "would go a hundred miles through sleet and snow, on the top of a coach, in a December night, to search a parish register, for the sake of showing that a man is illegitimate, or a woman older than she says she is."

Herschel Baker, in William Hazlitt, *The Belnap Press of Harvard University Press, 1962.*

John Gibson Lockhart (review essay date 1818)

SOURCE: "Cockney School of Poetry, No. IV," in *Blackwood's Edinburgh Magazine,* Vol. III, No. 17, August, 1818, pp. 519-24.

[*In the following review, Lockhart derides Keats' work, particularly his* Poems *and* Endymion, *as a symptom of what he calls "Metromanie," an "illness" that causes the Cockneys to write vulgar and unaccomplished poetry.*]

——OF KEATS,
THE MUSES' SON OF PROMISE, AND WHAT
FEATS
HE YET MAY DO, &C.

CORNELIUS WEBB.

Of all the manias of this mad age, the most incurable, as well as the most common, seems to be no other than the *Metromanie*. The just celebrity of Robert Burns and Miss Baillie has had the melancholy effect of turning the heads of we know not how many farm-servants and unmarried ladies; our very footmen compose tragedies, and there is scarcely a superannuated governess in the island that does not leave a roll of lyrics behind her in her band-box. To witness the disease of any human understanding, however feeble, is distressing; but the spectacle of an able mind reduced to a state of insanity is of course ten times more afflicting. It is with such sorrow as this that we have contemplated the case of Mr John Keats. This young man appears to have received from nature talents of an excellent, perhaps even of a superior order—talents which, devoted to the purposes of any useful profession, must have rendered him a respectable, if not an eminent citizen. His friends, we understand, destined him to the career of medicine, and he was bound apprentice some years ago to a worthy apothecary in town. But all has been undone by a sudden attack of the malady to which we have alluded. Whether Mr John had been sent home with a diuretic or composing draught to some patient far gone in the poetical mania, we have not heard. This much is certain, that he has caught the infection, and that thoroughly. For some time we were in hopes, that he might get off with a violent fit or two; but of late the symptoms are terrible. The phrenzy of the "Poems" was bad enough in its way; but it did not alarm us half so seriously as the calm, settled, imperturbable drivelling idiocy of "Endymion." We hope, however, that in so young a person, and with a constitution originally so good, even now the disease is not utterly incurable. Time, firm treatment, and rational restraint, do much for many apparently hopeless invalids; and if Mr Keats should happen, at some interval of reason, to cast his eye upon our pages, he may perhaps be convinced of the existence of his malady, which, in such cases, is often all that is necessary to put the patient in a fair way of being cured.

The readers of the Examiner newspaper were informed, some time ago, by a solemn paragraph, in Mr Hunt's best style, of the appearance of two new stars of glorious magnitude and splendour in the poetical horizon of the land of Cockaigne. One of these turned out, by and by, to be no other than Mr John Keats. This precocious adulation confirmed the wavering apprentice in his desire to quit the gallipots, and at the same time excited in his too susceptible mind a fatal admiration for the character and talents of the most worthless and affected of all the versifiers of our time. One of his first productions was the following sonnet, "*written on the day when Mr Leigh Hunt left prison.*" It will be recollected, that the cause of Hunt's confinement was a series of libels against his sovereign, and that its fruit was the odious and incestuous "Story of Rimini."

What though, for shewing truth to flattered state,
Kind Hunt was shut in prison, yet has he,
In his immortal spirit been as free
As the sky-searching lark, and as elate.
Minion of grandeur! think you he did wait?
Think you he nought but prison walls did see,
Till, so unwilling, thou unturn'dst the key?
Ah, no! far happier, nobler was his fate!
In Spenser's halls! he strayed, and bowers fair,
Culling enchanted flowers; and he flew
With daring Milton! through the fields of air;
To regions of his own his genius true
Took happy flights. Who shall his fame impair
When thou art dead, and all thy wretched crew?

The absurdity of the thought in this sonnet is, however, if possible, surpassed in another, *"addressed to Haydon"* the painter, that clever, but most affected artist, who as little resembles Raphael in genius as he does in person, notwithstanding the foppery of having his hair curled over his shoulders in the old Italian fashion. In this exquisite piece it will be observed, that Mr Keats classes together WORDSWORTH, HUNT, and HAYDON, as the three greatest spirits of the age, and that he alludes to himself, and some others of the rising brood of Cockneys, as likely to attain hereafter an equally honourable elevation. Wordsworth and Hunt! what a juxta-position! The purest, the loftiest, and, we do not fear to say it, the most classical of living English poets, joined together in the same compliment with the meanest, the filthiest, and the most vulgar of Cockney poetasters. No wonder that he who could be guilty of this should class Haydon with Raphael, and himself with Spencer.

Great spirits now on earth are sojourning;
He of the cloud, the cataract, the lake,
Who on Helvellyn's summit, wide awake,
Catches his freshness from Archangel's wing:
He of the rose, the violet, the spring,
The social smile, the chain for Freedom's sake:
And lo!—whose stedfastness would never take
A meaner sound than Raphael's whispering.
And other spirits there are standing apart
Upon the forehead of the age to come;
These, these will give the world another heart,
And other pulses. *Hear ye not the hum*
Of mighty workings?——
Listen awhile ye nations, and be dumb.

The nations are to listen and be dumb! and why, good Johnny Keats? because Leigh Hunt is editor of the Examiner, and Haydon has painted the judgment of Solomon, and you and Cornelius Webb, and a few more city sparks, are pleased to look upon yourselves as so many future Shakspeares and Miltons! The world has really some reason to look to its foundations! Here is a *tempestas in matulâ* with a vengeance. At the period when these sonnets were published, Mr Keats had no hesitation in saying, that he looked on himself as "*not yet* a glorious denizen of the wide heaven of poetry," but he had many fine soothing visions of coming greatness, and many rare plans of study to prepare him for it. The following we think is very pretty raving.

Why so sad a moan?
Life is the rose's hope while yet unblown;
The reading of an ever-changing tale;
The light uplifting of a maiden's veil;
A pigeon tumbling in clear summer air;
A laughing school-boy, without grief or care,
Riding the springing branches of an elm.

O for ten years, that I may overwhelm
Myself in poesy; so I may do the deed
That my own soul has to itself decreed.
Then will I pass the countries that I see
In long perspective, and continually
Taste their pure fountains. First the realm I'll pass
Of Flora, and old Pan: sleep in the grass,
Feed upon apples red, and strawberries,
And choose each pleasure that my fancy sees.
Catch the white-handed nymphs in shady places,
To woo sweet kisses from averted faces,—
Play with their fingers, touch their shoulders white
Into a pretty shrinking with a bite
As hard as lips can make it: till agreed,
A lovely tale of human life we'll read.
And one will teach a tame dove how it best
May fan the cool air gently o'er my rest;
Another, bending o'er her nimble tread,
Will set a green robe floating round her head,
And still will dance with ever varied ease,
Smiling upon the flowers and the trees:
Another will entice me on, and on
Through almond blossoms and rich cinnamon;
Till in the bosom of a leafy world
We rest in silence, like two gems upcurl'd
In the recesses of a pearly shell.

Having cooled a little from this "fine passion," our youthful poet passes very naturally into a long strain of foaming abuse against a certain class of English Poets, whom, with Pope at their head, it is much the fashion with the ignorant unsettled pretenders of the present time to undervalue. Begging these gentlemens' pardon, although Pope was not a poet of the same high order with some who are now living, yet, to deny his genius, is just about as absurd as to dispute that of Wordsworth, or to believe in that of Hunt. Above all things, it is most pitiably ridiculous to hear men, of whom their country will always have reason to be proud, reviled by uneducated and flimsy striplings, who are not capable of understanding either their merits, or those of any other *men of power*—fanciful dreaming tea-drinkers, who, without logic enough to analyse a single idea, or imagination enough to form one original image, or learning enough to distinguish between the written language of Englishmen and the spoken jargon of Cockneys, presume to talk with contempt of some of the most exquisite spirits the world ever produced, merely because they did not happen to exert their faculties in laborious affected descriptions of flowers seen in window-pots, or cascades heard at Vauxhall; in short, because they chose to be wits, philosophers, patriots, and poets, rather than to found the Cockney school of versification, morality, and politics, a century before its time. After blaspheming himself into a fury against Boileau, &c. Mr Keats comforts himself and his readers with a view of the present more promising aspect of affairs; above all, with the ripened glories of the poet of Rimini. Addressing the manes of the departed chiefs of English poetry, he informs them, in the following clear and touching manner, of the existence of "him of the Rose," &c.

From a thick brake,
Nested and quiet in a valley mild,
Bubbles a pipe; fine sounds are floating wild
About the earth. Happy are ye and glad.

From this he diverges into a view of "things in general." We smile when we think to ourselves how little most of our readers will understand of what follows.

Yet I rejoice: a myrtle fairer than
E'er grew in Paphos, from the bitter weeds
Lifts its sweet head into the air, and feeds
A silent space with ever sprouting green.
All tenderest birds there find a pleasant screen,
Creep through the shade with jaunty fluttering,
Nibble the little cupped flowers and sing.
Then let us clear away the choaking *thorns*
From round its gentle stem; let the young *fawns,*
Yeaned in after times, when we are flown,
Find a fresh sward beneath it, overgrown
With simple flowers: let there nothing be
More boisterous than a lover's bended knee;
Nought more ungentle than the placid look
Of one who leans upon a closed book;
Nought more untranquil than the grassy slopes
Between two hills. All hail delightful hopes!
As she was wont, th' imagination
Into most lovely labyrinths will be gone,
And they shall be accounted poet kings
Who simply tell the most heart-easing things.

O may these joys be ripe before I die.
Will not some say that I presumptuously
Have spoken? that from hastening disgrace
'Twere better far to hide my foolish face?
That whining boyhood should with reverence
bow
Ere the dread thunderbolt could reach? How!
If I do hide myself, it sure shall be
In the very fane, the light of poesy.

From some verses addressed to various amiable individuals of the other sex, it appears, notwithstanding all this gossamer-work, that Johnny's affections are not entirely confined to objects purely etherial. Take, by way of specimen, the following prurient and vulgar lines, evidently meant for some young lady east of Temple-bar.

Add too, the sweetness
Of thy honied voice; the neatness
Of thine ankle lightly turn'd:
With those beauties, scarce discern'd,
Kept with such sweet privacy,
That they seldom meet the eye
Of the little loves that fly
Round about with eager pry.
Saving when, with freshening lave,
Thou dipp'st them in the taintless wave;
Like twin water lilies, born
In the coolness of the morn.
O, if thou hadst breathed then,
Now the Muses had been ten.
Couldst thou wish for lineage *higher*
Than twin sister of *Thalia?*
At last for ever, evermore,
Will I call the Graces four.

Who will dispute that our poet, to use his own phrase (and rhyme),

Can mingle music fit for the soft *ear*
Of Lady *Cytherca.*

So much for the opening bud; now for the expanded flower. It is time to pass from the juvenile "Poems," to the mature and elaborate "Endymion, a Poetic Romance." The old story of the moon falling in love with a shepherd, so prettily told by a Roman Classic, and so exquisitely enlarged and adorned by one of the most elegant of German poets, has been seized upon by Mr John Keats, to be done with as might seem good unto the sickly fancy of one who never read a single line either of Ovid or of Wieland. If the quantity, not the quality, of the verses dedicated to the story is to be taken into account, there can be no doubt that Mr John Keats may now claim Endymion entirely to himself. To say the truth, we do not suppose either the Latin or the German poet would be very anxious to dispute about the property of the hero of the "Poetic Romance." Mr Keats has thoroughly appropriated the character, if not the name. His Endymion is not a Greek shepherd, loved by a Grecian goddess; he is merely a young Cockney rhymester, dreaming a phantastic dream at the full of the moon. Costume, were it worth while to notice such a trifle, is violated in every page of this goodly octavo. From his prototype Hunt, John Keats has acquired a sort of vague idea, that the Greeks were a most tasteful people, and that no mythology can be so finely adapted for the purposes of poetry as theirs. It is amusing to see what a hand the two Cockneys make of this mythology; the one confesses that he never read the Greek Tragedians, and the other knows Homer only from Chapman; and both of them write about Apollo, Pan, Nymphs, Muses, and Mysteries, as might be expected from persons of their education. We shall not, however, enlarge at present upon this subject, as we mean to dedicate an entire paper to the classical attainments and attempts of the Cockney poets. As for Mr Keats' "Endymion," it has just as much to do with Greece as it has with "old Tartary the fierce;" no man, whose mind has ever been imbued with the smallest knowledge or feeling of classical poetry or classical history, could have stooped to profane and vulgarise every association in the manner which has been adopted by this "son of promise." Before giving any extracts, we must inform our readers, that this romance is meant to be written in English heroic rhyme. To those who have read any of Hunt's poems, this hint might indeed be needless. Mr Keats has adopted the loose, nerveless versification, and Cockney rhymes of the poet of Rimini; but in fairness to that gentleman, we must add, that the defects of the system are tenfold more conspicuous in his disciple's work than in his own. Mr Hunt is a small poet, but he is a clever man. Mr Keats is a still smaller poet, and he is only a boy of pretty abilities, which he has done every thing in his power to spoil.

The poem sets out with the following exposition of the reasons which induced Mr Keats to compose it.

A thing of beauty is a joy for ever:
Its loveliness increases; it will never
Pass into nothingness; but still will keep
A bower quiet for us, and a sleep
Full of sweet dreams, and health, and quiet
breathing.
Therefore, on every morrow, are we wreathing
A flowery band to bind us to the earth,
Spite of despondence, of the inhuman dearth
Of noble natures, of the gloomy days,
Of all the unhealthy and o'er-darkened ways
Made for our searching: yes, in spite of all,
Some shape of beauty moves away the pall
From our dark spirits. Such the sun, the moon,
Trees old and young, sprouting a shady boon
For simple sheep; and such are daffodils
With the green world they live in; and clear rills
That for themselves a cooling covert make
'Gainst the hot season; the mid forest brake,
Rich with a sprinkling of fair musk-rose blooms:

And such too is the grandeur of the dooms
We have imagined for the mighty dead;
All lovely tales that we have heard or read;
An endless fountain of immortal drink,
Pouring unto us from the heaven's brink.

Nor do we merely feel these essences
For one short hour; no, even as the trees
That whisper round a temple become soon
Dear as the temple's self, so does the moon,
The passion poesy, glories infinite,
Haunt us till they become a cheering light
Unto our souls, and bound to us so fast,
That, whether there be shine, or gloom o'ercast,
They alway must be with us, or we die.

Therefore 'tis with full happiness that I
Will trace the story of Endymion!!!

After introducing his hero to us in a procession, and preparing us, by a few mystical lines, for believing that his destiny has in it some strange peculiarity, Mr Keats represents the beloved of the Moon as being conveyed by his sister Peona into an island in a river. This young lady has been alarmed by the appearance of the brother, and questioned him thus:

Brother, 'tis vain to hide
That thou dost know of things mysterious,
Immortal, starry; such alone could thus
Weigh down thy nature. Hast thou sinn'd in aught
Offensive to the heavenly powers? Caught
A Paphian dove upon a message sent?
Thy deathful bow against some deer-herd bent,
Sacred to Dian? Haply, thou hast seen
Her naked limbs among the alders green;
And that, alas! is death. No, I can trace
Something more high perplexing in thy face!

Endymion replies in a long speech, wherein he describes his first meeting with the Moon. We cannot make room for the whole of it, but shall take a few pages here and there.

There blossom'd suddenly a magic bed
Of sacred ditamy, and poppies red:
At which I wonder'd greatly, knowing well
That but one night had wrought this flowery spell;
And, sitting down close by, began to muse
What it might mean. Perhaps, thought I, Morpheus,
In passing here, his owlet pinions shook;
Or, it may be, ere matron Night uptook
Her ebon urn, young Mercury, by stealth,
Had dipt his rod in it: such garland wealth
Came not by common growth. Thus on I thought,
Until my head was dizzy and distraught.
Moreover, through the dancing poppies stole
A breeze, most softly lulling to my soul,

. . . . .

Methought the lidless-eyed train
Of planets all were in the blue again.
To commune with those orbs, once more I rais'd
My sight right upward: but it was quite dazed
By a bright something, sailing down apace,
Making me quickly veil my eyes and face:
Again I look'd, and, O ye deities,
Who from Olympus watch our destinies!
Whence that completed form of all completeness?
Whence came that high perfection of all sweetness?
Speak, stubborn earth, and tell me where, O where
Hast thou a symbol of her golden hair?
Not oat-sheaves drooping in the western sun;
Not—thy soft hand, fair sister! let me shun
Such follying before thee—yet she had,
Indeed, locks bright enough to make me mad;
And they were simply gordian'd up and braided,
Leaving, in naked comeliness, unshaded,
Her pearl round ears,'

. . . . .

She took an airy range,
And then, towards me, like a very maid,
Came blushing, waning, willing, and afraid,
And press'd me by the hand: Ah! 'twas too much;
Methought I fainted at the charmed touch,
Yet held my recollection, even as one
Who dives three fathoms where the waters run
Gurgling in beds of coral: for anon,
I felt upmounted in that region
Where falling stars dart their artillery forth,
And eagles struggle with the buffeting north
That balances the heavy meteor-stone;—
Felt too, I was not fearful, nor alone. . . .

Not content with the authentic love of the Moon, Keats makes his hero captivate another supernatural lady, of whom no notice occurs in any of his predecessors.

It was a nymph uprisen to the breast
In the fountain's pebbly margin, and she stood
Mong lilies, like the youngest of the brood.
To him her dripping hand she softly kist,
And anxiously began to plait and twist
Her ringlets round her fingers, saying, 'Youth!
Too long, alas, hast thou starv'd on the ruth,
The bitterness of love: too long indeed,
Seeing thou art so gentle. Could I weed
Thy soul of care, by Heavens, I would offer
All the bright riches of my crystal coffer
To Amphitrite; all my clear-eyed fish,
Golden, or rainbow-sided, or purplish,
Vermilion-tail'd, or finn'd with silvery gauze;
Yea, or my veined pebble-floor, that draws
A virgin light to the deep; my grotto-sands
Tawny and gold, ooz'd slowly from far lands
By my diligent springs; my level lilies, shells,
My charming rod, my potent river spells;

Yes, every thing, even to the pearly cup
Meander gave me,—for I bubbled up
To fainting creatures in a desert wild.
But woe is me, I am but as a child
To gladden thee; and all I dare to say,
Is, that I pity thee: that on this day
I've been thy guide; that thou must wander far

In other regions, past the scanty bar
To mortal steps, before thou can'st be ta'en
From every wasting sigh, from every pain,
Into the gentle bosom of thy love.
Why it is thus, one knows in heaven above:
But, a poor Naiad, I guess not. Farewell!
I have a ditty for my hollow cell.'

But we find that we really have no patience for going over four books filled with such amorous scenes as these, with subterraneous journeys equally amusing, and submarine processions equally beautiful; but we must not omit the most interesting scene of the whole piece.

Thus spake he, and that moment felt endued
With power to dream deliciously; so wound
Through a dim passage, searching till he found
The smoothest mossy bed and deepest, where
He threw himself, and just into the air
Stretching his indolent arms, he took, O bliss!
A naked waist: Fair Cupid, whence is this?
A well-known voice sigh'd, 'Sweetest, here am I!'
At which soft ravishment, with doting cry
They trembled to each other.—Helicon!
O fountain'd hill! Old Homer's Helicon!
That thou wouldst spout a little streamlet o'er
These sorry pages: then the verse would soar
And sing above this gentle pair, like lark
Over his nested young: but all is dark
Around thine aged top, and thy clear fount
Exhales in mists to heaven. Aye, the count
Of mighty poets is made up; the scroll
Is folded by the Muses; the bright roll
Is in Apollo's hand: our dazed eyes
Have seen a new tinge in the western skies:
The world has done its duty. Yet, oh yet,
Although the son of poesy is set,
These lovers did embrace, and we must weep
That there is no old power left to steep
A quill immortal in their joyous tears.
Long time in silence did their anxious fears
Question that thus it was; long time they lay
Fondling and kissing every doubt away;
Long time ere soft caressing sobs began
To mellow into words, and then there ran
Two bubbling springs of talk from their sweet lips.
'O known Unknown! from whom my being sips
Such darling essence, wherefore may I not
Be ever in these arms'. . . .

After all this, however, the "modesty," as Mr Keats expresses it, of the Lady Diana prevented her from owning in Olympus her passion for Endymion. Venus, as the most knowing in such matters, is the first to discover the change that has taken place in the temperament of the goddess. "An idle tale," says the laughter-loving dame,

A humid eye, and steps luxurious,
When these are new and strange, are ominous.

The inamorata, to vary the intrigue, carries on a romantic intercourse with Endymion, under the disguise of an Indian damsel. At last, however, her scruples, for some reason or other, are all overcome, and the Queen of Heaven owns her attachment.

She gave her fair hands to him, and behold,
Before three swiftest kisses he had told,
They vanish far away!—Peona went
Home through the gloomy wood in wonderment.

And so, like many other romances, terminates the "Poetic Romance" of Johnny Keats, in a patched-up wedding.

We had almost forgot to mention, that Keats belongs to the Cockney School of Politics, as well as the Cockney School of Poetry.

It is fit that he who holds Rimini to be the first poem, should believe the Examiner to be the first politician of the day. We admire consistency, even in folly. Hear how their bantling has already learned to lisp sedition.

There are who lord it o'er their fellow-men
With most prevailing tinsel: who unpen
Their baaing vanities, to browse away
The comfortable green and juicy hay
From human pastures; or, O torturing fact!
Who, through an idiot blink, will see unpack'd
Fire-branded foxes to sear up and singe
Our gold and ripe-ear'd hopes. With not one tinge
Of sanctuary splendour, not a sight
Able to face an owl's, they still are dight
By the blear-eyed nations in empurpled vests,
And crowns, and turbans. With unladen breasts,
Save of blown self-applause, they proudly mount
To their spirit's perch, their being's high account,
Their tiptop nothings, their dull skies, their thrones—
Amid the fierce intoxicating tones
Of trumpets, shoutings, and belaboured drums,
And sudden cannon. Ah! how all this hums,
In wakeful ears, like uproar past and gone—
Like thunder clouds that spake to Babylon,
And set those old Chaldeans to their tasks.—
Are then regalities all gilded masks?

And now, good-morrow to "the Muses' son of Promise;" as for "the feats he yet may do," as we do not pretend to say, like himself, "Muse of my native land am I inspired," we shall adhere to the safe old rule of *pauca verba.* We venture to make one small prophecy, that his bookseller will not a second time venture £50 upon any thing he can write. It is a better and a wiser thing to be a starved apothecary than a starved poet; so back to the shop Mr John, back to "plasters, pills, and ointment boxes," &c.

But, for Heaven's sake, young Sangrado, be a little more sparing of extenuatives and soporifics in your practice than you have been in your poetry.

From an unsigned review (by John Gibson Lockhart and possibly John Wilson) of Shelley's *Revolt of Islam* (1819):

Mr Shelly [*sic*] is devoting his mind to the same pernicious purposes which have recoiled in vengeance upon so many of his contemporaries; but he possesses the qualities of a powerful and vigorous intellect, and therefore his fate cannot be sealed so speedily as theirs. He also is of the "COCKNEY SCHOOL," so far as his opinions are concerned; but the base opinions of the sect have not as yet been able entirely to obscure in him the character, or take away from him the privileges of the genius born within him. Hunt and Keats, and some others of the School, are indeed men of considerable cleverness, but as poets, they are worthy of sheer and instant contempt, and therefore their opinions are in little danger of being widely or deeply circulated by their means. But the system, which found better champions than it deserved even in them, has now, it would appear, been taken up by one, of whom it is far more seriously, and deeply, and lamentably unworthy; and the poem before us bears unfortunately the clearest marks of its author's execrable system, but it is impressed every where with the more noble and majestic footsteps of his genius. It is to the operation of the painful feeling above alluded to, which attends the contemplation of perverted power—that we chiefly ascribe the silence observed by our professional critics, in regard to the *Revolt of Islam*. Some have held back in the fear that, by giving to his genius its due praise, they might only be lending the means of currency to the opinions in whose service he has unwisely enlisted its energies; while others, less able to appreciate his genius, and less likely to be anxious about suppressing his opinions, have been silent, by reason of their selfish fears—dreading, it may be, that by praising the *Revolt of Islam*, they might draw down upon their own heads some additional marks of that public disgust which followed their praises of *Rimini*.

John Gibson Lockhart and possibly John Wilson, in Blackwood's Edinburgh Magazine, *January 1819, reprinted in* The Young Romantics and Critical Opinion: 1807-1824, *by Theodore Redpath, Harrap, 1973.*

Ralph M. Wardle (essay date 1971)

SOURCE: "Moment of Triumph," in *Hazlitt*, University of Nebraska Press, 1971, pp. 211-41.

[*In the excerpt that follows, Wardle discusses Hazlitt's response to his* Blackwood *libelers and the essays that followed the critical attacks.*]

Soon afterwards [in 1818, Hazlitt] was back in London, probably not with his family at the York Street house, but in lodgings on King Street, Somers Town.[42] And just before or after his return he suffered an even more damaging personal attack—from a new source, *Blackwood's Magazine*. It probably came not as a complete surprise: the unscrupulous Tories on the *Black-wood's* staff had allowed Leigh Hunt and his friends no quarter; their "Cockney School" articles by "Z" [John Gibson Lockhart] had become notorious. Yet they had published Patmore's favorable reviews of Hazlitt's lectures and had included in their June issue an article "Jeffrey and Hazlitt," which, though not always complimentary, at least acknowledged the two to be the foremost critics of the age. But there were ominous clouds on the horizon. In the section "To Correspondents" included in the February issue the editors had commented: "We have no objection to insert Z.'s Remarks on Mr. Hazlitt's Lectures, after our pres-ent Correspondent's Notices are completed. If Mr. Hazlitt uttered personalities against the Poets of the Lake School, he reviled those who taught him all he knows about poetry." Then in the March issue the rhyming "Notices" alluded in passing to "pimpled Hazlitt's coxcomb lectures." And at the end of Pat-more's review of the lectures in April the editors inserted a cautionary note:

> When we undertook to give the foregoing abstract of Mr. Hazlitt's Lectures, it was not our intention to have accompanied it by a single observation in the shape of judgment, as to their merits or defects; but we find, that our own opinions have been strangely supposed to be identified with those we have done nothing more than detail. We choose, therefore, to say a few words on the impression we have received from these, and from Mr. Hazlitt's previous writings on similar subjects. . . .
>
> As we have not scrupled to declare, that we think Mr. Hazlitt is sometimes the very best living critic, we shall venture one step farther, and add, that we think he is sometimes the very worst. One would suppose he had a personal quarrel with all living writers, good, bad, or indifferent. In fact, he seems to know little about them, and to care less. With him, to be alive is not only a fault in itself, but it includes all other possible faults. He seems to consider life a disease, and death as your only doctor. He reverses the proverb, and thinks a dead ass is better than a living lion. In his eyes, death, like charity, "covereth a multitude of sins." In short, if you want his praise, you must die for it; and when such praise is deserved, and given really *con amore*, it is almost worth dying for.
>
> By the bye, what can our Editor's facetious friend mean by "pimpled Hazlitt?" if he knows that gentleman's person, he cannot intend the epithet to apply to *that;* and how "pimpled" may be interpreted with reference to *mind*, we are not able to divine.

In the May issue a "Letter from Z. to Leigh Hunt" referred to Hazlitt's pimpled nose, and the third Cockney school article in July mocked "Bill Hazlitt" as "that foundered artist"

> whose tact intellectual is such,
> That it seems to feel truth as one's fingers do touch.

Moreover, there was a clear threat in the final sentences of the article: "It was indeed a fatal day for Mr. Jeffrey, when he degraded both himself and his original coadjutors, by taking into pay such an unprincipled blunderer as Hazlitt. He is not a coadjutor, he is an accomplice. The day is perhaps not far distant, when the Charlatan shall be stripped to the naked skin, and made to swallow his own vile prescriptions."[43]

The threatened exposure came in the August issue of *Blackwood's,* which contained also the infamous Cockney school review of Keats's *Endymion.* The article, entitled "Hazlitt Cross-Questioned" and signed "An Old Friend with a New Face," consisted of eight direct questions. They began:

> Query I. Mr. William Hazlitt, ex-painter, theatrical critic, review, essay, and lecture manufacturer, London, Did you, or did you not, in the course of your late Lectures on Poetry, &c. infamously vituperate and sneer at the character of Mr. Wordsworth—I mean his personal character; his genius even you dare not deny?
>
> II. Is it, or is it not, true that you owe all your ideas about poetry or criticism to gross misconceptions of the meaning of his conversation; and that you once owed your personal safety, perhaps existence, to the humane and firm interference of that virtuous man, who rescued you from the hands of an indignant peasantry whose ideas of purity you, a cockney visitor, had dared to outrage?

The next five questions were focused on Hazlitt's published work, in effect accusing him of ignorance, dishonesty, and obscenity; the last read merely: "Do you know the Latin for a goose?"[44]

Obviously the editors of *Blackwood's* were athirst for blood. In the same issue, a review of Lamb's recently published works included the observation the Lamb "does not condescend to say one syllable" about "'pimpled Hazlitt,' notwithstanding his 'coxcomb lectures' on Poetry and Shakespeare." And, still in the August issue, the author of an article on Shakespeare's sonnets remarked of *The Characters of Shakespear's Plays:* "To [Hazlitt] truth and falsehood are indifferent. He cannot write one syllable on any subject, unless he has an opinion before him, and then he very magnanimously and intellectually contradicts that opinion. He stands with his back turned on the whole writing world, and need not therefore be surprised to get an occasional kick or two."

Hazlitt was stung by these remarks, so much bitterer and more personal than anything even the *Quarterly* had dealt him. J. A. Hessey sent his partner, John Taylor, a copy of the August *Blackwood's* and wrote him in a letter of September 5: " . . . Hazlitt has been here and he is very much moved—He thinks & so do I that he had better remain quiet and let them take their Course."[45] Within the next few days Hazlitt sent Archibald Constable a copy of the article, declaring that he did not "feel tempted to this kind of personal warfare," but promising to "see about it" if Constable so advised. In passing he remarked that he expected to receive two hundred, rather than one hundred, pounds for publication rights for his forthcoming lectures.[46]

But he spoke too soon. By September 16 he had conferred with Hessey and had learned that the publishers dared not risk so large an outlay for a book by a man recently under scandalous attack. Hessey complained to Taylor that Hazlitt was irked because they had not agreed to the original terms. He added that Hazlitt "says he is in better Health and Spirits than he has been for some years," that he was planning to go to the seaside to finish his lectures, and that (despite Jeffrey's advice) he hoped to repeat his lectures in Edinburgh.[47] He was in an aggressive mood.

On September 19 he wrote again to Constable. "In making my bargain the other day," he explained, "the various fabrications in [*Blackwood's*] article were objected to me as lessening the value of my literary e[state]." He had decided to take the matter to court and, by way of formality, he enclosed a note to William Blackwood threatening to sue him immediately if he did not supply the name of the author of the slanderous article.[48]

He had already taken steps to start proceedings. He had written to Francis Jeffrey asking him to act as his counsel in the suit, and Jeffrey replied on the twentieth that he would be glad to do so but could not recommend a solicitor for him because "I have no personal acquaintance with you." He had looked over the *Blackwood's* article and suspected that it was actionable; he warned, however, that Hazlitt must be able to disprove the statements in the article. Yet his tone was distinctly friendly: he assured Hazlitt that *Blackwood's* claim that he been "expelled" from the *Edinburgh Review* was *"quite false,"* though he could not provide "a formal warrant for saying so" because the *Edinburgh* never revealed authorship of its articles. And as if to prove his good faith he added that he would try to work Hazlitt's review of Reid's book into the next issue and asked him to send along "anything brilliant or striking" that he might have on other subjects. He suggested especially an article on the fine arts, since he had heard that Hazlitt was "profound" on that subject.[49]

The next day Keats wrote to C. W. Dilke: "I suppose you will have heard that Hazlitt has on foot a prosecution against Blackwood—I dined with him a few days sinc[e] at Hessey's—there was not a word said about [it], though I understand he is excessively vexed."[50] And the *Times* for the twenty-first contained a notice of the suit, describing *Blackwood's* as "a book filled with private slander." Hazlitt was gaining strong support.

News of the suit spread fast. Mrs. Sarah Coleridge wrote from Keswick to Thomas Poole before the end of the month:

> I understand Mr Wm Hazlitt is about to commence a prosecution against the Editor of [*Blackwood's*] for a libel. . . . I was annoyed at hearing of the intended prosecution, because Southey and Wordsworth may be troubled to give their evidence to the truth of the assertions in the article which would be very disagreeable, & as Master Hazlitt will cut a very ridiculous figure, I wonder he chuses to make a stir in it. I think I told you the ridiculous story of Hazlitt's behaviour to a Peasant Girl when he was here 12 or 14 years ago: some person has taken up this tale, mentioning the kindness of Mr Wordsworth and others to him on this occasion, & commenting on his ingratitude: W. spoke of it here last week & seemed vexed that his name was connected with the thing in any way; but so it is.[51]

Meanwhile William Blackwood had sent Hazlitt a curt note on the twenty-first refusing to divulge authorship of the article, and on the twenty-fifth Hazlitt wrote to James Balfour of Edinburgh authorizing him to bring suit against the publisher.[52]

At first Blackwood was scornful. When John Murray, a shareholder in the magazine, wrote in alarm that "the clamour against its personality [is] almost universal," Blackwood assured him that he supposed "this fellow merely means to make a little bluster, and try if he can pick up a little money"; and he promised a "most powerful" attack on Hazlitt as the lead article in the October issue of the magazine. He sent Murray a long letter composed by John Wilson and John Gibson Lockhart, the authors of "Hazlitt Cross-Questioned," assuring Murray that he had nothing to fear from Hazlitt. But by October 6, when he received a summons to appear before the Court of Sessions to defend himself against Hazlitt's suit for two thousand pounds' damages, Blackwood himself took fright. To add to his concern, an anonymous pamphlet, *Hypocrisy Unveiled, and Calumny Detected,* came out in the middle of the month, damning *Blackwood's* for its sins past and present, with special attention to its treatment of Hazlitt. "The libeller of MR. HAZLITT," wrote the author of the pamphlet,

> avows himself to be an *old friend* with a *new face,*—a face which certainly, whatever features it may have at one time displayed, exhibits only those of a demon. . . . The attack on Mr. Hazlitt comes with a worse grace from these persons, inasmuch as they praised him warmly in the outset, holding him up as the first poetical critic of the day, and afterwards devoting an article to a parallel between him and Mr. Jeffrey; but the secret of all is, that Mr. Hazlitt furnished several very able articles to the *Scots* or *Edinburgh Magazine;*—articles which display more original thinking than all that have yet appeared in Blackwood's work. . . . Hazlitt is an abomination in their sight because he is rising into consequence.[53]

At this point Wilson and Lockhart lost their heads and, by sending challenges to the publisher of the pamphlet, revealed that they were the authors of the offensive article. Murray was frantic. He assured Blackwood that "three fourths of the talent of the Bar are in hostility to you, and . . . any jury will be prejudiced against you." Then followed elaborate negotiations, carried on between Sharon Turner, acting for Murray, and P. G. Patmore, acting for Hazlitt. At length they came to terms, and Hazlitt agreed to drop the suit upon payment of one hundred pounds' damages and costs.[54] The *Scotsman* for January 30, 1819, announced that the case had been settled out of court.[55]

Inevitably the last months of the year 1818 had been an unpleasant period for Hazlitt. In spite of himself he had become a public figure: the forces of reaction seized upon his name as symbolic of all they regarded as most hateful. In October and November a writer for the *New Monthly Magazine* joined the general outcry with the first two installments of "The Cockney School of Prose," a nasty attack labeling Hazlitt as a "cankered Cockney," a "pimpled coxcomb," "the dirty dandy of literature," and so forth.[56] On October 22 Keats met Hazlitt on his way to a game of rackets—probably to work off some of his frustration.[57]

Yet there were compensations: his foes would never have been so vicious if they had not regarded him as a serious threat. As the author of *Hypocrisy Unveiled* had put it, he was "an abomination in their sight because he is rising into prominence." Accordingly, when he decided to prepare a written reply to *Blackwood's* in the midst of all the furor, he was able to express himself calmly, reasonably, and above all, with dignity. "Sir," he began,

> Before I answer your questions, give me leave to tell you my opinion of the person who asks them. I think then that you are a person of little understanding, with great impudence, a total want of principle, an utter disregard to truth or even to the character of common veracity, and a very strong ambition to be picked up and paid as a cat's paw. If I were in the habit of using the words, Liar, Fool, Coxcomb, Hypocrite, Scoundrel, Blackguard, &c.,

> I should apply them to you, but this would be degrading them still lower unnecessarily, for it is quite as easy to prove you the *things* as to call you the *names*. (9:3)

He depreciated his success as a popular writer, which his attacker had scorned; he pointed, proudly, instead, to his *Principles of Human Action,* a book which Coleridge had once praised. "When," he wrote,

> this gentleman, of whom I have at various times spoken the truth, the whole truth, and nothing but the truth, formerly knew me, when I passed for an idiot, he used to say of me (and by so doing he excited a Surprise and incredulity which only his eloquence and persuasive tones could overcome) that "I had the most metaphysical head he ever met with," and when by his advice, and in order as he said that I might laugh at the tittle-tattle about my private follies, I put my metaphysics on paper, answering for myself, he turned his back upon me. . . . This same person used at the same time to cocker me up with such expressions as these, that "if ever I got language for my ideas, the world would hear of it, for that I had guts in my brains." And now that I have got language for *my* ideas, he says they are *his* ideas, that my brains are in his and Mr. Wordsworth's head (I deprecate this last utterly) and he gets such a fellow as Z . . . to say that I am a charlatan. (9:3-4)

Then he turned to the specific questions directed at him in the *Blackwood's* article:

> 1. You ask me "if I do not infamously vituperate and sneer at the character of Mr. Wordsworth, *videlicet* his personal character; his genius even I dare not deny." Why not: because I dare not deny my own convictions: certainly I am bound by public opinion to acknowledge [it] in very unsparing terms, and I have in fact gone on the forlorn hope in praising him. As to his personal character, I have said nothing about it: I have spoken of his intellectual egotism (and truly and warrantably) as the bane of his talents and of his public principles. It is because you cannot answer what I have said on the Lake School of Poetry, that you ask me eight impertinent questions. . . .
>
> 3. You ask me whether I do not owe my personal safety, perhaps existence, to the interference of that virtuous man in my behalf, &c. I beg to be excused answering this question except as it relates to my supposed ingratitude, and on that subject my answer is as follows. (9:5-6)

And he told how pleased Wordsworth had reportedly been with the *Examiner* critique of *The Excursion* until he learned that Hazlitt had written it. The story was hardly relevant, but Hazlitt was wise to avoid reviving the details of the Keswick scandal. He answered the remaining questions clearly and decisively, and rested his case. But the reply was not published. He may have hoped to place it in a rival publication like the *Edinburgh Magazine*. But either he failed to place it or he decided, in the long run, to "remain quiet," as he had originally intended, rather than to draw further attention to the nasty interlude. He seems to have sent his reply to Jeffrey, adding marginal notes to aid Jeffrey in preparing his case against Blackwood.

During the autumn months he had three articles published in the *Edinburgh Magazine*—probably some of the "nonsense" that he had been writing at Winterslow during the summer. The September issue contained two: one "On Nicknames" and another "On Fashion." The first, a discussion of what would today be termed "name-calling," was undoubtedly prompted by *Blackwood's* writers' irresponsible use of "nicknames" to brand their foes. "No matter how undeserved the imputation," Hazlitt wrote, "it will stick; for, though it is sport to the bye-standers to see you bespattered, they will not stop to see you wipe out the stains" (17:48). The second article deplored the absurdity of constantly changing fashion and the vulgarity of those who take it seriously (17:51-56). Then in the October issue he offered the first installment of "Thoughts on Taste," a more penetrating essay in which he made the distinction: "Genius is the power of producing excellence; taste is the power of perceiving the excellence thus produced in its several sorts and degrees, with all their force, refinement, distinctions, and connections. In other words, taste (as it relates to the productions of art) is strictly the power of being properly affected by works of genius" (17:57). William Hazlitt, obviously, was a man of taste.

At about this same time he began writing the brief critical introductions which he provided for the plays included in William Oxberry's anthology, *New English Drama*.[58] Most of the plays were already familiar to him; he had read them, seen them, even reviewed many of them at one time or other, and occasionally he borrowed from his reviews. He was gaining a name for himself among the booksellers as a man of taste with a ready supply of literary lore which he could quickly turn to account. Even in mere hackwork like this he wrote with gusto, calling his readers' attention to the merits of each play and, always, sharing with them his delight in the characterization.

Most of his efforts during the last months of the year were directed to his new series of lectures on the English comic poets. On Tuesday, November 3, he gave the first lecture "On Wit and Humour," again at the Surrey Institution. "Man is the only animal that laughs and weeps," he stated at the outset, "for he is the only animal that is struck with the difference between what things are, and what they ought to be" (6:5). There were other remarks in a similar vein, perceptive, sometimes with wistful overtones; for example: "To explain the nature of laughter and tears, is to account for the condition of human life; for it is in a manner compounded of these two! It is a tragedy or a comedy—sad or merry as it happens" (6:5). But most of the lecture was given over to definition and analysis of wit and humor: "Humour," he stated, "is the describing the ludicrous as it is in itself; wit is the exposing it, by comparing or contrasting it with something else" (6:15). He obviously relished this sort of exercise: he could draw on his innate understanding of human nature, his reading and experience, and his skill in trenchant expression. He rounded out his remarks with capsule critiques of Aristophanes, Lucian, Molière, and Rabelais, candidly admitting that he said very little about the first two because he knew very little about them.

Faithful William Bewick attended the new series regularly and reported later with satisfaction that Hazlitt had recovered from his stage fright. Now when he called for Hazlitt before the lectures, "he would sip his cup of strong tea, and laugh and joke at the difficulty he had to surmount at his first series of lectures."[59] Another friend declared that Hazlitt "read his lectures in an abrupt yet somewhat monotonous voice, but they were very effective. If he failed in communicating by his manner, the lighter graces of his authors, he established their graver beauties, and impressed on his auditors a due sense of their power."[60]

The subject of the second lecture on November 10 was "On Shakspeare and Ben Jonson," and inevitably the section on Shakespeare outshone that on Jonson, whose plays, Hazlitt admitted, he had never enjoyed. Yet once again he stated his preference for Shakespeare's work in tragedy: his comedy is "too good-natured and magnanimous . . . ; it does not take the highest pleasure in making human nature look as mean, as ridiculous, and contemptible as possible" (6:35). Crabb Robinson was present, probably against his better judgment, and pronounced the lecture "a dull performance. He raised a tumult by abusing Gifford, which a few hissed at and many applauded; but the best thing he did was reading a glorious passage from Ben Jonson's *Alchemist.*"[61]

The third lecture, on the seventeenth, "On Cowley, Butler, Suckling, Etheredge, &c.," began with Dr. Johnson's definition of metaphysical poetry and proceeded with brief discussions of the poets named in the title, cursory glances at half a dozen others, and a final overview of minor seventeenth-century dramatists. Hazlitt had never before shown any real interest in or knowledge of this period; the writers who flourished then showed too little concern with the subtleties of human character to please him. Moreover, because he tried to touch on many writers rather than to concentrate on a few of the most rewarding, the lecture was superficial and incoherent. Crabb Robinson decided: "He is sinking as a lecturer very fast."[62]

Hazlitt took a two-week recess before the next lecture, ostensibly because of the death of Queen Charlotte, though he may have welcomed the chance to put in some additional preparation, realizing that he was not performing at his peak.[63] Fortunately he could feel sincere enthusiasm for his next subject, the Restoration comedy, which he discussed on December 8. He was dealing again with drama, with life; in fact he considered the comedies of Wycherely, Congreve, Vanbrugh, and Farquhar the finest of the genre in English, and he enlivened his lecture with animated accounts of the plays and generous excerpts. He could only deplore the reforming zeal of Jeremy Collier which led to the sentimental comedy of the next century. Crabb Robinson suspected him of deliberately "touching the sore spots of the saints" in the audience, "being always on the brink of obscenity and palpably recommending works of the most licentious character. . . . This lecture was, after all, but dull," he wrote, "and his audience grew thin."[64]

The lecture on December 15 "On the Periodical Essayists" had as its epigraph (at least in the printed version) a dictum which Hazlitt could approve wholeheartedly: "The proper study of mankind is man." Since the periodical essay was another of his favorites, he was again buoyed up as he discussed Addison and Steele (as usual, favoring Steele), Johnson (lauding his character, as revealed by Boswell, rather than his essays), and Goldsmith (declaring him "more observing, more original, more natural and picturesque" than Johnson). Crabb Robinson considered it "all for the greatest part a repetition of The *Round Table,*"[65] and in truth much of his discussion of Addison and Steele was lifted from his Round Table essay on the *Tatler*.

Hazlitt also drew liberally on his earlier writings in the next two lectures, "On the English Novelists" (December 22) and "On the Works of Hogarth—On the Grand and Familiar Style of Painting" (December 29).[66] In both, the subject was again human nature, realistically yet imaginatively drawn, and Hazlitt maintained a high pitch of enthusiasm throughout. He did not apologize for treating the novel as a serious literary form or for airing personal preferences. He rated Fielding's "superior insight into the springs of human character" (6:116) above Richardson's "artificial reality" (6:117), Ann Radcliffe's imaginative romances above Fanny Burney's detailed pictures of contemporary life. In the Hogarth lecture he praised the lifelike expressions of the figures in Hogarth's paintings, contrasting them with those of Wilkie, the "serious, prosaic, literal narrator of facts" (6:139). Yet he granted that Hogarth was not a painter to be compared with Rubens and he concluded with a nostalgic recollection of his days with the old masters in the Louvre.

The final lecture "On the Comic Writers of the Last Century" (January 5) was again anticlimactic. Hazlitt could generate little enthusiasm for the comic writers of the eighteenth century. Again he drew on materials already in print: his Round Table essay "On Modern Comedy" (attributing the decline of comedy to the tendency of literature and education to make people more alike), a critique of the actor Liston from a *Times* review, and a defense of Colley Cibber from the *Examiner.* The audience may have complained about his borrowings because he concluded his published lecture by admitting them—insisting, however, that they constituted "a very small proportion to the whole" (6:168). Except for his zestful remarks about Sheridan as dramatist and orator, this final lecture was commonplace; once again he filled out a meager sketch with odds and ends of information, rather ill digested, about minor playwrights and actors.

None the less the introductory lecture and those on Restoration drama, the novel, and Hogarth were ably handled, and few in the audience would have agreed with Crabb Robinson's sour comments on the series. Bewick left a quite different impression: "Hazlitt became a favourite at the Surrey Institution," he wrote,

> and stood up in his place at the lecture-table with all confidence, in the consciousness of having friends and admirers about him. In his flights of sarcasm, or bursts of censure upon the favourite authors of some of his hearers—Lord Byron, for instance—he would occasionally meet with disapprobation; and, as he calmly looked towards the place whence the hissing came, turning back the leaf of his copy, and deliberately repeating the sentiments with greater energy and a voice more determined than before, he exclaimed with slow emphasis, "If my Lord Byron will do these things, he must take the consequences; the acts of Napoleon Bonaparte are subjects of *history,* not for the disparagement of the Muse." Then tossing over the leaf with an air of independence and iron firmness, as if he was not to be influenced by opinions differing from his own on these subjects, he exhibited a striking contrast to the timidity and nervousness of his first appearance at the Surrey Institution.[67]

Although Keats did not attend these lectures, he arranged to borrow Hazlitt's manuscript copies of them.[68] They probably made no very lasting impression on him; after all, they had much less to offer him than did the lectures on the English poets. Yet he was sufficiently taken with Hazlitt's remarks about Godwin in the sixth lecture to copy them at some length in a letter to his brother and sister-in-law in America as "a specimen of [Hazlitt's] usual abrupt manner, and fiery laconiscism."[69]

The summary review of the series, probably by John Hamilton Reynolds, in the *Edinburgh Magazine* was, of course, highly commendatory, as were the reports in the *Examiner* and the *Morning Chronicle.* The *Monthly Review,* which considered these lectures along with *The Characters of Shakespear's Plays* and *Lectures on the English Poets* in their May, 1820, issue, hailed Hazlitt as "perhaps the most sparkling prose-writer of the present day" and prophesied: "All these volumes will be read with luxury on account of their brilliant execution, and with instruction on account of the many delicate remarks which are interspersed among the declamation." But most reviewers ignored the lectures, though they were duly published by Taylor and Hessey in the following year. They probably did not pay Hazlitt the two hundred pounds which he had asked for publication rights, and nothing came of his scheme to deliver them in Edinburgh. However, he was again asked to repeat the series at the Crown and Anchor Tavern, where Coleridge was still lecturing on Shakespeare.[70] He allowed himself only a week's respite, then gave his first lecture at the Crown and Anchor on January 10, 1819.

All in all, Hazlitt's fortunes had improved in the course of the year 1818. He rounded it out with a long review of Horace Walpole's recently published letters to George Montagu, a cheerful essay which appeared in the December issue of the *Edinburgh Review.* Although his earlier review of Reid's *Inquiry into the Human Mind* never appeared in the *Edinburgh* and the article on the fine arts, suggested by Jeffrey, seems never to have been written, he was back now in Jeffrey's fold. And his review of Walpole's letters glowed with pleasure; for although he recognized Walpole's shortcomings as a political thinker, his vanity, and his insensitivity, he praised him as "the very prince of Gossips." He quoted the letters at length, declaring that personal letters were "the honestest records of great minds" (16:141). He complained only about the cost of the book; it was a pity, he wrote, that so few readers could afford to enjoy, as he had, "this lively volume" (16:152).

In the terms of his lecture "On Wit and Humour" Hazlitt could look back on his life during the past twelve months as more comedy than tragedy, more merry than sad. He was still plagued by a loveless marriage and by open hostility from Tory critics. Yet he had made some gains: his health had improved during his summer at Winterslow, and the *Blackwood's* rascals were in retreat. Moreover, he seemed to be in a fair way to solving his perennial money problems; for though Hessey complained in his October 23 letter to Taylor that Hazlitt had called on him two days in succession "of course . . . for more money,"[71] he had found at last a decent livelihood. Lecturing had proved more profitable than he had anticipated; as he told Francis Jeffrey in his letter of May 12, he "got in all (Lectures & copyright included) 200 guineas for them, which is very well for ten weeks work."[72] It had other advantages too: it did not demand his constant presence in London, it involved a good deal of solitary reading and thinking such as he enjoyed, and it might, with luck, eventually free him from the abrasive warfare of contemporary journalism.

Notes

. . .[42] [W. Carew Hazlitt. *The Hazlitts: An Account of Their Origin and Descent*. Edinburgh: Ballantyne, Hanson and Co., 1911], p. 365.

[43] The verse was quoted from Leigh Hunt's poem "To W.H.". . . .

[44] Hazlitt was asked, among other questions, if he had not "wantonly and grossly and indecently insulted Mr. Conway the actor, and published a Retracting Lie in order to escape a caning.". . .

[45] [*The Keats Circle: Letters and Papers 1816-1878*. Edited by Hyder Edward Rollins. 2 vols. Cambridge, Mass.: Harvard University Press, 1948], 1:37.

[46] [*Times Literary Supplement* (London)], 21 March, 1936, p. 244.

[47] [Edmund Blunden. *Keats's Publisher: A Memoir of John Taylor (1781-1864)*. London: Jonathan Cape, 1936], p. 65.

[48] Jones, "Nine New Hazlitt Letters," pp. 276-77.

[49] Constable, *Archibald Constable and His Literary Correspondents,* 2:220-21.

[50] [*Letters of John Keats 1814-1821*. Edited by Hyder Edward Rollins. 2 vols. Cambridge, Mass.: Harvard University Press, 1958], 1:368.

[51] *Minnow Among Tritons,* ed. Stephen Potter (London: Nonesuch Press, 1934), p. 64.

[52] Jones, "Nine New Hazlitt Letters," p. 277.

[53] *Hypocrisy Unveiled and Calumny Detected* (London, 1818), quoted in [P. P. Howe. *Life of William Hazlitt*. New edition with an introduction by Frank Swinnerton. London: Hamish Hamilton, 1947], pp. 269-70.

[54] The complete texts of Blackwood's and Murray's letters appear in Margaret Oliphant, *Annals of a Publishing House: William Blackwood and His Sons,* 3 vols. (New York, 1897), 1:162-70, and Samuel Smiles, *A Publisher and His Friends,* 2 vols. (London, 1891), 1:482-93.

[55] See *TLS,* 22 August, 1935, p. 525.

[56] *New Monthly Magazine* 10 (1818): 198-202, 299-304.

[57] *Keats Letters,* 1:402.

[58] P. P. Howe reprints Hazlitt's eighteen introductions, written between 1818 and 1825, in volume 9 (pp. 63-94) of *Collected Works* and records Hazlitt's borrowing from his earlier works in the notes to the volume.

[59] [Thomas Landseer. *Life and Letters of William Bewick*. 2 vols. London, 1871], 1:145.

[60] *New Monthly Magazine* 29 (1830), pt. 2, p. 473.

[61] [*Henry Crabb Robinson Books and Their Writers*. Edited by Edith J. Morley. 3 vols. London: J. M. Dent and Sons, Ltd., 1938], 1:225. The lecture as published contained no reference to Gifford. Robinson may have been referring to the passage in the opening paragraphs where Hazlitt again cited Samuel Johnson's insensitivity to poetry. Gifford had castigated a similar passage in his review of *The Characters of Shakespear's Plays*. However, Catherine Macdonald Maclean (*Born under Saturn* [London: Collins, 1943], pp. 396-98) points out, from the *Examiner* report of the lecture, that Hazlitt introduced an attack on Canning by referring to him as dedicatee of Gifford's edition of Ben Jonson.

[62] Ibid.

[63] Eleven days before the beginning of the series Hazlitt had prepared little more than half the lectures. On October 23 J. A. Hessey reported to John Taylor that "he has got, he says, the first 4 Lectures written & much of the others" (*Keats Circle,* 1:53).

[64] Robinson, 1:225.

[65] Ibid., p. 226.

[66] In the notes to volume 6 of the *Complete Works,* Howe records Hazlitt's borrowing from his *Edinburgh Review* article "On Standard Novels and Romances" and his Round Table essay "On Hogarth's Marriage a la Mode."

[67] Landseer, 1:147-48.

[68] *Keats Letters,* 2:24 n. Cf. Leonidas M. Jones, "New Letters, Articles and Poems by John Hamilton Reynolds," *Keats-Shelley Journal* 6 (1957):102.

[69] Ibid., p. 24.

[70] Two newspaper articles of this period quoted by Kathleen Coburn in her edition of Coleridge's *Philosophical Lectures* ([London: Routledge and Kegan

Paul, 1949], pp. 34-35) seem to imply that Hazlitt and Cole-ridge were regarded as rival authorities on Shakespeare. In the *Champion* for January 10, 1819, John Thelwall wrote that Coleridge's interpretation of Hamlet "accords with, *if he has not availed himself of,* the opinions of Hazlitt and of another Lecturer [Thelwall himself] whose disquisitions on the character of Hamlet during the last season, excited very popular attention." And an anonymous writer in the *Courier* wrote after Coleridge's lecture on *Lear* on January 28, that he had "none of the glib nonsense of Mr. Hazlitt; no tinkling sentences of pretty phraseology, where big words ram-ble along without meaning, till the reader stares and wonders what it can be that is so utterly unintelligible. Mr. Hazlitt evidently never read a play of Shakespeare through, and the style in which he criticizes him, always reminds us of Bradbury, the clown, dancing upon stilts, where a great clutter, ungainly labour, and violent distortion, are substituted for agility, ease, and elegance."

[71] *Keats Circle,* 1:53.

[72] ALS, Yale University Library. Hazlitt was referring to the *Lectures on the English Poets.*

List of Short Titles Used in the Notes

When two arabic numbers are enclosed in parentheses within the body of the text (e.g., 12:234), they refer to the volume and page of the definitive edition of Hazlitt's works: *Complete Works of William Hazlitt,* ed. P. P. Howe, centenary ed., 21 vols. (London and Toronto: J. M. Dent and Sons, Ltd., 1930-34).

The Hazlitts—W. Carew Hazlitt. *The Hazlitts: An Account of Their Origin and Descent.* Edinburgh: Ballantyne, Hanson and Co., 1911.

Howe—P. P. Howe. *Life of William Hazlitt.* New edition with an introduction by Frank Swinnerton. London: Hamish Hamilton, 1947.

Keats Circle—The Keats Circle: Letters and Papers 1816-1878. Edited by Hyder Edward Rollins. 2 vols. Cambridge, Mass.: Harvard University Press, 1948.

Keats Letters—Letters of John Keats 1814-1821. Edited by Hyder Edward Rollins. 2 vols. Cambridge, Mass.: Harvard University Press, 1958.

Landseer—Thomas Landseer. *Life and Letters of William Bewick.* 2 vols. London, 1871.

Robinson—*Henry Crabb Robinson on Books and Their Writers.* Edited by Edith J. Morley. 3 vols. London: J. M. Dent and Sons, Ltd., 1938.

TLS—Times Literary Supplement (London).

THE POLITICAL AND SOCIAL IMPORT OF THE COCKNEYS AND THEIR CRITICS

Percy B. Shelley (preface date 1821)

SOURCE: Preface to *Adonais: An Elegy on the Death of John Keats, Author of Endymion, Hyperion, Etc.,* by Percy B. Shelley, Pisa, 1821, pp. 3-5.

[*The following is Shelley's Preface to his poem* Adonais: An Elegy on the Death of John Keats, *in which Shelley laments Keats' early death. Although Shelley does not mention John Wilson Croker by name in the Preface, he accuses the* Quarterly Review *critic—whose "savage criticism" of Keats'* Endymion *"produced the most violent effect on [Keats'] susceptible mind"—of precipitating the young poet's untimely death.*]

It is my intention to subjoin to the London edition of this poem, a criticism upon the claims of its lamented object to be classed among the writers of the highest genius who have adorned our age. My known repugnance to the narrow principles of taste on which several of his earlier compositions were modelled, prove, at least that I am an impartial judge. I consider the fragment of *Hyperion,* as second to nothing that was ever produced by a writer of the same years.

John Keats, died at Rome of a consumption, in his twenty-fourth year, on the—of—1821; and was buried in the romantic and lonely cemetery of the protestants in that city, under the pyramid which is the tomb of Cestius, and the massy walls and towers, now mouldering and desolate, which formed the circuit of ancient Rome. The cemetery is an open space among the ruins covered in winter with violets and daisies. It might make one in love with death, to think that one should be buried in so sweet a place.

The genius of the lamented person to whose memory I have dedicated these unworthy verses, was not less delicate and fragile than it was beautiful; and where canker-worms abound, what wonder, if it's young flower was blighted in the bud? The savage criticism on his "Endymion," which appeared in the *Quarterly Review,* produced the most violent effect on his susceptible mind; the agitation thus originated ended in the rupture of a blood-vessel in the lungs; a rapid consumption ensued, and the succeeding acknowledgements from more candid critics, of the true greatness of his powers, were ineffectual to heal the wound thus wantonly inflicted.

It may be well said, that these wretched men know not what they do. They scatter their insults and their slanders without heed as to whether the poisoned shaft lights on a heart made callous by many blows, or one, like Keats's composed of more penetrable stuff. One

Gravestone of John Keats, revealing the impact of critics on one member of the Cockney School

of their associates, is, to my knowledge, a most base and unprincipled calumniator. As to "Endymion"; was it a poem, whatever might be it's defects, to be treated contemptuously by those who had celebrated with various degrees of complacency and panegyric, "Paris," and "Woman", and a "Syrian Tale", and Mrs. Lefanu, and Mr. Barrett, and Mr. Howard Payne, and a long list of the illustrious obscure? Are these the men, who in their venal good nature, presumed to draw a parallel between the Rev. Mr. Milman and Lord Byron? What gnat did they strain at here, after having swallowed all those camels? Against what woman taken in adultery, dares the foremost of these literary prostitutes to cast his opprobrious stone? Miserable man! you, one of the meanest, have wantonly defaced one of the noblest specimens of the workmanship of God. Nor shall it be your excuse, that, murderer as you are, you have spoken daggers, but used none.

The circumstances of the closing scene of poor Keats's life were not made known to me until the "Elegy" was ready for the press. I am given to understand that the wound which his sensitive spirit had received from the criticism of "Endymion", was exasperated by the bitter sense of unrequited benefits; the poor fellow seems to have been hooted from the stage of life, no less by those on whom he had wasted the promise of his genius, than those on whom he had lavished his fortune and his care. He was accompanied to Rome, and attended in his last illness by Mr. Severn, a young artist of the highest promise, who, I have been informed "almost risked his own life," and "sacrificed every prospect to unwearied attendance upon his dying friend." Had I known these circumstances before the completion of my poem, I should have been tempted to add my feeble tribute of applause to the more solid recompense which the virtuous man finds in the recollection of his own motives. Mr. Severn can dispense with a reward from "such stuff as dreams are made of." His conduct is a golden augury of the success of his future career—may the unextinguished Spirit of his illustrious friend animate the creations of his pencil, and plead against Oblivion for his name!

Sidney Colvin (essay date 1917)

SOURCE: "September-December 1818: *Blackwood* and the *Quarterly*," in *John Keats: His Life and Poetry, His Friends, Critics, and After-Fame*, Charles Scribner's Sons, 1917, pp. 297-320.

[*In the following excerpt, Colvin describes the founders of* Blackwood's Magazine, *including their social and political motivations, and discusses the periodical's impact on Keats' professional and personal lives.*]

On the first of September, within a fortnight of Keats's return from the North, appeared the threatened attack on him in Blackwood's *Edinburgh Magazine*. Much as has been said and written on the history and effect of the 'Cockney School' articles, my task requires that the story should be retold, as accurately and fairly as may be, in the light of our present knowledge.

The Whig party in politics and letters had held full ascendency for half a generation in the periodical literature of Scotland by means of the *Edinburgh Review*, published by Archibald Constable and edited at this time by Jeffrey. The Tory rival, the *Quarterly*, was owned and published also by a Scotsman, but a Scotsman migrated to London, John Murray. Early in 1817 William Blackwood, an able Tory bookseller in Edinburgh, projected a new monthly review which should be a thorn in the side of his astute and ambitious trade rival, Constable, and at the same time should hold up the party flag against the blue and yellow Whig colours in the North, and show a livelier and lustier fighting temper than the *Quarterly*. The first number appeared in March under the title of *The Edinburgh Monthly Magazine*. The first editors were two insignificant men who proved neither competent nor loyal, and flat failure threatening the enterprise, Blackwood after six months got rid of the editors and determined to make a fresh start. He added his own name to the title of the magazine and called to his aid two brilliant young men who had been occasional contributors, John Wilson and John Gibson Lockhart, both sound Oxford scholars and Lockhart moreover a well-read modern linguist, both penmen of extraordinary facility and power of work, both at this period of their lives given, in a spirit partly of furious partisanship partly of reckless frolic, to a degree of licence in controversy and satire inconceivable to-day. Wilson, by birth the son of a rich Glasgow manufacturer but now reduced in fortune, was in person a magnificent, florid, blue-eyed athlete of thirty, and in literature the bully and Berserker of the pair. Lockhart, the scion of an ancient Lanarkshire house, a dark, proud, handsome and graceful youth of twenty-three, pensive and sardonically reserved, had a deadly gift of satire and caricature and a lust for exercising it which was for a time uncontrollable like a disease. Wilson had lived on Windermere in the intimacy of Wordsworth and his circle, and already made a certain mark in literature with his poem *The Isle of Palms*. Lockhart had made a few firm friends at Oxford and after his degree had frequented the Goethe circle at Weimar, but was otherwise without social or literary experience. Blackwood was the eager employer and unflinching backer of both. The trio were determined to push the magazine into notoriety by fair means or foul. Its management was informally divided between them, so that no one person could be held responsible. Of Wilson and Lockhart, each was at one time supposed to be editor, but neither ever admitted as much or received separate payment for editorial work. They were really chief contributors and trusted and insistent chief advisers, but Blackwood never let go his own control, and took upon himself, now with effrontery, now with evasion, occasionally with compromise made and satisfaction given, all the risks and rancours which the threefold management chose to incur.

Wilson's obstreperousness, even when he had in some degree sobered down as a university professor, was at all times irresponsible and irrepressible, but for some of the excesses of those days he expressed regret and tried to make atonement; while Lockhart, the vitriol gradually working out of his nature in the sunshine of domestic happiness and of Scott's genial and paternal influence, sincerely repented them when it was too late. But they lasted long enough to furnish one of the most deplorable chapters in our literary history. The fury of political party spirit, infesting the whole field of letters, accounts for, without excusing much. It was a rough unscrupulous time, the literary as well as the political atmosphere thick, as we have seen, with the mud and stones of controversy, flung often very much at random. The *Quarterly,* as conducted by the acrid and deformed pedant Gifford, had no mercy for opponents: and one of the harshest of its contributors was the virtuous Southey. On the other side the Edinburgh, under the more urbane and temperate Jeffrey, could sneer spitefully at all times and abuse savagely enough on occasion, especially when its contributor was Hazlitt. If a notorious Edinburgh attack on Coleridge's *Christabel* volume was really by Hazlitt, as Coleridge always believed and Hazlitt never denied, he in that instance added unpardonable personal ingratitude to a degree of critical blindness amazing in such a man. Even Leigh Hunt, in private life one of the most amiable of hearts, could in controversy on the liberal side be almost as good a damner (to use Keats's phrase) as his ally, the same Hazlitt himself. But nowhere else were such felon strokes dealt in pure wantonness of heart as in the early numbers of Blackwood. The notorious first number opened with an article on Coleridge's *Biographia Literaria* even more furiously insulting than the aforesaid Edinburgh article on *Christabel* attributed to Hazlitt. But for Hazlitt Coleridge was in politics an apostate not to be pardoned, while for the Blackwood group he was no enemy but an ally. Why treat him thus unless it were merely for the purpose of attracting a scandalized attention? More amazing even than the virulence of Black-wood was its waywardness and inconsistency. Will it be believed that less than three years later the same Cole-ridge was being praised and solicited—and what is more, successfully solicited—for contributions? Again, nothing is so much to the credit of Wilson and Lock-hart in those days as their admiration for Wordsworth. The sins of their first number are half redeemed by the article in Wordsworth's praise, a really fine, eloquent piece of work in Wilson's boisterous but not undiscriminating manner of laudation. But not even Wordsworth could long escape the random swash of Wilson's bludgeon, and a very few years later his friends were astonished to read a ferocious outbreak against him in one of the *Noctes* by the same hand. In regard even to the detested Hazlitt the magazine blew in some degree hot and cold, printing through several numbers a series of respectful summaries, supplied from London by Patmore, of his Surrey Institution lectures; in another number a courteous enough estimate of his and Jeffrey's comparative powers in criticism; and a little later taking him to task on one page rudely, but not quite unjustly, for his capricious treatment of Shakespeare's minor poems and on another page addressing to him an insulting catechism full of the vilest personal imputations.

The only contemporary whose treatment by the Blackwood trio is truly consistent was Leigh Hunt, and of him it was consistently blackguardly. To return to the first number of the new series, three articles were counted on to create an uproar. First, the aforesaid emptying of the critical slop-pail on Coleridge. Second, the *Translation from an ancient Chaldee Manuscript,* being a biting personal satire, in language parodied from the Bible, on noted Edinburgh characters, including the Blackwood group themselves, disguised under transparent nicknames that stuck, Blackwood as Ebony, Wilson as the Leopard, Lockhart as the Scorpion that delighteth to sting the faces of men. Third, the article on the Cockney School of Poetry, numbered as the first of the series, headed with a quotation from Cornelius Webb, and signed with the initial 'Z.' As a thing to hang gibes on, the quotation from the unlucky Webb is aptly enough chosen:—

> Our talk shall be (a theme we never tire on)
> Of Chaucer, Spenser, Shakespeare, Milton, Byron,
> (Our England's Dante)—Wordsworth, Hunt, and Keats,
> The Muses' son of promise, and what feats
> He yet may do—

Nor are the gibes themselves quite unjustified so far as they touch merely the underbred insipidities of Leigh Hunt's tea-party manner in *Rimini*. But they are as outrageously absurd as they are gross and libellous when they go on to assail both poem and author on the score of immorality.

> The extreme moral depravity of the Cockney School is another thing which is for ever thrusting itself upon the public attention, and convincing every man of sense who looks into their productions, that they who sport such sentiments can never be great poets. How could any man of high original genius ever stoop publicly, at the present day, to dip his fingers in the least of those glittering and rancid obscenities which float on the surface of Mr Hunt's *Hippocrene?* His poetry is that of a man who has kept company with kept-mistresses. He talks indelicately like a tea-sipping milliner girl. Some excuse for him there might have been, had he been hurried away by imagination or passion. But with him indecency is a disease, as he speaks unclean things from perfect inanition. The very concubine of so impure a wretch as Leigh Hunt would be to be pitied, but alas! for the wife of such a husband! For him there is no charm in simple seduction; and he gloats over it only when accompanied with adultery and incest.

Such is the manner in which these censors set about showing their superior breeding and scholarship. 'Z' was in most cases probably a composite and not a single personality, but the respective shares of Wilson and Lockhart can often be confidently enough disentangled by those who know their styles.

The scandal created by the first number exceeded what its authors had hoped or expected. All Edinburgh was in a turmoil about the *Chaldee Manuscript,* the victims writhing, their enemies chuckling, law-suits threatening right and left. In London the commotion was scarcely less. The London agents for the sale of the Magazine protested strongly, and Blackwood had to use some hard lying in order to pacify them. Murray, who had a share in the Magazine, soon began remonstrating against its scurrilities, and on their continuance withdrew his capital. Leigh Hunt in the *Examiner* retorted upon 'Z' with natural indignation and a peremptory demand for the disclosure of his name. The libellers hugged their anonymity, and at first showed some slight movement of panic. In a second edition of the first number the *Chaldee Manuscript* was omitted and the assault on Hunt made a little less gross and personal. For a while Hunt vigorously threatened legal proceedings, but after some time desisted, whether from lack of funds or doubt of a verdict or inability to identify his assailant we do not know, and declared, and stuck to the declaration, that he would take no farther notice. The attacks were soon renewed more savagely than ever. The second of the 'Z' papers alone is scholarly and relatively reasonable. Its phrase, 'the genteel comedy of incest,' fitly enough labels *Rimini* in contrast with the tragic treatment of kindred themes by real masters, as Sophocles, Dante, Ford, Alfieri, Schiller, even Byron in *Manfred* and *Parisina.* The third article, and two other attacks in the form of letters addressed directly to Hunt with the same signature, are merely rabid and outrageous. Correspondents having urged in protest that Hunt's domestic life was blameless, the assailant says in effect, so much the greater his offence for writing a profligate and demoralizing poem; and to this preposterous charge against one of the mildest pieces of milk-and-water sentimentality in all literature he returns (or they return) with furious iteration.

The reasons for this special savagery against Hunt have never been made fully clear. He and his circle used to think it was partly due to his slighting treatment of Scott in the *Feast of the Poets:* nay, they even idly imagined for a moment that Scott himself had been the writer,—Scott, than whom no man was ever more magnanimously and humorously indifferent to harsh criticism or less capable of lifting a finger to resent it. But some of Scott's friends and idolaters in Edinburgh were sensitive on his behalf as he never was on his own. Even for the Blackwood assault on Coleridge one rumoured reason was that Coleridge had rudely denounced a play, the *Bertram* of Maturin, admired and recommended to Drury Lane by Scott; and it is, as a matter of fact, conceivable that a similar excess of loyalty may have had something to do with the rancour of the 'Z' articles.

Looking back on the way in which the name of this great man got mixed up in some minds with matters so far beneath him, it seems worth while to set forth exactly what were his relations at this time to Blackwood and the Blackwood group. About 1816-1817 the two rival publishers, Blackwood and Constable, were hot competitors for Scott's favour, and Constable had lately scored a point in the game in the matter of the *Tales of my Landlord.* It became in the eyes of Blackwood and his associates a vital matter to secure some kind of countenance from Scott for their new venture. They knew they would never attach him as a partisan or secure a monopoly of his favours, and the authors of the *Chaldee Manuscript* divined his attitude wittily and shrewdly when they represented him as giving precisely the same answer to each of the two publishers who courted him, thus. (The man in plain apparel is Blackwood and the Jordan is the Tweed):—

> 44. Then spake the man clothed in plain apparel to the great magician who dwelleth in the old fastness, hard by the river Jordan, which is by the Border. And the magician opened his mouth, and said, Lo! my heart wisheth thy good, and let the thing prosper which is in thy hands to do it.
>
> 45. But thou seest that my hands are full of working and my labour is great. For lo I have to feed all the people of my land, and none knoweth whence his food cometh, but each man openeth his mouth, and my hand filleth it with pleasant things.
>
> 46. Moreover, thine adversary also is of my familiars.
>
> 47. The land is before thee, draw thou up thy hosts for the battle in the place of Princes, over against thine adversary, which hath his station near the mount of the Proclamation; quit ye as men, and let favour be shewn unto him which is most valiant.
>
> 48. Yet be thou silent, peradventure will I help thee some little.

More shrewdly still, Blackwood bethought himself of the one and only way of practically enlisting Scott, and that was by promising permanent work on the magazine for his friend, tenant, and dependent, William Laidlaw, whom he could never do enough to help. So it was arranged that Laidlaw should regularly contribute a chronicle on agricultural and antiquarian topics, and that Scott should touch it up and perhaps occasionally add a paragraph or short article of his own. In point of fact the peccant first number contains such an article, an entertaining enough little skit 'On the alarming Increase of Depravity among Animals.' After the number had appeared Scott wrote to Blackwood in tempered approval, but saying that he must withdraw his support if satire like that of the *Chaldee Manuscript* was to continue. He had been pleased and tickled with the prophetic picture of his own neutrality, but strongly disapproved the sting and malice of much of the rest.

One cannot but wish he had put his foot down in like manner about the 'Cockney School' and other excesses: but home—that is Edinburgh—affairs and personages interested him much more than those of London. Lockhart he did not yet personally know. They first met eight months later, in June 1818: the acquaintance ripened rapidly into firm devotion on Lockhart's part—for this young satirist could love as staunchly as he could stab unmercifully—a devotion requited with an answering warmth of affection on the part of Scott. At an early stage of their relations Scott, recognizing with regret that his young friend was 'as mischievous as a monkey,' got an offer for him of official work which would have freed him of his ties to Blackwood. In like manner two years later Scott threw himself heart and soul into the contest on behalf of Wilson for the Edinburgh chair of moral philosophy, not merely as the Tory candidate, but in the hope—never fully realised—that the office would tame his combative extravagances as well as give scope for his serious talents. And when the battle was won and Lockhart, now Scott's son-in-law, crowed over it in a set of verses which Scott thought too vindictive, he remonstrated in a strain of admirable grave and affectionate wisdom:—

> I have hitherto avoided saying anything on this subject, though some little turn towards personal satire is, I think, the only drawback to your great and powerful talents, and I think I may have hinted as much to you. But I wished to see how this matter of Wilson's would turn, before making a clean breast upon this subject. . . . Now that he has triumphed I think it would be bad taste to cry out—'Strike up our drums—pursue the scattered stray.' Besides, the natural consequence of his situation must be his relinquishing his share in these compositions—at least, he will injure himself in the opinion of many friends, and expose himself to a continuation of galling and vexatious disputes to the embittering of his life, should he do otherwise. In that case I really hope you will pause before you undertake to be the Boaz of the Maga; I mean in the personal and satirical department, when the Jachin has seceded.
>
> Besides all other objections of personal enemies, personal quarrels, constant obloquy, and all uncharitableness, such an occupation will fritter away your talents, hurt your reputation both as a lawyer and a literary man, and waste away your time in what at best will be but a monthly wonder. What has been done in this department will be very well as a frolic of young men, but let it suffice. . . . Remember it is to the *personal* satire I object, and to the horse-play of your raillery. . . . Revere yourself, my dear boy, and think you were born to do your country better service than in this species of warfare. I make no apology (I am sure you will require none) for speaking plainly what my anxious affection dictates. . . . I wish you to have the benefit of my experience without purchasing it; and be assured, that the consciousness of attaining complete superiority over your calumniators and enemies by the force of your general character, is worth a dozen of triumphs over them by the force of wit and raillery.

It took a longer time and harder lessons to cure Lockhart of the scorpion habit and wean him from the seductions of the 'Mother of Mischief,' as Scott in another place calls *Blackwood's Magazine*. Meantime he had in the case of Keats done as much harm as he could. He had not the excuse of entire ignorance. His intimate friend Christie (afterwards principal in the John Scott duel) was working at the bar in London and wrote to Lockhart in January 1818 that he had met Keats and been favourably impressed by him. In reply Lockhart writes: 'What you say of Keates (sic) is pleasing, and if you like to write a little review of him, in admonition to leave his ways, etc., and in praise of his natural genius, I shall be greatly obliged to you.' Later Benjamin Bailey had the opportunity of speaking with Lockhart in Keats's behalf. Bailey had by this time taken orders, and after publishing a friendly notice of *Endymion* in the *Oxford Herald* for June, had left the University and gone to settle in a curacy in Cumberland. In the course of the summer he staid at Stirling, at the house of Bishop Gleig; whose son, afterwards the well-known writer and chaplain-general to the forces, was his friend, and whose daughter he soon afterwards married. Here Bailey met Lockhart, and anxious to save Keats from the sort of treatment to which Hunt had already been exposed, took the opportunity of telling him in a friendly way Keats's circumstances and history, explaining at the same time that his attachment to Leigh Hunt was personal and not political; pleading that he should not be made an object of party denunciation; and ending with the request that at any rate what had been thus said in confidence should not be used to his disadvantage. To which Lockhart replied that certainly it should not be so used by *him*. Within three weeks the article appeared, making use to all appearance, and to Bailey's great indignation, of the very facts he had thus confidentially communicated.[1]

'That amiable but infatuated bardling, Mister John Keats,' had received a certain amount of attention from 'Z' already, both in the quotation from Cornelius Webb prefixed to the Cockney School articles, and in allusion to Hunt's pair of sonnets on the intercoronation scene which he had printed in his volume, *Foliage*, since the 'Z' series began. When now Keats's own turn came, in the fourth article of the series, his treatment was almost mild in comparison with that of his supposed leader. 'This young man appears to have received from nature talents of an excellent, perhaps even of a superior, order—talents which, devoted to the purposes of any useful profession, must have rendered him a respectable, if not an eminent citizen.' But, says the critic, he has unfortunately fallen a victim to the *metromania* of the hour; the wavering apprentice has been confirmed in his desire to quit the gallipots by his admiration for 'the most worthless and affected of all the versifiers of our time.' 'Mr Hunt is a small poet, but he is a clever man, Mr Keats is a still smaller poet, and he is only a boy of pretty abilities which he has done everything in his power to spoil.' And so on; and so on; not of course omitting to put a finger on real weaknesses, as lack of scholarship, the use of Cockney rimes like *higher, Thalia; ear, Cytherea; thorn, fawn;* deriding the Boileau passage in *Sleep and Poetry,* and perceiving nothing but laxity and nervelessness in the treatment of the metre. In the conceit of academic talent and training, the critic shows himself open-eyed to all the faults and stone-blind to all the beauty and genius and promise, and ends with a vulgarity of supercilious patronage beside which all the silly venial faults of taste in Leigh Hunt seem like good breeding itself.

> And now, good-morrow to 'the Muses' son of Promise;' as for 'the feats he yet may do,' as we do not pretend to say like himself, 'Muse of my native land am I inspired,' we shall adhere to the safe old rule of *pauca verba*. We venture to make one small prophecy, that his bookseller will not a second time venture £50 upon any thing he can write. It is a better and a wiser thing to be a starved apothecary than a starved poet; so back to the shop Mr John, back to 'plasters, pills, and ointment boxes,' etc. But, for Heaven's sake, young Sangrado, be a little more sparing of extenuatives and soporifics in your practice than you have been in your poetry.

There is a lesson in these things. I remember the late Mr Andrew Lang, one of the most variously gifted and richly equipped critical minds of our time, and under a surface vein of flippancy essentially kind-hearted,—I remember Mr Andrew Lang, in a candid mood of conversation, wondering whether in like circumstances he might not have himself committed a like offence, and with no *Hyperion* or *St Agnes' Eve* or *Odes* yet written and only the 1817 volume and *Endymion* before him, have dismissed Keats fastidiously and scoffingly. Who knows?—and let us all take warning. But now-a-days the errors of criticism are perhaps rather of an opposite kind, and any rashness and rawness of undisciplined novelty is apt to find itself indulged and fostered rather than repressed. What should at any time have saved *Endymion* from harsh judgment, if the quality of the poetry could not save it, was the quality of the preface. How could either carelessness or rancour not recognize, not augur the best from, its fine spirit of manliness and modesty and self-knowledge?

The responsibility for the gallipots article, as for so many others in the *Blackwood* of the time, may have been in some sort collective. But that Lockhart had the chief share in it is certain. According to Dilke, he in later life owned as much. To those who know his hand, he stands confessed not only in the general gist and style but in particular phrases. One is the use of Sangrado for doctor, a use which both Scott and Lock-hart had caught from *Gil Blas*.[2] Others are the allusions to the *Métromanie* of Piron and the *Endymion* of Wieland, particularly the latter. Wieland's *Oberon,* as we have seen, had made its mark in England through Sotheby's translation, but no other member of the Blackwood group is the least likely to have had any acquaintance with his untranslated minor works except Lockhart, whose stay at Weimar had given him a familiar knowledge of contemporary German literature. In the *Mad Banker of Amsterdam,* a comic poem in the vein of Frere's *Whistlecraft* and Byron's *Beppo,* contributed by him at this time to *Blackwood* under one of his Protean pseudonyms, as 'William Wastle Esq.,' Lockhart sketches his own likeness as follows:—

> Then touched I off friend Lockhart (Gibson John),
> So fond of jabbering about Tieck and Schlegel,
> Klopstock and *Wieland,* Kant and Mendelssohn,
> All High Dutch quacks, like Spurzheim or Feinagle—
> Him the Chaldee yclept the Scorpion.—
> The claws, but not the pinions, of the eagle,
> Are Jack's, but though I do not mean to flatter,
> Undoubtedly he has strong powers of satire.

Bailey to the end of his life never forgave Lockhart for what he held to be a base breach of faith after their conversation above mentioned, and his indignation communicated itself to the Keats circle and afterwards, as we shall see, to Keats himself. Mr Andrew Lang, in his excellent *Life* of Lockhart, making such defence as is candidly possible for his hero's share in the *Blackwood* scandals, urges justly enough that the only matter of fact divulged about Keats by 'Z' is that of his having been apprenticed to a surgeon ('Z' prefers to say an apothecary) and that thus much Lockhart could not well help knowing independently, either from his own friend Christie or from Bailey's friend and future brother-in-law Gleig, then living at Edinburgh and about to become one of *Blackwood's* chief supporters. When in farther defence of 'Z's' attacks on Hunt Mr Lang quotes from Keats's letters phrases in dispraise of Hunt almost as strong as those used by 'Z' himself, he forgets the world of difference there is between the confidential criticism, in a passing mood or whim of impatience, of a friend by a friend to a friend and the gross and reiterated public defamation of a political and literary opponent.

Lockhart in after life pleaded the rawness of youth, and also that in the random and incoherent violences of the early years of *Blackwood* there had been less of real and settled malice than in the *Quarterly Review* as at that time conducted. The plea may be partly admitted, but to forgive him we need all the gratitude which is his due for his filial devotion to and immortal biography of Scott, as well as all the allowance to be made for a dangerous gift and bias of nature.

The *Quarterly* article on *Endymion* followed in the last week of September (in the number dated April,—such in those days was editorial punctuality). It is now known to have been the work of John Wilson Croker, a man of many sterling gifts and honourable loyalties, unjustly blackened in the eyes of posterity by Macaulay's rancorous dislike and Disraeli's masterly caricature, but in literature as in politics the narrowest and stiffest of conservative partisans. Like his editor Gifford, he was trained in strict allegiance to eighteenth-century tradition and the school of Pope. His brief review of *Endymion* is that of a man insensible to the higher charm of poetry, incapable of judging it except by mechanical rule and precedent, and careless of the pain he gives. He professes to have been unable to read beyond the first canto, or to make head or tail of that, and what is worse, turns the frank avowals of Keats's preface foolishly and unfairly against him. At the same time, like Lockhart, he does not fail to point out and exaggerate real weaknesses of Keats's early manner, and the following, from the point of view of a critic who sees no salvation outside the closed couplet, is not unreasonable criticism:—

> He seems to us to write a line at random, and then he follows not the thought excited by this line, but that suggested by the *rhyme* with which it concludes. There is hardly a complete couplet inclosing a complete idea in the whole book. He wanders from one subject to another, from the association, not of ideas but of sounds, and the work is composed of hemistichs which, it is quite evident, have forced themselves upon the author by the mere force of the catchwords on which they turn.

In another of the established reviews, *The British Critic,* a third censor came out with a notice even more contemptuous than those of *Blackwood* and the *Quarterly.* For a moment Keats's pride winced, as any man's might, under the personal insults of the critics, and dining in the company of Hazlitt and Woodhouse with Mr Hessey, the publisher, he seems to have declared in Woodhouse's hearing that he would write no more. But he quickly recovered his balance, and in a letter to Dilke of a few days later, speaking of Hazlitt's wrath against the *Blackwood* scribes, is silent as to their treatment of himself. Meantime some of his friends and more than one stranger were actively sympathetic and indignant on his behalf. A just and vigorous expostulation appeared in the *Morning Chronicle* under the initials J. S.,—those in all likelihood of John Scott, then editor of the *London Magazine,* not long afterwards killed by Lockhart's friend Christie in a needless and blundering duel arising out of these very Blackwood brawls. Bailey, being in Edinburgh, had an interview with *Blackwood* and pleaded to be allowed to contribute a reply to his magazine; and this being refused, sought out Constable, who besides the *Edinburgh Review* conducted the monthly periodical which had been kind to Keats's first volume,[3] and proposed to publish in it an attack on Blackwood and the 'Z' articles: but Constable would not take the risk. Reynolds published in a west-country paper, the *Alfred,* a warm rejoinder to the *Quarterly* reviewer, containing a judicious criticism in brief of Keats's work, with remarks very much to the point on the contrast between his and the egotistical (meaning Wordsworth's) attitude to nature. This Leigh Hunt reprinted with some introductory words in the *Examiner,* and later in life regretted that he had not done more. But he could not have done more to any purpose. He was not himself an enthusiastic admirer of *Endymion,* had plainly said so to Keats and to his friends, and would have got out of his depth if he had tried to appreciate the intensity and complexity of symbolic and spiritual meaning which made that poem so different from his own shallow, self-pleasing metrical versions of classic or Italian tales. Reynolds's piece, which he re-printed, was quite effective and to the point as far as it went; and moreover any formal defence of Keats by Hunt would only have increased the virulence of his enemies, as they both perfectly well knew. Privately at the same time Reynolds, who had just been reading *The Pot of Basil* in manuscript, wrote to his friend with affectionate wisdom as follows:—

> As to the poem, I am of all things anxious that you should publish it, for its completeness will be a full answer to all the ignorant malevolence of cold, lying Scotchmen and stupid Englishmen. The overweening struggle to oppress you only shows the world that so much of endeavour cannot be directed to nothing. Men do not set their muscles and strain their sinews to break a straw. I am confident, Keats, that the 'Pot of Basil' hath that simplicity and quiet pathos which are of a sure sovereignty over all hearts. I must say that it would delight me to have you prove yourself to the world what we know you to be—to have you annul *The Quarterly Review* by the best of all answers. One or two of your sonnets you might print, I am sure. And I know that I may suggest to you which, because you can decide as you like afterward. You will remember that we were to print together. I give over all intention, and you ought to be alone. I can never write anything now—my mind is taken the other way. But I shall set my heart on having you high, as you ought to be. Do *you* get Fame, and I shall have it in being your affectionate and steady friend.

Woodhouse, in a correspondence with the unceasingly kind and loyal publishers Taylor and Hessey, shows himself as deeply moved as anyone, and Taylor in the course of the autumn sought to enlist on behalf of the victim the private sympathies of one of the most cultivated and influential Liberal thinkers and publicists of the time, Sir James Mackintosh. Sending him a copy of *Endymion,* Taylor writes:—'Its faults are numberless, but there are redeeming features in my opinion, and the faults are those of real Genius. Whatever this work is, its Author is a true poet.' After a few words as to Keats's family and circumstances he adds, 'These are odd particulars to give, when I am introducing the work and not the man to you,—but if you knew him, you would also feel that strange personal interest in all that concerns him.—Mr Gifford forgot his own early life when he tried to bear down this young man. Happily, it will not succeed. If he lives, Keats will be the brightest ornament of this Age.' In concluding Taylor recommends particularly to his correspondent's attention the hymn to Pan, the Glaucus episode, and above all the triumph of Bacchus.

Proud in the extreme, Keats had no irritable vanity; and aiming in his art, if not always steadily, yet always at the highest, he rather despised than courted such successes as he saw some of his contemporaries—Thomas Moore, for instance, with *Lalla Rookh*—enjoy. 'I hate,' he says, 'a mawkish popularity.' Wise recognition and encouragement would no doubt have helped and cheered him, but even in the hopes of permanent fame which he avowedly cherished, there was nothing intemperate or impatient; and he was conscious of perceiving his own shortcomings at least as clearly as his critics. Accordingly he took his treatment at their hands more coolly than older and more experienced men had taken the like. Hunt, as we have seen, had replied indignantly to his *Blackwood* traducers, repelling scorn with scorn, and he and Hazlitt were both at first red-hot to have the law of them. Keats after the first sting with great dignity and simplicity treated the annoyance as one merely temporary, indifferent, and external. When early in October Mr Hessey sent for his encouragement the extracts from the papers in which he had been defended, he wrote:—

> I cannot but feel indebted to those gentlemen who have taken my part. As for the rest, I begin to get a little acquainted with my own strength and weakness. Praise or blame has but a momentary effect on the man whose love of beauty in the abstract makes him a severe critic on his own works. My own domestic criticism has given me pain without comparison beyond what 'Blackwood' or the 'Quarterly' could possibly inflict—and also when I feel I am right, no external praise can give me such a glow as my own solitary re-perception and ratification of what is fine. J. S. is perfectly right in regard to the slip-shod *Endymion*. That it is so is no fault of mine. No!—though it may sound a little paradoxical. It is as good as I had power to make it—by myself. Had I been nervous about its being a perfect piece, and with that view asked advice, and trembled over every page, it would not have been written; for it is not in my nature to fumble—I will write independently.—I have written independently *without Judgment*. I may write independently, and *with Judgment,* hereafter. The Genius of Poetry must work out its own salvation in a man: It cannot be matured by law and precept, but by sensation and watchfulness in itself. That which is creative must create itself. In *Endymion* I leaped headlong into the sea, and thereby have become better acquainted with the Soundings, the quicksands, and the rocks, than if I had stayed upon the green shore, and piped a silly pipe, and took tea and comfortable advice. I was never afraid of failure;

> for I would sooner fail than not be among the greatest. But I am nigh getting into a rant.

Two or three weeks later, in answer to a similar encouraging letter from Woodhouse, he explains, in sentences luminous with self-knowledge, what he calls his own chameleon character as a poet, and the variable and impressionable temperament such a character implies. 'Where then,' he adds, 'is the wonder that I should say I would write no more? Might I not at that very instant have been cogitating on the characters of Saturn and Ops? . . . I know not whether I make myself wholly understood: I hope enough to make you see that no dependence is to be placed on what I said that day.' And again about the same time to his brother and sister-in-law:—

> There have been two letters in my defence in the 'Chronicle,' and one in the 'Examiner,' copied from the Exeter paper, and written by Reynolds. I don't know who wrote those in the 'Chronicle.' This is a mere matter of the moment: I think I shall be among the English Poets after my death. Even as a matter of present interest, the attempt to crush me in the 'Quarterly' has only brought me more into notice, and it is a common expression among bookmen, 'I wonder the "Quarterly" should cut its own throat.'
>
> It does me not the least harm in Society to make me appear little and ridiculous: I know when a man is superior to me and give him all due respect—he will be the last to laugh at me and as for the rest I feel that I make an impression upon them which ensures me personal respect while I am in sight whatever they may say when my back is turned.

Since these firm expressions of indifference to critical attack have been before the world, it has been too confidently assumed that Shelley and Byron were totally misled and wide of the mark when they believed that *Blackwood* and the *Quarterly* had killed Keats or even much hurt him. But the truth is that not they, but their consequences, did in their degree help to kill him. It must not be supposed that such words of wisdom and composure, manifestly sincere as they are, represent the whole of Keats, or anything like the whole. They represent, indeed, the admirably sound and manly elements which were a part of him: they show us the veins of what Matthew Arnold calls flint and iron in his nature uppermost. But he was no Wordsworth, to remain all flint and iron in indifference to derision and in the scorn of scorn. He had not only in a tenfold degree the ordinary acuteness of a poet's feelings: he had the variable and chameleon temperament of which he warns Woodhouse while in the very act of re-assuring him: he had along with the flint and iron a strong congenital tendency, against which he was always fighting but not always successfully, to fits of depression and self-torment. Moreover the reviews of those days, especially the *Edinburgh* and *Quarterly,* had a real power of barring the acceptance and checking the sale of an author's work. What actually happened was that when a year or so later Keats began to realise the harm which the reviews had done and were doing to his material prospects, these consequences in his darker hours preyed on him severely and conspired with the forces of disease and passion to his undoing. . . .

Notes

[1] Houghton MSS.

[2] The source is the Spanish *sangrador,* blood-letter; which Le Sage in *Gil Blas* converts into a proper name, Sangrado.

[3] The old *Scots Magazine* lately re-started under a new name. . . .

Keats to Benjamin Bailey, 3 November 1817, on the *Blackwood's* series "The Cockney School of Poetry":

There has been a flaming attack upon Hunt in the *Endinburgh Magazine* [October, 1817]—I never read any thing so virulent—accusing him of the greatest Crimes—de-p[r]eciating his Wife his Poetry—his Habits—his com-pany, his Conversation—These Philipics are to come out in Numbers—calld 'the Cockney School of Poetry' There has been but one Number published—that on Hunt to which they have prefixed a Motto from one Cornelius Webb Poetaster—who unfortunately was of our Party occasionally at Hampstead and took it into his head to write the following—something about—"we'll talk on Wordsworth Byron—a theme we never tire on and so forth till he comes to Hunt and Keats. In the Motto they have put Hunt and Keats in large Letters—I have no doubt that the second Number was intended for me: but have hopes of its non appearance from the following advertisement in last Sunday's *Examiner*. "To Z. The writer of the Article signed Z in *Blackwood's Ed[i]nburgh* magazine for October 1817 is invited to send his address to the printer of the *Examiner,* in order that Justice may be executed of the proper person" I dont mind the thing much—but if he should go to such lengths with me as he has done with Hunt I mu[s]t infalibly call him to an account—if he be a human being and appears in Squares and Theatres where we might possibly meet—I dont relish his abuse.

John Keats, in a letter to Benjamin Bailey, November 3, 1817, reprinted in The Letters of John Keats, 1814-1821, Volume I, *edited by Hyder Edward Rollins, Harvard University Press, 1958.*

John O. Hayden (essay date 1969)

SOURCE: "The Cockney School," in *The Romantic Reviewers: 1802-1824,* Routledge and Kegan Paul, 1969, pp. 176-215.

[*In the following excerpt, Hayden surveys the contemporary critical reviews of Leigh Hunt's poetry, which frequently focus on his expressed political views.*]

The idea of a 'Cockney School of Poetry' was originated by John Gibson Lockhart in *Blackwood's Magazine* in a scurrilous series of articles begun in October, 1817. In the same month, the *Edinburgh Magazine* recognized a literary group which included the same writers, Leigh Hunt, John Keats, and William Hazlitt. Thus it is evident that the grouping by *Blackwood's* is not ascribable solely to a desire for lumping together offensive writers for ease of attack, as was largely the case with Southey's vaguely descriptive 'Satanic School'.

The Cockney School was, in fact, the nearest approach to a literary school of any so denominated by the reviewers. The members lived in the London area and they were friends. More important, they shared certain attitudes toward life and literature, as well as certain peculiarities of style and sentiment. Ironically, Hazlitt's writings had the least of the vulgarity which the title 'Cockney' was meant to designate, but he was more often than Hunt or Keats attacked as a 'Cockney'.

Much of the abuse discharged at the Cockneys was, of course, political. With Leigh Hunt, who was in many ways the center of the group, editing the radical *Examiner* during most of the period, this should surprise no one. What is remarkable, however, was the extent to which their political affiliations were more an asset than a liability, as we shall see.

Leigh Hunt

In the light of Leigh Hunt's well-known skirmishes with *Blackwood's Magazine,* the relations of the 'King of the Cockneys' with his reviewers would most likely be thought to have been hostile, but such is not the case. The 'On the Cockney School of Poetry' series in that periodical, it is true, deal mainly with Hunt, but most of the articles are not reviews but invective of the lowest order. In any case, *Blackwood's* did not reflect the opinion of the reviewers as a whole, who rendered favorable judgments on most of Hunt's publications.

The first of these, the *Critical Essays on the Performers of the London Theatres* (1807), contained selections of Hunt's dramatic criticism as published in the *News*. It was in general well received, with particular approbation given to his judgment, impartiality, and taste. Qualifications took the form of censure of stylistic blemishes, such as quaint diction (for example, 'close wideness'), evident immaturity in thinking, and unsuccessful attempts at humor. Hunt's only other extensive prose publication in the period under study, *An Attempt to Shew the Folly and Danger of Methodism* (1809), was likewise a collection of articles published previously, this time in the *Examiner*. It received only two reviews, both favorable.

Discounting Hunt's verses in the *Examiner,* which received a gratuitous hostile review in the *Satirist,* his first poetic publication after 1802 was *The Feast of the Poets* (1814). As with the prose pieces, this satiric poem met with a majority of favorable verdicts though there was a good deal of adverse criticism of the slovenliness and vulgarity of the style. Hunt's vanity also came under good-humored fire in the *Critical Review,* which commented on Hunt's statement of reluctance, as a critic himself, to publish verse:

> There is a constitutional quality in this gentleman which operates so undisguisedly—a frankness of assumption, which proves him to be on such excellent terms with himself, that we hear of his perplexity with a most satisfied persuasion of its philosophical endurance. . . . [And yet] a little solemn coxcombry, when united to ability and good intention is pardonable enough; and possibly not the less palatable for a slight perception of the ridiculous which attends our regard of it.[1]

The *Critical Review* also observed that Hunt went too far in taking his attacks on the poets into their private lives; and the *Monthly Review* remarked: 'He plays the part of a critic with less mercy than the most merciless of reviewers. . . .'[2] A fit time for the *Satirist* to prefigure *Blackwood's* bitter, personal abuse: Hunt is 'in politics, a drivelling man-milliner; and in literature, an empty coxcomb'.[3]

In the following year, Hunt published *The Descent of Liberty,* an attempt to revive the form of the masque. Again the reception was more favorable than otherwise, but critical opposition was gaining momentum (with, however, only the monthlies and one weekly concerned). There was good reason for the increased hostility; for unlike the light-hearted satire which preceded it, the masque was a serious attempt to succeed with a difficult form and was a failure on many counts. Even John Scott in the *Champion,* who praised the poet and his work to the skies, had to condemn Hunt's affectation and familiarity, and, a more important failing, his allowance of 'a too licentious indulgence of the shadowy gleamings of his fancy, by permitting them to escape him in language like themselves, half-formed, new coined, and unsanctioned'.[4] Scott explained:

> The difficulty of finding words to represent all that passes within the poet's mind, is, in many respects, salutary;—it drives him to the necessity of selecting with some reference to the understandings, tastes, and habits of his readers; it forces him to define what he would otherwise leave vague,—and, in short, forms his and the public's best security, against his being seduced to outpour upon them the egotism, wildness, crudity, and rawness of his secret breast, instead of

> presenting a refined and assorted col-lection of what is truly valuable, suitable, and pleasing.

The best criticism of the masque, however, was delivered by the *Theatrical Inquisitor*. After praising Hunt's integrity and independence and censuring his egotism and over-confidence, the reviewer attacks the allegory, 'a species of writing much too abstracted to be entertaining', made even worse here by 'its making an improbable fiction of reality [the political situation on the Continent], and consequently destroying the interest of the tale'.[5] The long-winded, ludicrous stage directions are next ridiculed as they deserved. But the reviewer was just warming up to more serious charges: 'The language is often rugged, the metre in many lines is deficient, the ideas trite and quaintly expressed.' One of many stated examples of the latter is a *'Wrapping* looks and *balmy* tongue', and the comment on all the examples was:

> Surely no reader of taste or common understanding will accept of these unmeaning phrases as the genuine language of poetry. Even supposing, which is not the case, that the ideas were poetical, the want of just expression would still be felt as a most intolerable defect; for although it must be confessed that words are nothing more than the symbols of ideas, yet the beauty and appropriate use of these symbols form the second great source of the pleasure we receive from poetry.[6]

Then the meaning of passages is questioned: for example, airs 'feel as they were fit for *hearts* and eyes / To *breathe* and sparkle in' (italics added by the reviewer). 'The idea of hearts breathing', he commented, 'has at least the merit of novelty.'[7] Examples of rugged meter ('And summon from their waiting climes / The pleasures that perfect victorious times') and of familiarity ('Phaniel, if your cloud holds two, / I'll come up, and sit with you') were also given. The reviewer observed:

> By a strange contradiction of judgment, or of feeling, he has written on two very opposite principles; sometimes he has affected a homeliness of language and ideas, that is almost disgusting; and at other times he has heaped together, without any meaning, a parcel of high-sounding words. . . . [8]

The review ends with the hope that Hunt will abandon poetry and stick to politics: 'In the one he will only lose that credit which he has obtained in the other.'[9]

In the following year (1816), Hunt published what is easily his best original work in verse, *The Story of Rimini*. The reviewers certainly thought it was the best published to that point, and for the first time the quarterlies became involved. Only the *Quarterly Review* and the *New Monthly Magazine* were hostile, although all of those reviewing the poem had reservations of one kind or another.

But the freshness and vigor of the execution received a good deal of praise. Jeffrey (probably drawing upon a MS review by Hazlitt) in the *Edinburgh Review* thought the tone very like Chaucer's, except that Hunt's homeliness and directness often seemed forced. Hunt's vivid descriptions were praised by many reviewers, and Jeffrey noted that the activity being described in the opening account of the procession was reflected in the gaiety and movement of the verse. The progress of the passion of Paulo and Francesca also received favorable comment from many hands.

But then there was the obstacle of Hunt's style, which had, in the words of the *Literary Panorama,* 'imperfections easily pointed out, by men who possess no proportion of his powers'. In this review is also perhaps the best description of the effect of reading the poem:

> In this poem he indulges himself in description, and his ideas, his versification, his management are so lively, graceful, and applicable, that the reader shares with him in the delight of his composition, which, perhaps, is as great a compliment as words can utter. Amidst this gratification the reader detects in slovenly affectation of ease, the constraint of Art, a kind of occasional slipshod hitch in the verse. . . .[10]

Another incidental but discerning point was that

> In a short poem points of time, or incident, may occur, in which the mind feels the disadvantage resulting from early exhaustion. The mind feels that excessive labour has been bestowed on opening incidents, and to place this labour where it would be more effectual, a part at least of what has been read must be forgot; a new train of ideas, the same, yet not the same, demanded by the imagination, excite a dangerous kind of rivalship, and the poet must forego them, because he has already introduced others so nearly alike, that the most careless reader must detect the resemblance.[11]

The most important defect in the poem, however, was pointed out by Jeffrey in the *Edinburgh Review:* 'The diction of this little poem is among its chief beauties—and yet its greatest blemishes are faults in diction.—It is very English throughout—but often very affectedly negligent, and so extremely familiar as to be absolutely low and vulgar.'[12] Some examples given are 'a scattery light' and 'a clipsome waist'.

In the Preface to the poem, Hunt had echoed Wordsworth's Preface to the *Lyrical Ballads* of 1800: 'The proper language of poetry is in fact nothing different from that of real life. . . .' And thus the whole controversy in which the reviewers were still engaged at this time with respect to Wordsworth's theories was provoked for the moment in reviews of *The Story of Rimini.* Unfortunately—for those theories—Hunt's poetic practice made only too easy a mark for the opposition. It was so easy, in fact, that the controversy is uninteresting in comparison with the discussion of Wordsworth's theories and practice. John Wilson Croker in the *Quarterly Review* merely quotes from Hunt's Preface, which admits that 'of course mere vulgarisms and fugitive phrases' must be excluded, and comments:

> If there be one fault more eminently conspicuous and ridiculous in Mr. Hunt's work than another, it is,—that it is full of *mere vulgarisms* and *fugitive phrases,* and that in every page the language is—not only not *the actual, existing language,* but an ungrammatical, unauthorized, chaotic jargon, such as we believe was never before spoken; much less written.

> In what vernacular tongue, for instance, does Mr. Hunt find a lady's waist called *clipsome,* (p. 10.)—or the shout of a mob 'enormous', (p. 9.)—or a fit, *lightsome;*—or that a hero's nose is '*lightsomely* brought down from a forehead of clear-spirited thought', (p. 46.)—or that his back 'drops' *lightsomely in,* (p. 20).[13]

The question of morality was also raised. The plot of the poem turns on an incestuous liaison; yet it is notable that the reviewers did not object to the mere fact of the incest, although some felt a slight repugnance at the choice of theme. The *British Review* and the *Monthly Review* observed that the story was handled with all possible delicacy; the latter review further remarked, in a sort of inverted defense of the poem, that nevertheless, 'enough occurs to alarm the vigilant and perhaps fastidious supervisors of female reading in the present nice era'.[14] John Gibson Lockhart, on the other hand, in that part of his article on the poem in *Blackwood's* having pretensions to serious criticism, objected strongly to the light-hearted handling of the theme: 'It would fain be the genteel comedy of incest.'[15] And the *Eclectic Review* had its doubts:

> We give the Author full credit for the decency of his representations, for the absence of every thing that can disgust, or seduce, or inflame: but still we doubt whether such stories are not likely to do some hurt to the cause of morality; whether it is possible so to distinguish between the offence and the offender, as to render the one detestable, while the other is represented as so very amiable; and whether indeed this amiableness is not gotten by paring off sundry little portions of the sin; such as selfishness—that unheroic quality, on the part of the seducer; base infidelity on the part of the woman.[16]

The *Literary Panorama* offered a different sort of objection: 'The writer who attributes evils to fate, is not a moral writer.'[17]

Though the reviewers in general were not morally outraged, two hostile reviewers indulged in some vicious personal abuse. The Dedication to Lord Byron was the target; for example, Croker observed:

> We never, in so few lines, saw so many clear marks of the vulgar impatience of a low man, conscious and ashamed of his wretched vanity, and labouring, with coarse flippancy, to scramble over the bounds of birth and education, and fidget himself into the *stout-heartedness* of being familiar with a LORD.[18]

The Dedication, like so much of Hunt's writing, is indeed embarrassingly familiar, but such remarks as Croker's are, to say the least, inadmissible.

Faced with the vanity and familiarity of Hunt's dedications and prefaces, and the vulgarity and preciousness of his poetic diction, the reviewers turned more and more to humorous comment. Elements of the comic had been present in some of the earliest reviews of Hunt's works; but it was the totally serious review that was the exception in the criticism of *Foliage* (1818), a collection of original poems (or 'Greenwoods') and translations of classical poetry (or 'Evergreens'). (The *Literary Gazette* remarked on the puns: 'There is much silliness in such doings. . . .')[19] The review in the *Quarterly Review,* possibly by John Wilson Croker, opened on a facetious note:

> Winter has at length passed away: spring returns upon us, like a reconciled mistress, with redoubled smiles and graces; and even we poor critics, 'in populous city pent', feel a sort of ungainly inspiration from the starved leaflets and smutty buds in our window-pots; what, then, must be the feelings with which the Arcadian Hunt,
>
> 'half-stretched on the ground,
> With a *cheek-smoothing air coming taking*
> *him round,*'
>
> —p. lxxxi.
>
> must welcome the approach of the 'fair-limbed' goddess to his rural retreat at Hampstead? He owes her indeed especial gratitude; and it would be unpardonable in him to suffer his 'day-sweet' voice, and 'smoothing-on' 'sleeking-up' harp to be mute upon this occasion.[20]

The *Literary Gazette* was a little more serious:

> True poetry opens a nobler pursuit than this squirrel-hunting among bushes. . . . Many of our modern writers seem to imagine that poetic genius consists in the fanciful illustration of the most trite objects; that to call a tree leafy, and a bird hoppy, and a cat purry, is genuine nature; that to speak of brutes having '*lamping* eyes', . . . of rills among stones having 'little *whiffling* tones', . . . of 'sleek seas . . .', and

> similar fooleries, is pure unadulterated inspira-tion and not silly nonsense. They may be right: we are sceptics.[21]

Fair or not—legitimate critical style or mere abuse—such humorous comment must have been hard to stifle with respect to much of Hunt's verse.

But Hunt's slighting remarks about Christianity, abruptly obtruded into the Preface to the volume, occasioned some serious discussions. The *Eclectic Review* observed that it is very difficult to give oneself to poetry when offensive opinions get in the way—that consequently nothing is more impolitic for a poet than

> to obtrude upon his readers those points in his individual character, which relate to differences of religious creed or political opinion, thereby tending to awaken a class of associations opposite to those which it is the business of the poet to excite.
>
> Mr. Leigh Hunt has, in the present volume, been betrayed by his incurable egotism, into this capital error.[22]

The *Quarterly* was less circumspect in tendering its objections; Hunt and his associates were branded as Epicureans. And although Hunt is said to avoid in all likelihood the practice which he preaches, he is held accountable for the possible corruption of disciples—those 'who have neither the intellectual pride of a first discovery to compensate them for self-restriction, nor the ardent anxiety for the reputation of an infant sect to support them against their own principle. . . .'[23] This is at least taking Hunt's philosophy more seriously than anyone today would do; but any force the argument might have is invalidated by the vicious, personal attack, which follows, on one of Hunt's associates. It is Shelley, unnamed but unmistakable; and this is in a way ironic; for Shelley is often said to have suffered from his connection with Hunt. In this review, exactly the opposite is the case.

Nevertheless, the *Quarterly Review* in spite of its objections recognized Hunt's merits: 'a general richness of language, and a picturesque imagination; this last indeed, the faculty of placing before us, with considerable warmth of colouring, and truth of drawing, the groups which his fancy assembles, he possesses in an eminent degree. . . .'[24] But perhaps his scenes are a little too picturesque, too like paintings. This last comment, also made in the *Eclectic Review,* is remarkable, inasmuch as the capacity of a poetic scene for graphic transposition was almost always a form of praise used by reviewers.

And yet, the reviewer in the *Quarterly* continues, besides his dangerous philosophy and his stylistic defects Hunt presents, 'though it occurs but seldom, an impurity of both' language and sentiment.

> He may amuse or deceive himself with distinctions between voluptuousness and grossness, but will he never learn that things indifferent or innocent in themselves may become dangerous from the weakness or corruption of the recipient? . . . If the thing be practically pernicious, its abstract innocence is but a slight compensation. . . .[25]

What voluptuousness there is occurs mainly in the longest poem of the collection, 'The Nymphs', which received from the reviewers most attention and most praise. The chatty epistles to his friends were not so well received; the *Eclectic Review* briefly described the central problem: 'Mr. Hunt's attempts at playfulness are not graceful.'[26] The *British Critic* likewise summed up the defect in Hunt's exuberant translations: 'We will not call Mr. Hunt a mannerist, but he has the happy faculty of making all the poets whom he translates sing in strains very like his own', often with catastrophic results.[27]

Hunt's next original verse, *Hero and Leander; and Bacchus and Ariadne,* was published in the collected edition of his poetry in 1819. It received only one review, and that one was most strange. P. G. Patmore in the *London Magazine* begins by claiming that Hunt had been badly treated by the reviewers—a claim which can only refer to the reviews of *Foliage;* and yet after indulging in some enthusiastic praise of Hunt's poetry (for example, it is 'all over spots of sunshine'), he defends *The Story of Rimini,* which on the whole had received favorable reviews.[28] Then the strangeness increases as Patmore goes on to enumerate Hunt's stylistic faults, which he maintains are present in that poem as well as in *Hero and Leander:* 'The inveterate mannerism,—the familiarity reaching sometimes to vulgarity,—the recurrence of careless and prosaic lines, and even whole passages,—and the determination to use old and uncommon words in new and uncommon, and sometimes inappropriate and unintelligible senses.' And yet, 'in spite of all this, Hero and Leander in particular, is a very sweet little poem.'[21] It is difficult to understand exactly what caused such inconsistencies and reversals; perhaps the review had been heavily edited or maybe it was just that Patmore was sympathetic in general, becoming confused when faced with Hunt's shortcomings.

Another strange occurrence preceded this: a partly favorable reception in *Blackwood's,* Hunt's most relentless foe, of his annual *Literary Pocket-Book* of 1819 and 1820. The review, possibly by John Wilson, is actually a mixture of attacks on Hunt and Keats, of *Blackwood's* customary cloying, whimsical humor, and of praise and recommendation of the volumes. The *Literary Pocket-Book* of 1821 received a truly favorable review in the *London Magazine*.

Hunt was applauded more loudly by reviewers of his *Amyntas* (1820), a translation of Tasso's *Aminta.* Far and away the best work of Hunt published in the period under study, it received three enthusiastic reviews and only one unfavorable one (in the *Literary Gazette*). The *Monthly Magazine* summed up the general attitude:

> We . . . think this translation superior to any thing of Mr. Hunt's which we have seen: it has more of what is good in his manner, and abounds in fewer of his faults. It is written, too, quite *con amore*. We perceive our author is in his true element—for the original itself is simple and *affected* throughout.[30]

The reviewer in the *Monthly Review* agreed with this and offered some further observations of a more general nature. He maintained that the 'familiarity and quaintness both of thought and expression', notable in Hunt's previous poems, 'do not arise out of affectation and conceit, as we might first suppose: they are rather the offspring of necessity; of singular and somewhat confined powers both of mind and language. . . .'[31] In fact, 'his success, in the little work before us, is to be chiefly attributed to his want of capacity for greater things'.[32] The reviewer went on to disagree with 'the *dicta* of a modern critic [Hazlitt]: who, with latitudinarian kindness towards the world, maintains that *every thing is poetry,* and that *we are all poets',* by arguing for a more elevated content and form in poetry.[33] But in arguing such points in relation to Hunt's verse, the reviewer has too easy a time and does nothing but set forth his own views, which are not very profound. His remarks on Hunt's merits, after a discussion of his mannerisms, show more thought:

> Still this system is not without its use. It has beauties of its own, and of a peculiar kind; and it makes him notice objects that other poets have neglected, and describe them in words which though singular are often happy. There is a freshness of perception about his poetry, and his descriptions of scenery and character are given with ease. The lighter and more transient feelings are likewise under his controul, though the intenseness of the passions is exhibited with little effect.[34]

After years of relatively favorable and for the most part serious criticism, Hunt published *Ultra-Crepidarius* (1823), a satire on William Gifford, editor of the *Quarterly Review;* and the nature of the satire upset the equanimity of the critics. Some of the reviews were favorable and some hostile; but all of them were partisan and therefore uninteresting, except for the extent of their malignity. The reviewer in *Blackwood's,* possibly John Wilson, showed that magazine's usual flair along those lines. In referring to a passage describing the arising of Mercury and Venus from bed, he remarks: 'One thinks of some aged cur, with mangy back, glazed eyeballs dropping rheum, and with most disconsolate mazzard muzzling among the fleas of his abominable loins, by some accident lying upon the bed where love and beauty are embracing, and embraced.'[35]

Political bias is more obvious in reviews of Hunt's works than in those of most writers dealt with in this study. This should not be surprising in view of Hunt's political career as editor of the *Examiner.* What is remarkable is that the political bias worked largely in Hunt's favor. Periodicals run by Dissenters, such as the *Critical Review* and the *Eclectic Review,* and the liberal journals, such as the *Champion* and the *London Magazine,* gave Hunt critical support, which could scarcely have been offset by the hostility of periodicals of an opposite political persuasion, such as the *British Critic* and the *Literary Gazette.*

And the extent to which the bias affected the literary judgments is, in any case, difficult to determine in view of the unevenness of Hunt's work. His verse is not much esteemed today; there has, in fact, been no edition of his poetry since 1923. It is the incredible unevenness in its quality, I think, that accounts for Hunt's present unpopularity. The poet who could write

> Hallo!—what?—Where? What can it be
> That strikes up so deliciously?
> I never in my life—what? no!
> That little tin-box playing so?

could also pen the following speech of a shepherdess describing her conversion to the ranks of Love (translated from Tasso's *Aminta*):

> I yielded, I confess; and all that conquered me,
> What was it? patience and humility,
> And sighs, and soft laments, and asking pardon.
> Darkness, and one short night, then shewed me more,
> Than the long lustre of a thousand days.

Wordsworth, like Hunt, was dealing with emotions at the point where it becomes difficult to keep from crossing the thin line that separates sentiment from sentimentality—simple emotion from affectation; and Wordsworth sometimes crossed over. Hunt was forever skipping back and forth across that line.

Vulgarity, familiarity, bad taste: as terms of critical disapproval these are, I believe, valid and meaningful, although it is not often necessary to call them into use; for the occasion seldom arises when dealing with works of any literary value. When dealing with Hunt's works, some of which are well worth reading, the need for applying such terms is constant. They may at first seem to be mere abuse when encountered in contemporary reviews; but it is difficult to tell a writer he is being vulgar without sounding abusive, just as it is difficult to point out familiarity without restoring to humorous comment. *Blackwood's,* as usual, went too far and indulged in personal abuse, thereby creating a one-sided image of Hunt's contemporary critics. It is significant that the word 'Cockney', applied with such malignity by 'Blackwood's Merry Men', was almost never used by Hunt's reviewers in other periodicals. . . .

Notes

[1] *CR,* V 4s (Mar., 1814), 293-94.

[2] *MR,* LXXV (Sept., 1814), 100.

[3] *Sat.*, XIV (Apr., 1814), 327.

[4] *Champ,* Mar. 26, 1815, p. 102.

[5] *TI,* VI (Apr., 1815), 290.

[6] *Ibid.,* p. 294.

[7] *Ibid.,* p. 295.

[8] *Ibid.,* p. 297.

[9] *Ibid.,* p. 298.

[10] *LP,* IV 2s (Sept., 1816), 936.

[11] *Ibid.,* pp. 936-37.

[12] *ER,* XXVI (June, 1816), 491.

[13] *QR,* XIV (Jan., 1816), 477.

[14] *MR,* LXXX (June, 1816), 138.

[15] *BM,* II (Nov., 1817), 197.

[16] *EcR,* V 2s (Apr., 1816), 381.

[17] *LP,* IV 2s (Sept., 1816), 937.

[18] *QR,* XIV (Jan., 1816), 481. Hunt himself later admitted his guilt with regard to this charge. See Leigh Hunt, *Lord Byron and Some of His Contemporaries,* 2d ed. (London, 1828), I, 54-55.

[19] *LG,* Apr. 4, 1818, p. 212.

[20] *QR,* XVIII (Jan., 1818), 324-25.

[21] *LG,* Apr. 4, 1818, pp. 210-11.

[22] *EcR,* X 2s (Nov., 1818), 484-85.

[23] *QR,* XVIII (Jan., 1818), 327.

[24] *Ibid.,* pp. 329-30.

[25] *Ibid.,* p. 329.

[26] *EcR,* X 2s (Nov., 1818), 492.

[27] *BC,* X 2s (July, 1818), 95.

[28] *LM,* II (July, 1820), 46.

[29] *Ibid.,* p. 51.

[30] *MM,* L (Aug., 1820), 65.

[31] *MR,* XCIII (Sept., 1820), 18.

[32] *Ibid.,* p. 29.

[33] *Ibid.,* p. 19.

[34] *Ibid.,* p. 20.

[35] *BM,* XV (Jan., 1824), 87.

Works Cited

British Reviewing Periodicals 1802-24

BC British Critic (1793-1826). . . .

BM Blackwood's Edinburgh Magazine (1817-). . . .

Champ Champion (1814-22). . . .

CR Critical Review (1756-1817). . . .

EcR Eclectic Review (1805-68). . . .

ER Edinburgh Review (1802-1929). . . .

LG Literary Gazette (1817-62). . . .

LM London Magazine (1820-29). . . .

LP Literary Panorama (1806-19). . . .

MM Monthly Magazine (1796-1825). . . .

MR Monthly Review (1749-1845). . . .

QR Quarterly Review (1809-). . . .

Sat Satirist (1807-14). A monthly magazine of 112 pages first published in London (Vols. I-V) by Samuel Tipper, then (Vol. VI) by W. N. Jones, and finally by anonymous 'Proprietors'. Much more political than most magazines, the *Satirist's* literary reviews nevertheless contain indiscriminately unfavorable judgments, especially severe after George Manners, the original proprietor and editor, sold the magazine to William Jerdan (later editor of the *LG*) in 1812. Hewson Clarke was probably the reviewer of both editions of Byron's *Hours of Idleness;* at least Byron believed him to be the culprit (L. Marchand, *Byron* [New York, 1957], I, 155; R. E. Prothero, ed. *The Works of Lord Byron: Letters and Journals* [London, 1898-1901], I, 321n). The *Sat* contained political cartoons by George Cruikshank.

TI Theatrical Inquisitor (1812-21). A monthly magazine of eighty pages published in London by C. Chapple. It was conducted in 1814 by George Soane (L. M. Jones, 'The Essays and Critical Writing of John Hamilton Reynolds', Harvard diss. [1952], p. 11n. See also F. Sper, *The Periodical Press of London* [Boston, 1937], p. 15). It had the usual magazine features, except for chronicles, but was, as its title implies, weighted in the direction of drama. It nevertheless contained a considerable number of literary reviews.

Jerome McGann (essay date 1979)

SOURCE: "Keats and the Historical Method in Literary Criticism" in *Comparative Literature,* Vol. 94, No. 5, December, 1979, pp. 988-1032.

[*In this excerpt, McGann focuses on the quality of Keats' poetry alternatively known as colloquialism and vulgarity.*]

To see that the passage [from an 1815 verse epistle to George Felton Mathew] refers to specific historical events is perforce to be made aware of the extreme artificiality of the poetic style, and to be reminded as well how much of Keats's early verse typifies such a style. Throughout the poetry of 1814-1817 the men and women Keats actually moves among are variously called "fays," "elves," "nymphs," "swains," and he employs as well a whole array of related Aesopian language to speak of other, equally ordinary matters. Later, under Hunt's influence, this artificial manner began to develop along a number of other lines, and the result we have come to call the Cockney style, which dominates both the 1817 volume and *Endymion.*

Of course, the general characteristics of Keats's early verse are well enough known to academics. I raise the matter again, in this context, only because the significance of this Cockney style—its specifically poetic significance—is not very widely recognized, even among specialists. Only by reading such poetry in a sharply specified historical frame of reference are we able to see, at this date, the aesthetic domain which Cockney verse attempted to conquer, and hence to describe precisely not merely the abstract *characteristics,* but the felt *qualities* of its poetic structure.

When critics today talk about Keats's Cockney poetry they dismiss it as some sort of aberrant juvenile necessity, one of those odd preludes to genius with which the history of art is generally marked. Here is a good critic's good summary of the technical characteristics of that "precious, luscious, plaintively sentimental kind of verse" we call Cockney poetry:

> As experiments in what he calls 'unaffected' or artless language, his verses sometimes degenerate into colloquial chatter; and adopting the manner of Spenser and seventeenth-century Spenserians, he writes a precious, luscious, plaintively sentimental kind of verse. There is no fusion, but just a queer juxtaposition of the natural and the archaic. The other characteristics of Hunt's poetry—especially of his vocabulary and versification—stem from his desire to secure a medium of expression which is both luxurious and lively, and have been noted in detail by De Selincourt, Claude Finney, W. J. Bate, and other critics and commentators: use of abstract nouns expressing a concrete thing or idea; abundance of present participles; predilection for adverbs formed from present participles, and delight in the use of—y adjectives; divergence from the closed couplet resulting in extreme looseness of structure: liberal use of double rhymes, trisyllabic feet, and varied medial pauses; stress-failure; accentuation of final syllables of polysyllabic rhyme words. Hunt apparently confused freedom with laxity, and these stylistic devices—or aberrations—had undoubtedly a pernicious influence on the young Keats who studied *A Feast of the Poets* and the *Story of Rimini* with avidity.[20]

If we return to the early reviewers who named and defined the Cockneyism of Hunt and Keats, we find all of these qualities enumerated, and most of them deplored. We also find, however, a pattern of negative remarks on the "uncleanness of this school"[21] as well as recurrent references to the "slang" of its style and its general effort at a casual and colloquial manner. Indeed, the other recurrent charge, of vulgarity, is only explicable in such a context. The reviewers who make this charge are censuring not merely the erotic subjects in Keats's poetry but Keats's peculiarly mannered treatment of sexual images and subjects.

> Feed upon apples red and strawberries,
> And choose each pleasure that my fancy sees;
> Catch the white-handed nymphs in shady places
> To woo sweet kisses from averted faces
> Play with their fingers, touch their shoulders white
> Into a pretty shrinking with a bite
> As hard as lips can make it. . . .
> ("Sleep and Poetry," 103-109)

> I stood tip-toe upon a little hill,
> The air was cooling, and so very still
> That the sweet buds which with a modest pride
> Pull droopingly, in slanting curve aside,
> Their scantly leaved and finely tapering stems,
> Had not yet lost those starry diadems. . . .
> ("I Stood Tip-Toe," 1-6)

"Vulgar" is a precise and accurate description of passages like these. But we will not understand the *meaning* of that charge unless we see that it is delivered from a certain perspective. The reviewers who censure Keats's vulgarity consistently see him from a class-conscious perspective. Keats is low born and ought not to be writing poetry in the first place; he lacks the appropriate education for the office. That social judgment, as is well known, generates the notoriously *ad hominem* ridicule which some of the reviewers heaped upon Keats. But that social judgment also generates the related, and apparently "technical" point: that Keats's style violates poetic propriety by treating a "high" subject in a "low" diction and colloquial manner. In fact, the attack upon the Cockney School is in many respects a repetition of the attack upon Wordsworth's program in the *Lyrical Ballads*. In both cases the more traditional critics insist that a common lexicon and a colloquial style in poetry are only proper within certain prescribed—normally, comic—limits.

Against this background let us look at the following passage from the *Edinburgh Magazine's* review of the 1817 volume:

> He seems to have formed his poetical predilections in exactly the same direction as Mr. Hunt; and to write, from personal choice, as well as emulation, at all times, in that strain which can be most recommended to the favour of the general readers of poetry, only by the critical ingenuity and peculiar refinements of Mr. Hazlitt. That style is vivacious, smart, witty, changeful, sparkling, and learned—full of bright points and flashy expressions that strike and even seem to please by a sudden boldness of novelty,—rather abounding in familiarities of conception and oddnesses of manner which shew ingenuity, even though they be perverse, or common, or contemptuous. The writers themselves seem to be persons of considerable taste, and of comfortable pretensions, who really appear as much alive to the socialities and sensual enjoyments of life, as to the contemplative beauties of nature. In addition to their familiarity, though,—they appear to be too full of conceits and sparkling points, ever to excite any thing more than a cold approbation at the long-run—and too fond, even in their favourite descriptions of nature, of a reference to the factitious resemblances of society, ever to touch the heart. Their verse is straggling and uneven, without the lengthened flow of blank verse, or the pointed connection of couplets. They aim laudably enough at force and freshness, but are not so careful of the inlets of vulgarity, nor so self-denying to the temptations of indolence, as to make their force a merit.[22]

Certain phrases here are extremely interesting: the repeated comment on Keats's excessive "familiarity" and poetic colloquialism, as well as the recurrent sense that the poetry is also—perhaps paradoxically?—marked by a smart mannerism. The general view is that Keats's work is a tissue of self-conscious artifice and poetic conceits.

Today we do not think of Keats's early poetry as "vivacious, smart, witty, changeful, sparkling, and learned." But the early reviewers—whether they praised, censured, or merely described Keats's work—did see the poetry in this way. Such descriptive terms necessarily offer an odd contrast to the views of twentieth century critics, who customarily see Keats's early work as mawkish, self-indulgent, sentimental. The explanation of this notable difference of views is not my present concern, but it could be found through an analysis of the ideological structures of modern critical opinions.

For my present purposes, what I want to emphasize is this: that the Cockney style of Keats is sentimental to modern ears only *because* it is also, self-consciously, "smart, witty . . . and learned." As the reviewer notes, the style is marked by colloquialism and familiarity, and a lively, cosmopolitan chattiness. Indeed, this chattiness—recall the passage I quoted above from the verse epistle to Mathew—is directly, intimately related to the mannered and artificial style of the poetry. A close, modern analogue to the sort of work produced in Keats's early epistles, or in "Sleep and Poetry" and "I Stood Tip-toe," is the verse style recently cultivated by Frank O'Hara and the New York School in general. . . .

Notes

. . .[20] Bhabatosh Chatterjee, *John Keats: His Mind and Work* (Bombay, 1971), 211.

[21] My discussion here is in debt to John O. Hayden's fine synthetic description of contemporary reactions to "The Cockney School" in his *The Romantic Reviewers* (Chicago, 1968), pp. 176-215.

[22] "On the Cockney School of Poetry," *Edinburgh Magazine* (Oct. 1817), p. 256.

Patrick Story (essay date 1980)

SOURCE: "A Neglected Cockney School Parody of Hazlitt and Hunt," in *Keats-Shelley Journal,* Vol. XXIX, The Keats-Shelley Association of America, Inc., 1980, pp. 191-202.

[*In the following essay, Story analyzes the political assumptions and classism underlying* Blackwood's *attack on the Cockney School, focusing on a neglected review by Eyre Evans Crowe.*]

The fictitious "Cockney School of Poetry" was introduced by John Gibson Lockhart in the Tory *Blackwood's Magazine* of October 1817 as a burlesque counterpart to the by then respectable "Lake School" of poets.[1] This journalistic revival of Alexander Pope's proven tactic of identifying his London enemies as hacks and dunces initiated the most notorious controversy in British literary history. Continuing for over seven years, it included a successful libel suit by William Hazlitt and the 1821 duel in which Jonathan Henry Christie, originally acting for Lockhart, killed the editor of the *London Magazine,* John Scott. Some said the hostilities hastened the early death of John Keats.[2] One of the most revealing attacks that *Blackwood's* ever leveled against "pimpled" Hazlitt and Leigh Hunt was given the obscure title "Characters of Living Authors, By Themselves / No. I" (Vol. 10, part 2 [August 1821], 69-72). Though its existence is noted in Alan L. Strout's *Bibliography of Articles in* Blackwood's Magazine, which identifies it as the work of a regular contributor, Eyre Evans Crowe (1799-1868), a minor journalist and historical writer, it has never been considered as part of the controversy, perhaps because the victims themselves evidently chose to ignore it.[3] Nevertheless, this neglected parody not only sustains the usual themes of the Cockney School attack, it makes explicit the political assumptions not always apparent in the episodes previously considered. Crowe's political emphasis points beyond parties, toward the underlying *class* basis for the continuing reactionary attack, initiated with the sedition trials of 1794, upon those stubborn radicals and republicans whose opinions threatened what both sides called "existing institutions."

The principal members of this "School"—Hazlitt, Hunt with his hated weekly *Examiner,* and "Johnny" Keats—were also under a sustained attack by the more prestigious Tory journal the *Quarterly Review,* headed by William Gifford, whom Hazlitt described seriously as the "hidden link between literature and the police."[4] The *Quarterly* had gone about as far as it was possible to go with explicit political denunciation, and, without abandoning the charges of "sedition," *Blackwood's* took the only innovative path left open: reckless personal vilification. It is therefore all the more surprising that Crowe's attack should appear under a title so allusive as to appear unrelated to the others in the series. Certainly a dangerous atmosphere had been created by the Christie-Scott duel some six months earlier, but, as Herschel Baker has shown, *Blackwood's* had been studded nevertheless with Cockney School insults during that period.

By the standards of the Cockney School series, Crowe's attack was fullscale—four double-column pages—and he labored in both form and content to make his purpose unmistakable. The form of a parody in the first person had already been established in *Blackwood's* two years before. Lockhart's "Cockney School No. v" (April 1819) had ridiculed Hunt in "On Sonnet-Writing, and Sonnet-Writers in General," and had concluded with a "Sonnet on Myself." Crowe's title would also signal an attack upon the Cockney School to those who recognized the parody of two contemporary portrait series. The more recent, Hunt's "Sketches of the Living Poets" in the *Examiner,* had begun to appear just a few weeks before.[5] A character by Hazlitt, "Mr. Crabbe," had also appeared three months earlier in the *London Magazine* under the title "Living Authors, No. 4," a series originated by John Scott before his death in the duel.[6] In fact, Crowe may have intended to raise the cruel irony that Scott himself was literally no longer a "Living Author." Also, in the context of the duel, the otherwise conventional religious conclusion of Crowe's "personification" of Hazlitt seems heavy-handed and menacing: "often am I tempted to cry out, in the language of that book I have neglected, 'There is no peace for me but in the grave'" (p. 72).

Stylistically, Crowe parodies Hazlitt with deliberately trite quotations, stale allusions, and forced paradoxes. He also uses wittily altered and verbatim passages from recent works, especially the first volume of *Table Talk,* published four months before. For example, in "On Genius and Common Sense," Hazlitt had written, "Dr. Johnson was a fool to Goldsmith in the fine tact, the airy intuitive faculty with which he skimmed the surface of things, and unconsciously formed his opinions."[7] The term "fine tact" reflects, of course, Hazlitt's concern with the imagination's active response to sensory impressions, and it had been applied in praise of his own critical abilities by Hunt in "To W.H., Esq.," in the *Examiner* of 14 July 1816: "Dear Hazlitt, whose tact intellectual is such / That it seems to feel truth, as one's fingers do touch." A year later, a favorable *Monthly Magazine* review of the *Round Table* also referred to the "well-known fineness of tact of the two contributors."[8] Crowe had studied Hazlitt's works carefully (he reviewed both volumes of *Table-Talk* in *Blackwood's* the following year)[9] and, with the instinct of a good parodist, recognized how vulnerable the new critical vocabulary had become. He makes Hazlitt say here, "I shall be the half-Boswell, half-Johnson, of my age.—Not that I deign to compare myself with the first in dignity, or with the last in 'that fine tact, that airy intuitive faculty,' that purchases at half-price ready-made wisdom" (p. 72). With this duncelike self-condemnation, Crowe transforms Hazlitt's subjectivity into the combination of buffoonery and dogmatism that Boswell's and Johnson's names, especially when cited together, could evoke in the period.

Hazlitt's characteristic tone in familiar self-reference is also lowered into a cloying but sometimes witty parody of itself: "People call me egotist; but they don't know what they say. I never think of myself but as one among the many—a drop in the ocean of life. If I anatomize my own heart, 'tis that I can lay hands on no other so conveniently; and when I do even make use of the letter *I,* I merely mean by it, any highly-gifted and originally-minded individual" (p. 69).

In content, Crowe maintains and extends the Cockney School charges against Hazlitt personally: pimples, promiscuity, and plagiarism. (These in addition to the general charges against the "School" of presumption, ignorance, egotism, and especially Jacobinism.) The opening line of the parody, "I'm a philosopher of no philosophy," combines the charges by ridiculing Hazlitt's besieged defenses of his intellectual qualifications for addressing the public. But the introductory paragraph closes with a more specific allusion: "If a person can once enter into the receptacles of his own feelings, muse upon himself, . . . the Indian jugglers, with their brazen balls, were nothing to the style in which he can fling sentences about" (p. 69). The reference is to one of Hazlitt's best-known essays, also first published in Volume I of *Table-Talk,* "The Indian Jugglers." The word "brazen" does not appear in the original, and the daringly obscene pun on Hazlitt's presumption in writing reveals the hypocrisy in the *Blackwood's* stance of protecting an innocent public from Cockney School lewdness.

The most primitive charge in earlier attacks, that against Hazlitt's physical appearance, alleged a red nose and "rubicund swandrops."[10] Here he is made to complain, "they will have me pimpled in soul and body," and the cause of these imagined symptoms is disclosed: "It is a sorry look-out, though, to be dependent on [stimuli]—to owe every bright thought to 'mine host' or mine apothecary" (p. 72). "Stimuli" may pun upon Hazlitt's frequent attacks on the sensationalist school of philosophy, but as an allusion to artificial stimulants, it is the only place to my knowledge where he is charged not only with drunkenness but with narcotics addiction.

The charge of promiscuity, raised by John Wilson's reference, in "Hazlitt Cross-Questioned" (August 1818), to Hazlitt's notorious if somewhat obscure 1803 run-in with Lake-district peasants, was of course generally true, but it is only lightly alluded to here: "I hate 'the womankind'—I have reason" (p. 69). The perhaps more damaging allegation against a critic, that he plagiarized literary conversation, had also been raised in "Hazlitt Cross-Questioned" and eventually attained the permanence of art in the "Mr. Eavesdrop" of Thomas Love Peacock's *Crotchet Castle* (1831). Here, Crowe has him admit, "It is all very likely," but ask (approximating his real attitude), "why do they talk so much?" (p. 71).[11] Crowe's contribution to the subject is a claim that Hazlitt lifted his theory of comedy from Madame de Staël's "Essay on Fiction." Throughout, he maintains the corresponding assumption of Hazlitt's dunce-like ignorance: "Despise learning: never mind books but to borrow"; "it's Greek, Bill, read on," etc.

The egotism implied by Crowe's autobiographical-sounding title was a major theme in the Cockney School attacks: many reactionaries of the day presumed that egotism tended toward discontent and Jacobinism. Crowe implies this tendency, especially in broadening his attack to include Leigh Hunt. Hunt had been addressed as the "King of the Cockneys" by Lockhart in the "Letter from Z" of *Blackwood's,* May 1818, but here, echoing the squabbles of the *Dunciad,* Crowe's Hazlitt usurps authority:

> Enthroned between Addison and Bacon, my spirit shall wield the sceptre of Cockney philosophy. . . . From Winterston [*sic for* Winterslow] to Hampstead my name is known—at least, with respect. I am in literature the lord-mayor of the city—the Wood of Parnassus (what an idea!). . . . I am the prefect of all city critical gazettes; and L.H. for all his huffing and strutting, is but my deputy—my procounsul. . . . I blew into his nostrils all the genius he possesses, and introduced him to the honourable fraternity of washerwomen and the round-table. . . . (p. 172)

(Lockhart had already attacked Hunt's innovative *Round Table* essay on washerwomen in "Cockney School No. v.")

In keeping with the overall *Blackwood's* attack, Crowe suggests, sometimes indirectly but always ominously, that the upstart cockney egotism goes beyond the ridiculous to the subversive. For example, reinforcing his title, he provides an appropriate French motto for his "personification":

> Dans ce siècle de petits talen[t]s et de grands succès, mes chefs-d'oeuvre auront cent éditions, *s'il le faut.* Par-tout les sots crieront que je suis un grand homme, et si je n'ai contre moi que les gens de lettres et les gens de goût, j'arriverai peut-être à l'Académie.
>
> LOUVET

> [In this century of small talents and great successes, my works will have a hundred editions, *if necessary.* Every where, fools will proclaim that I am a great man, and if I have no one against me except men of letters and men of taste, I may arrive at the Academy.]

Jean Baptiste Louvet de Couvrai (1760-97) was a novelist and playwright, and a Girondist in the Revolution. Hazlitt had mentioned his name once in passing in *Table-Talk,* Volume I, evidently providing Crowe the opportunity he needed.[12] I have been unable to locate this fatuous and cynical passage in Louvet's works, and it may be spurious, but the effect here is plain in any case. Though a member of what was generally viewed as the moderate party, Louvet was associated in England with scandal and violence.[13] His romance, *Fabulas* (1786-89), was considered licentious, and his *Mémoires . . . sur la révolution française* (1795) united two themes, according to a recent commentator, which could be considered morally questionable in England: "the Revolution and the pangs of separated lovers." He had been mentioned amid scenes of horror and atrocity in well-known British eyewitness accounts by John

Adolphus and Dr. John Moore, and excoriated in the four-volume denunciation of the Revolution by the abbé Barruel, translated as *Memoirs Illustrating the History of Jacobinism* (1797-98).[14] His name, linked with the upstart motto, establishes a solid guilt by association with Hazlitt and Hunt.

As though Louvet were not sufficient, Crowe also invokes Rousseau, for whom Hazlitt of course had often expressed admiration, especially in his *Round Table* essay, "On the Character of Rousseau" (1816). Crowe's views, fully stated in *Blackwood's* six months after the parody in his "On the Character and Genius of Rousseau," were in the strongest anti-Jacobin tradition.[15] Rousseau, he argues, suffered from an almost congenital "mental egotism," which caused him to perceive "virtue" as "'but an empty name'"; religion as nonsense; laws as chains; and men as villains. Representing a "most abominable and unspeakable debauchery, atheism, and fanaticism," his influence was, Crowe implies, nevertheless mysteriously kept before the French people (by conspirators?) during the decade separating his death and the Revolution. At one point in the essay, Crowe comments that Rousseau's initial success "pointed out paradox to him as the easiest road to fame," an allegation which repeats the idea of the motto above. Predictably, he makes Hazlitt say in the "personification" (with "L.H.'s" encouragement), "I have always thought myself very like Rousseau" (p. 70). Crowe obviously attributes this dangerous "mental egotism" to his Cockney School subjects, and in his concluding sentence effectively links it to the real element of self-pity in Hazlitt:

> I . . . am too innocent for the world. After attacking private character and public virtue,—endeavoring to sap all principles of religion and government,—uttering whatever slander or blasphemy caprice suggested, or malice spurred me to,—yet I am surprised, and unable to discover, how or why anyone can be angry with me. (p. 72)

For his purpose in the satire, Crowe prudently avoids debating political ideas as such, having Hazlitt admit that "as to my politics, it would be a difficult matter to say what they were. I know not myself . . ." (p. 72). But the political implication of the attack as a whole touches fundamental issues about the period. What Crowe (representing *Blackwood's*) fears as aberrant "mental egotism" is what we recognize as precisely the most advanced and historically progressive form of bourgeois individualism, and identify as "Romantic." The Romantic artist, expressing the need of his class to overcome all remaining feudal encumbrances upon its development, believes that he feels and speaks for all mankind.[16] In the midst of economic, social, and political upheaval, he looks not to existing institutions but within himself for meaning, and creates, as M. H. Abrams has pointed out, the secularized spiritual autobiography—from Rousseau's *Confessions* to the *Prelude* to the familiar essay.[17]

Such self-referential, self-authenticated voices were either alienated and outcast from existing class society, or consciously fraternal and democratic in demanding more and more freedom for the individual. Writers like Hazlitt or Shelley could express both aspects by turns, and within the same essay or lyric. This was above all a time of postwar depression, unemployment, and hunger, and, in the teeming industrial slums of Manchester, the most violent class struggles to occur in England between Waterloo and the Reform Bill of 1832 erupted into the Peterloo Massacre of August 1819.[18] Under these circumstances, both liberal and conservative elements of the aristocracy and bourgeoisie were made conscious of the "destabilizing" social potential of egalitarian Romantic self-reference, especially when joined with explicit radical demands that could further incite the already threatening proletariat.

One way the situation was brought under control was through the establishment of the first mass medium for the molding of mass public opinion. The first modern British periodical in this sense was probably *The Anti-Jacobin* (1797-98), established by George Canning and William Gifford for obvious propaganda purposes. But the whiggish *Edinburgh Review,* founded in 1802, was more ideologically flexible and therefore more effective than the *Anti-Jacobin* in mediating on one hand the Tory administration's provocative reactionary excesses, and, on the other, in providing liberal restraint for seething mass opinion itself.[19] (As Hazlitt took pains to clarify in *The Spirit of the Age* [1825], the *Edinburgh*'s principles of free, impartial discussion of social issues "were by no means decidedly hostile to existing institutions.")[20] But the *Edinburgh* went too far in the celebrated "Don Cevallos" attack upon the administration's war effort, especially in arguing that British support of the Spanish uprising could be considered support for the right of a people to overthrow an unjust government! As a result, its more reactionary contributors, like Sir Walter Scott, withdrew to join with Canning and Gifford, who came together again to form the *Quarterly Review* (1809), an administration-sanctioned organ complete with "leaks" of secret information when needed. The rest of the new periodical press emerged through a continuing chain reaction between liberal and conservative interests, and the attack by *Blackwood's Magazine* a decade later upon what it took to be a radical and republican threat to class stability was an inevitable outgrowth of the process.

This familiar summary of periodical history may seem superfluous for the understanding of this thoroughly familiar controversy. But the controversy's larger significance in British literary history has been questioned in some of the most recent American criticism of the Romantic periodical reviews. To concentrate on one example: the Introduction to John O. Hayden's useful anthology, *Romantic Bards and British Reviewers* (1971), a distillation of his important study, cited earlier, *Romantic Reviewers, 1802-1824* (1968). The perspective in both seems to reflect two powerful influences upon the interpretation of literary history in the United States today: the prevailing nonhistorical, formalist (New Critical) theory of literature; and the dogma of "pluralism" in American political theory, which fragments class struggle into perceived rivalries and interest groups.[21]

In his Introduction, Hayden accurately notes that "in the wake of the French Revolution, with the Radicals clamoring for the reform of Parliament, political ideology was much more important than party affiliation," but adds that the *Edinburgh* and *Quarterly* accordingly "reflected the actual political cleavage of the times: liberal and conservative" (p. xii). Yet, as he indicates in context, this last amounts simply to saying that the two sides disagreed only on how to protect basically the *same* class interests. On fundamental social and political assumptions, they agreed, and in many cases used the same writers. As Hazlitt wrote in 1819, the two reviews, "as far as politics are concerned," remind one of "opposition coaches, that raise a great dust or spatter one another with mud, but both travel the same road, and arrive at the same destination."[22] Yet here is how Hayden describes the functioning of the consensual restraints upon opinions which threatened their common interest:

> the general political bias of the Romantic periodicals has in the past probably been exaggerated. . . . There were of course instances of politically biased reviews of literature. . . . And yet the writers mainly involved, Byron, Shelley, Keats, and Hazlitt, were more than merely liberal; they often obtruded into their works jacobinical or unpatriotic sentiments that were considered dangerous enough to call forth any kind of attack. (p. xiii)

The problem with such a perspective is that instead of really locating the periodical reviews within the posited historical context, it isolates them from it. The use of the term "obtruded" seems to imply that only the sociopolitical views of a few radicals—who turn out to be the most important writers of their generation—violate the (presumably) otherwise purely "aesthetic" quality of the literature of the period. But this is manifestly inaccurate in the face of all the reactionary works published at the time. The only alternative interpretation of the passage is to assume that "acceptable" political views, like those of the Laureate, Robert Southey, when expressed, were not "obtruded"—i.e., were aesthetically subsumed into the works. This is to use formalist critical presuppositions to shift the ostensible provocation in the works from the content to the form. But as Hayden elsewhere recognizes, the readers of the era readily understood the content of their contemporary literature in its political and historical dimensions.[23]

Hayden's use of the term "politically biased" likewise implies the assumption that normally the reviews in these journals were somehow "unbiased" (outside social conflict?) except for those deservedly "called forth" by the provocative works. This is simply to accept the pervasive and unexamined *class* bias of the reviewers themselves, which assumed that routine approval or narrow aesthetic consideration of works that supported currently permissible sentiments was not a form of bias.

Moreover, Hayden goes on to defend the reasonable generalization that the great reviews were not "citadels of reaction" with the questionable if not damaging evidence that we now know that the reviewers themselves were not stereotypical hired hacks. They were mostly well off, educated (i.e., had attended a university), and included, besides a lot of lawyers, "distinguished physicians, journalists, ministers [i.e., clergymen], and university professors" (p. xiv). Admittedly, they may not all have been reactionary, but such hopeful representatives of the *petite bourgeoisie,* with their great expectations of rising in "existing institutions," hardly required provocative radicals to elicit their routine consensual bias in the evaluation of contemporary literature. On the contrary, it was the radicals who exposed it. Traditional aesthetic expectations, of course, not to mention what Leigh Hunt called "favoritism, animosities, and hesitations," played important roles in the reviewing. But it is the obvious and overwhelming function of the journals to mold mass opinion within consensual class limitations that enables us to put these factors into perspective at all.

Methodological isolation of the reviews of Romantic literature from their larger social context either renders the vilification, wasted careers, and bloodshed of a phenomenon like the Cockney School controversy incomprehensible, or reduces it, and necessarily much of the greatest poetry and prose of the period, to mere personal eccentricity, "mental egotism." At stake here is not only an understanding of, in Eliot's phrase, "the pastness of the past." Since the end of the nineteenth century the Anglo-American mass media have been transformed financially into vast interlocking oligarchies, almost unrecognizable in contrast to the makeshift efforts of over a century and a half ago. Yet, as studies like Herbett Schiller's *The Mind Managers* (1973) show, they still carry out their essential function of manipulating mass opinion, and with ever-increasing efficiency.

Notes

1 "On the Cockney School of Poetry," *Blackwood's,* 2 (October 1817), 38. The most judicious overview

of the controversy is Herschel Baker's in *William Hazlitt* (Cambridge, Mass.: Harvard University Press, 1962), pp. 370-381. Alan Lang Strout's "Hunt, Hazlitt, and *Maga,*" *ELN,* 4 (June 1937), 151-159, is still useful on Hunt, and Keats's responses are detailed by W.J. Bate in *John Keats* (Cambridge, Mass.: Harvard University Press, 1963), pp. 224-226, 366-368. In *The Romantic Reviewers, 1802-1824* (Chicago: University of Chicago Press, 1968), pp. 176-215, John O. Hayden provides comparative discussions of the conventional literary reviews during the period, most of them favorable, of works by Hunt, Hazlitt, and Keats, and the fullest bibliographies available of all periodical reviews through 1824 (pp. 270ff.).

[2] Commentators on the impact of unfavorable reviews on Keats's health must necessarily range themselves between Shelley's exaggeration in the Preface to *Adonais* (1821), and Byron's incredulity in Canto XI of *Don Juan* (1823). In "On Living to One's-Self" (*Table-Talk,* 1821), Hazlitt's views come very close to Shelley's, but instead of the *Quarterly Review* attack on *Endymion,* Hazlitt blames the *Blackwood's* "epithet" of "cockney school." See *Complete Works of William Hazlitt,* ed. P. P. Howe (London: J. M. Dent and Sons, 1930-34), VIII, 99.

[3] On 4 August 1824, Crowe wrote to Blackwood, "My friend Anster transmitted to you last week an article of mine personifying Hazlitt." See Alan Lang Strout, *A Bibliography of Articles in* Blackwood's Magazine, *1817-25* (Lubbock, Texas: Library, Texas Technological College, 1959), p. 83. Since most of the themes are common to all the attacks, I have been unable to identify any contemporary responses limited to this one specifically.

[4] *Complete Works,* IX, 13; noted in Baker's *William Hazlitt,* p. 366.

[5] *Examiner* (15 July 1821), pp. 444-446.

[6] *London Magazine,* 3 (May 1821), 484-490. For background on Scott's editorship, see Josephine Bauer, *The London Magazine* (Copenhagen: Rosenkilde and Bagger, 1953).

[7] *Complete Works,* VIII, 32. The publication of *Table-Talk* in April 1821 may be dated by Hunt's shocked and angry letter to Hazlitt concerning references to himself. See P. P. Howe, *Life of William Hazlitt* (1922; London: Penguin, 1949), pp. 315-322.

[8] Both passages are quoted in Ralph M. Wardle's *Hazlitt* (Lincoln: University of Nebraska Press, 1971), pp. 171, 185.

[9] 12 (August 1822), 157ff. On attribution to Crowe, see Strout, *Bibliography,* p. 145.

[10] According to the *OED,* a *swandrop* is "the knob on a swan's bill." See especially *Blackwood's,* 2 (March 1818), "Notices" on unnumbered preliminary leaves; and 9 (April 1821), 62.

[11] In some essays, Hazlitt was clearly an early violator of the prevailing decorum concerning what Crabbe Robinson referred to as "private confidence in the detail of conversation" (quoted by Wardle in *Hazlitt,* p. 177). Hazlitt's only defense seems to have been that he did not plagiarize, but openly reported what he heard in order to expose hypocrisy. The eighteenth-century gentleman's agreement protecting private conversation from comparison with public statements was partly a matter of plain expediency, partly derived from the notion of the "dignity" of biography and history. (See Joseph W. Reed, Jr., *English Biography in the Early Nineteenth Century, 1801-1838* [New Haven: Yale University Press, 1966], pp. 39-40.) The "dignity" of biography had, of course, been violated notoriously by Boswell in his *Life of Johnson,* which provides another context for Crowe's above association Hazlitt with Boswell. Yet Hazlitt later made the most of the association by using the name "Boswell Redivivus" for his *Conversations with Northcote,* first serialized in 1826.

[12] *Complete Works,* VIII, 102.

[13] James M. Thompson, *Leaders of the French Revolution* (New York: D. Appleton, 1929), pp. 91-113.

[14] Gerald McNiece, *Shelley and the Revolutionary Idea* (Cambridge, Mass.: Harvard University Press, 1969), pp. 22-28.

[15] *Blackwood's,* 9 (February 1822), 137-153, esp. 138, 141.

[16] A brief analysis of the class basis of British Romantic literature is included in Chritopher Caudwell's *Illusion and Reality: A Study of the Sources of Poetry* (London: Macmillan and Co., 1937), especially in Chapter v, "English Poets: The Industrial Revolution." His comments are both criticized and developed by Manfred Wojcik, "In Defence of Shelley," *Zeitschrift für Anglistik und Amerikanistik,* 2 (1963), 157-159.

[17] See M. H. Abrams, *Natural Supernaturalism: Tradition and Revolution in Romantic Literature* (New York: Norton, 1971), pp. 84-87, 90.

[18] The best discussion of Peterloo and its social significance appears in Edward Palmer Thompson, *The Making of the English Working Class* (London: Gollancz, 1963), pp. 669-700.

[19] See Walter E. Houghton's magisterial brief histories, from a liberal perspective, of the founding of the *Edinburgh,* the *Quarterly,* and *Blackwood's* in *The*

Wellesley Index to Victorian Periodicals, 1824-1900 (Toronto: University of Toronto Press, 1966), I, 7-9, 416-421, 696-701. Hayden surveys much the same material from a more conservative perspective in *The Romantic Reviewers,* pp. 7-38, 60-63.

[20] *Complete Works,* XI, 127.

[21] For readable brief surveys of these influences, see Richard Ohmann, "Teaching and Studying Literature at the End of Ideology," in *The Politics of Literature: Dissenting Essays on the Teaching of English,* ed. Louis Kampf and Paul Lauter (New York: Pantheon Books, 1972); and "Where a Pluralist Goes Wrong," Chapter ix of G. William Domhoff's *The Higher Circles: The Governing Class in America* (New York: Random House, 1970).

[22] *Complete Works,* VII, 20; noted by Sir Llewellyn Woodward in *The Age of Reform 1815-1870* (Oxford: Clarendon Press, 1962), p. 58.

[23] See Hayden's discussion of reviewers' attitudes in *The Romantic Reviewers,* pp. 243ff., and Abrams, *Natural Supernaturalism,* pp. 11-14.

William Keach (essay date 1986)

SOURCE: "Cockney Couplets: Keats and the Politics of Style," in *Studies in Romanticism,* Vol. 25, No. 2, Summer, 1986, pp. 182-96.

[*In the essay that follows, Keach examines the couplets of Keats'* Poems *and* Endymion *as politically charged Cockney insurgences.*]

The focus of this paper—Keats's couplet writing in the *Poems* of 1817 and in *Endymion* of 1818—may seem less than inviting if you take the dim view of this poetry that still prevails. But the conspicuous influence of Leigh Hunt, together with the Tory attacks on Keats's "Cockney style" largely provoked by that influence, make it possible to reconstruct a more detailed political context for this poetry than for any other text or moment in Keats's career. I should acknowledge straightaway that the political implications of Keats's "Cockney style" have been recognized before by (among others) John Hayden, Theodore Redpath, and most recently Jerome McGann.[1] What I want to do is explore one aspect of those implications more intensively, speculating along the way about the difficulties as well as the possibilities of doing so. And I want to suggest that whatever you think about the couplets in *Sleep and Poetry* or *Endymion,* the critical questions they encourage aren't entirely dissolved in Keats's later stylistic achievements. McGann is right, I think, to say that "the significance of this Cockney style . . . is not very widely recognized,"[2] especially (I would add) its significance for Keats's own subsequent development.

In late July 1818, on a visit to Scotland, Benjamin Bailey dined at the house of Bishop George Glieg, his future father-in-law, and there met John Gibson Lock-hart, one of the main contributors to the new magazine recently founded by the Tory publisher and bookseller William Blackwood.[3] In August, Bailey wrote to Keats's new publisher, John Taylor, about this meeting:

> [Lockhart] abused poor Keats in a way that, although it was at the Bishop's table, I could hardly keep my temper. I said I supposed then [Keats] would be attacked in Blackwood's. He replied "not by *me*"; which would carry the insinuation he would by some one *else*. The objections he stated were frivolous in the extreme. They chiefly respected the *rhymes*.[4]

As it turned out, of course, Lockhart—and possibly his cohort John Wilson—did attack Keats in *Blackwood's Magazine,* in the last of a series of abusive articles begun in October 1817 on the "Cockney School of Poetry." For "Z," as the *Blackwood's* reviewers signed themselves, Keats's rhyme in his 1817 and 1818 volumes wasn't a frivolous matter at all. It epitomized the corruption of what *Blackwood's* called "the Cockney school of versification, morality, and politics":

> . . . this romance is meant to be written in English heroic rhyme. To those who have read any of Hunt's poems, this hint might indeed be needless. Mr Keats has adopted the loose, nerveless versification, and Cockney rhymes of the poet of Rimini.[5]

Lockhart's implication is clear: Keats's loose liberal couplets are the stylistic analogue of the loose liberal politics he had imbibed from Hunt. Near the end of the review Lockhart quotes twenty-two lines (exactly half of them enjambed) from Keats's denunciation of those "who lord it o'er their fellow-men / With most prevailing tinsel"[6] at the beginning of Book III of *Endymion.* He introduces this quotation by saying: "We had almost forgotten to mention, that Keats belongs to the Cockney School of Politics, as well as the Cockney School of Poetry."[7]

The same linking of politics and versification marks John Wilson Croker's attack on *Endymion* in the arch-Tory *Quarterly Review:*

> —At first it appeared to us, that Mr. Keats had been amusing himself and wearying his readers with an immeasurable game at *bouts-rimés*. . . . He seems to us to write a line at random, and then he follows not the thought excited by this line, but that suggested by the *rhyme* with which it concludes. There is hardly a complete couplet inclosing a complete idea in the whole book.[8]

For Croker, Keats's Cockney couplets are an affront to the orthodoxy of the closed Augustan couplet and to the social and moral traditions it symbolizes. Croker's reference to the game of *bouts-rimés,* although it doesn't exactly fit the compositional process he thinks he sees in Keats, is politically significant. Addison had defined the game in attacking its eighteenth-century vogue in one of his *Spectator* essays (No. 60) on forms of "False Wit": "They were a List of Words that rhyme to one another, drawn up by another Hand, and given to a Poet, who was to make a Poem to the Rhymes in the same Order that they were placed upon the List."[9] That this game was still fashionable in Regency society is evident from Byron's delightfully macaronic couplet in Canto 16 of *Don Juan,* where we hear about the Duchess of Fitz-Fulke's taste in poetry: "But of all verse, what most ensured her praise / Were sonnets to herself, or 'Bouts rimés'" (St. 50).[10] In accusing Keats of playing at *bouts rimés,* Croker insinuates that this low-born London "neophyte" of Leigh Hunt is abusing Pope by taking seriously a parlor game with which his aristocratic betters merely while away their time on country weekends. Like *Blackwood's* "Z," Croker ridicules other features of Keats's Cockney style as well: the meter, the diction, the erotic imagery. But it is the "Cockney rhymes" that most obviously betray what these Tory reviewers see as Keats's inseparable poetical and political vices.

Keats was caught up, then, in a squabble between Tory traditionalists, for whom the balanced and closed Augustan couplet had become something of a cultural fetish, and the liberal reformers who set out to establish "a freer spirit of versification," as Hunt says in the Preface to *The Story of Rimini,*[11] along with a freer society. So far this picture of the politics of Keats's "Cockney style" seems to be fairly predictable—but that's because it's still misleadingly simple.[12] Consider, for instance, the political ramifications of Hunt's developing the couplet, not blank verse, as an antithesis to what he saw as the monotonous regularity of "Pope and the French school of versification" (Preface, *The Story of Rimini*). Hunt's effort to reform the heroic couplet is an exact image of his reformist politics. There is a general formulation in Hunt's essay "What is Poetry?" that could characterize his ideal society almost as easily as his ideal couplet: "Poetry shapes this modulation into uniformity for its outline, and variety for its parts, because it thus realizes the last idea of beauty itself, which includes the charm of diversity within the flowing round of habit and ease."[13] Hunt loves "the flowing round of habit and ease" that marks the couplet as long as it is internally varied, diverse. And there is an undeniably conservative impulse in his desire, as he says in the Preface to the second edition of *The Feast of the Poets,* "to bring back the real harmonies of the English heroic, and to restore to it half the true principle of its music,—variety."[14]

But there may also be a specifically political anti-conservative impulse in Hunt's—and initially Keats's, before the unCockney Miltonic experiments of the first *Hyperion*—avoidance of blank verse. For by 1817-1818, blank verse had come to be inevitably associated with Wordsworth, whose political conservatism Hunt frequently criticized even as he made efforts to align himself with Wordsworth's power as a poet of nature.[15] We should note in this regard that when the *Blackwood's* review defends Pope against Keats's attack on "rocking Horse" couplets in *Sleep and Poetry,* it does so by proclaiming that "to deny [Pope's] genius, is just as absurd as to dispute that of Wordsworth, or to believe in that of Hunt."[16] Hunt and Keats may not have shared Shelley's judgment that the author of *The Excursion* was "a slave"[17] (Shelley himself countered *The Excursion* in *Alastor* by taking on its verse form as well as its argument), but their staying away from blank verse may have had a political motivation all the same. It was in the summer of 1818—the summer of the *Black-wood's* and *Quarterly Review* attacks—that Keats tried to visit Wordsworth at Rydal Mount, only to hear that he was out campaigning for the Tory Lowthers against the reformer Henry Brougham in the Westmoreland elections.[18]

While Keats praises Wordsworth in that section in *Sleep and Poetry* on the current state of English verse, he does so as part of a performance that suggests anything but a writer naive about or unaware of the politics of style. It's not just that 28 of the 49 lines in these two verse paragraphs are enjambed, in open defiance of the closed couplets savored by the likes of Croker. At several points Keats's couplets mock by mimicking the poetic conventions under scrutiny:

with a puling infant's force
They sway'd about upon a rocking horse,
And thought it Pegasus. Ah dismal soul'd!
(185-87)

The rhythm of "They sway'd about upon a rocking horse" rocks childishly along in satirical harmony with the rhyme ("infant's force"/ "rocking horse"), and then comes to an abrupt halt at the medial full-stop after "And thought it Pegasus."[19] Keats knew what he was about in attacking Pope's couplets with couplets of his own devising:

But ye were dead
To things ye knew not of,—were closely wed
To musty laws lined out with wretched rule
And compass vile: so that ye taught a school
Of dolts to smooth, inlay, and clip, and fit,
Till, like the certain wands of Jacob's wit,
Their verses tallied. Easy was the task:
(193-99)

Here Keats flouts the "wretched rules" of Augustan verse formally as well as argumentatively by refusing to pause grammatically for four consecutive line-endings (the doubly unstopped "rule"/"school" couplet is an act of open unruliness)—until he moves into the mincing steps of "to smooth, inlay, and clip, and fit," where he prosodically parodies the process he names. It was shrewd of Byron, in what would have been the first of his contributions to the "Pope controversy," to attack Keats's attack on Pope by referring sarcastically to Mr. Keats's "new 'Essay on Criticism.'"[20] Byron recognized Keats's polemical exploitation of making "The sound . . . seem an Echo to the sense" (*Essay on Criticism* II.365), and he knew that Keats learned to do that sort of thing from Pope himself.

Byron's response to Keats's parody of Pope's couplets suggests just how complicated and even contradictory the politics of style can become. He first mocks Keats's mockery in "Some Observations upon an Article in *Blackwood's Magazine,*" a rambling piece written in March 1820 and sent to Murray for immediate publication (Murray held it back, however, and did not publish it until 1833).[21] The *Blackwood's* article in question, published in August 1819, had nothing directly to do with Pope—it was a moralizing denuncation of Byron's private life as reflected in *Don Juan.* Byron thought the *Blackwood's* piece to have been authored by John Wilson,[22] who the previous summer had very likely collaborated in the attack on Hunt and Keats. So Byron's initial denuncation of Keats's writing appears as part of his assault on the same Tory magazine that had first derided Keats's "Cockney rhymes." The ironic political crossings get even more intricate. Byron dedicated his unpublished "Observations" to Isaac Disraeli, who just four months later defended Pope in a long review of two competing editions of Joseph Spence's *Anecdotes* and of William Lisle Bowles's *The Invariable Principles of Poetry* in *The Quarterly Review,*[23] which had of course published Croker's savaging of *Endymion.* It was Disraeli's review that elicited Byron's first public entry into the "Pope controversy" (the first, that is, since *English Bards and Scotch Reviewers*). "They support Pope I see in the Quarterly," he wrote to Murray. "Let them Continue to do so. . . ."[24] In his *Letter to*********[*John Murray*] . . . *on the Rev. W. L. Bowles's Strictures on the Life and Writings of Pope* (March 1821), Byron sides openly with the *Quar-terly*'s position in the "Pope controversy." In his *Second Letter* on the same subject (also written in March 1821 but not published until 1835), Byron has another go at Keats (or "Ketch," as he now calls him)—this time as part of a condescending dismissal of "my friend Leigh Hunt" and what "some one has maliciously called the 'Cockney School.'"[25]

Byron's willingness to side with the Tories in the "Pope controversy" against the liberal poetics of Hunt and Keats reflects interestingly on the politics of his own couplet style. As Peter Manning has recently shown in two excellent articles on the political context and significance of *The Corsair,*[26] Byron's writing appealed strongly to reformist and even to radical readers. Conrad's "anti-authoritarian" and "anarchic" behavior led to his being invoked as the type of Jeremiah Brandreth, one of the leaders of the Pentridge uprising of June 1817, and to a popular prose adaptation of *The Corsair* by the radical publisher William Hone. Byron himself had indicated his own ties to the reformist Whigs in the dedicatory letter to Thomas Moore which prefaced the first edition of *The Corsair* in 1814. By referring to "The wrongs of your own country" and "the magnificent and fiery spirit of her sons,"[27] Byron reaffirms his passionate appeal for Catholic emancipation in his second speech before the House of Lords (21 April 1813).[28] At the same time, as Manning demonstrates, there was much about *The Corsair* that contradicted its oppositional implications and made it appeal to conservative bourgeois readers: the volume's expensive production, the learned epigraphs and notes, the urbane authorial voice adopted in those notes and in the letter to Moore—and the versification, which Byron advertises as "the best adapted measure to our language, the good old and now neglected heroic couplet."[29]

The couplets of *The Corsair* provide a striking contemporary contrast to Keats's Cockney couplets in *Sleep and Poetry* and *Endymion.* Enjambment is rare; only two lines in the poem's opening 42-line section, for example, aren't strongly end-stopped. Croker could have found in Byron's couplets just what he missed in Keats's: "a complete couplet inclosing a complete idea." And the relation between couplet form and idea in *The Corsair* is politically suggestive. Consider the couplet that begins the opening song of Conrad's pirates: "'O'er the glad waters of the dark blue sea, / Our thoughts as boundless, and our souls as free,'" (1.1-2). Conrad and his followers may have "thoughts" that are "boundless" and "souls" that are "free," but the couplet which celebrates this spirit is neither—it is as carefully bound-ed and closed as a couplet from *The Essay on Man.* An even more arresting instance of the way in which Byron's heroic couplets check—and also give contrasting point to—the poem's appeal to a restless, rebellious energy appears later in this opening section, as the pirates distinguish their lives on the open sea from "him who crawls enamoured of decay": "'While gasp by gasp he faulters forth his soul, / Ours with one pang—one bound—escapes controul.'" (1.31-32). "Escapes controul" comes sharply up against the controlling closure of a full-stop. Manning's work on *The Corsair* helps us see that however anti-authoritarian and anarchic Byron's hero may be, he performs within stylistic terms as familiar and congenial to genteel Regency readers as Keats's Cockney couplets were strange and rebarbative.

Keats knew what he wanted to do in his 1817 Cockney couplets, and he knew how far beyond the "flowing round of habit and ease" characteristic of Hunt's liberal reform couplets he wanted to go. The *Blackwood's* review is right, given its basic assumption, to assert that "the defects of [Hunt's] system are tenfold more conspicuous in his disciple's work than in his own."[30] Tenfold may be an exaggeration, but anyone interested in the statistical evidence for just how much further

Keats went than Hunt in breaking the metrical and grammatical conventions of the Augustan couplet can look such evidence up in the studies of M. R. Ridley and W. J. Bate.[31] Hunt himself had complained about the excesses of Keats's couplet experiments in his *Examiner* review of the 1817 *Poems:*

> Mr. Keats' . . . fault, the one in his versification, arises from . . . contradicting over-zealously the fault on the opposite side. It is this which provokes him now and then into mere roughness and discords for their own sake, but not for that of variety and contrasted harmony.[32]

Keats's friend John Hamilton Reynolds had made much the same complaint a few months earlier in his unsigned review for the progressively liberal *Champion* (9 March 1817).[33] In fact the liberal reviewers, though quite favorably disposed towards Keats's early poem, had almost as many reservations about the couplets as their Tory counterparts. P. G. Patmore in *The London Magazine* (April 1820) praised the "freedom, sweetness, and variety" of Keats's rhythms in *Endymion* but admitted that "the verse frequently runs riot, and loses itself in air."[34]

Such responses ought to make us ask to what extent, and in just what ways, the stylistic choices and performances of the 1817 and 1818 volumes *are* political choices and performances. The broad relevance of a highly politicized context to Keats's early style is clear, but no one would want to argue that his extravagant experiments in couplet writing are in themselves expressive of political convictions more radical and anarchic than those of liberals like Hunt. If anything, Keats's stylistic extravagance might appear to be radically anti-political in its tendency to produce lines which, as Hunt said in 1832 of the more disciplined couplets of *Lamia,* "seem to take pleasure in the progress of their own beauty."[35] We seem to have arrived at a point where the explanatory usefulness of the political context for Keats's early couplet style breaks down. Or perhaps both that context and Keats's stylistic response to it are only complicating themselves beyond the level at which we usually work when we look at what McGann refers to as "the specific ways in which certain stylistic forms intersect and join with certain factual and cognitive points of reference."[36]

As a way of pushing on speculatively at this point, I want to turn to another moderately liberal reviewer, Francis Jeffrey, writing belatedly about *Endymion* in the August 1820 number of *The Edinburgh Review.* Jeffrey sees that if Keats is playing at *bouts rimés* in the couplets of *Endymion,* he is doing so in a distinctive and at least potentially fruitful way:

> A great part of the work indeed, is written in the strangest and most fantastical manner than can be imagined. It seems as if the author had ventured every thing that occurred to him in the shape of a glittering image or striking expression—taken the first word that presented itself to make up a rhyme, and then made that word the germ of a new cluster of images—a hint for a new excursion of the fancy—and so wandered on, equally forgetful whence he came, and heedless whither he was going, till he had covered his pages with an interminable arabesque of connected and incongruous figures, that multiplied as they extended, and were only harmonized by the brightness of their tints, and the graces of their forms.[37]

Some of Jeffrey's response is vaguely generalizing, but the part that's worth holding onto for the moment is the suggestion that Keats allows himself to be led (and also misled) by the rhyme as it generates a need for connection and development, as it provokes and then gives unexpected shape to figurative elaborations. At times in *Endymion* and in the 1817 volume, Keats seems to be doing just this, and with an air of self-delighting curiosity as to the consequences. There is an extraordinary moment in "I Stood Tip-toe" when Keats wanders off into a day-dream occasioned by the couplet that precedes it:

> Were I in such a place, I sure should pray
> That nought less sweet might call my thoughts
>   away,
> Than the soft rustle of a maiden's gown
> Fanning away the dandelion's down:
> (93-96)

He follows this figure for four more couplets before reluctantly letting her depart:

> And as she leaves me may she often turn
> Her fair eyes looking through her locks aubùrne.
>   What next? A tuft of evening primroses,
> O'er which the mind may hover till it dozes;
> (105-8)

The genial audacity of that "What next?" is winning in its way—it's hard not to read it as Keats's exclamation about having gotten by with a rhyme like "turn"/ "aubùrne," as well as an indication that he is letting himself be surprised by what turns up next.

The serious critical issue here is the extent to which Keats is willing to let the pressures and possibilities of rhyming, and thus of contending with arbitrary phonetic and semantic convergences, shape the development of his poem. Is this an issue with political implications, amenable to historical and political understanding? Or have we passed beyond the level at which politics and form intersect? It's one thing to accept, say, P. N. Medvedev's principle that "A linguistic form is only real in the concrete speech performance, in the social utterance,"[38] or David Simpson's insistence "on the historical grounds of [a] play of possibilities rendered into language."[39] It's quite another to make good on McGann's claim that "Only by reading [Keats's Cockney poetry] in a sharply specified historical frame of reference are we able to see . . . and hence to describe precisely not merely the abstract *characteristics,* but the felt *qualities* of its poetic structure."[40] Some of those "felt *qualities,*" as we have seen, yield amply to being understood "in a sharply specified historical" and political "frame of reference." But what about the quality Jeffrey felt in observing that Keats often allows the first rhyme-word in a couplet to become "the germ of a new cluster of images—a hint for a new excursion of the fancy"?

One initial response to these questions ought to be that they can't be settled theoretically, simply as points of principle. The degree to which historical and political circumstances are precisely useful in understanding matters of style, or the level at which they cease to become useful, isn't decidable in advance of our actually trying to think about a particular stylistic feature from a historical and political point of view. With this in mind, I want to look briefly at rhyme-induced figurative "excursions" from Keats's later poetry. That such "excursions" grow out of the sort of verbal opportunism in Keats's "Cockney style" that upset Tory and liberal reviewers alike was demonstrated years ago by Kingsley Amis, in the inaugural volume of *Essays in Criticism.* Amis complained that Keats's "hopelessly inadequate" rhyming of "my sole self" and "deceiving elf" in the last stanza of "Ode to a Nightingale" has its origin in one of the Cockney couplets of *Endymion,* when the narrator laments "The journey homeward to habitual self! / A mad-pursuing of the fogborn elf" (II.276-77).[41] Readers more interested than Amis apparently was in Keats's broodings about the self as a construct at once deceiving in its significance and yet hauntingly persistent may find that the rhyming precipitation of "elf" out of "self" (it's like a miniature of Blake's "spectre" and "emanation"), far from being "hopelessly inadequate," is intrinsic to Keats's thinking through the issue of poetic subjectivity. His attitude towards the self, as reading Hazlitt helps us see, is implicitly political in deep and complicated ways. Instead of trying to draw those implications out within the confines of this paper, however, I want to turn to another example which raises more immediate questions about the politics of style and impinges directly on the debate provoked by McGann's political reading of "To Autumn."

Here are the last seven lines of the poem's opening stanza, beginning with the second of that stanza's opulent infinitive clauses:

> To bend with apples the moss'd cottage-trees,
> And fill all fruit with ripeness to the core;
> To swell the gourd, and plump the hazel shells
> With a sweet kernel; to set budding more,
> And still more, later flowers for the bees,
> Until they think warm days will never cease,
> For summer has o'er-brimm'd their clammy cells.
>
> (5-11)

In this stanza of "To Autumn," where all is made to feel so inevitable, we feel an inevitable resistance to recognizing that anything as overtly arbitrary as the exigencies of rhyme could be involved in generating that culminating image. Yet the "bees" in "their clammy cells" are there in part to rhyme with "cottage-trees" and "hazel shells." And these very rhymes appear in *Endymion,* in Cockney couplets like the ones attacked by *Blackwood's* and the *Quarterly:*

> Just when the light of morn, with hum of bees,
> Stole through its verdurous matting of fresh trees.
>
> (111.419-20)

> And gather up all fancifullest shells
> For thee to tumble into Naiads' cells,
>
> (1.271-72)

It's plausible to think that Keats was led to the "cluster of images" that concludes the first stanza of "To Autumn" by, among other concerns, the suggestive pressure of rhyme, and by his recalling his own Cockney versification. But is there anything political about his being thus led?

As David Bromwich points out, Keats had already used a reference to bees to distinctive political effect in "Robin Hood" (1818), where it is followed in rhyming position by an aggressively Cockney couplet linking "honey" to "money." We know from a letter to Bailey shortly after his moving to Winchester that however pleased Keats may have been with this quiet retreat into solitude, the class-based slurs on his Cockney writing were still very much in his mind: "One of my Ambitions is . . . to upset the drawling of the blue stocking literary world" (14 August 1819).[42] And as both Bromwich and Paul Fry remind us, Keats was avidly keeping up with the current political turmoil in the country. He had gone back to London from Winchester for a few days (to try to arrange financial help for his brother George in America) just in time to see Orator Hunt's tumultuous return from Manchester and Peterloo. The *Examiner*'s reports on Peterloo, which Keats read during his Winchester stay, provide a dark backdrop to the "Season of mists and mellow fruitfulness" celebrated in "To Autumn." The number for Sunday, 5 September—the last number Keats would have seen before his trip to London—contains a particularly important linking of the month's political and literary significance. Following a series of letters reporting on the aftermath of Peterloo, including letters from Henry Hunt himself on his Manchester trial, and immediately following a piece entitled "Return of the Killed and Wounded at Manchester. Letter from Mr. Pearson," is an entry called "Calendar of Nature. (From the Literary Pocket-Book.) September." This item begins with the September stanza from the procession of the months in Spenser's Mutability Cantos (*The Faerie Queene* VII.vii.38), a stanza that contains iconographical de-

Percy Bysshe Shelley, English poet, 1792-1822.

tails to which Keats was clearly responding in "To Autumn."[43] Even more suggestive, however, are the details in the *Examiner*'s gloss on Spenser's stanza:

> The poet still takes advantage of the exuberance of harvest and the sign of the Zodiac in this month, to read us a lesson on justice.
>
> Autumn has now arrived. This is the month of the migration of birds, of the finished harvest, of nut-gathering, of cyder and perry-making. . . . The swallows . . . disappear for the warmer climates, leaving only a few stragglers behind, probably from weakness or sickness. . . .
>
> September, though its mornings and evenings are apt to be chill and foggy, and therefore not wholesome to those who either do not or cannot guard against them, is generally a serene and pleasant month, partaking of the warmth of summer and the vigour of autumn. . . . The feast, as the philosophic poet says on a higher occasion . . .[44]

Here the *Examiner* quotes a Spenserian stanza from Shelley's *The Revolt of Islam* (Hunt's extended enthusiastic review of the poem had appeared in February and March 1818) describing a victory feast held by the forces of liberation. The stanza is slightly misquoted to make it fit with the *Examiner*'s prose:

> The feast is such as earth, the general mother,
> Pours from her fairest bosom, when she smiles
> In the embrace of Autumn. To each other
> As some fond parent fondly reconciles
> Her warring children, she their wrath beguiles
> With their own sustenance; they, relenting, weep.
> Such is this festival, which from their isles,
> And continents, and winds, and oceans deep,
> All shapes may throng to share, that fly, or walk, or creep.
>
> (v.lv.2209-2307)

Is this Autumn's "lesson on justice," this image of a momentary natural bounty that "beguiles" the "wrath" of people previously oppressed? Hunt had not quoted the stanza in his review of Shelley's poem, but his summary of this phase of the narrative is pertinent: "a festival is held at which *Cythna* presides like a visible angel, and every thing seems happiness and security. The Revolters however are suddenly assailed by the allies of the tyrant; and the fortune of the contest is changed."[45]

All this contextual material may seem remote from Keats's bees in "To Autumn," but the *Examiner*'s quoting of Shelley suggests one way in which it may be pointedly relevant. When in his "Song to the Men of England" (1819) Shelley asks the "Bees of England" why they allow "these stingless drones" to "spoil / The forced produce of your toil" (the "spoil"/"toil" rhyme, incidentally, appears in the stanza from Spenser quoted in the *Examiner*), he is drawing upon a figurative tradition common in radical political writing of the later eighteenth and early nineteenth century.[46] True, Keats's imagery has an important Virgilian source, as editors have pointed out: even the rhyme-word "cells" has its antecedents in the "cellas" of Virgil's famous simile.[47] But knowing this doesn't preclude our thinking politically about Keats's image. After all, Virgil's early summer image ("aestate nova") of Dido's subjects joyfully laboring to build Carthage has complicated political resonances of its own, resonances carried over but transformed in Keats's early autumnal image of worker-bees whose momentary abundance makes them "*think* warm days will never cease" (my emphasis), and whose "o'er-brimm'd . . . cells" are disturbingly "clammy." A reader in 1819-1820 familiar with popular political pamphlets and songs might have found Keats's image of laboring bees political in ways that no blue stocking would have approved of.

I'm not arguing that all references to bees in romantic poems ask to be read politically, or that Keats's stylistic habits led him deliberately to focus his own and his readers' attention in these lines on the living conditions of real English gleaners in the autumn of 1819. But I am arguing that here as elsewhere, "To Autumn" presents us with an idealized, mythologized image of culminated and therefore death-set fruition that fends off but cannot finally exclude a negative historical actuality which Keats was certainly in touch with. His writing cannot free itself entirely from either the political reality or the political language that both McGann and Fry, in opposite ways, insist that he wants to avoid.

My larger point is that even at a level of performance where the specific political context of Keats's Cockney couplets ceases to be immediately instructive, the stylistic instincts encouraged and shaped by that context may produce writing with an important though momentarily suppressed political dimension. If our engagement with the "richer entanglements" of Keats's poetry is going to expand to include a fresh sense of that political dimension, we will need to make ourselves newly alert to the ways in which acts of writing and reading may be subject to historical and political circumstances quite remote from a poem's immediate field of reference.

Notes

[1] John O. Hayden, *The Romantic Reviewers, 1802-1824* (London: Routledge, 1969) 188-96; Theodore Redpath, *The Young Romantics and Critical Opinion 1807-1824* (London: Harrap, 1973) 418-21; Jerome McGann, "Keats and the Historical Method in Literary Criticism" *MLN* 94 (1979): 996-99.

[2] McGann, "Keats and the Historical Method" 996.

[3] Walter Jackson Bate, *John Keats* (Cambridge, Mass.: Harvard U P, 1963) 366-67.

[4] *The Keats Circle: Letters and Papers 1816-1878,* ed. Hyder Edward Rollins (Cambridge, Mass.: Harvard U P, 1948) 1: 34.

[5] "Cockney School of Poetry, No IV," *Blackwood's Edinburgh Magazine* 3 (August 1818): 522.

[6] All quotations are from *The Poems of John Keats,* ed. Jack Stillinger (Cambridge, Mass.: Harvard U P, 1978).

[7] "Cockney School of Poetry" 524.

[8] "Art. VII.—*Endymion: A Poetic Romance*. By John Keats," *The Quarterly Review* vol. 19, no. 37 (April 1818): 205-6.

[9] *The Spectator,* ed. Donald F. Bond (Oxford: Clarendon, 1965) 1: 256.

[10] All quotations of *Don Juan* are from *Byron's "Don Juan": A Variorum Edition,* ed. Truman Guy Steffan and Willis W. Pratt (Austin: U of Texas P, 1957).

[11] (London: J. Murray; W. Blackwood; Cumming, 1816) xv. Subsequent quotations are from this edition. In "The Return of the Enjambed Couplet" (*ELH* 7 [1940]: 239-52, Earl Wasserman argued that Hunt's and Keats's originality in opening up the closed Augustan couplet had been exaggerated, that "the versification of Keats and Hunt is . . . the fulfillment of a movement that had its beginnings in the last quarter of the eighteenth century" (251).

[12] We need to remember here that a majority of the reviewers of both Keats's early volumes were encouraging. See Hayden, *The Romantic Reviewers* 188, 190.

[13] "An Answer to the Question What is Poetry? Including Remarks on Versification," *Imagination and Fancy* (New York: Wiley and Putnam, 1845) 2.

[14] (London: Gale and Fenner, 1815) 32.

[15] See P. M. S. Dawson, "Byron, Shelley, and the 'new school,'" *Shelley Revalued: Essays from the Gregynog Conference,* ed. Kelvin Everest (Totowa, N.J.: Barnes, 1983) 89-108, esp. 91-101.

[16] "Cockney School of Poetry" 520.

[17] *Mary Shelley's Journal,* ed. Frederick L. Jones (Norman: U of Oklahoma P, 1947) 15.

[18] Bate, *John Keats* 349-50.

[19] Douglas Bush notes that the source of Keats's image here is Hazlitt's "On Milton's Versification" (1815): "Dr. Johnson and Pope would have converted his [Mil-ton's] vaulting Pegasus into a rocking-horse" (John Keats, *Selected Poems and Letters* [Boston: Houghton, 1959] 312).

[20] "Some Observations Upon an Article in *Blackwood's Magazine,*" Appendix IX in *Byron's Works: Letters and Journals,* ed. Rowland E. Prothero (London: John Murray, 1898-1901) IV: 493.

[21] See note 20 above and Leslie A. Marchand, *Byron: A Biography* (New York: Knopf, 1957) II: 845 and note.

[22] Prothero, *Letters and Journals* IV: 474, refers to Byron's letter to Murray of 10 December 1819 (see IV: 385 and note in Prothero's edition). Leslie Marchand, *Byron's Letters and Journals* (Cambridge, Mass.: Harvard U P, 1976) VI: 257n. says, "It is still a question as to whether John Wilson wrote the review."

[23] Vol. 23, no. 46 (July 1820): 400-34.

[24] *Byron's Letters and Journals* VII: 217 (4 November 1820). Bowles's own preference for the open, enjambed couplet is an aspect of the "Pope controversy" that doubtless exacerbated Byron's antipathy

to Bowles as it did his antipathy to Keats. See Wasserman, "The Return of the Enjambed Couplet" 248-49.

[25] Prothero, ed., *Letters and Journals* Appendix III, V: 588.

[26] "Tales and Politics: *The Corsair, Lara,* and *The White Doe of Rylstone,*" *Salzburger Studien zur Anglistik und Amerikanistik* 13 (1980): 204-30; and "The Hone-ing of Byron's *Corsair,*" chapter 6 in *Textual Criticism and Literary Interpretation,* ed. Jerome McGann (Chicago: U of Chicago P, 1985) 107-26.

[27] Quotations of *The Corsair* are from vol. III of *The Complete Poetical Works,* ed. Jerome J. McGann (Oxford: Clarendon, 1981). The references to Byron's Preface are on 111: 148.

[28] See Manning, "Tales and Politics" 209.

[29] *Complete Poetical Works* 111: 149.

[30] "Cockney School of Poetry" 522.

[31] M. R. Ridley, *Keats' Craftsmanship: A Study in Poetic Development* (London: Methuen, 1903) 241-49 and 305, Note J, and Walter Jackson Bate, *The Stylistic Development of John Keats* (New York: Humanities, 1945) 19-28, 147-55.

[32] 6 and 13 July 1817, reprinted in Redpath, *The Young Romantics and Critical Opinion* 455-56.

[33] Reprinted in Redpath, *The Young Romantics and Critical Opinion* 451-52.

[34] Vol. I, no. 4: 383.

[35] *The Poetical Works of Leigh Hunt* (London: Edward Moxon, 1832) xxxvi-xxxvii.

[36] "Romanticism and its Ideologies," *SiR* 21 (1982): 576.

[37] *The Edinburgh Review* vol. 34, no. 67 (August 1820): 204-5.

[38] P. N. Medvedev/M. M. Bakhtin, *The Formal Method in Literary Scholarship: A Critical Introduction to Sociological Poetics,* trans. Albert J. Wehrle (Baltimore: Johns Hopkins U P, 1978) 122. This passage is quoted by McGann in "Keats and the Historical Method" 990.

[39] "Criticism, Politics, and Style in Wordsworth's Poetry," *Critical Inquiry* 11 (1984): 67.

[40] "Keats and the Historical Method" 996-97.

[41] "The Curious Elf: A Note on Rhyme in Keats," *EIC* 1 (1951): 189-92.

[42] *The Letters of John Keats,* ed. Hyder Edward Rollins (Cambridge, Mass.: Harvard U P, 1958) 2:139.

[43] Helen Vendler emphasizes the influence of the Mutability Cantos on "To Autumn" in *The Odes of John Keats* (Cambridge, Mass.: Harvard U P, 1983) 242-43. She mentions the September stanza in passing but says nothing about its appearance in *The Examiner.*

[44] No. 610 (5 September 1819): 574.

[45] No. 527 (1 February 1818): 76.

[46] See P. M. S. Dawson, *The Unacknowledged Legislator: Shelley and Politics* (Oxford: Clarendon, 1980) 50-51. The quotation is from *Shelley: Poetical Works,* ed. Thomas Hutchinson, corrected by G. M. Matthews (Oxford: Oxford U P, 1970).

[47] References are to *Aeneid* 1.430-36 in the Loeb Classical Library edition (Cambridge, Mass.: Harvard U P, 1934).

John Gibson Lockhart, on the charge that John Wilson Croker's 1818 review of Keats' *Endymion* killed the poet:

As for the absurd story about Mr. John Keats having been *put to death* by the *Quarterly,* or by any other criticism, I confess I really did not expect to meet with a repetition of such stuff in the *Edinburgh Review.* If people die of these wounds, what a prince of killers, and king of murderers, must Mr. [Francis] Jeffrey [long-time editor of the *Edinburgh Review*] be! In law, the intention makes the crime, and he who fires a pistol at my body is a murderer, although he happens to miss me, or although I recover of the wound he inflicts. Granting, then, that this is the law, what are we to say to the man who cut up Byron's *Hours of Idleness?* That review, surely, was *meant* to be as severe as any review that was ever penned touching poor Johnny Keats. . . .

John Gibson Lockhart, in Blackwood's Edinburgh Magazine, *August, 1823, reprinted in* Lockhart's Literary Criticism, *Basil Blackwell, 1931.*

Richard Cronin (essay date 1996)

SOURCE: "Keats and the Politics of Cockney Style," in *Studies in English Literature 1500-1900,* Vol. 36, No. 4, Autumn, 1996, pp. 785-806.

[*In this essay, Cronin disputes the prevailing critical tendency to read Keats' poems as conveying explicit political opinions, insisting rather that his views are expressed in the nuances of the Cockney style.*]

On the evidence of the poems it might seem that John Keats's recent critics are a good deal more interested in politics than he was himself.[1] "At Dilkes I fall foul of Politics,"[2] Keats told his sister-in-law, representing it as a social danger on a level with Leigh Hunt's puns and the sentimentalism of John Hamilton Reynolds's sisters. But if his poems have similarly fallen foul of their modern readers, then there is at least good precedent for it. Contemporary reviewers shared with modern critics a sensitivity to the radical import of the poems curiously out of proportion to the provocation that the poems seem to offer. The opening of book 3 of *Endymion,* in which all the regalia of monarchy is dismissed as so much "tinsel," and the references to Isabella's brothers as "ledger-men" and "money-bags" were passages repeatedly cited as evidence that Keats was as cockney in his politics as his poetry. But the repetition works to undermine rather than to substantiate the charge. Tory reviewers had no need to characterize the politics of Percy Bysshe Shelley and Lord Byron on the basis of two passages.

G. M. Matthews sensibly explains the reception of Keats by pointing out that Keats's literary career coincided with a period in which the rival reviews had worked so to blur "literary and political opinion" that "it was hardly possible for a creative writer associated with one side to receive fair treatment from a reviewer employed by the other."[3] Keats was championed by Hunt, Hunt was the editor of the *Examiner,* and the reviewers needed no more to convince them that Keats's poems must be deeply tainted by his patron's politics. For the reviewers Keats was guilty by association, and the damning association was with Hunt. But Matthews, like Keats's friend Benjamin Bailey, assumes that the *Quarterly* and *Blackwood's* detestation for Hunt can be explained simply by reference to Hunt's being "so decidedly a party-man."[4] On the contrary, all evidence suggests that it was a detestation prompted more forcibly by Hunt's poetry than his politics, and by *The Story of Rimini* in particular, a poem almost entirely without political reference.[5]

MY DEAR BYRON

It has become conventional in modern criticism to insist on the relationship between cockney poetry and politics, to represent the attack on the closed couplet of the Augustans as an inflection of the political assault on a closed society. As William Keach, the most scrupulous of such critics, puts it, Hunt's claim in the preface to *The Story of Rimini* that he had attempted "'a freer spirit of versification'" is of a piece with his desire for a freer society.[6] But it is Keach's special virtue that he advances such claims only to put them into question. It may be that Hunt's "effort to reform the heroic couplet is an exact image of his reformist politics,"[7] but Keach is rightly chary of drawing the conclusion that Keats's far more radical experiments on the couplet form, from *Sleep and Poetry* to *Endymion,* indicate an analogous difference between Keats's politics and Hunt's liberal reformism.

From 1815 to 1819, the *Examiner* was a journal divided between literature and politics, and throughout those years it became increasingly difficult to reconcile its two dominant interests, with the result that in 1819 Hunt launched the *Indicator,* a move that amounts almost to a confession that the languages of literature and of politics could no longer be accommodated together within the same publication. Hunt devoted his own energies to the *Indicator,* as if in recognition that the political language that he had developed, a language that continued to invoke Charles James Fox as the ultimate political authority, and that found in Sir Francis Burdett its most congenial parliamentary spokesman, had become outmoded. It had been usurped by the quite different language spoken by Henry Hunt and written by William Cobbett and the group of radical journalists that Cobbett had inspired. Given this, it was natural that Leigh Hunt should respond by turning to the other language in which he was proficient, the language of literature. Keach asks what political statement can be deduced from Keats's habit in *Endymion* of allowing the exigencies of rhyme to determine the sequence of thought, and the value of his question is that it reveals on one level what Hunt's decision to establish the *Indicator* reveals on another. It shows that the languages of cockney politics and poetry were not one language but two. Hunt's political language was developed in the years of the Napoleonic wars. By 1810, in the series of articles that led to his imprisonment, it is fully formed. The language of cockney poetry, on the other hand, was a product of the peace. It was fully embodied for the first time in *The Story of Rimini,* published in 1816.[8]

Cockney poetry is most easily defined not as a style but as a relationship between a style and a subject matter. Hunt's poem tells the story of the ill-fated marriage between Francesca, daughter of Guido Novello da Polenta, duke of Ravenna, and Giovanni Malatesta, duke of Rimini. The bridegroom's procession with which it begins and the funeral procession with which it ends frame the tale within two pageants which embody the elaborate social hierarchy that establishes the place of the poem's chief characters at its apex. It is not a continuous but a fractured hierarchy. The nobility of Ravenna assembles in the palace square to welcome the bridegroom, while the townspeople, barred by the palace guards from entering the square, throng the doorways to catch a glimpse of the procession. But a single mood of joyful expectancy unites the nobles gracefully seated on the lawn with the "tip-toe" populace. The poet, Guy Cavalcanti, "the young father of Italian song," is one of the privileged, the center of an admiring circle among whom he dispenses courtly witticisms. Giovanni has agreed to marry by proxy, represented at the ceremony by his younger brother, Paulo, and when Paulo enters the courtyard he secures himself in the good graces of the bride and of all Ravenna by dropping into the hand of a follower a rich jewel, a gift for Cavalcanti. There is an obvious ironic discrepancy between Cavalcanti, blushingly and with a "lowly grace," accepting his princely gift, and Hunt, who wrote his poem as the autumn rains "[w]ash[ed] the dull bars" of the prison cell where he was imprisoned for his libel on the Prince Regent, but it is an irony that Hunt chooses not to point. He distinguishes himself from Cavalcanti more quietly, by surveying the bridal procession from the doorway, from amidst the "rude heave" of the populace.

At the climax of *The Story of Rimini* is an act of transgression, an act which disrupts the ideal chivalric order figured in the poem's processions. Paulo commits adultery with his sister-in-law. But in the funeral procession which closes the poem, the transgressive act is accommodated. Giovanni's jealous rage does not survive his brother's death: he arranges for Paulo and Francesca to be interred together, and by finding within himself this generosity of spirit, he re-institutes the ideal order that the events of the poem had threatened. It is in his style, not in his story, that Hunt overpowers the palace guards who prevent the common folk from mixing with the aristocratic wedding guests, and he does so by developing the poetic style that its detractors categorized as cockney.

On her journey to Rimini the newly married Francesca travels through a forest. The forest itself is a typically Huntian hybrid of wild wood and cottage garden, made up of pear trees, juniper, and oak, intermingled with bryony, honeysuckle, and ivy, but over it all towers the pine, "In lordly right, predominant o'er all." Hunt blandly overthrows what Keats calls the "grand democracy of Forest Trees" (*Letters,* 1:232), and establishes in its stead a woody hierarchy that exactly reflects the feudal order of the human society that he depicts. But as soon as he establishes the dominance of the pine, he diverts the attention from the tree to its cones, its "fruit with rough Mosaic rind." The epithets are at once awkward and exact, and the effect is to allow the claims of the large, "lordly right" to be challenged by the indecorous demand for attention made by the small. *The Story of Rimini* refuses in its style that graceful subordination of part to whole, and of the less to the more important that secures the economy of classical narrative. Similar effects are dispersed throughout the poem. In the square at Ravenna there is a fountain, and Hunt characteristically captures it at the point when the jets of water lose their shape and disintegrate into droplets, the moment at which the fountain begins to "shake its loosening silver in the sun." All through the tale there is a similar "loosening," as Hunt allows the narrative momentum to dissipate by removing attention from the story to details, from his characters to their appurtenances. When they emerge, as light fades, into a grassy clearing in the forest, the horsemen pause, and allow their mounts to graze, to "dip their warm mouths into the freshening grass." The steaming horses and the dew-cooled grass conspire to make an appeal to the sympathetic imagination stronger than seems the right of such incidental figures.

Hunt always looks at horses closely, imitating, I suppose, the connoisseurship natural to characters devoted to the pleasures of the chase and the tournament. But the effect is to mimic rather than to share their culture. Paulo brings with him, as a gift for the duke of Ravenna, a troop of Arabian steeds: "with quoit-like drop their steps they bear." This is exact—it works hard to capture the delicately vertical fall of the thoroughbred's hoof—but its awkwardness establishes Hunt's remove from any society where the finer points of horses are easily discussed. It establishes his role in relation to the society he writes about as that of the encroacher. Hunt has a clear sense of the manner of address that defines the gentleman. He knows that it is the product of a social confidence that the gentleman can transmit to all those who come into his presence. Paulo has it to perfection, the gentlemanly aura: "That air, in short, which sets you at your ease, / Without implying your perplexities." Hunt's style is remarkably easy, but its distinctive, its definingly cockney, characteristic is that its easiness always implies the perplexities of its reader.

Most reviewers located the origins of their perplexity in the poem's diction, in Hunt's strange habits of word formation. A waist is "clipsome," horsemen travel at a "pranksome" speed, trees are "darksome," and "lightsome" does for the sit of a cap, the fall of a man's back, the slope of his nose, and for the morning star. Items in the poem may be "streaky," "mellowy," "glary," "scattery." There are unusual comparatives: "martialler," "franklier," "tastefuller." Hunt likes adjectives formed from present participles: light conversation becomes "fluttering talk," the happy earth is rendered as the "warbling sphere." Some words just seem odd, as when the hindquarters of horses are praised for their "jauntiness."[9] These cockneyisms are not best defined linguistically, by calling attention, for example, to Hunt's habit of moving a word from one part of speech to another, so that sunlit patches become "flings of sunshine." Rather they are defined socially, by the perplexities, the awkward embarrassment, that they provoke in the reader. Hunt writes as if he had the freedom of an earlier poet, of Edmund Spenser, say, to invent his own poetic diction, as if he were unaware that poetic diction could no longer be defined by the character of the words used but by the cultural authority that had been invested in them, an authority that allows "finny tribe" to remain unobtrusive but exposes "glary yellow" as ludicrously affected.

Hunt, however, writes only "as if" he were unaware of these matters. His is always a knowing innocence, an "affectation of a bright-eyed ease." The character of the poem's style is fixed by a whole series of linguistic swoops, in which Hunt plunges from a precariously, even affectedly "poetic" diction toward a diction that is daringly colloquial. In the preface he defends the habit in formulations that echo William Wordsworth's preface to *Lyrical Ballads*. "The proper language of poetry," Hunt claims, "is in fact nothing different from that of real life." He positions his own "free and idiomatic cast of language" between the "cant of art" and "the cant of ordinary discourse,"[10] but the language of his poem reveals that between these two varieties of cant there is no longer any space. Wordsworth claims for the language of his own poems, the language of "[l]ow and rustic life,"[11] a natural authority. It may be a language that survives in the speech of a particular class, but that is because rustic speakers use a language that is protected from contamination by "arbitrary and capricious habits of expression."[12] Wordsworth values their language not because it is the expression of a particular locality and a particular social station, but, on the contrary, because it is "a far more philosophical language" than that often used by poets, and hence retains an affinity with the "pure and universally intelligible" language of Geoffrey Chaucer.[13]

Hunt replaces Wordsworth's key word, "natural," with the word "rural." The refinement of Francesca's sensibility is shown by her "books, her flowers, her taste for rural sights." Paulo is her proper mate because his taste can be summarized in the poem's most notorious couplet: "The two divinest things this world has got, / A lovely woman in a rural spot!" Hunt's "rural" is Wordsworth's "natural" debased from the status of moral principle to that of a variety of taste. "'Twas but the taste for what was natural," and the "taste for rural slights" is developed in the city rather than in the countryside. It has its origins in a childhood spent not in wandering "like a breeze" over the mountains, but in reading. Hence the propriety of Hunt's prefacing Francesca's enjoyment of "rural sights" by a reference to her "books," and hence the special potency for him of story in which the entry into the aristocratic world of high, forbidden passion comes through a book, when Paulo joins Francesca as she reaches that point in the tale of Launcelot when he begins to feel a guilty passion for the queen, at the moment when Francesca begins to feel "a growing interest in her reading."

That phrase does more to define cockney style than an expression such as "scattery light." It is "free and idiomatic," and yet it remains redolent of the "cant of ordinary discourse"; that is, it is an expression that betrays the social class of its user. Whenever the word "taste" is used in the poem, it carries the special charge that it has for a class who is always anxious that it may be betrayed by its predilections, the class that Thomas Moore sums up in his Fudge family. But Leigh Hunt relocates the Fudges in the palaces of thirteenth-century Italy, crediting the duke of Rimini with an ambition that his wife should "haunt his eye, like taste personified," or admiring a troop of knights with the kind of simper that Miss Biddy Fudge reserves for a particularly fashionable beau:

> But what is of the most accomplished air,
> All wear memorials of their lady's love,
> A ribbon, or a scarf, or silken glove.

The result is to superimpose Hampstead on Rimini, so that Francesca's falcon responds to her for all the world as if it has been a canary: he "sidled on his stand, / And twined his neck against her trembling hand." Paulo, meanwhile, trying to shrug off his suspicion that Francesca might have more than sisterly feelings for him, exerts himself to "look / About him for his falcon or his book." The courtly appurtenances, the falcon, for example, survive, but they are overpowered by a syntax that transforms the palace chamber into a suburban sitting room.

In *The Story of Rimini* Hunt invents cockney poetry as an inverted pastoral. Instead of courtly poets appropriating the language and sentiments of rustics, Hampstead poets appropriate the manners of the court, and infect its language with the cant terms of their own ordinary discourse; rural, tasteful, accomplished. To J. G. Lockhart the effect seemed self-evidently ridiculous, as it seems still to most modern readers. But for Lockhart laughter is not enough to dissolve the perplexities that the poem implies. Hunt's failure to find a style appropriate to his subject matter strikes him in the end not as a comedy of self-exposure but as a moral outrage. Hunt's theme, the incestuous love of a brother for his sister-in-law, stimulates a hysterically violent denunciation that Lockhart is never able fully to explain.[14] In *Parisina* Byron himself had, as Lockhart knew, chosen a similar topic, incest between a son and a stepmother, and Byron's poem, although Lockhart did not admit it, may have been indebted to Hunt's.[15] Lockhart tries to secure a distinction between the two by insisting that Byron, unlike Hunt, preserves a reverential horror at the breaking of the incest taboo. But his case seems thin. Byron is protected from Lockhart's indignation not by the soundness of his morals but by the soundness of his style, by an ease that remains gentlemanly without ever descending to jauntiness.

William Hazlitt was surely right to recognize that the judgments of the *Blackwood's* reviewers could be understood only by recognizing that for them the test of political opinion remained subordinate to a quite different test: "It is name, it is wealth, it is title and influence that mollifies the tender-hearted Cerebus of criticism . . . This is the reason why a certain Magazine praises Percy Bysshe Shelley, and villifies 'Johnny

Keats.'"[16] In other words, differences of political opinion might be more easily accommodated than differences of class. Hunt's political language remained firmly within an Enlightenment tradition that construed political difference as an opposition of ideas. In the years between 1815 and 1819 that language became increasingly irrelevant. Its place was usurped by the quite different language spoken by Henry Hunt and written by Cobbett, a language that construed political difference as the expression of class enmity. The politics that Hunt recognized, the battle between ideas, was being replaced by a different politics which hinged on the relationship between classes. Hunt found it all but impossible to address himself to this new phenomenon in his political prose. But in *The Story of Rimini* he had already developed a poetic style that had, as Lockhart's response reveals, a disruptive power precisely accommodated to the new politics of the peace.

In his preface Hunt wrote the manifesto for the new poetry. The preface recommends "'a freer spirit of versification,'" the use of a poetic language founded on "an actual, existing language" (p. xvi), and the repudiation of Alexander Pope as a model for versification in favor of Chaucer. But the radical import emerges from the social gestures that the preface makes rather than the critical precepts that it lays down. The preface parades a culture that is at once ostentatiously displayed and thin—"Homer abounds" with "exquisite specimens" of the "natural" style, "though, by the way, not in the translation"; "with the Greek dramatists I am ashamed to say I am unacquainted" (p. xvii). The preface simultaneously asserts a genial intimacy with the Western tradition of high culture, and exposes the fragile grounds on which that intimacy is claimed. It is at once an artistic credo and a social gaffe, or, better, it is the social gaffe offered as itself embodying a poetic manifesto. The whole preface is an elaboration of the address with which it begins, an address the temerity of which left Lockhart aghast: "My Dear Byron." It inaugurates a new school of poetry, defined, as Lockhart knew, by the class of its practitioners, a poetry that would at once lay claim to possession of a culture that had until then been the monopoly of the classically trained and university educated, and betray its lack of proper title to the culture that it claimed.

JOHNNY KEATS

From early on his career (1817), Keats made anxious efforts to free himself from Hunt's stylistic and social mannerisms, as many of his critics have noted.[17] By late 1818 he was able to write *Hyperion,* a poem as distant from any of Hunt's in its style as it is easy to imagine. But, in the wider sense in which I have defined the term, Keats remained throughout his career a cockney poet. The narrative poems dramatize tales of encroachment. Lorenzo and Porphyro are interlopers, the one contriving entry into the domestic circle of his employers, the other into the castle of his enemies. Elsewhere, as in *Endymion* or *Lamia,* the plot threatens the boundary between species, between a mortal and a goddess or a serpent and a woman. In the lyric poems Keats confronts some item so heavily freighted with cultural associations that it can serve as a metonym for the whole tradition of high culture. Keats stands in contemplation of the Elgin marbles, a Grecian urn, a nightingale, or melancholy, the emotion that beyond all others the poetic tradition has dignified as a badge of cultural attainment. The poems chart the fluctuations by which Keats successively demands his right to a place within that culture, and betrays his bitter sense that its boundaries are patrolled by cultural monitors such as J. W. Croker and Lockhart, whose function it is to preserve culture from the encroachments of those like Keats, whose education and social station do not qualify them for entry.

Of Keats's critics, only Marjorie Levinson has shown herself fully sensitive to the cultural predicament out of which the poems are produced: that is, Keats's intense consciousness of himself as belonging to a class that had no attributes other than its difference. On the one hand, there was the difference from Byron: "I superfine! rich or noble poets—ut Byron. 2 common ut egomet" (*Letters,* 1:368). On the other, there was the difference, that Keats insisted on, from the likes of Samuel Bamford, "the weaver poet": "I am a weaver boy to them," "the literary fashionables" (*Letters,* 2:186).[18] His was, as Levinson puts it, in the "neither/nor" position construed by the reviewers as "monstrous."[19] Levinson brilliantly offers "On First Looking into Chapman's Homer" as an epitome of Keats's whole enterprise, for it is a poem that at once celebrates Keats's enfranchisement, and confesses his lack of title to the enfranchisement he claims. His reading has made him a free citizen of the Homeric world, able to breathe for the first time "its pure serene,"[20] but the metaphor claims a natural ease that the poem's plot, with its ingenuous confession that Homer is available to Keats only in translation, denies. The poem's gestures cancel each other, so that it is predictable that the poem should end in silence. The wonder is that its silence should have been made eloquent, in this prefiguring Keats's whole achievement. He sought to inscribe his own name in the book of literature by the production of poems that betrayed the cultural disabilities that disqualified him from inclusion within it.

Levinson's book is important in part because it helps to explain the failure of those who have sought to address directly the question of Keats's political opinions. The evidence from the letters and the poems is clear: Keats placed himself firmly "on the liberal side of the question" (*Letters,* 2:176). He addresses politics at length in only two letters. In the letter of October 1818 to his brother and sister-in-law, he repudiates at once Napoleon and "the divine right Gentlemen": "All the departments of Government," and the "Madmen" who would seek to overthrow them, men "who would like to be beheaded on tower Hill merely for the sake of eclat" (*Letters,* 1:396-7). Between these opposing groups, he recognizes only Leigh Hunt "who from a principle of taste would like to see things go on better," and those "like Sir F. Burdett who like to sit at the head of political dinners." His own intervention is confined to expressions of nostalgia for the Commonwealth that seem rather too glibly to echo Wordsworth: "We have no Milton, no Algernon Sidney" (*Letters,* 1:396). In the letter of September 1819, he shares with the George Keatses an understanding of English history since Richard II that divides it into three stages. In the first the kings found common interest with the people in accomplishing "the gradual annihilation of the tyranny of the nobles." In the second, the kings turned on the people in an effort to "destroy all popular privileges." In the third, those privileges are reasserted. It is this third stage that has been "put a stop to" by the "unlucky termination" of the French Revolution, but Keats trusts that it will be no more than "a temporry stop" (*Letters,* 2:193-4). This is the familiar Whig view of history, lucidly and sensibly rehearsed, and it bears not the faintest stamp of the delicate, exploratory intelligence that is scarcely ever absent when Keats is thinking about poets, or poetry, or his own compositional processes.

Like Hunt, Keats had acquired a Whig political vocabulary, a vocabulary founded on an analysis of the nation into three distinct orders: the monarchy, the aristocracy, and the people. It was not, however, possible for him to express his own place within the public world in the terms that this political vocabulary allowed him. Keats was ungrateful to Hunt, but Hunt remains the single most important influence on his poetry because Hunt showed him the way out of his difficulty. Hunt showed him how to write a public poetry that derived its vigor not from the sentiments it expressed but from its style. He showed Keats, that is, how to become a cockney poet.

Morris Dickstein has proposed that the description of *Hyperion*'s "'transcendental cosmopolitics'" in Hunt's *Autobiography* should replace critical responses to the poem that confine attention to "its epic ambitions, its sonorous impersonality, and the Miltonic 'stationing' of the verse."[21] Dickstein suggests an analogy linking Saturn, the dying George III, and the deposed Napoleon. Alan J. Bewell notes that Keats associates his Titans with the art of Egypt, points out that Egyptian art was conventionally associated with tyrannical power and priestly mystery, and suggests an analogy between the action of Keats's poem and Napoleon's Egyptian campaign. A political allegory that allows Napoleon to be associated either with Hyperion and Saturn or with the Apollo who supersedes them seems unusually "transcendental," and neither reading accommodates easily the pathos with which Keats invests the downfall of the Titans. Bewell recognizes such difficulties, and suggests that *Hyperion* espouses a "political ideology,"[22] a Whig understanding of history as progress, only for Keats to find that this imposed on him a political language with which he was uncomfortable. In its "'cosmopolitics'" *Hyperion* remains incoherent: in its "epic ambitions," however, the poem vigorously places itself within the public world.

Keats seems not to have set about writing *Hyperion* in earnest until immediately after the attacks on *Endymion* by Lockhart and by Croker.[23] *Hyperion* is, in some sort, as Thomas A. Reed suggests, a response at once defiant and submissive.[24] Keats veers from Hunt to Milton: from couplets that risked "wearying his readers with an immeasurable game of bouts-rimes,"[25] he turns to blank verse, and for the anarchically episodic structure of romance he substitutes the more regular narrative sequence of epic. In all this a wish to placate his hostile critics is evident enough. But Lockhart had also derided Keats's lack of title to the subject matter he claimed: he and Hunt "write about Apollo, Pan, Nymphs, Muses, and Mysteries, as might be expected from persons of their education," from persons, that is, whose classical scholarship amounts to no more than "a sort of vague idea, that the Greeks were a most tasteful people."[26] In writing *Hyperion,* Keats defiantly persists in claiming a right to appropriate the mythological subject matter from which, according to Lockhart, his educational deficiencies debarred him.

The plot of *Hyperion,* in which Saturn and the Titans are ousted, and Hyperion is forced to recognize the nobler music of Apollo, seems designed to express Keats's heady sense of his own irresistible genius. "Byron, Scott, Southey, & Shelley think they are to lead the age," he once told Haydon, "but . . . ," and Haydon's anxiety not to compromise his young friend's reputation for modesty led him to erase the rest of the sentence.[27] But Keats was given just as often to intense self-doubt, a sense of himself as having been forcibly removed from the "strong identity," the "real self" that would permit him to fulfill his ambitions, which is surely one reason why Saturn's overthrow only serves to secure his place within Keats's imaginative sympathies. It is easy to speak of these Keatsian characteristics as defining a personality, but it would be more accurate, as Levinson realizes, to recognize them as defining the social class to which Keats belonged. They are characteristics that inform the style more completely than the plot of *Hyperion,* and hence it is in its style, in its "epic ambitions," that the poem makes its most forceful intervention in the public world.

More completely than any other of Keats's poems, *Hyperion* displays Keats's alternating reflexes, his capacity for "in-feeling" and his concern with "stationing." He inhabits Hyperion's mouth, when the taste of incense sours to the "[s]avour of poisonous brass and metal sick,"[28] and he freezes Thea, kneeling before Saturn, for a month in a single, mute posture of despair. So it is that the poem's characters are at once intimately possessed and yet remain immeasurably remote. The first two books are dominated by dialogue in which the "large utterance of the early Gods" is rendered into "our feeble tongue" (1.51, 49).[29] Keats can afford gracefully to assume the modesty of the translator in the knowledge that he has so amply recreated "that large utterance," but the apology works to alert the reader to a quality in the poem that aligns it with translation. It is as far as possible from Hunt's ideal of a "free and idiomatic cast of language." The poem displays to its reader the words from which it is made, offers them to be savored as sounds, as actions in the mouth, as the "ponderous syllables" of Enceladus (2.305), or the syllables that throb through Apollo's "white melodious throat" (3.81). We understand these words, and yet they retain a material opacity, like that of the "hieroglyphics old" that have survived the loss of their "import" (1.277, 282). Hence, as in the very best translations, the poem seems to reconcile two languages, the comfortably familiar language of "our feeble tongue" and another language that remains remote and unaccommodated. It is through its style that the poem articulates Keats's understanding of his own place in the social structure, the "neither/nor" place of a class that cannot claim, like Lockhart, the cultural attainments of the classically educated, and yet is unwilling to dispute a definition of culture that confines it to those who know Greek and Latin. But in *Hyperion* the plot and the style are at odds. The plot allies itself with an optimistic Whig view that understands history as a process in which one "power" succeeds another in obedience to a benevolent "eternal law," but the style gives voice to a social class that can take no part in such an evolutionary process.[30] It cannot achieve cultural power because it is defined by its aspiration toward it: it cannot arrive because it has its only being in becoming. In *Hyperion,* Keats generated a quite new kind of cockney poetry, distinguished from Hunt's cockney by its being not at all "rediculous." In *Hyperion,* Keats had found a way "to write fine things which cannot be laugh'd at in any way" (*Letters,* 2:174), but he had not found a plot. Hence his decision to abandon the poem and begin work on *The Fall of Hyperion.*

In the revised poem, Keats turns, as Hunt had turned in *The Story of Rimini,* to Dante. It seems, from a modern perspective, grotesque that the cockney poets should have nominated Dante as their ancestor, but it is less so than it seems. Hunt was drawn to a story in which desire is displaced from a book to the body, a story in which nature is a by-product of culture, and hence an appropriate story for a new kind of poetry which would take as its primary subject its own literariness. Keats seems to have been attracted by a poem that so transparently concerns itself with its own place within literary history. The Keats who represented himself as "cowering under the Wings of great Poets" would have responded immediately to Dante's Virgil (*Letters,* 1:239), at once so protective and so overawing a presence. "Those minute volumes of carey" that Keats carried with him to Scotland in the summer of 1818 were to provide him with the clue that he needed to reshape the material of *Hyperion* into an episode within a new plot (*Letters,* 1:294), the defining plot of cockney poetry. It would no longer be a poem about Hyperion ousted by Apollo, but a poem in which Keats explored his own entitlement to write about the wars of the gods.

In *The Fall of Hyperion* much more directly than in its predecessor, Keats confronts his own cultural position. Lockhart had summoned up a comic vision of a nation suffering from a rhyming plague, "Metromanie," a disease that has struck down farm-servants and unmarried ladies, footmen, governesses, and a young man "bound apprentice some years ago to a worthy apothecary in town."[31] Keats's first response is moving in its simplicity: "Who alive can say / 'Thou art no poet; may'st not tell thy dreams'?"[32] Poetry is not the preserve of the privileged few, but available to "every man," if only he "had lov'd / And been well nurtured in his mother tongue" (1.13-5). The condition seems anodyne enough until one remembers Lockhart's mockery of "two Cockneys," one of whom "confesses that he had never read the Greek Tragedians, and the other knows Homer only from Chapman."[33] The only "breeding" that a poet needs is a breeding in the mother-tongue, and yet within the poem the maternal presence, the figure whose "words / Could to a mother's soften" (1.249-50), is a goddess called Moneta or Mnemosyne, a muse as classical as even Lockhart could stipulate. The poem carefully places Keats in the "neither / nor" position that defines the cockney poet.

In the poem's first vision, the poet finds himself in a forest clearing where a feast is spread on a mossy mound: "Which, nearer seen, seem'd refuse of a meal / By angel tasted, or our mother Eve" (1.30-1). The poet standing amidst "empty shells" and "grape stalks but half bare" forms a tableau that, since Bate, has functioned as the primal scene of poetic belatedness (1.32-3);[34] but, as Bate notes, Keats emphasizes the "plenty" rather than the paucity of the "remnants" (1.35, 33). The poet has more than enough to eat and drink. The point, surely, is not at all the meagerness of the meal, but the undignified circumstances in which it is consumed. The poet's is precisely the position of the servant who gains entry to a costly banquet after the authentic guests have departed and gluts himself on the rich remains of a meal to which he was not invited. The passage identifies the poet as an interloper. When he wakens from his sleep. the scene has changed, but not his role within it. The "eternal domed monument" in which he finds himself is clearly a temple of culture

(1.71). The bric-a-brac strewn at his feet, the "draperies" and "strange vessels" (1.73), "[r]obes, golden tongs, censer and chafing dish. / Girdles, and chains, and holy jewelries" (1.79-80), suggest what Philip Larkin calls "the stuff up at the holy end," but more because of the reverence with which they are listed than the nature of the items themselves. The paraphernalia corresponds to the half-finished meal: it represents the detritus of a high culture, rich and enclosed, to which the poet has gained magical, guilty access. Moneta challenges him as a trespasser, as one attempting to "usurp this height'" (1.147).

K. K. Ruthven's observation that Moneta was, as Keats would have learned from Andrew Tooke's *Pantheon,* at once the supplier of "'wholesome counsel'" and "the goddess of *money*" has intrigued several recent critics, but, with the exception of Daniel P. Watkins, to oddly little effect.[35] The reason is, I suspect, that it has proved impossible to graft Ruthven's perception onto a view of Moneta that insists on representing her role within the poem as uncomplicatedly benign. The best antidote to such an assumption is to place side by side Moneta's remarks to the dreamer and Lockhart's remarks to the young Keats. Moneta accuses the poet of being "'a dreaming thing; / A fever of thyself'" (1.168-9). Lockhart had advised Keats that he was suffering from a "disease," and belonged to a "fanciful, dreaming" set. Lockhart describes a young man, stricken with a "poetical mania" that has unfitted him for the "useful profession" for which his friends had destined him, "the career of medicine."[36] Moneta distinguishes between those who "seek no wonder but the human face" (1.163), and those like Keats whose activities are of no social utility: "'What benefit canst thou do, or all thy tribe, / To the great world?'" (1.167-8). Lockhart offers his review as an astringent medicine that, if taken, will "put the patient in a fair way of being cured." The dreamer thanks Moneta for having "'medicin'd'" him (1.183). Finally, Lockhart castigates the presumption of "uneducated and flimsy striplings" such as Keats who dare to speak familiarly of their cultural superiors. The sonnet "Great Spirits Now on Earth Are Sojourning" is singled out as a particularly egregious example of Keats's daring to place "himself, and some others of the rising brood of Cockneys" on a level with "the most classical of living English poets": "Wordsworth and Hunt! what a juxtaposition!"[37] Compare Moneta:

> "Art thou not of the dreamer tribe?
> The poet and the dreamer are distinct,
> Diverse, sheer opposite, antipodes."
> (1.198-200)

Moneta's face, "deathwards progressing / To no death" (1.260-1), is itself a fit emblem of the notion of culture over which Lockhart claims guardianship, a notion that conceives culture as a condition of moribund immortality, as the spectral, unending afterlife of the dead civilizations of Greece and Rome, the essence of which is enclosed in the tomblike chambers of Moneta's "hollow brain" (1.276), as in a mausoleum.

At this point, Ruthven's perception becomes crucial, because the forces that guard Lockhart's cultural precincts are, as Lockhart boasts, economic. He ends his review smugly prophesying that no bookseller will "a second time venture £50 upon anything [Keats] can write."[38] In the months that Keats worked on *The Fall of Hyperion,* his true financial predicament seems to have been brought home to him for the first time. He began to cast about for some way of securing a competence: taking passage as a surgeon on an Indiaman, going to Edinburgh to qualify himself as a doctor, writing political articles "for whoever will pay me" (*Letters,* 2:176). The figure of Lockhart presided over his difficulties. As he told his sister, he would "try the fortune of [his] Pen once more," and should that fail, "I have enough knowledge of my gallipots to ensure me an employment & maintenance" (*Letters,* 2:124-5).[39]

Moneta stares at Keats with blank, blind eyes, "like two gold coins," as Ruthven has it,[40] a ghastly embodiment of the defensive alliance between culture and economics that worked to deny Keats's right of settlement in the "realms of gold."[41] But, as all the poem's critics have properly noted, Moneta's presence in the poem is monitory rather than minatory, her gaze benignant rather than baleful. She says hard words to the poet, too hard for many of the poem's critics,[42] but she is also "'kind'" to him (1.242), her voice like a "mother's" (1.250), and the poet responds to her with grateful reverence. In the confrontation of the poet with Moneta, Keats achieves his most complete expression of his cultural situation, for it accommodates fully both his capacity for reverence and his stinging sensitivity to ridicule. Keats's impulse is to keep the two responses apart, to maintain "'[t]he pain alone; the joy alone; distinct'" (1.174). He delights in fancying Shakespeare his "Presider" (*Letters,* 1:142), a cultural authority wholly different from the likes of Croker and Lockhart who preside over the reviews. Keats reverences "genius," and genius is measured in inverse proportion to the taste of the "literary world": "Just so much as I am humbled by the genius above my grasp, am I exalted and look with hate and contempt upon the literary world" (*Letters,* 2:144). But the distinction between "genius" and the cultural institutions that accredit it is precarious, secured only by the passage of time. Keats's acutely erratic responses to his contemporaries, to Hunt and to Wordsworth in particular, are controlled by conflicting needs to hail "genius," and to maintain a lofty contempt for "that most vulgar of all crowds the literary" (*Letters,* 2:43). He writes a poetry that is impelled at once by a "love of fame" and a defiantly maintained indifference to literary success (*Letters,* 2:116), and it is to the extent that this ambivalent stance "'venoms'" his poetry that it achieves political importance (*Fall of Hyperion,* 1.175). Jerome J. McGann has famously described Keats's 1820 volume as a self-conscious and determined attempt to "dissolve social and political conflicts in the mediations of art and beauty."[43] The evidence from both letters and poems establishes beyond possibility of argument Keats's passionate desire to find in the world of art a sphere independent of, and dissociated from, the corrupt spheres of power and of money, but just as clearly they record Keats's bitter recognition that the spheres are interlocked, near neighbors that there is no possibility of unperplexing.

OUR CLASSICAL EDUCATION

Modern critics interested in the relationship between poetry and politics have constructed the brief period of Keats's poetic activity, the years from 1816 to 1819, as a single narrative that reaches its catastrophe in Manchester on 16 August 1819 at Peterloo. Hence the oddity that the question of the political significance of Keats's poems has been disputed most keenly in discussions of a single poem, "To Autumn," a poem written just a month after the massacre.[44] The campaign that culminated at Peterloo had provoked a crisis of style. In these years Henry Hunt and Cobbett were involved in a determined attempt to wrest the radical leadership from the grasp of the radical Whigs, led by Burdett, and assume to themselves a quite different kind of leadership. Burdett and his associates, Douglas Kinnaird, John Cam Hobhouse, and Byron, wielded political power by virtue of their wealth and birth, and chose to place that power at the service of the people. Hunt and Cobbett opposed them with a power secured only by popular support, by the mass readership of Cobbett's *Political Register,* and by the hundreds of thousands that Hunt could summon to his open-air meetings. Burdett spoke for the people in parliament: Hunt and Cobbett devised a technique of mass protest that entirely by-passed parliament, and in doing so they devised a new political language, the enduring monument of which is Cobbett's prose. It was a language designed not to address fellow parliamentarians or electors, not designed even to address the well-off radical London merchants who determined the outcome of elections at Westminster, but to speak directly to weavers, shoemakers, millhands.[45] Shelley responded with the composition of a group of poems, chief among them *The Mask of Anarchy,* in which he makes a conscious decision to essay a poetical style that would proclaim his solidarity with the Manchester demonstrators, a style that required him to repudiate his own literariness as a necessary condition for repudiating the class of which that literariness was a badge. Byron saw what was at issue as clearly as Shelley, but responded with passionate outrage that men such as Hunt and Cobbett should dare to dispute with the Whig aristocracy its claim to be the people's true leaders. He wrote angrily to Hobhouse when he heard that his friend planned to attend a dinner given in Henry Hunt's honor: "Why our classical education alone—should teach us to trample on such unredeemed dirt."[46] He transmuted his own responses to Peterloo, the Cato Street conspiracy, and the Queen Caroline affair into the play *Marino Faliero,* and avoided the danger that he might be besmirched by intellectual contact with those lacking a proper education by his insistence on maintaining the rigid conventions of Italian classical drama.[47] Byron's and Shelley's responses to the political and stylistic crisis of 1819 could scarcely have been more divergent, and yet they have in common a certain theatricality. In Byron's case this is literally true: not only does he turn to drama, but in the protracted agony that he suffered over the staging of *Marino Faliero,* he contrived to rehearse the predicament of his doge. Just as his hero was forced to capitulate to the necessity of entering into a conspiracy with plebeians that he despised, so the poet was forced to surrender to the humiliation of public representation, and place the success of his tragedy in the hands of the vulgar populace. Shelley's gesture, too, is theatrical, turning from *Prometheus Unbound,* which was characterized in Mary Shelley's words by an "abstraction and delicacy of distinction" that was available only to minds "as subtle and penetrating as his own" to the direct broadside ballad style of *The Mask of Anarchy.*[48] Both Byron's classicism and Shelley's populism remain in their different ways feats of ventriloquism.

Their stylistic experiments serve to indicate a general awareness that by 1819 English politics had assumed a new character. The central political issues were no longer debated by individuals who differed in their views but shared a common language. Burdett and Cobbett both argued for a reform of parliament, but the antagonism between them was more implacable than that between, say, Burdett and George Canning. They differed in the language that they used, and difference in language had superseded difference in policy as the critical indicator. Byron and Shelley, however much the latter might try to mend himself, shared the language common to those who had enjoyed a "classical education." This is why, of course, a Tory critic such as Lockhart could admire their poems despite his dislike of their politics, but find nothing in the poetry of Hunt and Keats that did not inspire him to contempt. His aesthetic sense could transcend difference of opinion, but could not rise above difference of class.

Keats's modern critics have been right to insist on restoring the political import of Keats's poems, but they have not been very much more successful in locating that import than Keats's reviewers, and for the same reason. The attempt has been to deduce from the poems a set of political opinions; to read "To Autumn" as guiltily retreating from thoughts of the ill-fed weavers and millhands who assembled at Manchester into a visionary world of pastoral opulence, or alternatively as incorporating a system of allusions to Peterloo which places Keats firmly "on the liberal side of the question." Such readings do not so much straitjacket the poems as dress them in a jacket remarkable for being so neatly reversible.[49] The political resonance of Keats's poems has its origin not in their opinions but in their style, which is to say, not in their liberalism but in their cockneyism. It is through their style that the poems occupy the "neither/nor" position that defined Keats's class, and it is the very indeterminacy of that particular social class, its unfixed medical position, that enables the poems to express the new politics of the years between 1816 and 1819. This new politics was characterized less by a conflict of opinion than a conflict between languages, between styles. Keats's poems do not take a side in that conflict; rather they accommodate it, and in doing so they expose more clearly than was possible for Byron or Shelley the politics of "England in 1819."

Notes

[1] Current interest in the political significance of Keats's poems originated with Jerome J. MacGann's 1979 article, "Keats and the Historical Method in Literary Criticism," *The Beauty of Inflections: Literary Investigations in Historical Method and Theory* (Oxford: Clarendon Press, 1985), pp. 12-65; rprt. from *MLN* 94, 5 (December 1979): 988-1032. It was further developed in a special edition of *Studies in Romanticism,* "Keats and Politics: A Forum," *SiR* 25, 2 (Summer 1986): 171-229, and culminated in two book-length studies and a volume of essays: Daniel P. Watkins, *Keats's Poetry and the Politics of the Imagination* (London: Associated Univ. Presses, 1989); Marjorie Levinson, *Keats's Life of Allegory: The Origins of a Style* (Oxford: Basil Blackwell, 1988); and Nicholas Roe, ed., *Keats and History* (Cambridge: Cambridge Univ. Press, 1995), hereafter cited as *KH.*

[2] John Keats, *The Letters of John Keats,* ed. Hyder Edward Rollins, 2 vols. (Cambridge MA: Harvard Univ. Press, 1958), 2:244. Subsequent citations to *Letters* appear parenthetically in the text by volume and page number.

[3] G. M. Matthews, ed., introduction to *Keats: The Critical Heritage* (London: Routledge and Kegan Paul, 1971), pp. 1-37, 2.

[4] Walter Jackson Bate, *John Keats* (Cambridge MA: Harvard Univ. Press, 1963), p. 366; hereafter cited as *JK.*

[5] Vincent Newey makes the strongest possible case for the political import of the poem, offering it as "a critique of society," but even in this reading it does not appear to be a critique either powerful or pointed. See Newey, "Keats, History, and the Poets," in *KH,* pp. 165-193, 169.

[6] Quoted in William Keach, "Cockney Couplets: Keats and the Politics of Style," *SiR* 25, 2 (Summer 1986): 182-96, 184.

[7] Keach, pp. 184-5.

[8] Hunt continued to tinker with *The Story of Rimini* until 1844. Quotations are taken from the first edition (London: John Murray, 1816). In this edition the lines are not numbered.

[9] Hunt presumably derives his word from the verb "jaunce," which describes the prancing of a horse, but "jauntiness" already carried its modern sense (OED, s.v. "jauntiness").

[10] Hunt, preface to *The Story of Rimini,* pp. vii-xix. The quotations are from pp. xv-xvi. Subsequent page references will appear parenthetically in the text.

[11] William Wordsworth, preface to *Lyrical Ballads, with Pastoral and Other Poems* (1802), *William Wordsworth: The Poems,* ed. John O. Hayden, vol. 1 (New York: Penguin, 1982), pp. 867-96, 869.

[12] Wordsworth, p. 870.

[13] Ibid.

[14] J. G. Lockhart, signing himself "Z," "The Cockney School of Poetry, No. II," *Blackwood's Edinburgh Magazine* 2, 8 (November 1817): 194-201.

[15] In both poems the husband detects the crime when the wife speaks endearments to her lover in her sleep.

[16] William Hazlitt, "On the Qualifications Necessary to Success in Life," in *The Plain Speaker, The Complete Works of William Hazlitt,* ed. P. P. Howe, 21 vols. (London: J. M. Dent and Sons, 1930-4), 12:195-209, 208.

[17] See Bate, *The Stylistic Development of John Keats* (New York: Modern Language Association, 1945).

[18] Samuel Bamford published his first volume of verse, *The Weaver Boy,* in 1819. Keats seems to have been irked that Bamford was, like himself, given the advantage of Hunt's benevolent patronage in *The Examiner.*

[19] Levinson, p. 5.

[20] Keats, "On First Looking into Chapman's Homer," in *The Poems of John Keats,* ed. Jack Stillinger (Cambridge MA: Belknap Press, 1978), p. 64, line 7.

[21] Morris Dickstein, "Keats and Politics," *SiR* 25, 2 (Summer 1986): 175-81, 180.

[22] Alan Bewell, "The Political Implication of Keats's Classicist Aesthetics," *SiR* 25, 2 (Summer 1986): 220-9, 229. Bewell's conclusion, that "Keats's inability to speak in an assured political voice . . . represents an identification with those anonymous groups whose political voice cannot yet be heard in either poetry or English politics" (p. 229), is less convincing. It comes close to taking Keats for a "weaver boy."

[23] Lockhart as "Z," "The Cockney School of Poetry, No. IV," *Blackwood's Edinburgh Magazine* 3, 17 (August 1818): 519-24, and J. W. Croker, unsigned review, *Quarterly Review* 19, 37 (April 1818, although this issue was, in fact, published in September): 204-8.

[24] Thomas A. Reed, "Keats and the Gregarious Advance of Intellect in *Hyperion,*" *ELH* 55, 1 (Spring 1988): 195-232, 195.

[25] Croker, p. 206.

[26] Lockhart, "Cockney School, No. IV," p. 522.

[27] Bate, *JK,* p. 131.

[28] Keats, *Hyperion: A Fragment,* in *The Poems of John Keats,* pp. 329-56, bk. 1, line 189. Subsequent citations will be to this edition and appear parenthetically by book and line number.

[29] Bate notes that fifty-eight percent of the lines in the first two books consist of dialogue (*JK,* p. 391).

[30] Michael O'Neil shares my suspicion of the poem's inability "to believe full-bloodedly in a liberal, optimistic version of history," but would rather deny that this failure is "class-motivated." For him, it is a product of Keats's dawning recognition of the inevitable difference between imaginative and political value. See O'Neill, "'When this warm scribe my hand': Writing and History in *Hyperion* and *The Fall of Hyperion,*" in *KH,* pp. 143-64, 153.

[31] Lockhart, "Cockney School, No. IV," p. 519.

[32] Keats, *The Fall of Hyperion: A Dream,* in *The Poems of John Keats,* pp. 478-91, canto 1, lines 11-2. Subsequent references will be to this edition and appear parenthetically by canto and line number.

[33] Lockhart, "Cockney School, No. IV," p. 522.

[34] Bate, *JK,* p. 590. Bate extended and generalized his belief that Keats suffered from a sense of belatedness in *The Burden of the Past and the English Poet* (Cambridge MA: Belknap Press, 1970), which Harold Bloom acknowledges as supplying the germ of *The Anxiety of Influence* and its successors.

[35] K. K. Ruthven, "Keats's *Dea Moneta,*" *SiR* 15, 3 (Summer 1976): 445-59, 448 and 449. Levinson comments that Ruthven "does not do very much in a critical vein with his mythographic findings," only to agree that "there's not a great deal to do" (p. 257). She goes on to use Ruthven's perception in her discussion of *Lamia,* not *The Fall of Hyperion.* Watkins is unique in insisting on the complexity of Moneta's dialogue with the poet, a dialogue in which the poet is "belittled and maligned while at the same time being rewarded" (p. 168), and allowing that recognition to control his response to the poem. My difference with Watkins is that, in the end, he reads the poem as an allegory in which Moneta is the embodiment of the "marketplace" that is the governing power of Keats's world. The marketplace values poetry only as a "product" that functions to absorb the contradictions inherent in a capitalist society and to "soothe the frustrations of the alienated" (p. 169). Such a reading grants Keats a stable, ironic understanding of the poet's naiveté, establishing him as the authoritative analyst of his own cultural and historical predicament. See Watkins, pp. 156-76.

[36] Lockhart, "Cockney School, No. IV," p. 519.

[37] Lockhart, "Cockney School, No. IV," p. 520.

[38] Lockhart, "Cockney School, No. IV," p. 524.

[39] Compare Lockhart: "It is a better and wiser thing to be a starved apothecary than a starved poet; so back to the shop Mr John, back to 'plasters, pills, and ointment boxes,' &c." ("Cockney School, No. IV," p. 524).

[40] Ruthven, p. 450.

[41] Keats, "Chapman's Homer," line 1.

[42] Bate, for example, insists that lines 187-210, the lines in which Moneta denies the poet's title to the name of poet, should not be regarded as a part of the poem on the sole authority of a single memorandum by Richard Woodhouse: "'Keats seems to have intended to erase this and the next twenty-one lines'" (quoted in Bate, *JK,* pp. 599-600). But it is easy to understand Woodhouse's response as an attempt to save his friend from supplying, even after his death, ammunition of the kind that hostile critics had shown themselves so ready to use. Woodhouse would have had bitter memories of the critical response to the preface to *Endymion.* Stillinger seems right to argue that Woodhouse's note has the status of a "critical conjecture" rather than a record of an authorial decision. See Stillinger, *The Texts of Keats's Poems* (Cambridge MA: Harvard Univ. Press, 1974), p. 262.

[43] McGann, p. 53.

[44] See Geoffrey Hartman, "Poem and Ideology: A Study of Keats's 'To Autumn,'" *The Fate of Reading and Other Essays* (Chicago: Univ. of Chicago Press, 1975), pp. 124-46; McGann, pp. 48-65; Keach, pp. 192-6; Roe, "Keats's Commonwealth," in *KH*, pp. 194-211.

[45] In 1818 William Cobbett published an English grammar addressed to "Young Persons," and "more especially" to "Soldiers, Sailors, Apprentices and Plough-boys." Cobbett's design is to challenge the monopoly of literacy claimed by those who had enjoyed a classical education, and hence to challenge the monopoly of political power to which, they claimed, their education entitled them. On Cobbett's *Grammar,* see Olivia Smith, *The Politics of Language, 1791-1819* (Oxford: Clarendon Press, 1984), pp. 239-48.

[46] Lord Byron to John Cam Hobhouse, 22 April 1820, *"Between Two Worlds," 1820, Byron's Letters and Journals,* ed. Leslie A. Marchand, vol. 7 (Cambridge MA: Belknap Press, 1977), pp. 80-2, 81.

[47] On the topicality of *Marino Faliero,* see Malcolm Kelsall, *Byron's Politics* (Brighton, England: Harvester, 1987), pp. 89-109.

[48] Mary Shelley, quoted in *Shelley: Poetical Works,* ed. Thomas Hutchinson, rev. G. M. Matthews (Oxford: Oxford Univ. Press, 1978), pp. 270-4, 272.

[49] See Susan Wolfson's introduction to "Keats and Politics: A Forum," *SiR* 25, 2 (Summer 1986): 171-4. Wolfson contrasts George Bernard Shaw's appreciation of Keats's attack on the "avaricious capitalism" of the brothers in *Isabella; or the Pot of Basil* with John Scott's distaste for Keats's "'school-boy vituperation of trade and traders'" (pp. 172, 173). It is clear to me that Scott is offended not, as Wolfson would have it, by a proto-Marxist radicalism, but by what he takes to be an affected, genteel contempt for trade and traders. Again, one finds that the same passage offers itself to a reversible political understanding.

FURTHER READING

Baker, Herschel. "Politics and Literature." In his *William Hazlitt*, pp. 320-81. Cambridge, Mass.: Belknap Press of Harvard University Press, 1962.

Discusses Hazlitt's political commentary, especially in the *Examiner*, and his responses to politically motivated attacks by the *Blackwood* critics.

Barnard, John. "Charles Cowden Clarke's 'Cockney' Commonplace Book." In *Keats and History*, edited by Nicholas Roe, pp. 65-87. Cambridge: Cambridge University Press, 1995.

Considers Keats' poetry and political views as deeply indebted to the influence of Charles Cowden Clarke.

Lockhart, John Gibson. *Lockhart's Literary Criticism*. Edited by M. Clive Hildyard. Oxford: Basil Blackwell, 1931, 168 p.

Collection of Lockhart's criticism, especially from *Blackwood's Edinburgh Magazine*, grouped according to the figures discussed

Mugglestone, Lynda. "The Fallacy of the Cockney Rhyme: From Keats and Earlier to Auden." *The Review of English Studies* 42, No. 165 (February 1991): 57-66.

Explores the Cockneys' violation of grammatical convention and interprets the critics' charge of vulgarism as arising from the primacy given the written (rather than the spoken) language.

Death in Nineteenth-Century British Literature

INTRODUCTION

The subject of death and descriptions of deathbed scenes are nearly ubiquitous in nineteenth century British literature. Authors worked in an environment in which death was practically everywhere. Mortality rates were high among the young. One hundred and fifty out of every thousand births resulted in death for the newborn. Mortality rates were also high in urban areas. Massive migrations from farms to cities (with some cities doubling in population in just a few decades) were caused by the use of the steam engine and by the rise of industrialization in general in the early nineteenth century. And this rapid increase in urban population was attended by poor living conditions. Untreated sewage was dumped into the same water supplies used for drinking; severe overcrowding was the norm; and diseases spread easily in an environment of filthy living quarters, fume-filled workplaces, and graveyards that reeked of decaying flesh. Furthermore, since all but the penniless died at home, there was little separation of the living and the dying. Deathbed scenes and the final actions and words of the dying were commonly witnessed and then reported to fascinated listeners. The funerals that followed were not only a religious but also a social necessity—to maintain respectability, and sometimes even to advance the status of the departed in the society of the living. Indeed, a significant portion of Britain's economy involved funerals and mourning—it has been estimated that a third of the money deposited in banks was saved to pay for funerals. Many workers paid a percentage of their weekly wages in subscription to ensure proper burials eventually for themselves and their loved ones. This preoccupation with and exposure to death impacted the literature of the time.

Authors found death to be an important and versatile device in their works. Frequently death was used to reveal the moral character of the dying. How a person lived was reflected in how that person died: a good person would most likely die peacefully, a bad person painfully (or full of regret for a life not lived in the proper manner). And such deathbed scenes could serve as moral instruction on the right way to live. Charles Dickens, one of the most popular nineteenth century authors, typically used death scenes as representations of the final moral worth of the dying. For example, Quilp, in *The Old Curiosity Shop*, is seen suffering in his drowning, a just punishment for his wicked deeds. In contrast, Little Nell Trent, also in *The Old Curiosity Shop*, dies without a complaint, and her passing away is compared to a sunset. The death of Little Nell's grandfather from a broken heart just days after the death of Little Nell shows not only the character of the grandfather but also the worth of Little Nell. In general, children in nineteenth century novels represent innocence, and when they die, they are freed from living a hard life of toil and can be expected to go to a better world. Dickens, in the person of Sydney Carton in *A Tale of Two Cities,* also showed how a person can find solace even while laying down his life. As Carton goes to the guillotine in the place of another, he utters these famous words: "It is a far, far better thing that I do, than I have ever done; it is a far, far better rest that I go to, than I have ever known." Dickens, among others, also used deathbed scenes as settings for repentance. It was never too late to repent, and those who did, even though they were near death, as in the case of Alice Marwood in *Dombey and Son*, died peacefully. However, as John R. Reed points out, there were reactions against conventional deathbed scenes. For example, *Middlemarch* by George Eliot describes a death in an unprettified manner. *Woodlanders* by Thomas Hardy portrays Giles Winterborne dying realistically without fanfare, and *Jude the Obscure,* also by Hardy, shows Jude dying bitterly, unobserved by people outside celebrating a festival. *Jane Eyre* by Charlotte Brontë tells how the death of Mr. Rochester's wife allows two lovers to unite. And finally, *Wuthering Heights* by Emily Brontë shows how Heathcliff's obsession with Cathy Earnshaw persists even beyond her death, lasting until Heathcliff's own death.

Some critics consider the emphasis on death in nineteenth century British literature as simply a reflection of the realities of the time, as a warning that conditions must be improved, or as a means of providing moral instruction for the reader. However, Carol Hanbery MacKay suggests that certain descriptions of death illustrate the sublimation of sexual impulses and the influence of Victorian public morals. In addition, feminist scholars have explored other kinds of death including the social death that women can experience while living in a sexist society. For example, Beth Ann Bassein argues that the accidental death of Maggie in a George Eliot novel promotes the negation of the achievements and abilities of women. Elisabeth Bronfen, on the other hand, examines the process of the representation of a woman's death, the return of the woman from death as a revenant, and the detecting of the woman's secret truth, which brings about the second and final death of the woman. Still other scholars have been interested in studying aspects of life beyond death. Benjamin P. Kurtz traces the development in the thought of Percy Bysshe Shelley from a philosophy of materialism to a belief in the immortality of the spirit. And finally, Edward T. Hurley finds in the writings of George Eliot an emphasis on immortality through the family rather than on immortality for the individual through the intervention of God.

REPRESENTATIVE WORKS

Charlotte Brontë

Jane Eyre (novel) 1847
Shirley (novel) 1849
Villette (novel) 1853

Emily Brontë
Wuthering Heights (novel) 1847

Robert Browning
"My Last Duchess" (poem) 1842
"The Bishop Orders His Tomb at Saint Praxed's Church" (poem) 1845
The Ring and the Book (poem) 1869

Wilkie Collins
The Woman in White (novel) 1859-60

Charles Dickens
Oliver Twist (novel) 1838
The Old Curiosity Shop (novel) 1841
Dombey and Son (novel) 1848
David Copperfield (novel) 1850
A Tale of Two Cities (novel) 1859
Great Expectations (novel) 1860

George Eliot
The Mill on the Floss (novel) 1860
Middlemarch (novel) 1871-72
Daniel Deronda (novel) 1876

Thomas Hardy
The Woodlanders (novel) 1887
Jude the Obscure (novel) 1895

Percy Bysshe Shelley
"On Death" (poem) 1814
"Alastor; or, The Spirit of Solitude" (poem) 1815
"Mont Blanc" (poem) 1816
"Ozymandias" (poem) 1818
"Ode to the West Wind" (poem) 1820
"Adonais" (poem) 1821

William Makepeace Thackeray
Vanity Fair (novel) 1847-48

OVERVIEWS

John R. Reed (essay date 1975)

SOURCE: "Deathbeds," in *Victorian Conventions,* Ohio University Press, 1975, pp. 156-71.

[*In the following essay, Reed overviews of Victorian attitudes toward death and describes assorted uses of deathbed scenes in literature, including that of moral instruction for the reader.*]

Attitude Toward Dying

E. M. Forster observed that the Victorians had a strong affection for deathbeds,[1] and Elizabeth Longford in her biography of Victoria explained that "Frank interest in death-bed scenes was quite normal. Partly because Victorians cared passionately about religion, the moment of passing from this world to the next was not one to be hushed up. Only paupers died in hospital so opportunities for study were plentiful." She adds that "The young Victoria collected from Queen Adelaide the 'painfully interesting details of the King's last illness'."[2] J. F. Stephen was among those critics of the literature of his time who felt that deathbed scenes were abused, especially by a writer such as Dickens.[3] But on the whole deathbed scenes were common in Victorian literature because they were an important practical and moral feature of life. "The fetish of deep family mourning was encouraged by the tradesmen concerned; but it was also one of the most strongly entrenched customs of the age. Mourning the dead is an instinct as old as man, but in no era had it become such an iron-bound convention as in the Victorian age."[4] And deathbed scenes were a central part of the mourning tradition, which extended of course well beyond the actual interment.

George Eliot, identifying the books that Adam Bede read to improve himself, lists works that one might expect to have found in many an English home well into the nineteenth century. Among these books is "Taylor's 'Holy Living and Dying.' " (*Adam Bede,* Ch. 19)[5] In *The Rule and Exercises of Holy Dying* (1651), Jeremy Taylor provided prayers, forms of conduct, and attitudes of mind to meet the difficulties of one's own or another's temporary or fatal illness. At one point he gives a list of "Arguments and Exhortations to move the Sick Man to Confession of Sins," that a minister or other concerned person might employ. There are twenty-four separate items in the list; and most of those he mentioned would reappear often in some of the moving or bathetic deathbed scenes of Victorian literature.

In a subsection of *Holy Dying* entitled "The Circumstances of a Dying Man's Sorrow and Danger," Taylor also presented the traditional belief that a man who has led a sinful life will experience a painful and arduous death, accompanied by fear and remorse. "But when a good man dies," he says, "angels drive away the devils on his deathbed," and thus "joy breaks forth through the clouds of sickness" which does "but untie the soul from its chain, and let it go forth, first into liberty, and then into glory." (Ch. 2, sec. 4) Martin Tupper, in "Life's End," rephrased Taylor's thoughts for his own audience, declaring that "when the bad man dieth, all his sins rise up against him, / Clamouring at his memory with imprecated judgments; / But when the good departeth, all his noble deeds / Surround him like a cloud of light to sphere his soul in glory." George Borrow, describing his father's death in his arms, had similar traditional views in mind. "I make no doubt," Borrow declares, "that for a moment he was perfectly sensible, and it was then that, clasping his hands, he uttered another name clearly, distinctly—it was the name of Christ. With that name upon his lips, the brave soldier sank back upon my bosom, and, with his hands still clasped, yielded up his soul." (*Lavengro,* Ch. 28) This is the tone of most virtuous deathbed scenes. But upon occasion, it is not the Bible, or Christ, that is prominent, as in Dr. Dabbs' account of Tennyson's last moments.

> Nothing could have been more striking than the scene during the last few hours. On the bed a figure of breathing marble, flooded and bathed in the light of the full moon streaming through the oriel window; his hand clasping the Shakespeare which he had asked for but recently, and which he had kept by him to the end; the moonlight, the majestic figure as he lay there, "drawing thicker breath," irresistibly brought to our minds his own "Passing of Arthur."[6]

The sentimentalizing of a great poet's death might easily draw upon the secular deity of poetry, rather than the divine, but the scene is, one way or the other, clearly staged, as were so many deathbed scenes of the time. Henry Peach Robinson's popular photograph, "Fading Away," represents, perhaps, the common pictorial version of the scene. It is, therefore, refreshing to find a description such as Edward Fitzgerald's record of his father's death. There is no mention of Christ, Shakespeare, noble features, moonlight or other traditional trappings. Instead, Fitzgerald notes, of the father he loved, "He died in March, after an illness of three weeks, saying 'that engine works well' (meaning one of his Colliery steam engines) as he lay in the stupor of Death."[7]

Dickens employed the traditional warning tales of dying profligates in *Pickwick Papers,* but also utilized types who would reappear later in different guises. The Chancery prisoner's death in *Pickwick Papers* anticipates the death from inanition of Mr. Gridley, the man from Shropshire, and Richard Carstone, both victims of Chancery in *Bleak House.* Some deathbed scenes combine the innocence of childhood and pathos of adulthood, as with David Copperfield's mother, who "died like a child that had gone to sleep" in Peggoty's arms. (*David Copperfield,* Ch. 9) And other deathbed scenes, while being serious, also have a touch of the comic in them, like the death of Mr. Barkis. Hablot K. Browne captured this combination of sentiments in his illustration entitled "I find Mr. Barkis 'going out with the Tide' " in *David Copperfield,* where Barkis ludicrously embraces the chest containing his valuables, while the onlookers are all serious and sympathetic, and on the wall behind Barkis a picture shows Christ ascending into heaven.

Deathbed Scenes in Literature

In Victorian literature, deathbed scenes served every conceivable purpose. In Susan Ferrier's *Marriage,* Mary Douglas and Charles Lennox realize the depth of their love over the deathbed of Charles' blind mother. Deathbed scenes occur regularly whenever a moral pause is required in T. P. Prest's *The Gipsy Boy,* and Samuel Warren's "A Scholar's Death-Bed" is a typical sentimental set piece. Deathbed scenes are common in the poetry of the period, from Thomas Hood's thoroughly conventional, "The Deathbed," to Rossetti's subtley related poem, "My Sister's Sleep." The verse of "A Vagrant's Deathbed," describing the contrast between affluence and poverty, in *Household Words* (Vol. 3, no. 53) was complemented by more accomplished poems of established poets. Browning exploited the deathbed setting in "Evelyn Hope" and "The Bishop Orders His Tomb," while his wife wrote "A Thought for a Lonely Death-bed," a prayer requesting that nothing be interposed between the speaker and Christ when she comes to die. Tennyson used the device comically in "The Northern Farmer: Old Style" and melodramatically in "Rizpah."

The convention was obvious, in fiction as well as in poetry, though in fiction it appeared as part of a larger narrative, and therefore had a different function. In novels, for example, deathbed scenes are frequently instrumental in revealing the moral direction of the narrative. They become tests of character and turning points in action as much as dramatic scenes in their own right. The sentimental deathbed scene of Isabel Vane in *East Lynne* made a heavy moral point. Charlotte Brontë used a traditional deathbed scene to describe Helen Burns' passing in *Jane Eyre,* but was capable of a subtler utilization of the convention when, in *Shirley,* she employed all of the tricks of the deathbed scene and then had her heroine, Caroline Helstone, recover. Anthony Trollope was content to indicate predictable conditions in his deathbed scenes, and consequently, while the questionable Mrs. Proudie dies in bizarre circumstances, the good Mr. Harding dies mildly, and Bishop Grantly, in *Barchester Towers,* displays in death the attributes of his life, expiring in a mild and serene manner. Much of the last chapter of Froude's "The Spirit's Trial" (1847) is, in effect, a prolonged deathbed scene, at the end of which Edward Fowler has his friend read an account of a deathbed scene to him. As Edward is dying at Eastertime, the sun breaks out, and he exclaims, "See, see! he is coming!" (ch. 9) Playing to a somewhat different audience, Ouida employed deathbed scenes of a more piquant, though less meditative nature as with the death of Leon Ramon, or Rake's death in the desert in *Under Two Flags* (1867). And Allan Quatermain's prolonged deathbed scene in Rider Haggard's *Allan Quatermain* (1887), provides a typical picture of the clean-living adventurer's resigned and trusting acceptance of the end.

One commonplace use of the deathbed scene was to give a fallen sinner the opportunity to demonstrate rehabilitation and repentence. Dickens gave even the most conventional of these scenes his own transforming touch. Thus, although Alice Marwood's dying moments are little different from many others, they are nonetheless particularly Dickensian. Repenting her former life, and brought to an appreciation of Christian truths by Harriet Carker, Alice dies thankful of her friend's help. Alice's eyes follow Harriet as she leaves the room:

> and in their light, and on the tranquil face, there was a smile when it [the door] was closed.
>
> They never turned away. She laid her hand upon her breast, murmuring the sacred name that had been read to her; and life passed from her face, like light removed.
>
> Nothing lay there, any longer, but the ruin of the mortal house on which the rain had beaten, and the black hair that had fluttered in the wintry wind. (*Dombey and Son,* ch. 58)

If Alice's death demonstrates the redemption of a sinner on a personal level, Magwitch's death in *Great Expectations* indicates broader meanings, for his "deathbed scene" actually includes his courtroom denunciation of man's faulty justice and God's greater judgment. Afterward, Magwitch dies quietly, his last act being to kiss Pip's hand—a form of blessing and thanksgiving combined.

Deathbed scenes could also reveal the dreadful state of those who were remorseful, though not reformed. The drunkard tumbler's death in the "Stroller's Tale" in *Pickwick Papers* is a typical example. In this case the dying man is overcome with guilt, he fears the wife he has abused so long, and raves about the theatre and the public house. Finally he lapses into a fit of delirium tremens, and dies a convulsive and painful death. Similarly, in Anne Brontë's *The Tenant of Wildfell Hall,* Arthur Huntington's short, brutish life of intemperance leads to death, and his abused wife, Helen, returns to tend him in his final illness, happily reporting that on his deathbed Huntington was penitent at last.

There is a conscious exploitation of the deathbed scene in Miss Braddon's *Charlotte's Inheritance* when Captain Paget, who has been a petty swindler and rascal all his life, faces his last moments.

> Later, when the doctor had felt his pulse for the last time, he cried out suddenly, "I have made a statement of my affairs. The liabilities are numerous—the assets *nil;* but I rely on the clemency of this Court." (Book 10, ch. 6)[8]

And in G. P. R. James' *The Gipsy,* we learn something of why rascals might feel penitence on their deathbeds, though nowhere else. When Sir Roger Millington, a parasite who has assisted the evil Lord Dewry in his schemes, is dying, the local parson encourages him to repent and to help, with his dying breath, to undo some of his mischief. He fortifies his persuasion by reminding the dying scoundrel that man closes his eyes in death and wakes instantly in the other world stripped of his body, where the sins of his life are naked for all to see. Not surprisingly, the parson's argument succeeds. In Rossetti's "A Last Confession," a dying Italian, without repenting, regrets the loss of the woman he loved, but murdered. Still, the deathbed convention of the period contributes greater force to Rossetti's poem simply because his audience anticipates penitence. When it does not come, the poem becomes something sharper, perhaps more believable, than a mere deathbed confession with the normal pieties.[9] Roger Scatcherd, in Trollope's *Doctor Thorne,* is a forceful example of the debauchee who dies penitent. Despite being worth a half-million pounds, Scatcherd regrets his entire life of vindictiveness and intemperance. Nothing, the obvious moral shows, can shield a man from the truthful last moments of the deathbed.

Another example of deathbed remorse draws the theme of misspent and misvalued life closer to the artist himself, for Tennyson's "Romney's Remorse" deals with the painter George Romney's deathbed regret that he had abandoned his wife in order to pursue his career. His debauchery was an indulgence not of the body, like Dickens' pathetic tumbler, but of the spirit. At last, he has "stumbled back again / Into the common day, the sounder self." But he is dying and his humble wife returns to tend him at the last. Now he hates the word art and exclaims: "My curse upon the Master's apothegm, / That wife and children drag an artist down!" He now sees his error in leaving his wife to seek artistic fame, and fears that he has "lost / Salvation for a sketch." He has no alternative but to lament and hope for forgiveness. In Kingsley's *Two Years Ago* (1857), the poet Elsley Vavasour dies repenting his vanity and false jealousy. He urges his friends to burn all of his poems and to prevent his children from making verses. The poet in Owen Meredith's poem, "Last Words," also laments a life devoted to the pursuit of fame through art. He tells his friend Will, who attends him at the end, that death is actually easier than life, and, he begins to feel hope beyond this world in which he has known only failure.

> Already I feel, in a sort of
> still sweet awe,
> The great main current of all that I am
> beginning to draw and draw
> Into perfect peace. I attain at last! Life's a
> long, long reaching out
> Of the soul to something beyond her. Now
> comes the end of all doubt.

The poet in "Last Words" has failed in his ambition to fashion from common men, "Man, with his spirit sublime, / Man the great heir of Eternity, dragging the conquests of Time!" just as Browning's Paracelsus failed in his extravagant aims. But on his deathbed, Paracelsus conveys to his faithful friend, Festus, his hopes for the progress of Man. He dies not lamenting his wasted life and his obscurity, but hopeful that, in the future, men will come to understand the message of love he has won with such effort.

Customarily deathbed scenes sought to show the importance of being ready for death, and to justify the existence of this overpowering mystery. Consciousness of death runs throughout Charlotte Yonge's *The Heir of Redclyffe,* climaxing in Guy Morville's deathbed scene. Aware that death is imminent, he has Amabel recite some verses from *Sintram,* which conclude hopefully.

> Death comes to set thee free,
> Oh! meet him cheerily,
> As thy true friend:
> And all thy fears shall cease,
> And in eternal peace,
> Thy penance end.
>
> (vol. 2, ch. 13)

Guy, who has proved his noble and generous nature throughout his life, now dies a noble death. It is a typical picture.

> At that moment the sun was rising, and the light streamed in at the open window and over the bed; but it was "another dawn than ours" that he beheld, as his most beautiful of all smiles beamed over his face, and he said, "Glory in the Highest!—peace—good will"—a struggle for breath gave an instant's look of pain; then he whispered so that she could but just hear—"The last prayer." She read the Commendatory Prayer. She knew not the exact moment, but even as she said, "Amen," she perceived it was over. The soul was with Him, with whom dwell the spirits of just men made perfect; and there lay the earthly part with the smile on the face. She closed the dark fringed eyelids—saw him look more beautiful than in sleep,—then, laying her face down to the bed, she knelt on. (vol. 2, ch. 13)

In many deathbed scenes a dying one passes on a moral responsibility to others. Constance Brandon, in *Guy Livingstone,* conveys to her saddened lover both remorse for his behavior and a yearning to seek a higher meaning in life. In Kingsley's *Yeast,* Argemone Lavington on her deathbed not only acknowledges the appropriateness of her death from a fever contracted while tending the poor her wealthy family has hitherto neglected, but passes on a legacy of moral duty to her faithful lover, urging him to remember her and labor to achieve the noble aim of seeing the slums cleared and disease brought under control among the poor.

The death of a good woman, especially a mother, often called for a sentimental tableau in the popular literature of the Victorian period. Mrs. Aubrey in Samuel Warren's *Ten Thousand A-Year* recovers from a brand of madness just in time to die a good and inspiring death. On the other hand, Alice Wilson, in Mrs. Gaskell's *Mary Barton,* having lived a pious life, glides into death by way of a second childhood. "The firm faith which her mind had no longer power to grasp, had left its trail of glory; for by no other word can I call the bright happy look which illumined the old earth-worn face. Her talk, it is true, bore no more that constant earnest reference to God and His holy word which it had done in health, and there were no deathbed words of exhortation from the lips of one so habitually pious." (Ch. 33) Instead, Alice's mind dwells in the happy memories of her childhood. "And death came to her as a welcome blessing, like an evening comes to the weary child." (Ch. 33) The virtuous and long-suffering mother of the prodigal Paul Tatnall in Joseph H. Ingraham's *The Gipsy of the Highlands,* manages, on her deathbed, to convert the young woman who loves her son with forceful and sustained arguments. Having accomplished this, she prays that her son may repent and be saved, but "here her voice failed her, and her eyes, after steadfastly regarding heaven, slowly closed, while a smile came like sunlight to her features, and then a shadow passed slowly across her falling countenance—a sigh! and the pure spirit of the broken-hearted and pious widow took its flight to heaven!" (Ch. 9) In the popular literature of the time, "Purity and innocence always triumphed over the powers of evil, and the story ended with a betrothal, or, quite as often, with the sinner repentant on his deathbed," Janet Dunbar observes.[10]

In *The Ring and The Book* Browning wrote a memorable deathbed scene which, like Magwitch's in *Great Expectations,* was less the expression of an individual spirit than the exemplification of a way of life, correcting a faulty world with the intensity of vision given to those who are on the verge of a presumably higher and finer realm. Pompilia is the embodiment of innocence, and her proper home is not this world, but the next. "The hovel is life," she says, anticipating liberation from it. Like Little Nell, she does not fear death, but looks forward to it almost gladly, certainly with relief. Her last words are for those who must remain in the world, and, although she does not, like Kingsley's Argemone, have any specific social labor to recommend, she does cheer on the laborers left in the vineyard.

> So, let him wait God's instant men call years;
> Meantime hold hard by truth and his great soul,
> Do out the duty! Through such souls alone
> God stooping shows sufficient of His light
> For us i' the dark to rise by. And I rise.
> (Book 7)

Although Pompilia's virtue has earlier been questioned, there is little doubt in the reader's mind of her virtue. The same can be said of Mrs. Gaskell's Ruth. Although Ruth had lapsed from chastity in her youth, her adult life has been a series of virtuous triumphs, and her death represents the achievement of a higher virtue than that found in most of her neighbors, for she has contracted her own fatal illness while tending epidemic victims whose health concerns the entire community. Her death is an apotheosis of selfless dedication and it enjoys the appropriate furnishings.

> "I see the Light coming," she said. "The Light is coming," she said. And, raising herself slowly, she stretched out her arms, and then fell back, very still for evermore. (ch. 35, *Ruth*)

Less theatrical, but equally indicative of feminine virtue is the long "deathbed" letter that Jane Graham leaves for her husband to read after her death in Coventry Patmore's *The Angel in the House* (sections 7 through 9 of "The Victories of Love"). Jane includes expressions of her love for Frederick and her hope for their future, as well as a record of her vision of heaven. Although this is not a genuine deathbed scene, it achieves the same effects and draws upon the same conventional materials. In some ways it is even more demonstrative of what the virtuous deathbed scene meant to Victorians, since it avoids entirely the actual physical death by concentrating on the thoughts recorded while Jane gradually weakened, thus making her posthumous letter resemble a private prayer.

The Child.

If Charlotte Yonge had captured a prevailing sentiment about death in her picture of Guy Morville's end in *The Heir of Redclyffe,* she touched an equally evocative chord in her conventional account of the child, Felix Dixon's death. Gillian Avery has written that whereas Georgians tried to shock their readers into good behavior through the use of death, "the early Victorians strove to edify by recording pious deaths," and later Victorians became sentimental. In all cases, childhood death "tended to be linked with the themes of punishment and reward."[11] A disobedient child could be instructive to others. In tract stories, a child's death is quite openly a "holy example" required for the conversion of the remaining characters of the tale.[12] As the century progressed, the death of innocence was more markedly associated with the death of children. Peter Coveney writes of two popular novelists of the later Victorian period, "with Marie Corelli, as with Mrs. Henry Wood, death is never very far removed from her image of the child."[13]

Dying children were clearly representatives of innocence, but although "the child may die talking of heaven and angels, he does not seem to have heard of sin."[14] In *Misunderstood* (1869), Florence Montgomery exploited both the punishment of the disobedient child and the innocence of his death, combining them both into one character, young Humphrey Duncombe. Humphrey is not a bad boy, though he is thoughtless. Yet, when he is dying, the narrator remarks that "natures like Humphrey's are not fit for this rough world. Such a capacity for sorrow has no rest here, and such a capability for enjoyment is fittest to find its happiness in those all-perfect pleasures which are at God's right hand for evermore." (Ch. 16) Humphrey has been capable of one profound emotion—love for his dead mother, and, on his deathbed, beneath his mother's picture, he imagines she has come to claim him.

> Those who were standing round saw only the expression of pain change to the old sunny smile. His lips moved, and he lifted his arms, as his eyes were raised, for a moment, to the picture above him, on which the sun was pouring a dazzling light. They closed: but the smile, intensely radiant, lingered about the parted lips; the short breathing grew shorter . . . stopped . . . and then . . .
>
> "It's no use my saying the rest," said little Miles in a whisper, "for Humphie has gone to sleep." (ch. 17)

Gillian Avery comments that the death of Humphrey in *Misunderstood* is "shamelessly derived from the death of Paul Dombey,"[15] while Peter Coveney remarks that "William Carlyle of *East Lynne* is perhaps the most notorious of the Victorian dying children, whose ancestry lay in Little Nell and Paul Dombey." Coveney adds, however, that whereas such figures as Paul Dombey, and Eppie in *Silas Marner* are serious creations, William Carlyle's context "is no more than a moralizing melodrama, declaring the inevitable retributions of carnal sin."[16] Little Paul's death in *Dombey and Son* was one of the most famous deaths in Victorian fiction. The dying is prolonged, but the deathbed scene is relatively brief, terminating with the suggestion that little Paul already views his dead mother and his Savior before he dies. "Mama is like you, Floy," he says to his sister. "'I know her by the face! But tell them the print upon the stairs at school is not divine enough. The light about the head is shining on me as I go!'" (Ch. 16) A scene such as this could be viewed as moving and moral, or merely as sentimental trash, but it sold.

Dickens made frequent and varying use of the dying child. Little Johnny, in *Our Mutual Friend,* dies in a spirit of charity, bequeathing his toys to the ailing child in the bed near his own, but his death is merely one more in a sequence of touching childhood deathbed scenes. Dickens had used a child's deathbed to point a moral as early as *Pickwick Papers,* when Gabriel Grub was forced to witness the pathetic event. Later, Scrooge, though obliged to witness a similar scene, had the opportunity to forestall it. There are, of course, other dying youngsters of various ages in Dickens' works, including Smike in *Nicholas Nickleby* and Jo in *Bleak House,* but the most memorable children's deathbeds, aside from Paul Dombey's, appear in *The Old Curiosity Shop.* Long before her own decline, Little Nell witnesses the death of a young schoolboy, his schoolmaster's most promising student. The meaning of this death is not lost on Nell.

> But the sad scene she had witnessed, was not without its lesson of content and gratitude; of content with the lot which left her health and freedom; and gratitude that she was spared to the one relative and friend she loved, and to live and move in a beautiful world, when so many young creatures—as young and full of hope as she—were stricken and gathered to their graves. (Ch. 26)

There are other advantages to an early death that Nell does not consider, but some of them are indicated to her later by the schoolmaster who has learned to accept the death of the young and innocent through his faith in the triumph of good. "If the good deeds of human creatures could be traced to their source," he says, "how beautiful would even death appear; for how much charity, mercy and purified affection, would be seen to have their growth in dusty graves." (Ch. 54) Although we do not witness Nell's death, we see her soon after on her deathbed. She signifies death of innocence and her travail in this world is ended. "Sorrow was dead indeed in her, but peace and perfect happiness were born; imaged in her tranquil beauty and profound repose." (Ch. 71)

The consolation suggested by the schoolmaster's words and implied in Dickens' portrayal of Nell, is echoed in Archbishop Trench's poem, "On An Early Death": "Nothing is left or lost, nothing of good, / Or lovely; but whatever its first springs / Has drawn from God, returns to Him again." This view was commonplace, and yet, it is possible, beyond the Christian comfort for the loss of youth and innocence, there is a more ominous implication. Peter Coveney sees in the transformation of the image of the child, from life-bearer, to death-borne, a grim indication about the Victorian age. "It is as if so many placed on the image the weight of their own disquiet and dissatisfaction, their impulse to withdrawal, and, in extremity, their own wish for death. . . . It is a remarkable phenomenon, surely," he adds, "when a society takes the child (with all its potential significance as a symbol of fertility and growth) and creates of it a literary image, not only of frailty, but of life extinguished, of life that is better extinguished, of life, so to say, rejected, negated at its very root.[17]

For many writers, and doubtless some portion of their audience, the deathbed became a sanctuary, where the qualities of childhood could escape the effects of time and suffering. The poems of poets such as Francis Thompson and Ernest Dowson suggest the wistful desire to worship what children stand for, while hoping that life will not touch them. On a gayer note, but no less exclusive, the world of children is largely removed to the province of fantasy in the works of R. L. Stevenson, Sir James Barrie, Rudyard Kipling, and George MacDonald. This exclusion of the child from the corrupting ways of adulthood, suggests a growing conciousness of the nature of that society's failure and is, to a large extent, a confession of decline.

Conclusion

Despite its apparent sentimentality, the deathbed convention was much in keeping with the Victorian attitudes toward death, which, in general, would appear exaggerated and mawkish today. But some manifestations of the convention are truly memorable. It was not only women and children who could die deaths remarkable for their innocence and sweetness, for example. Though most adults were somehow qualified in their virtue by mere exposure to the world, some could transcend that sullying influence. Thackeray transformed the customary image of adult reconciliation with death into one of innocence more commonly associated with the deaths of children, and, in doing so, created one of the most famous deathbed scenes in Victorian literature. Old Colonel Newcome is wandering in his mind as the end draws near. He is a pensioner now of his old school, Grey Friars, but he feels no shame in his humble position. His concerns, even in his hallucinations, are for those he loves. Finally, the end comes.

> At the usual evening hour the chapel bell began to toll, and Thomas Newcome's hands outside the bed feebly beat time. And just as the last bell struck, a peculiar sweet smile shone over his face, and he

> lifted up his head a little, and quickly said, "Adsum!" and fell back. It was the word we used at school, when names were called; and lo, he, whose heart was as that of a little child, had answered to his name, and stood in the presence of The Master. (*The Newcomes,* Vol. 2, ch. 42)[18]

There is a general resemblance here to other concluding deathbed scenes. Mordecai's death, for example, closes *Daniel Deronda* like a sort of benediction.

The traditional moral significance of deathbed scenes persisted beyond the nineteenth century. The dying curses that echoed through the popular romances of the time, and modifications of them, as in Bulwer-Lytton's *A Strange Story,* where the dying Dr. Lloyd angrily foretells his professional antagonist, Dr. Fenwick's, suffering and doubt, did not disappear from adventure tales. And religious significance remained in such stories as Mrs. Opie's novel, *Adeline Mowbray* (1905), where a freethinker recants on his deathbed.[19] Some writers employed the convention merely as a technical convenience. Wilkie Collins opened *Armadale* with a prolonged deathbed scene, in which the older Allan Armadale, dying of a creeping paralysis, recounts the history of his misadventures with his antagonist, the other Allan Armadale. Collins realized that this was a strong scene, and used the technique in *The Dead Secret* as well. The device provides a forceful initiation to the story, but, aside from hinting of malign agencies at work and impending disasters prescribed by destiny, Collins did little to exploit the convention. There is a little more irony in Dutton Cook's *A Prodigal Son* (1863), where the first five chapters are taken up by the death of old George Hadfield. The tough old man dies with a smile on his lips and his doctor remarks that "He looked so grand and handsome, it was difficult to believe that he died cruel, and relentless, and unforgiving." (Vol. 1, ch. 5)

The deathbed convention was not a mere literary contrivance. Most families were acquainted with the fact of death near at hand. In "The Lifted Veil" (1859), George Eliot acknowledged, through the narrator of her story, the monumental importance of witnessing the dying moments of another being. Latimer, recounting how he had watched at his father's deathbed, exclaims, "What are all our personal loves when we have been sharing in that supreme agony? In the first moments when we come away from the presence of death, every other relation to the living is merged, to our feeling, in the great relation of a common nature and a common destiny." (Ch. 2) Possibly it was this sense of a common destiny, more than the attempt at moral persuasion, that was most captivating in the convention of the deathbed. Walter Houghton is, perhaps, too hasty in declaring that death scenes in Victorian novels "are intended to help the reader sustain his faith by dissolving religious doubts in a solution of warm sentiment."[20] A powerful passage from Robert Bell's *The Ladder of Gold* (1850) demonstrates that the Chamber of Death signified more to Victorian readers than a consoling reassurance about the next life. It was, as much or more, a reminder of the vanity of this life.

> Rich and poor, proud and humble, the wronged and the wrong-doer, are here brought to a common level. Their stormy passions, their grand projects, their great revenges,—what are they here in the Presence of the Dead—a breath of air which thrills a leaf and passes on. What are our loves and hates here? our honours, our humiliations?—a poor fading dream! Upon this threshold the unreality of life is made clear to us, and we see the pageant vanishing before our eyes. (Book 1, ch. 4)

Not all deathbed scenes were conventional. Many still appear faithful to the reality. There is the justly famous dramatic and realistic decease of Peter Featherstone in *Middlemarch,* where George Eliot actually seems to be taking pains to contradict the saccharine deathbed scenes which she herself was not totally innocent of using, as the death of Eppie in *Silas Marner* testifies. And Eliot's realism was in keeping with a growing tendency to resist the conventional form of the deathbed scene. As was so often the case, when conventions came to be attacked, Thomas Hardy was prominent in the assault. Not only does he introduce the bizarre deathbed sequence of old John South (who dies when the elm tree that has terrified him is cut down) into *The Woodlanders,* but in the death of Giles Winterborne in the same novel he presents a matter-of-fact exit, not a sentimental diminuendo. After becoming ill from exposure, Winterborne loses consciousness. "In less than an hour the delirium ceased; then there was an interval of somnolent painlessness and soft breathing, at the end of which Winterborne passed quietly away." (Ch. 43) This plain demise is in contrast to the brutal deathbed scene of Jude Fawley in *Jude the Obscure.* There Jude lies abandoned on his deathbed reciting to himself the lamentations of Job, while outside the crowds cheer on a festival day, and his wife sports with some gay associates. He dies alone and unheeded with only a wish never to have lived upon his lips. It is a bitter termination for a convention that had held the conviction of its readers throughout the century.

Deathbed scenes in Victorian literature could be moving or bathetic; they could be technically convenient or structurally important; but they were generally accepted and appreciated. The deathbed presented the last preserve of truth; it was a final opportunity to repent, admonish or encourage. As a result, it customarily bore, for Victorians, an importance far greater than what we place upon it. Very likely there were few of those staged deliveries of touching last words in reality. Perhaps those mortal scenes were uglier than writers cared to admit. But in literature they were an automatic means for conveying clearly and without reserve, the basic importance of the moral scheme which underlay so much of the writing of the time. As faith in a life after death waned, death could still be viewed as the touchstone of human vanities, but the deathbed scenes disappeared as mortuary practices changed and most deaths began to occur in hospitals rather than homes.[21] Offensive as many modern readers now find the deathbed convention, it was, for its time, a truly immediate reality that bound fictional convention and social fact together.

Notes

[1] E. M. Forster, *Marianne Thornton (1797-1887): A Domestic Biography* (London, 1956), see chapter four entitled "The Death Beds."

[2] Elizabeth Longford, *Queen Victoria: Born to Succeed* (New York, 1966), p. 310.

[3] See Sir James Fitzjames Stephen on *A Tale of Two Cities* in *Saturday Review*, 17 Dec. 1859; reprinted in *The Dickens Critics,* eds. George H. Ford and Lauriat Lane, Jr. (Ithaca, New York, 1961), pp. 38-46.

[4] Janet Dunbar, *The Early Victorian Woman: Some Aspects of Her Life (1837-57)* (London, 1953), p. 60. John Morley's *Death, Heaven and the Victorians* (Pittsburgh, 1971), describes in detail the Victorian preoccupation with death and burial, and the numerous moral, social, and economic implications that influenced mourning customs of the time.

[5] Coventry Patmore's wife, Emily, considered Taylor's *Holy Living and Holy Dying* her favorite book (Derek Patmore, *The Life and Times of Coventry Patmore* [London, 1949], p. 107). Since she died in 1863, it may be assumed that Taylor's work was still well known and respected. John Morley notes that Taylor was often quoted on matters concerning death and the rites of burial. (p. 21)

[6] Hallam Tennyson, *Alfred Lord Tennyson: A Memoir by His Son,* 2 vols. (New York, 1905), 2, pp. 428-29. Thomas Hardy supposedly asked to have stanza 81 of Fitzgerald's *Rubaiyat* read to him on his deathbed. Not all poets died grandly, though reports might make it seem so. B. R. Jerman has an interesting study, "The Death of Robert Browning" in the *University of Toronto Quarterly* 35, no. 1 (1965), pp. 47-74. In *The Brothers Karamazov,* Father Zossima's corpse causes a scandal, because his fellow monks have not expected such a saintly man's remains to stink of corruption. (Part 3, Book 7, ch. 1)

[7] Edward Fitzgerald, *Letters & Literary Remains of Edward Fitzgerald,* 7 vols. (New York, 1966: reprint), 2, p. 4; dated, 1852.

[8] An earlier reference to Colonel Newcome's "Adsum," shows that Braddon was fully conscious of Thackeray's earlier and more memorable employment of the convention.

[9] The crusty old character, Bernard Haldane, in George Alfred Lawrence's *Barren Honour. A Tale* (1868), does not die a calm and reconciled death, but remains bitter toward the woman who broke his heart.

[10] Dunbar, *Victorian Women,* p. 122.

[11] Gillian Avery, *Nineteenth Century Children: Heroes and Heroines in English Children's Stories 1780-1900* (London, 1965), p. 212.

[12] Ibid., p. 220.

[13] Peter Coveney, *The Image of Childhood: The Individual and Society: A Study of the Theme in English Literature* (Baltimore, 1967), p. 188.

[14] Avery, *Nineteenth Century Children,* p. 174.

[15] Ibid., p. 175.

[16] Coveney, *Image of Childhood,* p. 179.

[17] Ibid., p. 193. However, the negation of life in the child is intended to lead to positive results in the way that evil was, through the inscrutable ways of providence, meant to perpetrate a greater good. An example of this is in a tale published in the March, 1865 issue of the *Cornhill Magazine,* entitled "Willie Baird: a Winter Idyll," in which a little scholar dies, and his saddened teacher lives on with the boy's dog, who had tried to lead the teacher into the storm to save the dying boy. The teacher had not understood, and the boy had died. But the death has a moral effect upon the teacher. "I read my Bible more and Euclid less," he says.

[18] U. C. Knoepflmacher writes of *Vanity Fair* that "The novel's many death scenes are not due to a mawkish Victorian fascination with such situations, but rather stem from Thackeray's desire to remind the reader that death, the end of life, is the only true vanquisher of vanity" (*Laughter & Despair: Readings in Ten Novels of the Victorian Era* [Berkeley, 1971], p. 82).

[19] Patricia Thomson, *The Victorian Heroine: A Changing Ideal 1837-1873* (London, 1956), p. 158.

[20] Walter E. Houghton, *The Victorian Frame of Mind 1830-1870* (New Haven, 1964), p. 277.

[21] As one might expect, deathbed scenes retained an interest for spiritualists. Sophia Morgan wrote, in *From Matter to Spirit* (London, 1863): "The apparent recog-

nition by the dying of those who have gone before, is a common and notorious fact." (p. 176) She gives several instances in chapter ten of deathbed recognitions of dead beings.

Andrew Sanders on Dickens:

The prevalence of death in [Dickens'] fiction reflected a familiar enough reality to his readers; he neither killed characters for the market . . . nor for fictional convenience. . . . Dickens wrote of dying children because so many nineteenth-century families, including his own, lost children in infancy; he described pious adult deathbeds because he had attended them; he expressed grief at the loss of fictional characters because he so sorely felt the loss of friends and relatives. . . .

Andrew Sanders, in an introduction to Charles Dickens Resurrectionist, *The Macmillan Press, Ltd., 1982.*

Andrew Sanders (essay date 1982)

SOURCE: "They Dies Everywhere . . . ," in *Charles Dickens Resurrectionist,* The Macmillan Press, Ltd., 1982, pp.1-36.

[*In the following essay, Sanders examines Charles Dickens' portrayals of death and of deathbed scenes and asserts that they reflect both Victorian fascination with death and concern about the very high mortality rate of urban-dwellers in the nineteenth century.*]

The death-rate in *Bleak House,* John Ruskin argued, functions merely as 'a representative average of the statistics of civilian mortality in the centre of London'; it might therefore be further adduced that the substantial number of fatalities suffered during the span of Dickens's novels from *Pickwick* to *Edwin Drood* reflects that in the real urban world of the nineteenth century.[1] No major character dies in *Pickwick Papers,* though dark mortal shadows are cast over the story by deaths and hauntings in the interpolated tales and especially by the account of the death of the 'Chancery prisoner' in Chapter 44. From *Oliver Twist* onwards, however, characters, major and minor, are variously struck down in the course of narratives and their death-beds, or at least death-scenes, come to take on a considerable local or thematic importance in the development of a story. Oliver Twist's unmarried mother dies in childbed in the first chapter of the novel, to be followed by the news of little Dick's impending demise and by the violent deaths of Nancy, Sikes, and Fagin. Smike's deathbed, if we except those of the 'widow's son' in *Sketches by Boz* and the 'Chancery prisoner', effectively Dickens's first, haunts the closing chapters of *Nicholas Nickleby* and forms a striking contrast to the despairing last hours of Ralph Nickleby. Little Nell's death is virtually the goal of the progress traced in *The Old Curiosity Shop,* though her chief persecutor, Daniel Quilp, is to drown on 'a good, black, devil's night' and to be washed up, a glaring corpse, on a deserted mud-bank. *Barnaby Rudge* is pervaded by violence, and the unsolved murder at the Warren seems almost to presage the murderous actions of the mob during the Gordon Riots. If *Martin Chuzzlewit,* which displeased so many of its first readers, accounts for the death of no major character, it at least contains the murder of Tigg, the suicide of Jonas Chuzzlewit, and Mrs Gamp's superlative expatiations on the loveliness of corpses. *Dombey and Son* opens, like *Oliver Twist,* with the death of a mother and it goes on to describe the decline of its first protagonist, the death-beds of the newly-converted Alice Marwood and the desolate Mrs Skewton, and the violent end of Carker. Mrs Copperfield dies of the effects of bearing David's brother in Chapter 9 of *David Copperfield,* to be followed in due course by the roughly parallel death of Dora, by Barkis going out with the tide, and by the dramatic drownings of Ham and Steerforth. In *Bleak House,* Jo dies of the apparent effects of fever and neglect, Richard Carstone wastes away, his life-blood sucked by a vampire law-suit, Lady Dedlock is found dead at the gates of the squalid grave-yard where her former lover lies buried, Tulkinghorn is found shot, and Krook is the supposed victim of spontaneous combustion. Stephen Blackpool is mortally injured by falling down a disused mine-shaft in *Hard Times,* and Josiah Bounderby is to die after the novel's close of a fit in a Coketown street. Mr Dorrit declines into distraction and death and Merdle opens his jugular vein in his bath in *Little Dorrit,* while Blandois is killed in the collapse of the Clennam house, a collapse which also occasions Mrs Clennam's terminal stroke. *A Tale of Two Cities* opens with Dr Manette's recall to life and ends with Sydney Carton's anticipation of his resurrection from the steps of the scaffold, having meanwhile accounted for the identifiable deaths of the villainous Marquis St Evrémonde, and Mme Defarge and the numerous unnamed but innocent victims of the September massacres and the guillotine. *Great Expectations* opens in a grave-yard, moves to a London dominated by Newgate, and describes the diverse ends of Mrs Joe, Miss Havisham, Compeyson and Magwitch. *Our Mutual Friend* begins as a mangled corpse is dredged from the Thames and witnesses the peaceful deaths of little Johnny and Betty Higden, the violent ones of Gaffer Hexam, Rogue Riderhood and Bradley Headstone, and the attempted murders of John Harmon and Eugene Wrayburn. The unfinished *Edwin Drood* is centred on yet another murder, but the mystery of the novel will remain forever unsolved as a result of the intervening death of the only man ever able to solve it correctly.

Calculating the exact number who die in the course of Dickens's novels is as vain an exercise as estimating Lady Macbeth's fertility-rate, but it is none the less clear that the novelist was a man much preoccupied with mortality. As a recorder of his times he was also transcribing, and eventually transforming, the evidence of the urban civilisation around him, data which was as much relative to the facts of death as to those of life. Given the vast increase in the population of Victorian Britain, and its steady annual growth, Death posed questions which disturbed more than simply religious hope. The grave-yards groaned with a surplus worse than that of the slums, and Death as the ultimate *omnium gatherum* steadily undid more people than ever streamed optimistically through the crystal aisles of the Great Exhibition. The Victorians delighted in statistics, and if Dickens did not exactly share the delight in Benthamite cataloguing demonstrated by many of his contemporaries, he must at least have shared their shock at the published evidence of Parliamentary Commissions, conscientious journalists, Registrars General, and corresponding members of the Statistical Society of London. The thirst for knowledge, and for a scientific basis for reform, paralleled an increase in social ill, and a lack of social hygiene appalled men and women aware for the first time of the benefits of sanitary improvement. Although the bubonic plague had declined a century or more before as a basic condition of urban life, it was effectively replaced by epidemic waves of cholera, typhus, typhoid, dysentery and smallpox. If Samuel Pepys's fellow-citizens blindly shut their windows at night, burnt bonfires at street-corners and incense in their houses, the Victorians publicly fretted over the fact that their science seemed to explain the causes of infection without providing them with an effective means of combatting it. The catalogues of ill, from the opening of Tennyson's *Maud* to the reports which stimulated the Public Health Acts of 1866, 1871 and 1875, pointed to the fact that peace was proving a worse killer than war. As Edwin Chadwick soberly and unpoetically noted in his *Report on the Sanitary Condition of the Labouring Population* of 1842, 'the annual loss of life from filth and bad ventilation are greater than the loss from death or wounds in any wars in which this country has been engaged in modern times'. Yet more disturbingly, the evidence assembled by Chadwick's commissioners suggested that 'the ravages of epidemics and other diseases do not diminish but tend to increase the pressure of population'.[2]

Chadwick's report reminded early Victorians, as much as *Bleak House* reiterated the fact to mid-Victorians, that diseases bred in the slums took their revenge on society as a whole. A huge new urban population, in London and in the industrial cities of the Midlands and the North, transferred rural poverty into the cities and concentrated problems into smaller, but densely populated, areas. In a city of London's scale the classless effects of disease and death were accentuated by proximity. Castes separated from each other by hedges and park walls in the country shared the same water supply and drainage in the town; however much they endeavoured not to, they jostled each other in the central streets, and the mansion merely hid the tenement to its rear. If the juxtaposition of rich and poor, and of two distinct nations unknown to each other, has been exaggerated for propagandist reasons, in London at least, each class, and the infinite and often subtle gradations which blurred real class distinctions, shared a common geographical if not social setting. There was, nevertheless, as Dickens himself noted in 1863, a noticeable class distinction in the capital's mortality-rates. 'The most prosperous and best cared for among men and women', he told an audience at a banquet in aid of the Royal Free Hospital, 'know full well that whosoever is hit in this great and continuing battle of life . . . we must close up the ranks, and march on, and fight out the fight. But', he went on, extending his analogy, 'it happens that the rank and file are many in number, and the chances against them are many and hard, and they necessarily die by thousands, when the captains and standard-bearers only die by ones and twos.'[3] In 1830, for example, the average age at death for a gentleman or professional man and his family was forty-four; for a tradesman or clerk and his family it sunk dramatically to twenty-five, while for a labourer and his family it was only twenty-two.[4] Edwin Chadwick himself noted that in the socially mixed parish of St George, Hanover Square, in 1839, the average age at death was thirty-one, though that average was pulled down by the statistics for infant mortality amongst the poorer parishioners.[5] Such figures are deceptive in one important regard, for they are biased by the very fact of the inclusion of infant mortality-rates, and, as a result of better hygiene, nourishment and medical treatment, a child born into a middle-class family stood a marginally better chance of survival than one born lower down the social scale. If the figures are adjusted by placing infant deaths in a special category, a slightly brighter picture of average life-expectancy emerges. Between 1838 and 1854, statistics for England and Wales suggest that the average age at death for both men and women was 39.9 years; having survived the first fifteen of those years, however, life-expectancy could be extended to 58.2 years. After the age of twenty-five, it extended again to 61.1. For the period 1950 to 1952, by contrast, these averages read 66.4 years, 69.4 and 70 respectively.[6]

As the nineteenth century advanced into the twentieth, life-expectancy gradually extended, largely as a result of a more general application of precisely those benefits which once exclusively strengthened the middle-class infant. This improvement was noticeable to the Victorians themselves, and became a matter of some self-congratulatory relief and compensation for the frightening conclusions drawn by Chadwick and his fellow-statisticians in the early 1840s. There had been a general national decline in the death-rate in the period 1780-1810, but it had begun to rise again with the development of the large industrial towns, a factor which greatly disturbed the Census Commissioners in 1831.[7] The rate varied between regions, however, with London generally better off than the new northern cities.

By 1880, one can sense the relief of Thomas A. Welton who reported to the Statistical Society of London that over a twenty-five-year period the overall mortality-rate had declined by about 25 per cent.[8] The zymotic diseases (scarlatina, typhus, typhoid, and typhinia) and diseases of the lungs remained the biggest killers, but, Welton noted, the general risk of falling victim to one or the other was slowly diminishing, the rate in London (1.98 per cent) remaining appreciably less than that in Manchester (3.14 per cent) or Liverpool (3.10 per cent). Some fifteen years earlier the *Journal of the Statistical Society* had commented extensively on the findings of the twenty-fifth annual report of the Registrar General. So pervasive was the high rate of infant mortality in the period 1850-60 that the *Journal* did not bother to adduce reasons or to diagnose likely causes. In the age-group 5-10 years, however, it was noted that more than half the deaths of the children concerned were attributable to the zymotic diseases, while the remainder were supposed to be the various results of scrofula, tabes, phthisis, hydrocephalus and a category generally labelled 'diseases of the brain and lungs'. Amongst children aged between 10 and 15, the death-rate remained one in every two hundred, though consumption is now increasingly cited as the main cause of death, only marginally overtaking the fevers and diphtheria. In the age-group 15-25 it is noted that smallpox emerges as the biggest single killer, though half of the deaths of young women are attributed to consumption, and a significant proportion to the effects of childbirth. Two out of every hundred men aged between 25 and 35 and three out of every hundred women were left widowed. Only after reaching the age of 45 does it seem that the risk of dying from organic disease other than those of the lungs outbalances the dire effects of the zymotic diseases, diarrhoea, dysentery, phthisis and cholera.[9] It scarcely comes as a surprise to learn that in 1839, with a population approaching two million, there were 45,277 funerals in London, 21,471 of them being of children aged under ten years.[10] For infants the mortality-rate remained 150 in every 1000 births until the end of the century, only dropping to 138 in every 1000 births between 1901 and 1905.[11] Edwin Chadwick even estimated that of the £24 million deposited in savings banks in 1843, some £6-8 million was saved in order to meet the expenses of funerals, that is, extraordinarily enough, between a quarter and a third of saved capital.[12]

It is with these figures in mind that we can begin to grasp not only the alarming mortality-rate at Mrs Mann's baby-farm in *Oliver Twist,* and the death of the brickmaker's child in *Bleak House,* but also the sudden departure of little Johnny in *Our Mutual Friend,* and the slow declines of older children like Nell Trent and Paul Dombey. The deaths in childbed of the mothers of Oliver Twist and Philip Pirrip, of Mrs Dombey, and of the two Mrs Copperfields, equally have a perspective, as does the extensive use of the imagery of fever in *Bleak House.* Thrombosis, which kills, amongst others, Mrs Skewton, Mr Bounderby and Mrs Clennam, is a disease associated exclusively with old, or at least middle age. It was to kill Dickens himself at the age of 58. The vague, though once, it seems, definable 'brain fever', accounts, as one recent commentator has shown, for a substantial number of near fatalities in Victorian fiction, amongst them Pip's.[13] Tuberculosis, a familiar enough remover of the less robust characters of other contemporary novelists, seems comparatively rare in Dickens's novels, though it kills 'the widow's son' in one of the earlier *Sketches by Boz;* nevertheless, as several medically qualified Dickensians have noted, he is otherwise an excellent observer and recorder of symptoms.[14]

Bleak House remains, however, the most significant investigation amongst Dickens's works of the various effects of disease on urban life in the nineteenth century. An unspecified contagious disease, most probably, given the nature of Esther's subsequent scars, smallpox, becomes not only a uniting image for the story, but also a sign of the real destructiveness caused by the rottenness of society. It is, of course, useful that Dickens remains unspecific, for he is thereby able to exploit a more general Victorian concern with fever. The contemporary concern was well founded, for fevers, even those loosely diagnosed as 'brain fever' and likely to be the result of mental as much as physical disease, regularly reached epidemic proportions in the middle years of the century. It was not idly that George Eliot gave Lydgate an interest in 'special questions of disease, such as the nature of fever or fevers' in a novel set in the early 1830s, for the problem was very much associated with the growth in the urban population at the time. In larger concentrations of people than Middlemarch, most notably London, Glasgow and some of the northern manufacturing cities, typhus and typhoid were already endemic. Typhus, a sickness especially associated with poverty and dirt, produced severe epidemics in 1848, 1856 and 1861. Typhoid fever, recognised as a separate affliction after the middle of the century, was, by contrast, classless. It killed Prince Albert at the age of 42 in 1861, and very nearly killed his son Albert Edward, Prince of Wales, in 1871. Cholera first appeared in England in 1831-2, though a more serious outbreak occurred in September 1848, reaching its height during the following summer, and killing 52,293 people in 1849 alone.[15] It appeared again in the mid-summer of 1853, first in London, but gradually spreading throughout the kingdom and causing a total of 20,097 deaths in England and Wales by the end of 1854. A fourth epidemic began in July 1865 killing a further 14,378 men and women, 5548 of them in London.[16] Other contagious diseases were largely confined to children. The incidence of scarlet fever gradually increased; an outbreak of an especially malignant form occurred in Dublin in 1831, and by 1834 as many had died of it as had suffered during the cholera epidemic of 1832. It crossed to England in 1840, and reached epidemic proportions in 1844 and again in the terrible year of 1848. In the 1850s almost two thirds of the deaths were of children under five. Diphtheria, also only recognised as a separate disease in 1855, was endemic throughout Europe and North America for the remainder of the decade. An epidemic of smallpox is estimated to have killed an average of 12,000 people annually during the years 1837-40, though after the Vaccination Act of 1840 was enforced, incidence in the United Kingdom dropped to the none the less alarming figure of 5000 per annum.[17]

Medical observers shared with sanitary and social reformers the firm, and often justified belief, that the slums of the cities provided a breeding ground for contagious disease. The Thames, which had always functioned as London's main artery of traffic as much as its chief sewer, had become, by the 1850s, an offensively rank carrier of infection. During a period of speculation about appropriate mural decoration for the newly completed Houses of Parliament, *Punch* published a cartoon showing 'Father Thames introducing his offspring (Diphtheria, Scrofula and Cholera) to the Fair City of London', suggesting that the design, with its bloated and skeletal horrors, might be suited for a fresco.[18] At the time of the 'Great Stink' in the summer of 1858 Disraeli, an otherwise acclimatised Londoner, was driven out of a Commons Committee Room facing onto the river by the 'pestilential odour'.[19] Domestic sanitation, with sewage drained directly into the Thames, was often primitive even at the most august addresses in the capital. The relatively newly reconstructed Buckingham Palace reeked with 'filth and pestilential odours from the absence of proper sewage', and one of the workmen employed to improve matters in 1848 reported that he had hardly ever been in 'such a set of stinks'.[20] If one 'amazing Alderman' declared, according to the 1867 Preface to *Oliver Twist,* that the diseased slums of Jacob's Island did not exist, indeed had never existed, Dickens's description of the riverside squalor in the novel is fully justified in other near contemporary accounts. It in fact might seem that the novelist was suppressing some details which might have offended more sensitive noses and stomachs, an understandable precaution given his personal experience and that of official investigators of similar conditions. When in 1842, for example, Dickens, accompanied by Forster and Maclise, took the visiting Longfellow on a night tour of 'the worst haunts of the most dangerous classes' in London, Maclise was 'struck with

Charles Dickens, English novelist, 1812-1870

such a sickness on entering the first of the Mint lodging-houses . . . that he had to remain, for the time [they] were in them, under guardianship of the police outside'.[21] In his avowedly propagandist *Alton Locke* of 1850 Charles Kingsley was less circumspect. Kingsley's hero is led, during one of the worst epidemics of fever in the transpontine slums, into 'the wildernesses of Bermondsey' to

> a miserable blind alley, where a dirty gas-lamp just served to make darkness visible, and show the patched windows and rickety doorways of the crazy houses, whose upper stories were lost in a brooding cloud of fog; and the pools of stagnant water at our feet; and the huge heap of cinders which filled up the waste end of the alley—a dreary, black, formless mound, on which two or three spectral dogs prowled up and down after the offal, appearing and vanishing like dark imps in and out of the black misty chaos beyond.

Kingsley quite clearly intends us to see this blind alley as a living hell (his echoes of Milton tell us as much), though if it is compared with any of the flatter descriptions in Chadwick's *Report,* or even with Engels's appalled and impassioned account of Manchester at the same period, it can be appreciated that the only exaggeration consists in Alton Locke's 'pointing' of the incident. Victorian readers would readily have understood his shorthand use of words and phrases like 'stagnant water', 'cinders' and 'offal'. Like a Dantesque visitor to Hell, Alton is led further into the horror:

> Downes pushed past . . . unlocked a door at the end of the passage, thrust me in, locked it again, and then rushed across the room in chase of two or three rats, who vanished into cracks and holes. And what a room! A low lean-to with wooden walls, without a single article of furniture; and through the broad chinks of the floor shone up as it were ugly glaring eyes, staring at us.—They were the reflections of the rushlight in the sewer below. The stench was frightful—the air heavy with pestilence. The first breath I drew made my heart sink, and my stomach turn. But I forgot everything in the object which lay before me, as Downes tore a half-finished coat off three corpses laid side by side on the bare floor.
>
> There was his little Irish wife:—dead—and naked—the wasted white limbs gleamed in the lurid light; the unclosed eyes stared, as if reproachfully, at the husband whose drunkenness had brought her there to kill her with the pestilence; and on each side of her a little, shrivelled, impish, child-corpse—the wretched man had laid their arms round the dead mother's neck—and there they slept, their hungering and wailing over at last forever: the rats had been busy already with them—but what matter to them now?[22]

Kingsley is determined to prove his point that there is a fearful connection between the sanitary condition of the slums and disease, and that the unburied bodies of the dead continue to spread the contagion amongst the living. Downes, Alton's drunken Virgil, has even imagined in his delirium tremens that he has seen the fever devils coming up through the cracks in the floor 'like little maggots and beetles . . . I asked 'em and they said they were fever devils'. His medical science is in fact only marginally less developed than that of a Victorian doctor, but Kingsley's point is that poverty breeds not only ignorance but also the very causes of infection. The shanty, built over a sewer, both creates and is obliged to partake of the tainted water below and the pestilential air above.

The fate of the destitute Irish family in *Alton Locke* may have shocked both Charles Kingsley, in the persona of a self-educated tailor, and his predominantly middle-class readers, but the degradation that he describes does not seem to have been atypical of the desperately poor in the worst years of the cholera and typhus epidemics in London. But the concern with the idea that the living poor spread the contagion to their better-off brothers and sisters in a great sanitary chain of being was equalled by a very present fear that the living might be infected by the unburied dead, and even by the barely interred coffins in an overcrowded burial-ground. Downes's family, like the cases pungently described in Edwin Chadwick's supplementary report on *The Practice of Interment in Towns,* remain to decompose slowly in his lodgings simply because he is too poor to bury them. Even if he had been able to afford the not inconsiderable cost of a funeral, or had been forced to resort to the Parish as a pauper, it is likely that their place of burial would have resembled the urban grave-yard which lies at the centre of Dickens's *Bleak House.* Again, Dickens does not appear to have been exaggerating.[23]

The prejudice against 'intra-mural interment' was a relatively new one in early Victorian England, and the alternative, the establishment of extra-mural cemeteries, even newer. Both, suspiciously enough to traditionalists, had spread from rational France in the closing years of the eighteenth century, and both reversed an ancient Christian pattern. Jews and Romans had buried their dead without the city wall; early Christians, gathering for worship around the tombs of the martyrs, had gradually rejected earlier taboos, and then built their churches over the hallowed sites. The faithful chose in their due turn to be buried as close as possible to the saints. As the faith spread, so did the idea of a church with an attached burial-ground, and with the graves of the more influential parishioners actually under the flagstones of the nave and aisles of the building itself. The nineteenth-century Londoner's problem lay not only in his by now *damnosa haeritas* of the remains of his forbears, but also in the far more damnable problem of how to dispose of the increasing annual toll of his dead fellow-citizens. By the 1820s and 1830s even the vaults under newly constructed churches were full, as were suburban burial-grounds situated some distance away from the parish church itself. For Dissenters, with their own burial-grounds, the physical, and indeed sanitary, problem was just as disturbing. Nevertheless, by the 1870s the writer of a guidebook to London could remark on the happy, though recent enough, abandonment of what he refers to as 'the barbarous practice of interring human bodies within the precinct of the Metropolis'. In recommending visitors to London to see the new suburban cemeteries (Kensal Green, Highgate, Nunhead, Norwood, Abney Park and Brompton), he drew a clear distinction between their handsomeness and the old grave-yards—'the plague-spots of the population'.[24] The taste for metropolitan improvement, and the Victorian belief that all improvements were worth visiting, is matched by the new faith in the dignity and beauty of the cemeteries themselves. The sloping lawns of Highgate and the classical avenues of Kensal Green must have contrasted vividly with memories of the old burial grounds and with Dickens's imaginative vision of the hemmed-in grave-yard which festers at the core of *Bleak House.*[25]

By 1852 Dickens's comment on the 'pestiferous' and 'obscene' church-yard to which Captain Hawdon's body is borne may well have seemed outmoded to many of his readers and merely a further expression of the manner in which the novel is set back in the immediate past. In 1839, some thirteen years before the novel's publication, George Alfred Walker had described the horrifying state of forty-three metropolitan burial-grounds in his notorious *Gatherings from Grave-Yards,* or, to give the book its full propagandist title, *Gatherings from Grave-Yards, Particularly those of London: With a concise History of the Modes in Interment Among different Nations, from the earliest Periods. And a Detail of dangerous and fatal Results produced by the unwise and revolting Custom of inhuming the Dead in the midst of the Living.* Within a distance of two hundred yards in Clement's Lane off the Strand, and therefore close enough to the Hall of Lincoln's Inn, there were four burying-grounds from which, Walker recorded, 'the living breathe on all sides an atmosphere impregnated with the odour of the dead'. Of one he avowed that the soil was 'saturated, absolutely saturated, with human putrescence', and in another close by a local resident described how a grave had been dug under his window for a deceased neighbour: 'A poor fellow who died in this house, in the room above me: *he* died of typhus fever . . . *they have kept him twelve days,* and now they are going to put him under my nose, by way of warning to me.'[26] In 1843 the indefatigable Edwin Chadwick conducted a special Parliamentary enquiry into the practice of interment in towns and published a detailed report, based on the evidence of a wide range of witnesses from all over Britain, describing the likely risks to public health from both the state of the grave-yards and from delays in burying the dead. Chadwick himself summed up the nature of London's problem: overcrowding had left the city's church-yards tiered with coffins like geological or archaeological strata, and his ready statistics pointed the horror:

> In the metropolis, on spaces of ground which do not exceed 203 acres, closely surrounded by the abodes of the living, layer upon layer, each consisting of a population numerically equivalent to a large army of 20,000 adults, and nearly 30,000 youths and children, is every year imperfectly interred. Within the period of the existence of the present generation, upwards of a million of dead must have been interred in these same spaces.

The attendant risk of infection seemed self-evident:

> A layer of bodies is stated to be about seven years in decaying in the metropolis: to the extent that this is so, the decay must be by the conversion of the remains into gas, and its escape as a miasma, of many times the bulk of the body that has disappeared.[27]

Like Walker, Chadwick was intent on not sparing tender feelings in his campaign in favour of hygienic and dignified interment in suburban cemeteries. The nastiness of the urban burial-grounds is systematically catalogued and reported, and words like 'miasma', 'effluvia', 'emanation', and the less classical, but no less emotive, 'stench', run through the report and are reiterated as unpleasant reminders of the ever-present causes of disease. In some poor districts the smell of the decomposing dead was intermingled with the pervasive stink of sewerage, though local residents seemed frighteningly immune to the fact:

> The sense of smell in the majority of inhabitants seems to be destroyed, and having no perception even of stenches which are unsupportable to strangers, they must be unable to note the excessive escapes of miasma as antecedents to disease. Occasionally, however, some medical witnesses, who have been accustomed to the smell of the dissecting room, detect the smell of human remains from the grave-yards in crowded districts: and other witnesses have stated that they can distinguish what is called the 'dead man's smell' when no-one else can, and can distinguish it from the miasma of the sewers.[28]

Elsewhere, Chadwick's witnesses gave evidence of the supposedly dire effect of actually living near a grave-yard. One Mr Barnett, the medical officer for the parish of Stepney, testified to certain distressing incidents in his area which have the macabre overlaid with a new sense of the risk to the health, rather than simply to the sensibilities, of the living:

> Some years since a vault was opened in the church-yard and shortly after one of the coffins contained therein burst with so loud a report that hundreds flocked to the place to ascertain the cause. So intense was the poisonous nature of the effluvia arising therefrom, that a great number were attacked with sudden sickness and fainting, many of whom were a considerable period before they recovered their health.

> The vaults and burial ground attached to Brunswick chapel, Limehouse, are crowded with dead, and from the accounts of individuals residing in the adjoining houses, it would appear that the stench arising therefrom, particularly when a grave happens to be opened during the summer months, is most noxious. In one case it is described to have produced instant nausea and vomiting, and attacks of illness are frequently imputed to it. Some say they have never had a day's good health since they resided so near the chapel-ground.[29]

The pressure for official action to close the urban burial-grounds went hand-in-hand with a determined advocacy of the beauty and propriety of the new cemeteries. City church-yards not only seemed likely causes of infection for the living, they also removed any dignity from the dead. In 1848, for example, a substantial couplet poem, ponderously entitled 'The Cemetery: A

Brief appeal to the feelings of Society on Behalf of Extra Mural Burial', first evoked the horrors of interment in the city:

> Hark! cracks the mattock on a coffin lid,
> And earth gives up her injured dead, unbid.
> Wrought loose as mole-hill 'neath th'oft
> ent'ring tools,
> Each opening grave, a banquet meet for
> Ghoules,
> Bids yawn in livid heaps the quarried flesh;
> The plague-swoln charnel spreads its taint afresh.
> In foul accumulation, tier on tier,
> Each due instalment of the pauper bier,
> Crush'd in dense-pack'd corruption there they
> dwell,
> 'Mongst earthy rags of shroud, and splinter'd
> shell.

The anonymous versifier then waxed pastoral, contrasting such 'noisome vapours' to the kind of rustic church-yard doubtless familiar to his readers from the works of the elegiac eighteenth-century poets. It is a typical enough piece of city/country opposition, but the point of it is to stress the advantages offered to the city-dweller by the cemeteries, true expressions of the ideal of *rus in urbe* and yet as stately as the park of a great country-house:

> Let plumy pine with cedar blend, and yew,
> To tuft the walk, and fringe the avenue:
> But oh! let love be first, and second art,
> Let Cemeteries win the people's heart;
> Though lowly lay secure the weary head,
> And in the tomb domesticate the dead.[30]

The cemetery is then democratic, and should prove both acceptable and lovable to paupers as much as to the more substantial owners of plots in existing necropolises in the suburbs. A similar mood inspirited a visitor to Kensal Green in 1842 who later delightedly described his impressions in *Ainsworth's Magazine:* 'What an escape', he wrote, 'from the choked charnel house to that verdant wide expanse, studded with white tombs of infinite shapes, and stone marked graves covered with flowers of every brilliant dye!'[31] The architectural and horticultural potential of cemeteries was emphasised in the following year by a true inheritor of the picturesque tradition, the builder and landscape gardener, John Claudius Loudon:

> A church or church-yard in the country, or a general cemetery in the neighbourhood of a town, properly designed, laid out, ornamented with tombs, planted with trees, shrubs, and herbaceous plants, all named, and the whole properly kept, might become a school of instruction in architecture, sculpture, landscape-gardening, arboriculture, botany, and in those important parts of general gardening, neatness, order and high-keeping.[32]

Loudon's high sentiments derive not simply from a taste for Arcadian landscapes, but also from that other later development in the picturesque, an attachment to the contours of English scenery, and particularly to the melancholy beauty of the country church-yard. The cemetery might, for some, express an ideal of the Elysian Fields, or even an Egyptian tomb-scape, but for sentimental or empassioned Gothicists it needed to embody an English mediaeval tradition.

Gray's elegiac meditation on graves and worms and epitaphs remains the best-known example of a widespread enough eighteenth-century fashion for church-yards and church-yard poetry. To the Victorians, however, the contrast between G. A. Walker's observations in Clement's Lane and Gray's at Stoke Poges must have seemed both striking and provocative. Nevertheless, the ideal of burial in the country was too firmly established ever to be quite superseded in the literary imagination by cemeteries, however Arcadian their design and lay-out. In 1814, Wordsworth, another direct heir of the picturesque tradition, appended to *The Excursion* an 'Essay upon Epitaphs' which stressed the extent to which the living and the dead blessedly intermingled in a rural setting:

> A village church-yard, lying as it does in the lap of nature, may indeed be most favourably contrasted with that of a town of crowded population; and sepulture therein combines many of the best tendencies which belong to the mode practised by the Ancients, with others peculiar to itself. The sensations of pious cheerfulness, which attend the celebration of the sabbath-day in rural places, are profitably chastised by the sight of the graves of kindred and friends, gathered together in that general home towards which the thoughtful yet happy spectators themselves are journeying. Hence a parish-church, in the stillness of the country, is a visible centre of a community of the living and the dead; a point to which are habitually referred the nearest concerns of both.[33]

Wordsworth's church-yard stands properly in the midst of a community, reminding the living of the dead and of the fact of their being part of a continuous process of growth and decay; the epitaphs are imbued with meaning as engraved sermons in stones. The mood of the Essay was reflected as much in the pictorial arts as in the literature of the post-Romantic period. Benjamin W. Leader's 'The Churchyard at Bettwys-y-Coed', for example, remains, despite its Welsh setting, solidly in a Wordsworthian tradition though it was not exhibited at the Royal Academy until 1863. Children play amid the stillness of a grave-yard, the tomb-stones moulding into the mountain landscape. In Joshua Mann's 'The Child's Grave', painted in the mid-1850s, a family is seen visiting a country church-yard, the apparently bereaved mother accompanied both by an older woman and by a surprisingly large brood of surviving children. Millais's 'The Vale of Rest', which bore the inscription 'where the weary find repose' at its exhibition in 1858, shows a nun digging a grave at sunset while a contemplative sister beside her looks out at us from the canvas. Arthur Hughes's 'Home from Sea', exhibited in its final form five years later, has a young sailor lying weeping on his mother's grave in the then rural church-yard at Chingford in Essex, while his sister kneels beside him dressed in deep mourning. Yet more complex in its iconography is Henry Arthur Bowler's truly Tennysonian 'The Doubt: Can these dry bones live?' of 1853. The picture shows a lady leaning on the tombstone of one John Faithful and contemplating some recently disturbed bones. The answer to the lady's rhetorical question is provided by the words 'I am the Resurrection and the Life' inscribed on the stone, and by the single word 'Resurgam' on a nearby slab. A butterfly, the traditional emblem of the soul, has lighted on a skull in the foreground, while on the slab a chestnut, fallen from the overhanging tree, has begun to germinate.[34]

When Dickens leads his Little Nell, herself a popular enough subject with painters, into her first country church-yard, she, the town-bred and town-haunted child, is overcome by an almost instinctive wonder. It is a wonder doubtless cultivated in her by her creator's own reading of the Romantic poets:

> She walked out into the churchyard, brushing the dew from the long grass with her feet, and often turning aside into places where it grew longer than in others, that she might not tread upon the graves. She felt a curious kind of pleasure in lingering among these houses of the dead. . . . (ch. 17)

In Chapter 53 of *The Old Curiosity Shop,* when the evidently mortal Nell has reached the pleasantly decaying village in which it is clear that she too is to end her days, she once again lingers in the church-yard. As if in response to a Wordsworthian summons,

> Some young children sported among the tombs, and hid from each other, with laughing faces. They had an infant with them, and had laid it down asleep upon a child's grave, in a little bed of leaves. It was a new grave—the resting place, perhaps, of some little creature, who, meek and patient in its illness, had often sat and watched them, and now seemed to their minds scarcely changed.
>
> She drew near and asked one of them whose grave it was. The child answered that that was not its name; it was a garden—his brother's. It was greener, he said, than all the other gardens, and the birds loved it better because he had been used to feed them. When he had done speaking, he looked at her with a smile, and kneeling down and resting for a moment with his cheek against the turf, bounded merrily away.

Nell has already the mark of death upon her, but through the children, Dickens allows her one further lesson in patience before obliging her to listen to the somewhat more chilling doctrines of the old sexton whom she encounters immediately afterwards. Dickens's language may not be particularly resourceful here, for he is evidently ill at ease with an elegiac country church-yard mood, but it must none the less be appreciated that it is precisely because he finds the death of his heroine so painful a subject to talk about that he chooses to set it in a conventionally soothing context. Wordsworth's dead or dying children find, like the mysterious Lucy, a place in the natural scheme of things, and Dickens, by removing Nell from the man-made city, attempts to come to terms with the inevitability of her mortality by re-exploring an established literary convention. Nell at least seems to have no fear of death as she speaks to the equally fearless and trusting children; surrounded by a nature which is itself dying only to be reborn in spring, she sees life and death as a continuum. It is a hope that her creator too desperately holds to at this early point in his career. When Dickens visited Mary Hogarth's tomb at Kensal Green in June 1837 he found that the 'grass around it was green and the flowers as bright, as if nothing of the earth in which they grew could ever wither or fade'; only the poignantly fresh memory of his dead sister-in-law disrupted the illusion of a serene immortality in the natural world. But by allowing that Mary and Nell become part of a larger creative process, some meaning emerges in the face of loss. The suburban cemetery, like the church-yards in *The Old Curiosity Shop,* seemed to suggest that in Nature a vivid memory of the past united with a promise of continual growth. When Dickens later desired that 'a rose-tree or a few little flowers' be planted on Mary's grave he was expressing the same hope, a hope which was otherwise denied in the decaying burial-grounds of London.[35] In 1854, three years after the death of his infant daughter, the fatally named Dora, the novelist removed the child's body from a vault at Highgate and had it interred in 'a very small freehold' in the cemetery, 'to lie under the sun', later asking Angela Burdett Coutts to have a tree from her nearby estate planted beside the plot.[36]

Dickens's attachment to the tombs of Mary and Dora, and his concern to have them beautified in the most natural way possible, was not untypical of his times. The Victorian cemetery, like the lingering nostalgia for the countryside, expressed an idyllic and pastoral alternative to the spiritual emptiness of the city. Nature hallowed and comprehended Death. To many Victorian city-dwellers, mortality was no less a familiar phenomenon than it had been to their recent forbears, but a new insistence on commemorating the dead, and the inevitable pressure of population, demanded a dignified alternative to the evident unpleasantness of intra-mural interment. The Victorians were heirs not only to the invigorated pastoral tradition of the Romantics, but also to the new sensibility about death which had gradually established itself during the eighteenth century. As the nature of family relationships had developed, partly as a response to evolving economic conditions, so had a need to memorialise the beloved after death. The living justified their continuing love by celebrating it, both through the performance of an elaborate ritual of mourning and through the construction of a dignified funerary monument.[37] The Victorian celebration of death in art overlaps with, and draws from, an existing literary mode. Emotional shows, death-bed scenes, crêpe bands and black ostrich plumes were not, as has frequently been suggested, an outward and visible sign of a decline of faith, or of an increase in secularism, but of an increased attention to ordinary family relationships. If Dickens, for one, loathed the extravagance of bourgeois *pompes funèbres* and the whole panoply of the undertaker's shop, he did so largely because he found them *un*-natural and a false expression of a real enough grief. They intruded themselves between the mourner and the mourned, and, rather than helping to purge the sense of loss, they dramatised its horror and served as an affront to both commemoration and understanding. If, however, we can now begin to appreciate that some of the more pompous forms of Victorian mourning merely represented a democratisation of ceremonies once confined to the ritual funerals of kings and noblemen, we ought also to see that what has often been labelled 'the Victorian death-bed' is in fact an extension of a norm of aristocratic tragedy into the bourgeois novel. In its transference from the epic and from the stage into the novel the tragedy was redirected, defused, occasionally even transformed. Though comparatively few Victorian novels are directed exclusively towards a climactic death-bed, or even death-scene, the nature of dying has a crucial structural and emotional function in a wide range of important contemporary fiction.[38] Dickens's use of death, death-beds, and mourning in his novels reflects, therefore, not simply an established literary norm but also the social changes which contributed to the rise, and eventually to the triumph, of the novel as an art form.

The bonds of affection and love which bind husbands and wives, parents and children, brothers and sisters, friends and friends, lovers and lovers, are, it has been argued, conditioned as much by a social and cultural environment as by the dictates of the heart. To some important degree, the heart is cultivated by the world in which it seeks direction. The relationship between parent and child based on love rather than honour or duty marks a shift in socially acceptable norms between the seventeenth and eighteenth centuries. As Laurence Stone has recently suggested of the mid-seventeenth century, 'The key to all understanding of interpersonal relationships among the propertied classes . . . is a recognition of the fact that what mattered was not the individual but the family; younger sons, and particularly daughters, were often unwanted and might be regarded as no more than a tiresome drain on the economic resources of the family.'[39] Later in his lengthy study Stone notes the significant change in attitudes and emotions that had set in by the middle of the following century:

> The death of an infant or young child was no longer shrugged off as a common event on which it would be foolish to waste much emotion. A good example of the new response by a conventional eighteenth-century Christian is that of James Boswell to the death of his five-month-old son David in 1777 . . . Boswell carried the corpse upstairs and laid it on a table in the drawing-room. The next day, 'I was tenderer today then I imagined, for I cried over my little son, and shed many tears. At the same time I had a really pious delight in praying with the room locked, and leaning my hands on his alabaster frame as I knelt.' . . . The death of an adolescent child had inevitably always been far more traumatic for the parents, but even here there are changes. There was an intensification of grief in the eighteenth century, and it was expressed not only more openly and more bitterly, but also less ritually, in a more personal, more introspective manner. Members of the nuclear family now dramatized their sense of loss in violently expressive, and no doubt highly therapeutic ways. . . . At the height of the romantic period, the sufferings of parents at the death of a child reached an extreme intensity.[40]

Stone supports his contention by quoting examples of bereavement in both aristocratic and bourgeois households, and he thereby helps to establish a social basis from which we can draw literary conclusions for both the eighteenth and the nineteenth centuries. A similar argument, based largely on French evidence, runs through Philippe Ariès's study, *Western Attitudes toward Death from the Middle Ages to the Present Day.* Ariès notes a shift in the treatment of death in literature from the conventionally extended death-scenes in the *chansons de geste* and the ritual death-beds of the mediaeval Christian citizen on the one hand, and the eighteenth- and nineteenth-century dramatisation of dying on the other:

> Beginning with the eighteenth century, man in western societies tended to give death a new meaning. He exalted it, dramatized it, and thought of it as disquieting and greedy. But he already was less concerned with his own death than with *la mort de toi,* the death of the other person, whose loss and memory inspired in the nineteenth and twentieth centuries the new cult of tombs and cemeteries and the romantic, rhetorical treatment of death.[41]

Ariès traces a move away from the ritual death-bed of the Middle Ages, one based on an accepted *ars moriendi,* in which the dying man himself organised the scene, presided over it 'and knew its protocol', towards an almost dissociated interest in the deaths of others, an interest which partially served to deflect the knowledge of one's own mortality away from oneself. *La mort de toi* usefully veils *la mort de soi.* It is precisely the shock which hits Tolstoy's dying Ivan Ilyich:

> In the depths of his heart he knew he was dying but, so far from growing used to the idea, he simply did not and could not grasp it.
>
> The example of a syllogism which he had learned in Kiezewetter's *Logic:* 'Caius is a man, men are mortal, therefore Caius is mortal,' had seemed to him all his life to be true as applied to Caius but certainly not as regards himself. . . .
>
> And Caius was certainly mortal, and it was right for him to die; but for me, little Vanya, Ivan Ilyich, with all my thoughts and emotions—it's a different matter altogether. It cannot be that I ought to die. That would be too terrible.[42]

Tolstoy's story is scarcely paralleled in the literature of western Europe in the nineteenth century, and certainly not in England, for it examines the process of dying from the point of view of the dying man rather from that of the bystanders at the death-bed. Though it serves to justify Ariès's point, it ultimately also qualifies it. Nevertheless, much of what Ariès argues can usefuly be applied to the literature of Victorian England and especially to Dickens. Dickens was well aware that his treatment of death in his novels could prove therapeutic for novelist and reader alike; if the loss of Mary Hogarth lies behind the exposition of the sad fate of Little Nell in *The Old Curiosity Shop,* the novel was also intended to 'do something which might be read by people about whom Death had been,—with a softened feeling, and with consolation'.[43] When Dickens later extracted and adapted the scenes surrounding the death of little Paul Dombey for a public reading, he was much moved to find that 'mothers, and fathers, and sisters, and brothers in mourning' came up to him afterwards and thanked him for his seemingly intimate understanding of their loss.[44]

A novelist like Dickens could, however, draw on and adapt a pattern of the death-bed which was well enough established in literature and art. Although eighteenth-century models might seem the most obvious sources, two highly significant seventeenth-century models can be seen to have contributed to the tradition. Shakespeare's account of the dream of his pious Queen Katherine, a dream preparatory to a peaceful death, is elaborately choreographed and functions as the culmination of a line of meditations upon death in *Henry VIII.* After hearing quietly of the penitent death of Wolsey, and after duly forgiving her erstwhile enemy, Katherine falls asleep to the 'celestial harmony' of a 'sad and solemn music'. As she slumbers there enter to her

> solemnly tripping one after another, six Personages, clad in white robes, wearing on their heads garlands of bays, and golden vizards on their faces, branches of bays or palm in their hands. They first congee unto her, then dance: and, at certain changes, the first two hold a spare garland over her head, at which, the other four make reverend curtsies. Then the two that held the garland deliver the same to the other next two, who observe the same order in their changes, and holding the garland over her head. Which done, they deliver the same garland to the last two, who likewise observe the same order. At which (as it were by inspiration,) she makes (in her sleep) signs of rejoicing, and holdeth up her hands to heaven. And so in their dancing vanish, carrying the garland with them. The music continues. (IV. ii)

The scene might be paralleled in a Victorian lantern slide. The play itself steadily maintained its popularity on the nineteenth-century stage partly as a result of its demands for spectacle and suggestions of the supernatural. A production at Drury Lane in 1811, directed by and starring John Philip Kemble, was only outclassed in its effects by that of Samuel Phelps in 1848. But the most celebrated nineteenth-century production of *Henry VIII* was Charles Kean's of 1855 which ran for one hundred nights at the Princess's Theatre.[45] Kean had been determined to express his idea of 'the domestic habits of the English court' in spectacular terms, and Ellen Terry, who at ten played the topmost angel on a ladder in the vision scene, admitted in her autobiography that the play contained effects which she had never seen surpassed.[46] Queen Katherine's vision proved equally popular as a subject for Romantic artists, most significantly so for those who, like Fuseli and Blake, had mystical or religious leanings.[47]

Queen Katherine may, given the conventions of the Shakespearian theatre, have to be borne away to die off-stage, but the point about the nature of her going hence and her salvation is clearly made. She is absolute for death, and she has, like many of her Victorian descendants, already glimpsed the joys of heaven. If Katherine does not ritually organise her death-bed, she at least is seen to embrace two of its crucial stages—she forgives her enemies, and she is instructed in a due humility before God and man by the saintly Griffith. One further, and more certain, seventeenth-century influence on the nineteenth-century death-bed ought also to be cited here, that of the safely Protestant Jeremy Taylor's handbook *Holy Dying.* Taylor provided the literate common man with a manual of preparation for a good death in order to enable him to anticipate a bliss akin to the dying queen's. Shakespeare had proved theologically circumspect about Katherine's last hours, and Taylor too assumes that priestly assistance and the viaticum are inessential to the human passage between earth and heaven. *Holy Dying,* first published in 1651, maintained its steady popularity for the next two hundred years, having reached its twenty-eighth edition by 1810, and being reprinted at least twenty times again before the end of the century. The enterprising and scholarly printer, William Pickering, alone saw five separate finely produced editions through the press between 1840 and 1853.[48] Taylor had written in his dedicatory epistle to Richard, Earl of Carbery, of the vital relationship between holy dying and a preparatory holy living:

> My Lord, it is a great art to die well, and to be learnt by men in health, by them that can discourse and consider, by those whose understanding and acts of reason are not abated with fear or pains: and as the greatest part of Death is passed by the preceding years of our life, so also in those years are the greatest preparations to it; and he that prepares not for Death before his last sickness, is like him that begins to study Philosophy when he is going to dispute publicly in the Faculty. All that a sick and dying man can do is but to exercise those virtues which he before acquired, and to perfect that repentance which was begun more early.[49]

Holy Dying was to serve as a constant reminder of *la mort de soi,* and its accessibility to the devout Victorian should be remembered, for, despite other shifts in literary taste, established spiritual classics retained their power and influence. It should scarcely surprise us, for instance, that a copy of Taylor's work is listed amongst Adam Bede's books, and that he proves to be amongst Dorothea Brooke's favourite authors.

With the growth of evangelical discipline in the last years of the eighteenth century, new, and to some extent severer, manuals of death-bed devotion, doubtless intended as up-dated complements to Taylor's, appeared. Henry Venn's *The Complete Duty of Man* of 1812, for example, recommended more rigorous repentance in order to secure the promise of salvation, while a laxer, but none the less emotional and moral, High Church tradition was asserted in John Warton's two-volume didactic work *Death-bed Scenes,* published in 1827.[50] In his *Miscellanies on Various Subjects* of 1823, the Reverend William Hett of Lincoln reprinted meditations on the four last things which he had first written for his parishioners some seventeen years earlier. In the manner of a Baroque Emblem Book Hett outlined the subject of an engraving to be prefaced to his thoughts on the death-bed:

> The good man's sick chamber.—He is sitting in the middle of the bed, his back supported.—His wife hanging over the bed side, his left hand grasped in her two hands, her eyes fixed upon his face in a silent agony of distress.—The children near the mother all in tears: the two little ones clinging to her, and attentive to her only: the larger ones dividing their grief between each parent.—The servants, male and female, standing in a group, at a small distance from the bottom of the bed, in mute and serious attention to the last good words of their dying master, which he is in the act of uttering. In the features of his countenance, the inward sentiments of hope and joy rising, as far as is possible, superior to the appearance of languor and debility.—His medical friend, at a small distance from the wife, in an attentive posture, his face full of thought, indicating this sentiment, 'How nobly a Christian can die!'—In the window an hourglass nearly run out.—Upon a small round table, near the bed, on the right hand of the sick man, a Bible open at this passage of Job, which is legible, 'I know that my Redeemer liveth.' A prayer-book open at the Burial Service, with these words legible, 'I am the resurrection and the life.'[51]

If the *ars moriendi* is not strictly being practised as an art, at least this tableau suggests that there is an ideal to be aimed at, if not exactly lived up to. When, in 1779, John and Charles Wesley first published their collection of hymns 'for the use of the people called Methodists', they included some fourteen in the section 'describing Death'; nearly all eagerly look forward to the release of the spirit from its carnal prison, and express an earnest joy at the passage of the Christian soul out of the Vale of Tears and into the celestial kingdom. There is little room for mourning. One, which seems particularly alien to twentieth-century taste, delightedly contemplates a corpse, with a relish worthy of Mrs. Gamp:

> Ah, lovely appearance of death!
> What sight upon earth is so fair?
> Not all the gay pageants that breathe
> Can with a dead body compare:
> With a solemn delight I survey
> The corpse when the spirit is fled
> In love with the beautiful clay,
> And longing to lie in its stead.[52]

The hymn, which pursues the thought through a further five verses, was reprinted in the many subsequent editions of the Wesleys' poetry in the nineteenth century, and it serves to remind us that in one area, at least, a firmly mediaeval *contemplus mundi* could still effectively operate. If Venn's *The Complete Duty of Man,* Warton's *Death-bed Scenes,* and Hett's *Miscellanies* attempted to bring the sinner to repentance by meditating on the inevitable end of life, the Wesleys know that they are preaching to the converted. Nevertheless, by the end of the eighteenth century the moralistic contemplation of mortality no longer remained a clerical preserve. It was already firmly established in popular imaginative literature.

Edward Young's long-popular and esteemed *Night Thoughts on Life, Death and Immortality* was first published between 1742 and 1745; between 1800 and 1870 alone there were some eight collected editions of Young's works, and twenty-three of *Night Thoughts* as a separate poem. Despite Dr Johnson's *caveat* that Young's poetry abounds in thought 'without much accuracy or selection', its ten thousand thoughtful lines seem to have held the attention of generations of devout and discriminating readers.[53] In the second book, 'On Time, Death and Friendship', the poet describes a holy death-bed for the benefit of the worldly and impious Lorenzo:

> The chamber where the good man meets his fate
> Is privileged beyond the common walk
> Of virtuous life, quite in the verge of heav'n.
> Fly, ye profane! if not, draw near with awe,
> Receive the blessing, and adore the chance
> That threw in this Bethesda your disease:
> If unrestored by this, despair your cure;
> For here resistless demonstration dwells:
> A death-bed's a detector of the heart.
> Here tired dissimulation drops her mask
> Through life's grimace, that mistress of the scene!
> Here real and apparent are the same.
> You see the man, you see his hold on heav'n,
> If sound his virtue; as Philander's sound.
> Heav'n waits not the last moment; owns her friends
> On this side death, and points them out to men;
> A lecture silent, but of sov'reign pow'r!
> To vice confusion, and to virtue peace.[54]

The sovereign power of the death-bed to convert the unbeliever and the sinner had perhaps been suggested to Young by the action of the dying Addison who in 1719 had summoned Lord Warwick ('a young man of very irregular life, and perhaps of loose opinions') to see 'how a Christian can die'.[55] Although the effect of 'this awful scene' on the young earl is not known, Addison's action seems to have impressed his contemporaries as a pattern for the modern Christian's departure; his words were certainly in the Revd. William Hett's mind some hundred years later when he outlined the image of the ideal death-bed to his parishioners, and it is possible that the pious hope of contemporaries that David Hume would repent of his professed atheism when faced by death drew from a similar source.[56]

Of comparable influence was Samuel Richardson's *Clarissa,* the culminating volume of which appeared in 1748. *Clarissa* was, as Richardson reminded readers of the second edition, not to be considered 'a *light Novel,* or *transitory Romance*' but as an inculcator of 'the HIGHEST and *most* IMPORTANT *Doctrines*'; the highest and most important of these doctrines emerges as the heroine's ability to die as a Christian and thereby to move those who observe her to a true repentance. Although some impatient readers may be struck by the unconscionable time that Clarissa takes to die, Richardson endeavours to enliven the extended death-bed with exemplary instruction and incident. In Letter XXXII of the final volume, for example, Mr Belford writes to Lovelace describing the dying heroine's almost baroque preparations for her own burial; having, as a prelude, already dreamed of 'flying hour-glasses, death's heads, spades, mattocks, and Eternity', Belford describes Clarissa's personally designed coffin-plate, engraved with texts and ornaments, including a winged hour-glass, an urn, and a white lily 'snapt short off and just falling from the stalk'; her coffin, which she refers to as 'her palace', is ready by her bedside, her shroud draped over it. When in Letter LX Belford describes her last moments to Lovelace, he writes disjointedly with 'a weight of grief' upon his mind. It is a moving scene, even wrenched out of its context:

> Her sweet voice and broken periods methinks still fill my ears, and never will be out of my memory.
>
> After a short silence, in a more broken and faint accent;
>
> —And you, Mr Belford, pressing my hand, may God preserve you and make sensible of all your errors—You see, in me, how All ends—May *you* be
>
> —And down sunk her head upon her pillow, she fainting away, and drawing from us her hands.
>
> We thought she was gone; and each gave way to a violent burst of grief.
>
> But soon shewing signs of returning life, our attention was again engaged; and I besought her, when a little recovered, to complete in my favour her half-pronounced blessing. She waved her hand to us both, and bowed her head six several times, as we have since recollected, as if distinguishing every person present; not forgetting the nurse and the maid-servant; the latter having approached the bed, weeping, as if crowding in for the divine lady's last blessing; and she spoke faltering and inwardly,—Bless—bless—bless—you All—And now—And now—(holding up her almost lifeless hands for the last time) Come—O come—Blessed Lord—JESUS!
>
> And with these words, the last but half-pronounced, expired: Such a smile, such a charming serenity over-spreading her sweet face at the instant as seemed to manifest her eternal happiness already begun.
>
> O Lovelace!—But I can write no more![57]

Belford breaks down with emotion, and the hiatus in his manuscript is marked with printers' flowers. The hiatus doubtless also left time for more emotional readers to recover their composure before the narrative resumes. If Clarissa's preparations for death remind us of the seventeenth century, the manner of her death looks forward to the nineteenth. Like the Wesley hymn, she joyously contemplates her release from the body, but her creator bids us mourn with Belford, penitent certainly, but also involved imaginatively with the characters and their emotions. Richardson had also spoken in his 'Advertisement' of accommodating his moral message 'to the Taste of the Age', an age which was able to associate deep emotion as much as religious inspiration with a fictional death-bed.

The religiously charged death-bed, used as a moral exemplar, was therefore scarcely the invention of the Victorians. Even its exploitation in evangelical tracts, teetotal lantern-slides, popular ballads, and mawkishly sentimental poetry shows something of a continuity with the previous century. The image, once established, could serve the earnest moralist, just as it served Young and Richardson, as a 'detector of the heart' and an instructor in 'the highest and most important doctrines'. One just pre-Victorian example, intended for young children, might suffice to demonstrate a norm familiar enough to Dickens's contemporaries. Even if most English families of the first half of the nineteenth century must have been personally familiar with the painful frequency of child mortality, it must be admitted that *The Child's Companion or Sunday Scholar's Reward* somewhat exaggerates the phenomenon for the purposes of its moral argument. In the twelve monthly issues of the magazine intended for distribution amongst scholars at the newly established Sunday Schools in 1828 the death-beds of no fewer than four children are graphically described, and the threat of an early death is frequently posed as a warning to young readers. Susan Neate of Cheltenham dies in the June number at the age of six; Martha Kinsey of Manchester follows in July at the age of nine; the inaptly named George William Strong of Woodbridge dies in October, aged seven, followed in November by Francis Bartley of Rotherhithe, aged five. All were devout Sunday Scholars, deeply grateful to their instructors for their education, and sure and certain of their resurrection. In September, readers were advised by 'A Father' of the benefits to the soul of a sick-bed which afforded leisure 'for self-examination'. In November we are told of a boy called James, 'a thoughtful boy', who writes the word ETERNITY in a book while he is ill; James recovers, but the same issue contains the account of the premature death of Richmond Wilberforce who disappoints his grieving father by reaching eternity before his hoped-for ordination to the ministry. This is followed by further counsels from 'A Father', who begins a short sermon on Death with the advice 'sooner or later you must die, for "the wages of sin is death" ' December opens with the warning that some small readers may be in eternity before another year closes, and the number ends with an article, accompanied by a delightfully funereal woodcut, entitled 'That's a little baby's grave'.[58]

Lest we be persuaded to suppose that these childhood death-beds have been fictionalised, or at least piously tampered with, for the purposes of evangelical propaganda, it is worth comparing them with what purports to be the actual account of the death of the eighteen-year-old daughter of a High Church clergyman forty years later in the century. Agnes Skinner had proved to be as precocious a child as the smuggest of the Sunday Scholars or the most responsive of Mr Brocklehurst's protegées. She could sing the psalter in church without difficulty by the age of four, and before the service began she would thrust a Bible into her mother's hand, and whisper, 'Find me about the virgins, mamma.' At the age of eleven she prophetically drew a little tombstone on her slate, and 'as it were, in a fit of abstraction', put her name on it and added the date 1868. When the year 1868 duly came round, it was painfully obvious to her family that Agnes was dying of consumption. While she lay on her death-bed, the parish choir sang her favourite hymns in the hallway downstairs, she sent her savings from her pocket-money to help the poor, bade her cousin to try to take her place in her mother's affections, and meditated on what language was spoken in Paradise. Agnes died, like Clarissa, with the name of Jesus on her lips.[59]

It is nevertheless difficult to determine the extent to which the Victorian fascination with mortality, and the conduct of the death-bed, are instances of art imitating life or of virtuous life following patterns established and enshrined in its art. The assumption that Dickens in particular was to blame for the debasing of the sober art of fiction by over-indulging in death-bed sentimentality seems to have established itself early on. Despite the fact that in the 1840s Dickens's descriptions of the ends of Little Nell and Paul Dombey had reduced the otherwise harshly critical Francis Jeffrey to tears, the more hard-headed James Fitzjames Stephen, writing in the *Saturday Review* in 1858, found it proper to complain publicly of the nature and number of his fictional fatalities. Perversely enough, though, as the twentieth century has proved, prophetically, currency is first made of the contrast between English novels and French ones:

> The outrageous rants, surgical operations and *post mortem* examinations which afford such lively pleasure to Parisian readers, would be out of place here; but if anyone can get a pretty little girl to go to heaven prattling about her dolls, and her little brothers and sisters, and quoting texts of Scripture with appropriate gasps, dashes and broken sentences, he may send half the women in London, with tears in their eyes, to Mr Mudie's or Mr Booth's.

The reference to a Parisian taste for *post mortems* is doubtless derived from the continuing *succès de scandale* of *Madame Bovary,* but the reviewer has conveniently forgotten (again like his modern successors) both the romantic upsurge which produced *Paul et Virginie,* and more recent tear-jerkers, those potentially operatic classics, *La dame aux camélias* by Dumas fils and Henri Murger's *Scènes de la vie de Bohème.* Nevertheless, he goes on to roundly accuse Dickens with having both created and exploited the distressingly vulgar state of death-bed affairs in England:

> He is the intellectual parent of a whole class of fictions. . . . No man can offer to the public so large a stock of death-beds adapted for either sex and for any age from five-and-twenty downwards. There are idiot death-beds, where the patient cries ha! ha! and points wildly at vacancy—pauper death-beds, with unfeeling nurses to match—male and female children's death-beds, where the young ladies and gentlemen sit up in bed, pray to the angels and see golden water on the walls. In short, there never was a man to whom the King of Terrors was so useful a lay figure.[60]

It is amusing and vigorous criticism, but it is inevitably grossly unfair. Like the easy jests of critics since, it demonstrates a disturbing failure both to sympathise with the nature and intent of Dickens's art, and to grasp the tradition in which he is working. Dickens draws from and adapts a popular literary norm, and he does so in high seriousness. The springs of his moral art determine not only his treatment of life, but also his interest in death.

We need to draw a clear distinction between what many Victorians accepted as healthy enough 'sentiment', and what the post-Victorians suspect as an indulgence in 'sentimentality'. As has frequently been suggested, not all of the first readers of *The Old Curiosity Shop* were as lachrymatory in their enjoyment of the novel as Francis Jeffrey, but the greater number seem to have been genuinely and comparably moved. If the 'Nelly part' of the story struck Thackeray, for one, as 'lugubrious', it seems to have remained more consistently acceptable to the rest of his contemporaries than, for example, the 'weak and artificial' *Little Dorrit.*[61] Dickens may play on his readers' emotions, especially in his earlier novels, but his impulse to do so derives from a real enough emotional reaction within himself. It may well be that a subject is either too painful to him, as the account of Nell's demise certainly was, or that it strains his imaginative and verbal resources, but that should not suggest to us that he was insincere or lacking in full emotional and intellectual commitment. We often fail to appreciate the effect of Dickens's transitions, or occasionally lurches, between comedy and potential or realised tragedy. As the *Saturday Review* critic willingly granted, the novelist varies both the nature and the occupants of his death-beds, but if we look more closely at his developing art, it should also become evident that he moderates and shapes them to serve precise fictional, thematic, and indeed emotional, purposes. Death, which loomed so largely and oppressively as 'the King of Terrors' to his age, must also be allowed to be as much of a vital, as opposed to gratuitous, presence in his novels as it is in the work of his great contemporaries. If we except *The Old Curiosity Shop,* none of his novels moves as inexorably towards a culminating death-bed as had *Clarissa,* though all contain and imaginatively exploit mortality as an essential part of human experience, physical as much as spiritual. Dickens, like Mrs Gaskell, or the Brontë sisters, or even George Eliot, gives death both a fictional context within a realist scheme, and something of a moral force; in Dickens's case, however, it also has a crucial role in an evolving design.

As many contemporary biographies demonstrate, the concluding acts of a subject's life held a fascination for the Victorians which has been replaced in our own century by uneasiness and embarrasment. Details of the mortal sickness, death-bed confessions or professions, last words, and complex funerary arrangements, once considered an essential element in the exposition of character, are now likely to be suppressed or at least tainted with the pejorative overtones of the word 'Victorian'.[62] In the nineteenth century, however, the death-bed retained its ancient moral importance as the final tester of the soul, but as the F. D. Maurice affair of 1853 revealed, questions of the soul's ultimate destiny remained of prime public interest. To steadily Protestant England, the four last things—Death, Judgment, Heaven and Hell—were the only last things, and decisions concerning Heaven and Hell were fixed and eternal. The mortal soul, consigned to one or the other, was judged everlastingly without the doubtful benefit of a purgatorial middle way. If Jacobean playwrights, a steady stream of tract-writers and composers of sacred and profane lives, and a positive lava-flow of Hell-fire preachers had asserted the damnation not only of notorious sinners but also of the large body of men unfortunate enough not to be numbered amongst the elect, Victorian novelists generally speculated circumspectly or not at all. Having given life to characters and led them through temptation, few were prepared to continue judging them after death. F. D. Maurice attempted to voice publicly a churchman's honest doubts as to the doctrine of eternal damnation, but the arguments behind his case were not only current in liberal-Christian circles, they were often already accepted. Unitarians, at least, had long argued that a loving God could not properly abandon his creation so easily to the everlasting bonfire.[63] It was scarcely surprising that Maurice's *Theological Essays* should have been dedicated to his old friend Tennyson, for if a doubt about any life after death runs through *In Memoriam,* the idea of Hell certainly does not. Nevertheless, if the agnostic George Eliot found Maurice's argument 'muddy rather than profound', his fellow-churchmen were greatly disturbed by his supposedly reasoned challenge to orthodoxy.[64] The literature of the period suggests, however, that if an easy division of characters into sheep and goats was possible in this world, it was proper to relieve the pain of loss by assuming that in the next the sheep alone lived on. If Mrs Gaskell was already firmly established in the Unitarian theological tradition, it is perhaps significant to the nature of his death-beds that Dickens chose to worship as a Unitarian in the 1840s. Certainly, he allots extended death scenes only to his virtuous characters, and visions of eternal bliss only to his most innocent.

Although Nell's actual death takes place off-stage (Dickens's own grief seems to have insisted that it did), we are given sufficient assurances as to its divine nature. Nell bequeaths her love to the living, and her soul to the angels. Her creator, actively distressed by the death of one 'so young, so beautiful, so good', wrenches comfort from the idea of life going on in this world:

> Oh! it is hard to take to heart the lesson that such deaths will teach, but let no man reject it, for it is one that all must learn, and it is a mighty, universal Truth. When Death strikes down the innocent and young, for every fragile form from which he lets the panting spirit free, a hundred virtues rise, in shapes of mercy, charity, and love, to walk the world, and bless it. Of every tear that sorrowing shed on such green graves, some good is born, some gentler nature comes. In the Destroyer's steps there spring up bright creations that defy his power, and his dark path becomes a way of light to heaven. (*OCS,* ch. 72)

As Alexander Welsh has noted, memory seems to supply immortality and 'good deeds that spring from the wounds of the dead are deeds inspired in the living'.[65] This idea remains constant in Dickens's work, both as a form of comfort to the living and as a reassurance in the face of an actively encroaching death, but Welsh is surely too narrow in his fundamental assertion that 'Dickens does not believe in supernatural powers'.[66] His references to an afterlife may well suggest that they are merely 'intimations' of immortality, but the fact that 'none of [his] imputations of another existence is very definite' does not necessarily undermine their acceptability as statements of faith, or as testimony to an as yet veiled reality. In *The Old Curiosity Shop* the blessed memory of its dead heroine creates an active goodness in *this* world, while her continued existence as an angel in another is much more vaguely implied, but this superstitious, even gratuitous faith is one that seems to have answered a purely local need. As Dickens's art develops, so does his understanding. It is true that there is a steady belief in the fact that the kingdom of Heaven is made up of children, but it is scarcely an unorthodox or heretical faith. If heaven is made up of Nells, Paul Dombeys, Jos, and little Johnnys, it is better so than if it were a refuge for the likes of Harold Skimpole, who merely thinks of himself as a child. In his later novels the idea of memory as a guardian angel is not only developed, it is gradually allowed to become subsidiary to a grander assertion of resurrection, one which is not confined to children but which is open to all who accept the idea of rebirth in the spirit. Florence Dombey may be inspired by the memory of a dead mother and a dead brother, but that does not mean that the novel implies that that existence is stronger than one beyond the watery, rippling sunlight on the wall. If we cannot accept the promise held out to both Jo and to Richard Carstone in *Bleak House,* we will inevitably fail to understand what Dickens is saying in *A Tale of Two Cities, Great Expectations* and *Our Mutual Friend.* Dickens's 'implied' heaven is surely potent enough as Jo and Magwitch drift out to scriptural quotations, as Sydney Carton mounts the scaffold, or as Betty Higden is 'lifted up to Heaven' beside the rushing waters of the Thames.

This promise of salvation is held out even to some of the villains. Carker, run down by an avenging train, is given a glimmer of eternal hope, though it is no more than a glimmer amidst the encircling gloom, and it is posed as a rhetorical question—'who shall say that some weak sense of virtue upon Earth and its reward in Heaven, did not manifest itself, even to him'. Otherwise Carker's frantic wanderings, and his sudden, accidental destruction are almost a reprise of the demise of that most haunted, but unredeemed, of Dickens's villains, Bill Sikes. Sikes denies himself repentance, it seems; he is driven out like Cain, and drawn desperately to fire; his end, strangulation in a noose intended as his means of escape, leaves him no time to seek for redemption. His wanderings seem to have presented him only with a Dantesque reiteration of his crime, an agony or torment from which he cannot be released. Ralph Nickleby too dies suddenly, and alone, rejecting hope and decency 'with a wild look . . . in which frenzy, hatred, and despair, were horribly mingled' as a storm-cloud lowers above him. Quilp drowns with 'a yell, which seemed to make the hundred fires that danced before his eyes tremble'. Jonas Chuzzlewit poisons himself, while Steerforth (if he is to be classed amongst such villains) drowns at sea in yet another storm. Rigaud is killed in the collapse of the creaking Clennam house; Mme Defarge is accidentally shot as she struggles with Miss Pross; Compeyson dies as he wrestles in the water with Magwitch, and Rogue Riderhood and Bradley Headstone drag each other down, locked in an unyielding and deathly grip. Only Fagin, whose execution we do not witness, is allowed time to contemplate his impending end, and he, so long associated with the Devil, thrusts aside the kneeling, praying Oliver as he rejects the last chance of repentance; left alone in his cell as his visitors leave Newgate, 'he struggled with the power of desperation for an instant; and then sent up cry upon cry that penetrated even those massive walls, and rang in their ears'. Fagin, like Sikes, has made his own Hell.

The essence of Dickens's attitude to the death-bed can be seen in the letter he wrote in November 1840 in response to a request for an opinion of the work of an aspiring young poet, R. S. Horrell. Dickens's criticism of the submitted poems mixes muted praise with outright dissatisfaction, and he complains at length of one poem purporting to describe the despairing last hours of a painter haunted by the face of an imagined beloved. Horrell, he believed, had perverted the proper object and intention of a death-bed:

> To make that face his comfort and trust—to fill him with the assurance of meeting it one day in Heaven—to make him dying, attended, as it were, by an angel of his own creation—to inspire him with gentle visions of the reality sitting by his bedside and shedding a light even on the dark path of Death—and so to let him gently pass away, whispering of it and seeking the hand to clasp in his—would be to complete a very affecting and moving picture. But to have him struggling with Death in all its horrors, yelling about foul fiends and bats' wings, with starting eyes and rattles in his throat, is a ghastly, sickening, hideous end, with no beauty, no moral, nothing in it but a repulsive and most painful idea. If he had been the hero of an epic in seventy books, and had out-Lucifered Lucifer in every line of them, you could scarcely have punished him at last in a more revolting manner.[67]

Horrell's archly romantic account of a haunted death-bed had left no room for what Dickens seems to have regarded as essential: hope, comfort and room for repentance. The imagination rather than opening heaven to the dying man, served only to accentuate his despair, and Horrell seemed to have stifled any chance of the redemption of either a desolate past or a horrific present.

'Men's courses will foreshadow certain ends, to which, if persevered in, they must lead.' This proposition is desperately posed by Ebenezer Scrooge as the Ghost of Christmas Yet to Come points to his grave-stone in a gloomy and overgrown city church-yard. Scrooge is allowed to add a qualification, however: 'But if the courses be departed from, the ends will change.' The accompanying Spirit gives him no answer until he moves from the inspiration to the act of faith:

> 'Spirit!' he cried, tight clutching at its robe, 'hear me! I am not the man I was. I will not be the man I must have been but for this intercourse. Why show me this, if I am past all hope?'

The Spirit wavers, trembles, and then disappears as Scrooge's resolution translates itself into fervent prayer. The grave-yard 'walled in by houses, overrun by grass and weeds, the growth of vegetation's death, not life; choked up with too much burying; fat with repleted appetite', is suddenly transformed into Scrooge's familiar bedstead, and Time lies before its newly awakened occupant, offering him the chance of a fuller and happier life. *A Christmas Carol,* the first of the Christmas books, meditates like all of its successors, on time, past, present, and to come, and it sees death countered only by the hope of new life. Scrooge is allowed, unlike Dives in the parable, to come back to life, and he, unlike Lazarus too, is allowed to warn and to preach repentance. In changing from the man he was, he is not simply reborn, he is seen literally to defeat death. Earlier in the story, as he had been forced to contemplate his own unwanted corpse, Scrooge had been struck by the horror of death, a horror which Dickens stresses before he counters it:

> Oh cold, cold, rigid, dreadful Death, set up thine altar here, and dress it with such terrors as thou hast at thy command: for this is thy dominion! But of the loved, revered, and honoured head, thou canst not turn one hair to thy dread purposes, or make one feature odious. It is not that the hand is heavy and will fall down when released; it is not that the heart and pulse are still; but that the hand WAS open, generous, and true; the heart brave, warm, and tender; and the pulse a man's. Strike, Shadow, strike! And see his good deeds springing from the wound, to sow the world with life immortal![68]

Over the good man, though not yet over Ebenezer Scrooge, Death has no Dominion, however blighted the world in which he had his being, even a world dominated by a festering grave-yard. Good deeds, springing from the assured heart, redeem first the man, and, gradually, the world beyond him.

Notes

[1] 'Fiction, Fair and Foul' (*Nineteenth Century,* June 1880), vol. XXXIV of the Library Edition of the Works of John Ruskin, ed. E. T. Cook and Alexander Wedderburn, p. 272. For Dickens's death-rate see also William R. Clark, 'The Rationale of Dickens' Death Rate', *Boston University Studies in English,* vol. II, no. 6 (Autumn 1956) pp. 125-39.

[2] Edwin Chadwick, *Report on the Sanitary Condition of the Labouring Population of Great Britain* (1842), M. W. Flinn (ed.) (Edinburgh, 1965) pp. 422-3.

[3] 6 May 1863. *The Speeches of Charles Dickens,* K. J. Fielding (ed.), (Oxford, 1960) p. 320. For Dickens's interest in public health see also Norris Pope, *Dickens and Charity* (1978) ch. 5.

[4] These figures are based on those in Edwin Chadwick's *Supplementary Report on the Results of a Special Enquiry into the Practice of Interment in Towns* (1843)

p. 248. For further comment on this subject see John Morley's excellent study *Death, Heaven and the Victorians* (1971) p. 7.

[5] Edwin Chadwick, 'On the best Modes of representing accurately, by Statistical Returns, the Duration of Life', *Journal of the Statistical Society of London,* vol. VII (1844) p. 6.

[6] Quoted from B. Benjamin, *Health and Vital Statistics* (London, 1968) p. 115.

[7] See George Rosen, 'Disease, Debility, and Death' in H. J. Dyos and Michael Wolff (eds), *The Victorian City,* vol. 2 (1973) pp. 626-7.

[8] Thomas A. Welton, 'On Certain Changes in the English Rates of Mortality': A Paper read to the Statistical Society, 17 Feb. 1880, *Journal of the Statistical Society of London,* vol. XLIII (1880) pp. 65 ff.

[9] *Journal of the Statistical Society of London,* vol. XXVIII (1865) pp. 402 ff.

[10] Figures based on those in Chadwick's *Supplementary Report . . . On the Practice of Interment in Towns* (1843) pp. 256-66.

[11] Rosen, op. cit., p. 649.

[12] Chadwick's *Supplementary Report,* pp. 55-6.

[13] Audrey C. Peterson, 'Brain Fever in Nineteenth Century Literature: Fact and Fiction', *Victorian Studies,* vol. XIX (June 1976) pp. 445 ff.

[14] See for example Walter Russell Brain, 'Dickensian Diagnoses', *British Medical Journal* (1955), reprinted in *Some Reflexions on Genius and other Essays* (1960) pp. 123-36. See also the exhibition catalogue *Dickens and Medicine* (Wellcome Institute of the History of Medicine, June 1970).

[15] For Dickens's possible experience of the outbreak at Chatham in 1832 see W. J. Carlton, 'When the Cholera raged at Chatham', *The Dickensian* (June 1953).

[16] These figures are quoted from R. Thorne Thorne's *The Progress of Preventive Medicine during the Victorian Era 1837-1887* (1887) by George Rosen, op. cit., pp. 634-6.

[17] Ibid., pp. 652-5.

[18] *Punch,* vol. xxxv (1858) p. 5.

[19] Quoted by Denis Smith in his 'The Building Services' in M. H. Port, (ed.) *The Houses of Parliament* (New Haven and London, 1976) p. 226.

[20] Henry Mayhew, *London Labour and the London Poor,* vol. II (1851) p. 402.

[21] John Forster, *The Life of Charles Dickens,* ed. J. W. T. Ley (1928) p. 279.

[22] Charles Kingsley, *Alton Locke, Tailor and Poet: An Autobiography,* vol. II (1850) pp. 204-7.

[23] For the grave-yard in *Bleak House* see Trevor Blount, 'The Graveyard Satire of *Bleak House* in the context of 1850', *R. E. S.* New Series, vol. xiv, no. 56 (1963).

[24] *Black's Guide to London and its Environs,* fifth edition (1873) p. 19.

[25] The history of cemeteries in the nineteenth century has been excellently charted by James Stevens Curl in his *The Victorian Celebration of Death* (Newton Abbot, 1972). For cemeteries see also Chapters 3 and 4 of John Morley's *Death, Heaven and the Victorians,* and Philippe Ariès, *Western Attitudes towards Death from the Middle Ages to the Present,* trans. Patricia M. Ranum (Johns Hopkins UP, 1974) pp. 15-21, 70 ff. For Dickens's attitude to, and use of, urban graveyards see A. W. C. Brice and K. J. Fielding, '*Bleak House* and the Graveyard' in Robert B. Partlow Jr (ed.), *Dickens the Craftsman: Strategies of Presentation* (Carbondale, Illinois, 1970).

[26] G. A. Walker, *Gatherings from Graveyards* (1839) quoted by Morley, op. cit. pp. 35-6.

[27] Edwin Chadwick, *Supplementary Report on . . . the Practice of Interment in Towns,* p. 27.

[28] Ibid., pp. 23-4.

[29] Ibid., p. 15.

[30] 'The Cemetery: A Brief Appeal to the Feelings of Society on Behalf of Extra Mural Burial' (1848). Quoted by Curl, op. cit., pp. 136-7.

[31] Quoted by Morley, op. cit., pp. 42-3.

[32] J. C. Loudon, *On the Laying Out, Planting and Managing of Cemeteries and on the Improvement of Churchyards* (1843) p. 1.

[33] 'An Essay upon Epitaphs', *The Poetical Works of Wordsworth,* ed. Thomas Hutcheson, new edition revised by Ernest de Selincourt (Oxford, 1936) pp. 730-1.

[34] Leader's 'The Churchyard at Bettwys-y-Coed' is now in the Guildhall Art Gallery and Hughes's 'Home From Sea', thought to have been first exhibited (without the figure of the girl) in 1857, in the Ashmolean Museum. Both are reproduced in Jeremy Maas's *Victorian Paint-*

ers (1969) pp. 228 and 136. Bowler's 'The Doubt' is now in the Tate Gallery. Both it and Mann's 'The Child's Grave' are illustrated in Christopher Wood's *Victorian Panorama: Paintings of Victorian Life* (1976) pp. 105 and 106. Millais's 'The Vale of Rest' is also in the Tate Gallery.

[35] *The Pilgrim Edition of the Letters of Charles Dickens*, ed. Madeline House, Graham Storey and Kathleen Tillotson, vol. 1, pp. 268, 390.

[36] *Letters from Charles Dickens to Angela Burdett-Coutts 1841-1865*, selected and edited by Edgar Johnson (1953) pp. 264-5, 294. For the possible relationship between Nell's country grave and Mary's suburban one see F. S. Schwarzbach, *Dickens and the City* (1978) pp. 59-62.

In November 1831 Dickens had written a particularly weak eight-stanza poem entitled 'The Churchyard' in Maria Beadnell's album. It is largely a meditation on the contrast between the rich and the poor and on the equality enforced by death. See *Collected Papers* (Nonesuch Dickens) vol. II, pp. 281-2. The last illustration to *Nicholas Nickleby* ('The Children at their Cousin's Grave') also precisely reflects this mood.

[37] For Victorian funerary art see Morley, op. cit., and Curl, op. cit. See also Geoffrey Rowell, 'Nineteenth-century attitudes and practices' in G. Cope (ed.), *Dying, Death and Disposal* (1970).

[38] For a useful general survey of death-beds in Victorian fiction see Chapter 7 of John R. Reed's *Victorian Conventions* (Ohio University Press, 1975). See also Philip Collins's pamphlet, *From Manly Tear to Stiff Upper Lip: The Victorians and Pathos* (Victoria University Press, Wellington, New Zealand, 1974).

[39] Laurence Stone, *The Family, Sex and Marriage in England 1500-1800* (1977) p. 112.

[40] Ibid., pp. 257-9.

[41] Ariès, op. cit., pp. 55-6.

[42] *The Death of Ivan Ilyich*, trans. Rosemary Edmonds in *The Cossacks and Other Stories* (Penguin Classics, 1960).

[43] *Pilgrim Letters* vol. II, p. 188. See below Chapter 3.

[44] *The Letters of Charles Dickens* (Nonesuch Edition), ed. Walter Dexter (1938), vol. III, pp. 61-2. See below Chapter 4.

[45] See the introduction by R. A. Foakes to the Arden Edition of *Henry VIII* (1957). See also the *Revels History of Drama in English vol. IV 1750-1880*, p. 20.

[46] Ellen Terry, *The Story of my Life* (1908) p. 21.

[47] See W. Moelwyn Merchant, *Shakespeare and the Artist* (1959) pp. 84-6. See also Peter Tomory, *The Life and Art of Henry Fuseli* (1972) p. 33.

[48] See Geoffrey Keynes, *William Pickering, Publisher: A Memoir and A Checklist of His Publications* (rev. edn, 1969) p. 91.

[49] Jeremy Taylor, *The Rule and Exercises of Holy Dying, with Prayers and Acts of Virtue To Be Used by Sick and Dying Persons and Rules for the Visitation of the Sick* (1847) p. xi. There was a copy of the *Beauties of Taylor* (1845) in Dickens's library at Gad's Hill Place.

[50] For Venn and Watson, and for a masterly general survey of Victorian attitudes to the four last things, see Geoffrey Rowell, *Hell and the Victorians* (Oxford, 1974) pp. 7-8.

[51] William Hett, *Miscellanies on Various Subjects, in Prose and Verse* (1823) pp. 21-2.

[52] *A Collection of Hymns, for the Use of the People Called Methodists* (1830) pp. 50-1.

[53] *The Lives of the Most Eminent English Poets*, 4 vols (Edinburgh, 1815) vol. 3, p. 265.

[54] Edward Young, *Night Thoughts on Life, Death and Immortality* (1821) p. 28. In a footnote in his *The Childhood and Youth of Charles Dickens* (1891) Robert Langton notes a slight, and perhaps joking parallel between Young and Dickens (p. 222).

[55] Samuel Johnson, *The Lives of the Most Eminent English Poets*, vol. 2, pp. 210-11.

[56] James Boswell visited the dying Hume on 7 July 1776, who professed to him that he 'had never entertained any belief in Religion since he began to read Locke and Clarke' and that he 'did not wish to be immortal'. The prospect of meeting friends again in Heaven seemed to Hume 'a foolish and absurd notion'. Boswell left him 'with impressions which disturbed [him] for some time'. See Boswell on Hume: 'An Account of my last interview with David Hume Esq.', printed in Norman Kemp Smith's edition of Hume's *Dialogue concerning Natural Religion* (Oxford, 1935).

[57] Samuel Richardson, *Clarissa, or the History of a Young Lady*, vol. VII (1748) pp. 129-30, 218-19. Dickens had a copy of the 1810 edition of *Clarissa* [8 vols] in his library at Gad's Hill Place. He also saw a French stage-adaptation of the novel in Paris in 1847, at the time of the composition of the death-bed of little

Paul Dombey. He found that in the play Clarissa died 'better than the original'. *Nonesuch Letters,* vol. II, p. 10.

[58] *The Child's Companion, or Sunday Scholar's Reward,* vol. VI (1828).

[59] (Maria Towle), *James Skinner: A Memoir* (1883) pp. 254-72. The states of mind of the Sunday Scholars and of Agnes Skinner are wonderfully, if irreverently caught by Mark Twain in his account of Huckleberry Finn's visit to the Mississippi home of the recently deceased Emmeline Grangerford (*Huckleberry Finn,* Chapter 17). Although the novel dates only from 1884, Emmeline's Crayon drawings of funereal subjects exactly reflect the sentimental art of the first half of the nineteenth century. It is small wonder that the pictures give Huck the 'Fan-tods', and that his unease is accentuated once he learns that she had also kept a scrap-book in which she collected obituaries, notices of accidents, and 'cases of patient suffering' snipped from the *Presbyterian Observer.*

For the eighteenth-century and Romantic interest in children see also Peter Coveney's *The Image of Childhood: The Individual and Society: A Study of the Theme in English Literature* (1967) and Gillian Avery's *Nineteenth-Century Children: Heroes and Heroines in English Children's Stories 1780-1900* (1965).

[60] Sir James Fitzjames Stephen, *Saturday Review,* vol. 5 (8 May 1858).

[61] W. M. Thackeray in a review of Reybaud's *Jerome Paturot, Fraser's Magazine,* vol. XXVIII, pp. 349-62. John Hollingshead, 'Mr Dickens and his Critics', *The Train,* August 1857. Reprinted in Philip Collins (ed.), *Dickens: The Critical Heritage* (1971) p. 376.

[62] For the use of the death-bed in Victorian biography see Chapter 3 of A. O. J. Cockshut's *Truth to Life: The Art of Biography in the Nineteenth Century* (1974).

[63] For the Maurice affair and its place in the general Victorian discussion of Hell see Rowell, op. cit., pp. 76-89. See also W. O. Chadwick, *The Victorian Church,* part one (1966) pp. 545-50.

[64] *The George Eliot Letters,* ed. G. S. Haight, vol. II, p. 125.

[65] Alexander Welsh, *The City of Dickens* (Oxford, 1971) ch. XII, pp. 196 ff. My debt to Professor Welsh's study is considerable.

[66] Ibid., p. 196.

[67] To R. S. Horrell, 25 November 1840. *Pilgrim Letters,* vol. 2, p. 155.

[68] All quotations from *A Christmas Carol* (1843) are from vol. I of the Penguin English Library Edition of the Christmas Books edited by Michael Slater.

RESPONSES TO DEATH

Fred Kaplan (essay date 1987)

SOURCE: "Are You Sentimental?" in *Sacred Tears: Sentimentality in Victorian Literature,* Princeton University Press, 1987, pp.39-70.

[*In the excerpt below, Kaplan contends that Charles Dickens' depictions of death were deliberately sentimental so as to arouse and encourage the public's sense of morality.*]

. . . In his depiction of the deaths of Little Nell and Paul Dombey, Dickens dramatizes his belief in the innate moral sentiments and in sentimentality as morally instructive. "Yet nothing teacheth like death," one of Dickens' predecessors, whose works he owned, preached. William Dodd's widely read *Reflections on Death* (1763) is representative of hundreds of similar volumes whose depiction and evaluation of death the Victorians read. Dickens would have agreed with Dodd that

> it is too commonly found, that a familiarity with death, and a frequent recurrency of funerals, graces, and church-yards, serve to harden rather than humanize the mind, and deaden rather than excite those becoming reflections which such objects seem calculated to produce. Hence the physician enters, without the least emotion, the gloomy chambers of expiring life; the undertaker handles, without concern, the clay-cold limbs; and the sexton whistles unappalled, while the spade casts forth from the earth the mingled bones and dust of his fellow creatures.[9]

In *Oliver Twist,* Dickens contrasts the easy familiarity and insensitivity toward death of Noah Claypool with Oliver's alertness to the inherent moral lessons in the coffin and the tomb. *Nicholas Nickleby, Barnaby Rudge,* and *Martin Chuzzlewit* also contain effective dramatizations of the moral significance of death, vivid embodiments of the Victorian concern with the potential devitalization of that powerful teacher of moral lessons and Christian virtues. To Dickens and his contemporaries, strong emotional response to death seemed more desirable than the all-too-common callousness, the kind of hardening of the feelings, that Dodd warns against. In a scene in *Reflections on Death,* which may have directly influenced Dickens' depiction of the death of Little Nell, Dodd dramatizes the death of a paragon of Christian virtue, a young mother who on her deathbed consoles her own parents, claiming that she is "wholly resigned" to God's will.

"I am on the brink of eternity, and now see clearly the importance of it—Remember, oh remember, that every thing in time is insignificant to the awful concerns of—" Eternity, she would have said; but her breath failed; she fainted a second time; and when all our labours to recover her, seemed just effectual, and she appeared returning to life, a deep sob alarmed us—and the lovely body was left untenanted by its immortal inhabitant! NOW SHE IS NUMBER'D AMONG THE CHILDREN OF GOD, AND HER LOT IS AMONG THE SAINTS.[10]

For her mourners, Nell provides a similar example of the lesson that death is a reminder to the living to allow their innate moral sentiments to flourish. To linger with expressive sentiment over the deathbeds or the graves of the departing or departed is to stand, even if prematurely, at the portals of paradise, being reminded that death is not only the mother of beauty but also that the moral sentiments that death evokes are the fountainhead of our feelings about the soul and about eternity. Dickens lingers for some time over Nell's deathbed, partly to affirm his commitment to Dodd's "important truth: The abuse of life proceeds from the forgetfulness of death." "Oh thank God, all who see it," Dickens writes of Paul Dombey's death, "for that older fashion yet, of Immortality! And look upon us, angels of young children, with Regards not quite estranged, when the swift river bears us to the ocean" ([*Dombey and Son*], chap. 16). Though some modern readers may be uncomfortable with the emotional intensity and the rhetoric with which Dickens describes such dyings, and may elevate discomfort and misunderstanding into an accusation of insincerity, Dickens is attempting purposely to arouse his readers' innate moral sentiments, reminding them that the more emotionally sensitive they are to death the more morally attentive they will be to the values of life. In the early stages of his career, Dickens felt optimistic that such dramatizations would stir the world's conscience as well as its fears. The suppressed and the exploited would benefit. He believed that fictional presentations of the deaths of children had extraordinary corrective potential. Such deaths appealed powerfully to the moral sentiments both because they seem against "nature" and "human nature" and because children are more vulnerable than adults. Intensely aware of children dead and dying, Dickens and many of his contemporaries thought it impossible to be excessively feeling or "sentimental" in any pejorative way about such losses. Attempts to curb the expression of such feeling denied human nature and human need. . . .

Carol Hanbery MacKay (essay date 1990)

SOURCE: "Controlling Death and Sex: Magnification v. the Rhetoric of Rules in Dickens and Thackeray," in *Sex and Death in Victorian Literature,* edited by Regina Barreca, The Macmillan Press, Ltd., 1990, pp. 120-39.

[*In the following essay, MacKay explores the strong erotic elements in depictions of death found in particular works of Charles Dickens, George Eliot, and William Makepeace Thackeray.*]

Shall I believe
That unsubstantial Death is amorous,
And that the lean abhorrèd monster keeps
Thee here in dark to be his paramour?
(Shakespeare, *Romeo and Juliet,* 5.3.102-5)[1]

He held her, almost as if she were sanctified to him by death, and kissed her, once, almost as he might have kissed the dead. (Dickens, *Our Mutual Friend,* p. 764)

Perhaps because sex and death involve such intense, primal emotions, the rhetoric of each often comes to resemble that of the other—that is, an intense poetic rendering of death may assume an erotic cast, while a rhetorical amplification of sexual desire frequently evokes images of death and dying. From Cupid's arrow to the Elizabethan slang term for sexual climax, 'to die', we witness this melding. My point here is primarily a rhetorical one, borne out especially well by Victorian fiction, but we can recognise a similar psychological tension existing in both desire and death—the tension between attenuation and completion—and presume that rhetoric, faced with the problem of expressing such opposite extremes in human experience, might be forced to conflate the two. Georges Bataille pursues the connection one step further in his basic formulation: 'eroticism is assenting to life even in the face of death' (Bataille, p. 11). By eroticising death, an author makes of death not an ending but something that is a part of the life process, itself endlessly repeated. And when death is rendered at moments which otherwise impose closure, this strategy becomes especially tempting, for it permits an author to resist an ending that implies the 'death' of his or her connection with the reading audience; in effect, this treatment allows the author to seduce the reader into a living, ongoing relationship.

But the desire to embellish death also presented a challenge to Victorian novelists, who—on some level of consciousness—sought to make death an aesthetic act without giving free rein to its erotic component. Garrett Stewart's full-length study of death scenes in British fiction confirms this concern with 'styles of dying'—or dying 'aestheticized'—while John Kucich's close analysis of Charles Dickens' *The Old Curiosity Shop* points equally well to how 'the eroticizing of death' can establish a conjunction that still keeps sexuality in check (Kucich, 1980, p. 64). Thus, our goal is to be alert to forms of control or distancing of death in Victorian fiction. Note, for example, how often Victorian novels focus on childhood mortality or death in old age. Even when these deaths are introduced primarily for mimetic purposes, they also provide Victorian novelists with a relative degree of asexuality or, at the very least, with a way of apparently introducing eroticism more safely.[2]

The favoured method for attempting this de-eroticisation involved a manipulation of time, which could reduce the tension between attenuation and completion. Besides making the victim very old or very young, the novelist could attenuate death in such a manner that the sexual element apparently disappears—as is the case in Dickens' *Great Expectations* with Miss Havisham, who seems to be living a perpetual, attenuated death-in-life, its erotic component buried in the dust and decay of time. Of course, to twentieth-century minds—aware of unconscious psychological mechanisms such as transferral, sublimation and repression—these efforts may sometimes seem less than wholly successful.[3] At the same time, however, such efforts and our attention to them can equally well remind us of our continuity with our Victorian predecessors regarding both obsession with and repression of sexuality, as the work of Michel Foucault and the recent collections edited by Martha Vicinus, Donald Cox, and Catherine Gallagher and Thomas Laqueur have attested.

Through Miss Havisham we can also read another major means of restraining the sexual aspect of death, often employed in conjunction with manipulations of time: the use of social rules and boundaries—power and powerlessness—to pre-empt the erotic through depersonalisation, isolation, and the dampening effect of ethical considerations or religious language.[4] One can try to lose the sexual element of death either through the powerlessness of the masses or through the extreme isolation of status, both of which are depersonalising. Specifically, Miss Havisham's powerlessness—her isolation and position as a social outcast—denies her sexual possibilities. At the same time, however, she exercises power by perpetuating through Estella her death-in-life, transferring the contained erotic component so effectively that Estella becomes the cold-hearted temptress, who in turn manipulates social rules and boundaries to self-destructive ends.

Social boundaries likewise de-eroticise death in Thomas Hardy's *Jude the Obscure* and Anthony Trollope's *Barchester Towers.* In Hardy's novel, eroticism is dispersed: Little Father Time commits murder and suicide 'because we are too menny' (Hardy, p. 266). And in Trollope's text, Bishop Grantly's all-too-unique social status dilutes the emotional component of his death by blending it with power machinations, as his son tries not to hope too fervently for the old man's timely demise (Trollope, pp. 1-9). Here we can recognise another example of eroticism transferred. Although the son's emotional intensity almost parallels the energy of sexual desire, his emotions are confused, ambivalent, and ultimately denied. Both of these cases also convey strong moral or ethical considerations—variations on the theme of social power—whose presence tends to defuse erotic potential.

With George Eliot and the ending of *The Mill on the Floss,* we witness a typically aesthetic treatment of death that reveals an almost overwhelming erotic component. Up until this point in the novel, the erotic has been kept fairly well in check, emerging briefly in the imagery of the Red Deeps and in Maggie Tulliver's 'electrical' response to Stephen Guest. Only at the moment of closure is the erotic allowed to dominate—in this case in an image of dissolved boundaries, of brother and sister dying in each other's arms. Maggie and Tom Tulliver are at the mercy of the raging floodwaters of the river Floss, its fatal vehicle inevitably 'hurrying on in hideous triumph'. Suffused with foreboding, the scene is rife with erotic overtones, which Eliot tries to control:

> They sat mutely gazing at each other: Maggie with eyes of intense life looking out from a weary beaten face—Tom pale with a certain awe and humiliation. Thought was busy though the lips were silent: and though he could ask no question, he guessed a story of almost miraculous divinely-protected effort. But at last a mist gathered over the blue-gray eyes, and the lips found a word they could utter: the old childish—'Magsie!' (Eliot, pp. 455-6)

At this intimate moment, Eliot evokes the power of time to contain the erotic element. Maggie's 'weary beaten face' and the reversion to childhood both offset the building intensity, while 'awe and humilation' suggest a degree of social and religious distancing. The erotic bursts forth in the line, 'Maggie could make no answer but a long deep sob of that mysterious wondrous happiness that is one with pain', but it is immediately suppressed by her invocation of duty: ' "We will go to Lucy, Tom" ' she says; ' "we'll go and see if she is safe, and then we can help the rest." ' The wooden machinery, 'clinging together in fatal fellowship', also serves as a social image, pointing back toward the social boundaries that constrain Maggie and limit Tom's capacity to accept her freely.

The sexual implications of this scene are so strong that Eliot's rhetorical attempts at control barely restrain them. Even Victorians had to bow to the conflation of the rhetorics of sex and death during times of great emotional intensity, as in the flood scene, or when the moment of death itself was at hand and needed to be given a full poetic treatment. One solution to this dilemma seemed to involve the use of religious language and imagery, in which the sensual qualities were sanctioned—'de-psychologized', as it were—by time and longstanding tradition. Eliot seeks to control the flow of eroticism by a sustained use of this Victorian technique of last resort:

> [The full meaning of what had happened to Tom and Maggie] came with so overpowering a force—it was a new revelation to his spirit of the depths in life, that had lain beyond his vision which he had fancied so keen and clear—that he was unable to ask a question.

Ultimately, this technique depicts brother and sister reliving together 'one supreme moment', their tandem death transforming the physicality of 'two bodies that were found in close embrace' into the transcendent epitaph: 'In their death they were not divided' (p. 457).[5]

As might be expected, we find some of the most intriguing examples of rhetorical attempts to control sex and death in the work of the two leading male novelists of the Victorian era, Charles Dickens and William Makepeace Thackeray. Whereas Dickens magnifies and then tries to de-eroticise death through extreme attenuation, displacement and isolation—of either character or psychological conflict—Thackeray puts boundaries between sex and death from the outset by setting up ironic parallels between them. In this manner, he plays on the social rules and power relationships themselves, employing them as a form of parodic negation. In particular, Thackeray replaces the usual rhapsodic rhetoric of death with the rhetoric of his own rules, which allow him to 'put away' his puppets and draw lines between layers of the text.

I

Dickens typically magnifies death through an extreme attenuation of time, only to de-eroticise it through a process of rhetorical or psychological dispersal, which separates and isolates the erotic elements. *Dombey and Son* enacts for young Paul a very sensual death, its attenuation emblematic of erotic death in literature—making it an especially fitting climax to Dickens' public reading, 'The Story of Little Dombey'. In fact, this reading so condenses the rendition of Paul's death as to make it appear even more erotic than it seems to be in the novel. In this case, Dickens could perhaps be adjudged a fairly conscious manipulator of his elements, for we know how carefully he revised and shaped his public readings from their published originals. And in this respect, he was already building on what many readers of his letters have concluded was a highly calculated incident: in *Dombey and Son,* with the death of Little Dombey, Dickens was attempting a 'repeat performance' of the 'popular' death of Little Nell. As George Ford observes, elements of Dickens the rhetorician blend with those of Dickens the artist in the conscious manipulation of this death scene.[6]

Through Paul's impressionistic view of time slowly passing, Dickens renders his death attractive, even beautiful. Spatial configurations and posture set up and frame the erotic imagery, which pours in just before the moment of death:

> Sister and brother wound their arms around each other, and the golden light came streaming in, and fell upon them, locked together.
>
> 'How fast the river runs, between its green banks and the rushes, Floy! But it's very near the sea. I hear the waves! They always said so!' (*Dombey and Son,* p. 297)

Here Dickens reaches the height of sensuality, his rhetorical energy infused by typical erotic imagery in the conjunction of rhythmic waves, rocking boat, and golden light. Thus, we should not be surprised to discover that when a popular song of the day, 'What Are the Wild Waves Saying', drew upon this imagery, its lyricist was quick to counter the eroticism with his own brand of religiosity in the refrain: 'The voice of the great Creator/ Dwells in that mighty tone!' (Glover, p. 9) And as Alexander Welsh notes about Florence Dombey's role in this intimate scene, it too creates an antithetical effect: Dickens has been grooming her to be one of his 'Angels of Death'.[7]

But most significantly, extreme attenuation in this version of death enables Dickens to disperse the sensual elements, temporally and spatially (in effect, Paul can be said to be 'dying' over the space of some 100 pages.) If we take key words and phrases from a single extended passage towards the end of this process—about two pages of the text—we can see the erotic element only too clearly: 'quivered', 'rolled', 'resistless, he cried out!', 'leaning his poor head upon her breast', 'rising up', 'reviving, waking, starting into life once more', 'glistening as it rolled', 'roused', 'the flush', 'again the golden water would be dancing on the wall' (*Dombey and Son,* pp. 292-4). Yet Dickens not only dissipates these sensual terms over time; he also shunts them aside by making them poetic descriptions of the environment as the boy perceives it. All the while, death is spoken of and treated as part of nature, implying the conjoinment of sensual and morbid qualities, despite their rhetorical dispersal. At the same time, the isolation of Paul reveals Dickens' characteristic use of psychological and social isolation to de-eroticise his scenes. When death finally does arrive, it comes to the old-young boy who epitomises—through the aesthetic power of repeated parallelism—the 'old old fashion—Death!'[8]

Any discussion of death in Dickens' fiction must eventually address his presentation of Little Nell in *The Old Curiosity Shop* and the immense interest her death has generated—in both the author and his reading public. Little Nell's death also disperses and displaces the erotic—this time into both the framing narration and her grandfather's romantic rhetoric, which

Ronald Colman in the 1935 film version of Charles Dickens's A Tale of Two Cities, *playing Sidney Carton on his way to the guillotine.*

dramatises the lover's insistence that he is not separated from his beloved:

> 'You plot among you to wean my heart from her. You never will do that—never while I have life. I have no relative or friend but her—I never had—I never will have. She is all in all to me. It is too late to part us now.' (*The Old Curiosity Shop*, p. 652)

These words asserting love's union occur in the context of a novel which has portrayed the villainous Quilp as relentlessly pursuing Nell—the eroticism of his pursuit barely concealed—and they were written by an author who admitted to the childhood desire of wanting to marry Little Red Riding Hood when he grew up.[9] Trying to deny fourteen-year-old Nell's sexuality by direct ascription throughout the novel, Dickens finally protests too much. At this point, it is impossible to resist the temptation to read into this scene some of Dickens's own biography. Writing to John Forster about the difficulty of performing what he would two months later call his 'Nellicide', he comments, 'Dear Mary died yesterday when I think of this sad story' (*Letters*, vol. 2, pp. 228 and 182).[10] Mary is, of course, Mary Hogarth, Dickens' teenaged sister-in-law who died in his arms in 1837; not only did he wear her ring for the rest of his life, but he hoped to be buried next to her as well. Given this insight, we would not be amiss to read into the rhetoric of Nell's grandfather some of Dickens' own sentiments.

As Dickens approaches Nell's death—not something absolutely demanded by the plot—he succumbs to another form of rhetorical attentuation and temporal avoidance: he presents her death after the fact. Nonetheless, the surrounding rhetoric of the characters extols and glorifies Nell, each character jealously vying with her grandfather to apotheosise her the more. Finally, based on Dickens' explicit instructions, George Cattermole's illustration presents us with the pubescent 'bride' on her death-'bed': 'upon her breast, and pillow, and about her bed, there may be slips of holly, and berries, and such free green things' (*Letters*, p. 172). Flirting with necrophilia as he earlier has with paedophilia, Dickens' interest here may seem inappropriate to our twentieth-century readership, but it did not seem so to his Victorian audience, for many of whom personal connotations (and perhaps suppressed eroticism) were released. While we might expect such a popular incident to result in one of Dickens' public reading texts, we can also recognise that—for both author and auditor—the emotional intensity might well have been excessive.[11]

But Dickens also tries to delimit the erotic element by setting Nell's grandfather in conflict with other characters and isolating him through his apparent insanity. Her grandfather's denial of death—'She is sleeping soundly' (*The Old Curiosity Shop,* p. 648)—is further contradicted by the narrator's litany, 'She was dead. . . . She was dead' (pp. 652-4). Moreover, we can actually see the physical separation of the fulminating old man and Nell herself during the height of his rhetoric: not only is she already dead, but she is also sealed off in another room. Once again, Dickens illustrates for us the twin motifs of excess and restraint that Kucich has so appropriately employed in his full-length study to characterise the opposing forces of Dickensian energy.

In *Oliver Twist,* with the overt sexual overtones of Sikes killing Nancy, we uncover a treatment of death which is strikingly atypical for Dickens. A violent murder leaves no scope for languid attenuation or sentimentalisation of death. Victorian authors generally favoured the erotic over the merely lustful side of sexuality, and the spiritual over the violent aspect of death—but here those preferences cannot hold sway. At the same time, Sikes's murder of Nancy employs in concentrated form some of the same rhetorical techniques we have recognised in other fictional scenes of death. This passage gains its phenomenal intensity precisely because of the pressure it places on the very Victorian desire to keep things discrete. The rhetorical tools used to offset the sex-death conflation must be economical and powerful, eschewing the sort of slow dispersal that Dickens generally espoused.

Although time is limited, Dickens still tries to keep his characters' sexuality in complete isolation—from one another as much as possible, and from the Victorian reader as well. Note, for example, that the violent death itself occurs between two members of the lower classes, to some degree isolating it from its presumed Victorian audience. The graphic description of Sikes as he blindly rushes home to do the deed—with his blood-engorged muscles fairly bursting through his skin—presents a rare glimpse of murderous lust:

> Without one pause, or moment's consideration; without once turning his head to the right or left, or raising his eyes to the sky, or lowering them to the ground, but looking straight before him with savage resolution: his teeth so tightly compressed that the strained jaw seemed starting through his skin; the robber held on his headlong course, nor muttered a word, nor relaxed a muscle, until he reached the door. (*Oliver Twist,* p. 421)

But this vividness is altered when Sikes comes upon Nancy and their physical separateness ends. The descriptions of Sikes are greatly reduced and depersonalised. He douses the only candle in the room and prevents Nancy from opening the curtain on the faint light of day, and what we see of him from then on are murky glimpses of hands and arms committing the murder. He is depersonalised—referred to as 'the man' and 'the housebreaker'—while Nancy's words enhance the negative quality, as she cries, 'You cannot have the heart to kill me. . . . I will not loose my hold, you cannot throw me off' (p. 422).

The murder itself is rife with forms of isolation. Sikes and Nancy speak in ways that indicate their contrasting perceptions—like a meeting of two opposite worlds—the social and perceptual boundaries rendered all the more emphatic because they are *not* dispersed or attenuated. Once these separate beings begin to talk and interact, Nancy's words take on some of the spiritual or aesthetic quality we have witnessed in more typical death scenes, but her attempts to 'aestheticise' the scene only isolate her further. The rhetoric negates light and time, typical aesthetic images and motifs of natural death. Knocking down the candle, Sikes denies even its faint light. Time, too, is negated—an inversion of Dickens's usual technique to de-eroticise death—as Nancy helplessly pleads for time: 'It's never too late to repent. . . . We must have time—a little, little time!' Finally, Dickens completes this complex and difficult isolation of murderer from victim as Nancy breathes 'one prayer for mercy to her Maker!' (p. 423)—so that Sikes becomes the profane representative of death, Nancy the transcendent victim.

Yet this is not the final word on this infamous murder, for Dickens resurrected it for his reading audiences. Recast as 'Sikes and Nancy', the reading text develops through a series of parallel structures, thus attempting to highlight the aesthetic as a counter to its eventual acts of violence. Then, as he begins to recount the murder scene, Dickens almost reproduces it from the novel exactly. This in itself is unusual, for it points to the highly condensed nature of the original—creating the intensity that has already challenged the author to offset it. But Dickens also performs several key acts of omission, which force us to return to the novel and to read its murder more as an implicit rape. Unlike the reading text, the novel's text continues to affirm Nancy's sexuality as it describes her greeting Bill 'with an expression of pleasure at his return' (p. 421).[12] The novel further provides Nancy with the very words a rape victim might utter to pacify her attacker: 'I—I won't scream or cry—not once—hear me—speak to me—tell me what I have done!' (p. 422) Deleting these sexual overtones from his reading text hardly left Dickens with an expurgated passage, but he did reduce some of its over-charged nature. There would be difficulty enough in his repeatedly performing the roles of murderer and victim—the very performance which from most reports constituted his self-murder.[13]

II

Dealing more overtly with the erotic than Dickens, Thackeray in *Vanity Fair* draws a satiric contrast between the rigidified, death-oriented (i.e. military and legal) rules of male society and the diffuse, unspoken rules of the suppressed subculture of women. Here the parallels between sex and death are consciously depicted and constitute part of the novel's structure, yet the very highlighting of the parallels emphasises their separateness and distinction. Thackeray recognises that he cannot talk about either male or female sexuality directly, so his viewpoint is distanced, avoiding, by and large, aestheticisation. In the preface to his next novel, *Pendennis,* he would make his famous pronouncement on the limits dictated by middle-class morality: 'Since the author of Tom Jones was buried, no writer of fiction among us has been permitted to depict to his utmost power a MAN' (*Pendennis,* p. xi). Thackeray tends to be blunt about death—recall the sudden, anti-erotic revelation of George Osborne 'lying on his face, dead, with a bullet through his heart' (*Vanity Fair,* p. 315)—and ambivalent about sex, rather than engaging in the rapturous time-dilation and dissolution of boundaries that we encounter in Eliot, Dickens and many other Victorian novelists. We do not, in other words, uncover in Thackeray a rhetorical struggle against the conflation of sex and death, but rather an intellectual acknowledgement and manipulation of their parallels. Instead of invoking rhetorical forms of isolation, Thackeray depi ts the two elements as occurring in different spheres and according to different rules from the outset: isolation exists as the fabric of his fictional world.

When Becky Sharp appears in the charade as Clytemnestra, Thackeray seems willing to concede the connection between sex and death, but he carefully encapsulates the scene, almost parodying his own aestheticising of it: it is a tableau—outside the temporal flow of the plot and with no causal relationship to the rest of the story:

> Aegisthus steals in pale and on tiptoe. What is that ghastly face looking out balefully after him from behind the arras? He raises his dagger to strike the sleeper [Agamemnon, played by Rawdon Crawley, Becky's husband], who turns in his bed, and opens his broad chest as if for the blow. He cannot strike the noble slumbering chieftan. Clytemnestra glides swiftly into the room like an apparition—her arms are bare and white,—her tawny hair floats down her shoulders,—her face is deadly pale,—and her eyes are lighted up with a smile so ghastly, that people quake as they look at her. (p. 494)

At the height of the murderous illusion, someone shouts out his recognition that Clytemnestra is indeed Becky, and then 'scornfully she snatches the dagger out of Aegisthus's hand, and advances to the bed'. The scene has sensational power—'a thrill of terror and delight runs through the assembly' (p. 492)—but we end up feeling that Thackeray, as usual, remains relatively free of these disturbing forces and is using them intellectually as a discrete comment on his text, rather than as a symbolic statement of what really goes on at the heart of his novel.[14] This scene is to *Vanity Fair* what Sikes killing Nancy is to *Oliver Twist:* in Dickens, the result is shattering, a release of repressed emotional power; in Thackeray, it is an entertainment, once again deliberately highlighting the boundaries that keep sex and death separate in his world. This is Thackeray's intellectual means of isolating these elements. Cooler and more distanced than Dickens in his approach, he draws parallels and keeps his forces—like puppets—under control.

Thackeray can even be blunt about death when he chooses to attenuate its presentation. Chapter 61 of *Vanity Fair*—'In Which Two Lights Are Put Out'—juxtaposes the deaths of the two patriarchs, Mr Sedley and Mr Osborne.[15] In the first case, a dissolution of old emotional boundaries and an expansion of time occur, as they frequently do in Dickens. But when death finally comes, the sexual angle is more anti-erotic than anything else, for Thackeray treats death almost wholly in terms of satiric negation—i.e. by the setting up of ironic parallels:

> So there came one morning and sunrise, when all the world got up and set about its various works and pleasures, with the exception of old John Sedley, who was not to fight with fortune, or to hope or scheme any more: but to go and take up a quiet and utterly unknown residence in a churchyard at Brompton by the side of his old wife. (p. 587)

Moreover, as Mr Osborne's death is compared with Mr Sedley's—and we realise that there will never be a reconciliation between the two former friends—we recognise that Thackeray has consciously set up this contrast, again maintaining his intellectual control: 'One day when he should have come down to breakfast, his servant, missing him went into his dressing-room, and found him lying at the foot of the dressing-table, in a fit' (p. 591). Indeed, Thackeray's use of parallelism could be said to constitute his rhetorical manipulation of time—his technique for allaying the sex-death conflation.

Elsewhere in Thackeray's canon, when he magnifies death, as in the case of Helen Pendennis or Colonel Newcome, he continues to exert his control through satirical framing or drawing an actual line between death and imaginary sexual fulfilment. For example, as Helen's impending death leads to a mother-son reconciliation, the narration leaps ahead in time to observe, in the context of religious discourse, that ever after, in his best moments and worst trials, Pen would know that 'his mother's face looked down upon him, and blessed him with its gaze of pity and purity' (*Pendennis,* p. 213). Time also stretches backwards, to encompass Pen's youthful repetition of his 'Our Father', recited 'at his mother's sacred knees' (p. 214). On the one hand, when this earlier period is recalled, the alert reader can hardly deny the incestuous overtones at both periods, for Helen has ever desired of Pen that she be 'his all in all' (p. 196). On the other hand, these overtones also provoke a more incisive narrative commentary that undermines both Helen's death scene and the sexual connotations of her 'poor' individual story.[16] In the chapter immediately preceding the one that narrates her death, Helen's 'devouring care' prompts the narrator to turn her into a representative 'type', who perpetuates—in co-conspiracy with her male partner—the tyranny of gendered role differentiation:

> Is it not your nature [Delia] to creep about his feet and kiss them, to twine round his trunk and hang there; and Damon's to stand like a British man with his hands in his breeches pocket, while the pretty fond parasite clings round him? (p. 197)

In many ways, Colonel Newcome's death recalls Little Nell's: it is Thackeray's old-age counterpart to Dickens' treatment of death claiming the innocence of youth.[17] In fact, when the Colonel becomes a poor brother at Grey Friars, time expands to encompass him as both 'a youth all love and hope' and 'a stricken old man, with a beard as white as snow covering the noble care-worn face' (*The Newcomes,* p. 443). But any sexuality raised by his excited, romantic rhetoric is displaced by Thackeray's rhetorical handling of the attenuated death scene: the Colonel's age and delirium isolate him from the other characters (as they do Nell's grandfather); his repeated reunions with Madame de Florac recall only unfulfilled love; and we are further distanced from his courtly discourse because it is not directly quoted. Moreover, the conclusion itself cuts both ways:

> And just as the last bell struck, a peculiar sweet smile shone over his face, and he lifted up his head a little, and quickly said, 'Adsum!' and fell back. It was the word we used at school, when names were called; and lo, he, whose heart was as that of a little child, had answered to his name, and stood in the presence of The Master. (pp. 444-5)

Here we can recognise emotional magnification as time expands to convey the old man once again as a young boy. Yet 'Adsum' also recalls rules, and 'Master' implies hierarchies. Then the 'real' conclusion appears as Thackeray draws a literal line across his text, thereby foregrounding his own artistry and reminding us that he can make his own rules: now we are in the author's, not the narrator's, time frame, where the fulfilment of erotic passions is merely a speculative venture—'for you, dear friend, it is as you like' (p. 446).

Such boundarylines and rule-making return us to *Vanity Fair,* where we can note that even when Becky is depicted as a mermaid—as a death-in-life siren—and Thackeray evokes some of the disturbing, unconscious disgust at the conjunction of death and sexuality, his whole rhetorical approach involves drawing ironic parallels, playing on the dividing line that the water makes—and on his intention to keep clear of it:

> Those who like may peep down under waves that are pretty transparent, and see [the monster's tail] writhing and twirling, diabolically hideous and slimy, flapping amongst bones, or curling round corpses; but above the water line, I ask, has not everything been proper, agreeable, and decorous, and has any the most squeamish immoralist in Vanity Fair a right to cry fie? (*Vanity Fair,* p. 617)

The passage that follows continues to deliver negations. Whenever Thackeray touches on this sort of charged material, he launches into either controlled, intellectual parallels or else a series of parodic denials: now we learn that 'we had best not examine the fiendish marine cannibals, revelling and feasting on their wretched pickled victims'. Cannibalism combines with sexuality to suggest all the attendant horrors of vampirism raised by Nina Auerbach in *Woman and the Demon,* yet Thackeray still maintains 'the laws of politeness' and invokes the power of his own negating rhetoric.[18]

Given his usual separation of death and sex, it is intriguing to note that in order to illustrate how Becky refuses to confront the implications of her own sexuality, Thackeray uses a metaphor of death: 'But,—just as the children of Queen's Crawley went round the room where the body of their father lay;—if ever Becky had these thoughts [of leading a straightforward life], she was accustomed to walk round them, and not look in' (pp. 410-11). In fact, she pointedly avoids examining thoughts about an alternative existence: 'She eluded them, and despised them—or at least she was committed to the other path from which retreat was now impossible.' But Becky circling round a corpse at a great distance is equally an appropriate symbol for the author's own reluctance to confront death *or* sex, his distanced, manipulative treatment of both contrasting with Dickens' tendency to immerse himself in the magnification of death, while concurrently trying to de-eroticise the subject. Thackeray's enforced 'bachelorhood' due to his wife's mental illness, and Dickens' attraction to younger women, made sexuality a highly charged subject for both of them—and hence something they were more comfortable positing in their female characters. In this respect, both also evince a fear of female sexuality. Yet while Dickens kills off or deports a number of his most erotic female characters, Thackeray persists in examining Becky Sharp—his epitome of female eroticism—from the admittedly safe distance implied by ironic parallels with death and destruction.

Finally, at the end of *Vanity Fair,* death once more occurs within a context that seems to invoke sexuality. In stark terms, Jos Sedley is reported to have died. But instead of learning any details about his demise, we are confronted with speculation, innuendo, and insurance companies—death and sex completely bureaucratised, which at the same time might be considered as the most extreme form of dispassionate separation. In the midst of this controversy, Thackeray makes it clear that the insurance companies are very suspicious about the cause of Joseph's death, with foul play on Becky's part being the implication. On this occasion, for such a specific insinuation about sex and death, Thackeray employs some of his most powerful negating rhetoric: 'it was the blackest case'; Becky's lawyers, 'of Thaives Inn', are named after three notorious murderers; and they in turn declare her 'the object of an infamous conspiracy' (pp. 664-6). Yet Thackeray does not stop with the power of language: he carries his argument into the visual arts, where his accompanying illustration depicts Becky lurking behind a curtain while Jos pleads with Dobbin not to reveal his intention of leaving her. Entitled 'Becky's second appearance in the character of Clytemnestra', this illustration is teasingly ambiguous: does Becky hold a knife in her hand, or is that just a trick of the light? Thackeray obviously intends this ambivalence to extend to her sexual power over Jos as well: she may be using her (and his) sexuality to bring about his death, but we will never know for certain since she is always allowed to operate 'below the water line'.

The whole subject of *rules,* especially social and artistic ones, is central to this topic. Victorians were very involved with social regulations—particularly those involving sex and death—yet the foregrounding of either sex or death tends also to involve a questioning or loosening of rules. This condition created another link (besides what I have been calling 'aestheticisation') between the rhetorics of sex and death. It provided Thackeray with a perfect fulcrum for dealing with both sex and death, not in terms of the usual rapturous rhetoric, but in terms of *artistic* rules—disposing of puppets ('Come children, let us shut up the box and the puppets, for our play is played out', p. 666) and drawing lines between layers of the text. And Becky Sharp works in the limbo between these two realms (which may be the true import of the mermaid symbol, a sexually enticing yet sexually censored figuration) as does the novelist himself. If neither Dickens nor Thackeray could articulate sexuality without invoking controls (after all, neither could transcend both personal and societally imposed proscriptions), Thackeray's artistry was the more daring, allowing him to layer private and public sublimation in ways that are particularly amenable to twentieth-century narrative analysis. Ultimately, it is Thackeray's use of his own artistic rules to explore societal rules that makes *Vanity Fair* one of the most innovative Victorian novels on the twin subjects of sex and death.

Notes

[1] All references given in the text are to titles and editions given in the Bibliography following these Notes.

[2] Kucich's article provides a good introduction to how the literature of the period reflected the Victorian 'climate' of death (see especially pp. 58-9), while Kincaid's paper, as well as his work in progress on paedophilia, alerts us to how Victorian discourse on child sexuality operates within and exposes models of play and power.

[3] For example, David Lean's film of *Great Expectations* (1946) justifies its 'happy ending' by having Pip save Estella—who has just been jilted by Bentley Drummle in the rewritten script—from becoming another Miss Havisham. Polhemus develops his argument by concentrating on Pip's symbolic 'rape' of Miss Havisham, finding in it 'the tension and energy latent in the nineteenth-century drive to reconcile the desire and the prohibition [against incest] without diminishing the power of either' (Polhemus, p. 1). And Eigner's study demonstrates how David Copperfield's suppression of both death and sex results in the formulation of his doubles, Steerforth and Heep.

[4] The contributors to the collection of Gallagher and Laqueur, originally published as *Representations,* No. 14 (1986), build especially on the work of Foucault to illustrate how Victorian agencies of power began to redirect their energies to evidence concern about and then control of various aspects of sexual behaviour.

[5] Stewart's book is certainly required reading for anyone studying about death in Victorian fiction, while his article is of particular interest on the subject of death by drowning.

[6] Ford continues: 'Even on Dickens' own terms, there was an ironical aftermath to his bid for favor. . . . After the death of Paul, the later numbers of *Dombey* seemed anti-climactic' (Ford, p. 59).

[7] In his chapter, 'Two Angels of Death' (Welsh, pp. 180-95), Welsh presents Florence Dombey and Agnes Wickfield in the context of nineteenth-century allegorical representations of the female angel of death. This presentation is a prelude to the argument that 'sexuality in a heroine biologically implies the hero's death as an individual' (p. 210). Thus, the strategy of Dickens and his contemporaries was 'to domesticate death, to wrest it from the city and take it in by the fireside' (p.

212). As a result, Welsh concludes, 'the institution of marriage and the institution of the novel deserve credit for so adroitly converting the sexual relation that implies death into a relation that saves from death' (p. 228). Of course, Florence as a representative of woman's regenerative power can produce another Little Paul; in Bataille's terms, 'Reproduction leads to the discontinuity of beings, but brings into play their continuity; that is to say, it is intimately linked with death' (Bataille, p. 13).

[8] As I argue in my article on the rhetoric of soliloquy, Dickens is particularly adept at utilising structural and imagistic parallelism at moments that transcend closure. The concluding words of *A Tale of Two Cities* speak this point eloquently, creating foreshadowing that crosses the boundaries of time and consciousness: 'It is a far, far better thing I do than I have ever done; it is a far, far better rest that I go to than I have ever known' (*A Tale of Two Cities,* p. 403).

[9] Kucich cites the Little Red Riding Hood anecdote as taken from Dickens' short story, 'A Christmas Tree' (Kucich, 'Death Worship', p. 71 note 20). He goes on to discuss *The Old Curiosity Shop*'s 'explicit experience of violence' as a project that dramatises violation as eroticised death (p. 68). Mark Spilka, on the other hand, reads the text as releasing 'neurotic rather than erotic violation'. 'How else', he argues, 'can we explain such related phenomena as the cult called Love of Little Girls . . . or the increased popularity of child-prostitutes . . . ?' (See p. 175 of his article, 'On the Enrichment of Poor Monkeys by Myth and Dream; or, How Dickens Rousseauisticized and Pre-Freudianized Victorian Views of Childhood', in Cox, pp. 161-79.)

[10] Letters to and from Dickens during the months preceding and following Nell's death confirm his shared preoccupation with the death of this girl-child. Ford devotes an entire chapter to the Nell phenomenon, 'Little Nell: The Limits of Explanatory Criticism' (Ford, pp. 55-71).

[11] William Macready's letter of 25 January 1841 may be representative of this degree of feeling: 'This beautiful fiction comes too close upon what is miserably real to me [the death of his own daughter two months earlier] to enable me to taste that portion of pleasure, which we can often extract (and you so beautifully do) from reasoning on the effect of pain, when we feel it through the sufferings of others' (*Letters,* p. 193). Weinstein picks up on the recurrence of father-daughter relations in Dickens within a context of illicit sexuality (Weinstein, p. 32), noting that he is 'unable to abandon or endorse this fantasy-desire [of father/husbands]' (p. 39).

[12] Langbauer's article demonstrates that Dickens grounds erotics in woman—making *her* the seductress.

[13] Collins' introduction to 'Sikes and Nancy' describes how Dickens developed this last addition to his repertoire—now he revelled in its horror, passion and drama. His friends and family found such 'outright histrionic violence disquieting'—and he went on to become obsessed by it, to the point of jeopardising his health (Dickens, *The Public Readings,* pp. 465-71). We must not forget, either, that the murder of Nancy serves as a prelude to the pursuit and death of Sikes, rendered subjectively in the rewritten version. Thus, Dickens' most dramatic tie with his living audiences was also intimately linked on multiple levels with acts of dying.

[14] Of course, the charade does provoke Lord Steyne's intense admiration of Becky and foreshadows elements of the triangular confrontation scene that follows their interlude. DiBattista also argues persuasively that the Clytemnestra myth 'serves as a psychological and *historical* commentary on the unexamined delusions of the Victorian's sexual ideology' (DiBattista, p. 833). But both points simply confirm my assertion that Thackeray has moved our considerations to an intellectual plane.

[15] Another old patriarch's death deserves comparison here because it is so totally negated and anti-eroticised: Thackeray completely elides the death of Sir Pitt Crawley; it apparently occurs within the interstices of the text: 'there was a great hurry and bustle'; 'lights went about'; 'a boy on a pony went galloping off'—and then the Bute Crawleys arrive to ascertain that no one falsely lay claim to family property (*Vanity Fair,* pp. 390-1).

[16] Bledsoe's article makes a good case for the novel's careful balancing between 'Helen the self-styled middle-aged martyr' and 'Helen the sympathetic young wife' (Bledsoe, pp. 871-2), but she finally devolves into an embodiment of all pure but possessive women (p. 875). In this respect, she rather accurately reflects Thackeray's intense ambivalence about his mother. In contrast, Dickens tends to create split characters to represent his mother, e.g. Mrs Micawber and Miss Murdstone.

[17] Stewart's discussion of Colonel Newcome's death also suggests its affinities with Dickensian death scenes by raising the issue of sentimentality but then qualifying it with reference to contrivance and irony (Stewart, p. 132); in general, Stewart's study demonstrates how much less sentimental both of their death scenes are than is usually presumed. In this respect, Barickman *et al.* have not analysed the specific conjunction of death and the erotic when they too easily generalise about 'the eroticism that is diluted into sentimental rhetoric in Dickens' (Barickman *et al.,* p. 93).

[18] Mermaids and serpent-women, vampires and monsters blend angel and demon in Auerbach's discussion

of characters like Becky Sharp and Beatrix Castlewood (from Thackeray's *Henry Esmond*); see *Woman and the Demon,* especially pp. 88-101. The figures of angel and demon inform Auerbach's earlier studies of Florence Dombey and Maggie Tulliver as well; see her reprinted essays in *Romantic Imprisonment,* pp. 107-29 and 230-49. For his last completed novel, *Philip,* Thackeray was prepared to conjoin motherhood, self-sacrifice, and cannibalism within his opening pages (*Philip,* p. 106).

Works Cited

Auerbach, Nina, *Romantic Imprisonment: Women and Other Glorified Outcasts* (New York: Columbia University Press, 1985).

Auerbach, Nina, *Woman and the Demon: The Life of a Victorian Myth* (Cambridge, Massachusetts: Harvard University Press, 1982).

Barickman, Richard, Susan MacDonald, and Myra Stark, *Corrupt Relations: Dickens, Thackeray, Trollope, Collins and the Victorian Sexual System* (New York: Columbia University Press, 1982).

Bataille, Georges, *Death and Sensuality* (New York: Walker, 1965).

Bledsoe, Robert, '*Pendennis* and the Power of Sentimentality: A Study of Motherly Love', *PMLA,* vol. 91 (1976) pp. 871-83.

Cox, Don Richard (ed.) *Sexuality and Victorian Literature. Tennessee Studies in Literature,* vol. 27 (1984).

DiBattista, Maria, 'The Triumph of Clytemnestra: The Charades in *Vanity Fair*', *PMLA,* vol. 95 (1980) pp. 827-37.

Dickens, Charles, *Dombey and Son,* introduction by Raymond Williams (Harmondsworth: Penguin, 1970).

Dickens, Charles, *Great Expectations,* edited by Angus Calder (Harmondsworth: Penguin, 1965).

Dickens, Charles, *The Letters of Charles Dickens,* edited by Madeline House and Graham Storey, vol. 2: 1840-1841 (Oxford: Clarendon Press, 1969).

Dickens, Charles, *The Old Curiosity Shop,* introduced by Malcolm Andrews (Harmondsworth: Penguin, 1972).

Dickens, Charles, *Oliver Twist,* introduced by Angus Wilson (Harmondsworth: Penguin, 1966).

Dickens, Charles, *Our Mutual Friend,* edited by Stephen Gill (Harmondsworth: Penguin, 1971).

Dickens, Charles, *The Public Readings,* edited by Philip Collins (Oxford: Clarendon Press, 1983).

Dickens, Charles, *A Tale of Two Cities,* edited by George Woodcock (Harmondsworth: Penguin, 1970).

Eigner, Edwin, 'Death and the Gentleman: Charles Dickens as Elegiac Romancer', unpublished essay, 1985.

Eliot, George, *The Mill on the Floss,* edited by Gordon Haight (Boston: Houghton Mifflin, 1961).

Ford, George, *Dickens and His Readers: Aspects of Novel-Criticism Since 1836* (New York: Norton, 1965).

Foucault, Michel, *The History of Sexuality. Vol. 1: An Introduction,* translated by Robert Hurley (New York: Random House, 1978).

Gallagher, Catherine, and Thomas Laqueur (eds) *The Making of the Modern Body: Sexuality and Society in the Nineteenth Century* (Berkeley: University of California Press, 1987).

Glover, Stephen, 'What Are the Wild Waves Saying'. Lyrics by Joseph Edwards Carpenter (London: Robert Cocks, [1850]).

Hardy, Thomas, *Jude the Obscure,* edited by Irving Howe (Boston: Houghton Mifflin, 1965).

Kincaid, James, 'Dickens, Discourse Analysis, and the Sexuality of the Child', MLA Convention, Chicago, 30 December 1985.

Kucich, John, 'Death Worship among the Victorians: *The Old Curiosity Shop*', *PMLA,* vol. 95 (1980) pp. 58-72.

Kucich, John, *Excess and Restraint in the Novels of Charles Dickens* (Athens: University of Georgia Press, 1981).

Langbauer, Laurie, 'Dickens's Streetwalkers: Women and the Forms of Romance', *English Literary History,* vol. 53 (1986) pp. 411-31.

MacKay, Carol Hanbery, 'The Rhetoric of Soliloquy in *The French Revolution* and *A Tale of Two Cities*', *Dickens Studies Annual,* vol. 12 (1983) pp. 197-207.

Polhemus, Robert. 'The Burning of Miss Havisham: The Oedipal Dickens and the Victorian Incestual Bias.' MLA Convention. New York, 29 Dec. 1986.

Shakespeare, William, *Romeo and Juliet,* in John E. Hankins (ed.) *The Complete Works* (New York: Viking, 1969) pp. 855-94.

Stewart, Garrett, *Death Sentences: Styles of Dying in British Fiction* (Cambridge, Massachusetts: Harvard University Press, 1984).

Stewart, Garrett, 'The Secret Life of Death in Dickens', *Dickens Studies Annual,* vol. 11 (1983) pp. 177-207.

Thackeray, William Makepeace, *Vanity Fair: A Novel Without a Hero,* edited by Geoffrey and Kathleen Tillotson (Boston: Houghton Mifflin, 1963).

Thackeray, William Makepeace, *The Newcomes* (London: Smith, Elder, 1878).

Thackeray, William Makepeace, *Pendennis* (London: Smith, Elder, 1878).

Thackeray, William Makepeace, *Philip* (London: Smith, Elder, 1879).

Trollope, Anthony, *Barchester Towers,* introduced by Robin Gilmour (Harmondsworth: Penguin, 1983).

Vicinus, Martha (ed.) *A Widening Sphere: Changing Roles of Victorian Women* (Bloomington: Indiana University Press, 1977).

Weinstein, Philip M., *The Semantics of Desire: Changing Models of Identity from Dickens to Joyce* (Princeton: Princeton University Press, 1984).

Welsh, Alexander *The City of Dickens* (Oxford: Clarendon Press, 1971).

FEMINIST PERSPECTIVES

Elisabeth Bronfen (essay date 1992)

SOURCE: "Necromancy, or Closing the Crack on the Gravestone," in *Over Her Dead Body: Death, Feminity, and the Aesthetic,* Manchester University Press, 1992, pp. 291-323.

[*In the following excerpt, focusing on Wilkie Collins'* The Woman in White *and Emily Brontë's* Wuthering Heights, *Bronfen explores how the disrupting presence of the revenant—one who returns from death—poses questions concerning identity and the nature of death.*]

> If we could be sure of the difference between the determinable and the undeterminable, the undeterminable would be comprehended within the determinable. What is undecidable is whether a thing is decidable or not. *Barbara Johnson*

Certainly one of the more perturbing Victorian examples of the interstice between feminine speech and death is Robert Browning's poetic rendition of the Roman trial and execution in 1698 of Guido Franchescini, *The Ring and the Book* (1869). The accused nobleman had stabbed his wife's adoptive mother and father and then inflicted twenty-two dagger wounds on his wife Pompilia herself, five of them deadly. He claimed she had committed adultery with the priest Caponsacchi, who had assisted her in her unsuccessful flight from his house eight months earlier. The Roman court had allowed Pompilia to return to her parents' house, where she gave birth to a son two weeks prior to the event of her husband's assault, though it had left the verdict dangerously unclear, with neither party guilty nor a divorce granted. On her dying bed Pompilia, about to fall completely silent, articulates her lack of a public voice by accusing the court as it documents her testimony, 'Oh yes, patient this long while / Listening and Understanding, I am sure! / Four days ago, when I was sound and well / And like to live, no one would understand' (VII, 906-9). If Guido's fatal assault on his wife's body signifies an effort to put an end to a case the court left undecided, death also produces a moment of transition in which everything is called into question. The sheer materiality of Pompilia's body liminally suspended between life and death, the threat of its irrevocable absence, lets her pose as a hermeneutic task and serve as the site of its truth.[1]

Browning's text records the way this dying body provokes discrepant explanatory narratives before its actual death for although the facts of the case are clear, closure can be put on the disruption death causes only when the right interpretation engenders the establishment of a new order; when the somatic closure, the body safely interred beneath the earth, corresponds to a semiotic closure, the case's 'truth . . . grasped and gained' (I, 471). Browning records narratives that defend Guido for having saved his honour, fought for his property and executed his husband's rights along with those that defend Pompilia's purity, invoking her despair due to her husband's cruelty and due to her own motherhood. These recounts hover between reading the husband's murder as 'vindictive jealousy' or 'justified revenge' and the wife's flight as the gesture of 'a saint, a martyr' or 'an adulteress'. They also use her murder to debate the status of marriage, the deficiency of the Roman legal system and the crisis in belief into which Christianity had fallen.

Leaving aside issues I have already discussed—Pompilia as the object of a financial exchange between parents and husband, her marriage as a form of death with real death her desired apotheosis, her sacrificial death as the sign of her purity with her blood 'washing the parchment white' (VII, 1781), her union with her forbidden beloved Caponsacchi in heaven—I point to the representation of the dying Pompilia as a structural paragon of the themes to be discussed in this chapter. For the 'one beauty more' of her story is that on the fatal night she 'simulated death . . . obtained herself a respite, four days' grace / Whereby she told her story to the world' (IX, 1421-2), embodied 'the miracle of continued life'. Not only does the public listen to her precisely because she is dying, not only does her impending death imbue the search for the correct representation of her death with urgency, but death restrained authorises the truthfulness of her speech and the idea that truth can be found even if only over a dying feminine body. The public claims, 'Confession of the moribund is true' (IV, 1478). Pompilia seeks time not simply 'to confess and get her own soul saved— / But time to make the truth apparent . . . lest men should believe a lie' (IV, 1428-30). She uses the knowledge of impending death to fashion her story into its final version and in so doing she can control her public representation after her death, even if she could not design her existence as a living woman.

Pompilia's dying body and its generation of solutions to the 'mystery of the murder' is paradigmatic in two ways. The disruption that death incites must be resolved in a semiotic as well as a physical sense; the deceased and her story must receive a stable meaning even as the grave is closed to assure that the process of mourning is complete. But narratives aimed at solving the ambivalence death poses also emerge from the site of liminality, emerge precisely because Pompilia is a kind of revenant, so that representations seem inextricable from the resurrection of the dead. Guido in fact emphasises that Pompilia speaks as her own uncanny double: 'she too must shimmer through the gloom o'the grave . . . o'the death-bed . . . Tell her own story her own way, and turn / My plausibility to nothingness! . . . Four whole extravagant impossible days . . . Had she been found dead as I left her dead / I should have told a tale brooked no reply' (XI, 1680-703).

Resurrection is also a stake on the narrative level of Browning's poem. Though Pope Innocent XII closes the case by affixing to Guido the signifier 'guilty,' and to Pompilia the signifiers 'perfect in whiteness', he admits that 'truth, nowhere, lies yet everywhere . . . evolvable from the whole' (X, 228-30). A fixed representation, though grounded on disjunctions, emerges from their elimination. Browning's narrator supports the Pope's verdict that while each individual testimony contains falsehood the synthesis art presents 'may tell a truth obliquely' (XII, 856), yet his text is also explicitly uncanny. For at the start of the narration Browning describes his poetic gesture as a reopening of the exchange between the living and the dead, 'the life in me abolished the death of things . . . as then and there acted itself over again once more / The tragic piece' (I, 520-3). Not only does this imply an analogy between Pompilia's desire to speak as a means of abolishing her death for four days. It also suggests that with the resurrected dead, the narrative discrepancies, which the Pope's final reading buried along with the bodies of the husband and wife, return as well. This raises the question whether symbolic replacement of the dead body in the form of gravestone inscriptions and narrative documentation truly produces a canny representation or whether the representational process doesn't irrevocably return to uncanny difference, by returning the dead back to the living.

Pompilia is the crux of a mystery story precisely because she is a revenant and as such figures as a nodal point in two distinct though enmeshed plots—that of detection and that of mourning. If the living woman is unstable because ambivalent in her meaning, seemingly dissimulating (adulteress, saint, both, neither), her death affords somatic fixture, resolves the lies and intrigues with which her existence was inscribed. It figures as an enigma whose solution implies a second semiotic fixture, the binding of a univocal signifer to the signified body. If the living woman threatens that truth is nowhere, a reading of her death allows truth obliquely to emerge at the hands of the survivors. Dressed in the solution imposed from outside (the Pope's, the poet's), the dead Pompilia confirms that in a world of disjunctions and lies, truth can be found. Her dying body is in fact transmitted as its incarnated emblem, the martyred saint whose death speaks her truth and thus truth *per se*.

Yet the explanation of her murder not only solves the meaning of her story retrospectively by translating the disjunction her femininity traced into a stable figure, 'perfect in whiteness'. Rather, in that the detective story traces the uncovering of hidden facts about an event of death, hidden truths about characters' motivations in relation to death, what it in fact must solve is death itself.[2] The dead woman who remains and in so doing engenders narratives, functions as a body at which death is once again coupled to the other central enigma of western cultural representation—femininity. The solution of her death is a form of documenting both of these unknowns. The dead woman, embodying a secret, harbours a truth others want and since the dead body is feminine, with death and femininity metonymies of each other, the condensation of the two allows one and the same gesture to uncover a stable, determinate answer for this double enigma.

As Todorov notes, detective fiction tells two stories, the story of the crime and the story of the investigation. As such it depicts two murders, the first committed by the actual murderer, the second by the pure and unpunishable murderer, the detective.[3] In the texts to be discussed—Wilkie Collins' *The Woman in White* (1859-60), Emily Brontë's *Wuthering Heights* (1847) and Bram Stoker's *Dracula* (1897)—the duality of these two plots is such that two events collapse. Unearthing the answer posed by a woman's death becomes coterminous with placing the dead feminine body into the earth. A corpse spurs on the urge to detect missing facts with death explained by virtue of a reconstruction of the events—the doubled narrative imitating the uncanny position of the dead / remaining woman. Once her death has been explained the corpse can lie peacefully, the end of the narrative double plot equal to the end of her revenant position. The divided woman poses questions which are resolved as her division is undone, as the uncanny double is transformed into the canny division between buried corpse and transmitted emblem. By solving the murder, the detecting survivors can re-establish the illusory belief that they have expelled the uncanny difference that woman's duplicity and death's disjunction traced in their lives. If in the last chapter I discussed the feminine position as one posed between bride and dead girl, I will now turn to the masculine position as that of the mourner as detective.

In that each of these women, in the guise of the double, preserves a corpse (literally as vampire woman or phantom, figurally by virtue of resemblance), each stages the uncanny. As harbingers of death the double incarnates the end of bodily existence, figures ephemerality and contradicts notions of wholeness and uniqueness due to the division of the self it traces, even as the double also incarnates the notion of endless preservation of the body, the beginning of immaterial existence. The revenant, occupying the interstice between two forms of existence—a celebration and a triumph over death—calls forth two forms of anxiety, i.e. the anxiety that death is finitude and the anxiety that death may not be the end. Because the heroines are revenants of sorts, because their appearance deceives, they function as living tropes for the notion that a secret, a truth, lies hidden beneath the surface of the body. They embody the site of two disjunctions—a dead body remaining in the guise of a living one, a feminine body dissimulating an identity which hides her true being—and both ambivalences are brought to rest when, in the instance of their second death, ambivalent doubleness is brought into a transparent relation of signifier and signified (the dead body no longer remains, the woman's appearance no longer dissimulates a false identity). The logic these narratives unfold is that to attribute a fixed meaning to a woman, to solve the mystery of her duplicity is coterminous with killing her, so that her death can be read in part as a trope for the fatality with which any hermeneutic enterprise is inscribed. The achievement of a stable semiotic meaning, which excludes semantic difference and ambivalence, is debated over the establishment of another stable division—that between the living and the dead.

Precisely because it involves two deaths, however, the detective plot can be seen analogous to another plot beginning in death—the trajectory of the mourning process. For the purpose of mourning is to kill the dead by ceasing to reanimate psychically a body physically absent; by withdrawing one's libidinal investment in a lost love object, forgetting or preserving it as dead.[4] While the solution of the detective plot is to kill the 'dead' woman twice by virtue of deciphering and affixing a truth to her duplicitous body, the solution of a successful mourning plot is to kill the lost woman psychically preserved as a phantom, by virtue of decathexis. The solution of death that both detection and mourning provide in part serves to avert the idea that the death of another in fact threateningly signifies the presence of death in oneself. Mourning is a way to repress the threatening realisation that death can never be solved except in the form of one's own demise. Mourning allows one to retrieve those parts of the investment made in the lost object.[5]

Before the detection plot has found its end, however, those related to the murdered body are like mourners, the corpse not yet safely beneath the graveplate, the survivors not yet severed from the dead, the detecting survivors like the revenant in liminality. Only the psychic solution (successful disinvestment of the dead beloved) and the hermeneutic solution (successful deciphering of the enigma) arrests an uncanny body into a recuperated stable division between living and dead, between fluidity of appearance and fixed answer. Mourning requires a participation of the living in the mortuary state of the deceased. A process of mental disintegration precipitates the closure of the case which occurs when society triumphs over death and recovers its peace by assuring itself that the dead are univocally beyond or beneath the worldly realm.[6]

The newly dead are conceived of as double, simultaneously present in the tomb and in some spiritual realms.[7] In this liminal position they are regarded as dangerous and polluted because they appear between all pure classifications and unambiguous concepts.[8] The social group has a vested interest in hastening along the liberation of the soul from the corpse in order to eliminate the impurity and duplicity of the decomposing body. Mourning and funeral rites were originally determined by decomposition and by the desire to protect the living and assure the double's liberation. They aimed at preserving of the corpse only the bones or replacing it by a symbolic substitute—in the form of an effigy or a gravestone.

Vampires in turn were understood as doubles that were not successfully delivered from the corpse, as animated corpses preserved in the dangerous liminal realm, as moments of failed decomposition that consequently also meant an arrestation of decathexis on the part of the mourners.[9] The intact corpse of the revenant, artificially reanimated, has a correlative in the Christian saint, immune to decay. A rational explanation for the image of the vampire in folklore is that it was merely an exhumed dead body, monstrously threatening because still undergoing a process of decomposition. The killing of the revenant, a second killing of a corpse, a second burial, indicates the end of mourning and marks an attempt to bind the corpse in place, so as to protect the living from the dead. Revenant tales feed off the notion that after death the body has a second destructive life, that while it is decomposing, it is still changing, and still involved in the world. If they remain, the dead are a potential source of danger because death is thought to come from the dead body. The second killing puts an end to this double's life by holding the dead body in one place and rendering it inert, incapable of undergoing further changes.

Paul Barber reads the revenant as a trope for the fear of contagion transmitted by the corpse and the destabilisation of notions of the intact body that decomposition figures.[10] He distinguishes between two versions of the corpse—the monster or bad corpse (the body in the early stages of decomposition), and the good corpse (the body successfully decayed into harmless bones). In that the first body is in the liminal position, it corresponds to that of the premarital bride, dangerous due to her indefinite state, while the good corpse implies the canny rigidity of mature femininity. The fear of the somatically contagious and semiotically indeterminate revenant provokes a desire to neutralise the corpse; to 'kill' it a second time; to solve its death and preserve not the body but its appearance; to replace the dead body double (the revenant that in decomposing keeps changing, the phantom that inhabits the mourner's mental realm), with a fixed, unchanging form of double, a grave inscription, unambiguous, marking a clear distinction between living and dead. A protection of the living from the dead requires repetition not on the indexic/somatic but on the arbitrary/symbolic level. It prescribes a translation from body to skeleton, from unconscious memory representations to culturally controlled ones.

The deceased is no longer dangerous when its body stops undergoing change, stabilised into its last ossified state and when its image has receded and stops entering the survivor's dreams and memories, stabilised into a commemorative representation. To delineate how the feminine revenant serves as a trope for the conceptual enmeshment of mourning, detection and representation, I will problematise the notion that a stable closure of the crack the revenant opens is achieved through the second killing. Though the dangerously fluid revenant's body which dissimulates death may find some stability in the written documentation and gravestone ornaments meant to replace it, the rhetoric of any pictorial or textual representation is also based on difference and semantic indeterminacy or duplicity and transforms into a disturbing double in its own right. Finally, one can define the vampire as 'a dead body that appears to be dead except that it doesn't decay' so as to conjoin it to my definition of the hysteric as being someone whose appearance or self-representation is other than she in fact truly is. In these texts the heroine's chosen or induced duplicity is such that she appears as dead, but without a body to prove her death, so that the revenant emerges as yet another aspect of the hysteric's rhetoric of dissimulation.

The exposition of *The Woman in White* presents a woman bearing a secret, socially dead because buried alive in an insane asylum to procure her silence, literally dying of a heart disease, as she escapes her confinement and returns to the world of the living. As Walter Hartright walks home along the lonely road to London at the 'dead of the night', about to embark for Cumberland to begin work as a drawing master for the daughters of Mr Fairlie, the 'touch of a hand laid lightly and suddenly' on his shoulder from behind petrifies him 'from head to foot' (47). What he sees as he turns instantly, 'with my fingers tightening round the handle of my stick', is an apparition which 'seriously startled' him because of the suddenness of its appearance, 'as if it had sprung out of the earth or dropped from the heaven' and because of its extraordinary guise—'a solitary Woman, dressed from head to foot in white garments'. Like Medusa, she fascinates and terrifies, because her femininity is not only doubly encoded but also resonates death. She is thought to emerge from the beyond (angel) or beneath (demon), while the whiteness of her clothes refers simultaneously to a bridal gown or a shroud. The touch of her hand laid with 'a sudden gentle stealthiness' elicits a sexual response. He notes it was a 'cold hand' when he 'removed it with mine', and excuses himself by claiming 'I was young . . . the hand which touched me was a woman's' (50). The woman's touch, however, also effects a death-like experience in the touched masculine body—'in one moment every drop of blood in my body was brought to a stop'.[11]

The feminine figure appears at precisely the moment when Walter wonders 'what the Cumberland young ladies would look like.' Her uncanny touch initiates a first enigma, which in turn generates a plethora of secrets and detections that propel this tale of sensation and mystery but which itself remains undecided even after the diverse plots and conspiracies have been resolved. This nocturnal walk towards London with a woman 'whose name, whose character, whose story, whose objects in life, whose very presence by my side, at that moment, were fathomless mysteries to me', arouses a sensation in Walter which is so perturbing because strangely undefined. An erotic desire is displaced on to a curiosity to penetrate her social identity, 'to lift the veil that hung between this woman and me' (52). Yet the eroticised form of detective desire further displaces the fact that the initial sensation was one of death. What is left open is whether the plot of detection arising from this uncanny encounter is erotically encoded merely to displace the anxiety of death her touch produced or precisely to occlude a forbidden desire for the death this woman seemingly incarnates.

A second indeterminacy is maintained throughout Collins's text, namely the fact that along with Walter's motivation, the feminine object of his desire is not entirely clear. The entire narrative is constructed around the seeming coincidence that one of the Cumberland ladies, Laura Fairlie, looks like the mysterious woman in white, who withholds her identity, who preserves her secret—Anne Catherick. Even before Walter has seen the woman he will eventually marry and for whose sake he undertakes the dangerous and cumbersome task of detection, the other woman has inscribed herself in his imaginary register. She disturbs his drawing and his reading and is the object of his first conversation with Laura's companion Marion. Given the extraordinary physical and psychic similarity between Anne and Laura (who herself is 'rather nervous and sensitive' (63)), the question Collins raises is whether Walter doesn't in fact love Anne in Laura. Within such a scenario, his wife serves as the repetition and displacement of the startling woman, and the domestic happiness repeatedly invoked as the context from which he writes veils the fact that his initial object of desire was the death-like Anne not the bride Laura. Walter desires Laura precisely because she recalls the other woman who, insane and dying, is an impossible choice, with his choice of Laura denying even as it affirms that what initiated desire in him was this impossible woman on the edge of death. That the ambivalent desire for Laura veils the desire for Anne as she represents the trauma of a death sensation, finds implicit articulation in the first description Walter gives of Laura. He argues that the 'mystery which underlies the beauty of women', of which Laura's is the paragon, is such that it touches sympathies other than the charm the senses feel, that it is the 'visionary nurseling' of the viewer's 'fancy'. Yet his first sight of Laura is mingled with a sensation that 'troubled and perplexed' him, with the impression of 'something wanting'. Significantly the source of this lack is undetermined—'At one time it seemed like something wanting in *her:* at another, like something wanting in myself.' Like Georgiana's birthmark it articulates itself in a contradictory manner, a sense of incompleteness troubling the harmony and charm of her face, eluding his discovery (77).

Only when Marion reads the part of Mrs Fairlie's letter pertaining to the accidental resemblance between Anne and her daughter can Walter affix a signifier to the 'something wanting', namely that of 'ominous likeness'. More importantly, only when looking down at Laura from a window, while she, dressed in white, walks in the moonlight, when he sees her *as* 'the living image . . . of the woman in white', (the word living implying he fancied the original as a dead image), is Walter chilled again by a 'thrill of the same feeling which ran through me when the touch was laid upon my shoulder on the lonely high-road' (86). While Laura's type of beauty can claim kin with the 'deeper mystery in our souls' (76), in her function as Anne's double she induces those other charms which Walter feels with the senses.

Solving the uncanny relation of ominous likeness between these two women by cleanly severing the one from the other may as much involve a foreclosure of the necrophilic thrill of the senses that the one feminine figure of death evokes, as it involves the social restitution of the other. While Walter can allow himself to want woman as the visionary nurseling of his fancy, he must repress his desire for woman as an uncanny apparition, who thrills him even as she must be forbidden precisely because she evokes the presence of death in life, because she represents what lies beneath the veil of Laura's bright, innocent beauty, because she enacts the decaying body not the beautiful body masking its mortality. As Walter calls out 'let me lose the impression again as soon as possible. Call her in', he refers to the twofold threat this instance of uncanny doubling poses. He literally sees that Laura is divided, is more and other than her fair, sweet and simple appearance, and he figurally sees her as a double of Anne. If to see one's double is a harbinger of death, the twist Collins gives to this folklore motif is that Laura does indeed herald Anne's death. She will herself experience a form of death due to this duplicity, even as she will also be the living image that death has not taken place.

From the moment of her escape from the asylum Anne traces the figure of death in more than one sense. Given that she appears only to disappear and reappear again elsewhere, as the material bearer of a secret, as elusive in body as the truth she can not tell, incessantly receding from the grasp of those who seek her until death fixes her in place, she enacts the figure of *aphanisis;* a paragon of the rhetoric of death. She is also the image Walter compulsively returns to in his fantasies, whereby compulsive repetition functions as another sign of the death drive. She causes difference to emerge in Walter's imaginary relation with Laura because speaking of Miss Fairlie repeatedly raises the memory of Anne Catherick, 'setting her between us like a fatality that it was hopeless to avoid' (97). When Marion trusts Walter she does so because of his conduct towards 'that unhappy woman'; when she asks him to leave because Laura is engaged she appeals to the same honest, manly consideration for his pupil which he had once showed to 'the stranger and the outcast'. The mention of Sir Percival Glyde as Laura's betrothed reinvokes 'again, and yet again, the woman in white. There *was* fatality in it' (100). His farewell from his mother and sister are irrevocably connected with 'that other memory of the moonlight walk', and even as he leaves England with the image of Laura Fairlie 'a memory of the past', the name of Anne Catherick remains present, 'pronounced behind him as he got into the boat' (205).

In a less rhetorical and a more literal sense, Anne appears and fades in Laura's proximity as an overdetermined figure of death. She is literally dying and shows Laura what she will look like when death sets in. Her letter warning her of Sir Percival's fiendish nature beneath his fair appearance implies that Laura's 'beautiful white silk dress' and bridal veil could by virtue of marriage turn into a shroud, and in so doing confirms the bride's own nervous premonitions. Her proclivity toward Mrs Fairlie's grave and her choice to wear only white lets her appearance be interpreted by spectators such as the schoolboy Jacob Postlewaite as that not merely of a ghost but 't' ghaist of Mistress Fairlie'. The brilliant turn on which the other villain Count Fosco's masterful death plot hinges is that by turning the bride Laura into the dead girl Anne, the former will become her own ghost, will literally repeat at her own body what the schoolboy saw. As Laura's double, then, Anne is a figure of death in life on several scores—she literally signifies a dying body, her repeated appearance is a trope for fatality and, though she means to warn against danger, she will be the concrete instrument by which Laura's figural burial succeeds, by which the trope becomes materialised reality.

Significantly this image of the 'ghost of Miss Fairlie' standing beside the marble cross over Mrs Fairlie's grave repeatedly draws Walter to the graveyard, first to meet Anne a second and last time and then, upon his return to England, to see her double, the 'dead' Laura. At the grave Walter himself consciously reverses the relation between the two half-sisters, sees not Anne in Laura, but 'Miss Fairlie's likeness in Anne Catherick'. Even more startling, analogous to the thrill he felt standing at the window, is the dissimilarity this likeness articulates, because it imposes the hateful thought that if 'ever sorrow and suffering set their profaning mark on the youth and beauty' of Laura, the two would be 'the living reflections of one another' (120). Given that he never fancies what Anne would look like in health, his interest is clearly in the common denominator he finds in the process of dying. What startles him is not merely the issue of likeness but the way likeness points to the figure of death. The effect of this body double is contrary to that of the gravestone. Rather than indicating the presence of the dead in the beyond she represents uncanny difference, as a figure of death, in the realm of the living.[12]

Anne's own desire for death articulates itself in her longing to clean Mrs Fairlie's grave, to whose memory she clings as the one kind person in her youth. Kissing the gravestone, she expresses the wish to die so as to 'be hidden and at rest with *you*' (127), with death understood as a closure of the gap, as the release from tension. It is precisely this desire which Fosco, having overheard Anne repeat it to Laura, will fulfil as he exchanges the identities of the two women, so that his plot merely materialises what the mentally unbalanced Anne enacts and fancies. Walter's and later Laura's attraction to Anne, nominally because she harbours the secret of Glyde's past which could destroy him, draws both towards the realm of the dead. Walter meets this woman a second time at an equally lonely, nocturnal site, 'a grave between us, the dead about us' (119). When Laura is faced with her double, with the 'sight of her own face in the glass after a long illness', she too experiences a death-like shock, incapable of speaking for the moment. What she elicits from Anne is, however, not the secret that would empower her against Glyde but rather the madwoman's fantasies about being buried with her mother, to 'wake at her side, when the angel's trumpet sounds, and the graves give up their dead at the resurrection' (302). Like Walter, Laura is startled not only at the likeness between herself and a dying woman but also because this sight is duplicated by a spoken representation of death and its encroachment on life—'I trembled from head to foot—it was so horrible to hear her.'

As Walter's later investigation shows, Anne serves as the embodiment of two enigmas—of dying and of Sir Percival's secret. Yet while she has a true knowledge of dying, the truth of Glyde's illegitimacy is only in her mother's possession and inaccessible to her. In a manner fatal to her, she mimicks possessing the truth of his past, has the signifier (her mother's threat to expose Sir Percival's secret) but not the signified. Given that the answers Walter and Laura receive from her only pertain to her fantasies of death and resurrection, Collins's narrative implies that the search for a truth to the mystery of a man's past as it relates to a woman's future materialises another desire—the search for a contact with those on the edge of death, with the fantasy of Christian resurrection as a counter-image to that of the socially-dead returned, the revenant. Under the influence of Walter and Laura's contact with Anne even the reasonable Marion, supposedly beyond superstition, repeatedly dreams of death in the form of the representation of Walter 'kneeling by a tomb of white marble', and the shadow of a veiled woman, or 'the veiled woman rising out of the grave and waiting by his side' (296, 310). This dream representation connects the schoolboy's fanciful vision with Anne's fantasies of resurrection and will, owing to Fosco's brilliant creation of death and resurrection, find a materialised representative in Laura's body. In the figure of the woman in white, haunting the fantasies of all those involved with her, death is given a representation before its occurrence and preserved even after the event, because the revenant remains in a double guise—in the body of the living-dead Laura and in the survivors' memory of Anne.

Though the narrative privileges Walter's relation to this revenant, Anne continues to appear and disappear even after he has left England. By dissimulating that she could disclose a powerful secret she poses as a threat to Glyde and Fosco while figuring the sign of hope for the two sisters. By simulating a form of living death, she serves as a source of inspiration for the villains and a source of anxiety for Laura and Marion. For the two sisters, catching Anne's incessantly eluding body means disclosing the secret it bears, while for the two villains tracing Anne means preserving the secret. While she haunts in the double guise of a harbinger of death and a bearer of a secret, her detection offers Fosco the possibility of yet another form of double plot, in which mourning hides an economic speculation. Because Laura's sole heir is her husband, the conspiracy he devises is such that Glyde can pay his bills with his wife's fictional death.

For the three detectives in the narrative, Marion, Walter and Fosco, disclosure is meant either to ward off death, to distance death from life or to create it in life. Marion writes in her diary, spurred on by 'a fear beyond all other fears', the fear of impending death. Walter collects written narratives from all those involved owing to the desire to put closure on the event of death that has occurred. Fosco traces Anne in order to create a death artificially, to give a fatal fixture to the doubleness her body staged. Having been tricked into entering his London home, Anne dies of a heart attack under the false name Laura Glyde and is buried ironically where she wished, in the grave with Mrs Fairlie, while Laura, passed off as Anne Catterick, is returned to the asylum. Although the enigma she falsely signified, Glyde's past, seems to be buried with her body, the other, death, is precisely what does not remain under ground, for in the body of Laura, Anne continues to haunt until the headstone inscription has been undone, fixing the ghost of Anne in place and separating a living from a dead woman.

There are, then, two sets of doubles. Firstly, the somatic double of one woman by another resulting in a fatal exchange which leaves Laura socially dead, psychically numb and without a will of her own. Secondly, two semiotic doubles, the gravestone inscribed 'Sacred to the memory of Laura, Lady Glyde', which restitutes her in the beyond as well as Walter's collection of narratives meant to undo the false inscription and give Laura a second symbolic birth. While the first leaves death present in life, the second marks an effort to sever death from life cleanly.

Upon his hearing of Laura's death Walter is drawn to her grave, yet as he approaches he recalls not only his lost beloved but also that this was the site where he watched 'for the coming of the woman in white', so that once again the one woman covers the other, the knowledge of the disappearance of the former recalling the uncanny apparition of the latter. The headstone inscription is the sema replacing the absent soma, a form of biography 'which told the story of her life and death', meant to preserve the individual in the collective memory. Michel Serres notes that the designation of the gravestone *ci-gît,* 'here lies', generalises and combines two other designations of place—'subject' (*subjacere*) as something lying or thrown beneath and 'object' (*objacere*) as something thrown before. While the designation 'here lies' is self-reflexive, designs and stabilises the sense of place in that the tombstone has death define the concept of 'here', the other two designations demand a missing reference. They raise questions such as, placed before or beneath whom, beneath what, in relation to whom, to what, to where? The object before and the subject beneath are non-referential, insisting on, requiring spacial fixture. In the form of the revenant this triadic issue of placement in reference to the site death marks is given a curious figuration, for the resuscitated dead body lies here, beneath the ground and is thrown before the founding mark of death, the tombstone; the subject (beneath) becomes the object (before). In relation to their reference to death, object and subject can be substituted for one another. The object (the double as image) becomes equivalent with the body returned, the subject resuscitated (the double as apparition or revenant).[13]

It is this triadic relation—an inscription of death marking the *here,* with a body split *beneath* and *before* this reference to death—which Collins represents in the *peripeteia* of his narrative. As Walter kneels by the tomb, wearily recalling his lost love—'I . . . closed my weary eyes on the earth around, on the light above. I let her come back to me'—a veiled woman approaches him. Analogously to the apparition at the crossroads, she takes possession of him 'body and soul'. Standing 'close to the inscription on the side of the pedestal . . . the black letters' she lifts her veil. Walter is faced with a superlatively uncanny moment, a multipled love object collapsing all points of reference into one site—Laura recalled in his memory, a headstone inscription 'Sacred to the memory of Laura, Lady Glyde' assuring her doubled restitution in the beyond; i.e. the same body beneath and thrown before him (subject collapsing with object), for 'Laura, Lady Glyde . . . was standing by the inscription, and was looking at me over the grave' (430f.). Like the apparition that initiated the plot, 'sprung out of the earth or dropped from the heaven', this Laura as figure of death in life marks the site where the two half-sisters can stand in for each other perfectly; where in an uncanny sense their difference collapses; where Laura as social subject/heiress and Anne as desired object/madwoman merge; where Walter can have both, just as, in reference to death, object/revenant (before) and subject/corpse (beneath) merge.

While Anne as Laura's double served as a harbinger of death, signified what Laura would look like dying, Laura as Anne's double signifies that death has only taken place in an uncanny sense, with a body beneath connected to its double before rather than beyond. By virtue of death exchangeable with Anne, Laura is forced to retrace the social and psychic death of her double, must duplicate the socially hidden, mad and dying Anne in the guise of the symbolically dead Laura, with a confused and weakened memory, without strength, without any will of her own, her mental faculties shaken and weakened. The fatal resemblance that had thrilled Walter earlier, as an idea only, is now by virtue of death realised—now 'a real and living resemblance which asserted itself before my own eyes' (454)—the subject become object.

Because Laura is symbolically designated as dead, none of her community will recognise her. Because she wears Anne's clothes, the director of the asylum accepts her back. Once she has, like her double, escaped, she strikes all others as a mad impostress who is dissimulating 'the living personality of the dead Lady Glyde' (434); an excessive figure of duplicity in that she dissimulates herself as dead and living alike. Though Walter claims that, unlike all the others who refuse to recognise Laura, no suspicion crossed his mind from the moment she lifed her veil, the scene of recognition can be interpreted in a more complex manner. If to lift the veil is understood as a cultural sign for the disclosure of truth, the truth Walter sees is not only that Laura is alive, in contradiction to the headstone, but that the beloved he invoked, with his head on the grave, and that means in relation to death, is precisely the uncanny merger of the two—the figure of fatality that had initially thrilled him; the feminine body which merges object (thrown before) and subject (thrown beneath) in its relation to death; the revenant. For significantly he affixes his claim of possession 'mine at last' to the description of a woman more like Anne than Miss Fairlie, 'Forlorn and disowned, sorely tried and sadly changed—her beauty faded, her mind clouded—robbed of her station in the world, of her place among living creatures' (435).

The mourning and the detection plot merge in such a way that the object of mourning must be exchanged, Anne's death acknowledged and Laura's life reconfirmed. Death is in this case literally solved when it is proved that it did not occur. The trajectory of the investigation is twofold. Firstly, there is the investigation of the conspiracy, discovering and convicting the guilty. Secondly, there is the denial that death has occurred by healing Laura's psychic/physical feebleness and by symbolically healing her social loss of place produced by the false headstone inscription. The veil Laura lifts to expose an uncanny figure, the 'dead-alive', the Laura-Anne now united at one and the same body, must fall again. The dead girl once again becomes a bride, Mrs Hartright socially reaggregated. In the course of a dual social ritual, a second burial/birth and second marriage, the revenant is undone, the doubled body cleanly split into two separate beings. Until this solution has been found, however, the twofold revenant remains in the form of Laura impersonating Anne, and Anne mentally reanimated as the woman in white through whose mystery the way to the secret lies (475). The urgency to restore the one to the living is coterminous with restoring the other to death and both acts hinge on solving the secret that her first appearance in their midst heralded. The doubled bride/dead girl engenders two plots. The one an economic speculation of a husband fulfilled by virtue of dissimulating death, the other the spectacle of an uncanny resemblance transformed into a living trope for fatality. Both plots, however, use the likeness achieved by the double to articulate death in a manner where the literal and the rhetorical merge. The literal death of Anne evokes a conspiracy of dissimulation, where the dead body serves as instrument to victimise a second body into living death, while the rhetoric of the double as harbinger of death finds a 'living resemblance' when Laura equals the dead Anne.

In that sense Fosco's conspiracy is the acme of the chain of uncanny double events, a masterful creation of death in life, with the gravestone precisely not dividing the two. Indeed his plot uncannily blurs another opposition, that between life and art, when he compares his grand scheme to 'the modern Rembrandt' and suggests in his narrative testimony that the situation he created in life—the resurrection of the woman who was dead in the person of the woman who was living—might serve as model for the 'rising romance writers of England' (630). He takes particular pride in his function as the resurrectionist of the dead Anne in Laura and privileges this part of the conspiracy over the production, even if accidental, of Anne's real death. Solving Laura's fictional death also means resolving what was intertwined with her by Fosco's plot and by Walter's eroticised fancy, the ghostly figure of Anne, which, in Walter's words, 'has haunted these pages, as it haunted by life' (576). If Fosco turns death into an artwork, Anne even before her entanglement with Laura's story, served as a living emblem of death, so that her second burial implicitly buries the body that thrills as a figure of death in life.

The final opposition, then, is between two forms of creating signs out of death, between Fosco's creation of death in life and life out of death, with women's bodies his instruments, and Walter's retracing of events in the form of collecting and combining documents that are meant to double the absent like the headstone, and to restitute the absent not here but beyond. Both men represent themselves in relation to death with women's bodies as the site of this exchange. Fosco, the creator of a fatal conspiracy plot, employs the indexic/iconic mode of semiosis when he uses two women's bodies as his material, and turns his written confession of the crime into a remarkable creation meant to represent 'my own ingenuity, my own humanity' (632). Walter represents himself in the collection of testimonies as the one who resuscitated Laura, as the one who repeats and surpasses the maternal by giving a symbolic rebirth to his wife.

Installing the ritual of second burial, Walter calls together Laura's community before which he leads her back into the home from which she had left as bride and was later expelled as a madwoman. Before the collected audience he presents a public disclosure of the funereal conspiracy, outlines its course and the motives behind it, only to close the proceeding by informing those present of Sir Percival's death and his own marriage. Once the symbolic recognition has occurred, Laura is socially reaggregated. Raised by her husband's arm 'so that she was plainly visible to everyone in the room' the community responds by declaring her regained identity—'there she is, alive and hearty'. Though the grave is not reopened, the disjunction it signified is obliterated, the false inscription erased and replaced with Anne Catherick's name and date of death. This socially sanctioned burial of Anne resolves the uncanny likeness between the two half-sisters, and with it one aspect of death's rhetoric in life. It also fixes the ghost which had haunted Walter independently of Fosco's conspiracy plot, and resolves the uncanny desire for/anxiety about death, puts closure on his compulsive return to Anne as the figure whose sudden appearance had initially brought every drop of blood in his body to a stop. In the end he has successfully decathected Anne, by symbolically severing the woman whose appearance thrills from the innocent beauty of his restored wife. Second burial puts an end to the bad corpse of Anne's ghostly haunting figure and Laura's simulation of a revenant, by disjoining the bride's name from the tombstone and inscribing it so that it truly doubles a woman restituted in the beyond. In an analogous manner, Fosco's bad art, using women's bodies to materialise death and resurrection, to produce uncanny representations is exchanged for the stable art of narrative documentation that results in a recuperation of canny division.

Emily Brontë's *Wuthering Heights* also revolves around an imperfectly closed grave, owing to which the buried woman remains among the living. Though Catherine Earnshaw-Linton's body lies beneath the headstone bearing her name, she is repeatedly resurrected imaginarily by two survivors—by her lover Heathcliff and by her servant Nelly Dean. The former preserves her as a libidinal revenant, as part of his process of mourning, in fact literally loosens one side of her coffin to keep the borders of her burial site open. The latter preserves her as a representational revenant, with her narrative of the past events meant as a strategy by which to find a husband for her mistress's daughter Cathy Heathcliff. Because he is both the spectator of Heathcliff's mourning and the chosen addressee of Nelly's tale, Lockwood, the tenant at Thrushcross Grange, not only offers the narrative frame of the text

Haworth Parsonage, in Haworth Village, Yorkshire, England, home of the Brontë family

but is also the interstice between these two processes of resuscitation.

Visiting his landlord at Wuthering Heights he encounters two women liminally positioned and doubles of each other in so far as the daughter Cathy has exactly the same eyes and the same appearance of haughtiness as her mother Catherine. This daughter, left a disinherited widow by her husband's death, strikes Lockwood as 'being buried alive' (55) and herself remarks that she is locked in, forbidden to go beyond the garden wall. The mother, in turn, appears to him first in the form of a triple signature scratched repeatedly onto the ledge of a couch window where he is to spend the night, so that as he closes his eyes, 'white letters . . . as vivid as spectres' haunt him—'the air swarmed with Catherines' (61). Finding her writing covering the white blanks of nearly all the books stored in this bed-couch, an interest for the 'unknown Catherine's is kindled in Lockwood, and he reads bits of her autobiographical sketches until he falls asleep and is befallen by the intense horror of nightmare. The touch of a child's 'little, ice-cold hand' as it tries to get in through the window, wailing to be let in, complaining of its twenty-year waifdom, so maddens him with fear that he yells out in 'a frenzy of fright' (67). He had rubbed the ghost's wrist on the broken glass pane to keep it out, for the fancied touch is implicitly understood as a threat of death.

To Heathcliff, who responds to his cry, he describes her as a spectre 'who probably would have strangled me' (69). Yet not only the true nature of this ancestor but also Heathcliff's agony—he tears open the lattice, calls the absent Catherine to come in—leaves Lockwood faced with an enigma. While the daughter appears to him locked in and buried alive in her widowhood, the mother appears as an unburied ghost, locked out yet resuscitable over her signature and her diary. She further returns as the object of anxiety in Lockwood's nightmare visions and as the object of desire in Heathcliff's anguished mourning. While Lockwood tries to partition off the ghost and with it the presence of death, Heathcliff desires precisely to undo this division; with a desire for the return of his lost beloved and for death interchangeable.

Though it does not bring him death, Catherine's spectral appearance is one of the causes for Lockwood's five weeks of 'torture, tossing and sickness' (130). During this period of confinement she returns yet again, in Nelly's relation of the past, in which the plot of the spectral bride is used uncannily by the narrator to foster her listener's interest in 'that pretty girl-widow', accompanied by hanging her picture over his fireplace, hoping her story will induce him to 'win Mrs Heathcliff's heart' (346). Yet the opposite occurs, for in the same manner that he locked out the ghost of Catherine Linton, Lockwood shields himself from the 'fascination that lurks in Catherine Heathcliff's brilliant eyes', fearing an uncanny repetition, 'the daughter . . . a second edition of the mother' (191).

The frame Brontë's text sets up revolves around two instabilities—Heathcliff's mourning which preserves Catherine's ghost on earth and the daughter Cathy's widowhood, which has her liminally positioned between two marriages. The mourning and the detective plot are enmeshed in such a way that Heathcliff seeks to retain Catherine's ghost, seeks to view her corpse, to preserve the dead woman and with it death's presence in life. Lockwood seeks Nelly's narrative to decipher the fascination that the girl-widow, and the horror that the spectral-mother provoked. By not choosing the beautiful Cathy he also rejects the notion of death's presence in life. At the end of the plot, Heathcliff's death and Cathy's betrothal to her cousin affords fixture to these diametrically opposed responses to death. Heathcliff, who has "a strong faith in ghosts", designs his funeral in such a way that his partly opened coffin will face the opening he made on Catherine's, so that he can walk the earth after death united with his spectral bride. Lockwood's solution is to exclude all belief in ghosts, to divide death from life. He not only rejects the daughter but also denies, in the presence of the graves, that 'anyone could ever imagine unquiet slumbers for the sleepers in that quiet earth' (367).

Before the resolution of these two plots—of mourning and of marriage—the dead Catherine Linton remains present, however, in the shape of two doubles. On the one hand, she returns as the ghost her forbidden lover clings to, since he conceives of the dead woman as holding his soul. Their relation is that of a symbiotic imaginary duality, where the beloved other is the same as the self, present as long as the survivor exists, absent or lost only over his absence. Their love embodies a notion of oneness that allows for difference only in the sense of annihilation. On the other hand, the mother returns in the shape of her daughter who repeats her, but with a life-sustaining difference.[14] The fatality of repetition traced by the plot occurs not at the site of the body double but rather of the mourner. Heathcliff's death puts closure on the disruption or gap engendered by the mother's death. He severs the maternal revenant from the daughter by reuniting him with her instead. In that death is repeated at Heathcliff's body, Cathy is prevented from repeating her mother's self-destructive fate. Not unlike Laura, Cathy's possible identity with a dead girl is foreclosed by virtue of a second burial, which lets her in turn re-emerge as a bride. In contrast to Nelly's uncanny narration—in which both the ghost of the dead mother and the daughter as its double are invoked—the bride of Hareton Earnshaw can dispel any fear that fatality may be inscribed in her life because an arrestation of repetition has occured. With her second social birth (her second marriage) occurring over the mourning lover and the maternal spectres' expulsion, her new life will be undisturbed by revenants. Like Lockwood she can reject the uncanny double and with it the rhetoric death traces in life.[15]

The story Brontë frames with Lockwood's detective and Cathy's marriage plots, and which like these finds its resolution in Heathcliff's death, traces the diametrically opposed articulation of death's rhetoric in life: a symbiotic love which cannot be sustained within the 'castrative' subjugation and prohibitions that the social order requires but rather must annihilate itself. While Catherine enacts the hysteric's choice of self-destruction against the fear of being divided from her lover, shows the bride becoming a dead girl rather than dividing herself in childbirth, Heathcliff desires death as an undoing of the divisions and differences that sustain life and invokes the dead girl as his revenant bride. The teller of this uncanny tale, Nelly, hesitates between both attitudes—the expulsion of death from life and the embrace of death against life. Though her common sense assures her that the 'dead are at peace' she fears to be out at night. Though her aim is the closure marriage puts on death, her tale uncannily raises the dead to contradict the 'three headstones on the slope next the moor', whose sight so reassures Lockwood.

From the start she depicts Catherine's relation to Heathcliff as one placing them beyond the social law—implicitly forbidden because incestuous, explicitly because a misalliance between a landowner's daughter and a servant. The fact that they resist any separation implies a narcissistic bond which tries to obliterate difference by insisting on an absolute oneness or an absolute non-existence. Catherine explains to Nelly, she loves Heathcliff 'because he's more myself than I am', because whatever 'souls are made of, his and mine are the same,' because he is 'always in my mind . . . as my own being' (121f.). Though set against death as a force causing separations and divisions,

Catherine sees her love in light of two other aspects of death—a notion of eternal fixture against temporality ('my love . . . resembles the eternal rocks beneath') and the uncanny lack of position belonging to the revenant. Equating a marriage to Edgar with being in heaven, she recounts a dream in which she wept to come back to earth and was flung back on to the heath by the angels.

Against the wound to her narcissism which a division from Heathcliff implies, she retaliates in the form of self-destruction, much as Heathcliff responds to loss by directing his aggressive energies against others. During the period Edgar woos Catherine, she threatens to go with her illict lover, should her brother send him away. Her immediate response to Heathcliff's departure is a psychosomatic enactment of the unconscious knowledge of her non-existence. She falls into a delirium that turns into a fever, abstains from eating and becomes suicidal. Because the presence of her lover, who gives her the sense that she is whole, sustains her life, his absence makes death the object of her desire.

The hysteric knows that she is inscribed by a lack and seeks an alternate ego or double as representative of herself. Catherine, however, designs this double not as a version of herself but precisely in the shape of another. The hysteric's knowledge that she is no-body means that she spends her life in proximity to symptomatisation and annihilation—histrionic when she tries to capture the masculine gaze, suicidal when she loses it. In moments of transition, where a position of security is disrupted and transformed, she is confronted with the knowledge that she signifies a lack of being, with the real void of death located beneath all gestures of dissimulation that keep her within the symbolic order. Transitional moments such as marriage and motherhood are dangerous, and it is precisely these that bring on Catherine's fevers and suicidal desires.

Her very first separation from Heathcliff had occurred when a wounded ankle forced her to stay with the Lintons, only to learn at Thrushcross Grange the prohibitions and restrictions of the cultured social world. Her first exposure to social prohibitions was concomitant with not only a somatic wound but also a wound to her narcissism, embodied in the absence of her companion. Their second separation brings her into a proximity of real death (her fever), turns her into an agent of death (she fatally infects the Linton parents), and encourages her marriage, which is later described as a form of living death, her body a 'corpse' because its soul (Heathcliff) has been severed from her. Heathcliff's response to the loss of his beloved is also 'violent exertions', but turned outward, a carefully designed strategy of getting 'levers and mattocks to demolish the two houses' (352). Whenever the two lovers reunite, this violence is abated.

In that the force of their love seeks a complete imaginary unity of total sameness or complete annihilation it disrupts social codes, transgresses taboos, disrupts family structures even as it destroys the lovers' bodies and as such can be seen as a trace of the semiotic chora. In that their love aims to attain the static union before and beyond social divisions and compromises, it transforms into a love for death. Because it resists the mitigated death drive embodied in the agency of the superego, of cultural laws, it transforms into an articulation of the unrestrained pure death drive, located in the primary processes, in the unconscious. Whenever the threat of division re-emerges, that of the real void of death reappears as well. Fearing a repeated disappearance of Heathcliff after a fight with Edgar, Cathy once again falls ill and this brain fever, which now cannot be deflected on to others, is the main cause of her subsequent death in childbirth. Her hysterical symptomatisation signifies the recognition of her non-existence, given that it is induced by the fear that she will lose her alternate ego. Her 'fit of frenzy', her rage, 'dashing her head against the arm of the sofa, and grinding her teeth' (156), her three-day confinement behind a barred door, her refusal of food, are in part consciously designed to direct aggressive passions against others. She wishes to frighten her husband and her lover by using her own destruction as punishment—'I'll try to break their hearts by breaking my own' (155). Forced by her husband to make a choice between him and her illicit lover, the former implying the irrevocable acknowledgment of a split within herself, Catherine chooses death, as a movement beyond divisions.

The scene describing the acme of her fit of frenzy, which Nelly and her doctor understand as a repetition of her 'former illness', is a return to consciousness after a near-death experience of 'utter blackness'. In a manner that will prove fatal, Nelly decides that Catherine 'acted a part of her disorder'. Because she does not comprehend that a hysterical simulation always also signifies real pain she remains blind to the 'true condition', which her mistress's 'ghastly countenance, and strange exaggerated manner', bespeaks (159). Catherine splits into various persons, vacillating between violent, feverish bewilderment and an absent-minded return to childhood memories. She notes a division between herself and her mirrored image, asking 'Is that Catherine Linton'. Later she is unable to recognise her mirrored face and associates this image instead with a ghost haunting her, until she finally gasps at the realisation that what she sees is 'myself'. This forced recognition of herself as being other than the image of the beautiful, loved and undivided self she has fashioned for herself articulates on several scores that the mirrored double signifies death. Rhetorically in the manner Blanchot describes, this distinction between self and self-designation evokes the absence of the speaker. Figurally the fact that she can't recognise herself can be seen as a trope for the alienation her married life entails, for the absence of her true self in the role of wife and mother. It can also be read as a trope for her desire to return to a symbiotic unity before the mirror stage, given that the latter always implies the division of the dyad by a third agency (father, language, absence). Literally the image she sees in the mirror is that of a dying woman, much as Laura saw an image of her dying self reflected in her double Anne's face.

The fact that she will not accept the split in herself, which every division form Heathcliff as her 'all in all' gives figure to, that she will prefer a real non-existence over being no whole body in her social world, entertains an aspect of duplicity. Her madness is such that she hovers between her present condition of illness and memories of her youth; between being 'the wife of a stranger; an exile and outcast' and the recollection of the first time she 'laid alone', separated from Heathcliff by her brother's interdiction. Her hysterical simulation of death is brilliantly doubled, for not only does she alternate between raving and half-dreaming, but she is also simultaneously in two places, 'knows those about her' even as her mind is filled 'with all sorts of strange ideas and illusions' (167). Against these images of repeated experiences of the loss of the positive double and of her married self as an embodiment of a negative division, she posits an image of death as a return to the sense of total unity, as a return home. Its completion involves another aspect of the double in that a release from the psychic death becomes coterminous with the state of the revenant.

Opening the window, implicitly a call for death, she recalls her childhood games when she and her companion stood 'among the graves' and asked the ghosts to come. Calling Heathcliff, so as to undo the 'abyss' their separation draws, becomes a double call—she calls herself to death so as to call him to follow her—'I'll keep you . . . they may bury me twelve feet deep, and throw the church down over me; but I won't rest till you are with me' (164). This image of the restless deceased is a chiasmic reversal of her married existence, conceived by her as a separation of her body (belonging to her husband) and her soul (belonging to her lover). Threatening Edgar that she will 'spring from the window! What you touch at present, you may have; but my soul will be on that hill top before you lay hands on me again' (165) retrospectively implies that what he had all along was merely the 'corpse' of her body. Her death is merely the exchange of one form of revenant existence for another. The division her marriage signified not only finds an apotheosis in her hysterical fit, where with her body as medium she writes her sense of social non-existence and her proximity to death. Rather it is also chiasmically repeated in the division she imagines to embody after death. At the origin and the end of this divided or doubled existence stands the union with her alternate ego, the release of all tension possible only, in Freud's terminology, in the inanimation of the pre-organic state.

Even her actual death is divided in the sense that it has a dual cause—the brain fever, with the 'permanent alienation of intellect' it induces and the pregnancy from which a 'puny, seven month's child' is born over her dying body.[16] The former responds to the fear that by losing Heathcliff a division of the self and a loss of her soul will be repeated yet again, and her madness duplicates this split in that her body is present while her mind wanders; her eyes with 'dreamy and melancholy softness,' vague, distant, always gazing beyond. The latter instead responds to the fear of literally splitting her body in two by giving birth, a somatic repetition and reinforcement of her psychic division. Her death also articulates that the perfect identity of two bodies is a form of love which transgresses social laws, outside marriage, even outside the realm of the living. Against the notions previously discussed that death reunites the lovers in heaven, this love can also not be restituted in the beyond, but must remain located in between, in the transgressive and liminal position of the ghost.

The scene initiating her death repeats and condenses these themes of duplicty and division into one final image. As the two lovers fall into their embrace, from which Catherine emerges 'a lifeless-looking form,' (199), she accuses him of murder ('You have killed me'), desires his death ('I wish I could hold you . . . till we were both dead'), invokes her postmortal unrest ('I shall not be at peace'), curses him to feel the same distress she will feel 'underground', even as she invokes death one last time as a form of liberation from the 'shattered prison' of her married existence. Death will fulfil her supreme desire, 'never to be parted', because once dead she can call him as she can't in life: 'my Heathcliff. I shall love mine yet, and take him with me—he's in my soul' (196). Her death is a doubly directed act of aggression. Though it destroys her, it also inflicts on her lover a renewal of the 'hell' of division, so that he conceives of his mourning as a slow form of being murdered by the ghost of the deceased, a 'strange way of killing' (321). Catherine's death-like loss of consciousness during her last embrace, from which she emerges bewildered—'she sighed, and moaned, and knew nobody'—significantly occurs as Edgar's approach threatens to break the symbiotic dyad and finalises her hysteric desire to repress all signs of division. She dies without recovering 'sufficient consciousness to miss Heathcliff and to know Edgar', without being forced to acknowledge that she is divided in the two senses discussed—lacking her lover and delivered of a daughter.

Nelly sees her corpse as the semblance of 'perfect peace' and tranquillity, her body an 'untroubled image of Divine rest.' Implicitly she misreads her mistress's belief that in death she would be 'incomparably beyond and above' her survivors, much as she misread her earlier fit of frenzy. In support of the double attitude toward death that the novel's frame exhibits, Brontë leaves the question undecided whether Nelly's view that 'her spirit is at home with God' is adequate, whether she fully condones Nelly's allegorisation of the corpse into a figure legitimising a belief in 'the endless and shadowless hereafter—the Eternity . . . when life is boundless in its duration and love in its sympathy, and joy in its fullness' (201). Or whether she also recognises Heathcliff's contrary assurance that the dead woman is not beyond, 'not *there*—not in heaven'.

While for Nelly a narcissistically informed desire for wholeness requires that the dead be fully restituted in the beyond, Heathcliff's same desire requires an obliteration of the division between the living and the dead. He calls to the absent to haunt him, to wander on earth, not to leave him alive alone. While Nelly sees the corpse as a figure whose peace assures the division of death from life and supports a canny notion of a peaceful existence after wordly strife,—Heathcliff wishes to see her corpse as a sign that death can uncannily be preserved in life, that the absence death causes is incomplete. While for Catherine death signifies the liberation from an enclosure, for Heathcliff the corpse remains a signifer of a gap. The ghost of his beloved tempts and recedes from his grasp, just as the forbidden wife of Edgar Linton had, and her death is not a release of tensions but merely a shift in its manner of articulation.

The first of several instances of tampering with her corpse so as to assure an exchange is that he places a lock of his hair into a locket around her neck to be buried with her. On the day of her burial he tries to undo the division that the grave affords by literally uncovering the coffin, wishing to have her in 'his arms again'. Yet his necrophilic desire turns into mourning because his 'strong faith in ghosts' lets him sense the spectral presence of Catherine 'there, not under me, but on the earth'. Relinquishing his initial desire to embrace the corpse initiates 'that strange feeling' which shapes the next eighteen years of mourning until he does indeed open the coffin. This uncanniness, spurred on by a refusal to see the corpse, lets her remain as an immaterial body, present though absent in body. In his psychic reanimation, she traces the figure of *aphanisis,* an 'intolerable torture', because constantly oscillating between fading from his view and returning in his sensation and imagination. At Wuthering Heights, Heathcliff 'felt her by me—I could *almost* see her, and yet I *could* not!' When he closes his eyes she is there—outside the window, entering the room, resting her head next to his, yet once he opens his eyes she is again gone. This uncanny preservation, the woman simultaneously *da* and *fort,* remaining yet receding from any concrete vision and grasp, keeping him alive yet in constant relation to death, is what Heathcliff ultimately calls 'a strange way of killing . . . to beguile me with the spectre of hope'. While he defines his mourning as a form of murder, with the revenant bringing him death by 'fractions of hair-breadths', what remains undecided is whether the hope he refers to is her complete resurrection in body or his complete physical annihilation. His mourning represents the lost beloved in the image of the female vampire, who returns to bring death to her bridegroom. The indeterminacies this motive is inscribed with are such that the relation of signifer to signified is opaque. Does death desire him because she desires him? Does he, by desiring her, desire death? Or does he desire her as a displaced desire for death?

Emily Brontë (1818-1848), painted by Bramwell Brontë

The liminal phase of mourning—in which he retains her on earth as the revenant who haunts him—finds closure when Heathcliff does indeed open the coffin, for the sight of the dead body affords 'some ease'. Concomitant with the invoked revenant theme, her body has not decomposed. Implicitly, because he has preserved her mentally, her body will begin to dissolve only when he too shares this process. The vampirisation is such that her uncanny presence strangely kills him, sucks his life even as his psychic clinging to her sustains her body, with his mental anguish serving as the blood that arrests her bodily dissolution and precludes any form of dissolution. The sight of the corpse, 'the distinct impression of her passionless features,' removes that 'strange feeling' of her intangible presence, assures him that she is indeed dead. The tranquillity he gains from this sight closes the uncertainty that the thwarted first disinterment provoked, because it discloses a repressed knowledge—the truth of her death. Had he initially aimed at literally lying with the corpse, disregarding whether she be cold or motionless, as an act of defying the gap death produced, he now imagines such a necrophilic embrace as a trope for his own demise—'I dreamt I was sleeping the last sleep, by the sleeper, with my heart stopped, and my cheek frozen against hers' (320).

Though Catherine's second burial does not put closure on her revenant status, but on the contrary fixes it (Heathcliff has used the opening of the grave to loosen one side of her coffin), it does terminate the spectrality that fed his mourning and introduces his dying. The second burial terminates his fetishistic position of mourning, his hesitation between a denial of her disappearance and the fact that the intangibility of her ghost forced him to acknowledge her bodily absence. Before he saw the corpse he could still conceive of his beloved in terms of the living, could sustain his life uncannily over her psychic reanimation. Once he has seen her corpse, her death is certain, and in his invocations he now does not ask her to return but rather to help him be gone as well. Because he can no longer focus his attention on the one image of her spectral body, he sees her everywhere, 'in every object . . . the entire world a dreadful collection of memoranda that she did exist and that I have lost her' (353). His form of death is a repetition of Catherine's—abstaining from food, he stares beyond into 'a vacant space'. All absorbed by the dead woman, he bars himself from the living, withdraws into the panelled bed of their childhood unity. Where she died so as not to 'miss Heathcliff', he hopes death will assuage this lived lack.

Though Heathcliff understands this death as an irrevocable obliteration of the division between himself and his other, Brontë's text ends on a note which embellishes the crack of duplicity—thematically and structurally. For the heaven Heathcliff has 'nearly attained' is their spectral reunion, their wandering between earth and heaven, not a fixture in a grave and in the beyond (the heaven of Christianity 'altogether unvalued, and uncoveted'). Rhetorically the doubled narrative, the frame and its embedded tale, remains split between a notion that the dead are cleanly severed from the living and one that locates the dead on their margins—in the room at Wuthering Heights closed to signify their absence but just as plausibly shut up 'for the use of such ghosts as choose to inhabit it' (366) and in the tome of their textual representation serving either as a repetition of the gravestone, assuring the quiet slumbers of the dead or as the correlative of the panel oak bed, to whose inhabitant Catherine's ghost so tauntingly will reappear. . . .

Notes

[1] See N. Auerbach, 1982, who emphasises that Pompilia is perfect in whiteness and exemplifies truth because her death enables her to speak with purity.

[2] M. Holquist, 1983.

[3] T. Todorov, 1977.

[4] J.B. Pontalis, 1978.

[5] H. Cixous, 1981.

[6] R. Hertz, 1960.

[7] M. Eliade, 1977.

[8] V. Turner, 1977.

[9] E. Morin, 1970.

[10] See P. Barber, 1988.

[11] D. A. Miller, 1988, argues that this scene is the novel's 'primal scene which it obsessively repeats and remembers . . . as though this were the trauma it needed to work through,' p. 152. He emphasizes that the protagonist is nervous about the possibility of being contaminated by virtue of the unknown woman's touch, whereas I will argue that this touch elicits an uncanny desire for and anxiety about death.

[12] J.-L. Vernant, 1988, argues that the gravestone holds the place of the deceased as a double, incarnating its life in the beyond. It marks a clear opposition between the world of the living and the world of the dead. As sign of an absence, it signifies that death reveals itself precisely as something which is not of this world. Though this double marks the site where the dead are present in the world of the living or the living project themselves on to the universe of the dead, it makes the invisible visible even as it reveals that death belongs to an inaccesible mysterious realm beyond, fundamentally Other.

[13] M. Serres, 1987.

[14] S. Gilbert and S. Gubar, 1979, argue that Heathcliff is Catherine's almost identical double, while Cathy is her mother's non-identical double, because a more genteel version, of her.

[15] For a similar plot resolution see Daphne Du Maurier's modern gothic romance *Rebecca* (1938), where a sec-

ond wife must 'kill' the revenant of a first wife, lest she be completely absorbed by the image of her predecessor. In my next chapter, the solution of the mourning process will be shown to resort to the [opposite] choice—the double sacrificed so as to preserve the mourner from death.

[16] See also M. Homans, 1986, who discusses Brontë's novel as an example of how the mother's death is a prerequisite for the daughter's entrance into the social order. S. Gilbert and S. Gubar, 1979, read the novel as delineating the movement from nature to culture. J. Boone, 1987, discusses her death as the only liberation from a fragmented existence, found especially in mariage. See also E. Lemoine-Luccione's, 1976, psychoanalytic discussion of pregnancy as one of the crucial moments of self-division in the feminine life cycle.

Works Cited

Primary literature

Brontë, Emily (1847). *Wuthering Heights.* Harmondsworth: Penguin (1965).

Browning, Robert (1869). *The Ring and the Book.* Harmondsworth: Penguin (1971).

Collins, Wilkie (1859-60). *The Woman in White.* Harmondsworth: Penguin (1974).

Stoker, Bram (1897). *Dracula.* Oxford: Oxford University Press (1983).

Secondary literature

Auerbach, Nina (1982). *Woman and the Demon. The Life of a Victorian Myth.* Cambridge, Harvard University Press.

Barber, Paul (1988). *Vampires, Burial, and Death. Folklore and Reality.* New Haven: Yale University Press.

Boone, Joseph Allen (1987). *Tradition Counter Tradition. Love and the Form of Fiction.* Chicago: Chicago University Press.

Cixous, Hélène (1981). 'Castration or Decapitation'. *Signs 7,* pp. 41-55.

Eliade, Mircea (1977). 'Mythologies of Death: An Introduction'. *Religious Encounters with Death* ed. Frank E. Reynolds and Earle H. Waugh. University Park: Pennsylvania State University Press, pp. 13-23.

Gilbert, Sandra M. and Susan Gubar (1979). *The Madwoman in the Attic. The Woman Writer and the Nineteenth-Century Literary Imagination.* New Haven: Yale University Press.

Hertz, Robert (1960). *Death and The Right Hand.* Glencoe: The Free Press.

Holquist, Michael (1983). 'Whodunit and Other Questions: Metaphysical Detective Stories in Postwar Fiction'. *The Poetics of Murder. Detective Fiction and Literary Theory* ed. Gleen W. Most and William W. Stowe. New York: Harcourt Brace Jovanovich, pp. 149-74.

Homans, Margaret (1986). *Bearing the World. Language and Female Experience in Nineteenth-Century Women's Writing.* Chicago: University of Chicago Press.

Lemoine-Luccioni, Eugénie (1976). *Partages des femmes.* Paris: Seuil.

Miller, D. A. (1988). *The Novel and the Police.* Berkeley: University of California Press.

Morin, Edgar (1970). *L'Homme et la Mort.* Paris: Seuil.

Pontalis, J.-B. (1978). 'On Death-Work in Freud, in the Self, in Culture'. *Psychoanalysis, Creativity and Literature* ed. Alan Roland. New York: Columbia University Press, pp. 85-95.

Serres, Michel (1987). *Statues. Le second livre des fondations.* Paris: Éditions François Bourin.

Todorov, Tzvetan (1977). *The Poetics of Prose.* Ithaca: Cornell University Press.

Turner, Victor (1977a). 'Death and the Dead in the Pilgrimage Process'. *Religious Encounters with Death* ed. Frank E. Reynolds and Earle H. Waugh. University Park: Pennsylvania State University Press, pp. 24-39.

Vernant, Jean-Louis (1988). 'Figuration de l'invisible et catégoire psychologique du double: le colossos'. *Mythes & pensée chez les Grecs.* Paris: La Découverte, pp. 325-38.

STRIVING FOR IMMORTALITY

Edward T. Hurley (essay date 1969)

SOURCE: "Death and Immortality: George Eliot's Solution," in *Nineteenth-Century Fiction,* Vol. 24, No. 2, September, 1969, pp. 222-6.

[*In the following essay, Hurley contends that George Eliot's characters seek immortality through the family rather than through religion.*]

If the novelist seeks to explain life, one of the things he must also explain is death. The question of life is, how am I to satisfy my desire to live? Given a historical realization of death, the desire to live must somehow accommodate the challenge that apparently ends that life and frustrates the desire. Thus each change in man's explanation of life has been accompanied by a change in his explanation of death, and each literature has its distinctive approach to death as well as to life.[1] No literary period since the Elizabethan had its inherited explanation of life challenged so profoundly as the Victorian, and it is natural that its later and more intellectual novelists should reflect the unrest in seeking to face anew the problem of life through the solution to the problem of death. George Eliot furnishes a notable example.

Writing in 1848 Elizabeth Gaskell had ended *Mary Barton* with a Christian reconciliation between the working class (John Barton) and the capitalist employer (Mr. Carson). In the spirit of Christ Mr. Carson forgives the murder of his son, and out of the acceptance of his son's death a new social order arises. This is a remnant of the Christian solution to death where man lives on after death by the spirit of the living God. Here the continued life is represented in the fruit of Harry Carson's death, which resolves the social and personal conflicts in the story. In more orthodox fashion, the spirit would have ascended to God to live again in the life of God. Instead, heaven is brought to earth and Harry Carson lives on in the new social order of peace and understanding that his death makes possible. God is the charismatic source of this blessing, the action taking place on earth rather than in heaven. George Eliot gave her guarded approval to Mrs. Gaskell for her depiction of the dissolving social order in the opening of *Mary Barton,* while carefully dissociating herself from Mrs. Gaskell's solution. " 'I was conscious, while the question of my power was still undecided for me, that my feeling toward Life and Art had some affinity with the feeling which had inspired "Cranford" and the earlier chapters of "Mary Barton." ' "[2] George Eliot also recognized that Victorian society had lost its old certainties about life, but denied that one surmounted its chaos (represented in Harry Carson's death) by the intervention of the living, transcendent God. " 'There is no just God that governs the earth righteously, but a God of lies, that bears witness against the innocent,' " says Silas Marner in his bewildered fury at being framed for a crime he did not commit (I). He overcomes this bitterness not by discovering a just God but by discovering Eppie, a human through whom he can make contact with other humans. There is neither a God of righteousness nor a God of lies. At the end of the novel, Silas tries to return to the site of his early evangelical enthusiasm, Lantern Yard, where his coreligionists had betrayed him. We, the readers, given a God-like perspective by the omniscient narrator, know the "objective truth" of this betrayal, but we are powerless to help Silas. He finds that Lantern Yard is gone and he must return to what the present and future have to offer. God vanishes. The insight of art becomes the closest approach to his knowledge, but the participator in art is removed from any effective action by the artistic distance that George Eliot maintained so insistently in her didacticism.

If a God beyond our mortal life no longer conquers death by bequeathing his life on man, then death assumes a new and terrifying importance. George Eliot represented this in death by drowning, a recurrent event in her fiction. She defined the experience in one of her earliest stories, "Janet's Repentance."

> The drowning man, urged by the supreme agony, lives in an instant through all his happy and unhappy past: when the dark flood has fallen like a curtain, memory, in a single moment, sees the drama acted over again. And even in those earlier crises, which are but types of death—when we are cut off abruptly from the life we have known, when we can no longer expect to-morrow to resemble yesterday, and find ourselves by some sudden shock on the confines of the unknown—there is often the same sort of lightning-flash through the dark and unfrequented chambers of memory. (XV)

Man is alone, cut off from heaven and earth, with nothing but his own past to accompany him into an unknown tomorrow. The unknown, beyond death, formerly defined by life with God, now has no comparable myth to explain it, to rationalize it, and make it acceptable as a part of life. Even the most perfect human knowledge cannot face it. Latimer, the narrator of "The Lifted Veil," has perfect insight and foresight into humans and events, but is terrified of death. Through his unique psychic powers, he sees that humans are depraved "even to the heart strings." Yet he clings to life. He recognizes that his desire is irrational and inexplicable. It has become so because he can find no explanation in life and so no explanation in death. An intolerable life will allow for an intelligible death on the premise of a happy after-life, but for Latimer the after-life only extends the present depravity. With no happy after-life Latimer must conquer death in this life, also an impossibility. Thus the deaths by accidental drowning of Thias Bede in *Adam Bede,* Dunstan Cass in *Silas Marner* and Henleigh Grandcourt in *Daniel Deronda* all are the expressions of personal and social absurdity, man cut off from meaning and society in death. *The Mill on the Floss* completes its pattern of irrational clinging to a nonexistent ideal by a triumphant drowning, an effort by George Eliot to conquer the most extreme form of death by blindly embracing it.

Outside *The Mill on the Floss,* no hero or heroine dies by drowning. Romola, when she despairs of ever finding a way of life that will satisfy her desire to live, thinks briefly of drowning herself but at best can only drift out to sea, allowing nature to take her course. Romola's actions show George Eliot's determination to find life and to reject inadequate solutions. When Romola rejects drowning, she rejects despair over the meaning of life. When she earlier rejected her father's classical stoicism, she rejected the idea that life was solipsistic and that one surmounted death by refusing to desire the life which made death a problem. When she rejected Savonarola, she rejected a transcendental God as the solution to death. If the transcendental order of St. Theresa (*Middlemarch*) and the transcendental God of Savonarola have ceased to exist, then a solution must be found in a new social order and in a new immanentism that survives all changes, including the change of death. The fictional device that George Eliot uses to embody her new myth is the family, as another near-drowning shows.

In *Daniel Deronda* Mirah Cohen attempts to drown herself in despair of finding her lost mother and brother. Deronda rescues her, identifies his own search for lost parentage with hers, and ultimately marries her. Death and despair, then, are associated with the lost family. Discovery of the old family and the formation of a new one, however, provide a reason for living.

As the narrator of *Romola* stands overlooking present-day Florence with a spirit from the Renaissance city, she warns him of the physical changes he would find should he go down into the city. But despite historical changes "the little children are still the symbol of the eternal marriage between love and duty . . ." (Proem). The family has survived the ages as the reconciliation and fruit of the drives of life: love and duty. At the close of *Middlemarch* Dorothea Brooke's two marriages are named "the determining acts of her life." The one is sterile, a false step whose fruit was death. The second, to Will Ladislaw, bears two children and continues into the indeterminate future as Dorothea's son inherits the Brooke estate. The family becomes throughout the novels the focus and bearer of continuing life, which masters time, history, and death.

The family has a past and a future and under the proper conditions both are immortal. The family's past is immortal when it is a continuous chain stretching back into the past, carrying out a common task or occupying the same land. In *Adam Bede* there are three Martin Poysers at Hall Farm: the grandfather, the father, and the son. The one has finished the task of caring for the land and his family and peacefully awaits death; the second Martin is tilling the soil and raising a family to take his place; the third Martin is a sturdy young boy growing up to be like his father. Where this chain is threatened it means disaster, and the old go to their graves restless and embittered, their hopes gone. In *The Mill on the Floss* Edward Tulliver makes his son, Tom, swear to carry out his vengeance, and Tom single-mindedly works to regain the hereditary Tulliver mill. In *Felix Holt* Mrs. Holt is disconsolate when Felix deserts the quack profession of his father, and she is not content until he has formed his own family in the end, which perpetuates itself in turn with Felix Jr.

This immortality is a specific manifestation of the more general doctrine of the immortal deed. Any action, once done, bears its fruit inevitably: "the seed brings forth a crop after its kind" (*Silas Marner,* IX). The child is the fruit of the deed of parenthood, so that the child carries its father's image and the obligation to perpetuate it. Harold Transome tries to set himself up independent of his mother in *Felix Holt,* only to discover his illegitimate birth and the burden it carries. Tito Melema tries to disavow his foster-father in *Romola,* but that father seeks him out by a series of providential strokes. Daniel Deronda does not know his parentage but his mother, despite herself, seeks him out from the compulsion she feels to pass her father's mission on to her son.

But if the past is immortal and the past of the family is a heritage that stretches back indefinitely, it will move forward indefinitely only on the free choice of its members acknowledging their place in the family and their duty to pass on the heritage. Those who make this choice almost invariably end the novels in marriage and with children: Adam Bede with Adam Jr., Felix Holt with Felix Jr., Dorothea Brooke with her son; even Romola has Tito's bastard son, Lillo. But those who choose to disavow their family position die sterile and their memory fades as their line ceases. In *Silas Marner* Godfrey Cass, Eppie's real father, says to his wife late in life, " 'I wanted to pass for childless once, Nancy—I shall pass for childless now against my wish' " (XIX). Tito Melema's children do not bear his name and are instructed by Romola to model their lives on her father, Bardo de' Bardi. The past is irrevocable but will be extended into the future only by the free choice of father and child. By this method George Eliot circumvents her own doctrine of determinism and makes immortality a personal choice within the family.

The concern with death and the limits it places on the individual seems to have grown as George Eliot grew older. To counteract death, the role of the family expanded and began to transform the past into a new, ever widening future. In *Felix Holt* (1866) both Felix and Esther Lyon consciously select elements from their varied heritage to make a new social order, of which their small family will be a model. *Middlemarch* (1871-1872) pauses for a skeptical, satiric criticism of Casaubon's system-building and misbegotten effort to immortalize his dead marriage by "willing" it to continue after his death. But *Daniel Deronda* (1876) returns to *Felix Holt's* idealism on a world-wide scale. When Deronda discovers his past he discovers a mission, and his marriage to Mirah Cohen is the beginning of a new nation, the bridge between Jew and Gentile that will usher in a new age. The nation is greater than Deronda and Deronda is greater than his grandfather. One not only becomes immortal, but one's heritage grows with the future when each generation bears out its duty to the past and the future.

In George Eliot's fiction, then, one overcomes death and satisfies the desire to live by performing one's role within the instrument of immortality, the family. The family carries on despite time, despite history. It has an irrevocable past, a series of deeds done by a series of ancestors that offer to the present generation all the potentialities of that past. If the individual is faithful to the essence of that past, he himself will become a part of it and in turn his image will be carried forward in his children or in the transformation of the past that he achieves. In the earlier, more modest novels, this is simply a family that carries on the family work on the family land. In the later novels it becomes a broader social revolution, culminating in the transcendental nation of *Daniel Deronda.*

George Eliot tried to retain the principal values and beliefs of her Evangelical, Victorian upbringing, but gave them a new foundation within history. She felt her obligation to the past, to orderly, rational transformation of personal life and the social order. Thus her pronounced sense of history in each of her novels and her concern to maintain what was essentially a Victorian solution to death, modified by forming it on the individual and the family within history rather than on religion and God.

Notes

[1] Cf. John S. Dunne, *The City of the Gods* (New York, 1965) for the development of this idea and its application to Homer (pp. 30-79), Dante (pp. 162-172) and Shakespeare (pp. 172-181). The present essay is deeply indebted to this study.

[2] *The George Eliot Letters,* ed. Gordon S. Haight (New Haven, 1954-55), III, 198.

Benjamin P. Kurtz (essay date 1970)

SOURCE: "Romantic Death: Real Death," in *The Pursuit of Death: A Study of Shelly's Poetry,* Octagon Books, 1970, pp. 82-142.

[*In the following essay, Kurtz examines the many varied attitudes towards death that Percy Bysshe Shelley expressed in his poetry and traces the influences that led to the development of these attitudes.*]

The failure of the quest for an embodied ideal is the great romantic failure. But some romanticists pass through this failure and come out on the further side. Their dreams, modified by the experience, become visions which are contagious to the world. If the romanticist is he who lives hugely in his dream and emotion, with more or less of Rousseau's suspicion of mere reason, and who trusts his imagination and emotion for guidance in affairs and for revelation of reality, his weakness will lie in emotionally running away from facts, his strength in critically correcting dream by fact and purifying fact by dream. The dream may be a supposititious escape from fact, because it has lost contact with fact and is illusory, as is the case with the Gothic romances; or it may be an ideal end, or vision, toward which facts are manipulated, an eternal and wise ideal discoverably and significantly related to the actual, though it always is a receding horizon, as is the case with the humanism of whatever epoch. In Shelley's poetry for the next four years (1814-1817), there is discernible a mutual purgation of romantic dream and real experience, making definitely for greater strength of idea and greater power of utterance. In no other phase of his work is this process more noticeable than in his changing attitude toward death. During these four years he definitely anticipates the three victories over death—the moral, aesthetic, and mystical victories—which he is fully to achieve in the last five years of his life.

I

Two brief poems commence the new artistry: *Oh, there are spirits of the air,* and *Stanzas. April, 1814.* Written early in 1814, while the rift between Harriet and himself was tragically widening, they seem to have sprung from real and poignant suffering; the former, in particular, having an effect of desperate actuality, as against the make-believe tragics of the juvenilia.

With their relation to Shelley's marital experience, the evidence they may give of his conduct in the troubles with Harriet, I am not here concerned. I am not taking sides either for or against Shelley. I am not pretending to know exactly what happened, what Shelley did, what Harriet did. A few unchronicled words spoken impetuously and later respoken in deliberation may have had more effect than all the known events. They do, with sensitive people. And Shelley was preternaturally sensitive; Harriet not so much. I am not preaching what Shelley or Harriet should or should not have done. The story has been told gently by some biographers, ungently by others; but neither apology and sentimentalism, nor innuendo, suspicion, and sarcasm, make impartial biography. So far as I am here concerned, "the book's the man." All that I am noting is that in these few heartbroken lines there is a new strength of passion, simple and unaffected; and, especially, that an important mood of his early affectation—the exuberant insistence upon death—is missing. The younger, inexperienced Shelley, imagining the failure of love, would have had recourse to the melodrama of death. Its macabre rhetoric would have tintinnabulated from the mouths of the two erstwhile lovers, as it did from the lips of the "victim of grief" in the *Dialogue* written five years before, when he was seventeen:

Oh, Death! oh, my friend! snatch this form to
 thy shrine
And I fear, dear destroyer, I shall not repine.

Now, in the suffocation of reality, the expression is tragically quiet, a line in each poem:

The glory of the moon is dead.

Thou [the poet, himself] in the grave shalt
 rest. . . .

Two poems curiously mark the transition to this strength in passion. One carries the new tone clearly; but the other sounds only a slight echo of it, the effect being primarily that of some reworking of an earlier poem that had been written originally in his worst style. In *Mutability,* developing his favourite theme that all things change and go down in death while only mutability endures, Shelley achieves verbal harmony and a real fingering of the lines, in place of intolerable jingling. Indeed, most of the poems after *Mab,* from 1813 on, gain suddenly in harmony and melody, the combined result, perhaps, of the opening of his eyes in Wales and Lynmouth to the mysterious beauty of nature, of the access of strength that may come with sorrow, of the music, literal and spiritual, at the Boinvilles, of the reading of Coleridge and Wordsworth, and of the practice-work in *Queen Mab.* The thought itself has nothing of the doctrinaire quality of *Mab.* Mutability is not related grandiosely to any Spirit of Nature, or Necessity. But a sensitive heart, uttering its accustomed instinctive lament for the change of all fair things, is now especially saddened by the failure of its own love. The dream woven around the heart of a child-wife is dead. This is the most extended and imaginative expression, so far, of Shelley's elegiac mood. Less of stock romantic melancholy and more of what appears to be genuine, personal experience make it a poem of some real rank.

The other poem, *On Death,* is a revision of the only verses Shelley cared to preserve from the Esdaile manuscript. It retains some of the jingle and declamation of its first form; yet neither thought nor mood nor music is entirely Gothic. There is even a reminiscence of the great and mournful oratory of *Ecclesiastes,* growing out of the verse prefixed to the poem: "There is no work, nor device, nor knowledge, nor wisdom in the grave, whither thou goest." At any rate, the political and religious anarchism of his earlier lyrics on death, *A Dialogue* and *To Death,* which gave so radical and raucous a tone to them, is absent.

Yet a third pair of poems, the brief elegy on the Lechlade churchyard, and the long blank-verse *Alastor* written after his return from an excursion up the Thames with Peacock, reveals another phase of his deepening regard of death. Early in 1815, after he had come back from his first trip abroad with Mary, he had been told that he was a victim of tuberculosis. He thought he had but a little while to live. This belief called forth in these two poems a mood of somewhat sombre but decidedly romantic contemplation of the lovely solemnity of euthanasia. Already, in *Mab,* as we have seen, he had eagerly declaimed that although even in a perfected world death is inescapable, yet there it will come upon good men like a mild and gradual sleep. Now, in a graver and more self-conscious, rather Wordsworthian mood, he acclaims the mortal loveliness of such a death in an actual and imperfect world.

In the little elegy, which Matthew Arnold used to pronounce Shelley's "first entire poem of value," the treatment is more gently solemn and less dramatic than in *Alastor.* Here we have his first notable achievement in that *triste* autumnal theme he was so especially to make his own. He pictures the stillness of a September day dying along the river banks, the sere and motionless grasses in the graveyard, the church-spires aflame in the sunset and then slowly effaced in the lessening twilight, and the gathering of darkness among the first stars, while in the little yard the dead sleep on in their sepulchres. The quiet scene stimulates an intuition, "half sense, half thought," of the awful hush and the mild and terrorless serenity of great death, and even a child-like hope that death hides sweet secrets, or that loveliest dreams keep a perpetual watch beside its breathless sleep. Yet the old theme of loathly decay intrudes. It is from the mouldering sleep of the dead on their wormy beds that the mysterious voice of hope arises! The old theme dies hard. The conversion to beauty is incomplete. It is interesting, too, to note an allusion to his boyhood habit of haunting graves in quest of revelation.

The euthanasia in *Alastor* is dramatic, pathetic, self-conscious, and romantic. It is the crest of the poem, for a handsome young idealist, gentle, brave, and generous, wandering abroad to worship beauty, perishes in the solitude of the mountains. The influence of Scott's *Helvellyn* is again obvious.

Hutton, long ago, in what is one of the earliest and best essays upon Shelley's poetry, pointed out that the mere framework of the poem is a romantic absurdity. A lone poet walks from Cashmere across Asia Minor (*not* the steppes of southern Russia, as Hutton has it), traverses Balk (Hutton says the Balkans!), rushing wildly by the desolate tombs of the ancient Parthian kings, arrives at the Black Sea, finds a small, leaky boat, sets up his coat for a sail, voyages two days (while his hair turns grey), sails up a river into the heart of the Caucasus Mountains, and dies in a place of impossible geography—all in search of two eyes he saw in a dream. But, penetrative as most of Hutton's essay is, here it fails to perceive the romantic symbolism of the poem. Indeed, many of Shelley's descriptions of persons and places—a notable instance is the chief character and the scenery of his *Witch of Atlas*—become absurd if applied to mere tangible realities, instead of being regarded as symbolic of mental states. Shelley himself, once for all, in his preface to *Prometheus Unbound,* has called attention to his half-mythopoeic fashion of animating mental experiences in the guise of personages, situations, and even, it should be added, the forms and events of nature. He consciously employed this device, and held it to be a method that, though strange to modern poetry, was used repeatedly by Shakespeare, habitually by the Greek poets, and most of all and with greatest success by Dante. In *The Tempest,* Prospero, Caliban, and most of the other characters, as well as the storm itself, are symbolic, but by no means allegorical, presentations of great-mindedness and brutishness in struggle one with the other. Goethe's *Faust* is replete with such symbolism, the second part even more so than the first. Every stage, though not every detail, of *The Divine Comedy* is a story figuring mental experience. The odes of Pindar and many of the scenes and choral odes of the Greek tragedians, more especially Aeschylus and Sophocles, reach their fullness of meaning in such symbolism, where characters and scenes display not so much different individualities and their operations as different phases of the mental activity of one mind. In *Alastor* the description of the itinerary of the poet is only a way of marking out the mind-history of a poet, of Shelley himself: his glamorous, imaginative youth, his enthusiastic reading, his passionate preoccupation with a higher reality, his deep sensitiveness to all noble ideas and to the incommunicable suggestions of natural beauty, his piercing need of truly beautiful human companionship, his hopeless search for the ideal love, his loneliness, failure, illness, and his solemn anticipation of an early death. The hero of *Alastor* had nurtured his youth with the solemn visions of the ancient philosophers and the choicest responses to natural beauty. He had left a "cold fireside and alienated house" to seek abroad the truths that are all too strange to the conventional minds of father, mother, friends, and wife. He would make in the wilderness a home, "inaccessible to avarice or pride," where

> Nature's most secret steps
> He like her shadow . . . pursued.

Thus the tutelage of the poetic mind by literature and nature is imaged. Its fecundation by the lore of the past is represented by the poet's wandering, "obedient to high thoughts," in the ruins of Athens and Tyre, Balbec and Jerusalem and Babylon, and Æthiopia and Egypt, among the stupendous columns of Ozymandias and the remains of ancient temples,

> and wild images
> Of more than man, where marble dæmons watch
> The Zodiac's brazen mystery, and dead men
> Hang their mute thoughts on the mute
> walls around.

From the past, much as in the second part of *Queen Mab,* a great lesson is learned of man's cruelty to man, of superstitions, and of the ever-enduring search for a supreme reality. His exultant education continues through the strange places of Arabia and Persia,

> And o'er the aërial mountains which pour down
> Indus and Oxus from their icy caves.

Then, resting in the vale of Cashmère, he has the vision of ideal beauty, which gathers into itself and climaxes all the fine, fair learning from nature and man. This spiritual beauty is a woman seen in a dream, that feminine alter-ego of the romantic poet, of whom he ever after dreams, and for some adequate embodiment of whom in an actual woman the rest of his life is a ceaseless quest. This is the "beauty afar," *La Princess Lointaine,* of Jaufre Rudel. This is that romantic worship of beauty, and far, strange search for it, with which Keats endowed Endymion, and of which Rossetti sang so well:

> This is that Lady Beauty, in whose praise
> Thy voice and hand shake still,—long
> known to thee
> By flying hair and fluttering hem,—the
> beat
> Following her daily of thy heart and feet,
> How passionately and irretrievably,
> In what fond flight, how many ways and days!

In *Alastor* the search becomes a wild wandering through Asia Minor and a voyage into the Caucasus. The wilderness, the various stream and devious river, and dark, mysterious gorges, are, as the wanderer himself declares, the image of the poet's mental life. The scenes are at once descriptive and interpretive, animistically identifying the experiences of mind with the life of nature. Such dreams of loveliness drive the Actaeon-poet restlessly to his death. Therefore the issue of the quest is in the figure of a romantic euthanasia under a waning moon, with autumnal mountain-winds heaping dead leaves over the corpse of the wanderer.

Death here is no mere Gothic horror. It is the inevitable close of the romantic pursuit of the beautiful, the pathetic mystery that ends the dramatic failure to find the ideal embodied in the actual. Characteristically, for Shelley, this beauty stimulates a ceaseless, febrile pursuit of an ideal which is both a supreme social good and need, and also a personal need and good. His is not a flight from the world to a sequestered beauty, but the pursuit and preaching of a panacea. He cannot lose himself even temporarily, as Endymion did, in the ecstasy of the senses and in the delight of merely imaging the spirit-beauty. He cannot hypnotize himself, as Rossetti did so often, with a haunted contemplation of dead beauty, extinct ecstasies, and desolate eyes. Rather, with native Platonic bent for abstracting eternal invisibles from actual love and concrete beauty, he must at once pass beyond sensuous joy to philosophical meaning. To be sure, the great Wordsworthian invocation of Nature, with which the poem opens, pulses with a passionate love of the things of earth, ocean, and air; and in obvious reminiscence of *Tintern Abbey,* the reading of which must have deepened his sensibility, opened a door of his own spirit, he prays that his verses, breathing the natural magic of air and forest and sea, may become "woven hymns of night and day." This is rich testimony to that poetic baptism in nature which has been the second birth of so many poets. Nevertheless, beside his love of the thing there always exists his love of the idea. He must sanctify the fact by truth. Then, turning back, he searches for the ideal in the concrete, but never finds a perfect incarnation. Thus, almost insensibly, he is forced into that dualistic and dramatic antithesis of spirit and sense that has already been noted in some of his earlier poems.

This failure of the romantic quest for an embodied ideal is the natural catastrophe of a dualism and antithesis of spirit and sense. All such dualism has always resulted in defeated hopes of finding or founding a kingdom of heaven upon this earth. The defeat has been disguised as a mere delay until the kingdom shall be accomplished by the slow evolution of society; or the hopes have been postponed to the realization of a spirit-kingdom hereafter, not made with hands; or, often in unconscious surrender of the dualism, the hopes have been turned individually inward, transmuted into an asseveration that the kingdom of God is within one's self, or that the Kingdom is the community of those hearts in which the ideal has been achieved. Young Keats, too intoxicated with sensuous beauty to face hard facts definitely, removed the ideal pursuit to Endymion's unreal world, where by a boudoir-miracle the dusky, Ganges maid could be transformed to the golden-haired Diana of the quest. Again, the surrender may be conscious and pessimistic, as in Cabell's *Way of Ecben.* It is of the essence of Mr. Cabell's thought that no distinction between the heavenly and the common Aphrodite should be drawn. The Uranian love is but a rarefied and very self-deceiving variety of the common passion; and when old age meets the Uranian ideal it finds only a commonplace girl's body, after all. In spite of faithfulness, all love shrivels with age, and the dream is dead. Thus, in one way or another, failure is the necessary end, intuitively recognized by the poet, of his quest for an objectively realized ideal. Because Shelley had long been preoccupied with death, this failure is at once symbolized as death. However, 'symbolized' is too weak a word to express his conviction that in the theatre of this life death inevitably puts a *Finis* to the beautiful eagerness of the youthful poet, of himself.

But if the parts of the poem are really symbolical of states of mind, it should be noted that the poet curiously fails to understand that the object of his quest is, properly, too, a state of his own mind. Instead, the end remains an ideal realized in an object external to him, and so forever elusive.

What is *Alastor* without death? What would be the search for perfection, or even for a near-perfect mutual understanding, without disappointment, failure, loneliness, and a new, intimate awareness of the immanence of death? *Alastor* is that romantic dream of youth which time and night must quench forever; or, at any rate, always. Over against the pursuit of a dream of an absolute ideal, youth discovers, there is set a universal drama of perpetual change. All lovely things go down into death, exit into mystery. In the midst of that drama the lonely, eager, puzzled soul itself perishes also, while fallen leaves are spectrally driven by autumn winds. The first part of the great *Ode to the West Wind* will state this theme yet more powerfully, beginning where *Alastor* ends.

More powerfully, yes. For, however sympathetically one may read the romantic symbolism of *Alastor,* the poem leaves him with some sense of a decoration of reality, instead of a mature and resolute grappling with it. Reality is handled picturesquely and immaturely, with the fevered intensity of one expecting to be cut off while life is still a daily miracle, long before it has become customary, and dull with age. The poem, therefore, is really a romantic fantasia of the triumph of death over youthful dreams. Indeed, the smaller and weaker one's individual life may seem, the more incongruous is this sentimentally pathetic euthanasia, so romantically staged, so grandiosely gestured.

Death, to be sure, has now been poetized more completely than ever before in Shelley's verses. There is an access of vivid doubt, won from his experiences with love, as to love's persistence beyond the grave, quite in contrast to the facile faith expressed in some half-dozen previous poems.

He eagerly pursues
Beyond the realms of dream that fleeting shade;
He overleaps the bounds. Alas! alas!
Were limbs and breath and being intertwined
Thus treacherously? Lost, lost, forever lost
In the wide pathless desert of dim sleep,
That beautiful shape! Does the dark gate of death
Conduct to thy mysterious paradise,
O Sleep? Does the bright arch of rainbow clouds
And pendent mountains seen in the calm lake

Lead only to a black and watery depth,
While death's blue vault with loathliest
vapors hung,
Where every shade which the foul grave exhales
Hides its dead eye from the detested day,
Conducts, O Sleep, to thy delightful realms?
This doubt with sudden tide flowed on his heart;
The insatiate hope which it awakened stung
His brain even like despair.

The hope of finding the perfection of love beyond death is gloomy and desperate. Fear of delusion dogs the young romantic, as it is bound to if he really thinks, instead of allowing sensations completely (*Gefühl ist alles!*) to take the place of thought. Moreover, the adolescent, languorous delight in imaginary dying has lost a part of its lenitive charm with the near approach of the reality. All this is true. Yet the poem is a poem of the triumph of death, not of life or hope or faith. And the triumph is rendered with no courageous tragic force, but with a melodramatic, self-conscious pathos, and the nearest approach to Byronic theatricality anywhere to be found in Shelley's treatment of his own fate, whether figured in another's, as here, or rendered directly, as in some of his great odes and in *Adonais.*

The chief advance in artistry remains to be mentioned. At last the poet has turned from the causes he has been advocating to the enforced contemplation of life itself. It is his own life, to be sure; and self-pity plays the usual role, so disconcerting to penetrative self-analysis. But the gain is certain, nevertheless. From rhetorical radicalism to romantic mystery, with a greater sensitiveness to nature, and a new verbal harmony, and some infiltration of the sincerity of Wordsworth and the sorcery of Coleridge, is no slight poetic advance. Nor is there a better measure of the improvement than the incongruity with which one passage on political fear and ruin interrupts the peaceful, moonlit solitude of the poet's death, toward the end of the poem. Yet even it borrows from its context a quieter tone than can be found in the earlier fulminations against tyranny.

The few poems of the eventful and fateful year, 1816, show a remarkable development in Shelley's realization of death. But the mood of romantic peace that he had elaborated to soothe himself in the anticipation of an early death carries over, slightly, into the first poem, *Sunset,* where again death and genius contend in a young poet's "subtle being." Though the poet's death and the grief of the lady of his love, who through the tragic succeeding years patiently tended her aged father, are done with a truer dramatic pathos, yet the enervating spice of romantic self-consciousness is not altogether rejected. The reader is aware of a sad, half-hid delight with which the poet dreams that a fair maid will mourn *him* after he is gone, like the virgins who pined and wasted for the always gentle, brave, and solitary, but never lingering, hero of *Alastor.* Nor does he realize the possibilities of the theme that is actually broached. In one of the best passages it is said of the lady's deep grief that

. . . but to see her were to read the tale
Woven by some subtlest bard to make hard hearts
Dissolve away in wisdom-working grief.

But if this wisdom-working grief were to accomplish anything more than to bring tears to hard eyes, it might be expected to amend her own state of mind with some high faith in the triumph of spirit over death, after the fashion of the teaching of *Adonais.* Instead, the only moan she makes is a despairing cry for the passionless calm and silence of death, whether the dead live or die "in the deep sea of Love."

The first important event of the year for Shelley, after the birth of a son in January, and not taking into account the sordid, long drawn out story of Godwin's debts, was the trip to Switzerland, May to September, with the sojourn at Geneva with Byron. It stimulated a stronger, serener mood and freed Shelley from all sickly sentimentalism in the contemplation of death. Again the mountains tutored the poet, as the impressive poems of these months, the *Hymn to Intellectual Beauty* and the *Mont Blanc,* testify.

What is accomplished in the *Hymn* is in one way not very notable, in another way highly remarkable. As a reasoned teaching the poem is as unsatisfactory as Wordsworth's *Intimations;* as a figuration of mood it belongs with the greatest mystical poems of the language. We must consider it at some length, for it contains a key to much of Shelley's later thought.

The thought is Platonic, coming straight from the *Phaedrus* and the *Symposium.* This "intellectual beauty," a phrase Shelley used two years later in translating the *Symposium,* though there is no original for it in the Greek, is a happy naming of that supreme beauty, or love, to the worship of which Diotima is supposed to have converted Socrates. It is, in fact, a name for one of the Platonic Forms, or Ideas—the eternal archetype of beauty from which, somehow, according to Plato's dream, all beauty in all beautiful things derives. It is the central term in a more or less transcendental explanation of the beautiful.

The method of becoming aware of the archetype is a progressive generalization of our love for beautiful particulars. From a love of one beautiful being men may proceed to that of two, because of the one beauty that is in both; then they may ascend to the love of all forms that are beautiful, because they realize the general beauty in them all; from beautiful forms they pass to beautiful habits and institutions, thence to beautiful doctrines—"until, from the meditation of many doctrines, they arrive at that which is nothing else than the doctrine of the supreme beauty itself." This merely rationalized beauty, as the modern realist would call it, is regarded transcendentally by Diotima as a supreme reality, to which is ascribed the origin of beautiful objects of sense-perception. It is perfect, eternal, and absolute; not subject to change, to increase or decay; not subjective, not varying with different subjectivities; not figurable to the imagination; not subsisting in particular things.

> Nor does it subsist in any other that lives or is, either in earth, or in heaven, or in any other place; but it is eternally uniform and consistent, and monoeidic with itself. All other things are beautiful through a participation of it, with this condition, that although they are subject to production and decay, it never becomes more or less, or endures any change.

This is Shelley's own translation, important to be cited because it gives in his own words his understanding of a Platonic doctrine that repeatedly appears in his poetry from now on, particularly in *Mont Blanc, Prometheus Unbound,* and *The Witch of Atlas.*

The run of the thought is, exoterically at least, dualistic. Plato, as Bosanquet observed, was indeed the prophet of a dualism between nature and intelligence, or spirit. Over against all beautiful appearances is set an unapparent beauty, intellectual in its nature, but unlimited, not subjective, of which we become aware by an intellectual discipline that carries us from the contemplation of the many to the one. However, both here and in the *Phaedrus,* there are sentences that supplement this intellectual dualism with that sort of emotional mysticism against which Hegel was wont to protest. From the gradual contemplation of beautiful objects, the disciplined lover comes *suddenly* to his vision of this supreme and sublime beauty. In the knowledge and contemplation of it a rapturous shudder and a great awe pass through him, and at last he reposes in deep, ineffable joy. "He is in contact not with a shadow but with reality," and his human nature puts on 'immortality.'

Here was a union of idea and mood that fitted in perfectly with the unusual personality of the young poet. It appealed to his flair for analyzing the intellectual life, to his love of philosophical synthesis, to his deep emotionalism, his constructive imagination, to his ingrained habit of seeing invisibles, to his native mysticism. Moreover, it ratified his view of mutability as a process somehow set over against perfection, and thus provocative, turn by turn, both of the immediate, tense grief at a loss, and of time's softening of the grief into a perduring sorrow, or general sadness. And it offered a comfort for these elegiac moods by confirming his faith in a real perfection existing outside change yet related to it either as source or as a final cause. Shelley's deep, intuitive assent to Platonism in general, and to the Platonic Idea of the beautiful in particular, is one of those intricate assents of the total individual which modern slang calls a "click."

Shelley had early begun the reading of Plato in French and English translations. Medwin says he studied the *Symposium* at Eton (1804-1810) with Dr. Lind. At Oxford (1810-1811) he read Dacier's translation, and some of the works of Thomas Taylor the Platonist. Plato's works were sent him at Tanyrallt in 1812. Hogg and Lady Shelley refer to his reading the *Phaedrus* and the *Symposium* at Marlow.

Plato and Godwin were his great books. Back and forth between them repeatedly he passed in his reading, excited both by the transcendental realism of the one and the philosophical radicalism of the other, and deriving mixed nutriment from the confusion. Both Godwin's necessity and subjectivism of good and evil, and Plato's unresolved dualism of natural appearances and their ideal Forms, filled his mind with images of perfectibility and perfection, the one contributing to his political, the other to his religious, or poetic, ideals. In both he found a dualistic *Weltanschauung.* In Godwin, it took the form of a constant struggle to render the higher motives operative in the mind and thus, out of the conflict of lower and higher impulses, to hasten the advent of a perfect political state. In Plato, it took the form of a partly rational, partly intuitive recognition of a metaphysical reality, by which the ugliness of commonplace reality is overcome and a perfect intellectual-mystical state is achieved.

As he sailed about Lake Geneva with Byron, the marvellous blue of the lake, the purple of the mountainsides, the far snow-capped summits, the flush of sunrise over the white peaks, and the solemn beauty of Alpine sunsets, readily stirred his memories of the *Symposium* and the *Phaedrus.* He must have recalled with awe, and with a thrilling recognition of its spiritual appropriateness, Plato's remark that of all the ideal Forms, that of visible beauty "shines through the clearest aperture of sense":

> For sight is the most piercing of our bodily senses; though not by that is wisdom seen; her loveliness would have been transporting if there had been a visible image of her, and the other ideas, if they had visible counterparts, would be equally lovely. But this is the privilege of beauty, that being the loveliest she is also the most palpable to sight. . . . He . . . who has been the spectator of many glories in the other world, is amazed when he sees any . . . form which is the expression of divine beauty; and at first a shudder runs through him, and again the old awe steals over him; then looking upon the face of his beloved as of a god he reverences him, and if he

> were not afraid of being thought a downright madman, he would sacrifice to his beloved as to the image of a god. (*Phaedrus,* 250-251. Jowett's translation.)

Shelley's sacrifice was a Hymn to this divine, or intellectual, beauty.

The *Hymn* preserves and animates the Platonic dualism, for the idea-form becomes the Spirit of Beauty, itself the shadow of an Unknown Power which is the metaphysical absolute, even as all the Ideas emanate somehow from an Absolute. This Spirit comes and goes in the intellectual life of man, as Plato hints in his description of the recurring vision. Its elusiveness and mysterious subtlety, for mortal mind, are symbolized in images of evanescent moonbeams showering behind a pine-clad mountain, of the tenuous hues and harmonies of evening, of the memory of music that has ceased, of

> . . . aught that for its grace may be
> Dear, and yet dearer for its mystery.

While one is aware of it, everything human is consecrated; and "like moonlight on a midnight stream," it "gives grace and truth to life's unquiet dream."

But the *Hymn* is both a pæan and an elegy. It is a song of joyful discovery of a sentiment, or attitude, that resolves for a moment the ugliness of experience. It is a song of regret at the failure, or, rather, evanescence, of that transforming sentiment. The pæan prevails over the elegy in stanzas one, and five to seven, thus enveloping with a kind of mystical rapture the elegiac regret sounding in the three central stanzas.

With this elegiac regret at the passing of the Spirit of Divine Beauty, the unsatisfactory character of the thought, with which both Plato and Shelley must be charged, is apparent. The Spirit is not regarded as being always immanent in nature, but as being, when we are aware of it, only a shadow of some perfection afar. That is, mind conceives a remote, ideal perfection incompletely and inconstantly. To be sure, there is a vague, misleading statement, in the third verse, to the effect that this Shadow "visits the various world." But the opening lines of the second stanza make it clear that this "various world" is the world of "human thought," and in the first stanza it is clearly asserted that the inconstant visitor comes to "each human heart and countenance." If Shelley meant to say that this Spirit resides, but not subsists, in nature, he does not say so clearly, and certainly does not represent it as permanently present there. At any rate, be that as it may, he goes on to deplore that when this inconstant spirit passes away, our commonplace reality, "this dim vast vale of tears, . . . of fear, and hate and despondency, and death," is left doubly vacant and desolate. Now, most characteristically, Shelley's depression recurs, with further reference to death. No other faith—not all the superstitious names of "Dæmon, Ghost, and Heaven"—avail to sever

> From all we hear and all we see,
> Doubt, chance, and mutability.

When the Spirit has passed, the grave, like life and fear, remains a dark reality. Metaphysical Reality, then, is a far God, or Spirit, elusive to mind. And if it is present in things, it is not always present, and is only partially suggested, message-like, by their beauty. Phenomena are declensions from Reality. The implication is that life, or commonplace reality, is a kind of evil, over against the ideal good. Only a vision of the greater reality can hide, and then for but a moment, the gloom and misery of immediate reality.

The need of some resolution of this sulky Platonic dualism becomes disquietingly apparent. A more monistic, even Aristotelian, generalization is required; some archæsthetism, which recognizes consciousness as a primitive attribute of 'matter,' and as the cause of evolution toward ever more perfect forms, instead of a crude dualism that sees human life as a gloom miserably consummated in death. Death and mutability are not absorbed, as they are in a monistic theory, into the process of evolution; they still stand forth, in this *Hymn* to perfection, as negations of, or at least antitheses to, an elusive perfection.

Analysis of the thought of the poem provokes disappointment. But a poem's meaning is not limited to thought that can be paraphrased in abstract terms. If it were so, there would be less need of poetry than there is. As a unique configuration of profoundly impressive images, intuitive thought, and an ecstatic mood, the poem has an incommensurable meaning. And it is with the fifth stanza, as, the more consciously learned, Platonic address finished, Shelley begins to speak more directly from his own, original experiences, that the greater meaning appears. It is from one's very own imaginative and emotional syntheses of beautiful things, passionate sacraments of love, that the finer meaning always springs, rather than from any reframing, poetic or otherwise, of book-learning. Suddenly Shelley becomes retrospective, linking to his boyhood's extravagant awareness of the unknown, of which we have spoken above, a later insight, or vision, which is the real ground of the poem. In a passage already quoted he recalls his graveyard wanderings and ghost-hunts, and describes his young failure to uncover a true spiritual life either in the grave or in the poisonous conventional religion which youth is taught. These failures left him yet more curious about the invisibles. Then, of a spring day, while he was musing on the mystery, something in the vital, genial warmth of spring's rebirth stirred that glorious intuition of the oneness of all the life-processes which always has been the vision of those greatly endowed with the poetic, animistic imagination. What young Shelley saw on that spring-day was, I am sure, essentially identical with the central visions of Vaughan and Wordsworth, Blake and Tennyson, and all the poets of second sight, or insight. It was what Dante called the universal form of the life-complex,

> *La forma universal di questo nodo,—*

what he endeavoured to symbolize under the figure of the scattered leaves of all the universe bound by love in one volume. Indeed, the *Divina Commedia,* in its three major parts and all the circles and subdivisions of each, is Dante's attempt to unite, through a schematic gradation, all other experience to this central, unique experience. The entire poem leads up to this supreme moment of poetic insight. For Shelley, too, this is the central vision that alone gives meaning to all the rest of experience. He tells us with what ecstasy he welcomed the vision, with what devotion he dedicated his powers to its service, with what faithfulness he has kept the vow in all zeal of study and delight of love, and with what solemn hope he prays that the deep harmony of this vision which descended on his passive youth will supply to his onward life a spiritual serenity, binding him

> To fear himself, and love all human kind.

Now this deep faith in a spiritual reality is essentially monistic, escaping that dualism with which Shelley has associated it in the first four, more Platonic, and less personal and original, stanzas of the *Hymn.* Dante speaks for the monistic truth of this by no means uncommon mysticism, which grows nevertheless from a unique experience with a special meaning of its own, when he stresses love as binding the scattered leaves. Love brings all together in one beautiful whole—substance and accidents and their relations fused in one simple flame. In these magnanimous lines he is perilously close to the alleged heresy of Origen, salvation for all through the divine justice and love:

> *Sustanzia ed accidenti, e lor costume,*
> *Quasi conflati insieme per tal modo,*
> *Che ciò ch'io dico è un semplice lume.*

Implicit, therefore, in that generalization is the beauty of mutability and death, and a complete conquest of the fear and the distaste of all kinds of change. But these implications Shelley has not yet definitively conceived. Future pain and sorrow and beauty must teach him. At present, he can associate the crude dualism of the first four stanzas with the poetic monism of the last three, as though the former were but a personification of the latter. Intuition really outran conception. Poetry anticipated reason.

But it is significant that in a previous, blank-verse rendering of the *Hymn* this dualism is not present. The noble address to the "mother of this unfathomable world," at the beginning of *Alastor* (lines 18-49), contains in close composition all the essential ideas of the *Hymn.* The Mother is analogous to the Spirit of the later poem; her shadow and the darkness of her steps, upon which he has ever gazed, become in the *Hymn* the shadow of an Unseen Power; in both cases the story of his youthful search for spiritual manifestation at dead of night in the graveyard is connected with his later divination of nature; in both the fruitless faith of popular superstition is deplored; in both the inability completely to grasp the spiritual reality is lamented; in *Alastor* the intuitions of incommunicable dreams, twilight phantasms, and deep noonday thought correspond to the spring-day vision of the *Hymn;* a mood of dedication pervades both; and, finally, the acme of each is reached in a mystic serenity and an ideal love of humankind. The correspondence of ideas is very striking. But the dualism is absent in the *Alastor* passage. Instead, it concludes with what is almost an identification of the great parent-spirit with natural appearances: at any rate, the spirit is so pervasive that, like the supreme Brahma, speaking to the poet in all the voices of living things, it modulates his own recording of what he hears:

> . . . serenely now
> And moveless, as a long-forgotten lyre
> Suspended in the solitary dome
> Of some mysterious and deserted fane,
> I wait thy breath, Great Parent, that my strain
> May modulate with murmurs of the air,
> And motions of the forests and the sea,
> And voice of living beings, and woven hymns
> Of night and day, and the deep heart of man.

Such a *"woven hymn"*—perhaps in this phrase is the very anticipation of the later poem—is the *Hymn to Intellectual Beauty;* but into the weaving was introduced the old Platonic dualism, not too happily. It is as though in this earlier passage we had the truer, more immediate expression of his divination of a reality always at one with nature, whereas in the *Hymn* the experience is Platonically mediated, bookishly divided.

Not the least important phase of this self-revealing *Hymn* is the method of fusing metaphysics with politics. For all of Shelley is here, as in most of his greater poems from now on: both his poetic religion and his ideal anarchism. Never, he avers, since that vision, even in his greatest joys, has he been without hope

> . . . that thou wouldst free
> This world from its dark slavery,
> That thou—O awful loveliness,
> Wouldst give whate'er these words cannot express.

Selfish politics, no less than death and all mutability, makes for this "dark slavery." But all ugliness may some day yield to the ideal loveliness. Again the inveterate dualism! Again the postponed Kingdom of Heaven! Dualism must always sacrifice the present to the future.

However, the fusion of death and politics in the concept of ugliness makes clear the essentially aesthetic movement of Shelley's thought. This aesthetic quality, as yet incompletely and even crudely philosophized, is the secret, or originative principle, of his intellectual life. It is what constitutes him a poet. It is that phase of his genius by which he converts into one complex whole physics, politics, religion, love, and poetry. It is the dynamics of his strangely unified interest in all these. His economics is fundamentally aesthetic; so, too, are his politics and religion, his philosophy and love. Therefore, to criticize them from any other point of view, as has often been attempted, is to misunderstand and misrepresent them. The history of his thought in general, as well as of his view of death in particular, is the progressive adjustment of this innate, radical tendency, "soul of his soul," to all his experiences. Therefore his life-long struggle was a struggle to conquer the pain with which he witnessed all ugliness and the fading and death of all fair things. Therefore he loved Plato, and was attracted to Lucretius and Goethe. Therefore, reading Godwin and the French materialists, he transfigured them with a beauty of which their actual thought was scarcely susceptible, and so incurred the superficial inconsistencies of *Queen Mab* and *Prometheus.* Many of the inconsistencies in his work spring from the beauty he imports into thoughts not his own, seeing them thus as somewhat other, and more, than they are. But with time and practice the inconsistencies are burned away by the growing flame of his own thought, his originative aestheticism.

Equally important is the forward-looking, almost practical, faith implicit in this aesthetic fusion of metaphysics and politics. Shelley remains true to his social programme. His vision gives courage to his political faith. The Utopian vision, then, is no mere self-satisfying, sequestered dream. It is not a substitute for action. The poem does not belong to the poetry of escape from a life poets fail to face. It is a poem not of flight but of rescue, giving the very grounds of faith, and of courage to persist in stimulating men to the attainment of the humane ideal. Shelley's visions of loveliness, whether political or metaphysical, are not the reveries of one who has given up the human struggle. They are visions, with the social purpose of freeing men from their banal self-satisfaction in the commonplace. Therein lies the spiritual identity of *Queen Mab* and the *Hymn to Intellectual Beauty,* however great their difference in artistry.

In *Mont Blanc,* properly called by Shelley "an undisciplined overflowing of the soul," for it lacks both clearness and structural unity, the dualism that has been noted, once more obtains. Shelley's own explanation of the poem discloses it. He was concerned to read symbolically "the inaccessible solemnity" of Mont Blanc. The surrounding wilderness becomes a symbol of universal change, of the universe of things that live and die and live again:

> All things that move and breathe with toil
> and sound
> Are born and die, revolve, subside, and swell.

But the Mountain, gleaming high above all else, still and solemn, is the symbol of the secret, governing strength of things, of both matter and mind. And this hidden strength, like the Mountain, and like the Spirit of the *Hymn,* dwells apart:

> Power dwells apart in its tranquillity,
> Remote, serene, and inaccessible.

The fear and disgust of death, too, reappear, almost like condign punishment for the violence inherent in the dualism. For in a truly eloquent and no longer merely rhetorical dramatizing of the vast effort of change, which is likened to a restless tumult of winds swirling around the serene king of mountains, death is called a "detested trance"; and the destruction that overtakes the homes of insects, beasts and birds, and men—"and their place is not known"—is a thing of dread, the tragic loss of so much life and joy. Yet the poetic animism is so pervasive of the scene, the sense of a presence everywhere is so deeply felt, the veil is so far lifted from the hidden beauty of the world, and the skill of the music is so enchanting, that unless one reads the poem ever so attentively he feels its general trend and meaning are pantheistic. It is as though Shelley's reason had here, too, failed to grasp the full implication of his mood.

In these two mountain-poems, one written among, the other about mountains, death has been set in melancholy, or even tragic, antithesis to a great serenity. There is an advance beyond the sentimental play with death in *Alastor.* Bookishness early developed in Shelley a power of expression out of proportion to his first-hand knowledge of life. A sporting, juvenile Gothicism, an earnest, excited, tumid anarchism, and a personal, sentimental romanticism were effects of that inequality. Then the mountains, and other impressive rhythms of nature, vastly enriched his experience, developing his sensitiveness, deepening his moods, fecundating his imagination. He divined vaster meaning. Correspondingly, his verse-music was modulated by the verbal equivalents of the rhythms of ocean and earth and air. A serener and more solemn, more nearly sublime, reading of himself and humankind was an effect of this advance in experience. But death, and all change, remained something ugly, apart from serenity and beauty.

II

And now, two actual tragedies, in the closest circle of his human intimacies, were to add their deep, immediate teaching, through suffering, through personal grief and sorrow.

Fanny Imlay, whom Shelley loved almost as a sister, committed suicide the ninth of October, 1816. A month later, one winter day, or night, no human being knows exactly when, Harriet Shelley threw herself into the Serpentine.

Shelley did not write a long poem on either tragedy: only three brief, heartbroken lyrics.

Editors agree that the little *pallida-mors* ballad of twenty-eight lines beginning, *The cold earth slept below,* refers to the death of Harriet. There are several striking contemporary reports of how poignantly Shelley suffered, but this poem is the sole poetic memorial of his grief. Its brevity is significant. The last stanza is heart-rending. No declamation. Stark lyric simplicity. No rhetoric, no tumult, no grandeur. But a new restraint; and a transparent objectivity—the terrible contrast between the fresh, girlish beauty he had once sheltered, and loved so keenly, and the pale, dead face, gleaming in the moonlit water:

> The moon made thy lips pale, belovèd;
> The wind made thy bosom chill;
> The night did shed
> On thy dear head
> Its frozen dew, and thou didst lie
> Where the bitter breath of the naked sky
> Might visit thee at will.

Such a lament! The dear dead under the naked sky; the once beloved body in the sluggish stream: the horrible, unchangeable fact, beyond embroidery of mood and image. It is Shelley's first truly pathetic treatment of death; really, his first actual experience of death. Harriet and Fanny doubly taught the simple, tragic fact.

In 1817 two other very short poems express the same reality of grief. Six little lines on Fanny, recalling his last parting with her, speak his regret that he did not then guess the misery that already had broken her heart. It is a well-known kind of regret—that regret at heedlessness and lack of sympathy, which comes upon us afterwards and leaves us wondering whether, had we been less obtuse, we could have spoken the word that would have meant comfort and have averted catastrophe. Poor Fanny Imlay! Sweet, frail flower! Her mother, Mary Wollstonecraft, had once attempted suicide. Her stepfather, Godwin, preached it. When affairs in the Godwin household grew unbearable to this sensitive spirit, she accomplished it. For her sort of suffering the world, knowing it too well, has a sharp, bitter name—Misery—and too much room for it:

> Misery—O Misery,
> This world is all too wide for thee.

The other poem, entitled *Death,* makes a refrain of the misery of parting. For Shelley, it contains an unusually large number of the common, universal themes of grief: that death is final and the dead return not, that pain remains and goes on and on, that the old familiar scenes remind one poignantly of the dead, that the routine we lived with them is broken forever, that all we have of them is the grave. This access of the all too well-worn, primitive topics of grief, very simply taking the place of the grandiose theorems characteristic of his inexperience, is another sign of the reality of his grief. The would-be sophisticated ideas and moods give way to the primitive when hard experience supervenes. One picture, however, a picture of himself as a youth with hoary hair and haggard eye, sitting beside an open grave, is a romantic intrusion from the *Alastor* phase.

At the same time, his dreams are dying, his dreams of any immediate political revolution, of his power, like an Illuminatus or Eleutherarch, to effect a sudden change in the minds of men. The sanguine hopes give place to despondency and are assimilated somehow to his personal misfortunes, so that one vocabulary serves for his affliction and his dejection:

> That time is dead forever, child,
> Drowned, frozen, dead forever!
> We look on the past,
> And start aghast
> At the spectres wailing, pale and ghast,
> Of hopes which thou and I beguiled
> To death on life's dark river.

There is much meaning in that word "beguiled," as though all his excited mental adventuring had rushed on heedless of its real effect upon human hearts, until the interruptions of death taught regret too late.

Every part of his life seemed infected with failure, loss, and death. Death surrounded him. The very trance of music seemed a trance of death. Constantia's singing moved him to such a trance as sensitives have always known in the presence of beautiful sound, none more than Spenser:

> The whiles a most delitious harmony
> In full straunge notes was sweetly heard to sound,
> That the rare sweetnesse of the melody
> The feeble sences wholy did confound,
> And the frayle soule in deepe delight nigh drownd.

But the stunning familiarity with death at this time must have given special significance to his imaging that swooning trance of delight as the soul's swooning through death into the arms of spiritual reality. In this poem, indeed, *To Constantia Singing,* in which the stanza usually printed first should always be read last, Shelley has united the moods of affliction and dejection with the promise, the comfort, of the serene Reality of *Mont Blanc* and the last part of the *Hymn.* This were death, indeed, he cries, to be dissolved in such ecstasies and pass thence, traversing (there is here a reminiscence of the flight in *Queen Mab*) the "mighty moons that wane upon Nature's utmost sphere," to the realm of perfected, or intellectual, beauty. Out of effects of voluptuous, sensuous beauty, he distils, through yet another euthanasia, the spiritual beauty the contemplation of which had wrought serenity only the year before.

It is very characteristic of Shelley, this reunion in a new and fairer form and lovelier music, of many of his old ideas and moods: translated echoes of *Queen Mab* and the *Dœmon of the World,* of *Alastor* (the dying poet), the *Hymn,* and *Mont Blanc,* and of the terse tragic lyrics of his personal affliction. Already, in his juvenile anticipations of his later, well-known themes and characters, and in imperfect dislodgment in *Queen Mab* of mystic moods by incongruous ideas, Shelley's characteristic method of intellectual and artistic growth has been noted: a growth evident not so much in the appearance of new ideas as in the richer reworking of old ones—new learning about old ideas. Here, again, in *Constantia,* he is advancing old themes or parts of old themes, into new beauty, new imaginative and emotional realization. Really, his thought advances not so much through analysis and dissection, a scrupulous criticism of the philosophical propositions he loved so well, as by the natural, primitive, and poetic method of constantly reanimating old ideas with new experience, carrying the symbol further in expressiveness as experience itself developed. And the rich increase of music at each transformation is precisely the sign and measure of the advance in realization, the music being, of course, at once the soul and life-garment of the vision.

III

But it would be a mistake to consider the year 1817 entirely one of dejection, relieved only by this marvellous lyric to Constantia that almost translates music into imagery. The truth is far otherwise. All Shelley's poems of dejection are short. Nearly all his long poems pulsate with hope and courage. The chief work of the year is the longest of all his poems, *The Revolt of Islam,* and in it he valiantly reasserts his social credo. It is, in a way, a companion piece to his *Ozymandias,* also of this year. The sonnet epitomizes what the epic discourses, the colossal wreck of tyranny.

The Revolt of Islam, an apology for the French Revolution, is a poem of political idealism, of hope, suffering, failure, and death, but eventual triumph: a projection, in all these respects, of Shelley's interests upon an epic canvas. It is a story of violence and revolution. But a mood of peace pervades it; for its comfort for failure and its prophecy of success proceed from a faith in the power of love to survive suffering, lost causes, and death. This faith, in turn, though another example of the repetition of a previous and favourite theme, is here in particular a reflection of the deep, passionate love with which the life of Shelley and Mary was at this time suffused. Moreover, it was written under that new awareness of suffering which had come at the end of the previous year, and the heedful sympathy he learned in that actuality he here began to teach in song. Finally, the precariousness of life, especially of his own life, which influenced him so strongly in *Alastor,* was his constant thought while he sat in Bisham Wood morning after morning, composing this new poem. He tells us this himself. Much of the poem was written, he says, "with the same feeling, as real, though not so prophetic, as the communications of a dying man." How strange it is, this constant genius of death in the work of Shelley! In the *Revolt* that genius is present in added strength, a new lenity, and greater tenderness. Shelley's politics and private life are inextricably interwoven.

These points require substantiation.

But at first, as one reads the poem, and discovers the recrudescence of the old political themes of death, there is disappointment; for there seems to be no advance in treatment, and the serener vision of the *Hymn* and *Mont Blanc* seem nowhere to be found. The four ideas involving death and politics, which we have traced through the juvenilia, enter in unabashed tumidity. Again the tyrant is hurling death upon a bleeding world, again the patriot declaims that death is preferable to loss of liberty, again we behold the grandeur of the past fallen into decay and ruin; and again the poet prophesies the tortured death of the tyrants, but with a difference.

Again, personified Fear, Hatred, Bigotry, and Tyranny spread pestilence, decay, and death. Horrors are described with increased vigour; now in connection with the supernatural, as in his earliest poems; now in a conjunction of nature and death, as in this view of a rotting battle-field, which obviously owes much to Coleridge:

> Day after day the burning Sun rolled on
> Over the death-polluted land. It came
> Out of the east like fire, and fiercely shone
> A lamp of autumn, ripening with its flame
> The few lone ears of corn; the sky became
> Stagnate with heat, so that each cloud and blast
> Languished and died; the thirsting air did claim

All moisture, and a rotting vapour passed
From the unburied dead, invisible and fast.
(X.13)

The death of a slave condemned to torture is pictured deliberately. The tyrant is a murderer who

Slaked his thirsting soul as from a well
Of blood and tears, with ruin.
(V.31)

"He murders, for his chiefs delight in ruin." (VIII.14) The king passes surrounded by the steel

Of hired assassins, through the public way
Choked with his country's dead.
(X.8)

One recalls two lines in *Queen Mab:*

War is the statesman's game, the priest's delight,
The lawyer's jest, the hired assassin's trade.
(IV.167-168)

Again, the martyr welcomes death in the cause of liberty. Laon braves one for the other, and invokes his countrymen to do the same. Cythna hopes for either liberty or death. The death of the patriot is a "glorious doom." In the cause of liberty sweet maidens die happily and sentimentally, singing

. . . a low sweet song, of which alone
One word was heard, and that was Liberty.
(X.48)

The patriot-protagonists, Laon and Cythna, face martyrdom joyfully, though even here Shelley could not but lament that one so young and fair as Cythna should die. Again, the dungeons, palaces, and temples of the past fade like vapour, leaving not a rack behind. But man, with his heritage of perfectibility,

Remains, whose will has power when all
beside is gone.
(VIII.16)

However, it is when the fourth accustomed theme enters that the new learning becomes apparent. Just what quality in the poem is the effect of the deeper knowledge of life Shelley has been acquiring? I think it is a chastening of the young extremism which first created the romantic villains of *Zastrozzi* and then converted them into the political villains of *Queen Mab.* Hitherto Shelley has exulted in the painful death of bigots and tyrants, and has found therein the cure of all evils. But now he recognizes the fallacy of this hopeful killing off of his personified evils. The tyrants, somehow, must be reconciled with the kingdom of love. Inevitably their evil deeds will draw on punishment, as they sit "aghast amid the ruins [they themselves] have made." Mere self-realization is their inevitable punishment. Yet, they are men—individual, actual men—and as such must have their part in a universe of love, in the theatre of redemption. Merely to avenge the misdeed on the misdoer is only to increase the misery in a world "all too wide for it."

At last, the contradiction of ideas that we have suspected in *Queen Mab* is removed. Necessity, we heard, governs every working of the tyrant's moody mind; the soul of the universe foresees "the events chaining every will" (VI.181-190): yet the tyrant and bigot were in that poem objects of unmitigated scorn. But in the meantime the poet, standing before Mont Blanc, has heard voices that "repeal large codes of fraud and woe," has hymned a wise serenity of the spirit, has been in disgrace with fortune and men's eyes, and has seen despair lead to tragic death. These experiences have softened the indignations of the young idealist, and he learns how to pity, if not to love, the enemies of the public good. The confusion is thereby obliterated.

It is death that teaches tolerance. His young, wild passions and hopes, his disdains and hatreds of unreal, set villains of tyranny, and his hopes of impossible perfections, had indeed beguiled Shelley into the very presence of death. Harriet's death, and Fanny's, too, were tragic commentaries on Godwin's teachings. The logical abstractions and classifications of that strange philosopher, even when they passed into the ardent rhetoric of his chief disciple, were not fitted to the commonplace realities of human nature. Their practice in a perfectly logical world might be undeleterious. But in the actual world of Harriets and Fannies their practice got mixed up with the unpredictable results of passionate weakness and despair. It is in the face of these mixed personal equations that the ideologist learns tolerance through suffering. Classifications of good and evil, and personifications of them as patriots and tyrants, become vanities before the face of individual suffering. Shelley was learning more about individuals, and placing a higher value upon the tragic little theatre that each one is. He no longer could hate even a personification.

The rationale of this moral development, then, perhaps was something like this: Godwin's dream of perfectibility "clicked" with Shelley's ardent, innate benevolence; Godwin's cool logic, satisfying Shelley's conscientious impulse always to appeal to reason when dealing with human affairs, seemed to ratify the dream; his own ardent imagination animated Godwin's theorems into personifications, and insensibly the human quality of the personification was confused with human beings themselves, and he was convinced that his masquerade of personifications was a true picture of persons; then came misfortunes—the loss of his wife's love, the two suicides, the loss of his children by Harriet—at the same time that he was learning more of human sympathy from the Boinvilles and from Mary. He began to learn the difference between the personifications and actual persons. It was what he had to learn in order to proceed poet, for the poet gives us not propositions, even personified, about life, but the very life itself, deepened by a most sensitive, imaginative awareness of actual men and women. After his juvenile practice in themes derived from hearsay, he faces sorrow and derives his major themes from life itself. Then his imagination draws him more and more into concrete, commonplace reality, and passes on intuitively to a knowledge of spiritual, all-unifying reality, so that he feels each individual *sub specie aeternitatis.* So Shelley proceeds, uniting himself in love with persons, listening, though not in Wordsworth's contemplative fashion, to the "deep, sad music of humanity."

In *Islam,* then, Shelley's new learning is evident as a broadening of the power to love, as a more sympathetic understanding of human nature, and as the consequent moderation of his political hatreds. To be sure, the theme of *Islam* is still romantically idealistic, wildly emotional. To be sure, the dream that a perfect and bloodless revolution may result from the contagious genius of beautiful young eleutherarchs, like Laon and Cythna, who preach a gospel of love, is so much sentimentality. These moods leave the political realist cold indeed. But when their tolerance is set over against the fanaticism of *Queen Mab,* a growth in understanding is apparent. It is an advance from hate to love; from u[illegible]ness to a measure of beauty; from a crude dualism o[illegible] evil and good issuing in a fanatical rejection of impossibly wicked villains, toward that deeper and more hopeful humanism which issues in the injunction, "Love thine enemies." It is a step toward that repentant renunciation of hate with which Prometheus opens Shelley's greatest long poem, and which constitutes the spiritual unbinding of the Titan. The beginning of Shelley's own unbinding from extremism is in *The Revolt of Islam.*

Herein, too, lies Shelley's apology for the French Revolution, for in his preface to *Islam* he avers that the failure of the Revolution was not the failure of the ideas upon which it rested, but of the prosecution of its programme by the very means of hatred, murder, and vengeance that were opprobriated in tyranny. His patient, brave words deserve quotation:

> The panic which, like an epidemic transport, seized upon all classes of men during the excesses consequent upon the French Revolution, is gradually giving place to sanity. It has ceased to be believed that whole generations of mankind ought to consign themselves to a hopeless inheritance of ignorance and misery because a nation of men who had been dupes and slaves for centuries were incapable of conducting themselves with the wisdom and tranquillity of freemen so soon as some of their fetters were partially loosened. That their conduct could not have been marked by any other characters than ferocity and thoughtlessness is the historical fact from which liberty derives all its recommendations, and falsehood the worst features of its deformity. There is a reflux in the tide of human things which bears the shipwrecked hopes of men into a secure haven after the storms are past. Methinks those who now live have survived an age of despair.

Islam is the symbolic presentation of these ideas: the great hopes of Laon and Cythna, their initial successes, the magnificent rejoicing and the *Champ-de-Mars* festival of the benevolent new order, the return of the tyrants, the failure of the Revolution, and the hope of a later and more perfect event, embody these principles. Wordsworth and Coleridge, older contemporaries, who directly witnessed the shipwreck of liberal hopes in the storm of The Terror, made no sufficient distinction between means and end, and with that natural confusion lost faith in revolution; Shelley, escaping the crisis (he was only two years old at the close of The Terror), was free twenty-three years later to make the necessary distinction and realize the eternal nature of the struggle for freedom. Wordsworth's *The Borderers* and Shelley's *Revolt of Islam,* Professor Koszul reminds us, mark the difference in reaction.

But in this poem love defeats a thing less avoidable than hatred. It conquers the ugliness of death, though temporarily, conditionally. The strength for that conquest was the gift of the union with Mary. There we touch upon the other great plastic power of the poem, one that has kneaded its matter into a human beauty that is a companion-picture to the natural beauty of *Alastor.* Its presence is felt at the very beginning, in the seventh and eighth stanzas of the Dedication to Mary. Her loving companionship and the blessing of the "two gentle babes born from her side" are the very parents of this song, he says. It is the love of Shelley and Mary that makes the love of Laon and Cythna, their children that make the child of the lovers in the poem. The undaunted, winding way of the human fellowship of lovers and their children leads everywhere through the ideal story, from the beginning in love, through the suffering and disgrace at the hands of men, to the immolation of the lovers and their reunion in a heavenly paradise. Their revolutionary daring is that of Mary and Shelley, their rending of the mortal chains of custom, their high hopes for mankind's regeneration, their fortitude in seeming failure, their wisdom of stern contentment the while they are mocked by poverty and infamy, are the very things of which Shelley makes his love-song for Mary in the Dedication.

But it is in the last five stanzas of the ninth canto that the ecstasy of this love belittles death. The thought is a truism, like the thought of so many great poems; the mood and its music are very nearly sublime. The thought is as follows: the senses and reason discover nought in death but decay and extinction; but the world is full of delusion, and we know nought of the Power behind each thing; the mind faints, realizing its impotence to grasp the full nature of things, but this we know, that extinction is dearer than a life apart from the beloved; everything is darkly driven toward the abyss of death, but all change is as nothing *if* only love be not changed. There is the run of ideas. Now read them in the suggestivity of mood and image and music. Cythna is speaking to Laon:

"The while we too, belovèd, must depart,
And Sense and Reason, those enchanters fair,
Whose wand of power is hope, would bid the heart
That gazed beyond the wormy grave despair;
These eyes, these lips, this blood, seems darkly there
To fade in hideous ruin; no calm sleep,
Peopling with golden dreams the stagnant air,
Seems our obscure and rotting eyes to steep
In joy;—but senseless death—a ruin dark and deep!

"These are blind fancies. Reason cannot know
What sense can neither feel nor thought conceive;
There is delusion in the world—and woe,
And fear, and pain—we know not whence we live,
Or why, or how, or what mute Power may give
Their being to each plant, and star, and beast,
Or even these thoughts.—Come near me! I do weave
A chain I cannot break—I am possessed
With thoughts too swift and strong for one lone human breast.

"Yes, yes—thy kiss is sweet, thy lips are warm—
Oh, willingly, belovèd, would these eyes
Might they no more drink being from thy form,
Even as to sleep whence we again arise,
Close their faint orbs in death. I fear nor prize
Aught that can now betide, unshared by thee.
Yes, Love when Wisdom fails makes Cythna wise;
Darkness and death, if death be true, must be
Dearer than life and hope if unenjoyed with thee.

"Alas! our thoughts flow on with stream whose waters
Return not to their fountain; Earth and Heaven,
The Ocean and the Sun, the clouds their daughters,
Winter, and Spring, and Morn, and Noon, and Even—
All that we are or know, is darkly driven
Towards one gulf.—Lo! what a change is come
Since I first spake—but time shall be forgiven,
Though it change all but thee!" She ceased—night's gloom
Meanwhile had fallen on earth from the sky's sunless dome.

Though she had ceased, her countenance uplifted
To Heaven still spake with solemn glory bright;
Her dark deep eyes, her lips, whose motions gifted
The air they breathed with love, her locks undight;
"Fair star of life and love," I cried, "my soul's delight,
Why lookest thou on the crystalline skies?
Oh, that my spirit were yon Heaven of night,
Which gazes on thee with its thousand eyes!"
She turned to me and smiled—that smile was Paradise!

(IX.32-36)

Thus death, extinction, immortality, love, and mutability are woven into a beautiful and tragic whole, with love dominating fear and hope. Strong, varied, impassioned, undidactic, this is one of Shelley's most direct and powerful utterances on love and death—the most immediately human so far. Here even the old coffin-worm theme is mitigated into something effective, as, too, are all the other vapid anticipations to which we have listened in the poems of the first two decades. One previous theme is only dimly suggested: that great gate-theme, *mors janua vitae,* that stands at the end of *Queen Mab.* Perhaps even it takes second place to this attitude. Here most of us, at any rate, will pause in admiration, even though the Gate glisten afar in the *Hymn,* in *Mont Blanc,* and in *Adonais* itself.

For a victorious attitude, at least its promise, is indubitably present. *Its promise,* because the victory is conditional on the possibility of love's surviving the mutability of all else. This themendous *if* makes the beauty of the address a tragic beauty, by constraining the dream to a doubt of its fulfilment. The assertion is no mere ecstatic conversion of hope to fact; it is at once both stronger and more contingent than if it were outright delusion emotionally promoted to conviction. Its tragic contingency, indeed, gives it a touch of sublimity; and all moral sublimity conquers the fear and ugliness of death. Sublimity of heroism and sacrifice and courageous self-dependence, of faith and vision, of beauty and love—all these make death small, in very fact negligible.

But, finally, there is even more of comfort than is contained in this moral disregard of death; for in the supreme moment of love, as Shelley says toward the very end of the poem, describing the last great love-moment of the dying lovers,

> . . . the mighty veil
> Which doth divide the living and the dead
> Was almost rent, the world grew dim and pale—
> All light in Heaven or Earth beside our love
> did fail.
>
> (XII.15)

That assertion rises above contingency by substituting a present value for all fact and possibility—

> All light in Heaven or Earth beside our love
> did fail.

The experience is so supreme that it all but synthesizes within itself the antithesis of life and death—"the veil was almost rent." This intense, mystical annihilation of the dualism of matter and spirit, of life and death, of all such opposites, is the mark of the highest aesthetic moment, as Coleridge long ago pointed out in his doctrine of poetic unity. Moreover, the passage is an anticipation of another such moment, yet more splendidly realized, at the very close of *Adonais.* Shelley's aesthetic mysticism is most fully released, indeed, near the inspired close of certain of his poems: a first release in the great passage in *Queen Mab,* which has been discussed; a second, here; a third at the very end of the *Ode to the West Wind;* the greatest, in the last stanza of *Adonais.* Each of these passages is an impressive example of what James Mark Baldwin meant by his definition of the aesthetic moment: a moment of immediate contemplation in which the dualism of the inner and outer controls is annihilated in a higher reality embracing both. Here the outer control is the fact of life and death; the inner, the dream of survival; and the higher reality is the mystical faith that annihilates the difference between fact and dream. The contrast is annihilated, and a greater reality, including the fact and the dream in its higher synthesis, is ours for a moment. Afterwards we may wonder where we may find the faith to believe in the vision. But the poet, remaking the vision, re-instating the moment, comes ever to our aid.

After the successful portrayal of this great mood and attitude, dwarfing all else, the picture of the lovers' reunion in the heaven-palace of the Spirit is but so much dramatic myth and symbol. Heaven, rather, in reality is in the moment of unfathomable beauty: our moment, here and now. The rest can be taken on trust. Nay, like Dante in beatitude of the vision of God, we are content then to be nothing.

IV

Perhaps it is an anticlimax to consider what of precision there was in Shelley's ideas of immortality up to this time. It is unnecessary to point out again the earliest, flimsy passages on the subject, in *The Wandering Jew,* in which, before he had begun original thought, he merely reflected the conventional Christian belief he had been taught as a child; or to trace the rise of his distrust of that too easy faith in a definitely personal immortality. For a while French materialism, which later he rejected, threatened the promptings of his imagination, and at times he thought death ended all. But his considered opinion at the time he wrote *Islam* was a mixture of impersonal but intense idealism making for impersonal, or at least inconceivable, survival, with an impassioned hope, converted at certain great moments into an impassioned faith, that in eternity lovers will not be lost to each other.

For these beliefs Shelley argued in various ways, and repeatedly he imaged them in poetic figures. Six years earlier, in letters to Elizabeth Hitchener (June 20, June 25, 1811), he had rather speciously contended that the laws of conservation of energy and imperishability of matter assured the soul against perishing; and then had suggested that as the soul's faculties are temporarily suspended during sleep, so they may be in death, and that in its future state the soul will begin life anew, possibly under an inconceivable shape, but forgetful of its previous existence. A few months later in the same year (Oct. 15?, Nov. 24, 1811), he had ingenuously confided to her that though his reason told him death closes all, yet feeling made him believe directly the contrary, and that this deep feeling, or "inward sense," seemed to him a very proof of the soul's immortality. While admitting what so many others, from Cicero to Emerson, have asserted, that the desire for a future state may be a proof of it, Shelley remembers that the wish may prejudice us in favour of the argument. But he thinks that everything lives again, and that the soul of anything, even of a flower, being but the force which makes it what it is (as Aristotle would say, its function or end), cannot be conceived as perishing utterly. Yet where it exists and how we cannot discover. "Have not flowers also some end which Nature destines their being to answer?" he asks. The closeness of this train of thought to Aristotle's teleology of the soul is remarkable. Early in the next year (Jan. 7, 1812), he wrote in a postscript: "I find you begin to doubt the eternity of the soul: I do not"; adding, rather ambiguously, "More of that hereafter"!

In *Queen Mab,* for all its appeal to reason and its *quasi* materialism, the "inward sense" triumphs quite Platonically: soul is the only true reality, animating every atom (IV.139-146). This faith he had put forward tentatively in the letter to Miss Hitchener, dated November 24, 1811. Now he asserts it roundly, and adds that a soul though spoiled by earth may regain its original perfection—

> Soul is not more polluted than the beams
> Of Heaven's pure orb, ere round their rapid lines
> The taint of earth-born atmospheres arise.
>
> (IV.151-153)

One recalls a passage in the tenth book of the *Republic:* "Soul does not perish like the body, because its characteristic evil, sin or wickedness, does not kill it as the diseases of the body wear out the bodily life." Moreover, through death's dark gate the soul passes to a greater glory:

> Fear not then, Spirit, death's disrobing
>   hand, . . .
> 'Tis but the voyage of a darksome hour,
> The transient gulf-stream of a startling sleep.
> (IX.171-175)

The Universal Spirit, called also Spirit of Nature, Necessity, Soul of the Universe, carefully distinguished from the unreal God of human error and superstition, is represented as ceaselessly active, and as never interrupted by the temporary failure of earthly life in the grave (VI.146-238), though the problem of the exact nature of the relation between the universal mind and the individual, both before birth, during life, and after death, is deliberately avoided. But a positive and fairly definite answer to the question of personal survival was elaborated, we have seen, in connection with his love for Harriet, based again upon feeling. Our best and rarest emotional feelings, especially love, urge us to believe in something beyond death (*Q.M.* IX. 171-184). Birth, on the other hand, is regarded in the *Dæmon of the World* as the means of waking the universal mind to "individual sense of outward shows." *Alastor* develops this transcendentalism in a series of romantic images, and then it is presented with a new awe and serenity in the *Hymn* and *Mont Blanc.*

Intensity of feeling, then, or, rather, of love in particular, as well as a certain deep "inward sense," led Shelley to believe, even against reason, in some kind of persistence beyond the grave. The "inward sense" inclined him to a general and vague conception of that persistence; love in its passionate moments wrung from him a belief in the persistence of the individual, or, at least, of something equal, or finer, in its power to satisfy the desire for the perpetuation of ecstatic states.

But there is a curious relation, partly of contradiction, partly of agreement, between the ideas in *Queen Mab* and the ideas on survival contained in certain prose essays and fragments written subsequent to the poem. In the first two of these prose pieces, he argues against survival, in the third he becomes doubtful of his ground, in the fourth he disclaims personal survival but argues for some sort of persistence, and in the fifth he rationalizes the Christian teachings of personal survival and Heaven.

Queen Mab was published in 1813. The date of the brief prose tract, *On a Future State,* is uncertain, but in all probability it is not later than the following year, 1814. The tract is written under the influence of the French materialists he had been reading. It contains some ten chief arguments against survival of any sort, and includes reversals of the assumptions he had adopted in the Hitchener letters and in *Queen Mab.* (a) The imperishability of matter is now put forward not as a justification of the belief in immortality, but as an analogy destructive of the grounds of that belief. All matter divides and changes, and therefore gives no warrant for the assumption that spirit (defined as a mere name given to sensibility and thought to distinguish them from their objects) never changes, never divides, never loses a given personal identity. (b) Those philosophers to whom we are most indebted for discoveries in the physical sciences suppose that intelligence, or 'spirit,' is the "mere result of certain combinations among the particles of its objects," and that therefore it must cease with the inevitable dispersal of those particles and consequent annihilation of the combinations. If, then, these natural philosophers wish to believe in survival, it becomes necessary for them to assume the interposition of a supernatural power which overcomes the law of division and change in all matter. (c) The actual decay of the mind during life, seen in madness, idiocy, and old age, does not justify a presumption of changelessness and survival. (d) If mind is a special substance, which permeates, and is the cause of, the animation of living beings, there is no warrant for supposing that this substance is exempt from the general law of substance, viz., decay and change into other forms. (e) The condition of the body at death—the organs of sense destroyed and the intellectual operations dependent on them inoperative—offers no ground for an argument for survival of intelligence. (f) No valid argument for persistence can be drawn from an assumption of preëxistence, for the assumption cannot be supported. The argument that in each living being there is a prior and indestructible generative principle which converts surrounding substances into a substance homogeneous with itself (another of the arguments in the Hitchener letters) is untenable, because this so-called 'principle' does not really exist, but is only an hypostasis of an observed process, or, rather, of an observed coëxistence of certain phenomena.—These six arguments rest on the naturalistic definitions of spirit as intelligence and of intelligence as entirely dependent on the senses. In the remaining four arguments, an attack is made upon the immaterialistic grounds of belief.—(g) The idea of a survival in a mode of being totally inconceivable to us at present, which had been mentioned in the Hitchener letters and which is developed in some later poems, is called an unreasonable presumption, because it is not supported by a single analogy and because by its very transcendental nature it cannot be brought to the bar of reason. "It is sufficiently easy, indeed, to form any proposition, concerning which we are ignorant, just not so absurd as not to be contradictory in itself, and defy refutation." (h) The argument drawn from the Divine Justice—that a just

Deity must compensate the virtuous who suffer during life by providing them with eternal happiness—is lightly dismissed as satisfying no one! (i) Moreover, were it proved that a Divine Power rules the world, survival would not follow as a necessary inference. (j) The secret and real cause of the belief in survival is merely the wish to survive. "This desire to be forever as we are; the reluctance to a violent and unexperienced change, which is common to all the animated and inanimate combinations of the universe, is, indeed, the secret persuasion which has given birth to the opinions of a future state." So he disposes of the argument from the heart, which he has used in his earliest poems, in the Hitchener letters, in *Mab,* and in *Islam,* and which he continues to use in many a later poem. If only that enthusiastic rhetorician, W.R. Alger, had written his *Critical History of the Doctrine of a Future Life* before 1814, what meat he would have been for the Shelley of *On a Future State!* What fun Shelley would have made, for instance, of Alger's picture of mighty man walking the universe, supported by his inalienable instinct for immortality: "Crowned with free will, walking on the crest of the world, enfeoffed with individual faculties, served by vassal nature with tributes of various joy, he cannot bear the thought of losing himself, of sliding into the general abyss of matter"!

In the second pamphlet, the ironical *Refutation of Deism* (1814), the Christian doctrine of the eternal damnation or salvation of souls by an all-foreseeing, all-causing God is ridiculed as inconsistent with any but a savage and obscene conception of deity.

With the fragment *On the Punishment of Death* (1814 or 1815), a change of opinion begins. After asserting that it is quite impossible to know whether death be good, evil, or indifferent, a punishment or a reward, he admits that he thinks the common idea of the survival of "that within us which thinks and feels" is supported by "the accurate philosophy of . . . the modern Academy." This complete reversal in interpreting the French Encyclopedists is made to turn upon a phase of their own teaching, viz., the "prodigious depth and extent of our ignorance respecting the causes and nature of sensation." Shelley has come to realize that the materialists' assumption that sensations are irreducible, or pure, minima of consciousness is highly questionable. In turn, he has recourse to a conception against which he had argued, speciously, to be sure, in the first of these essays: that if we do survive, the manner of our existence must be such as no earthly experience can conceive or understand. But he concludes the matter by observing that if at death the individual soul is merely absorbed in the universal soul, death can be pronounced neither good nor evil, but only indifferent.

The fourth paper is the fragment, *On Life* (1815). Now, definitely renouncing and attacking the materialistic psychology, Shelley tends to take his stand with the idealists. The mind naturally disclaims alliance with transience and decay, and cannot conceive annihilation (this dogma is close to that of the "inward sense" noted above); but idealism leads the mind to such a conception of the unity of all life that the common, intense, and exclusive meaning of individuality is destroyed. Out of this annihilation of the antithesis of the individual and the universal, the poetry of the *Adonais* is to be forged by the heat of tragic experience. But at the close of the fragment Shelley moves away from the idealists, holding that it is "infinitely improbable that the cause of mind, i.e. of existence, is similar to mind," because mind cannot create, but can only perceive.

The last of these prose pieces, the *Essay on Christianity* (1815? 1817?), has definite relations to *The Revolt of Islam.* Christ's traditional teaching concerning the future life is rationalized. The promise that the pure in heart shall see God is understood, not as a reference to a literal beholding of God, after death, but as a poetic way of referring to the blessed and beautiful inner experience of the simple, sincere, and virtuous man: the ideal 'natural' man of Rousseau. The beatitude is strictly equivalent to the saying that virtue is its own reward. Similarly, Christ's description of the bliss of the soul in Heaven is to be taken as a poetic and enthusiastic hyperbole for the heavenly beauty of the inner life of the good man. Presently we shall have occasion to quote extensively the eloquent exposition of this point, and then its relation to *Islam* will become clear. For the rest of the *Essay,* it need only be remarked that in the course of it are to be found in several places the assumption of an over-ruling Power, by which we are surrounded, from which we experience "benignant visitings." The step from that last phrase to the Spirit of the *Hymn to Intellectual Beauty* and of the *Mont Blanc* is obvious.

These five essays, then, give us some faint and, we may say, in view of their fragmentary, hurried nature, some erratic, suggestions of the change in mind by which Shelley passed from the materialistic psychology of Locke and the Encyclopedists back to the faith expressed in the Hitchener letters and forward to the faith of the *Hymn, Mont Blanc,* and all his later poems. Death and immortality and the nature of God were the crucial problems through which he progressed in making the change from his temporary materialism back to his native gift for the invisible and forward to his more or less reasoned idealism. But it is particularly noticeable that in *Queen Mab,* although it was composed during the materialistic period, the native gift finally triumphed over the acquired materialism, even though the materialistic arguments were resumed in the essay *On a Future State.* His own spirit, when thoroughly aroused, as toward the end of *Mab,* burst through the psychology imported from France or found at home in Locke.

In *Islam,* according to Professor Woodberry, "the expressions with respect to the immortality of the spirit are perceptibly more strong and favorable" than in *Queen Mab* and *Alastor.* I am not sure that this is a true statement. But, at any rate, most of Shelley's previous ideas upon the subject are repeated—the more general ones with greater conviction, perhaps; those dealing more particularly with personal survival, with rather less, it seems to me. For here, again, there is certainty with regard to the existence of a higher power, called both Necessity (IX.27) and Spirit (XII.31.41), which, in a phrase recalling the *Hymn,* is said to "float unseen, but not unfelt, o'er blind mortality" (VI.37). Again, as in *Queen Mab,* and as later in the *Ode to the West Wind,* we are reminded of the social, or influential, immortality of our good deeds and thoughts. The good who die beneath the tyrant's rod are as autumn, dying before winter; but like autumn, they sow in their good works the seeds which spring shall bring to leaf and flower:

> Our many thoughts and deeds, our life and
> love,
> Our happiness, and all that we have been,
> Immortally must live and burn and move
> When we shall be no more.
>
> (IX.30)

Now we live in the winter of the world's discontent, and die therein, even as the winds of autumn expire in the frore and foggy air. But a glorious spring of perfected moral life awaits society, though the good who give promise and prophecy of it must pass. But if the good would behold the glory of that great dawn, they have but to look at the Paradise of their own hearts, which is "the earnest of the hope which made them great" (IX.25-27). Again, mere reason makes him believe in oblivion (IX.32), the extinction of personality (IX.29). But, and, once more, again, reason and the senses cannot give the final answer, and therefore we doubt the blank answer of reason, though we cannot know what mute Power may animate the universe of mind and matter (IX.33, as quoted above). The last recourse, then, is to feeling, especially love,

> Yes, Love when Wisdom fails makes
> Cythna wise.
>
> (IX.34)

The love she feels for Laon, typical of all great love, is the only certainty which she knows—the only certainty by which she can interpret death. Because of this greatness and this certainty she is unwilling to believe that Laon's personality and her love for him will be annihilated. Cythna is Love's prophetess of a more perfect life beyond the grave (IX.20). Here is the reversal of the last argument in *On a Future State.*

What persuaded Professor Woodberry that Shelley had reached in this poem a stronger conviction of the personal immortality of the soul was, probably, the definite depiction, in Cantos I and XII, of a paradise for the souls of the good and great. But the very definiteness of these pictures, the wealth of concrete detail lavished on them, their sheer extravagance of imagery, might lead another reader to suspect Shelley never meant them to be taken literally, especially in view of his known objections, both now and later, to confusing such anthropomorphic religious fairy-tales with fact. Rather their very extravagance of bliss is a symbol of the beauty these spirits attained in life, a beauty that cannot die among men, but grows fragrant with time and memory; and a poetic way of suggesting not what does actually lie beyond death, but what is the best possible idea a mortal mind can achieve of a perfect mind. At any rate, they are a part of the fairy-machinery of the poem, floating lightly in the romantic and sentimental atmosphere. Like other marvels in the poem—the child with the silver wings, the boat of hollow pearl, the eagle who refused to bring ropes, and the Tartarean steed—they are properties of the romantic theatre, to be interpreted figuratively, rather than literally.

But Shelley's attitude toward these pictures of heavenly bliss may be gathered pretty definitely from his interpretation of Christ's utterances on a similar theme. I quote, as I promised, from the *Essay on Christianity:*

> We die, says Jesus Christ, and when we awaken from the languor of disease the glories and the happiness of Paradise are around us. All evil and pain have ceased forever. Our happiness also corresponds with, and is adapted to, the nature of what is most excellent in our being. We see God, and we see that he is good. How delightful a picture, even if it be not true! How magnificent and illustrious is the conception which this bold theory suggests to the contemplation, even if it be no more than the imagination of some sublimest and most holy poet, who impressed with the loveliness and majesty of his own nature, is impatient and discontented, with the narrow limits which this imperfect life and the dark grave have assigned forever as his melancholy portion.

So, too, Shelley into his poetry boldly projects the paradise of his own best ideas, making a symbolic external Heaven out of the Kingdom within him, moved thereto by discontent with the imperfections of life and the ugliness of the grave. Of course, such a process again and again must fling out a bolder figurative statement, whether of Utopias or Heavens, than sober sense would allow in reasoned prose. Poetry is a kind, the highest and most natural kind, of intoxication.

Of the classic arguments for the immortality of the soul, which, then, has Shelley, up to this time, put forward? Though Voltaire's epigram, that the problem of immortality has been "discussed for four thousand years in four thousand different ways," well sets out the confusion as well as the indeterminate nature of the discussion—in 1878 Ezra Abbot of Harvard College went Voltaire 977 times better by compiling a list of 4977 books "relating to the nature, origin, and destiny of the soul"—nevertheless some few arguments are outstanding. They are outstanding not because they are convincing, but because they are common or typical, occurring repeatedly in the logomachy, with great variety of specific traits at each occurrence, to be sure. Following Dr. Garvie's admirable *Britannica* article on immortality, I shall pick out five of these common, typical approaches. There is the argument from metaphysics: that the soul, being indivisible and independent of the body cannot perish with the latter—the favourite teaching of Leibnitz and Ernst Platner, to say nothing of many a scholastic, with Albertus Magnus at their head. There is the juridical argument, represented by Kant and Bishop Butler: that the present life is so imperfect there must be another, perfect existence. There is the ethical argument, well developed by Hugo Münsterberg: the more lofty a man's aims, the more incomplete is his life on the earth; therefore there must be another, complete life. There is the religious (Christian) argument: man, being created in God's image, cannot be death's victim. God is the God of the living, not of the dead, as Christ is reported to have said (Matthew 22.32). Finally, there is the argument from the emotions: the heart protests against severance from its love by death, and as man feels love is his most godlike characteristic, love's claim has supreme authority. This is the argument of *In Memoriam.* Now, of these five, the only one that Shelley definitely and directly stresses is the last, the argument from feeling: it is his first argument, in *The Drowned Lover* and the lines *To Harriet;* it survives determinism in *Queen Mab;* it comes back to its own in *The Revolt of Islam,* first with tragic contingency, then with mystic faith; it continues through poems not yet considered in this essay, such as *Prometheus Unbound* and *Adonais;* as late as *Hellas* (1821-22), in a note to that poem, Shelley says that the desire for immortality "must remain the strongest and the only presumption that eternity is the inheritance of every thinking being." This is the only argument for personal survival that he at any time admits, and he stresses it, as is natural, far more in the passion of poetry than in the reflection of prose. Of the four other arguments, the Christian-religious does not at all appear; the ethical and juridical appear only very indeterminately and imperfectly, or figuratively, in scattered suggestions of the hope of final blessedness for the world's political martyrs; and the metaphysical can only with difficulty be read into one or two ambiguous passages.

The other arguments for survival that Shelley has used can properly be taken only as arguments against personal immortality. His idealistic utterances in *On Life* are connected with a persuasion that personality is a sort of fallacy; and the suggestion that survival must be in an inconceivable mode of being negatives, by implication at least, the definite concept of separate entity. I must conclude, therefore, that Mrs. Shelley's summary of his belief does not fit the state of his published opinions at the time he wrote *Islam,* for in this summary, which follows, she has certainly thrown far more emphasis upon individual survival than appears in these writings, or, for that matter, in his later writings. Perhaps in her eagerness to bridge the gulf between Shelley and the public she unconsciously overestimated the personal element in his opinions or took too literally the Heaven of *Islam;* or, perhaps, she did not fully grasp the impersonality of his idealism. Here, at any rate, is what she wrote:

> Considering his individual mind as a unit divided from a mighty whole, to which it was united by restless sympathies and an eager desire for knowledge, he assuredly believed that hereafter, as now, he would form a portion of that whole—and a portion less imperfect, less suffering, than the shackles inseparable from humanity impose on all who live beneath the moon. (Essays, Letters from Abroad, etc. 1840. I.xiv)

The difficulty lies in the phrase "hereafter, as now," for it seems to designate a survival as personal as is the present life. The rest of the summary is fairly accurate. But it is high time to hold our tongues concerning these endless speculations. By way of relief, let us remember another of Voltaire's satirical remarks:

> "Hold your tongue," said the dervise. "I promised myself the pleasure," said Pangloss, "of reasoning with you upon effects and causes, the best possible of worlds, the origin of evil, the nature of the soul, and the pre-established harmony."—The dervise, at these words, shut the door in their faces.

V

Now the story turns back to moods of grief and dejection. *Prince Athanase,* the next document, is a fragment. As it stands it has little about death. Had it been completed, death would have been its pathetic *dénouement.* It is a revised *Alastor,* involving a significant addition. The romantic, hoary-headed young poet of *Alastor,* pursuing his dream of a divine beauty and love, hoping to find it in the actual world, failed in the pursuit, and died in solitude at the touch of winter's changing hand. *Alastor* is a lyric solo of an impossible quest, a failure doomed by the nature of things. But in *Athanase* the poet-prince, also young, hoary-headed, and romantic, was to have won the body-beauty of an earthly love, finding out, too late, that this was not the heavenly love for which he searched. Then, at his death-bed, the spirit-beauty of his quest was to have appeared, to kiss his dying lips. It would have been a lyric drama of pursuit, mistake and repentance, failure, and dying vision.

The theme of the two loves, earthly and heavenly, is taken from Pausanias's speech in Plato's *Symposium.* There are two Aphrodites, said Pausanias, the heavenly, which is pure and noble, called Urania, and the earthly, which is physical and ignoble, called Pandemos. It is natural, and perhaps all too easy, to identify the Aphrodite Pandemos, in the scheme of the proposed poem, with Harriet. The ugly change in her love, at any rate, and the ensuing disappointment and failure, are parallel to the tragic disillusionment of the poem. That Mary was the Uranian love appears from the description of her, as the heavenly love, at the end of the fragment. That she comes too late, while the individual dies, is perhaps a dramatic parallel to actuality—Shelley again, while he wrote this poem, thought he was dying of a consumption—rather than a symbol of some teaching that perfection belongs only to the moment, that all moments in their death give birth to others. That teaching of how to be reconciled with mutability's theft of all beautiful things—that each moment is fulfilled of beauty—was Keats's instinctive teaching; or, at least, an idea his instinct for sensuous beauty demanded of his intellect, so that he need not admit a serpent of ugliness into his young Eden of delight. But it is not yet Shelley's teaching, or realization.

Thus death, dramatic and pathetic, would have been the catastrophe of the poem; but a death true, at least, to Shelley's mournful preoccupation with the failure of loveliness, the brightness of the world ever in eclipse.

But it would have been true, too, to the grief, hardly yet turned through reconciliation into sorrow, which pulses in the poem itself. And, though the actual fragment has so little of death in it, yet for this weight of real grief it becomes an important witness to the growth of Shelley's ideas on death. Athanase is described as bowed with a secret sadness, one that he himself scarcely understands, which his friends emptily conjecture, and which he himself never confesses to them. But the nature of the burden is nevertheless made fairly clear: a deep, almost subconscious intuition of all the evils done under the sun, intensified by a particular, personal tragedy:

> . . . 'Tis the shadow of a dream
> Which the veiled eye of memory never saw,
> But through the soul's abyss, like some dark stream
> Through shattered mines and caverns underground,
> Rolls, shaking its foundations; and no beam
> Of joy may rise but it is quenched and drowned
> In the dim whirlpools of this dream obscure.

This woe for the deep-seated evils of the world was indeed for Shelley embittered to grief by many particulars which had come close to him. We have already rehearsed most of the catalogue. The cruel political persecutions of the time, the causes of some of them deliberately manufactured by the government's nefarious and shameless *agents provocateurs,* inspired him with horror; the loss of his elder children by the court's decision that he was an unfit father to care for them, was the cause of a continual, inexpressible anguish, as both Mrs. Shelley and Leigh Hunt have testified; his fears that little William, his son by Mary, might also be torn from him by the law, embittered him; the loss of friends, the public opprobrium which followed upon the affair with Mary, the deaths of Harriet and Fanny, and his own health failing, as he believed, day by day, filled him with grief, "withering up his prime." Loss of political dreams, loss of family, love, friends, loss of health and hope, the threatened loss of Mary and the new and greater love:—his little immediate world repeated the evils and anguish of the great world. But, most of all, the tragic mistake shared between Harriet and himself shook the foundations of his mental life.

There was this intense mental agony, from which there seemed no escape: "like an eyeless nightmare grief did sit upon his being." That was one half of him, a half that remained untold, except in the disguise of *Athanase.* The other half of him, also pictured in the poem, was the unresting multitude of thoughts driven tumultuously through his mind, a feverish mental activity alternating, in manic-depression fashion, with "lethargy and inanimation." His reason and his feelings, though in some particulars interfused, as in his theory and practice of marriage, led separate but fevered lives, and, like the Prince, he was always disquieted, shaken with "spasms of silent passion."

> . . . there was an adamantine veil
> Between his heart and mind,—both unrelieved
> Wrought in his brain and bosom separate strife.

His mind was indeed in a state of insurrection and terrible confusion. He saw nothing that might help to lighten the load. It must be borne alone and silently. He felt a solemn duty, to keep the worst of it from Mary. "Let it remain—untold," were the words with which he concluded the description of his hero's agony.

The poem, then, is a veiled confession of agony, of tumults of feeling and reason. Shelley, in a note, says he gave up completing it because he feared he "might be betrayed into the assuming a morbid character." There was in Shelley the moral strength that sometimes accompanies sensitiveness. He fought manfully and successfully against his depression in the heroic days before psycho-analysis made paying patients of us all. But the poem is a prelude to the veiled agony of *Julian and Maddalo.*

Nearly all the major themes of death thus far traced reappear in a new unity in the partly autobiographical poem, *Rosalind and Helen,* a poem of love and death, founded on an experience of one of Mary's friends, but amplified to give a picture of Shelley himself under the guise of the dead lover, Lionel. Lionel, like Shelley and the youth in *Alastor,* had looked forward to an early death, a slow wasting away, like a too early blooming flower that droops in an April frost. Something of the romantic self-pity of *Alastor* intrudes again. Like Laon and Shelley, Lionel was a dreamer of Utopias; like Shelley he was for a while crushed by the failure of his political hopes, which were

> Like the life of youth
> Within him, and when dead became
> A spirit of unresting flame
> Which goaded him in his distress.

That is one of the clearest of Shelley's poetic confessions of his political despair, revealing as it does the emotional intensity of his dreams—"like the life of youth within him." Shelley's political theories, be it said again, were not to him mere abstract ideas; they were sensations of the nervous system, ideas that were tied into all the privacies of his emotional life.

Next comes the story of Lionel's death. His widow, Helen, tells it. The almost unrelieved grief and melancholy of this first part of the poem again reflects the new contact with reality. The pain of utter despair which the death of a loved one unseals, until agony obliterates even the hope of rest in death, is presented simply and poignantly, as of one

> Walking beneath the night of life,
> Where hours extinguished, like slow rain
> Falling forever, pain by pain,
> The very hope of death's dear rest.

Yet he cannot resist using his old theme of the ugliness of death, the coffin-worm, though he no longer employs it to create a mood of horror. It becomes expressive of the bitter despair with which the living contemplate the physical failure called death; even of the hideousness of life itself that must experience grief and go down to obscenity. Then, after the pessimistic gloom has settled over poet and reader, almost unbearably, there comes that optimistic turn, toward the end of the poem, which one finds so often in Christian elegy, and in so many of Shelley's poems—in *Queen Mab, The Revolt of Islam,* and, finest of all, *Adonais.* It is, once again, the conviction that love dies not with the dead. The very passion of Helen's love for Lionel leads her to feel, like Cythna, that the thing which she loves and finds so beautiful must be eternal:

> And in my soul I dared to say
> Nothing so bright can pass away;
> Death is dark and foul and dull,
> But he is—Oh, how beautiful!

Once more death is defeated through desire, by the emotion of personal love, by the intensity of the sacrament of the union of two individuals. That sacrament is too exquisite to mean nothing; it is the incandescence in which what all life burns toward, is realized. But from this passionate conviction the thought rises to the serener perception of a universal beauty which includes and answers death. This is the mood of the *Hymn* and *Mont Blanc.* But this serenity is here united with that special intensity which impassions the lyric to Constantia. Lionel, speaking comfort, had said in a kind of revelation:

> Heard'st thou not that those who die
> Awake in a world of ecstasy?
> That love, when limbs are interwoven,
> And sleep, when the night of life is cloven,
> And thought, to the world's dim
>   boundaries clinging,
> And music, when one beloved is singing,
> Is death? Let us drain right joyously
> The cup which the sweet bird fills for me.

All these figures—the intense union of love, the intense vision in dream, the intense abstraction of thought, the intense ecstasy of music—are figures of those uttermost moods of which we are capable, which seem to have a unique and mystical meaning of their own, and which persuade us, at least momentarily, that all beauty is but an anticipation, in comparison dull enough, of the perfect beauty of a reality that encompasses death serenely. "Perchance this were death indeed."

This aesthetic ecstasy in which Lionel dies is a kind of death, i.e., it transcends the common and false antithesis of life and death in a more than ordinary, or mystical, state of awareness, wherein thought clings "to the world's dim boundaries" as it all but escapes those boundaries. This ecstasy is the 'death' of the misleading antithesis. Hence it is that, as Shelley himself enters this ecstasy while he is composing *Adonais,* he cries "Die, if thou wouldst be with that which thou dost seek." Lionel's death, in its mystical consummation, is an anticipation of the central theme of *Adonais.*

In *Rosalind and Helen,* moreover, a remarkable link between the pathetic death of the poet in *Alastor* and the comfort of death in *Adonais,* is discoverable. Rosalind's description of the place where she wishes to be buried is distinctly reminiscent of the burial of the poet in the former poem. She wishes her grave may be on some Alp, whose snowy head is islanded in the azure air (the *Mont Blanc* theme), for, as her lover had said,

'T were sweet
'Mid stars and lightnings to abide,
And winds, and lulling snows that beat
With their soft flakes the mountain wide . . .

Similarly the leaves of the mountain wilderness had covered the body of the *Alastor* poet. But the quiet union with nature thus accomplished in a romantic solitude had carried with it, even in *Alastor,* some undersong of natural, or even spiritual, deathlessness. Here the undersong sounds forth more clearly:

Who knows, if one were buried there,
But these things might our spirits make,
Amid the all-surrounding air,
Their own eternity partake?

Surely the next link in this chain of thought, which with each link becomes more masterfully conceived and beautifully fashioned, is the famous metamorphosis of the poet in *Adonais:*

He is made one with nature; there is heard
His voice in all her music, from the moan
Of thunder to the song of night's sweet bird.

Thus Shelley's poems are continually, not merely echoing each other, but striking each into each with such an ever deepening harmony as makes all seem one increasing composition of ever repeated themes.

Rosalind and Helen is one of Shelley's many minor, second or third rate, poems. It largely though not entirely lacks his distinctive race—his special excitement that springs from the union of mystical abstraction and sensuous vividness, as though Brahma should become an impassioned lover, dancing like Siva, or even Kali. It is probably the most pedestrian of any of Shelley's poems of equal or greater length. It seems an exercise faithfully fulfilled for the less intuitive mind of Mary, who asked him to tell the story. But it is a peculiarly interesting poem for the student of Shelley's thought. For in it, for the first time after his contact with tragic reality in his own life, and after the maturing process of composing the long *Islam,* he has united his old book-bred ideas about life in general with his new realization of it through particular personal happenings, in an extended scale of finished composition. And something new has descended upon him: the fructification of ideas by pain, the humanizing of his youthful, inexperienced tragic gloom, the poignancy of realized grief, the quite genuine submersion in sorrow, and then a sincere revulsion to hope and faith.

Such is the result of the alternation of moods and ideas during these four years, 1814-1817; such is the mutual purgation of romantic dream and real experience. Shocked out of the romantic self-pity of *Alastor* by real tragedies, converted in *Islam* from vituperation to sympathy and pity, plunged into despair by the wreck of his hopes, reaching uncertainly toward serenity in the *Hymn* and *Mont Blanc,* stifling his agony in *Athanase,* making a new love into a spiritual dream of personal immortality, manfully re-creating hope and faith out of their own wrecks, Shelley is becoming acquainted with the burden of life—its many kinds of death.

FURTHER READING

Bassein, Beth Ann. "Adultery and Death: Clarissa, Emma, Maggie, Anna, Tess, Edna." In *Women and Death: Linkages in Western Thought and Literature,* pp. 58-127. Westport, CT: Greenwood Press, 1984.

Faults George Eliot's expediency in *The Mill on the Floss* in having Maggie die an accidental death, an ending deemed damaging to women readers seeking inspiration and hope in characters.

Bewell, Alan. "The History of Death." In his *Wordsworth and the Enlightenment: Nature, Man, and Society in the Experimental Poetry*, pp. 187-234. New Haven: Yale University Press, 1989.

Contrasts William Wordsworth's writings on death with Enlightenment thought on the subject and examines Wordsworth's views on immortality and the origins of burial.

Bronfen, Elisabeth. "Risky Resemblances: On Repetition, Mourning, and Representation." *In Death and Representation,* pp. 103-29. Edited by Sarah Webster Goodwin and Elisabeth Bronfen. Baltimore: The Johns Hopkins University Press, 1993.

Explores resurrection in Edgar Allan Poe's "Ligeia."

Curl, James Stevens. *The Victorian Celebration of Death.* Detroit: The Partridge Press, 1972, 222 p.

Includes a discussion about Victorian views on death in addition to the central study of the Victorian cemetery.

Edmond, Rod. "Death Sequences: Patmore, Hardy, and the New Domestic Elegy." *Victorian Poetry* 19, No. 2 (Summer 1981): 151-65.

Compares the poetic sequences of Coventry Patmore and Thomas Hardy on the subject of the death of their respective wives and assesses the contributions of the poets.

Ermarth, Elizabeth. "Maggie Tulliver's Long Suicide." *Studies in English Literature 1500-1900* XIV, No. 4 (Autumn 1974): 587-601.

Considers the life of George Eliot's Maggie to be a type of death, one caused in part by internalizing sexist norms.

Keefe, Robert. *Charlotte Brontë's World of Death.* Austin: University of Texas Press, 1979, 224 p.

Studies the impact that the death of Charlotte Brontë's mother had upon Charlotte's writings.

Morley, John. *Death, Heaven, and the Victorians.* Pittsburgh: University of Pittsburgh Press, 1971, 208 p.

Provides background on nineteenth-century mortality rates and death customs.

Robison, Roselee. "Time, Death, and the River in Dickens' Novels." *English Studies* 53, No. 4 (August 1972): 436-54.

Examines the maturation of Dickens's use of river imagery in writing about death.

Stewart, Garrett. "The Secret Life of Death in Dickens." *Dickens Studies Annual* 11 (1983): 177-207.

Explores the narrative importance of the deaths by drowning in Charles Dickens's novels.

———. "Traversing the Interval." In his *Death Sentences: Styles of Dying in British Fiction*, pp. 53-97. Cambridge: Harvard University Press, 1984.

Surveys in chronological order some of Charles Dickens's important death scenes.

Stone, Harry. *The Night Side of Dickens: Cannibalism, Passion, Necessity.* Columbus: Ohio State University Press, 1994, 726 p.

Traces how these more-concealed aspects of Charles Dickens appear in Dickens's writings, how they influence his work, and what works best represent these aspects of Dickens's dark side.

Wheeler, Michael. *Death and the Future Life in Victorian Literature and Theology.* Cambridge: Cambridge University Press, 1990, 456 p.

Examines how theological questions of death, judgment, heaven, and hell are considered in nineteenth-century literature.

English Romantic Hellenism

INTRODUCTION

The relationship between the literary Romantic movement and the growing interest in ancient Greek literature, mythology, art, and culture in nineteenth-century England is a complex one; scholars rarely agree on which development is an offshoot of the other. While Harry Levin (1931), in the first major study of English Romantic Hellenism, maintained that the "cult of Greece" became a "mere enthusiasm" among a "long series of romantic obsessions," James Osborn (1963) pinpoints Romantic Hellenism as a part of the larger Neo-Hellenism movement. While the boundaries of these movements remain blurred, it is clear that during the late eighteenth century and early nineteenth century, in the aftermath of the eighteenth century's neo-classicism, England became increasingly enamored of Greece, and the Romantic poets—most notably Lord Byron, Percy Bysshe Shelley, and John Keats—turned to the past and to the East for inspiration.

Several concurrent developments influenced a shift in English attention from Rome to Greece during the eighteenth and nineteenth centuries. In terms of literature, the writings of ancient Rome and Greece had long been lumped together under the rubric of "classical studies." Typically, Latin translations of Greek works served as the basis of such studies, due in part, John Churton Collins (1910) notes, to the difficulty of the Greek language. But gradually, a separation of Roman and Greek cultures began to occur, resulting in a new respect for Greek works as the models on which subsequent Roman literature was based. At the same time, Greece was experiencing a new wave of travelers to its shores. French and English travelers to Greece published accounts of their observations, and in the mid-eighteenth century, two British artists, James Stuart and Nicholas Revett, set out to measure the Parthenon and other Greek structures. James Osborn notes that with the publication of their *The Antiquities of Athens, Measured and Delineated* (1762), a new Grecian fashion in architecture and decoration took hold in England. Countless similar excursions to Greece followed, and soon overlapped with interest in Greek literature, as scholars sought to investigate the veracity of Homer and his works. Finally, it must be noted that in 1800, Thomas Bruce, seventh Earl of Elgin, had plaster casts made of Greek statues of the Parthenon. Elgin was also authorized to remove pieces of statuary on which there appeared inscriptions. The "Elgin marbles," as they became known, soon arrived in England (many by 1804) and in 1816 were purchased for the country by the British government.

The late eighteenth and early nineteenth centuries also saw numerous developments within the field of mythography. Throughout most of the eighteenth century, explains Alex Zwerdling (1964), mythographers were primarily concerned with making pagan "idolotary" acceptable to a Christian audience. While the typical eighteenth-century attitude toward Greek mythology was a negative one, it remained a source of interest, mainly out of a sense of obligation to classical studies. By the late eighteenth century, the distortion of Greek myth for the sake of Christian sensibilities was becoming increasingly unpalatable to the growing Romantic movement. Greek mythology underwent a revival in which it was presented factually and objectively, rather than being reduced to Christian allegory. These more "scientific" treatments, as well as more comprehensive studies of lesser known myths, became the point-of-entry into Greek myth for many Romantics. Edward B. Hungerford (1941) stresses that for Shelley and Keats, as well as other Romantics, mythology became a "new language" for exploring religious and spiritual themes.

Before long, such shifts in attitudes were reflected in the works of England's Romantic poets. Lord Byron, just prior to his departure for Greece in 1809, disparaged the Elgin marbles as "freaks" and "mutilated blocks of art." After having traveled in Greece, Byron published the first two cantos of his *Childe Harold's Pilgrimage* in 1812, which included passages glorifying Grecian ruins. In *The Curse of Minerva* (1815), Byron berated Lord Elgin for his vandalism of Grecian statuary. Byron treats Greek themes in other poems as well, including *The Bride of Abydos* (1813) and *The Giaour* (1813). Byron, Shelley, and Keats are acknowledged by modern critics to be the best representatives of English Romantic Hellenism; as Levin notes, the three poets "are very near the centre of romantic Hellenism in England." Yet Byron is often characterized as Philhellenic, in that his interests toward the end of his career turned away from ancient Greece and toward the political issues surrounding contemporary Greece. In fact, Byron died at the age of 36 when he was killed fighting for Greek independence from the Turks.

The works of Shelley and Keats, on the other hand, continue to be examined as more purely Hellenic. William Wordsworth, as well, has been identified as a Romantic Hellenic, with Douglas Bush (1937) describing him as "the fountain-head of nineteenth-century poetry on mythological themes." Bush points to such poems as "Laodamia" (1815) as evidence of Wordsworth's embracing of myth as a symbol of religious imagination, and credits the poet with establishing mythology as the "language of poetic idealism." Bush further maintains that Wordsworth "passed on to younger poets . . . a noble and poetic conception of mythology as a treasury of symbols rich enough to embody not only the finest sensual experience but the highest aspirations of man." One of these "younger poets" was Shelley. Levin describes Shelley's Hellenism as "sentimental." Shelley's most noted Hellenistic work is *Prometheus Unbound* (1820), in which he reworks the ancient myth of Prometheus. Modern critics observe a number of significant differences between the classic and romantic versions. Levin describes the poem as abstract and as "pure allegory, with little immediate or symbolic significance." Frederick Pierce (1917) finds that the "ancient models" for the poetic drama are only followed in the first act, yet "unquestionably Greek elements" flow throughout the poem. However, Collins states that while Shelley's poem "is a magnificent varient" of the myth, he charges that "its florid beauty and philanthropic enthusiasm are far from being Greek."

Bush identifies John Keats as the poet most influenced by Wordsworth; Levin describes him as "the most Grecian of modern poets." Keats's inspiration includes Grecian sculpture and art, as in "Ode on a Grecian Urn" (1820), as well as mythology, as in *Endymion* (1818). Pierce notes that poems such as "Ode on a Grecian Urn" and *Hyperion* (1820) are "classic in the noblest sense of the word, as nobly Grecian as anything in our language."

Wordsworth, Byron, Shelley, and Keats, like many minor poets, were inspired in a variety of different ways by ancient Greece. Stephen Larrabee (1943), in concluding his analyses of the influence of Greek sculpture on the Romantics, summarizes what is perhaps the main thrust of English Romantic Hellenism when he notes that the Romantic poets "wished to emulate the Greeks in making great art from the circumstances of their time."

REPRESENTATIVE POETRY

Lord Byron
Childe Harold's Pilgrimage (Cantos 1 and 2) 1812
The Bride of Abydos 1813
The Giaour 1813
The Curse of Minerva (written in 1811) 1815
"Prometheus" 1816

Leigh Hunt
Foliage 1818
"The Nymphs" 1818
Hero and Leander 1819

John Keats
Endymion 1818
Hyperion 1820
"Ode on a Grecian Urn" 1820
The Fall of Hyperion. A Dream (written in 1819) 1856

Thomas Love Peacock
Rhododaphne 1818

Percy Bysshe Shelley
Prometheus Unbound 1820
Adonais 1821
Hellas 1821
The Witch of Atlas 1824

William Wordsworth
"Laodamia" (written in 1814) 1815
"Dion" (written in 1816) 1820
"Ode to Lycoris" (written in 1817) 1820

OVERVIEWS

Harry Levin (essay date 1931)

SOURCE: *The Broken Column: A Study in Romantic Hellenism,* Harvard University Press, 1931, pp. 29-76.

[*In the excerpt that follows, Levin analyzes the characteristics of Romantic Hellenism and discusses the poetry of Byron, Shelley, and Keats as representative of various types of Romantic Hellenism.*]

An Anatomy of Romantic Hellenism

Before we proceed on our quest for the amaranth flower, it may be well for us to fix firmly in mind the characteristics of romantic Hellenism. I shall therefore attempt, very briefly, to anatomize the subject in its successive stages. It begins, as I have indicated, in a complete distrust of the classics, which are associated with the neo-classical period of western European literature. Gradually Greece is dissociated from the rest and converted into an Arcadia for the romanticists. World-weary denizens of the drawing-rooms are ready to divide the world, with Schiller, into naïve and sentimental peoples, and to yearn for the primitive, simple, and idyllic society of the Greeks.

They proclaim that the world was young in those days, that the Greeks were the children of nature. "The mental culture of the Greeks was a finished education in the school of nature," we hear, in ringing falsetto, from the lecture platform of Herr Dr. Professor Schlegel. "Sie haben die Poetik der Freude ersinnen." Hereafter we shall not be surprised to learn that the masterpieces of Greek literature were the spontaneous outpourings of an artless and unsophisticated folk, who performed their greatest achievements for no other purpose than to express themselves. The Spartans followed their rigorous discipline, as Pater explains, so that they might become "a spectacle æsthetically interesting to the rest of Greece." The assumption is by no means uncommon today. M. Salomon Reinach, for example, seems to think that Atticism blossomed into "the unique and immortal flower of human genius" for no other purpose than to provide him with material for the opening chapters of his handbook on art.

It is but a step from the mythological attitude to the historical. The new historical attitude, instead of seeking the relationships between past and present, emphasizes their points of variance. The romanticists have discovered that the supposed simplicity of Greek life disagrees with their own experience of life. Rather than change their interpretation, they conclude that they are undergoing a phase of experience which the Greeks did not know. They have forgotten that Attic Greek and Ciceronian Latin were not dead languages to those who spoke them, that the Greeks did not look upon themselves as figures in a history book, that their sculptors did not chisel their statues for us to put in our museums. So the Greeks become a static people and life to them is, according to Browning, "an eternal petrification." They are not even allowed to have feelings; Herder, Winckelmann, and Schlegel all join arms against Lessing for suggesting that poor Philoctetes experienced any agony.

When Renan stood upon the Acropolis, in 1865, he felt the spirit of Greece as "a fresh, penetrating breeze from very far away." He saluted the goddess and went through a wavering litany, but in confessing his sins—as he says—he became enamored of them. "Une littérature qui, comme la tienne, serait saine de tout point, n'exciterait plus maintenant que l'ennui." Classic perfection bores him, so he embraces the romantic abyss. Indeed, many of the romanticists, in their distrust of perfection, seem to have done their utmost to escape from it.

This eternally rapt repose, on the one hand, and a self-consciously rampant voluptuousness, on the other, are contrasted by Nietzsche as the Apollonian and Dionysiac souls. His disciple Spengler, the provocative critic of history, sets up an Apollinian man as a symbol of the static Greek soul, and opposes to him the modern or Faustian man, a dynamic creature, who strives and strays, knows infinitesimal calculus, and loves Beethoven. It is difficult to keep from being misled by distorted comparisons and, at the same time, from disregarding the grain of truth in a strained distinction. Stevenson, in one of his *New Poems,* rebukes the "greenspectacled Wordsworth" for his sentimental evocation of youth. In his own youth, Stevenson recalls, he was an Indian (full of "feverish questionings" in the "widening well of space"); in his old age he will be a St. Francis. Meanwhile, between the extremes of life, he is a Greek,

> White-robed among the sunshine and the
>   statues
> And the fair porticoes of carven marble—
> Fond of olives and dry sherry,
> Good tobacco and clever talk with my
>   fellows,
> Free from inordinate cravings.

From Schiller to Spengler, the romanticists show increasing dissatisfaction with the complacency which they find in the Greeks, and growing appreciation of the infinite longings which they discover in themselves. Victor Hugo, for whom traditional Greece lacks in color, is forced to turn to the oriental elements in modern Greece. The sentimental travellers have come across the modern Hellenes and tricked Greece out in a new nationalism and a colorful orientalism. At this point, romantic Hellenism coalesces with the romantic passion for liberty, and we have philhellenism.

A casual passage from Bryon's *Curse of Minerva* will aptly illustrate how many extraneous influences—nature, sentiment, oriental atmosphere, moonlight, and nationalism—have colored the romantic conception of Greece.

> With cornice glimmering as the moonbeams
>   play,
> There the white column greets her grateful
>   ray,
> And bright around, with quivering beams
>   beset,
> Her emblem sparkles o'er the minaret:
> The groves of olive scatter'd dark and wide,
> Where meek Cephisus sheds his scanty tide,
> The cypress saddening by the sacred mosque,
> The gleaming turret of the gay kiosk,
> And sad and sombre 'mid the holy calm,
> Near Theseus' fane, yon solitary palm;
> All, tinged with varied hues, arrest the eye;—
> And dull were his that pass'd them heedless
>   by.

Here, in some dozen lines, blended with appropriate emotions, we have the typical scenery of romantic Hellas. In our wanderings through this region, we shall be constantly stumbling upon crumbling columns, shattered pillars, and single solitary plinths. It might be estimated that, if all the broken columns that figure in this movement were collected and repaired, we should have a colonnade extending from the Victor Emmanuel II. Monument in Rome to the Brandenburger Tor in Berlin, by way of the Madeleine in Paris.

Let us pass on to consider our stylites. Criticism which consists merely of facile generalizations and exhaustive tabulations is a thoroughly desiccating procedure. Let us keep our eyes on the object and not forget that we are concerned primarily with literary values. It is absurd to rake over a whole literature ruthlessly in an effort to destroy its fundamental doctrines, and then to admit, in conciliating tones, that nevertheless much of that literature may be very beautiful. It is just as foolish to insist that this incidental beauty is all that matters and that the ideas in question are of no importance. The very greatest literature has always contrived to put beautiful ideas into beautiful forms, and I believe that undue emphasis upon the one element or the other is responsible for the present aberrations of critical taste.

We shall find it most profitable to avoid abstractions or catalogues and to turn to the actual pages of romantic writers for illustrations of the ideas that we are following. The works of Byron, Shelley, and Keats present a body of poetry which is unified, full, and extraordinarily fruitful for an inquiry of this sort. The three poets are close contemporaries, if not good friends, and their paths meet—not in Greece, to be sure, but in Rome (now pardoned by the romanticists and set up as the museum of the world).

Their respective styles and backgrounds supplement each other, so that a comprehensive view of much that is typical in romantic poetry may be gained from studying them. Byron, for example, has much in common with the writers of the eighteenth century, Keats is often akin to the Elizabethans, while Shelley is the most purely romantic of the three. Byron, again, has important relations with the continent, Keats is very English, and Shelley has as little as possible to do with this earth. The philhellenism of Byron, the sentimental Hellenism of Shelley, and the more or less genuine naïveté of Keats invite comment. All three, it will be acknowledged, are typical romanticists and poets of approved worth.

The course of romantic Hellenism in England has not yet been explored or chronicled. The philologists of Germany and the literary historians of France have traced the broken column to its plinth, and recorded the development of nineteenth-century classicism in their respective countries, although, in many cases, they have neglected to examine the authenticity of its claims or to show its connexion with the romantic movement. Specimens might be culled from Hölderlin's *Hyperion* or Lamartine's *Mort de Socrate,* from the life of Alfieri or the works of the *Parnasse,* to show the full flowering of Neo-Hellenism in its literary form on the continent. We must hope that a capable critic will some day treat this important chapter of English intellectual history. His amply documented pages will remind us of the once famous travels of "Athenian" Stuart. They will explain the Greek façades in St. James's Square. They will gossip of bands of dilettanti, like the Hellenic Society, and pause to admire collections of virtu, like Lord Hamilton's ceramics. They will find evidence in unsuspected places. Few of us were aware that Oxford's poetry prize was awarded, according to the terms laid down by Sir Roger Newdigate in 1806, for "fifty lines and no more in recommendation of the ancient Greek and Roman remains of architecture, sculpture, and painting."

Meanwhile, for our purposes, Byron, Shelley, and Keats are very near the centre of romantic Hellenism in England. Their poetic forbears are singularly free from any vestiges of classicism—Wordsworth and Coleridge through conscious reaction, Burns and Blake through ignorance. Their poetic posterity has inherited its attitude toward Greece from the second romantic generation. Their near contemporary, Landor, may well stand aloof on this question, as he did on every other. On him Mr. Oliver Elton has pronounced the final word: "His *Hellenics* are not really like anything ancient or modern, except the rare imitations of themselves."

In one of the letters of William Beckford, that esoteric describes the mildly diabolical festivities that celebrated his coming-of-age:

> On the left of the house rises a lofty steep mantled with tall oaks amongst which a temple of truly classical design discovers itself. This building (sacred to the Lares) presented a continued glow of saffron-coloured flame, and the throng assembled before it looked devilish by contrast.

I am afraid that we shall witness many such incongruous scenes and encounter many such contrasts. Let us take care that we neither do irreverence to the Lares nor view the devilish throng in too lurid a light.

The Isles of Greece

Byron, in some late verses, confides to us that his style is the romantic,

> Which some call fine, and some call frantic;
> While others are or would seem *as* sick
> Of repetitions nicknamed Classic.
> For my part all men must avow
> Whatever I was, I'm classic now.

Both the finely frantic and the narrowly classic are distinctly discernible in his poetry. He may have repudiated the classical studies of his youth, but he never forgot them. The curriculum appears to have been thorough, if not sympathetic. Byron's early collections are full of translations and paraphrases from the Greek and Latin, evident relics of Harrow and Cambridge. And he has nothing but disgust for the student

> Who, scarcely skill'd an English line to pen,
> Seans Attic metres with a critic's ken.

The unfortunate result of this kind of schooling was a purely superficial familiarity with the classics. The very word "classic," in Byron, seems to be synonymous with "dull," and is applied to such writers as Hallam and Sheffield. "Attic wit" is no wit at all. Homer is never mentioned, except in astonishment that men should continue to be interested in those crude chronicles of obsolete battles. Byron's conception of Plato, like Shelley's, is colored by the Petrarchans, but, unlike Shelley, he has no patience with this airy Platonism.

The quality of his appreciation of classical art is indicated by his preferences—the *Laocoön* and the *Apollo Belvidere.* He had been brought up under a regimen of the most hollow and uninspired neo-classicism, to which the new, ameliorated views had not penetrated, and in his ardent reaction he was ready to damn the classics as "faint fictitious flames, pastoral passions and cold compositions of art." Under the circumstances, he counselled wisely in *English Bards and Scotch Reviewers:*

> And you, associate bards! who snatch'd to light
> Those gems too long withheld from modern sight;
> Whose mingling taste combined to cull the wreath
> Where Attic flowers Aonian odours breathe,
> And all their renovated fragrance flung
> To grace the beauties of your native tongue;
> Now let those minds, that nobly could transfuse
> The glorious spirit of the Grecian muse,
> Though soft the echo, scorn a borrow'd tone:
> Resign Achaia's lyre, and strike your own.

One of the principal difficulties in dealing with Byron is the fact that, at some time or other, he almost invariably contradicts every statement he makes. Thus we find the converse of this proposition:

> Ye who seek finish'd models, never cease,
> By day and night, to read the works of Greece.

The couplet is from a paraphrase of Horace, composed in spare moments snatched from *English Bards.* The ambidexterous poet was able to translate the *nocturna versate* with his right hand and to pen a denunciation of the Greekling poetasters with his left.

Byron is still, in many ways, a good Horatian. He is the sole champion of Dryden and Pope in his age, and a frequent assailant of the Lakists on grounds of which Dr. Johnson himself might have approved. His satires and many of the early pieces (*An Occasional Prologue,* for example) show him as the legitimate heir of the English Augustans. They have bequeathed to him much of the conventional frippery of eighteenth-century poetry. Yet Byron lacks the neat precision and subtle grace of Pope and his school; their kind of rhetoric seldom becomes profuse or expansive.

To understand this phase of Byron, we must remember that English poetry, after Gray, did not turn romantic overnight, but that the old satirical tradition continued into the nineteenth century, considerably inflated with poetic bombast and political bias. We must recall much occasional and journalistic verse, many forgotten album-pieces, and a great deal of oratorical poetry. Byron has a close kinship with parliamentary poets like Churchill, Frere, Gifford, and the writers of the *Anti-Jacobin.*

Just as in Byron's attitude toward the classics, so in his poetry itself there is an eternal warfare of heart and head. The witty and rationalistic Augustan strain is counter-pointed by an elegiac and introspective romantic mood. Like many fellow-poets, he kept a skull about, but this skull was useful as well as ornamental—Byron drank beer out of it. "Today I have boxed one hour," he notes in his diary for April 10, 1814, "written an ode to Napoleon Bonaparte, copied it, eaten six biscuits, drunk four bottles of soda water, and redde [*sic*] away the rest of my time." The very virility that drove him to rebel against a pallid classicism also saved him from a neurasthenic romanticism.

> I've seen much finer women, ripe and real,
> Than all the beauty of their stone ideal.

This is the strain that develops into many fine lyrics, full of lips and loves and last long fond farewells. It also develops into the very theatrical eastern tales and the not very theatrical dramas. For it was this *Doppelgängerei,* this curious dissociation of intellect and emotion, that enabled him to dramatize himself, to posture before the rest of the world in his life and poetry. It also made it impossible for him to penetrate beyond his own egoism and to look objectively upon life as a whole. So we have, in the dramas, feeble and unintelligent echoes of *Faust,* such as *Manfred,* a monologue on the heights.

Despite his youthful excursions into the spluttering and ejaculatory style of Ossian, and his admiration for the early romanticists, it is in his life and mood, rather than in his style, that Byron is romantic. His language is always concrete; he employs without compunction the standard poetic diction, well seasoned with colloquialisms and occasionally spiced with a dash of color; he is never as vulgar as Wordsworth, as vague as Shelley, or as fond of images as Keats. He retains a sense of form and recognizes

> What Nature *could,* but *would not,* do,
> And Beauty and Canova *can.*

But, abandoning more general considerations, we must seek "the land of the cypress and myrtle" and hearken to the Æolian strains. Byron occasionally follows the "self-torturing sophist, wild Rousseau," and discovers an idyllic Greece where everything is natural and expansive and beautiful. Thus he characterizes one of Don Juan's and Haidée's more intimate moments as "Half-naked, loving, natural, and Greek." Yet it was the North and Nature, he tells us, in *The Island,* that had taught him to adore these sublime southern scenes. The primitive Greeks, we learn from one of the freest passages in his free translation of the *Ars Poetica,* did not narrow their hearts with commerce, but were "given alone to arms and arts" in true æsthetic fashion. Like Juan, when he awoke to find Haidée addressing him, we cannot understand this kind of Greek, but it all sounds very beautiful.

> Cold is the heart, fair Greece! that looks on
> thee,
> Nor feels as lovers o'er the dust they loved,

sighs Childe Harold's companion, although Harold (heartless wretch) is able to depart without a tear. To the companion a little urn says more than a thousand homilies. He loves to linger by the Ilissus, amid the ruins of the temple of Zeus Olympius, in full view of the Acropolis, with a sepulchral urn before him, and, not far off, a skull from a neighboring burial-ground. How different this lonely figure from the pair that walked and talked there beneath the plane tree many centuries before—the youth Phædrus and the sage Socrates. What would they have thought of this soul-stricken stranger, posing before his solitary column?

Travel is a hereditary privilege of the Englishman, whether his invasions of the continent take the form of a grand tour, a sentimental journey, or a search for the picturesque. The sentimental traveller of the Regency was a great-grandson of the cosmopolite in the reign of the first George, but Childe Harold's wanderings had a new sort of restlessness that distinguished them from the ramblings of Jack Wilton or even Mr. Yorick and Dr. Syntax. Part of Byron's predilection for Greece was due to the fact that he was forever seeking appropriate settings for the continuous monologue of his life. Part was due to his characteristic nostalgia and weariness; he loved, he says, in *The Siege of Corinth,* to be among

> Remnants of things that have pass'd away,
> Fragments of stone, rear'd by creatures of clay!

So it was Rome that finally became the city of his soul. Greece, with its oriental traits, nourished his taste for the exotic, but Greece was so far away that his pilgrimage ended in *Sehnsucht nach Italien.* Rome had later associations which made it holy land, and a soft lunar haze blended its temples with its castles and *palazzi.* St. Peter's was the very height of sublimity. Rome's columns, in the light of the moon, were more eloquent than Tully. And nature was necessary to complete the spell, for Byron abhorred the Phidian peaks of museums and continually reviled Lord Elgin.

> Art, glory, freedom fail, but Nature still is
> fair.

Yet Byron's landscapes are seldom complete without a ruin in the corner. The declaration, "I love not man the less, but Nature more," must be interpreted in the light of the poet's subjectivity; he was man, and nature was his mirror. In his verse the mountains, rivers, hills, and lakes always turn out to be Byron in disguise. Now and again we have a plea for pantheism that has in it true poetic insight, as in the fragment *Aristomenes:*

> False or true, the dream
> Was beautiful, which peopled every stream. . . .

Most typical, however, is the Byron who hymns the beauty of Greece in its age of woe. He sings a mingled measure. Childe Harold identifies Hellas not only with the orient, but even with—of all places—Andalusia. His Romaic love songs are no more classical than his *Hebrew Melodies* are biblical. "Could I scale," he stipulates, in *Beppo,*

> Parnassus, where the Muses sit inditing
> Those pretty poems never known to fail,
> How quickly would I print (the world
> delighting)
> A Grecian, Syrian, or Assyrian tale;
> And sell you, mix'd with western
> sentimentalism,
> Some samples of the finest Orientalism!

Ultimately, Byron's philhellenism contributed to the success of the Greek Revolution in 1821-33, one of the most significant practical results of the romantic movement. Did he realize how far from ancient Hellas all this was? Again we have the *Doppelgänger.* For the sentimental poet, the modern Greeks, though degenerated into "craven, crawling slaves," were still the legitimate heirs of the ancient glory; there was "the same light in each eye." For the satirical letter-writer, they were "plausible rascals, with all the Turkish vices, but without their courage." The question is easily settled. It was already a settled question to Tacitus, who records Piso's rebuke to the romantic Hellenist, Germanicus, for honoring "non Atheniensis tot cladibus extinctos, sed conluviem illam nationum." The issue has more to do with Pan-Slavism than with any sort of classicism.

Greece had taken its place along with Byron's other Arcadias of liberty—Venice, Switzerland, America. It is a long way from the liberty of Milton to the liberty of Byron and Shelley. The romantic conception of liberty is temperamental rather than ethical. Attractive and indefinite phrases about liberty are too readily employed to lend a meaning and a philosophy to a libertine life. Periclean Athens had very little freedom in our modern sense. Byron's activities did not revive the old Hellas; they complicated the Near Eastern question.

Missolonghi was the final compromise that put an end to the quarrel between Byron's two selves. At last he had to leave his drawing-rooms and charming ladies for miserable huts and ragged rebels, and at last he became a romantic hero. Head followed heart into the Greek cause, and, although the experience may have been disagreeable to Byron, it left a theatrical tale to the world. The world, however, is better pleased with the compromise of his two selves in Byron's poetry, which gave us that masterpiece of romantic irony, *Don Juan.* In this ranging and chatty picaresque epic, we frankly accept the fact that the form is sprawling and the story subjective, because the raconteur is so amusing. A moral, a plot, or even an ending would be entirely irrelevant.

All irony is based on the relationship of the real and the ideal. With Byron, Heine, and Jean Paul, the disillusioning facts of life obtrude themselves upon the unrestrained flights of the poet's fancy. With Socrates, the contrast is between petty actualities and universal truths. Romantic irony vacillates from pole to pole without direction. Socratic irony is governed by standards, or at least by logic (Socrates occasionally exhibits an almost Shavian perversity). The Greek ironist never parodies himself. The romantic ironist delights in sharp antitheses. Hardly has the metallic ring of the pseudo-Alcaic ode to "The Isles of Greece" stopped echoing before the author resumes his leisurely manner:

> Thus sung, or would, or could, or should have sung,
> The modern Greek, in tolerable verse;
> If not like Orpheus quite, when Greece was young
> Yet in these times he might have done much worse:
> His strain display'd some feeling—right or wrong;
> And feeling, in a poet, is the source
> Of others' feeling; but they are such liars,
> And take all colours—like the hands of dyers.

Feeling, to be sure, had been brought back into poetry and life, but in the process control had been eliminated, and either is vain without the other. Byron was acutely aware that he was the puppet of his feelings. In the poem generally quoted as his last, he sounds a clarion call, not to Greece ("she *is* awake!"), but to his soul:

> Tread those reviving passions down,
> Unworthy manhood! . . .

But there is a later fragment, a single stanza published in 1887 as *Last Words on Greece:*

> What are to me those honours or renown
> Past or to come, a new-born people's cry? . . .
> I am a fool of passion, and a frown
> Of thine to me is as an adder's eye. . . .
> Such is this maddening fascination grown,
> So strong thy magic or so weak am I.

So Byron continued to play the rôle of the weary Titan, chained to his *papier-mâché* Caucasus by shackles of his own forging, with the tragic fire preying eternally on his heart.

The Poet Unbound

"As he wandered among the ruins made one with Nature in their decay, or gazed on the Praxitelean shapes that throng the Vatican, the Capitol, and the palaces of Rome, his soul imbibed forms of loveliness which became a portion of itself." The soul is Shelley's and the speaker is the second Mrs. Shelley, in one of the marginal dithyrambs with which she has lovingly glossed her husband's works. It will be our part to inquire whether the soul really assimilated the loveliness, or whether it simply projected itself upon all beautiful forms that came in its way. Or again, how far did Shelley's classical background affect his ideas, and how far did his ideas affect his classical background?

The Hellenism of Shelley is complicated by the fact that he had a deeper interest in Greek literature and a wider knowledge of it than any of his contemporaries. Most of his familiarity with the classics was acquired, as his wife records, after his early departure from Oxford and during his travels on the continent. The circumstance is highly significant. It means that Shelley did not have the opportunity to be repelled by the classical curriculum, that his approach to the classics was wayward and unacademic, and that his subsequent reading was influenced by his political and philosophical obsessions.

"The poetry of ancient Greece and Rome, and modern Italy, and our own country," he confesses, in the preface to *The Revolt of Islam,* "has been to me, like external nature, a passion and an enjoyment." (O soul of

Sir John Cheke!) The collected poems include translations of Plato, Euripides, the Homeric Hymns, and the pastoral poets, among others. Some of them sound enough like Shelley to raise our suspicions. We turn, quite at random, to the rendering of Vergil's tenth *Eclogue.*

> . . . the wild woods knew
> His sufferings, and their echoes

is Shelley's version of the three simple Vergilian words, "respondent omnia silvæ."

To read Shelley is to become conscious of the vast distance between the modern poet and those ancients whom he continually evokes. He is a poet of the averted gaze; we never know for sure what he is writing about. Mary Shelley praises him for "discarding human interest and passion to revel in the fantastic ideas that his imagination suggested." "As to real flesh and blood," he wrote, to his friend Gisbourne, "you know that I do not deal in those articles." What are your wares, then, Mr. Shelley? Many will answer for the poet that he is a dealer in ideas, a philosopher. Professor Elton, for example, a stalwart champion, enshrines Shelley on high, with Plato on his right hand and Ruskin on his left.

The name of Plato has been shamelessly abused by twenty-odd centuries of poets and philosophers. As Shelley puts it, with unconscious aptness,

> "Then Plato's words of light in thee and me
> Lingered like moonlight."

Hellas has a lyric scene in which Christianity and Platonism are reconciled by the simple dramatic expedient of having Christ praise Plato. A more familiar kind of Platonizing ensues when Shelley invokes his "moth-like muse" in *Epipsychidion.* The result is more like a Petrarchan sequence than the *Symposium.* Emilia is "Spouse, Sister, Angel," but Shelley's love for her, like Tristan's for Isolde, goes beyond the sonneteers and seeks to consummate itself in annihilation. "I pant, I sink, I tremble, I expire."

Shelley does not deal in thoughts, but in "the shadow of the idol of a thought." He has the romantic wish to be infinite, so he seeks the mazes and mists of a vaporish philosophy. His idealism expresses moods instead of expounding ideas. In *Prince Athanase,* when he quotes the philosopher,

> "The mind becomes that which it
> contemplates,"

we are tempted to recall the occasion on which he contemplated the wind ("Be thou me, impetuous one"), and to consider him eminently successful in becoming the object of his contemplation. For Shelley, to put it baldly, is all fire and air, without much fire.

If Shelley deals neither in flesh and blood nor in ideas, what—we rudely repeat—is his merchandise? Again the never-failing Mrs. Shelley has a ready answer. He had, she tells us, in her preface to the first 1839 edition of his poems, "the luxury of imagination, which sought nothing beyond itself (as a child burdens itself with spring flowers, thinking of no use beyond the enjoyment of gathering them)." Apparently the garden of poetry has become so overgrown that our later poets have only to linger in the shade of its trees, languidly culling poetic conventions and dallying with poetic devices.

Her husband preludes his *Hellas* with the announcement that "the subject, in its present state, is incapable of being treated otherwise than lyrically." But it is Shelley, as we have reason to believe, who is incapable of treating any subject otherwise than lyrically. This is undoubtedly true of his treatment of Greece. "The modern Greek," he claims, "is the descendant of those glorious beings whom the imagination almost refuses to figure to itself as belonging to our kind, and he inherits much of their sensibility, their rapidity of conception, their enthusiasm, and their courage."

We recognize the purest sentiments of romantic Hellenism—the identification of ancient and modern Greece, the isolation of ancient Greece as an Arcadia in "the world's golden dawn," and the purely romantic emotional coloring. They are to be expected from the man who found Priapus "quaint" and Pan "melancholy." By now these concepts are familiar, and perhaps tiresome, to us. We are chiefly interested in the essential quality which Shelley attributes to Greece and in his explanation of the golden age.

"If England were divided into forty republics, each equal in population and extent to Athens," he writes, in one of his introductions, "there is no reason to suppose but that, under institutions not more perfect than those of Athens, each would produce philosophers and poets equal to those who (if we except Shakespeare) have never been surpassed." Liberty, then, is the sole reason for this superiority of the ancient Greeks. "If not for Rome and Christianity," he informs a correspondent, "we should all have been Greeks—without their prejudices." Is liberty enough? Shelley reveals not only a superficial conception of liberty, but also a superficial conception of genius. An age of genius has seldom been an age of liberty. We are reminded of Chénier's couplet:

> Les poètes anglais, trop fiers pour être
> esclaves,
> Ont même de la raison rejeté les entraves.

An examination of the lyric drama *Prometheus Unbound* will serve to bring out many of the differences between classical tragedian and romantic lyricist. The lost tragedy of Æschylus was set apart in the catalogue because it dealt with gods rather than with men. To Fontenelle, Metastasio, and Voltaire it seemed a violation of the principles of taste. Shelley has forsaken both gods and men to concern himself with continents, spheres, and elements. Against a background of ravines and icy rocks in the Indian Caucasus, the protagonist calls in turn upon mountains, springs, and air, while "Asia waits in that far Indian vale."

The Prometheus of Greek drama, in his misery, invokes first the lands of the earth and finally the waves of the sea, but we must bear in mind that he is addressing the dwellers in those lands and that the personification of the ocean was a climax intended to impress Greek audiences with the dire extent of his woes. Æschylus has relieved the super-human argument by introducing Io and her very human plight. Even Power and Force show a crude characterization. The modern play has none of the cruelty of the ancient; where the classical Titan agonizes, the romantic Titan rhapsodizes. Although the modern poet has no more sympathy for his subject than the ancient poet, the duty of Æschylus is to perceive and acknowledge the necessary outcome of the struggle. Shelley rebels against the inevitable and, by refusing to recognize the common lot of man, casts off the ties that bind literature to life.

His preface not only points to Prometheus as the champion of mankind and to Zeus as its oppressor, but goes a step farther and identifies Prometheus with Satan, "the Hero of *Paradise Lost.*" On this romantic diabolism, Shelley builds a labyrinth of pure allegory, with little immediate or symbolic significance. It is a compound of Plato and Godwin, Milton and Mist. The sense of necessity and the deep awe of the *Prometheus Vinctus* are dispelled. The mystical machinery is inconceivable, the action beyond human emotions (nay, even beyond the chain of cause and effect), and our interest languishes, save when revived by the grace or skill exhibited in a chorus.

It is not easy to follow the misty dramatis personæ. The Earth is the daughter of Asia, who is the daughter of Oceanus. Somehow or other, the rebellious phantasm of Zeus abjures him. Eternity is rebuked and the Spirit of the Hour quotes Dante. No more abstract poetic language could be imagined than such a figure as "cancelled cycles." In the midst of this potpourri of abstractions, Shelley comes down in a machine and proclaims the Millennium, which is celebrated in a carnival of adjectives. He has progressed from the triumph of evil in *The Revolt of Islam* to the return of the golden age in *Hellas.*

This, like thy glory, Titan, is to be
Good, great and joyous, beautiful and free;
This is alone Life, Joy, Empire, and Victory.

But Shelley, after all, was a human being, and for that reason his Titanism is unconvincing. Milton and Æschylus succeeded in creating superhuman figures by drawing men on a vast scale. Shelley lacked the power of characterization (*The Cenci* reveals him as a wooden Webster), and so he sought to convince by imagery and allegory. Occasionally the contrast between his characters and the things which they symbolize becomes amusing; thus Asia instructs the Spirit of the Earth in what every young sphere ought to know:

Peace, wanton, thou art yet not old enough.
Think ye by gazing on each other's eyes
To multiply your lovely selves, and fill
With spherèd fires the interlunar air?

How fair these air-born shapes? You are nothing—we are tempted to say—but a pack of words. It takes only a single phrase to dethrone Jupiter and his dynasty. Symbolism carried beyond a certain stage loses all significance. See, then, how easy is it to have a man walk out on the stage and say, "I am Eternity!" Shelley discovered that it was no more trouble to write hymns on mountains and chasms than to write homilies on stones and brooks, thereby reducing Wordsworth to absurdity. In a passage like the following, he develops a veritable apotheosis of the "pathetic fallacy":

The tongueless Caverns of the craggy hills
Cried, "Misery!" then; the hollow Heaven
  replied,
"Misery!" and the Ocean's purple waves,
Climbing the land, howled to the lashing
  winds,
And the pale nations heard it, "Misery!"

When Shaftesbury defined the poet as "a second maker, a just Prometheus under Jove," he was heralding a host of romantic poets, with Byron at their head, who sought out lonely rocks and raged at the heavens. Yet Byron realized the inevitability of the Titan's fate and did not attempt to overthrow the order of things:

Like thee, Man is in part divine,
 A troubled stream from a pure source;
And man in portions can foresee
His own funereal destiny;
His wretchedness and his resistance,
And his sad unallied existence.

Byron knew more of the world than Shelley, and had a sounder sense of human values. Still, he lacked the lighter touch of the younger poet. Byron's verse often sounds rhetorical and commonplace when compared with the smoothness and exquisite finish of Shelley's.

But Shelley lacked the elder poet's sense of humor. In his pseudo-Aristophanic comedy, *Swellfoot the Tyrant,* the chorus of swine grunts out such fanciful lines that the satire against George IV. and Castlereagh loses point. Now and again Shelley restrained this profusion and produced a poem of the true Greek epigrammatic quality, like the sonnet *Ozymandias,* so effective in its refusal to point a moral. Often, too, he found a becoming subject for his customarily atmospheric and evocative style, as in *Adonais,* one of the happiest examples of "reflective" poetry.

"Why, did you ever hear any people in clouds speak plain?" asks Mr. Bayes, in *The Rehearsal.* "They must be all for flight of fancy, at its full range, without the least check or control upon it. When once you tie up spirits and people in clouds to speak plain, you spoil all." The present attitude toward Shelley resembles the viewpoint of Mr. Bayes. Shelley could not have been tied up and made to speak plain, but many of his admirers prefer him untied and in the clouds. They are apostles of what the French literary critics call *lyrisme.*

Lyricism is the practise of poetry for poetry's sake. Poetry originated before the days of writing, when men adapted their sayings to rhythm in order to make them memorable. Then it is developed to a high degree of art and performs a lofty function in the life of a people. But sooner or later there comes an Alexandrian period, when men feel that the normal possibilities of literature have been exhausted, and take to experimenting with novel forms and recherché emotions. *Belles-lettres* become a mere drawing-room accomplishment.

Lyricism is a very late stage in the history of poetry. It is a reaction against undue didacticism, against formalism of all sorts. The western civilization is more prone to it than the classic, because its melody is more obvious and because accent and rhyme often dictate the sentiment. When our critics read a poem which rhymes and scans and apparently has nothing to say, they speak of its lyricism. Human character and emotion have been fully exploited in narrative and drama, the lyricist feels; the only thing left for him to do is to summon up, in lyric snatches, vague moods, embellished by the approved poetic conventions. His art is suggestive and literary to the extreme. We have the impression that he is writing about poetry rather than life.

Byron, Shelley, and Keats can show us aspects which are typical of romantic poetry and quite foreign to the best classical poetry with which we are familiar. With Byron it is subjectivity; the author's personality is more important than his theme, and he is unable to look upon life objectively. With Shelley it is lyricism; he is interested in words for their own sake and substitutes moods for ideas. With Keats, as we shall see, it is imagism; the trappings of poetry are for him its chief charm, and his verse becomes a kind of decoration.

Beauty or Truth?

> John Keats, who was killed off by one critique,
> Just as he really promised something great,
> If not intelligible, without Greek
> Contrived to talk about the gods of late,
> Much as they might have been supposed to speak.

Or, at least, that is what Byron has to say about it. Keats himself says (to Charles Cowden Clarke) that

> . . . my thoughts were never free, and clear,
> And little fit to please a classic ear.

Despite this confession, Keats has been pointed out as the most Grecian of modern poets. If he had been subjected to irregular verbs, perhaps his longing for Homer's wide demesne might have been tempered somewhat. Because he knew the classics at second hand, his attitude toward them is purely conventional. Thus we find pale reflections of the various phases of romantic Hellenism in his poems—the rocking-horse Pegasus of neo-classicism, the mythological echoes, the early Greeks unconsciously culling Time's sweet first fruits,

> . . . with as sunburned looks
> As may be read of in Arcadian books.

"I hope I have not in too late a day touched the beautiful mythology of Greece, and dulled its brightness," Keats writes, in the preface to *Endymion.* The mythology of Greece continues to shine, although it is not certain whether Keats has attained his pious hope in *Endymion.* Certainly he has attained it in the charming verses beginning, "I stood tiptoe upon a little hill," which present a delightful picture of the reveries of the romantic Hellenist. "Pan is no longer sought," complains the poet, in his fresh and vivid delineation of the hillside scene. Then there follows an evocation of several Greek myths suggested by the landscape, and the poet finally dedicates himself to the tale of Endymion. Such verses go far to justify the romantic conception of Greece or to suggest that there were Neo-Hellenists who held a wider and clearer outlook than their neo-classic predecessors.

But Keats' poetry abounds in a profusion very unlike the Greek. He was unable to sustain the statuesque style of *Hyperion.* The more characteristic *Endymion* is suffused with Spenser, and it betrays the touch of Archimago's wand. The poet longs for the moon, in four cantos. His Endymion is constantly falling into swoons, heretofore the peculiar privilege of men of feeling or the heroes of mediæval romance. The poppies and lilies with which the poem is redolent are no Grecian flora. The style is Elizabethan, although Keats makes embellishment his *raison d'être.* He preferred to look back to the golden age in the literature of his own people, rather than to follow the classical tradition. He says little of Homer and a great deal about Chapman.

Keats is the laureate of bric-à-brac. "Lo, I must tell a tale of chivalry!" he announces. He must not, he will not, he cannot. He will simply talk about plumes and chargers and glittering trappings. *St. Agnes' Eve* and the other tales show that his chief concern was with stage settings. Had he actually been an Elizabethan, he would have written masques instead of dramas. Images alone suffice, for Keats is in love with sense impressions. But it is wrong to call Keats a child of nature; he is really a connoisseur. He betrays at times an almost morbid delight in things physical, and his interest in nature is not marked by the wholesome pleasure of the sportsman, but by the wistful regret of the consumptive. It is conceivable that his Greeks should sleep in the grass, feed upon red apples and strawberries, catch nymphs, and even bite their white shoulders,—as they do in *Sleep and Poetry,*—but the dove-wings, the dancing-girls, the almond blossoms, and the cinnamon betray the connoisseur. It is the poor cockney from Moorfields who speaks.

When the poet is a voluptuary, it is natural that poetry should be treated as a narcotic. The poetry of Keats is heavy, sweet, languorous, and soporific. There is a sense of fatigue and romantic melancholy, a feeling that the scroll of mighty poets has been made up and rolled away. Everyone is tired in this tragic century. Newman felt a sense of "pain and weariness" which he found elsewhere only in the pages of Vergil. That is the strain of Tennyson's *Lotus-Eaters* and the sad, faint harmonies of Swinburne, who inherited Shelley's lyricism and Hellenism. The great end of poetry, for Keats, was "to soothe the cares, and lift the thoughts of man," but he was only successful in achieving the first of his aims.

When he comes to apostrophize the Grecian urn in terms of pure lyric speculation, Keats realizes that nothing in this life endures save what is crystallized by art into a work of beauty. The symbolism of the poem is indisputable. Sappho, however, would draw her distinctions with greater nicety. . . .

And that is not all ye need to know; ye need to know what is truth and what is beauty. Plato could not have quarrelled with the idea expressed in the *Ode,* but if he had read it in the light of Keats' other poems he would have rebuked Keats for exalting beauty of so purely sensuous a character. In another ode (the one addressed to Psyche) the poet speaks of his "soul" when he is really talking about his sensibility. The beauty of his work is ultimately achieved through the play of his fancy, which he ever allows to roam, rather than through the deliberations of that austerer faculty, the imagination. Lamia is apparently beautiful, but not true, and yet the poet will not recognize the reality and would embrace the serpent. "Græcum est, non potest legi." Poor Keats never learned Greek. . . .

Romanticism arose as a protest against the neo-classicism into which the humanistic tradition had frozen. But let us not make the mistake of judging romantic Hellenism from the neo-classical viewpoint. It is doubtful if the neo-classicists always had a sounder apprehension of the classics than their romantic Hellenist successors. It is very likely that they, too, often saw the reflected ideals of their own age in ancient Greece, when they adapted Homer for the drawing-rooms, made "Caton galant et Brutus dameret," and turned a hero of ancient tragedy—according to Dryden's taunt—into "Monsieur Hippolyte." Every young lady was a nymph, muses and lyres were the indispensable equipment of the poet, and writers put the pantheon in their pages. "Mes belles dames," was their query, "voulez-vous des éventails à la grecque?" Yet their appreciation of the classics developed to such a degree of nicety that La Harpe could attack Homer for violating classical taste and Chesterfield could sneer at the Homeric heroes as porters. *Don Juan* strays no farther from the *Odyssey* in one direction than *Télêmaque* does in the other.

The Greeks, unfortunately, were unable to have such a thing as a classical education. Subsequent civilization was able to codify their experience and to depend upon it for authority during the course of many centuries. The Greeks, perhaps for historical reasons, did not have our habit of turning back, at every step, to consult the past. It has been said that the Greek language was pure because the Greeks read and spoke no other. It may be that this principle can explain the clarity which we find in classical times and the confusion which we see, at present, in our own age. Whether or not that is true, we may be sure, when we look back to the past, that the Greeks were ever looking forward to the future; Pericles' funeral oration or the epitaphs at Marathon or Andromache's farewell to Hector should teach us that. Up to this late day, when we are depending more and more upon that vast tradition of our own which we have accumulated, and less and less upon our inheritance from the more remote past, each successive age has interpreted Hellas anew.

Timothy Webb (essay date 1982)

SOURCE: Introduction to *English Romantic Hellenism: 1700-1824,* edited by Timothy Webb, Manchester University Press and Barnes and Noble Books, 1982, p. 35.

[*In the following essay, Webb traces the English rediscovery of interest in Greece from the eighteenth century to the mid-nineteenth century, exploring both the influences and the impact of this renewed fascination on English culture and literature.*]

I

In 1675 a French writer described his feelings on first seeing the city of Athens:

> At the first sight of this Famous Town . . . I started immediately, and was taken with an universal shivering all over my Body. Nor was I Singular in my Commotion, we all of us stared, but could see nothing, our imaginations were too full of the Great Men which that City had produced.[1]

The sentimental traveller called himself de la Guilletière but his real name was Georges Guillet de Saint-George and, in spite of the vivid catalogue of physical symptoms, he had never been to Athens. His travels were fictional but his picture of the city was based on a variety of sources including eye-witness accounts provided by the French Capuchins who had settled in Athens. This curious gallimaufry of fact and fiction was reprinted several times and was regarded as authoritative by more than one unsuspecting scholar who had no opportunity of testing its veracity. *Athènes ancienne et nouvelle* marks the end of one phase of writing about Greece and heralds the beginning of another; the factual basis of de la Guilletière's account was soon to be tested in person by travellers of a more empirical temperament, while his emotional prostration at the sight of Athens was to be echoed in a variety of postures by a long succession of Romantic Hellenists.

Of course, as Dr Charles Perry was to point out nearly seventy years later, first-hand experience did not always guarantee accuracy of observation. The emotional impact of an encounter with the classical past sometimes distorted the vision.[2] Travellers to Greece could rarely avoid the sigh of regret for the departed glories of the past or the strong tug of identification with the Greeks of the present day, miserably subservient to the tyranny of the Ottoman Empire. A century and a half of these responses was later to receive its most complete and most powerful expression in Byron's *Childe Harold:*

> Fair Greece! sad relic of departed worth!
> Immortal, though no more; though fallen, great!
> Who now shall lead thy scatter'd children forth,
> And long accustom'd bondage uncreate?[3]

Yet the attractions of the landscape, the suggestiveness of ruins and the touching political plight of the Greeks were also to be held in balance by an increasing desire to discover the truth, a scientific curiosity to collect and assess the evidence of Greece both as it had been in the days of its glory and as it now was in the time of its sad decline.

In the year in which *Athènes ancienne et nouvelle* appeared, another Frenchman, Jacob Spon, and an Englishman, George Wheler, were touring Greece and the Levant and recording their impressions in some detail; in particular, they were able to present a first-hand account of Athens and to report on the Parthenon, part of which was to be destroyed in an explosion in 1687. Spon's book appeared between 1678 and 1680, Wheler's in 1682; together they provided the first extensive, authoritative description of modern Greece. Spon's account, in particular, became an important work of reference for later travellers and archaeologists. They were not without prejudices; Wheler offered an emotional dedication to Charles II, which looked over its shoulder at the Civil War and which helped to procure a knighthood for its author. Yet although they were not always objective, Spon was a doctor and antiquarian and Wheler a zoologist and botanist and they approached their subject with a curiosity not unallied to the spirit of scientific enquiry. The keynote was stuck by Wheler when he complained that previous travellers 'have perhaps seen it [Athens] only from Sea, through the wrong end of their Perspective-Glass'.[4] Whatever the motes in their respective eyes, Spon and Wheler did make their own observations and their enquiries were not conditioned by the goals of a simple-minded search for the picturesque.

In their emphasis on the pragmatic, Spon and Wheler might be regarded as the originators of a new and influential approach to the understanding of Greece. Undoubtedly, the history of neo-classicism and of its close relation Romantic Hellenism was partly shaped by subjectivity, emotionalism and a predilection for *lontani* and the wrong end of the perspective-glass; but the eighteenth and early nineteenth-century view of Greece was also firmly grounded on the endeavours of travellers, archaeologists, cultural historians and scholars. Although Athens retained its potency as an ideal city of the mind 'Based on the crystàlline sea / Of thought and its eternity'[5] and although neo-classical theory consistently propounded the virtues of ideal beauty, there was an increasing interest in discovering the reality of Greece both past and present.

This interest can be traced very clearly in the epoch-making *Antiquities of Athens* by James Stuart and

Nicholas Revett (first vol. 1762, second vol. 1789, three other vols. to 1830): these beautifully-produced volumes which were sponsored by the aristocratic art-lovers of the Society of Dilettanti . . . provided the first adequately detailed and accurate visual record of Greek architectural remains at Athens and in Asia Minor . . . . Stuart and Revett were impelled not only by the desire to elevate Greece at the expense of Rome but also by their concern to establish the architectural and archaeological facts:

> We have carefully examined as low as to the Foundation of every Building that we have copied, tho' to perform this, it was generally necessary to get a great quantity of earth and rubbish removed; an operation which was sometimes attended with very considerable expence.

When they found that they could not get an unobstructed view of the Tower of the Winds, they arranged to have an interfering building demolished and rebuilt after they had finished their investigation. Even the six engaging plates in the first volume which are based on the drawings of Stuart were conditioned by the pursuit of accuracy:

> The Views were also finished on the spot; and in these, preferring Truth to every other consideration, I have taken none of the Liberties with which Painters are apt to indulge themselves, from a desire of rendering their representation of Places more agreeable to the Eye and better Pictures. Not an object is here embellished by strokes of Fancy.

This scrupulous exactitude exerted its influence on the Ionian Mission which was officially sponsored by the Society of Dilettanti and whose members were Revett, Richard Chandler and the artist William Pars. The Mission eventually resulted in the *Ionian Antiquities* (first vol. 1769, second vol. 1797) which, like the *Antiquities of Athens,* was elegant and influential . . . . Like its predecessor, it helped to create a new taste for Grecian architecture and decoration which appealed to the aesthetic sensibility but which was founded on a scientific attention to fact. Together with the *Antiquities of Athens* it provided a detailed reservoir not only of architectural ideas but of the precise details and measurements of the elevations. The joint impact of these publications made its mark both on interior decoration and more gradually on architecture; some of the resulting buildings at first appeared exotically inappropriate to the English scene but by the early years of the nineteenth century the Greek style had been established as one of the dominant standards of architectural excellence.

Ionian Antiquities included a number of engravings from the sensitive watercolours of William Pars (the younger brother of Blake's drawing master) which removed the architectural remains from the scientific vacuum in which they were presented for architectural purposes and portrayed them as buildings in a landscape. While the linear purity of the designs and elevations was certainly inspiring to architects and neo-classical seekers after the pleasures of contour or outline, the engravings provided a balance by introducing the narrative, the human and the exotic. Without these softening influences, the *Antiquities* would be a work of almost abstract severity, an act of homage to intellectual beauty as well as to archaeographical and architectural exactitude. The contribution of Pars is to remind the reader or the student of architecture that the antiquities of Ionia were originally designed to interpenetrate with the landscapes and to draw attention to the present state of the buildings, many of which were ruined. Pars was obviously influenced by James Stuart who, for all his dedication to Nature and Truth as opposed to Fancy, introduced into his pictures some splashes of local colour and a number of figures, including members of his own party variously equipped with tape-measures and sketching materials.

If *Ionian Antiquities* maintains a balance between the imaginative and the scientific response, so does the individual work of its leading contributor, Richard Chandler . . . . Chandler is not primarily concerned with the aesthetic delights of the picturesque or the exotic, or with the pleasurable sadness pursued by the sentimental traveller; instead, he exhibits an almost puritanical dedication to the correction of poetic misapprehensions. Athens, for example, has encouraged extravagant flights of the imagination from those who have never seen it . . . ; in deliberate contrast, Chandler asserts the supremacy of empirically tested reality and of local truth.

Similar corrections are made by other writers such as J. B. S. Morritt . . . , though sometimes in a different spirit and with different intentions. Many of the pioneering travellers had taken in Greece as part of their travels in the Levant (indeed a number of them had worked for the Levant Company or had been attached to the embassies at the Sublime Porte). As a result, the earlier narratives usually devoted more attention to wet Greece than to dry (or mainland) Greece. After the great artistic/archaeographic expeditions and towards the end of the eighteenth century, there was an increase in the number of travellers to the mainland; this was to culminate in the activities of the topographers in the early nineteenth century. One consequence was that the poets' evocations of the Golden Age could be set more clearly against the criteria of those who had actually travelled in Greece. On one occasion we even find a painter approaching Athens and matching the colours of the landscape and the buildings against the palettes of Poussin, Lodovico Caracci and Titian.[6]

The most celebrated of these later travellers was, of course, Lord Byron, whose first-hand experience of

Greece and Asia Minor entitled him to the pleasures of correcting 'poetic geography'; the correction was given added piquancy because it provided an opportunity to find Wordsworth at fault both in his idealization of the 'still seclusion' of Turkish cemeteries and in his sense of place:

> He says of Greece in the body of his book—that it is a land of
>
> *rivers—fertile* plains—& *sounding* shores
> Under a cope of *variegated* sky
>
> The rivers are dry half the year—the plains are barren—and shores *still & tideless* as the Mediterranean can make them—the Sky is anything but variegated—being for months & months—but "darkly—deeply—beautifully blue."

Here Byron is exhibiting his own predilection for fact while he gleefully accuses Wordsworth of substituting a soft and charming English pastoral for the vivid but harsher realities of the Greek landscape. Yet, although Byron generally employs his experiences of Greece to satisfy a highly personal need to deflate the falsely 'poetic' and the complacent, he also uses his knowledge to defend Pope's Homer against ignorant detractors. Having 'read it on the spot', he records authoritatively that 'there is a burst—and a lightness—and a glow—about the night in the Troad'.[7] In such consultations of the realities, Byron is part of a tradition which goes back to the eighteenth-century travellers, to *Antiquities of Athens* and to its successors.

These travellers included poets as well as prose writers and students of history and manners. As a poet, Byron was in a position to draw, directly or indirectly, on the Greek experiences of predecessors such as William Falconer, W. R. Wright, Richard Polwhele and J. D. Carlyle. He had a particular regard for Falconer, a sailor who produced the first extensive treatment of modern Greece in English poetry. Byron admired Falconer because of 'the strength and reality of his poem'[8] but, although the topographical passages of *The Shipwreck* (1762) are tinged with a precise evocativeness derived from genuine experience, they remain somewhat idealized. In contrast the success of the Greek passages in *Childe Harold* is based on Byron's ability to present a powerful and convincing picture of the present-day country set against glimpses and nostalgic intimations of its past. Byron's sentiment is kept in check by the sharpness and the authenticity of his observations, while the topographical descriptions of the traveller and the political reflections of the Philhellene are animated by the drive of the verse and the immediacy of the feeling. It was a balance achieved by few of his predecessors or his contemporaries in the tradition of Greek travel.

Lord Byron, costumed in Greek attire.

II

The search for truth also played an important part in the revaluation of Homer. Much of the early interpretation tended to isolate the poems both from social and cultural circumstances and from their geographical settings. Few scholars were personally familiar with the geography of the *Iliad* or of those sections of the *Odyssey* which are set in Greece. Gradually, a shift in thinking began to take place as it was recognized that Homer was the product of a specific environment and that a careful study of the Greek landscape and of those factors which had helped to produce him could throw much light both on the details and perhaps on the very nature of his poetry.

One of the first writers to make first-hand use of local evidence was Lady Mary Wortley Montagu. . . . Writing to Alexander Pope from Adrianople in 1717 she noted that she was living 'in a place where Truth for once furnishes all the Ideas of Pastorall'. She had been reading the latest volume of Pope's translation and had been struck by the exact correspondences between certain descriptions in Homer and contemporary Turkish life. In a second letter Lady Mary reports on her visit to Troy in a manner which is commonsensical and robustly humorous but which remains susceptible to the spirit of place and the promptings of the historical imagination. Her respect for Homer is enhanced by her observations: 'While I view'd these celebrated Fields and Rivers, I admir'd the exact Geography of Homer, whom I had in my hand'. This letter was not published till 1763 but the tribute to Homer is significant; it marks the prelude to a fresh series of attempts to match the poem to the available facts, an investigation which perhaps reached its climax with Schliemann's excavations of Troy and Mycenae but which is still continuing today.

One of the most important contributions to the rediscovery of Homer in this period was made by Robert Wood. . . . Wood's travels in Greece and Asia Minor had convinced him that 'the Iliad has new beauties on the banks of the Scamander; and the Odyssey is most pleasing in the countries where Ulysses travelled and Homer sung'. Experience of the classical sites was a pleasure in itself but Wood recognized that its implications reached beyond the sentimental indulgences of the tourist and could sometimes 'help us to understand them [the poet or historian] better'. Little allowance is made for originality or poetic imagination: Wood's *Essay on the Original Genius of Homer* (1767) is based on the premise that Homer's poems are an accurate representation of reality. Unlike Le Bossu and many of the French critics, Wood sees the *Iliad* as a work without moral design; instead, it is 'an exact transcript' both geographically and in matters of history. Wood finds fault with Pope's translation because it ignores these facts and treats Homer's geographical precisions as if they were arbitrary adjectival decorations. His lengthy account of the geographical details of the Catalogue of Ships . . . is intended to show how Pope's poetical liberties have distorted and sometimes confused the particularities of Homeric geography; Wood acknowledges that some of these deviations can be attributed to the imperatives of the rhyme scheme but he insists that, for all its spirit, Pope's translation perverts the verisimilitude of the original.

Not everyone agreed: as late as 1808, Anna Seward observed that Pope's version of the Catalogue of Ships 'shows what genius and judgement can do with the most *barren* materials'. The Swan of Lichfield maintained that it was better to sin against truth than against beauty and she had no doubt that 'Pope's Homer was, as *poetry,* very superior to its Original . . .'.[9] Yet, in spite of such firmly asserted preferences, there was a growing tendency to apply the criteria of verifiable reality. Homer was no longer regarded primarily as an allegorist or a master of mythological generalities but as a clear-eyed observer of the world around him. Writing in 1771 P.-A. Guys insisted on the value of reading Homer and the Greek poets on Greek soil where one can recover even the smallest details by using one's eyes—'C'est en Grèce qu'il faut relire l'Iliade & l'Odyssée . . .'; after a visit to Troy in the company of the *Iliad,* he responded enthusiastically: 'Quelle vérité! quelle énergie! quel choix dans toutes ses images!'[10] Travelling in Greece in 1776 the Comte de Choiseul-Gouffier also attempted to relate the landscape to the Homeric poems; the result was a beautifully produced folio, the first volume of which appeared in 1782. A similar enlightenment came to Goethe, who never visited Greece but who discovered that the landscape of Magna Graecia brought Homer vividly to life. He told Herder:

> A word about Homer. The scales have fallen from my eyes. His descriptions, his similes, etc., which to us seem merely poetic, are in fact utterly natural though drawn, of course, with an inner comprehension which takes one's breath away. Even when the events he narrates are fabulous and fictitious, they have a naturalness about them which I have never felt so strongly as in the presence of the settings he describes. Let me say briefly what I think about the ancient writers and us moderns. *They* represented things and persons as they are in themselves, *we* usually represent only their subjective effect . . . [11]

Perhaps the most popular site for the student of Homer was the plain of Troy. Robert Wood had experienced some difficulty in identifying the site of the city and later visitors and classical scholars were not slow to put forward rival theories. Le Chevalier, Jacob Bryant, Gilbert Wakefield, James Dallaway, J. B. S. Morritt, William Francklin and Henry Hope among others all expressed their views before 1800; the early nineteenth century saw the productions of Edward Clarke, Edward Dodwell, J. Rennell and C. Maclaren, and of eminent topographers such as William Gell and William Leake. Some found fault with Homer, and Bryant even concluded that the Trojan War had not taken place and that the city of Troy had never existed. Bryant had never been to Troy and was firmly refuted by others who had. Among the believers was Lord Byron. For him, as for Robert Wood, Mary Wortley Montagu and others, one of the prime virtues of Homer was his veracity: ' . . . we *do* care about "the authenticity of the tale of Troy". I have stood upon that plain *daily,* for more than a month, in 1810; and, if any thing diminished my pleasure, it was that the blackguard Bryant had impugned its veracity . . . I still venerated the grand original as the truth of *history* (in the material *facts*) and of *place.* Otherwise, it would have given me no delight.'[12]

This gradual discovery of Homer's veracity makes an interesting counterpoint to the views of the eighteenth-century novelists. The novel was establishing itself at this time by creating its own identity and teleology; this involved an emphasis on realism as opposed to romance, and on contemporary relevance and immediacy rather than adherence to classical models. One result was an attempt to discredit the classics in general and Homer in particular. For instance, Daniel Defoe diagnosed a damaging lack of morality in classical literature: the siege of Troy was all for 'the Rescue of a Whore' and there was 'not a Moralist among the *Greeks* but *Plutarch*'. Homer was a superstitious wandering bard who had transformed the story of 'the Wars of the Greeks . . . from a Reality, into a meer Fiction . . .'.[13]

Henry Fielding's views were more complex. He admired classical literature and recognized that it still had its uses: as he explains in *Tom Jones* (xii. 1), the ancients are 'to be esteemed among us writers as so many wealthy squires, from whom we, the poor of Parnassus, claim an immemorial custom of taking whatever we can come at'. Homer was a particular favourite: Parson Adams's discourse on his virtues (*Joseph Andrews,* iii.2) is not uninfluenced by Fielding's own preferences. Fielding employs Homer as a model in *Joseph Andrews,* for structural and thematic purposes, while in *Tom Jones* he uses the epic both as a subject for burlesque and as a standard by which the action of the novel may be measured. Fielding began by equating *Joseph Andrews* with the *Odyssey* and Fénelon's *Télémaque* as opposed to the French romance (Preface to *Joseph Andrews,* 1742). By the time he came to write *The Journal of a Voyage to Lisbon* (1755) he had completely reversed his position:

> But in reality, the *Odyssey,* the *Telemachus,* and all of that kind, are to the voyage-writing I here intend, what romance is to true history, the former being the confounder and corrupter of the latter . . . (Preface).

However one may wish to qualify this statement by noting, for example, that it does not mention the *Iliad* and that the needs of a journal are different from those of a novel, it is clear that Fielding sides with Defoe in finding Homer wanting by the criteria of the historian and the realist.

Thirty years later, this point was developed by the novelist Clara Reeve in *The Progress of Romance* (1785) where she draws parallels between the *Odyssey* and the adventures of Sinbad the Sailor and declares that, in spite of her veneration for Homer, she finds little to choose between the two narratives. One of the speakers in the dialogue makes a claim which is disputed but never successfully controverted: 'Homer was the parent of Romance; where ever his works have been known, they have been imitated by the Poets and Romance writers.'[14]

Clearly, there were two ways of seeing Homer. For the novelists, he was a writer of outmoded romances, the product of a barbarous age which had little interest or relevance for the recorders and analysts of contemporary British society; for many poets, travellers and men of letters, he was not only the most meticulous of observers but the historian of a world which, though undoubtedly alien, was irresistibly attractive.

III

The fluctuating reputation of Homer is a useful index of changing (and sometimes conflicting) attitudes towards Greece and the classical past. The French scholars, critics and writers who engaged in the Battle of the Ancients and the Moderns devoted much of their energy to discussing his faults and virtues. Many of them showed a tendency to idealize Homer and to concentrate on the simplicity of heroic manners. Fénelon believed that 'Rien n'est si aimable que cette vie des premiers hommes';[15] for him, as for Mme Anne Dacier, the simplicity of Homeric manners seemed to bring back the Golden Age. Fénelon's influential didactic romance *Télémaque* (1699 . . .) was designed to reproach his courtly contemporaries for their luxury and corruption by presenting an idealized narrative which distils a pastoral serenity from passages in the *Odyssey,* while Mme Dacier's view was based on an unfavourable contrast with her own times ('Pour moy, . . . je trouve ces temps anciens d'autant plus beaux, qu'ils ressemblent moins au nostre').[16] The calmer episodes of the *Odyssey* provided the main imaginative stimulus for those who preferred to idealize the Homeric world; both the *Iliad* and the more violent incidents of the *Odyssey* were usually ignored or tactfully kept in the background. Conversely, those who found fault with Homer tended to concentrate on the *Iliad* and on the barbarity and uncouthness of its heroes and their language. Both sides acknowledged that Homer's society bore only the slightest resemblance to their own. One of the most significant effects of the Battle was to bring out more clearly the importance of understanding the true nature of that ancient society: the Battle 'emphasized uniqueness, difference, change, and development, not permanence or universality'.[17]

In English criticism an early example of the developing historical sense can be found in Pope's Preface . . . and Notes, in marked contrast to the translations themselves which tend to transmogrify Homer in conformity to the principles of Augustan taste. In the translations, the harsher or cruder or 'lower' aspects of Homeric life, language and style are either omitted or elevated by the use of elegant poetic diction so that they lose their capacity to shock or to arrest us by their strangeness. Pope's prose accounts of Homer are sympathetic and alert us to the cultural differences between Homeric society and his own, though this sense of difference sometimes leads him to emphasize the virtues of a pastoral way of life. Like Fénelon and Mme Dacier, he responds to the intimations of a Golden Age with an enthusiasm which may seem uncritical: 'There is a Pleasure in taking a View of that Simplicity in Opposition to the Luxury of succeeding Ages . . .' The Notes are marked by a tendency to allegorize but they also display a willingness to explain what may seem disturbingly alien to the modern reader. Pope's admiration for Homer leads him to acknowledge qualities which lie beyond the precincts of Augustan decorum. He also refuses to idealize the Homeric world by ignoring those features which are more brutal and less comfortably 'uncivilized':

> Who can be so prejudiced in their Favour as to magnify the Felicity of those Ages, when a Spirit of Revenge and Cruelty, join'd with the practice of Rapine and Robbery, reign'd thro' the World, when no Mercy was shown but for the sake of Lucre, when the greatest Princes were put to the Sword, and their Wives and Daughters made Slaves and Concubines?

Pope's commentary is often revealing but it remains subsidiary to the translation. The historical approach was given a more continuous and extensive formulation in Thomas Blackwell's *An Enquiry into the Life and Writings of Homer* (1735 . . .). According to Blackwell, the life of the wandering bard was 'the likest to the plentiful state of the Golden Age'. Blackwell's attractive representation of the bardic life was influential both among the Scottish primitivists, who detected parallels with Macpherson's Ossian (Macpherson himself translated the *Iliad*) and among the German critics. Blackwell's Homer was the product of the society he portrayed and for whom he performed—not the 'Inhabitants of a *great luxurious City*' but smaller groups not far removed from the nomadic, balanced between total barbarism and the more settled institutions associated with commercial prosperity. The Greeks '*lived naturally,* and were governed by the *natural Poise* of the Passions, as it is settled in every human Breast'; their language was artless and unaffected, far removed from the verbal dexterities of more sophisticated societies. Blackwell insists on the naturalness of this society which he contrasts with the greenhouse artificialities of his own. Yet, although the whole trend of this argument would seem to align Blackwell with Fénelon and other seekers after the Golden Age, he is alert to the price exacted by the 'natural' and the primitive. If Homer had the advantage of living at a time when men's passions were close to the surface, he suffered the disadvantage of living in a violent and warlike society. If 'polishing diminishes a Language' and 'coops a Man up in a Corner', it also marks his separation from a society in which 'living by Plunder gave a Reputation for Spirit and Bravery'.

Blackwell's book derives much of its impetus from the contrast between the Greek way of life as portrayed by Homer and the life of contemporary Western Europe. His investigations were conducted from Aberdeen and based on the authority of his library but their implications were confirmed by more adventurous students. For example, Robert Wood (whose geographical findings we have already encountered) travelled both in Greece and the Near East and was able to record from personal experience the manners of the Arabs which so closely resembled those of the Homeric poems and which represented 'a perpetual and inexhaustible store of the aboriginal modes and customs of primeval life'. In listing the main features of these societies, he exposes not only their deficiencies and crudities according to the criteria of contemporary 'polite' society, but also their cruelty and violence and their cheap regard for women, for heterosexual love and for human life. If judged by the standards of Wood's own society, 'the courage of Achilles must appear brutal ferocity, and the wisdom of Ulysses low cunning'.

While Homer was being reinterpreted in the light of these new contexts, travel writers and missionaries were gradually working their way towards the science of comparative ethnology. The first stirrings can be traced back as far as the seventeenth century when a number of travellers (most of them missionaries) began to record their experiences in various parts of the world: among them were Richard Blome (America; 1687), Abraham Roger (India; 1670), Arnoldus Montanus (China and Japan; tr. 1670–1), Joannes Schefferus (Lapland; tr. 1674), Willem Bosman (Guinea; tr. 1705) and La Créquinière (India; tr. 1705). One of their main concerns was the savage customs and cult practices which they encountered and which as missionaries they were anxious to eradicate. Their accounts of these practices consistently invoke the ancient world by way of analogy: it was, says Frank E. Manuel, 'virtually impossible to examine a strange savage religion without noting disparities and conformities with what one knew about ancient paganism'.[18]

Such comparisons can be found, for example, in the letters and reports of Jesuit missionaries, most notably perhaps in the highly important account by Joseph François Lafitau of his experiences among the Iroquois (*Moeurs des sauvages amériquains comparées aux moeurs des premiers temps* (1724)). Lafitau's book was designed to destroy the atheistical notion that there were many primitive nations who had no religion at all, and no knowledge of divinity. For such purposes, the Iroquois and the ancient Greeks threw a revealing light on one another. The sacrifices, initiations and rituals of the Indians brought to mind what he had read about similar practices among the Pelasgians. For instance, the myth of the satyr was given a plausible origin in the Indian custom of wearing the skins and horns of animals; the connection was illustrated by an engraving which placed two satyrs between an ancient German and an American Indian. Here and elsewhere the illustrations represent the Indians in the posture of classical sculpture. When confronted with naked flesh, Europeans often tended to invoke the Greco-Roman tradition; long before Lafitau, the explorer Verrazzano had seen in the Indians an 'aria dolcie e suave imitando molto l'antico' (a judgement which was ironically qualified when the Indians abandoned their classical poses to eat him).[19] The same artistic influences can be found in J. G. Forster's account of the inhabitants of Tahiti whom he observed on Cook's expedition to the South Seas. . . . In Lafitau's case the engravings conferred on his subjects a dignity and nobility which seems rather oddly to transcend those brutal tendencies which he acknowledged both in the Indians and the Homeric warriors ('Quoi de plus inhumain que les Héros de l'Iliade?')[20]

An even more illuminating perspective on the Greeks was advanced in an essay which appeared in the same year as Lafitau's book, the *Discours sur l'origine des fables* by Fontenelle. Like Lafitau, Fontenelle compared the ancient Greeks to the American Indians; the idea had occurred to him as early as 1680 and the essay had originally been written in the 1690s. He made a number of comparisons between the myths of the Greeks and the American Indians and concluded that the Greeks had once been as savage and uncivilized as the Indians were now. What distinguished Fontenelle's approach from that of Lafitau and other predecessors and contemporaries was his premise of a progressive paganism. Fontenelle was especially concerned to trace the origins of myth by examining the operations of the primitive mind; his examination was based not only on Homer and the Greek writers and on the reports of travellers but also on observations of peasants and children. Fontenelle concluded that the Homeric gods were crude, brutal and warlike because they reflected the minds of their creators. He did not idealize: his Greeks were neither love-lorn shepherds nor gentlemen in pastoral disguises.[21]

The gradual recognition of the less civilized aspects of the Homeric poems was partly responsible for the declining popularity of Pope's translation and the rediscovery by the Romantics of the virtues of George Chapman. Even as late as the Romantic period, Pope still had his champions and defenders (Byron combatively declared that the Pope version had 'more of the spirit of Homer than all the other translations . . . put together')[22] but by the second half of the eighteenth century his translation seemed increasingly vulnerable to a variety of criticisms. Many critics found that their newly developed historical sense was offended by the way in which Pope had transformed the simplicity and natural vigour of the original into the fop-finery of a gentleman of the eighteenth century. Some, such as William Cowper, objected to Pope's tying the bells of rhyme round Homer's neck so that Pope's Homer resembled Homer just as Homer resembled himself when dead. 'I never', said Cowper, 'saw a copy so unlike the original.'[23] Others, such as Wordsworth and Coleridge, objected to Pope's poetic diction which, in their view, was intimately connected with his failure to observe even the most obvious natural phenomena.[24] Yet other readers objected specifically that Pope had deprived the original of its primitive brutality. Lord Kames complained that Pope considered it below the dignity of Achilles to 'act the butcher', forgetting that one of our greatest pleasures in reading Homer arises from his 'lively picture of ancient manners'.[25] Charles Lamb expressed a similar point of view in a letter to his friend Charles Lloyd, who had attempted to translate some Homer. Lamb suspected that Lloyd's principles and turn of mind would lead him 'to *civilize* his [Homer's] phrases, and sometimes to *half christen* them'. The deficiencies in his work in progress were obvious:

> What I seem to miss, and what certainly everybody misses in Pope, is a certain savage-like plainness of speaking in Achilles—a sort of indelicacy—the heroes in Homer are not half-civilised, they utter all the cruel, all the selfish, all the *mean thoughts* even of their nature, which it is the fashion of our great men to keep in.[26]

Taste had changed dramatically since Lord Chesterfield had told his son that 'Achilles, was both a brute and a scoundrel, and, consequently, an improper character for the hero of an epic poem' and had spoken disparagingly of 'the porter-like language of Homer's heroes . . .'.[27]

The dwindling popularity of Pope's Homer was balanced by a rise in the fortunes of George Chapman, whose translation was much less concerned with the 'milkiness of the best good manners' . . . and much more accommodating to the savage vitality of the original. Pope himself had acknowledged in Chapman a 'daring fiery Spirit that animates his Translation, which is something like what one might imagine *Homer* himself would have writ before he arriv'd to Years of Discretion' (Preface). That child-like forthrightness and animation must have recommended Chapman to the poets and critics of the Romantic age, who showed remarkable unanimity in their admiration for his poetic achievements. Coleridge: ' . . . it has no look, no air, of a translation. It is as truly an original poem as the Fairy Queen'. Lamb: 'Chapman gallops off with you his own free pace . . . (what *Endless egression of phrases* the Dog commands)!' and later: 'I shall die in the belief that he has improved upon Homer, in the Odyssey in particular . . .' Keats borrowed a copy from Haydon, and was inspired to write his famous sonnet when he first read Chapman in 1816. Shelley ordered Chapman's *Homeric Hymns* in 1818 and adopted several turns of phrase in his own translation of the Hymns. Even Blake had his own copy of Chapman. The main feature which everyone remarked about this extraordinary translator was that he was 'thoroughly invested and penetrated with the sacredness of the poetic character'.[28] His poetic gifts compensated to all but the niggling few for the occasional harshness of his verse, for his interpolations, and for his frequent departures from the original Greek.

IV

At the beginning of the eighteenth century the status of mythology was precarious. Under pressure from the growing tendency to value the factual and the verifiable, defenders of mythology often resorted to allegorical interpretation and claimed that the stories concealed significant moral truths; but this did not satisfy hardheaded interpreters such as Pierre Bayle who claimed that the Greek myths were literally true and whose interpretations were deliberately calculated to deflate. An English equivalent can be found in Daniel Defoe, whose version of the Prometheus myth involves a well-meaning but absent-minded astronomer who contracts consumption by staying out at night on Mount Caucasus.[29] This bluntly reductive reading is not uncharacteristic of a number of English mythographers in the first half of the eighteenth century who approached the subject with heavy-handed rationality and deprived it of any imaginative appeal.

In spite of these pressures, classical mythology was still very much in evidence, especially in the earlier stages of the century. The main influences were still Roman: Virgil and Ovid were an important part of the mental furniture of the cultured man. The prestige of Ovid had declined since the Elizabethan period yet, as Douglas Bush records, 'every gentleman of letters translated parts of the *Metamorphoses* or the *Heroides* or the *Ars Amatoria'*.[30] The classical gods could still be encountered regularly in the immensely popular *Pantheon* which Andrew Tooke had translated from the French of Fr F. A. Pomey in 1698 and which was to appear in twenty-three editions by 1771. The divinities received further publicity from Pope's friend Joseph Spence, whose *Polymetis* first appeared in 1747. . . . This detailed and didactic work attempted to examine the connections between Roman poetry and 'the remains of the antient artists': its emphasis on the picturesque qualities of Roman poetry accorded well with the taste of many of Spence's contemporaries. Outside literature, classical mythology exerted its influence in a variety of locations. One observer noted in 1756: 'While infidelity has expunged the Christian theology from our creed, taste has introduced the heathen mythology into our gardens';[31] the gods could still be detected in paintings, in the details of interior decoration and occasionally even in church.

In poetry and in prose, classical mythology was a rich source of vitality for the mock-heroic; otherwise its vigour was greatly diminished and the purposes it served were mostly decorative or superficial. Poetry, in particular, was debilitated by the system of poetic diction which Lord Chesterfield explained in an approving letter to his son.[32] This predilection for making 'translations of prose thoughts into poetic language', as Coleridge called it,[33] usually involved a thin coating of mythological varnish and produced results which were often grotesquely inappropriate. The habit must still have been infectious when Coleridge was at school since his teacher delivered a vigorous denunciation of mythological periphrasis.[34] It is easy to understand why William Blake could lament in 1783 the cessation of ancient melody in a poem which itself invokes the world of classical mythology as a beautiful but distant reality: 'The languid strings do scarcely move! / The sound is forc'd, the notes are few!'[35]

Not surprisingly, the novelists kept their distance. Daniel Defoe, who prided himself on his veracity and unassuming style, had no sympathy with the mythological method. Surveying the Thames from Hampton Court, he assures his readers: 'I shall sing you no Songs here of the River in the first Person of a Water Nymph, a Goddess, (and I know not what) according to the Humour of the ancient Poets.'[36] Here Defoe is in reaction not only against topographical writers such as Camden and Drayton but against mythology and the deceptive delights of the pastoral setting which so often accompanied it. Fielding's mythological burlesques in *Joseph Andrews* and *Tom Jones* are affectionate but their potency is generated by forcing a gap between the sublimity of the diction and the inescapably mundane nature of the subject matter. (Byron was later to follow this example in *Don Juan.*) Nearly forty years after Fielding and sixty years after Defoe, Henry Mackenzie, author of *The Man of Feeling,* objected to the continuing recourse to mythology in terms which seem to anticipate Wordsworth's attack on Pope's poetical diction in the Preface to *Lyrical Ballads:* 'Another bad consequence of this servile imitation of the ancients . . . has been to prevent modern authors from studying nature as it is, from attempting to draw it as it really appears; and, instead of giving genuine descriptions, it leads them to give those only which are false and artificial.'[37]

In criticizing the prevalence of classical myth, the novelists were issuing a declaration of independence which helped to define the territory of the novel and to mark it off from the realm of poetry. Yet the shortcomings of classical mythology were equally evident to many poets. William Blake, for instance, provides a short and telling history of the subject in Plate 11 of *The Marriage of Heaven and Hell.* His analysis owes an obvious debt to the eighteenth-century debates on polytheism, on the origins of religion and on the dangerous potency of priestly imposture. Directly or indirectly, Blake's ideas can be traced to the concerns of Bayle, Fontenelle, Hume, and Holbach in *L'Enfer détruit* (1769). Yet there is a crucial divergence in emphasis. Fontenelle, for example, was interested in the way in which Greek myths had taken root in the imagination with such tenacity that even contemporary Christians resorted to them continually in art and literature: 'Nothing proves better that imagination and reason hardly have converse with each other and things of which reason is completely disabused lose none of their attractions for the imagination.'[38] It is at this point that Blake takes leave of the philosophers; where Fontenelle had regretted the failure of the reason to triumph over the imagination, the emphasis of Blake's compressed history is on the creative faculty of mind as opposed to the disabling constraints of system. Blake's own poetic career was to provide one of the most remarkable examples of one man's attempt to create a personal mythology of cosmic significance; his objection was not to the mythological method but to the unimaginative application of a prefabricated system of ciphers.

In a letter of 1802 Coleridge addresses himself to the same problem. Like Blake, he detects a dearth of imaginative involvement but, where Blake is partly concerned with the manipulation of power, Coleridge invokes those critical/psychological standards which were to be formulated so powerfully in *Biographia Literaria:*

> It must occur to every Reader that the Greeks in their religious poems address always the Numina Loci, the Genii, the Dryads, the Naiads, &c &c—All natural objects were *dead*—mere hollow Statues—but there was a Godkin or Goddessling *included* in each—In the Hebrew Poetry you find nothing of this poor Stuff—as poor in genuine Imagination, as it is mean in Intellect—At best, it is but Fancy, or the aggregating Faculty of the mind—not *Imagination,* or the *modifying,* and *co-adunating* Faculty.[39]

Here, as in his criticism of Gray, and as in Wordsworth's Preface, there is a close connection between the use of an inherited mythology and the employment of a traditional poetic diction: both imply a failure to observe accurately and a crippling deficiency of the imagination. The social implications of adhering to classical mythology were also evident to the Romantic poets: in particular, the connections between the delusions of mythology and the complacencies of pastoral were examined by poets who knew the countryside at first hand. The Arcadian idyll, the image of the country as a garden populated by nymphs, shepherds and classical divinities, was just as offensive to George Crabbe as it had been to Daniel Defoe. Crabbe refuses to hide the 'real ills' of the 'poor laborious natives' in the 'tinsel trappings of poetic pride'; his aim is to 'paint the Cot, / As Truth will paint it, and as Bards will not' (*The Village*).[40] Much of Wordsworth's poetry could be said to pursue the same goals; the insensitivity and selfishness of his own age may have caused him to think regretfully of pagan times when one might 'Have sight of Proteus rising from the sea; / Or hear old Triton blow his wreathed horn' yet he too rejected the temptations of classical pastoral, and the rich mythology of his poetry is the product of his own imagination working on personal experience. Like Crabbe and Wordsworth, John Clare also rejected the conventions and chose instead 'A language that is ever green / That feelings unto all impart'.[41]

A number of writers were also exercized by an uneasy feeling that Greek mythology was the product of paganism and therefore unsuitable for the poetry of a Christian country. Several valiant scholars attempted to close the breach, working from the assumption that 'whenever there was any resemblance between classical and sacred literature the former had borrowed from the latter'.[42] The results were often preposterously unhistorical: for instance, in *Omeros Ebraios: sive historia Hebraeorum ab Homero conscripta* (1704) Gerhard Croese claimed that the *Iliad* was a pagan version of Joshua's attack on Jericho and that the story of Odysseus was derived from the wanderings of the patriarchs. The gardens of Alcinous he equated with Eden, while Mars and Venus suggested Samson and Delilah, and the fall of Troy represented the destruction of Sodom and Gomorrah. Fanciful theories such as this probably resulted from a desire to discover an underlying principle of unity, perhaps even a universal religion, behind the seeming heterogeneity of myth.

Many Christian writers were unimpressed. Joseph Spence advised in *Polymetis* that pagan mythology should be segregated from Christian truth in poetry to avoid the dangers of contamination. Coleridge and Wordsworth were much more sympathetic to the spirit of Greek poetry but, in the end, they too found that its religious implications were unacceptable, and its artistic achievements correspondingly limited. Clearly, they were both profoundly attracted by the beauty they found it necessary to reject. There are at least three passages in *The Excursion* (1804) and one in *The Prelude* where Wordsworth reveals his affection for Greek mythology and for its pastoral setting.[43] One of the passages irritated Byron by its idealization of the Greek landscape and its susceptibility to the Mediterranean dream . . . ; much more important is its account of the workings of the mythological imagination:

> And doubtless, sometimes, when the hair was shed
> Upon the flowing stream, a thought arose
> Of Life continuous, Being unimpaired;
> That hath been, is, and where it was and is
> There shall endure . . . [44]

Wordsworth here acknowledges the creative origins of Greek mythology yet, for his own purposes, the pastoral 'pleasure-ground' was less inviting than the moors, mountains, headlands and hollow vales of his own bleaker northern landscape which 'seize / The heart with firmer grasp'. Finally, Wordsworth was repelled by 'the anthropomorphitism of the Pagan religion'.[45]

The drift of Coleridge's sympathies was not dissimilar. The lines he freely translated from Schiller for *The*

Piccolomini (1800) evoke the world of Greek mythology with an almost wistful sense of loss:

> The intelligible forms of ancient poets,
> The fair humanities of old religion,
> The Power, the Beauty, and the Majesty,
> That had their haunts in dale, or piny
> mountain,
> Or forest by slow stream, or pebbly spring,
> Or chasms and wat'ry depths; all those have
> vanished;
> They live no longer in the faith of reason!

Yet Coleridge maintained that Greek poetry was inferior both to Hebrew poetry and to English because it lacked imaginative force. This point he often repeated, discriminating between the limitations of the Greek mythology and the infinite suggestiveness of the Christian:

> The Greeks changed the ideas into finites, and these finites into *anthropomorphi,* or forms of men. Hence their religion, their poetry, nay, their very pictures, became statuesque. With them the form was the end. The reverse of this was the natural effect of Christianity; in which finites, even the human form, must, in order to satisfy the mind, be brought into connexion with, and be in fact symbolical of, the infinite; and must be considered in some enduring, however shadowy and indistinct, point of view, as the vehicle or representative of moral truth.[46]

It would appear that the seam of classical mythology had been exhausted and that poetry could expect no further enrichment from that source. Yet when Joseph Cottle pronounced in the Preface to the second edition of *Alfred* (1804) 'whoever in these times, founds a machinery on the mythology of the Greeks, will do so at his peril', he was not delivering an epitaph; perilous though the enterprise might be, Greek mythology was about to enjoy a rich poetic revival. In retrospect, it appears that, although it was much weakened, it had never really died even in the eighteenth century. The first stirrings of a new life can be identified in the work of Mark Akenside (1721-70) and William Collins (1721-59). Neither achieved major poetic significance yet both produced poetry which was traditional and inventive. Akenside acknowledged a debt to the Greek lyric poets in his shorter works while he based the *Hymn to the Naiads* (1746) on the model of Callimachus, whose hymns he admired for 'the mysterious solemnity with which they affect the mind'. Characteristically, Akenside experiences no Keatsian delight at the appearance of Bacchus and his pards who are dismissed in favour of the cool and unimpassioned serenities represented by the Naiads; yet, for all its restraint, his *Hymn* demonstrates the rich potential of Greek mythology. Collins shared Akenside's preference for the neo-classical; he even composed an ode to simplicity in which that poetic ideal appeared as 'a decent maid / In Attic robe arrayed'. His odes are abstract in conception yet they often exhibit a sensuousness, an imaginative power and an instinct for the suggestive and the undefined which transcends the limitations of their allegorical framework and which seems to look forward to the symbolic creations of the Romantics. Collins, like Akenside, finds his inspiration in Greece rather than in Rome—this gradual tilt of favour is an important feature of the second half of the eighteenth century.

It seems clear that the interest of Shelley and Keats in the possibilities of Greek mythology can be traced back in part at least to those eighteenth-century forebears. But there were other factors which helped directly or indirectly to create a favourable climate of thought for the production of *Endymion,* the two versions of *Hyperion,* 'Ode on a Grecian Urn', *Prometheus Unbound, The Witch of Atlas,* and many shorter poems and translations. One of these was the work of Thomas Taylor, who not only translated Plato and many of the Neoplatonists but who provided a key for the reading of symbolic narrative. . . . Plato's reputation had been depressed throughout the eighteenth century. In 1700 Matthieu Souverain had denounced him in *Le Platonisme dévoilé,* dismissing his doctrine because it was as 'absurd as the Theology of the Poets, and as unpolish'd as the Religion of the most superstitious vulgar' (English tr., 1700). Eighteenth-century rationalism found little to admire in what Monboddo described as 'the enthusiasm and mystic genius of Plato'.[47] Taylor's rediscovery of Plato and the Platonic tradition marked the slow reemergence of a sense of the mysterious and the numinous which was to characterize the Romantic movement. It also heralded a shift from the frozen clarity of the eighteenth-century personification to the more suggestive connotations of the symbol. Although it was derided by many of his contemporaries, Taylor's work seems to be intuitively in touch with the direction which poetry was to take; in spite of his pedantry and his awkward style, he seems to have possessed some creative insight and his translations and essays were harbingers, if not necessarily promoters, of the symbolic narratives of the great Romantic poets.

The significance of Greek mythology was further underlined by the mythological handbooks of Lemprière (1788) and John Bell (1790), by William Godwin's book for children (published under the name of Edward Baldwin, 1806) and by interpretative works such as Richard Payne Knight's *An Inquiry* (1818). The two dictionaries are more objective and less opinionated than most of their predecessors in the art of interpretation; here, the nature of Greek mythology is accepted rather than attacked for its immorality or idolatry or explained away through various interpretative devices. Godwin's study displays a distinct sympathy with the Greek outlook, while Knight eludes the old-fashioned ethical emphases and devotes himself to unravelling cosmological and metaphysical symbols. The same period witnessed the growth of the rather speculative science of syncretic mythology which was based on the premise that 'beneath the seemingly disparate and heterogeneous elements of ancient universal mythico-religious and historical traditions there lay a harmonious tradition'.[48] George Eliot's Mr Casaubon was a late follower of this system; its best known exemplar was Jacob Bryant, who began to publish *A New System; or, An Analysis of Ancient Mythology* in 1774. Studies such as these were often absurdly fanciful or misguided yet they were part of a movement of thought which accorded significance and value to Greek mythology.

Greek influences also made themselves felt in the world of art: *The Antiquities of Athens* and *Ionian Antiquities* had helped to create a new interest in Greek design and architecture, while Winckelmann celebrated the achievements of Greek sculpture as the products of a happy climate and a favonian democracy. . . . A variety of illustrated books on Pompeii, Herculaneum, Paestum and Magna Graecia as well as on Greece itself continued to shift the balance of attention from Rome to Greece in spite of the resistance of Piranesi, Robert Adam, William Chambers and others. . . . The arrival in London of the Elgin Marbles confirmed the trend and provided tangible manifestations of the Greek spirit which had a profound effect on artists such as Haydon . . . and on his friend Keats. Greek pottery also emerged from obscurity through books and collections and through the artistic enterprise of Josiah Wedgwood and his protégé John Flaxman. . . .

Of course, Shelley and Keats came to discover Greek mythology by routes which were highly personal and which cannot be adequately accounted for in terms of this brief and general perspective. Yet their poetry was written in an age which abandoned the preconceptions of eighteenth-century poetry, preconceptions founded, as Leigh Hunt expressed it, on 'their gross mistake about what they called classical, which was Horace and the Latin breeding, instead of the elementary inspiration of Greece'.[49] What liberated their imaginations was the discovery that mythology need not be merely decorative or superficial but that it could be used to investigate the deepest human concerns. Byron, who had little sympathy either for the implications of Greek mythology or for his social 'inferiors', observed condescendingly of Keats that he had 'without Greek / Contrived to talk about the Gods of late'.[50] Francis Jeffrey was more understanding, and in an extremely perceptive essay in *The Edinburgh Review* for August 1820 acknowledged Keats's originality in his exploration of 'the loves and sorrows and perplexities' of mythological beings. As Jeffrey recognized, Greek mythology was no longer a fixed pantheon of marble postures but a point of entry to a world of moral and psychological significance. *Endymion, Lamia* and the two *Hyperions* go some way towards repairing that damaging dissociation of sensibility so precisely diagnosed by Coleridge: they combine the picturesque elements of Greek mythology with the 'inwardness or subjectivity, which principally and most fundamentally distinguishes all the classic from all the modern poetry'.[51] In the case of Keats, Greek mythology was also closely associated with his own feeling for natural beauty (as in 'I stood tip-toe') and with his delight in the combination of mythological story and natural setting in the works of Claude, Poussin and his other favourite artists. The conjunction between myth and the beauties of nature also made its impact on Keats's friends and contemporaries: Hazlitt, Wordsworth and Leigh Hunt all recorded the attractions of what Hunt described as 'the fair forms and leafy luxuries of ancient imagination'.[52]

Shelley, too, was susceptible to these attractions and his later poetry is often centred on a pastoral world which owes much to his constant recourse to Greek literature as 'the only sure remedy' for diseases of the mind. Shelley's search for a New Jerusalem involves a return to the image of the Golden Age: he did not share the nostalgic resignation of friends like Peacock, Hunt and Thomas Jefferson Hogg to the death of the mythological faculty but found that Greek mythology and Greek literature afforded satisfying images both of what man had achieved in the past and of a potential which might yet be realized again. If Keats's use of Greek mythology in *Hyperion* is focused on the problems of poetry and on the harsh but necessary processes of evolution, Shelley's characteristic focus is often related to his political concerns and to his deep and much challenged allegiance to Hope. Shelley was interested in the past largely because of its implications for the future: 'What the Greeks were, was a reality, not a promise. And what we are and hope to be, is derived, as it were, from the influence and inspiration of these glorious generations.'[53] Both *Hellas* and, particularly and outstandingly, *Prometheus Unbound,* take Aeschylus as their starting point and evolve into highly complex revisionary versions of their originals. Here Shelley is rescuing Greek literature from the confines of classicism and liberating the positive potential which is trapped within. Just as the Promethean trilogy had been used as a pretext for justifying the *status quo,* so Greek mythology had been wilfully misunderstood by Christian interpreters who had 'contrived to turn the wrecks of the Greek mythology, as well as the little they understood of their philosophy, to purposes of deformity and falsehood'.[54]

Shelley's affirmation of the power of mythology is both a refusal to accept the grim orthodoxies of Christianity with its degrading notion of eternal punishment in hell and an expression of the spirit of joy as manifested in the powers and forces of nature. This involves his translations from the Homeric Hymns, the crystalline neo-classical clarity of 'Arethusa', the sensuously realized dialectical balance of the Hymns of Pan and Apollo (intended for his wife's play *Midas*), the visionary invention of *The Witch of Atlas* and the Ionian island-paradise which marks the climax of *Epipsychidion.* Shelley also produced a number of poems in which the mythological imagination is allowed to work directly on the phenomena of the natural world without the intervening influence of a Greek original. Both 'Ode to the West Wind' and 'The Cloud' are freshly observed and both display a vivid use of mythological invention which has been informed by the example of Greek art and literature but which is never derivative or heavy-footed. Shelley's own desire to capture and to express 'the animation of delight' was reinforced and its achievement made possible by his sympathetic response to the joyous creativity of the Greeks. In contrast to a system centred on the image of a tyrannical and elderly father . . . , Shelley envisages a world informed by divinities who are young and beautiful and whose energy never deprives them of that serene poise and self-confidence which is aesthetically as well as morally pleasing. These poems give vital embodiment to 'the Religion of the Beautiful, the Religion of Joy' as Keats used to call it. Shelley would have been in sympathy with Keats's remarks to the painter Joseph Severn. 'Keats', said Severn, 'made me in love with the real living Spirit of the past.' '"It's an immortal youth", he would say, "just as there is no *Now* or *Then* for the Holy Ghost".'[55]

V

If mythology could give rise to such varying interpretations, so too could the record of Greek literature and history. The Greek tradition was used not only as an encouraging pretext for reform but as an endorsement and justification of the *status quo.* This might seem surprising to the modern reader who is likely to remember the enthusiastic support which the Greeks received from the English Philhellenes during the War of Independence, Shelley's prophetic anticipation of a Greek victory in *Hellas,* and Byron's death in the Greek cause at Missolonghi. Yet in England it was always clear that a love of the classics was not necessarily associated with a love of liberty or a desire for social equality. Certainly, a knowledge of the classics and of Greek in particular was often associated with feelings of superiority—see Lord Chesterfield's advice to his son on the social value of Greek[56] and, eighty years later, the reactions of Lord Byron and the reviewers to Keats's attempt to revive Greek mythology without the advantages of a classical education.

The compliment could, of course, be reversed: although one of his contemporaries considered it a 'misfortune' for Samuel Richardson that 'he did not know the Antients',[57] the novelist prized his originality and cultivated a freedom from tradition whose consequences were ethical as well as aesthetic. Richardson vehemently disapproved of the morality of classical literature and of the epic in particular: the *Iliad* and the *Aeneid* were largely responsible for 'the savage spirit that has actuated, from the earliest ages to this time, the fighting fellows, that, worse than lions or tigers, have ravaged the earth, and made it a field of blood'.[58] Similar views can be found not only among the novelists, who may have connected the classics with a world of privilege and power from which they were excluded, but among poets of a radical persuasion. Blake, for example, identified the classics with military imperialism: 'The Classics! it is the Classics, & not Goths nor Monks, that Desolate Europe with Wars.'[59]

Some admirers of Greece seem to have combined their admiration with a dislike for the changing society in which they lived, finding in Greek literature either a refuge from unpleasant social and political realities or a justification of things as they were. Shelley's friends Peacock and Hogg both had recourse to Greek as an antidote. Peacock's response was less reactionary and more intelligently flexible than that of Hogg, as his novels show, but he too was somewhat susceptible to the allure of the pastoral idyll. A much more extreme interpreter of the Greek tradition was Thomas Taylor, the Platonist. His attempt to restore the lost philosophy of Greece may have helped the progress of poetry and may even have appealed to radical poets such as Shelley and Blake but Taylor himself was profoundly anti-democratic and his researches into Greek literature and philosophy only confirmed his prejudice. The main trend of his thinking emerges very clearly in a passage in the preface to his translation of Pausanias, which was printed in 1794 . . . . Here the formal excellence of Greek style is set in counterpoint to those licences which have helped to cause the French Revolution: for Taylor the best safeguard against the horrors of anarchy was the cultivation of the classics. Perhaps it is no accident that John Flaxman, who helped to popularize Greek mythology through the neo-classical finesse of his engravings and of his designs for Wedgwood, was also out of sympathy with the Revolution.

If literature and philosophy could be so interpreted, it is only to be expected that Greek history would provide anti-democratic lessons for those who were anxious to find them. John Gillies, whose two-volume study appeared in 1786, expressed some admiration for Athens and its democracy but also pointed out 'the evils inherent in every form of Republican policy', an interpretation which was fittingly embellished by a dedication to George III . . . . In his view, Britain had a more stable and desirable system because of the emphasis it placed on the 'lawful dominion of hereditary Kings'. There are times when his account of Athenian society seems to be directed at the political reformers of his own age. Gillies' history was soon translated into French and German but it was overshadowed by the larger achievement of William

Mitford (1744–1827) whose history appeared in five volumes between 1784 and 1810. If Gillies preferred the stability of constitutional monarchy to the turbulence of democracy, Mitford earned the title of 'the Tory historian of Greece'. Byron, who did not approve of his habit of 'praising tyrants', granted him the ambivalent virtues of 'learning, labour, research, wrath, and partiality'.[60] Mitford was certainly partial. The Athenian people he caricatured as a 'complex Nero' while in Macedon he discovered 'that popular attachment to the constitution and to the reigning family, the firmest support of political arrangement'. What Coleridge saw as his 'zeal against democratic government'[61] became more attractive to many readers as the French Revolution took its troubled course: the parallel between Athens and revolutionary France could be used to potent effect.

Greek history, it would seem, was by no means a simple advertisement for the virtues of democracy. The historical record was ambiguous and, as with every other aspect of Greek civilization, a great deal depended on the eye of the interpreter. If Gillies and Mitford interpreted the history of Greek democracy as a terrible warning, more radical thinkers were eager to seize on its happier aspects. It is ironical that while Mitford employed Athens as a grim illustration of what was to be avoided, Thomas Paine used the same example to illuminate the value of democracy: 'We see more to admire, and less to condemn, in that great, extraordinary people, than in anything which history affords.'[62]

Yet the English concern with Greek liberty was centred not so much on the rights of man as on a sympathetic identification with the struggle to break free from Turkish rule. English travellers tended to lament the decline of Greek fortunes so vividly symbolized by the Turkish occupation of the Acropolis, where a mosque had been built inside the Parthenon, and to hope that one day the Greeks would regain their independence; there were many who considered this a distant possibility because the modern Greeks seemed to have sunk into an unattractive apathy. Although these feelings were often aroused by first-hand observation, the sympathetic impulse was frequently stimulated not by travel but by the reading of Greek history and literature and by a strong belief that Greece was the home not simply of democratic politics but of liberty itself. Not surprisingly, this theme can be detected at the height of the period of Philhellenism when, for example, a poem in the workers' newspaper *Black Dwarf* interprets Peterloo in terms of the struggle between Turks and Greeks: the crowds now become 'each helpless Greek' while the yeomanry are transformed into 'ye English Janizaries of the *north*' (1 December 1819). This attitude can be traced back throughout much of the eighteenth century. It appears in Samuel Johnson who was stirred by the philhellenic spirit when he revised his play *Irene* (produced in 1749) and developed the theme of conflict between Grecian liberty and Turkish tyranny. It is prominent in Thomson's *Liberty,* in Glover's *Leonidas* and in Collins's 'Ode to Liberty' but it can also be found in the poetry of Thomas Warton, of Gray and of Falconer, and in Sir William Young's *The Spirit of Athens* (1777). Glover's interest suggests some of the political complications of the subject: although he later composed *The Athenaid* (posthumously published in 1787) his fame was based on *Leonidas* (1737). This lengthy poem was directed against the administration of Sir Robert Walpole but its political message was linked with the celebration of the Spartan virtues and the endorsement of their value in the struggle for liberty. The emphasis is significant: although Athens was a regular focus of sympathetic interest, oligarchic Sparta was also much admired, not least because of its contribution to the struggle against the Persians. English supporters of the Greek claim for independence could hardly fail to be moved by the heroism of the Spartans: 'Of the three hundred give but three, / To make a new Thermopylae.'[63] Sometimes the equation was altered so that the French rather than the Turks were identified with the Persians. A revival of interest in *Leonidas* may be traced to the Napoleonic threat: there were new editions in 1798 and 1804, a broadsheet of 1803 entitled *The Briton's Prayer* (which was based on passages from Glover's poem) and a dramatized 'enlargement' of 1792.[64] Classical history still had its uses.

In England, of course, an admiration for Sparta never fuelled a revolution as it seems to have done in France but the Spartan example remained very attractive, especially to the Whigs. This is probably symptomatic: the British tendency was to identify not with democratic Athens but with Greece as a whole in its struggle for liberty in which the Spartans had played a celebrated part. The positive values which could be deduced from the Greek example were elevated and rather generalized in their application. Perhaps the finest example is provided by an anecdote concerning the Earl of Granville told by Robert Wood in his book on Homer:

> Being directed to wait upon his Lordship, a few days before he died, with the preliminary articles of the Treaty of Paris, I found him so languid, that I proposed postponing my business for another time; but he insisted that I should stay, saying, it could not prolong his life, to neglect his duty; and repeating the following passage, out of Sarpedon's speech [*Iliad,* xii. 310-28], he dwelled with particular emphasis on the third line, which recalled to his mind the distinguishing part he had taken in public affairs . . . His Lordship repeated the last word [let us go] several times with a calm and determinate resignation; and after a serious pause of some minutes, he desired to hear the treaty read . . .

Homer, it would seem could offer lessons in morality which raised him far above the status of the vigorous recorder of a primitive society and the celebrator of its heroes. It was precisely this quality of moral grandeur which caused William Pitt to recommend to his nephew the study of Homer (significantly coupled with Virgil):

> You cannot read them too much: they are not only the two greatest poets, but they contain the finest lessons for your age to imbibe: lessons of honour, courage, disinterestedness, love of truth, command of temper, gentleness of behaviour, humanity, and in one word, virtue in its true signification.[65]

Such moral fervour might easily cause us to forget that, as we have seen, many writers were prepared to draw comparisons between the Homeric warriors and the American Indians which were not entirely flattering.

The contrast is emblematic. If Homer could be many things to many men, so too could the Greek example. The fascination of Romantic Hellenism is in its endless variety, in the scope which it offers for views which are often radically opposed. Throughout the eighteenth and in the early years of the nineteenth century the image of Greece was constantly refined, revised, refuted or reinterpreted: what we have briefly examined in this introduction is a complex and continuous process of redefinition. Greece provided a pretext for revolutionary politics and for rigid conservatism; it acted as an inhibiting example to writers and artists and as a liberating possibility; sometimes it stimulated, sometimes it provoked angry and dismissive reactions. Through all the changes, political and aesthetic, which mark this period of history, Greece remained a rich imaginative matrix either as an ideal toward which one might aspire or as a false example which must be repudiated: it was a mirror in which the age could see itself.

Notes

[1] *An Account of a late Voyage to Athens,* 1676, pp. 123-4.

[2] Charles Perry, *A View of the Levant,* 1743, pp. 504-5.

[3] II. lxxiii (ll. 693-6).

[4] *A Journey into Greece,* 1682, p. 347. For the close connections between travel and scientific enquiry, see R. W. Frantz, *The English Traveller and the Movement of Ideas 1660–1732,* Lincoln, Nebr., 1934.

[5] Shelley, *Hellas,* ll. 698-9.

[6] 'Extract of a Letter from an English Historical Painter at Rome', *Annals of the Fine Arts,* v (1820), 102-5.

[7] *Byron's Letters and Journals,* ed. Leslie E. Marchand, 1973-iv. 325. . . .

[8] *The Works of Lord Byron: Letters and Journals,* ed. R. E. Prothero, 1898–1901, v. 551.

[9] E. V. Lucas, *Charles Lamb and the Lloyds,* 1898, pp. 190, 183.

[10] P.-A. Guys, *Voyage littéraire de la Grèce,* Paris, 1771, ii. 56. Like Mary Wortley Montagu, to whose letters he refers (ii. 79), Guys compares contemporary customs and dress to those described in Homer and other classical writers.

[11] *Italian Journey [1786–1788],* tr. W. H. Auden and Elizabeth Mayer, Penguin Books, Harmondsworth, 1970, p. 310.

[12] *Byron's Letters and Journals,* ed. Marchand, viii.21-2. The phrase about 'authenticity' comes from Thomas Campbell's comment on the *Oriental Eclogues* of Collins; Bryant's book is obliquely referred to in *Don Juan,* IV.ci. For Troy, see SPENCER (*Fair Greece, Sad Relic*), pp. 203-5 and SPENCER ('Robert Wood and the Problem of Troy in the Eighteenth Century'), CLARKE, pp. 183-5.

[13] *Essay upon Literature,* 1726, pp. 118, 117; the final quotation is cited by Ian Watt, *The Rise of the Novel,* 1957, p. 242, a study to which I am much indebted in this survey.

[14] i.19.

[15] *Lettre sur les occupations de l'Académie française,* v, pp. 107, 50.

[16] *L'Iliade d'Homère,* Paris, 1711, i.xxvi.

[17] FOERSTER, pp. 9-10.

[18] MANUEL, p. 16.

[19] Hugh Honour, *The New Golden Land: European Images of America from the Discoveries to the Present Time,* 1976, p. 277.

[20] *Moeurs des sauvages amériquains,* Paris, ii.428. See Margaret T. Hodgen, *Early Anthropology in the Sixteenth and Seventeenth Centuries,* Philadelphia, Pa., 1964.

[21] Cf. 'I have known the poet blamed for the insolent and abusive language which he puts into the mouths of his heroes, both in their assemblies and in the heat of battle: I then cast my eyes on children who approach much nearer to nature than ourselves, on the vulgar always in a state of childhood, on savages who are always the vulgar; and have observed in all these, that their anger constantly expresses itself in insolence and outrage, previous to producing any other effect.' Jean-Jacques Barthélemy, *Les Voyages du jeune Anacharsis en Grèce,* Paris, 1788; English. tr. by W. Beaumont, 2nd ed. 1794, i.109.

[22] *Lady Blessington's Conversations of Lord Byron*, ed. Ernest J. Lovell, Jr., Princeton, N.J., 1969, p.141.

[23] . . . *Correspondence*, ed. T. Wright, 1904, ii.404.

[24] See *Essay Supplementary to the Preface, The Prose Works of William Wordsworth*, ed. W. J. B. Owen and J. Smyser, Oxford, 1974, ii.73-4; Coleridge, *Biographia Literaria*, ed. George Watson, 1975, p. 22n.; Southey, review of *Works of the English Poets, Quarterly Review*, xii (1814) which includes this judgement: 'The astronomy in these lines would not appear more extraordinary to Dr. Herschell than the imagery to every person who has observed moonlight scenes' (87). For a detailed account of Romantic reactions to Pope, see Upali Amarasinghe, *Dryden and Pope in the Early Nineteenth Century*, Cambridge, 1962.

[25] *Sketches of the History of Man*, Edinburgh, 1778, i.366n., cited by FOERSTER, p. 44n.

[26] *The Letters of Charles and Mary Anne Lamb*, ed. Edwin W. Marrs, Jr., Ithaca, Cal., and London, 1975—, iii.17.

[27] *The Letters of Philip Dormer Stanhope*, ed. Bonamy Dobrée, 1932, iv.1306, 1610.

[28] . . . Lamb, *Letters*, ed. Marrs, ii.82; *The Letters of John Keats*, 1814-21, ed. H. E. Rollins, Cambridge, Mass., 1958, ii.308, 326; see Timothy Webb (*The Violet in the Crucible*), pp. 137-40; Geoffrey Keynes, *Blake Studies*, Oxford, 1971, p. 161; Godwin quoted in *Shelley Memorials*, 3rd. ed. 1875, p. 47.

[29] *Essay upon Literature*, pp. 115-16.

[30] BUSH (*Mythology*), p. 32.

[31] Cited in James Sutherland, *A Preface to Eighteenth Century Poetry* [1949], repr. 1966, p. 142. Cf. Pluche's comment in MANUEL, p. 5.

[32] *Letters*, ed. Dobreé, ii. 362.

[33] *Biographia Literaria*, p. 10.

[34] *Biographia Literaria*, p. 4.

[35] 'To the Muses'.

[36] *A Tour thro' the Whole Island of Great Britain*, ed. G. D. H. Cole, 1927, i.173.

[37] *The Lounger*, 37 (10 October 1785) cited in Sutherland, *A Preface*, p. 143.

[38] Cited in MANUEL, p. 52.

[39] *Collected Letters*, ii.865-6.

[40] i.39ff.

[41] 'Pastoral Poesy', ll. 13-14.

[42] By Milton's time the idea was commonplace (see *Paradise Regained*, iv. 336 ff.). In his later years, Blake claimed that Greek art derived from the Cherubim of Solomon's temple (*Complete Writings*, ed. G. Keynes, 1966, pp. 565, 775).

[43] *Excursion*, iv.718-62, 847-87; vi.52-57; *Prelude*, viii.312ff. (1805-6), 173ff. (1850). See also *Excursion*, vii.728-40.

[44] iv.718-62.

[45] Preface of 1815, *Prose Works*, iii.34.

[46] *Coleridge's Miscellaneous Criticism*, ed. Thomas Middleton Raysor, 1936, p. 148. . . .

[47] Cited in CLARKE, p. 116n.

[48] KUHN, p. 1094.

[49] Preface to *Foliage, Literary Criticism*, ed. L. H. and C. W. Houthchens, Columbia University Press, New York and London, 1956, p. 130.

[50] *Don Juan*, XI.1x.

[51] *Miscellaneous Criticism*, p. 148.

[52] *Literary Criticism*, p. 135.

[53] *Shelley's Prose*, ed. David Lee Clark, Albuquerque, N. Mex., corr. ed., 1966, p. 219 (corrected). See, in particular, Peacock's 'Sir Calidore' (1818) and Hunt's Preface to *Foliage* (1818). For further discussion, see WEBB (*The Violet in the Crucible*), chapter II.

[54] *Shelley's Prose*, p. 274.

[55] William Sharp, *The Life and Letters of Joseph Severn*, 1892, p. 29.

[56] *Letters*, ed. Dobrée, iii.1155.

[57] See John Nichols, *Literary Anecdotes of the Eighteenth Century*, 1812-15, iv. 585.

[58] *Selected Letters of Samuel Richardson*, ed. John Carroll, Oxford, 1964, p. 134 (?late 1749).

[59] *Complete Writings*, ed. Geoffrey Keynes, 1966, p. 778.

[60] Note to *Don Juan*, XII.19.

[61] *Miscellaneous Criticism*, pp. 146-7.

[62] *The Rights of Man* [1792], Everyman ed., 1915, p. 177.

[63] 'The Isles of Greece', *Don Juan,* III. 86, stanza 7.

[64] RAWSON, pp. 357-8.

[65] *Correspondence of William Pitt, Earl of Chatham,* 1838, i.62-3.

HISTORICAL DEVELOPMENT OF ENGLISH ROMANTIC HELLENISM

Harry Levin (essay date 1931)

SOURCE: "The Romanticists and the Classical Tradition," in *The Broken Column: A Study in Romantic Hellenism,* Harvard University Press, 1931, pp. 18-28.

[*In the excerpt below, Levin offers a brief account of Romantic Hellenism as a reaction against eighteenth-century neo-classicism.*]

The Romanticists and the Classical Tradition

Although we ordinarily expect to find the man reflected in the books that he reads, what are we to judge from the classical tastes of Émile, the romantic child of nature? "En général, Émile prendra plus de goût pour les livres des anciens, que pour les nôtres," explains his godfather, Rousseau, "par cela seul qu'étant les premiers, les anciens sont le plus près de la nature, et que leur génie est plus à eux." Emile, then, took his books along with him into the thicket and the shadows of leaves sifted over the pages as he read them. They reflected him in the sense that the whole world became, for the romantic egoist, a dim gallery of mirrors. The classical tradition, in a civilization which had hesitated to take a single step without looking back to Greece and Rome, was too strong to be swept aside, but men can always put new interpretations upon a body of laws too venerable to be flouted or abolished.

There were, early in the romantic movement, various attempts to flout and abolish the classics, and the literatures of Greece and Rome were, for a time, completely obscured by the literatures of the north. Battles of books and *querelles des anciens et des modernes* had been fought at the very height of neo-classic dominance, but both parties had then stood behind the ensign of correctness, and prominent classical scholars had engaged on the side of the moderns. The early romanticists attacked both the ancients and the correct moderns, and allied themselves to the primitives of their own respective races. It was, no doubt, a protest against the cast of formalism into which the classics had firmly settled during the period from the middle ages to the eighteenth century. We have only to recall Rousseau's youthful struggles with Vergil or Byron's confession (to Horace) that he abhorred

> Too much, to conquer for the Poet's sake,
> The drilled dull lesson, forced down word by
> word
> In my repugnant youth. . . .

So they turned from these formalized studies to more novel explorations. The individualistic doctrines of Rousseau had undergone a new development when Herder and the German romanticists placed them on a collective and national scale. New self-conscious nationalisms supplanted the old commonwealth of nations, cosmopolitanism took on an imperialistic taint, nations went digging after their origins, and Latin was no longer the language of Europe. Universality gave way to particularism. And the course of classical studies, hitherto on the main road of European culture, was forced into a bypath down which it is still straying.

The Renaissance has been described as the addition of a new Hellenism to the old Latinity of the schoolmen. It was the claim of the romanticists that their school had purified the Greek tradition by repudiating Rome. There never was a time, during the romantic movement, when the classics were completely disregarded. Greek and Latin were still the staple of education and most of the romantic writers were brought up on them, although poetry may have been obscured by pedagogy, as Byron charges. But there is no sharp cessation or sudden revolution in the general attitude toward the classics; very gradually the formalistic and pedantic elements come to be identified with Latin culture.

The second romantic generation, no longer under the necessity of reacting to a Latinized neo-classicism, held no bias against the glory that was Greece. Schooled in the fundamental tenets of their predecessors, and yet weary of the mediæval tinsel, they proclaimed a renaissance of ancient Greece. It was to be, in the paradoxical and confusing terminology of the literary historian, "the end of classicism and the return to the antique." The function of the classics as an intellectual discipline came to be neglected, and the cult of Greece became a mere enthusiasm in the long series of romantic obsessions. Poets began to indulge in Hellenic nostalgia. "La Grèce apparaît toujours comme un des cercles éclatants qu'on aperçoit en fermant les yeux," sighed Chateaubriand, the high priest of mediævalism, in a letter to the Hellenist Marcellus. "Quand retrouverai-je les lauriers-roses de l'Eurotas et le thym de l'Hymette?"

The manifesto of the new point of view had been the *Geschichte der Kunst des Alterthums* which appeared in 1764. Madame de Staël sensed its significance when she wrote, "L'homme qui fit une véritable revolution

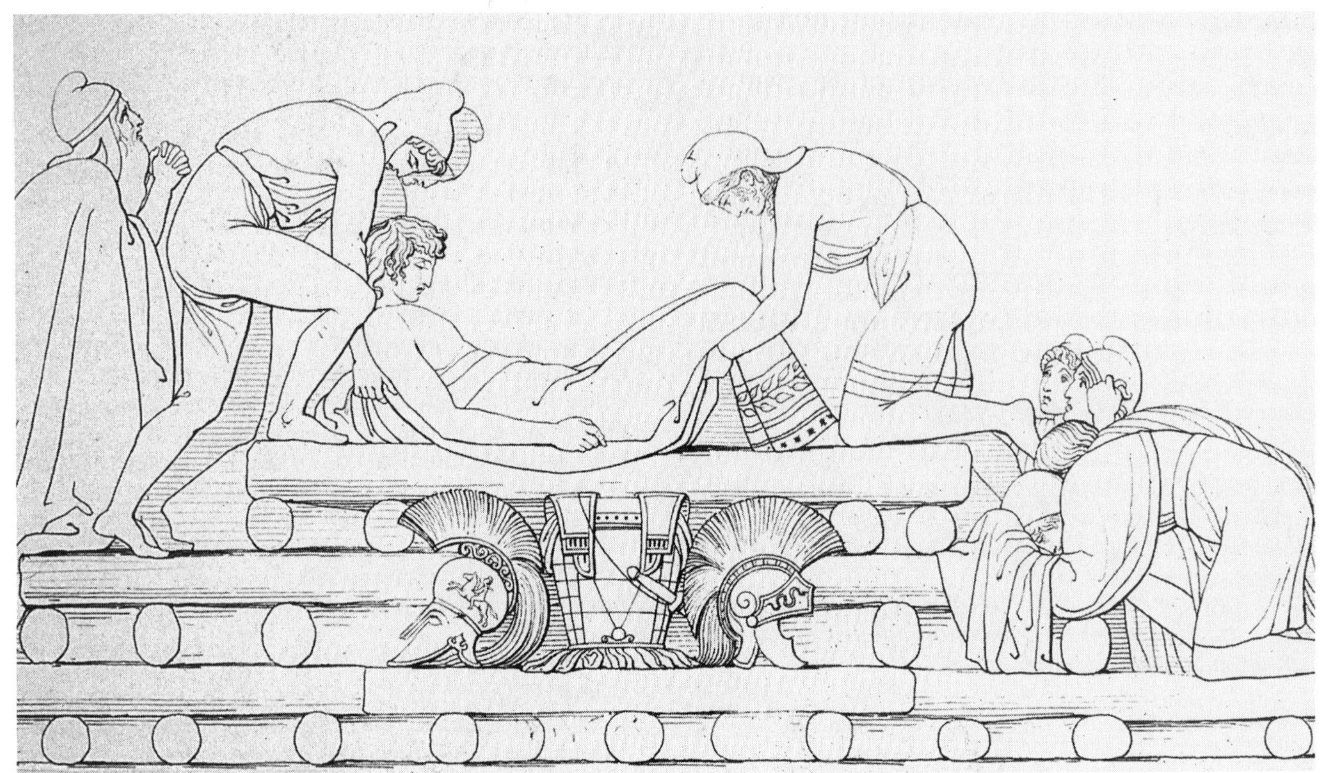

The funeral of the Trojan hero Hector, as depicted in Homer's epic poem The Iliad.

de la manière de considérer les arts, et par les arts la littérature, c'est Winckelmann." And indeed it was Winckelmann who crystallized in his studies the scientific approach to Greece made by the antiquarians, the sentimental approach of the travellers, and the aesthetic approach of the poets. Winckelmann's glorious task, in the opinion of Walter Pater, was to supplant a "flimsier, more artificial classical tradition" by "the clear ring, the eternal outline of the genuine antique." Although the infancy of his new spade-and-footrule Hellenism forced him to over-emphasize Roman civilization and to draw inspiration from masterpieces at third hand, still his chest heaved and fell when he viewed the *Apollo Belvidere.*

Winckelmann's generation was intermediate between the neo-classicists and the romantic Hellenists. Like those of the editors and grammarians who heralded the Renaissance, the names of these scholars and enthusiasts are mostly forgotten. It is hard to pass judgment upon individual figures in the movement, or to do anything but trace a general progression from the one point of view to the other. The travels of "rapid Gell" (the epithet is Byron's), Chandler, Wilkins, Colonel Leake, and Fauvet, the archæological endeavors of Humboldt, Cockerell, Raoul-Rochette, and Elgin, the philological studies of Boeckh, Matthaei, Gesner, and Heyne, and the doctrines of Quatremère De Quincey, Mengs, Quinet, and Cousin contributed to this development. There was a great deal of talk about "New Humanism" (*absit nomen!*), preached by Christ in Germany, and later by Villemain in France, and by certain obscure Russian cults. Lectures and *feuilletons* announced the marriage of Faust and Helena, and celebrated the coming of the Hellenic angel of peace to reconcile Latin-French classicism with English-Teutonic romanticism. At the very outset, Diderot had ranked Æschylus with Shakspere, and compared Sophocles favorably to George Lillo. A copy of the Abbé Barthélemy's *Voyages du jeune Anacharsis* lay on every boudoir table in France, although a more thoroughgoing romantic Hellenist, August Wilhelm von Schlegel, was to label these the travels not of a young Scythian, but of an old Parisian. Considering this current of thought in the light of the contemporary Industrial Revolution and of the social consequences of the romantic movement, we may call it a bourgeois classicism.

Such a spirit is present in the art and architecture of the period. It reveals itself in Empire and "Biedermeier" furniture. Imported by Thomas Jefferson in a convoy of romantic ideas, it makes itself evident in American homes built at the time. It calls to mind the demagogues of the French Revolution, and how they were constantly likening themselves to Greek and Roman heroes. We find Neo-Hellenism on the one hand in the pompous vulgarity of David, and on the other in the fragile idealism of Canova. Piranesi, Fragonard, Thorwaldsen, Flaxman, and Danneker may be summoned up to show the extent of its artistic ramifications. Many contemporary manifestations, such as "physical culture" or the late Miss Isadora Duncan, continue to remind us of the pervasive influence of romantic Hellenism.

What classics—it will be inquired—did these admirers of the classics read? Homer, Sophocles, and Plato did not hold sway as undisputed favorites. They read such authors as reflected their own feelings: Demosthenes for his rhetoric and republican sentiments, Herodotus for his narratives of marvels, *Daphnis and Chloe* for its languorous eroticism, Anacreon for his trivial lyrics, and Plutarch for his mysticism, his idealism, and his religious liberalism. Of the Latin writers, Seneca found the least disfavor. Few of these authors or the qualities for which they were read, obviously, are in the main stream of the classical tradition.

An inherent change in the nature and scope of classical studies becomes apparent before the end of the eighteenth century. The Greek culture had been codified and vulgarized by Rome, which in turn supplied the intellectual framework of the middle ages. Down to the beginning of the eighteenth century, education and the classics meant almost the same thing, and successive generations of minds were molded by this unchanged discipline. It may have been perverted by involution and pedantry, but it remained essentially humanistic, because it placed authority in tradition, and accepted a body of human experience as evidence. The modern, naturalistic point of view accepts nothing but physical phenomena.

Scholarship has reversed its methods and turned from internal to external evidence. The early eighteenth-century scholar pored over his texts of Homer, which the approval of the past had bequeathed to him for their just representation of life as a whole, until he was rewarded by his discovery of the digamma and thereby enabled to recover many forgotten felicities of poetic style. The late nineteenth-century scholar rolled up his manuscripts and his sleeves, took down his pickaxe, and clambered over the Troad in search of the actual remains of that small tribe from Asia Minor whose particular activities had set Homer singing. He found his reward in a half-defaced inscription or the fragment of a drinking-bowl.

Centuries of Homeric doubts culminated in the attempt of romantic scholarship to settle a question which had wearied generations of scholiasts. The contentions of the Chorizontes and the Peisistratidean tradition attest the fact that the Greeks themselves were conscious of the obscurity which surrounds the origin of the *Iliad* and the *Odyssey.* European classicism was not untroubled by this problem; Perrault had attacked Homer in the name of good taste, D'Aubignac had denied his very existence, and Vico had begun to suspect that all epics were derived from ballads. Still the prevailing pre-romantic attitude is better expressed by Dr. Johnson, with his complete faith in Homer as a real poet and his utter contempt for the "sequel of songs and rhapsodies" theory.

It remained for Wolf, basing his *Prolegomena* of 1795 upon the accumulated arguments of the disintegrating crities, to lay down the principles for a completely romantic reinterpretation of Homer. His task had been facilitated by Villoisin's edition of the Scholia, and anticipated by the essays of Blackwell and Wood, which had laid great stress upon the oral character of the epics and crowned Homer with the newly garnered laurels of the original genius, the bard of the soil, warbling his native woodnotes wild after the manner of Ossian. But Wolf, in attacking the unity of the *Iliad,* went a step farther and argued that the Homeric epic was no polished production, deliberately planned and carefully executed by a skilled poet, but a mere potpourri of the random utterances of any number of rustic bards and rhapsodes.

Thus Herder, in *Homer und das Epos,* had only to draw the moral: that the epic was the haphazard, vegetative outgrowth of the folk themselves, and, as such, was chiefly remarkable for its national idiosyncrasies. This conclusion is perhaps most significant of the many changes which affected the humanities under the influence of the new ideas. Modern criticism has rejected the authority of the classics and split up classical studies into such categories as archæology, epigraphy, palæography, economic history, and comparative philology. If anything is left, it may be served up as pure æsthetics. The critical tendencies of the eighteenth century must account for the wide gulf between a pair of classicists like Bentley and Mommsen in their aims, methods, and intellectual outlook. The international republic of letters was no more, learned treatises were written not in Latin but in German, and classical study became the expert's research and the dilettante's diversion. . . .

Terence Spencer (essay date 1954)

SOURCE: "Hellenism and Philhellenism," in *Fair Greece, Sad Relic: Literary Philhellenism from Shakespeare to Byron,* Weidenfeld and Nicolson, 1954, pp. 194-211.

[*In the following essay, Spencer discusses the factors that influenced the growing interest of late eighteenth- and early nineteenth-century interest in Greece, and analyzes the gradual shift in attention from the spirit of ancient Greece to the political situation of modern Greece.*]

> It is one thing to read the *Iliad* at Sigaeum and on the tumuli, or by the springs with Mount Ida above,

> and the plain and rivers and Archipelago around you; and another to trim your taper over it in a snug library—*this* I know.
>
> *Childe Harold's Pilgrimage,* canto iii, note 19.

> Ah, Athens! scarce escaped from Turk and Goth,
> Hell sends a paltry Scotchman worse than both.
>
> *The Curse of Minerva* (1811), a cancelled couplet.

> I cannot forbear mentioning a singular speech of a learned Greek of Ioannina, who said to me, "You English are carrying off the works of *the Greeks,* our forefathers—preserve them well—we Greeks will come and re-demand them!"
>
> John Cam Hobhouse, *A Journey through Albania and other Provinces of Turkey in Europe and Asia* (1813).

Although our view nowadays of Greek civilization may be very different from that current at the beginning of the nineteenth century, there can be no doubt that the eighteenth century enjoyed a fuller appreciation of ancient Greece and her achievement than had existed since Roman times; and the result was an enthusiasm that was both intense and contagious. Greece was the new focus of attention for classical studies. The "second Renaissance" which took place in the later eighteenth century and which both stimulated and was nourished by the researches of ardent antiquaries, above all, Winckelmann, made the very word "Grecian" full of emotional overtones. The Abbé Barthélemy's *Anacharsis,* and its imitators, were educating Europe to an appreciation of the life and "sensibility" of the ancient Greek. The background to the more generous attitude to the modern Greeks was the idealization of the ancient Greeks. The new Hellenism was, in England and in France, but not in Germany, a powerful companion of Philhellenism, principally because it took the enthusiasts to Greece and created a demand for information about the country.

What had been recovered during the Renaissance in the fifteenth and sixteenth centuries was more of a Roman culture than a Greek culture. It was generally assumed that the Romans had learnt their arts from the Greeks; and that therefore the accessible Roman remains of sculpture, architecture and literature were adequate models of Greek excellence. Classical enthusiasm hardly distinguished between Greek and Roman. It took several centuries to discover that Greek art and literature, and Roman art and literature, were fundamentally different from each other. The discovery came first, of course, in literature; as regards the fine arts, it was necessary to reveal the survivals in Greece itself. The growing enthusiasm for the Greek arts meant an expanding interest in Greece.

In architecture the first stage in the revelation of "the true Greek genius" was the discovery of Doric. When at Verona, Addison had noticed "the ruin of a triumphal arch erected to Flaminius, where one sees old Doric pillars without any pedestal or basis, as Vitruvius has described them";[1] but the modern world knew practically nothing of the Doric order (except from the descriptions of Vitruvius and from travellers' inadequate accounts of the Parthenon) until the discovery of Paestum about the middle of the eighteenth century[2] and the increase in the number of visitors to the Grecian temples of Sicily. Although the toast of the Society of Dilettanti was, from its earliest days, "Grecian Taste and Roman Spirit", the first part of this aspiration was imperfectly or negligibly realized for some years. Only after they had organized their expeditions to Greece and Ionia and arranged for their magnificent publications, did the Dilettanti reveal to themselves and to the world what Grecian Taste was. The notion of "The Antique" was undergoing a fundamental change. "Classicism" gradually came to mean a devotion to purely Greek ideals, in so far as those ideals could be discovered. The taste for Roman antiques, although still widespread, became much more discriminating. It was a common opinion that Rome had been inferior to Greece in all spheres of the arts; and Roman objects were of interest only so far as they could be relied upon as a just reflection of Greek art. The Portland Vase could be regarded as sufficiently Hellenic to provide patterns for decorative porcelain and the background to an ode on a Grecian Urn. The reputation of the Apollo Belvedere, the Venus dei Medici, and the Discobolus could be saved because they were supposed to be examples of Greek workmanship.

The new Hellenism, which developed in the latter part of the eighteenth century, thus directed towards Greece a good deal of the enthusiasm which had hitherto been concentrated upon Rome. The movement which Stuart and Revett had accelerated by their important pioneer publications had provoked, in many quarters, an enthusiasm for "pure Grecian" architecture. Some eminent architects, it is true, warmly opposed the growing fashion. The Grecian style did not grow up unopposed or uncondemned. Sir William Chambers, trained in the old Vitruvian and Palladian styles, emphatically rejected this new classicism, and proclaimed the superiority of the Roman remains in Italy and France over any surviving examples of Grecian architecture in Greece; and, without, of course, having seen any of the Athenian buildings, he ventured to assert that St. Martin-in-the-Fields was superior to the Parthenon. It should be remembered, however, that the source of information about the Doric order was, for many years, Le Roy's *Ruines des plus beaux Monuments de la Grèce* (1758), the incorrectness of which is obvious to modern eyes. . . . The first volume of the Society of Dilettanti's work on Athens by Stuart and Revett (1762) contained no important specimen of Doric. It was not until the second volume (twenty years after Le Roy's

Ruines) that the world had an accurate account of Doric monuments. The rejection and contemptuous treatment of "Grecian" by many artists who were trained in the Palladian style becomes more intelligible when we remember that they had no material more authentic or accurate than Le Roy's to base their opinions upon. But the third volume of Stuart's work (1794) contained, for the first time, full delineations of Doric architecture; and this may be regarded as marking the turning-point in the reputation of "Grecian". After that date a visit to Greek lands and the careful study of the surviving monuments came to be regarded as an important part of the training of a young architect. With the decline of the taste for the Palladian style, the authority of the *dicta* of the Italian architects of the Renaissance weighed less heavily. Greater emphasis was placed on the actual study of extant remains. The Buildings of the Ancients, Robert Adam had written, "are in Architecture, what the works of Nature are with respect to the other Arts; they serve as models which we should imitate, and as standards by which we ought to judge: for this reason, they who aim at eminence, either in the knowledge or in the practice of Architecture, find it necessary to view with their own eyes the works of the Ancients which remain, that they may catch from them those ideas of grandeur and beauty, which nothing, perhaps, but such observation can suggest".[3] Fired with ideas like these, a visit to Greece for the purpose of studying the extant remains became the ambition of all the more adventurous young architects; and those who were unable to make the journey studied the records which had been made by others. The result is the large number of buildings in London and elsewhere based on Hellenic models, and incorporating memories and motifs brought back from Greece. Of course, the arguments against the adoption of an authentic Grecian style were strong. The method of construction which was appropriate to the climate of Greece is hardly suitable, or rarely suitable, in England. The porticos are unattractive and wasteful in a country where the inhabitants look for sunshine not shade. The pitch of the roof is not high enough to get rid of the snowfall in northern latitudes. The windows characteristic of pure Grecian buildings are ludicrously inadequate on the frequent sunless days. Yet none of these practical objections was sufficiently strong to overcome the romantic appeal of the Grecian manner; and buildings deriving their form from the Parthenon, the Erectheum, etc., filled the towns of Europe. It was a startling new architectural style. We have forgotten how strongly it once stirred the imagination.

Willey Revelly (d. 1799), one of Chambers's pupils, accompanied Sir Richard Worsley, the great collector of antiquities, during his tour of Greece in 1785–7, as architect and draughtsman; and on his return immediately began producing buildings in the Grecian style. It was he who edited the third volume of Stuart's *Antiquities of Athens* (1794), and in the preface he replied to Chambers's strictures on Greek architecture. Sir Robert Smirke was in Greece in 1802, before he was twenty-one; published his *Specimens of Continental Architecture* 1806, and later designed the British Museum and the Royal College of Physicians in Trafalgar Square in the new Greek style. William Wilkins, in his early twenties, was also in Athens; he published his *Atheniensia, or Remarks on the Topography and Buildings of Athens* in 1812, and later designed the façade of the National Gallery and University College, London, where he reproduced the Choragic Monument of Lysicrates on the top of the dome. These are some famous characteristic London buildings. But there were many other architects in the first two decades of the nineteenth century, whose travels to Greece gave them a style which filled town and country with romantically Grecian buildings.

It was the architect Thomas Harrison (1744–1829) who urged Lord Elgin, on his appointment as British Ambassador at Constantinople in 1799, to obtain casts and drawings of works of art at Athens and other places in Greece. For during the first few years of the nineteenth century conditions in the Turkish dominions gradually became especially advantageous to the English. The favourable issue of the struggle against Napoleon impressed the Porte, which became anxious to placate the government of the nation whose sea-power was dominant in the Mediterranean. Nelson was already a popular hero amongst the Greeks. He was presented with a golden-headed sword by the people of the Zante, together with a truncheon studded with all the diamonds that the island could furnish. It was on account of the enhanced prestige of Britain after the Battle of Copenhagen (1801) that Elgin was eventually able to obtain a firman from the Porte which allowed his agents to "fix scaffolding round the ancient Temple of the Idols [i.e. the Parthenon], and to mould the ornamental sculpture and visible figures thereon in plaster and gypsum". This was not all. They were also given permission "to take away from the Acropolis any pieces of stone with old inscriptions or figures thereon". Elgin wrote in his report: "In proportion with the change of affairs in our relations towards Turkey, the facilities of access to the Acropolis were increased to me and to all English travellers, and about the middle of the summer of 1801 all difficulties were removed." The story of the removal of the sculptures from the Parthenon, their shipment to England, their shipwreck off Cerigo and recovery after three years, and the eventual purchase for the British Museum for £35,000, is well known.[4] It was one of the events which were bringing Greece into the English imagination in the early years of the nineteenth century. Plaster casts of most of the frieze were probably to be seen in London before Elgin's cases were unpacked. For W. R. Hamilton (who was Elgin's secretary during his embassy, and later minister at Naples, secretary of the Society of Dilettanti, and a trustee of the British Museum) had had casts made of the marbles before they were dispatched to England and these casts were visible in London before the marbles.[5]

Elgin's activities in Greece were notorious before Byron went to Athens and wrote his scathing attacks on the second destroyer of the Parthenon. Already in *English Bards, and Scotch Reviewers* (1809) he had expressed his derision of the Grecian cult:

> Let ABERDEEN and ELGIN still pursue
> The shades of fame through regions of Virtù;
> Waste useless thousands on their Phidian freaks,
> Misshapen monuments and maim'd antiques . . .
> (1027-30).

Thus Byron joined in the fashionable contempt for the Elgin marbles, which, led by Payne Knight, was then usual in England. But after he had lived in Athens and could see with his own eyes the devastation that Elgin's agents had caused, his language acquired a personal bitterness:

> Come then, ye classic Thieves of each degree,
> Dark Hamilton and sullen Aberdeen,
> Come pilfer all the Pilgrim loves to see,
> All that yet consecrates the fading scene.[6]

But we need not trouble to come to Elgin's defence; it is clear that, during the first twenty years of the nineteenth century, the eagerness to obtain genuine examples of Grecian sculpture was so great that, if one despoiler had not succeeded, another would have taken his place. The sentiments of the Greeks on the matter were noted, but not taken very seriously. Hobhouse, who was in Athens in 1810 with Byron, gave his readers a thoughtful discussion of the rights and wrongs of removing the sculptures, but concluded:

> I have said nothing of the possibility of the ruins of Athens being, in event of a revolution in the favour of the Greeks, restored and put into a condition capable of resisting the ravages of decay; for an event of that nature cannot, it strikes me, have ever entered the head of any one who has seen Athens, and the Modern Athenians. Yet I cannot forbear mentioning a singular speech of a learned Greek of Ioannina, who said to me, "You English are carrying off the works of *the Greeks,* our forefathers—preserve them well—we Greeks will come and re-demand them!"[7]

"No circumstance", wrote James Dallaway, "has tended so much to improve the national style of design and painting as the introduction of so many genuine antiques or correct copies of them."[8] But until towards the end of the eighteenth century, Italy, and Rome in particular, had remained the principal source of antiquities for the English collectors. The ancient marbles derived from Italy were almost all late copies of Greek originals or mere imitations by sculptors of the Roman period. From the beginning of the nineteenth century, however, Greek sculpture of the finest periods (according to nineteenth-century taste) began to arrive in the country; and the British Museum acquired a series of marbles which have made it one of the greatest depositories of Greek art in the world. More and more did Greece romantically fill the imagination. "My spirit is too weak", wrote the Greekless poet contemplating the wonders of Greek sculpture:

> Such dim-conceived glories of the brain
> Bring round the heart an indescribable feud;
> So do these wonders a most dizzy pain,
> That mingles Grecian grandeur with the rude
> Wasting of old Time—with a billowy main
> A sun, a shadow of a magnitude.[9]

Moreover, new Greek arts were being discovered and appreciated. The vases which for long had been known as "Etruscan" and collected by English connoisseurs in Italy, such as Sir William Hamilton, were now recognized as Greek. An English gentleman called Stephen Graham was noted as a highly successful excavator, having secured nearly a thousand vases near Athens.[10] Another collector was a merchant of the Levant Company, Thomas Burgon (1787–1858), the nephew of that Greek lady, Mrs. Baldwin, whom Reynolds painted in 1782,[11] and father of the author of *Petra* ("a rose-red city half as old as time"). Burgon made an important collection of vases, and conducted excavations on Melos. Two travellers named Berners and Tilson returned from Greece about 1795 with a large collection of vases. The old error, that the pottery which we know as a characteristic product of Greek art of its finest periods was of "Etruscan" origin, was soon exploded; and the way was prepared for the interpretation of Greek literature and culture with the help of ancient vase-painting, a field of scholarship that has borne fruit ever since.

The idea that the library of the Grand Seraglio contained some valuable Greek manuscripts had long been held;[12] it was thought, too, that the libraries of some of the mosques which had been converted from Christian Churches, especially that of Aya Sophia, might contain lost treasures of Greek literature. It had also been reported, at various times, that the monasteries of the Levant contained manuscripts, which might represent unknown and important ancient writings. When Elgin was sent out as British ambassador in 1799, it was decided, therefore, that a suitably erudite person should accompany him who might explore these unknown literary treasures. "The plan originated with Mr. Pitt and the Bishop of Lincoln, who thought that an embassy sent at a time when Great Britain was on the most friendly terms with the Porte, would afford great facilities for ascertaining how far these hopes of literary discovery were well founded. They trusted that the ambassador's influence would obtain permission for the transmission at least, if not for the acquisition of any unpublished work that might be found."[13] The choice fell upon the professor of Arabic at Cambridge, Joseph Dacre Carlyle, who joined Elgin's entourage as his official chaplain,[14] and it was he who by an extraordinary concession, the result of Elgin's pressure and the prestige of the English at the Porte, was admitted to the sealed library of the Seraglio. A full account of his remarkable achievement was sent home by Carlyle to the Bishop of Durham and the Bishop of Lincoln; and his letters make amusing reading. He was interviewed by Youssouf Aga, probably the most influential person at the Porte at that time; and Carlyle had to persuade the Turk that this activity of hunting for old books was of great importance to the Franks, even to the politicians. "I observed" (Carlyle wrote home) "that different nations possessed different customs; that my discovery of one of these ancient authors would be looked upon in England as very important; and I took the liberty of adding, that no person felt more interested in subjects of this kind than Mr. Pitt. Youssouf Aga replied, that nothing could give them greater pleasure than to gratify the British nation, and particularly Mr. Pitt; and that if they could give any intelligence where such books were deposited, I should not only have the liberty of inspecting them, but of carrying them along with me to England."

Thus fortified, and trembling with anticipation, Carlyle was ushered into the room which no infidel (it was supposed) had entered since the Turk had been at Constantinople; and there he found, amid large numbers of Persian and Arabic books, not one manuscript in Greek or Latin. The dream was at an end. Had he come upon the poems of Sappho or a codex of the comedies of Menander, Carlyle would have been famous; and Elgin would have been better known for his success in bringing Greek literature to England than in bringing Greek sculpture. But not a single classical fragment of a Greek or Latin author was found in any of these vast collections.[15]

Topographical investigation became especially important during the last decade of the eighteenth century and the beginning of the nineteenth century owing to the rise of the great Homeric Problem or Trojan Puzzle. The trouble began with Robert Wood, whose tour of Greece and Asia Minor in 1750–51 resulted in his book *A Comparative View of the Antient and present State of the Troade. To which is prefixed an Essay on the Original Genius of Homer* (1767). In this work (which went through five editions and was translated into French, German, Italian, and Spanish) Wood discussed, among other things, whether the art of writing was known to Homer; and he came to the conclusion that it was not. His book was well received in Germany and enthusiastically reviewed by Heyne, the foremost German humanist; and Wood's view of writing became the chief evidence on which F. A. Wolf, in his *Prolegomena* (Halle, 1795), based his theory of multiple authorship of the Homeric poems. Meanwhile in 1775, Wood's book was edited by his untravelled friend, Jacob Bryant, a somewhat disputatious scholar, known in literary history as the author of a strongly written defence of the authenticity of the Rowley poems. But other travellers were visiting the Troad and coming to conclusions about the topography, in relation to Homer's poems, very different from the opinions of Wood. The French traveller Choiseul-Gouffier made an important survey of the region, and concluded that Homer's Troy was not at New Ilium but at Bunarbashi. These ideas were communicated, without acknowledgement, to the Royal Society of Edinburgh by another Frenchman, J. B. Le Chevalier; and the account was translated, with annotations by Andrew Dalzel, the respected Professor of Greek at Edinburgh, as a *Description of the Plain of Troy, translated from the original not yet published* (Edinburgh, 1791), in which Wood's account was condemned. Bryant responded not merely with his *Observations* (Eton, 1795) on Le Chevalier's treatise, but followed this by a work which began an acrimonious controversy lasting for many years, *A Dissertation concerning the War of Troy, and the Expedition of the Grecians as described by Homer. Showing that No Such Expedition Was Ever Undertaken, and that No Such City of Phrygia Existed* (1796). The title explains itself. Naturally Bryant was immediately attacked, both by those who (like himself) had never seen the Troad with their own eyes and by those who brought their first-hand impressions to the problem. The impetuous Gilbert Wakefield hastily produced a pamphlet (*A Letter to Jacob Bryant, Esq.*, 1797) and William Vincent reviewed Bryant's book unfavourably in *The British Critic* (January 1 and March 1, 1799; the reviews were also printed separately as a pamphlet). Meanwhile, James Dallaway in his important and veracious book *Constantinople, Ancient and Modern, with Excursions to the Shores and Islands of the Archipelago and to the Troad,* had written agreeing with Le Chevalier on the topography of Troy; and J. B. S. Morritt of Rokeby, fresh from his adventurous tour in the Levant (1794–6), leaped to Homer's defence in his *Vindication of Homer and of the Ancient Poets and Historians who have recorded the Siege and Fall of Troy* (York, 1798). Bryant replied to all attacks, often with great bitterness of tone, and republished his book in 1799 with corrections and additions. Replies, Vindications, Observations, and further Observations followed one another. New topographers set out to examine the evidence once again. William Francklin, in company with Henry Philip Hope, the brother of the author of *Anastasius,* re-surveyed the site and published his *Remarks and Observations on the Plain of Troy, made during an Excursion in June 1799* (1800), corroborating Morritt's views. In 1804 Sir William Gell produced his folio *Topography of Troy;* Edward Clarke, Dodwell, Leake, and many others during the next few years gave the world the benefit of their observations on the problem.

"These tedious and pedantic productions" are the words used by one of the few modern scholars who have had occasion to mention the series of books and pamphlets which Wood and Bryant provoked.[16] This judgment is unfair. Of course, any entirely obsolete controversy will seem tedious to later generations. But the Troy Problem was an exciting development in Homeric studies in those years; and, so far from being pedantic, the whole movement to relate the Homeric poems to a real environment was the very opposite of pedantry. Pedants did not make the difficult, troublesome, and sometimes dangerous journeys to the Trojan plain. It mattered intensely to many people of the time—and not merely to scholars—whether or not the Homeric environment could be made to fit the actual topography. Suggestions to the contrary provoked a characteristic outburst from Byron, who was not one to waste energy on pedantic controversies and who detested "antiquarian twaddle". To those who declared that it did not really matter whether the tale of Troy was authentic or not, Byron had nothing but scorn.

> We *do* care about 'the authenticity of the tale of Troy'. I have stood upon that plain *daily,* for more than a month in 1810; and if any thing diminished my pleasure, it was that the blackguard Bryant impugned its veracity. . . . I venerated the grand original as the truth of *history* . . . and of *place;* otherwise it would have given me no delight.[17]

It is this reborn Troy-sentiment—now Homeric, no longer Virgilian—which provides one of the most telling poetical localizations in Byron's poetry:

> The winds are high on Helle's wave,
> As on that night of stormy water
> When Love, who sent, forgot to save
> The young—the beautiful—the brave—
> The lonely hope of Sestos' daughter. . . .
>
> The winds are high, and Helle's tide
> Rolls darkly heaving to the main;
> And Night's descending shadows hide
> That field with blood bedew'd in vain,
> The desert of old Priam's pride;
> The tombs, sole relics of his reign,
> All—save immortal dreams that could beguile
> The blind old man of Scio's rocky isle.
>
> Oh! yet—for there my steps have been;
> These feet have pressed the sacred shore,
> These limbs that buoyant wave hath borne—
> Minstrel! with thee to muse, to mourn,
> To trace again those fields of yore,
> Believing every hillock green
> Contains no fabled hero's ashes,
> And that around the undoubted scene
> Thine own "broad Hellespont" still dashes,
> Be long my lot! and cold were he
> Who there could gaze denying thee.[18]

Nor was his experience of the Troad forgotten when Byron was writing *Don Juan:*

> High barrows, without marble, or a name,
> A vast, untill'd, and mountain-skirted plain,
> And Ida in the distance, still the same,
> And old Scamander (if 'tis he), remain;
> The situation seems still form'd for fame—
> A hundred thousand men might fight again
> With ease; but where I sought for Ilion's walls,
> The quiet sheep feeds, and the tortoise crawls. . . .
>
> (IV, lxxvii)

Although Troy provided the most interesting problem of topography, the whole of Greek studies, both history and poetry, was being enlightened by the detailed inquiries into the country of Greece and the remains of antiquity which were conducted during the dozen years before the arrival of Byron in Greece. By the end of the eighteenth century it was still possible for those who concerned themselves with classical geography to present their ideas to the world without having seen the places they were writing about. Thus, Jacob Bryant evolved his ideas about the topography of Troy without any personal experience; and one of his opponents, Thomas Falconer, later to be celebrated as a student of Strabo, produced *Remarks on some Passages in Mr. Bryant's Publications respecting the War of Troy* (1799), being equally inexperienced. Occasionally a brilliant guess might be made by an untravelled scholar, as, for example, when Arthur Browne revealed the situation of the Vale of Tempe in his *Miscellaneous Sketches, or Hints for Essays* (2 vols., 1798). But on the whole the time had passed when the learned could write about the geography and topography of Greece as if it were a place built to music, therefore never built at all, and therefore built for ever; and it was now fully appreciated that the country itself must be investigated for the light it might be expected to throw on the history and literature of the ancients.

The most ardent and assiduous of those who came to Greece in these years left his bones in Athens. Among all the Englishmen in Greece none seems to have caught the imagination of the learned world like the unfortunate and all-accomplished Tweddell. His was a name (it is accented on the first syllable) which once, whatever it may sound like now, was associated with every pathos and every grace. John Tweddell, fellow of Trinity College, Cambridge, having been crossed in love,[19] set out on his European travels in September 1795, at the age of twenty-six. He traversed the north of Europe and parts of the Near East, and arrived in Greece. "Athens especially, is my great object", he wrote in a letter from Tenos in December 1798. "I promise you that those who come after me shall have nothing to glean. Not only every temple, but every stone, and every inscription, shall be copied with the most scrupulous fidelity."[20] He had engaged the French artist Preaux, whom he had met in Constantinople, to accompany him through Greece as his draughtsman and artist. They reached Athens early in 1799. Tweddell was there for four months, diligently pursuing his researches. He died on July 25th 1799, in the arms of the faithful Fauvel, in the house of Spiridion Logothete, of a "double tertian fever". Tweddell seems to have been genuinely regretted in Athens. The Turkish commandant of the city wished his funeral to be accompanied by his own guard. He was buried in the Theseum, at his own request—precisely in the middle, because Fauvel hoped to find some traces of Theseus while Tweddell's grave was being dug. The Archbishop of Athens, the Archons, and a great crowd of people, formed the funeral procession; and as it was lowered into the grave, three salvos of musketry saluted his corpse—an unprecedented honour.[21] The arrangements for a monument were a topic of discussion and rivalry among the Englishmen in Athens for several years. When Edward Clarke was there in 1801, he found that the burial had been carelessly made. Fearing foraging animals, he had the coffin re-interred more efficiently; and a lump of Pentelic marble from the Parthenon, left by Elgin's agents, was used for a tombstone. A creditable epitaph in Greek was written by Robert Walpole in 1805 as an inscription, concluding that it was some solace to his friends that Athenian dust was strewn upon this cultivated Briton's head.[22] Although the poem was certainly inscribed on the marble soon afterwards (Edward Clarke, who has preserved it, says so), the tombstone itself appears to have now disappeared. When Byron was in Athens in 1810, he and one of his friends, John Fiott of St. John's, exerted themselves to get something done about Tweddell's grave. Eventually a Latin inscription also was placed in the Theseum. Fragments of this Latin monument are still preserved in the English Church at Athens, whither they have been removed from the Theseum.[23] Many memorial verses were composed in his honour by scholars of both Universities. Among the prettiest was that of his friend Abraham Moore in 1799. If Tweddell must die, where but in his beloved Athens would he wish to rest? "Happy art thou, if perchance it is permitted to thee to retain any feelings in the grave; for the bones of how many great men rest here! and does not thine own Athens cover thee too?"[24] Yet in spite of the interest and affection Tweddell had aroused, all the papers which he had collected, all his journals and drawings, unaccountably disappeared, after being sent by the British consul in Athens to the ambassador at the Porte. The loss was regarded as a severe one to the cause of learning, and for the next twenty years it provoked an acrimonious controversy. Tweddell's friends demanded some explanation from Elgin, who, however, denied all knowledge and resented the accusations made by Clarke, Thornton, Spencer Smith, and others. The complete loss of all Tweddell's extensive literary labours seemed a cruel blow after his unhappy death; and this, too, encouraged the University Muses to deplore "the exemplary and lamented Tweddell".[25]

Others, however, were more fortunate. William Martin Leake, the most accurate and indefatigable of the old topographers of Greece, was in 1799 sent on a military mission to Constantinople to instruct the Turkish troops in the use of modern artillery; for the Porte was anticipating aggression from the French. It was a time when, as we have seen above, in every province of the Turkish Empire, the English had an advantageous position; and Leake as a topographer (like Elgin as a collector) seized the favourable opportunity and travelled extensively throughout Greece and Asia Minor. In 1802 he was in Athens; and in September that year he sailed with Hamilton from the Piraeus in the boat which was conveying the Parthenon marbles from Athens and which was wrecked off Cythera. In 1809–10 he was British Resident in Yannina, much respected by Ali Pasha. Here Byron met him.[26] He returned to England in 1815 and henceforth devoted himself to the preparation of a series of topographical writings on Greece, which are still of the greatest value to the modern scholarly traveller, for Leake records much that has now been destroyed.

Another serious and voluminous traveller was Edward Daniel Clarke, who, as the travelling tutor to a succession of young noblemen, made extensive journeys in the Levant. He was in Greece in 1801–2, collecting coins, ancient manuscripts (of which he secured some great prizes), statues (his colossal "Ceres" now in the Fitzwilliam Museum was his greatest achievement), pottery, and other antiquities. It is said that, when Clarke published his *Travels* in 1810 and the following years, he made nearly £7,000 from the sale. Greece and the Near East were certainly the subjects of popular interest. Byron rarely spoke with much enthusiasm of his fellow-travellers in the Levant; but a letter to Clarke dated December 15th 1813, is highly complimentary.[27]

The year 1801 was indeed a remarkable one for the English in Greece. In that year William Wilkins began his four years' tour in the Levant, preparing material for his *Antiquities of Magna Graecia* (Cambridge, 1807) and his *Atheniensia, or Remarks on the Topography and Buildings of Athens* (1812). Edward Dodwell arrived in Greece in 1801 and made a second journey in 1805–6. He was a prisoner-of-war in the hands of the French government, and, through the good offices of Le Chevalier, the topographer of Troy, he had been granted leave of absence to travel. Dodwell was a cultivated traveller and an ardent collector of the usual type in those years. It took him some years to get his travel-book ready for the press; it eventually appeared in 1819 as *A Classical and Topographical Tour through Greece,* in two quarto volumes. Sir William Gell accompanied Dodwell from Trieste to Greece in April 1801,[28] and began a great series of topographical surveys, which, but for the fact that he has been somewhat outshone by Leake, would be regarded as a remarkable contribution to classical studies.

> Of Dardan tours let Dilettanti tell,
> I leave topography to classic Gell,

wrote Byron in *English Bards, and Scotch Reviewers* (1809), although his manuscript originally referred to him as "coxcomb".[29] Gell was among the first seriously to study the topography of Ithaca for the sake of its Homeric associations and elucidations. He went to the island, in company with Dodwell, in 1806 and published his *Geography and Antiquities of Ithaca* in 1807, the first attempt to localize the Homeric descriptions. Gell, of course, carried to impossible lengths his identifications of the smallest allusions by the poet to the topography of Odysseus's kingdom. His *Ithaca* and his *Itinerary of Greece* (1810) had the honour of a detailed and skilful review by Byron in *The Monthly Review* for August 1811.[30] From Patras in October 1810 Byron had written to Hobhouse, "I have some idea of purchasing the Island of Ithaca; I suppose you will add me to the Levant lunatics."[31]

Robert Walpole returned from extensive travels, apparently about 1808, and began his collection of papers on the antiquities and modern conditions of Greece and the Greeks which appeared in two parts in 1817 and 1820 (*Memoirs relating to European and Asiatic Turkey; edited from manuscript journals* and *Travels in Various Countries in the East; being a continuation of Memoirs relating to European and Asiatic Turkey*). Most of this impressive collection of essays and journals belongs to the pre-Byronic years. Here were printed papers by many of those Englishmen who had devoted themselves to the study of modern Greece in the early years of the century; the Earl of Aberdeen, John Sibthorp, John Hawkins, W. M. Leake, John Squire, C. R. Cockerell, William Wilkins, Henry Raikes, J. B. S. Morritt, W. G. Browne, William Haygarth, and others. Here, too, appeared a street-plan of contemporary Athens which had been prepared by the industrious and amiable Louis-François-Sébastien Fauvel (1753–1838), the cicerone of every learned traveller to Athens in those years. Fauvel had been taken into his service by Choiseul-Gouffier, the French ambassador, and eventually became consul.[32] He was an eager and skilful excavator (by the standards of the age), and a paper on his work around Athens was printed in Robert Walpole's *Memoirs* in 1817. Among his many talents was some skill in landscape painting, in which he is no inconsiderable figure.[33] Fauvel was Byron's guide to the antiquities of Athens and its neighbourhood, as he was for many others.

Byron, of course, had his joke against all this devoted inquiry into ancient Greek ruins; and he is reputed to have said, when standing before the Parthenon, "Very like the Mansion House".[34] In some cancelled lines, which originally formed part of his allusion to the celebrated temple of Corinth in *The Siege of Corinth,* he wrote of

> Monuments that the coming age
> Leaves to the spoil of the season's rage—
> Till Ruin makes the relics scarce,
> Then Learning acts her solemn farce,
> And, roaming through the marble waste,
> Prates of beauty, art, and taste.[35]

But, as a matter of fact, Byron saw all the usual things, and made all the usual expeditions as well as several unusual ones. Moreover, he employed a "famous Bavarian artist taking some views of Athens, etc., etc." for him, as he wrote home to his mother.[36] He was sufficiently proud of his painter (Jacob Linckh) to mention the fact in a note to *Childe Harold's Pilgrimage:* "I was fortunate to engage a very superior German artist, and hope to renew my acquaintance with [Cape Colonna], and many other Levantine scenes, by the arrival of his performances."[37] Nearly all the travellers in Greece took with them their own draughtsman, or employed one of those who had settled in the Levant, whose task it was to record the beauties of Nature and the relics of Antiquity. Fauvel played his part in this pictorial record of Greece, although he was not a professional artist; and many of his representations were engraved in the travel-books of the time. But there were several professionals who made their living by accompanying English gentlemen on their travels in Greece. Most of these were of Italian origin, but there were some Frenchmen and others. Dawkins and Wood had an Italian named Borra. Sir Robert Ainslie, who was ambassador at the Porte 1776 to 1792, employed Luigi Mayer to make drawings, which were subsequently engraved in a splendid series of books which Ainslie sponsored. Gaetano Mercati accompanied Liston on his embassy to the Porte 1793 to 1796; and from his drawings the engravings in Dallaway's book were made.[38] John Sibthorp the botanist, who in 1794 began his second extensive tour of Greece collecting materials for his famous *Flora Graeca* (1806, etc.) had with him one Francis Borone. J. B. S. Morritt in 1794–6 had a Viennese artist (unnamed).[39] Tweddell employed Preaux, who, on Tweddell's death in 1799, was taken over by Thomas Hope of Deepdene.[40] Many of Preaux's drawings were engraved in Clarke's *Travels.* Agostino Aglio was met by Wilkins in Rome in 1801, travelled with him in Greece, and subsequently came to England to help Wilkins in the production of his *Magna Graecia* (1807), in which the illustrations were executed in aquatint by Aglio. A Neapolitan draughtsman, Lusieri, was employed by Elgin and Hamilton in Athens after they had failed to enlist the services of Turner for the task; Turner proved to be too expensive. Dodwell was accompanied by Pomardi, who made 600 drawings while in Greece; Dodwell himself made 400.[41]

In 1634, Henry Peacham had praised the Earl of Arundel for transplanting old Greece into England . . . , but the transplantation really took place in the latter years of the eighteenth century and the early years of the nineteenth century. This eager exploring, excavating, transcribing, depicting, and collecting was fully developed before Byron went to Greece; and it forms the background, and the explanation, of many of his most characteristic utterances and attitudes while he was there. The revival of the Greek nation was taking place at a time when ancient Greece had become, more than it had ever been before, vividly resurrected in the imagination of Europe. There were thus many Englishmen in Greece to observe the stirrings of Greek national consciousness, and to form their opinions about the nature of a Greek revival, the possibility of a revolution, and the consequences of political independence. Some of the Englishmen were champions of the modern Greeks; some were sceptical of the Greek capacity for self-government. But both enthusiastic champions and cynical sceptics were expressing their opinions against a background of romantic attitudes to the ancient Greeks, as well as of the social and commercial advances which were being made by the modern Greeks. . . .

Notes

[1] *Remarks on several parts of Italy . . . in the years 1701, 1702, 1703.* (*Works,* ed. Hurd, Bohn's Library (1854), i, 378.)

[2] See S. Lang, "The Early Publications of the Temples at Paestum" (*Journal of the Warburg and Courtauld Institutes,* XIII (1950), 48-64).

[3] *Spalatro* (1764) (ad init.).

[4] See Courtenay Pollock, "Lord Elgin and the Marbles" in *Essays by Divers Hands being Transactions of the Royal Society of Literature,* New Series, vol. XI (1932), pp. 41-67; Michaelis, pp. 132 ff.; A. Hamilton Smith in *The Journal of Hellenic Studies,* XXXVI (1916).

[5] Hamilton purchased Stanley Grove in Chelsea about 1815 and added a large East Room to accommodate them. They are still there, now that the house has become part of the College of St. Mark and St. John.

[6] *Childe Harold's Pilgrimage,* from a cancelled stanza after II, xiii. (*Poetical Works,* ed. E. H. Coleridge, ii, 108.)

[7] *A Journey through Albania and other Provinces of Turkey in Europe and Asia* (2 vols., 1813), i, 347-8.

[8] *Anecdotes* (1800), p. 269.

[9] Keats, Sonnet v, "On seeing the Elgin Marbles for the first time", *Poems,* ed. de Sélincourt, p. 275.

[10] Clarke, *Travels in Various Countries* (1810, etc.), 2nd ed., 1816, IV, preface and p. 25. . . .

[13] Robert Walpole, *Memoirs* (1817), p. 84.

[14] Carlyle is in the *Dictionary of National Biography;* but this episode is misunderstood and slighted because the author (Stanley Lane-Poole, who should have known better) has missed the letters of Carlyle printed in Robert Walpole's *Memoirs* (1817).

[15] Walpole, *Memoirs,* pp. 86, 173.

[16] M. L. Clarke, *Greek Studies in England, 1700-1830* (Cambridge, 1945), p. 184.

[17] Diary, January 11, 1821; *Letters and Journals,* ed. Prothero, v, 165-6.

[18] *The Bride of Abydos,* canto the second, i-iii, 483-7, 502-20.

[19] Some love-letters are printed by "George Paston" in *Little Memoirs of the Eighteenth Century* (1901).

[20] *Remains of the late John Tweddell Fellow of Trinity College Cambridge* (1815), p. 268.

[21] Letter from Preaux to Spencer Smythe, *Remains,* p. 395.

[22] Printed in Edward Clarke, *Travels,* iii, 534.

[23] The following can be read:

> O H S S (=Ossa Hic Sita Sunt)
> Johannis Tweddell An(gli)
> Provincia Northumbria
> Canta(bri)giae Literis in
> (Thomas de Elgi)n Comes
> (Amico Optimo Op)timeq(ue) Merito
> (M. C. F.) C.

I adopt the reconstruction of the late William Miller.

[24]
> Felix! si tibi forsan inter umbras
> Persentiscere fas sit, ossa tecum
> Illo marmore quanta conquiescant,
> Tuae te quoque quod tegant Athenae!
>
> *Remains,* p. 23.

[25] Edward Clarke, *Travels,* iii, 532.

[26] *Childe Harold's Pilgrimage,* ii, note B.

[27] *Letters and Journals,* ed. Prothero, ii, 308-11; a better text is in *Byron, A Self Portrait; Letters and Diaries,* edited by Peter Quennell (1950), i, 204-5.

[28] Dodwell, *Tour,* i, 2.

[29] 1033-4. In the fifth edition of the poem, Byron, now better acquainted with Greece, again altered the epithet, this time to "rapid Gell", with the note: "Rapid indeed! He topographized and typographized King Priam's dominions in three days!" (*Poetical Works,* ed. E. H. Coleridge, i, 379.)

[30] Reprinted in *Letters and Journals,* ed. Prothero, i, Appendix III (pp. 350 sqq.).

[31] *Op. cit.,* i, 305.

[32] See an account of him by Phillipe Ernest Legrand, "Biographie de Louis-François-Sébastien Fauvel, Antiquaire et Consul", in *Revue Archaeologique,* Ser. 3, XXX and XXXI (1897).

[33] Two of his water-colours were exhibited at Burlington House in the Exhibition of French Landscape Painting 1950 (nos. 432, 442, representing the east front of the Parthenon and the temple of Bassae).

[34] *Recollections of the Table-Talk of Samuel Rogers* (1856), p. 238.

[35] *Poetical Works,* ed. E. H. Coleridge, iii, 470; the lines follow section xviii.

[36] A letter dated January 14th 1811; *Letters and Journals,* ed. Prothero, i, 309-10.

[37] Note 6 to Canto ii (*Poetical Works,* ed. E. H. Coleridge, ii, 170).

[38] *Constantinople,* Advertisement, p. xii.

[39] Some feeble drawings are reproduced in Morritt's *Letters* (1914).

[40] *Remains,* pp. 402, 440.

[41] *Tour,* preface, p. ix.

James M. Osborn (essay date 1963)

SOURCE: "Travel Literature and the Rise of Neo-Hellenism in England," in *Bulletin of the New York Public Library,* Vol. 67, No. 5, May, 1963, pp. 279-300.

[*In the following essay, Osborn offers a detailed outline of the development of "Neo-Hellenism," identifying Romantic Hellenism as a part of this larger movement.*]

Appropriately, this paper begins with a quotation from Sir George Wheler. For two centuries the mainland of Greece had been virtually sealed off from the states of Europe when in 1675 Wheler, a young Oxford graduate on the Grand Tour, accompanied by a French travelling companion, ventured to land in Attica where he filled notebooks with accounts of the antiquities and the present state of the Greek people. To their surprise, though some voyagers had asserted that little besides the Acropolis remained, they found Athens to be a populous and comparatively well organized city. Wheler complained that these travellers "perhaps have seen it [Athens] only from the Sea, through the wrong end of their Perspective-Glass." The thesis offered in this paper is similar—that writers on Neo-Hellenism in England also have tended to look "through the wrong end of the Perspective-Glass."[1]

Despite the extensive list of writings on Neo-Hellenism in France and Germany,[2] no book on Neo-Hellenism in England appeared until 1931, when Harvard University published the Bowdoin Prize Essay for that year, written by an undergraduate named Harry Levin. Titled *The Broken Column, A Study in Romantic Hellenism,* the essay is an inquiry into the changes that affected the classical tradition in the romantic age. By examining the concept of Greece held by various Germans from Winckelmann to Herder, and French writers from the Abbé Barthélémy to Renan, and in more detail the attitudes of Byron, Keats and Shelley, the young author provided a comprehensive panorama of the subject. The essay made a welcome contribution to the study of romanticism, within the limitations of its size and scope.

Levin's influence is acknowledged in the opening sentence of Bernard H. Stern's *The Rise of Romantic Hellenism in English Literature 1732–1786* (1940). Although only fifty years are staked out for examination, Stern's study ranges beyond the announced dates, and also beyond English literature to archeology and the aesthetics of Winckelmann. He also has a chapter on "Romantic Hellenism and the Literature of Travel to the East," most of which consists of quotations.

The next important book appeared in 1943, Stephen A. Larrabee's *English Bards and Grecian Marbles.* The rest of the title indicates the special area covered: "The Relationship Between Sculpture and Poetry, Especially in the Romantic Period." Although thus limited to one aspect of the larger subject, Larrabee provides many perceptive remarks on the history of taste.

The fourth book (and the first outside America) is Terence Spencer's *Fair Greece, Sad Relic,* published in 1954. The subtitle describes its scope as "Literary Philhellenism from Shakespeare to Byron," which the Introduction explains as "a survey of the literary contacts between England and the modern country of

Greece during the three centuries preceding the romantic enthusiasm which greeted the Greek national revival in the early nineteenth century." The author has thrown his net far and wide (no reference to a Turk in early drama escapes him) but has synthesized well the broad aspects of his subject. Spencer stands on the shoulders of his American predecessors, and *Fair Greece, Sad Relic* may be considered the definitive book on Philhellenism.

To return to "the wrong end of the Perspective-Glass" my contention is that Levin, Stern, Larrabee and Spencer have looked at Neo-Hellenism through the reverse end of the historical telescope. Their books are concerned with romanticism first and with Neo-Hellenism primarly as an aspect of romanticism. Moreover, being literary critics, these four authors discuss Neo-Hellenism chiefly as a literary event. Their attitude can even be called belletristic, for they focus on the best poets, though poetry represents only one of the manifestations of Neo-Hellenism.

My reading of the subject has led to several conclusions: first that Neo-Hellenism passed through three recognizable phases. The "bookish" Hellenism of neoclassicism, which characterized the seventeenth century gave way to the first phase of Neo-Hellenism, which may be called Archaeography, the systematic description of antiquities. (Archaeology, the term used by some writers, is unsatisfactory because of its implication of excavations, particularly in prehistorical sites). The Archaeographical phase lasted well into the second half of the eighteenth century, when the romantic element, present from the beginning, became dominant. This second phase is Romantic Hellenism, so named by Levin and his followers. The third phase occurred when Philhellenism became the foremost element: romantic sentiments towards the ancient Greeks were superseded by political sentiments towards the modern Greeks, sympathy for them in their struggle for independence from the Turks. In all three phases, each of the three elements is found; though each in turn becomes dominant.

My second contention is that Neo-Hellenism should be viewed in a chronological perspective, beginning with the renewal of contact with Greece by travellers in the seventeenth century and continuing with their followers in succeeding generations.

Thirdly, I believe that Neo-Hellenism is best understood by focusing on the means by which these travellers communicated with the general public, namely through the books they wrote about Greece, for travel literature was then, as it is now, a popular literary genre.

The first phase in "the rise of Neo-Hellenism in England" begins with the hero of our opening paragraph, Sir George Wheler. Before he set foot on the Greek mainland ("dry Greece" as it is called, in contrast to "wet Greece," the myriad Greek islands) English travellers had been rare indeed. Although ships visited Zante, Crete, Rhodes, Cyprus, Chios and other islands, as well as Smyrna and other Asia Minor ports, few of them risked calls on the mainland of Greece, especially the peninsular areas south of the Dus massif, where most of the history celebrated as the "glory that was Greece" took place. Professor Warner G. Rice, in his pioneering study of "Early English Travellers to Greece and the Levant,"[3] written earlier than Levin's *Broken Column* though published two years later, reports only six Englishmen who visited Athens or the peninsular mainland, some of them on second-hand evidence.[4] To these I can add only three others who were there before 1675.[5] That year marks a milestone, for in June of that year Wheler, the young Oxford graduate, having sometime earlier parted company with George Hickes, his learned tutor while at Lincoln College, teamed up with a new travelling companion, Jacob Spon, a Doctor of the Faculty of Paris, who had practised medicine in Lyons, but had spent half a year in Rome studying antiquities. In fact, before leaving Lyons in 1674 Spon had published the first account of Athens by any eyewitness among the early travellers. This was in the form of a long letter from the French Jesuit, Jacques Paul Babin, dated 8 October from Smyrna, addressed to the Abbé Pecoil of Lyons. Spon supplied some notes and a preface and published the letter as *Relation de l'État Présent de la Ville d'Athènes.* It fired the French physician with a desire to visit Greece, an ardor which he communicated to Wheler. The young Englishman had inherited a modest income, sufficient to allow him to concur in the venture to Greece and Constantinople, and to pay the expenses of the "discreet and ingenious" Dr Spon.[6]

Two circumstances serve as concomitants to make 1675 a felicitous time for Wheler and Spon to have embarked on their journey. The first concerns the French Ambassador to the Porte, the Marquis de Nointel, who had visited Athens in the previous year. Thus when Wheler and Spon reached Constantinople in the autumn of 1675, the French Ambassador was able to describe to them in detail the present state of Athens and the Acropolis. Their eyes must have blazed when he showed them the drawings of the frieze on the Parthenon, executed at the Ambassador's direction by an artist named Jacques Carrey.[7] Here was first hand evidence of what the young travellers could expect to find, and practical advice about how to venture into this Turkish stronghold: evidence and advice of equal value they could not have found elsewhere, or at any earlier time.

The second concomitant circumstance was the acquisition of a book recently arrived from Paris,[8] which Wheler and Spon pored over while awaiting departure in Venice, and studied repeatedly as they voyaged among the Greek islands and the cities of Asia Minor before they finally landed on the mainland of Greece about New Year's day, 1676. Published under the name of Monsieur de la Guilletière and with the title *Athènes ancienne et nouvelle* (1675) the book gave a remarkable account of the city, its people and its antiquities. The young travellers hung on every point, of which only a few can be quoted here.[9]

The narrative whisks the reader about from one detail to another that twentieth-century travellers may recognize: one street, he tells us, is occupied mainly by shoemakers; the list of chief families reads like a directory of streets in modern Athens; the bright Greek schoolboys excel at their lessons; the conversational vivacity of the citizens prompted the remark, "We attributed much of their vigour to their diet, and their use of Honey, which the Athenians use very frequently, being excellently good. Their physicians account their Honey the wholsomest of their food . . ." (p 147).

Thus Wheler and Spon were well prepared when in January 1676 they approached Athens. Fortunately, they were able to stay with Jean Giraud, a Frenchman who served as the British consul. Wheler and Spon remained a month, each day crammed with observing details about Greek people, Greek antiquities and local botany.[10] But it did not take these two keen-eyed travellers long—especially Dr Spon—to ascertain that Monsieur de la Guilletière was a literary fiction, and the book a fake. The author, one Guillet,[11] possessed a gift of style, thanks to which the book has a vivacity, a narrative flow, and sense of veracity that remind one of Defoe. Sooner or later someone would have exposed the fraud, though if Wheler and Spon had not arrived so promptly on the classic ground with their measuring rods, while their host, the worthy consul Giraud, was still alive, the exposure of the fabrication might have been more difficult.

After returning to their respective homelands both young men published accounts of their travels. Dr Spon, who wrote with an easy flow of mind, produced in 1678 three volumes under the title, *Voyage d'Italie, de Dalmatie, de Grèce et du Levant . . . par Iacob Spon, Docteur Médecin Aggregé à Lyon, & avec George Wheler Gentilhomme Anglois.* Wheler, more phlegmatic as well as more naive than his Gallic companion, did not bestir himself until the success of Spon's book brought the threat of an English translation. Wheler's response, with a reciprocal bow to his French colleague, appeared as a folio volume published in November 1682 with the title *A Journey into Greece . . . In Company of Dr Spon of Lyons.* In his preface Wheler states that he found Spon's text so consistent with his own notebooks that he had been content to translate with few changes, principally the addition of many botanical observations. The book was dedicated to Charles II, who responded by conferring a knighthood on the author. Its publication was indeed a noteworthy event, for Spon and Wheler were the first travellers since Pausanias in the second century A D to give a careful description of Greek antiquities. Later generations are particularly indebted to their description of the Parthenon before bombardment by the Venetians reduced it to ruins in 1686. The books were deservedly popular and remained authoritative for over a century. Spon's volumes were reprinted six times, including editions in Dutch, German, and Italian. Despite the availability of the French editions of Spon, Wheler's book was translated into French in 1689 and republished in 1734.

The significance of this travel book (for it is essentially one book, published in two versions) as an event in the origins of Neo-Hellenism in Europe cannot be overestimated. Of the two travellers, the precedence undoubtedly belongs to Dr Spon. Indeed, as noted earlier, Spon's edition of Brother Babin's report on Athens in 1674, before he met Wheler in Rome, with his preface and notes, may be cited as the overture to the whole Neo-Hellenic revival. Spon's published account of his travels influenced at first or second hand every serious student of Greek antiquities for four generations, and it is still a source book that cannot be neglected. Further, his exposure of the faked narrative of Guillet resulted in fanning interest in Athens. Thus Spon's and Wheler's report offered the fresh interest of travellers into unexplored territories, into what had been a virtually blank space on the map.[12]

In the first half of the eighteenth century many Englishmen visited the Levant, for the rise of British sea power during the war of the Spanish Succession opened up the Mediterranean to trade, especially for the sale of English cloth. The Embassy at Constantinople was considered the highest diplomatic post under the British Crown, both in importance and emoluments. The English factory at Smyrna, the chief center of the Levant Company, even in Wheler's day, consisted of about a hundred persons, many of them sons of gentlemen apprenticed to merchants. In their goings and comings they visited many of the islands, and from Smyrna they made excursions to Ephesus and other nearby ruins in Asia Minor,[13] but very few of them visited "dry Greece." Perhaps the most surprising example is Aaron Hill, the future projector and pompous dramatist, who at the age of fifteen voyaged to Constantinople to visit his relative, Lord Paget, the British Ambassador to the Porte. Hill returned with Lord Paget three years later (1703) and in 1709 published *A Full Account of the Present State of the Ottoman Empire,* a volume of florid writing that went into a second edition, but is worthless as a source of information. Similarly, Lady Mary Wortley Montagu, on the return journey in 1718 after her husband's term as Ambassador, had their fifty-gun frigate anchor off the Troad. Afterwards she sailed among the Isles of Greece, but did not stop on the mainland, then newly reconquered by the Turks from the Venetians. Lady Mary's emotive response to reading Homer on the Trojan plains was not available to readers, however, until after her death five decades later.[14]

Two young aristocrats followed Wheler's example and extended the Grand Tour to include Greece. In 1738 another Montagu, John, fourth Earl of Sandwich (1718–1792) embarked with a company of friends on a voyage that brought them to Athens. The twenty-year-old Earl had the foresight to bring along the French artist, Jean Étienne Liotard, "to preserve in their memories, by the help of painting, these noble remains of antiquity they went in quest of." Here again, the printed account of *A Voyage Performed by the late Earl of Sandwich round the Mediterranean in the Years 1738 and 1739. Written by himself,* did not reach the public until 1799, seven years after the Earl's death. A similar expedition was made in 1749 by another future statesman, James Caulfield (1728–1799) fourth Viscount and later first Earl of Charlemont. Like Sandwich, Charlemont was accompanied by young friends, a classical tutor and an artist named Richard Dalton. The latter's folio volume of *Views in Greece, Egypt and Italy,* published in 1752, provided Englishmen with their first engravings of the Parthenon sculptures. Charlemont himself published nothing on Greece until 1790, when after years in the center of Irish politics, he gave one paper at the Royal Irish Academy.

The only important published travel book during this period was *A View of the Levant: particularly of Constantinople, Syria, Egypt and Greece,* 1743, reporting the first-hand observations of Charles Perry M D (1698–1780) in the years 1739–1742. His full description of the ruins of Greece was the first since those of Spon and Wheler to be written by an actual observer.

Less significant than Perry's book are the two volumes of Richard Pococke's *Description of the East* (1743, 1745). He had visited Athens for ten days in 1740, and the nine-page description in his second volume brings to mind Gibbon's remark that Pococke "too often confounded what he had seen with what he had heard." The plates are particularly inept: he shows the Thesium with tall thin pillars, and the westernmost caryatid of the Erechtheum facing west, with her back turned to her sisters.

The year 1744 saw the publication of *The Travels of the late Charles Thompson Esq; Containing his Observations on . . . Turkey in Europe . . . and Many parts of the World,* a work so popular that four more editions were called for within the next few decades. But like his predecessor, Monsieur de la Guilletière, Thompson is a fictional character. The book reminds us that we are discussing the age of *Robinson Crusoe* and George Psalamanzar; it is a cento of paraphrased passages from other authors, especially the French. For it should not be forgotten that the English were eager readers of French travel books, both in the original language and in translation, though none of them aside from Dr Spon's is significant enough to examine here.

The most important event of the Archaeographic phase had its beginnings in 1748. Rome was then the mecca for students of the arts who flocked there from all parts of Europe, especially from England. The neo-classical style of the French Academy was dying, and the young men either looked more deeply into the classic ideal, or turned away from it entirely. The shift from neo-classicism to the antique was stimulated by the spade, for Cardinal Albani and a number of other arbiters of taste learned how to turn marble into gold. The new excavations at Herculaneum in 1738 fanned a flame of interest in the antique that was augmented by the treasures uncovered at Pompeii a decade later. Sometime earlier, connoisseurs had adopted the attitude that Greek artists were superior to their Roman followers, and the architecture and art objects found at Herculaneum and Pompeii deflated the grandeur of Augustan Rome that the Renaissance had dreamed of. The time had come to look back to the origins of classicism, to Greece from whence Roman art and architecture were now recognized to have derived.

This was the situation in 1748 when two young British artists in Rome, James Stuart and Nicholas Revett, issued proposals for an expedition to Greece to measure exactly the Parthenon and other buildings. With the financial help of several wealthy members of the Society of Dilettanti (a club comprised of English veterans of the Grand Tour,[15] whose toast was "To Grecian Taste and Roman Spirit") Stuart and Revett finally reached Athens in March 1751. While Stuart made sketches of the buildings, Revett recorded the dimensions of every architectural detail, using "a Rod of Brass, three feet long, most accurately divided."

They finished in 1753, and after barely escaping with their lives, reached England in 1755. Following delays due both to careful preparation of the plates and to Stuart's indolence, their superb elephant folio finally appeared in 1762, with a dedication to the King, bearing the title, *The Antiquities of Athens, Measured and Delineated.* Anticipation had been built up over so many years (the proposals were issued in London in 1751 and in Venice in 1753) that publication was a major event. The list of subscribers reads like a *Who's Who* of the world of taste, containing besides the aristocrats, Sir Joshua Reynolds, David Garrick, Horace Walpole, Laurence Sterne, Benjamin Franklin and the Abbé Barthélémy (of whom more in proper time). Of equal significance, the leading men in the building trades had also subscribed their four guineas in advance. Stuart, now a famous man, was overwhelmed with commissions and henceforth was known as "Athenian Stuart." "Grecian Gusto" became the fashionable style in architecture both in London and the provinces. Ten years later the author of *Letters concerning the Present State of England* reported:

> There is now a purity and Grecian elegance diffused through every part of the edifices erected in the present age; the ornaments of the ceilings, walls, and chimney-pieces, are in a stile unknown to the last age; instead of the heavy, clumsey exertions of blundering artists, whose utmost efforts of finery reached no higher than much gilding, we now see the choicest remnants of the finest ages of antiquity made the standard of our taste. The rooms fitted up from the designs of Mr. Stuart, have an elegance unrivaled in all the p[a]laces of Europe.[16]

Parenthetically it should be remarked that the Grecian style in the eighteenth century was primarily in decorative details; the Greek revival in architectural structure did not occur until the nineteenth century. In point of fact the second (1789) and third (1794) volumes of Stuart and Revett first revealed the Doric style to the world in full detail.

In the interval between the issuing of Stuart and Revett's Proposals in 1748 and publication in 1762 the new taste had been furthered by the publications of other travellers. Only two months after they had begun work in Athens two Englishmen turned up, James Dawkins and Robert Wood, on their way to Palmyra and Baalbec. When Wood's beautifully illustrated *Ruins of Palmyra or Tedmor in the Desart* came out in 1753 it carried a handsome compliment to Stuart and Revett that heightened eagerness among those who had read their original proposals. Dawkins, the silent but wealthy partner, subscribed for twenty copies of *The Antiquities of Athens,* to follow his earlier help, for he had issued the 1751 London proposals.

Another traveller in Greece who had read the 1748 proposals was the Frenchman, Julien Davide LeRoy. LeRoy got to Greece in 1754, the year after Stuart and Revett had left, and on the basis that national honor was at stake with the help of friends at the French court managed to publish in 1758 *Les Ruines des plus beaux Monuments de la Grèce.* The book was warmly received and promptly translated into English (1759). Stuart and Revett were piqued because LeRoy nowhere mentioned them or their project, but particularly because he had tried to steal their market. Consequently, when the first volume of *The Antiquities of Athens* made its tardy appearance in 1762, Stuart took pains to point out the mistakes in LeRoy's plates as well as the errors that LeRoy had taken over from Spon and Wheler. The controversy was not left unnoticed by reviewers, and the aspect of national rivalry added to the widening interest in Hellenic antiquities.

The Society of Dilettanti was so impressed with the value of Stuart and Revett's first volume that they decided to send out an expedition to measure and delineate antiquities in other parts of Greece. Revett agreed to go again to do the measuring, a youthful artist named William Pars was employed to sketch and paint, and for the learned descriptions they engaged on Robert Wood's recommendation Richard Chandler, a young Oxonian who had already earned a reputation in archaeography with *Marmora Oxonensia* (1763), a careful account of the specimens owned by the University, including those brought back by Sir George Wheler. The book produced by this team, *Ionian Antiquities: or Ruins of Magnificent and Famous Buildings in Ionia* (1769), lived up to the expected standards, combining the virtues that Revett had displayed in the 1762 *Athens* with the vivid detail of Spon and Wheler. Chandler followed with two volumes of excerpts from his journals, the first being *Travels in Asia Minor* (1775) and the second, *Travels in Greece* (1776). These volumes served as the well of knowledge about modern Greece for the next two generations.

The archaeographical phase of Neo-Hellenism had now reached its crest. Stuart became involved in politics with his patron, the Marquis of Rockingham, who gathered a group of aristocrats and gentlemen weekly at Stuart's house on Leicester Square. The professed purpose of these meetings was to discuss Greek literature and antiquities, though skeptics whispered that the business of the Rockingham party was the chief topic of conversation.

Stuart dawdled so long with the important second volume, showing the "Buildings erected while the Athenians were a free people," that at the time of his death in 1788, sixteen years after the first volume, it was not yet ready for publication, though his widow managed to put it into the hands of the public in the following year. The third volume followed in 1794 with a preface by Willey Revelly, notable for its answer to the posthumous attack which Sir William Chambers, champion of the Vitruvian and Palladian schools of architecture, had made on Stuart. Chambers considered that the Parthenon appeared deformed by "gouty columns"; he stated that it was less attractive and smaller than the church of St Martin in the Fields, and that its appearance would be improved by the addition of a steeple! Revelly retorted that Chamber's ignorance of the Parthenon derived from his friend and correspondent LeRoy, that the Parthenon was about a third larger than St Martin in the Fields, and he asked why Sir Robert (author of a book on Chinoiserie) had not suggested adding a pagoda instead of a steeple? Revelly concluded, " . . . the popularity into which Grecian principles are daily growing, in spite of the feeble attempts that have been made to decry them, is the best answer to such undistinguishing assailants" (p 19-26). An unstated irony is that "Athenian" Stuart had been buried in St Martin in the Fields shortly before Chambers published his attack.

Remaining events in the archaeographic phase of the Greek Revival can be summarized briefly without the need for detailed comment. In 1806 the Newdigate Poetry Prize at Oxford was first put on a regular footing; the chosen subject was "A Recommendation of the Study of the Remains of Ancient Grecian and Roman Architecture, Sculpture and Painting," and the contestants were restricted to only fifty lines of verse in covering this broad subject. The winner, a young Scot named John Wilson, survived to enjoy a literary career under the pseudonym of "Christopher North." The fourth and last volume of Stuart's *Antiquities of Athens* did not appear until 1816, edited by Joseph Woods, and consisting mainly of odds and ends from Stuart's papers, along with a biographical memoir.[17]

In the meantime, thanks to Lord Elgin's having in 1801 convinced the Sultan to allow Englishmen easy access to Greece, travellers began to come in droves. Thus Goethe, in setting the third act of the second part of *Faust* in Greece, has Mephistopheles ask the Sphinx,

> Are Britons here? So round the world they wheel,
> To stare at battlefields, historic traces,
> Cascades, old walls and classic dreary places;
> And here were something worthy of their zeal.[18]

By now the Greek war for independence was just around the corner, and when peace came, Prince Otho of Bavaria had been crowned King of the Hellenes and a century of German archaeology had begun.

Before leaving this scientific phase of Neo-Hellenism, a comment is in order concerning the state of Greek studies in England. Aside from the efforts of Richard Bentley, Greek scholarship lay quiescent. The universities remained in the state so well described by Gibbon, when the dons were "sunk in prejudice and port," and professorships were regarded as little more than livings. In 1779 when Andrew Dalzel was appointed to the Greek professorship at Edinburgh the status of his chair was at the lowest ebb. Philological studies were far behind archaeographical in concept: in 1783 when Richard Porson was invited by the Cambridge University Press to prepare a new text of Aeschylus and replied that the manuscript in the Laurentian Library at Florence should be collated, the syndics of the Press gravely suggested that "Mr. Porson might *collect* his manuscripts at home."[19] A new era in Greek studies was clearly overdue. It began in 1793 when Porson was appointed Regius Professor at Cambridge.

Long before Neo-Hellenism reached its Romantic phase, romantic elements occurred abundantly in the early travel books. Indeed, the fictional Monsieur de la Guilletière set the tone in *Athènes ancienne et nouvelle* (1675) when he described his sentiments on approaching the city, a passage overlooked by writers on Romantic Hellenism:

> And here I cannot but acknowledge my own weakness, you may call it folly if you please: At the first sight of this Famous Town (struck as it were with a sentiment of Veneration for those Miracles of Antiquity which were Recorded of it) I started immediately, and was taken with an universal shivering all over my Body. Nor was I singular in my Commotion, we all of us stared, but could see nothing, our imaginations were too full of the Great Men which that City had produced. (p 123-124)

In turn, Spon and Wheler echoed this attitude, though with proper restraint. When the adolescent Aaron Hill reached Greece he "found a certain pleasure in the very looking at a Place of such *Antiquity*."

Lady Mary Wortley Montagu, equally moved, enshrined her sentiments in verse:

> Warm'd with poetic transport I survey
> Th' immortal islands, and the well-known sea;
> For here so oft the muse her heart has strung,
> And not a mountain rears his head unsung.[20]

From Troy she wrote to Alexander Pope, "I read over your Homer here with an infinite pleasure, and find several little passages explained, that I did not before entirely comprehend the beauty of." Pope responded, ". . . you may lay the immortal work on some broken column of a hero's sepulchre, and read the fall of Troy in the shade of a Trojan ruin."[21]

As the century progressed and romantic sentiments became more common the very word "Grecian" produced an emotional response in the minds of all who had read Homer, even Pope's translation into heroic couplets which Bentley had decried for its lack of Homeric quality. Like Pope, other writers who had not visited Greece in the flesh travelled there in spirit, and poured their emotional response into their writings. First (and least romantic) is that strange Scotsman, Andrew Ramsay, who spent most of his life in France in the service of the exiled Stuarts, where he was known as Le Chevalier Ramsay. In 1727 Ramsay published *Les Voyages de Cyrus,* an imaginary account of the education of Cyrus, prince of Persia in the time of Xenophon, as he travelled with a philosophical tutor on a Grand Tour of the eastern Mediterranean. Book IV describes Cyrus's experiences in Greece, where Solon shows him around Athens, explains its laws and describes the life of the citizens. Cyrus is also taken to a performance at the theatre and given a lecture on Greek tragic drama. *Les Voyages de Cyrus* immediately became a best seller, and went through over thirty editions in English and French before the end of the century, not to mention translations into German, Italian, Spanish, and ultimately into modern Greek. Space does not permit detailed discussion of its content or influence, except to remark that it demonstrates the existence of a wide audience eager for information about life in antiquity. (Remember, the novel had not yet come into being, so travel books attracted readers hungry for narrative fiction.)

Perhaps the most lasting effect of Ramsay's *Les Voyages de Cyrus* was that it prepared the way for *Les Voyages du Jeune Anacharsis,* published after thirty years of incubation in 1789 by the Abbé Barthélémy. Although Barthélémy had traveled no farther than Rome, he was a keen student of Greek antiquity (we have noted earlier that he was a subscriber to Stuart's and Revett's *Antiquities of Athens*). Despite the fact that eight volumes were required to recount the *Travels of Anacharsis the Younger, in Greece,* ten editions were called for in the first ten years, not to mention translations into English and other languages, extending to Danish, Dutch, Armenian, and modern Greek. It tells how the young philosopher, Anacharsis, comes from Scythia to Greece in the middle of the fourth century and visits all the famous places. Anacharsis first learns about earlier events of Greek history. He then describes with proper romantic sentiments the appearance of Greek cities, temples, and statues; he inquires particularly into the laws and forms of government, and warms to the praise of democracy and the glorious state of liberty.

That publication of this book coincided with the dawn of the French Revolution accounts for some of its phenomenal success, and also for the enthusiasm with which the Revolutionists identified themselves with the ancient Greeks. Political leaders enjoyed comparing themselves with heroes of the age of Pericles, for democracy and liberty were now revived in Paris, along with other Athenian virtues. The women of fashion followed the example, and modeled their dress on that of the ancient Greeks; they wore sandals and tunics, cut their hair in imitation of statues or bound it with fillets over which they wore hats constructed to look like classic helmets. Carlyle's graphic description comes to mind, "Behold her, that beautiful adventurous Citoyenne: in costume of the Ancient Greeks, such Greek as Painter David could teach; her sweeping tresses snooded by glittering antique fillet; bright-dyed tunic of the Greek women; her little feet naked, as in Antique Statues, with mere sandals, and winding-strings of riband—defying the frost."[22] Barthélémy's *Travels of Anacharsis* was only one cause behind this sentimental enthusiasm for ancient Greece, but the importance of the book in the rise of Romantic Hellenism in Europe can scarcely be exaggerated.

To return to Britons in Greece, one of the accidents of fate was the survival of a Scottish sailor named William Falconer when his ship went down in a storm off the ruined temple on Cape Sunium, an experience which he versified and published in 1762 as *The Shipwreck.* Present day literary historians look down their noses at Falconer's didactic verses, but they moved a generation of readers, and influenced poems as recent as Masefield's *Dauber.* Falconer contributed to the rising stream of Romantic Hellenism by interrupting his narrative to describe the ruins of Greece in sentimental terms, thus becoming the first traveller to do so in verse.

Surprisingly, the last quarter of the eighteenth century saw only a dozen or so British travellers in "dry Greece," aside from the archaeographers already mentioned and others on official missions. One of the most devout was Thomas Watkins in 1788, who on landing at Piraeus kissed the classic ground. In the meantime a controversy raged at home that involved numerous Hellenists, the "Troy Controversy." In brief it concerned the problem of locating the Homeric city, but expanded to the question of whether the Trojan war was merely a creation of the poet's imagination.[23] A dozen learned men published tracts or dissertations on the subject, the academics' arguments being based on writings of the ancient geographers, and the travellers' on their actual visits to the Troade. In 1804 Sir William Gell settled the matter with his *Topography of Troy and its Vicinity.*

The year 1800 marks the beginning of another controversy, for in that year another Scot, Thomas Bruce, seventh Earl of Elgin, having recently been appointed (at the age of thirty-three) Ambassador to the Porte, sent before him a group of technicians to make plaster casts of statuary in "the Temple of the Idols" as the Turkish authorities called the Parthenon. The following year permission was granted "to take away any pieces of stone with old inscriptions or figures thereon." During the next two years Elgin's "predatory band" were busily at work, and included such distinguished visitors as his Lordship's father and mother-in-law and Dr Carlyle, Professor of Arabic at Cambridge. The story is well known of the transportation of the Elgin Marbles to London and of the long controversy over their merits, before Parliament in 1816 finally purchased them for the nation (at £35,000, less than half the amount Elgin had invested in them). The British public, stimulated by the controversy, flocked to see the sculptures. Whether the stones were authentic works of Phidias or were merely Roman copies became the foremost artistic issue of the day, and ultimately became a political issue as well, the Liberals taking the opposition. Once the marbles were ensconced in the British Museum they became the most popular exhibit, and we read that the cows of the Athenian hectacomb excited the admiration of English cattle breeders and that a riding master decided to bring his pupils to study the marbles in preference to giving them a riding lesson, so that they might contemplate for an hour these riders.[24] The glories of the Phidean school were now open for the eyes of all to see. The result was a revolution in taste; the delicate, polished style of the Hellenistic Venuses and Apollos (complete to their fingertips) was gradually replaced by the rough, energetic, fragmentary style of the age of Pericles. Ancient Greek art became established on the pinnacle already occupied by Greek philosophy and Greek poetry—the pinnacle of perfection beyond all emulation. Romantic Hellenism had reached its zenith.

So far there has been no occasion to mention Lord Byron. As we have seen, by 1810 the path up the Acropolis was well trodden by the boots of English travellers, most of whom wrote up their experiences in one form or another. Before the adolescent Byron entered Cambridge (1805) the public had received poetical descriptions of Greece written by Dr Carlyle (already mentioned), including one titled "On Viewing Athens from the Pnyx, by the light of a waning moon." The bulk of the Elgin marbles had already arrived in London in 1804. Indeed, Byron took a reactionary attitude towards them, and before he set out for Greece in 1809 condemned them as "freaks . . . misshapen monuments and maim'd antiques . . . mutilated blocks of art."[25]

A few months before Byron left England he read a book of poems entitled *Horae Ionicae* written by W. R. Wright, sometime Consul General of the Ionian Isles. Greatly impressed, he inserted a passage praising the book into *English Bards and Scotch Reviewers:*

> . . . doubly blest is he whose heart expands
> With hallowed feelings for those classic lands.
> Who rends the veil of ages long gone by,
> And views the remnants with a poet's eye!
> WRIGHT! 'Twas thy happy lot at once to view
> Those shores of glory, and to sing them too;
> And sure no common Muse inspired thy pen
> To hail the land of Gods and Godlike men.
> (lines 873-880)

Here, indeed, was a program for Byron to follow; to write not another travel book in prose (that task was left to his companion, Hobhouse[26]) but to write poetical travels centering on a fictional character. Thus when the first two books of *Childe Harold's Pilgrimage* were published in March 1812, the world welcomed it as a poetical travel book by a new major poet. But when the Grecian canto (the second) is read with the earlier travel books and poems in mind, we see that Byron had little new to say, regardless of the emotional and poetic power with which he said it. The Greek canto begins by lashing his whipping boy, Lord Elgin, then, after taking us to Albania, Istanbul, and the Bosphorus, returns to wallop the despoilers of Greek statuary. Childe Harold does not reach Greece proper until the 73d stanza, so that only a third of the canto is actually given to Greece. The principal idea expressed by Byron's "gloomy wanderer" is a lament on the old theme of lost liberty; the modern Greeks he considered "a degenerated horde," "From birth to death enslaved; in word, in deed, unmann'd." There are even indications that at this time Byron preferred the Turks to the Greeks, an attitude common among English merchants in the Levant.[27]

During the next ten years Byron returned again and again to Greek scenes for his poems. Like other writers of travel books, histories, and poems he ranged beyond Greece to other areas of the Levant, for the whole Near East had become popular subject matter. W. C. Cable who studied "The Popularity of English Travel Books about the Near East, 1775–1825,"[28] has supplied impressive evidence, especially from contemporary magazines, remarking, "It is hardly possible to open a single issue of a periodical of the time without encountering a review or a listing of some new travel account of the Near East" (p 74). His subsequent study of minor poetry of the same fifty years led to the following conclusions:

> First, the application of these contemporary ideas to the Near East obviously originated in the travel books. Second, the popularity of the travel-book material made these themes easily accessible to the minor poets at home. Third . . . the minor poets not only read extensively in the travel books, but . . . appropriated the travellers' dominant ideas. Finally, by so doing the minor poets helped to reinforce the vogue of these ideas in England and the association of them with the Near East. Thus the minor poetry, as well as the travel books, played an important part in creating the milieu of English interest in the Near East.[29]

Of all the areas in the Near East it was Greece, of course, that excited the most emotion.

As noted earlier, the French were second only to the British in producing travel books about Greece. Pierre Guys set the tone with his *Voyage Littéraire de la Grèce* in 1771, which promptly appeared in an English translation with the Sternian title, *A Sentimental Journey Through Greece.* These books, like the *Travels of Anacharsis* already mentioned, were widely circulated in England. Byron, a voracious reader, had gulped down the literature of Near Eastern travel from boyhood on. He scribbled, "Knolles, Cantemir, De Tott, Lady M. W. Montagu, Hawkins's translation from Mignot's History of the Turks, the Arabian Nights—all travels or histories, or books upon the East, I could meet with, I had read, as well as Ricaut, before I was ten years old."[30]

The idea that the Greeks should once again become free goes back at least to the early seventeenth century. Terence Spencer has chronicled the subject so thoroughly that here a nutshell summary will suffice. In short, after 1687 when the Venetians briefly occupied Athens and the Peloponnesus, the population began to be stirred from the hopeless state they had known for two hundred years. In 1770 an abortive revolt occurred inspired by Catherine of Russia, which drew world wide attention to Greece. By the 1790s Turkey was recognized as the "sick man of Europe" and the great powers—Russia, Britain, and Napoleonic France—each feared that the others might take advantage of the situation. The emergence of a modern Greek literary revival led by Rhegas (d.1798) crystallized nationalist sentiment, and simultaneously the "fallout" of the French Revolution carried to distant lands. The revolt of Byron's friend the Ali Pasha of Albania in 1820 touched off the action in Greece proper. Once it had begun, the interests of the Great Powers, however tardy in participation, made the outcome certain.

Byron, in the meantime, followed the shift in attitude towards the Greek people, albeit somewhat belatedly. In the eyes of all Europe he had become the image of the Philhellene; thus an inevitability of fate called him to join in the cause with which, somewhat paradoxically, he was identified. Sir Harold Nicholson in *Byron: the Last Journey* has described in detail the personal factors in his decision and the magnificent courage he displayed during the nine months before his death at Missolonghi. From that day onward travel books had a new tone, for Philhellenism, especially fascination with the birth of a new nation that had won liberty on classic ground where liberty (according to accepted myth) first grew, now reached its crest. Of course, the romantic tone persisted, and archaeography also, though it became transposed to archaeology as digging became a science, especially after the Germans (to the annoyance of the British) took over under the patronage of King Otho.

Once peace broke out Greece became for the prosperous British a popular extension of the Grand Tour. Athens was now as accessible as Avignon had been a few generations earlier. Journals, diaries, and other travel books proliferated from the pens of the classical Dr Syntaxes who set out "to make a tour and write it." The successful development of the steam printing press drastically reduced publishing costs; so travel books along with all others poured forth in an expanding flood.

Only a few events remain to be mentioned. First, let us salute a milestone in the annals of the travel industry: in April of 1833, less than a year after Otho had been crowned, the first organized cruise ship, the *SS Francois Premier,* sailed for Greece. The passenger list signifies the importance of this enterprise, for it includes several ambassadors, the brother of King Otho, Madame la Duchesse de Berry, and, as might be expected, sundry English travellers.[31]

A second event, equally notable as a portent of a whole future industry, was the publication in 1840 of Murray's *Handbook for Travellers in the Ionian Isles, Greece,* etc. Ostensibly this should have eliminated the need for further travel books, but no change in the output can be noted. Actually, so many tourists were crawling over the Greek landscape, a writer in the *Quarterly Review* in 1842 complained, that Greece was being westernized and romance had gone out of the Hellenic pilgrimage.[32] Only four years later, in 1846, Thackeray found his visit to Athens a subject ripe for satire in his burlesque of travel books, *Notes of a Journey from Cornhill to Grand Cairo by Michel Angelo Titmarsh:*

> Not feeling any enthusiasm myself about Athens, my bounden duty of course is clear, to sneer and laugh heartily at all who have. . . . What call have young ladies to consider Greece "romantic"—they who get their notions of mythology from the well-known pages of Tooke's *Pantheon?* What is the reason that blundering Yorkshire squires, young dandies from Corfu regiments, jolly sailors from ships in the harbour, and yellow old Indians from Bundelcund, should think proper to be enthusiastic about a country of which they know nothing; the physical beauty of which they cannot, for the most part, comprehend; and because certain characters lived in it two thousand four hundred years ago? What have these people in common with Pericles, what have these ladies in common with Aspasia (O fie)? Of the race of Englishmen who come wandering about the tomb of Socrates, do you think the majority would not have voted to hemlock him? Yes; for the very same superstition which leads men by the nose now, drove them onward in the days when the lowly husband of Xantippe died for daring to think simply and to speak the truth.[33]

By this time the scribbling travellers had done their work, and Philhellenism had grown beyond the measuring and delineating into an understanding of the principles of Greek architecture and how they could be used in northern Europe. Similarly, classical scholars who had visited Greece were illuminating the texts and the literature. Grote and Finlay were writing the history of Greece with authority, especially Finlay, who invested his inherited capital in Greek real estate and penned his pages in the ashes of disillusionment.

Thus Neo-Hellenism can be seen as a phenomenon, in both intellectual history and the history of taste, that passed through several phases. Just as reading of the classics had prepared earlier generations to think of Greece as the homeland of the greatest poets and philosophers, so the books written by successive generations of travellers—once such travel became possible—prepared the public for successive new attitudes towards things Greek. In a nation where prose fiction commonly utilized travel plots and situations (*Robinson Crusoe, Gulliver, Tom Jones, Humphrey Clinker, Rasselas,* etc, etc) it is not surprising that travel books rivalled fiction in popularity, as library records show.[34] Indeed, the books by travellers to Greece prepared the audience for *Childe Harold's*

Thomas Love Peacock, Enlgish novelist and poet, 1785-1866.

Pilgrimage, itself in turn a travel book that created a wave of sympathy for Greece just before the struggle for independence.

Before the nineteenth century had ended, Neo-Hellenism passed into a new phase. The romantic view became superseded by a relatively clear-eyed objectivity, based on scholarship. The emotion-charged image of Greece became transformed into a rational understanding of actualities. (Emotional attitudes towards Greece will, of course, persist, but the actualities have become available for those who wish to know them.) With the founding of the British School in Athens in 1886, British archaeologists began to regain their laurels usurped by the Germans. And with Arnold, Jebb, Jowett, Gilbert Murray, and others, Hellenism became a vital factor in English culture. The "Greek way of life" came to be a phrase spoken with comprehension and conviction.

Notes

[1] Sir George Wheler, *A Journey into Greece* (1682) 347.

[2] Neo-Hellenism may be defined as the revival of interest in ancient Greek civilization, based on the conviction that it made a peculiar and lasting contribution to Western culture. Among studies on French aspects, the following may be mentioned: Louis Bertrand, *La fin du classicisme et le retour à l'antique dans la seconde moitié du XVIIIe siècle et les premières années du XIXe, en France* (Paris 1897); Demetrius Bikélas, "Le Philhellénisme en France," *Revue d'Histoire Diplomatique* v 346-365 (Paris 1891); René Bray, *La formation de la doctrine classique en France* (Paris 1927); Nicholas Torga, *Les voyageurs Français dans l'Orient Européen* (Paris 1928); Le Comte de Laborde, *Athènes aux XVe, XVIe, et XVIIe siècles,* 2 vols (Paris 1854); Jean Longnon, "Quatre siècles de philhellénisme français," *La Revue de France* I (No 6) 512-542; Émile Malakis, *French Travellers in Greece, 1770–1820: An Early Phase of French Philhellenism* (Philadelphia 1925). For Neo-Hellenism in Germany see: Karl Borinski, *Die Antike in Poetik und Kunsttheorie von Ausgang des klassischen Altertums bis auf Goethe und Wilhelm von Humboldt* (Leipzig 1914–24); E. M. Butler, *The Tyranny of Greece over Germany* (London 1935); Humphrey Trevelyan, *The Popular Background of Goethe's Hellenism* (London 1934); Hans Meyer, et al, *Kulturwissenschaftliche Bibliographie zum Nachleben der Antike* (Leipzig and Berlin 1931–34).

[3] University of Michigan *Essays and Studies in English and Comparative Literature* (Ann Arbor 1933).

[4] John Erigena in the ninth century, on the testimony of William of Malmesbury (p 206); Anthony Jenkinson and John Sanderson in Elizabethan times (p 213); the painful perigrine, William Lithgow who was in Greece about 1610; William Petty, sent by Sir Thomas Roe to look for marbles in Athens; and another agent (or Petty?) dispatched by Sir Thomas to the Peloponnese (p 252, 255).

[5] Master John of Basingstoke, Archdeacon of Leicester in the early thirteenth century, is said by Matthew Paris to have studied in Athens. Lord Winchelsea, Ambassador to the Sublime Porte, stopped there late in 1668 and a few months later sent a frieze to England. The traveller Bernard Randolph, who cruised about the Levant on several voyages, visited the mainland in 1674, though his *Present State of the Morea* did not reach print until 1686. Quite possibly three other Englishmen also visited Athens: Sir Paul Rycaut, while secretary to Lord Winchelsea, Lord Henry Howard (later sixth Duke of Norfolk) on his return from a visit to Constantinople in 1664, and the traveller Edward Brown.

[6] Besides their enthusiasm for antiquities the friends had at least two other bonds of interest. The first, surprisingly, was religion, for Dr Spon held strong Protestant views and Wheler had decided before embarking on his travels to enter Holy Orders on his return. He ultimately became a Prebendary of Durham Cathedral and the author, among other worthy works,

of *The Protestant Monastery; or Christian Oeconomicks, containing Directions for the Religious Conduct of a Family* (1698). The second, perhaps equally surprising, was science, for Wheler had been from childhood an ardent and observant botanist.

[7] Wheler, *Journey,* p 362. Carrey's drawings were first reproduced in the Abbé Barthélémy's *Les Voyages du jeune Anacharsis* in 1791, in miniature. The first enlarged reproductions were in Vol IV of the *Antiquities of Athens,* 1816.

[8] It was licensed 13 Dec 1674 and registered 4 Jan 1675.

[9] From the English translation that appeared promptly in 1676 under the title, *An Account of a Late Voyage to Athens, Containing the Estate both Ancient and Modern of that Famous City . . . now Englished.*

[10] In his preface Wheler observed, *"I know some will say, why does he treat us with insiped descriptions of Weeds, and make us hobble after him over broken stones, decayed buildings, and old rubbish?"*

[11] He had developed a correspondence with the Capuchin missionaries in Athens, and based his account on information received from them, printing for the first time a map of Athens that had been sent to the Capuchin headquarters in Paris. Guillet also had corresponded with Giraud, who had been consul to the French before he shifted his services to the British. He then embellished the current information with details gleaned from the ancients. (Fortunately these had been collected by Johannes Meiersuis, professor of Greek at Leyden, in his *Athenae Atticae,* 1624.)

[12] Guillet, who had already profited from three editions of his book in 1675, did not retreat before Spon's exposé, but counterattacked in a booklet that questioned whether Spon himself had ever been in Greece. In the exchanges that followed Guillet managed to obscure the issue so successfully that his fraudulent travel book was cited seriously by a learned British Hellenist as late as 1810 (Edward Clarke, in his *Travels* III ii sec 2, 472).

[13] For example, Edmund Chishull, British Chaplain at Smyrna, 1698-1702, whose *Travels in Turkey and back to England* were not published until 1747.

[14] Her *Letters* were first published in 1763, the year after her death.

[15] Lionel Cust, *A History of the Society of Dilettanti,* 1914.

[16] 1772, p 244-245.

[17] Beginning in 1810 classical topography became a popular branch of archaeography with Sir William Gell's *Itinerary of Greece,* a sub-genre that he exploited to the full. In 1812 William Wilkins, the future architect of Downing College, Cambridge, of University College, London, and the National Gallery, whose career is linked with the Greek Revival, published *Atheniensia, or Remarks on the Topography and Buildings of Athens.* Edward Dodwell's *Classical and Topographical Tour through Greece,* in two volumes quarto, followed in 1819. Two years earlier the Dilettanti Society had published an *omnium gatherum,* entitled *Unedited Antiquities of Attica.*

[18] From Bayard Taylor's translation, Act III scene i.

[19] J. E. Sandys, *History of Classical Scholarship* (1908) II 427.

[20] *Letters and Works of Lady Mary Wortley Montagu* (1893) I 300

[21] *Correspondence of Alexander Pope,* ed G. Sherburn (1956) I 440.

[22] *The French Revolution,* ed C. R. L. Fletcher (1902) III 223.

[23] M. L. Clarke, *Greek Studies in England, 1700–1830* (1945) 184 et passim.

[24] J. T. Smith, *Nollekens and His Times* (1829) chapter 11.

[25] *English Bards and Scotch Reviewers,* lines 1027-32. In 1810, visiting the Acropolis daily, he came to take a different view. "These relics that were being carried away were not now in his eyes worthless stones . . . but the heritage of the finest culture of the Greek race. . . ." Leslie A. Marchand, *Byron* (1957) I 224-225.

[26] Hobhouse carried a large supply of paper and ink, as well as the standard books on Greece. He would spend his mornings studying the classic sites while Byron was poetizing, and then take Byron back to the site in the afternoon. Hobhouse's *Journey through Albania* was published in 1813. See Marchand I 266, 268, III 1107, 1115-16.

[27] See his letter of 3 May 1810: "I see not much difference between ourselves and the Turks. . . . I like the Greeks, who are plausible rascals,—with all the Turkish vices, without their courage." But he was superior to, and amused by, the merchants' contempt of those they exploited. See Marchand I 226 and Byron's note on stanza 73.

[28] *Philological Quarterly* XV (Jan 1936) 70-80.

[29] *Philological Quarterly* XVI (July 1937) 271.

[30] Moore's *Life of Byron* (1830) I 255.

[31] Two printed accounts exist in the Gennadius Library at Athens, and doubtless elsewhere; the first by J. Girandeau (1835) and the second by someone who wrote under the pseudonym, Marchebeus (1839).

[32] *Quarterly Review* LXXX No. cxxxix 130-131.

[33] *Burlesques; From Cornhill to Grand Cairo* (1903) 271.

[34] Paul Fussell, Jr, "Patrick Brydone; The Eighteenth Century Traveller as Representative Man," *Bulletin of The New York Public Library* LXVI (1962) 349-350.

INFLUENCE OF GREEK MYTHOLOGY ON THE ROMANTICS

Douglas Bush (essay date 1937)

SOURCE: "Coleridge: Wordsworth: Byron," in *Mythology and the Romantic Tradition in English Poetry,* 1937. Reprint, Harvard University Press, 1969, pp. 51-80.

[*In the following essay, Bush examines the influence of Greek mythology on Coleridge, Wordsworth, and Byron. Bush argues that Christian ideas dominate "Hellenic impulses" in Coleridge's poetry; maintains that Wordsworth "re-created mythological poetry for the nineteenth century"; and asserts that Byron's use of myth is most effective in his satires.*]

I. *Coleridge*

Before we come to Wordsworth, who has been described as Coleridge's greatest work, and, like all his other works, left unfinished, a few pages must be given to Coleridge's writings. Mythology is perhaps not to be counted among the first score or two of his major interests, but some of his allusions to the subject in both prose and verse are very suggestive and important. He touched everything, and seldom touched anything that he did not either illuminate or befog. For an example of the latter result, it is enough to refer to the extraordinary essay "On the Prometheus of Aeschylus" (1825).[1] Much briefer and somewhat more lucid are his remarks on Asiatic and Greek mythologies. Whatever his immediate sources of information, ancient and modern, Coleridge might be summarizing Blackwell (not to mention the Germans) when he describes Greek mythology as being "in itself fundamentally allegorical, and typical of the powers and functions of nature, but subsequently mixed up with a deification of great men and hero-worship."[2] It is in harmony with such ideas that Coleridge takes Bacchus not merely as the jolly god of wine but as "the symbol of that power which acts without our consciousness from the vital energies of nature, as Apollo was the symbol of our intellectual consciousness."[3] Here also he is in agreement with Schlegel and Heyne—and Nietzsche—though it is doubtful "whether Heyne taught Coleridge anything that he did not know before he went to Germany."[4]

Coleridge's scattered and of course repeated observations on the finite, anthropomorphic, and statuesque quality of the Greek gods and Greek art are more familiar and perhaps more significant. In his lecture on Dante he compares these Greek "finites," in which the form was the end, with their opposites, Christian symbols of moral truth and infinity:

> Hence resulted two great effects; a combination of poetry with doctrine, and, by turning the mind inward on its own essence instead of letting it act only on its outward circumstances and communities, a combination of poetry with sentiment. And it is this inwardness or subjectivity, which principally and most fundamentally distinguishes all the classic from all the modern poetry.[5]

It may be said in the first place that this whole passage seems to be mainly a reproduction of Schiller and Schlegel, though the general distinction between the finiteness of the Greek mind and the insatiable longing for the infinite characteristic of Christianity was a commonplace of German romanticism;[6] we shall encounter the idea throughout the nineteenth century. Secondly, if we take Coleridge's definition of the two attitudes of mind without questioning its entire validity, it may be said that it is the union of those attitudes which distinguishes the mythological poetry of Keats and Shelley; for they (along with Elizabethan opulence of expression) combine, in different ways and degrees, this outwardness and inwardness, they make the beautiful forms of Greek myth symbols of infinity and progress.

Coleridge's comment on Gray's unfortunate "Phoebus" has a much wider bearing than its immediate topic:

> That it is part of an exploded mythology, is an objection more deeply grounded. Yet when the torch of ancient learning was rekindled, so cheering were its beams, that our eldest poets, cut off by Christianity from all *accredited* machinery, and deprived of all *acknowledged* guardians and symbols of the great objects of nature, were naturally induced to adopt, as a *poetic* language, those fabulous personages, those forms of the supernatural in nature, which had given them such dear delight in the poems of their great masters. Nay, even at this day what scholar of genial taste will not so far sympathize with them, as to read with pleasure in Petrarch, Chaucer, or Spenser, what he would perhaps condemn as puerile in a modern poet?[7]

Coleridge (above) described Greek mythology as being "fundamentally allegorical" but "mixed up with a deification of great men and hero worship."

In a footnote Coleridge mentions the desiccating agent that we have noticed already, "the mechanical system of philosophy" which had made the world in relation to God like a building in relation to its mason, and had left "the idea of omnipresence a mere abstract notion in the state-room of our reason." In a similar, though more poetic and nostalgic, mood he had written the beautiful passage in *The Piccolomini* (1799–1800):

> The intelligible forms of ancient poets,
> The fair humanities of old religion,
> The Power, the Beauty, and the Majesty,
> That had their haunts in dale, or piny mountain,
> Or forest by slow stream, or pebbly spring,
> Or chasms and wat'ry depths; all these have
> vanished.
> They live no longer in the faith of reason!
> But still the heart doth need a language, still
> Doth the old instinct bring back the old
> names. . . .[8]

These lines are written, in a sense, from the outside, they are an expression of wistful regret, a comment, not a recreation; yet Coleridge has so rich an understanding of beauty, both sensuous and philosophic, that in his religious imagination the figures of mythology can become symbols of divine omnipresence in nature and in the heart of man.

One reason for the nature and the uniqueness of that mood is that Coleridge was not "primitive" or "pagan" enough in temperament to have an instinctively mythological intuition of the natural world such as, in varying degrees, Wordsworth, Keats, and Shelley had. A more positive reason we have met already, in the contrast between Greek finiteness and Christian ideas of infinity. It would be pleasanter to end this sketch with a memory of the fair humanities of old religion, yet one would give an inadequate picture of Coleridge, and an inadequate introduction to much later verse and prose of the century, if one failed to emphasize the dominance of his Christian over his Hellenic impulses, of his philosophic desire for unity over what he conceived to be the Greek contentment with multiplicity. In such moods he could be astringently and unpoetically hostile to Greek religion and myth.[9]

II. *Wordsworth*

The Victorians, beset by science and skepticism, and groping for an undogmatic faith, reverenced the poet who gave them a natural religion. We, who have got far beyond such naïve gropings, and recoil from a plaster embodiment of virtue and nobility, have acquired a new respect for the poet who gave to society a natural daughter. Wordsworth has become, so to speak, one of ourselves; "Daddy Wordsworth" is, for a distinguished modern critic, "a reformed rake." Although the poet has been so happily revived and rehabilitated, the limitations of our subject forbid chatter about Annette and compel attention to what he wrote, and only a small portion of that. Nowadays we recognize Wordsworth, no matter how great his debt to Coleridge, as the most richly germinal of all the romantic poets, as the fountain-head from which flowed the main stream of nineteenth-century poetry. It is an obvious but less familiar fact that the poet of nature and the humble man was also the fountain-head of nineteenth-century poetry on mythological themes. In *Laodamia* he re-established the classical genre, and in the extended passages on the origins of myth in *The Excursion* he brought back to life what had been dead. When we think of the body of poetry which we call Wordsworth, we may be inclined to regard the offspring of his mythological Muse as another natural child, but his ideas of Greek myth were really rooted in his deepest intuitions.

Wordsworth was not a mere ruminating cow; he was from youth up, at least until weak eyes hampered him, an ardent reader of English and foreign literature; in his increasing preference for books of his own writing he was only more candid than most poets. Even as a child of the mountains, he says in the eleventh book of *The Prelude,* and before he had read the classics, he had "learnt to dream of Sicily," and he goes on to salute Theocritus. The boy who loved the *Arabian Nights* was the boy who reveled in their Roman counterpart, Ovid's *Metamorphoses,* who was later thankful that his early passion for romance had not been snuffed out by Rousseauistic educators, and who, later still, protested against Niebuhr's scientific destruction of the heroic legends of Rome.[10] His note on the *Ode to Lycoris* (1817) is too important not to be quoted at length:

> But surely one who has written so much in verse as I have done may be allowed to retrace his steps in the regions of fancy which delighted him in his boyhood, when he first became acquainted with the Greek and Roman poets. Before I read Virgil I was so strongly attached to Ovid, whose *Metamorphoses* I read at school, that I was quite in a passion whenever I found him, in books of criticism, placed below Virgil. As to Homer, I was never weary of travelling over the scenes through which he led me. Classical literature affected me by its own beauty. But the truths of Scripture having been entrusted to the dead languages, and these fountains having recently been laid open at the Reformation, an importance and a sanctity were at that period attached to classical literature that extended, as is obvious in Milton's *Lycidas* for example, both to its spirit and form in a degree that can never be revived. No doubt the hacknied and lifeless use into which mythology fell towards the close of the 17th century, and which continued through the eighteenth, disgusted the general reader with all allusion to it in modern verse; and though, in deference to this disgust, and also in a measure participating in it, I abstained in my earlier writings from all introduction of pagan fable, surely, even in its humble form, it may ally itself with real sentiment, as I can truly affirm it did in the present case.[11]

It was quite natural that the younger Wordsworth should prefer to sit on old gray stones rather than on "parlor" furniture of faded plush (though the *Evening Walk* and *Descriptive Sketches* exhibit every other vice of eighteenth-century style). But, like most artists who have rebelled against effete conventions of the immediate past, Wordsworth was in touch with an older and richer tradition. His chosen masters, Chaucer, Shakespeare, Spenser, and Milton, had all delighted in Ovid and classic story, and, apart from other reasons, it was inevitable that under their influence, especially that of Milton, Wordsworth's initial antipathy to myth should diminish. The poetry of his great decade certainly contains very little mythology in comparison with his later and generally inferior work, but what there is is important; and his increasing use of myth is partly but not wholly explained by age and failing inspiration, since he wrote more good stuff after 1807 than he is always given credit for.

The finest and most familiar of Wordsworth's mythological allusions is the impassioned outburst in *The world is too much with us:*

> Great God! I'd rather be
> A Pagan suckled in a creed outworn;
> So might I, standing on this pleasant lea,
> Have glimpses that would make me less forlorn;
> Have sight of Proteus rising from the sea;
> Or hear old Triton blow his wreathèd horn.

We have here a Miltonic complexity of literary reminiscence. Although Wordsworth was a reader of Plato, the Platonism of the *Intimations of Immortality* is rather that of Proclus and Coleridge. The sonnet was apparently written in 1802, at the same time as most of the *Ode,* and this sentence from Proclus, translated in Thomas Taylor's *Plato,* has connections with both the *Ode* and the sonnet:

> It is requisite therefore that the soul which is about to be led properly from hence to that ever vigilant nature, should amputate those second and third powers which are suspended from its essence, in the same manner as weeds, stones, and shells, from the marine Glaucus; should restrain its externally proceeding impulses and recollect true beings and a divine essence, from which it descended, and to which it is fit that the whole of our life should hasten.[12]

Wordsworth's "Pagan" is of course a general symbol, but he undoubtedly is thinking of Proclus, one of the last opponents of Christianity; and Glaucus, who belongs originally to Plato's *Republic,* has become Proteus, a sea-god made more familiar by *Paradise Lost, The Faerie Queene,* and *Colin Clout;* this last poem furnishes also Triton's wreathed horn and, less happily, the pleasant lea.[13] But these borrowings are fused into a completely original whole, and the classical allusions, though beautifully decorative, are essential to the rendering of the idea. In this sonnet we may find the keynote of a mass of mythological poetry of the nineteenth and twentieth centuries; the old antagonism between Pan and Christ has become a contrast between the ugly materialism of our commercial and industrial civilization and the natural religion, the ideal beauty and harmony, of Hellenic life. Unlike many later poets, however, Wordsworth does not fall into sentimentalism.

In a similar though a more calm and philosophic mood Wordsworth wrote the passages on the origin and significance of myth in the fourth book of *The Excursion.*[14] Reacting, like Coleridge, against eighteenth-century rationalism, and, like Coleridge, putting his faith in imagination (as they understood that faculty), Wordsworth could not despise ancient mythological religions as idle superstitions; they were testimonies, however imperfect, of the divine presence and of man's endeavor to apprehend it. Here, then, for the first time in many generations a great English poet set forth a really glowing conception of pagan myths as vital symbols of the religious imagination and established mythology as the language of poetic idealism. The passages are too long for quotation, but the substance, bereft of its beauty, is this. The Solitary, the disciple of Voltaire, overcome by disillusionment and despair of truth, has cut himself off from man and nature, has taken refuge in cynical apathy. But, declares the Wanderer, even humble children of the ancient east possessed a natural piety, a religious imagination. The rustic Greek, however ignorant and superstitious, lived close to the spirit of nature, in intimate communion with the deities of sun and moon and wood and stream. Through such forms of the divine were nourished the admiration, hope, and love by which we live, and perhaps too that faith in "Life continuous, Being unimpaired," which strengthens and sustains the frail creatures of a day.[15] When the mind admits the law of duty, man gains dominion over experience, ascends in dignity of being and in spiritual power. As the moon rises behind a grove and turns all the dark foliage to silver,

> Like power abides
> In man's celestial spirit; virtue thus
> Sets forth and magnifies herself; thus feeds
> A calm, a beautiful, and silent fire.

The ethical import of this passage, of the whole poem in fact, was fully absorbed by Keats, and re-expressed particularly in *Hyperion.* It is more obvious that his senses and imagination would be delighted by Wordsworth's account of the way in which the myth-making faculty of the Greeks peopled heaven and earth with radiant or shaggy deities, from Apollo and Diana, naiads and oreads, to satyrs and Pan himself, "The simple shepherd's awe-inspiring God!"[16] It is doubtless an insoluble problem how much Wordsworth's general conception may have owed to Coleridge and, directly or through Coleridge, to such German Hellenists as Schiller.[17] At any rate he was not writing under any neo-pagan impulse. Though classic myth may seem remote from the Wordsworth we usually think of, it is not at all remote if we remember the animism which was for him, as it could not be for Coleridge, almost a religious faith.[18] For one who held such conceptions of nature and of imaginative intuition, myths inevitably embodied authentic tidings of invisible things.[19]

Laodamia (1814) was the chief poetic fruit of Wordsworth's renewed reading, with his son, of some ancient authors. Ovid supplied a few details, though his epistle of course could not treat the return of Protesilaus, and Ovid's heroine, while not without pathos, comes dangerously close to comedy when she urges her husband to remember that his prowess should be displayed not in war but in love. Catullus, one of the Roman poets with whom Wordsworth's acquaintance was "intimate," emphasizes the passion of Laodamia. But the essential classical source was the sixth book of the *Aeneid.*[20] While Tennyson is commonly accepted as the most Virgilian of nineteenth-century English poets, it is a less familiar fact that his nearest rival is the supposedly unbookish Wordsworth. The few lines in *Laodamia* are enough to convince one that no poet has absorbed with finer understanding, or rendered with more wistful beauty, the spirit of Virgil's picture of Elysium:

> In his deportment, shape, and mien, appeared
> Elysian beauty, melancholy grace,
> Brought from a pensive though a happy place.
>
> He spake of love, such love as Spirits feel
> In worlds whose course is equable and pure;
> No fears to beat away—no strife to heal—
> The past unsighed for, and the future sure;
> Spake of heroic arts in graver mood
> Revived, with finer harmony pursued;
>
> Of all that is most beauteous—imaged there
> In happier beauty; more pellucid streams,
> An ampler ether, a diviner air,
> And fields invested with purpureal gleams;
> Climes which the sun, who sheds the brightest
> day
> Earth knows, is all unworthy to survey.[21]

"An ampler ether, a diviner air" is Virgil rendered with literal felicity, but touched also with the Platonic radiance which illumines this and other parts of the poem; and the second and third lines of the quotation, though not directly Virgilian, are the distilled essence of Virgil's melancholy grace of style, his high, grave pity, tenderness, and hope.

Wordsworth's treatment of his heroine is not altogether Virgilian. Laodamia, like Dido, is passionate, and, so far as conventions go, with more justification (though her vulgar outspokenness offended the modesty of that British matron, Sara Coleridge).[22] But Dido captured Virgil's sympathy to such a degree that for most modern readers she throws the poem out of focus—and perhaps did so for the author. Wordsworth, though at first lenient, grew more severe, as later versions of the ending show, in meting out punishment to Laodamia. And while Protesilaus has a sense of duty and discipline that is worthy of Aeneas, his moral seriousness, with its emphasis on chastity, is perhaps more puritan than Roman. His discourse on self-control and on the higher objects of love is partly Platonic, but it is Platonism that has, one may think, filtered through Milton.[23] The name of Milton suggests a central question in regard to *Laodamia.* Milton treated the conflict between human reason and mainly sensual temptation in his four long poems. In *Comus* and *Paradise Regained* there is no struggle and no sin, while in *Paradise Lost* and still more in *Samson Agonistes* it is only after defeat that erring human beings win the victory which is a vindication of man's divine gifts and possibilities. Hence the one pair of poems (though their power has until lately been underestimated) do stir us less profoundly than the others. With which group does *Laodamia* belong? Did Wordsworth conceive of his heroine as a woman or as an object lesson, a sort of female Byron who dared to take "Life's rule from passion craved for passion's sake"?[24] There is an obvious gulf between the poet's appeal to rational self-control and his early reliance for moral wisdom upon emotional intuitions of nature, between the condemnation of Laodamia's ardor and the ecstasies of *Vaudracour and Julia,* though the change is not in itself evidence of decline. Does Wordsworth's faith in reason and discipline mean that the romanticist has become classical (whatever that means!), or is this "classicism" a reversion to the mingled timidity and moralizing of the eighteenth-century classicist, a mark of the poet's own advancing years? Has he achieved a Sophoclean grasp of law and imaginative reason, or has he only put off the old man to put on the old woman?[25]

Such questions are perhaps unanswerable, but an increasing distrust of spontaneous emotion and impulse, an increasing desire for rational self-discipline, are clearly revealed in many poems of the great decade, in *Ruth* (1799), in *Resolution and Independence* (1802), in the noble series of patriotic sonnets, where Wordsworth appeals to heroic minds and careers and to "pure religion breathing household laws," in the 1805–06 version of *The Prelude.*[26] Then there is the notable group of poems of 1804–06, the *Ode to Duty, Elegiac Stanzas Suggested by a Picture of Peele Castle,* and the *Character of the Happy Warrior.* The last two were written, like the conclusion of *The Prelude,* under the shadow of his brother's death, a loss which had thrown Wordsworth back upon his ultimate resources; to meet such a test the healing power of nature was not enough. In the reality of grief he submitted to a new control, the law of reason. The same lesson of high and composed endurance, with more religious coloring, is learned by the heroine of *The White Doe of Rylstone* (1807–08).[27] Some relevant sentiments in *The Excursion* have already been touched upon, and that poem is so largely concerned with "reason's steadfast rule" over passions that "hold a fluctuating seat," with submission to the law of conscience, with the search for the central peace that subsists at the heart of endless agitation, that it would be idle to cite passages.[28] Thus the doctrine which receives such stately expression in *Laodamia* does not represent a unique or isolated mood. Wordsworth did not, during some years at least, merely grow old and timid. Under the shock of grief especially, he fought a real battle to arrive at "the top of sovereignty"—to quote, for variety, the words of Keats—the power

> to bear all naked truths,
> And to envisage circumstance, all calm.

The trouble is that in a number of Wordsworth's later poems, including *Laodamia,* that genuine struggle seems to have receded into the past, and a "classical" faith in reason, order, moderation, becomes at times indistinguishable from copy-book morality and conventional pietism. At any rate, whatever motives really prompted the final ending of *Laodamia,* it has been, since Arnold, too readily accepted as inferior to the first one; some readers may prefer not to have a marmoreal poem suddenly lapse into softness.[29]

Dion (1816) ought to be more satisfying than *Laodamia,* for the hero is an indubitable sinner. In *The Prelude,* Dion had been linked with Beaupuy.[30] Now he has, though with good intentions, "overleaped the eternal bars" of wisdom and moderation, and has "stained the robes of civil power with blood." But if we are to be moved by the workings of eternal justice we must be made to realize the behavior of the offender who is punished; and Dion is little more than a name, the lesson of his fate is not "carried alive into the heart by passion." Thus if the two poems are to be called partial failures, the cause is not so much lack of passion, for Wordsworth's half-mystical elevation of moral wisdom surely deserves that name, but the fact that the passion lacks an "objective correlative," that the *raison d'être* is inadequately conceived.

Laodamia and *Dion* are often spoken of, and were in their own day, as *tours de force,* and certainly they appear un-Wordsworthian in style if one comes to them directly from the Lucy poems or *Michael.* But if we had time to trace Wordsworth's stylistic evolution through the splendors of *Intimations of Immortality* and the frequent sublimities of *The Excursion,* we should find a fairly steady increase in the amount of classicized diction. Sometimes there is a truly Miltonic afflatus, sometimes only pseudo-Miltonic inflation. The Miltonic Wordsworth can now and then gain effects impossible for the Wordsworth of homespun, and we could ill spare the ornate dignity of the best parts of these poems, and such scattered beauties as "An incommunicable sleep" and "the unimaginable touch of Time."[31] Not that Wordsworth lost his command of pregnant simplicity:

> How fast has brother followed brother,
> From sunshine to the sunless land!

The last phrase carries an aura of classical suggestion like that of Housman's "strengthless dead."

We cannot linger over the mythological allusions in Wordsworth's later verse. The imagination which had called up Proteus and Triton from the sea dwindled for the most part into uninspired bookishness, serious or playful; the poet who had been content with a simple Highland girl and a solitary reaper began to think of rustic maidens in terms of dryads.[32] But that the aging Wordsworth was capable of genuine mythological and sensuous ardor we have Hazlitt's testimony, in his account of the poet's glowing talk about Bacchus and Titian's painting; and we have such a surprising and pretty piece of paganism as the Bacchic procession in *On the Power of Sound* (1828).[33] It was not, however, pagan enough for Landor, who declared in his Landorian way that "after eight most noble Pindaric verses on Pan and the Fawns and Satyrs, he lays hold on a coffin and a convict, and ends in a flirtation with a steeple. We must never say all we think, and least so in poetry."[34] In general, Wordsworth's nymphs, unlike Swinburne's, are clothed to the neck in British woolens, and they haunt, not an antique brake, nor the Mount Ida of the nude goddesses, but "The chaster coverts of a British hill."[35]

The consciousness of an antithesis between Christianity and paganism seems to have grown upon Wordsworth; in a more pallid way, for the question was not central in him, he went through a sort of Miltonic cycle. Even in *The Excursion,* the poem in which he had given new life to myth by treating it as a manifestation of natural religion, he could, like Milton, reveal in the same passage his love of myth and his fear of it.[36] And in his preface of 1815 he expresses sentiments partly similar to those we have met in Coleridge. He names, as "the grand store-houses of enthusiastic and meditative Imagination," the prophetic and lyrical parts of the Bible, and Milton, and he cannot forbear to add Spenser:

> I select these writers in preference to those of ancient Greece and Rome, because the anthropomorphitism of the Pagan religion subjected the minds of the greatest poets in those countries too much to the bondage of definite form; from which the Hebrews were preserved by their abhorrence of idolatry. This abhorrence was almost as strong in our great epic Poet, both from circumstances of his life, and from the constitution of his mind. However imbued the surface might be with classical literature, he was a Hebrew in soul; and all things tended in him towards the sublime.[37]

If, in regard to classic myth, the visionary gleam had fled in Wordsworth's old age, if he was in that as in other affairs a lost leader, at least he had been a leader. Whatever he may have owed to Coleridge or Germany, it was he who re-created mythological poetry for the nineteenth century. He passed on to the younger generation, especially to Keats, its most influential representative, a noble and poetic conception of mythology as a treasury of symbols rich enough to embody not only the finest sensuous experience but the highest aspirations of man. And it was Wordsworth who created a style, or rather styles, fit for the treatment of such subjects. Of course Keats and Shelley absorbed Shakespeare, Spenser, Milton, and others of the Renaissance tradition, but in the matter of mythology the earlier masters were not enough. After the eighteenth century the vitality of serious poetic myth needed to be demonstrated by a great poet who belonged to their own age, who wrote under similar conditions, and who wrestled with similar problems in philosophy and poetry.

William Wordworth

III. *Byron*

Byron's classical mythology was mainly so remote from the idealistic symbolism of his contemporaries that a discussion of him at this point amounts to a digression. But his use of myth has some lively aspects, and, besides, such a book as this could not pass by "Euphorion," the poet whose name and whose death are bound up with the revival of Hellenism and the cause of Greek freedom. Only one whole poem, *Prometheus,* comes within our range—since we cannot take account of the drama *Sardanapalus*—and though mythological allusions are abundant, a glance at this peripheral aspect of Byron's work must be in the nature of a squint, for it excludes a view of wholes and misses the earth-shaking power and spacious sweep which animate pages or cantos but are rarely concentrated in single unforgettable images and phrases. We are all agreed that Byron was a volcano; it is not agreed whether he is an extinct one. However, his mythology mostly belongs to that part of him which still lives, the eighteenth-century part.

Although Byron's early education left him with a "sickening memory" of "the daily drug," "the drilled dull lesson,"[38] his writing owed a great deal to his knowledge of ancient literature and history. One genuine passion was early kindled and never extinguished, a passion for the *Prometheus Bound.* The Donna Inez who "dreaded the Mythology" resembled Lady Byron more than Mrs. Byron, and the "filthy loves of gods and goddesses" which embarrassed Juan's tutors were not all that the young Byron absorbed:

> The infant rapture still survived the boy,
> And Loch-na-gar with Ida looked o'er Troy,
> Mixed Celtic memories with the Phrygian
> mount,
> And Highland linns with Castalie's clear
> fount.[39]

Whatever the sufferings involved in the process, Byron learned about as much of the classics "as most schoolboys after a discipline of thirteen years,"[40] as much at least as sat gracefully on a peer. In literary matters the great rebel was always a thorough conservative and well-bred man of the world. To vary a phrase of Georg Brandes' about Voltaire, the man who had little respect for anything in heaven or earth respected the dramatic unities. Byron never forgot his rank, and social prejudice apparently counted as much as critical taste in aligning him with Moore, Campbell, Rogers—"the last Argonaut of classic English poetry"[41]—and the gentlemanly Popeian tradition; the Lake poets, clothed in homespun and moonshine, were not familiar denizens of St. James's Street and Pall Mall, and they undervalued Pope.

The romantics generally, even Keats, started out in the eighteenth-century manner, but all except Byron soon cast it off. While his non-satirical poems were seldom free from the glossy and rhetorical, he was, as a hard-headed man of this world commenting on society with realistic vigor, a truer and more masculine heir of Dryden and Pope.[42] From almost the beginning to the end of his career Byron employed myth both seriously and facetiously. Most allusions of the former kind are conventional tags, though a few reach the level of memorable rhetoric or even poetry. The flippant and satirical ones are nearly all good, very often among the best of their kind; and when Byron uses the same reference in both ways, the witty one is almost invariably superior. The second canto of *The Bride of Abydos* opens with a serious, romantic recollection of the tale of Hero and Leander which might have been written by any poetaster; the humorous poem on his emulation of Leander (of which feat he was genuinely and inordinately proud) is at least worthy of Prior.[43] In the first canto of *Childe Harold,* Byron writes of Phoebus and "his amorous clutch"—a mauling, perhaps, of "Phoebus' amorous pinches"—but the deity is more than a verbal counter in the famous apostrophe: "Oh, Amos Cottle!—Phoebus! what a name. . . ."[44]

We shall not try to follow Childe Harold as, with the brand of Cain on his brow and the taste of Dead Sea fruit in his mouth, he moved slowly about Europe, sighing or spouting before the appropriate landmarks. (It is true, as Mr. Grierson has said, "that Byron made his readers feel that he was large enough to stand thus face to face with these sublime topics—the Alps, Venice, Rome, the Sea—and comment in passionate tones, and in a single breath, on them and on himself.")[45] There were good reasons for his fame. He was a peer, a rake, and a romantic misanthrope; his impressionistic guide-book in verse had more animation than the placid pages of Eustace, Clarke, and Gell; and in taste and style he was, unlike Shelley and Keats, in happy accord with the mass of readers. We can praise an image (borrowed from Sabellicus) as worthy of Venice—

> She looks a sea Cybele, fresh from Ocean,
> Rising with her tiara of proud towers—[46]

yet here, as often, we feel how completely Byron's style was lacking in distinction, magic, finality of phrase and rhythm.

His rhetorical energy appears in the faded purple patches on works of art. Byron's esthetic opinions were largely a compound of untutored instinct and personal or popular prejudice. Following in the wake of Payne Knight, he had gibed at Lord Elgin's "Phidian freaks," and in *The Curse of Minerva* prejudice was mingled with genuine devotion to Greece, of which Byron had a tendency to regard himself as proprietor.[47] But a literary member of the House of Lords had to combine correct taste with the good sense of the cosmopolite, he had to walk the zigzag path between "artiness" and Philistinism. Accordingly Childe Harold was bound to pause at intervals and declaim before the well-known statues, and he did so in the style of an admirer of Canova. In the dubiously Lucretian picture of Venus, whose "lava kisses" pour on Mars "as from an urn," we feel that we are reading "made" poetry, and we prefer the easy spontaneity, half idyllic, half mocking, of the lines on Haidée and Juan:

> And thus they form a group that's quite
> antique,
> Half naked, loving, natural, and Greek.[48]

In a stanza on "the Lord of the unerring bow" the Pythian of the age is seeing and feeling, yet we are still uncomfortably aware of being addressed by an unusually eloquent guide-lecturer.[49]

Now and then Byron's passion for freedom burns into a memorable phrase, as in the apostrophe to Rome, "The Niobe of nations! . . . Childless and crownless, in her voiceless woe." Not many poets could equal his nonchalance in striking a different note; the Church, "Like Niobe, weeps o'er her offspring—Tithes."[50] So too we may pass from the romantic grandeur and solitude of Childe Harold's ocean, where "the dark Euxine rolled Upon the blue Symplegades," to "The new Symplegades—the crushing Stocks," or to the passage in *Don Juan* where the Symplegades are still blue but where "Euxine" rhymes with "pukes in."[51] If we had time to run through *The Island* (1823), Byron's chief contribution to romantic primitivism, we should observe how jejune and colorless the serious mythological allusions are when put beside satirical parallels in *Don Juan.*[52] Indeed it would add a welcome sparkle to these pages to quote dozens of bits from that great epic, such as the original euhemeristic interpretation of Pasiphae, or the linking of Castlereagh with Ixion in the savage stanzas of the Dedication,[53] but we have had more than enough evidence of the superiority of Byron's facetious over his serious mythology. The large element of earth and prose in Byron did not prevent his using myth with fluent triteness, but it contributed to his robust common sense, his firm grasp of realities. His cynicism was not unmixed with Calvinism. If we turn from *Epipsychidion* to *Don Juan,* we may at times recoil in disgust; but there are moods, not necessarily baser ones, in which we prefer Byron's anti-Platonic mockery. And however enraptured we may be by Shelley's visions of a golden age, we may find wisdom in such a stanza as this:

> Oh, Mirth and Innocence! Oh, Milk and Water!
> Ye happy mixtures of more happy days!
> In these sad centuries of sin and slaughter,
> Abominable Man no more allays
> His thirst with such pure beverage. No matter,
> I love you both, and both shall have my praise:
> Oh, for old Saturn's reign of sugar-candy!—
> Meantime I drink to your return in brandy.[54]

Byron's last expedition to Greece was inspired partly by the desire of a man who was only half a poet to express in action an impulse worthier of his better self than his recent life had been. Like his own Sardanapalus, he "springs up a Hercules at once." It was with more than an aristocratic disdain for Grub Street that Byron insisted that he did not rank poetry and poets high in the scale of intellect. He praised the few authors, from Aeschylus down, who had been brave and active citizens, and preferred the capacity for doing to all the speculations of mere dreamers and observers.[55] The desire to let inward lava erupt in action was of course coupled with Byron's zeal for freedom and his old love of Greece, "the only place," as he wrote to Trelawny, that he "was ever contented in." Trelawny records too that "he often said, if he had ever written a line worth preserving, it was Greece that inspired it."[56] Yet even in these last days Byron still possessed the two pairs of lenses through which, according to his mood, he surveyed the world. "If things are farcical, they will do for *Don Juan;* if heroical, you shall have another canto of *Childe Harold.*"[57] One example must serve. When, at Ithaca, Trelawny wanted Byron to visit the scenes supposedly connected with Odysseus, he became the exasperated man of the world who detested "antiquarian twaddle." Yet it was during this very time that he wrote, at Cephalonia, the fragment *Aristomenes* which laments the death of Pan and other ancient deities.[58] Even if the lines seem little more than a halting imitation of Coleridge's regrets for the fair humanities of old religion, their testimony to a genuine vein of sentiment is borne out by many other things in Byron. Finally, there is no better illustration of the poet's two sides than *The Isles of Greece.* Here passion kindles rhetoric into poetry, yet Byron is so afraid of being caught shedding manly tears that he puts the poem into a flippant frame.[59]

If one who knew a good deal of Byron were told that he had written only one poem on a mythological character, a character into whom he could project himself, the answer would be an easy guess. As Mr. Garrod says, "Of this new Prometheus, all the world was the Caucasus, and all the men and women in it vultures; and the part of first vulture was taken by a preposterous mother."[60] *Prometheus* was written in Switzerland in 1816, during the days of Byron's companionship with Shelley, and the modern significance of the myth must have been a topic of conversation. While there was doubtless mutual influence, Shelley had so far used Prometheus only as an example of the ills that came with the cooking and eating of flesh, and Byron in 1814 had recorded his view of "him, the unforgiven," who "in his fall preserved his pride."[61] Moreover, Byron said that Aeschylus' drama, of which he "was passionately fond as a boy," was always so much in his head that he could easily conceive its influence over all or anything that he had written; his works contain some seventeen allusions to Prometheus, of varying length and seriousness.[62]

The *Prometheus Bound* had been too vast and explosive for neoclassic taste—Dacier, for instance, comments on its monstrosities[63]—but as in the course of the eighteenth century the formal and the rococo gave way to the wild and strong and rebellious, Prometheus (like Milton's Satan) came to be a symbol of heroic individualism, of revolt against divine or human tyranny. The development of the theme followed two main lines, which were sometimes separate, sometimes united. One starts (if a scholar may safely use the word "start" about any idea) from Shaftesbury's description of the true poet or artist who imitates the Creator, who "is indeed a second *Maker;* a just Prometheus under Jove."[64] This partly esthetic conception, growing with the doctrine of original genius, may be said to culminate in the brief drama of Goethe (1773). Here Prometheus is more or less Goethe himself, a type of the free spirit of the artist who, emancipated from fear of the dull and idle gods, rejoices in the fullness of life as it is and in the exercise of his creative powers.[65]

The other main line of evolution, less esthetic than rebellious or humanitarian or both, is represented by Byron's poem and Shelley's drama, and also by Goethe's great monologue, "Bedecke deinen Himmel, Zeus."[66] Byron's poem is of only fifty-nine lines, but he seldom maintains through even that space such unfaltering dignity of thought and expression. His Prometheus is a Titan, and the poem, for all its brevity, has a massive effect. Byron's hero is not Goethe's intellectual and creative spirit, nor is he Shelley's humanitarian idealist and lover of Asia. He embodies part of the conception that we have in Shelley, of the god who endures punishment for befriending man, but he is the Prometheus of Shelley's opening lines; he would have uttered the curse against Jupiter, he would never have retracted it. Byron's Prometheus is of course as much of a self-portrait as the works of Goethe and Shelley, and, though calm and restrained in manner, he anticipates the heaven-storming rebellion of *Manfred, Cain,* and *Heaven and Earth.* The poem "is a defiant and unshakeable arraignment of the conception of Providence taught him by Orthodox Evangelicalism," and Prometheus "becomes the symbol of humanity, humanity more sinned against than sinning."[67] But though Byron denies the Calvinistic God and the Calvinistic conviction of sin and personal responsibility, he cannot find relief in a Shelleyan gospel of love, for the sense of inward discord and the reality of evil is in his bones. A stanza on life and evil in *Childe Harold* is echoed in *Prometheus Unbound,* and the iron lines at the end of Byron's *Prometheus* are echoed in Shelley's last stanza, but Byron cannot escape from his realistic dualism to rejoice in the triumphant and harmonious soul of man.[68]

Notes

[1] *Miscellanies, Aesthetic and Literary,* ed. T. Ashe (1885), pp. 55 ff. Along with Coleridge's own rueful account of the lecture (*Letters,* ed. E. H. Coleridge, 1895, II, 740) one should mention Hazlitt's eloquent report of the poet's eloquent talk on the *Prometheus* and Greek tragedy in general (*The Spirit of the Age*). See also *Unpublished Letters of Samuel Taylor Coleridge,* ed. Earl L. Griggs (1932), II, 281-82, 336.

[2] *Miscellanies,* p. 150; *Coleridge's Miscellaneous Criticism,* ed. Thomas M. Raysor (Harvard University Press, 1936), p. 191. Cf. Blackwell, *Letters Concerning Mythology* (1748), pp. 171, 207 ff., and above, ch. I, part v. Coleridge goes on to discuss ancient mysteries, the Cabiri, and other twilight topics which attracted Blackwell also (*Letters,* pp. 277 ff.), but he seems here to be following the mazy track of Friedrich Schelling, *Ueber die Gottheiten von Samothrace* (Stuttgart and Tübingen, 1815).

[3] *Coleridge's Shakespearean Criticism,* ed. Thomas M. Raysor (Harvard University Press, 1930), II, 263; cf. *ibid.,* I, 184-85, II, 7. See also *Lectures and Notes on Shakspere and Other English Poets,* ed. T. Ashe (1908), pp. 234, 462; *Lectures and Notes on Shakespeare and Other Dramatists* (World's Classics ed.), p. 60. The phrase "vinum mundi" as applied to Bacchus occurs in the older texts of Coleridge, though not in Mr. Raysor's. While criticizing other Hellenic notions of Coleridge's, Mr. Gilbert Murray endorses his idea of the god as the wine of the world; see "What English Poetry May Still Learn from Greek," *Essays and Studies by Members of the English Association,* III (1912), 10.

[4] A. C. Dunstan, "The German Influence on Coleridge," *M.L.R.,* XVIII (1923), 196. Both Coleridge and Schlegel heard the lectures of Heyne. For Schlegel's conception of Bacchus as a symbol of higher aspirations, see Anna A. Helmholtz (Mrs. A. A. von Helmholtz Phelan), *The Indebtedness of Samuel Taylor Coleridge to August Wilhelm von Schlegel, Bulletin of the University of Wisconsin, Philology and Literature Series,* III (1907), 365 (and also p. 299); and Dunstan, pp. 194-95. Dunstan also quotes Heyne.

[5] *Miscellanies,* pp. 140-41; *Coleridge's Miscellaneous Criticism,* ed. Raysor, p. 148. Cf. *Lectures and Notes,* ed. Ashe, pp. 233 ff.; *Coleridge's Shakespearean Criticism,* ed. Raysor, I, 176, 222, II, 262-63; *Unpublished Letters,* ed. Griggs, II, 336.

[6] A. C. Dunstan (*M.L.R.,* XVII [1922], 274-75) quotes Schiller's *Über naive und sentimentalische Dichtung;* see *Schillers Sämtliche Werke* (Säkular-Ausgabe), XII, 184 (and 179 ff., 247 ff.). For Coleridge and Schlegel, see Mrs. von Helmholtz Phelan, pp. 310 ff., 326, 337, 365 ff. According to Dunstan (*M.L.R.,* XVIII, 193), both Schlegel and Coleridge drew their comparisons of classical and Gothic architecture and drama from Goethe's *Deutsche Baukunst.* See also Arthur O. Lovejoy, *P.M.L.A.,* XXXIX (1924), 243-46, and *M.L.N.,* XXXV (1920), 139.

[7] *Biographia Literaria,* ch. XVIII (ed. Shawcross, Clarendon Press, 1907, II, 58). Cf. Dryden, *Essays,* ed. Ker, II, 30-33; and Wordsworth's note on his *Ode to Lycoris,* quoted below.

We may recall the conclusion of Coleridge's *The Garden of Boccaccio* (1828), and the characterization, both charming and true, of Renaissance mythologizing—Boccaccio with his manuscript of Homer, and "Ovid's Holy Book of Love's sweet smart," and the all-enjoying, all-blending fancy which mingles "fauns, nymphs, and wingéd saints."

[8] *Wallenstein,* Part II (*The Piccolomini*), II. iv. 123 ff. In the fourth line of the extract, "their" was "her" in the 1829 text; see *Complete Poetical Works,* ed. E. H. Coleridge (Clarendon Press, 1912), II, 649. For the German text, as we have it now, see Schiller's *Werke,* V, 132, *Die Piccolomini,* III. iv, ll. 1632 ff. In considering Coleridge's very free adaptation we may remember that "the manuscript used by Coleridge was carefully prepared by Schiller and differed in some respects from the text that has since become the standard" (John L. Haney, *The German Influence on Coleridge,* Philadelphia, 1902, p. 21). And then, as Mr. Haney remarked in a letter to me, Coleridge "had too lively a poetic imagination to stick very closely to any original that he translated."

One may wonder if the rendering of these lines was colored by recollections of Schiller's *Die Götter Griechenlands,* a poem that he must surely have known. He translated Schiller's *Dithyrambe* (*Gedichte,* I, 7) as *The Visit of the Gods.* See Haney, p. 14; and F. W. Stokoe, *German Influence in the English Romantic Period* (Cambridge University Press, 1926), p. 122, note 4.

[9] In a letter to Sotheby, September 10, 1802, Coleridge writes: "It must occur to every reader that the Greeks in their religious poems address always the Numina Loci, the Genii, the Dryads, the Naiads, etc., etc. All natural objects were *dead,* mere hollow statues, but there was a Godkin or Goddessling *included* in each. In the Hebrew poetry you find nothing of this poor stuff, as poor in genuine imagination as it is mean in intellect. At best, it is but fancy, or the aggregating faculty of the mind, not imagination or the *modifying* and coadunating faculty. This the Hebrew poets appear to me to have possessed beyond all others, and next to them the English. In the Hebrew poets each thing has a life of its own, and yet they are all our life" (*Letters,* ed. E. H. Coleridge, I, 405-06). See the severe condemnation of mythology in comparison with Christianity in a letter of December 17, 1796 (*ibid.,* I, 199-200).

[10] *Memorials of a Tour in Italy* (1837), sonnets iv-vi (*Poems of Wordsworth,* ed. T. Hutchinson, Oxford University Press, 1926, p. 359). Unless some other reference is given, Wordsworth is regularly quoted from this edition.

[11] *Poetical Works,* ed. W. Knight (1896), VI, 145-46. . . .

[12] Frederick E. Pierce, "Wordsworth and Thomas Taylor," *P.Q.,* VII (1928), 62. For the Latin text see John D. Rea, "Coleridge's Intimations of Immortality from Proclus," *M.P.,* XXVI (1928–29), 208-09. See also Herbert Hartman, "The 'Intimations' of Wordsworth's *Ode,*" *R.E.S.,* VI (1930), 1-20.

[13] Rea, p. 211; *Republic,* bk. x, 611; *Paradise Lost,* iii. 604; *Faerie Queene,* III. viii, IV. xii; *Colin Clout,* ll. 245, 248 ff., 283. For Triton see also *Comus,* l. 873.

Miss Abbie F. Potts has pointed out many reminiscences of Spenser and Milton in the *Ode;* see *S.P.,* XXIX (1932), 607 ff.

[14] Ll. 717 ff., 847 ff. Later (vi. 538 ff.) Wordsworth mentions the stories of Prometheus, Tantalus, and the line of Thebes, as fictions in form, but in their substance tremendous truths.

[15] The image reminds us of the last sonnet of the Duddon series, where Wordsworth splendidly echoes Milton and Moschus (*Poems,* pp. 384, 915).

For the lines in *The Excursion* on the casting of a lock of hair into the river, Wordsworth would have found suggestions in various books that he possessed, such as Taylor's translation of Pausanias (I. xxxvii. 3) and Pope's *Iliad,* xxiii.175, note; see *Works,* ed. Knight, V, 396-97. For a parallel idea in Wordsworth's *Essay upon Epitaphs,* see *Poems,* p. 928, col. 2; or *Prose Works,* ed. Knight (1896), II, 128. He might also have got hints, especially for "Life continuous, Being unimpaired" (l. 755), from Potter's *Archaeologia Graeca* (ed. Edinburgh, 1818), II, 278. His library in 1859 contained Potter's first volume (*Transactions of the Wordsworth Society,* VI, 206, item 61); presumably he had owned the second, and possibly he had lent it to Coleridge. Potter says that both the watery deities and the sun were thought to deserve gratitude "for the first gift, as well as continuance of life."

[16] See also the perfect lines on Pan in *The Prelude,* viii. 180 ff. Except for one word they are the same in the version of 1805–06 as in the later one.

[17] Some scholars have found echoes of Schiller's *Gods of Greece* in these mythological passages of *The Excursion,* but the resemblances seem too slight and general to prove anything. Wordsworth of course knew, and admired, Coleridge's lines on the fair humanities of old religion (see *The Correspondence of Henry Crabb Robinson with the Wordsworth Circle,* ed. Edith J. Morley, Clarendon Press, 1927, I, 402), and they may well have been in his mind, but he is less close to Coleridge in *The Excursion* than in the fifth section of the *Ode* of 1816 (*Poems,* p. 325: "And ye, Pierian Sisters. . . ."). For various opinions on these points see, for example, Theodor Zeiger, *Studien zur vergleichenden Litteraturgeschichte,* I (1901), 287-89; Thomas Rea, *Schiller's Dramas and Poems in England* (1906), pp.

74-75; Max J. Herzberg, "William Wordsworth and German Literature," *P.M.L.A.*, XL (1925), 339-42; F. W. Stokoe, *German Influence in the English Romantic Period* (1926), p. 116; A. C. Bradley, "English Poetry and German Philosophy in the Age of Wordsworth," *A Miscellany* (1929), pp. 126-27; Frederic Ewen, *The Prestige of Schiller in England 1788-1859* (Columbia University Press, 1932), p. 80, note 154.

[18] "It is interesting to notice that when Wordsworth began to write *The Prelude* he still delighted to conceive of Nature not merely as the expression of one divine spirit, but as in its several parts animated by individual spirits who had, like human beings, an independent life and power of action. This was obviously his firm belief in the primitive paganism of his boyhood . . . and long after he had given up definite belief in it, he cherished it as more than mere poetic fancy" (E. de Selincourt, *The Prelude*, Clarendon Press, 1926, p. 506). Cf. Melvin M. Rader, *Presiding Ideas in Wordsworth's Poetry* (*University of Washington Publications in Language and Literature*, VIII, 1931), especially pp. 175 ff., 186 ff.

[19] For one expression of Wordsworth's belief in the religious character of all true poetry, see his letter in reply to Landor's strictures on *Laodamia* (*Works*, ed. Knight, 1896, VI, 9; *Letters of the Wordsworth Family*, ed. Knight, 1907, II, 214-15).

[20] An obvious initial suggestion for the poem was the appearance of Laodamia among the shades of unhappy lovers. Some other items derived from the sixth book are the opening sacrifices to the infernal gods, the attitude of the suppliant Laodamia (modeled on that of the priestess), her vain attempt to embrace the ghost of her husband, and of course the passage quoted in the text. . . .

See Catullus, lxviii; and *Letters of the Wordsworth Family*, II, 179. In Hyginus (*Fab.* ciii-iv) Laodamia wins the favor from the gods; in Lucian (*Dialogues of the Dead*, xxiii) it is the ardent Protesilaus. In Propertius (I. xix) Protesilaus is the passionate one of the pair. See also Servius, on *Aen.* vi. 447. For details about Ovid, Euripides, and Virgil, see *Works*, ed. Knight, VI, 11 ff.

[21] Cf. *Aen.* vi. 637 ff.:

> "His demum exactis, perfecto munere divae,
> devenere locos laetos et amoena virecta
> fortunatorum nemorum sedesque beatas.
> largior hic campos aether et lumine vestit
> purpureo, solemque suum, sua sidera norunt.
> pars in gramineis exercent membra palaestris,
> contendunt ludo et fulva luctantur harena;
> pars pedibus plaudunt choreas et carmina
> dicunt."

One might add two passages which show the difference between a dead convention and a convention brought to life. In *Descriptive Sketches* (1793 version, *Poems*, p. 613), Wordsworth echoes a hundred eighteenth-century versifiers:

> "For come Diseases on, and Penury's rage,
> Labour, and Pain, and Grief, and joyless Age,
> And Conscience dogging close his bleeding
> way. . . ."

This is from *Yew-Trees* (1803; *Poems*, p. 185):

> ". . . ghostly Shapes
> May meet at noontide; Fear and trembling Hope,
> Silence and Foresight; Death the Skeleton
> And Time the Shadow. . . ."

Cf. *Aen.* vi. 273 ff.

[22] *Memoir and Letters* (1873), I, 396 ff.

[23] Compare *Laodamia*, ll. 73 ff., 145 ff., and *Paradise Lost*, viii. 586 ff. For the alterations in the conclusion see Wordsworth's *Poems*, p. 901.

[24] *Evening Voluntaries*, iv (1834), *Poems*, p. 455.

[25] . . . See Dean Inge's remarks, quoted by Miss Edith C. Batho, *The Later Wordsworth* (Cambridge University Press, 1933), p. 307; and Aubrey de Vere, *Essays Chiefly on Poetry* (1887), I, 186-88.

Mr. Herbert Read (*Wordsworth*, 1930, pp. 214 ff.) and Mr. Hugh Fausset (*The Lost Leader*, 1933, p. 443) are very severe upon *Laodamia;* they both see behind the hero and heroine the figures of Wordsworth and Annette. It may be so, but one has grown weary of Annette as the one key to the poetry of Wordsworth, and the tone of critics who lecture him is not entirely unlike that of the Protesilaus they detest.

[26] See, for example, book xiii, ll. 160 ff., 261 ff., pp. 482 and 488 in *The Prelude*, ed. De Selincourt (1926).

While in his early prime Wordsworth often disparaged books and reason, such sentiments were sometimes dramatic or playful, and sometimes they were the natural reaction of a man who had turned for salvation to Godwinism, the intellectual system *par excellence*, and had found it both inadequate and dangerous. Moreover, at the time of *Laodamia* or later he could on occasion cherish his early faith in impulses from the vernal wood.

[27] Canto vii, ll. 1621-28 (*Poems*, p. 414).

[28] See, for example, iv. 1270 ff., v. 1011 ff., and below, ch. III, notes 63-64.

[29] For Arnold's complaint about Wordsworth's tinkering see his *Letters,* ed. G. W. E. Russell (1895), II, 182-83.

[30] *The Prelude,* ix. 408 ff. See De Selincourt's edition, pp. 570, 589. For Wordsworth's use of Plutarch in the poem, see *Works,* ed. Knight, VI, 125 ff. The most detailed criticism of *Dion,* and the highest eulogy, that I have seen is that of Mr. Sturge Moore ("The Best Poetry," *Transactions of the Royal Society of Literature,* Second Series, XXXI [1912], 36 ff.).

[31] This last phrase may be a reminiscence of the "unimaginable touches" of Milton's remarks on music in his *Of Education* (*Prose Works,* Bohn ed., III, 476). On the next page Milton says that in the spring "it were an injury and sullenness against nature, not to go out and see her riches"; with this compare *Excursion,* iv. 1190-91; *Intimations of Immortality,* l. 42.

[32] See, for example, the Miltonic conclusion of *The Brownie's Cell* (1814); *The Excursion,* vi. 826 ff.; *The Three Cottage Girls* (1821); the opening of the third part of *The Russian Fugitive* (1830).

[33] See Hazlitt's *The Spirit of the Age.* Mr. De Selincourt has suggested that Hazlitt's account is colored by recollections of Keats's Bacchic lines (*Poems of John Keats,* 1926, p. 572).

[34] John Forster, *Walter Savage Landor* (1869), II, 323.

[35] *The Triad* (1828); see *Poems,* p. 220. One of the triad, Sara Coleridge, thought the poem "artificial and unreal" (*Memoir and Letters,* 1873, II, 352), but Wordsworth liked it (*Letters of the Wordsworth Family,* II, 351).

[36] Book vii, ll. 728 ff. The lines are uttered by the Pastor.

Doubtless too much should not be made of the anecdote told by Haydon and by Hazlitt, especially since both were masters of vivid corroborative detail. At Christie's, apparently in 1824, Wordsworth looked for some time, says Haydon, at "the group of Cupid and Psyche kissing," and then "he turned round to me with an expression I shall never forget, and said, 'The Dev-ils!'" (See *Autobiography and Memoirs of Benjamin Robert Haydon,* ed. Aldous Huxley, 1926, I, xviii, 351; *Works of William Hazlitt,* ed. P. P. Howe, VIII [1931], 343.) Miss Batho (*The Later Wordsworth,* p. 84) insists that "there are at least two impossible interpretations, that he hated art and hated or was afraid of passionate love."

[37] *Poems,* p. 957.

[38] *Works of Lord Byron. Poetry,* ed. E. H. Coleridge (1903–04), I, 405, 424 (*Hints from Horace,* ll. 225-26, 513-14); II, 386-88 (*Childe Harold's Pilgrimage,* IV. lxxv ff.).

[39] *The Island,* ii. 290-93 (*Works,* V, 609-10); *Don Juan,* I. xli (*Works,* VI, 26).

[40] *Works. Letters and Journals,* ed. R. E. Prothero (1902–04), I, 172.

[41] *Ibid.,* V, 270, note; V, 274.

[42] The early paraphrase, in *Hours of Idleness* (1807), of the Virgilian episode of Nisus and Euryalus often reads like an awkwardly heightened imitation of Dryden's rendering, which in fact it sometimes echoes. An odd conjunction of stars, by the way, was responsible for Byron's imitation of Ossian, *The Death of Calmar and Orla* (*Works,* I, 177-83), which is based on the Virgilian story.

[43] *Works,* III, 13. Cf. *Don Juan,* II. cv. In *Don Juan,* II. cciv, Byron seems to echo the passage in the *Hero and Leander* of Musaeus which describes the uncanonical union of the lovers.

[44] *Childe Harold,* I. lviii; *English Bards, and Scotch Reviewers,* l. 399; *Antony and Cleopatra,* I. v. 28.

[45] "Lord Byron: Arnold & Swinburne," *The Background of English Literature* (1925), p. 89.

[46] *Childe Harold,* IV. ii (*Works,* II, 328).

[47] See, for instance, his defence of Pope's translation of the moonlight scene in Homer, and his strictures on Wordsworth's geography in the passage on Greece in *The Excursion* (*Letters,* III, 239 ff.). And see the remarks of Apollo-Byron in Disraeli's skit *Ixion in Heaven* (ed. 1927, p. 15).

[48] *Childe Harold,* IV. li; *Don Juan,* II. cxciv.

[49] *Childe Harold,* IV. clxi. Cf. Thomson, *Liberty,* iv. 163 ff.

[50] *Childe Harold,* IV. lxxix; *The Age of Bronze,* ll. 642-43.

[51] *Childe Harold,* IV. clxxv-clxxvi; *The Age of Bronze,* ll. 658-59; *Don Juan,* V. v. In this as in other respects Byron may have owed something to Frere, though he went far beyond him. See *The Monks and the Giants,* ed. R. D. Waller (Manchester University Press, 1926), II. li, III. ix and xi, IV. xiv-xv, xxxiii ff.

[52] For example, compare the allusions to the *Argo* in *The Island,* i. 229-30 (*Works,* V, 597), and *Don Juan,*

II. lxvi, XIV. lxxvi; or the allusions to Aphrodite and Venus in *The Island,* ii. 132-33, and *Don Juan,* I. lv.

[53] *Don Juan,* II. clv; Dedication, xiii.

[54] *Beppo,* lxxx (*Works,* IV, 185).

[55] *Letters,* II, 345, III, 405.

[56] *Trelawny's Recollections of the Last Days of Shelley and Byron,* ed. Dowden (Oxford University Press, 1923), pp. 107, 22.

[57] *Ibid.,* p. 142.

[58] *Trelawny's Recollections,* pp. 136-37 (and cf. *Letters,* VI, 242); *Works,* IV, 566. The autograph manuscript of the fragment is dated September 10, 1823.

[59] *Don Juan,* III. lxxxvi, lxxxvii.

[60] *The Profession of Poetry* (Clarendon Press, 1929), p. 52.

[61] *Ode to Napoleon Buonaparte,* xvi (*Works,* III, 312).

[62] See notes on *Prometheus* (*Works,* IV, 48); *Letters,* IV, 174 (1817). Nearly all the allusions are collected by Mr. Chew, *M.L.N.,* XXXIII (1918), 306-09. One might refer to the Promethean ejaculation uttered by Byron when ill after a swim (*Trelawny's Recollections,* p. 101).

[63] *La poëtique d'Aristote traduite en françois* (Paris, 1692), p. 205.

[64] "Soliloquy or Advice to an Author," *Characteristics,* ed. J. M. Robertson (1900), I, 136; and see II, 15-16. For some studies of the Prometheus theme in modern literature, see the writings of John Bailey, Arturo Graf, Karl Heinemann, and Oskar Walzel, in my bibliography, "General."

[65] *Goethes Sämtliche Werke,* Jubiläums-Ausgabe (Stuttgart and Berlin, 1902–07), XV, 11 ff. As Strich observes, "dieses Gedicht bringt ein neues Element in die mythologische Dichtkunst: den Mythos als Erlebnis des Dichters" (*Die Mythologie in der deutschen Literatur,* I, 235).

[66] *Werke,* II, 59. It is uncertain whether this monologue was intended for incorporation in the play or not (J. G. Robertson, *Life and Work of Goethe,* 1932, pp. 44-45). As Robertson remarks elsewhere, this magnificent *Prometheus* was Goethe's "real reply to Wieland, a reply before which Wieland's whole would-be Greek world shrivelled up" (*The Gods of Greece,* p. 10; *Essays and Addresses,* p. 125).

[67] H. J. C. Grierson, "Byron and English Society," *The Background of English Literature,* pp. 184-86.

[68] *Childe Harold,* IV. cxxvi; *Prometheus Unbound,* II. iv. 100 ff.

Bibliography

. . . In the bibliography, as in the footnotes, the place of publication of books is London, unless another place is named. Abbreviations used here and in footnotes are these:

A.J.P., American Journal of Philology; ELH, English Literary History; J.E.G.P., Journal of English and Germanic Philology; M.L.N., Modern Language Notes; M.L.R., Modern Language Review; M.P., Modern Philology; P.M.L.A., Publications of the Modern Language Association of America; P.Q., Philological Quarterly; R.E.S., Review of English Studies; S.P., Studies in Philology; T.L.S., London Times Literary Supplement. . . .

(*a*) Coleridge and Wordsworth

Leslie N. Broughton, *The Theocritean Element in the Works of William Wordsworth.* Halle, 1920.

Douglas Bush, "Wordsworth and the Classics." *University of Toronto Quarterly,* II (1933), 359-79.

C. C. Bushnell, "A Parallelism between Lucan and Lines in *Tintern Abbey.*" *J.E.G.P.,* IV (1902), 58.

Lane Cooper, "Wordsworth's Knowledge of Plato." *M.L.N.,* XXXIII (1918), 497-99.

A. C. Dunstan, "The German Influence on Coleridge." *M.L.R.,* XVII (1922), 272-81; XVIII (1923), 183-201.

John L. Haney, *The German Influence on Samuel Taylor Coleridge.* Philadelphia, 1902.

Herbert Hartman, "The 'Intimations' of Wordsworth's *Ode.*" *R.E.S.,* VI (1930), 1-20.

Anna A. Helmholtz (Mrs. A. A. von Helmholtz Phelan), *The Indebtedness of Samuel Taylor Coleridge to August Wilhelm Schlegel. Bulletin of the University of Wisconsin, Philology and Literature Series,* III (1907), 273-370.

William Knight, "A Lost Wordsworthian Fragment" [On Harmodius and Aristogeiton]. *Classical Review,* XV (1901), 82.

K. Lienemann, *Die Belesenheit von William Wordsworth.* Berlin, 1908.

Frederick E. Pierce, "Wordsworth and Thomas Taylor." *P.Q.,* VII (1928), 60-64.

J. P. Postgate, "Two Classical Parallels [Lucan, v. 219 ff., and *Intimations of Immortality*]." *Classical Review,* XXIII (1909), 42.

John D. Rea, "Coleridge's Intimations of Immortality from Proclus." *M.P.,* XXVI (1928-29), 201-13.

F. W. Stokoe, *German Influence in the English Romantic Period.* Cambridge University Press, 1926.

Una V. Tuckerman, "Wordsworth's Plan for his Imitation of Juvenal." *M.L.N.,* XLV (1930), 209-15.

James W. Tupper, "The Growth of the Classical in Wordsworth's Poetry." *Sewanee Review,* XXIII (1915), 95-107.

(*b*) BYRON

Karl Brunner, "Griechenland in Byrons Dichtung." *Anglia,* LX (1936), 203-10.

L. M. Buell, "Byron and Shelley [Prometheus]." *M.L.N.,* XXXII (1917), 312-13.

Samuel C. Chew, "Byroniana." [Cf. Buell above.] *M.L.N.,* XXXIII (1918), 306-09.

E. S. De Beer and Walter Seton, "Byroniana: The Archives of the London Greek Committee." *Nineteenth Century,* C (1926), 396 ff.

O. E., "Byron and Canova's Helen." *T.L.S.,* September 23, 1926, p. 632.

H. J. C. Grierson, "Byron and English Society." *The Background of English Literature* (1925), p. 167-99; *Byron, the Poet,* ed. Walter A. Briscoe (1924), pp. 55-85.

R. G. Howarth, "Byron's Reading." *T.L.S.,* March 15, 1934, p. 194.

Sir Richard Jebb, "Byron in Greece." *Modern Greece* (1880), pp. 143-83.

F. Maychrzak, "Lord Byron als Übersetzer." *Englische Studien,* XXI (1895), 384-430.

F. H. Pughe, "Byron, Wordsworth und die Antike." *Studien über Byron und Wordsworth,* ch. III. *Anglistische Forschungen,* VIII (1902), 40-54.

Helene Richter, "Byron. Klassizismus und Romantik." *Anglia,* XLVIII (1924), 209-57; *Lord Byron* (Halle, 1929), pp. 126 ff.

Walter F. Schirmer, "Zu Byrons 'klassizistischer Theorie.'" *Archiv,* CLI (1926), 84-85.

Harold Spender, *Byron and Greece.* 1924.

Douglas Bush (essay date 1937)

SOURCE: "Minor Poets of the Early Nineteenth Century," in *Mythology and the Romantic Tradition in English Poetry,* 1937. Reprint, Harvard University Press, 1969, pp. 169-96.

[*In the essay below, Bush traces the Greek influence among the works of minor nineteenth-century poets—notably Leigh Hunt, Thomas Love Peacock, Hartley Coleridge, Thomas Hood, and Thomas Lovell Beddoes—and stresses that these poets helped to nurture the growth of Romantic Hellenism.*]

While we look back to Wordsworth, Keats, and Shelley as the creators of the mythological genre in the nineteenth century, many smaller poets reflected and in some degree fostered the growth of romantic Hellenism. Indeed some of the poorest of them were popular when the great poets were not. However, the reader will not be asked to crawl with me through the endless underbrush which envelops the foothills of Parnassus . . . and most of this chapter, after the first few pages, is concerned with such more or less important minor poets as Hunt, Peacock, Hartley Coleridge, Hood, and Beddoes. We may observe, among other things, how constantly the mythological impulse is accompanied by, or springs from, Elizabethan enthusiasms. That note is dominant in such pioneers as Mrs. Tighe and Lord Thurlow. Mrs. Tighe, said Christopher North, was an angel on earth, "evanescent as her own immortal Psyche"; she was celebrated by Moore, and, in Mooreish strains, by the young Keats. In her long and languid allegorical poem of 1805 . . . , Mrs. Tighe was more of an eighteenth-century Spenserian than a true romantic, though her sensuous coloring was softer and warmer than that of her predecessors. If Elizabethan ardor, and adaptations of Shakespeare and Spenser, could alone make a poet, Lord Thurlow, the author of *Ariadne* (1814) and *Angelica* (1822), would have been one, and a man who thought the golden age of our language was that of Elizabeth was not entirely the fool Byron called him; but his *Ariadne* is as fantastic a romance as Henry Petowe's continuation of Marlowe's *Hero and Leander.*

A few better-known writers belong to the Hellenic rather than the Elizabethan revival. Mrs. Hemans, whose first volume appeared in 1808, began to celebrate Greek themes when still in pinafores. Her very literary Muse ranged far and wide, and might have groaned, with Aeneas, that the whole earth—and a large tract of heaven—was full of her labors. In her tepidly idealistic and romantic way Mrs. Hemans versified numerous bits of Plutarch, Mitford's *History of Greece,* Potter's *Archaeologica Graeca,* and similar books; her *Elysium* is headed by a quotation from Chateaubriand's *La génie du christianisme.* In *Modern Greece* (1817) she sang, a fluent, feminine, decorous Byron, of Greek freedom, art, and antiquities; the noble lord resented the infringement of his monopoly by a writer who had never been in Greece. Campbell eulogized the past, in his lectures on the poetry of Greece (1812), and to the modern struggle for independence he paid a tribute, not unworthy of his martial fire, in his *Song of the Greeks.* That charming friend of all the world, Tom Moore, translated Anacreon in 1800, with some aid from "Thomas Little," and then, as Thomas Little, drew from Anacreon a warmth of amorous sentiment which maintained his reputation for naughtiness well through the strict period of the Regency. No such adventitious interest helps to carry one through his *Evenings in Greece* (1825) and *Legendary Ballads* (1830). The thin treble of the songs is accompanied by a ponderous bass in the form of footnotes which testify to the multiplication of books of travel and antiquities, but Moore's reading did not prevent his Greece from bearing a close resemblance to the Orient of *Lalla Rookh.* His cheerfully inadequate notions of ancient Epicureanism were demolished by Peacock.

Three other writers must be included in these preliminary paragraphs, Thomas Wade, Mary Shelley, and Bryan Waller Procter. Of these the best poet was Wade, one of the earliest poetic admirers and imitators of Shelley; Keats also he admired, and Shakespeare's narrative poems.[1] As one would expect, his long *Nuptials of Juno* (1825) was what, since the time of Shelley and Keats, has been called a typical young man's poem, an exuberant mythological tapestry of rich color and sensuous warmth. This last phrase should be partly qualified with reference to the opening episode, based on a rather obscure myth; a cuckoo, after being fondled by Juno, turns into Jove, and there follow fourteen blameless lines of asterisks.

Mary Shelley's little dramas, *Proserpine* and *Midas,* were probably written in 1820; the former was first printed in 1832, the latter in 1922, in M. Koszul's excellent edition. They are not important, but they enable us to read Shelley's lovely lyrics in the setting for which they were designed. Apart from the question of comparative quality, the lyrics harmonize with the context, though the conclusion at least of the *Hymn of Pan* hardly warrants the adjectives of Tmolus and Midas, "blithe," "merry," "springhtly," and "gay." The fable of each drama sticks pretty closely to Ovid (whom Mary read with Shelley); there is the usual fanciful and descriptive elaboration. In *Midas* there is also a moral, that only a man who preferred earthly to divine music would be fool enough to crave unlimited gold. (If Mary had not been a devoted daughter, one might be tempted to see behind Midas the figure of her father, who for some time cared less for Shelley's poetry than for negotiable bits of his formal prose.) But Midas learns his lesson, and the conclusion anticipates the era when man, having lost the curse of gold, shall be "Rich, happy, free & great." In *Proserpine* Mrs. Shelley expresses her own spontaneous pleasure in the beauties of nature and myth, and, while she cannot take wing like her husband, she does at moments catch something of the pure Shelleyan limpidity.

The amiable gentleman of letters, Bryan Waller Procter, long outlived the numerous mythological poems of "Barry Cornwall." In his Elizabethan and Italian sympathies, and in his soft, smooth, luscious manner, he was closer to Hunt than to his great contemporaries. The effort to be Miltonic, in *The Flood of Thessaly* (1823), did something to brace his nerveless and invertebrate style, but the poem was a comparative failure. *Blackwood's,* which had praised Procter's early work, now reluctantly linked him with the "Greekish" Cockneys, "the lieges of Leigh the First."[2] In general Procter turned myths into pretty tapestries of descriptive luxuriance and delicate amorousness.[3] Mrs. Browning acknowledged his "genius," but said he had done a good deal "to emasculate the poetry of the passing age."[4] Both Shelley and Keats spoke well of Procter and ill of Barry Cornwall; Keats's words are kind and final.[5] But I may quote a more formal judgment from the *pontifex maximus* of criticism because it is a general characterization of the new mode in mythological poetry. In his belated review Jeffrey praised Keats highly, and linked him as a mythological poet with Barry Cornwall. These and other recent poets, he says,

> sheltering the violence of the fiction under the ancient traditionary fable, have in reality created and imagined an entire new set of characters; and brought closely and minutely before us the loves and sorrows and perplexities of beings, with whose names and supernatural attributes we had long been familiar, without any sense or feeling of their personal character. We have more than doubts of the fitness of such personages to maintain a permanent interest with the modern public;—but the way in which they are here managed certainly gives them the best chance that now remains for them; and; at all events, it cannot be denied that the effect is striking and graceful.[6]

I. *Leigh Hunt (1784–1859)*

Our memory of Leigh Hunt's verse is often limited to *Abou Ben Adhem* and a bad couplet or two from *The Story of Rimini*—the damned "rural spot" will not out—but he wrote, to mention only what concerns us, one charming poem, *The Nymphs* (1818), and two partly good narratives, *Hero and Leander* and *Bacchus and Ariadne,* both of 1819. Though his instinct for mythological luxuries had appeared as early as his *Juvenilia* (1801), Hunt may, in this group of poems, have been emulating Keats.[7] We do not regret that, on hearing of Shelley's work, he abandoned a projected *Prometheus Throned,* since, as he wrote to Shelley, he was "rather the son of one of Atlas's daughters, than of Atlas himself."[8] But if Hunt the romantic and mythological poet flowered and died early, Hunt the critic, essayist, and book-maker continued to testify to his faith, for the endless misfortunes and endless labor of his later life seem hardly to have dimmed his youthful vision of the radiant antique world.

Before we consider Hunt's notions of myth a word should be said of *The Story of Rimini* (1816) because of its general influence on mythological poetry. Taking as his model the English poet whom at that time he found most delightful, John Dryden, Hunt set out, with a stronger sense of "the tender and the pathetic," and a more sensuous pleasure in nature and color, to tell a romantic story in verse of informal flexibility, which should combine rich decoration with something of realism in tone and sentiment.[9] As he candidly acknowledged later, *Rimini* was pitched in the wrong key—he was Ariosto's man, not Dante's—but, when all his lapses have been duly condemned and when the poem is compared with what had gone before rather than with what came after, it remains a notable piece of romantic narrative. For young writers of luscious tastes who inclined to the antique, *Laodamia* was too austere in form and style, and *Rimini* did more than any other single work to create the convention which Hunt himself, Keats, and others more or less followed in their mythological verse. If the fruits of that convention were sometimes over-ripe, they were sometimes beautiful too.

While Hunt was grateful to Christ's Hospital (if not especially to the renowned Boyer) for making him "acquainted with the languages of Homer and Ovid," gerund-grinding developed no immediate love for any of the classics except Virgil (and one episode in him, that of Nisus and Euryalus). His saturation in mythology began as a boyish and extra-curricular enthusiasm, that kind of enthusiasm which seems so often to have been engendered by primitive educational systems. Like Keats, Hunt reveled in a trinity which look drab enough now, Lempriere's *Classical Dictionary,* Spence's *Polymetis* (this for its plates rather than its text), and above all Tooke's *Pantheon,* over which he dreamed in the fields as well as in school.[10] Later came such poetry as Spenser and the fifty-six volumes of the *Parnaso Italiano* (which the cheerful martyr bought while in prison) to fill his imagination with gods and nymphs. In addition to the classical and modern literature that he might be expected to know, Hunt could quote familiarly from such formidable mythographers as Boccaccio, Natalis Comes, George Sandys, Bochart, and others.[11] More important than knowledge was his rich appreciation of mythology and the older poetic tradition, and no critic of his time set forth with such full and intuitive sympathy the esthetic and spiritual values which the romantic poets had re-discovered in myth. In the preface to *Foliage* (1818) Hunt expanded, with special reference to mythology, the anti-classicist doctrine of the preface to *Rimini.* Shakespeare

> felt the Grecian mythology not as a set of school-boy common-places which it was thought manly to give up, but as something which it requires more than mere scholarship to understand,—as the elevation of the external world and of accomplished humanity to the highest pitch of the graceful, and as embodied essences of all the grand and lovely qualities of nature.

Hunt rejoiced, then, that the living and life-giving tradition of Shakespeare, Spenser, and the rest had come up, on the other side of the eighteenth-century desert, in romantic poetry. In its serious essence Hunt's interpretation of myth is in harmony with that of *The Excursion:*[12] "There is a deeper sense of another world, precisely because there is a deeper sense of the present; of its varieties, its benignities, its mystery."[13] But, as we should expect, Hunt feels more esthetic and sensuous enjoyment than religious or mystical aspiration. Like Francis Thompson toward the end of the century, he was well aware of what modern poets, because of their very remoteness from pagan religion, added in the way of refinement and nobility to ancient conceptions.[14] Moreover, his approach to the subject was not merely bookish:

> He that would run the whole round of the spirit of heathenism to perfection [a phrase impossible for Coleridge, Wordsworth, or Keats or Shelley!], must become intimate with the poetry of Milton and Spenser; of Ovid, Homer, Theocritus, and the Greek tragedians; with the novels of Wieland, the sculptures of Phidias and others, and the pictures of Raphael, and the Caraccis, and Nicholas Poussin. But *a single page of Spenser or one morning at the Angerstein Gallery,* will make him better acquainted with it than a dozen such folios as Spence's Polymetis, or all the mythologists and book-poets who have attempted to draw Greek inspiration from a Latin fount.[15]

I have emphasized Hunt's views of myth because they are such a clear summary of what his betters were doing in poetry, and because he exerted so much personal influence; his influence as a noted liberal is another story. His poem *The Nymphs* is not altogether unworthy of his critical ideals. Indeed it may be counted Hunt's best poem, though he left it out of the canon. It delighted Shelley, and we can hardly read the song of the Nepheliads without feeling that it contributed something to the richer music and imagery of *The Cloud* and *Arethusa.*[16] The poem requires no investigation of sources; except for the names of the classes of nymphs and their general functions, it grows out of Hunt's lively senses.[17] "I write to enjoy myself," he says in the preface to *Foliage,* and the statement indicates both his virtues and his limitations. "The main features of the book are a love of sociality, of the country, and of the fine imagination of the Greeks." Nowhere else does Hunt express so poetically, and with so few of his irritating faults, his sensitive joy in all the bright and happy phenomena of nature, his loving observation of wood and field and stream and sky, and, one may add, the female form. There is no explicit symbolism in the poem; it is mainly "a now" in luxuriant verse. To use a formula of the age which Hunt the critic handled with insight, *The Nymphs* has more of fancy than imagination; but there is visual imagination at least, and in peopling the natural world with lovely nymphs Hunt is true to his own conception of the Greeks and their direct, unsophisticated response to nature. He does achieve something of a primitive outlook,[18] though his more or less authentic tidings are of visible things. Hunt never wearied of quoting "Great God! I'd rather be . . . ," and he hazarded the guess that he had had far more sights of Proteus than Wordsworth; for Wordsworth, in occasional revulsions from ugly actuality, was only escaping into the world of imagination where he, Hunt, had habitually lived.[19] Granted the possible truth of the claim, it would help to account for Hunt's rank as a poet. He was a more active and courageous publicist than his great elders and juniors, and in his personal experience of life he bore perhaps as much trouble as any of them, yet his sunny temperament seems to have banished clouds, and his writing to a large extent remained outside the world of reality.

Such a lover of the Elizabethans as Hunt should have had qualms in undertaking to re-tell the story of Hero and Leander. He made no such additions to the legend as Marlowe had, though he treated it freely enough and apparently with little thought of reproducing the antique.[20] Indeed his sense of the modernity, or the timelessness, of the tale, which dictated his style and tone, is revealed in his thinking of the star-crossed lovers as he "would of two that died last night."[21] The manner is much like that of *Rimini,* though nothing is so good or perhaps quite so bad. Such lines as "And after months of mutual admiration" and "Strained to his heart the cordial shapeliness" represent the obverse side of Hunt's attempt at unaffected ease. There is compensation in some half-Tennysonian lines like that about the crane which "Began to clang against the coming rain," or "All but the washing of the eternal seas."

The first part of *Bacchus and Ariadne,* which narrates the heroine's discovery of Theseus' desertion, is mainly adapted from the tenth epistle of the *Heroides.* Hunt softens the high-pitched rhetoric of the original into his own key of pathetic sentiment, and pleasantly amplifies Ovid's touches of nature; a happy example is the picture of Ariadne in her leafy bower, wakening out of her dreams to the chirp of birds. But if the poem has any claim upon the modern reader, it is by virtue of a long and fine bravura passage on the arrival of Bacchus and his throng. Though marred of course by bits of flat or inept phrasing, and though far inferior to Keats's Bacchic procession, it stands comparison better than most of Hunt's work because Hunt is at his best and Keats, while splendid, is merely descriptive. As for sources, Hunt would know Ovid and Catullus and other renderings in verse and prose, not to mention such paintings as Titian's and Poussin's.[22]

One cannot take leave of Hunt without quoting the finest mythological image he ever struck out, one that his greatest contemporaries might have been glad to own. In the essay "A Walk from Dulwich to Brockham" he described a bed of poppies with dark ruby cups and crowned heads, glowing with melancholy beauty in the setting sun: "They look as if they held a mystery at their hearts, like sleeping kings of Lethe."[23] Francis Thompson did not equal that.

II. *Thomas Love Peacock (1785–1866)*

Rhododaphne (1818) is an attractive if not important poem, and it partly expresses an element in Peacock which the reader of his lively prose might overlook. Though his literary career covered the first two thirds of the nineteenth century, Peacock was always an eighteenth-century aristocrat. His mellow (and sometimes belligerent) classical scholarship, his Epicurean creed, which was both gustatory and philosophic, his infinite common sense, his skeptical mockery of all forms of irrationality and "enthusiasm," these things are of the eighteenth century, and, along with his mental agility and high spirits, they give to his books their unique sanity and sparkle and tang. As a largely self-trained classic, Peacock united to more than donnish crotchets the more than donnish passion for Greek with which he endowed such fine old pagan clerics as Dr. Folliott. In temperament he was closer to Lucian than to Plato, and, like most satirists, he attacked his own age because he had visions of a better one. But he was no martyr or crusader because, again like most satirists', his visions were of the past, not of the future. Greece, however, is not a mere refuge from reality, it is reality; it is the touchstone of truth and simplicity, of rational wisdom. In the Aristophanic comedy in *Gryll Grange,* Peacock, like Spenser, makes use of Plutarch's Gryllus, the victim of Circe who preferred to retain his hoggish nature; for the man of the Renaissance such porcine contentment is an affront to the dignity of the human soul, in Peacock it expresses a resolute Tory's contempt for modern boasts of progress.[24] If Gryllus belongs to the backyard of the Pantheon, Peacock employs mythology proper, along with medieval romance, in the prose fragment *Calidore* (1816). In this fantasy, which reminds us of Heine's *The Gods in Exile,* we learn that the Olympian deities were happy in their relations with humanity until men degenerated and began to call the gods Beelzebub and Astaroth, to sigh and groan and turn up the whites of their eyes. The Nonconformist conscience, as Mr. Beerbohm would say, had made cowards of them all, and the gods, disgusted with so unpleasant a race, retired to an undisturbed island.

The harmony which soon prevailed between the Olympians and their Arthurian visitors might be taken, allegorically, as a symbol of Peacock's combination of Hellenic rationalism with a genuine romantic strain. When in *The Four Ages of Poetry* (1820) he says, "We know too that there are no Dryads in Hyde-park nor Naiads in the Regent's-canal," he is not a rationalist rejoicing in the march of mind but a romantic mourning the decay of the spirit of wonder and mystery that progress has brought about. He feels, like Arnold thirty years later, how unpoetical the age is. And at the end of his life he was not merely the "whiteheaded jolly old worldling" whom Thackeray saw. The confession of faith that he put into the mouth of Mr. Falconer may stand as essentially his own; Peacock himself, strange as it seems, was a devotee of St. Catherine. Mr. Falconer feels the need of believing in some local spiritual influence, genius or nymph, to link him with the spirit of the universe, for the world of things "is too deeply tinged with sordid vulgarity."

> There can be no intellectual power resident in a wood, where the only inscription is not *"Genio loci,"* but "Trespassers will be prosecuted"; no Naiad in a stream that turns a cotton-mill; no Oread in a mountain dell, where a railway train deposits a cargo of vandals; no Nereids or Oceanitides along the sea-shore, where a coastguard is watching for smugglers. No; the intellectual life of the material world is dead. Imagination cannot replace it. But the intercession of saints still forms a link between the visible and invisible. . . . [25]

If this complaint has a touch of elderly sentimental peevishness—like "By the Ilissus there was no Wragg, poor thing"—Peacock's fundamental attitude, like the much more philosophic Arnold's, was sincere. His half-primitive and pagan belief, or desire to believe, was the closest approach to religious sentiment that his irresponsible intelligence permitted. But while in mythological poems Keats and Shelley, with their larger vision, did not lose sight of the modern world, Peacock did in *Rhododaphne.* The critic of modernity who wrote the novels owed much to his commerce with the ancients; the Hellenism of the poem is wholly a romantic dream, a way of escape.

The fable of the seven cantos can be briefly summarized. The maiden Calliroë suffers from a strange disease, and her lover Anthemion goes to a festival in honor of Love to make an offering on her behalf. He is enthralled by the beauty and magical power of Rhododaphne. He escapes to his own home, to find Calliroë well and radiant, but when he kisses her with the lips that have been kissed by the enchantress, she swoons, apparently in death. The stricken Anthemion rushes away. He is recaptured by Rhododaphne, who passionately insists that she holds sway over all things but his heart, and she must possess it. They live together in a magic palace, until Rhododaphne is slain by Uranian Love for profaning his altars. The palace vanishes, and Anthemion awakens to find himself at home in Arcadia, with the dead Rhododaphne beside him. But Calliroë appears, alive and lovely, to be reunited with him, and to weep for the fate of the loving Rhododaphne.

Peacock's main interest was in a tale of ancient magic and mystery and beauty. His imagination was too concrete, too simply romantic, for the symbolism that Keats and Shelley instinctively found in the antique, yet he went some way in that direction. The poem commences with a differentiation of threefold love, creative, heavenly, and earthly, and at the beginning of the last canto we are reminded that "Love's first flame," Anthemion's love for Calliroë, is "of heavenly birth," while the passion between him and the enchantress is earthly. The story of a young man torn between a supernatural and a human love will have recalled Keats's *Endymion,* which appeared a few months after *Rhododaphne,* and which Peacock did not like.[26] But Peacock did not work out his parable with anything like Keats's seriousness, so that his critics have generally failed to observe that he has one. The episode of the magic palace reminds us at once of *Lamia,* and, as we have seen, Keats apparently gathered some hints from Peacock.

Rhododaphne contains, as Shelley said, "the transfused essence of Lucian, Petronius, and Apuleius," and the author's classical learning appears, unobtrusively, in and between the lines.[27] In comparison with *Endymion* and *Prometheus Unbound,* if not in an absolute sense, the poem deserves Shelley's epithets, not yet overworn, of "Greek and Pagan," although, as Shelley went on to say, the love story is more modern than the spirit and scenery. The "strong *religio loci*" is partly in the substance of the tale, and so far may be called Hellenic, and partly it is in the way of modern and nostalgic comment. The most genuine emotion in the poem is felt in the expressions of wistful regret for the passing of the infant world and its divinities:

> The life, the intellectual soul
> Of vale, and grove, and stream, has fled
> For ever with the creed sublime
> That nursed the Muse of earlier time.[28]

Peacock's classical taste is everywhere apparent, not merely in the use of local color but in the crystalline clarity, definiteness, and objectivity of his narrative method, style, and imagery. We have no vagueness or fumbling, no Keatsian lapses in taste, no beating of Shelleyan wings. That is a merit, and it belongs partly to the ancients and partly to the eighteenth century; one may say of the poem what the East India Company's officials said of the author's examination papers, "Nothing superfluous and nothing wanting." But one is compelled to add that Peacock is not struggling to utter anything of much difficulty or importance. If we happen to begin *Rhododaphne,* we yield at once to its melodious charm and the freshness of its bright water-color pictures, but we retain no memory of it, and we may forget to pick it up again; the story of human love stirs no emotion, the diablerie causes no *frisson.* If we compare the description of Rhododaphne in the moonlit grove with parallel scenes in *Christabel,* we feel at once what the former lacks, or avoids.[29] When Peacock uses the simile "like the phantom of a dream," it has in its context something of Greek externality and distinctness which is quite different from the inwardness, the suggestion of reverie, in Shelley's "As suddenly Thou comest as the memory of a dream."[30] There seem to be echoes of the poem in Shelley's work, and it was doubtless association with Shelley that kindled a genuine poetic flame from the ashes of *Palmyra* and *The Genius of the Thames.* Yet Peacock remained himself, a modern Ovid.

III. *Hartley Coleridge (1796–1849)*

Hartley Coleridge discussed mythology in a prose essay much more lucid than his father's speculations.[31] Like Jeffrey, he linked together "Keats, Cornwall, and Shelley"—and he added Wordsworth—as poets who had breathed a new life into dry bones. Like Jeffrey also, he observed that the stern, simple gods of ancient paganism had acquired "new manners, and almost new faces"; they have become tender, radiant beings allied with "the gentler parts of nature." The most eloquent bits of the essay are largely an elaboration of the mythological passages in *The Excursion* and *The Piccolomini,* both of which are quoted. In Hartley's sympathetic view Greek myth lives on, at least for poets, because of its very humanity; it once was, and may still be, the beautiful or terrible expression of man's unchanging loves and fears, his yearnings and his passions. From a gifted poet thus inclined toward the symbolic use of myth, a poet with a keen love of nature and one who went up to Oxford, as Southey said, with Greek enough for a whole college, we might expect something distinctive. If Hartley's verse on classical themes (like much of his other verse) does not seem worthy of his powers, still we have such things as the sonnets on Homer,[32] *The Vale of Tempe, Diana and Endymion,* and the fragment of a dramatic poem, *Prometheus.*

In addition to the general causes which hindered the fulfilment of Hartley's poetic promise there was the fact that, in spite of his imaginative sympathy with mythology, his heart was divided. In the first place he inherited the paternal doctrine of the finite quality of Greek anthropomorphism.[33] That idea is touched, quite beautifully, in *The Vale of Tempe,* but at least between the lines of the sonnet appears a related and more fundamental anti-mythological instinct, also paternal, the religious pietism which found such sincere and usually unpoetic expression in Hartley's later poems. For a full statement of it we may turn back to the very essay in which he celebrated the poetic possibilities of myth:

> Oh! what a faith were this, if human life indeed were but a summer's dream, and sin and sorrow but a beldame's tale, and death the fading of a rainbow, or the sinking of a breeze into quiet air; if all mankind were lovers and poets, and there were no truer pain than the first sigh of love, or the yearning after ideal beauty; if there were no dark misgivings, no obstinate questionings, no age to freeze the springs of life, and no remorse to taint them.[34]

Such words, from Hartley Coleridge, are not mere rhetoric, and some of them have a parallel in the *Prometheus* which, in ignorance of Shelley's drama, he had begun at Oxford, apparently in 1820.[35] His scholarly equipment was admirable; he translated the *Medea* in 1820 and planned a prose version of Aeschylus. For many years he hoped to finish *Prometheus,* but of course he never did, partly on account of his constitutional infirmities and partly, perhaps, because he sank under the formidable exposition of the myth which his zealous father unloaded upon him.[36] The fragment, which has something over six hundred lines, consists mainly of a dialogue between the unconquerable Prometheus and a chorus of sylphs who wish to be allowed to plead with Jupiter on his behalf. As "a lovely child, a boy divine," Jupiter had sworn to make his reign a golden age, and the sylphs had sung of it. It is their music, says Prometheus, which deludes mortals into dreaming of a new world of peace

> Where beauty feads not, love is ever true,
> And life immortal like a summer day.

How the drama would have evolved we cannot tell, but the separate "Conclusion" gives a hint:

> Mortal! fear no more,—
> The reign is past of ancient violence;
> And Jove hath sworn that time shall not
> deface,
> Nor death destroy, nor mutability
> Perplex the truth of love.

The reign of love sounds Shelleyan, though not the idea of a reformed and beneficent Jupiter.[37] Hartley may have intended something like the Aeschylean solution, or, more probably, a development of the contrast between pagan and Christian ideals. In Bagehot's judgment the poem had no Greek severity of style, no defined outline, but one may think that in general concreteness and humanity of feeling it is closer to Greek drama than most English imitations except those whose severity is indistinguishable from *rigor mortis.*[38]

IV. *Thomas Hood (1799–1845)*

Hood's arduous maturity allowed little time for classical reading, but he must have absorbed some mythological lore during his brief schooldays.[39] The poems of his which concern us are notable examples of Elizabethan influence combined with that of some moderns, especially Keats. The least happy example is *Lamia,* which is Keats's poem made over into an Elizabethan play.[40] In the charming *Plea of the Midsummer Fairies* (1827) we are reminded not only of Shakespeare but of Spenser and Marlowe, and of Keats by the rich coloring and the "hoary majesty" of Saturn.[41] The feeling that Hood here expressed for the old divinities of tree and stream[42] found further expression in the two classical narratives, *Lycus, the Centaur* (1822) and *Hero and Leander* (1827).

Both the theme and the sensuous detail of the former poem show the influence of Keats. The nymph who loves Lycus procures a charm from Circe to make him immortal, but, as she utters it and sees him becoming a horse, she breaks off in horror, and he remains a centaur. One thinks at once of the episode of Glaucus, Scylla, and Circe in the third book of *Endymion;* though Hood is concerned with the sensations of Lycus and not with humanitarian and ethical symbolism, he is closer to Keats than to Ovid.[43] Besides, as Mr. Elton remarks, *Lycus* seems to be influenced, in its slow-galloping meter, by Shelley's *Vision of the Sea,* and "perhaps also in its highly charged attempt at dreadfulness."[44] Hartley Coleridge wrote to Hood that the poem was "a work absolutely unique in its line, such as no man has written, or could have written, but yourself," and John Clare could not understand a word of it.[45] Something can be said for both opinions. The utterance of a man changed into a centaur may well be somewhat distraught and incoherent. But if Hood has the imagination, he has not the style to sustain horror and pity at the level he sometimes reaches.

Hero and Leander contains some beauties, and its faults may be less irritating than those of Hunt's version. Hood avoided direct competition with Marlowe by inventing a large part of his story. He begins with the parting of the lovers in the morning. Leander, on his way back to Abydos, encounters a sea nymph who carries him down to her home, not knowing that gratification of her love means death to him; in the hope of restoring his life she brings him up to the shore, but the body is removed by fishermen and she returns to the water. This episode occupies ninety out of the hundred and thirty stanzas; only at the end does Hood resume the original tale in describing the grief and suicide of Hero. The theme of the episode is common property—it had been used lately by Hood's friend, J. H. Reynolds, in *The Naiad* (1816), and by Hood himself in *Lycus*—but the initial hint might have come from Marlowe's lines about Neptune's pulling Leander down to the depths where sweet singing mermaids sported with their loves. Hood's poem has some clear echoes of Marlowe.[46]

There are also clear echoes of *Venus and Adonis*—not to mention the sixain stanza—and of *The Rape of Lucrece.* The nymph's invitation to love, and her efforts to revive the drowned Leander, recall Shakespeare's Venus.[47] When she sees that Leander is dead, she denounces Night in a series of conceits parallel to those of Lucrece on the same theme, and her address to Death, in the latter part of the same speech, was doubtless suggested by the tirade of Venus.[48] But no list of actual reminiscences or imitations could begin to indicate the Elizabethan quality of the rhetorical speeches, conceits, gnomic lines, and the diction generally. The poem is probably the most remarkable example in modern verse of almost complete reproduction of the narrative manner of the Elizabethan Ovidians. One cannot quite dismiss as *pastiche* what is written with the youthful freshness and spontaneity of a contemporary of Shakespeare and Marlowe. Of course there is some obvious modernity of spirit and expression—and Keats is not forgotten[49]—but in general Hood seems to see and think and feel in the Elizabethan way, and he is as unconscious as Shakespeare and Marlowe were that it is often a bad way.

V. *Thomas Lovell Beddoes (1803–49)*

That Beddoes was the last Elizabethan—more properly the last Jacobean—has long been a cliché of criticism, and the incidental mythology of the dramas recalls the main varieties of Elizabethan style. He can be soft and idyllic, in the Elizabethan-Romantic convention of his own day, though he seldom lapses into mere prettiness; he can let himself go in boyishly flamboyant rhetoric, like Marlowe and Shakespeare; or, like Donne, he can divest a decorative mythological image of its traditional glamor and give us an anti-romantic or ghoulish shock. Though Beddoes took classical prizes at school, and in later life continued to read Greek along with anatomy and German, most of his writing was decidedly "Gothic." And, for all his strange Elizabethan quality, his distinctive mythological allusions could not be mistaken for early work; whether quiet or turbid, they are of the nineteenth century. Every critic quotes these lovely lines:

> Here's the blue violet, like Pandora's eye,
> When first it darkened with immortal life.[50]

The first line might have been uttered by Perdita, but not the second. For a less serene image, take the lines on Night with giant strides stalking over the world

> Like a swart Cyclops, on its hideous front
> One round, red, thunderswollen eye ablaze.[51]

While the Elizabethans and Jacobeans loved such large personifications, there is here a modern touch of conscious composition or aggregation. Beddoes is more characteristic in his sardonic or macabre vein. It is a far cry from, say, Portia's "Peace, ho! the moon sleeps with Endymion," to Isbrand's

> That wolf-howled, witch-prayed,
> owl-sung fool,
> Fat mother moon . . . ,

or from Shakespeare's or even Hunt's Cleopatra—"The laughing queen that caught the world's great hands"—to Beddoes' lines on the queen's cracked and battered skull.[52]

In addition to many allusions, Beddoes has some poems on classical subjects, from the genial, robust, and grotesque *Silenus in Proteus* to such a romantic whimsy as the *Song of the Stygian Naiades.*[53] His most ambitious effort in that vein was *Pygmalion* (1825), which most of his critics have united in ignoring, perhaps in the belief that the author, who liked it at first, was right in looking back on it as "considerable trash."[54] In style the poem reminds one sometimes of Landor's *Hellenics,* sometimes of Keats;[55] it is at any rate not Elizabethan, unless the largely imagined and energetic conceits and the occasionally knotty texture have a parallel in Chapman. All that Beddoes retains of the Ovidian myth is the first part—how Pygmalion, scorning the women around him, made a statue and fell in love with it—and even that part is re-created; the conclusion, and the interpretation, are entirely modern. This poem is Beddoes' *Alastor* or *Endymion.* Pygmalion is a type of the lonely artist, the artist of an age of idealism, frustration, and *Weltschmerz,* whose life is apart from the world about him. The statue is so beautiful that its maker must be called divine, a giver of immortality greater than Jove, but he cannot pass the bars between his mortal self and the fragment of reality he has created. He prays that he may be spared from death and the grave, that the figure into which he has poured his soul may be endowed with life by the gods who have often wasted life "On the deformed, the hideous and the vile."[56] But the statue remains stone and the sculptor pines away; as his body dies the statue comes to life. Artist and work of art are united only in the immaterial world of eternity.[57]

As poetry, *Pygmalion* is not one of the things by which Beddoes lives, yet as a document at least it is worth something. His skeptical, disillusioned brain and soul harbored a tormenting conviction of the emptiness of life, and he searched "with avidity for every shadow of a proof or probability of an after-existence, both in the material & immaterial nature of man." Nothing else could "satisfy the claims of the oppressed on nature, satiate endless & admirable love & humanity, & quench the greediness of the spirit for existence."[58] One other passage from a letter brings us close to the specific theme of *Pygmalion:*

> Shakspeare, Dante, Milton, all who have come next to the human heart, had found no object in life to satiate the restless yearnings of their hearts & appease at the same time the fastidious cravings of their imaginations. Dissatisfaction is the lot of the poet, if it be that of any being; & therefore the gushings of the spirit, these pourings out of their innermost on imaginary topics, because there was no altar in their home worthy of the libation.[59]

And the conclusion of the last letter Beddoes wrote is the ultimate comment on *Pygmalion:* "I ought to have been among other things a good poet; Life was too great a bore on one peg & that a bad one. . . ."

These various minor writers show how ready the poetic soil was to foster the mythological seed sown by Keats and Shelley (and Wordsworth), and no one dropped more gentle rain from heaven upon it than Leigh Hunt. Besides the abundant evidence in print of these young men's interests, it is pleasant to hear of Hunt, Peacock, and Hogg on Sunday afternoons "talking of mythology, and the Greeks, and our old friends."[60] Some of these poets are original and important figures, others, like Barry Cornwall and Mrs. Shelley, only testify to the ease with which, after a fashion, the new mythological conventions could be worked. Nearly all of them showed in their writing the influence of their Elizabethan enthusiasms. With such exceptions as Hartley Coleridge and Beddoes, they generally lacked the philosophic depth and symbolic power of Keats and Shelley, and were content, like most of the Elizabethans, with decorative story-telling and picture-making. And only one, Hartley Coleridge, revealed the cleavage, apparent in his father and in Wordsworth, between Christian and pagan ideals, a cleavage which was to persist and to widen during the rest of the century.

Notes

[1] In addition to internal evidence in Wade's volumes of 1825 and 1835, see, in the latter, pp. 120-22, 234. This volume, *Mundi et Cordis,* was dedicated to Procter.

[2] *Blackwood's Magazine,* XIII (1823), 534; Richard W. Armour, *Barry Cornwall* (Boston, 1935), pp. 158-59.

[3] It was not always quite delicate, and Shelley was roused to unnecessary vehemence by Procter's imitation of *Beppo* and *Don Juan,* the pertly arch and vulgar *Gyges* (published in *A Sicilian Story,* 1820); see Shelley's *Letters,* ed. Ingpen (1914), II, 839, 847, 860. The birthmark with which Procter endows the queen,

and which he compares with that of Imogen, seems to be a reminiscence of Spenser's tale of Pastorella (*Faerie Queene,* VI. xii. 7). It is to Procter's credit as an Elizabethan student, if not as a poet, that he quotes a "moral" from the story of Gyges in Painter's *Palace of Pleasure.*

[4] *Letters of Elizabeth Barrett Browning Addressed to Richard Hengist Horne,* ed. S. R. Townshend Mayer (1877), I, 233. See Procter's retrospective words, in *The Browning Box,* ed. H. W. Donner (Oxford University Press, 1935), p. 50.

[5] *Letters,* ed. M. B. Forman (1935), p. 471.

[6] *Jeffrey's Literary Criticism,* ed. D. Nichol Smith (Oxford University Press, 1910), pp. 183-84; *Edinburgh Review,* XXXIV (1820), 206-07.

[7] Louis Landré, *Leigh Hunt* (Paris, 1936), II, 287; for a discussion of Hunt's mythological essays and sketches in prose, see II, 370 ff. M. Landré's study appeared too late to allow more than a last-minute perusal—since there comes a time when one does have to stop reading—but I am glad to find that my few pages, so far as they go, are in sufficient accord with that massive and admirable work.

[8] Edmund Blunden, *Leigh Hunt and His Circle* (1930), pp. 140-41; *Correspondence of Leigh Hunt* (1862), I, 132.

Any reader of Hunt's original verse might predict the varying degrees of success he would attain in his numerous translations—that he would be happy in rendering most of the Italians (such as Tasso's *Aminta* and Redi's *Bacco in Toscana*), the Greek pastorals and Anacreontics, and similar congenial things, and that he would be less happy with Homer. (Hunt infuriated Byron, of course, by referring, in the preface to *Foliage,* to Pope's *Iliad* as an elegant mistake in two volumes octavo; see Byron's *Letters and Journals,* IV, 238.) Perhaps the only real anomaly is Hunt's unexpectedly virile rendering of Catullus' *Attis,* done in 1810.

[9] *Autobiography of Leigh Hunt* (World's Classics ed.), p. 310.

[10] *Autobiography,* pp. 98-101, 108, 126, 138, 492.

[11] See especially the mythological papers included in the volume *A Day by the Fire,* ed. J. E. Babson (Boston, 1870). These had appeared in *The New Monthly Magazine* for 1835-36, and in other journals; see Luther A. Brewer, *My Leigh Hunt Library* (Cedar Rapids, Iowa, 1932), pp. 96, 127, 165, etc. Hunt's references to Sandys' *Ovid* in *A Day by the Fire* (pp. 195, 214) show that he used the edition of 1640, the one Keats also referred to.

[12] He refers admiringly to this passage in connection with his own poem of 1836, *Apollo and the Sunbeams* (*Poetical Works,* ed. H. S. Milford, Oxford University Press, 1923, p. 262). He had mentioned it in 1817 as the basis of Keats's myths in *I Stood Tip-toe;* see Edmund Blunden, *Leigh Hunt's "Examiner" Examined* (1928), p. 134; *Poems of John Keats,* ed. De Selincourt (1926), p. 390. Cf. Hazlitt, "On the Love of the Country" (*Works,* ed. Waller and Glover, 1902, I, 19), and Mr. C. D. Thorpe's edition of Keats (New York, 1935), pp. 56-57.

[13] "Spirit of the Ancient Mythology," *The Indicator,* January 19, 1820; *Essays. By Leigh Hunt* (Moxon, 1842); *Essays by Leigh Hunt,* ed. Arthur Symons (1888). This is one of a number of mythological pieces in prose which appeared in *The Indicator* during 1819–20.

[14] *Ibid.;* and *A Day by the Fire,* pp. 58-59.

[15] "A Popular View of the Heathen Mythology," *A Day by the Fire,* p. 59.

[16] *Works,* pp. 328-30, ll. 135 ff.; and p. 322, ll. 131-33. See *Letters of Shelley* (1914), II, 589, 909; for a report of Shelley's less favorable opinion of Hunt's work in general, see Peck, *Shelley,* II, 409. Although, or because, *The Nymphs* so much resembles the early verse of Keats, the more philosophic Keats found it inadequate; see the *Letters* (1935), pp. 16, 25-26, 96.

[17] The less common as well as the common names and functions (apart from the Nepheliads) were described in a number of books Hunt was familiar with, from Tooke's *Pantheon* (ed. 1781, pp. 223-24) and Natalis Comes, *Mythologiae,* V, xi-xii (ed. Padua, 1616, pp. 254-55), to the *Parnaso Italiano;* in this vast anthology, see, for instance, XVI, 197-98, 249, and XXIV, 194 (ed. Venice, 1784 *et seq.*). A prose analogue to the poem is Hunt's essay of 1836, "The Nymphs of Antiquity and of the Poets" (*A Day by the Fire*). A brief passage on nymphs in *Rimini* was based, Hunt says, partly on Poussin's picture of Polyphemus; see *Works,* p. 23, ll. 470 ff., and the preface to *The Story of Rimini,* 1817, p. xiii.

[18] Many years later Hunt remarked that the supernatural should not be weakly and mistakenly humanized by a poet: "His nymphs will have no taste of their woods and waters; his gods and goddesses be only so many fair or frowning ladies and gentlemen. . . ." (*Imagination and Fancy,* ed. 1870, p. 17.)

[19] *Autobiography,* pp. 492-93.

[20] In *Imagination and Fancy* (p. 122) Hunt mentions Marlowe's poem as "not comparable with his plays." In the same book (pp. 255, 263) he cites Coleridge's mythological paraphrases from Schiller, and he may

have known Schiller's *Hero und Leander.* There is some resemblance, for example, between Hunt's *Hero and Leander,* ll. 179 ff., and Schiller, ll. 65 ff. (*Werke, Säkular-Ausgabe,* I, 79), but it may be only coincidence.

[21] *Works,* p. 683.

[22] In *Sleep and Poetry,* Keats alluded to the prints on Hunt's walls, among them "several, probably, of his [Poussin's] various 'Bacchanals,' with the god and his leopard-drawn car, and groups of nymphs dancing with fauns or strewn upon the foreground to right or left" (Colvin, *John Keats,* 1917, p. 54).

[23] *The Companion. By Leigh Hunt* (1828), p. 361; *Essays,* ed. Symons, pp. 309-10; *Essays* (Everyman ed.), p. 85.

[24] *Faerie Queene,* II. xii. 86-87. See *Plutarch's Morals,* ed. W. W. Goodwin (Boston, 1878), V, 218 ff. ("That Brute Beasts Make Use of Reason").

[25] *Gryll Grange* (1861), ch. IX. See Carl Van Doren, *Life of Thomas Love Peacock* (1911), pp. 245-46; Jean-Jacques Mayoux, *Un épicurien anglais: Thomas Love Peacock* (Paris, 1933), p. 499.

[26] He complained because Keats's hero, instead of having an eternal sleep, went questing after shadows; see Peacock's *Works,* Halliford Edition, ed. H. F. B. Brett-Smith and C. E. Jones (1924-34), I, lxxxii. M. Mayoux (p. 317, note) says that to Peacock Keats would seem to have done violence to the classic ideal of repose, but Peacock's own narrative is hardly reposeful, and he was, moreover, contemptuous of *Hyperion* (*Works, loc. cit.*). In connection with Peacock's parable of love in *Rhododaphne,* M. Mayoux (p. 134) cites Shelley's *Prince Athanase.*

Peacock planned a nympholeptic tale, which "would obviously have been a second *Rhododaphne*" (Van Doren, pp. 110-11), but he gave it up on the announcement of Horace Smith's *Amarynthus, the Nympholept* (*Works,* I, lxxix).

[27] Shelley's *Letters,* II, 995; *Works,* ed. Ingpen and Peck (1926-30), VI, 273 ff. Peacock discusses these three and other ancient authorities in his preface and notes. He remarks that the song about Bacchus and the pirates in the fifth canto is based on the Homeric *Hymn to Dionysus;* see, to cite the most accessible edition, pp. 137 and 205 in *The Misfortunes of Elphin and Rhododaphne,* ed. G. Saintsbury (London, 1927). In the opening of the sixth canto Peacock paraphrases at length the reflections in Petronius (*Satyricon,* cxv) on a man lost at sea and the vicissitudes of human life (cf. the first section of Taylor's *Holy Dying*). A sentence from this passage of Petronius is the motto for the tenth chapter of *Gryll Grange.*

I cannot claim a close acquaintance with Peacock's beloved Nonnus—probably he did not wish that anyone should—but his animated description of Bacchic revels (p. 239), though the theme was stereotyped, may owe something to the *Dionysiaca,* xxii. I ff.; and see his reference to the twelfth book in a letter to Shelley (*Works,* VIII, 203). Magic palaces are also somewhat stereotyped, and Rhododaphne's apparently includes items from those of Alcinous (*Od.* vii. 100-02) and Psyche (*Rhododaphne,* canto vi, pp. 222, 225). For an account of similar palaces and gardens in Nonnus, see Lewis P. Chamberlayne, "A Study of Nonnus," *S.P.,* XIII (1916), 63-65. The transformation of a pirate crew into animals who prowl around the gardens (canto vii, p. 234) is an obvious reminiscence of Circe (*Od.* x. 212 ff.). The picture of Rhododaphne hurling the javelin (canto vii, p. 240) embodies some lines from Peacock's unpublished version of the dialogue *Phaedra and Nurse,* from Euripides (*Works,* VII, 413, 442).

[28] Canto iii, ll. I ff., and iv. 13 ff. Part of the former passage was quoted by Poe, who found the poem "brimfull of music"; see his *Works,* ed. E. C. Stedman and G. E. Woodberry (New York, 1914), VII, 314.

[29] *Rhododaphne,* canto iii; *Christabel,* ll. 58 ff., 279 ff.

[30] *Rhododaphne,* canto ii, l. 17; *Prometheus Unbound,* II. i. 7-8. Cf. also Peacock's lines on love, which rhyme "ocean" and "emotion" (canto vii, ed. Saintsbury, p. 245), and Shelley's use of the words and idea (*P.U.,* IV. 96-98). The second stanza of the *Hymn of Pan* seems to have echoes of Peacock's "Down Pindus' steep . . ." (canto iii, p. 176); see *Works of Shelley,* ed. Ingpen and Peck, IV, 402, and the opening of Shelley's review of *Rhododaphne.* For possible echoes in *Adonais,* see Peck, *Shelley,* II, 221, note 11 (and also I, 426, note 71).

[31] "On the Poetical Use of the Heathen Mythology," *London Magazine,* February, 1822, pp. 113 ff.; reprinted in *Essays and Marginalia,* ed. Derwent Coleridge (1851), I, 18 ff. The essay gave much pleasure to the Wordsworths (*Letters of the Wordsworth Family,* ed. Knight, II, 173).

[32] *Poems,* ed. Derwent Coleridge (1851), I, 144, II, 16. While Hartley's father, Wordsworth, and Southey "all leant to the Wolfian, or, as my brother called it, Wolfish and Heinous (Heyne) hypothesis respecting the origin of the Homeric poems, Hartley was always a stout and vehement upholder of the orthodox opinion" (*ibid.,* I, clvi). He said he had witnessed the Trojan war, being then "an insect which in these days is nameless," that took refuge in Helen's hair (Earl L. Griggs, *Hartley Coleridge,* University of London Press, 1929, p. 168).

[33] See *Essays,* I, 37; *Poems,* I, 37, 162, II, 212; Herbert Hartman, *Hartley Coleridge* (Oxford University Press, 1931), pp. 109-10.

[34] Cf. *Poems,* I, 117, and a piece in lighter vein, I, 152.

[35] See *Poems,* I, xciii, II, 280; Griggs, p. 93; Hartman, p. 81.

[36] That is, the lecture on the *Prometheus* of Aeschylus mentioned at the beginning of my second chapter. See *Unpublished Letters of Samuel Taylor Coleridge,* ed. E. L. Griggs (1932), II, 281, 336; and Derwent Coleridge's summary of the relevant part of the lecture (*Poems,* II, 282).

Apart from echoes of Aeschylus' Promethean drama in Hartley's poem, compare *Agam.,* ll. 717 ff., and *Poems,* II, 301; *Paradise Regained,* ii. 178 ff., and *Poems,* II, 295.

[37] Richard Garnett said that "although his brother attributes it to an earlier period, it is plainly composed under the influence of Shelley" (*D.N.B.* [*Dictionary of National Biography*]). Allowing for the identity of the fables, I do not think the internal evidence is so plain.

[38] See Bagehot's *Literary Studies* (Everyman ed.), I, 64. A reviewer in *Fraser's Magazine* (XLIII [1851], 611) complained, not quite justly, that the theme required an Aeschylus, not a Theocritus.

[39] See *The Irish Schoolmaster,* stanzas 22-23 (*Poetical Works of Thomas Hood,* ed. Walter Jerrold, Oxford University Press, 1920, pp. 64-65).

[40] The date of composition is uncertain; see my Appendix, under 1822. The allusion to the poor maiden that adored Apollo (i. 27; *Works,* p. 675) suggests *The Girl of Provence,* by Hood's friend Procter, which appeared in *The Flood of Thessaly* (1823), though the story was well known.

[41] For Spenser and Marlowe, see stanzas cxii and lx. While Saturn is altered to suit a fanciful poem, such stanzas as lxiii-lxv, including the borrowed phrase, recall *Hyperion* (cf. i. 59 in particular). Keats's general influence on Hood was discussed, rather inadequately, by Federico Olivero, in *M.L.N.* [*Modern Language Notes*], XXVIII (1913), 233-35.

[42] P. 116, st. xxiv.

[43] Cf. the myth of Cronus and Philyra in Apollonius Rhodius, *Argonautica,* ii. 1231 ff. Keats's *Lamia* is remembered in *Lycus,* ll. 56-57, and probably the first line of *Endymion* in ll. 154-55.

[44] *Survey of English Literature, 1780–1880* (1920), II, 288.

[45] Walter Jerrold, *Thomas Hood: His Life and Times* (New York, 1909), p. 197.

[46] E.g., Hood, ll. 403 ff., Marlowe, i. 347-48; Hood, ll. 493 ff., Marlowe, i. 375-76.

[47] See especially Hood, ll. 447-48, and Shakespeare, ll. 1127-28. In *Bianca's Dream* (*Works,* p. 76, l. 233) there is an acknowledged echo (see l. 234) of Shakespeare, l. 231.

[48] Hood, ll. 499 ff.; *Lucrece,* ll. 764 ff.; *Venus and Adonis,* ll. 931 ff. Hood doubtless knew the original of Lucrece's declamation on Night, *Faerie Queene,* III. iv. 55 ff. Hood's detailed description of the attitudes of the people watching the nymph (ll. 667 ff.) appears to be an imitation of Lucrece's account of the painting of Trojan scenes.

[49] For probable or possible echoes, see Hood, ll. 226-28, and *Isabella,* st. xxxiv; Hood, ll. 269-70, and Keats's sonnet on Leander (cf. Hood's sonnet and a comic piece on Hero and Leander, *Works,* pp. 194, 436); Hood, l. 376, and *Eve of St. Agnes,* st. xxxiii-xxxv; Hood, l. 620, and *Lamia,* i. 8.

[50] *The Brides' Tragedy* (1822), I. 1 (*Works,* ed. H. W. Donner, Oxford University Press, 1935, p. 174; ed. Gosse, 1928, II, 406).

[51] *Ibid.,* III. iii (Donner, p. 204; Gosse, II, 442-43).

[52] *Death's Jest-Book,* III. iii and V. iv (Donner, pp. 423, 479-80; Gosse, I, 184, 246). In Isbrand's lyric on Harpagus and Astyages, which has nothing lyrical but the meter, a sufficiently grim incident from Herodotus (i. 119) is elaborated with gruesomely jocular details (Donner, pp. 90, 466; Gosse, I, 230).

[53] Donner, pp. 136-37; Gosse, II, 375, 398.

[54] A letter of 1837 (Donner, pp. 662, 664; Gosse, I, 103, 105). For the poem, see Donner, pp. 78-83; Gosse, II, 346-52.

[55] Kelsall spoke of the "peculiar fascination" Keats had for Beddoes, and found "traces" of his influence in *Pygmalion,* "the sole instance of a direct impress from another mind, in the whole compass" of his friend's poetry; see his edition of the *Poems* (1851), pp. xxii-xxiii. Cf. Kelsall's letter of 1869, in *The Browning Box,* ed. H. W. Donner (Oxford University Press, 1935), pp. 85-86.

[56] In a letter of August 25, 1824, Beddoes wrote of Shelley: "What would he not have done, if ten years more, that will be wasted upon the lives of unprofitable knaves and fools, had been given to him" (Donner, p. 590; Gosse, I, 18).

[57] Though Beddoes went much beyond Rousseau's "Pygmalion," I think he owed somewhat more to it than

Mr. Donner admits. See Rousseau's *Œuvres complètes* (Paris, 1870-74), V, 232-36; Donner, pp. 601, 754, and his *Thomas Lovell Beddoes: The Making of a Poet* (Oxford, 1935), p. 174. Leigh Hunt, in his version of Rousseau's work, remarked that the author "was a kind of Pygmalion himself, disgusted with the world, and perpetually yet hopelessly endeavouring to realize the dreams of his imagination" (*The Indicator,* May 10, 1820, pp. 241 ff.). Compare Beddoes' "Translation of the Philosophic Letters of Schiller," published in 1825 (Donner, pp. 549 ff.).

[58] A letter of April 20, 1827 (Donner, p. 630; Gosse, I, 64-65). For this question as a motive in his medical studies see Donner, *Thomas Lovell Beddoes,* p. 187.

[59] October 21, 1827 (Donner, p. 635; Gosse, I, 71).

[60] Blunden, *Leigh Hunt and His Circle,* p. 139; *Correspondence of Leigh Hunt* (1862), I, 129 (March 9, 1819).

Bibliography

Edmund Blunden, "Leigh Hunt." *T.L.S.* [*London Times Literary Supplement*], November 16, 1922, pp. 733-34; reprinted, as "Leigh Hunt's Poetry," in *Votive Tablets* (1931), pp. 205-18.

Leigh Hunt, *A Day by the Fire; And Other Papers, Hitherto Uncollected,* ed. J. E. B[abson]. Boston, 1870.

Louis Landré, *Leigh Hunt (1784–1859): Contribution à l'histoire du romantisme anglais.* Paris, 1936.

Jean-Jacques Mayoux, *Un épicurien anglais: Thomas Love Peacock.* Paris, 1933.

Grete Moldauer, *Thomas Lovell Beddoes. Wiener Beiträge,* LII (1924).

Federico Olivero, "Hood and Keats." *M.L.N.* [*Modern Language Notes*], XXVIII (1913), 233-35.

Proserpine and Midas: Two unpublished Mythological Dramas by Mary Shelley, ed. A. Koszul. Oxford University Press, 1922.

Edward B. Hungerford (essay date 1941)

SOURCE: "Myths and Mythagogues," in *Shores of Darkness,* Columbia University Press, 1941, pp. 3-34.

[*In the following excerpt, Hungerford discusses the ways in which Greek mythology was researched and presented in the eighteenth through the early nineteenth century. The critic argues that nineteenth-century poets were influenced not only by the Euhemeristic and rationalistic treatments of mythology—which attempted to explain myths as covers for historical fact—but also by the works of "speculative mythologists," in which "new modes of treating the myths" were propounded.*]

Whoever has read carefully the mythological poems of the early decades of the nineteenth century has been aware of dead presences among them, of vague and nameless influences so remote and shapeless that the mind can scarcely define them. These spectres are no imaginary ones. They are ghosts indeed—the ghosts of a forgotten generation of men who once spoke of each other respectfully as "the learned," of men who believed that by the evidences of elephants' bones, the skeletons of giants, the roots of Greek verbs, Phoenician place names, Druids, and gods, they had traced man and his society and his religion to a pristine time—not more than a very few thousand years ago—when all was in a state of fresh wonder and men walked with God. These men were the speculative mythologists of the latter half of the eighteenth century and of the early years of the nineteenth. They rose quickly from obscurity and plunged so completely into oblivion that they have left scarcely an acknowledged trace upon intellectual history. Yet their pallid and disembodied shades walk with the living poets, like the unburied dead of ancient times who, for the want of a handful of dust thrown upon their bodies, could not descend to the abode of the dead. This chapter shall be that handful of dust which will give them decent burial.

My attention was first attracted toward these speculative mythologists by noticing that in the more ambitious mythological poetry of the early nineteenth century there were unusual departures from conventional myth which were certainly not authorized by classical mythology but which did not seem to be wholly inventions. A case in point is Keats's picture of the Titaness Asia in *Hyperion.* Instead of having Asia born of the usual mythological personifications which provided the Titans with parents in Greek myth, Keats names the father of his Titaness as Caf. No such figure, of course, appears in classical myth. In the *Oriental Library* of Herbelot some legends respecting a mountain named Caf are preserved, and William Beckford knew about them when he wrote *Vathek;* but Herbelot's legends do not explain Keats's use of the name. When I encountered the mythological speculations of Jean Sylvain Bailly, however, the allusion was made clear. Bailly had conceived a remarkable theory concerning the descent of culture, in which he imagined a prehistoric Atlantean people to have existed for many centuries in the region of Caf in the Caucasus Mountains. From this giant race, Asiatic culture had taken its origin. Keats, as I shall later point out in more detail, had seized hold of the picturesque theory and employed it as a means of prophesying the rise of Asiatic culture. The circumstance throws considerable light upon his plans for the story of *Hyperion,* and indicates that not merely classical mythology but contemporary speculations upon mythology found a place in the poetry which he based upon classical fable.

Others of the poets were reading not merely the classical authors and the mythological handbooks based upon them, but the highly speculative treatises whose brief vogue I shall describe. Blake in particular was affected by them so much that they constitute a kind of revelation of the world in which his imagination was operating, and it is worth reflecting that, in his poetry and in that of many other poets, ideas which seem mystical and scraps of erudition which seem profound may have been caught up from no more dignified source than Hancarville's ridiculous *Researches* or Wilford's "An Essay on the Sacred Isles in the West."

Who were these "speculative mythologists?" Most of them were men now so completely forgotten that the repetition of their names will not wake many echoes in the mind of the modern reader. The Abbés Pluche and Banier, Dom Antoine Pernety, Court de Gebelin, Charles François Dupuis, Jacob Bryant, Jean Sylvain Bailly, Hancarville, Francis Wilford, Georg Friedrich Creuzer, George Faber, Colonel Vallancey—these are but a few of the legion who made mythology their province. Most of them are too inconsequential to mention. The names of a truly imposing number are embedded in the list of "authorities" which Charles Anthon attached to his great mythological dictionary, and there I shall leave most of them. To review them all in detail might reveal a number of minute particulars in which they had exerted an influence upon the poets, but these "minute particulars," of which William Blake was so fond of speaking, would in the bulk be trivial compared to certain general tendencies in which their influence was most felt. At a time when the conventional myths had become too shopworn for literary fashion, the imaginative and exciting speculations of "the learned" introduced new modes of treating the myths.

It is a curious fact that the Greek Renaissance of the eighteenth and early nineteenth centuries did not express itself in literature as in the other arts. For a period of about seventy-five years, beginning near the middle of the eighteenth century with the excavations at Herculaneum and the publications of Winckelmann and subsiding with the setting up of the Elgin marbles in England and the revolution in Greece, there flourished an intense interest in the classical "antique." The diverse impulses of this latter Renaissance had a common denominator, the influence upon European taste not of a Greece preserved in books, but of an extant Greece surviving in the land itself and in its physical monuments. The fever of archaeological recovery burned high, and the contagion of a new classicism spread even to Russia and America. Never wholly Greek in character, the new classicism nevertheless shook off the rich adornment of the Renaissance and betook itself to what it regarded as a "purer" antique style. There emerged distinguishable styles in architecture, in sculpture, in painting, and in the arts of decoration. But the prevailing influences did not operate in literature in quite the same fashion as in the other arts. Keats's *Ode on a Grecian Urn* and the brief poems of André Chénier, true reflections of the Graeco-Roman taste of the era, did not strike the dominant note in poetry.

The truth of the matter is that men of letters from Dr. Johnson to William Blake had tired of the ancients as a too constant literary theme. The mythology of Greece and Rome had been so steadily exploited ever since the early Renaissance that its freshness as literary material had disappeared. The mythological theme had degenerated into its worst absurdity in the opera, and as Dr. Johnson pointed out, the mythological allusion had too often exhausted itself in puerilities. Mythological allusions were usually, he found, absurd, inappropriate, and dull. Reflecting the weariness of contemporary taste, Johnson resented the intrusion of "heathen fable" in poems dealing with religious themes, and modern attempts to revive mythological stories he regarded as properly doomed to neglect. Writing of Rowe's *Ulysses,* he observed shrewdly: "We have been too early acquainted with the poetical heroes to expect any pleasure from their revival: to shew them as they have already been shewn is to disgust by repetition; to give them new qualities or new adventures is to offend by violating received notions."

Laodamia, Endymion, Adonis, Albion, Prometheus, Helen, and Hyperion might well have been doomed, despite the ever-increasing Greek gusto, to the neglect which Dr. Johnson predicted for them had it not been that the study of mythology took a remarkable turn which was to fasten the minds of the poets upon it again as a new and different material.

After the early Renaissance the study of mythology had taken a fairly pedestrian course. At first books on mythology were concerned primarily with making an adjustment of fables which was satisfactory to the teachings of the Christian faith and the authority of the Bible, and secondly with providing a ready means for the acquisition of that intimate knowledge of the gods and heroes which superficially distinguished the lettered from the unlettered. But with the rise of an independent spirit of inquiry, mythologists followed the increasing rationalism of scientific thought in imposing systems upon inchoate knowledge, and throughout the latter seventeenth and early eighteenth centuries there appeared a wide diversity of treatises upon myth, each with a special theory to plead. When in 1765 the Chevalier de Jaucourt endeavored to survey for Diderot's *Encyclopédie* the great body of this

The Parthenon, temple of the Greek goddess Athena, on the Acropolis of Athens, Greece.

literature, he was forced to declare: "Each man has uncovered in myth what his own particular genius and the plan of his studies have led him to look for. The physician finds by allegory the mysteries of nature; the political scientist, the refinements of the wisdom of government; the philosopher, the most beautiful morals; the chemist, the secrets of his art. Each has regarded fable as a country to be invaded, where he has believed that he had the right to make expeditions conforming to his taste and to his interests."

The spirit of this literature was for the most part Euhemeristic or rationalistic; that is, it was concerned to demonstrate that the myths were covers for some historical or natural facts. Thus the Cyclops were lighthouse builders, and their one eye was the beacon. Endymion was an early astronomer who observed the courses of the moon. Neither of these schools of interpretation was particularly stimulating to the poetic imagination, but both were to evolve in directions which eventually provided the strongest sort of stimulation.

The Euhemerists were attempting to resolve myth into the corrupted record of historical fact, explaining the gods and heroes as having had an actual human origin. This was no modern form of mythological interpretation, for the Euhemerists were followers of an ancient mythographer, Euhemerus, whose work has survived only in fragments. But the motive of modern Euhemerism was different from that of the ancient world. Modern Euhemerism commenced with the effort to explain the myths of antiquity as corrupted records of persons and events mentioned in the Old Testament. It is no accident that old Samuel Bochart, the most celebrated and most eccentric of seventeenth-century mythologists, commenced his studies in the field by lectures designed to support the authority of the book of Genesis. But a study which commenced with the effort to explain the myths of the ancient world as corruptions of facts recorded in the Bible ended in the eighteenth century by questioning whether the events recorded in the Bible were not merely myths. Bochart's original effort to turn the gods into patriarchs resulted in turning the patriarchs into myths. Hence the suspicion with which mythology came to be regarded, and the unexpected alliances which we find between the mythologists and liberal thinkers who were advancing in various directions. Just as it was no accident that Bochart's speculations began with his lectures on the book of Genesis, so it was no accident that the unreligious Bailly formulated his Euhemeristic system in a set of letters to Voltaire.

What happened was this: Whether men were disposed to defend or to attack the authority of the Bible, the way was opened for a new consideration of all the evidences bearing on the earliest history of man, and in this study the mythologist assumed a position of unaccustomed and unexpected authority. Hence the excitement which greeted the rapid succession of new and, from a modern point of view, preposterous systems embracing theories of the origin and dissemination of culture, such as those of Bryant, Bailly, Davies, and Wilford. It is difficult for the modern mind to realize how central a position the mythologist assumed for a brief period in scientific inquiry, or to believe that men like Bailly could receive the approbation of such bodies as the Academy in France or that Wilford's effusions could be received with profound attention by sober men like Sir William Jones, president of the Asiatic Society. Shortly after the beginning of the nineteenth century "evidences" had accumulated in such great quantity that the theories of what we may now think of as a lunatic fringe of mythologists were swept into oblivion. The statement of Grimm's Law took linguistic science out of the hands of amateurs, and it was no longer possible to speculate wildly about the Phoenician origin of the Celts or the British origin of the Hindus. Evidences as to the antiquity of human society ended efforts to trace all civilizations to the scattering of the peoples after the destruction of the tower of Babel or to describe society in such simple terms as ante- and postdiluvian. Knowledge of the immense antiquity of the earth itself made the oldest myths seem recent. And the Darwinian theory of an upward evolution disposed forever of the widely held belief that society and man himself had degenerated from a Golden Age in which the first institutions of God had been perfect and those which we now possess are, as Volney described them, mere ruins.

The Euhemerism of the middle of the eighteenth century had led, by the beginning of the nineteenth, to a situation in which the mythologist exercised authority over speculation relating to the origin of culture. At the same time, mythology had been advancing in another direction. The fashion of the middle of the eighteenth century had been both Euhemeristic and rationalistic. From the efforts to explain myth in rational terms arose that diversity of special systems of which the Chevalier de Jaucourt complained. No matter how cogently each specialist pleaded his cause, it was apparent that not every system could be correct. Common to each was the everpresent conviction that the myths rested upon some natural fact, and gradually, without controversy, the doctrine that the myths were embodiments of natural phenomena gained ground. The most interesting development in this direction began in France with Hancarville's theory that most of the myths were merely variants of each other and that basically they were allegories of the procreative powers. The detection of sexual symbolism in the myths became fashionable; in England the work of Richard Payne Knight, who developed Hancarville's theories, caused a suppressed scandal. A development from the new form of speculation was the unsavory recognition of survivals of sexual symbolism in still revered religious forms, and adherents of nature myth found themselves under suspicion as antireligionists. Less preoccupied with sex was another school of symbolists who discovered in myth the primitive language of men who had attempted to express in symbolic language their awe before the face of unknown powers. The increasing recognition, as the study of comparative mythology developed, that the natural language of the myths of one country was common to all, led even to the assumption that in primitive times men had been in a direct relationship to God and that the myths contained a vague but high theosophic knowledge communicated directly in pristine revelation. In Germany it was the mystical feature of the new symbolism which became most significant. The mystic revelation, clothed in the symbols of ancient myth, was of the same character as the mystery of Christianity. The symbolists supported the new movement toward Catholicism in Germany. Voss attacked savagely on this ground. Symbolism became the foe of Protestantism, at least in Voss's attack upon Heyne, Hermann, and Creuzer. Even the moderate Keightley in England pointed out that if the symbolists were right, Christianity became unnecessary.

The Euhemerism and rationalism which prevailed at the middle of the eighteenth century had provided little to stimulate the imagination of the poets. But the subsequent developments, which I have perhaps too hastily surveyed, were of a far different sort. In these was matter for the poetic mind to take hold of. The study of mythology ceased to be, for the poets, merely the instrument of a polite and conventional erudition. It became, indeed, a new sphere in which each, according to his capacities and disposition, could operate. From the eccentric systems of Wilford and Davies it was but a step to that of Blake, and if Blake chose to metamorphose the nebulous figures of mythological personages into equally nebulous figures of his visions, the contemporary reader would at least have recognized the misty region in which he trod. If a mythical Arthur faded into the outlines of an equally mythical Albion, there was little to be astonished at, and Los and Urizen were no more implausible than Bryant's Noah and Bailly's Atlas. Compared to the wild fancies of George Faber and Colonel Vallancey, Blake's work was that of a rigidly disciplined scientist.

To men like Shelley, who had grown mistrustful of what they regarded as the hypocrisy of conventional religion, myth became a new language in which the essential religious truths could be reëxpressed. To the poets of England as to the symbolists of Germany, myth was the vehicle of religious utterance. It was no accident that when Blake and Shelley desired to give utterance to the yearning for a regeneration of mankind through love neither chose the figure of Christ for the sufferer and the redeemer; the one took the figure of Albion who should awake from his sleep, and the other the figure of Prometheus tortured upon his rock. Even the young John Keats strove to instill into his *Endymion* an aspiration of the soul for some higher good; if he failed to give the poem a convincing spiritual meaning, it was the fault of his youth, not of his desire.

Those mythologists who had attempted to trace, by their tenuous "evidences," the origin of the races had felt that they had made important and exciting discoveries. They had gazed with a wild surmise upon the Golden Age, and they trembled with the excitement of the explorer. To the poets they communicated not so much their wild surmises as their exhilaration. Blake's visions took him to the origin of things. He saw the giants of antediluvian creation, and he moved backwards in time through the epochs which had preceded man. Shelley and Keats lived in a world of myth, and Goethe drew the vanished beauty of the age of myth down through the centuries with Helena. Shelley conceived the primordial Demogorgon, and his imagination dwelt upon the age when Prometheus brought down the gift of fire. Keats's Endymion was of a generation before the heroes, and Hyperion drove his orb of fire to light a world of elementary forms. Mythologist and poet alike shared the mystery of the remote and the original. As Creuzer, the most mystic of the scholars, declared that the mythologist must have the mind of a poet, so the poet found himself at home in the realm of the mythologist.

If the intellectual interpretations of myth in the eighteenth century had given the poet little stimulation, such was no longer the case. In the poetry of Keats the new nature myth found an inspired utterance. No poet was more skillful than Keats in merging the personages of his mythological poems with the elements which they represent. The most beautiful passages of *Endymion* are of this sort. Sleep (Hypnos), Ocean, the rivers Alpheus and Arethusa are magical translations of personages into natural forms. In *Hyperion* the manner in which the older myth of the sun dies into the rising splendor of Apollo is infinitely subtle and beautiful. Brilliant also is the ingenious manner in which Keats was shaping Enceladus to represent—as he must eventually, had the poem been completed—the volcanic eruptions of Mount Aetna.

Shelley's complex and mercurial mind asserted itself in another direction. Capable of dealing with intricate moral and intellectual allegories, Shelley seized hold of Hancarville and Knight's thesis of the double symbol in myth of the generative powers of nature. The ingenuity with which he applied this theory to his poetic conception of Adonais and Urania, sustaining the allegory in terms applicable to the quickening influence of the poet Keats, gave his peculiar stamp to a mythographical fashion. The immense failure of Goethe's *Second Part of Faust* came from the superabundant diversity of subtle allegories which he attempted to apply to an incongruous mythological theme.

One of the notable influences of the new mythology upon the poets was the growth of interest in very obscure mythological documents containing unconventional variants of the myths. Dr. Johnson's prediction that to give the poetical heroes new qualities or new adventures would offend by violating received notions was met in a curious fashion.

In the effort to foist new theories upon an overworked mass of mythology, each expounder of a new system had to present fresh evidences. The result was a thorough but uncritical exploration of a vast number of doubtful "authorities." Homer, Hesiod, Vergil, and Ovid gave way before a host of minor personages and unfamiliar variants of well-known legends. Recondite notions buried in the most obscure of writings became more important than the usual and the well known. Early Greek logographers and late Byzantine poets, reputed Babylonian priests and nameless mediaeval scholiasts—these became the authorities whose alleged knowledge was cited in support of new theories. In the footnotes of "the learned," Euhemerus, Philo of Biblis, Sanchuniathon, and even the pseudo-Berotus awoke to a brief second life. One encounters names which only the very doughtiest has met upon the verges of bibliography—names like Dionysius Skytobrachion—he of the leather arm—revived for his account of the Atlanteans. Pherecydes, Harpocration, Sallust the Gaul surnamed the Philosopher, Ptolemy Chennus, Antoninus Liberalis—these are names as remote from the course of things as the dwellings of the Cimmerians or Homer's Ethiopians. Minor writers on mythological topics, such as Conon, Parthenius, Hyginus, Heraclides of Pontus, Cornutus (or Phurnutus), Fulgentius, Apollodorus the

Athenian, Palaephatus, even the doubtful, but certainly mediaeval, Albricus, became familiar names. Obscure writers on special subjects became fashionable, such as the astronomical writers Eratosthenes, Aratus, Manilius, and the pseudo-Hyginus. Poets as little read today as the pompous Tzetzes, the dull Nonnus, and the obscure Lykophron assumed a place among the sons of light. Even Theodontius, whom Boccaccio mentioned and perhaps invented, was revived, and with him that Pronapides, the tutor of Homer, from whom Theodontius received much valuable information, but whose works, unhappily, have perished.

The great Winckelmann once declared that the Greeks had one vanity the less, the vanity of knowing many books. From that modern vanity the Romantic poets were not exempted. Since the works of the mythologists bristled with the names of obscure authors, it is not surprising to find that the poets followed them in their erudite excursions. The insipidity and banality of mythological material was corrected by novelty. The vigorous research of the mythologists out from the conventional into the adumbral regions of myth drew new facts and new ideas from the shadows. Freshness of theme became possible by developing unusual variants of old legends, and worn classical figures were reinvigorated by unfamiliar circumstance.

Thus the theme of Keats's *Hyperion* was intended to turn, as I shall point out later, on an obscure circumstance hinted by Procopius and Tzetzes. The action concerning Demogorgon in Shelley's *Prometheus Unbound* rests upon traditions preserved by the doubtful Theodontius, who had them from who knows what sources—from that mythical Pronapides, from Conradus de Mure, from Janibiceps (whom Conrad cites but about whom nothing else is preserved but his astonishing name) and from the nameless scholiasts upon Lucan and Statius. In his *Achilleis* Goethe was plotting merely a single part of his action by putting together hints from a fragment of the Cyprian poems preserved by Proclus, a prophecy reported by Lykophron in the *Alexandra,* another from Quintus Smyrnaeus, a story in Pausanias, and an unusual and otherwise unrecorded piece of information in Ptolemy Chennus.

Even the most unostentatious of the poets drew, in matters pertaining to classical myth, upon circumstances far outside the limits of information which the ordinarily well-read man might be expected to possess. Thus a stanza of Wordsworth's *Laodamia* seems to have been suggested by a passage in Tzetzes' *Antehomerica.* Several of the Titans in Keats's *Hyperion* stepped from the pages of Hyginus. Keats's friend Woodhouse speaks of "the very dark hints in the mythological poets of Greece and Rome" which went into the making of *Hyperion.* Shelley turned a whole scene in *Prometheus Unbound* upon a trivial piece of information contained in a scholium upon Aristophanes. The classical erudition necessary to design Goethe's plans for the activities of the Thessalian witches in the *Second Part of Faust* is bewilderingly minute. In one case—in his choice of Manto—the identification as a Thessalian sibyl rests only upon an insignificant notice by Suidas.

There was, perhaps, an element of vanity involved in the display of the most minute classical erudition. When Byron confessed to reading Diodorus Siculus in preparation for writing *Sardanapalus,* he explained that it was merely to refresh his memory, as he had long been familiar with the story. Goethe's humor in the Classical Walpurgis Night and in the reproaches leveled against the character of Helen of Troy depends upon such out-of-the-way information as to make one suspect that the poet was deliberately puzzling and confounding the learned among his readers. But there was more than vanity involved. The poets had invented a new kind of pleasure. The thing was to take the most daring liberties with the received notion of well-known myths and yet not really depart from the authority of ancient texts. There was a challenge to the reader to detect that the writer had kept his fable within authorized limits. The critic who failed to discern might easily make a fool of himself. Shelley, for instance, could have cited reputable authority for every circumstance of his barely discernible identification of the cave of Prometheus with Colonus. Novelty was combined with authority, and the learned reader might have the additional pleasure of perceiving the deft manner in which a new turn to a mythological fable had been executed upon an old fact. Much of the action of the last book of *Endymion* depends upon a story recorded briefly in one of the fragments of a mainly lost work of Hesiod, a story amplified by a scholiast upon Apollonius of Rhodes. The reader's pleasure was intended to be increased by perceiving that although the story had departed far from the well-known story concerning Endymion, it was yet operating within limits allowed by the Hesiodic story. The extraordinary flights of Euphorion in the *Second Part of Faust* are quite puzzling unless one has turned to Ptolemy Chennus to discover that Helen's child was born with wings. . . .

Alex Zwerdling (essay date 1964)

SOURCE: "The Mythographers and the Romantic Revival of Greek Myth," in *PMLA,* Vol. LXXIX, No. 4, September, 1964, pp. 447-56.

[*In this essay, Zwerdling surveys the changing attitude toward Greek mythology from the eighteenth century through the early nineteenth century, noting that the Romantic poets contributed to the popularization of Greek myth, as did the mythographers of the eighteenth century.*]

That the English Romantic poets were much more seriously interested in Greek myth, both in itself and as a subject for poetry, than their eighteenth-century predecessors hardly requires demonstration.[1] The divergence may be suggested, admittedly in somewhat exaggerated form, by juxtaposing two quotations: Addison (in *Spectator* 523) congratulates a new poet because he "had not amused himself with Fables out of the Pagan Theology," unlike the fashionable poetasters who filled their works with the exploits of river gods; and Keats hopes (in the Preface to *Endymion*) that he had "not in too late a day touched the beautiful mythology of Greece, and dulled its brightness." The poet who uses the "pagan fables," Addison suggests, can only be amusing himself; while for Keats those fables have become "the beautiful mythology of Greece," which the poet scarcely feels himself worthy to touch.

Such a considerable shift in attitude, in "tone," is usually gradual and not exclusively the work of great minds. This is not to minimize the importance of the Keatses and the Wordsworths of any generation, but to acknowledge the fact that the new ideas of such men are frequently the complex products of controversies which only the historian can now trace. Such a controversy is recorded in the writings of those who, in the eighteenth and early nineteenth centuries, would have been considered the authorities on the subject: the mythographers.

The disrepute into which Greek myth had fallen by the eighteenth century did not of course extend to classical literature itself, and this presented something of a problem. How was one to read Homer and Virgil intelligently without knowing a good deal about the "Pagan Theology"? This need for adequate works of reference was filled by the "Pantheons" of the mythographers, factual and interpretative books on classical mythology primarily designed to help the modern reader who had only a limited familiarity with the writings of the ancients. Such handbooks were very popular in England, clearly indispensable in the schools, and an essential item in any good private library. The work of such mythographers, as may be imagined, is hardly likely to be very radical, and yet books like these create the taste of their times at least as much as they reflect it. The break with tradition which we find in a writer like Keats is made easier by the gradual transformation of the tradition itself by lesser minds moving, however clumsily, in the same direction. It is important to see the way in which Greek mythology was brought back into repute towards the end of the eighteenth century if we want to understand how one gets, so to speak, from Addison to Keats.

The mythographers of the eighteenth century were carrying on a medieval and renaissance tradition of commentary on classical myth which is discussed at length in Jean Seznec's *Survival of the Pagan Gods.* In continuing that tradition, these writers were still concerned with the problem of how to make pagan "idolatry" palatable to a Christian audience. For the uneasiness with which most commentators approached Greek myth in these later centuries suggests that the problem was still very real and that the two religions were to a significant extent still considered "rivals." The general attitude toward Greek myth in eighteenth-century England may be seen as the product of several opposing forces: a poetic tradition which had become largely decorative, a continuing (if not increasing) respect for the classical writers themselves, and a general uneasiness about the danger of exposing the true Christian to the pagan idolaters. The balance of these forces at the beginning of the eighteenth century made the predominant attitude more negative than positive, but if we look at the works of the mythographers and of other writers on Greek myth during the later eighteenth and early nineteenth centuries, we will begin to see a gradual shift in attitude which may be said to have cleared the way for the more positive evaluation of classical mythology during the Romantic period.

In their approach to classical fable, the mythographers of the early eighteenth century were following a tradition which in actuality goes back to classical times. The basic problem was how to make a theology which was apparently polytheistic and grossly immoral palatable to the Christian reader, and in confronting this problem the eighteenth-century writers on myth to a large extent turned to "solutions" which their medieval and renaissance counterparts had used before them. Seznec describes three basic theories which the mythographers used to de-emphasize the seeming immorality and polytheism of Greek fable: "(1) the myths are a more or less distorted account of historical facts, in which the characters are mere men who have been raised to the rank of the immortals; or (2) they express the union or conflict of the elementary powers which constitute the universe, the gods then being cosmic symbols; or (3) they are merely the expression in fable of moral and philosophical ideas, in which case the gods are allegories."[2] It will be apparent that each of these explanations actually de-emphasizes the primary, obvious meaning of any particular myth in favor of some less controversial meaning which is considered to lie behind it. The gods are not really gods; they are mortal men, or they are natural forces, or they are personifications of moral qualities; and therefore the events which the classical myths record are deceptive, and the only way to understand them properly is to look beneath the surface.

At least two of these methods of rehabilitating the gods survived into the eighteenth century: the euhemerism of the first and the allegorizing of the third. Euhemerism, the theory that the gods were in fact deified human beings, goes back at least to the fourth century B.C., to the Sicilian philosopher after whom it is named. Here, for example, is an explanation of the division of the universe among Jupiter, Neptune, and Pluto in

Andrew Tooke's famous *Pantheon,* a book which first appeared in 1698 but was constantly used, in later editions, throughout the eighteenth century: "*Jupiter* was King of *Crete,* and, according to *Eusebius,* contemporary with the Patriarch *Abraham.* This Jupiter deposed his Father, and afterwards divided by Lot the Kingdom with his two Brothers *Neptune* and *Pluto.* And, because the Eastern Part of the Country was by Lot given to *Jupiter,* the Western to *Pluto,* and the Maritime Parts to *Neptune;* they took Occasion from hence to feign, that *Jupiter* was the God and king of the Heavens, *Neptune* of the Sea, and *Pluto* of Hell."[3] The explanation of a myth which seemed to suggest the autonomy of at least three different gods by making it merely a disguised version of an actual event in the history of Crete thus allows the Christian reader to examine the myth without paying serious attention to the Manichean suggestiveness of its polytheism. But of course it does so at a price, for the euhemeristic explanation degrades the tale to the level of some rather sordid political machinations and makes it almost inconceivable that such "gods" could ever have been worshipped.

The myth of Endymion is one of the favorite provinces of the euhemeristic mythographer. The earthly paramour of the moon-goddess, Dr. King tells us in his *Historical Account of the Heathen Gods* (third edition, 1722), was, in reality, "a just King of Elis, and a famous Astronomer, who studied the Motions of the *Moon,* and therefore pass'd the Nights in retir'd Places, to observe her with less Interruption."[4] Samuel Boyse, on the other hand, in his *A New Pantheon* (1753), suggests that the Endymion fable "had its Origin in *Egypt.* These people in the *Neomenia* or Feast, in which they celebrated the antient State of Mankind, chose a Grove, or some retir'd shady Grotto, where they plac'd an *Isis* with her Crescent or Moon, and by her Side an *Horus* asleep, to denote the Security and Repose which Mankind then enjoy'd. This Figure they call'd Endymion, and these Symbolical Figures, like the rest, degenerated into Idolatry, and became the Materials for fabulous History."[5]

The explanation of this euhemeristic process was usually highly unflattering both to the predeified mortals and to the poets who were responsible for the fabrications. Boyse, for example, has a very ungallant explanation of the many myths in which a god seduces a mortal woman: "Sometimes a Concern for the Honour of the Ladies became the Source of Fables. If a Princess prov'd too frail to withstand the Attempts of her Lover, her Flatterer, to skreen her Reputation, immediately called in the Assistance of some enamour'd God; this was easily believed by the ignorant Vulgar; for they could suppose none but a divine Person could presume to attempt one of her Rank, or could be able to thaw the Coldness of the insensible Fair. Thus her Reputation was unsullied, and instead of becoming infamous, she was highly honoured, and the Husband himself, instead of being offended, partook of her Glory."[6] But the poets were the real villains, content to pervert the truth in order to satisfy the taste for entertainment or to flatter a patron. They were "meant rather to amuse than to instruct," Blackwell explains in the *Letters Concerning Mythology* (1748), "and therefore selected the most striking Tales for the Entertainment of their Audience, and dwelt upon the most wondrous Circumstances of these Tales, with little regard to the Truth of the original Doctrine, or Justness of the Application."[7] The very nature of literary art seems to encourage the confusion of deity and mortal. As Ramsay says in "A Discourse upon the Theology and Mythology of the Ancients" (second edition, 1728), poets "pass in a Moment from Allegory to the literal Sense, and from the literal Sense to Allegory; from real Gods to fabulous Deities: and this occasions that Jumble of their Images, that Absurdity in their Fictions, and that Indecorum in their Expressions, which are so justly condemned by the Philosophers."[8] In this way, the poet often becomes the scapegoat on whom the seeming idolatry (and even the immorality) of pagan myth can be blamed. This may seem to suggest that there is a less objectionable realm of classical religious thought which exists until the poets begin to corrupt it, and such an analysis of the mythopoetic process is actually found in many of the eighteenth-century mythographers.

The basic theory of these mythographers is that in the beginning Greek religious thought was monotheistic and thus not radically opposed to Christianity, and that its seeming polytheism is merely the result of the accretion of centuries of poetic flattery or vulgar superstition. One of his principal discoveries, Joseph Spence says in his *Polymetis* (1747), is that even the Roman religion is only seemingly polytheistic, that actually the more "thinking part of them believed that there was but one great Being, that made, and preserved, and actuated all things: which is just as much as to say that they believed there was but one God, in our sense of the word. . . . When they considered this one great Being as influencing the affairs of the world in different manners, they gave him as many different names; and hence came all their variety of nominal gods. When he thundered or lightened, they called him Jupiter, when he calmed the seas, Neptune; when he guided their councils, it was Minerva; and when he gave them strength in battle, it was Mars."[9] And Blackwell says that the source of the idolatrous proliferation of gods in heathen mythology was the literal-mindedness of the common people, "the blind and credulous Vulgar, always apt to take Representations for Things, as we see daily happen in Popish Countries" (p. 176). The comparison of the idolatry of the later stages of Greek religion with Catholicism was in fact fairly common in England: the minor deity was considered the equivalent of the Catholic saint.

It will be readily apparent that the euhemeristic explanation could be used either to attack or to defend Greek myths. When it was used to defend them, the basis of the argument was usually the contrast of two religions, one which the writers insisted was held by the "ignorant Vulgar," the other which was the province of the learned and intelligent members of the same society. This theory of "the double truth," as Frank Manuel has called it,[10] was extremely influential among the eighteenth-century mythographers. Ramsay insists that we must distinguish between the religion of the poets and the religion of the philosophers (p. 22), and Spence explains that the heathens had two beliefs, "1. That there was but one supreme God; and 2. They believed, or rather talked of a multitude of ministers, deputies, or inferior gods; as acting under this supreme. The first may be called the philosophical belief; and the second, the vulgar belief of the heathens" (p. 47). Blackwell combines this idea with an attack on Catholicism in the following passage: "Are there not many Parables and Prophecies well understood and justly explained by the wise and knowing, that are grossly shocking, in their literal Signification, and yet greedily so swallowed by the unthinking Vulgar? Are there not many Images, Relicks, Wafers, Agnus-Dei's, and other sacred Utensils among the Appendages of Devotion, that were never worshipped by a *Bessarion* nor a *Bembo,* by a *Borromeo* nor a *Sarpi;* but which the far greater Part of those who arrogate to themselves the Name of *Catholics* absurdly adore?" (p. 63). The price of making Greek religion respectable in this way, however, was the necessity of assuming that almost everything which distinguishes it from Christianity was mere vulgar accretion, and since most readers would have purchased such books because they wanted to know something about those distinctive characteristics, the mythographers were in a sense casting aspersions on their own wares.

Idolatry, however, was not the only thing which the modern Christian reader was likely to find objectionable in Greek myth. Even granted that polytheism could be explained away, what possible excuse was there for the gross immorality of these pagan gods and goddesses? Tooke's *Pantheon* illustrates this sense of outrage. The Romans, he says, were even worse than the Greeks, for they worshipped not only beasts but also "Adulterers, Thieves, Drunkards, Robbers, and such-like *Pests* of Mankind" (p. 5). And the exploits of Jupiter unleash a real verbal storm: "For, was there any Kind of Lewdness of which he was not guilty! or any Mark of Infamy that is not branded upon his Name?" Tooke then lists these exploits, being careful to use a different verb for each one: Jupiter "ruined his Sister," "corrupted Leda," "abused Antiope," "defiled Alcmena," "inflamed Aegina," "deflowered Clytoris," "debauched Calisto," and "undid Europa" (pp. 14-16). How could one possibly explain such immoral ity? One of the answers to this question had also been used by the medieval and renaissance mythographers: the stories have an allegorical meaning which the alert reader can discover. Allegorical interpretation, then, became essential if some of the Greek myths were to survive, and the commentators in adopting this method were merely following in the tradition of the moralizing mythographers since the time of the medieval *Ovide Moralisé.* King, for example, reminds his readers that "it is a well-grounded Opinion of Learned Men, that many Principles of Morality and Policy may be gather'd from the ancient Fables" (Preface, paragraph 3). Blackwell refuses to grant the title of myth to any tale which can not be so interpreted: "MYTHOLOGY in general, is *Instruction conveyed in a Tale.* A Fable or meer [sic] Legend without a Moral, or if you please without a Meaning, can with little Propriety deserve the Name" (p. 70). And his epigraph is a hortatory quotation from Dante (*Inferno* IX.61-63):

> O Voi! c'havete gl' Intelletti sani,
> Mirate la Dottrina, che s'asconde
> Sott'il Velame de gli Versi strani.

One of the best examples of this allegorizing technique is Tooke's explanation of the story of Venus' adulterous love for Mars: "Let us explain this Fable. Indeed when a *Venus* is married to a *Vulcan,* that is, a very handsome Woman to a very ugly Man, it is a great Occasion of Adultery. But neither can that Dishonesty, or any other, escape the Knowledge of the *Sun* of *Righteousness* although they may be done in the obscurest Darkness; though they be with the utmost Care guarded by the trustiest Pimps in the World; though they be committed in the privatest Retirement, and concealed with the greatest Art, they will at one Time or other be exposed to both the Infernal and Celestial Regions, in the brightest Light; when the Offenders shall be set in the Midst, bound by the Chains of their Conscience, by that fallen *Vulcan,* who is the Instrument of the Terrors of the true *Jupiter;* and then they shall hear and suffer the Sentence, that was formerly threatened to *David,* in this Life, *Thou didst this Thing secretly; but I will do this Thing before all* Israel, *and before the Sun*" (pp. 82-83). In this way, the fable of Venus and Mars becomes a highly moral tale, Jupiter is transformed into a Hebraic-Christian God of justice, and the Greek myth becomes an example of one of the universal Christian truths. The mythographer too can cite scripture to his purpose.

It must, however, be admitted that the method of allegorical interpretation seems to have fallen into relative disrepute during the eighteenth century. The simple fact that so many of the interpretations of the same fable put forward by earlier mythographers often flatly contradicted each other eventually gave rise to a more sophisticated and sceptical attitude which assumed that the variety of meanings could only be accounted for by ascribing the interpretation to the mythographer, rather than to the fable itself. So that, although someone like King will still explain some of the myths in an allegorical fashion, he warns us that "in these sort of Interpretations, Authors have been so various and fanciful, and even contradictory, that it were in vain to pretend to enumerate them" (Preface, paragraph 3).

It should be mentioned that the other category of interpretation which Seznec lists—the gods seen as natural or cosmic forces—is occasionally also found among the eighteenth-century mythographers, but even more rarely than the allegorical explanation. It may be useful to quote at length a passage from Boyse's *New Pantheon* which combines all three of these methods—euhemeristic, naturalistic, and allegorical—and at the same time reveals the effect of interpreting Greek myth in this way:

> Who would imagine that by the Wings of *Dedalus* and *Icarus,* were signify'd a Ship under Sail? That all the Changes of *Achelous* were only frequent Inundations? That by the Combat of *Hercules* with the God of that River, was only meant a Bank that was raised to prevent its Overflowing? That *Hercules* encountering the *Hydra* of *Lerna,* signified no more than a Man's draining a marshy Country; or, that *Hercules* separating with his Hands the two Mountains *Calpe* and *Abyla,* when the Ocean rush'd in with Violence, and found a Passage into the Mediterranean, meant no more, perhaps, than that in the Time of one *Hercules,* the Ocean, by the Assistance of an Earthquake, broke a Neck of Land, and form'd the Straits of *Gibraltar?* Or that the Fable of *Pasiphae* contains nothing but an Intrigue of the Queen of *Crete* with a Captain nam'd *Taurus?*

> Who could believe that *Scylla* and *Charybdis,* those dreadful Monsters that devour'd all Passengers, were only two dangerous Rocks near the Island of *Sicily,* render'd famous by their being frequently fatal to Mariners? That the frightful Monster which ravaged the Plains of *Troy,* was the Inundations of the Sea; or that *Hesione's* being expos'ed to this Monster, meant no more than that she was to be given to him, who put a Stop to these Inundations?

> Thus, says the *Abbe Banier,* if we would distinguish Truth from Fiction, whenever a Poet brings a God upon the Stage, he ought to be set aside: What *Homer* and *Virgil* ascribe to *Minerva,* is to be attributed to Prudence and good Conduct. It is no longer the Exhalations that produce Thunder, but *Jupiter* armed to affright Mortals. If a Mariner perceives a rising Storm, it is angry *Neptune* swelling the Waves. *Echo* ceases to be a mere Sound, and becomes Nymph bewailing the Loss of her *Narcissus.* (pp. 236-237)

The passage suggests exactly how Greek myth is preserved for the eighteenth-century reader. Pasiphae's bull is merely a captain named Taurus; Scylla and Charybdis have become a couple of Sicilian rocks; and the goddess Minerva is only Prudence in fancy dress. The shrewd reader, according to Boyse, is the one who can see through the absurd fictions of Greek myth to the simple truths which inspired them. He is not fooled by the poet's deceptions; he can tell Truth from Fiction and does not confuse mere sounds for wailing nymphs. The only thing which is sacrificed in the process is the idea of imaginative truth, the idea which the Romantic poets were to find so important: "What the imagination seizes as Beauty must be truth,"[11] Keats insists; but it is a statement which is flatly denied in the work of the eighteenth-century mythographer. For we are dealing here with a world in which the two must constantly be separated. If it is imaginative, it is false. It is only when we have penetrated to the core of truth that all imaginative "trappings" fall away.

It should be obvious, then, that in temporarily rescuing Greek mythology from oblivion, the mythographers of the eighteenth century were doing so at a price which the Romantic poets would not be willing to pay. For the final attitude which these mythographers wish to create in their readers is that Greek myth—if properly understood—may not be shocking or bad, but neither is it to be taken very seriously. The result is what one might call a decorative theory of mythology. As Thomas Blackwell writes to the young gentleman to whom he addresses his *Letters Concerning Mythology:* "I would not, you well know, altogether follow the old Sages in their Philosophy, how much soever I may admire their Morals. . . . These things, when set about in earnest, must be taken in other Lights. All the Use I wou'd have you to make of them, is *a little innocent Speculation,* whose sole Effect, as *Jack Anvil* says of all the fine things you can write, is *to make you simper a little, shake your Head, say it is a pretty, ingenious kind of a Thing, and so have done*" (p. 6).

Joseph Spence, who was particularly interested in the use which a modern poet might make of classical fable, is careful to insist that the most important rule to follow is *never* to mix Christian truth with pagan fable in the same poem. The trouble with so much modern poetry, he says, is that "The poet generally sits down wholly undetermined, whether Furies, or Devils, are to be the executioners he will make use of: and brings in either the one or the other, just as the humour takes; or, as the verse demands. If two syllables are wanting, it is Satan; but if four, you are sure of meeting with Tisiphone" (p. 300). One of the real failings of Spenser as a poet, he says, is "that poet's mixing the fables of heathenism, with the truths of christianity" (p. 302). The modern poet must be uniform, he must never "mix any one name of the gods of the heathens, with the names of the ministers of blessings and vengeance used in our sacred writings" (p. 320). This is a "rule" which has of course been broken not only by Spenser, but by

Chaucer, Shakespeare, and Milton; and it crystallizes for us the disrepute into which classical mythology had fallen in England since the Renaissance. For what worries Spence is not the problem of literary decorum, that Christ and Hyperion are the products of different cultures and should therefore be kept separate. Rather, what concerns him is the mixing of truth and falsehood and the possibility that Christian truth will be adulterated and devalued by being used side by side with pagan fiction. He is really suggesting that we approach these two realms in completely different ways: the world of Christian reference is true, therefore serious and worthy of the most complete attention; the world of pagan reference, on the other hand, is the world of the literary *exercise,* and it therefore can hardly be treated with comparable seriousness. When Keats says that "what the imagination seizes as Beauty must be truth," it seems likely that what he means is not that an imaginative world exhibits exactly the same *kind* of "truth" as the one which the physical eye can see, but rather that the products of man's imagination are to be given the *sort* of serious and unapologetic consideration which the eighteenth-century mythographer denied them. In the next three-quarters of a century, from about 1750 on, there was to be a shift in attitude which made Keats's view considerably less outrageous or absurd than it would have seemed to a Blackwell.

What elements contributed to the more positive evaluation of Greek mythology in the early nineteenth century? To answer this question, we should look at the traditional mythographers and the new "scientific" students of classical myth, as well as at the poets themselves; we have, on the whole, looked only at the poets. In the years between 1775 and 1825, there appeared in England a number of works on Greek myth which prepare the way for a genuinely new evaluation of the subject: Lempriere's *Bibliotheca Classica* or "Classical Dictionary" (1788), *Bell's New Pantheon* (1790), William Godwin's *The Pantheon* (1806), and R. P. Knight's *An Inquiry into the Symbolical Language of Ancient Art and Mythology* (1818). In many respects, these books seem to be based on the same principles and to use the same methods as their eighteenth-century predecessors, but a more careful examination also reveals some important divergences from the traditional practices of the early mythographers. In a sense the most important difference is also the most superficial. It is perfectly obvious, for example, that Lempriere and Bell are different in format from the books which we have just been considering. They are, in effect, dictionaries of classical fact, arranged alphabetically, and clearly designed as works of reference. Although this may seem to be a minor difference, it has this important effect: that the author of the work has considerably less opportunity to inculcate a specific approach to his subject. In reading an encyclopedia, for example, we are less likely to consider what the *general* attitudes of the "author" of any particular piece are likely to be. In effect, the author disappears as a potent force in his work: the more reliable such a work of reference is likely to be, the less conscious are we of the peculiar prejudices and attitudes of the writer. The form of the encyclopedic work encourages objectivity and anonymity.

Bell's New Pantheon is an example of such relative objectivity and anonymity. It is interesting that this enormous two-volume work should have no preface (except the publisher's note of self-congratulation because the work proved less costly than anticipated), and that it seems to have no author. John Bell is the publisher, but the book itself is anonymous: we are presumably expected to care as little about who is responsible for the various entries as we care about the "authors" of the telephone book. The entries themselves also reveal, on the whole, no central attitudes or points of view. There is little in the way of interpretation to get between the reader and the details of the myth he may be interested in. This is not to say, of course, that there are no allegorical or euhemeristic explanations. But usually such interpretations are qualified by a phrase like "some scholars have said," or "according to some mythologists." The Endymion legend, for example, is explained in this way: "According to some mythologists this fable had its origin from the Neomenia, or feast in which the Egyptians celebrated the ancient state of mankind; for which purpose, it is said, they chose a retired grotto, wherein they placed an Isis with her crescent, and by her side an Horus, asleep, to denote the repose and security mankind then enjoyed. This figure they called *Endymion,* or the *grotto of the representation.* Others affirm that Endymion was the 12th king of Elis, who being expelled his [sic] kingdom, retired to Mount Latmos, in Curia, where applying himself to the study of the heavenly bodies, but chiefly the moon, it was feigned that he was beloved by Luna, who visited him every night, as he lay asleep on the top of that mountain."[12] Now we have encountered both of these explanations before, it is true, but in two different works, and in each case as the *authoritative* explanation. Here they are presented merely as two contradictory explanations, and without any attempt to convince the reader of the truth of either one. In fact, the introductory phrases, "according to some mythologists," "it is said," and "others affirm that," create a more or less sceptical awareness of the nature of most mythological "interpretations," and focus attention on the story itself. But the most important differences which we find here are those of omission rather than of commission. There are no tirades against Catholicism; there is no sense of shock about the adulterous doings of the gods; there are no sermons about the superiority of Christian revelation to pagan idolatry. For the first time since the classical age itself, it seems to be possible to look at the realm of Greek mythology as a province of *fact,* to be dealt with as objectively as the historian would try to deal with the facts, say, of the Peloponnesian War.

Lempriere's *Classical Dictionary,* the standard handbook of the early nineteenth century on the subject, is the most famous example of the methods of the encyclopedia applied to the province of classical lore. Lempriere goes a step further in the direction of treating mythological subject matter as simply a part of the realm of fact. His book is an attempt to identify *all* the proper names mentioned by all classical writers, and as a result we find the figures of Greek mythology side by side with historical personages and geographical names.[13] Lempriere's work prospered. By 1809 it had gone through seven editions, and by 1831, 30,000 copies had been printed and sold, according to a contemporary estimate. It was "in the hands of every schoolboy. . . . The young and the old, the pupil and the master would be eager to possess a book, which promised to give 'a copious account of all the proper names mentioned in ancient authors'."[14] No library was complete without a copy.

Two other important works on classical mythology published in the early nineteenth century began by attacking some of the traditional methods and assumptions of the early mythographers. William Godwin's *The Pantheon* (written under the pseudonym of Edward Baldwin) is organized in the older non-encyclopedic fashion; though it uses the allegorical method of interpretation and assures its readers "that nothing will be found in it, to administer libertinism to the fancy of the stripling, or to sully the whiteness of mind of the purest virgin,"[15] it sounds one very new note. Godwin begins with an attack on Tooke's *Pantheon* and on the methods of the older mythographers in general:

> The dulness of the compilers in some instances, and still more extraordinary, their malice in others, have combined to place Pantheons and Histories of the Heathen Gods among the most repulsive articles of the juvenile library. The book in particular, written in Latin by the Jesuit Pomoy, and known among us by the name of Tooke, contains in every page an elaborate calumny upon the Gods of the Greeks, and that in the coarsest thoughts and words that rancour could furnish. The author seems continually haunted by the fear that his pupil might prefer the religion of Jupiter to the religion of Christ. (p. vi)

But such methods are surely no longer necessary, says Godwin, if indeed they ever were. Christianity "fears no comparison with the mythology of ancient Greece. It looks something like blasphemy for a Christian to think it necessary to the cause in which he is engaged, to inveigh against the amours of Jupiter, and to revive all the libels of the ancient Fathers against the religion of the government under which they lived. I felt no apprehension, that while I vindicated the Heathen mythology from misrepresentation . . . I should risk the seducing one votary from the cross of Christ" (pp. vi-vii).

Of course it is possible to interpret such a statement as a confirmation of an even more anti-mythological prejudice. It may be that Baldwin is merely saying the Greek religion is so totally inferior to Christianity that it degrades Christianity itself even to be mentioned in the same breath. But we soon begin to see that these are not his feelings, and that in fact he is making more of a case for the basic similarity of some of the elements of Christian and pagan belief. For the Greek mind, he says in a very unconventional passage, is genuinely religious, and Greek "myth" is a real religion:

> Every one must feel how superior this state of mind is to that of the atheist: if the Greeks were unacquainted with the Christian God, the "Father Almighty, maker of heaven and earth," the omniscient author and governor of the universe; if their Gods appear limited, fantastic, and in this tremendous comparison contemptible;—yet they had the happiness to regard all nature, even the most solitary scenes, as animated and alive, to see every where around them a kind and benevolent agency, and to find on every side motives for contentment, reliance and gratitude. (p. 101)

In its small way, Godwin's *Pantheon* proposed views almost as extraordinary as those of his better-known writings, ideas which were to find a place in the famous passage on Greek myth in Wordsworth's *Excursion.*

Another highly unconventional work on Greek mythology was Richard Payne Knight's *An Inquiry into the Symbolical Language of Ancient Art and Mythology,* first published in 1818. The 1836 edition of this book has a very interesting preface by E. H. Barker in defense of Knight, who seems to have come in for a considerable amount of hostile criticism. Barker contrasts Knight's objective methods with those of previous writers on the subject: "Disregarding the vain imaginations, and the wild speculations of Writers, who have discussed ancient mythology with more zeal than knowledge,—with more prejudice than judgment,—with more religion than piety,—Mr. KNIGHT has surveyed her not through a colored medium, but with the naked eye."[16] But surveying classical myth "with the naked eye" seems to have inspired the attacks of the more traditionally minded, those who felt that the mythographer must preach against the heresy he describes. This alone can account for the impassioned tone of Barker's remarks. True Christianity, he says, does not concern itself with such issues: "the words *sectarianism* and *heresy* are no terms in her vocabulary,—censure and persecution make no part of her business; exclusiveness is no sentiment of her mind, and bigotry no feeling of her heart" (p. iv).

If we turn to Knight's *Inquiry* itself, we see that though he is basically still using the methods of the allegorists, there are also a number of important variations in his approach to the subject. For one thing, he is violently opposed to the euhemeristic methods of his predecessors, not because their kind of speculation is unscholarly and inaccurate, but rather because the idea that the gods are merely mortals with a desire for attention succeeds only in degrading and discrediting the essentially religious truth of the ancient myths. Such mythographers "inferred that, because some of the objects of public worship had been mortal men, they had all been equally so; for which purpose, they rejected the authority of the mysteries, where the various gradations of gods, daemons, and heroes, with all the metaphysical distinctions of emanated, personified, and canonised beings, were taught" (p. 67). Perhaps it was understandable that these methods were used in early Christian times by the patristic writers, "Because it favored that system, which, by degrading the old, facilitated the progress of the new religion" (p. 67), but it was certainly no longer necessary to use such dishonest methods.

Although he attacks euhemerism, Knight continues to allegorize classical myths; and yet even here we can see an important change of method. For Knight does not interpret these fables as veiled moral allegories, nor does he treat Olympian gods as abstract virtues and vices. It is difficult to imagine him using the Venus and Mars story to prove that adultery does not pay. Rather, Knight is concerned with cosmological and metaphysical symbolism: the truths behind the fictions of Greek mythology are concerned with the creation of the world, the relationship between Time and Matter, the nature of Being, and so on. His Greek mythology is veiled metaphysics, not ethics. Here, for example, is his interpretation of the Saturn story: "The allegory of . . . Saturn devouring his own children seems to allude to the rapid succession of creation and destruction before the world had acquired a permanent constitution" (p. 11). This manner of "conveying knowledge by symbols, and its long-established appropriation to religious subjects, had given it a character of sanctity unknown to any other mode of writing" (p. 3).

Whether this form of allegorical interpretation represents any kind of advance over the methods of the older mythographers is indeed an open question. It seems quite possible that the results are just as arbitrary and just as untrue to the primitive mythological imagination. But the assumptions behind the method are of considerable importance, for Greek mythology is here being treated as a religion, to be taken with complete seriousness since it seeks answers to the basic religious questions. Furthermore, Knight's methods go hand in hand with the growing interest in metaphysical as opposed to ethical inquiry in the early nineteenth century. If the rehabilitation of Greek myth in the Romantic period was very largely a matter of raising it to the status of respectability, Knight's *Inquiry* was certainly an important step in that direction.

We have been considering, in these pages, a shift in attitude toward classical myth primarily among the writers of the handbooks of Greek mythology used during the eighteenth and early nineteenth centuries. Such books are reliable indicators of the general current of opinion, since any book designed to a great extent for use in schools is unlikely to offer shockingly unorthodox opinions. But in popularizing the academically respectable opinions of the day, the mythographers were also highly influential in creating a larger acceptance for these ideas during the formative years of the students who used such works. Among those students were the great Romantic poets who were later to popularize Greek mythology in their own way. Tooke's *Pantheon* "was one of the favorite books of Keats's boyhood."[17] His friend Charles Cowden Clarke tells us that the young poet seemed to be memorizing Lempriere: "The books, however, that were his constantly recurrent sources of attraction were Tooke's 'Pantheon,' Lempriere's 'Classical Dictionary,' which he appeared to *learn,* and Spence's 'Polymetis.' This was the store whence he acquired his intimacy with the Greek mythology."[18] And Wordsworth's library, according to the Rydal Mount Sale Catalogue, contained Tindal's *Polymetis Abridged,* Tooke's *Pantheon,* and two copies of Lempriere's *Classical Dictionary.*[19]

Nevertheless, it is important to emphasize that these writers were not the only students of mythology during the late eighteenth and early nineteenth centuries responsible for the gradual acceptance of Greek mythology as a legitimate and important realm of inquiry and as a possible subject for poetry. There were at least two other groups of writers directly concerned with this shift in taste: the so-called syncretic mythographers, and the new breed of scientific historians of Greek myth. Although these groups worked with very different methods, they are also partially responsible for the Romantic rehabilitation of classical fable.

The syncretic mythographers have already been discussed at length in Edward Hungerford's *Shores of Darkness* and in a recent article by Albert J. Kuhn.[20] The works of Jacob Bryant, George Stanley Faber, Edward Davies, and other syncretic mythographers differed from the more traditional books by being far more speculative and fantastic. Their subject matter was not restricted to classical mythology but rather extended to *all* myths, since most of the writers were arguing that "beneath the seemingly disparate and heterogeneous elements of ancient universal mythico-religious and historical traditions there lay a harmonious tradition" (Kuhn, p. 1094), which the student of mythology then set out to discover.

In a completely different way, the study of Greek mythology was being revitalized in Germany by scholars like Karl Otfried Müller and Chr. Augustus Lobeck. Müller's *Prolegomena zu einer wissenschaftlichen*

Mythologie, which might be translated as "An Introduction to a Scientific Study of Mythology," was published in Göttingen in 1825, and though it was not translated into English for some twenty years, the British public had been informed of its conclusions in a long article in *The Foreign Quarterly Review* in 1831.[21] Müller's is a revolutionary book, an attempt to formulate the general principles of a scientific study of mythology, and as such it may be said to represent the wave of the future. He attacks most euhemeristic interpretations on the grounds that they are not historically convincing, and that a proper knowledge of Greek philology, history, and geography makes most of the previous interpretations of specific myths seem highly inaccurate.[22] The first task for the serious student of Greek myth is to separate the primitive myths from the various interpretations which have been accumulating since the more sophisticated commentators of classical times began to turn their attention to them. In order to accomplish that, we must rid ourselves of any private interpretations or prejudices we may have. The new student of Greek myth, it seems, should have the qualities of mind which the *Foreign Quarterly Review* article finds in the German mythographers: "learning and industry . . . a cool discriminating judgment, a power of original investigation, a disregard for the authority of great names, and perfect controul over his imagination."[23]

With the perfection of this new thoroughly professional attitude toward the study of Greek mythology, the respectability of the subject matter may be said to have been finally demonstrated. Unlike the critics of and apologists for classical fable whom we have been investigating, the work of the scientific mythographer is totally unpolemical and reveals no attitude towards its subject whatsoever, though it is presumably based on the assumption that the subject is worthy of close investigation. But the important point is that such an assumption could not have been made in the early eighteenth century. The academic respectability which the province of Greek mythology had finally achieved is the direct result of the writings of many men, not least among them, presumably, the poets themselves, but also the mythographers writing around the turn of the century.

The historical interest created by the scientific mythologists combines with the poetical interest which is the product of the attitudes of the Romantic poets to make the province of Greek mythology completely respected by the middle of the nineteenth century. An anonymous pantheon published in 1842, for example, nostalgically suggests that there "was something very pleasing and poetical in the thought, that each river had its nymph, and every wood its god: that a visible power watched over even the domestic duties of the people, ready to punish and reward."[24] And in an article on the "Mythological System of the Hellenes" which appeared in *Fraser's* in 1847, the author praises Greek mythology because it is the province of pure, unsophisticated religious faith and thus in its way superior to the sceptical world which we see around us.[25]

Like almost any major shift in taste, the rehabilitation of Greek mythology was the product of many different but clearly related forces. Direct influences are difficult to establish; but the fact remains that in the century following Addison's attempt to convince his readers that the use of classical fable in serious verse was "down-right Puerility, and unpardonable in a Poet that is past Sixteen,"[26] Greek mythology had once again become an absorbing, important, imaginative world not only for the poet but for the audience which he addressed.

Notes

[1] Douglas Bush's *Mythology and the Romantic Tradition in English Poetry* (Cambridge, Mass., 1937) deals with the subject in full. See especially pp. 20-26 on the status of mythology in the eighteenth century. While there have been many discussions of the treatment of Greek myth by the Romantic poets (see especially Edward Hungerford's *Shores of Darkness,* New York, 1941, and Edward S. LeComte's *Endymion in England,* New York, 1944), the mythographers discussed in this article have received little attention. Seznec's *The Survival of the Pagan Gods* stops far short of the period, and Manuel's *The Eighteenth Century Confronts the Gods* deals primarily with the sources in continental philosophy of the attitudes toward Greek myth.

[2] Jean Seznec, *The Survival of the Pagan Gods* (New York, 1940), p. 4.

[3] Andrew Tooke, *The Pantheon, Representing the Fabulous Histories of the Heathen Gods, and Most Illustrious Heroes* (London, 1781), p. 26.

[4] [William] King, *An Historical Account of the Heathen Gods and Heroes; Necessary for the Understanding of the Ancient Poets* (London, 1722), p. 91.

[5] Samuel Boyse, *A New Pantheon: or, Fabulous History of the Heathen Gods, Heroes, Goddesses, &c.* (London, 1753), p. 94.

[6] Ibid., p. 239.

[7] [Thomas Blackwell], *Letters Concerning Mythology* (London, 1748), p. 178.

[8] The Chevalier Ramsay, "A Discourse upon the Theology and Mythology of the Ancients," *The Travels of Cyrus* (London, 1727–28), II, 23.

[9] Joseph Spence, *Polymetis: or, An Enquiry Concerning the Agreement Between the Works of the Roman Poets, and the Remains of the Antient Artists* (London, 1747), p. 47.

[10] Frank E. Manuel, *The Eighteenth Century Confronts the Gods* (Cambridge, Mass., 1959), p. 65.

[11] *The Letters of John Keats,* ed. Maurice Buxton Forman (London, 1952), p. 67.

[12] John Bell, *Bell's New Pantheon; or, Historical Dictionary of the Gods, Demi-gods, Heroes, and Fabulous Personages of Antiquity* (London, 1790), I, 287.

[13] It is interesting that when a heavily revised edition appeared in America in 1837, the editors proudly announced that they had separated the historical and geographical parts of the work from the mythological parts and relegated the mythological section to the last part of the book, presumably so that its imaginative "facts" would not be confused with the genuine facts of Greek history and geography. Furthermore, the editors of this edition informed their readers, they were particularly pleased that they had "removed from their pages the offensive matter with which those of the first author were so profusely stained," those "grosser failings, to pervert the moral sense and feeling of the youthful inquirer who may have recourse to its pages." [J. Lempriere, *Bibliotheca Classica: or, a Dictionary of All the Principal Names and Terms Relating to the Geography, Topography, History, Literature, and Mythology of Antiquity and of the Ancients. Revised and Corrected, and Divided . . . by Lorenzo L. DaPonte and John D. Ogilby* (New York, 1837), p. 5.] The America of 1837 sounds oddly like the England of 1737.

[14] "Lempriere's Dictionary," *The Quarterly Journal of Education,* I (1831), 297.

[15] Edward Baldwin (pseud.), *The Pantheon: or Ancient History of the Gods of Greece and Rome* (London, 1806), p. vii.

[16] R. P. Knight, *An Inquiry into the Symbolical Language of Ancient Art and Mythology* (London, 1836), p. iii.

[17] Douglas Bush, "Notes on Keats's Reading," *PMLA* [*Publications of the Modern Language Association*], L (1935), 796.

[18] Charles and Mary Cowden Clarke, *Recollections of Writers* (New York, [1878]), p. 124.

[19] Lots 673, 170, 321, and 449. *Transactions of the Wordsworth Society,* VI (1884), 195-257.

[20] "English Deism and the Development of Mythological Syncretism," *PMLA,* LXXI (1956), 1094-1116.

[21] "Mythology and Religion of Ancient Greece," *The Foreign Quarterly Review,* VII (1831), 33-52.

[22] Karl Otfried Müller, *Prolegomena zu einer wissenschaftlichen Mythologie* (Göttingen, 1825), pp. 61-62.

[23] "Mythology and Religion of Ancient Greece," p. 51.

[24] *Heathen Mythology. Illustrated by Extracts from the Most Celebrated Writers, Both Ancient and Modern* (London, [1842]), p. v.

[25] "Mythological System of the Hellenes," *Fraser's,* xxxv (1847), 304-305.

[26] *Spectator* 523. Addison does accept the use of the fables in the mock epic, however.

INFLUENCE OF GREEK LITERATURE, ART, AND CULTURE ON THE ROMANTICS

August Wilhelm von Schlegel (lecture date 1809)

SOURCE: "Vorlesungen über dramatische Kunst und Literatur," 1809, translated by J. Black, 1815. Reprinted in *English Romantic Hellenism, 1700-1824,* edited by Timothy Webb, Manchester University Press and Barnes and Noble Books, 1982, pp. 213-19.

[*In the following excerpt from a lecture, Schlegel enthusiastically praises Grecian art, poetry, and drama.*]

The formation of the Greeks was a natural education in its utmost perfection. Of a beautiful and noble race, endowed with susceptible senses and a clear understanding, placed beneath a mild heaven, they lived and bloomed in full health of existence; and, under a singular coincidence of favourable circumstances, performed all of which our circumscribed nature is capable. The whole of their art and their poetry is expressive of the consciousness of this harmony of all their faculties. They have invented the poetry of gladness.

Their religion was the deification of the powers of nature and of the earthly life: but this worship, which, among other nations, clouded the imagination with images of horror, and filled the heart with unrelenting cruelty, assumed, among the Greeks, a mild, a grand, and a dignified form. Superstition, too often the tyrant of the human faculties, seemed to have here contributed to their freest development. It cherished the arts by which it was ornamented, and the idols became models of ideal beauty.

But however far the Greeks may have carried beauty, and even morality, we cannot allow any higher character to their formation than that of a refined and ennobled sensuality. Let it not be understood that I assert this to be true in every instance. The conjectures of a few philosophers, and the irradiations of poetical inspiration, constitute an exception. Man can never altogether turn aside his thoughts from infinity, and some obscure recollections will always remind him of his original home; but we are now speaking of the principal object towards which his endeavours are directed.

Religion is the root of human existence. Were it possible for man to renounce all religion, including that of which he is unconscious, and over which he has no control, he would become a mere surface without any internal substance. When this centre is disturbed the whole system of the mental faculties must receive another direction . . .

Among the Greeks human nature was in itself all-sufficient; they were conscious of no wants, and aspired at no higher perfection than that which they could actually attain by the exercise of their own faculties. We, however, are taught by superior wisdom that man, through a high offence, forfeited the place for which he was originally destined; and that the whole object of his earthly existence is to strive to regain that situation, which, if left to his own strength, he could never accomplish. The religion of the senses had only in view the possession of outward and perishable blessings; and immortality, insofar as it was believed, appeared in an obscure distance like a shadow, a faint dream of this bright and vivid futurity. The very reverse of all this is the case with the Christian: every thing finite and mortal is lost in the contemplation of infinity; life has become shadow and darkness, and the first dawning of our real existence opens in the world beyond the grave. Such a religion must waken the foreboding, which slumbers in every feeling heart, to the most thorough consciousness, that the happiness after which we strive we can never here attain; that no external object can ever entirely fill our souls; and that every mortal enjoyment is but a fleeting and momentary deception. When the soul, resting as it were under the willows of exile, breathes out its longing for its distant home, the prevailing character of its songs must be melancholy. Hence the poetry of the ancients was the poetry of enjoyment, and ours is that of desire: the former has its foundation in the scene which is present, while the latter hovers betwixt recollection and hope. Let me not be understood to affirm that every thing flows in one strain of wailing and complaint, and that the voice of melancholy must always be loudly heard. As the austerity of tragedy was not incompatible with the joyous views of the Greeks, so the romantic poetry can assume every tone, even that of the most lively gladness; but still it will always, in some shape or other, bear traces of the source from which it originated. The feeling of the moderns is, upon the whole, more intense, their fancy more incorporeal, and their thoughts more contemplative. In nature, it is true, the boundaries of objects run more into one another, and things are not so distinctly separated as we must exhibit them for the sake of producing a distinct impression.

The Grecian idea of humanity consisted in a perfect concord and proportion between all the powers,—a natural harmony. The moderns again have arrived at the consciousness of the internal discord which renders such an idea impossible; and hence the endeavour of their poetry is to reconcile these two worlds between which we find ourselves divided, and to melt them indissolubly into one another. The impressions of the senses are consecrated, as it were, from their mysterious connexion with higher feelings; and the soul, on the other hand, embodies its forebodings, or nameless visions of infinity, in the phenomena of the senses.

In the Grecian art and poetry we find an original and unconscious unity of form and subject; in the modern, so far as it has remained true to its own spirit, we observe a keen struggle to unite the two, as being naturally in opposition to each other. The Grecian executed what it proposed in the utmost perfection; but the modern can only do justice to its endeavours after what is infinite by approximation; and, from a certain appearance of imperfection, is in greater danger of not being duly appreciated.

. . . . .

The theatres of the Greeks were quite open above, and their dramas were always acted in open day, and beneath the canopy of heaven. The Romans, at an after period, endeavoured by a covering to shelter the audience from the rays of the sun; but this degree of luxury was hardly ever enjoyed by the Greeks. Such a state of things appears very inconvenient to us; but the Greeks had nothing of effeminacy about them, and we must not forget, too, the beauty of their climate. When they were overtaken by a storm or a shower, the play was of course interrupted; and they would much rather expose themselves to an accidental inconvenience, than, by shutting themselves up in a close and crowded house, entirely destroy the serenity of a religious solemnity, which their plays certainly were. To have covered in the scene itself, and imprisoned gods and heroes in dark and gloomy apartments with difficulty lighted up, would have appeared still more ridiculous to them. An action which so nobly served to establish the belief of the relation with heaven could only be exhibited under an unobstructed heaven, and under the very eyes of the gods as it were, for whom, according to Seneca, the sight of a brave man struggling with adversity is a becoming spectacle.[1] With respect to the supposed inconvenience, which, according to the assertion of many modern critics, was felt by the poets from the necessity of always laying the scene of their pieces before houses, a circumstance that often forced them to violate probability, this inconvenience was very little felt by tragedy and the older comedy. The Greeks, like many southern nations of the present day, lived much more in the open air than we do, and transacted many things in public places which usually take place with us in houses. For the theatre did not represent the street, but a place before the house belonging to it, where the altar stood on which sacrifices to the household gods were offered up. Here the women, who lived in so retired a manner among the Greeks, even those who were unmarried, might appear without any impropriety. Neither was it impossible for them to give a view of the interior of the houses; and this was effected, as we shall immediately see by means of the encyclema.

But the principal reason for this observance was that publicity, according to the republican notion of the Greeks was essential to a grave and important transaction. This is clearly proved by the presence of the chorus, whose remaining on many occasions when secret transactions were going on has been judged of according to rules of propriety inapplicable to that country, and most undeservedly censured . . .

We come now to the essence of the Greek tragedy itself. In stating that the conception was ideal, we are not to understand that the different characters were all morally perfect. In this case what room could there be for such an opposition or conflict, as the plot of a drama requires?—Weaknesses, errors, and even crimes, were pourtrayed in them but the manners were always elevated above reality, and every person was invested with such a portion of dignity and grandeur as was compatible with the share which he possessed in the action. The ideality of the representation chiefly consisted in the elevation to a higher sphere. The tragical poetry wished wholly to separate the image of humanity which it exhibited to us, from the ground of nature to which man is in reality chained down, like a feudal slave. How was this to be accomplished? By exhibiting to us an image hovering in the air? But this would have been incompatible with the law of gravitation and with the earthly materials of which our bodies are framed. Frequently, what we praise in art as ideal is really nothing more. But the production of airy floating shadows can make no durable impression on the mind. The Greeks, however, succeeded in combining in the most perfect manner in their art ideality with reality, or, dropping school terms, an elevation more than human with all the truth of life, and all the energy of bodily qualities. They did not allow their figures to flutter without consistency in empty space, but they fixed the statue of humanity on the eternal and immoveable basis of moral liberty; and that it might stand there unshaken, being formed of stone or brass, or some more solid mass than the living human bodies, it made an impression by its own weight, and from its very elevation and magnificence it was only the more decidedly subjected to the law of gravity.

Inward liberty and external necessity are the two poles of the tragic world. Each of these ideas can only appear in the most perfect manner by the contrast of the other. As the feeling of internal dignity elevates the man above the unlimited dominion of impulse and native instinct, and in a word absolves him from the guardianship of nature, so the necessity which he must also recognize ought to be no mere natural necessity, but to lie beyond the world of sense in the abyss of infinitude; and it must consequently be represented as the invincible power of fate. Hence it extends also to the world of the gods: for the Grecian gods are mere powers of nature; and although immeasurably higher than any mortal man, yet, compared with infinitude, they are on an equal footing with himself. In Homer and the tragedians, the gods are introduced in a manner altogether different. In the former their appearance is arbitrary and accidental, and can communicate no higher interest to the epic poem than the charm of the wonderful. But in tragedy the gods either enter in obedience to fate, and to carry its decrees into execution; or they endeavour in a godlike manner to assert their liberty of action, and appear involved in the same struggles with destiny which man has to encounter. . . .

Notes

[1] *De Providentia.*

Thomas Campbell (essay date 1814)

SOURCE: From *Life and Letters,* edited by William Beattie, 1849. Reprinted in *English Romantic Hellenism, 1700-1824,* edited by Timothy Webb, Manchester University Press and Barnes and Noble Books, 1982, pp. 227-30.

[*In the excerpt below, written in 1814, Campbell rhapsodizes about the Greek sculptures he viewed at the Louvre, remarking that upon seeing the sculptures, he felt "suddenly transported . . . into a new world."*]

I write this after returning from the Louvre . . . You may imagine with what feelings I caught the first sight of Paris, and passed under Montmartre, the scene of the last battle between the French and Allies. . . . It was evening when we entered Paris. Next morning I met Mrs. Siddons; walked about with her, and then visited the Louvre together . . . Oh, how that immortal youth—Apollo! in all his splendour—majesty—divinity—flashed upon us from the end of the gallery! What a torrent of ideas—classically associated with this godlike form—rushed upon me at this moment! My heart palpitated—my eyes filled with tears—I was dumb with emotion.

Here are a hundred other splendid statues—the Venus—the Menander—the Pericles—Cato and Portia—the father and daughter in an attitude of melting tenderness . . . I wrote on the table where I stood with Mrs. Siddons, the *first* part of this letter in pencil—a record of the strange moments in which I felt myself suddenly transported, as it were, into a new world, and while standing between the Apollo and the Venus . . .

Coming home I conclude a transcript of the day:—The effect of the statue gallery was quite overwhelming—it was even distracting; for the secondary statues are things on which you might dote for a whole day; and while you are admiring one, you seem to grudge the time, because it is not spent in admiring something else. Mrs. Siddons is a judge of statuary; but I thought I could boast of a triumph over them—in point of taste—when she and some others of our party preferred another Venus to '*the* statue that enchants the world.' I bade them recollect the waist of the true Venus—the chest and the shoulders. We returned, and they gave in to my opinion, that these parts were beyond all expression. It was really a day of tremulous ecstacy. The young and glorious Apollo is happily still white in colour. He seems as if he had just leapt from the sun! All pedantic knowledge of statuary falls away, when the most ignorant in the arts finds a divine presence in this great created form. Mrs. Siddons justly observed, that it gives one an idea of God himself having given power to catch, in such imitation, a ray of celestial beauty.

The Apollo is not perfect; some parts are modern, and he is not quite placed on his perpendicular by his French transporters; but his head, his breast, and one entire thigh and leg are indubitable. The whole is so perfect, that, at the full distance of the hall, it seems to blaze with proportion. The muscle that supports the head thrown back—the mouth, the brow, the soul that is in the marble, are not to be expressed.

After such a subject, what a falling off it is to tell you I dined with human beings! yea, verily, at a hotel . . .

I was one of the many English who availed themselves of the first short peace to get a sight of the Continent. The Louvre was at that time in possession of its fullest wealth. In the Statuary-hall of that place I had the honour of giving Mrs. Siddons my arm the first time she walked through it, and the first in both our lives that we saw the Apollo Belvidere. From the farthest end of that spacious room, the god seemed to look down like a president on the chosen assembly of sculptured forms; and his glowing marble, unstained by time, appeared to my imagination as if he had stepped freshly from the sun. I had seen casts of the glorious statue with scarcely any admiration; and I must undoubtedly impute that circumstance, in part, to my inexperience in art, and to my taste having till then lain torpid. But still I prize the recollected impressions of that day too dearly to call them fanciful. They seemed to give my mind a new sense of the harmony of Art—a new visual power of enjoying beauty. Nor is it mere fancy that makes the difference between the Apollo himself and his plaster casts. The dead whiteness of the *stucco* copies is glaringly monotonous; whilst the diaphanous surface of the *original* seems to soften the light which it reflects.[1]

Every particular of that hour is written indelibly on my memory. I remember entering the Louvre with a latent suspicion on my mind, that a good deal of the rapture expressed at the sight of superlative sculptures was exaggerated or affected; but as we passed through the vestibule of the hall, there was a Greek figure, I think that of Pericles, with a chlamys[2] and helmet, which John Kemble desired me to notice; and it instantly struck me with wonder at the gentleman-like grace which Art could give to a human form, with so simple a vesture. It was not, however, until we reached the grand saloon, that the first sight of the god overawed my incredulity. Every step of approach to his presence added to my sensations; and all recollections of his name in classic poetry swarmed on my mind as spontaneously as the associations that are conjured up by the sweetest music. . . .

Engrossed as I was with the Apollo, I could not forget the honour of being before him in the company of so august a worshipper, and it certainly increased my enjoyment to see the first interview between the paragon of Art and that of Nature. Mrs. Siddons was evidently much struck, and remained a long time before the statue; but, like a true admirer, she was not loquacious. I remember, she said—'What a great idea it gives us of God to think that he has made a human being capable of fashioning so divine a form!' When we walked round to other sculptures, I observed that almost every eye in the Hall was fixed upon her and followed her: yet I could perceive that she was not known, as I heard the spectators say—'Who is she? Is she not an English woman?' At this time, though in her fifty-ninth year, her looks were so noble, that she made you proud of English beauty—even in the presence of Grecian sculpture. . . .

Notes

. . . [2] *Chlamys:* short mantle or cloak.

Percy Bysshe Shelley (essay date 1819)

SOURCE: "Letter from Naples," 1819. Reprinted in *English Romantic Hellenism, 1700-1824,* edited by Timothy Webb, Manchester University Press and Barnes and Noble Books, 1982, pp. 232-4.

[*In the following excerpt from a letter, Shelley discusses in detail the ruins of Pompeii—an area that the editor notes "was powerfully suggestive of the Greek tradition"—describing it as a Romantic would describe a Greek city, observing, for example, the relationship between the ruins and the landscape.*]

At the upper end, supported on an elevated platform stands the temple of Jupiter. Under the colonnade of its portico we sate & pulled out our oranges & figs & bread & [?soil] apples (sorry fare you will say) & rested to eat. There was a magnificent spectacle. Above & between the multitudinous shafts of the [?sunshiny] columns, was seen the blue sea reflecting the purple heaven of noon above it, & supporting as it were on its line the dark lofty mountains of Sorrento, of a blue inexpressibly deep, & tinged towards their summits with streaks of new-fallen snow. Between was one small green island. To the right was Capua, Inarime, Prochyta and Miseno. Behind was the single summit of Vesuvius rolling forth volumes of thick white smoke whose foamlike column was sometimes darted into the clear dark sky & fell in little streaks along the wind. Between Vesuvius & the nearer mountains, as thro a chasm was seen the main line of the loftiest Apennines to the east. The day was radiant & warm. Every now & then we heard the subterranean thunder of Vesuvius; its distant deep peals seemed to shake the very air & light of day which interpenetrated our frames with the sullen & tremendous sound. This scene was what the Greeks beheld. (Pompeii you know was a Greek city.) They lived in harmony with nature, & the interstices of their incomparable columns, were portals as it were to admit the spirit of beauty which animates this glorious universe to visit those whom it inspired. If such is Pompeii, what was Athens? what scene was exhibited from its Acropolis? The Parthenon and the temples of Hercules & Theseus & the Winds? The islands of the Ægean Sea, the mountains of Argolis & the peaks of Pindus & Olympus, & the darkness of the Beotian forests interspersed? From the forum we went to another public place a triangular portico half inclosing the ruins of an enormous temple. It is built on the edge of the hill overlooking the sea. . . . In the apex of the triangle stands an altar & a fountain; & before the altar once stood the statue of the builder of the portico.—Returning hence & following the consular road we came to the eastern gate of the city. The walls are of enormous strength, & inclose a space of three miles. On each side of the road beyond the gate are built the tombs. How unlike ours! They seem not so much hiding places for that which must decay as voluptuous chamber[s] for immortal spirits. They are of marble radiantly white, & two especially beautiful are loaded with exquisite bas reliefs. On the stucco wall which incloses them are little emblematic figures of a relief exceedingly low, of dead or dying animals & little winged genii, & female forms bending in groupes in some funeral office. The higher reliefs, represent one a nautical subject & the other a bacchanalian one. Within the cell, stand the cinerary urns, sometimes one, sometimes more. It is said that paintings were found within, which are now—as has been every thing moveable in Pompeii—been removed & scattered about in Royal Museums. These tombs were the most impressive things of all. The wild woods surround them on either side and along the broad stones of the paved road which divides them, you hear the late leaves of autumn shiver & rustle in the stream of the inconstant wind as it were like the step of ghosts. The radiance & magnificence of these dwellings of the dead, the white freshness of the scarcely finished marble, the impassioned or imaginative life of the figures which adorn them contrast strangely with the simplicity of the houses of those who were living when Vesuvius overwhelmed their city. I have forgotten the Amphitheatre, which is of great magnitude, tho' much inferior to the Coliseum.—I now understand why the Greeks were such great Poets, & above all I can account, it seems to me, for the harmony the unity the perfection the uniform excellence of all their works of art. They lived in a perpetual commerce with external nature and nourished themselves upon the spirit of its forms. Their theatres were all open to the mountains & the sky. Their columns that ideal type of a sacred forest with its roof of interwoven tracery admitted the light & wind, the odour & the freshness of the country penetrated the cities. Their temples were mostly upaithric; & the flying clouds the stars or the deep sky were seen above. O, but for that series of wretched wars which terminated in the Roman conquest of the world, but for the Christian religion which put a finishing stroke to the antient system; but for those changes which conducted Athens to its ruin, to what an eminence might not humanity have arrived!

John Churton Collins (essay date 1910)

SOURCE: "Influence of Greek Poetry," in *Greek Influence on English Poetry,* edited by Michael Macmillan, Sir Isaac Pitman and Sons, Ltd., 1910, pp. 53-77.

[*In this excerpt, Collins analyzes the ways in which Greek poetry—often through the medium of Roman literature—influenced English poetry, and identifies the most influential Greek poetic forms.*]

It would not be too much to say that the history of the development and characteristics of two-thirds of what is most valuable in English poetry is the history of the modification of Celtic and Teutonic elements by Classical elements.

These classical elements are almost entirely Greek, being derived either directly or indirectly from Greek Literature.

It is first necessary to distinguish between the direct influence of Greek Literature on our poetry and the indirect influence that came through a Roman medium. It must be clearly understood that Roman Literature was mainly an imitation of Greek Literature. What the moon is to the sun, that Roman is to Greek poetry. There was an indigenous literature in Rome and Latium up to about 240 B.C. Then came contact with Greece between the first and second Punic wars (242-218 B.C.). The result was that for the rude native plays represented by the Saturae and the Fabulae Atellanae were substituted tragedies and comedies, modelled in the main on the Attic tragedies and on the comedies of Philemon and Menander and their followers. The Saturnian metre gave place to the hexameter, which became in Rome, as it had been in Greece, the recognized metre of epic poetry.

In a word, in every species of poetry the Romans followed Greek models. The Roman Epics, the 'Æneid,' the 'Thebaid,' the *Argonautica* of Valerius Flaccus are modelled on the 'Iliad,' the 'Odyssey' and the *Argonautica* of Apollonius Rhodius. The first six books of the 'Æneid' are based on the 'Iliad,' the last six on the 'Odyssey.' It is the same with the Roman drama. The Roman tragedies were purely Greek. The older Roman dramatists, whose works have been lost, imitated Æschylus, Sophocles, and Euripides. The tragedies of Seneca, the sole intact remains of Roman tragedy, were modelled not on Attic tragedies, but on the later degenerate drama of Alexandria. . . . In comedy Plautus was largely and Terence wholly Greek. In didactic poetry the title of the Georgics is taken from one Greek poet, Nicander, and the matter largely from the 'Works and Days' of Hesiod and partly from the poems of Aratus and Nicander. Lucretius took his philosophy from Epicurus, Xenophanes and Empedocles. In lyric poetry Horace and Catullus imitated Alcaeus, Sappho and Archilochus. The title of Ovid's 'Metamorphoses' was taken from Parthenius, and probably much of the matter came from the same poet, and from the *Heterœumena* of Nicander. Roman elegies imitated Greek elegies, especially those of Callimachus and Philetas. Latin pastorals followed the 'Idylls' of Theocritus. All the measures of classical Latin poetry were Greek, as is clear from their names, hexameter, pentameter, Sapphic, Alcaic, hendecasyllabic, iambic. Indeed, Rome took from Greece all the nomenclature of poetry, even including the term for poet. The only important contribution to poetic literature made by the Romans was satire. "Satira tota nostra est," says Quintilian, and even this claim cannot be accepted without modification. Speaking generally, then, the whole of Roman Literature is derived from Greek Literature. As Horace says, "Captive Greece led captive her barbarous conqueror, and brought her refinements to rustic Latium." The Roman poets not only acknowledged, but even boasted of their indebtedness to Greek models.

Of course, the tone and colour of Roman poetry, imitative and reflective though it was, took its peculiarities from the Roman national character. The Greeks, that is those Greeks who produced and represented the master poets of the race, were essentially a poetical people, imaginative, emotional, exquisitely sensitive to æsthetic impression, finely touched, artistic. The Romans, on the contrary, were not a poetical people. They had not even a native word for a poet nor any proper common term to denote the class till they came into contact with Greece, for *vates* means soothsayer. Nay, their name for the poet was *grassator*—a vagabond or idler.[1] Their genius was essentially unimaginative, practical and political; their temper from an æsthetic point of view was coarse-fibred; the finer aroma of poetry escaped them. And a curious illustration of this is that they were not so much attracted by the great Greek poets—by Homer, Pindar, Æschylus, Sophocles—as by the later poets of the Alexandrian schools, poets who stand pretty much in the same relation to the great masters as Dryden and Pope stand to Shakespeare and Milton.

The note of Roman poetry is rhetoric. Magnificent rhetoric was its glory and ornament, second and third-rate rhetoric was its defect and vice. As was their character, so was their literature and their language, "the voice of empire and of war"—let me quote Nelson Coleridge's words—"of law and of the state; inferior to its half parent and rival in the embodying of passion and in the distinguishing of thought, but equal to it in sustaining the measured march of history, and superior to it in the indignant declamation of moral satire."

And now we must proceed to the consideration of what we must carefully discriminate, the indirect influence of Greek on our poetry, and the direct influence. Indirectly, as we have seen, we must attribute to Greek influence almost all, so far as form is concerned, which directly we must attribute to Roman influence. Take, for example, first our "classical" tragic drama as represented by 'Gorboduc,' our first formulated tragedy. 'Gorboduc' is modelled on the Latin tragedies of Seneca or possibly on Italian imitations of those tragedies; but the Latin tragedies of Seneca were modelled on the Greek tragedies and so, of course, by implication, were the Italian imitations of Seneca. Take, secondly, our romantic tragedy, the drama culminating in the tragedies of Shakespeare. Our romantic tragedies also originated in the imitation of the Latin tragedies of Seneca, and of Italian imitations of those tragedies; but those in their turn were modelled on the Greek tragedies. So that back we have to go again historically to the Greek tragedies. Take comedy. The first formulated comedies, both in Italy and England, were modelled on Plautus and Terence; but the comedies of Plautus and Terence were modelled on the New Comedy, as it was called, of the Greeks. Our romantic comedy, 'Twelfth Night,' for example, or 'As You Like It,' was, historically explained, a modification of Italian classical comedy; but Italian classical comedy was a modification of the comedies of Plautus and Terence, and these, as we have seen, were modelled on the Greek comedies. So, back we have to go once more to the Attic stage here. And so it is with the epic. We may trace the English epic to the Roman epic, but what is the Roman epic but an imitation and copy of the Greek? Ultimately then in this, and in other branches of poetry, the pastoral, for instance, we have to go back to Greece, even though immediately we need not go further than Rome.

Now, taking the whole mass of our poetry, it is undoubtedly true that Greece has to a very considerable extent influenced us indirectly through Rome. We may explain the architecture of the English classical epic by reference to the 'Æneid,' not to the 'Iliad,' the 'Odyssey' and the *Argonautica.* Similarly we may trace the genesis of our eighteenth century pastoral to Virgil's Bucolics, not to Theocritus. But for all that, we have historically to go back to Virgil's models. I have said that Greece has influenced a vast mass of our poetry indirectly through Rome, and the reasons have been these. The Latin language has always come home to us more than the Greek, and Latin authors have always been better known in England than Greek authors. It is not difficult to see why this should have been so. In the first place, the English genius is much more in affinity with Rome than with Greece. Secondly, the difficulty of the Greek language has always been an impediment in the way of knowledge of Greek Literature, and this difficulty was for a long time aggravated in England by want of lexicons, grammars, and good texts, so that an intimate critical acquaintance with it was impossible till late in the eighteenth century. It may be doubted whether before Milton any of our poets, except perhaps Spenser, Chapman and Ben Jonson, travelled further in Greek scholarship than being able to follow Greek texts in Latin translations, and it may be doubted whether any other of our poets, except Congreve, between Milton and Akenside (who was certainly a fair Greek scholar, as his 'Hymn to the Naiads' shows) had made much way in this study. Among the Elizabethan poets there is no poet so Greek in style as Marlowe. His 'Hero and Leander' is thoroughly Hellenic, and it is not so because it is on a Greek subject, but simply because of its architecture and style, for it is an original poem, not, as it is always described, a translation of the poem ascribed to Musaeus—for it is not even a paraphrase of that poem. But Marlowe's Hellenism was probably not the result of an intimate acquaintance with Greek, but was like that of Keats the result of natural temper and sympathy. On the whole, we may say with safety that familiarity with Greek poetry in the original was a rare accomplishment among English poets till about the middle of the eighteenth century, when there was a Greek Renaissance marked by Akenside, Collins, Gray, Mason, Glover and Thomas Warton.

Distinguishing, therefore, between the indirect influence of Greece and its ambiguous manifestations, I mean where it may be attributed to second-hand knowledge, let us note where it is direct and unmistakable. Perhaps the best way of dealing with it will be to trace its influence through the various branches of poetry. . . . Passing by the 'Davideis' of Cowley, which is modelled on Virgil, and owes nothing directly to Greek, and Davenant's 'Gondibert,' which was written with the intention of emancipating the epic from the canons of classicism, we come to that interesting epic of Richard Glover's, 'Leonidas,' published in 1737. Warton, a very competent judge, tells us that Glover was one of the best and most accurate Greek scholars of his time. 'Leonidas' was once, for a short time, the most popular poem in English literature, but that was for political reasons, because Glover was the poet laureate of the Patriots, as they were called, that is to say, of the Opposition at the time of Walpole's ministry. But his 'Leonidas' is now forgotten, and the world is always right in these matters, seldom losing its memory without good reason. The truth is that Glover was one of those poets who just stop short of genius. But in style and tone 'Leonidas' is thoroughly Greek. The poem is modelled on Homer and occasionally, though not often, catches the Homeric note; the style severely simple, terse, chaste, lucid and precise, is Greek in the true sense of the term. But these qualities are carried too far; its simplicity degenerates too often into baldness; its terseness into abrupt, jerky brevity, and its lucidity and precision are acquired at the expense of charm, of flexibility, variety, grandeur. In choosing a Spartan subject it would seem that Glover affected a Spartan style. It is just such a poem as a Spartan Homer, without genius, might have written. It is like Homer's style in shorthand. What life the poem has is in its vindication of liberty, and we may note in passing that it was as the eulogists, vindicators and prophets of liberty that the Greek poets and orators especially attracted Akenside, Collins, and even Gray, the poets, so to speak, of the Second Greek Renaissance. Glover left another epic, the 'Athenaid,' in thirty books, which was a continuation of 'Leonidas.' But it is much inferior, less Greek in style, and probably represents only the first draft of a poem which his severe taste would have greatly curtailed had he lived to revise it.

Southey's Epics, 'Roderick' and 'Madoc,' come next. They owe nothing to Greek and little, if anything, to classical influence. A man who preferred Lucan and Statius to Virgil in Latin literature is not likely to have resorted to Greek models, or in any case to have profited much from them. But in Landor's 'Gebir' we are again with the Greeks and the Homeric poems. Landor's robust and original genius always revolted from servile imitation, but its chief impulse and nutriment came from the Greeks. He is one of the most Greek of English poets. If not in architecture, at any rate in tone, colour and style, 'Gebir' is thoroughly Homeric, however much Landor's own genius has modified, and modified it has importantly, Homeric qualities. And what is true of 'Gebir' is true in a still greater degree, we may note in passing, of Landor's 'Hellenics.' But for the Greeks, we should not have had the best poetry of Landor; and most of his best poetry is found in these 'Hellenics.'

Next, chronologically, to 'Gebir' comes the magnificent epic fragment of Keats, the *Hyperion*. Nothing could be more Greek in some important respects than this poem, but it is Hellenism tempered slightly with the Elizabethan note and more potently with the Miltonic note. It is remarkable that Keats could not read Greek poetry in the original; he was too lazy and dissolute to undertake the drudgery necessary for the task; but, as in the case of Marlowe, natural affinity, instinctive sympathy, enabled him to get at Greek genius and art through translations, so that sometimes in his poetry we find the pure Greek spirit as in his 'Ode on a Grecian Urn':—

> Who are these coming to the sacrifice?
> To what green altar, O mysterious priest,
> Leadst thou that heifer lowing at the skies
> And all her silken flanks with garlands drest?
> What little town by river or sea-shore,
> Or mountain-built with peaceful citadel,
> Is emptied of its folk this pious morn?

Landor and Keats lead us, as transition links, to the poets with whom we conclude this brief review of the influence of Greek on our epic poets—Tennyson and Matthew Arnold.

The 'Idylls of the King' was a new experiment in epic poetry, which may be called the Idyllic Epic—a continuous epic story, presented in a series of idylls—pictures, frescoes as it were. Now it is not unlikely that Theocritus designed an epic on a similar plan. Among his idylls are two, the 'Infant Hercules' and 'Hercules the Lion-slayer,' both apparently fragments. It might have been that he designed an epic on the career of Hercules, intending to present it in a series of idylls, not in continuous epic narrative. Such an idea would be exactly in accordance with the spirit and taste of the Alexandrian age, an age like our own, when short works, especially in poetry, were more to people's liking than long ones. . . . [T]he great book is tantamount to a great evil, said the typical man of that age, Callimachus. And there are, moreover, other indications in Alexandrian Literature of epics being designed on that popular plan. No doubt they talked—those degenerate, hurriedly living Alexandrians—of 'wading' through the 'Iliad' and 'Odyssey' much as we talk of wading through 'Paradise Lost.' It is probable, then, that the idyllic epic, which we have seen realized by Tennyson, was originated by the Alexandrian poets, and it was from them that Tennyson got the idea.

The Homeric influence on the 'Idylls of the King' is immense, and it is quite impossible here to touch on it in detail. Similes, phrases, epithets, idioms are transferred from 'Iliad' and 'Odyssey' alike. For illustrations I may be allowed perhaps to refer to my 'Illustrations of Tennyson.' Tennyson, being mainly in essence a reflective and artificial poet, resembles Virgil much more than he resembles Homer. But it may safely be said that there is more of the race and flavour of Homer's style in these idylls than there is in the 'Æneid.' Virgil never got as near Homer as Tennyson does in a passage like this:—

> They couch'd their spears and prick'd their steeds and thus
> Their plumes, driv'n backward by the wind they made
> In moving, all together down upon him
> Bare, as a wild wave in the wide North Sea
> Green glimmering toward the summit bears, with all
> Its stormy crests that smoke against the skies,
> Down on a bark and overbears the bark
> And him that helms it, so they overbore
> Sir Lancelot and his charger.

And so, in the 'Morte d'Arthur,' which the poet himself described as a faint Homeric echo, the opening lines are truly Homeric:—

> So all day long the noise of battle roll'd
> Among the mountains by the wintry shore.

But Homer would never have described a moustache as "the knightly growth that fring'd his lips," and the poem, as a whole, is far more Virgilian than Homeric.

And lastly we come to the most comprehensively faithful Homeric echo in our language, Matthew Arnold's episode of 'Sohrab and Rustum.' This is pure Homer, the exact counterpart of the ordinary level and cast of the Homeric style and temper, not rising as Tennyson rises in the passages just quoted to the very grandest of his notes, but faithfully catching and preserving all but those. Matthew Arnold most accurately defined and indicated Homer's characteristics, when he said they were majesty, simplicity, rapidity and radiance. Read 'Sohrab and Rustum,' and you will understand in English illustration what he meant. There is also much of the Homeric spirit in his 'Balder Dead,' but this is not equal to 'Sohrab and Rustum.' Matthew Arnold's poetry, as a whole, is the nearest approach our English language and poetry has ever made in point of style to the style of Greek poetry. Here we must conclude this very brief sketch of the influence of Greek on our epic poetry, and turn to the consideration of the Drama. . . .

Between 1751 and 1759 William Mason made a second attempt to naturalize Greek tragedy in English in his two dramas, 'Elfrida' and 'Caractacus.' The latter was translated into Greek by G. H. Glasse. Then came Richard Glover with his 'Medea' in 1761. Here we have a slight variety from the Greek model in its being divided into acts and scenes, but with this exception it is purely Greek. The lyrics of the chorus, in one or two of which he anticipates Matthew Arnold, are unrhymed and are strictly arranged in strophe and antistrophe. Just noticing William Sotheby's 'Orestes' in 1802, we come to Matthew Arnold's 'Merope' (1858), which is an exact counterpart of the Greek drama, not only in form, but also in its ethical characteristics. Last of all, we have Swinburne's brilliant dramas, 'Atalanta in Calydon,' and 'Erechtheus.' Such have been the attempts to naturalize the Greek drama in its rigid form in our literature.

Of modified forms of the Greek drama in English one of the most important is Milton's 'Comus.' Shelley's 'Prometheus Unbound' is a magnificent variant on the 'Prometheus Bound' of Æschylus, but its florid beauty and philanthropic enthusiasm are far from being Greek. Mrs. Browning's 'Drama of Exile' is another modification of the Greek dramatic form. Nor must we forget Robert Browning's fine setting of the 'Alcestis' in 'Balaustion's Adventure,' and of the *Hercules Furens* in his 'Aristophanes' Apology.'

Satan's address to the sun in the beginning of the fourth book of 'Paradise Lost' was originally intended to be the prologue to a drama in the Greek style. Like other soliloquies in 'Paradise Lost' and 'Paradise Regained,'[2] it is an imitation of the soliloquies found in the Greek dramas. On those soliloquies have also been modelled such noble poems as Browning's 'Artemis Prologizes' and Tennyson's 'Ulysses,' 'Tithonus,' 'Teiresias,' 'Demeter and Persephone,' which are tempered sometimes with a Homeric sometimes with a Theocritean note. It should be added, too, that the Greek choruses have been the models on which some of our finest poetry has been constructed. From them sprang such lyrics as Collins' 'Ode to Fear' and Shelley's 'Worlds on Worlds' in 'Hellas.'

The old Greek comedy, as represented by Aristophanes, has for the most part influenced English Literature only indirectly. Ben Jonson imitated the Parabases of Aristophanes. Foote, owing to the violent personality of the satire in his dramas, was called, not without reason, the English Aristophanes. Richard Cumberland, another playwright who had studied Greek at the University, translated the 'Clouds' into English, and no doubt in his own dramas owed something to his knowledge of the old Attic comedy. Four unsuccessful attempts which are not worth mentioning have been made in recent years to present counterparts to Aristophanic comedy in English. The influence of the New Comedy through Plautus and Terence has, of course, been immense, but we are not concerned at present with what has come to us indirectly through Rome.[3]

Bucolic poetry and idyllic poetry, the creations of the Alexandrian school, are represented to us by the idylls of Theocritus, Bion and Moschus, which have influenced English poetry so immensely that I have only space to indicate that influence by one illustration, the Funeral Poem. From the dirge over Daphnis in the first

British diplomat James Bruce, son of Thomas Bruce, 7th Earl of Elgin. Thomas Bruce was responsible for transferring the "Elgin Marbles" from Greece to the British Museum.

idyll of Theocritus, from Bion's dirge over Adonis and from Moschus' funeral poem on Bion have flowed (other rills, of course, contributing, and various modifications taking place), Spenser's 'Astrophel' and 'Mourning Muse of Thestylis,' Drummond's 'Pastoral Elegy,' Milton's 'Lycidas,' Congreve's 'Mourning Muse of Alexis,' Mason's 'Musæus,' Shelley's 'Adonais,' Matthew Arnold's 'Thyrsis' and innumerable other elegies: I have only selected one, as you will see, from each era.

Again, Theocritus suggested the form and gave the keynote for the style of 'Œnone,' for such idylls as the 'Gardener's Daughter,' and 'Walking to the Mail,' and for the superb lyric in the 'Princess,' "Come down, O maid." Turn where we will in Tennyson's poetry, we are never long without perceiving the perfume of this sweetest of Greek poets. And here we may notice that it is not so much in what is formal and susceptible of exact estimation that the influence of poetry on poetry is most real. The indebtedness of our poets to Greece, where that indebtedness is greatest, is often such as evades illustrative definition.

And now let us turn to another branch of poetry, and notice the influence which the Greek hymns have had on our poetry. These are represented by the Homeric hymns, the hymns of Callimachus and the Orphic hymns. Our poetical literature is full of poems, or of passages in poems, which have been modelled on them, which are sometimes simply parodies of them. We have first of all Spenser's four hymns, to Love, to Beauty, to Heavenly Love, to Heavenly Beauty. To these we shall have again . . . to recur, because they are steeped in Platonism. These do not, of course, borrow their form from the Greek hymns, but they derived their origin from them and much of their inspiration, and are constructed on their model. Chapman, who translated the Homeric hymns, modelled on them his 'Hymn to Christ upon the Cross.' If the Psalms gave the main inspiration, the hymns in 'Paradise Lost' owed much in the formal moulding to the Homeric hymns and to those of Callimachus. Henry More's philosophical poems are penetrated with the influence of the Orphic hymns. Two of the hymns of Callimachus have been paraphrased by Prior. Akenside, who, by the way, was saturated with Greek, has given us in his 'Hymn to the Naiads' the exact counterpart in English of the Callimachan hymn, and in several of his inscriptions we have the pure Greek note.

In William Whitehead's 'Hymn to the Nymph of the Bristol Spring' we have another imitation of Callimachus. Warton's 'Pleasures of Melancholy,' which would have been more correctly entitled 'A Hymn to Melancholy,' is but an ornate and picturesque variation of the Callimachan hymn. What are Keats' 'Hymn to Neptune,' Shelley's 'Hymn of Apollo,' Coleridge's 'Hymn to the Earth,' Wordsworth's 'Hymn to the Moon,' and innumerable others, but glorious echoes of the old Greek strains?

Now passing over the influence of the Greek minor poetry—the elegiac poetry and the epigram, which from the Elizabethan Age downwards has penetrated our poetry, giving us directly or indirectly many precious gems—we come to the great Greek Lyric Poets. To Anacreon, or rather to the Pseudo-Anacreon, we owe the charming Anacreontic, which, since Cowley naturalized it, has gone on repeating itself in every generation of our poets. To Sappho we owe innumerable poems or passages of poems of which Tennyson's 'Eleanore' and Swinburne's 'Anactoria' may be taken as illustrations. On Dionysius' 'Ode to Nemesis' Gray modelled his noble 'Ode to Adversity,' which became in its turn the model for Wordsworth's as noble 'Ode to Duty.' And who that is familiar with the fragments of other Greek lyric poetry, with those of Alcæus and Simonides especially, does not find their perfume and their echo in the lyrics of Akenside, Collins, Gray, Shelley, Landor, Tennyson, Arnold and Swinburne?

But our grandest inheritance from the Lyric of Greece is the Pindaric Ode—the ode modelled on the Epinikian Odes of Pindar. To deal adequately with the influence of Pindar on English poetry would require a volume. Let me only touch on the subject generally. And let us take first the direct imitations of Pindar; then the various modifications; and we shall find famous masterpieces of English lyric poetry.

The odes of Pindar are constructed on a very rigidly metrical system, among both the former and the latter, and in the full scheme consist of strophe, antistrophe and epode. The first poet who attempted to naturalize the Pindaric ode in English was Ben Jonson in his Pindaric ode on the death of Sir Henry Morison, and this regards faithfully the metrical scheme of strophe, antistrophe and epode. Next came Cowley in his 'Pindarique Odes,' as he calls them, two of which are adaptations of Pindar, one of Horace, one a paraphrase of part of Isaiah, and the others are original. But Cowley does not regard the strophe, antistrophe and epode, though there is a certain regularity about his metre. The consequence of this was that he called into being the pseudo-Pindaric or irregular ode, which, from his time to the death of Dryden, became one of the most popular forms of lyric poetry, and the works of the minor poets of that time abound in these so-called Pindaric odes, wild and licentious compositions in verses of every variety of syllables and feet, from verses of two feet to verses of sixteen. Some memorable odes were written in this pseudo-Pindaric style, such as Dryden's 'Song for St. Cecilia's Day,' his 'Ode to the Memory of Mrs. Anne Killigrew,' and his 'Alexander's Feast.' Dryden's contemporary, John Oldham, produced one of the most remarkable of the pseudo-Pindaric odes in his dithyramb in praise of Bacchus. Cowley's tradition was also kept up by the Pindarics of Dr. Thomas Sprat and by Thomas Yalden in his 'Hymn to Darkness.' Then came Congreve, who, after writing some of these irregular pseudo-Pindaric odes, acknowledged his error and wrote two in which he restored the strophe, antistrophe and epode, prefixing to them an interesting preface, in which he explained the metrical regularity of Pindar. Nevertheless, Swift, Pope, Addison, Prior and innumerable others went on producing their irregular Pindarics. But one poet of that age, Elijah Fenton, wrote in the regular style and produced a really fine Pindaric ode, dashed with Horatian influence—his 'Ode to Lord Gower,' which contains such powerful lines as these:—

> Shall man from Nature's sanction stray,
> With blind opinion for his guide,
> And rebel to her rightful sway,
> Leave all her bounties unenjoy'd?
> Fool! Time no change of motion knows
> With equal speed the torrent flows,
> To sweep Fame, Power, and Wealth away:
> The past is all by Death possess'd,
> And frugal Fate that guards the rest,
> By giving, bids him live to-day.

Passing by Akenside, whose Pindarics are more than respectable, we come to two immortal lyric poets, Collins and Gray. Collins' odes to Fear, to Mercy and to Liberty are three of the finest lyrics in our language, and are modelled partly on Pindar and partly on the Greek choruses. The ode to the Passions is not in strophe, antistrophe and epode, but an irregular and noble variation of the Pindaric ode. Then come Gray's 'Bard' and 'Progress of Poesy' which, though strongly flavoured with Latin rhetoric, are attempts to produce in English exact counterparts of Pindar, and so also is his fine Installation Ode. Then, passing over minor illustrations, we come to Shelley's grand Pindaric 'Ode to Naples.' And how splendid have been the modern variants of the Pindaric, Coleridge's Odes on France and the Departing Year, Shelley's 'Ode to Liberty,' Wordsworth's 'Intimations of Immortality' and 'Vernal Ode,' Tennyson's 'Ode to Memory' and 'On the Death of the Duke of Wellington'! So remarkable has been the history of Pindar's direct and indirect influence on our lyric poetry.

On Greek lyric poetry, simple or choric, have been modelled such gems as Ben Jonson's 'Queen and Huntress Chaste and Fair,' as the second and third song in Milton's 'Arcades,' as the Echo Song and the Sabrina Song in 'Comus.' Of Matthew Arnold's most delicious lyrics some are purely Greek, faithful Greek echoes, and, even where the modern note predominates, the Greek note is always there. But turn where we will in English lyric and elegiac poetry, we shall never wander very far without catching the breath and savour of the lyric genius of Greece. Nor must we omit to notice the enormous influence, both direct and indirect, which the Greek anthology has exercised on our minor poetry. From the time of the Renaissance there were innumerable selections from this collection generally accompanied with a Latin version, and it would literally fill a substantial volume adequately to indicate the influence of these poems on our minor poetry from, say, Shakespeare's last sonnet, which is a version of one of these poems, Ben Jonson's imitations, and onward through the Elizabethan Age in unbroken tradition to the poetry of to-day. The form of these poems has seldom or never been borrowed, but the matter, the sentiment, the imagery, the ideas have been a common treasury.

I have exceeded the time allotted to me, and yet I have not touched on what is perhaps the most important part of this subject, I mean the influence which Greek poetry has, as it were, insensibly exercised, exercised not formally on expression but as an inspiring, tempering, modifying, educative power, by which our poetry has been imperceptibly affected much as our minds are unconsciously affected by the air and character of those with whom we associate. And this constitutes perhaps our most real and important debt to Greece. But I have said enough to indicate, though I have only grazed the surface of the subject, how vast and complex is the indebtedness of English poetry to the poetry of Greece.

Notes

[1] Poeticae arti honos non erat: si qui in eâ re studebat aut sese ad convivia adplicabat, grassator vocabatur.—Cato apud Aulum Gellium xi, 2, 5.

[2] See P. L. iv, 358, 505. P. R. i, 196.

[3] On the influence of Plautus in modern literature see Reinhardstöttner, *Spätere Bearbeitungen plautinscher Lustspiele* (1886).

Frederick E. Pierce (essay date 1917)

SOURCE: "The Hellenic Current in English Nineteenth-Century Poetry," in *The Journal of English and Germanic Philology,* Vol. XVI, No. 1, January, 1917, pp. 103-35.

[*In the excerpt below, Pierce traces the "reasonably distinct Hellenic current" in English poetry from 1812 through the nineteenth century. Pierce discusses the Greek themes and forms of the poetry of this time, and credits several forces—including an increase in travel literature about Greece and Byron's journey to and writings about Greece—with developing the Greek "spirit" in nineteenth-century poetry.*]

I

There are two ways in which the literature of a foreign country may influence our own poetry: as a forming spirit, molding any material either that of its own or that of another nation; or as a source of material, molded by any forming spirit, whether Greek, Roman, or medieval. The two methods are often distinct and often merge. William Mason's *Elfrida* is Greek in spirit, medieval in subject matter. The Hellenic tales of William Morris's *Earthly Paradise* are Greek in material, medieval-romantic in atmosphere. Wordsworth's *Laodamia* is Greek in both.

The problems raised by a discussion of these two influences are also different. In studying the working of the Hellenic or the medieval spirit we must ask ourselves whether we have truly comprehended or misconceived it; whether it will assimilate with our existing culture; whether it is the element best fitted to maintain artistic balance in our national life. In tracing the use of Hellenic material by modern poets, the exploiting of ancient history, legend, and mythology, we are confronted by other questions. Does the richness of association investing these tales make them still especially fit for poetry, or are they becoming shopworn from overuse? Does continual association with events caused by an obsolete social system tend to expand our horizon; or does it, on the contrary, tend to produce certain stereotyped faults, akin to those of decadent neo-classicism, in the handling of both incident and phraseology? So distinct are the two sets of problems that a critic might with perfect consistency advocate for our modern poetry a great increase in the Hellenic spirit and a great decrease in the use of Hellenic legend.

In his *Greek Influence on English Poetry* the late J. Churton Collins has recently discussed the first and more difficult problem. We wish to supplement his work by tracing the use of Greek material through the nineteenth century, drawing some conclusions and leaving others for our readers. Occasionally we may have gone too far into the limbo of forgotten rhymers; but for the modern poet and critic failure at times has its lesson as well as success.

Although we have heard repeatedly that English neo-classicism was Latin rather than Greek, it is something of a revelation to analyze our writers from 1700 to 1812 and find how indifferent they seemed to the narrative possibilities of the chief classical literature. Pope, Thomson, Collins, Gray, Chatterton, the Wartons, Dr. Johnson, Goldsmith, Cowper, Crabbe, Burns, Blake, have not left us a single great original poem located on Greek soil or drawn from Greek mythology. This is the more marked when we remember that Gray and Thomas Warton were eminent Greek scholars, and that the poems of Collins teem with Grecian allusions. There were evidently counter influences in the air. The few versifications based on Hellenic material during that long period are now almost unreadable. Thomson's *Liberty* and *Agamemnon,* Home's *Agis,* Glover's *Leonidas,* Beattie's *Judgment of Paris,*—who outside of specialists as much as hears their names? Even Akenside's *Hymn to the Naiads* and the digression on Greece in the last book of Falconer's *Shipwreck* are following their less deserving comrades into oblivion.

The early nineteenth century writers before 1812 make only a little better showing. The poems of Wordsworth published before 1814, the earlier works of Coleridge, Southey, Scott, Campbell, and of the more poetical minors, such as Hogg and Leyden, almost ignore Hellas. Moore's paraphrase of *Anacreon* (1800), though well received, was essentially a schoolboy's exercise. Two or three early minor poems of his on Greek themes are short and insignificant. Some of Landor's early poems might be mentioned; but these were unknown and still are. His *Count Julian* and *Gebir* are Spanish in location, whatever they may be in spirit.

To find much in this decade we must go down among the minors. William Sotheby, Byron's pet aversion, "that Itch of Scribbling personified,"[1] in 1802 published his *Orestes,* a crude play mixing a melodramatic ghost crying "Vengeance" with classic antiquity. Mrs. Tighe's *Psyche* (1805) was on a Greek theme and influenced Keats's *Endymion;* but, aside from the fact that it is a minor work, it speedily drifts away from an earthly Hellas into a medieval dreamland, with a feudal knight, a "Gothic castle", and all the allegorical machinery of Spenser. W. R. Wright in 1809 published his *Horae Ionicae,* written partly in Greece, partly from memory in England. The book is full of first-hand, though badly worded, descriptions of Greek scenes, but in meter and diction represents the most decadent stage of the Pope tradition.

From 1812 on we find a reasonably distinct Hellenic current, turning both major and minor poets to Grecian themes, increasing or lessening from time to time, but continuing practically unbroken to the present day. That contemporaries felt this rise of a new stream is shown by a quotation from the *Edinburgh Review*[2] for 1813: "Greece, the mother of freedom and poetry in the West, which had long employed only the antiquary, the artist, and the philologist, was at length destined, after an interval of many silent and inglorious ages, to awaken the genius of a poet."

Before tracing this current we may pause to consider its causes. One of these was obviously the world-ransacking curiosity of the romantic generation. Another was the growing realization among the romanticists, after their first reaction against neo-classicism, that Greek literature[3] was not neo-classic. Another was the intrinsic beauty of that literature, which even in the garbled versions of the eighteenth century

> Would plead like angels trumpet-tongued
> against
> The deep damnation of its taking off.

But back of these, and stimulating them, lay the great revival in Greek scholarship near the turn of the century. "As in the seventeenth, so in the eighteenth century, Greek had not much hold on the many. Neglected in the public schools, neglected in the universities, not required either for degrees or for ordination, it was the rarest of accomplishments."[4] "The difficulty of the Greek language has always been an impediment in the way of knowledge of Greek literature, and this difficulty was for a long time aggravated in England by want of lexicons, grammars, and good texts, so that an intimate critical acquaintance with it was impossible till late in the eighteenth century."[5] For the cure of the latter evil, the world owes a lasting debt to Richard Porson, the greatest Greek scholar of his age, and far superior in that particular field to his eighteenth century predecessors. In textual criticism, comment, etc., his editions of the ancients were epoch-making, and they came just in time to influence the younger generation of the romantic poets. Byron studied Porson's edition of *Hecuba* at Harrow, and afterward bequeathed his copy to the library there.[6] "The prince of Grecians," drunken and untidy, was no *arbiter elegantiarum,* but the effect of his work on poetry is unquestionable.

Profoundly skill'd,—in learning deeply read,
He form'd the *judgment,* while the *taste* he
led. . . .
In Grecian learning he was deeply vers'd,
The best of Grecians, he was *own'd* the first,

wrote a minor poet[7] in 1808, the year of his death. And De Quincey[8] reminds us that "as a Grecian, Coleridge must be estimated with a reference to the state and standard of Greek literature at that time and in this country. Porson had not yet raised our ideal." "Classical scholarship had not been represented by a single man of mark since the death of the learned Richard Bentley in 1742, and Porson, the eminent Greek scholar by whom it was revived, did not receive his appointment as professor until 1793,"[9] says Professor Legouis; and he adds that at Cambridge, Porson's university, "The[10] mathematical tripos, or principal competitive examination was instituted in 1747, the classical tripos not until 1824," which was just about the time that the Tennyson brothers began to come to Cambridge.

Increasing knowledge of Hellas itself went hand in hand with increasing knowledge of Hellenic literature. Between 1784 and 1818 Mitford was publishing in various installments his *History of Greece.* In spite of its faults it opened to the public a field which had not before been even respectably presented to them. In his Advertisement to the first edition Mitford declared that his errors could only be excused by "The reality of the want," and a very stern, anti-literary reality that was. Mitford, at the suggestion of Gibbon, took this subject, not because he was especially in sympathy with it, but because it had been so glaringly neglected. The effect of such a work on a curious age craving for novelty and beauty, must have been considerable. Mrs. Hemans' *Storm of Delphi,* as she tells us in a footnote, was suggested by Mitford's citations from Herodotus; and other better poems must have had a similar origin.

The great increase in books of travel discussing Greece was also unquestionably a factor. The footnotes to Grecian poems by Moore and Mrs. Hemans refer repeatedly to many such books, most of which appeared between 1760 and 1830. A number of other works on scholarship and travel in Greece during this period are cited by Professor H. T. Peck in his *History of Classic Philology* (p. 380). *The Monthly Review* for August, 1811, reviewing books of Sir William Gell, (*The Topography of Troy* (1804), *Geography and Antiquities of Ithaca* (1807, etc.) mentions "that laudable curiosity concerning the remains of classical antiquity, which has of late years increased among our countrymen."[11]

Another cause was Byron's journey to Greece—in itself part of the increasing tourist current turning there—and the sudden popularity in 1812 of his poetry describing it (*Childe Harold,* Canto II). The purely Hellenic current was also at first associated with, and encouraged by, the great Orientalizing movement led by Byron and Moore. Between 1812 and 1840 at least many poets saw in all Greece what Lord Houghton saw specially in Corfu,

A portal, whence the Orient,
The long-desired, long-dreamt of, Orient,
Opens upon us, with its stranger forms,
Outlines immense and gleaming distances,
And all the circumstance of faery-land.[12]

By the irony of destiny, the movement that Byron precipitated was additionally furthered by an act which he himself in *The Curse of Minerva* had denounced as vandalism. Not far from the time when the great poet returned to England with *Childe Harold* in his portmanteau, Lord Elgin brought to the same shores from Greece the famous Elgin Marbles; and in 1816 they were purchased by the government and put on public exhibition in the British Museum. The Hellenizing influence of so much beautiful sculpture in a place so easily accessible could not but have its effect. Both Keats and Mary Shelley[13] speak of spending an afternoon in the Museum with the Elgin Marbles. Keats wrote two sonnets on them, in one of which he says:

So do these wonders [bring] a most dizzy
pain,
That mingles Grecian grandeur with the rude
Wasting of old Time—with a billowy main—
A sun—a shadow of a magnitude.

These sonnets were addressed to Keats's friend, the painter Haydon, who had published an essay pointing out the beauties of the sculptures in question, and done all in his power to spread their influence. Hazlitt[14] in *Table Talk* says of statues that he "never liked any till I saw the Elgin marbles." The mood which they would tend to develop in a man is exactly that found in Keats's *Ode on a Grecian Urn.* Less important, though of the same nature, was the greater accesibility to Englishmen after 1814 of the classic art treasures of the Louvre, treasures which had been almost closed to them for two decades by the French wars. "The reader may remember," says Beattie,[15] "the enthusiasm with which Campbell had visited the antique statues in the Louvre [in 1814]. The effect was still fresh in his mind, and when he resumed his lectures on the Poetry of Greece [in 1818], his prose was enriched by frequent allusions to her sculptures."

The last and most obvious of the causes we are discussing was the revolt of the Greeks against Turkey in 1821, which turned on them the eyes of all Europe. The connection of this war with literature is patent, and needs no discussion except a reminder that "coming events cast their shadows before," and that the strain and unrest of the Greeks—their longing for liberty in an age when the French Revolution had set every one dreaming of liberty—must have influenced English poetry long before the first cannon was fired.

Bearing these causes in mind, let us take up the beginning and first broadening of the current, the period from 1812 to 1830. By a strange mockery of fate, the great original impetus came from a spirit in some ways the very opposite to Athenian art, from Byron. But that Byron became an innovator was not due merely to the fact that he happened to travel in modern Attica. Deep in his heart he admired and longed for the very elements he lacked. We feel this in *Manfred,* where the stormy Byronic hero confronts the Witch of the Alps, with her calm brow, "Whereon is glassed serenity of soul." And Byron loved the country of Hellas, with its associations. His "longings constantly turned toward Greece. Even before the actual publication of *Childe Harold* Dallas and other friends pressed him to continue it; this, he replied, was impossible in England, he could only do it under the blue skies of Greece."[16] Hence it was not so strange that the "rhyming peer" should lead in the revival under discussion. His second canto of *Childe Harold,* written largely on Grecian soil, was filled with existing ruins and the glory of past associations,

> When wandering slow by Delphi's sacred side,
> Or gazing o'er the plains where Greek and Persian died.
>
> And yet how lovely in thine age of woe,
> Land of lost gods and godlike men, art thou.
>
> Where'er we tread 'tis haunted, holy ground.

Then followed *The Giaour,* and *The Bride of Abydos,* which, though Oriental tales, contain long interpolated passages on the past glory of Hellas and the Trojan war.

> "Clime of the unforgotten brave!" says *The Giaour*
> "Shrine of the mighty! can it be,
> That this is all remains of thee? . . .
> Say, is not this Thermopylae? . . .
> Pronounce what sea, what shore is this?
> The gulf, the rock of Salamis!"

The second canto of *The Bride of Abydos* devotes over fifty lines to musings on the plain of Troy, memories of Leander, Priam, Achilles, Alexander, and Homer. *The Corsair* and *The Siege of Corinth* are located on Grecian soil, and though little connected with the great past suggest it occasionally. Byron's *Prometheus* is a Promethean theft from the mythology of Aeschylus; and in his poem on his thirty-sixth year he cries:

> The sword, the banner, and the field,
> Glory and Greece, around me see!
> The Spartan borne upon his shield,
> Was not more free.

Most intense of all in its Hellenism is "The isles of Greece" in Canto III of *Don Juan:*

> Where burning Sappho loved and sung,
> Where grew the arts of war and peace,
> Where Delos rose, and Phoebus sprung.

If we should say that Byron is praising the land of poets whose thought and style were utterly unlike his own, he would be first to acknowledge it and point to his own lines:

> And must their lyre so long divine,
> Degenerate into hands like mine.

The two great products of this current before 1830 were Keats and Shelley, but others around and before them were touched by it. Mrs. Hemans, significant through popularity if not through merit, turns from domesticity and medievalism to write *Modern Greece* (1817), a poem of a thousand lines in imitation of *Childe Harold.*

> "Oh! who hath trod thy consecrated clime,
> Fair land of Phidias! theme of lofty strains!
> And traced each scene, that, 'midst the wrecks of time,
> The print of Glory's parting step retains," etc.

The same author gives us over a dozen scattering short poems on Grecian themes: *The Last Song of Sappho; The Spartan's March,* etc.

Her *Tombs of Platea* begins:

> And there they sleep!—the men who stood
> In arms before the exulting sun,
> And bathed their spears in Persian blood,
> And taught the earth how freedom might be won.

In 1818 T. L. Peacock, soaked for years in the best literature of antiquity, printed his one masterly poem, *Rhododaphne,* Grecian in story, and Attic in its polished style, wildly romantic as are its incidents.

Tom Moore's *Evenings in Greece* (1826) is very feeble poetry; but its length shows that the author felt the growing current. The scene is modern, but, like all descriptions of modern Greece, tinged with some past associations. Moore's *Legendary Ballads* (1828) contain short poems on the Greek themes of *Cupid* and *Psyche, Hero and Leander,* and *Cephalus* and *Procris.* His *Memoirs* (published by Lord John Russell) show that the Irish lyrist during this period read many books or articles about Greece and Greek literature, among them Fouriel's *Chantes Populaires de la Gréce.*[17] Campbell in 1822 wrote his *Song of the Greeks,*

Again to the battle, Achaians!

and in 1828 his *Stanzas on the Battle of Navarino,*

Hearts of oak that have bravely delivered the brave,
And uplifted old Greece from the brink of the grave.

Barry Cornwall in 1823 published his *Flood of Thessaly,* a poem of over a thousand lines developing in fair Miltonic verse the story of Deucalion and Pyrrha. It ends with Deucalion's Miltonic vision of the coming glories of ancient Hellas. Barry Cornwall also, in his *Dramatic Scenes* (1819) includes *Lysander and Ione* "a pastoral" with "something of the familiarity of a common dialogue," like the more playful style of Landor. Lysander's description of a waterfall, "Rich as Dorado's paradise," shows a romantic mercy toward anachronisms.

The current produced from Wordsworth one classic masterpiece, *Laodamia* (1815), located in the Greece of the Trojan wars and celebrating "calm pleasures" and "majestic pains." Lamb felt that a change had come over the poet of the *Lyrical Ballads,* and wrote to Wordsworth: "*Laodamia* is a very original poem; I mean original with reference to your own manner. You have nothing like it. I should have seen it in a strange place, and greatly admired it, but not suspected its derivation."[18] The same atmosphere appears in his *Dion* (1820):

Mourn, hills and groves of Attica! and mourn
Ilissus, bending o'er thy classic urn.

Wordsworth also produced three mediocre sonnets on Greek themes: "When Philoctetes in the Lemnian isle" (1827); and the two sonnets *On a Celebrated Event in Ancient History,* published 1815 but written 1810. Beddoes, probably not long after 1820, turned from his haunted charnel-house to write *Pygmalion,* a Greek theme handled somewhat in the style of Keats's *Lamia.* Leigh Hunt in 1819 published his *Hero and Leander.* The same subject was treated more at length and with more success by Tom Hood in 1827. In the same volume with the latter Hood published his charming *Lycus, the Centaur,* which portrays the terrible effects of Circe's power with romantic horror sufficiently unlike *Comus.* Passing mention can also be afforded to *Ariadne* (1814) by Edward, Baron Thurlow, *The Naiad* (1816) by Keats's friend and one time poetic rival, J. H. Reynolds, and Praed's prize poem *Athens* (1824).

Enough has been said to show that in the decade and a half following 1812 there was a widespread Hellenic tendency. In the midst of this current rise, as its two chief exponents, Keats and Shelley. In Keats's first volume the Greek element is slight, and is completely overshadowed by pseudo-medievalism. But in his second work the growing tide has caught him. *Endymion* in mood and style is distinctly Spenserian, not Homeric; but its subject matter is wholly Attic and is regarded through a loving though uncritical eye. In the third or 1820 book of poems *Lamia,* the *Ode on a Grecian Urn, Ode to Psyche,* and the unfinished *Hyperion* are classic in the noblest sense of the word, and as nobly Grecian as anything in our language.

The Greek element in Keats is the instinctive answer of deep to deep, and by no means confined to poems on Greek mythology. Compare with his well known *Ode To Autumn* the following lines from Pater's[19] translation of Theocritus:

"The scent of late summer and of the fall of the year was everywhere; the pears fell from the trees at our feet, and apples in number rolled down at our sides. . . . A cup like this ye poured out now upon the altar of Demeter, who presides over the threshing-floor. May it be mine, once more, to dig my big winnowing-fan through her heaps of corn; and may I see her smile upon me, holding poppies and handfuls of corn in her two hands!"

Shelley, like Keats, was drawn in among the Hellenists after he had already appeared as an author, although a love for things Grecian seems always to have existed in both. *Queen Mab, The Revolt of Islam,* and *Rosalind and Helen* have nothing especially Greek either in spirit or matter, nor is any such element sharply prominent in *Alastor.* The *Cenci* is Elizabethan rather than Greek, and full of verbal echoes from Shakespeare. *Swellfoot the Tyrant* (1820) though redolent of Aristophanes, is not a great drama. It is in *Prometheus Unbound* (1820) and scattering poems, chiefly posthumous, which follow it, that Shelley's discipleship to the ancients becomes mature. *Hellas* (1821) was suggested by the *Persians* of Aeschylus; and, imperfect as it is, reveals its great model in the noble closing chorus. The following short poems, all written after 1819, are thoroughly Greek: *Arethusa; Song of Proserpine, while gathering flowers; Hymn of Apollo; Hymn of Pan; Orpheus.* At least three of these belong to the highest order of poetry. The *Prometheus Unbound,* by the direct comparison which it invites with Aeschylus, shows what the Hellenic current in English poetry before 1830 was and what it was not. Attic symmetry is found only fitfully in the short poems and almost never in the long ones. The action of *Prometheus Unbound* is dramatic and Aeschylean only in the first act, where the ancient models are most closely followed. The rest of the poem, like a river released from its levees, spreads out into a meandering, beautiful, uncharted marsh, with water lilies and moonshine and music across the waves. Yet certain unquestionably Greek elements are there; the pure sense of beauty, the avoidance of the medieval grotesque, the world of the calm superman as opposed to the stormy superman of Byron. All of these elements appear also in *Hyperion,* and the first two in *Endymion.*

The Hellenic current was an outgrowth of the romantic movement. In its own productions it was sometimes thoroughly romantic, sometimes doubtfully so; but it was never neo-classic. It is perhaps significant that no poems on Grecian themes were produced by either Crabbe or Rogers, although the latter locates his most lengthy poem in the country of the ancient Romans. In general the writers of the romantic generation saw the light of Hellas as they did that of the Middle Ages, through the stained glass of a temperament, which sometimes resulted in a startling juxtaposition of the words *classic* and *romantic.* Mrs. Hemans in Modern Greece (xxiii) addresses a Greek ruin as "romantic temple," and adds two lines below:

> Years, that have changed thy river's *classic* name,
> Have left thee still in savage pomp sublime.
>
> lxvii: Thebes, Corinth, Argos!—ye, renoun'd of old,
> Where are your chiefs of high *romantic* name?

Campbell in his lectures on Greek poetry said that "scarce any conception of romantic poetry existed, the germ of which might not be traced to the Odyssey."[20] K. H. Digby in his *Broad Stone of Honour* emphasizes the fact that Greek poets loved remote lands and ages: "Of all the Grecian princes who went to Troy, Ulysses was from the country most remote from the land of Homer. The heroes of the Athenian tragic drama, the Pelopidae, and the Labdacidae, were all foreigners. Pausanias remarks that the Greeks must always have more admired the wonders of foreign countries than of their own; since their most celebrated historians have described the pyramids of Egypt with the greatest exactness, and have said nothing of the royal treasury of Minyas, nor of the walls of Tirynthus, no less admirable than the pyramids."[21] But a less romantic, more truly classic note often appears, as, for example in Hazlitt's *Round Table,*[22] a quotation from which may be compared with Keats's *Grecian Urn:* "The gusto in the Greek statues is of a very singular kind. The sense of perfect form nearly occupies the whole mind, and hardly suffers it to dwell on any other feeling. It seems enough for them *to be,* without acting or suffering. Their forms are ideal, spiritual. Their beauty is power. By their beauty they are raised above the frailties of pain or passion; by their beauty they are deified." Shelley writes:[23] "Could a Grecian architect have commanded all the labour and money which are expended on Versailles, he would have produced a fabric which the whole world has never equalled."

The less romantic attitude toward Greece was not a less enthusiastic one. "Rome and Athens,"[24] declared Hazlitt, "filled a place in the history of mankind, which can never be occupied again." In his posthumous Essay on the Revival of Literature (1832) Shelley speaks of "Grecian literature,—the finest the world has ever produced." Unlike Hazlitt, however, he admired Greece at the expense of Rome. In a letter to Peacock, January 26th, 1819, he cries: "O, but for that series of wretched wars which terminated in the Roman conquest of the world; but for the Christian religion, which put the finishing stroke on the ancient system; but for those changes which conducted Athens to its ruin,—to what an eminence might not humanity have arrived!" He writes again to John Gisborne, November 16, 1819: "Were not the Greeks a glorious people? What is there, as Job says of the Leviathan, like unto them? If the army of Nicias had not been defeated under the walls of Syracuse; if the Athenians had, acquiring Sicily, held the balance between Rome and Carthage, sent garrisons to the Greek colonies in the South of Italy, Rome might have been all that its intellectual condition entitled it to be, a tributary, not the conqueror of Greece."

Notes

[1] Prothero's *Byron's Letters,* IV, 228.

[2] Vol. XXII, p. 37.

[3] "The machinery of early romance writers," wrote Southey in the Preface to his *Amadis of Gaul,* "is probably rather of classical than of Oriental origin. . . . Enchanted weapons may be traced to the workshop of Vulcan as easily as to the dwarfs of Scandinavia. The tales of dragons may be originally oriental; but the adventures of Jason and Hercules were popular tales in Europe, long before the supposed migration of Odin, or the birth of Mohammed. If magical rings were invented in Asia, it was Herodotus, who introduced the fashion into Europe? The fairies and ladies of the lake bear a closer resemblance to the nymphs and naiads of Rome and Greece, than to the peris of the East."

[4] J. Churton Collins' *Greek Influence on English Poetry,* p. 51.

[5] J. Churton Collins' *Greek Influence on English Poetry,* p. 58.

[6] Lord Russell's *Memoirs of Moore,* II, 624.

[7] Barker's *Anecdotes,* II, 6.

[8] *Coleridge and Opium Eating.*

[9] Legouis' *William Wordsworth,* Matthews' translation, p. 72.

[10] *Ibid.,* p. 74.

[11] P. 371.

[12] *Corfu* (written 1832).

[13] Dowden's *Life of Shelley,* II, 183.

[14] Waller and Glover's ed., VI, 16.

[15] Beattie's *Life and Letters of Thomas Campbell,* II, 93.

[16] Elze's *Life of Byron,* p. 130 of Eng. Translation.

[17] Russell II, 515.

[18] Lucas's Lamb's Works, VI, 457.

[19] In *Demeter and Persephone.*

[20] Redding's *Literary Reminiscences,* I, 113.

[21] Godefridus, p. 19, ed. of 1844.

[22] Waller and Glover's ed., I, 79.

[23] Dowden's *Life of Shelley,* II, 43.

[24] Waller and Glover's ed., I, 4.

Stephen A. Larrabee (essay date 1943)

SOURCE: Conclusion to *English Bards and Grecian Marbles: The Relationship Between Sculpture and Poetry, Especially in the Romantic Period,* Columbia University Press, 1943, pp. 277-88.

[*In the following essay, Larrabee reviews the reaction of Romantic poets to Greek sculpture, and argues that the Romantic poets "wished to emulate the Greeks in making great art from the circumstances of their time."*]

During the Romantic period in England poets responded to the sculpture of Greece in a variety of ways. Many of them stated directly the sensations felt when they beheld works of art. In recording in verse the actual experience of seeing sculptured works, Byron and Keats surpassed other poets of the time. A man of taste almost in spite of himself, in *Childe Harold* Byron described the "old antique" in the visits of his hero to the Italian galleries. The familiar Greco-Roman works had been somewhat staled by countless gentlemen who had marveled at their canons of proportion and Ideal Beauty. None the less, Byron gave the Apollo and the Venus a show of significance through his easy rhetoric and passionate sentimentality. In *The Curse of Minerva* a different method of statement appeared, with the imagined sensations of prize fighters and dainty maidens reflecting the poet's own experience and opinion of the Elgin Marbles. Keats, on the other hand, in the "Haydon" sonnets reported almost too accurately his experiencing of the "mighty things" from the Parthenon. A young poet untutored in the arts, he transferred to paper the dizzying rush of sensations with which he saw before him a new realm of artistic achievement in the grand style of the Greek sculptures.

Two lesser poets offered parallel statements. In *Paris in 1815* George Croly, a disciple of Byron, enumerated the antiques in the Halls of Sculpture at the Louvre and minutely described their appearance. William Haygarth in *Greece* imagined the Elgin friezes in their original places on the Parthenon, even turning his eyes upward to gaze upon the "long procession" of marble men and maidens moving to the sacrifice.

Other poets left glowing accounts of their "soul-adventures" in the presence of Greek sculpture, but more often in letters or journals, in criticism, or in miscellaneous prose than in poetry. Again Keats and, in a lesser degree, Byron gave very personal reports, though Shelley easily outdid them in prose statements of his interest in ancient art. The comments in Shelley's *Notes on Sculptures in Rome and Florence* were the most vivid record by any Romantic poet of stimulating hours in galleries. Shelley represented all poets, perhaps, when he remarked, "These things are best spoken of when the mind has drunk in the spirit of their forms."[1]

For "romantic" poets, as indeed for certain poets as far back as the twelfth century, the most exciting element in seeing Grecian statuary was the feeling that the forms or figures of sculpture were expressive. Statues were not "bodies" but "breathers." After making that discovery, the poets went beyond their own sensations to revel in and to describe the "life" of the sculptured forms. To show the vitality and lifelike qualities of a statue, the "romantic" poet often termed it a "breathing stone" in the manner of earlier poets. He was more likely, however, to grant the statue a more complex set of activities than merely being a counterfeit of nature or the embodiment of a typical trait or characteristic. Many statues were imagined as enjoying finer lives than those of human beings, in passionate moments made enduring in the lasting material of marble. Whether stones "warmed to life," whether "incarnations," in the language of Shelley, "of all the finest minds have conceived of beauty," or whether "cold pastoral" scenes of bacchanales or sacrifices, Greek sculpture had to reveal vital or living or emotional qualities in order to stir the feelings and imaginations of poets.

The discovery of "life" in statues was the prerequisite of poetry throughout the long tradition of interest in Greek sculpture among English poets. In the Romantic period the imaginative "animation" or "energizing" or "emotionalizing" of Grecian statues took a greater variety of forms than previously. There was little evidence of aesthetic appreciation of sculpture, of course, in the factual or informational accounts, which remained fairly numerous. The minor poets, such as the collegiate winners of Newdigate Prizes and Chancellor's Medals, tended to assert the "life" of sculptures and to describe little more than the positions of the figures and the activities represented. Byron, Wordsworth, and Coleridge at times wrote verse of this more rhetorical and "academic" nature.

The emphasis on the "life" of statuary also led to a rehearsal of episodes from the mythological history of the subject. In the Romantic period poets turned on many occasions from statues to mythological tales, legends, and fancies. Procter's "Theseus" was perhaps the finest example of a purely mythological sketch suggested by a statue. The Pygmalion myth still attracted the poets, along with a somewhat similar modern story of the maid of France who died from unrequited love for the Apollo Belvedere.

As far as the description in poetry of the "life" found in sculpture was concerned, Keats held the foremost position among "romantic" poets, largely because he vitalized the sculpture itself instead of presenting incidents and episodes other than those represented in the subjects of his poems. In the "Ode on a Grecian Urn" and the "Ode on Indolence," for example, he concerned himself with the emotions and passions of the figures, in other words, with the drama arrested in the sculpture instead of with extraneous incidents. The continuously blissful future of the lovers (along with the "happy boughs" and the "melodist, unwearied,") was mentioned, to be sure, but always as an ever living, because sculptured, passionate activity. Since Keats kept his attention on the figures themselves as they were upon the urn and the vase, the two odes approached the ideal of the poetic endowing of sculpture with "life," the re-creation of the feeling of sculpture in the medium of poetry.

The identification of himself with a sculptural figure imagined to possess great vitality and emotional activity was easy for almost every "romantic" poet. At some time all the major poets except Wordsworth and Coleridge identified their own feelings with the "life" in Grecian statues. The Apollo statues, especially the Belvedere figure whose arrow has perhaps just felled a tyrant, was a particular favorite. Apollo also symbolized various aspects of the beau ideal of manly beauty for Shelley, Byron, and Hunt. The statue was admired, too, as the form of the poet's god, the symbol of poesy, reason, thought, and everything muselike. Byron saw the love of Juan and Haidée in a sculptured group as an idealized version of one of his own amours. Shelley identified himself with Bacchus; Byron associated himself sometimes with Hercules and again with Apollo. Blake could find in the Laocoön group an allegory of his struggles with the world of art. Keats interpreted figures on vases in relation to his personal problems.

"Romantic" poets likewise gave peculiarly personal descriptions of Grecian statues. The Venus de Medici still served for the beau ideal of feminine grace. Byron in particular tended to judge many of his friends by their similarity to the darling of the Uffizi. Shelley responded to Praxitelean shapes of an eager lightness and a soft ideality. Landor's feeling in sculpture was for coldness, grandeur, and restraint. Hunt, Keats, De Quincey, and Hazlitt carried their ideas of sculpture into the theater, writing criticism of actors and acting in the terms of sculpture.

Yet the imaginative re-creation of sculptural scenes and figures presented the best reflection of the interest of poets of the Romantic period in the "life" which they found in ancient art. These re-creations of the feeling of sculpture ranged from Byron's Zuleika postured as a younger Niobe to Shelley's hermaphrodites in *The Witch of Atlas* and *Epipsychidion;* from Keats's statuesque "stationings" in *Hyperion* and *Endymion* to the flower in Wordsworth's "Love Lies Bleeding" drooping in the fashion of the Dying Gladiator, or to Moore's "Kiss" *à la* Cupid and Psyche; and from the sculpturesque scenes in the poetry of Keats and Landor to the visionary sculptures of Blake and the linear, dreamlike reliefs seen by Shelley.

Landor, Keats, and Shelley excelled in re-creating sculptural scenes and relief-like figures, with Hunt and Byron nearest them, though at some distance. Somewhat apart from the other poets in his conscious checking of emotional suggestiveness, Landor was most nearly the "classical" sculptor. Nevertheless, he was only slightly more appreciative of the decorative values of sculpture than were Keats and Shelley. The three of them were the early nineteenth-century poets most concerned with sculpturesque qualities. Keats possessed the ability to make his descriptions of sculpture convey the feeling of the art to a degree unequaled by any contemporary English poet. Shelley had similar powers of intuition and expression, but he often clothed his figures in Shelleyan garments. His sculptural figures became rather too unsubstantial, too dreamlike, or too linear for sculpture. Byron was sensitive to sculptural qualities, though he was inclined either to be too serious and too sentimental or else to distrust his feelings. His imaginative use of sculptures for comical and satirical purposes was unequaled in Romantic poetry. In a few lines Hunt alone rivaled him in poetry of this kind.

A similar richness and variety appeared in the poetry of the Romantic period which dealt with the complex group of "ideas" concerning society, the arts, and culture associated, as we have seen, with Greek sculpture by poets from the seventeenth century onward. The Grecian enthusiasm of Shelley, Byron, Hunt, and Landor led them to relate social and political ideals to sculpture more often than the other poets. They were the leading Hellenists of the Romantic period in respect to social and political matters, and they admired the state where sculpture had flourished under the tutelage of Liberty.

Blake, Shelley (and through him Byron to a small degree), Landor, Wordsworth, and Coleridge were interested in the Grecian workmanship revealed in sculpture for the light shed upon the poetical faculty or power and upon the nature of the artistic or creative processes Landor again stood somewhat apart from the other poets in that he failed to advance the distinctive "romantic" theory of art, namely, the theory in which the stress fell upon the inner meaning and organic form of the ancient statues. Shelley more than compensated for Landor's silence, however, in his numerous treatments in poetry of various aspects of that view of the Antique.

Excluding Landor, then, these poets might be called Hellenists in regard to morality and aesthetics, were it not that one hesitates to apply the term to Blake, Wordsworth, and Coleridge. The three poets were such staunch defenders of the Christian and the Modern against the Pagan and the Ancient that they scarcely merit the label of Hellenist. They would probably have agreed with Horace Smith, whose "Moral Ruins" related a kind of "progress" of sculpture and the other arts in the light of their morality, in which the highest and the one true and abiding religion proved to be the Christian.

> The marble miracles of Greece and Rome,
> Temple and Dome,
> Art's masterpieces, awful in the excess
> Of loveliness,
> Hallowed by statued Gods which might be thought
> To be themselves by the Celestials wrought,—
> Where are they now?—their majesty august
> Grovels in dust.[2]

However, they were concerned with the moral and religious influences upon Grecian art almost as much as Shelley. Though convinced that the mythological fables of Greece expressed pagan creeds and outworn sentiments, this trio might have been willing occasionally to join the poetaster T. K. Hervey, whom Williams's *Select Views in Greece* (1829) moved to exclaim,

> The heart that owns a better faith may kneel,
> Nor wrong his creed, while bending o'er the sod
> Where gods—and men *like* gods, in act and will,—
> Are made immortal, by the wizard rod
> Of him whose every thought aspired to be a god![3]

Moreover, like Shelley, each poet interpreted the Greek works as illustrating his personal and "romantic" conceptions of the creative power. Blake imagined that the Grecian artists had sculptured visions. Wordsworth and Coleridge saw in Grecian art the working of the Neo-Platonic plastic process by which spiritual belief reveals itself in sensuous and intelligible material forms. Shelley felt that the ancient artists had made sculpture into a vehicle for the expression of thought and intellectual beauty. The Greek statues were of great beauty and external loveliness; but, for all four poets, their true glory lay in the mental or intellectual or spiritual elements which the sculptors had expressed in "fixed shapes" of stone.

Great artists, the Greek sculptors too, apparently, had been "romantic." In the words of Blake, they had bodied forth "spiritual existences." Or, as a minor "romantic" poet, Charles Lloyd, succinctly stated this view of art:

> 'Tis not the form that is th' essential thing,
> It is the soul, the spirit, that is there.[4]

Yet the all-important spirit or soul needed a shape or material form in which to reveal itself, and the statues of Greece presented something close to an ideal fusion of spirit and matter, the Idea made manifest in sensible form. In sculpture, as practised by the Greeks in particular, Coleridge found that "the perfection of form is an outward symbol of inward perfection and the most elevated ideas, where the body is wholly penetrated by the soul, and spiritualized even to a state of glory." Expressive symbols, the statues were living forms whose external beauty resulted from the spirit within.

With such a view of art, the admiration of external forms is already on the decline. Their praise of the spirit of Grecian workmanship actually led Blake, Wordsworth, and Coleridge away from the Antique—to such an extent that one ordinarily excludes them from the ranks of the Hellenists. These "romantic" poets valued statues, not for their perfect forms—whether reposeful or grandly simple or teeming with emotional activity—but for the spirit or soul operating within the marble forms. Wordsworth gave the finest statement in poetry of this view of sculpture in *The Excursion,* where he explicitly turned from the "fixed shapes" of statuary to the spiritual or immaterial essence. Coleridge expressed a similar view in his carefully worded warning against excessive imitation of the Antique in *On Poesy or Art.* Clearly the stress on the spirit operating within a work of sculpture—both the plastic power felt by Shelley and the organic or inner form in the aesthetics of Wordsworth and Coleridge—tended to make poets slight the individual masterpieces of sculpture.

Only Shelley, the thoroughgoing Hellenist of this group of Romantic poets, failed to warn against too great a liking for the "fixed shapes" of the Antique. In his poetry, however, Shelley showed more often than either Wordsworth or Coleridge how a poet would use this theory; for he always read the spiritual (and intellectual and emotional) qualities expressed in a statue from its external form. Under the influence of both Shelley and Wordsworth, Byron also reflected at times a somewhat similar feeling for the spirit of ancient statues. Keats presented in his re-creations of sculpture an even finer illustration of the ways in which a poet imaginatively seizes upon the spirit operating within external appearances. Accordingly, had he explicitly stated a theory of sculpture, he would probably have equated the spirit in statues with emotions and passions or sensations rather than with intellectual and spiritual elements. Yet Keats, too, wished to explore

> all forms and substances
> Straight homeward to their symbol-essences.

Strange as it seems, the Elgin Marbles were yet another influence which, to some extent, at least, directed poets away from the Antique. At the time of the controversy over their merit in 1815 and 1816, critics like Hazlitt, artists like Canova, West, and Haydon, and poets like Keats regarded the sculptures as "natural" in contrast to the "old antique" of the idealized Greco-Roman figures. The Elgin Marbles presented the forms of nature. The great beauty of the Parthenon sculptures resulted from a grandeur of style employed in displaying actual human beings engaged in the activities of real life. This "naturalness" showed that the Greek sculptors had made beautiful sculpture out of the circumstances of their age and out of the deeds of heroes and the actions of gods which were instinct with meaning for the Greeks. The lesson taught by the Elgin Marbles was that "romantic" poets should treat the life of the early nineteenth century in the spirit of the Greek artists, or in the "naked and Grecian manner" of grand design achieved with care and precision in detail. Thus the Elgin Marbles contributed the force of their antique example to the "romantic" theories about art: fifth-century Greece joined hands with Wordsworth and Coleridge in urging writers to use the circumstances and spirit of their own age.

Yet the familiar forms of Ideal Beauty of the "old antique" lingered in the minds of many Romantic poets even after the "new antique" of the Elgin Marbles had been placed in the British Museum. The opposition between the Greco-Roman and the Parthenon figures remained, for the most part, a subject for discussion among critics and gentlemen rather than poets, with the notable exceptions of Keats and Byron. Although Haydon belabored the Greco-Roman favorites of the connoisseurs, and although Hazlitt and other critics ridiculed the Ideal Beauty of the Neo-Classical and Academic theorists, the Elgin Marbles failed to displace the "old antique" from the affections of the English poets. Most of them continued to think of the statues which they had seen in books like Spence's *Polymetis* at school or at the universities and elsewhere. In Italy the poets, like Shelley and Byron and Landor, still studied the Greco-Roman works after the Elgin Marbles had been accepted in England.

Of course, a good deal of the Romantic poetry inspired by Greek statuary was primarily sculpturesque decoration, in which poets were little concerned, if at all, with theories of art. Interested in the poetic or imaginative and emotional values in the sculpture of Greece, Landor, Hunt, Shelley, and especially Keats liked to describe the beautiful objects of the art of the sculptor—from gems to friezes, from urns and vases to heroic statues. They were the heirs of the Alexandrian poets of classical antiquity and of the Renaissance. Landor, Keats, and, to a lesser degree, Shelley took pleasure in ornamenting and adorning the stages upon which occurred the moving drama of their poetry.

But classical details and architectural and sculptural effects alone satisfied few Romantic poets. Landor, Keats, Byron, Shelley—in fact, almost every poet of the time—poured modern feelings into ancient forms, since they felt that the forms or "fixed shapes" of classical sculpture, history, mythology, and poetry offered poor vehicles for modern themes and feelings. Largely for that very reason, Wordsworth and Coleridge pointed out the difference between the fancy, with which a poet might treat classical motifs, and a higher power, the imagination, with which he expressed the vital articles of his beliefs. Their analysis of the opposition between fancy and the imagination reflected the growing realization among "romantic" writers of the conflict between

> the Grecian dream
> Of Beauty perfect in a finite mould[5]

and the indefinable, intangible, and spiritual sentiments of the Christian and modern (or "romantic") genius—the conflict which profoundly disturbed the poets of the later nineteenth century.

What these foreshadowings of the conflict between the Grecian or pagan and the modern or Christian meant in the Romantic period may be seen by reference to two admirers of Wordsworth and Coleridge. Charles Lloyd versified the opposition between fancy and imagination in relation to sculpture thus:

Beauty, to the ancients, was a love, devotion:
 Power was their symbol of sublimity!
Attitude, Passion, Symmetry, and Motion,
 With them were fix'd in forms of statuary!

. . . . .

But, at the same time, howe'er much I prize,
 And much I prize it, classical tradition,
I still must feel what difference there lies
 'Twixt it, and gospel truth's sublimer
  mission.
From one for fancy many charms may rise;
 To the sense grateful is its exhibition!

. . . . .

But, in the gospel page, Imagination.[6]

George Dyer announced that he could feel the spirit or soul or genius of the lakes of Westmoreland and Cumberland, which he had visited with Wordsworth and Southey, with greater force

'Mid falling water's solemn sound,
'Mid pathless rocks, and mountains rude,
  And all yon deep opaque of wood,
 Than if, enshrin'd aloft I saw thee stand,
Glittering in robes of gold, and shap'd by
  Phidias' hand.[7]

Moreover, though they had inherited a preference for things classical, especially Grecian, "romantic" poets and critics determined to find subject matter and means of presentation appropriate to their age. Because the Greeks and Romans had been silent concerning many emotions, sentiments, and experiences which were of great importance and of frequent occurrence in the nineteenth century, these writers found it difficult to "coöperate" fully with the Ancients. "Romantic" poets must create the forms which would possess significance for their own age.

The "romantic" poets in England continued, nevertheless, to look to the past and to Greek sculpture, but not as their immediate predecessors of the Academies had turned to antiquity. Many gentlemen, connoisseurs, and poets of the eighteenth century had refined themselves according to classical antiquity, where they found the perfect or correct taste—first of Rome and then of Greece—by which they became urbane, reasonable, and enlightened. "Romantic" poets saw themselves, rather, as links new-forged in the golden chain of poets; and they hailed the sculpture of Greece as a stimulus to creative activity on their own part. They wished to emulate the Greeks in making great art from the circumstances of their time. In other words, they were to do "for Britain what the artists of old did for Greece: their works are classical—not from being the offspring of a classic land, but because they were the embodied poetry of its actual beauty and sentiment."[8]

Among the poets and critics of the Romantic period, therefore, description of antique forms was supplemented and largely replaced by imaginative and poetic interpretation, and admiration of the canons of proportion of the Antique gave way to study of the inner harmony and organic form. Wordsworth and Coleridge presented this position most clearly—a position which had developed almost inevitably from the Platonic theories of Shaftesbury, Winckelmann, and Reynolds and from the pioneer versification of an aesthetic response to sculpture by Thomson and Akenside. Accordingly the "romantic" poets treated the spirit of works of ancient art more often than their external forms.

At the same time that Wordsworth and Coleridge, through their stress upon the inner qualities of art, to some extent directed poets away from the Antique, they encouraged the study of the nature of the artistic processes, including what they considered to have been the spirit of the Grecian workmanship. The finest poetic re-creations of sculpture in the Romantic period sprang, indeed, from the concern with the spirit within the ancient works—that is, with the intellectual and mental and emotional qualities which poets imaginatively discovered in sculpture. The emphasis upon the internal and poetic and imaginative qualities in Greek sculpture paralleled the renewed interest in the spirit of ancient religion and mythology. Again, poets sometimes sought to understand the Ancients by studying how the sculptors had presented the beliefs of Greece in their statues, vases, and friezes of gods and men and heroes.

Wordsworth set the pattern for succeeding poets—with his early toying with classical motifs in the manner of the Academic poets; with his original creations of the great decade from 1798 to 1807 in which he showed how a modern poet made poetry from the familiar matter of his day with a "classical" simplicity inherited from the eighteenth century; with his analysis in *The Excursion* and elsewhere of a spirit within the "fixed shapes" of Grecian sculpture which possessed more beauty than stone or marble; and, finally, with several poems on classical subjects where his fancy could make use of the forms of ancient art.

Then, too, Wordsworth joined with Coleridge in advancing the "romantic" theory by which the two of them as well as other poets, both in the Romantic period and later, might hope to create works of art comparable in formal beauty and spiritual significance to

  the works
Of Grecian Art and purest Poetry.

Notes

[1] See letter to Peacock, March 23, 1819 (*Letters,* X, 37), and above, pp. 167 ff.

[2] *Poetical Works* (1857 ed.), pp. 40-41.

[3] See "The Temple of Jupiter Olympius at Athens" and "The Acropolis, at Athens," *The Poetical Sketch-Book* (1829), pp. 14, 120-21. Hervey's note explained that the wielder of the "wizard rod" was none other than Phidias!

[4] *Desultory Thoughts in London* (1821), p. 41.

[5] Aubrey de Vere, *The Waldenses* (1842), p. 292.

[6] *Desultory Thoughts in London,* "On the Connection between Different Degrees of Spiritualization, in Religion, and a Taste for the Arts in General, and a Material or Metaphysical Taste in Poetry," and "Parallel between the Imagery of Heathenism and That of the Bible," pp. 71, 155. Lloyd had in mind *The Excursion* (see above, pp. 124 ff.) and Coleridge's lines on mythology in *The Piccolomini* (see above, pp. 143-44).

[7] *Poetics; or, A Series of Poems, and Disquisitions on Poetry* (1812), p. 231. See above, pp. 127 ff.

[8] Allan Cunningham, criticizing the classicistic forms painted by James Barry, *Lives of the Most Eminent British Painters, Sculptors, and Architects* (2d ed., 1830), II, 140.

FURTHER READING

Arnold, Matthew. "Hebraism and Hellenism." In *Culture and Anarchy: An Essay in Political and Social Criticism*, pp. 109-27. New York: Macmillan and Co., 1883.

Discusses Hebraism and Hellenism as forces or influences that need to be balanced in English society in order to ensure the stability of the state. Arnold equates Hebraism with religious authority and moral conduct and stresses the overly Hebraic nature of England, maintaining that the influences of Greek philosophy and art (Hellenism) are required to rectify this imbalance. Arnold's views on the subject reflect a debate in later-nineteenth-century England that was becoming increasingly racial in tone, pitting Aryan against Semite, due in part to a reaction to the growing Jewish population in nineteenth-century England.

Chislett, William, Jr. "The Romantic Revolt." In *The Classical Influence in English Literature in the Nineteenth Century*, pp. 8-10. Boston: The Stratford Co., 1918.

Provides a brief list of nineteenth-century poets who were inspired by Grecian themes.

Clarke, G. W., ed. *Rediscovering Hellenism: The Hellenic Inheritance and the English Imagination.* Cambridge: Cambridge University Press, 1989, 264 p.

A collection of essays discussing the various ways in which Greek philosophy, literature, and art influenced English society and culture during the nineteenth century.

Le Comte, Edward S. *Endymion in England: The Literary History of A Greek Myth.* New York: King's Crown Press, 1944, 189 p.

Traces the course and influence of the Greek myth of Endymion in English literature, ending with a discussion of Keats's treatment of the myth.

Stern, Bernard Herbert. *The Rise of Romantic Hellenism in English Literature, 1732-1786.* Menasha, Wisc.: George Banta Publishing Co., 1940, 182 p.

Studies the development of romantic Hellenism in the eighteenth century, including the influences of increased interest in Greek archaeology and renewed interest in Eastern travel and in travel literature.

Stevenson, Warren. "Hebraism and Hellenism in the Poetry of Byron." In *Byron, the Bible, and Religion: Essays from the Twelfth International Byron Seminar*, edited by Wolf Z. Hirst, pp. 136-52. Newark: University of Delaware Press, 1991.

Analyzes literary evidence in an attempt to determine whether Byron was essentially a Hebraist or a Hellenist.

Victorian Hellenism

INTRODUCTION

In English and American culture today it is conventional wisdom to think of ancient Greece, c. 500 B.C., as the birthplace of Western civilization and to attribute the qualities associated with the flowering of Western European culture—especially those of secular humanism—to the inheritance, more or less direct, from the great flowering of art, philosophy, and especially democracy in ancient Athens. These beliefs do not take into account, however, the inheritance of Victorian values, for it was nineteenth-century Britain that initiated the valorization of all things Hellenic (relating to ancient Greece), manifested largely in the Victorians' desire to see themselves as the resurrection of Hellenic Greece. In Victorian England one aspect of the rich and complicated culture was an enthusiastic self-identification with ancient Greece. While men of the ruling classes were steeped in the study of classical literature—and its associated values—as the basis of their education, popular notions of Hellenism, of its superiority and relevance, spread throughout the culture at large.

As many scholars of Victorian culture have argued, eras preceding the Romantic and Victorian took only an occasional interest in Greece. Instead, Europeans of the Renaissance and Enlightenment viewed themselves in a line of descent from the Roman republic, extolling its politics, philosophies, and aesthetics. In the years that bridged the late eighteenth and early nineteenth centuries, however, certain threads in European culture—particularly in Germany and England—prompted a desire to diverge from that Roman image. Where studies of ancient Greece occupied only a corner of scholarship and publication in the centuries preceding the nineteenth, by the end of that century such publications had far outstripped the focus on Rome. Hundreds of books, articles, and pamphlets celebrated ancient Greece's philosophy, literature, mythology, art, religion, and politics. New translations of all the major authors and many minor ones became available. Rome took on an image of decadence and insincerity, while Greece illustrated the first burgeoning of democracy, lyric poetry, humanism—all elements appealing to rising currents in Victorian culture.

England's enthusiasm for Hellenism had roots in eighteenth-century Germany, where scholars studied ancient Greek texts and culture in such earnest that it had a tremendous and far-reaching impact on the country's educational system, as well as on the later development of scholarship in general. By the beginning of the nineteenth century, this rather specialized interest in classical studies had a marked growth in England. One of the most important texts of the revival, K. O. Müller's *History of Greek Literature*, came from Germany, but in fact appeared in translation in England in 1840 even before it reached publication in Germany.

The Victorian take on Hellenism, which both inherited and diverged from the early nineteenth-century Hellenism of the English Romantics, germinated very concretely in curricular changes at Oxford University. Long-standing language requirements for admission at both Oxford and Cambridge insured that every university educated man—as well as every man educated at schools hoping to send their students to Oxford or Cambridge—would know Latin and Greek. In the mid-nineteenth century, Oxford's curriculum changes outstripped this traditional focus on language and brought Greek history, literature, and philosophy much more pervasively into the education of all its students.

From this primary training site, the country's future leaders--in politics, letters, business, and religion--acquired a shared set of values such that even where they debated specific issues, a certain frame of reference, distilled from the prevailing interpretations of classical texts, permeated the dominant culture in all fields. As these men set the standard for their culture, the values that they embraced filtered through the country at large, no longer just in the specialized fields of history or philology. Greek myth and imagery became common in literature, in the most popular poetry as well as the most specialized texts, and in the visual arts. The presence of Hellenism in political and economic discourse was also substantial. George Grote's *History of Greece*, published in twelve volumes between 1846 and 1856, not only contributed to the Hellenic passion, it also put forward one of the most influential notions of ancient Greece: the belief that classical Athens had realized the greatest potential of democracy. In the mid-nineteenth century, this argument had a significant place in heated contemporary debates over the direction and nature of an expanding liberal democracy.

Frank M. Turner, one of the first specialists to study Victorian Hellenism, has frequently remarked that Victorian writers appropriated ancient Greece in particularly self-serving fashions, exploiting it as a vessel for containing an unlimited array of images or messages. Consequently, the reasons that Victorians embraced ancient Greece with such affinity, argues Turner and others, had much more to do with certain forces bearing on Victorian culture than with the history of Greece itself. Economic and political changes presented England's ruling classes with new challenges, and, as commentators from Friedrich Nietzsche to Turner have argued, they fortified themselves for this challenge with new self images borrowed from ancient Greece. Nietzsche identified the urge as one prompted by the limitations of the modern world, which sent his fellows in search of the succor of a meaningful past and mythology. When the late eighteenth century bore witness to two major revolutions, in America and France, one sympathetic response came from Romanticism. Douglas Bush ascribes the initial nineteenth-century revival of Hellenism to "the Romantic reaction against a rationalistic and mechanistic view of the world and man"—a rationalism largely exemplified by the leading poets of the eighteenth century, including Alexander Pope. The considerable room for interpretation embedded in Hellenism ultimately allowed it to assume divergent functions—from the relatively radical to the relatively conservative. For example, thinkers used Hellenism both as a mode for pushing away the traditional religious values that had held sway in England since the Restoration and as a new justification and explanation of those values.

In the 1980s, Turner noted the dearth of significant criticism on Victorian Hellenism. At the beginning of the century, Edwardian critics looking back at the Victorians—the generation just preceding their own—painted that culture over with their own need to reject its values. Consequently, previous to the wave of fresh analyses concurrent with Turner's own work, scholars either failed to look at Hellenism as a significant facet of Victorian culture or flatly accepted the Edwardian assessment at face value. Not until the 1980s did scholars begin to challenge the absence of more thoughtful inquiries and contend, as Turner did in his groundbreaking *Greek Heritage in Victorian Britain* (1981), that Victorians avidly created ancient Greece in their image—or in their own desire to see themselves in a particular image. Since that time, many articles and books have appeared examining the motives and meanings of Hellenism in Victorian politics, philosophy, theology, education, and arts.

REPRESENTATIVE WORKS

Matthew Arnold
Culture and Anarchy 1883

James Frazer
The Golden Bough 1890

William Gladstone
Studies in Homer and the Homeric Age 1858

Alexander Grant
The Ethics of Aristotle 1858

George Grote
History of Greece 1856

Benjamin Jowett
The Dialogues of Plato 1871

J. P. Mahaffy
Social Life in Greece from Homer to Menander 1874

K. O. Müller
History of Greek Literature 1840

Walter Pater
Greek Studies 1895

J. A. Symonds
Greek Poets 1876

Oscar Wilde
Picture of Dorian Gray 1891

OVERVIEWS

Frank M. Turner (essay date 1981)

SOURCE: "The Victorians and Greek Antiquity," in *The Greek Heritage in Victorian Britain,* Yale University Press, 1981, pp. 1-14.

[*In the following essay, Turner illustrates the pervasiveness of the Victorian fascination with classical Greece. Briefly tracing the history and breadth of that fascination, he focuses primarily on the various concepts of Greece that became most influential in British culture and stresses four concepts of history that undergirded the fascination.*]

Throughout much of the European intellectual community of the last century there flourished an immense fascination for ancient Greece. From Goethe, Hegel, and Shelley to Kierkegaard, Arnold, Grote, and Fouillée, through Nietzsche, Fustel de Coulanges, and Frazer, the list of poets, critics, philosophers, historians, and scholars concerned at one time or another with the Greeks reads like an index of the major contributors to the intellectual life of the age. The results of their probing of the Greek experience were impressive on every score. Greek revival buildings came to dot the rural and urban landscape from Ireland to Russia. Ancient temples, theaters, marketplaces, palaces, and tombs buried for over two millennia were unearthed and their remains transported hundreds of miles to the west for display in museums designed to resemble Greek temples and dedicated to the modern muses of popular enlightenment. Whole fields of learning, scholarship, and teaching about Greek antiquity entered the life of European universities for the first time. New scholarly societies and schools for archaeology were established. In libraries and on private bookshelves there slowly accumulated a vast array of books and journals concerned with Greece. And in the learned imagination of Europe the ancient Hellenic achievement assumed a vitality and sense of relevance previously entertained in the minds of only a fewscore Renaissance humanists.

The extensive nineteenth-century concern with ancient Greece was essentially a novel factor in modern European intellectual life. Although Greek philosophy had influenced some Renaissance writers and Aristotelian categories still informed science and logic, until the late eighteenth century most educated Europeans regarded their culture as Roman and Christian in origin, with merely peripheral roots in Greece. Europe had a Roman past, and European civilization was congruent with Latin Christendom. Caesar had recorded the conquest of Gaul and the invasion of Britain, and Tacitus had described the life of the ancient Germans. Roman law and Roman literature, as well as the Latin church fathers, had dominated Europe's cultural experience. Roman walls, forts, bridges, baths, theaters, roads, and aqueducts could be found in Britain and across the Continent. In contrast to this visible, tangible, and pervasive Roman influence, the Greeks simply had not directly touched the life of Western Europe. Even the broad Enlightenment appeal to antiquity had concentrated on Rome.

Greek antiquity began to absorb the interest of Europeans in the second half of the eighteenth century when the values, ideas, and institutions inherited from the Roman and Christian past became problematical. The search for new cultural roots and alternative cultural patterns developed out of the need to understand and articulate the disruptive political, social, and intellectual experience that Europeans confronted in the wake of the Enlightenment and of revolution. In some cases the appeal to Greece served to foster further change, in others to combat the forces of disruption. In both cases the turn to Greece on the part of scholars, critics, and literary figures constituted an attempt to discern prescriptive signposts for the present age in the European past that predated Rome and Christianity. These writers were, of course, actually erecting new landmarks.

Greek antiquity first assumed major intellectual significance in Germany. There, from approximately 1750 on, poets, literary critics, and historians of art looked to ancient Greece as an imaginative landscape on which they might discover artistic patterns, ethical values, and concepts of human nature that could displace those of Christianity and ossified French classicism.[1] The discontinuity between Greece and modern Christian Europe rendered the Greek experience all the more valuable and useful. Greece could represent almost any value or outlook that a writer wished to ascribe to it. The moral variety in Greek culture, which was fully recognized at the time, further contributed to the breadth of its perceived relevance, as in the works of Winckelmann, Lessing, Goethe, Schiller, Hölderlin, and others. Writers used the values they discerned in the Greek experience either to throw off the asceticism of the Christian tradition and the restraints of French academic rules or to find an alternative secular confirmation for modes of taste and moral experience that were normally buttressed by Christianity or modern aesthetics. Things Greek thus contributed both to the devising of new myths and to the sustaining of old values in novel guises.

Contemporary with this well-known German literary activity there arose the less familiar but ultimately perhaps more important early historical and philological scholarship of the University of Göttingen. From it developed the major critical approaches to both pagan and Christian antiquity that characterized German theological and historical endeavors for the next century and that became models for other European and American scholars.[2] Following the lead of Christian Gottlieb Heyne, German scholars began to study ancient texts in a critical manner that took into consideration questions of linguistics, history, and textual integrity. The flowering of this *Neue Humanismus* opened fundamentally new dimensions to the understanding of the classical past and to the criticism of its literature. Those same methods held shattering implications for the study of the Bible and the historical origins of Christianity. The classical and religious studies were repeatedly to become intertwined.

A third factor independently contributing to the sense of the relevance of ancient Greece to modern Europe was the stirring of liberal democracy that began with the American Revolution. Whether the age of revolution between 1760 and 1815 was one of genuinely democratic revolution may remain a vexing question, but there can be no doubt that the revolutionary experience roused on an unprecedented scale the intensive examination of the ancient Greek democracies and particularly that of Athens. The polemical writing of Greek history began in England in the 1780s, well before the expeditions of the Philhellenes in aid of the Greek revolution. The specter of a contemporary Greek democracy fascinated and inspired the romantic liberals who went to fight in its cause, but it was the possibility for conservative polemic presented by the turbulent history of the ancient Athenian democracy that occasioned the first major studies of that subject and that often determined the framework for later studies as well.

Although the focus on Greece was a change from the previous emphasis on Rome, the reorientation was a relatively simple cultural accomplishment because it occurred within literate classes already familiar with the ancient world as a source of prescriptive values and of illustrative moral and political allusions. The inheritance of the humanist education enjoyed by the educated classes in Britain since the Renaissance made the appeal to and the use of Greek antiquity both possible and effective. In 1856 John Grote, professor of moral philosophy at Cambridge and the brother of the Greek historian, observed,

> Classical study . . . is a point of intellectual sympathy among men over a considerable surface of the world, for those who have forgotten their actual Greek and Latin bear still generally with them many traces of its influence, and in fact it is this which, more than anything, makes them, in common parlance, educated men. That any one subject should be thus extensively cultivated, so as to make such sympathy possible, is a most happy circumstance, supposing it simply historical and accidental. The destruction or disuse of it will destroy one bond of intellectual communion among civilized men, and will be, in this respect, a step not of improvement. And though studies more definitely useful might succeed it, there is an utility lost, and one which will hardly be considered trifling.[3]

That now dissipated general familiarity with the classics was once one of the distinguishing and self-defining marks of the social and intellectual elite of Europe. It had originated in thoroughly aristocratic times and endured through the first century of the liberal democratic age. To no small extent knowledge of the classical world and acquaintance with the values communicated through the vehicle of classical education informed the mind and provided much of the intellectual confidence of the ruling political classes of Europe. The great enterprises of translation undertaken during the nineteenth century in part represented attempts to preserve that frame of cultural and intellectual reference for an expanding, but not always classically trained, political elite. And the effort succeeded well until the social and political impact of the First World War thoroughly undermined the vestiges of the aristocratic life in Europe.

The structures of classical education made possible and largely sustained the study of Greek civilization and the application of that study to contemporary life. In England until after World War I a knowledge of Greek was required for admission to both Oxford and Cambridge.[4] This requirement set the major pedagogical pattern for the public schools and all other secondary institutions that hoped to send students to those universities or to provide the veneer of an elite education. The examinations for the Home Civil Service, the Indian Civil Service, and the Royal Military Academy afforded considerable advantage to students who could score well in Greek. Consequently, a knowledge of Greek (even if rarely mastery) and a familiarity with Greek culture were characteristic of a large portion of the British political elite as well as of the leaders and clergy of the Church of England. So long as this educational situation prevailed, discussions of Greek history, religion, literature, and philosophy provided ready vehicles for addressing the governing classes of the country and could be expected to find in them a potentially receptive and possibly responsive audience. Indeed, in 1865 the major commentator on Homer as well as a major translator of the poet, the chief critic and historian of Greek literature, the most significant political historians of Greece, and the authors of the then most extensive commentaries on Greek philosophy either were or had recently been members of the House of Commons or the House of Lords.

Throughout the century the profound influence on the English educated classes of the Oxford school of *Literae Humaniores* reenforced the use of both Greece and Rome as points of cultural and intellectual self-reference. This deservedly famous program of study involved then, as now, the careful, detailed translation and criticism of a set list of texts—the Greats—that changed somewhat during the course of the century. The program required two different sets of examinations. The first, known as Moderations, was taken at the end of the two years and tested primarily linguistic ability and knowledge of Greek and Latin literature. The second examination, written at the end of four years, was topically oriented and covered history, ethics, metaphysics, and political philosophy. One result of the character of the latter examination was, as R. W. Livingstone observed in 1932, a "tendency to study the classics not in and for themselves, but in relation to modern thought and modern life."[5]

During the nineteenth century the modern thought to which the classics were related at Oxford and elsewhere changed from decade to decade. As Francis Cornford of Cambridge wrote in 1903; "The ancient classics resemble the universe. They are always there, and they are very much the same as ever. But as the philosophy of every new age puts a fresh construction on the universe, so in the classics scholarship finds a perennial object for ever fresh and original interpretation."[6] Early in the century the Greeks and their philosophy were often related to the thought of Anglican theologians, such as Bishop Butler. By the thirties the patristic revival associated primarily with the Tractarian movement at Oxford stimulated interest in the relationship of Greek and Christian thought and helped to foster new approaches to the study of Plato. The same decade witnessed the major impact of German scholarship in the British universities and the publication in English in 1840 of Müller's *History of Greek Literature,* even before it was published in German. The scholarship of the Continent also led to a more critical tone in the writing of Greek history in Britain. At mid-century utilitarian and rationalist writers established a major claim to Greek studies with the publication of George Grote's *History of Greece.* The German influence reappeared in the sixties with the Aryanism of F. Max Müller's theories of myth and, more important, in the Hegelianism of Jowett's introductions to Plato. Thereafter, archaeology and anthropology began to transform Greek studies, and by the turn of the century social psychology and French sociology had begun to make themselves felt in works on Greek religion, philosophy, and politics. Throughout the century the tradition of critical editing and commentary, inherited from Richard Porson as much as anyone, continued to be influential in the publication of Greek texts that permitted new and often revisionist commentary and emendation. In this regard one thinks of James Frazer's editing of Pausanias and the latter's attention to varieties of ritual observance that would become so important for Frazer's later work.

A final reason for the impact of contemporary concerns on the British evaluation of Greece was the largely undefined nature of classics as a discipline. Except for linguistic ability in Greek and Latin, the analytical tools and categories employed to examine a question or problem from Greek antiquity were almost invariably derived from other modern disciplines or modern religious and philosophical outlooks. Modern aesthetics guided the consideration of Greek sculpture. Modern religious sensibilities and anthropological theories determined the interpretation of Greek myths. Modern biblical scholarship influenced the reading of Homer. Modern political thought and anxieties were brought to bear on the Athenian democratic experience. Greek philosophers were judged before the bar of modern epistemology and political philosophy.

The overwhelmingly amateur character of the Victorian scholars who undertook the enterprise exacerbated this use of modern nonclassical disciplines for interpreting the Greek experience. Their work in the classics was almost always derivative of theological or ecclesiastical concerns or related directly to matters of current politics, morals, or aesthetics. A Hampshire squire, an Anglican bishop, and a City of London banker pioneered the study of Greek political history. A chancellor of the exchequer contributed the major mid-century study of Homer. A school inspector made "Hellenism" and "Hebraism" terms of common literary and cultural usage. These and others who wrote and commented on Greece approached their subjects less from an interest in the past for its own sake than from a firm conviction that what they said about Greece would have an impact on contemporary political, religious, philosophical, and moral discourse. The paradox of professional humanistic scholarship—a growing body of knowledge attained by precise methodology but tied to a shrinking sense of its perceived relevance—had happily not overtaken the Victorian study of Greece.

For all of these reasons the nineteenth-century exploration of Greek antiquity constantly manifested the wider intellectual life of the day and opens the latter for more complete consideration. Writing about Greece was in part a way for the Victorians to write about themselves. The most famous and perhaps still the most widely consulted book in English on nineteenth-century Hellenism bears the title of *The Tyranny of Greece over Germany.*[7] Whatever the merits or faults of the rest of that volume, its title has fundamentally misled most subsequent consideration of the subject. What actually constituted the primary and most striking feature of Victorian Hellenism wherever it appeared was the tyranny of the ninetenth-century European experience over that of Greek antiquity. In a perceptive essay written shortly after World War II, W. H. Auden noted, "It is the unlikeness of the Greeks to ourselves, the gulf between the kind of assumptions they made, the kind of questions they asked and our own that strikes us more than anything else."[8] The reaction of nineteenth-century writers to ancient Greece had been just the opposite as again and again, in the most unexpected and sometimes perverse manner, Greek subjects were made to conform to contemporary categories of thought, culture, and morality. Across the Western world Victorian authors and readers were determined to find the Greeks as much as possible like themselves and to rationalize away fundamental differences.

Although the Hellenic revival of the nineteenth century involved an international community of scholars and writers, many of whom appealed to the wisdom of Greece in terms of a universal human experience or some concept of uniform human nature, the study and interpretation of Greek antiquity nonetheless occurred within the context of national intellectual communities whose characters bore the distinctive imprints of their respective political structures, university organization, and religious confession. In each of these intellectual communities the exploration and criticism of Greek life reflected the particular political, religious, and philosophical preoccupations of the national culture. Scholars in the various European countries read each other's books and articles, but the manner in which they evaluated those ideas and incorporated them into their own work often depended on factors outside the realm of classical scholarship proper. For this reason, as well as because of the sheer mass of evidence and documentation, the present volume will be devoted exclusively to the study of Greek antiquity in nineteenth-century Britain. It may, however, also prepare the way for similar studies of other nations so that in time a comparative understanding of the role of antiquity in the intellectual life of the century may emerge.

Thus far, the words *Greeks, Greek antiquity,* and *the classics* have been used as general terms. Some important Victorian critics, such as Matthew Arnold and his disciples, did regard them in this way. Because Arnold's prose, especially portions of *Culture and Anarchy,* have entered the literary canon, there has been a tendency to equate his version of Hellenism—one often imperfectly understood—with the entire British and European consideration of Greece. This interest in Arnold has obscured broader, more important explorations of Greek civilization by other Victorian commentators. Most nineteenth-century scholars and critics of Greece, in contrast to Arnold, dealt with specific and well-defined areas of Greek life rather than with general phenomena or an extracted Hellenic essence. The self-generating engines of critical scholarship and political controversy assured a more differentiated portrayal of Greece than the one that flowed from the German literary Hellenists to whom Arnold was so much indebted.

To become more adequately acquainted with the Victorian use and abuse of Greek antiquity, one must perform an exegesis upon an exegesis. That is, one must look at the literature in which nineteenth-century critics, historians, editors, and commentators actually discussed Greek topics. This large body of materials includes histories of Greece, formal commentaries on Greek literature, authors and philosophers, the extensive introductions and footnotes to editions of the texts and translations of major Greek works, university lectures, textbooks, review essays, major encyclopedia articles, and discussions of archaeology, anthropology, and comparative religion. When these little-examined documents are studied, they reveal a world of Victorian discourse possessing considerable integrated unity and one replete with surprises and unexpected intellectual twists and turns. To read these now neglected and frequently dust-covered volumes is also to discover how correctly John Grote grasped the cultural and intellectual function of classical studies in his society. Discussions of Greek antiquity provided a forum wherein Victorian writers could and did debate all manner of contemporary questions of taste, morality, politics, religion, and philosophy.

The university-educated and other widely read classes of Great Britain often felt that a profoundly intimate relationship existed between themselves and the ancient Greeks. In a typical statement of that sentiment J. P. Mahaffy, an Anglo-Irish scholar of Trinity College, Dublin, wrote in 1874:

> Every thinking man who becomes acquainted with the masterpieces of Greek writing, must see plainly that they stand to us in a far closer relation than the other remains of antiquity. They are not mere objects of curiosity to the archaeologist, not mere treasure-houses of roots and forms to be sought out by comparative grammarians. They are the writings of men of like culture with ourselves, who argue with the same logic, who reflect with kindred feelings. They have worked out social and moral problems like ourselves, they have expressed them in such language as we should desire to use. In a word, they are thoroughly modern, more modern than the epochs quite proximate to our own.

A few paragraphs later Mahaffy continued in the same vein.

> If one of us were transported to Periclean Athens, provided he were a man of high culture, he would find life and manners strangely like our own, strangely modern, as he might term it. The thoughts and feelings of modern life would be there without the appliances, and the high standard of general culture would more than counter balance sundry wants of material comfort. . . . Some of the problems which are still agitating our minds were settled by the Greeks, others, if not settled, were at least discussed with a freedom and acuteness now unattainable. Others, again, were solved in strange violation of our notions of morals and good taste; and when such a people as the Greeks stand opposed to us, even in vital principles, we cannot reject their verdict without weighing their reasons.[9]

What is of particular significance about Mahaffy's statement and what can be replicated from scores of other writers was the conviction that the Greeks had been like the Victorians and that the historical situations of the two civilizations were essentially similar. Although this attitude did not survive much beyond the first quarter of the twentieth century, it was fundamental to Victorian intellectual life and determined the outlook of much Victorian scholarship, criticism, and commentary on the Greeks.

The appeal to the affinity between the Victorian and the Greek experience was rarely made in a casual manner. There almost always existed a particular motivation for drawing the direct relationship. There was, however, no single motivating interest but rather a cluster of them, many of which were quite unrelated. Furthermore, writers convinced of one set of relationships often remained unconvinced by other approaches and uninfluenced by the authors who pursued them. For example, numerous Victorian commentators sought in one way or another to relate Greek antiquity to Christianity. They had virtually no impact on other scholars whose concerns lay with the implications of Athenian democracy for modern politics. Yet both groups were part of the larger picture of the Victorians and Greek culture. Because of the diverse approaches of the nineteenth century to the study of ancient Greece, two questions repeatedly present themselves: Why the Greeks? and Which Greeks?

The question Why the Greeks? has a fairly straightforward answer. The political parallel between ancient democracy and modern democracy established in English writing by 1790 was of major significance, as was the possibility of contrasting the ideal of Greek heroism and the Greek appreciation for beauty with bourgeois humdrum and philistinism. But authors who made these uses of Greek culture and those who appealed to Greek antiquity for other polemical purposes usually believed their analysis appropriate because of one of four general philosophical approaches to the past. These concepts of history gave them the confidence to draw the parallels. From the viewpoint of Christian providential history, the Greeks had played an important linguistic and philosophical role in preparing the world for the Gospel. Christian writers also often regarded the Greeks as having displayed the highest moral character that human nature could assume without the light of the Gospel. The second theory, which informed several significant discussions, was a version of Viconian cycles in which certain ages of Greek history (usually the fifth century B.C.) were seen as analogous to certain periods of modern history—and thus subject to the drawing of relevant parallels. This view was particularly attractive to liberal Anglicans about the middle of the century. A third idea that defined the Victorians' approach to the Greeks was Auguste Comte's law of the three stages of intellectual development. Adherents to this theory, or to a modified version thereof, tended to conceive Greek religious and philosophical life as a microcosm of the Comtean pattern of development. These writers invariably favored positivistic epistemology and chose their intellectual heroes among the Greeks according to that standard. Finally, Hegel's concept of the historical development of Greek philosophy also suggested that Greek thought and culture held particular relevance for the Victorian experience. Nineteenth-century writers who accepted his view of the passage from *Sittlichkeit* to *Moralität* in Greek civilization discerned a similar development in their own time.

These several philosophies of history did not function in hermetically sealed compartments. For example, Benjamin Jowett seems to have found the Hegelian pattern operative because he also accepted the Viconian concept of analogous ages. Some writers adhered to the connection between Greece and Britain without a specific understanding of the theory of history from which their views derived or that informed the thought of another scholar upon whose thought they drew. Yet, however construed or misconstrued, these theories provided the major framework by means of which Victorian writers sustained their belief that the experience of Greece was directly significant for their own culture.

The answer to the question Which Greeks? is more difficult and elusive. In 1939 George Boas noted, "Every age of European culture, like every individual of the intellectual classes, has gone back to the Greeks for inspiration ever since there were any Greeks to go back to. But what Greeks they selected as *'The Greeks,'* and what ideas and manners and standards they chose as typically Hellenic have varied from age to age and from individual to individual."[10] Boas's claim to the timeless appeal of the Greeks is much exaggerated but not his assertion about the variety of human experience they have been used to illustrate. Which Greeks a Victorian writer intended to denote frequently depended on which secondary authors he had read as much as upon his familiarity with the ancient Greek literary sources. The image projected upon the Hellenes also changed with the discovery of new evidence and with the application of new conceptual frameworks. The Greeks of Matthew Arnold were simply not those of James Frazer.

Victorian and Edwardian commentators were generally aware of these changing perceptions. In 1897, looking back over the past century of British and continental Greek studies, Gilbert Murray commented:

> The "serene and classical" Greek of Winckelmann and Goethe did good service to the world in his day, though we now feel him to be mainly a phantom. He has been succeeded, especially in the works of painters and poets, by an aesthetic and fleshly Greek in fine raiment, an abstract Pagan who lives to be contrasted with an equally abstract early Christian or Puritan, and to be glorified or mishandled according to the sentiments of his critics. He is a phantom too, as unreal as those marble palaces in which he habitually takes his ease. . . . There is more flesh and blood in the Greek of the anthropologist, the foster-brother of Kaffirs and Hairy Ainos. He is at least human and simple and emotional, and free from irrelevant trappings. His fault, of course, is that he is not the man we want, but only the raw material out of which that man was formed; a Hellene without beauty, without the spiritual life, without the Hellenism. Many other abstract Greeks are about us, no one perhaps greatly better than another; yet each has served to correct and complement his predecessor; and in the long-run there can be little doubt that our conceptions have become more adequate.[11]

There had not been and there could not have been a single Victorian image of Greece and the Greeks. Considerable variety was inherent in the Greek experience itself. The several Victorian concepts of Greek culture represented appeals to different portions of that experience and the assimilation of new evidence, but they also embodied transformations in Victorian moral and religious sensibilities that permitted a new appreciation for evidence previously available. The Victorians' conceptions of what the Greeks had been or should have been changed as their own comprehension of the physical world, of history, and of human nature changed; and as educated Victorians began to understand themselves in more complex terms, they came to ascribe a similar complexity to the Greeks.

Notes

[1] Henry Hatfield, *Aesthetic Paganism in German Literature from Winckelmann to the Death of Goethe* (Cambridge, Mass.: Harvard University Press, 1964); Walter Rehm, *Griechentum und Goethezeit* (Bern: Francke Verlage, 1952); Humphrey Trevelyan, *Goethe and the Greeks* (Cambridge: Cambridge University Press, 1952); Martin Vogel, *Apollinisch und Dionysisch: Geschichte eines genialen Irrtums* (Regensburg: Bustav Bosse Verlag, 1966), pp. 37-94.

[2] Herbert Butterfield, *Man on His Past: The Study of the History of Historical Scholarship* (Boston: Beacon Press, 1960), pp. 32-61; Christian Hartlich and Walter Sachs, *Der Ursprung des Mythosbegriffes in der Modernen Bibelwissenschaft* (Tübingen: J. C. B. Mohr, 1952); Carl Diehl, *Americans and German Scholarship,* 1770-1870, (New Haven: Yale University Press, 1978), pp. 6-48.

[3] John Grote, "Old Studies and New," in *Cambridge Essays: 1856* (London: John W. Parker and Son, 1856), p. 114.

[4] See "Memorandum of the Council of the Society for the Promotion of Hellenic Studies on the Place of Greek in Education," *Journal of Hellenic Studies* 36 (1916): lxix-lxxii.

[5] Richard W. Livingstone, "The Position and Function of Classical Studies in Modern English Education," *Vorträge der Bibliothek Warburg* (1930-31), p. 258.

[6] Francis Macdonald Cornford, *The Cambridge Classical Course: An Essay in Anticipation of Further Reform* (Cambridge: W.H. Heffer & Sons, 1903), p. 19.

[7] Eliza Marian Butler, *The Tyranny of Greece over Germany* (Boston: Beacon Press, 1958; first published, 1935).

[8] W.H. Auden, "Introduction," W.H. Auden, ed., *The Portable Greek Reader* (1948; reprint ed., New York: The Viking Press, 1955), p. 16.

[9] John Pentland Mahaffy, *Social Life in Greece from Homer to Menander* (London: Macmillan and Co., 1874), pp. 1, 2-3.

[10] George Boas, "Preface," George Boas, ed., *The Greek Tradition* (Baltimore: The Johns Hopkins Press, 1939), p. v.

[11] Gilbert Murray, *A History of Ancient Greek Literature* (London: William Heinemann, 1897), pp. xiv-xv.

Frank M. Turner (essay date 1989)

SOURCE: "Why the Greeks and Not the Romans in Victorian Britain?," in *Rediscovering Hellenism: The Hellenic Inheritance and the English Imagination,* edited by G. W. Clarke, Cambridge University Press, 1989, pp. 61-81.

[*In the essay that follows, Turner contrasts the nineteenth-century enthusiasm for classical Greece with preceding eras' valorization of all things Roman in order to demonstrate significant Victorian differences in self-perception. Asserting that Victorians sought a mirror in the distant past so as to distinguish themselves from their immediate history, and from that era's identification with Rome, he stresses a central change in political and class values.*]

The event I wish to examine here—and for which I hope to suggest a series of explanations—is the emergence within the intellectual life of nineteenth-century Britain of a predominating concern with Greek over Roman antiquity. In 1903 Francis Cornford declared, "The ancient classics resemble the universe. They are always there, and they are very much the same as ever. But as the philosophy of every new age puts a fresh construction on the universe, so in the classics scholarship finds a perennial object for ever fresh and original interpretation."[1] Around the close of the eighteenth century British scholars not only came to reinterpret that classical universe, but they sharply shifted their field of interest from Rome to Greece. This development was not inevitable; nor was it, in 1750, even predictable: it is an event within intellectual history that begs for an explanation.

The nineteenth-century interest in things Greek did not, of course, preclude concern for Roman culture. Schoolboys continued to study Caesar, Cicero, Virgil and Horace, though rather to the exclusion of Ovid. But in most respects the continuing interest in things Roman was a vestige of both the previous century and the Renaissance programme of humanist education. Late in the Victorian age W.Y. Sellar wrote, "Familiarity with Latin literature is probably not less common relatively to familiarity with the older [Greek] literature. The attraction of the latter has been greater from its novelty, its originality, its higher intrinsic excellence, its profounder relation to the heart and mind of man."[2] This observation illustrates the remarkable character of the shift to Greece as well as its intensity: to appeal to Rome was to draw upon a line of continuous cultural influence within Europe; to appeal to Greece was to appropriate and domesticate a culture of the past with which there had been, particularly in Britain, a discontinuous relationship. And that very discontinuity may have been part of the attraction for nineteenth-century writers who regarded much of their own experience as discontinuous with the recent past.

Three broad examples will illustrate the character and the extent of the rise of Greek and the decline of Roman concerns. The first is in the area of narrative history.

Between the 1690s and 1780s there were published numerous Roman histories including works by Laurence Echard, Thomas Middleton, Nathaniel Hooke, Thomas Blackwell, Oliver Goldsmith, Adam Ferguson and, of course, Edward Gibbon. There were, in addition, numerous political pamphlets by writers such as Swift and Bolingbroke, in which the Roman example was related to modern British politics. Allusions to ancient Roman history, especially that of the Republic, were frequent in both Britain and in the North American colonies.[3]

If one turns to the nineteenth century, a startling change has occurred. Between the publication of the revised edition of Ferguson's history of the Republic in 1799 and the appearance of William Heitland's three-volume history in 1902, no other major study of the Roman Republic appeared in Britain—George Long's being only a non-interpretive paraphrase of ancient sources. Furthermore, the Victorian age produced no successor to Gibbon's history. The only major Victorian history of Rome was Charles Merivale's *History of the Romans under the Empire* (1850-64) in eight volumes. It covered the period of the late Republic through the point where Gibbon's narrative commenced. Thomas Arnold had begun a history of Rome in the late 1830s, but the work was not taken up by another writer after Arnold's death in 1842.

This paucity of Roman history contrasts with the ever expanding bookshelf of Greek history. William Mitford had begun to publish his ten-volume history of Greece in 1784. It was republished several times, the last being in 1835. Mitford's work was followed in the nineteenth century by the eight volumes of Connop Thirlwall, the two volumes of Bulwer-Lytton, the twelve volumes of George Grote, the three volumes of Evelyn Abbott, and the several volumes of E.B. Grundy after the turn of the century, as well as by a large number of one-volume histories.

The same pattern emerges in nineteenth-century writing devoted to Roman and Greek literature and philosophy. In the eighteenth century Virgil and Horace served as prescriptive literary models, and Cicero was regarded by many (though certainly not by all) as a sound philosopher of public life and a sober religious thinker. But already in the eighteenth century Homeric studies had begun to generate broad interest, and the next hundred years might be considered Homer's century. The Greek tragedies also came into their own during the Victorian age. Cicero fell by the wayside in the wake of the multifaceted Platonic revival of the mid nineteenth century and the emergence of Aristotle's *Ethics* as a key Oxford University text. Plato came to be translated into English as never before.

A third indication of the predominant stature of Greek studies is the public and scholarly distinction of the persons conducting them. One need only mention the names of Connop Thirlwall, George Grote, William Gladstone, Matthew Arnold, Benjamin Jowett, John Ruskin, Alexander Grant, Walter Pater, Samuel Butler, Edward Caird, John Burnet, A.E. Taylor and Alfred Zimmern to establish the eminence of the coterie of Victorian Hellenists. All of them knew that the pursuit of Hellenism held forth the possibility of influencing their contemporaries in a manner in which Roman studies did not.

The reason why intellectuals and persons in public life were interested in classics in the first place derives from the educational system of the British elite. For better or worse the undergraduate education at the two ancient universities was centred on training in the classics. The system worked in two directions. First, the language requirements for admission to Oxford and Cambridge meant that the public and grammar schools dedicated to sending students to Oxbridge weighted their curricula toward the classics. This training continued to serve students well after their university years, because from mid century onward the civil service examinations which led to government posts favoured persons well trained in the ancient languages. Consequently, the relatively small educated British elite, which was largely coterminous with the social and political elite, shared as a cultural trait familiarity with the ancient world. The importance of this fact cannot be overemphasized. As John Grote wrote in 1856:

> Classical study . . . is a point of intellectual sympathy among men over a considerable surface of the world, for those who have forgotten their actual Greek and Latin bear still generally with them many traces of its influence, and in fact it is this which, more than anything, makes them, in common parlance, educated men.

This bond "of intellectual communion among civilized men" allowed the classics to provide a frame of cultural reference for discussion and debate.[4] It was more useful and self-limiting than the Christian heritage, which extended over class lines and stirred profound contemporary divisiveness. In that respect debate over the classics provided a relatively safe forum wherein the educated elite could in a more or less exclusive manner explore potentially disruptive modern public topics that were carefully concealed in the garb of the ancients.

To be more specific, a topic from antiquity genuinely engaged a Victorian writer only if it was perceived as more or less immediately relevant to his own day. Usually one of three reasons accounted for this perception of relevance. First, the classical subject or question might have a simple and direct polemical application. Such was the case of the ongoing nineteenth-century debate over Athenian democracy.

Second, in a more subtle and indirect fashion, disagreement in the ancient sources themselves could invite the attention of a commentator because a particular interpretation might support his views of a particular modern problem. This was the situation in regard to discrepancies about Socrates in the testimony of Plato, Xenophon, Aristophanes and Aristotle. Depending upon which source one most highly valued, Socrates could be drawn into either the idealist or positivist camp. Furthermore, the problems of the four accounts of the historical Socrates suggested ways for scholars to extricate themselves from the troubling issues surrounding the four Gospels and the problem of the historical Jesus.

Finally, an issue drawn from antiquity could become unexpectedly relevant because of the stature of the modern writer who first broached the subject. Such was clearly the situation created by Hegel's interpretation of Socrates, Grote's discussion of Athens, Benjamin Jowett's rendering of Plato, and physicist John Tyndall's comments on Lucretius.[5] In each case the eminence of the writer and the contemporary school or philosophy with which he was associated evoked criticism and debate over the classical subject he had discussed.

During the nineteenth century these factors of direct perception of relevance, the problematic character of documents, and the distinction of the scholars engaged in classical studies all shifted the balance of interest away from the Romans and toward the Greeks. This change may be seen in regard to the writing of political history, the evaluation of ancient epic poetry, and the appreciation of Roman and Greek philosophy and religion.

Political history

Throughout the eighteenth century commentators on British politics and historians of ancient Rome perceived a very close affinity between the ancient Roman Republic and the modern British polity since the Glorious Revolution of 1688. An essayist in the *Monthly Review* of 1764 succinctly stated the assumptions that informed such consideration of the Republic:

> It is certain, that a thorough acquaintance with the Roman government, must afford the most useful information to the subjects of a free State, and more especially to our own: for there is undoubtedly a very strong resemblance between the general forms of each: both being of a mixed nature, compounded of royalty, aristocracy, and democracy, though the respective powers of these three orders were, in each constitution, blended together in very different proportions. The fundamental principles in each, however, being so nearly similar, many profitable conclusions may be drawn from a comparison between the Roman State and our own; and from the fatal effects of party zeal, public corruption, and popular licentiousness in the one, we may form probable conjectures with regard to the consequences which the same circumstances must produce in the other.[6]

The perceived analogy between the two nations stemmed from the allegedly mixed constitution of each. Ancient political philosophers had written extensively about mixed polities consisting of elements of monarchy, oligarchy and democracy. Polybius had specifically analysed the Roman republican constitution in those terms. Then Renaissance civic humanists, particularly Machiavelli, had drawn the ancient concept of the mixed polity into modern political thought. From at least the middle of the seventeenth century English political thinkers—often indebted to Machiavelli—had discussed English political structures in terms of a mixed constitution. By the early eighteenth century the metaphors of the mixed and balanced constitution had become central to British political discourse.

In the wake of the events of 1688 and the Revolution Settlement, some English political commentators saw a clear resemblance between early republican Rome liberated from its tyrannical kings and modern England freed from the absolutism of the Stuarts. Like republican Rome, modern Britain enjoyed a mixed constitution guarded by wise aristocrats in Parliament. During the first half of the century several major political pamphlets explored the character of the Roman Senate and made explicit comparison with the composition of Parliament and in particular the House of Lords.

The interpretation of Roman history informing all these speculations was that of Machiavelli's *Discourses* with its moral explanation of the collapse of ancient Roman republican liberty. Machiavelli, like the ancient sources upon which he drew, had ascribed the loss of Roman freedom to the impact of luxury following the victory over Carthage. Luxury had fostered individual selfishness and had thereby displaced patriotic virtue. Those moral developments in turn had fostered the establishment of personally independent military commanders no longer obedient to the Senate. Consequently the later Roman Republic lacked the political balance that Polybius had perceived to function so wisely and efficaciously in an earlier age.

The British context for establishing the analogy between the fate of the Roman Republic and that of modern Britain in these Machiavellian terms was the country-party critique of the court—Whig political supermacy under the leadership of Robert Walpole.[7] The spokesmen for the country-party ideology were Tories proscribed from office by Walpole and Whigs more radical than he. These pamphleteers urged that the proper balance of the British constitution (and thus the essential guarantee of liberty) had been undermined since the settlement of 1688, first by William and his ministers, then by the Whigs of the court of Queen Anne, and finally (and most despicably) by Walpole under the first two Hanoverians. The indications of this corruption and of the betrayal of liberty were excessive commercialism, a large national debt, a standing army, placemen in Parliament and an overly strong central executive authority sustained by patronage and novel financial structures. The new forms of commercial wealth and crown monetary resources were overwhelming the political influence of the genuinely independent men of landed wealth in Parliament and thereby the balance of the British polity.

The country-party Roman polemic appeared in numerous political pamphlets, but most extensively in Nathaniel Hooke's *The Roman History from the Building of Rome to the Ruin of the Commonwealth* (4 vols., 1738-71). Although a Tory, Hooke took the side of all the major republican heroes who had challenged the corrupt Senate of the late Republic. It was essential to his purposes that an opposition critical of a senatorial order that claimed to protect liberty be given legitimacy. He praised the Gracchi for having attempted to create a stabilizing class of small landowners, and he described the senators who had crushed the two brothers as 'the oppressors of their country, men determined to enslave Rome'. He heaped contempt on the ancient senatorial order for having illicitly used the word *liberty* to describe a state in which "the bulk of the people have neither property, nor the privilege of living by their labour". He also argued that from the time of Sulla's restoration onward "the Freedom of the Roman People . . . was surely, at best, no better than the freedom of outlaws and banditti". By the closing years of the Republic Pompey and Caesar had stepped forth to lead respectively "the two permanent and distinct parties in the Republic, the Aristocracy and the People".[8] Once triumphant from the civil wars, Caesar had ruled wisely and benevolently and without monarchical ambition. In Hooke's narrative Caesar stood as one of those heroic figures of the Renaissance civic humanist tradition of political thought who possess the capacity, if permitted to exercise it, of restoring a state to its original principles. The most familiar eighteenth-century version of this ideal was Bolingbroke's Patriot King.

Court-oriented writers found themselves compelled to answer these country-party charges. The major spokesmen for the court were Conyers Middleton in *The History of the Life of Marcus Tullius Cicero* (2 vols., 1741); Thomas Blackwell in *Memoirs of the Court of Augustus* (3 vols., 1753-63); and Adam Ferguson in *The History of the Progress and Termination of the Roman Republic* (4 vols., 1783: 5 vols., 1799). The general strategy of these court-oriented histories was to attack those Romans who had challenged the authority of the Senate and to praise those (most particularly Cicero) who had tried to protect the structures of the Republic and to defend traditional republican liberty. For example, Middleton's biography of Cicero established a close parallel between the Cicero who had attempted to protect the Republic against the wiles of Catiline, Caesar and Octavian and the Walpole attempting to preserve English liberty against the plots of the Jacobites, disaffected Tories and radical Whigs. Blackwell drew a strong and sharply hostile parallel between Caesar and the Stuart Pretender.[9]

Ferguson's history was the most reasoned of the court-oriented works. He criticized the Gracchi for not having understood the function of property in a free state and for having attempted to impose inappropriate political structures. He praised Sulla for having rescued Rome from the "scene of wild devastation, attended with murders, rapes, and every species of outrage" that had prevailed under Marius. Sulla's restoration of order might have saved Roman liberty "if the spirit of legal monarchy could at once have been infused into every part of the commonwealth; or if, without further pangs or convulsions, the authority of a Prince, tempered with that of a Senate, had been firmly established".[10] In other words, republican liberty might have been preserved had its ancient aristocracy been wise enough to establish the kind of political structure that Britain enjoyed under the Hanoverians.

Instead, what the Roman Republic experienced was a contest among self-aggrandizing aristocratic leaders. The evil genius behind that tumult was, of course, Caesar. In Ferguson's view, Caesar had rejected alliances with his own social class and had chosen to court "the populace in preference to the Senate or better sort of the People". He had decided to make himself "the chief among those who, being abandoned to every vice, saw the remains of virtue in their country with distaste and aversion". Capable of receiving public honour equal to Cato's, Cicero's or the Scipios", he had "preferred being a superior among profligate men, the leader of soldiers of fortune".[11]

Ferguson's characterization of Caesar begins to explain why the Roman example would cease to be useful for later British commentators. Whereas previous writers had equated Caesar with the Stuart Pretender, Ferguson's Caesar bore a close resemblance to the late eighteenth-century members of the aristocracy, gentry or respectable commercial classes who had made common cause with the lower social order to challenge the authority of the Hanoverian monarchy and the British Parliament during the Wilkesite protests, the American Revolution, the Yorkshire Association Movement, the Irish troubles and the Gordon riots. This shift in polemical emphasis and target was not accidental. From the 1760s through to the 1780s the country party's ideology, identified earlier in the century with Tories seeking position, place and patronage, had been appropriated by more radical political groups in both Britain and America.[12] The radicals of the later part of the century pointed to the alleged corruption of the British government and particularly of Parliament as a basis, not for replacing one group of aristocrats with another, but for direct appeals to the authority of the people and the recognition of popular leaders.

The Roman example adduced by the early eighteenth-century writers in the name of a balanced constitution was stolen by genuine modern republicans, first in the American colonies and then in France. Early in the century the Roman Republic had functioned as an ideal of balance and restraint: but the reality of modern republicanism in America and France, and then the emergence of Napoleonic Caesarism, turned all forms of republicanism ancient or modern into a terrifying spectre. The history of the Roman Republic was no longer useful even as a warning, because the forces of tumult and military monarchy had triumphed, and the old senatorial order had either perished or become politically impotent.

The appeal to the Roman Republic had been possible because it occurred in the context of the country-party ideology mediated by the influence of Renaissance civic humanism. The ideological reaction to the French Revolution set forth by Burke largely supplanted this outlook with its concern for the experience of the ancient republic and revived instead the ideal of the ancient English constitution. Moreover, the secular view of politics associated with the appeal to the pagan Republic gave way to a view of political life in a distinctly religious setting. The Roman polemic had first been used by British political figures who wished to oppose the government; it came virtually to an end when, in the wake of the French wars, all opposition came to be suspect and subject to government persecution.

Beginning with Mitford's *History of Greece* (1784), the example of the turmoil of Greek democracy came to be the ancient political case to which polemical appeal was most useful.[13] Initially the Greek example portrayed the problems of democracy and the conquest of unruly democracies by a monarchy. But as the political structures of Britain became more liberal in the 1830s, and as the discussion of the positive as well as the negative aspects of democracy became politically possible, the Greek example continued to be regarded as relevant, most especially in the mid century volumes of George Grote's *History of Greece.* There he pointed to the wise and beneficient features of Athenian democracy and to the "constitutional morality" he saw it fostering. And by the close of the nineteenth century, as new doubts arose within the British intellectual community about liberal democracy, the Athenian case remained applicable to such scholars as Abbott and Grundy.

The Roman political story could serve none of these Victorian purposes. A few historians inspired by Bonapartism and Carlyle's heroes did praise Julius Caesar and use him as a foil against partisan democracy; but they never provoked the controversy stirred by Greece. The austerity of early republican Rome had no appeal to an age dedicated to improvement and economic growth. Caesarism was attractive to only a few more or less isolated intellectuals who never really contemplated it for Britain. The Roman Empire in its power was not the empire that mid Victorians wished to establish. The Roman Empire in its decline was not a spectacle that the British intellectual nation wished to contemplate. Thus for the best part of a century Roman history languished in Britain, as Greek history waxed ever stronger.

Virgil and Homer

Whereas Roman history was often just ignored in the nineteenth century, Virgil was strongly attacked. Even during the eighteenth century his reputation had begun to wane. As R.D. Williams has pointed out, "The English Augustan Age was the high noon of admiration for Horace and Virgil."[14] The most outspoken of Virgil's late seventeenth and early eighteenth-century advocates was John Dryden. He admired both Virgil's poetry and, as a royalist supporter himself, the political message of the *Aeneid.* Virgil's political stance rendered his epic less than popular among eighteenth-century Whigs and political radicals. None the less, as long as epic poems were evaluated by neo-classical standards that emphasized established standards of refinement and gave only minimal concern to questions of history and original genius, Virgil held his own against Homer.

But toward the close of the eighteenth century several factors combined to displace Virgil in critical estimation and to raise Homer to unprecedented heights.[15] First, Thomas Blackwell's *An Enquiry into the Life and Writings of Homer* (1735) and Robert Wood's *Essay upon the Original Genius and Writings of Homer* (1775) had persuaded critics that Homer provided a vivid and historically accurate portrait of his age. To read and study Homer was actually to enter the life of a primitive epoch, a knowledge of which could also be used for comparative purposes when reading the Old Testament. Second, the emphasis on original genius that characterized romantic criticism in general led to Virgil being seen simply as an imitator of Homer. The romantic emphasis on heroes and great men similarly led to a higher estimation of Achilles than of Aeneas. Achilles really did seem larger than life, and more fully tragic. Finally, as had been often pointed out, Virgil's reputation suffered because he was so closely associated with the English Augustan poets against whom the Romantics rebelled.

The Victorian estimation of Virgil was not, however, simply critical; it was genuinely hostile. The article in the seventh edition of the *Encyclopaedia Britannica* (1842) condemns the *Eclogues* as imitations amounting to little more than translations of Theocritus. Virgil's deficiency "in the power of creating and bodying forth original compositions" could not be compensated for by his strength "in soundness of judgment and correctness of taste; in depth of tenderness of feeling; in chastened fancy and imagination; in vivid and picturesque description; in the power of appreciating and portraying the beauty, whether in nature or art; of depicting passion and touching the chords of human sympathy; in matchless beauty of diction and in harmony and splendour of versification". Without the presence of original genius and creativity, all of those other very considerable poetic virtues commanded acknowledgement but neither respect nor admiration. Furthermore, Virgil had been ill-advised to undertake an epic poem because "neither the age which produced it, nor the genius of the poet, was favourable to such an achievement". The political goal of the poem—"the exaltation of Augustus"—led to fatal flaws in composition. Such was especially the situation with the portrayal of Aeneas whom Virgil had necessarily "represented as the mere passive instrument of fate", and "there is consequently little about him of heroic daring".[16]

William Ewart Gladstone, 1809-1898, English essayist and statesman

Other lesser histories and commentaries on Roman literature echoed these sentiments, but the single harshest attack came from William Gladstone, the author of more commentary on Homer than any other Victorian writer. Gladstone's polemic appeared in *The Quarterly Review* of 1857, one year before he published his three-volume *Studies in Homer and the Homeric Age* (1858). Except for the power of Virgil's poetic language, Gladstone could find nothing to admire about the *Aeneid.* The politics of the epic alone had proved "fatal to the attainment of the very highest excellence". Gladstone reminded his readers, "While Homer sang for national glory, the poem of Virgil is toned throughout to a spirit of courtier-like adulation. No muse, however vigorous, can maintain an upright gait under so base a burden." Furthermore, Virgil's admittedly majestic poem suffered from flaws in its diction, which was "more like the performance of a trained athlete, between trick and strength, than the grandeur of free and simple Nature, as it is seen in the ancient warrior, in Diomed or Achilles; or in Homer, the ancient warrior's only bard".[17]

However the main object of Gladstone's very considerable scorn was the hero of the Virgilian epic of whom he declared: "It is perhaps hardly possible to exhaust the topics of censure which may be justly used against the Aeneas of Virgil." Aeneas presented to readers moral deficiencies" and "intellectual mediocrity" unredeemed by other virtues. He stands forth as neither a true statesman nor a warrior, but merely as the creation of the poet. His conduct toward Dido is nothing less than "vile", and the excuses he offers for this action are "wretched". These deficiencies reflect a "feeble and deteriorated conception of human nature at large". The poet has treated mankind as "but a shallow being", and "had not sounded the depths of the heart, nor measured either the strength of good or the strength of evil that may abide in it".[18]

The real problem, though, was Virgil's insincerity. In contrast to Homer, Virgil never appeared to be forthright, authentic or personally sincere. Gladstone contended that since Virgil had constructed his work for "a corrupt court, and not for mankind at large", it had been impossible for him to "take his stand upon those deep and broad foundations in human nature which gave Homer a position of universal command". Virgil had also laboured under the disadvantage of a prevailing religion that stood "undermined at once by philosophy and by licentiousness, and subsisted only as machinery, and that terribly discredited, for civil ends". Consequently there ran through the *Aeneid* "a vein of untruthfulness" that was "as strong and as remarkable as is the genuineness of thought and feeling in the

Homeric poems".[19] The intensity of Gladstone's polemic against Virgil must be read in the context of his self-proclaimed mission to bring Homer into the Oxford curriculum.[20] But while those private religious and political ends account for Gladstone's article and its timing, those eccentric purposes do not account for the absence of substantial protests against his condemnation of Virgil. Gladstone would seem to have epitomized mid Victorian distaste for the *Aeneid:* it was imitative, lifeless and insincere. Virgil's epic revealed neither the mind of a great poetic genius nor the customs of an age from which the Victorians felt they could learn new insights into the human condition.

Three major attempts were made in the last quarter of the century to defend Virgil and to accommodate him to the Victorian poetic audience. These were W.Y. Sellar's *Roman Poets of the Augustan Age* (1877), Henry Nettleship's *Lectures and Essays on Subjects Connected with Latin Literature and Scholarship* (1885), and T.R. Glover's *Studies in Virgil* (1904). Their treatments demonstrate that the best way for a Victorian critic to save Virgil was by making him appear to resemble Homer.

Sellar pointed out in considerable detail why Rome generally, and Virgil in particular, might have welcomed the Principate as a release from turmoil, war and destruction. That peace under an admittedly questionable political regime had fostered new patronage of poetry. It was this very close relationship of the poets to the new society that "tended to make literature tamer in spirit and thought, perhaps also less original in invention, more bounded in its range of human interest". Sellar also went so far as to confess that Virgil "never again can enter into rivalry with Homer as the inspired poet of heroic action".[21] Homer alone could reveal the heroic age of humankind.

Sellar then assigned to Virgil a different poetic and literary mission: he must in the future be regarded "as a representative writer—representative both of the general national idea and of the sentiment and culture of his own age". In this manner the late Victorian Virgil became, like the late eighteenth-century Homer, a spokesman of his own day and the provider of an important historical record, though of a civilized rather than a primitive age.

> His poems, better than any other witnesses, enable us to understand how weary the Roman world was of the wars, disturbances, and anarchy of the preceding century, how ardently it longed for the restoration of order and national unity, how thankfully it accepted the rule of the man who could alone effect this restoration and how hopefully it looked forward to a new era of peace and prosperity, of glory and empire, under his administration.[22]

Virgil was more than the kept poet of a despotic regime; he was the writer who makes us understand why many people praised and supported that regime. Gladstone had portrayed Homer as carrying out a somewhat similar empathetic function in his portrayal of Greek and Trojan politics.

Sellar also attempted to draw Virgil directly into Matthew Arnold's strain of cultural Hellenism. Virgil stood forth as "pre-eminently the most cultivated man belonging to the age". As such he had appropriated "all the past wisdom of the ancient world". Although his verse may never have reached the heights of the Greek poetry, "the deep and tranquil charm of Virgil may prove some antidote to the excitement, the restlessness, the unsettlement of opinion in the present day". These remarks echo Matthew Arnold's Preface of 1854, and his later discussions of Hellenism. Sellar is clearly attempting to associate Virgil, if not with Homer, at least with the sweetness and light of culture that Arnold ascribed to fifth-century Greek intellectual and artistic life. Sellar claims for Virgil what Arnold might have claimed for Hellenism over Hebraism: " . . . the nobleness of Virgil's nature is not the nobleness of those qualities which make men great in resistance to wrong but the nobleness of a gentle and gracious spirit".[23]

Henry Nettleship, the Corpus Professor of Latin Literature at Oxford, continued this effort to Hellenize Virgil. In his "Suggestions Introductory to a Study of the Aeneid" (1875; published 1885) he contended that the emphasis on Homer had led to an undervaluing of Virgil's achievement. But once he began to discuss the achievement, a somewhat Homeric Virgil emerged. Virgil is portrayed as having put before his readers "the primitive condition of Italy and of the characters with whom Aeneas is brought into contact". Virgil seeks to present "the idea of the subjugation of semi-barbarous tribes under a high civilization and religion". Virgil's imitative qualities reflected the character of Roman poetry, not a lack of genius. Moreover, even if he was imitative, he rose higher in the quality of his poetry than any other Roman. But most important, the spiritual and religious concepts that inform Virgil are "very like the spirit which animates the action and play of character with which Greek tragedy has made us familiar". And Virgil has portrayed human passions in conflict with divine purposes and providence "with all the dignity and purity of Sophocles". In particular the Dido episode is "worked out very much in the spirit of Greek tragedy, the confused moral conflicts of which it thoroughly recalls".[24] In this manner Nettleship accepted the imitative character of Virgil and transformed it into an assimilative genius.

By the opening of the new century T.R. Glover set forth a strong secular defence of Virgil. He declared that " . . . the Aeneid is one, it is 'grand', it interests, it expresses the Roman people, and it rises from time to time to be the utterance of humanity". For Glover the subject of Virgil's epic is "the birth of a great people, of a great work done to found a great race, of a spirit and temper brought into the world which should in time enable that race to hold sway over the whole world and to be the whole world, with all its tribes and tongues, the pledge and the symbol of its union and its peace". In the story of Aeneas, Virgil had discovered a "clue to the story of every man, the linking of divine decree with human suffering, something to explain waste of life and failure of hope by a broader view of heaven's purpose and earth's needs, a justification of the ways of God to men, not complete, only tentative, but yet an anodyne and an encouragement in an unintelligible world". Virgil's originality lay in his "conscious appeal to a nation, as we understand the word 'nation' today, to a people of one blood living within well-defined but broad limits, a people with various traditions all fusing in common tradition". Virgil was the poet who "gave for the first time its literary expression to the triumph of a nation, politically, racially, and geographically one, over the clan and over the city-state". In doing so, Virgil stood as the poet who expressed a collective nation and the ideal best self of "the ideal Roman temper".[25]

Glover's remarks are curious on a number of levels, including his ascription of blood nationhood to the polyglot Augustan empire. There is little or no evidence that the Romans under the Principate looked to Virgil as having set forth their ideal temper. But there is, of course, overwhelming evidence that the Greeks in various ages and cities saw Homer as their common bond, and as having expressed values to which they all ascribed. Homer and the Olympian religion did to some extent overcome political and religious localism in Greece, and that role for Homer was well known and widely acknowledged. Glover was simply attempting to appropriate that Homeric role to Virgil.

Glover's praise for Virgil and for the emperor Virgil lauded was characteristic of the Edwardian age and beyond. With the turn of the century Rome did begin to reassert itself over Greece with new appreciation appearing for empire, efficiency and administration.[26]

Religion and philosophy

The hegemony of Greek religion and philosophy over Roman in the nineteenth century was no less remarkable than the apotheosis of Homer. During the early eighteenth century Cicero for all his indecision and vacillation had been intensely admired for his philosophy of public life and conduct. His religious and philosophical speculation was also compatible with the tolerant religious spirit of the Enlightenment and the strongly Erastian character of the eighteenth-century Church of England. During these same years both Aristotle and Plato received rather minimal attention.

During the Victorian age interest in both Greek religion and mythology and in Greek philosophy came into its own.[27] Aristotle's *Ethics* became the major common text studied at Oxford, and a Platonic revival began, the force of which is still felt. The intensification of British religious life associated with evangelicalism and other modes of romantic religion had differentiated between real religion and nominal religion, or between real Christianity and nominal Christianity. Roman religion had widely been regarded as shallow, insincere and political in character: Greek religion and its myths seemed, in contrast, to be sincere, lyrical and serious—frighteningly so in some regards. Also, as the Victorians became concerned with the origins of religion, the antiquity of Greek myth and ritual made them more interesting than a Roman religion manifested in a decadent society. In the hands of Grote, Mueller, Pater, Frazer, Cornford and Harrison the exploration of Greek religion became an exploration of an ancient, primeval stage of human intellectual development. Finally, it was possible to interpret Greek religion as an earlier stage of a human perception of the divine that was in certain respects compatible with, if not admittedly identical with, Christianity. The Greek sense of fate appealed to Christians familiar from childhood with the idea of predestination, and familiar in adulthood with evolutionary or scientific determinism.

The beauty, intensity, seriousness and antiquity of Greek religion reflected qualities that the Victorians wished to attach to their own religious life. A similar situation prevailed with Greek philosophy. Within the British universities Greek philosophy became a means of defence against utilitarianism and other rationalistic philosophies derived from the eighteenth century. Here, as with the appreciation of Homer, a determining influence was the thought of modern Germany. German idealism, Greek philosophy and liberal Anglicanism could be combined to forge an ethical and metaphysical outlook that for over a century prevented utilitarianism and rationalism from significantly intruding upon any British university except the utilitarian foundation of University College, London.

Not only did Victorian scholars regard Greek philosophy as very useful, but they saw themselves as uniquely qualified to comprehend its character. As Alexander Grant wrote in 1858:

> With the present century fresh lights have gradually dawned upon the world, and we now look with different eyes upon antiquity. We bring to the remains of the ancient philosophers new ideas to guide us in our study. First among these is the historical spirit, the axiom that human thought can only be known by knowing its antecedents; second, is the critical spirit, which is neither hasty to accept nor to reject, but which weighs and discriminates; third, is the philosophical spirit, which has a certain sympathy and affinity for the speculation of the Greeks. It requires some philosophy to interpret a philosopher. Modern German thought, whatever may

> have been its extravagances, has, to say the least, this advantage, that it puts those who have to the slightest degree caught its influence on a better level for understanding Parmenides and Heraclitus, Plato and Aristotle. And thus it is only in the present century that the history of Grecian philosophy has been adequately written.[28]

German idealism and historicism, then, as infused into the British university system and into theological speculation from Coleridge's later writings onward, convinced Victorian intellectuals that they possessed previously undiscovered insights whereby they could make Greek philosophy their own. Indeed, virtually all the nineteenth-century philosophies of history—Hegelian, Comtean, Viconian and Christian providential—could appropriate the Greek experience more easily than the Roman. Nowhere was this more true than in regard to Greek philosophy.

First, Greek political and ethical thought could help to define elite civic life in a liberal democracy. Ciceronian public philosophy had been suited to a republic of hereditary senators possessing immense privilege, or to an aristocracy facing the emergence of a tyrannical monarchy. Neither situation obtained in Victorian Britain. By contrast, both Aristotle and Plato portrayed a social and intellectual elite functioning and maintaining itself in the face of democracy. They provided a philosophy for a political elite legitimated by merit and by moral and intellectual superiority. Moreover this public philosophy was one that could be taught in the universities, and its propagation gave university intellectuals a real *raisón d'être* in an age of levelling liberal democracy. As Benjamin Jowett described the true statesman in his commentary on the *Gorgias:*

> A true statesman is he who brings order out of disorder; who first organizes and then administers the government of his own country; and having made a nation, seeks to reconcile the national interests with those of Europe and mankind . . . Although obliged to descend to the world, he is not of the world. His thoughts are fixed not on power or riches or extension of territory, but on an ideal state, in which all the citizens have an equal chance of health and life, and the highest education is within the reach of all, and the moral and intellectual qualities of every individual are freely developed, and "the idea of the good" is the animating principle of the whole. Not the attainment of freedom alone, or of order alone, but how to unite freedom with order is the problem which he has to solve.[29]

In the hands of Jowett and other late century Victorian dons, the philosophy of Aristotle and Plato became a pedagogical vehicle that taught this lesson to two generations of young men who would enter the civil service and other areas of public life.

Second, Greek philosophy provided both a surrogate for Christianity and a foil against Victorian utilitarianism and scientific naturalism. No doubt the most brilliant Victorian interpretation of Plato was Grote's *Plato, and the other Companions of Socrates* (1865); but the dominant interpretation was that contained in Jowett's translations and commentaries.[30] Jowett translated Plato's dialogues into the cadences of the authorized version of the Bible and the Book of Common Prayer. His commentaries included paraphrases of the dialogues and his own comments, with no indication being given for over twenty years as to which was which. His Plato was a proto-Christian whose ethic was that of Christian duty and self-sacrifice. There was, for Jowett, no sharp break between the emergence and diffusion of Greek ethical thought and the later rise of Christianity. The message of the Christian faith, under siege from science and historical criticism in its biblical mode, was thus preserved by being transferred to Plato. The protection of the core of Christianity—which Jowett had attempted in his contribution to the theologically liberal *Essays and Reviews,* only to confront persecution and failure—he actually achieved by his appropriation of Plato to liberal Anglican idealism.

No Roman philosopher could serve that same function. All were too close to the life and events of early Christianity to serve as prescriptive models. It was, after all, the paganism of the Roman world that Christianity had displaced and eventually conquered. This was why the very discontinuity between Greek and Victorian culture was so important. Only one Roman writer could even possibly seem useful: Marcus Aurelius. But Mathew Arnold's remarks on the philosopher-emperor displayed the distinct limits to Victorian appreciation of any Roman ethical thought.

In his essay of 1863 Arnold asserted that Marcus Aurelius was one of the very great moralists, an acquaintance with whom was "an imperishable benefit". Furthermore, he described Marcus Aurelius as "perhaps the most beautiful figure in history" and as "one of those consoling and hope-inspiring marks, which stand for ever to remind our weak and easily discouraged race how high human goodness and perseverance have once been carried, and may be carried again". Marcus Aurelius had prescribed right actions and assigned motives "which every clear reason must recognise as valid". What Arnold found especially attractive in this philosopher's morality was "its clear accent of emotion . . . [that] reminds one of Christian morality". This element of the *Meditations* gave to its author a genuinely religious quality and a moral quality that raised him above utilitarianism or scientific naturalism in Arnold's eyes. But the most admirable feature of his writing was his clear yearning for something which he could not attain through mere human means.

> What an affinity for Christianity had this persecutor of the Christians! The effusion of Christianity, its relieving tears, its happy self-sacrifice, were the very element, one feels for which his soul longed; they were near him, they brushed him, he touched them, he passed them by . . . We see him wise, just, self-governed, tender, thankful, blameless; yet, with all this, agitated, stretching out his arms for something beyond.[31]

The great charm of Marcus Aurelius was not that he was a Roman but rather that he might have been a Christian. Not only had he passed by the opportunity, but also he had persecuted the Christians. To state both the attractions of Marcus Aurelius and the faults was to undermine his role as a model. Both the Greek philosophers and Marcus Aurelius were viewed by their Victorian commentators as having sought the light; but the Greeks, unlike the Romans, had not sinned against the light.

Notes

[1] Frances Macdonald Cornford, *The Cambridge Classical Course: An Essay in Anticipation of Further Reform* (Cambridge, 1903), p. 19.

[2] W.Y. Sellar, *Roman Poets of the Augustan Age,* 2nd edn (Oxford, 1892), p. 74; 1st edn (1877).

[3] Frank M. Turner, 'British Politics and the Demise of the Roman Republic', *The Historical Journal,* 29 (1986), 577-99; John M.G. Pocock, *The Machiavellian Moment: Florentine Political Thought and the Atlantic Republican Tradition* (Princeton, 1975), pp. 333-552; Gordon S. Wood, *The Creation of the American Republic, 1776-1787* (New York, 1972), pp. 3-70.

[4] John Grote, 'Old Studies and New', in *Cambridge Essays: 1856* (London, 1856), p. 114.

[5] Frank M. Turner, 'Antiquity in Victorian Contexts', *Browning Institute Studies,* 10 (1982), 1-14; 'Lucretius among the Victorians', *Victorian Studies,* 16 (1973), 229-348.

[6] *Monthly Review,* 30 (1764), 107-8. This entire section of the present essay is drawn from my article on 'British Politics and the Demise of the Roman Republic', *The Historical Journal,* 29 (1986), 577-99.

[7] See works cited in n.3, and Caroline Robbins, *The Eighteenth-Century Commonwealthman: Studies in the Transmission, Development and Circumstance of English Liberal Thought from the Restoration of Charles II until the War with the Thirteen Colonies* (Cambridge, 1959); Isaac Kramnick, *Bolingbroke and His Circle: The Politics of Nostalgia in the Age of Walpole* (Cambridge, 1968); J.A.W. Gunn, *Beyond Liberty and Property: The Process of Self Recognition in Eighteenth Century Political Thought* (Montreal, 1983), pp. 1-42.

[8] Nathaniel Hooke, *The Roman History from the Building of Rome to the Ruin of the Commonwealth* (London, 1738-71), II. 534; III. 223n.; IV. 4. For more details on Hooke's history see my 'British Politics', and Addison Ward, 'The Tory View of Roman History', *Studies in English Literature, 1500-1900,* 4 (1964), 413-56.

[9] See my 'British Politics', and Reed Browning, *Political and Constitutional Ideas of the Court Whigs* (Baton Rouge, 1982), pp. 1-34, 210-56.

[10] Adam Ferguson, *The History of the Progress and Termination of the Roman Republic,* new edn (Edinburgh, 1799), II. 170, IV. 140.

[11] Ibid., IV. 140; II. 369; IV. 101.

[12] See J.G.A. Pocock, '1776: The Revolution against Parliament', Alison Gilbert Olson, 'Parliament, Empire, and Parliamentary Law, 1776', and John Brewer, 'English Radicalism in the Age of George III', in J.G.A. Pocock (ed.), *Three British Revolutions: 1641, 1688, and 1776* (Princeton, 1980), pp. 265-367.

[13] See my study, *The Greek Heritage in Victorian Britain* (New Haven, 1981), pp. 187-263.

[14] R.D. Williams, 'Changing Attitudes to Virgil: A Study in the History of Taste from Dryden to Tennyson', in D.R. Dudley (ed.), *Virgil* (New York, 1968), p. 123. See also T.W. Harrison, 'English Virgil: The Aeneid in the XVIII Century', *Philologica Pragensia,* 10 (1967), 1-11, 80-91; Donald M. Foerster, *The Fortunes of Epic Poetry: A Study in English and American Criticism, 1750-1950* (Washington, 1962), pp. 15-29, 76, 134-9; Howard D. Weinbrot, *Augustus Caesar in 'Augustan' England* (Princeton, 1978), *passim.*

[15] Donald M. Foerster, *Homer in English Criticism: The Historical Approach in the Eighteenth Century* (New Haven, 1947).

[16] 'Virgil', *Encyclopaedia Britannica* (7th edn).

[17] William Gladstone, 'Homer and His Successors in Epic Poetry', *Quarterly Review,* 10 (1857), 82, 84.

[18] Ibid., 84, 85.

[19] Ibid., 88, 89.

[20] Turner, *Greek Heritage,* pp. 159-77, 236-43.

[21] Sellar, *Roman Poets of the Augustan Age,* pp. 31, 78.

22 Ibid., pp. 78, 81.

23 Ibid., pp. 84, 91-2, 129-30; see also, Turner, *Greek Heritage,* pp. 17-36.

24 Henry Nettleship, *Lectures and Essays on Subjects Connected with Latin Literature and Scholarship* (Oxford, 1885), pp. 106, 108, 125, 129.

25 T.R. Glover, *Virgil,* 2nd edn (London, 1912), pp. 83, 105, 106, 141. Glover entitled the first edition of this work *Studies in Virgil.*

26 See Turner, 'British Politics', and Raymond F. Betts, 'The Allusion to Rome in British Imperialist Thought of the Late Nineteenth and Early Twentieth Centuries', *Victorian Studies,* 15 (1971), 149-60.

27 Turner, *Greek Heritage,* pp. 77-134.

28 Alexander Grant, *The 'Ethics' of Aristotle Illustrated with Essays and Notes* (London, 1857, 1858), II. xi-xii.

29 Benjamin Jowett, *The Dialogues of Plato, Translated into English with Analyses and Introductions* (Oxford, 1871), II. 308-9.

30 Turner, *Greek Heritage,* pp. 383-446.

31 Matthew Arnold, 'Marcus Aurelius', in Whitney J. Oates (ed.), *The Stoic and Epicurean Philosophers* (New York, 1940), pp. 596, 598, 609, 610.

Anthony Grafton (essay date 1992)

"Germany and the West, 1830-1900," in *Perceptions of the Ancient Greeks,* edited by K. J. Dover, Basil Blackwell, Ltd., 1992, pp. 225-45.

[*In the following essay, Grafton examines the development of Hellenism in eighteenth- and nineteenth-century Germany, which contributed to the later and more pervasive growth in England. He delineates two competing strains of methodology in the German universities: one advocating the most precise forms of philology, with its narrow focus on language; the other expounding the effort to evoke ancient Greece in a more broad and holistic fashion.*]

Confronting the Greeks

Early in the 1860s two *Untersekundaner* (fourth-formers) wandered in the fields outside their gymnasium, reciting Anacreon as they went, "filled with all the more enthusiasm for his poems as their easy Greek presented few obstacles to the understanding."[1] Their friendship continued after their departure from school in 1864, and they rented rooms together at the romantic University of Bonn, where both registered to study theology—but in the event, like many of their contemporaries, studied philology. One of them soon decided that his life's vocation lay with the science of antiquity. He attached himself to Friedrich Ritschl, leaving with him for Leipzig when the Bonn philological school exploded in a famous quarrel in 1865. Once there he lost no opportunity to berate his friend for his failure to dedicate himself also to philology, and thus make productive use of his youthful years, when he could still hope to do original work.

The young *Philolog* discoursed at length about the value of philology: "This is a study in which one must pay with many a drop of sweat, but also one that really rewards every effort." But he also admitted that the philologist was a very different animal from the schoolboy who light-heartedly recited Greek lyrics in the fields. He needed "erudition and routine—that is, experience and practice" to make any progress at all; and "for that one needs time, much time." And he confessed that the real philologist might have to swallow a peck of scholarly dust as the price of entrance to the professional study of the eternally wise and luminous texts of the Greeks.[2] Thus he discouraged his friend from entering what seemed a deeply important but also a heavily trodden area of study, the development of Plato's thought. Such a field might offer rich rewards for one's *Geist,* but it presented few possibilities for one's career, since one could hardly hope to exhaust it or arrive at genuinely new results. Something narrower and duller would be preferable: "For your general formation [*Bildung*] choose the hardest and most attractive problems, but for the purpose of a dissertation a modest little out-of-the-way corner, nothing more."[3]

The relationship seems typical of its moment and milieu. Two young German students consider embracing *scholarship as a profession.* Both men encounter the Greek classics, in the original, at the newly rigorous gymnasium of the mid nineteenth century. They are charmed by simple, late poems, which appeal to their adolescent sentimentality with their idealized Fragonard imagery of lovers in a classical landscape. Both learn to read a far wider range of texts, and to do so methodically, at university, thanks to the equally new and even more rigorous research seminars which required them not only to master a range of scholarly tools and materials but also to use these to produce original arguments. Both are invited by their teachers to grasp the goals and ideals of that proudest and newest of nineteenth-century sciences, *Altertumswissenschaft,* the rigorous and comprehensive study of the ancient world. This interdisciplinary enterprise, designed by Heyne, Wolf and Böckh, sought both to establish the texts of all works of Greek literature critically and to understand them historically, as their authors themselves had, in the light of the context in which they were first produced and read. And both are forced by their situation to confront the process of professionalization that characterized the practice of this science by the middle of the nineteenth century.

To be a professional student of Greek, a true philologist, one had to "produce" original interpretations; and to find texts from which one could produce them one might have to move from classical to late texts, from the literary to the technical, from the interesting to the unrewarding. The philologist's picture of classical Greece, in short, might show little of that noble simplicity which had inspired the Hellenic revival of the end of the eighteenth century; might, indeed, reveal nothing but a cliff-face of disparate data, *loci difficiliores* and conflicting traditions to be scaled competitively by young men in search of jobs rather than enlightenment. So much for the effort to provide *Bildung* (education) through *Wissenschaft* (science) that had inspired Wolf and Humboldt to reform the German universities by example and regulation. So much also for the enterprise of understanding the great ancient writers not anachronistically, as the *philosophes* had read them, but historically, in the light of the full matrix of social, personal, institutional and literary factors within which their works took shape. The modern hunt for a subject boring enough to lack an existing literature had begun; and the older boy explained its rules to the younger one with skill and zest. One apprentice initiated another into the most characteristic intellectual craft of post-revolutionary Europe: the philology that provided a new career for many sons of pastors and a safely unpolitical general education for the broad new group of *Gebildete* (educated). The tyranny of Germany over Greece seems well established, comfortable, safe.

In fact, however, there is a good deal wrong with this picture. The younger, hesitant partner in these discussions was Paul Deussen, who eventually became a famous and productive Indologist. The older, confident one, the professional philologist smoothly ascending the ladder until he won a chair while in his twenties, was Friedrich Nietzsche—whose later career would see the smooth upward arc of his early professional success sharply broken off, and whose later writing would include many denunciations of the smugly limited aspirations he had urged his friend to accept at the *conditio sine qua non* of the study of antiquity.[4] In eavesdropping on their intercourse we certainly do not overhear two normal young upwardly mobile philologists.

Even more surprising is the picture of a German classical training that emerges from the records they left. Normal histories of German classical scholarship in the nineteenth century insist that one great set of fighting issues clove the profession as a whole into warring camps: textual critics bent on clarifying and emending works of literature and cultural historians bent on evoking the life of Greece as a whole. The great quarrel that drove Ritschl from Bonn was inspired by this division. He was the leading younger proponent of the textualist school of Hermann, and his opponents at Bonn repeatedly ridiculed his obsession with petty textual details and his students' disdain for and ignorance of wider issues:

> He keeps his students busy exclusively with the formal exercises of philological criticism. Knowledge of the real life of antiquity, its history, its conditions, its literature, is on so low a level as it is here at no other German university. No semester passes without the promotion *multa cum laude* of some philologist who knows nothing of the existence of Thucydides, confuses Ammianus with Appian, makes conjectures on Livy but doesn't know the content of the chapters in question. . . .[5]

Jahn, his opponent, stood by contrast for a far wider and more engaged concept of classical studies, for the direct study of ancient art as well as the correction of ancient texts and for the drawing of political lessons from the past. So much the adult participants in these quarrels knew.

At the time, however, things looked entirely different and far less clear-cut to the student pygmies who stood amazed as their gigantic professors built and broke their theoretical Valhallas. Nietzsche saw his teacher's brand of philology as relevant to far more than textual criticism. In summer 1871, instructing his Basle students about the study of the classics in general, Nietzsche defined the field as springing from the "the wish to understand a classical *Dasein*".[6] He found it perfectly reasonable to insist that a rigorous training in source-criticism and textual emendation made the best of preparations for what sounds like a holistic, intuitive enterprise. For all classical scholarship rested on the systematic philological criticism that Ritschl had inherited, ultimately, from Richard Bentley, with its firm injunction "to test every fact and every passage with mistrust." And though Nietzsche prophesied the arrival of an "age of synthesis" in scholarship, he warned his students that they could not synthesize until they had shown themselves worthy of the existing "age of analysis". Though trained by the great textual critic, Nietzsche assumed that philology was a historical and interpretative enterprise—a thesis his teacher sometimes downplayed and sometimes attacked. Deussen saw even less difference than Nietzsche did between Ritschl and Jahn. Both had proved excruciating bores in the classroom, the one obsessed with variants and the other with bibliography. The rigorous philology of the professionals seemed to Deussen to obscure, not illuminate, the classical texts they were supposed to interpret: "their manner . . . alienated me, with my soul full as it was with the splendour of classical antiquity, more and more from classical philology".[7] Evidently, then as now, the experience of study in a school or university could differ sharply in its texture not only from one cohort, but also from one student to the next—far more so than one could possibly suspect from a distance. That limitation must be borne in mind throughout this chapter.[8]

Mastering the Greeks

It is possible, to be sure, to describe some aspects of the nineteenth century vision of the Greek past with an appearance of rigour. To begin, in period fashion, with what are usually taken as the facts: this was the second great age of discovery and consolidation of the Greek heritage, one of scholarly achievements more astounding in scale and more sweeping in effect than any since the sixteenth century. In Germany the Humboldtian programme for university reform, which insisted that independent research into the classical past was the best form of mental discipline and should become the central occupation of both professors (*selbständig Forschende*) and students (*geleitet Forschende*), had profound, if equivocal, effects. Humboldt, Niebuhr and others convinced university administrators and state ministers to offer scholars and students financial support for travel, collection of information, and publication of results.[9] Some of this support took traditional forms. The Berlin Academy of Sciences, long a centre of debate about important philological issues, continued to propose prize essay topics for debate and to reward the winners with bursaries and publication of their essays. But it also began to offer support for large-scale, long-term enterprises. In 1815 it provided a first grant of 6,000 talers for a corpus of Greek inscriptions, to be supervised by a committee headed by Böckh and including Bekker, Buttmann, Niebuhr and Schleiermacher. The first, enormous volume appeared in 1828; the fourth and last in 1877.[10] This vast array of texts and commentaries represented a first effort at what became one characteristic form of German philology: large-scale scholarly enterprises resembling the new corporations of the day in their substantial capital foundations, large boards of directors, long-term planning, and spectacular creative energies. The results were dramatic: this new *Corpus* displaced the standard one produced more than two centuries before by two great late Renaissance scholars, Joseph Scaliger and Janus Gruter. The new *Corpus* was specialized where the old had included both Greek and Latin. The new one exploited the sources intensively, subjecting them to intense philological dissection, where the old had printed bare texts with only a small number of text-critical remarks. And the new one paid special attention to questions of authenticity, rejecting many reported texts as Renaissance and later fakes, where the old one had exiled only a few pages' worth of "spuria" to an isolation ward at the end of the book, and had admitted such evidently problematic texts as the Greek epitaph of one Chyndonax the Druid, found in Dijon just before 1600. Professional philology, with its dedication to pruning the record of late and faked evidence, thus visibly replaced an older humanism. And this process repeated itself in field after field, as editions of Greek texts ceased to include the Latin translations on facing pages that had made them familiar and accessible since the mid sixteenth century, and as histories of ancient Greece came to deal with strange issues, alien to the humanist tradition, such as the silver mines that had supported what Böckh reconstructed as *The Public Economy of Athens.* The Greek world stood forth far more clearly than ever before, in three dimensions and with many shadows; and in some lights it resembled a Daumier print more than *The School of Athens.*

The German scholars attacked the data in a variety of ways. Sometimes they went in for a sort of philological booty capitalism, amassing new resources in vast quantity but not processing them with equal subtlety. Immanuel Bekker, for sixty years ordinarius in Greek at Berlin, proved the great exponent of this style of work. He showed himself dazzlingly adept at avoiding the necessity to lecture and obtaining travel funds from the Prussian government, and profited from this ability to explore libraries everywhere in Europe, collating hundreds of manuscripts and producing vastly improved texts of more than 100 Greek and Latin authors not by the sophistication of his critical method but by the new richness of his materials—though his improved Aristotle would have been an admirable life's work in itself for an ordinary scholar.[11] The sedentary scholars of the late eighteenth and early nineteenth centuries had understood as clearly as Bekker that all texts should be established only after intensive study of the manuscript tradition. Some grasped that this process should result in the elimination of most witnesses as derivative witnesses; Wolf's famous *Prolegomena to Homer* began with a brilliant demonstration of precisely this point. But they had been harnessed to teaching posts that required as many as twenty hours of lectures a week, hampered by low salaries, and often required to supplement their salaries by writing enormous numbers of reviews or large works of reference. They could never have amassed materials as Bekker did—or as his Bavarian contemporary Friedrich Thiersch amassed them for analysis and partial publication in the *Acta Philologorum Monacensium,* with which he introduced the new methods to the southern areas of the German-speaking lands, or as the far less accurate and honest, but incredibly diligent Wilhelm Dindorf did with his Bonn corpus of Byzantine historians. As Germany gradually became industrialized, moreover, classical publishers shared the new prosperity, expanding in scale and ambition to match the efforts of the scholars. As early as 1825 Ludwig Dindorf founded that most expansive and enduring of all enterprises in publishing the classics, the *Bibliotheca Teubneriana,* which gradually replaced the traditional, neo-classically elegant eighteenth-century Greek texts with their austere modern counterparts, more solid of apparatus if devoid of helpful Latin translations. The Berlin houses of Weidmann and Calvary were equally indispensable parts of the material base of the new *Geisteswissenschaften.*

Often the new scholarship rose from primitive accumulation to sophisticated exploitation. Hellenists had known since the Renaissance that one could not trace the history of any Greek literary genre, from lyric poetry to philosophy, except by reconstructing lost texts by the patient tracing and reassembly of their fragments. By the late eighteenth century, again, all Hellenists knew that sort of work was vitally needed, and the more ambitious of them assigned the collection of the fragments of one author to their best students as an appropriate dissertation topic. The enterprise had many advantages. It forced the young man who undertook it to work through the whole range of Greek literary texts, and many other, less appealing works as well: the scholiasts, lexicographers, and compilers whose tedious (and sometimes unedited) works were marbled with the richest veins of quotation, and whom any philologist had to know if he really hoped to be a Hellenist. Heyne's son-in-law Heeren described this process vividly: "I went about it with the enthusiasm of youth. I read and excerpted all the grammarians and scholiasts in print, without exception (afterwards also some in manuscript at the Royal Library in Paris . . .) until, half-blind, I could shut my Eustathius. The fruit of this was a—perhaps fairly complete—collection of the fragments of the Greek lyric poets," which never reached print because of Heeren's ineptitude at metrics.[12] Heyne had a more gifted pupil to edit Stesichorus, and Wolf another to edit Antimachus of Colophon. Many prose authors received similar treatment in the transitional years around 1800. Schleiermacher helped to begin the first great modern philological journal, the *Rheinisches Museum für Philologie,* with an elaborate treatment of "The fragments of Heraclitus the obscure", and Gottfried Bernhardy, moving from poetry to prose and literature to science, began his distinguished career as a literary historian of Greece with a systematic collection of *Eratosthenica* (1824).

In the course of the nineteenth century, however, the enterprise of fragment-hunting underwent a change of state. Scholars now set out on safaris instead of butterfly-hunts: they assemble not a hundred pages of bits and pieces by one writer but the entire records of whole genres. Between the 1830s and the 1850s Theodor Bergk edited the *Poetae lyrici Graeci* (1834), August Meineke the five volumes of the *Fragmenta Comicorum Graecorum,* and "Charles" Müller (a political exile supported by his publishers, the Didot, rather than by government subsidy) the four volumes of *Fragmenta historicorum Graecorum* (1841-51). In the second half of the century Hermann Diels would reorient the early history of philosophy with his *Fragmente der Vorsokratiker.* As the century ended, new projects arose in which the zeal to discover new material and the effort to interpret it in depth intersected fruitfully. The *Inscriptiones Graecae* offered a sprawling home for the wide range of new texts turned up by systematic investigation of Greek sites; and even the vast technical works of the Empire and later ones still, such as the works of the commentators on Aristotle, began to be attacked, explored, and edited. A third wave of new editions began to replace some of what now seemed the traditional, even humanistic, and uncritical editions of the early nineteenth century—an effort necessarily partial but vastly impressive, as when the *Corpus medicorum Graecorum* finally began to supplant the handy but often flawed tomes of Kühn's Galen, with its unsatisfactory (and sometimes forged) texts and old-fashioned (and often problematic) Latin translations.

The rest of the West early recognized German supremacy in the production of large-scale scholarship based on solid research. As early as 1809, the *Edinburgh Review* remarked of the Clarendon Press that "though this learned body have occasionally availed themselves of the sagacity and erudition of Ruhnken, Wyttenbach, Heyné and other *foreign* professors, they have, of late, added nothing of their own, except what they derived from the superior skill of British Manufacturers, and the superior wealth of their establishment; namely, whiter paper, blacker ink, and neater types." The reports of Charles Villers and Mme de Stael drove home the point that—as the *Eclectic Review* put it in the 1830s—"philology itself" had become a "science" not in Oxford but "in the hands of the inquisitive Germans."[13] Americans, for political as well as cultural reasons, saw as early as the beginning of the century that their own classical curriculum could not be nourished except from German sources, and intrepid pioneers from both countries visited German universities, learned the German language, and reported back on their findings. Short-lived but learned journals, the *Museum Criticum* and the *Philological Museum,* reported on the doings of the German literati (even if, being English rather than German, they juxtaposed their articles on Hermann and Aeschylus with Walter Savage Landor's imaginary dialogues of the ancients in Latin). And some members of the elite in both countries showed considered willingness to combine the grammatical and literary skills they had mastered at home with the wider historical interests of the Germans.

The American George Bancroft, later an influential historian and diplomat, went as a student to Göttingen in the second decade of the century. There he read the classic, founding text of German scholarship, "Wolf & yet Wolf & yet Wolf."[14] He took elaborate notes on Dissen's lectures at Göttingen on the entire encyclopaedia of classical studies, from chronology to mythology and art to metrics. His notes, which survive, show that his teacher's course combined elaborate lists of references to *Literatur* with capsule judgments on every disputed problem imaginable—which may explain why Bancroft found them as emotionally depressing to sit through as they were intellectually absorbing.[15] None the less he would translate and expand on Böckh for an American audience in the *North American Review.* And, if fewer Britons took German degrees, British publishers did more than Americans to bring some results of German scholarship to their readers: the works of Otfried Müller on tragedy and mythology, the history of the Dorians and the development of Greek literature were all translated into English—the last, indeed was even written at the request of a British publisher.

On the other hand, few scholars in America or Britain could hope to do the sort of original research that German scholars practised on their own account. The Americans lacked adequate libraries; the English if not the Scots lacked any system of rewards, since professorships were almost non-existent, and college fellowships existed to support young bachelors until they received the offer of a good living and could marry and retire to the country. And both countries harboured many scoffers at the impiety, pedantry or both that seemed the dark side of German learning. As late as the 1870s, only a few Britons shared Mark Pattison's understanding of and admiration for German skills in source criticism and dedication to research—though, to be sure, the opening of the first deposits of papyri in Egypt would enable the British to make their own particular contribution to the stock of Greek learning, with such startling new texts as *The Constitution of Athens* to be edited and such skilled—if sometimes eccentric—Hellenists as Jebb and Mahaffy to correct and print them.[16]

France played an intermediary position. The university system remained deeply conservative, committed to Latin humanism and scholastic philosophy. But individual scholars mastered the language and method of *Altertumswissenschaft*—above all Ernest Renan, who greeted the revolution of 1848 with blazing enthusiasm and urged his countrymen to reform their intellectual as well as their social world by remodelling it on the basis of German philology, which he took to be the characteristic, liberating science of the nineteenth century.[17] Translators made much German work available, and the great French periodicals—above all the *Revue des deux mondes*—discussed Homeric criticism and scientific mythology in long but accessible articles. And German classicists of a liberal bent, like so many other Germans, found Paris their safe harbour in times of repression at home. Karl-Benedikt Hase, that engaging figure who wandered the slums, encountering prostitutes two at a time and recording what he did with them in a diary kept in Greek, and "Charles" Müller, among others, supported themselves working for the firm of Didot, reworking the great sixteenth-century Greek *Thesaurus* of Henri Estienne to meet modern needs, as it still more or less does, and editing many Greek texts (at least one of which, a Byzantine account of Russia, Hase forged).[18]

As German scholarship drove deeper, wider, and generally firmer foundations under its historical reconstructions of Greek society, literature, and thought, German education created a wider and wider basis for classical studies by ensuring that far larger numbers of young men than ever before could actually read Greek with ease and comfort. Greek had always been taught in the Latin schools and universities, to be sure. But the level of competence most students attained was hardly high. As late as 1811, when Wolf was shown Süvern's plan for the reform of the Prussian Gymnasien, with its suggested requirement that "In Greek, Attic prose and Homer must be understood at sight and a tragic chorus with the help of a dictionary" he reacted with scorn: "Given the want of time, Sophocles, Euripides and their consorts are really read in only a tiny number of gymnasien. It's hardly possible for anyone to hear three prose authors and a good piece of Homer. A tragic chorus! The whole proposal makes an indescribable impression on anyone who knows the world as it really is."[19] After all, Wolf argued, few teachers could read the harder sections of Greek tragedy or prose; one should hardly expect their pupils to do what they could not.

Gradually, however, conditions altered for the better in many individual cases.[20] When E. Poppo, student of Hermann and editor of Thucydides, headed the gymnasium at Frankfurt am Oder, he saw to it that pupils had eight and a half years of Greek, that they read comedy and bucolic as well as epic, and wound up with perhaps the most difficult of all Greek authors, Aeschylus and Pindar. Substantial amounts of time were devoted to prose and verse composition, prepared and extemporaneous, as well. And even less ambitious teachers managed to establish, first in Prussia and then in other kingdoms and in some of the old free cities, impressive regimens of Greek study. Ministerial regulations determined the curriculum year by year; the state-administered test, the *Abitur,* ensured that the quality of instruction was more uniform. The time needed to finish a gymnasium course rose as the demands it made increased; by the 1860s most graduates were over twenty years old. And as one might expect, the newly rigorous course proved far more socially exclusive than the old and lenient humanistic one. It thus neatly matched the desires of those who sent their sons to wear the uniforms and fill the benches of the classical gymnasium: the merchants, noblemen and officials whose children would become, by virtue of their shared eight years before the classical mast, equally cultured people despite their unequal birth and upbringing, the *Bildungsbürgertum* (educated bourgeoisie). By mid-century the classical gymnasium had established itself as *the* school for well-born young men, excluding the barefoot poor boys who had once starved their way through the Latin schools to become pastors. The new scholarship and new education, working together, had produced what amounted to a new society defined by its common ability to read Greek: one of 'Homer-reading lawyers and Sophocles-quoting merchants'.[21] Facility in Latin remained the central, testable result of classical schooling, and Greek accordingly never received nearly as much space as Latin in the curriculum. But the universities had an adequate supply of young men ready and able to penetrate the mysteries of the new many-volumed fragment collections that threatened to overwhelm the canonical curriculum authors on the shelves of seminar libraries. The most diverse of nineteenth-century German-speaking intellectuals, moreover, from Marx to Freud and Nietzsche to Lagarde, used the terms and images familiar from their classical educations to describe what they saw as their own deepest insights into the human condition. Freud's *Interpretation of Dreams,* for example, seems to transgress every imaginable canon of nineteenth-century good taste in its ascription of unimaginable desires to ordinary children and of explanatory weight to dreams. Yet it is deeply conventional in one basic respect: Freud's certainty that *Oedipus Rex* moves a modern audience no less than it did the contemporary Greek one, because it embodied a myth with "profound and universal power to move".[22] Even this greatest of revolutionaries, the man who tore the fabric of Viennese good taste into shreds—even Freud retained his culture's reverence for Greek wisdom and art, as his terrifyingly cluttered consulting room, with its classical fragments and relief of Gradiva, clearly shows.[23]

In Britain, too, a rigorous education in Greek became the mark of membership in an elite which had once been indifferent to the refinements of scholarship and far more concerned with Latin literature and precedent than with Greek. The examination systems that came into effect in both Oxford and Cambridge in the first half of the nineteenth century imposed a higher standard of linguistic knowledge on those who hoped for fellowships, and the public and grammar schools responded by emphasizing the reading and composition of Greek, above all Greek verse, at a level not previously institutionalized. By mid-century ancient history and philosophy had also entered the Oxford curriculum, as Greats took on its canonical form.[24] But the emphasis lay always on texts, not contexts; false quantities were penalized while the anachronistic belief that the Athenian empire could serve as a model for the British was rewarded, and the most influential of Oxford Greek professors, Jowett, translated and explicated Plato as a liberal Anglican who had happened to write Greek.[25] It thus seems only reasonable that even those Britons who studied the classics with the greatest intensity at university and found the deepest and most problematic personal lessons in ancient texts did not fully connect the two activities. Gilbert Murray's translations of Euripides, not the Oxford Classical Texts he studied for Mods, gave Julian Grenfell the terms with which he tried to decipher his intense and difficult relations with his mother.[26] Still, the British schools and universities did produce vast flocks of young men who could translate leaders from the *Scotsman* into the Greek of Xenophon, record the activities of the wet-bobs at Eton in that of Thucydides, or even imagine Herodotus reporting on the London Zoo—even if it never became proper to quote untranslated Greek in the House of Commons.

Conflicts and Fissures

Yet this apparently solid, factual record of territories conquered by individual scholars and cultivated by teams of docile pupils makes no accurate map of the always uneven, sometimes tragic history of the Greek heritage. The smooth lists of manuscripts collated, fragments unearthed and editions published obscure a deeper, problematic history, a matter of fragments and fissures rather than continuous forward motion. The very nature of Hellenic scholarship and education—as well as the turbulent context of German history in which both were conducted—seemed far more complex and questionable to those who created them than we are liable to suspect as we look back in admiration to the patient and meticulous skills of the nineteenth century.

Even the stateliest and most objective-seeming products of nineteenth-century scholarship were as much the products of speculation as of erudition—and as much the result of controversy as of contemplation. Consider, for example, the *Corpus* of Greek inscriptions. This huge and heavy Latin book looks like an objective collection of primary sources—as cool and austere a product as one could imagine of the philologist's basic, uncontentious enterprise. But it begins with a sharply-worded preface by Böckh, in which he sets out to define the nature of philology itself. He begins by insisting that philology is not a mere congeries of unrelated disciplines, connected only by the fact that they deal with the ancient world. Instead, it is a "historical and philosophical understanding of antiquity," one which sought to work out the basic *notiones,* or "ideas," that expressed themselves within the culture and society of each people.[27] In making this argument, Böckh situated his enterprise on a complex map of contemporary debate about classical philology. He showed its independence from that of his teacher, Wolf, whose encyclopaedia had not been defined as a coherent effort to capture the *Geist* of the Greek nation as a whole. He showed its immunity from the attacks of his Berlin rival, the philosopher Hegel, who argued that philology was a mere "aggregate" rather than a coherent spiritual and intellectual enterprise. And he showed its difference from the editorial enterprises of his contemporary Gottfried Hermann, who saw the establishing of critical Greek texts, rather than the reconstructing of vague Greek "ideas", as the philologist's only real task.[28] The *Corpus* of Greek inscriptions, in short, was anything but what it seemed, a vast but neutral storehouse of building-blocks for some future structure. It was at once the result of, and a move in, widespread existing controversies about the whole basis of Greek studies—which soon blazed up anew as Böckh's own editorial methods came under sharp scrutiny from Hermann and his pupils. And its reader was less likely to receive a panoramic impression of the nature of Greek society than to find his attention caught by technical problems of source criticism and chronology.

The situation of the reader of the *Corpus* mirrors in little the experience of many of those who tried, as Deussen did, to enter the philologist's *hortus conclusus*. One came seeking scientific method and exact knowledge: that *Wissenschaft* of which philology provided the basic model. On arrival, one found learned armies clashing by day. In general, as we have already seen, German scholars saw themselves as divided into two camps, both stemming to some extent from Wolf and Humboldt. One group, headed by Böckh and Karl Otfried Müller, saw Greek studies as holistic and intuitive. They wished less to establish critical texts or historical facts than to evoke the central, ordering themes and rules of Greek culture as a whole. Their enterprise was meant to end less in a set of permanently established readings than in an empathetic evocation of the spirit of an earlier age. Müller, for example, ended his elaborated study of the history and institutions of the Dorians with a bold effort to "furnish a complete and accurate idea of their nature and peculiarities. That this cannot be done in a few words is evident; but that it can be done *at all,* I consider equally clear; I by no means agree with those who deny that a whole nation, like an individual, can have one character—an error which is perhaps best refuted by consideration of the different tribes of Greece."[29] Böckh intended his culminating masterpiece to be the *Hellen*—a comprehensive evocation of the Greek spirit that expressed itself partially in every aspect of antiquity from social organization and military technology to art and literature.

The other group—headed by Hermann—defined philology as concerned above all with language: establishing the rules of grammar, syntax, metre, and applying these to the criticism and explication of specific texts, line by line and word by word. Only a severely limited Greek philology of this kind, they held, could serve as a mental discipline for students or arrive at rigorous conclusions about the Greeks. And it must eventuate not in the foggy guesses of their opponents but in sharp, shiny new laws about the behaviour of the Greek language.

Two groups who offered such radically different portraits of the Greek world to students and readers could hardly leave one another in peace or let their readers superimpose the two visions on one another. As early as 1833 Müller made the *Eumenides* of Aeschylus the object of a programmatic commentary, one in which he did not comment line by line but added treatises which set the text as a whole into the literary history of Greek drama and the political history of Athens. He imaginatively reconstructed the original staging of the play, arguing that Aeschylus had treated the Athenians in his audience as the public assembly called to attend the trial of Orestes in the play, thus drawing them into the drama and making them "bear a part in the action".[30] And he insisted, in an angry preface, that this approach was characteristic of the historical school to which he belonged and far too sophisticated to be grasped by the followers of Hermann on the other side: "There is a class of scholars who raise questions about the ancient world too profound to be answered by mere word-for-word commentary [*Notengelehrsamkeit*]; the present work may perhaps give them material for fruitful consideration".[31] This attempt at a pre-emptive attack only enraged its object, Hermann, who replied in an incendiary review some 207 pages long, and was echoed by his pupil Fritzsche. The controversy raged in *Kritik* and *Anti-Kritik, Anhang* and *Erklärung,* until Müller's early death from sunstroke put an end to it. A generation later, as we have already seen, it would flare up again in Bonn.[32]

Debate raged within many fields as well as between the followers of different camps. No subject proved more attractive to explore, none more rife with deadly pitfalls, than classical mythology. Everyone agreed that ancient myth must be treated with more historical sympathy than the mythographers of the eighteenth century had shown; that it must be explained in its own terms, as the product of a habit of mind and speech alien from those of the modern world, not explained away by the methods of Euhemerus or Palaephatus. But the key to Greek mythologies proved evasive. Were they symbols or allegories? Could they be tied to local rituals, and thus set into place as part of the history of the wanderings and the formation of the Greek nations, as Müller held? Or should they be tied to the longer history of Indo-European thought and religion, which glimmered alluringly, or so some thought, in the newly accessible Sanskrit literature of India? Or should one simply follow Lobeck and demolish all these elaborate constructions by the application of a philologist's razor, insisting that they—not the myths they interpreted—rested on errors and confusions of thought? Or should one—as Jane Harrison and others would, towards the end of the century—use the flickering new torch of anthropology to reveal the ritual origins and religious feelings that underlay the transmitted myths? Each version had its exponents, each of whom claimed rigour for his own reconstruction of the gods of Greece and denounced the fantasies of his opponents.[33] And similarly sharp debates clouded the facts—if facts there were—about every point in Greek literary and civil history from the origins of Athens to the historicity of Homer.

Efforts were made to stem this acrid tide of debate. From 1838 onwards, the German philologists held national congresses, in which as many as 436 professors and gymnasium teachers assembled to hear papers and hold banquets. Their proceedings stressed unity and pluralism; they honoured both Müller (posthumously) and Hermann, and sponsored public debates far less vicious in tone than the written ones in the learned journals. But nothing could produce consensus on many of the points at issue, or reconcile those who had been joined by *Wahlverwandtschaft* (elective affinity) into parties, and plotted vigorously against one another when chairs were to be filled or editorial assignments to be parcelled out.[34]

Moreover, one basic contradiction stuck like a canker in the very heart of German Greek scholarship: a contradiction between the educational ideals it espoused and the scientific method it applied. The scholars of the nineteenth century normally claimed to use a purely historical approach to Greek antiquity. If analysis showed that the *Iliad* and *Odyssey* contained flaws and lacunae, and these in turn revealed the work of more than one author, the scholar might regret his conclusions but must certainly report them. "Our whole investigation," Wolf wrote in the preface to his own Homer edition of 1795, "is historical and critical; it deals not with what we would like to have happened but with what did happen."[35] The ability of the scholars to cut the Homeric epics into their original strata seemed the guarantee of the scientific character of their work: Schelling, among others, hoped that a geologist might be found who could analyse the earth as Wolf had analysed Homer.

But when scholars argued for the pre-eminence of Greek in secondary and university education, they rested their case less on the method they applied—which, could, after all, be applied as well to Rome or Israel—than on the object to which they applied it. They argued that Greek culture was more coherent, more original, more orderly, or more free than any other—choosing the epithet that qualified it as their prejudices and the needs of the moment dictated. From Wolf at the beginning of the century to Wilamowitz at the end, influential scholars set out research programmes that called for a rigorous historicism, but insisted on their personal allegiance to the unique superiority of Hellenism. No *Greek History* was more severely technical and critical, more insistent on the need for philological rigour and more devoid of romance, than that of K. J. Beloch. Yet Beloch, captivated both by his idealized vision of the Greeks and by the anthropology and liguistics of his day, which seemed to him to provide scientific support for his prejudices, began by arguing that only "we Aryans" could have brought forth, even in the magically splendid land of Greece, "a culture in the full sense"—an argument as dependent on dubious historical theses as it was on value-laden terms and vague epithets.[36]

The problem here was simple. When classical scholars insisted that their own method was historical, they were perfectly sincere. But in so far as they idealized the classics they contradicted themselves; for the past, once idealized, had to be cleansed of any literary work that did not meet the proper aesthetic standards, and any historical fact that did not meet the proper moral ones. Reconstruction and rejection, construction and demolition, were thus dictated not only by solid evidence and rigorous method, but also by assumptions that could not bear historical scrutiny. If F. G. Welcker wished to rehabilitate the fatherly, pure-minded homosexuality of Greek men, their ability to regard their lovers with a "blameless eros", he had to distinguish their relationships and emotions from those that seemed to connect Sappho with her female loved ones. He could do so easily, by ignoring all textual details and variants that told against him and insisting that Sappho's culture could not have tolerated—far less admired—a female homosexual: "no educated Greek would have thought these were beautiful love poems if something monstrous and disgusting had been going on in them".[37] If G. F. Schoemann wished to show that Aeschylus had never suggested, even in the *Prometheus Bound,* that Zeus could be unjust and Prometheus' resistance justified, he had to explain away the apparent evidence of the text before him, which he considered genuine. This was no aporia, however. Schoemann simply reconstructed the lost *Prometheus Unbound* which had been performed with the extant play, and which showed that Prometheus had been clearly in the wrong. He knew the lost play said this because he knew its author was a religious man, and "all true religious experience is related to Christianity."[38] And if Wilamowitz had to explain how the wonderful Greek spirit had been able to produce so bitter and mocking a specimen as Lucian, he could do so more easily still, not by attacking the genuineness of the large corpus of Lucian's writing but by identifying the racial origins of the writer. Lucian, Wilamowitz argued, was not Greek but Asian; only thus could one explain his work—or explain it away.[39] The German scholars who advanced and accepted such views of the ancient world did so because they were conservative by temperament, monarchical by politics and racist (to use an anachronistic, but not an inaccurate term) by prejudice, and found statements like these plausible and attractive—not because the evidence and the philological method underpinned them.

Two areas of nineteenth-century classical studies then seemed most glamorous and accessible and now seem most attractive and original: archaeology and anthropology. Both fields became part of institutionalized in scholarship as the great imperialist powers founded schools and supported excavations in Greek soil; anthropology even became part of classical education, at Cambridge and in Paris if not in Oxford or Berlin. And brilliant lecturers—such as Jane Harrison, that glamorous "green beetle" as she seemed to one young hearer—converted many nonspecialists to the belief that the contours of Greek sites and the customs of non-Greeks could shed a vast amount of light on Greek festivals and on the tragedies performed in them.[40] In the great age of the *Gesamtkunstwerk,* nineteenth-century opera, Greek tragedy too came to be imagined in three dimensions and many colours. Yet both studies were injured by the reluctance of many members of the classical establishment to come to terms with their more radical conclusions—especially those of Schliemann's digs—and by the sometimes wilful assurance of their proponents that small doses of evidence and large hypotheses could yield certain truths.

Given the contradictions between classicism and historicism, given the tensions and fissures within historicism, it is not surprising that what seems in retrospect a time of dizzying increase in knowledge about Greece seemed to many of those who lived through it a time of dizzying competition between hypotheses, which tended to replace once-solid texts with risky analytical theories, elaborate historical arguments, and—most problematic of all—proliferating secondary literature. And it seems unsurprising, too, that most efforts to produce an acceptable synthesis of a major field drew brickbats rather than bouquets from their reviewers as the century wore one. Böckh's effort to create an up-to-date encyclopaedia, though revised over and over through more than twenty cycles of lectures, fell dead when it appeared in the 1870s, and hardly anyone reviewed it.[41]

More independent and more critical reactions were always to be found—especially among the students, always less reverent and often more perceptive than their elders. A young student of history at Berlin, Jacob Burckhardt, was inflamed with admiration for the great Berlin lectures he encountered in 1840: "When I had heard my first lectures from Ranke, Droysen, and Böckh, I opened my eyes wide indeed. I saw that I had previously had the same experience as those knights in *Don Quixote* with their ladies, I had loved my science by hearsay".[24] He eagerly read Herodotus, Greek poetry, even Berosus on Babylon. And he remained deeply impressed all his life by Böckh's lectures on Greek antiquity, from which he took away essential ideals and information. Böckh taught him—as Wolf had taught Böckh—that the ancients drew a clear distinction between narrative history in the style of Thucydides and antiquarian scholarship in the style of Varro that described institutions and customs—a distinction crucial to his whole life's work.[43] But the deeper Burckhardt penetrated into the actual fabric of Greek history as the great man and their epigoni had reconstructed it, the more he became convinced that their work could never live up to its holistic ideal: "Is it not a pity", he asked in 1842 "that after three centuries of tyrannical assertions of classical education there is still no reasonable history of Greece? I once asked a reputable philologist about this and received the answer: "Views on myth had not arrived at nearly a sufficient state of clarity".[44] His own *Griechische Kulturgeschichte* would attempt to reconstruct the central characteristic of the Greek spirit as the professionals had failed to do, using a few outmoded secondary sources and the original texts to describe the "agonal" men of early Greece with incomparable eloquence. The book was, of course, notoriously a total professional failure when it appeared, declared dead on arrival by Wilamowitz. But it had a deep impact on young students and the reading public nonetheless.[45] Nietzsche's *Birth of Tragedy* had already had a similar fate; largely ignored by the professionals (except for his fellow graduate of Pforta, Wilamowitz, who lacerated the work in a brilliant pamphlet) the book gradually gathered momentum, inspiring more and more readers, notably Burckhardt, to look for the depths of emotion that neo-classical doctrines about the Greeks had obscured and denied.[46]

More than half a century after Burckhardt's Berlin years, another young student, Ludwig Hatvany, a Hungarian, published his account of his experiences as a young classicist. He did so in a pamphlet that took the form of mock notes on a year's work in classics in Berlin and bore the brilliant title *Die Wissenschaft des nicht Wissenswerten* (Berlin, 1911)—"The science of what is not worth knowing". With splendid brutality he pilloried his teacher, the infamous "Woepke," who took the passage in the *Protagoras* where the porter shuts the gate on Socrates and his companions as the pretext for a discourse on "the important and still unsolved question of door-shutting in antiquity". He ransacked the seminar libraries for evidence of the folly of the *Philologen,* their fruitless and repetitive disputes over the existence of Homer and the analysis of his poems into their original content. And he demanded a reform of classical studies which would somehow enable teachers and students to gain access to the human and emotional content of the ancient texts—a positive recommendation as vague as those of the apostles of the Third Humanism, Jaeger and Spranger, who would try to argue after the First World War that one could somehow combine the philologist's now traditional creed, "even the minutest details are worth knowing", with aesthetic and normative judgements about the value of texts.

Evidently a century's vast progress in knowledge and method, the vast tides of effort and erudition that break on any modern consulter of Pauly-Wissowa's great encyclopaedia of *Altertumswissenschaft,* had left the classics not only in high honour but also in deep ideological disarray. Scholarship seemed mired in controversy. A purely classical education might seem comprehensive and fulfilling to English schoolboys penned in their monastic establishments, but it seemed frustrating and absurd to young men in Vienna and Paris such as Stefan Zweig or Alfred Jarry. And on all sides competition loomed, as the votaries of "stinks" and science won the right to have their subjects taught in schools and to degree level at universities—to the immense gratification of patrons as different as the business elite of Manchester and the German Kaiser.

No formula can sum up, no summary do justice to the perpetual revolution that was the nineteenth century's contact with the Greeks. Perhaps an image can be more effective. As a young man, Toulouse-Lautrec painted a brilliant but highly uncharacteristic picture, parodying Puvis de Chavannes: a classical panorama of nymphs and satyrs, lawns and temples. Into it comes a procession of bearded men dressed in ugly modern clothing, among them Lautrec himself (who is urinating); a modern world obsessed by and transgressing on an ancient one which it can only imagine as an impossible ideal or recreate in its own up-to-date image. Prosaic though they may have seemed to those who sat through their lectures, the scholars and teachers who attacked the Greek heritage in nineteenth-century Berlin and Paris would also make appropriate figures in Lautrec's panorama of an impossible meeting.

Notes

[1] P. Deussen, *Erinnerungen an Friedrich Nietzsche* (Leipzig, 1901), p. 3.

[2] Ibid., pp. 30, 29.

[3] Ibid., p. 51; significantly chosen by Rudolf Pfeiffer as the epigraph for his doctoral dissertation.

[4] See already ibid., pp. 48-9.

[5] Sybel to Twesten, 13 May 1865, in P. E. Hübinger, 'Heinrich v. Sybel und der Bonner Philologenkrieg', *Historisches Jahrbuch* 83 (1964), 210.

[6] F. Nietzsche, *Gesammelte Werke* (Musarion Ausgabe), II (Munich, 1920), p. 339.

[7] Deussen, *Erinnerungen,* p. 25.

[8] Memoirs and polemics also often misrepresent the lived experience of a long-ago schooling; see M. Landfester, *Humanismus und Gesellschaft im 19. Jarhundert* (Göttingen, 1988) for the exemplary case of Kaiser Wilhelm.

[9] R. S. Turner, 'The Prussian Universities and the Concept of Research', *Internationales Archiv für Sozialgeschichte der deutschen Literatur* 5 (1980), 68-93.

[10] H. Kreissig, 'Einleitung,' *Die Altertumswissenschaft an der Berliner Akademie* (Darmstadt, 1985), p. 25.

[11] S. Timpanaro, *La genesi del metodo del Lachmann* (repr. of 2nd edn.; Padua, 1985), pp. 35-9.

[12] A. H. L. Heeren, *Christian Gottlob Heyne biographisch dargestellt* (Göttingen, 1813), pp. 189-90.

[13] A. Engel, 'The Emerging Concept of the Academic Profession at Oxford 1800-1854', *The University in Society,* ed. L. Stone (Princeton, 1974), I, pp. 311, 315.

[14] C. Diehl, *Americans and German Scholarship 1770-1870* (New Haven, 1978), p. 71.

[15] Bancroft's notes, in both German and English, are in the Bancroft Collection, New York Public Library. Naturally, other American scholars had far more inspiring experiences: above all B. L. Gildersleeve, for whom see *Basil Lanneau Gildersleeve. An American Classicist,* ed. W. W. Briggs jr. et al. (Baltimore and London, 1986).

[16] For the work of German and French as well as English pioneers, see E. G. Turner, *Greek Papyri: an Introduction* (Oxford, 1968), pp. 22-4; for one fascinating case see W. B. Stanford and R. B. McDowell, *Mahaffy: A Biography of an Anglo-Irishman* (London, 1971), pp. 183-7.

[17] For Renan's engagement with Greece—and his passage from his early view of Athens as a city like Revolutionary Paris, in which political crisis and cultural creativity co-existed, to the idealist racism of his *Prayer on the Acropolis*—see P. Vidal-Naquet, *La démocratie grecque vue d'ailleurs* (Paris, 1990), pp. 245-65.

[18] See P. Petitmengin's article in *Philologie und Hermeneutik im 19. Jahrhundert,* II (Göttingen, 1983).

[19] F. Paulsen, *Geschichte des gelehrten Unterrichts auf den deutschen Schulen und Universitäten* (Leipzig, 1885), p. 575.

[20] For what follows cf. Paulsen with Landfester, *Humanismus* (n. 8 above).

[21] W. Jens, 'The Classical Tradition in Germany: Grandeur and Decay', *Upheaval and Continuity: A Century of German History,* ed. E. J. Feuchtwanger (London, 1973), p. 69.

[22] S. Freud, *The Interpretation of Dreams,* tr. J. Strachey (New York, 1965), pp. 294-8.

[23] See *Berggasse 19* (New York, 1976), for the photographic record made by Edmund Engelman in 1938.

[24] See Engel, note 13.

[25] For a sensitive account, emphasizing the complexities of Jowett's private and public responses to Plato, see R. Jenkyns, *The Victorians and Ancient Greece* (London, 1980), ch. 10.

[26] N. Mosley, *Julian Grenfell* (New York, 1976), pp. 120-3.

[27] *Corpus inscriptionum graecarum,* I (Berlin, 1828), p. vii ff.

[28] See B. Bravo, *Philologie, histoire, philosophie d'histoire* (repr. Hildesheim, 1988).

[29] C. O. Müller, *The History and Antiquities of the Dorian Race,* tr. Tafnell and Lewis (Oxford, 1930), II, 405. See E. Rawson, *The Spartan Tradition in European Thought* (Oxford, 1969), pp. 322-4.

[30] *Dissertations on the Eumenides of Aeschylus* (London and Cambridge, 1853), pp. 60-1.

[31] *Aeschylos Eumeniden* (Göttingen, 1833), p. iv.

[32] See E. Vogt in *Philologie und Hermeneutik im 19. Jahrhundert,* ed. H. Flashar (Göttingen, 1979), pp. 103-21.

[33] O. Gruppe, *Geschichte der klassischen Mythologie und Religionsgeschichte* (Leipzig, 1921); B. Feldman and B. D. Richardson, *The Rise of Modern Mythology* (Bloomington and London, 1972); A. Henrichs, 'Welckers Götterlehre', *Friedrich Gottlieb Welcker. Werk und Wirkung,* ed. W. M. Calder III et al. (Stuttgart, 1986), pp. 179-229; W. Burkert, 'Griechische Mythologie und die Geistesgeschichte der Moderne', *Les études classiques aux xixe et xxe siècles* (Geneva, 1980), pp. 159-99.

[34] A. Grafton, 'Polyhistor into *Philolog,' History of Universities* 3 (1983 [1984]), 159-92.

[35] *Homeri et Homeridarum opera et reliquiae* (Leipzig, 1804), I, p. xxv.

[36] R. Drews, *The Coming of the Greeks* (Princeton, 1988), p. 7.

[37] J. DeJean, *Fictions of Sappho* (Chicago and London, 1989), 208. Welcker's argument was in other respects a masterly piece of historical inference; see the powerful *Ehrenrettung* by W. M. Calder III, 'F. G. Welckers *Sapphobild* and its Reception in Wilamowitz,' *Welcker: Werk und Wirkung,* pp. 131-56.

[38] G. F. Schoemann, *Opuscula academica,* III (Berlin, 1858), p. 136; see E. R. Dodds, 'The *Prometheus Vinctus* and the progress of Scholarship', *The Ancient Concept of Progress* (Oxford, 1973), pp. 31-2; H. Lloyd-Jones, 'Zeus in Aeschylus', *Journal of Hellenic Studies* 76 (1956), 55-67.

[39] N. Holzberg, 'Lucian and the Germans', *The Uses of Greek and Latin,* ed. A. C. Dionisotti et al. (London, 1988), pp. 205-9.

[40] J. E. Harrison, *Reminiscences of a Student's Life* (London, 1925), p. 59.

[41] J. Whitman, 'Nietzsche in the Magisterial Tradition of German Classical Philology', *Journal of the History of Ideas* 47 (1986), 453-68.

[42] J. Burckhardt, *Briefe,* I (Basel, 1949), p. 131.

[43] F. Gilbert, 'Jacob Burckhardt's Student Years,' *Journal of the History of Ideas* 47 (1986), 249-74.

[44] Burckhardt, *Briefe,* I, p. 218. Cf. ibid., IV (Basel, 1961), p. 198.

[45] A. Momigliano, 'Introduction to the *Griechische Kulturgeschichte* by Jacob Burckhardt', *Essays in Ancient and Modern Historiography* (Oxford, 1977), pp. 295-305; F. Gilbert, *History: Politics or Culture* (Princeton, 1990), pp. 69-80.

[46] Opinions on the value of Nietzsche's *Birth* for classical scholarship remain sharply divided. On the controversy with Wilamowitz see above all W. M. Calder III, 'The Wilamowitz-Nietzsche Struggle: New documents and a reappraisal', *Nietzsche-Studien* 12 (1983), 214-54. For Nietzsche's vast if subterranean impact see A. Henrichs, 'Loss of Self, Suffering, Violence: The Modern View of Dionysus from Nietzsche to Girard', *Harvard Studies in Classical Philology* 88 (1984), 205-40.

THE MEANINGS OF HELLENISM

Matthew Arnold (essay date 1883)

"Hebraism and Hellenism," in *Culture and Anarchy: An Essay in Political and Social Criticism; and Friendship's Garland: Being the Conversations, Letters, and Opinions of the Late Arminius, Baron von Thunder-Ten-Tronckh,* Macmillan and Co., 1883, pp. 109-27.

[*In one of the most persistently influential works of the Victorian age, Arnold characterizes his culture according to two complementary principles: Hebraism and Hellenism. Equating Hellenism with the humanist consciousness of the Renaissance, Arnold both stresses its centrality to modern civilization and warns against what he sees to be an inherent "moral weakness."*]

This fundamental ground is our preference of doing to thinking. Now this preference is a main element in our nature, and as we study it we find ourselves opening up a number of large questions on every side.

Let me go back for a moment to Bishop Wilson, who says: "First, never go against the best light you have; secondly, take care that your light be not darkness." We show, as a nation, laudable energy and persistence in walking according to the best light we have, but are not quite careful enough, perhaps, to see that our light be not darkness. This is only another version of the old story that energy is our strong point and favourable characteristic, rather than intelligence. But we may give to this idea a more general form still, in which it will have a yet larger range of application. We may regard this energy driving at practice, this paramount sense of the obligation of duty, self-control, and work, this earnestness in going manfully with the best light we have, as one force. And we may regard the intelligence driving at those ideas which are, after all, the basis of right practice, the ardent sense for all the new and changing combinations of them which man's development brings with it, the indomitable impulse to know and adjust them perfectly, as another force. And these two forces we may regard as in some sense rivals,—rivals not by the necessity of their own nature, but as exhibited in man and his history,—and rivals dividing the empire of the world between them. And to give these forces names from the two races of men who have supplied the most signal and splendid manifestations of them, we may call them respectively the forces of Hebraism and Hellenism. Hebraism and Hellenism,—between these two points of influence moves our world. At one time it feels more powerfully the attraction of one of them, at another time of the other; and it ought to be, though it never is, evenly and happily balanced between them.

The final aim of both Hellenism and Hebraism, as of all great spiritual disciplines, is no doubt the same: man's perfection or salvation. The very language which they both of them use in schooling us to reach this aim is often identical. Even when their language indicates by variation,—sometimes a broad variation, often a but slight and subtle variation,—the different courses of thought which are uppermost in each discipline, even then the unity of the final end and aim is still apparent. To employ the actual words of that discipline with which we ourselves are all of us most familiar, and the words of which, therefore, come most home to us, that final end and aim is "that we might be partakers of the divine nature." These are the words of a Hebrew apostle, but of Hellenism and Hebraism alike this is, I say, the aim. When the two are confronted, as they very often are confronted, it is nearly always with what I may call a rhetorical purpose; the speaker's whole design is to exalt and enthrone one of the two, and he uses the other only as a foil and to enable him the better to give

Matthew Arnold, 1822-1888, English poet and critic.

effect to his purpose. Obviously, with us, it is usually Hellenism which is thus reduced to minister to the triumph of Hebraism. There is a sermon on Greece and the Greek spirit by a man never to be mentioned without interest and respect, Frederick Robertson, in which this rhetorical use of Greece and the Greek spirit, and the inadequate exhibition of them necessarily consequent upon this, is almost ludicrous, and would be censurable if it were not to be explained by the exigencies of a sermon. On the other hand, Heinrich Heine, and other writers of his sort, give us the spectacle of the tables completely turned, and of Hebraism brought in just as a foil and contrast to Hellenism, and to make the superiority of Hellenism more manifest. In both these cases there is injustice and misrepresentation. The aim and end of both Hebraism and Hellenism is, as I have said, one and the same, and this aim and end is august and admirable.

Still, they pursue this aim by very different courses. The uppermost idea with Hellenism is to see things as they really are; the uppermost idea with Hebraism is conduct and obedience. Nothing can do away with this ineffaceable difference. The Greek quarrel with the body and its desires is, that they hinder right thinking; the Hebrew quarrel with them is, that they hinder right acting. "He that keepeth the law, happy is he;" "Blessed is the man that feareth the Eternal, that delighteth greatly in his commandments;"—that is the Hebrew notion of felicity; and, pursued with passion and tenacity, this notion would not let the Hebrew rest till, as is well known, he had at last got out of the law a network of prescriptions to enwrap his whole life, to govern every moment of it, every impulse, every action. The Greek notion of felicity, on the other hand, is perfectly conveyed in these words of a great French moralist: *"C'est le bonheur des hommes,"*—when? when they abhor that which is evil?—no; when they exercise themselves in the law of the Lord day and night?—no; when they die daily?—no; when they walk about the New Jerusalem with palms in their hands?—no; but when they think aright, when their thought hits: *"quand ils pensent juste."* At the bottom of both the Greek and the Hebrew notion is the desire, native in man, for reason and the will of God, the feeling after the universal order,—in a word, the love of God. But, while Hebraism seizes upon certain plain, capital intimations of the universal order, and rivets itself, one may say, with unequalled grandeur of earnestness and intensity on the study and observance of them, the bent of Hellenism is to follow, with flexible activity, the whole play of the universal order, to be apprehensive of missing any part of it, of sacrificing one part to another, to slip away from resting in this or that intimation of it, however capital. An unclouded clearness of mind, an unimpeded play of thought, is what this bent drives at. The governing idea of Hellenism is *spontaneity of consciousness;* that of Hebraism, *strictness of conscience.*

Christianity changed nothing in this essential bent of Hebraism to set doing above knowing. Self-conquest, self-devotion, the following not our own individual will, but the will of God, *obedience,* is the fundamental idea of this form, also, of the discipline to which we have attached the general name of Hebraism. Only, as the old law and the network of prescriptions with which it enveloped human life were evidently a motive-power not driving and searching enough to produce the result aimed at,—patient continuance in well-doing, self-conquest,—Christianity substituted for them boundless devotion to that inspiring and affecting pattern of self-conquest offered by Jesus Christ; and by the new motive-power, of which the essence was this, though the love and admiration of Christian churches have for centuries been employed in varying, amplifying, and adorning the plain description of it, Christianity, as St. Paul truly says, "establishes the law," and in the strength of the ampler power which she has thus supplied to fulfil it, has accomplished the miracles, which we all see, of her history.

So long as we do not forget that both Hellenism and Hebraism are profound and admirable manifestations of man's life, tendencies, and powers, and that both of them aim at a like final result, we can hardly insist too strongly on the divergence of line and of operation with which they proceed. It is a divergence so great that it most truly, as the prophet Zechariah says, "has raised up thy sons, O Zion, against thy sons, O Greece!" The difference whether it is by doing or by knowing that we set most store, and the practical consequences which follow from this difference, leave their mark on all the history of our race and of its development. Language may be abundantly quoted from both Hellenism and Hebraism to make it seem that one follows the same current as the other towards the same goal. They are, truly, borne towards the same goal; but the currents which bear them are infinitely different. It is true, Solomon will praise knowing: "Understanding is a well-spring of life unto him that hath it." And in the New Testament, again, Jesus Christ is a "light," and "truth makes us free." It is true, Aristotle will undervalue knowing: "In what concerns virtue," says he, "three things are necessary—knowledge, deliberate will, and perseverance; but, whereas the two last are all-important, the first is a matter of little importance." It is true that with the same impatience with which St. James enjoins a man to be not a forgetful hearer, but a *doer of the work,* Epictetus exhorts us to *do* what we have demonstrated to ourselves we ought to do; or he taunts us with futility, for being armed at all points to prove that lying is wrong, yet all the time continuing to lie. It is true, Plato, in words which are almost the words of the New Testament or the Imitation, calls life a learning to die. But underneath the superficial agreement the fundamental divergence still subsists. The understanding of Solomon is "the walking in the way of the commandments;" this is "the way of peace," and it is of this that blessedness comes. In the New Testament, the truth which gives us the peace of God and makes us free, is the love of Christ constraining us to crucify, as he did, and with a like purpose of moral regeneration, the flesh with its affections and lusts, and thus establishing, as we have seen, the law. The moral virtues, on the other hand, are with Aristotle but the porch and access to the intellectual, and with these last is blessedness. That partaking of the divine life, which both Hellenism and Hebraism, as we have said, fix as their crowning aim, Plato expressly denies to the man of practical virtue merely, of self-conquest with any other motive than that of perfect intellectual vision. He reserves it for the lover of pure knowledge, of seeing things as they really are. . . .

Both Hellenism and Hebraism arise out of the wants of human nature, and address themselves to satisfying those wants. But their methods are so different, they lay stress on such different points, and call into being by their respective disciplines such different activities, that the face which human nature presents when it passes from the hands of one of them to those of the other, is no longer the same. To get rid of one's ignorance, to see things as they are, and by seeing them as they are to see them in their beauty, is the simple and attractive ideal which Hellenism holds out before human nature; and from the simplicity and charm of this ideal, Hellenism, and human life in the hands of Hellenism, is invested with a kind of aërial ease, clearness, and radiancy; they are full of what we call sweetness and light. Difficulties are kept out of view, and the beauty and rationalness of the ideal have all our thoughts. "The best man is he who most tries to perfect himself, and the happiest man is he who most feels that he *is* perfecting himself,"—this account of the matter by Socrates, the true Socrates of the *Memorabilia,* has something so simple, spontaneous, and unsophisticated about it, that it seems to fill us with clearness and hope when we hear it. But there is a saying which I have heard attributed to Mr. Carlyle about Socrates,—a very happy saying, whether it is really Mr. Carlyle's or not,—which excellently marks the essential point in which Hebraism differs from Hellenism. "Socrates," this saying goes, "is terribly *at ease in Zion.*" Hebraism,—and here is the source of its wonderful strength,—has always been severely preoccupied with an awful sense of the impossibility of being at ease in Zion; of the difficulties which oppose themselves to man's pursuit or attainment of that perfection of which Socrates talks so hopefully, and, as from this point of view one might almost say, so glibly. It is all very well to talk of getting rid of one's ignorance, of seeing things in their reality, seeing them in their beauty; but how is this to be done when there is something which thwarts and spoils all our efforts?

This something is *sin;* and the space which sin fills in Hebraism, as compared with Hellenism, is indeed prodigious. This obstacle to perfection fills the whole scene, and perfection appears remote and rising away from earth, in the background. Under the name of sin, the difficulties of knowing oneself and conquering oneself which impede man's passage to perfection, become, for Hebraism, a positive, active entity hostile to man, a mysterious power which I heard Dr. Pusey the other day, in one of his impressive sermons, compare to a hideous hunchback seated on our shoulders, and which it is the main business of our lives to hate and oppose. The discipline of the Old Testament may be summed up as a discipline teaching us to abhor and flee from sin; the discipline of the New Testament, as a discipline teaching us to die to it. As Hellenism speaks of thinking clearly, seeing things in their essence and beauty, as a grand and precious feat for man to achieve, so Hebraism speaks of becoming conscious of sin, of awakening to a sense of sin, as a feat of this kind. It is obvious to what wide divergence these differing tendencies, actively followed, must lead. As one passes and repasses from Hellenism to Hebraism, from Plato to St. Paul, one feels inclined to rub one's eyes and ask oneself whether man is indeed a gentle and simple being, showing the traces of a noble and divine nature; or an unhappy chained captive, labouring with groanings that cannot be uttered to free himself from the body of this death.

Apparently it was the Hellenic conception of human nature which was unsound, for the world could not live by it. Absolutely to call it unsound, however, is to fall into the common error of its Hebraising enemies; but it was unsound at that particular moment of man's development, it was premature. The indispensable basis of conduct and self-control, the platform upon which alone the perfection aimed at by Greece can come into bloom, was not to be reached by our race so easily; centuries of probation and discipline were needed to bring us to it. Therefore the bright promise of Hellenism faded, and Hebraism ruled the world. Then was seen that astonishing spectacle, so well marked by the often-quoted words of the prophet Zechariah, when men of all languages and nations took hold of the skirt of him that was a Jew, saying:—*"We will go with you, for we have heard that God is with you."* And the Hebraism which thus received and ruled a world all gone out of the way and altogether become unprofitable, was, and could not but be, the later, the more spiritual, the more attractive development of Hebraism. It was Christianity; that is to say, Hebraism aiming at self-conquest and rescue from the thrall of vile affections, not by obedience to the letter of a law, but by conformity to the image of a self-sacrificing example. To a world stricken with moral enervation Christianity offered its spectacle of an inspired self-sacrifice; to men who refused themselves nothing, it showed one who refused himself everything;—*"my Saviour banished joy!"* says George Herbert. When the *alma Venus,* the life-giving and joy-giving power of nature, so fondly cherished by the Pagan world, could not save her followers from self-dissatisfaction and ennui, the severe words of the apostle came bracingly and refreshingly: "Let no man deceive you with vain words, for because of these things cometh the wrath of God upon the children of disobedience." Through age after age and generation after generation, our race, or all that part of our race which was most living and progressive, was *baptized into a death;* and endeavoured, by suffering in the flesh, to cease from sin. Of this endeavour, the animating labours and afflictions of early Christianity, the touching asceticism of mediæval Christianity, are the great historical manifestations. Literary monuments of it, each in its own way incomparable, remain in the Epistles of St. Paul, in St. Augustine's Confessions, and in the two original and simplest books of the Imitation.

Of two disciplines laying their main stress, the one, on clear intelligence, the other, on firm obedience; the one, on comprehensively knowing the grounds of one's duty, the other, on diligently practising it; the one, on taking all possible care (to use Bishop Wilson's words again) that the light we have be not darkness, the other, that according to the best light we have we diligently walk,—the priority naturally belongs to that discipline which braces all man's moral powers, and founds for him an indispensable basis of character. And, therefore, it is justly said of the Jewish people, who were charged with setting powerfully forth that side of the divine order to which the words *conscience* and *self-conquest* point, that they were "entrusted with the oracles of God;" as it is justly said of Christianity, which followed Judaism and which set forth this side with a much deeper effectiveness and a much wider influence, that the wisdom of the old Pagan world was foolishness compared to it. No words of devotion and admiration can be too strong to render thanks to these beneficent forces which have so borne forward humanity in its appointed work of coming to the knowledge and possession of itself; above all, in those great moments when their action was the wholesomest and the most necessary.

But the evolution of these forces, separately and in themselves, is not the whole evolution of humanity,—their single history is not the whole history of man; whereas their admirers are always apt to make it stand for the whole history. Hebraism and Hellenism are, neither of them, the *law* of human development, as their admirers are prone to make them; they are, each of them, *contributions* to human development,—august contributions, invaluable contributions; and each showing itself to us more august, more invaluable, more preponderant over the other, according to the moment in which we take them, and the relation in which we stand to them. The nations of our modern world, children of that immense and salutary movement which broke up the Pagan world, inevitably stand to Hellenism in a relation which dwarfs it, and to Hebraism in a relation which magnifies it. They are inevitably prone to take Hebraism as the law of human development, and not as simply a contribution to it, however precious. And yet the lesson must perforce be learned, that the human spirit is wider than the most priceless of the forces which bear it onward, and that to the whole development of man Hebraism itself is, like Hellenism, but a contribution.

Perhaps we may help ourselves to see this clearer by an illustration drawn from the treatment of a single great idea which has profoundly engaged the human spirit, and has given it eminent opportunities for showing its nobleness and energy. It surely must be perceived that the idea of immortality, as this idea rises in its generality before the human spirit, is something grander, truer, and more satisfying, than it is in the particular forms by which St. Paul, in the famous fifteenth chapter of the Epistle to the Corinthians, and Plato, in the *Phœdo,* endeavour to develop and establish it. Surely we cannot but feel, that the argumentation with which the Hebrew apostle goes about to expound this great idea is, after all, confused and inconclusive; and that the reasoning, drawn from analogies of likeness and equality, which is employed upon it by the Greek philosopher, is over-subtle and sterile. Above and beyond the inadequate solutions which Hebraism and Hellenism here attempt, extends the immense and august problem itself, and the human spirit which gave birth to it. And this single illustration may suggest to us how the same thing happens in other cases also.

But meanwhile, by alternations of Hebraism and Hellenism, of a man's intellectual and moral impulses, of the effort to see things as they really are, and the effort to win peace by self-conquest, the human spirit proceeds; and each of these two forces has its appointed hours of culmination and seasons of rule. As the great movement of Christianity was a triumph of Hebraism and man's moral impulses, so the great movement which goes by the name of the Renascence [I have ventured to give to the foreign word *Renaissance,*—destined to become of more common use amongst us as the movement which it denotes comes, as it will come, increasingly to interest us,—an English form.] was an uprising and re-instatement of man's intellectual impulses and of Hellenism. We in England, the devoted children of Protestantism, chiefly know the Renascence by its subordinate and secondary side of the Reformation. The Reformation has been often called a Hebraising revival, a return to the ardour and sincereness of primitive Christianity. No one, however, can study the development of Protestantism and of Protestant churches without feeling that into the Reformation too,—Hebraising child of the Renascence and offspring of its fervour, rather than its intelligence, as it undoubtedly was,—the subtle Hellenic leaven of the Renascence found its way, and that the exact respective parts, in the Reformation, of Hebraism and of Hellenism, are not easy to separate. But what we may with truth say is, that all which Protestantism was to itself clearly conscious of, all which it succeeded in clearly setting forth in words, had the characters of Hebraism rather than of Hellenism. The Reformation was strong, in that it was an earnest return to the Bible and to doing from the heart the will of God as there written. It was weak, in that it never consciously grasped or applied the central idea of the Renascence,—the Hellenic idea of pursuing, in all lines of activity, the law and science, to use Plato's words, of things as they really are. Whatever direct superiority, therefore, Protestantism had over Catholicism was a moral superiority, a superiority arising out of its greater sincerity and earnestness,—at the moment of its apparition at any rate,—in dealing with the heart and conscience. Its pretensions to an intellectual superiority are in general quite illusory. For Hellenism, for the thinking side in man as distinguished from the acting side, the attitude of mind of Protestantism towards the Bible in no respect differs from the attitude of mind of Catholicism towards the Church. The mental habit of him who imagines that Balaam's ass spoke, in no respect differs from the mental habit of him who imagines that a Madonna of wood or stone winked; and the one, who says that God's Church makes him believe what he believes, and the other, who says that God's Word makes him believe what he believes, are for the philosopher perfectly alike in not really and truly knowing, when they say *God's Church* and *God's Word,* what it is they say, or whereof they affirm.

In the sixteenth century, therefore, Hellenism re-entered the world, and again stood in presence of Hebraism,—a Hebraism renewed and purged. Now, it has not been enough observed, how, in the seventeenth century, a fate befell Hellenism in some respects analogous to that which befell it at the commencement of our era. The Renascence, that great re-awakening of Hellenism, that irresistible return of humanity to nature and to seeing things as they are, which in art, in literature, and in physics, produced such splendid fruits, had, like the anterior Hellenism of the Pagan world, a side of moral weakness and of relaxation or insensibility of the moral fibre, which in Italy showed itself with the most startling plainness, but which in France, England, and other countries was very apparent too. Again this loss of spiritual balance, this exclusive preponderance given to man's perceiving and knowing side, this unnatural defect of his feeling and acting side, provoked a reaction. Let us trace that reaction where it most nearly concerns us.

Science has now made visible to everybody the great and pregnant elements of difference which lie in race, and in how signal a manner they make the genius and history of an Indo-European people vary from those of a Semitic people. Hellenism is of Indo-European growth, Hebraism is of Semitic growth; and we English, a nation of Indo-European stock, seem to belong naturally to the movement of Hellenism. But nothing more strongly marks the essential unity of man, than the affinities we can perceive, in this point or that, between members of one family of peoples and members of another. And no affinity of this kind is more strongly marked than that likeness in the strength and prominence of the moral fibre, which, notwithstanding immense elements of difference, knits in some special sort the genius and history of us English, and our American descendants across the Atlantic, to the genius and history of the Hebrew people. Puritanism, which has been so great a power in the English nation, and in the strongest part of the English nation, was originally the reaction in the seventeenth century of the conscience and moral sense of our race, against the moral indifference and lax rule of conduct which in the sixteenth century came in with the Renascence. It was a reaction of Hebraism against Hellenism; and it powerfully manifested itself, as was natural, in a people with much of what we call a Hebraising turn, with a signal affinity for the bent which was the master-bent of Hebrew life. Eminently Indo-European by its *humour,* by the power it shows, through this gift, of imaginatively acknowledging the multiform aspects of the problem of life, and of thus getting itself unfixed from its own over-certainty, of smiling at its own over-tenacity, our race has yet (and a great part of its strength lies here), in matters of practical life and moral conduct, a strong share of the assuredness, the tenacity, the intensity of the Hebrews. This turn manifested itself in Puritanism, and has had a great part in shaping our history for the last two hundred years. Undoubtedly it checked and changed amongst us that movement of the Renascence which we see producing in the reign of Elizabeth such wonderful fruits. Undoubtedly it stopped the prominent rule and direct development of that order of ideas which we call by the name of Hellenism, and gave the first rank to a different order of ideas. Apparently, too, as we said of the former defeat of Hellenism, if Hellenism was defeated, this shows that Hellenism was imperfect, and that its ascendency at that moment would not have been for the world's good.

Yet there is a very important difference between the defeat inflicted on Hellenism by Christianity eighteen hundred years ago, and the check given to the Renascence by Puritanism. The greatness of the difference is well measured by the difference in force, beauty, significance, and usefulness, between primitive Christianity and Protestantism. Eighteen hundred years ago it was altogether the hour of Hebraism. Primitive Christianity was legitimately and truly the ascendant force in the world at that time, and the way of mankind's progress lay through its full development. Another hour in man's development began in the fifteenth century, and the main road of his progress then lay for a time through Hellenism. Puritanism was no longer the central current of the world's progress, it was a side stream crossing the central current and checking it. The cross and the check may have been necessary and salutary, but that does not do away with the essential difference between the main stream of man's advance and a cross or side stream. For more than two hundred years the main stream of man's advance has moved towards knowing himself and the world, seeing things as they are, spontaneity of consciousness; the main impulse of a great part, and that the strongest part, of our nation has been towards strictness of conscience. They have made the secondary the principal at the wrong moment, and the principal they have at the wrong moment treated as secondary. This contravention of the natural order has produced, as such contravention always must produce, a certain confusion and false movement, of which we are now beginning to feel, in almost every direction, the inconvenience. In all directions our habitual causes of action seem to be losing efficaciousness, credit, and control, both with others and even with ourselves. Everywhere we see the beginnings of confusion, and we want a clue to some sound order and authority. This we can only get by going back upon the actual instincts and forces which rule our life, seeing them as they really are, connecting them with other instincts and forces, and enlarging our whole view and rule of life.

R. M. Ogilvie (essay date 1964)

SOURCE: "Plato, Thucydides and the Victorians," in *Latin and Greek: A History of the Influence of the Classics on English Life from 1600 to 1918,* Routledge and Kegan Paul, 1964, pp. 91-133.

[*In the essay that follows, Ogilvie presents Victorian trends in the study of history and philosophy, epitomized by Thucydides and Plato, as a response among the more liberal members of the ruling classes to the social upheaval that threatened England at the beginning of the nineteenth century.*]

The exhaustion of the Napoleonic Wars and the lethargy of their aftermath allowed many social problems to proliferate unchecked or even unperceived. In the years 1795-1825 modern industrial society took shape, but it was a shape which was neither planned by forward-looking self-interest nor ameliorated by altruistic concern for the well-being of the working classes. The dense centres of industry concealed unnumbered thousands herded together in unimaginable squalor without any recreations except to reproduce their kind (birth-control was still neither respectable nor reliable) and to die (the expectation of life at birth in Liverpool in 1820 was fifteen years). As G. M. Young wrote in 1936, we

> can hardly apprehend the horror in which thousands of families a hundred years ago, were born, dragged out their ghastly lives, and died: the drinking water brown with faecal particles, the corpses kept unburied for a fortnight in a festering London August; mortified limbs quivering with maggots; courts where not a weed would grow, and sleeping-dens afloat with sewage.

There was no education, no health-service, not even the most rudimentary policing. There were no consolations except sex, crime and drink and no expectations except work and disease, or poverty and starvation.

Such conditions would be unendurable in a flourishing economy. In a depression they were explosive, and there were many moments in these and the succeeding years when commercial collapse threatened to unleash the savage forces of the unemployed. This threat loomed large in 1819 and again in the Labourers' Rising of 1830. It became insistent after the slump of 1836 and the failure of 1838. It found violent expression in the more hysterical utterances of the Chartists. It is the ever-present background to the novels of Disraeli and Dickens. The working classes, cut off from any hope of improvement, were a dangerous necessity and the memory of 1792 disquieted even the most sanguine. Any day the masses might rise and succeed in gratifying their pent-up misery in indiscriminate destruction. Dr. Arnold could write in 1834: "The disorders in our social state appear to me to continue unabated. You have heard, I doubt not, of the Trade Unions; a fearful engine of mischief, ready to riot or to assassinate; and I see no counteracting power." And Mr. Bingley in Disraeli's *Sybil* surveys a recent incident of rick-burning with the foreboding: "The temper of the people alarms me. Do you know, sir, there were two or three score of them here, and, except my own farm-workers, not one of them would lend a helping hand." *Sybil,* set in 1837, is, like the Silver Fork novels, an excellent mirror of the times.

The instinctive reaction of the upper classes to the dilemma that their prosperity depended upon an industrial proletariat which might at any moment erupt and engulf them was to pretend that such unpleasantness simply did not exist. It is often better for one's peace of mind to ignore the public and a true appreciation of the life of the poor would have caused many vainly sleepless nights. But the facility with which the educated classes were able to shut their eyes to the horrors around them was an excess of self-deception. Apart from a pious insistence upon the value of soap and cleanliness, they preferred not to talk about or refer to indecorous topics. Young cites as a characteristic instance the anger of *The Times* at a Parliamentary Committee, "who asked a factory woman if she had ever had a miscarriage . . . for violating the principles which should preside over such inquiries, 'a dread of ridicule and an anxious avoidance of indecency'". The refusal to call a spade a spade, and the consequent reluctance to believe in it as a serviceable implement, was one of the least estimable hangovers from the Horatian age. It was not "good form" to speak about the atrocities of the poor and hence there was no incentive to investigate them or to initiate any action to improve them.

England was in the grip not so much of complacency as of obtuseness. She was unaware of the true nature of the menaces that lurked underground: she felt only a nameless fear. Society continued much as before. Government rested in the hands of the same great families: the Universities furnished the same dilettante accomplishments to the same undergraduates and sent into the world the same orthodox clergymen and lettered politicians. But it was all increasingly irrelevant to the real needs of the country. England was no longer a rural aristocracy. Benevolent Anglicanism did not minister to the spiritual anguish of the unprivileged. A governing society "where mediaeval prejudice, Tudor Law, Stuart economics and Hanoverian patronage still luxuriated in wild confusion" was singularly ill-equipped to tackle, let alone to solve, the problems of the nineteenth century.

The first reaction of the more sensitive among the intellectuals was, as has been seen, one of revolt. They seized on the example of Greece as an inspiration to break away from the political and social restrictions of the old generation and to assert an artistic and philosophical liberty of their own. Such a reaction by its very nature was negative, selfish and anarchical. It was the reaction of men secure of their own position in the world who were resolved to disrupt current ways of thinking but were less disposed to engage in the practical measures required to change society's ways of living. They did much to quicken social imagination; they made novel and daring speculation permissible; but they were more concerned to shatter the idols of the upper classes than they were to succour the plight of the poor. Their break-away led to nothing: for such freedom is irresponsible.

Others, however, were more positive and it was from the Utilitarian and Evangelical movements that a new spirit of public concern was born. The Evangelicals, with their emphasis on temperance and earnestness, preached a gospel of redemption which was simple to comprehend and which offered hope even to the most abject, and they were not ashamed to preach it in the heart of the slums. Their insistence on the brotherhood of man, which was to triumph in the Anti-Slavery legislation of 1833, when uttered by a man of the standing and character of Wilberforce could not but shake the barriers which the gentility erected between themselves and the submerged population. If God can love the poor, should not the Levite as well as the Samaritan? From a very different stand-point, the Utilitarians worked towards the same result. Theirs was a doctrine of economic advancement. Progress was hindered by privilege and by ignorance. The greatest happiness of the greatest number was a goal which could be reached only by the abolition of privilege that stunted the natural fruits of competition and industry and by the dissemination of useful knowledge which would reveal to the workman the value of hard work and self-improvement. The brotherhood of man and universal suffrage were both assertions that the working classes must be treated as men and that it was the duty of the more fortunate to promote the reconciliation between the privileged and the deprived.

The dissatisfaction with the irrelevance of contemporary attitudes and the growing social conscience fostered by the Evangelicals and Benthamites inspired among the intelligent young a sense of mission. The feeling that there was work to be done, a feeling which became stereotyped in the late Victorian age into the avowal of public service, is the most conspicuous aspiration of the time. Bonamy Price wrote of Dr. Arnold's method of education: "Every pupil was made to feel that there was a work for him to do—that his happiness as well as his duty lay in doing that work well. Hence an indescribable zest was communicated to a young man's feeling about life; a strange joy came over him on discovering that he had the means of being useful and thus of being happy." Similarly Jowett believed that "privilege whether inherited or acquired means responsibility and that responsibility means hard work." "What does matter is the sense of power which comes from steady working." In the face of the prevailing frivolity of the Court, a "fancy dress court", as Sir Geoffrey Faber has called it, where "authority was more often animated—so far as it was animated at all—by a sense of privilege than by a sense of responsibility", young men wanted to be useful, to feel that they were labourers called to a harvest.

Nowhere is this preoccupation with work, this moral earnestness of social conscience, more evidently seen than in the revived interest in history. It is not just that new techniques of historiography, in particular the scientific rationalism of Wolf, Niebuhr and Ranke, had revolutionized the approach to historical evidence. Such advances did indeed have the effect of making most eighteenth-century work out of date, but it is the awareness that history should be more than the elegant narration of events that made men regard study and the writing of it as of intimate importance to the world in which they lived and popularized the vogue alike for historical treatises and historical romances. The lessons of history, whether they be the understanding of social and political movements, the elementary realization of economic factors or the effects of moral law, were topical and instructive. Grote writes of framing to himself "more complete and full-bodied ideas of the social phenomena of [the age of the Persian Wars] than are presented in other histories". Elsewhere he argues that the duty of a historian of Greece should be "to unfold the mechanism of society, and to bring into view the numerous illustrations which Grecian phenomena afford of the principles of human nature". In his own history he endeavoured to infuse "some useful doctrines, both as to political economy and the principles of population". From Grote to Arnold, from the Utilitarian pedant to the Christian pedagogue, is a far cry, but Arnold echoes the same conviction about the utility of history. He held that in the study of classical history "with a perfect abstraction from those particular names and associations, which are for ever biassing our judgement in modern and domestic instances, the great principles of all political questions, whether civil or ecclesiastical" can be grasped. Stanley writes of Arnold's "anxiety to call public attention to the social evils of the lower classes in England which [in his lectures as Professor of Modern History] he would have tried to analyse and expose in the process of their formation and growth—his interest in tracing the general laws of social and political science". The early Victorians looked to the past to provide them with some key to the bewildering complexities of the present. They read the great histories of antiquity—Thirlwall's *History of Greece* (1835-47) as well as Grote's, Arnold's *History of Rome* and Milman's *History of the Jews* (1830). In the field of modern history Carlyle's *French Revolution* (1837) and *Oliver Cromwell* (1845) led the way to Macaulay's *History of England* (1849). In the shade of these giants flowered and withered a host of lesser historians—Hallam, Markham, Priestley, Russell. For less chalcenteric readers there were the historical novelists, above all Scott and Lytton, who offered social analysis and moral enlightenment in a predigested form. It was the age of huge historical paintings and elaborate historical dramas.

It would have been unaccountable if these trends had not had repercussions on education in the schools and Universities; 150 years before, the cry had gone up that education should impart useful knowledge. So now critics asked whether the traditional classical training was adequate to prepare men for the conditions of an industrial civilization. It was all very well to commend "some longs and shorts about the Calydonian Boar which were not bad" and to claim that a classical curriculum "braced the mind for future acquisition" but did not Archimedes Silverpump, PH.D., the principal of Lycurgus House Academy, dispense the education that the times required? "We must be men of our age. Useful knowledge, living languages, and the forming of the mind through observation and experiment, these are the fundamental articles of my educational creed." The creed was articulated by many other reformers. It was the fault, they urged, of the traditional system that the nation's eyes had for so long been blind to social developments: there was nothing in the study of the classics that enabled men either to diagnose or to heal the sickness of the country. The long campaign, which has been admirably charted by Brian Simon in his *Studies in the History of Education, 1780-1870,* was conducted largely in the pages of the *Edinburgh Review,* the *Westminster Review* and the *Quarterly Journal of Education.*[1] Some of the earliest and ablest shots were fired by Sydney Smith in a review of R. L. Edgeworth's *Essays on Professional Education* (1809) which was part of a series of critical articles in the *Edinburgh Review* between January 1808 and April 1810. "The bias given to men's minds", Sydney Smith wrote about the classics, "is so strong that it is no uncommon thing to meet with Englishmen whom but for their grey hairs and wrinkles we might easily mistake for school-boys. Their talk is of Latin verses; and it is quite clear, if men's ages are to be dated from the state of their mental progress, that such men are 18 years of age and not a day older." He recalled the serious doubts of Dr. Georg about the Great King of Prussia "whether with all his victories he knew how to conjugate a Greek verb in μι." He proceeded to outline his own blue-print.

> We should deem it of the utmost importance that attention was directed to the true principles of legislation—what effects laws can produce upon opinions, and opinions upon laws—what subjects are fit for legislative interference, and what men may be left to the management of their own interests. The mischief occasioned by bad laws and the perplexity which arises from numerous laws—the causes of national wealth—the relations of foreign trades—the encouragement of manufactures and agriculture—the fictitious wealth occasioned by paper credit—the laws of population—the management of poverty and mendicity—the use and abuse of monopoly, the theory of taxation—the consequences of public debt. These are some of the subjects, and some of the branches of civil education, to which we would turn the minds of future judges, future senators and future noblemen.

It was not sufficient that Crumpet should spend the best years of his life in making Latin verses and should know that the *crum* in *crum-pet* is long and the *pet* short.

This was the criticism often and clamorously voiced. It is interesting to observe how closely it reflects the passion for sociological enquiry which, it has been suggested above, animated the spurt of historical curiosity in the same period. In 1750 education was asked to provide a code for living; now it was asked to provide a philosophy for understanding and regulating an intricate and potentially combustible society. The clear-cut discipline of Horatian *moderatio* was obviously incapable of providing such a philosophy. Its inflexibility is witnessed both by its failure to act as a seed-bed in which the spirit of neo-Hellenism could germinate and take root and by the cataclysmic decline of the Grammar Schools where its irrelevance to contemporary life was most damagingly displayed. Verbal elegance and the allied virtues in manners and behaviour were of singularly little profit to the mercantile and trading classes of the early nineteenth century. The classics had always been the principal study in the Grammar Schools and an obligation to teach Latin and Greek was included in the foundation statutes of many of them. It was particularly difficult for them to adjust themselves to the demands of a utilitarian age. On the whole they continued to teach Latin and Greek as they had always been taught, but badly and half-heartedly. Clarke mentions one school in London where "the highest class read aloud the beginning of the Latin grammar for an hour a week without explanation or knowledge of the meaning in order to satisfy founder's intention" and one of the Commissioners of the Schools Enquiry Commission set up in 1864 reported that "in eight schools where he examined no boy could give correctly the Latin for 'He was a good boy'". But the Grammar Schools had nothing constructive to put in the place of the old discipline. As soon as the traditional pattern of classical education based on the imitation and study of Horace and the Latin poet was exposed as obsolete, the Grammar Schools which did not move with the times lost ground both to new private schools, like Lycurgus Academy, which offered practical or vocational instruction, and to the Public Schools which, as will be seen, drew fresh life from the classics. Much of the subsequent bitterness of class-feeling stems from the failure of the Grammar Schools to keep pace with the Public Schools in these years and the failure was largely caused by their reluctance to revise their approach to the classics.

Education was at the cross-roads. The growing social concern, seen in the agitation of the Utilitarians and the Evangelicals and more widely in the public interest in history, was increasingly at variance with the old-style education which gave no insight into social or moral problems. In this predicament three courses were open. The schools and Universities might have done nothing. That way, as the Grammar Schools found to their cost, lay ruin and desolation. They might have abandoned the classics altogether and replaced them by some syllabus of modern subjects. The effects of such a solution can only be conjectured. What in fact they did was to reorientate the study of the classics towards Greek and, above all, towards the masters of philosophy and history, Plato and Thucydides. The results of this reorientation, which was so clearly in keeping with the tendencies of the age, were to prove of incalculable benefit.[2]

To Arnold is due much of the credit for originating the change. As an undergraduate at Oriel in 1812 he already gave a "decided preference to philosophers and historians of antiquity over the poets" and distinguished forcefully between "words and things". His passion was for Aristotle and Thucydides. When he obtained the power to put his ideas into practice, he altered or discarded much that was the legacy of tradition. Latin verse composition he regarded as "one of the most contemptible prettinesses of the understanding" and "it was an old opinion of his", according to Stanley, "which, though much modified, was never altogether abandoned, that the mass of boys had not a sufficient appreciation of poetry to make it worth while for them to read so much of the ancient poets, in proportion to the prose-writers, as was usual when he came to Rugby". In their place he read Demosthenes and Aristotle in school, but above all Thucydides and Plato. Former pupils recalled "the affectionate familiarity which he used to show to Thucydides knowing as he did the substance of every single chapter by itself" and "the keen sense of a new world opening before him with which he entered into the works of Plato".

If Arnold at Rugby, by his prestige and authority, was instrumental in popularizing the study of Plato and Thucydides in schools, it was Butler, during his long reign at Shrewsbury (1798-1836), who did most to extend the knowledge of the Greek language. Like Arnold, Butler favoured prose authors (Demosthenes and Thucydides for choice), but he also insisted on translation into Greek prose and Greek verse. The rigorous training in translation and composition gave Shrewsbury a unique standing in the academic world. In 1831 a Salopian still at school won the Ireland Scholarship at Oxford, defeating, amongst other candidates, W. E. Gladstone.

B. H. Kennedy, who had been a pupil of Butler's at Shrewsbury, had read all Aeschylus, Sophocles, Thucydides and Tacitus as well as much of Demosthenes, Plato, Herodotus, Pindar and Aristophanes before he went to Cambridge. Under Frederick Temple at Rugby (1857-69), Lucretius, Thucydides and Plato were the favourite authors. Temple even read the *Philebus* with the Upper Bench, a dialogue of little charm and great obscurity. The example set at these two schools was speedily copied. At St. Paul's in the 1830s Demosthenes and Thucydides were studied and more time was devoted to the teaching of Greek than of Latin. At Sedbergh it was expected in the 1850s that boys should have read all Homer, Thucydides and Sophocles before they went to the University. Rugby ideas were propagated by Rugbeian headmasters. Vaughan introduced the study of Plato to Harrow by 1859. At King Edward's, Birmingham, James Prince Lee, one of the great Victorian headmasters, stimulated his form by his burning love and phenomenal memory of Thucydides. B. R. Westcott recorded "the richness and force of the illustrations by which he brought home to us a battle-piece of Thucydides or a sketch of Tacitus" and another of his pupils, E. W. Benson, had read in his private work the whole of Livy, Herodotus and Thucydides by the time that he left the school. Only Eton and Winchester were unaffected by the great change of taste. Although Moberly numbered Thucydides among the elect, Wykehamists still devoted most of their energies to original verse compositions in Latin. Little Greek prose was either read or written. Eton, surviving the onslaught of the *Edinburgh Review* in 1830, slept the sleep of the unreformed until the Public Schools Commission of 1861.

These examples illustrate how the emphasis in school curricula had switched from Latin to Greek and how, in particular, it was concentrated on the study of Thucydides and Plato. The same trend is evident at the Universities. The study of Aristotle and the ancient historians had been part of Litterae Humaniores since its inception in 1807, but the course was slow to bear fruit and to have any effect on national life. This was partly because Oxford only became a serious place of study where most young gentlemen were expected to work and win honours as a result of the increased liberalization of the University and the pressure of the threatened and actual Royal Commissions of 1837 and 1851. The progress of Colleges like Balliol, Oriel and Lincoln is symptomatic of the change. Lincoln, which had for long been in the shadows, emerged under the guidance of Mark Pattison to win sixteen Firsts in the years 1834-51. The same period marked the beginning of Jowett's Tutorship. Partly, however, it was the lack of unity in the course. A syllabus which comprises most of the classical texts without any specified focus is aimless. The statute of 1850 which separated off the literary side of classical studies into a preliminary examination (Honour Moderations) and left the student to devote his energies thereafter single-mindedly to the study of ancient history and philosophy for the final degree (Greats) was a great step forward. It enabled him to move from the acquisition of linguistic facility to the employment of that facility in the serious appreciation of ancient civilization. The result of this simple organization was instantaneous. Greats became the premier University course. The merits of Greats are still valid. It does offer a study in depth of a society which is both intrinsically fascinating and educationally manageable in that the sources are adequate to make inferences from but not too numerous for an undergraduate to control. If the study of a different civilization is a help to the understanding of one's own, then Greats was one of the most valuable institutions of the Victorians. Partly, Litterae Humaniores only became popular when Plato had displaced Aristotle. As was seen earlier, in the original course Plato was not obligatory. But despite Arnold's determination not to send his son to a University where the Stagyrite was not studied (Cambridge), to most early Victorians Aristotle was *vieux jeu.* He had been studied by every generation of Oxford students since mediaeval times and, however novel the interpretations that might be propounded about him, he savoured too much of the old order of things. As Jowett said, "Aristotle is dead but Plato is alive". The change came in the 1830s when William Sewell, Professor of Moral Philosophy, began to lecture on Plato's *Republic.* Sewell was a tortuous and disorganized lecturer—one of his audience recalled that "he would commence a lecture on Aristotle in the usual way but would end with, perhaps, the Athanasian creed or the beauties of Gothic architecture"—but as Jowett was to fill Balliol hall with his lectures on Plato after 1847, so Sewell drew crowds of excited undergraduates to Exeter. Plato had arrived. The *Republic* took its place in the set books for Greats.

Two further considerations help to account for the success of Litterae Humaniores and for the resulting devotion to Thucydides and Plato at Oxford in the second half of the century. For fifteen years, from Keble's Assize Sermon to Newman's conversion and the Gorham Case, Oxford was preoccupied with theological controversy. It is hard for us, as it was for Lytton Strachey, to conceive how deeply men worried about doctrinal difficulties. The incoherent flutter excited by *Honest to God* does not compare with the sincere scandal of *Essays and Reviews.* But intelligent and thoughtful men, Gladstone and Acton as well as Newman and Arnold, were racked by religious doubts, which, as Pattison said, "had entirely diverted our thoughts from the true business of the place." It was, therefore, with an almost conscious relief that Oxford turned from theological speculation to the safer and less contentious waters of philosophical and historical research. Secondly, it is not possible to study ancient history solely through the medium of ancient texts. Until scholarly histories were available for reference, Greats was not able to progress beyond translation and interpretation of Thucydides or Tacitus. Thirlwall and Grote, Niebuhr and Arnold supplied the necessary tools.

By 1860 every Oxford Greats man would be reading Plato and Thucydides and nearly everyone at Oxford was reading Greats. Cambridge presents a less enlightened aspect. The Classical Tripos, instituted in 1824, consisted of composition in prose and verse and translation from the "best classical authors". It contained no philosophy and no history. If Plato and Thucydides were read, they were read purely for translation purposes. The Cambridge undergraduates gained no serious understanding of them, for that was of no assistance towards getting a good degree. The only palliative was the lectures of Julius Hare and Connop Thirlwall who around 1830 stimulated some more general interest in Plato's thought. A "Platonist Club" was founded. But all the time the emphasis was on the ability to construe and compose. The Royal Commission of 1850 isolated the weakness and in the same year Whewell openly charged that "it was possible to obtain high honours without acquiring any real knowledge of antiquity". Conservatism in Cambridge was firmly entrenched. An attempt to add a paper on ancient philosophy was defeated in 1849 and it was not until 1872 that one of three extra papers was approved involving questions on certain, mainly philosophical, set books. It was a very modest advance and the division of the tripos into two parts in 1882 did much to reverse it. Part I, the only compulsory part, contained the traditional translation and composition, with a further paper on questions on "History, Literature and Antiquities" which was a joke then and was still a joke in 1957. Part II allowed a candidate to read one optional special subject (ancient philosophy, history, archaeology or language): it was highly specialized and, in consequence, of little educational value. The failure of Cambridge, as of the Grammar Schools, to move with the times had a deleterious effect on the unity of classical education in England. It might not have been lethal but for the false glamour with which the leading scholar was to be invested.

A better idea of the popularity of Plato and Thucydides can be gained from casual references than from formal requirements. A. J. Ashton, who went up to Balliol in 1874, recounted an anecdote about Edward Harrison. A Jewish scholar of another College was reading aloud to a group of fellow-undergraduates the diary he had written about his Scandinavian travels. He ended one night's tale with the note "Painted Beauty £2". Harrison flung out of the room with an indignant "φιλοκαλοῦμεν μετ' εὐτελείᾱς," "we are lovers of beauty without expense". "The audience were all men to whom the second book of Thucydides was familiar and the speech of Pericles like household words. To such an audience nothing could have been more brilliant. At any rate I know a former Prime Minister who thought so". Or take the expostulation in *Tom Brown at Oxford:* "Reader! had you not ever a friend a few years older than yourselves, whose good opinion you were anxious to keep. A fellow *teres atque rotundus;* who could do everything better than you, from Plato and tennis down to singing a comic song." Cobden complained how preposterous it was that youths in the Universities who knew nothing about the Mississippi should know all about the little Athenian stream called the Ilissus (the opening scene of the *Phaedrus*), while Haldane, in an address at Liverpool in October 1901, contrasted the criticism of Greek philosophy of the day with "the shallow formalities which did duty in the English Universities" fifty years before.

The love of Plato and Thucydides outlasted the exigencies of schools' and Universities' curricula. In every walk of life we find men reading and re-reading the two great classics during the half-century that begins in 1830. Macaulay, "who loved Plato for the sake of what he called the 'setting' of the dialogues and ranked them according to their literary beauty rather than their philosophical excellence", defined an educated gentleman as a man who read Plato with his feet on the fender. Macaulay himself read the philosopher in a ponderous folio, sixteen inches long by ten broad, weighing twelve pounds, which had been published at Frankfurt in 1602. In 1853 he writes that he had "determined to read through Plato again" and in the course of the next few weeks his progress can be traced. He began with the *Phaedrus* "one of the most elegant, ingenious, fantastic and delicately ironical of the dialogues" and persevered until only the *Philebus, Sophist* and *Laws* were left. The *Phaedrus, Lysis* and *Protagoras* remained his favourites throughout his life. When Grote was a Member of Parliament "he found time to read through most of Plato in a committee room while waiting for his less punctual colleagues". Leslie Stephen had a little "Plato" which being of a convenient size for his pocket went with him on all his journeys and even travelled to America and back. Plato was indeed a popular journey-book. Dr. Alexander Robertson read the *Republic* on a Mediterranean cruise "wondering gratefully at its wisdom and reverence. There are flashes of insight into the human and divine of a truly wonderful kind and the tone of calm orderliness is exactly what we require. I had really not forgotten much of it, it was so well soaked into us at Balliol". Robertson was born in 1851. But few could equal the enthusiasm of J. A. Symonds who went to London "taking a crib of Plato with him. After seeing a play, he started the crib in bed and the sun was shining before he could put it down. 'It was as though the voice of my own soul spoke to me through Plato'." Later, in 1885, Symonds is found at Davos in Switzerland, reading the *Dialogues* with Margot Tennant (Asquith), that remarkable person to whom Jowett presented a copy of his *Republic* ("I wonder if it will have any meaning or interest for you") and who rebuked Lord Salisbury for not caring "fanatically about literature or culture . . . for Plato or any of the classics". Many returned to read Plato in their old age. Arthur Marshall took him up again in his eighty-second year, and Lord Dufferin, who as a young man had delivered the peerlessly classic speech to the assembled dignitaries of Iceland, beginning *"insolitus ut sum ad publicum loquendum"*, succeeded in 1895 at the age of seventy in rereading the Greek tragedians, Herodotus, Thucydides, Plato and much of Plutarch and Lucian—"no inconsiderable performance for a man who never neglected official business". It is a pretty scene to picture Sir Edward Grey, who left Balliol for idleness, and Sir Henry Newbolt, lunching at Itchen Abbas on "Wordsworth and Plato" and "discussing the Platonic transmigration of souls in the great lime avenue of Avington Park".

The sheer difficulty of Thucydides might seem at first sight to debar him from such casual perusal but, in fact, letters and memoirs provide continual references to his public popularity. Cobden's angry sneer that "one copy of *The Times* contains more useful information than the whole of Thucydides" is the natural outcome of Jowett's desire that every educated man should be able to read Thucydides in an armchair. Sir George Cornewall Lewis, Chancellor of the Exchequer under Palmerston and subsequently Home Secretary, corresponded regularly with Grote on the interpretation and text of Thucydides and such avocations were not the prerogative of the state. The Church too kept up its scholarship. Benson, when Bishop of Truro, wrote to his Wykehamist son to strengthen his resolve:

> You must be first soaked with the spirit and handling of Thucydides. The determination to take into account all the phenomena which were real and the insight into the first principles of action and the modification of high aims by inferior and selfish ones, and the perception that there are laws under which societies may be traced as acting. I am not at all surprised that you have not got yet into the sense of devotion to that mighty man which will, I think, soon seize your historical sense. . . . I do distinctly recollect the day and hour when I exclaimed sitting over my Thucydides, 'Why I am beginning to comprehend exactly what he means! I can understand all this as he goes on, slowly but really'.

Bishop Wilberforce was so steeped in Thucydides that he could transform Pericles' argument in the Funeral Speech that Athens was the educator of the rest of Greece into a plea that the Indian Civil Service should be open to competition from the Universities. Later Victorians were apt to view British history in the light of Athenian history and there were many solemn voices raised which claimed that the Boer War was Britain's "Sicilian Expedition". C. E. Montague wrote:

> I suppose all the big struggles everywhere looked pretty much the same in their time, except in superficials, for Thucydides gives a description of the effects of party feeling in Athens and the way it made people lose the meaning of words etc., which is beautifully appropriate now. He even described the Jingo press during the Boer war with great minuteness.

It was the influence of Arnold more than anyone else which kept men reverting to their Thucydides: Arnold who in the disturbances of 1819 thought "daily of Thucydides and the Corcyrean sedition, and of the story of the French Revolution, and the Cassandra-like fate of history, whose lessons are read in vain even to the very next generation"; Arnold who in the Preface of his Thucydides avowed that he was engaged "not on an idle inquiry about remote ages and forgotten institutions but a living picture of things present, fitted not so much for the curiosity of the scholar as for the instruction of the statesman and the citizen". All who came under his spell and many who entered on his inheritance were "disposed", in Young's phrase, "to bring everything in the state of England to the test of Isaiah and Thucydides".

Wherein lay the kinship of Victorian England and the Athenian city-state of the last years of the fifth century B.C.? Some contemporary estimates emerge from the quotations given above but since men of all stations, if less intensely than their "Augustan" predecessors, tended to visualize themselves as acting on the stage of antiquity, it is worth while examining the similarities between the two societies at closer view. Britain and Athens were small maritime nations which against formidable odds had unexpectedly conquered in a land war the greatest military power of the world. Waterloo, like Marathon and Plataea, was as much a spur to self-confidence as it was a triumph of arms. As a result of the Persian Wars Athens had acquired an empire: Britain's victory in the Napoleonic Wars allowed her to retain and consolidate hers. The possession of an empire resting on the command of the sea had similar consequences for both countries. As Pericles had said and the old Oligarch had cynically admitted, Athens became the centre of world trade . . . and the commercial prosperity which attended Britain, as seen both in the range of manufactured goods and in the wealth of imports and exports, was due to her fleet, to her overseas markets and to her command of raw materials. Military success and commercial prosperity widen the demand for education and education excites political awareness. In Athens and in Britain a radical extension of the franchise to include in the governing class the strata of society upon whom the welfare of the state depended was a natural corollary of their success. The responsible officer and the wealthy industrialist seek by education to raise their fortunes still higher and expect as of right some say in the management of a nation to whose service they have contributed so much. Pericles' measure in the 450s to extend the franchise is the counterpart of the Reform Bill of 1832 and widespread demand for Public School and University education is matched by the remarkable literacy of the audiences that could appreciate the drama of Sophocles, the wit of Aristophanes and the speculation of Euripides. In both countries there existed a well-educated and highly articulate minority "democracy": it was a democracy in that the actual rulers were directly chosen as representatives by the electorate but a minority since in England the total registration of votes was a mere 620,000 and in Athens perhaps not more than 40,000, while in both the vast majority of the populations, women and slaves/workers, was unrepresented. It was characteristic of the two democracies that members of the old aristocratic families should be eager to win political power through the suffrage. Lord John Russell, Lord Rosebery or Lord Randolph Churchill followed the tradition of Callias, Alcibiades and Pericles himself. Democracy, as Grote stressed, fostered the development of individual talent. Englishmen and Athenians could take pride in their cultivation of the arts, in their appreciation of music and poetry, in their taste for architecture and their courage in philosophic speculation. Moreover they lived in times when emotions were passionately felt and friendships intensely cultivated, when there was no inhibition on the open display of feeling, when strong men wept and embraced and walked together arm-in-arm.

The similarity was arresting but it was exaggerated by the euhemeristic ability of the Victorians to confuse the real world which can be unearthed from the pages of Thucydides and Aristophanes with the ideal world of Plato's *Republic.* They were too inclined to assume that most of the institutions which Plato advocated for his Utopian society actually existed in Athens and hence to create in their minds an imaginary picture of Athenian life on which they could model their own conduct and attitudes. For the differences were very great. England was a vast industrial country, Athens a small commercial city, and however little distinction in condition there might be between the slave and the worker (although, in fact, the slave was the better situated), there was a vital distinction of status. The worker was a citizen, an Englishman. The difference of size in itself is crucial, for in Athens direct democracy with the active participation of all citizens in the day-to-day running of affairs was possible, whereas, as the Utilitarians quickly realized, in a country as large as England only representative government was feasible. It is one thing to attend the assembly in person and vote on decisive issues: it is another to elect a Member of Parliament every three years. A further aspect—and in the character of a nation it is a determinant aspect—which the Victorians conscientiously eradicated from their view of Athenian life was its basis in homosexuality. Macaulay was repelled by it ("What a state of morals! What a distortion of the imagination"), Jowett managed to rationalize it ("What Plato says of the loves of men must be transferred to the loves of women before we can attach any serious meaning to his words. Had he lived in our times, he would have made the transposition himself." For Jowett, Plato could never be fundamentally un-Victorian), but most Victorians glossed placidly over it.

Taken all in all, however, there was enough in the resemblance between the situations of England and Athens to tempt the Victorians into feeling a spiritual kinship. With particular schools of nineteenth-century thought the ties were even closer. To the Utilitarians Plato was an attractive master. James Mill considered that "he was more indebted intellectually to Plato than to any other writer" and his son, J. S. Mill, wrote that "mankind could not be reminded too often that there was once a man called Socrates". One of the noblest memorials of the philosophical Radical movement was Grote's *Plato* ("the greatest intellectual gratification I have had in the long course of my sick years", as Harriet Martineau praised it). The Utilitarians had studied Plato long before he had become the fashionable author of the schools and Universities. They admired him primarily for his destructive approach to philosophical questions and for his harrying of every proposed solution or definition by remorseless cross-examination. J. S. Mill described it as "the close, searching elenchus by which the man of vague generalities is constrained either to express his meaning to himself in definite terms or to confess that he does not know what he is talking about". The Platonic-Socratic mode of enquiry was essential to the Utilitarians if the stored-up prejudices of centuries were to be swept away. But their debt to Plato went further than that. Although they utterly rejected Plato's Theory of Ideas, their own theory of knowledge owes much to views which Plato propounds if only to refute. The *Theaetetus* offers a criticism of Protagoras' doctrine that everything perceived must be relative to the perceiver ("Man is the measure of all things"). The Utilitarians preferred Protagoras to Plato but much of their impetus towards phenomenalism stemmed from the arguments which Plato deployed. Similarly, although Plato even in the *Protagoras* never espouses the Utilitarian or hedonistic cause in ethics, he often worries over the relationship between goodness and pleasure and his discussions of the problem in the *Republic* and *Philebus* as well as in the *Protagoras* laid the foundations on which the Utilitarians built. Chiefly, however, it was Plato's view of the state which appealed to them. Plato, intellectualizing the practice of Athenian democracy, held that society should be planned on strict rules and that the government of the state should rest with a specially educated class of Guardians. The theory of their education, that the people who have been taught how to rule are the right people to rule, is patently circular: the practice, as prescribed in the *Republic,* is a humane education on a high level. The man who has been taught how to rule merges into the broadly educated man. Thus while Bentham, Grote and the Mills rejected the stratification of society, the notions of justice and punishment, the censorship and the regimentation, they found much to admire in the general principle that prudent government was the fruit of education and in the particular recommendations of limiting the birth-rate (an old Malthusian ideal) and distributing property. The differences between the two conceptions of the state amounts to little more than the fact that Plato's is based on *a priori* and the Utilitarians' on economic organization.

On the other front the heirs of the Evangelical movement, men like Charles Kingsley and Charles Mansfield, scrupulously avoiding the disputes of the Tractarians, followed the lead of F. D. Maurice and dedicated themselves to humanitarian work among the poor. They believed in action, manly and robust action, to improve the lot of their fellow-men rather than in debilitating controversies. Maurice, a "learned Platonist", evolved an Anglican theology which combined the rational idealism and the reforming zeal of Plato. This union of common sense in theological matters and energetic philanthropy was the hall-mark of Christian Socialism and of the Broad Church Party.

Plato was, therefore, fertile in inspiration for much of the creative thinking of the age and the Athens which was synthesized from the study of him and Thucydides served as a pattern for Victorian England. The Victorians felt themselves to be like the Athenians: they strove to become more like. Is it possible to isolate any significant consequences of this conscious assimilation?

Plato was interpreted as believing that government should be in the hands of educated men rather than of technical experts. The philosopher king was a philosopher, not an economist or a career diplomat. Moreover, Athenian experience as documented by Thucydides and the visionary organization recommended by Plato in the *Republic* taught that the only system of government compatible both with democracy and efficiency was a committee system on which the educated served. It was the merit, in particular, of the Constitution of the 5,000 that elicited Thucydides's praise and he is never tired of insisting on the opposite dangers of personal rule (Alcibiades) or popular anarchy. It was, in reality, a long-established feature of the Athenian constitution where Boards of Archons, Logistai, Colacretai and so forth conducted the day-to-day administration. These two features constitute the two distinctive innovations of the nineteenth century. G. M. Young singled out Representative Institutions as one of the marks by which we may know the Victorians". By this we are to understand not merely the emergence of the House of Commons as a truly representative body and the evolution of the Cabinet as the recognized organ of government, but also the establishment of County and

Municipal Councils to have charge over local administration. We should include the creation of an organized Civil Service to replace the haphazard establishment of clerks and under-secretaries who had previously dealt single-handed with business. But principally we notice the proliferation of committees and commissions to investigate social problems. They were manned by ordinary men from every walk of life and, even if their secretaries were people, like Chadwick and Kay-Shuttleworth, of informed dedication, the credit for the improvements which they brought about rests on the disinterested intelligence of the Board-members as a whole. The list of major committees is impressive: The Poor Law Commission, Open Spaces (1833), Agriculture (1833), Inebriety (1834), Criminal Law (1834), Trade Unions (1838), Police (1839), Health of Towns (1840), Factories (1841), Town Housing and Sanitation (1842), Smoke Abatement (1843), Health of Towns (1844), Metropolitan Improvements (1844), Railway Navvies (1846), Universities (1851), Charities (1853), Elementary Education (1861), Public Schools (1864), Housing of the Poor (1884). Society has at its disposal many means of arriving at recommendations. The choice of the committee, rather than the deputed commissioner, and its method of operation are characteristically Athenian. It was Benthamite in conception and the Benthamites looked to Plato.

The second feature of the age was the conviction that unexpert intelligence was the best quality to bring to the problems of government of any degree. Consider some of the prominent administrators: Leonard Horner, who was responsible for many of the Factory Acts, had distinguished himself in the fields of science and education before he embarked in middle age on an administrative career. Southwood Smith, who deserves much of the credit for the measures adopted by the Poor Law Commission to combat cholera and typhus, was a Unitarian minister "whose devotional writings must have had some singular quality to be admired both by Wordsworth and Byron". It was the example of these men and of others like Grote and Hassall which pointed the way to the establishment of a regular Civil Service to which entry should be by academic competition rather than by patronage, birth, wealth or expertise. This was the great principle behind the Northcote-Trevelyan reforms of the Home Civil Service in 1853 and the parallel liberalization of the Indian Civil Service. Macaulay had attempted to introduce competitive entry into the India Bill of 1833. On that occasion he had urged: "whatever be the languages, whatever be the sciences, which it is in any age or country the fashion to teach, the persons who become the greatest proficients in these languages and these sciences will generally be the flower of youth; the most acute, the most industrious, the most ambitious of honourable distinction". In 1833 he felt that the character of the education was immaterial: suitability could be shown by the composition of "the most correct and melodious Greek or, for that matter, Cherokee verses". It is amusing and relevant to note that in 1850 the proposal to found a Fourth School (Modern History) at Oxford was opposed by the argument: "Is it a convenient subject for examination? Where is the standard author like Thucydides?" In 1853 Macaulay went further: "nor is there any reason to believe that they would have been greater lawyers if they had passed in drawing pleas and conveyances the time which they gave to Thucydides to Cicero, and to Newton". A liberal education imparted breadth of vision, intolerance of falsehood and clarity of thought. No other attainments were needed in public life. The dedicated amateur has lately come under much criticism. It is alleged that it is wrong that scientific policy or educational developments or economic decisions should rest with men whose only qualifications may be a First in Greats and an interest in politics. Conversely it is contended that higher education ought (and a moral "ought" is meant) to equip men with technical skills for their career or profession rather than develop a cultivated taste for thought and a sense of history. It is not here relevant to probe the purpose of higher education. Perhaps, in any case, there is no such absolute "purpose": it has always varied with the climate of the times. What is to be noted is that the Victorians of set intent fostered the humane administrator in order to secure disinterested judgement and nothing that has been preached in any of the sermons of Sir Charles Snow or his disciples has yet suggested an answer to the questions that puzzled Plato and the Victorians: Who can best adjudicate between the authority of rival experts? Who can best estimate the rival claims of different groups and needs in society? Whatever the answer, it is not another expert, be he sociologist or governmentalist.

The mixture of English society was being diversified with the rise of new classes. Merchant, industrialist, business man were aspiring to the ranks of the upper middle classes to join the cleric, scholar and professional. The liberal education which they all shared helped to identify their tastes and to forge common links between them which saved England from the exclusive snobberies of Germany. Mark Pattison and others might admire the academic productivity of the German schools and Universities but to have imported their system of narrowly specialized education into this country would have delayed, and perhaps prevented, the fusion of the gentry. The merchant's son was brought up with the statesman's son at the same school in the same learning and that learning abetted daily intercourse in breaking down the barriers of ignorance or prejudice between them.

Arnold had transformed the prefectorial system which he had inherited at Rugby into a missionary organization. The sixth form were entrusted with the responsibility of looking after the smaller boys in the school. The maintenance of order and discipline through the sanctions of corporal punishment was, of course, an element in that responsibility but Arnold envisaged it as a moral rather than a disciplinary task. He was obsessed by the sense of moral evil. He saw Satan lurking in every corner of the school. "When the spring and activity of youth is altogether unsanctified by anything pure and elevated in its desires, it becomes a spectacle that is as dizzying and almost more morally distressing than the shouts and gambols of a set of lunatics." His whole conduct of the school was directed to eradicating the evil in boys and to producing "Christian gentlemen". This was the burden of his preaching, this the aim of his educational reforms with their bias towards historical and philosophical substance, this the charge, often too heavy to bear, that he laid upon his sixth form.

But as the image of Plato took a firmer hold on the minds of mid-Victorian educators, the moral earnestness which was at the heart of Arnold's system was gradually superseded. The educational set-up which Plato advocated in the *Republic* and the *Laws* may have owed much in practical details to the example of the Lycurgan system at Sparta but it shared important common assumptions with the Public Schools. It was designed to educate a governing élite. Children were to be segregated from their families and educated together. The older were to supervise the younger. The principal exercise was the study of literature. . . . But the requirements of Plato's ideal state demanded other qualities from his pupils. Above all he insists on the importance of athletics . . . as the counterpart to literature . . . and the desirability of strengthening character through discipline and games. . . . Games are the twin sister of work: together they train the soul. . . . Frivolous recreations cannot produce responsible men. . . . It is by their prowess in physical and military training and by their reverence for authority that future Guardians are to be selected for further education.

Games and character. These were the two novelties that the cult of manliness and muscular Christianity, which we associate with the name of Charles Kingsley and the pen of Thomas Hughes, introduced into the more ingenuous and individual world of Arnold's Rugby. In the early nineteenth century schoolboys spent their leisure in going for walks—Shelley versifying by the Thames, Martin bird-nesting near Rugby, Bonney collecting fossils round Uppingham—or in unorganized sports and rough-and-tumble. After the middle of the century games were regimented under the official blessing of masters who saw in them a potent force for the development of "character". Charles Wordsworth had blazed the trail at Harrow. By 1870 Cotton and Bradley at Marlborough had succeeded in realizing "their leading endeavour to make the playing fields the chief centre of outdoor attraction for the School". To Temple at Rugby "games were part of the training of character". Edward Thring, who was headmaster of Uppingham from 1853 to 1887, was himself an athlete of outstanding distinction. He regarded games both as in themselves character-building and as a sphere in which the less intelligent could gain self-confidence and standing. So it came about that between 1860 and 1880 games became a compulsory and dominant part of the life of the leading Public Schools, and character rather than intellect the end of education. The new foundations were cast in the same mould. The ideal is enshrined by Newbolt in his poem, *Clifton Chapel:*

> To set the cause above renown,
> To love the game beyond the prize,
> To honour, while you strike him down,
> The foe that comes with fearless eyes;
> To count the life of battle good
> And dear the land that gave you birth,
> And dearer yet the brotherhood
> That binds the brave of all the earth.

What a contrast to Matthew Arnold's vision of his father in *Rugby Chapel:*

> Still thou upraisest with zeal
> The humble good from the ground,
> Sternly represseth the bad!
> Still, like a trumpet, does rouse
> Those who with half-open eyes
> Tread the border-land dim
> 'Twixt vice and virtue; reviv'st,
> Succourest!—this was thy worth,
> This was thy life upon earth.

England was in tune with Plato and the education which she evolved under the influence of Plato's vision was an education well calculated to serve her purposes. It inculcated loyalty, courage, responsibility and truthfulness: four virtues indispensable to the new governing class of a great empire. It produced over the years a steady stream of young men with good manners and a strong sense of public duty. "It taught boys how to obey and how to command."

Sir Harold Nicolson has epitomized the product of that education.

> As an ideal [the Public School Boy] was unique and may be obsolescent. But as a phenomenon he represents a rather grubby reversion to the Greek ideal of Lysis or Charmides. There was nothing banausic about him since he was a child of the rich: between the ages of nine and seventeen he was withdrawn from female influence and his instruction entrusted to males: he mixed on easy terms with his contemporaries, competing with them in sport and games: he was supposed to achieve an equal balance between music and gymnastics: and from time to time, in the form of chapel sermons and private tuitions, he could absorb the wisdom of his elders.

Athenian education had never in practice instilled responsibility; Plato's ideal was never put to the trial of actual experiment. The Public Schools of the Late Victorian period combining Athenian practice with Platonic theory redeemed the former and justified the latter and the result was the spring of England's greatness. If the Public Schools are to remain a creative force in English education in the future they must evolve a new goal to strive towards as well as resolve the social (and less important) problem of their membership. They must begin with attention to the mind rather than to the character.

A curious side-effect of Greek influence is the otherwise incomprehensible popularity of organized rowing.[3] Until the late 1830s rowing was an occasional pastime. The Fourth of June celebrations at Eton contained a regatta in 1793 which was made a regular fixture by 1805, but there is no other record of serious rowing at that time either at Eton or at other schools. Butler and Kennedy frowned even on casual sculling at Shrewsbury. So too at Oxford; Southey writes of "the caps and tassels of the students forming a curious contrast with their employment at the oars" and G. V. Cox describes rare parties to Nuneham in six-oared boats. In general, as Tuckwell remembered, "comparatively few men boated".

How different from the scene forty years later when the headmaster of Westminster had to lock some of his boys in to prevent them from racing against Eton at Putney, when *The Times* could write of "the great improvement rowing provided as a replacement for the evils of the turf", and when Edmund Warre, the future headmaster of Eton, would convince Jowett of the "social and even moral, as well as physical value of rowing as part of College life", and when Mark Pattison could lament that undergraduates dissipated all their energies on the river. The Boat Race was first held in 1829. The Procession of Boats became the climax of Cambridge Commemoration Week in 1842. Henley Royal Regatta was founded in 1839. Most of the school boatclubs date from the same period (e.g. Winchester in 1836). Rowing became a part of academic life, as a cursory glance at *Tom Brown at Oxford* reveals. The Hon. L. W. Denman at Shrewsbury recalled "the delight of rowing up to the Wheel at Berwick and on to Lloyd's of the Knowles who always gave us a good luncheon of beef and beer", and "the new pleasures of boating" seemed to bring to the young Dalmeny (Rosebery) at Eton "a special enlargement of mind and consciousness of promotion". T. K. Selwyn wrote a diary of boating at Eton (1829-30) in Greek under the name of Σέλφυν ὁ ʿΑμστεδικᾳς. It is one of the curios of the age. Leslie Stephen at Cambridge made rowing into so venerable a cult that Sir Charles Dilke who rowed in the Trinity Hall Head of the River Boat in 1864 "piously kept a piece of the boat hanging against the wall of his study in Sloane St. until the end of his life". Their prophet was William Cory (Johnson), the author of the *Eton Boating Song* (1863).

No one would deny that rowing, like all forms of pointless exertion, has a physical satisfaction of its own. Perhaps, however, the craze for rowing in nineteenth-century England was less naïvely engendered. The champions of it—Charles Wordsworth, second master of Winchester in 1833, Leslie Stephen, Edmund Warre and William Cory himself—were, of course, prominent "muscular Christians". Three of them were also Platonists. We have met Stephen's pocket "Plato": Cory slaked his thirst for Platonic friendships at the fountain itself; W. E. Gladstone, a private pupil of Wordsworth's, wrote to him anxiously in 1830, to elucidate the exact meaning of "τὸ ἄπειρον" as used in the early part of the treatise' (the *Philebus*). But the appeal which eight men propelling a boat through the water with precise discipline had for them was unquestionably that the oarsmen re-enacted the special skill of the Athenians, just as Kingsley's advocacy of the cold bath in *Great Cities* ("the morning cold bath which foreigners consider as Young England's strangest superstition") derives from Attic rigour commended by Aristophanes (*Clouds* 1043 . . .). It was Pericles' boast that rowing had made the Athenians what they were (Thucydides 1.143 . . .). England, too, was a naval empire and, although her strength depended on the power of wind and steam, something perhaps of the confident spirit of the Athenians could be acquired by daily outings on the Isis.

The spell exerted by Thucydides and Plato was sometimes insidious, sometimes ridiculous, but often unreservedly beneficial, and in no particular was it seen to more advantage than in the influence which it had over British Imperialism. The private enterprise of the East India Company and other bodies gave way to public administration, as the scandals became too monstrous to overlook and the colonies too important to neglect. Slowly and reluctantly Government had to replace the old adventurers and nabobs with Government servants. The new administrators took on a task in which there were no precedents, no principles, no instructions to help them. It was, therefore, not altogether quixotic of them to have turned to the pages of Thucydides for guidance. For the Athenian and British empires had resemblances and Thucydides had expressed many of the salient arguments which had swayed Athenian policy. The British in India never travelled without a copy of Thucydides. Hobbes' translation is prominent among the books of Nicholas Clarembault, and Mountstuart Elphinstone throughout his thirty-two years' service in India immersed himself in the Greek historian and thought of Indian problems in Attic terms. According to Lord Radcliffe, "his dispatches from Poona are consciously modelled on Thucydides". Macaulay read Thucydides twice at Calcutta (February 1835 and March 1836) and jotted down: "I finished Thucydides, after reading him with inexpressible interest and admiration. He is the greatest historian that ever lived." Of the theorists of imperialism, James, Viscount Boyce, the author of *Studies in History and Jurisprudence,* a seminal work of imperialist thought, was a connoisseur of Thucydides (as an undergraduate he had won the Gaisford Greek Prose Prize with an imitation of the Plague) and, while his examples tend to be Roman, most of his ideas are Greek. Evelyn Baring, 1st Earl of Cromer, who for long, by a mixture of cunning and passivity, was virtual master of Egypt, published after his retirement a revealing lecture, *Ancient and Modern Imperialism,* in which the comparison is made explicit. The list could be lengthened but it is more satisfying to isolate a few principles which seem to rest ultimately on the authority of Thucydides.

Once a nation has acquired, for whatever reason or by whatever accident, overseas possessions her first consideration must be, as Curzon pointed out in his lecture on *Frontiers,* to ensure that the territory is a self-contained unit. It has been the misfortune of a country like the Congo that it was a paper-entity not a natural unit. Whether the limits will be geographical (e.g. the Himalayas in India or the Limpopo in Africa) or ethnic, an imperial power must secure control of the whole extent up to the natural perimeter. It was this that the Liberal Imperialists realized when Gladstone and Lord Granville were mistakenly trying to rid themselves of the Egyptian encumbrance in 1882. It was this that led the Athenians to attack the island of Melos, a potential threat to their sea-lanes (Thucydides 5.97 . . .). The coherence of their empire was always a pressing concern. A second threat to the security of overseas possessions may come from the ambitions of other powers. An empire may be defended by the strength of its natural boundaries but the occasion can arise when further annexations have to be made to prevent strategic land falling into the hands of potential enemies. The operations of Clive against Dupleix in India, or the manœuvring of England and Germany in East Africa, were motivated by just this fear. The policy had been enunciated 2,000 years earlier by the Athenians in Sicily who argued that the justification of their expedition against Syracuse was 'to build up our security with the help of our friends' and to prevent Syracuse from reaching a position which could menace Athenian interests (Thucydides 6.83). The quest for internal security by establishing natural frontiers and eliminating prospective intruders was a cardinal policy of the early imperialists. To us it may seem an obvious quest which commonsense would have dictated without recourse to the advice of Thucydides, but the early Victorian administrators had not the benefit of our experience and hind-sight. They did know Thucydides.

The English, unlike the French or Germans, never attempted to assimilate themselves to their colonial subjects or their colonials to themselves. Therein lay the secret of their success. As far as possible, they relied on indigenous institutions for the running of the country and kept themselves apart. The doctrinaire character of the French Revolution entailed that French institutions were imposed upon the French empire. The Italians too readily melted into the social pattern of their colonies. But the English, preserving their own identity and respecting that of their subjects, governed, and the three distinctive traits of their government, the use of native troops, the preservation of existing institutions and the exploitation of internal politics, were all techniques which Thucydides had singled out as contributing to Athenian supremacy. Especially in India, the limitations of English man-power and the unpopularity of foreign service among English troops meant that the Government had to rely on native auxiliaries for the protection of the state and the maintenance of order. The same policy was adopted in Africa (e.g. the King's African Rifles) and, above all, in Egypt. Despite occasional disasters which, as in the Sudan and at the time of the Indian Mutiny, were due less to the disloyalty of the native troops than to the misjudgement of the central Government, the system worked and did much to dispel the impression of foreign tyranny. The Athenians, for the same reasons, adopted the same policy. Small settlements of Athenian colonists (cleruchies) might be planted in strategic spots as the English had their garrisons of British regulars in India, and Athens, like England, policed the seas. But the main business of providing troops devolved upon the allies. Local operations throughout the empire were officered by Athenians but the troops were native and the money found within the region. The Athenian Tribute Lists preserve records of these minor transactions. The large members of the empire were required to provide ships, smaller communities contributed military contingents: in the Sicilian Expedition more than half of the soldiers engaged on the Athenian side came from the 'allies' (Thucydides 6.43). Where a subject-state has had a long tradition of civilized government, as in India or in the majority of the Greek cities, confidence is increased and self-esteem shielded if the imperial power does not attempt to supersede the existing customs, laws and institutions. Where no such tradition exists, the arbitrary imposition of a foreign code, which has been evolved in a different historical context, is in the long run always futile and in the short run usually catastrophic. With few exceptions the English have been content to accept what they found and to use it for their will. Elphinstone wrote to the first District Commissioner at Poona: "In all cases you will endeavour to enforce the existing laws and customs unless where they are clearly repugnant to reason and natural equity." It was not until this century that egotism led the British to attribute their imperial success to some heaven-sent qualities of their own political system—representative government, the Parliamentary model, the independence of the judiciary, etc.—and to prescribe these panaceas for the government of backward tribes. In the Victorian hey-day, administrators, like Canning, accepted the wisdom of Thucydides who had argued that the minimum disturbance of prevailing laws was essential for political well-being (Thucydides 3.37.3 . . . ; cf. 1.71.3 et al.). Finally, the art of maintaining control consists very largely of exploiting the political differences within a community, of playing one party off against another and of preventing native politicians from forming a united front against the imperial power. This policy was triumphant in India; it would have been triumphant more recently in Africa if it had been carried through with adequate consistency, discretion and lack of scruple. It was second nature to the Athenians, as Hermocrates forcefully reminded the Sicilians (Thucydides 4.59-64).

The English acquired their empire, like the Romans, reluctantly and fortuitously. Having acquired it, how did they seek to use it? The enlightened aim of bringing her subjects by education and the efficient administration of justice to a pitch of civilization at which they could be trusted once more to govern themselves never, I think, seriously occurred to the Victorian proconsuls. Cromer, as late as 1909, could write: "It will be well for England, better for India and best for the cause of progressive civilization in general if it be clearly understood that however liberal may be the concessions . . . we have not the slightest intention of abandoning our Indian possessions and that it is highly improbable that any such intention will be entertained by our posterity." This view the country at large endorsed. The empire was a permanency. Our duty was to govern, our reward was trade not gratitude (cf. Thucydides 2.37 ff.).

Thus despite the fundamental difference that the Athenians were ruling fellow-Greeks of equal intelligence and culture, whereas the English governed heterogeneous and, in many respects, inferior races, the attitude of both states could be summed up in the words of Thucydides (1.76):

> We have done nothing extraordinary, nothing contrary to human nature in accepting an empire . . . and in refusing to give it up. Three very powerful motives prevent us from doing so—security, honour and self-interest. . . . Those who really deserve praise are the people who, while human enough to enjoy power, nevertheless pay more attention to justice than they are compelled to do by their situation. Certainly we think that if anyone else was in our position, it would soon be evident whether we act with moderation or not. . . .

The fatal weakness of the British empire was exposed by those very problems to which the Athenian empire provided no parallels. The Athenians did not have to surmount the obstacles of race, religion and colour.

So far we have considered the impact which the idolization of the Athenians had on educational ideals and public life. Scratch a Victorian and you will find an Athenian underneath, or at least what the Victorians beguiled by Thucydides and Plato would have liked an Athenian to be. The characteristic elements of nineteenth-century England—liberal education, committee administration, the Public School system, imperialism—were all the result of various combinations of historical circumstances, but the particular forms which they took were consciously moulded by the tendency of educated Englishmen to view themselves and their country in the mirror of ancient Athens. The feeling that there was an historical pattern for England's destiny, an "example laid up in heaven", which a classical education enabled them to perceive and to imitate, gave men a sense of direction which was badly needed in an age of rapid progress. The pervasive appeal of Plato helped them to formulate common and coherent attitudes of their own.

But unlike Ovid and Horace, Plato is a many-sided and contradictory figure. He is part logician, part mystic, part educationalist, part artist, part liberal, part authoritarian. Even in philosophy he was the intellectual progenitor both of the Utilitarians and of the Idealists. Whereas the common image of Ovid and Horace in the seventeenth and eighteenth centuries omitted few of their actual features, the Victorian conception of Plato excluded at least two facets of his enigmatic personality, and since these were the inspiration of two minor but crucial movements in the last quarter of the century it is worth examining them separately through the eyes of the men who led the movements and who responded most warmly to Plato's call.

To Mark Pattison, Jowett was no more than the headmaster of an enviably successful Public School, but Jowett believed in more than the production of good Civil Servants and Christian gentlemen.[4] He had always revered Plato, and the alliance of public furore over his part in *Essays and Reviews* and the Colenso Case with personal dissatisfaction in his relationship with Florence Nightingale drove him to take increasing refuge in the study and translation of the *Dialogues.* He wrote in 1862 to Dean Elliot: "You greatly undervalue Plato who is a most faithful friend to me—too faithful for indeed I can't get rid of him." Plato did indeed enlighten his Anglicanism but the voice of Plato that spoke most persuasively in Jowett's ear was the voice of success. Walter Sichel, who was up at Balliol in the 1870s, wrote that "the middling sort of man never appealed to him. He preferred extremes, cultivating either the young Alcibiades or the incipient Cleon. Like Socrates, his function was 'to rouse, persuade and rebuke'." So, more naïvely, Almond commented: "He was a Platonist all over and from Plato I never could extract more than one graspable idea, and that was the education of his ideal governors." While most Victorians nourished the conception of an educated, if narrow, democracy ("the muscular Christian"),

Jowett worked towards a more stringent end, that of a dedicated élite. It was the Guardians in the *Republic* that he sought to train, not the upper middle classes, as the parody in Mallock's *New Republic* makes all too clear. The success of his mission was to have a profound effect on the character of the succeeding generation; for Jowett encouraged a small but decisive section of the flower of England in a certain way of thinking and because that section was conspicuous and powerful its attitude, which in the final analysis amounted to the pursuit of personal excellence (the Homeric ἀρετη), tended to permeate downwards throughout society. The history of Jowett's proselytism has been too well documented in individual biographies and in Sir Geoffrey Faber's life of Jowett to merit elaboration here.

A very different reading of Plato was made by Walter Pater (1839-1894). Pater, like Jowett and Pattison, had attempted to reconcile Christianity and Platonism and in his *Pico della Mirandola* had adumbrated a reinterpretation of ancient philosophy in the belief that "nothing which has interested the human mind could wholly lose its vitality", but, as Benson wrote, "at bottom Jowett was a man of the world and valued effectiveness above most qualities, while Pater set no particular value upon administrative energy. Jowett was indifferent to art, except in so far as it ministered to agreeable social intercourse; with Pater art provided what were the deepest and most sacred experiences of his life." Jowett was blind to aesthetic sensibility; in Sichel's words, "though Plato formed the refrain of his life, there was little Hellenic about him—none of the glow for beauty". But Plato was a great artist, an artist both in his use of language and in the range and intensity of his vision. Macaulay believed that "the merit of Plato lies in his talent for narrative and description, in his rhetoric, in his humour, and in his exquisite Greek", and Pater, steeped in the *Phaedrus,* the *Symposium* and the myths, was touched by a still warmer enthusiasm. Pater lectured at Oxford on Plato and his lectures, like those of Sewell a generation earlier, were notorious for their artistic digressions. Humphrey Ward recalled: "I remember as we went out a senior man who used to amaze us with his ready translations of Thucydides . . . threw down his note-book with the cry 'No more of that for me; if Greats means that, I'll cut 'em' (which he wisely did)." But his interpretation of Plato was perhaps more faithful than Jowett's. He saw Plato not as a systematic philosopher with a defined creed but as a highly sensitive artist on whom the impressions of beauty and emotion acted to excite an awareness of some deeper beauty beyond. "We are not", he said, "naturally formed to love or be interested in, or attracted towards the abstract as such. We cannot love or live upon genus and species, accident or substance, but for our minds, as for our bodies, need an orchard or a garden with fruit and roses." In revolt from the continued ugliness of Victorian Utilitarianism, Pater preached the anti-creed of the aesthete.

Walter Pater, 1839-1894, English essayist and critic.

Plato and Platonism (1893) is a turning point in late Victorian thinking; it voiced the discontent of the younger generation with the means that society took for granted—prosperity, character, religion—and attracted attention to the question of ends. What should men aim at? Money? Position? Respectability? Or Beauty? Integrity? Communism? Plato became the hero of the aesthete (the Rossettis and Oscar Wilde as much as William Morris and Swinburne) and the god of the agnostics (Morley no less than Meredith). Thus F. W. H. Myers writes of Rossetti's sonnet *Under the Arch:*

> Rossetti was ignorant of Greek . . . but his idealizing spirit has reproduced the myth of the *Phaedrus*—even to the τρέφεταῖ καὶ εὐπᾷθεῖ—the words that affirm the repose and well-being of the soul when she perceives beneath the arch of heaven the pure Idea which is at once her sustenance and her lord . . . for Beauty, as Plato has told us, is of all the divine ideas at once most manifest and most lovable to men.

The sonnet itself is a precious example of aesthetic Platonism:

> Under the arch of Life, where love and death,
> Terror and mystery, guard her shrine, I saw
> Beauty enthroned; and though her gaze
> struck awe,

I drew it in as simply as my breath.
Hers are the eyes which, over and beneath,
The sky and sea bend on thee; which can draw,
By sea or sky or woman, to one law
The allotted bondman of her palm and wreath.
This is that Lady Beauty, in whose praise
Thy voice and hand shake still—long known to thee
By flying hair and fluttering hem—the best
Following her daily of thy heart and feet
How passionately and irretrievably,
In what fond flight, how many ways and days!

It is a strange testimony to the gregarious nature of human thought that Plato should have wielded so much posthumous power in so many different forms.

The activity of scholars takes its direction from the prevailing interests of the age. The intellectual atmosphere dictates the syllabus and the syllabus prescribes research. So there is always an underlying connection between what the lady of fashion reads in her boudoir and what the scholar writes in his study. The early nineteenth century, dominated by an awareness of social problems, had turned to history as offering an insight into the present through the comparable movements of the past. If the appreciation of ancient history was to be advanced by more than elegance of style or political interpretation, it was necessary both to evaluate critically the worth of the ancient sources and to supplement those sources by external evidence. The Germans had done pioneering work in the former and their work is mirrored in the popular essay of Sir George Cornewall Lewis on the *Credibility of Early Roman History* (1855) and in the incomplete but forceful *History of Rome* written by Thomas Arnold (1838-43), in the *History of the Decline of the Roman Republic* (1864-74), by George Long, who as a Professor of Greek and then of Latin at University College, London, had edited Cicero's *Speeches* and Caesar's *Gallic War* and had translated Plutarch's *Roman Lives,* and in the two masterpieces of Charles Merivale (1808-1894), Dean of Ely, the *History of the Romans under the Empire* and the *History of the Roman Republic.* Grote was the champion of this approach to Greek history.

These scholars brought rational scepticism to bear upon the testimony of the ancient historians. They asked what evidence could Herodotus or Thucydides have had for this or that assertion. They attempted to distinguish myth from legend and to account for the development of both. One of the best specimens of their method is Grote's article on *Early Grecian Legends* in the *Westminster Review* of 1843. The profits of such investigations, as of the exhaustive chronological researches of H. F. Clinton (*Fasti Hellenici,* 1824-32; *Fasti Romani,* 1845-50), are inevitably limited. The capital from which they are derived, the classical historians, is not expansible. A far wider prospect was opened up by the exploration of the ancient lands themselves. Grote had never travelled farther than Paestum and did not regard firsthand knowledge of Greece as being a prerequisite for writing Greek history. In this he was already old-fashioned; economic and political trends in antiquity were largely conditioned by geographical factors. The outburst of colonizing activity from 750-550 B.C. should be viewed with the Greek countryside in mind. The valleys of mainland Greece have a strictly limited area of cultivatable land: when that is all in use, there are no reserves to provide extra food for an increased population. The role of Megara in the fifth century can be appreciated only by a traveller who has seen that the routes from the Peloponnese to the north lead through the Megarid, and that there is no natural boundary between Attica and the Peloponnese except to the west of the Megarid. The systematic survey of classical lands was carried out by Colonel W. M. Leake who, even before retiring from the army and being invited by the Foreign Office to undertake the task, had published *Researches in Greece* (1814). He followed this with four definitive works—*Topography of Athens and the Demi* (1821), *Journal of a Tour in Asia Minor* (1824), *The Morea* (1830) and *Travels in Northern Greece* (1835-41). Important contributions were made by J. A. Cramer (1793-1843), Professor of Modern History at Oxford, with his *Geographical and Historical Description of Greece* (1823) and *Asia* (1832), and by Christopher Wordsworth (1808-1885), Bishop of Lincoln, who discovered the site of Dodona (*Athens and Attica,* 1836; *Greece* 1839). Lycia was surveyed by Charles Fellows (1838-40) and Crete by Captain T. A. B. Spratt (1851-3). The Greek East was inevitably less familiar than Roman Italy but even there much lay uncharted beyond the well-worn routes of the tourist. Many important sites were identified and recorded in Dennis's *Cities and Cemeteries of Etruria* (1848) and Burn's *Rome and the Campagna* (1871).

The interest in geography which had prompted these explorers and the discoveries which they published found their place in the commentaries and histories. Arnold brought new light to many of the geographical questions in Thucydides, and Herodotus was well served by J. W. Blakesley (1808-1885), Dean of Lincoln, whose edition (1852-4) paid particular attention to geography, and by G. Rawlinson (1815-1902), who enlisted the aid of his brother, Sir Henry Rawlinson, a distinguished Assyriologist, in the compilation of notes and essays to accompany his translation published in 1858. William More (1799-1860), Member of Parliament for Renfrewshire, visited Greece in 1838 and his *Critical History of the Literature of Ancient Greece* (1850-7) benefits both from his personal acquaintance with the country and from the methodological agnosticism of the Germans. E. A. Freeman (1823-1892),

Regius Professor of Modern History at Oxford, based his *History of Sicily from the Earliest Times* (1891-4) on scrupulous examination of the ancient texts and intimate knowledge gleaned from four long visits to the island. Among Roman historians the most notable exponent of the two new advances was Henry Pelham (1846-1907), President of Trinity College, Oxford, a great teacher in an age of great teaching, whose *Outlines of Roman History* (1890) combined a succinct and able résumé of Mommsen's monumental study of the Roman constitution with a sure grasp of the Italian scene.

Towards the end of the century archaeology began to supplant topography as the chief source of new light on the ancient past. One of the earliest and most enterprising archaeologists, C. T. Newton, was appointed Keeper to the Department of Greek and Roman Antiquities in 1861 after ten years in the Consular Service which he had spent excavating and exploring in Ionia and the Aegean Islands (*History of Discoveries at Halicarnassus, Cnidus and Branchidae,* 1862; *Travels and Discoveries in the Levant,* 1865; *Essays in Art and Archaeology,* 1880). Newton laboured to promote archaeology and the excavations at Priene, Ephesus and Rhodes owed much to his support. Sandys writes that "his appointment [as Keeper] marked the dawn of a true interest in classical archaeology in England". The British School of Archaeology at Athens was founded in 1879 and, at Oxford, a new chair in classical archaeology was instituted, despite the opposition of Jowett, in 1885. P. Gardner and Farnell began to give lectures which aroused considerable interest, but these enthusiasms belonged rather to the new generation, to the rediscovery of Homer, than to the old world of Greats. In the period under review it was not the subterranean disclosures of archaeology but the visible monuments of art and perception of geographical phenomena which added to the range and profundity of classical scholarship.

On Thucydides was unleashed the full force of this combination of scholarly activities. S. T. Bloomfield, of Sidney Sussex College, Cambridge, followed an edition of the Greek Testament with an annotated translation of Thucydides (1829). Richard Shilleto, who was for many years a private tutor in Cambridge and who coached many of the most successful candidates in the Tripos, was, as an education at Shrewsbury and Cambridge predisposed, primarily a writer of Latin and Greek verse, and the promise which a masterly edition of Demosthenes' *de Falsa Legatione* (1844) held out for the success of his long-projected commentary on Thucydides was never fulfilled. Like many other tutors he found that teaching increasingly absorbed his time and energies—and would not have had it otherwise. In the event only two Books saw the light (1872-80). J. W. Donaldson (1811-1861), headmaster of Bury St. Edmunds until forced to resign by an ill-judged attempt to prove that "the lost book of Jasher constituted 'the religious marrow of the Scriptures'", is remembered chiefly for his part in introducing the study of comparative philology to England (*New Cratylus,* 1839), but, besides editions of Pindar (1841) and Sophocles' *Antigone* he was also responsible for a text of Thucydides (1859). Another East Anglian headmaster, H. A. Holden (1822-1896), who taught at Ipswich for twenty-five years after resigning a Fellowship at Trinity College, Cambridge, crowned a scholarly career which had embraced editions of Xenophon and Plutarch's *Lives* and a text of Aristophanes with a detailed and thorough commentary on the Seventh Book of Thucydides. W. Y. Sellar, for many years Professor of Humanity at Edinburgh, whose *Roman Poets of the Republic* and *Virgil* graced the bookshelves of every cultured home, had made his name with an essay on *The Characteristics of Thucydides* (1855). The outstanding Greek scholar of the second half of the century, Sir Richard Jebb (1841-1905), Regius Professor of Greek at Cambridge from 1888 to 1905 and Member of Parliament for the University, was that rare combination a man of letters who was also a disciplined scholar. His place in scholarship is assured by his *Attic Orators* (1876) and his series of commentaries on the plays of Sophocles (1883-96) but he had first achieved notice by an essay on *The Speeches of Thucydides* which he contributed to Evelyn Abbott's volume *Hellenica* (1866). This was to be expected of a man with his broad humanism and concern for contemporary educational issues (cf. his *Essays and Addresses*), whose life-work united monographs on Erasmus, Bentley and Porson with a translation of Theophrastus and an edition of Bacchylides. As will be seen in the next chapter, Jebb bridged the period of two tastes. Perhaps the most striking case is W. G. Rutherford (1853-1907), headmaster of Westminster School for eighteen years. Rutherford's talent for language had been "discovered" by Jowett and his finest achievements in scholarship were the analytical study of Attic Greek (*New Phrynichus,* 1881) and the appraisal of the methods used by ancient commentators, especially the scholiasts on Aristophanes (*Scholia Aristophanica,* 1896; *A Chapter in the History of Annotation,* 1905). Yet current taste—or was it piety to Jowett?—led him to produce an edition of the Fourth Book of Thucydides (1889). As an edition it is a curiosity: all the linguistic difficulties are eliminated as interpolations ("adscripts"). In 1891 E. C. Marchant began to publish his serviceable school-editions of separate books on Thucydides.

It is noteworthy that almost all the leading scholars devoted a major part of their working lives to the understanding either of Thucydides or Plato. The secondary study of Plato as a creative philosopher and the impulse which that gave to the development of English philosophy would go beyond the limits of the present essay. Grote had intended to include a chapter on Plato in his *History of Greece* but finding that the subject outgrew the scope of the *History* he laid it aside to be treated fully in a three-volume treatise, *Plato and the other Companions of Socrates,* published in 1865. For a generation it was the standard textbook on the philosopher and its ruthless criticism was a foil to the broader sweep of introductions and interpretative essays that accompanied Jowett's complete translation (1871). Between them Grote and Jowett supplied a comprehensive survey of Plato's philosophy. The catalogue of classical exegeses of Plato is in itself equally as impressive. B. H. Kennedy, the schoolboy's grammarian, who ended his life as Regius Professor of Greek at Cambridge (1867-89), had continued Butler's work as headmaster of Shrewsbury in encouraging the study of Greek. Although his forte was the composition of Latin verse, he did much, if in a somewhat pedagogic spirit, for the elucidation of the Greek poets (*Studia Sophoclea,* 1874, 1884). His best work, however, is perhaps the translation of Plato's *Theaetetus* with annotations. Kennedy's predecessor as Regius Professor, W. H. Thompson, who resigned in 1866 on election to the Mastership of Trinity College which he held for the next twenty years, was a copious contributor to the study of Plato. In addition to writing judicious commentaries on the *Phaedrus* (1868) and the *Gorgias* (1872) and essays on Platonic topics in the *Journal of Philology,* he stimulated more general interest in Plato by wide-ranging and original lectures on Greek philosophy at Cambridge. A friend and contemporary of Thompson, Charles Badham, mitigated the restlessness of a nature that drove him from Oxford across half Europe to Cambridge and eventually led him through three brief headmasterships to the chair of classics in Sydney, Australia, sufficiently to produce editions of the *Phaedrus, Philebus, Euthydemus, Laches* and *Symposium.* Badham's inclination, as his career reveals, was towards the Porsonian school of textual criticism rather than the contemporary fashion for philosophical comment, but the text of Plato had been little studied and required the healing hand of a critic. The soundest Platonic scholar of the age was probably James Adam (1860-1907). After a stern training in the classics at Aberdeen University where he imbibed a love of Plato from W. G. Geddes, the editor of the *Phaedo* (1863), Adam came down to Cambridge to broaden his erudition with the study of philosophy and philology. The fruits of this wide education were divulged in his brilliant lectures and in a line of editions of Plato. The *Apology, Crito, Euthyphro* and *Protagoras* led up to the monumental commentary on the *Republic* (1902), which, recently reprinted, remains the standard English commentary. An obsession with the problem of the Platonic number (which he argued to be 12,960,000) did not impair his singularly balanced judgement of ancient and modern speculation. Of less accomplished scholars E. H. Gifford should be mentioned for his *Euthydemus* (1901). E. M. Cope, a pupil of Kennedy and an unsuccessful rival for the Regius chair in 1867, made his name by an *Introduction to Aristotle's Rhetoric* (1867) but advanced Platonic studies by creative and illuminating translations of the *Gorgias* (1864) and the *Phaedo.* Since Plato occupied such a central place in the Greats syllabus, it was natural that Oxford should conceive of a series of commentaries on the principal *Dialogues.* The inspiration was Jowett's and most of the collaborators were Balliol men: James Riddell edited the *Apology* (1867), Lewis Campbell, better known as the editor of Sophocles, the *Theaetetus* (1861), *Sophistes* and *Politicus* (1867), and Edward Poste the *Philebus* (1860). Jowett and Campbell, after long delays, produced a jointly ephemeral *Republic* (1894) which was quickly superseded by Adam's. A more enduring study was *Essays on Plato's Republic* by the ill-fated Balliol scholar, R. L. Nettleship, who lost his life on Mount Blanc in 1892.

There were few scholars who were untouched by the fever of the age and only three whose names still add lustre to the history of learning in England. It may be that they were the natural scholars, men who, whatever the atmosphere and interests of their generation, would have done what they did regardless, as distinct from the professional scholars who take their colour from the world around them and bend their intellectual energies as fashion directs. The latter must always make up the majority. For every ten people of ability there is only one with an original sense of purpose, and just as some momentum, born of inertia, led intellectuals unthinkingly 200 years ago towards the "purple power and profit" of the Church, and leads them today towards the sanctuary of the Senior Common Room, so the habit of conformity induced all but the few to research into Plato and Thucydides in the nineteenth century and induces them to investigate the social background of nonentities today. Latin studies were comparatively neglected and their prestige was enhanced by the timely creation of new chairs of Latin at Oxford (1854) and Cambridge (1869). The first holders were both remarkable men. John Conington represented an old-world type of scholarship. He was not interested in philosophy, in religious controversy or in social diagnosis. He brought to the study of Virgil an appreciation of literature, and his edition, however deficient it may be in "higher scholarship", is one of the few sensitive and acute pieces of Victorian literary criticism (1863-71). Conington died at the age of forty-four. The first Latin professor at Cambridge was H. A. J. Munro (1819-1885), a man of stalwart energy, whose researches ranged from Euripides and Aristotle to Lucilius and Catullus but whose main work was concentrated on the interpretation of Lucretius. Lucretius, since his brief blaze of popularity in the late seventeenth century, was an author almost unread in England. His atheism commended him even less to public taste than the crudity of his verse and the unevenness of his style. Munro's edition (1884)—which was unrivalled for nearly a century until Cyril Bailey's in

1949—restored Lucretius to his true place in popular esteem as one of the most forceful of Latin poets. Henry Nettleship, elder brother of R. L., who succeeded Conington as Latin professor in 1870, after a nine-year interregnum during which the chair was filled by Edwin Palmer, had been inspired by affection to complete his predecessor's editions of Virgil and Persius (1872) but there could hardly have been two more different men. Nettleship had studied under Haupt in Germany and sought to introduce to Oxford the full apparatus of German higher criticism, with its attention to philological and textual criticism. He himself broke new ground with his investigation into the ancient grammarians, Verrius Flaccus and Nonius, but the response which his lexicographical zeal evoked is a mute testimony to his originality: no one attended his lectures. He died before his influence could make itself felt in the University and left only scattered publications most of which were posthumously assembled in two stimulating volumes of *Lectures* and *Essays* (1885, 1895).

These were exceptional and individual men. Over the age as a whole, over its thought as well as its scholarship, brooded the spirits of Plato and Thucydides, and Arnold and Jowett were their appointed spokesmen. Neither was an exact scholar (Arnold's enthusiasm for philology was amateurish: A. E. Housman gave up attending Jowett's lectures because he was 'disgusted by his disregard for the niceties of scholarship') but both left fitting memorials, in the part they played in the redirection of classical education and national character and in their published works. Arnold had for many years worked on a *Lexicon Thucydideum* and on a commentary on Thucydides (1830-5), which illustrated 'his belief in the progress and inherent excellence of popular principles [and] in the distinct stages of civilization through which nations have to pass'. Jowett followed his translation of Plato with a lucid and moving translation of Thucydides (1881).

> If Greek literature is not to pass away, it seems to be necessary that in every age some one who has drunk deeply from the original fountain should renew the love of it in the world and once more present that old life with its great ideas and great actions, its creations in politics and in art, like the distant remembrance of youth, before the delighted eyes of mankind.
>
> (Jowett, from the *Preface* to *Thucydides*)[5]

English scholars could pride themselves that by their efforts at least two authors had been conjured back to life in the nineteenth century.

Notes

[1] A highlight of the campaign was Hazlitt's essay, *On the Ignorance of the Learned.*

[2] The Victorian regard for Plato is the subject of an essay entitled 'New Hellenic Renaissance' in J. E. Baker's *Reinterpretation of Victorian Literature* (Princeton, 1950).

[3] I have myself heard a Head of a House describe rowing as "more than a religion, a way of life".

[4] Balliol has always been a microcosm of England in cultural taste. Two centuries before Jowett, Henry, Savage, Master of Balliol, had published *Ballio fergus* (1661), the first history of a College in either Oxford or Cambridge. This is redolent of Ovid. Discussing the mismanagement of the College estates at Old Woodstock he assails Mr. Chapman who "tempted us with a handsome well-situated house: not forgetting that of the Poet

> Aspicis ut veniant ad candida tecta columbae
> Accipiat nullos sordida turris oves,
> [=*Tristia* 1.9.7-8]

A hundred years later the extensive Mastership of Theophilus Leigh, who had owed his election more to his connections than his talents, was drawing to a close. Leigh wrote to a correspondent: "I would have every young gentleman read Horace. It will keep him from the town and may improve his mind." Jowett's love of Plato was continued into this century by Lord Lindsay. The cultural disunity which prevails in 1963 is precisely symbolized by the fact that most men appointed today as heads of Colleges of Universities are in no sense preachers of an educational gospel but are qualified, by capacity or by inclination, as administrators.

[5] It was this translation that Mr. Asquith gave Lady Ottoline Bentinck (Morrell) to take and read at Syracuse.

Richard Jenkyns (essay date 1980)

SOURCE: "The Interpretation of Greece," in *The Victorians and Ancient Greece,* Harvard University Press, 1980, pp. 155-91.

[*In the essay that follows, which ranges broadly through academic and popular Victorian culture, Jenkyns demonstrates how Victorians depicted ancient Greece according to the desire to see themselves in certain lights.*]

The Greek Language

From Coleridge to Kingsley, from Sydney Smith to Wilde, writers loved to declare that the very language of Greece was an enchantment, and far superior even to the Latin tongue. "You have come to hear my ode!" says a Roman poet in Lytton's *Last Days of Pompeii.* "That is indeed an honour; you, a Greek—to whom the very language of common life is poetry." Macaulay decided, "The Latin language is principally valuable as an introduction to the Greek. . . . We cannot refuse our admiration to that . . . perfect machine of human thought, to the flexibility, the harmony, the gigantic power, the exquisite delicacy, the infinite wealth of words".[1]

As a boy Winckelmann was thrilled by the mere sight of Greek lettering;[2] the enticement of those symbols drew him on to the studies that were to govern his life. Children love runes and codes and cabbalistic signs; even in adult life there is perhaps a childlike pleasure, as Tolkien discovered to his profit, to be derived from the exploration of unfamiliar letter-forms, the sense of initiation into a secret or a mystery. Now of all the languages that a western European in the last century might expect to use only Greek was not written in the Roman script. In *Romola* Baldassarre's recovery of power is symbolized by his recovery of Greek letters, "magic signs", and George Eliot stresses her point by writing them in big black capitals on their own. Hardy is still more typographically emphatic: in a single chapter of *Jude the Obscure* H KAINH ΛΙΑΘΗΚΗ is written three times, and every time in capital letters.[3] These words, Greek for "The New Testament", unite Jude's religious emotions and his classical studies; they represent to him his Christian duty and, at the same time, the worldly ambitions that he hopes to realize through an education in the ancient tongues. He stares at the letters; then, conquered by the lusts of the flesh, rushes off to the voluptuous Arabella. When he returns,

> There lay his book . . . , and the capital letters . . . regarded him with fixed reproach . . . , like the unclosed eyes of a dead man:
>
> H KAINH ΛΙΑΘΗΚΗ
>
> The sheer sound of Greek is also a delight to Jude:[4]
>
> The policemen and belated citizens passing along under his window might have heard . . . strange syllables mumbled with fervour within—words that had for Jude an indescribable enchantment: . . .
>
> 'All hemin heis Theos ho Pater, ex hou ta panta, kai hemeis eis auton.'

We can hardly doubt that the enchantment was as strong upon Hardy as upon his Jude Fawley. It was even stronger upon Schliemann, whose story might seem to belong more to hagiography than to real life. He was fourteen years old and a grocer's apprentice when he heard a man reciting Homer and prayed to have the happiness of learning Greek. Later he made his fortune in the indigo trade, but threw it up at the age of thirty-six in order to devote the rest of his life to archaeology. He had been learning Greek for two years, not daring to begin earlier for fear of falling under the spell of Homer and neglecting his livelihood.[5] No doubt the words that he heard in the grocer's shop were wrongly pronounced; none the less, the beauty that he found there need not have been the product of self-deception. Greek is exceptionally abundant in short, light syllables; its fluidity and grace are qualities that hardly any pronunciation can destroy. It is equally fluid as a medium of expression; MacNeice explained,

> There are things you can do in Greek you never could do in English. The two negatives for instance—*ou* and *mē*—and even more the exquisite subtlety of the double negative *mē ou.* And the wealth of particles. . . . And that wonderful Greek word *an* which you can even tack on to a participle . . . the same with hockey; we learnt the economy of the wrist-flick, began to aspire in all things to a grace that was apparently effortless.

Virginia Woolf attempted to analyse the special quality of Greek:

> Every ounce of fat has been pared off. . . . Then, spare and bare as it is, no language can move more quickly. . . . Then there are the words themselves which . . . we have made expressive to us of our own emotions, *thalassa, thanatos, anthos* [sea, death, flower] . . . so clear, so hard, so intense, that to speak plainly yet fittingly without blurring the outline . . . , Greek is the only expression. It is useless, then, [she added with crushing certitude] to read Greek in translation.[6]

She brought out the taut simplicity of the Greek by attacking a recent translation: "Professor Mackail says 'wan', and the age of Burne-Jones and Morris is at once evoked." No doubt she was right; but did she manage any better herself? Her metaphors of clear waters, bright sunlight, sharp outlines, and naked athletic bodies evoke the age of Arnold and Pater, overlaid with the fastidiousness of an upper-class Englishwoman: "Greek is the only expression"—"Liberty's is the only shop." Perhaps she gives a fair impression of the language of Sophocles, but her account is hopelessly inapplicable to Aeschylus or Thucydides or almost any other Greek writer. It is probably impossible to define in words the distinctive character of any language, not least because one of the qualities of any good language is the capacity to be used in very different ways. A lady is alleged to have said, "It's a funny thing. The French call it a couteau and the Germans call it a Messer, but we call it a knife, which after all is what it really *is.*" She had a point; somehow we feel that *thalassa* is not quite the same thing as sea. Perhaps this is a sentimental feeling; at least it can easily become so. "Oh, Chronos, Chronos, this is too bad of you!" exclaims Bunthorne in Gilbert's *Patience. Chronos* simply means "time;" the aesthete uses a Greek word to disguise the banality of what he says. Beerbohm lists the works of Enoch Soames: "Next, a dialogue between Pan and St. Ursula—lacking, I rather felt, in 'snap.' Next, some aphorisms (entitled ἀφορςσμᾷτᾷν [aphorismata])."[7] Again, the Greek word, and still more the Greek script, add a touch of spurious distinction.

Gilbert and Beerbohm were plainly satirical, but when Wilde wrote *The Critic as Artist,* he may not have known himself whether he was in jest or in earnest. Pater had discovered how a foreign word or two could be used to season the dish: "It has been said that all the great Florentines were preoccupied with death. *Outre-tombe! Outre-tombe!*—is the burden of their thoughts."[8] A tart, paradoxical savour comes from the application of words so richly redolent of French romanticism to the fresh world of an earlier Italy. Wilde goes a step further, blending Greece with both France and Germany: speaking of the overture to *Tannhäuser* (a work which itself puts pagan Venus into northern, Christian Europe), his Gilbert says, "To-night it may fill one with that *erōs tōn adunatōn,* that Amour de l'Impossible . . ." Pater is again in Wilde's mind when Gilbert lights a cigarette. Marius took "for his philosophic ideal the *monochronos hēdonē* of Aristippus—the pleasure . . . of the mystic *now.*" Gilbert remarks, "There is nothing left for me now but the divine *monochronos hēdonē* of another cigarette." There is a piquancy about using a Greek expression to describe a uniquely modern pleasure. Brooke found a piquancy of a different but kindred kind when he wrote from Berlin,[9]

> *eithe genoimēn* . . . would I were
> In Grantchester, in Grantchester!

The Greek words are simply the equivalent of the English "would I were"; but the mere sound of those lucid syllables is enough to intensify the poet's yearning. He contrasts them with the ponderous words, oppressive both in sound and meaning, that he hears and sees about him, words such as *temperamentvoll* and *verboten.* He feels confined and constricted, but his longing to escape from his Teutonic surroundings, though expressed in Greek words, is directed not towards Greece itself, as it would have been in Pater, but rather—and here is the tang of paradox—to his native England. That is his land of lost content; familiar, undramatic countryside, though there glows upon its surface the bloom of a Hellenic loveliness:

> Is dawn a secret shy and cold
> Anadyomene, silver-gold?

anaduomenē, "arising"—the epithet of Aphrodite, born from the sea to be goddess of love and beauty.

Confined at Reading in no merely metaphorical sense, Wilde revelled in reading his Greek Testament, deriving a special pleasure from the erroneous belief that the Galilean peasants were bilingual and that Christ spoke Greek:

> It is a delight to me to think that . . . Charmides might have listened to him, and Socrates reasoned with him . . . : that he really said *egō eimi ho poimēn ho kalos* ['I am the good shepherd.'] . . . and that his last word when he cried out "My life has been completed, has reached its fulfilment, has been perfected" was exactly as St. John tells us it was: *tetelestai:* no more.[10]

Wilde points to the pregnant concision of Greek: the single word *tetelestai* contains all that is in his English paraphrase. Overcome by the charm of the language, he could not resist slipping in simple Greek words as he wrote: "the Greek woman—the *gunē Hellēnis*", "'God's Kingdom'—*hē basileia tou theou*". The game that he played in *The Critic as Artist* had grown serious.

A taste for Greek vocabulary was a conspicuous feature of decadent sensibility, and words such as "sardonyx" and "asphodel" were freely employed by aesthetic individuals, who sometimes, one suspects, had very vague ideas about what the stone or the flower looked like. A less elevated but no less sincere tribute to the attraction of the Greek language was paid by the banausic world that the aesthetes so despised. The slang of the educated classes included words like nous, kudos and hoi polloi; lawn tennis was first introduced as Sphairistike; a new board game was named Halma; galoshes were called antigropelos, an expression allegedly derived from the Greek words for "against wet mud". These are but distant echoes from the heights of Parnassus, where a single word might be a talisman. Byron wrote of the day "When Marathon became a magic *word*"; Cory, bitterly grieved by his dismissal from Eton, planned by way of consolation to write a little book of Greek Iambics and call it Iophon. Nothing but the name would carry me through."[11]

Euphony plays only a small part in such emotions. Most obviously, Marathon became a magic word because the Persians were defeated there. Wilde is pleased to think that Jesus spoke Greek partly because he associates the language with Athens, with Socrates and the fair Charmides. No doubt Cory's feelings were similar, while Brooke in his Berlin café was probably remembering those odes of tragedy in which the chorus yearn to escape from the sorrows around them to a land of bliss and quietude. We cannot entirely separate the way a word sounds to us from the associations that it suggests; perhaps that is part of what Virginia Woolf meant when she said that we have made Greek words "expressive to us of our own emotions". The word "sardonyx", for instance, appeals to a certain cast of mind because it is exotic; the exoticism derives partly from the spelling of the word, partly from its Greek etymology, partly from the nature of what it denotes (a jewel), partly from the contexts in which it has been used in modern literature. This does not mean that no word is intrinsically more euphonious than any other. MacNeice described his first sight of the Atlantic from the hills of Connemara: "Something rose inside me and shouted 'The Sea!' Thalassa! Thalassa! to hell with all the bivouacs in the desert; . . . the endless parasangs have ended."[12] But why does every schoolboy know that Xenophon's soldiers cried "Thalassa, thalassa" when they saw the sea? Because of the unforgettable sound of the words, the sound of the sea itself.

Leafing through any anthology of Victorian verse, one finds numbers of Greek names—Apollo, Hermione, Naiads and Dryads—starting from the pages. This is a tribute to their magic, but a limited tribute. We see Greek mythology hazily, through the veils successively laid over it by the Romans, the Renaissance and the classicism of the eighteenth century. "Now lies the earth all Danaë to the stars," says Tennyson in a line that conjures up the hushed expectancy of a wide, quiet land and marvellously suggests the night's strange mingling of peace with ecstacy; and we think not of ancient Greece but of the Italian Renaissance, of Titian's great evocations of voluptuous calm.[13] Earnest efforts were made to strip Greek names and stories of associative accretions. People had been accustomed to call the gods by their Roman names, even when they were talking about Greek history and literature; but in the course of the century this custom gradually died out. As Arnold said, "Hera and Juno are actually, to every scholar's imagination, two different people." Even the spelling of words could make a difference. "When we employ our C to designate the Greek K," Grote declared, " . . . we mar the unrivalled euphony of the Greek language." But Macaulay "never could reconcile himself to seeing the friends of his boyhood figure as Kleon, and Alkibiadês, and Poseidôn"; and Matthew Arnold felt that the reformed spelling led into "a wilderness of pedantry".[14] Even Grote allowed a few names to retain their familiar form; Browning was more ruthless:

> Aischulos' bronze-throat eagle-bark at blood
> Has somehow spoilt my taste for twitterings.[15]

The difficulty is that the reformed spelling carries with it as many overtones as the old. We are scarcely surprised that the radical, utilitarian Grote adopts a "rational" orthography, while the whig historian clings to "the friends of his boyhood". Equally Arnold's aspirations to a calm classicism lead him naturally to choose the time-honoured forms, whereas the new spelling seems to suit Browning's picture of Aeschylus' rugged genius. The eye plays a part in our perceptions of euphony, and the syllables that sound melodious when we read them in the original lettering can come to seem rough and barbarous if they are transliterated into our own script. The objection to Latinate spellings is that they blur the edges of Greek names, so that they resemble those statues which Pater valued the more because time had softened their outlines; the objection to the reformed spelling is that it makes the Greeks seem outlandish. Arnold put his case well: "The real question is this: whether our living apprehension of the Greek world is more checked by meeting . . . names not spelt letter for letter as in the original Greek, or by meeting names which make us rub our eyes and call out, 'How exceedingly odd!'" Even now the scholars who examine the Greeks from an anthropological or psychoanalytical standpoint tend to eschew Latinized spellings and the literary critics to retain them.

Greek names were often contrasted with dull, unromantic English names. Byron takes leave to praise Don Juan's friend Johnson,

> though his name, than Ajax or Achilles
> Sounds less harmonious.

And Thackeray declares, "One would fancy fate was of an aristocratic turn, and took especial delight in combats with princely houses—the Atridae, the Borbonidae, the Ivrys; the Browns and Joneses being of no account." Place-names could be used as well (to this day the English find the mention of Wigan or Neasden irresistibly comic): Mallock's Mr. Rose contrasts the Hellenic elegance of his ideal society with "abominable advertisements of excursion trains to Brighton, or of Horniman's cheap tea".[16] He concedes that even in his utopia there will be "the necessary *kapēloi*", but they will be "out of the way, in a sort of Piraeus". *Kapēloi* simply means "retailers"; the Greek word purifies the sordidness of trade, while "Piraeus" sounds better than "Surrey Docks".

Mr. Rose is fictional; but Arnold could be a great deal more extraordinary in real life. "The Function of Criticism at the Present Time" was written under sore provocation; one gentleman had asserted that the Anglo-Saxon race were "the best breed in the whole world", another that they had achieved a degree of happiness unrivalled in the world's history. Arnold ventured to dissent, quoting a recent newspaper report: "A shocking child murder has just been committed at Northampton. A girl named Wragg left the workhouse . . . with her young illegitimate child. The child was . . . found dead on Mapperley Hills . . . Wragg is in custody." This was a bitter and effective riposte; but almost immediately Arnold's eloquence veered in a startling direction: "Wragg! . . . Has anyone reflected what a touch of grossness in our race . . . is shown by the natural growth amongst us of such hideous names. Higginbottom, Stiggins, Bugg! In Ionia and Attica they were luckier . . . ; by the Ilissus there was no Wragg, poor thing!"[17]

Arnold's sense of euphony was affected by his eye. Surely he would not have found "rag" so objectionable a word as "Wragg", though the pronunciation is identical; the w looks harsh because it suggests wringing and twisting. Besides, there is something both homely and Anglo-Saxon, it appears, about names with a g and especially a double g in them. By inventing Mr. Baggins of Bag End, Tolkien brought out the humble Englishness of his Shire. What would happen to a tragedy in blank verse, G. H. Lewes asked, if the hero's name were Wiggins?[18] Lady Glenmire in Mrs. Gaskell's *Cranford* loses status by her second marriage: "Mrs. Hoggins! Had she . . . cut the aristocracy to become a Hoggins!"[19] The termination-ins would seem to be an extra cause of offence; the lady would have done a little better to marry a Mr. Hogg. The English feel that surnames can be a badge of class. Scots names are different; a Campbell may be a peasant or a peer.

These analogies suggest that Arnold was unconsciously affected by social feelings. No doubt the names Wragg and Stiggins do sound less melodious than Ilissus, but part of their offence is that they are plebeian. Likewise, when Byron said that Johnson was a less harmonious name than Ajax, he really meant that it was less noble. And Arnold was evidently influenced by yet other associations, for after mentioning the Ilissus, he continues, "'Our unrivalled happiness';—what an element of grimness, bareness, and hideousness mixes with it . . . ; the workhouse, the dismal Mapperley Hills, . . . the gloom, the smoke, the cold, the strangled illegitimate child!" He connects the sound of the name Wragg with both the grimness of a northern climate and the ugliness of an industrial landscape; correspondingly, the mere mention of the Ilissus conjures up the brightness and beauty of an idealized Athens. This stream stirred fewer romantic sentiments in the Athenians themselves; their poets never praised it, reserving their eulogies for the more ample river Cephisus. Early travellers in Greece noted ironically that the banks of the Ilissus were bare and its bed dry as a bone in summer. There is, in fact, a touch of sentimentality in Arnold's too easy contrast between the horrors of the present and the perfection of the past.

In *Culture and Anarchy* he replied to his critics with admirable humour, picturing their caricature of himself as "me, in the midst of the general tribulation, handing out my pouncet-box".[20] But this would not be a bad description of his earlier essay. Arnold was a decent and kindly man, who had no wish to mock the sufferings of the wretched Wragg; yet the moment is sad at which he turns from excoriating the complacency of his contemporaries to lamenting the inelegance of English appellations. There is no better testimony than Arnold's to the power of Greek words over the Victorian imagination; but that very power contained the seeds of its own destruction. The magic of Greek names was like one of those legendary enchantments that sap a man's acuity and vigour, and there was a danger that Hellenism itself would come to seem merely limp and querulous. When David Jones came to write his epic of the First World War, he threw commonplace English names into his Homeric catalogue of warriors:[21]

> from Islington and Hackney
> and the purlieus of Walworth
> flashers from Surbiton . . .
> Bates and Coldpepper . . .
> Fowler from Harrow and the House . . .

By this time the intrusion of Greek into a passage of English could only seem precious. In *Mr. Eliot's Sunday Morning Service* it indicates the churchgoer's etiolated refinement:

> In the beginning was the Word.
> Superfetation of *to hen.*

The witticism is thin, donnish. And the subsequent history of the poem has added a further irony that its author never intended: in every collected edition of his poetry the Greek has been misprinted.

The Victorian Vision of Greece

The eighteenth century saw the beginnings of a great change in the way history was written; historians, once concerned almost entirely with political and military events, began to investigate such things as commerce, religion and social habits. In a sense they were returning to the infancy of their art; the word history originally meant nothing more than "inquiry", and the early Greek historians had mixed topography, ethnography and travellers' tales with cheerful insouciance. Herodotus began the disciplining of history by directing these diverse elements towards the service of a unified and dramatic narrative; a process completed by the immensely tough intellect of Thucydides, who ruthlessly excised the decorative features of history and concentrated upon an account of events, chronologically arranged and keenly analysed. He stamped upon historiography the pattern that it was to bear throughout antiquity; indeed history is still in the popular mind the story of what happened in the past, and it is essentially to Thucydides that we owe this conception of it. His reputation stood very high in the last century; yet in a way there had never been a time when historiography was less Thucydidean: Macaulay, who adored him, felt none the less that his work afforded "less knowledge of the most important particulars relating to Athens than Plato or Aristophanes", and urged the future historians of Greece to turn from war and politics to a province that had so far been left to the "negligent administration of writers of fiction".[22]

Buckle considered the human race to be chiefly influenced by four physical agents, "Climate, Food, Soil, and the General Aspect of Nature"; the history of

Greece provided a testing ground for most of these. The topographical work of Leake and Gell had given the historian a new instrument, and it is a part of human nature to claim for any new instrument an exaggerated importance. Thirlwall began his history, "The character of every people is more or less closely connected with that of its land." George Eliot let a revealing anachronism into *Romola* when she made Bardo maintain that a "new . . . era would open for learning when men should . . . look for their commentaries on the ancient writers . . . in the paths of the rivers and on the face of the valleys and mountains";[23] such opinions do not belong in the fifteenth century. In Wordsworth's sonnet liberty has two voices: "One is of the sea, One of the mountains; each a mighty Voice"—a theory gratifying to the sea-girt British.[24] Greece had both sea and mountain, and so Greece was again the test. Grote remarked that the Greeks' position "made them at once mountaineers and mariners, thus supplying them with great variety of objects . . . and adventures"; their cities, separated from each other by the rocky terrain, but not so far as to destroy a sense of Hellenic identity, gave the Greeks "access to a larger mass of social and political experience" than any other race.

Henry Tozer, agreeing that the Greeks owed much of their adventurous and democratic temper to the combination of sea and mountain, added to Grote's arguments others less easy to assess: the sea teaches courage and hardiness, but also by its extent and changeful motion "expands the thoughts and inspires the feeling of restless activity"; mountainous terrain is easy to defend, but equally it "elevates the mind and inspires it with a sense of independence". Such views had a powerful hold upon the literary imagination; in an age when the beauty of natural scenery was more highly prized than ever before, it was agreeable to think that it might have shaped the destinies of nations. Symonds held that Athens was predestined to be the mother of reason "by virtue of scenery and situation"; the radiance of the Athenian landscape had "all the clearness . . . of the Attic intellect".[25] When Ruskin suggested that the Greeks had no taste for picturesque landscape, he started an agitated controversy, in which even Gladstone joined.

Gillies cited Isocrates and Aristotle to show how the Greeks themselves believed that they owed the character of their civilization to their climate. Aristotle said that those who lived in the cold of northern Europe were full of spirit, but short of intelligence; they were free, therefore, but without political organization. The natives of Asia were intelligent but wanting in spirit, and therefore always in subjection. "But the Hellenic race, which is situated between them, is likewise intermediate in character, being high-spirited and also intelligent. Hence it continues free, and is the best governed of any nation, and, if it could be formed into one state, would be able to rule the world."[26] These opinions were much quoted in the last century, and for an understandable reason: they could be adapted to apply neatly to Britain. The British stood amazed at their own achievements. What was the source of their energy? Perhaps the climate gave the answer. Charles Adderley declared that "the absence of a too enervating climate, too unclouded skies" had made the Anglo-Saxon race superior to all the world.[27] In fact the argument was more plausible in the nineteenth century than it had been in Aristotle's time: the climate of Asia is not so very different from that of Attica, but the English could look to the lazy Latins to the south of them and the sluggish Scandinavians to the north, and attribute their own good fortune to the laws of nature. Others, less sanguine, accounted for English philistinism on the same grounds. Religions could be similarly explained; "They brighten under a bright sky," Pater said. Disraeli's evangelical Mrs. Giles hopes that the Gulf Stream will change course: "Severe winters at Rome might put an end to Romanism." And surely the climate affected morals too. "We will bless God for our English homes," said the Rev. F. W. Robertson, thanking the Almighty for the climate with which He has been pleased to afflict us: "Its gloom . . . making life more necessarily spent within doors than it is among continental nations, our life is domestic and theirs is social. When England shall learn domestic maxims from strangers, as Rome from Greece, her ruin is accomplished."[28] (The Romans were granted the status of honorary northerners.) Such arguments were common—in those days France and Italy, not Scandinavia, were the "wicked" countries *par excellence*—and they had already been satirized by Byron:[29]

> What men call gallantry, and gods adultery,
> Is much more common where the climate's
> sultry.
>
> Happy the nations of the moral North!
> Where all is virtue, and the winter season
> Sends sin, without a rag on, shivering forth . . .

But Byron himself claimed to find in Attica and Ionia an excellence of climate strikingly different from the rest of the Mediterranean; a claim echoed by Symonds later.[30] Both men had travelled in Greece; and yet they let fantasy overcome experience. That compelling sense of the polarity between north and south fed a belief in the importance of climate and was fed by it in turn.

Many Victorians liked also to explain history in racial terms. All over Europe nationalism was waxing strong; while in imperial England it was hard to resist the sense of a special Anglo-Saxon destiny. Thomas Arnold used his inaugural lecture from the Regius chair at Oxford to argue that civilization progressed by being transmitted from one race to another: Greece fed the intellect, Rome established the rule of law, Christianity gave the perfection of spiritual truth. The changes of the last eighteen hundred years had been wrought by "the reception of these elements by new races", principally the German peoples, of whom the English were one. Arnold was typical of his age, both in his sense of a Germanic distinctness and in his desire to claim a kinship with the old Mediterranean world. The English were not descended from the Greek or Jewish races, he admitted, and hardly at all from the Roman, but "morally how much do we derive from all three". The "element of our English race" was the distinctively modern element in English history, and yet "here . . . we have . . . the ancient world still existing".[31]

And racial arguments gave a quasi-scientific backing to what might otherwise seem mere speculation. Lecturing at the Royal Academy, Leighton contrasted Assyria and Egypt with the Aryan spirit of fifth-century Greece—and then went on to talk a great deal of nonsense about Pelasgians and Autochthons. Disraeli made fun of Leighton's Aryanism, but he was no less addicted to racial arguments himself. Scott had drawn attention to the existence of two races, Saxon and Norman, in medieval England, and Disraeli used this idea, despite fantastic inconsistencies, to account for the "two nations" into which modern England was divided;[32] and he was particularly interested in the destiny of the Jews. Greece was once again the place where the significance of racial differences seemed most sharply visible, for in Greece there had been two main races, Ionians and Dorians, whose contrasting characters were symbolized by Athens and Sparta. Such ideas were further stimulated by the success of Mueller's *Dorians,* first translated in 1839, a book whose effect, through its influence on Ruskin and Pater, was still felt in the late Victorian age.

The subject was particularly interesting to the British, who could not rid themselves of the idea that the Dorians were the Scotsmen of the south. In translations Doric dialect was represented by Scotticisms; thus in Rogers's version of the *Lysistrata:*[33]

> Our hizzies, a'
> Risin' like rinners at ane signal word,
> Loupit, an' jibbed, an' dang the men awa'.

More than one reader has turned gratefully to the Greek to find out what the translation means. The use of "Doric" as a synonym for Scottish began as a jibe at the uncouthness of North Britain, but the Scots themselves started to take a pride in the epithet. Meanwhile, Edinburgh was being filled with solemn Doric-columned buildings. To Taine's Gallic eye they seemed ludicrously out of place in the cold, windy north; but had not Mueller said that the Doric character created the Doric architecture?[34] And was not the Doric character known to have been dour and phlegmatic? The analogy between Scots and Dorians was not openly argued for, but its insidious influence betrays itself from time to time. Matthew Arnold speaks of "Dorian highlanders", contrasting the "mobile Ionians" with the "steadfast mountaineers of northern Greece". Pater, too, contrasts the Dorian "spirit of the highlands" with "the mobile, the marine, and fluid temper" of the Ionians, whose tendency is "Asiatic" and "irresponsible"; and there is a flavour of Protestantism when he praises "the saving Dorian soul".[35] The old dichotomy of north and south has been transferred into a Greek setting, with the Dorians as stalwart northerners and the Ionians as feckless but artistic Latins. But in reality Sparta was not, as Pater claimed, a "little mountain town"; it lies low in a wide sleepy valley in the southernmost part of Greece. And in attributing the Ionian character to the fact that they were coastal people with the "roaming thoughts of sailors", Pater forgot that Dorian Corinth was for centuries the greatest port in Greece, and the home of its finest art.[36]

Mill protested unavailingly against the vulgar fondness for "attributing the diversities of conduct and character to inherent natural differences between races".[37] The opposite view is given by Disraeli's Contarini Fleming, who contrasts the naturally artistic Greeks with the "flat-nosed Franks": "They . . . invent theories to account for their own incompetence. Now it is the climate, now the religion . . . everything but the truth, . . . the mortifying suspicion that their organization may be different." Tozer compromised; the Hellenes would not have achieved greatness on the plains of Hungary, he suggested, but then nor would the Mongols in the land of Greece.[38] Usually the issue was less plainly put, and the effects of landscape, climate and race were not clearly distinguished; all three were already jumbled up in Schlegel's lectures. What did Adderley mean when he claimed that the Anglo-Saxons were 'the best breed in the world' because of their cloudy skies? Or Pater when he said that the landscape around Sparta was a type of the Dorian purpose in life?[39] Did he know himself? A sense of the distinct identity of the breed (a favourite Victorian word) was emotional rather than logical. After all, the Victorians were not to know the perils of what they were doing. They toyed with racial ideas casually and uncomprehendingly, like children playing by the power lines.

The Victorians, and especially the later Victorians, thickened the fog of vagueness surrounding the Greeks by the persistent use of themes which easily degenerated into clichés: light, youth, calm. The idea of Greek serenity derived from Winckelmann; so too perhaps did the metaphor of youth, for it was he who developed the theory that the fine arts wax and decay like a living organism: "Arts have their infancy as well as men."[40] But to trace these ideas back to their German origins is to give a false impression, for the secret of their power over the Victorian mind was that those origins were unappreciated. Calm, radiance and childlikeness seemed to be qualities inherent in the Greek genius, plainly perceived across a distance of two thousand years; if the Victorians had distinctly told themselves that these ideas were merely the products of an outdated scholarship, they would not have accepted them so tamely.

"O Solon, Solon, you Greeks are always children," said the Egyptian priest, contrasting the adventurous newness of Hellenic thought with the mysterious and immemorial depths of his native religion.[41] The passage was often cited, but in such a way that its meaning was changed. Pater's recurrent theme, repeated endlessly by his disciples, was that the Greeks had a child's unreflecting superficiality: "This unperplexed youth of humanity . . . passed, at the due moment, into a mournful maturity." The cult of athletics was "such worship as Greece, still in its superficial youth, found itself best capable of". This idea was made the more enticing by the belief that sculpture was the ruling art-form of the ancient world, as music of the modern; for sculpture deals necessarily with surfaces. "Our art," Symonds wrote, "appeals . . . to the emotions, disclosing . . . spiritual reality . . . Greek art remains upon the surface, and translates into marble . . . the external world."[42]

Many of the aesthetes liked the metaphor of youth because it allowed them to slip into talking about the cult of handsome young men. At the same time, it could be put to the service of a sentimental paganism which blamed the cold breath of the Galilean for blasting a world of joyous innocence. This idea underlies Pater's picture of Greece, but he was himself too subtle to take it over wholesale. Instead, he hints at a delicate, uncertain balance of loss and gain. To be sure, the Greeks had not known the maladies of the soul; and yet Marius finds in the Christians a mystic charm which makes him "doubt whether that famed Greek "blitheness" . . . had been, after all, an unrivalled success".[43] In *Denys l'Auxerrois,* a fable about the return of the god Dionysus in the Middle Ages, Pater contrasts a happy but too simple paganism with the Christian world, in which people have a larger spiritual capacity and . . . a larger capacity for melancholy"; in fact, the pains and privileges of adulthood. We may have been better or happier in our infancy, but do we wish to return to that state? Or as Pater puts it, "Since we are no longer children, we might well question the advantage of the return to us of a condition of life in which . . . the value of things would . . . lie wholly on their surfaces, unless we could regain also the childish consciousness, or rather unconsciousness, in ourselves."

As a literary conception these ideas have their charm, but with the Greeks themselves they have nothing to do. None the less, the metaphor of youth has great power; it was connected with a seductively simple theory of history, which has persisted into our own century in the works of Spengler and Toynbee, and a hundred years ago it overcame not only agnostics but even a future Archbishop of Canterbury. Frederick Temple maintained that "We may . . . rightly speak of a childhood, a youth, and a manhood of the world. The men of the earliest ages were . . . still children as compared with ourselves, with all the blessings and . . . disadvantages that belong to childhood."[44] The argument is muddled: at one time we are told that the Greeks were children being educated in preparation for the coming of Jesus, whose time on earth represented the world's adolescence; at another that the Greeks themselves had "the grace of the prime of manhood . . . the pervading sense of youthful beauty".[45] Today Temple's piece seems very dated, very "Victorian", jarring against the liberal, commonsense tone of the other contributions to *Essays and Reviews.* But the impression is mistaken, for another Victorian who delighted to see the Greeks as sweet simple children was that "cultured Anglo-German gentleman", Karl Marx.[46] How far, we may speculate, was Marx's naïve vision of the future founded upon his naïve picture of the ancient world? And with consequences for our own times, how great?

Quietly, almost imperceptibly, the metaphors of youth and light merged into one. We catch murmurs: "the Hellenic genius, radiant, adolescent" (Symonds), "radiance of fresh life" (Temple), "the first glow of a youth which has proved immortal" (Jebb); and from Pater, more suggestively, "They are at play . . . in the sun; but a little cloud passes over it now and then."[47] Hazlitt contrasted early Italian paintings "covered with the marks of . . . antiquity", with the far more ancient Greek statues which still "shine in glossy, undiminished splendour, and flourish in immortal youth and beauty".[48] This is emotion, not logic, for he bases his idea of Greece on the physical properties of stone and varnish. It was fatally easy to confuse symbolism with geographical fact; the brilliance of the Greek climate seemed to prove that Hellenism stood for the principle of intellectual light. Pater describes Winckelmann passing from "the tarnished intellectual world of Germany" into the "happy light of the antique"; that is a metaphor, but in the very next sentence Pater speaks literally of "the dusky precincts of a Germany school".[49] In *Duke Carl* we are told, "The god of light, coming to Germany . . . over leagues of rainy hill . . . had ever been the dream of the . . . German soul." The duke desires to bring "the daylight, the Apolline aurora . . . to his candle-lit people", but he abandons his journey to Greece on deciding that the true light is to be found in Germany itself, "the real need being that of an interpreter—Apollo, illuminant rather as the revealer than as the bringer of light". Thus Pater's fictional creature escapes from the confusion between physical and metaphorical light; but we may doubt, strange as it seems, whether Pater himself ever did so.

Youth, light and clear southern skies were blent together to represent the Greek genius as a kind of lithe, buoyant athleticism. In the age of muscular Christianity the Greeks became muscular pagans; clean fresh air became a symbol of the Hellenic spirit. Pater spoke of Greece winning "liberty, political standing-ground and a really social air to breathe in". "On the high places . . . of Greek . . . art," Jebb said, "those who are worn with . . . modern civilisation can breathe an atmosphere which, like that of Greece itself, has the freshness of the mountains and the sea." Henry Jenkyns argued that the classics increased men's moral excellence and invigorated their nature; especially, he added, since no land "can be visited with greater advantage than that of classical antiquity. By an abode in its clear and bracing climate the mind becomes more healthy . . . it acquires an elasticity, a gracefulness . . ."[50]

As northerners, the Victorians felt themselves inferior to the south; as moderns, to the past. When they contemplated the glories of Hellas, these two feelings fused into one. Greece was perfect, the past was perfect; must not the Greek climate have been perfect too? According to Symonds the Greeks lived amid "perpetual sunshine and perpetual ease—no work . . . that might degrade the body . . . no dread of hell, no yearning after heaven." As for the Greeks' modern descendants, "Their labours are lighter than in northern climes and their food more plentiful. . . . Summer leaves them not. . . . There is surely some difference between hoeing turnips and trimming olive boughs; between tending turkeys on a Norfolk common and leading goats to browse on cytisus beside the shore." He need only have read Hesiod to learn that labour can be heavy in Mediterranean lands, winters bitter, and food scarce; but he preferred to view the southern landscape with the impercipience of the milord for whom the peasants are picturesque objects in the middle distance: "The poetry of rustic life is more evident upon Mediterranean shores than in England."[51]

Pater had been less crude, but hardly less fanciful: "That delicate air . . . the finer aspects of nature, the finer . . . clay of the human form, and modelling . . . of the human countenance—these are the good luck of the Greek." As the Greeks exercised in the clear sunlight their forms and features seemed to become as perfect as their climate. Hazlitt had already wondered, paraphrasing Schlegel, whether the Greeks, "born of a beautiful . . . race . . . and placed under a mild heaven", might not have had "a natural organization . . . more perfect . . . than ours, who have not the same advantages of climate and constitution". Symonds contrasted the vast interior gloom of Milan Cathedral with the open air and "perfect human forms" of the Panathenaic procession. Pater could even tell that the Spartans were "visibly . . . the most beautiful of all people, in Greece, in the world". Visibly! How did he know?[52]

Justification might sometimes be found for associating the character of Greek art with the climate. Virginia Woolf claimed that the nature of Attic tragedy was determined by its performance in the open on a hot day. Or as Symonds said, "If the hero of a modern play . . . calls the sun to witness, he must point to a tissue-paper transparency. . . . But Ajax or Electra could raise their hands to the actual sun . . . nearly all the scenes of the Greek tragedies are laid in daytime and in the open air."[53] But what is remarkable is that there should be any impressive scenes—the opening of *Antigone,* the opening of *Agamemnon*—laid in the night at all. The furtive meeting in the darkness before dawn, the loneliness of the watchman under the stars—these are important parts of the theatrical effect. "Put out the light," says Othello; the candle is quenched, and the Globe Theatre is not a whit darker. Aeschylus, like Shakespeare, had to lure his audience by the power of poetry into resisting the plain evidence of their senses. It is ironic that the self-taught Hardy should appreciate "the triumphs of the Hellenic and Elizabethan theatre in exhibiting scenes laid 'far in the Unapparent'" at a time when his highly educated contemporaries did not.[54] Even their notion of the climate was wrong: the greatest theatrical festival was held in late March or thereabouts, when the Attic weather is uncertain; on one occasion the procession had to be cancelled because of snow.[55] But from Victorian Hellenists one sometimes gets the impression that not only were there no Higginbottoms by the Ilissus, but no rain ever fell there either.

"When we read their poems," Symonds wrote, "we seem to have the perfumes . . . and lights of that luxurious land distilled in verse. . . . In reading Aristophanes we seem to have the serene skies of Attica above our heads"—such sentiments are the staple of aesthetic criticism. They are symptoms of a process by which the Greek character was flattened out into a clear dull uniformity, ever sunny and simple and calm. Naturally enough, the Greeks themselves often failed to fit this picture; in which case the Victorians were liable to decide that they were no longer truly Greek. "In the best Greek work," Ruskin said, "you will find some things that are still false, or fanciful; but whatever in it is false, or fanciful, is not the Greek part of it. . . . The essential Hellenic stamp is veracity." Pater blandly observed that Botticelli's Venus offered "a more direct inlet into the Greek temper than the works of the Greeks themselves even of the finest period". Mallock parodied him—"Ah, they are sweet verses; a little too ascetic, perhaps, to be quite Greek. They are from Euripides, I see . . ."—but the parody is barely distinguishable from its model.[56] "Greek" and "Hellenic" could henceforth be applied as labels to things that had no connection with the historic Greece. Tovey detected "Greek simplicities" in Beethoven's later music and protested against the nickname of the Jupiter Symphony on the grounds that Mozart was "as Greek as Keats.

He might have written a Zeus symphony. He never did. . . ."[57] This is not meaningless talk, indeed it is all too suggestive; the usefulness of Hellenism as a metaphor reveals its decline as a living and complex force.

In the heyday of Arnold and Pater there was, as it so happened, no classical scholar in England of genuine originality of mind. The literary men set the tone, and the professional scholars followed tamely behind them. Jebb insisted that there was no conflict between "true Hellenism" and Hebraism: "The best Greek work . . . is essentially pure; to conceive it as necessarily entangled with the baser elements of paganism is to confound the accidents with the essence; the accidents have passed away; the essence is imperishable."[58] The Hellenic spirit seems to be a sort of 100% pure alcohol, to be distilled, by some unexplained process, out of what the Greeks actually said and did. The depth and variety of Greek art and belief were being forgotten, and thus at the very moment that Nietzsche was revealing to Germany the fierce, Dionysiac side of the Greek soul the English were marching boldly backwards towards Winckelmann and Goethe. Pater himself did once write, in a moment of insight, that the view of Greek religion as a religion of art and beauty was only a partial one: "The eye is fixed on the sharp, bright edge of high Hellenic culture, but loses sight of the sombre world across which it strikes." But one glance into the dizzy depths is enough for him, for he goes on immediately to say that religions brighten under a bright sky, and concludes that the Greeks' achievement was to brush the dark side of their beliefs under the carpet: "The Dorian worship of Apollo . . . with his unbroken daylight, always opposed to the sad Chthonian divinities, is the aspiring element, by force . . . of which Greek religion sublimes itself. . . . It was the privilege of Greek religion to be able to transform itself into an artistic ideal."[59] Such, certainly, was the transformation which Hellenism underwent at Pater's hands. Yet even where Nietzsche's influence has been strong, the feeling has persisted that the distinguishing characteristic of Greek art is a calm, balanced lucidity. Music again provides the test. Stravinsky liked to talk about the Apolline and Dionysian elements of art; there is nothing Greek about his most Dionysiac ballet, *The Rite of Spring,* whereas *Apollon Musagète* is consciously Hellenic in the lucid texture of its string orchestra and the austere purity of its clean, astringent discords. And when Sibelius described his plan for a symphony as "Joy of life and vitality. . . . In three movements—the last an Hellenic rondo",[60] we can guess what he had in mind: a fresh healthy animalism, vigorous but spare.

Despite its great influence on England Hellenism oddly refused to blend easily with the other influences acting upon art and thought. As Pater said, "The spiritual forces of the past, which have . . . informed the culture of a succeeding age, live indeed, within that culture, but with an absorbed, underground life. The Hellenic element alone has not been so absorbed . . . Hellenism is not merely an absorbed element in our intellectual life; it is a conscious tradition in it."[61] In Pater's time Hellenism was beginning to seem highbrow and alien. Once its independence had been a source of strength to it; now, in an age of eclecticism, it was becoming a weakness.

The Gods

> Where are they, the half-deceivers,
> Statue-forms and young men's fancies,
> Gods of Greece?
>
> Flecker, *Donde Estan?*

One of the rarest events in history is the death of a religion. Once any new system of belief has commended itself to a considerable body of people it is seldom altogether eradicated; Zoroastrianism, founded more than two and a half thousand years ago, has survived for the past millennium or so with less than 150,000 adherents. Even the small, eccentric sects that spin off the edges of the great religions have great powers of endurance, unless they are extirpated by persecutions of the utmost savagery and efficiency; even the half-religions—spiritualism, occultism, astrology, neoplatonism—seldom perish entirely: they are merely forgotten for a while, to be revived again whenever traditional means of comfort and edification seem to have lost their efficacy. Religions do not die; they become cataleptic.

To this general rule there is one enormous exception. The growth of Christianity completely destroyed the great Indo-European pantheons, Norse, German and Greco-Roman. Some time in about the sixth century A.D. the last man died who believed in the existence of Juno and Venus and Apollo, and in the succeeding centuries Asgard and Niflheim went the way of Olympus. The old gods faded quietly away and their disappearance was virtually unregretted until the later part of the eighteenth century, when the German Hellenists, eager to revive every aspect of Greek culture, were brought up against the impossibility of summoning the old religion back to life. Their disappointment was summed up by Schiller in *The Gods of Greece,* perhaps the most influential single poem ever written by a German. This was a lament for the disappearance of a mythology which portrayed the gods as serene, happy beings, and at the same time invested everyday sights with a portion of the divine: "Where now, so our wise men say, there is only a soulless ball of fire revolving, once Helios used to drive his golden chariot in calm majesty. Oreads thronged these heights, a Dryad perished with that tree . . ."

The Gods of Greece appeared in 1788. Its evocative power is shown by Mrs. Browning's attempt, more than fifty years later, to combat it in *The Dead Pan.* Teutonic melancholy was not for her:

O ye vain false gods of Hellas,
Ye are silent evermore! . . .

Get to dust, as common mortals,
By a common doom and track!
Let no Schiller from the portals
Of that Hades, call you back . . .

O brave poets, keep back nothing;
Nor mix falsehood with the whole!
Look up Godward! speak the truth in
Worthy song from earnest soul!

Despite the pious sentiments and the hearty, blustery tone, the poem has the ring of insincerity. Schiller does not mention Pan, but Mrs. Browning seems to have had a weakness for him. One of her most popular poems begins, "What was he doing, the great god Pan . . . ?"[62] Another describes how she was woken from sleep by her dog; for a moment she thought that he was Faunus, and started, "as some Arcadian, Amazed by goatly god in twilight grove". A pleasing fancy, it would appear; but the poetess has to overcome her "surprise and sadness" at losing the vision before ending very properly by thanking Christ, "the true PAN, Who, by low creatures, leads to heights of love."[63] With these other poems in mind we may find it hard to believe her when she writes in *The Dead Pan,*

Earth outgrows the mythic fancies
Sung beside her in her youth:
And those debonair romances
Sound but dull beside the truth.

Do they? Even Mrs. Browning seems to feel in her own despite the sadness of the old deities' defeat:

Have ye left the mountain places,
Oreads wild, for other tryst?
Shall we see no sudden faces
Strike a glory through the mist?
Not a sound the silence thrills,
On the everlasting hills.
  Pan, Pan is dead.

When *The Gods of Greece* was first published, it was taken to be an attack on Christianity, but Schiller blames the spiritual deadness of his age at least as much upon science; the "wise men" who have told us that the sun is merely a ball of fire are the physicists and astronomers. This aspect of Schiller's ideas was appreciated in England where the Industrial Revolution was making the destructive effects of science more obvious than they could possibly have been in Weimar. And the English romantics added the further idea that the loss of gods and nymphs had made the writing of poetry difficult or impossible. Mrs. Browning herself thought Schiller's doctrine "still more dishonouring to poetry than to Christianity".[64] But such thoughts were far from the doctrine's originator, who was writing at a time when German poetry was rising to heights that it had never reached before.

Compared to Schiller Wordsworth relied more on feeling, less on thought. Whereas the German regretted the loss of the Greek gods because it impoverished the life of the mind and removed an incentive to nobility of thought and action, the English poet mourned it because it diminished the pleasure and consolation to be got from nature:[65]

  Great God! I'd rather be
A Pagan suckled in a creed outworn;
So might I, standing on this pleasant lea,
Have glimpses that would make me less forlorn;
Have sight of Proteus rising from the sea;
Or hear old Triton blow his wreathed horn.

"Little we see in Nature that is ours," Wordsworth says; even the sea "moves us not". And this is the fault not of Christianity or the Enlightenment but of the modern money-grubbing world in which "getting and spending we lay waste our powers".

Wordsworth's influence was great; still greater was Byron's. Childe Harold grieved for the vanished Olympians:

Oh! where, Dodona! is thine aged grove,
Prophetic fount and oracle divine? . . .
All, all forgotten . . .

Byron enraptured the public with his picture of a "land of lost gods"; and yet, illogically but evocatively, he portrayed Greece as a place filled with divine presences: "Where'er we tread, 'tis haunted, holy ground." The very phrase "land of lost gods" is resplendently ambivalent: have the gods disappeared altogether, or does the poet imply that Greece is still haunted by melancholy divinities, bewildered survivors of a classical Götterdämmerung? Byron seems unable to decide whether the gods have gone or no: in a single stanza he tells us that the olive is still "ripe as when Minerva smiled" and that Apollo still gilds the long, long Grecian summer.[66] But the very equivocation adds to the poetic charm; the evanescence of the Grecian gods—no sooner are they espied than they seem never to have been present at all—is wistfully suggestive. Schiller, too, had celebrated the springlike beauty of Greece: "Lovely world, where art thou?—return again, gracious blossom time of nature! . . . All these blossoms have fallen at the wintry blast of the north." But his love for Greece was purely cerebral; those blossoms are the burgeonings of art and thought. Byron gave actuality to Schiller's "lovely world".

The chorus in Shelley's *Hellas* lament for Apollo, Pan and Jove, routed by the "killing truth" of Christianity:

Our hill and seas and streams,
Dispeopled of their dreams . . .
Wailed for the golden years.

These sentiments come incongruously from Greek women captured by the Turks; they are the poet's own. "I am glad to hear that you do not neglect the rites of the true religion," he wrote to Hogg from Italy. "Your letter awakened my sleeping devotion, and . . . I . . . suspended a garland, & raised a small turf altar to the mountain-walking Pan"—and here Shelley added in brackets, with an endearing touch of pedantry, the title of the mountain-walking Pan in Greek. Pan, indeed, was something of a favourite in Shelley's circle. Peacock signed a letter "in the name of Pan", and Leigh Hunt wrote to Hogg at Marlow, "I hope you paid your devotions as usual to the Religio Loci, and hung up an evergreen. If you go on so, there will be a hope . . . that a voice will be heard along the water saying 'The great God Pan is alive again'—upon which the villagers will leave off starving, and singing profane hymns, and fall to dancing again."[67]

How serious were Shelley and his friends about these devotions? Surely not at all, we tell ourselves; these rites were an amusing way of cocking a snook at the orthodox, and of satisfying, if only in play, the atavistic appetite of humankind for the performance of ritual acts. Surely it was only a game, we say, a pleasing flight of fancy: at best the gods of Greece are, in Flecker's phrase, but "half-deceivers". This answer may be right and yet a little facile; men do not always know themselves whether they are joking or in earnest. Edward Calvert, one of that group of painters nicknamed "the Ancients" because of their adoration of antiquity, erected in his little back garden an altar to Pan. W. B. Richmond, who used to receive from him "many picturesque vision in words of the relationship of the ancient gods with the modern world", did not doubt that he was serious. Dickens imagined many fantastic eccentricities flourishing in and around the metropolis—Wemmick in his castle, Venus in his shop—but he never pictured anything so extraordinary as the worship of a Peloponnesian goat god in a London suburb.

No doubt Calvert was exceptional, but the question remains: why did Pan in particular have such a hold upon the romantic imagination? Pan was not one of the Olympian gods, who had already been frozen by Goethe and Winckelmann into poses of statuesque calm. He had a dual character, both parts of which were attractive to a generation born at about the time of the French Revolution. On the one hand, he was a naughty, goatish creature, gloriously free from the restraints imposed by civilization or Christian morality; on the other, he became in late Greek theology the god of universal nature. The Greeks themselves accepted the false etymology which connected the name of Pan with the Greek word for "all", and Pan became the god of the pantheists. The romantics wanted to get back to nature, but "nature" is a word with many meanings. In part they wanted to escape from cities, from the artificiality of society, from the cycle of "getting and spending"; Pan god of the countryside was a symbol of their nostalgia and their hopes. But at the same time they wanted to study the natural world more deeply, to understand its quiddity, to penetrate to its essence, to make a primrose more than just a yellow primrose. Wordsworth accordingly adopted a form of pantheism. Richmond accounted for Calvert's religion by saying, "Pantheism . . . had gripped the intelligence . . . of a very highly-strung, poetical nature." Naturally Pan was his god.

Hunt spoke to Hogg of the "Religio Loci". He too was drawn to the old paganism not by abstract cogitation but by a feeling for nature and, more especially, for the particular quality of particular landscapes. It was landscape, again, that led Ruskin to discuss the nature of the Greek gods and their place in modern literature; and his chapters on this subject in *Modern Painters* are still illuminating after more than a hundred years. He once wrote that no day passed "without convincing every honest student of antiquity of some partial error, and showing him better how to think";[68] he did not approach the ancient Greeks armoured in the hard shell of self-confidence with which he came to art and architecture, and he was all the better for this lack.

He took as an example two lines from a poem by Kingsley:

They rowed her in across the rolling foam—
The cruel, crawling foam.

He comments, "The foam is not cruel, neither does it crawl. The state of mind which attributes to it these characters of a living creature is one in which the reason is unhinged by grief. All violent feelings . . . produce in us a falseness in all our impressions of external things." To this "falseness" Ruskin gave a name that has since become famous: the "pathetic fallacy". This fallacy, he claims, is "eminently characteristic of the modern mind" and he skilfully argues the point with the help of a comparison between Keats and Homer. He quotes Keats's description of a wave breaking out at sea:

Down whose green back the short-lived foam,
 all hoar,
Bursts gradual, with a wayward indolence.

"That," he says, "is quite perfect, as an example of the modern manner. . . . But Homer would never have written such words. He could not have lost sight of the great fact that salt water could not be either wayward or indolent. He will call the waves 'over-roofed', 'full-charged', 'monstrous', 'compact-black' . . . But every one of these epithets is descriptive of pure physical nature . . ."[69] This was very acute. Ruskin implied, it is true, that the Greeks never used the pathetic fallacy, which is an exaggeration; but in general his contrast between Greek and modern attitudes was both original and just.

Does the absence of the pathetic fallacy in Homer mean that Keats is the greater writer?

> Stay a moment. Homer *had* some feeling about the sea; a faith in the animation of it much stronger than Keats's. But all this sense of something living in it, he separates in his mind into a great abstract image of a Sea Power. He never says the waves rage, or the waves are idle. But he says there is somewhat in, and greater than, the waves, which rages, and is idle, and *that* he calls a god.

"What is Apollo," asked Symonds rhetorically and foolishly, "but the magic of the sun whose soul is light? . . . What is Pan but the mystery of nature . . . ?" He was trying to turn the Greeks into a whole nation of Wordsworths, a race for whom nature was "the secret of their sympathies, the wellspring of their deepest thoughts".[70] But precisely because they lived closer to nature than Symonds they were less eager to commune with it. As Ruskin had already shown, their preferred scenery consisted of gardens and cultivated land, where nature was safely under control.[71] If Symonds had read *Modern Painters,* he would have found his feeble question rebuked:

> I do not think we ever enough endeavour to enter into what a Greek's real notion of a god was. We are so accustomed to the modern mockeries of the classical religion . . . that we seem to have infected the Greek ages themselves with the breath . . . of our hypocrisy; and are apt to think that Homer, as we know that Pope, was merely an ingenious fabulist.[72]

These sentences are a fascinating mixture of good sense and eccentricity. Ruskin realized that Greek religion was utterly unlike romantic pantheism and that it is hard to imagine the beliefs and emotions associated with it; on the other hand, there is a certain absurdity in his picture of Homer as the representative of an age of faith, rebuking modern Europe for its infidelity. On the same page we find him anxiously exonerating the Greeks from the charge of idolatry, which was, he says, "neither the whole, nor the principal part, of Pagan worship. Pallas was not, in the pure Greek mind, merely a powerful piece of ivory in a temple at Athens."[73] The Greeks were not Romanists, so to speak, but good sound Protestants.

Ruskin was led into this earnest defence of Greek beliefs because like Wordsworth and his followers he passionately desired to invest nature with religious associations. "You have despised . . . all the deep and sacred sensations of natural scenery," he told his public,

> . . . You have made racecourses of the cathedrals of the earth. Your *one* conception of pleasure is to drive in railway carriages round their aisles, and eat off their altars . . . the beautiful places of the world . . . are, indeed, the truest cathedrals—places . . . to worship in; and . . . we only care . . . to eat and drink at their most sacred places.[74]

But unfortunately talk about nature's cathedrals and the sacred emotions inspired by mountain scenery was commonplace among gushing tourists who had dipped into the lake poets. How was Ruskin to convince these enthusiastic people of the sacrilegiousness of picnics? A remark in *Sesame and Lilies* suggests that he perceived an answer: modern Christians could be taught a proper reverence by the Greeks. Speaking of North Wales he declares, "These are the hills, and these the bays . . . , which, among the Greeks, would have been . . . faithful in influence on the national mind. That Snowdon is your Parnassus; but where are its Muses? that Holyhead mountain is your Island of Aegina; but where is its Temple to Minerva?"[75] This is unreasonable: Victorian Welshmen can hardly be blamed for failing to worship a set of pagan goddesses. Did Ruskin seriously regret the passing of Greek religion? Strange as it may seem, a part of him did.

The construction of a railway through Monsal Dale in Derbyshire provoked him to a protest which among even his writings is outstanding for mingled vigour and delicacy:

> There was a rocky valley between Buxton and Bakewell, once upon a time, divine as the vale of Tempe; you might have seen the gods there morning and evening—Apollo and all the sweet Muses of Light, walking in fair procession on the lawns of it. . . . You cared neither for gods nor grass, but for cash . . . You enterprised a railroad through the valley. . . . The valley is gone, and the gods with it; and now, every fool in Buxton can be at Bakewell in half-an-hour, and every fool in Bakewell at Buxton.[76]

Ironically, when the railway line was closed some years back, the viaduct over the River Wye, now much admired, was carefully preserved.

This talk of gods and muses was charmingly poetic, no doubt, but Ruskin wanted it to be something more. In the final chapter of *Praeterita,* the last of all his writings, he announced,

> I must here once for all explain distinctly . . . the sense in which throughout all my earnest writing of the last twenty years I use the plural word "gods".

> I mean by it, the totality of spiritual powers, delegated by the Lord of the universe to do . . . parts of His will . . . in meekness accepting the testimony and belief of all ages, to the presence, in heaven and earth, of angels and the like,—with genii, fairies, or spirits. . . . For all these, I take the general word "gods" as the best understood in all languages.

Finally he quotes, with understandable pride, his denunciation of the Buxton and Bakewell railway, introducing the passage with these astounding words:

> No true happiness exists, nor is any good work ever done . . . , but in the sense or imagination of such presences. The following passage . . . gives example of the sense in which I most literally and earnestly refer to them.[77]

In other words, he *literally* believes in Apollo and the Muses. We react with incredulity; yet that is what Ruskin emphatically and explicitly declares. More than thirty years earlier he had counted among the uses of the imagination its power to refresh the weary mind

> with such innocent play as shall be most in harmony with the suggestive voices of natural things, permitting it to possess living companionship . . . and to create for itself fairies in the grass and naiads in the wave.[78]

Now, in his old age, he could no longer distinguish fact from fantasy.

Greek mythology fascinated him throughout his life, but only once did he devote an entire book to it, and this, *The Queen of the Air,* is one of his maddest works. It is eloquent, however, because he was trying to reconcile in it the conflict between the view expressed in *Modern Painters*—that nowadays the Greek deities can be no more than an imaginative decoration of nature—and the feeling ultimately to be summed up in *Praeterita* by the plain statement that the gods actually exist. On the one hand, he insists that Greek mythology is "literal belief", "deeply rooted" in the mind of the general people and "vitally religious";[79] and there are one or two moments of startling insight that seem almost to anticipate Frazer or Freud. On the other hand, much of the book is devoted to the rationalization of Greek myth. Athena, for example, is the goddess of fresh air, and so when Homer says that she laid Penelope into deep sleep, "and made her taller, and made her smoother, . . . and breathed ambrosial brightness over her face", he means that the lady went to bed early and left the window open. To us such allegorical interpretations seem to be not only wrong but prosaic, robbing the *Odyssey* of its magic, but Ruskin would have viewed the matter the other way round; he was bringing magic back to the experiences of everyday life. "Whenever you throw your window wide open . . . ," he wrote, "you let in Athena, as wisdom and fresh air at the same instant; and whenever you draw a . . . full breath . . . , you take Athena into your heart, through your blood; and with the blood, into the thoughts of your brain."[80] One would normally assume that such language is figurative, but with Ruskin one can never be quite sure; throughout this book he is striving to reconcile Greek myth with modern science. In later life he moralized the natural world as he had earlier moralized art. On his last visit to Venice he was impressed with the sadness and even weakness of the Mediterranean coasts" and in *The Queen of the Air* not even vegetables escape moral scrutiny: beans are commended as "the most entirely serviceable and human"—human!—"of all orders of plants", and the hapless potato is denounced as "the scarcely innocent underground stem of one of a tribe set aside for evil".[81]

Such bizarre assertions are the extreme consequence of his attempt to do under modern conditions what the Greeks, as he thought, did spontaneously, by the very nature of their beliefs. In *Modern Painters* he had not been so foolhardy; he envied the Greeks, but he did not think to imitate them. His achievement there was to recognize how difficult it was to enter imaginatively into the spirit of Greek religion, and to perceive how greatly the Greek attitude to nature differed from the superficially similar pantheism of the romantic age. He saw that Greek beliefs were complex, and he expounded these complexities with both subtlety and lucidity. After offering allegorical interpretations of parts of the *Iliad,* he added, "But I do not believe that the idea ever weakens itself down to mere allegory. When Pallas is said to . . . strike down Mars, it does not mean merely that Wisdom . . . prevailed against Wrath. It means that there are, indeed, two great spirits, one entrusted to guide the human soul to wisdom and chastity, the other to kindle wrath and prompt to battle."[82] In other words, the allegorical element is only one part of Greek religion; and stressing the vitality of that religion, Ruskin rejected the simple schematism that opposed Hellenism and Hebraism:

> There is not the smallest . . . unspirituality in this conception. If there was, it would attach equally to the appearance of the angels to Jacob . . . or Manoah . . . the highest authority which governs our own faith requires us to conceive divine power clothed with a human form . . . , and retaining, nevertheless, sovereignty and omnipresence in all the world. This is . . . the heathen idea of a God; and it is impossible to comprehend . . . the Greek mind until we grasp this faithfully.[83]

Ruskin believed the Greek gods to be both abstract and actual; and he was thus able to give a more convincing account than could his contemporaries of how the Greeks conceived the relation between their deities and the natural world. "With us," he concluded, " . . . the idea of the Divinity is apt to get separated from the life of nature; and imagining our God . . . far above the earth, and not in the flowers or waters, we approach those visible things with a theory that they are dead; governed by physical laws, and so forth. But coming to them, we find the theory fail." We cannot, he says, resist the feeling that the fountain sings and the flowers rejoice, and so we fall "into the curious web of hesitating sentiment, pathetic fallacy, and wandering fancy, which form a great part of our modern view of nature." The Greek felt otherwise: "'The tree *is* glad,' said he, 'I know it is; I can cut it down: no matter, there was a nymph in it'."[84] In this way Ruskin could explain, what most Victorian scholars could but weakly deny, how the Greeks could believe that the visible world was filled with divine presences and yet have little or none of the modern feeling of love for nature. This much was shrewd; the strange feature of Ruskin's exposition is the apparent implication that Greek beliefs were in some respects truer than those of the nineteenth century. The theories of the scientists "fail"; Christian beliefs in transcendence and monotheism seem inadequate. Though Ruskin's passionate adherence to Christianity was at times shaken to its foundations, his love and admiration for Greek beliefs never wavered.

His temperament led him to give a strongly moralistic tone to his account of Greek religion: Athene is the spirit of Wisdom, Ares of Wrath. But it was his interest in classical and modern landscape that drew him to investigate Greek beliefs in the first place, and throughout his life he loved Greek mythology above all because it enabled him to invest the British landscape with a numinous splendour, and, at the same time, to express his feeling for the *genius loci.* He liked to distinguish "the fishermen and ocean Gods of Solway" from "the marchmen and mountain Gods of Cheviot": he liked to "think of the Tay as a goddess river, as Greta a nymph one".[85] Symonds too enjoyed imagining that the landscape was charged with numinous presences; unlike Ruskin, though, he could not manage this in Derbyshire or Northumberland, but only in southern landscapes, where, he said, "The oread dwellers of the hills, and dryads . . . seem possible . . . men themselves are more a part of nature here than in the North, more fit for companionship with deities of stream and hill."[86]

The south was an unsullied region where antiquity survived; even, perhaps, in the people's religious practices. Wilde felt it "always a source of pleasure . . . to remember that the ultimate survival of the Greek Chorus is to be found in the servitor answering the priest at Mass". Baron Corvo, fantastical, Catholic, and decadent, imagined in *Stories Toto Told Me* an Italian peasant boy relating tales in which Christian tradition and pagan legend were curiously intermingled. So charming, the ignorance of these simple folk! Symonds might well have entered into this spirit, had not his agnosticism led him in a different direction. In one of his essays he describes a Sunday walk near Menton:

> Everything fits in to complete the reproduction of Greek pastoral life. The goats eat cytisus. . . . Pan sleeps in noontide heat. . . . Nothing is changed—except ourselves. I expect to find a statue of Priapus or pastoral Pan. . . . Surely, in some far-off glade . . . there must still be a pagan remnant of glad Nature worship. . . . So I dream until I come upon a Calvary. . . . There is the iron cross . . . the nails, the crown of thorns. . . . Nothing can take us back to Phoebus or Pan. Nothing can identify us with the simple natural earth.[87]

These are again second-hand sentiments, but this time the influence is Heine's. As a German and a Jew, Heine felt the contrast between the ancient and modern worlds acutely, seeing it also as a contrast between Hellenism and Hebraism. In his *Pictures of Travel* he quoted one of Homer's descriptions of the gods feasting. Then he continued, "Suddenly there came gasping towards them a pale Jew . . . bearing a great cross of wood . . . and he cast the cross on the high table of the gods . . . and the gods . . . melted in utter mist."[88] In a poem called *The Gods of Greece* he combated Schiller's appeal to the ancient deities to come back: "I have never loved you, ye gods! For the Greeks are repugnant to me." Zeus is now white-haired and miserable, Apollo's lyre is silent; younger gods have driven out the old, who are now exiled and defeated. He reverted to this theme in some of his last prose writings. Part of *The Goddess Diana* describes how Diana, Apollo and Dionysus invade a gothic castle. In *The Gods in Exile* he discusses the fates of the pagan deities in the Middle Ages; Mercury set himself up as a merchant; Apollo became a shepherd in Austria, but was executed by the church authorities because his singing shocked them. Bacchus became Father Superior of a monastery in the Tyrol, with Silenus and Pan for cook and cellarer, and once a year they would throw off their monkish robes and hold a Dionysiac revel.

Thespis; or, the Gods Grown Old was the first collaboration between Gilbert and Sullivan; so far had Heine's theme penetrated the English consciousness. Arnold had popularized the dichotomy between Hellenism and Hebraism; and Pater developed Heine's witty fictions, composing two stories about the return of pagan gods in the Middle Ages, both of them set in France: *Denys l'Auxerrois,* in which the hero proves to be an avatar of Dionysus, and *Apollo in Picardy.*[89] But Heine has suffered a sea-change in the course of crossing the Channel. In the first place, Pater does not draw a sharp dividing line between antiquity and the Middle Ages; his eclectic temper sought for strange similarities in dissimilar things, and he brings out the resemblances, as well as the conflict, between ancient Greece and the Christian centuries. Secondly, whereas Heine is interested only in the great abstract question of the change that came over culture and civilization with the victory of Christianity, Pater's concern, like that of the English romantics before him, is more concrete and visual, being largely with art and landscape. When Dionysus comes, the ancient and medieval worlds are blended together; therefore the miracle must happen in the distinctive scenery of "midland France", a "happy mean between northern earnestness and the luxury of the south". Under the god's influence the sculptors working on the cathedral develop a new style, combining the seriousness of the Middle Ages with the greater technical assurance of the Greeks. When Apollo comes to Picardy, it is the architecture that he affects: a barn is being built, and though gothic, it acquires a "classical harmony"; the stone has the texture of antique marble, and the gable is "almost a classic pediment".

In the middle of the last century there was a vogue for paintings of elves and fairies. Often these were mildly titillating (fairies do not wear clothes), but they were popular also because they offered a British equivalent to the nymphs and sylvans of antiquity. Wishing to invest their native landscape with an atmosphere of numinous wonder, the Victorians liked to pretend that there were fairies (or rather faeries) at the bottom of their gardens. Pater had many imitators because he (and Ruskin) showed that there was a more sophisticated way of indulging this fancy, by setting Greek gods among English scenery. Flecker carried this theme off with some verve in *The Ballad of Hampstead Heath,* which relates how Bacchus descended upon London:

> He spake in Greek, which Britons speak
>   Seldom, and circumspectly;
> But Mr. Judd, that man of mud,
>   Translated it correctly.
>
> And when they heard that happy word,
>   Policemen leapt and ambled:
> The busmen pranced, the maidens danced,
>   The men in bowlers gambolled.

But in *Oak and Olive* he was flimsily whimsical:

> When I go down the Gloucester lanes
>   My friends are deaf and blind:
> Fast as they turn their foolish eyes
>   The Maenads leap behind . . .
>
> Have I not chased the fluting Pan
>   Through Cranham's sober trees?
> Have I not sat on Painswick Hill
>   With a nymph upon my knees . . . ?

This theme is markedly Edwardian; even the sardonic Saki composed a story about Pan-worship in the English countryside. Sometimes the tone is hushed and reverent. In Grahame's *Wind in the Willows* the Rat and the Mole come to a "holy place" where they behold Pan: "The Mole felt a great Awe fall upon him . . . some august Presence was very, very near . . . he . . . saw the backward sweep of the curved horns . . . saw . . . the long supple hand still holding the pan-pipes. . . ." Most adults today are unimpressed by this sort of holy whimsy; but it still holds many children spellbound.

Most of the littérateurs who practised this genre have been forgotten; but Beerbohm's skit upon them survives.[90] The protagonists of *Hilary Maltby and Stephen Braxton* are rivals; each has produced a first novel which is competing with the other to be the most successful book of 1895. Maltby's *Ariel in Mayfair* is described as delicate and fanciful; it tells how "Ariel re-embodied himself . . . , leased a small house in Chesterfield Street, was presented at a Levée . . . , and worked meanwhile all manner of amusing changes among the aristocracy." Braxton's novel is called *A Faun on the Cotswolds;* Beerbohm comments, "From the time of Nathaniel Hawthorne to the outbreak of the War, current literature did not suffer from any lack of fauns. But when Braxton's first book appeared fauns had still an air of novelty about them. We had not yet tired of them and their hoofs and their slanting eyes and their way of coming suddenly out of woods to wean quiet English villages from respectability. We did tire later."

Beerbohm's satire is exceedingly acute; he appreciated that the advent of gods (or fairies) was a theme that had been used for different ends. Maltby exploits it for the purpose of comic fantasy; so in real life did Flecker, and Beerbohm himself. Indeed, is not Maltby, small, dapper, an exile in Italy, a fastidious stylist, in part a parody of his own creator? Towards the end of the nineteenth century the supernatural suddenly became respectable in literature: Wilde and even Henry James were prepared to use it to express symbolic truths about society and its members. Braxton, however, is somewhat different. A city-dweller like Saki was pleased to think that the countryside was seething with dark superstitions and volcanic passions; some recent films have shown that this fantasy still appeals to the urban mind. Beerbohm delicately insinuates that Braxton's rustics are preposterously earthy. "There remains deep down within our souls," said Symonds in his usual refined tones, "some primal sympathies with nature, some instincts of the Faun, or Satyr, or Sylvan, which education has not quite eradicated."[91]

In his *Four Quartets* Eliot describes a visit to Little Gidding in midwinter. It is not a beautiful spot: the road is rough, and the dull façade of the church is hidden behind a pigsty. Yet this is a holy place; God is present in the flat, sodden countryside of Huntingdonshire, "Now and in England".[92] It may seem inept to compare Eliot with Flecker and Grahame, and yet they have much in common; in all three there is a concern with landscape and its supernatural associations. Beerbohm was shrewd to make Braxton's faun appear in the Cotswolds: Gloucestershire was a favoured setting for such Hellenic intrusions, because it was felt to be so quintessentially English; this is where Flecker saw the Maenads. The poet enjoys the piquant contrast between exotic Greece and the everyday English scene, between goatish Pan and the "sober" trees. The proper nouns, Cranham and Painswick, are important: sturdy, solid English names. And yet they evoke one of the more romantic regions of the country. Flecker's attitude is complex: at the very moment that he stresses the ordinariness of the English landscape, he is asserting with Ruskin that "you might have seen the gods there morning and evening". The same complexity is to be found in Eliot: on one level "Now and in England" means "in our familiar, commonplace circumstances", and yet as he repeats the word "England" we realize that it reverberates with heroic associations, recalling the history of which the community at Little Gidding was a small but glorious part. We sense the throb of patriotism, the sudden catch at the heart. Unlike Flecker, Eliot does not find his Deity in a conventionally picturesque setting; but like him, he extols the magical beauty of the ordinary English countryside:

> If you came this way in may time, you would
> find the hedges
> White again, in May, with voluptuary
> sweetness.

Grahame, for his part, uses the names of flowers to stress the Englishry of the place where Pan is seen. "The rich meadow-grass seemed . . . of a freshness and greenness unsurpassable. Never had they noticed the roses so vivid, the willow-herb so riotous . . . they stood on a little lawn of marvellous green, set round with . . . crab-apple, wild cherry, and sloe." This is not a Grecian scene.

No more Greek is the watery landscape in J. W. Waterhouse's picture of "Hylas and the Nymphs". Here is a good old English pond with muddy, sludgy banks and greeny-brown waters; just the sort of place where Tom Brown might be angling or Jeremy Fisher propelling his punt. (On another canvas Waterhouse set the indubitably northern Ophelia in much the same marshy world of reeds and weeds and squashy vegetation.) It is a sunless summer day. We can even determine the time of year within quite narrow limits: it is late June or July, since there are water-lilies and the yellow flags are in flower. The nymphs are rising from the waters, pubertal, unmistakably English, and naked. And they have shed their inhibitions with their clothes; despite their shy, wistful expressions, there is a gleam of invitation in their eyes, and two of them reach out their arms to the young man. Here Greece and England are blended pictorially, as elsewhere in verse and prose.

It was best for the gods to go by their Greek names, which sounded grand and elemental, whereas the Roman names merely brought to mind the tame classicism of the eighteenth century. Besides, had the Romans themselves really believed in their gods? "No passing beggar or fiddler . . . ," said Yeats, "has ever . . . been awe-struck by nymph-haunted or Fury-haunted wood described in Roman poetry. Roman poetry is founded upon documents, not upon belief." But Greek poetry could be genuinely spooky: "When I prepared *Oedipus at Colonus* for the Abbey stage I saw that the wood of the Furies . . . was any Irish haunted wood."[93] It is Eros, not Cupid, who stands in the middle of Piccadilly Circus; a period piece, since only perhaps in the 1890s would anyone have thought to commemorate the evangelical Lord Shaftesbury with a statue of a pagan god of sexual desire. However, Londoners quickly took their revenge on this intrusion of an alien culture by pronouncing him Eeross.

For Pan *was* dead, and all the preciosities and poetasteries of the *fin de siècle* could not make the old gods live. Forster made the point in *The Longest Journey*. "I had a great idea," says Rickie Elliot, "of getting into touch with Nature, just as the Greeks were in touch; and seeing England so beautiful, I used to pretend that her trees and coppices and summer fields of parsley were alive. . . . I got in such a state that I believed, actually believed, that Fauns lived in a certain double hedgerow near the Gog Magogs." In consequence, he takes to writing short stories of the whimsically numinous kind. One of them, as he tells Agnes Pembroke, is about a girl who rebels against her fiancé's vulgar materialism and rushes into the woods, where she turns into a dryad; or so the story implies, for the word "dryad" is never used. Agnes objects: "You ought to put that part plainly. Otherwise, with such an original story, people might miss the point." Forster portrays her as silly and shallow throughout the novel, but we are meant to feel in this case that her commonsense philistinism has exposed the artificiality of Rickie's Hellenism. There is an irony too in her belief that this hackneyed theme is so original. Forster returns to this motif later, when Rickie is dead and Mr. Pembroke is proposing to issue his stories posthumously under the title *Pan Pipes*. Wonham asks, more shrewdly perhaps than he realizes, "Are you sure 'Pan Pipes' haven't been used up already?"[94] And here there is a further irony still: Pan's pipes are "used up" because Greek religion is used up. Eliot is immeasurably superior to Flecker not least because his God is or has been authentically a part of English belief.

Wilde addressed a villanelle to Pan:[95]

> No nymph or Faun indeed have we,
> For Faun and nymph are old and grey, . . .
>
> Ah, leave the hills of Arcady!
> This modern world hath need of thee!

In one of his earliest poems, written at about the same date, Yeats uttered a conventional lament over the greyness of the modern world, beginning, "The woods of Arcady are dead."[96] But now it has changed its meaning: standing first among his collected poems, it seems to rebuke Wilde's appeal with the stern voice of the new century.

Notes

[1] *The Table Talk . . . of . . . Coleridge* (1917), p. 184; Kingsley, *The Heroes,* preface; *The Works of . . . Smith* (1859) I, p. 169; Wilde, *De Profundis;* Lytton, [*Last Days of Pompeii*] bk. 1, ch. 7; Macaulay, 'Thoughts on the Advancement of Academical Education . . .', *Ed. Rev.* XLIII (1826), 331.

[2] E. M. Butler, *The Tyranny of Greece over Germany* (Cambridge, 1935), p. 11.

[3] *Romola,* ch. 38; *Jude,* pt. 1, ch. 7.

[4] Pt. 2, ch. 3.

[5] J. E. Sandys, *A History of Classical Scholarship* (Cambridge 1903-8) III, p. 234.

[6] MacNeice, *The Strings Are False* (1965), p. 87; Woolf, *Collected Essays* (1966-7) I, p. 11 f.

[7] *Seven Men,* 'Enoch Soames'.

[8] *The Renaissance,* 'The Poetry of Michelangelo'.

[9] *The Old Vicarage, Grantchester.*

[10] *De Profundis.*

[11] *Childe Harold's Pilgrimage,* canto 2, st. 89; *Extracts from the Letters and Journal of William Cory,* ed. F. Warre Cornish (Oxford, 1897), p. 282.

[12] Op. cit., p. 111.

[13] *The Princess,* sect. 7, l. 167.

[14] Arnold, *On Translating Homer* (*Prose Works,* ed. Super, I, p. 150); Grote, *History of Greece,* prefatory note; G. O. Trevelyan, *The Life . . . of Lord Macaulay,* ch. 11; Arnold, ib.

[15] Browning, *Aristophanes' Apology.*

[16] *Don Juan,* canto 8, st. 39; *The Newcomes,* ch. 31; Mallock, *The New Republic,* bk. 4, ch. 1.

[17] Super III, p. 272 f.

[18] W. J. Bate, *The Burden of the Past . . .* (1971), p. 74.

[19] *Cranford,* ch. 15.

[20] Ch. 2 (Super V, p. 116).

[21] *In Parenthesis* (1937), p. 160 f.

[22] 'On Mitford's History of Greece'.

[23] Buckle, *History of Civilization in England* I, ch. 2; *Romola,* ch. 6.

[24] *Thoughts of a Briton on the Subjugation of Switzerland.*

[25] Grote, *History of Greece,* pt. 2, ch. 1; Tozer, *Lectures on the Geography of Greece* (1873), p. 177; Symonds, *Sketches in Italy and Greece* (1874), p. 207.

[26] Gillies, *The History of Ancient Greece* (1786) I, p. 36; Aristotle *Pol.* 1327 b.

[27] See Arnold, 'The Function of Criticism . . .' (Super III, p. 272).

[28] Pater, *The Renaissance,* 'Winckelmann'; Disraeli, *Lothair,* ch. 8; Robertson, *Sermons on Christian Doctrine* (1906), p. 298.

[29] *Don Juan,* canto 1, st. 63.

[30] *Childe Harold's Pilgrimage,* canto 2, st. 73; Symonds, op. cit., p. 207 f.

[31] *Introductory Lectures on Modern History* (Oxford, 1842), pp. 36 f., 33.

[32] Leighton, *Addresses Delivered to the Students of the Royal Academy* (1896), address of 1883; Disraeli, *Sybil, passim.*

[33] Ar. *Lys.* 998 ff.

[34] *Taine's Notes on England,* tr. E. Hyams (1957), p. 286; Mueller, *Dorians,* bk. 4, ch. 1, sect. 4.

[35] Arnold, 'A New History of Greece' (Super V, p. 263); Pater, *Plato and Platonism,* chs. 8, 1.

[36] Pater, ib., ch. 8.

[37] Buckle, loc. cit.

[38] *Contarini Fleming,* pt. 5, ch. 8; Tozer, op. cit., p. 175.

[39] Pater, op. cit., ch. 8.

[40] *Writings on Art,* ed. D. Irwin (1972), p. 73.

[41] Plato, *Tim.* 22b.

[42] Pater, *The Renaissance,* 'Winckelmann'; *Greek Studies,* 'The Age of Athletic Prizemen'; Symonds, *Studies of the Greek Poets,* ch. 21.

[43] *Marius the Epicurean,* ch. 22.

[44] *Essays and Reviews,* p. 4.

[45] Ib., pp. 24, 27.

[46] Kovalevsky's description (S. S. Prawer, *Karl Marx and World Literature* (Oxford, 1966), p. 395).

[47] Symonds, *Studies . . . ,* ch. 1; *Essays and Reviews,* p. 27; Jebb, *Essays and Addresses* (Cambridge, 1907), p. 560; Pater, *Greek Studies,* loc. cit.

[48] 'On Antiquity' (*Complete Works,* ed. P. P. Howe, XII, p. 254 f.).

[49] *The Renaissance,* 'Winckelmann'.

[50] Pater, *Greek Studies,* loc. cit.; Jebb, op. cit., p. 570; Jenkyns, *A Lecture on the Advantages of Classical Studies* (Durham, 1834), p. 10 f.

[51] *Studies . . . ,* chs. 24, 21.

[52] *The Renaissance,* 'Winckelmann'; Hazlitt, 'Schlegel on the Drama' (Howe XVI, p. 64); Symonds, *Sketches . . .* p. 216 f.; Pater, *Plato and Platonism,* ch. 8.

[53] Woolf, op. cit. I, p. 3; Symonds, *Studies . . . ,* ch. 17.

[54] *The Dynasts,* preface.

[55] Plut. *Demetr.* 12.

[56] Symonds, *Studies . . . ,* chs. 18, 10; Ruskin, *Aratra Pentelici,* § 200; Pater, *The Renaissance,* 'Sandro Botticelli'; Mallock, op. cit., bk. 3, ch. 4.

[57] Edn. of Beethoven, op. 110 ad loc.; *Essays in Musical Analysis* (1935-9) I, p. 195.

[58] Op. cit., p. 569.

[59] *The Renaissance,* 'Winckelmann'.

[60] R. Hill (ed.), *The Symphony* (1949), p. 349.

[61] *The Renaissance,* 'Winckelmann'.

[62] *A Musical Instrument.*

[63] *Flush or Faunus.*

[64] *The Dead Pan,* headnote.

[65] 'The world is too much with us . . .'

[66] *Childe Harold's Pilgrimage,* canto 2, sts. 53, 85, 88, 87.

[67] *Hellas,* l. 230 ff.; *Shelley at Oxford,* ed. W. S. Scott (1944), pp. 64 f., 61; *The Athenians,* ed. Scott (1943), p. 44.

[68] *The Queen of the Air,* preface.

[69] *Modern Painters* III (pt. 4), ch. 12, § 5; ch. 13, § 1 f.

[70] Ib. III, ch. 13, § 3; Symonds, *Studies of the Greek Poets,* ch. 24.

[71] *Modern Painters* III, ch. 13, § 15 ff.

[72] Ib., § 4.

[73] Ib., § 5.

[74] *Sesame and Lilies,* § 35.

[75] Ib., § 84.

[76] *Fors Clavigera,* letter 5.

[77] *Praeterita* III, § 84.

[78] *Modern Painters* III, ch. 4, § 5.

[79] Op. cit., § 3.

[80] Ib., § 32.

[81] *Praeterita* III, § 70; *The Queen of the Air,* § 75 f.

[82] *Modern Painters,* III ch. 13, § 7.

[83] Ib., § 8.

[84] Ib., § 13.

[85] *Praeterita* III, § 84; I, § 75.

[86] *Sketches in Italy and Greece* (1874), p. 21.

[87] Wilde, *De Profundis;* Symonds, *Sketches . . . ,* p. 6 f.

[88] Op. cit., *The City of Lucca,* ch. 6 (tr. C. G. Leland).

[89] In *Imaginary Portraits* and *Miscellaneous Studies.*

[90] In *Seven Men.*

[91] *Studies . . . ,* ch. 21.

[92] *Little Gidding,* sect. 1.

[93] *Explorations* (1962), p. 438.

[94] Chs. 7, 35.

[95] *Pan.*

[96] *The Song of the Happy Shepherd.*

Linda Dowling (essay date 1994)

SOURCE: "Victorian Manhood and the Warrior Ideal," in *Hellenism and Homosexuality in Victorian Oxford,* Cornell University Press, 1994, pp. 32-66.

[*In the essay that follows, Dowling provides an extensive account of the shift to a classical curriculum at Oxford in the mid-nineteenth century. With her exploration of the cultural motivation for these changes, she lays the groundwork for her larger thesis, in which she contends that the Hellenism revived to provide a new model of masculinity also provided the model for the first true "homosexual" identity.*]

The most memorable figure of J. A. Symonds's Oxford career, the man he met weekly for almost two years, and into whose beloved presence he never stepped without acute emotion, was Benjamin Jowett, Tutor of Balliol and Regius Professor of Greek. As Jowett supervised the younger man's preparation for the crucial final honors examination in classical philosophy and history, the course of study known at Oxford as *Literae humaniores* or Greats, Symonds found himself by turns crushed and uplifted by the intense experience of these tutorials, "feeling myself indescribably stupid, and utterly beneath my own high level," as he recalled, "but quitting the beloved presence with no diminution of an almost fanatical respect" (Brown 1:226). By the time such undergraduates as Symonds and Pater were coaching with him in the early 1860s, Jowett had become a celebrated tutor, whose students' brilliant successes in the examination schools so repeatedly foretold their subsequent achievements in the sphere of national and imperial affairs—in the Church, the Foreign Office, and Parliament—the worldly realm of power and duty which Jowett himself rated so high.

Yet it was not the worldly advantage unlocked by his teaching and sponsorship which Jowett's students would remember with such vividness, but instead the intensity of the tutorial itself, with its racking silences, penetrating queries, quenching utterances. Whatever were the pains inflicted by this experience, its pleasures seemed to the young men to be unexampled. Symonds, paralyzed by the conviction of his own complete inadequacy, nonetheless left the tutor's room feeling "obscurely yet vividly" that "my soul [had] grown by his contact, as it had never grown before" (1:226). This note is sounded repeatedly in the memoirs left by Jowett's pupils, of a moral counsel so capacious in its scope that it became a "pastoral supervision" (Campbell 203), of an intellectual stimulus that seemingly produced the requisite abilities in the very men from whom they were so harrowingly demanded, Jowett's labors as tutor always implying, as one Balliol student remembered, "a belief in powers hereafter to be developed, and the belief seemed to create the thing believed in" (200).

It was this intense Oxford "tutor worship," centering in Jowett especially but involving other dons as well, that contemporary Cambridge men regarded as so peculiarly Oxonian, a species of devotion, as one graduate insisted, which "does not flourish on the banks of the Cam" (Tollemache 181). Such modern commentators as Geoffrey Faber would seek to account for the peculiar intensity of Jowett's tutorial relationships by projecting upon it the categories of Freudian psychology, positing in Jowett a homosexual "sublimation" which early became for him "not only possible but necessary" (84). Yet it is only when we attend to the specific Victorian context of these Oxford tutorials, to their historical enmeshment in a series of urgent questions and fears about Britain's national survival, that the larger meaning of Oxford tutor worship, as well as its complex relationship to the emergence of homosexuality in the twentieth-century sense, becomes genuinely clear. For when we view it against its original mid-nineteenth-century background of deep and conflicting sociopolitical anxieties, Jowett's tutorial becomes visible as an instrument of profound ideological change, as a traditional structure now deployed to new purpose, effectively channeling a saving new secular gospel of intellectual self-development and diversity into the souls of the civic elite who would guide Britain, as Jowett believed, through the darkening wilderness of the century's end.

College tutorials had been conducted in some form at Oxford during the preceding two centuries. Only in the years following 1825, however, would this generally dry and formulaic interchange between tutor and pupil begin to assume a larger significance in English cultural life. For with its reinvention as a tradition by J. H. Newman and Hurrell Froude during the Anglican religious insurgency to be known as Tractarianism, the college tutorial began to function at Oxford as a vehicle for the intensifying reciprocal bonds of masculine interest, affection, and obligation to which modern cultural theory has given the name "male homosociality." In the hands of a few Tractarian teachers conversing with a few responsive undergraduates, the Oxford tutorial would become part of an ethos in which intellectual growth was to merge with religious awakening, and instruction would verge on intimacy. When in turn Jowett's no less insurgent generation of liberal dons later sought a vehicle for their own very different reforms, the Tractarian tutorial lay ready to hand. Coming to power through the revolution of university reform in the 1850s and 1860s, Jowett and the university liberals were to commandeer the Oxford tutorial, recommissioning it in the name of "mental illumination," Greek studies, and more generally, Hellenism.

Immediately after Oscar Wilde's trial for sodomic indecency, of course, it would be difficult to pronounce the word "Hellenism" without an insinuating leer. Behind that semantic corruption, however, lies a larger and more significant story of cultural transformation and unintended consequences. For so great was the success of Victorian liberal Hellenism in coming to represent all the dimensions of human experience denied under the Calvinist dispensation of religious fundamentalism or starved under the materialist regime of industrial modernity that it would open—in a way wholly unanticipated by the liberals themselves—the possibility of legitimating male love. Liberal partisans of Greek studies had instead been intent upon deploying Hellenism as a discursive language of sociocultural renewal. For by the 1860s such liberals as Jowett and Arnold, Gladstone and Mill would come to sense that the older ideological structures of public life were no longer capable of sustaining Britain in the struggle among nations. Precisely as such structures as the warrior ideal underlying classical republicanism came to seem increasingly irrelevant to the actual conditions imposed upon Britain by industrial modernity did the alternative values Victorian liberals located in Hellenism seem to promise the hope of cultural transformation. The great irony would thus always be that the mid-Victorian liberals, struggling in the face of the apparent powerlessness of classical republican "manliness" to rescue Britain from stagnation and future decay, would so far succeed in their polemical work on behalf of Hellenism as quite unexpectedly to persuade the late-Victorian homosexual apologists that in Hellenism they themselves would find a no less powerful, no less liberal language, a legitimating counterdiscourse of social identity and erotic liberation.

To speak of Tractarianism by its other customary name as the Oxford Movement is to see the University of Oxford as a decisive battleground in the Victorian struggle over the sociopolitical order being brought forth by secular materialism and industrial modernity. As an episcopal seat and the leading school of the Anglican church, Oxford would inevitably experience any changes in the relationship between church and state with the sharpest immediacy. With the tumultuous onset of political reform in Britain during the 1820s and 1830s, however, constitutional change seemed to those resisting it to bear a frighteningly revolutionary, even "Jacobinical" face. "Three of the great embankments of our Constitution have recently been cut through," declared Sir Thomas Acland, referring to the repeal of the Test and Corporation Acts in 1828, the Catholic Emancipation of 1829, and the great Reform Bill of 1832. "The first broke down the long established qualification for office in our Christian state," he continued, "the second *let in, as legislators,* men implacably hostile to the great living principle of all our institutions; the third, as a natural consequence of the two former poured into the House of Commons . . . the turbid waters of sheer *mammonry,* democracy and republicanism" (Brendon xv).

Inside the space of four short years, the hegemony of the Church of England, theoretically intact since the seventeenth century, had thus been broken. For after 1828 the Parliament that was constitutionally permitted to intervene in church affairs was no longer exclusively Anglican in membership; after 1829, it was no longer exclusively Protestant; and in 1830 a bill was introduced to admit Jews, Macaulay arguing with incomparable brio that there was no argument against admitting Jews which did not hold at least as strongly against seating Christians.[1] The violent agitation of 1831-32 over the Reform Bill saw outbreaks of hostility against the Church for its role as traditional ally of Tory intransigence. After 1832 the unmistakable momentum of reform suggested that disestablishment itself was near, with matriculations at Oxford falling by 20 percent as young men doubted there would still be a Church of England into which to be ordained (*Report* 17). Then, in the culminating event of the series, the new Parliament that had been elected by the tradesmen and tenant farmers enfranchised through the Reform Bill voted in 1833 to abolish ten bishoprics in Ireland. What could be the future of the Church, many Anglicans asked themselves, if powers so alien and antagonistic to it were allowed so large a share in determining its future?

Against this background of constitutional revolution and "national apostasy," Oxford became the center of the impassioned counterrevolution known as Tractarianism. Hurrell Froude and John Henry Newman, electrified by John Keble's "national apostasy" sermon of July 1833, and stirred by the example of the French bishops persecuted during the July Revolution of 1830 in France, joined their voices to reassert the ancient powers and privilege of the Church. Together they raised the cry of "The Church in danger!" not hurled in such vehemence since the Sacheverell crisis of 1710. "Open your eyes to the fearful change which has been so noiselessly effected," as Froude now commanded, "and acknowledge that BY STANDING STILL YOU BECOME A PARTY TO REVOLUTION" (8).

Within the fiery Tractarian insistence on reasserting the supernatural authority and agency of the Church, in turn, there surged a darker apprehension, the fear that the hectically "commercial" statecraft employed to secure the passage of the recent reforms in Parliament (Mozley 1:141) was but the sign of a larger bankruptcy. Looking on in anger as essential religious principle was crassly exchanged for profitable or peaceful relations with powerful interest groups, the Tractarians became convinced that these greasy machinations—for which Sir Robert Peel's stunning reversal on the Catholic Emancipation he had originally opposed had become the unforgettable, unforgivable symbol—would soon obliterate the way to a higher, purer life. We have always understood that what Samuel Taylor Coleridge refers to in his brilliant and influential *Lay Sermon* of 1817 as the "overbalance of the commercial system" (117-18) was nothing other than the consequences of nineteenth-century modernity itself: the complex socioeconomic formation that was daily remaking Britain through the secularizing, materializing, and alienating effects of the cash nexus and urbanization, swelling population, social mobility, and class competition, the centralization, democratization, and homogenization produced through widening literacy and the new systems of transport and communication. Yet such Victorian movements as Tractarianism become fully intelligible only when we also see that this moment was still one in which modernity could not yet be grasped in secular terms. This is why Coleridge's *Lay Sermon* had been, in some sense, intended as an actual homily or sermon, and it is why his argument had been so concerned to offer the Church, conceived in somewhat altered terms, as a counterpoise to the "Commercial System."

The earliest stirrings of Tractarianism may thus be glimpsed in the growing conviction that Coleridge's vision of the Church partaking "not merely of a better but of an *other* life," regenerating the English community as "not so properly better as *other* men" (126), had instead been itself reduced to a passive instrument of the "Commercial Spirit." In the same way, Peel's pursuit of compromise and accommodation in Parliament had seemed to reduce his followers to contemptible puppets, each knowing that "whoever bound themselves to him might any day be called on to unsay all they had been saying and undo all they had been doing" (Mozley 1:141). This picture convinced the Tractarians that both the Church of England and English society as a whole were becoming dangerously unmoored from the realm of the transcendental—the domain of honor and ideals where men were, as Coleridge had said, "weighed not counted" (140). It was in this critical moment that Newman at Oxford would issue his thrilling call to arms in the first of the *Tracts for the Times:* "CHOOSE YOUR SIDE. To remain neuter much longer will be itself to take a part" ("Tract" 10).

Newman grasped from the first that the Oxford Movement involved far more than just the hopes of those young men specifically intending to take Anglican orders, his genius perceiving the hunger among so many other impressionable and idealistic Oxford undergraduates for some higher rule of life. Like its equivalents at Harvard, Heidelberg, and Salamanca, a significant portion of the rising Oxford generation had felt "the deeper seriousness," as Arthur Stanley was to call it, "breathed into the minds of men . . . by the great convulsion of the French Revolution" (158). During this time, the English youths' sense of the apocalyptic immediacy of change was repeatedly sharpened by fears of rebellion by radicals, by the Irish, and later by the Chartists, just as their sense of the living alternative reality of the medieval past was heightened by Robert Southey's *Colloquies* (1829), Kenelm Digby's *Broad Stone of Honour* (1822), and the novels of Walter Scott, to whom Newman, as he would say in later years, owed his very self.

Newman's keen sense of the ardor and sincerity alive within the younger men with whom he dealt as tutor of Oriel and rector of St. Mary's, was in turn heightened by his indignant awareness that their idealism went unanswered—worse, was throttled into conformity or condemned as fanaticism by the conventional society of the day. Driven by the widening prosperity spread through the railway and shipbuilding boom of the 1830s, the demand for social acceptance on the part of hitherto disdained or excluded social classes was, he saw, at once encouraging and calcifying a regime of respectability. It was "a narrow and shallow system, that Protestant philosophy," as Newman called it, and it "forbids all the higher and more noble impulses of the mind, and forces men to eat, drink, and be merry, whether they will or no" ("Antony" 93).

What indeed, asked Newman, would have been the fate of a Saint Antony or any of the early church fathers had he to live instead according to the cramping formulas of present-day English existence? "Longing for some higher rule of life than any which the ordinary forms of society admit, and finding our present lines too rigidly drawn to include any character of mind that is much out of the way, any rule that is not 'gentlemanlike,' 'comfortable' and 'established'" (95), as Newman declared, such a man would have become a renegade to the craven society of "*sensible* Protestants" who will "not let a man do anything out of the way without stamping him with the name of fanatic" (93).

Profoundly, even contemptuously aware of the ignobly deforming powers exerted by social and commercial modernity, Newman perceived in the same moment that a single counterpoise to that modernity lay all about him, in the visible spires and invisible traditions of Oxford. Looking out upon his alma mater through the imaginative historical vision he had gained from Scott, he saw that "her present life is but the continuation of the life of past ages, and that her constituent members are, after all, in a new form and with new names, the Benedictines and Augustinians of a former day ("Oxford" 331). This monastic principle, exercrated and defamed in the tradition of anti-Catholicism which had flourished in England ever since the expropriation of the monasteries under Henry VIII, was lingering still at Oxford and Cambridge. Absorbed everywhere else in the nation into "the frivolous or selfish tempers and opinions of an advanced civilization" (331), the monastic principle constituted nothing less than a vital principle of opposition to modernity, and Newman now called upon the ancient universities, "as being out of the world, to measure and expose the world, and, as being in the heart of the Church, to strengthen the Church to resist it" (331).

The specific staging ground for Newman's campaign to recover the ancient religious power lying latent within Oxford was the college rather than the university, for colleges constituted better, other "homes," as Newman said ("Rise" 189), and could function as intimate moral communities for each resident, "where his better thoughts will find countenance, and his good resolutions support" (189-90). Newman began by working to restore his own college, Oriel, to its medieval condition under the founding statutes as a body of resident fellows devoted to both educating younger students and pursuing their own studies. To recover the genuine educational function of the college was to strip structures such as the college tutorial of all their old accreted crust of condescension, impersonality and sloth, that eighteenth-century tradition of donnish coldness and indolence immortalized in Gibbon's *Autobiography* as the "almost incredible neglect" of pupils by tutors and the utterly "impassable gulf" lying between them (82).

Newman's idea of the tutorial connection, by contrast, insisted on its nature as a pastoral relationship, a cure of souls. Because by collegiate statute every tutor was a fellow, and every fellow was either in Anglican orders or preparing for them, Newman could insist that "a Tutor's profession was of a religious nature" (Culler 72) and could defend his claim by appealing to the statutes through which flowed the transcendental authority of the visible Church. In this way his reform in college teaching could be accomplished, not by proposing any new change, but simply by recalling the tutorial to its original religious purpose.

The pastoral relationship in turn supplied the metaphysical basis for what Newman himself recognized were the extraordinary new relations "not only of intimacy, and friendship, and almost of equality" (Faber, *Apostles* 166) arising between the Oriel tutors and their pupils, for Newman and Froude had come to stand "in the place of a father, or an elder and affectionate brother" to the younger men (Mozley 1:181). In Newman's hands the reformed tutorial represented the institutionalization of his doctrine of "personality" or personal influence, that "sovereign compulsory sway" which a "single individual, trained to practise what he teaches" may in a spirit of unconscious holiness exercise over "the weak, the timid, the wavering, and the inquiring" ("Personal" 94-95). Sustained and purified by the ideal disinterestedness of the pastoral bond, the tutorial relationship became a channel through which the presence and personality of the teacher—"the living voice, the breathing form, the expressive countenance"—could perform the "living and bodily communication of knowledge" ("Rise" 14, 13). Frustrated and short-lived as this tutorial experiment at Oriel proved to be, it yet became the core of a compelling pedagogical ideal, of teaching as a mode of intercourse comprehending the student in the full range of his humanity and potentiality, that would in the years to come remain at the heart of Oxford's institutional identity.

The tutorial revolution itself, however, comprised only one-half of Newman's effort to reconstitute Oriel on the lines of the medieval statutes. The other half was to recover the old monastic principle as a living motive for the tutors and fellows themselves. Newman's celebrated gift for friendship, coupled with the conditions of political threat outside Oxford as well as institutional persecution within, combined to generate around the Tractarians an exhilerating ethos of struggle, danger, sacrifice, and vital common purpose. Deeply moved by the ascetic example of the early fathers, Newman regarded monachism as a mode of life consisting "not in solitariness, but in austerities" ("Antony" 94), and perceived that such austerities as the celibacy requirement traditionally imposed on holders of college fellowships could contribute to their sense of community and solidarity, fellows wordlessly being encouraged to remain not only unmarried but resident in the college.[2]

If to shrink from celibacy, as R. W. Church would later say, was considered within Tractarian circles "a mark of want of strength or intelligence, of an unmanly preference for English home life, of insensibility to the generous devotion and purity of the saints" (321), celibacy itself gleamed outside those circles as the pattern for a high and noble sacrifice realizable within the limits of actual English life. This belief that an unseen, transcendent world just as utterly real and immediately present as the visible one could be approached through simple gestures of self-restraint is why the Tractarian practices of fasting and chastisement or the Tractarian desire "to live a virgin life, and to die a virgin," as one of Newman's younger colleagues, F. W. Faber, expressed the celibate ideal (Bowden 79), would move so many non-Tractarians to admiration. Tennyson, for example, otherwise so indifferent to theological controversy, would embody the celibate ideal in his 1834 poem "Sir Galahad," where the virgin knight's ecstatic vision of lilies and angels is shown to possess exactly the same degree of phenomenological reality as the driving hail that "crackles on the leads."

In this context an intense language of religious inwardness and confession would begin to operate as the idiom of daily life, first among the Tractarian partisans, and later among other disaffected and sensitive young men who were not of the Tractarian party. For the momentous questions concerning the survival of the Church in a hostile age were paralleled on the personal level among the more serious Oxford undergraduates by no less momentous questions concerning each man's belief and vocation, every commitment and every renunciation demanding an examination of conscience which was pitiless in its scrutiny and all but limitless in its scope. In these exigencies of conscience, a religious man would turn to the confidential society of his friends, because his heart, as Faber explained, "is teeming with a thousand high themes; and utterance brings the same kind of relief to him that tears do to the stupified heart-bursting mourner" (Bowden 12-13). Here the traditional religious vocabulary of bitter self-reproach and headlong emotional avowal, of "seaméd souls" and "filthy imaginings" and "love," becomes detached from its wholly inward bearing on the soul or God. Merging with a Wordsworthian idiom of emotional crisis and expressive relief, this religious language is now made to incorporate an outward orientation toward the friend, as when Faber, for instance, addresses a trusted companion:

> Now thou has seen my heart. Was it too near?
> Didst thou recoil from the o'erpowering sight;
> That vision of a scarred and seaméd soul?
> Ah! yes: thy gentle eyes were filled with fear
>
> . . . . .
>
> Well, be it so, dear friend! it was but right
> That thou shouldst learn where blossoms yet
> may bless,
>
> . . . . .
>
> Thou saw'st my heart: and didst not love me
> less.
>
> (Faber 68)

At any such moment as this we hear expressed the Tractarian ideal of friendship as spiritual communion which would so deeply color Oxford sociality in later years, prompting both A. H. Clough and G. M. Hopkins to fill their Oxford diaries with brief but impassioned notations of the ebb and flow in friendships. Even men at several removes of age or religious allegiance from the Tractarians would feel the power of its ideal of religious friendship—Jowett, for example, apologizing in an 1842 letter for not having written more about religion because "it seems so cold and prosy to write to an intimate friend about anything else" (Campbell 109-10). The same impulse would prompt R. L. Nettleship in 1869 to remind Henry Scott Holland of their Oxford years together, with their "memories of God approached together" in the "communion of souls" (Paget 37). As its original religious matrix receded, the Tractarian ideal of a friendship sealed in religion was to become instead simply an intense but secular religion of friendship at Oxford, while its defining assumption—that in the communion of souls one friend could show another the truth of his own "scarred and seaméd soul"—would become simply a plot device in Wilde's *Picture of Dorian Gray.* All these later developments would belong, however, to the interior history of Oxford. The great consequence of Tractarianism for the world outside Oxford, by contrast, lay upon a more immediate horizon.

With the dismaying conversion of Newman and other Tractarians to Roman Catholicism in the years around 1845, his enemies' darkest predictions of apostasy and betrayal were confirmed. Newman's "perversion" to Rome compelled the nation to accept as a fact, the *Oxford Protestant Magazine* insisted, "that for years the Universities have been the seat of a dangerous, and too successful conspiracy against the faith of which they were supposed to be the bulwarks" (Engel 23). The violently anti-Tractarian reaction that followed found its classic literary expression in the "muscular Christianity" of Charles Kingsley and J. A. Froude. This reaction arose, it is usually said, out of specifically religious and sexual anxieties, the sort of embittered panic that, for example, Kingsley underwent when he feared that his fiancée might be lost first to Tractarian "fanaticism" and then to Rome, or that Froude suffered when his early zeal for his elder brother Hurrell's Tractarianism wavered and reversed field at Newman's desertion, leading him into skepticism and heresy.[3]

In this view, the ten years following 1845 witnessed virtual hysteria over the growing power of the Roman church. The Tractarian "perverts" were succeeded by the inrush of Catholic immigrants fleeing the potato famine in Ireland. And the savage "anti-Maynooth campaign" against increasing a parliamentary grant to an Irish Catholic seminary was followed by volcanic indignation at the "papal aggression" of 1850-51, when Pius IX, appropriating ancient English names for modern Roman purposes, presumed to create an "archbishop of Westminster." In that moment, "No Popery" frenzy reached its highest pitch since the Gordon Riots of 1780 (Wolffe 2).

Yet virulent and widespread as this anti-Catholic feeling undeniably was, especially among Dissenting and Evangelical Protestants, the response among such Victorians as Kingsley and Froude involved far more than religious prejudice alone. If Kingsley could contemptuously dismiss the vulgar fear that "Popery will in a few years become the popular religion of these realms" ("Fear" 467), he could not regard with the same equanimity the cultural transformations being wrought by Tractarianism—in particular, its legions of "sleek passionless men, who are too refined to be manly, and measure their grace by their effeminacy" (*Tragedy* 82). Intense, remote, ostentatiously pious, and most of all, flagrantly, inhumanly celibate, the new masculine ideal encouraged first by Tractarianism and then by the Roman Catholic converts had become the *beau idéal,* as Kingsley insisted, of a "mesmerizing, table-turning, spirit-rapping, Spiritualizing, Romanizing generation" ("Thoughts" 571). Everything he read, everywhere he looked, from the diseased poetic preference for Shelley over Byron, to the inexplicable success of the Spasmodic poets—convinced Kingsley that "the age is an effeminate one" (571).

Such fears, as David Newsome and Norman Vance have so well described, were to leap into apocalyptic vividness when viewed against the fiery backdrop of war and war scares which the decade of the 1850s was to supply—the French invasion scare of 1852, the Crimean War of 1854-56, the Indian Mutiny of 1857, and the renewed fright over French invasion in 1859-60. In the face of these dangers, Kingsley declared, the nation required "Tyrtaean strains" from its poets ("Alexander" 459), not the flaccid introspection of the Spasmodics or the "denationalized" maunderings of "those who have lately joined, or are inclined to join, the Church of Rome" ("Froude" 224). Such Tractarians as Frederick Faber had already hailed the decline in martial fervor among young men as a sign of spiritual growth; he declared, "I joy for the young that they lay not [England's] honour . . . in that which mere blood of her sons hath won her, / Her world-wide name of glory. / I joy for the loss of the noisy gladness / That hath made late ages dull" (293). To Kingsley and Froude, however, that noisy gladness was nothing less than the war cries of England's victorious sailors and soldiers at the Armada and at Waterloo. In the immensely popular works each man wrote during this time—Kingsley's *Westward Ho!* (1855) and Froude's *History of England from the Fall of Wolsey to the Defeat of the Spanish Armada* (1856-70)—they sought to reawaken English patriotism and make it noisier still.

It is precisely here, as Kingsley and Froude glory in the blood sacrifice of England's armies and navies, that the "muscularity" of "muscular Christianity" demands to be seen as a specifically civic response. For when Kingsley protests that the age is "an effeminate one" or warns that in Spasmodic poetry "the manhood, the 'virtus' is small" ("Thoughts" 576), we instantly recognize the old language of classical republicanism, invoked as it had been by John Brown a hundred years before when effeminate manners and heated nurseries appeared to be pushing England toward defeat in war. In the same way, we understand that Kingsley's indignation at the "sleek passionless men" brought forth from Anglo- and Roman Catholicism is nothing other than the ancient voice of civic alarm as it confronts the approach of dangers threatening the nation at its most fundamental level as a polity. For garbed in a Tractarian cassock, the effeminatus has reappeared upon the national stage, taking up from the fop, the eunuch, and the molly its traditional role within classical republican discourse as the invariable sign of onrushing civic debility and ruin.

The primordial anxiety underlying this language of civic alarm expresses itself, as we have seen in Chapter 1, in a sustained tendency among Western nations of the republican tradition to identify the very safety and stability of a human community with the warrior ideal. Almost as though it belonged to an archaic level of consciousness capable under the right conditions of generating seismic tremors of sociocultural dismay, this anxiety reads any signs of "effeminacy" as evidence that the deepest mental or spiritual foundations of the polity—the willingness and ability of its citizens to defend it even unto death—are threatened with collapse. This is why civic dread can be focused, even so late as the mid-nineteenth century, upon the figure of the warrior, and specifically on the citizen-soldier who embodies the political collectivity, both in war, when "the nation inscribes itself in the body . . . in the wound" (Scarry 112), and in peace, when the nation repays its obligation to the soldier's sacrifice by bestowing upon him the civic powers most completely defining citizenship in the polity.

The earliest and most memorable expression of this symbolic relation between citizen-soldier and polity is made in the Western political tradition by the seventh-century B.C.E. Greek poet Tyrtaeus:

> Here is courage [*aretē*], mankind's finest possession, here is
> the noblest prize that a young man can endeavor to win,
> and it is a good thing [*xūnon*] his city and all the people share
> with him
> when a man plants his feet and stands in the foremost spears
>
> (Lattimore 14)

Thus does Tyrtaeus capture in a single image the symbolic or synecdochic relation between the collectivity and the hoplite warrior—the *xūnon* or good shared in common—which had come to birth in the historical moment when the older Homeric mode of warfare, consisting mainly of the berserk martial frenzy of a relatively small number of individual heroes engaged in single combat, was giving way to that new coordination of large numbers of soldiers, weaponry, and collective strategy called by historians of ancient Greece the "hoplite reform."

As the more expensive weapons and more difficult martial skills demanded in Homeric combat were replaced by the simpler panoply and skills of hoplite warfare, more men were enabled to fight. With the shift in tactics dictated by this increase in numbers, everything could now be seen to depend on the coordination and the self-discipline or restraint (*sōphrosynē*) of the Greek citizen-soldier acting as a part of a larger group or phalanx. For every hoplite was armed with a large round shield and spear, and, joining in the long, closely massed lines of his fellow hoplites, each man bore his shield overlapped to the left so as to protect his neighbor's unshielded right side. Mustered into battle by cadenced music, the entire phalanx thus moved as a single body, and the experience of this physical and tactical solidarity in combat generated, as Marcel Detienne has so brilliantly described, the very experience of collectivity and the common good which was to constitute the new Greek idea of political community.

Writing in the first moment when the experience of the phalanx and the polis began to coalesce as a sense of political communality, Tyrtaeus celebrates excellence or virtue (*aretē*) as a complex of specifically martial qualities. Emphasizing not only the physical courage required in hand-to-hand combat, when the hoplites had to stand and slash at their opponents, fighting "toe to toe and shield against shield hard driven, / crest against crest and helmet on helmet, chest against chest" (16), Tyrtaeus insists as well upon the psychic firmness and solidarity needed to sustain the phalanx in the bloody throes of battle: "All thought of foul flight completely forgotten, / [the hoplite] has well trained his heart to be steadfast and to endure, / and with words encourages the man who is stationed beside him" (14).

When Aristotle relocates this *aretē* within the ethical system of the *Politics,* the martial dimension to "virtue," even as it is subsumed within a larger morality of citizenship, will never be forgotten: the fighting qualities required by the hoplite phalanx remain the general or symbolic type of excellence to be aspired to by every citizen (3:7). In Aristotelian theory, the stark physical need of the polis for defense thus comes to be completed by the ethical need of the citizen to fulfill his telos as a man (*zōon politikon*) through the pursuit of civic excellence. In the republican tradition of succeeding centuries, this archaic warrior core will always retain something of its original potency. For Machiavelli, for Harrington, for John Brown, it is as crucial as for Aristotle, a psycho-cultural substrate that when disturbed never fails to respond with shattering force.

This is the buried level of martial consciousness stirred so powerfully in Kingsley and Tennyson during the war and invasion-scare years of the 1850s. It imparts in turn to such furiously topical anti-French poems of 1852 as Tennyson's "Form, Riflemen, Form" a deeper resonance with John Brown's dire warnings about the unmanned English coasts, and endows Tennyson's famous "Charge of the Light Brigade" of 1854 with its preeminent symbolic status as a poem of war. With its dactyllic rhythms summoning up the rigorously controlled canter of the British cavalrymen as they rode directly into the murderous cannon fire at the battle of Balaclava, Tennyson's "Charge of the Light Brigade" re-creates the primal scene of republican polity—soldiers' lives volunteered in blood sacrifice for the common good—and portrays that sacrifice under its Tyrtaean conditions.

The extraordinary compression in Tennyson's description of the actual fighting at Balaclava has helped obscure this point in much modern commentary on the poem (see, for example, McGann), so it may be well to emphasize it here. For the description,

> Flashed all their sabres bare,
> Flashed as they turned in air
> Sabring the gunners there
>
> (*Tennyson* 510)

is precise in its detail and specifically military in its reference, depicting not the static pose of some Romantic hussar out of Géricault, but instead the urgently mobile action of the cavalrymen's sabers as they execute the sword stroke known as the *moulinet,* that "almost ceaseless play . . . whirling round and round overhead" (Kinglake 4:169) which helps riders desperately beset on all sides keep their attackers at bay. "Sabring the gunners there"—the enemy whose bodies are "Shattered and sundered"—Tennyson's cavalrymen thus are fighting with all the relentless violence amid all the hideous visceral havoc of Tyrtaeus's hoplites fighting "toe to toe" so many centuries before.

This sudden and shocking reappearance, in the middle of the nineteenth century, of the Tyrtaean aspect of war is what would give the charge of the Light Brigade its enormous symbolic importance for Victorian civilization. It explains in turn why Kingsley would first have to struggle with disbelief and amazement ("I tell you the whole thing stuns me") before he could recognize that his own earlier call for "Tyrtaean strains" in poetry had in fact been answered by Tennyson, who, as Kingsley now said upon reading "Charge of the Light Brigade," "has a glimpse of what Tyrtaeus ought to be" (F. Kingsley 180-81). Through an extraordinary chance of war, topography, and human "blunder," the conditions of ancient warfare had resurfaced in a valley of the Crimea, tragically entrapping in anachronistic hand-to-hand combat a modern brigade of British cavalrymen whose normal military function was to harry the enemy, not attack fixed-gun emplacements.

The self-discipline—the *sōphrosynē*—and solidarity of these cavalrymen as they preserved the set pace and order of their lines down the long valley under deadly crossfire was breathtaking. Continuously closing up their ranks each time a rider fell so that "to distant observers, the alternate distension and contraction of the line seemed to have the precision and sameness which belong to mechanic contrivance," the measured advance of the Light Brigade under the hellish fire moved the French general Pierre Bosquet to protest in admiration, "C'est magnifique; mais ce n'est pas la guerre" (quoted in Kinglake 4:265-66 n.369). Yet it was precisely because it was war, war thrown so far back upon its ancient political premise as no longer to resemble any enterprise of modern military science, that the charge of the Light Brigade transfixed Tennyson, Kingsley, and the breathless Victorian public.

This in turn is why Tennyson's speaker, in recounting the approach, attack, and retreat of the brigade, is able to accomplish the complex illocutionary act Christopher Ricks and Edgar Shannon have noted as one of the great achievements of the poem, his "combining the immediacy of an eyewitness with the respectful distance of the acknowledged non-combattant" (18). For the speaker understands and keenly feels his own direct civic involvement in the distant battle, and does so according to the ancient terms of republican discourse: these young men have represented *him,* just as they have represented or taken the place of all the others too young or old or weak to go to war. The young men have suffered and died on behalf of the polity and the common good, and so the speaker concludes by calling on the polity to complete the circuit of civic excellence: to acknowledge the greatness of the young men's sacrifice, and the corresponding magnitude of its own debt: "Honour the charge they made! / Honour the Light Brigade" (*Tennyson* 511).

Yet "Charge of the Light Brigade" also contains a disquieting sign that all this courage and glory are mere illusion. For the display of archaic *aretē* and *sōphrosynē* embodied in the famous six hundred cavalrymen comes to light on this occasion only as the result of a grotesque series of errors—"Some one had blundered." The textual history of this famous line underscores its problematic relationship to the "glory"—the *aretē*—the poet wishes to celebrate, for Tennyson originally included, then excluded, then restored it, as if detesting the fact of the appalling "blunder" yet aware that it finally could not be separated from the extraordinary act of courage which was its outcome and very antithesis. Taking over "blunder" from a lead story in the *Times,* Tennyson makes use of a word rich in connotations of heavy clumsiness, and gross blindness, to convey the heedlessly unseeing, namelessly bureaucratic mentality that originated the fatal order. This fumbling stupidity he then contrasts to the brilliant grace and poise of the Light Brigade—smaller-made men, lightly armed, mounted on lighter-weight horses—who had with such a fearsomely clear-eyed devotion looked into the eyes of their own individual deaths and nonetheless carried the order out.

In fact, as such episodes as Florence Nightingale's struggle to establish a barrack hospital at Scutari made clear, the Crimean War itself belonged not to the world of Tyrtaeus at all but to the incomparably more complicated, bureaucratic world of modern war. This sphere was filled with professionalized cadres of officers and enlisted men, geopolitical strategic considerations, impersonal deployment of forces, complex logistical, support and resupply problems, tactical theories, interally diplomacy, inter-service rivalry, press and public relations—to name merely those aspects playing a role at Balaclava. It is this bureaucratized world in all its baffling and unmartial complexity which first presses into view behind the line "Some one had blundered," only to resurface again in Tennyson's uneasy awareness that he could keep this world neither out of his poem nor from enmeshing its brilliant Tyrtaean moment in an enormously complex web of material relations and civilian considerations wholly removed from the clear and noble imperatives of the ancient martial ideal.

The crucial poem for understanding the paradox of an archaic warrior ideal surfacing in the midst of a bewilderingly complex modernity thus becomes Tennyson's *Maud* (1855). In that work the Crimean War both is and is not the solution to the maddened narrator's misery. For it restores him to relative mental stability and function in the world as he goes off to fight at the end of the poem, yet it is at the same time clearly powerless to sweep the world clean of all the evils of modernity which have combined with the narrator's morbid temperament and his personal losses—his father's suicide, his mother's death, the duel with Maud's brother, Maud's death—to push him to, and then over, the brink of madness. The massive disparity between the speaker's belief that the war will bring beneficial change to the world and the likelihood of any genuine amelioration actually coming from war is one Tennyson's critics have from the first been keenly attentive to, in recent years arguing that the speaker's faith in war is proof of his continuing madness or of some obscurer satiric purpose or of a lobotomized jingoism, in Herbert Tucker's pungent phrase, so massive as to constitute a complete moral abdication (429).

The great virtue of this critical response has been that it underscores the degree of disjunction and tension between two competing sociocultural systems, whether these are termed realist versus romantic, or middle class versus aristocratic, or modern versus traditional. Its limitation, however, has been to identify the speaker's martial commitment at the end of *Maud* with an aristocratic or medieval-chivalric ideal of war. Instead, the martial ideal voiced in Maud's song—and hence in the speaker's decision to go to war which is shown to flow directly from her song—demands to be understood within the context of civic republicanism. For when the song tells of men who "March with banner and bugle and fife / To the death, for their native land,"[4] it refers not to any medieval campaigns or chivalric crusades but to a mode of combat in defense of the *patria* arising out of the Renaissance effort, so closely identified with Machiavelli's *Discourses* and *Art of War,* to revive the citizen militias of the classical republics. Here lies the great significance of so seemingly minor a detail as the fife music the soldiers march to in Maud's song. For the fife had first been adopted as a military instrument in England at the initiative of Henry VIII (Schlesinger 331), and thereafter became quite literally the instrument of the revived citizen militia ideal.

"Gallant and gay," Maud's song thus belongs to the frank, daylight world of such broadside ballads as "Duke William" (1746) or "Brave Wolfe" (1759) with their vivid retelling of the English victories at Culloden and Quebec[5] rather than to the eerie, mournful realm summoned up by a Border ballad such as "Sir Patrick Spens." In the same way, it is only within the ideological universe of classical republicanism that the "readiness" of the soldiers ("Ready in heart and ready in hand" [I:170]) can ever be a matter of genuine praise, for only citizen-soldiers are free to choose to fight—medieval fighting men, by contrast, having been stripped of such voluntary agency either by their oaths of fealty or by their pay as mercenaries.

Viewed against the background of classical republican assumptions, Maud's song thus becomes the voice ("Not her, not her, but a voice" [I:189]) of the archaic martial ethos that undergirds, as we have seen, the reciprocity and interdependence of polity and citizen at the deepest level of Western political experience. Taking Maud as its mouthpiece, this ancient ethos speaks to the narrator "an air that is known to me," and this responsive substrate of martial consciousness within him, once touched, continues to reverberate throughout the rest of the poem. At first paining him with the contrast between its "glory" (I:183) and his own languor and baseness (I:179), then rousing him to less self-centered and self-exculpatory thoughts (I:382-97), this ancient martial mentality finally moves the young man to the selflessness of enlisting to fight for the *patria* ("I have felt with my native land, I am one with my kind" [III:58]).

In this context, the speaker's concluding hope that, with the onset of war, the "glory of manhood" will "stand on his ancient height" (III:21) must be identified, not merely with some local anxiety about sex or gender in the twentieth-century sense, but with *virtus* or *aretē.* For that complex of martial and civic excellences will now be restored to a site that is "ancient" in the sense of "former" as well as in the sense of "extremely old," at least as old as Tennyson's source for this image in the early fifth-century B.C.E. Greek poet Simonides:

> There is one story
> that Virtue [*aretē,* feminine noun] has her
>   dwelling place above
> rock walls hard to climb
>
> . . . . .
>
> and she is not to be looked upon by the eyes
>   of every mortal,
> only by one who with sweat, with clenched
>   concentration
> and courage, climbs to the peak [*akron* = the
>   highest point or height]
>
> (Lattimore 55)

—lines Tennyson himself had copied into a volume in 1851 as the motto for his laureateship (Francis 123).

Even to glance through Tennyson's *Maud* is to see how deeply the categories of classical republican or Country-party ideology supply at each crucial juncture of the poem materials for the speaker's impassioned critique of commercial modernity. For such famous party rallying cries as the "paper credit" of Davenant and Pope, the "oriental despotism" of Trenchard and Gordon, the "master-miss" and "effeminacy" of Pulteney and Brown still may be heard resounding within Tennyson's poem, from the "vast speculation" that drives the speaker's ruined father to suicide, to Maud's "Sultan" brother who would marry her to a rich suitor, to the monied suitor himself, a "wanton, dissolute" and, in an earlier version of the poem, "effeminate" boy (I:387). The speaker himself, so shrunken by isolation, poverty, and misanthropy as to have become a bitterly inarticulate monad of Mandevillian egoism and Ricardian self-interest ("A wounded thing with a rancorous cry" [I:363]), can find a vocabulary with which to arraign the age for its monstrous selfishness only because he can still recall the classical republican language of commonality with its ideal of the *xūnon,* "the public good" (II:283).

At the same time, however, a fundamental tension persists throughout the poem between this ancient "voice" of martial citizenship and its modern incarnation in Maud, the beautiful young girl who opens to the speaker a private world of intimacy, sympathy, and erotic bliss so much more genuine and intensely real to him ("I have led her home, my love, my only friend. / There is none like her, none" [I:599-600]), as we are likely to believe, than any counterworld of the res publica summoned up by bugle and fife. The symptoms of an underlying tension or instability of values in both *Maud* and "Charge of the Light Brigade" thus reveal the degree to which the classical republican ideal of martial and civic "virtue" by the middle of the nineteenth century belonged to a discourse no longer answering to any lived historical reality.

Thus, as the equation of martial and civic competence at its core proved ever less relevant to the emergent modernity signaled by Coleridge's "Commercial System," the language of classical republicanism becomes so obviously reduced, as in *Maud,* to the status of a merely critical language, useful in sounding a certain sort of civic alarm but now only residually or intermittently capable of enunciating a positive ideal. For though such isolated and anomalous moments as "Charge of the Light Brigade" might for an instant restore its urgency, its power to comprehend the historical process had long since been negated by that "spirit which the ancients did not recognize," as Coleridge had long ago called it, "namely the Spirit of Commerce" (149). In this sense Macaulay's brilliant insight into the martial reality underlying and shaping Greek political ideals ("to be butchered on the smoking ruins of their city, to be dragged in chains") achieves its superb clarity precisely because it comes at the *end* of the historical stage of which it speaks, and hence can see it whole.

Yet the sense of civic danger or crisis so evident in Tennyson's Crimean War poems would remain at the center of Victorian intellectual consciousness, giving us the corresponding sense in which Victorian liberalism would arise as the project of mastering the crisis through an alternative system of thought or discourse adequate to the bewilderments of modernity in its unending social transformations. The great representative figure in this enterprise is, as we have always recognized, John Stuart Mill. Deeply responsive to the critique of commercial society developed by Adam Smith and Adam Ferguson in the Scottish Enlightenment, and powerfully influenced as well by Alexis de Tocqueville's analysis of democratic polities, Mill's writings give us, as John Burrow and Stefan Collini have so suggestively conveyed, something like the precise moment when English cultural analysis would turn away from an ethical perspective and toward a sociological one. For an account of Hellenism and homosexuality in Victorian Oxford, the crucial point lies in the way Mill's liberalism takes over the insight of such theorists as Smith and Ferguson into the dialectical nature of historical progress—that civilization must produce, as the very price of its advance, uncivilizing effects that in their turn retard or undermine the very civilization that had produced the progress.

The great difficulty Mill confronted was thus to reassert the genuine progressiveness of human progress, in the face of its regressive consequences in the nineteenth century, by recovering some compensatory power to offset or overcome those regressive effects. To find Mill in this posture regarding progress and social modernity is to see him once again as what he acknowledged he was—Coleridge's intellectual heir as much as Jeremy Bentham's. For by the 1850s as Mill prepared to write *On Liberty,* his enormously influential analysis of social and industrial modernity, he found himself in the position Coleridge had earlier occupied in the *Lay Sermon* of 1817—searching for a "counterpoise", indeed, Mill will borrow the very word, to the excesses of the "Commercial System."

At the same time, the situation of such Victorian liberal intellectuals as Mill had become much more difficult by the 1850s, because now there could be no more appeal to the counterpoise of the Church or religious belief of the sort Newman and the Tractarians had once raised. For by the 1850s it had become clear that at a deep and unsuspected level of cultural formation, religion itself was contributing to the problem of commercial modernity, not to its solution. From the Ritualist movement that was succeeding to the place of Tractarianism within the Anglican church to the Dissenting sects outside the Church so mindlessly agitated by the battle against "popery," the apparent resurgence of Victorian religious belief was providing a convenient screen for the demigod of respectability and the goddess of getting-on, whose worship was resulting, as Mill warned in *On Liberty,* in "a low, abject, servile type of character" (256). This character was, for Mill, precisely the reverse of the psychic and intellectual qualities now so urgently needed: that ideal of a rich individuality, as John Burrow has described it, "nurtured by free exposure to 'variety of experience' and diverse modes of life, issuing in an independence of mind and spirit which Mill presents both as the goal of individual human self-development and the guarantee of future social progress" (*Whigs* 81).

By contrast, the most regressive of the Victorian religious groups—the growing body of fundamentalist believers newly empowered by prosperity and political privilege—were able to impart energy to their money-making activities alone. Everywhere else—in science, in art, in society—the pinched and hidebound Calvinist character Matthew Arnold was to call Philistinism, and Dickens would depict under a myriad of fictional guises as the deadliest enemy to joy, sought to inhibit and constrain energy, wherever it could not utterly crush it as the irrefutable evidence of evil human self-will.

The stultifying effect of this narrow religious character, in turn, was being intensified and extended by other consequences of industrial modernity. From the civil servant's craven self-effacement within a torpid bureaucracy, to the silent assimilation of "different ranks, different neighborhoods, different trades and professions" (274) into the stupefying homogeneities of mass society, to the invasive psychosocial regimentation imposed by the burgeoning movements intent on the improvement of morals, the new conditions bred of industrial modernity were generating forces, as Mill believed, that would eventually crush out the independence and free creative powers of the gifted individual. It was precisely these qualities which were so necessary, in his view, to the further development of society as a whole. In an economic order increasingly determined by ideas rather than material resources or physical power, any deficit or stagnation in intellectual force must inevitably assume a great and ominous significance for Britain's future. Presided over by men and women too fearful "of doing 'what nobody does,' or of not doing 'what everybody does'" (270), the nation would lose its way, as Mill warned, unless individuals "of another stamp" arose to prevent its decline (272).

At this point in Mill's cultural analysis of modernity he resorts to a vocabulary of "Chinese stationariness" and "stagnation" to express his anxious sense of sociocultural crisis. For with the massive change in underlying historiographical paradigms which had begun to gather force in the later eighteenth century came a shift away from the cyclical model of history so central to classical republican thought, with its recurrent rise and fall of polities as each in its turn plays out the four-act Polybian drama of virtue, luxury, corruption, and ruin—and toward the model of progressive linearism, with its story of a single, cumulative ascent from barbarism to enlightenment. With this paradigm shift, in turn, must come a correlative shift away from the old explanatory categories of classical republican discourse—"virtue" "effeminacy" "corruption"—toward a conceptual idiom that is, as Burrow has so persuasively described in *Whigs and Liberals,* only residually civic humanist if indeed it is at all—the idiom of "stagnation" and "stationariness" and "uniformity."

Mill thus grasped with a clairvoyance born of genius and reading Tocqueville what Kingsley was constitutionally unable to see—that in an age when Britain's gravest danger lay in the weakness of its ideas rather than its defenses, the nation's central excellence—its *aretē*—could no longer be vested in any simply martial or muscular notion of "manliness." In the same way, Mill grasped through the medium of rational discourse what Tennyson was able to intuit only through the incomparably sensitive instrument of his poetry—that the old conceptual categories made available through classical republicanism were emptying and thinning out, slipping away from the new formations being raised throughout mid-Victorian culture by the forces of commercial and industrial modernity.

As soon as the crisis Mill identified in mid-Victorian Britain was perceived by his contemporaries as centering in the spread of social and intellectual "stagnation" and "uniformity," and no longer in civic "corruption," the compensatory excellence needed to oppose it could not longer be located in simple "manliness" but must be looked for in something like "energy" and "individuality" and "diversity." As soon as the residually Calvinist religious fundamentalism—what Mill now termed "this narrow theory of life" (256) and Newman had earlier called the "shallow and narrow system, that Protestant philosophy"—could no longer be restored to civic usefulness as a counterpoise to modernity by a simple resurgence of religious faith, there must be found elsewhere an alternative, secular ideal, and a conceptual language through which to express it. This positive ideal and conceptual language Mill and other Victorian liberals discovered in Hellenism.

A fierce struggle of antagonistic or competing discourses thus underlies the emergence of Hellenism as a major element in Victorian culture. For the burden assumed by Victorian liberalism was not merely that of inventing some alternative discourse adequate to the complexities of the modern age, but also of demonstrating, through the very form of its own discourse, why the great heritage of classical republican thought was no longer relevant to the modern world. The solution of Mill, Grote, Arnold, and other liberals would be precisely to counterpose to the Graeco-Roman model of classical republicanism its own image of a far different Greece, to challenge the authority of the classical republican model of the recurrent rise and fall of polities by insisting on Attic or Athenian Greece as the earliest embodiment of an enlightened rational progressiveness, the very engine of all subsequent Western advance. Without the momentous 150-year interval of high Athenian civilization, declared Mill as he reviewed Grote's *History of Greece,* the work that so massively transformed the Victorians' view of Athens, there would have been no other source "from which freedom and intellectual cultivation could have come, any other means by which the light never since extinguished might have been kindled" ("Grote II" 313).

Yet as the epigraph Mill chose for *On Liberty*—"the absolute and essential importance of human development in its richest diversity" (215)—would always suggest, Mill's Hellenic ideal represented no direct recovery of an ancient model so much as the powerfully mediated version of Greece produced by eighteenth-century German Hellenism. Behind this epigraph to *On Liberty,* which Mill is borrowing from Wilhelm von Humboldt's essay on the powers of government, lies the enormously rich idea of *Bildung*—of autonomous self-cultivation directed toward the end of a fully rounded and harmonious development of individual human potentiality—as it had been elucidated and enlarged for over fifty years by J. J. Winckelmann, J. G. Herder, Goethe, Schiller, Humboldt, and a score of others. Thus what Stefan Collini has called the distinctively Millian note of "variety, not uniformity" ("Introduction" lii) will always be heard to ring most immediately with echoes of a German *Kultur, Bildung,* and *Vielseitigkeit* (many-sidedness).

This German reinterpretation of Greece is in turn why the words of Pericles' Funeral Oration, to which Grote and Mill were both wont to appeal as the authorizing text for their ideal of Hellenism, would come to assume this particular aspect of "variety not uniformity" only during the later nineteenth century, after the influence of Germano-Hellenism had been diffused throughout Victorian literary culture. For the knotty Greek shorthand of Thucydides' account of the Periclean oration admits of many interpretative readings, and the word *eutrapelōs* (2.41.1), which such Victorian translators as Benjamin Jowett and Henry Dale, working by the light of liberal Hellenism, would render as "with versatility" or "versatile," had earlier been translated in a far less positive sense. When Samuel Bloomfield had translated the passage in 1828, for instance, his version clearly suggested that the flexibility or suppleness of character which Pericles so praised in the Athenians as *eutrapelōs* might to an Englishman writing thirteen years after Waterloo in fact resemble nothing so much as the volatility and perfidy of the French (Bloomfield 1:383n).

Only now, looking back on the founding moment of Victorian liberalism and Victorian Hellenism from a historical standpoint well beyond them, can we grasp the justice of Isaiah Berlin's observation that "variety as a positive value is a new idea. . . . Some think that Pericles said something of this kind in his famous Funeral Speech. He came close to it but does not reach it" (53). For the Hellenic ideal Mill and Grote found in fifth-century Athens, that "picture of generous tolerance towards social dissent, and spontaneity of individual taste, which we read in the speech of the Athenian statesman" ("Grote II" 320), and all Mill meant by "variety not uniformity" and "human development in its richest diversity" belong preeminently to the midcentury moment of the Victorian sociocultural crisis. Only then, during the anxious transition when culture, as Pocock has noted, finally replaced property as the qualifying characteristic of the civic elite, did the Funeral Oration of Pericles come to be ranked among the sacred writings of Western civilization (500).

Within Mill's call for a new ideal of individuality and diversity, for a modern-day Hellenism encompassing such elements as "pagan self-assertion," "nonconformity," "freedom," and "variety of situations," there may already be glimpsed the outlines of a late-Victorian counter-discourse of sensuous diversity and homosexual dissent. Yet a more immediate question arises: on what basis could the new discourse of liberal Hellenism, unmartial, aesthetic, and inward-turning as it seemed to be, engage the allegiance of a Victorian civic elite whose instinctive psychosocial responses had been, as we have seen, so deeply molded by the martial, arms-bearing traditions of classical republicanism and Country-party ideology?

The answer in turn is that Victorian Hellenism could supplement, and in time come so largely to supplant, the older republican ideal of martial and civic *virtus* because at the deepest level of its own discursive genealogy it encompassed a position understood to be no less martial and essential to the polity: civic diversity. The doctrine of civic diversity, brought to something like classic formulation by Machiavelli during the "nightmare of degradation and imminent ruin" (de Grazia 16) imposed on Florence in 1494 by Charles VIII's invading mercenary armies, referred to two crucial centers of concern: first, to the variety of citizens inhabiting a polity. For it was only this "diversità de' cittadini," as Machiavelli said (*Discorsi* 3:9), which would allow the polity to adapt to the changing circumstances imposed by fortune—producing a bold general like Scipio or a temporizing one like Fabius as the occasion might require. Second, there needed to be a variety of talents within the individual citizen, for only this "anima ad omnia versatilia," as the character was described in Leonardo Bruni's *De Militia* (Bayley 199), could so easily shift from civilian to military roles and back again as to preserve the polity not only from its external enemies but also from subjection at the hands of the mercenary army it would otherwise have to employ for its own defense.

When the notion of civic diversity is relocated within German and later Victorian liberal Hellenism, this underlying martial dimension to diversity and versatility, even as they both are being deployed in a larger campaign against the psychic fragmentation and cultural stagnation produced by social and industrial modernity, continues on a buried level of psychocultural implication to impart a public and civic orientation to a Hellenism that might otherwise seem to be entirely private and aesthetic. Seamlessly meshing with the native emphasis on diversity within both the English tradition of religious Dissent and the newer discourse of biological or Darwinistic evolution, the diversity ideal within Victorian Hellenism thus allows Hellenism silently to fulfill one of the central sociopolitical functions of the fading older discourse of classical republicanism. At the same time, Hellenism is explicitly embraced by such liberals as Mill and Matthew Arnold as the solution to the problems raised by industrial modernity, which classical republicanism can now no longer grasp.[6]

Viewed against this background of the Victorian liberals' argument for Hellenism as the means of rescuing England from the uniformity and stagnation of industrial modernity, the Oxford university-reform movement of the 1850s and 1860s thus becomes visible as the translation of that abstract or theoretical argument into specific curricular or institutional terms. For the whole effort of the reformers was to reintegrate Oxford into the national life, "opening the University to the nation and to the world," as Mark Pattison was to declare in an influential statement of the reformers' goal, "allowing the full and entire play of free competition in instruction" which would, as he said, "increase our power and elasticity" (*Report* 44). Critics outside Oxford called for the admission of more poor students and, for the first time, of non-Anglicans as the best ways of breaking up the intellectually desolating regime of snobbery and extravagance encouraged by the traditional predominance within Oxford's undergraduate body of orthodox and aristocratic elements.

In the same way, critics inside Oxford urged toughening undergraduate curricular requirements, and opening the competition for college fellowships to all candidates, rather than just the descendants of the founder's kin or residents of a specific county or graduates of a certain school or whatever else might be specified by the college statutes. Such changes as these, the liberal reformers declared, were the way to spread throughout the institutionally crucial echelon of college fellows the intellectual vibrancy and comprehensiveness of mind which had hitherto prevailed at scarcely more than two colleges: Oriel and Balliol. So pervasive did the liberal vocabulary of energy versus stagnation become that one Victorian, surveying the long struggle for Oxford reform in 1869, was to use Mill's language without any sense of its ideological innovativeness as he recounted the story of "a stagnant and aimless University [that] has been shaken out of its torpor and inspired with new hopes and a new life" (Fyffe 187).

By contrast, the Tractarian movement of the 1830s and 1840s now seemed to the academic liberals like a temporary and incomprehensible episode, a passage verging on institutional nightmare in the larger life of Oxford. "It seemed incredible," as Pattison was to recall in mock amazement, "that we had been spending years in debating any matter so flimsy as whether England was in a state of schism or no" (*Memoirs* 123). Once the hurricane of Tractarianism had blown itself out and the all-absorbing vortex of its exclusively theological concerns had dispersed, broader, fresher intellectual currents flooded in from the Continent and especially from Germany: B. G. Niebuhr, Hegel, Comte, Ferdinand Baur. Much of the new and invigorating intellectual atmosphere at Oxford, as one graduate remarked, was due to Thomas Arnold and his Rugby pupils, much of it to the introduction of new books and the general advance of knowledge. But no less influential than these, he noted, were "the genius and energy of a living professor, and the interest in German literature which he has awakened" (Fyffe 185). This man was Benjamin Jowett.

Jowett's role as an agent of revolutionary change at Oxford, especially as that change was to flow through the Greats curriculum, can scarcely be overestimated. First exerting a politic but insistent pressure during the lull after the Tractarian storm, he was able to shift the curricular bias of Greats both away from Latin and toward Greek, and away from the narrowly grammatical emphasis in reading ancient texts and toward a powerfully engaged mode of reading which insisted on the vivid contemporaneity and philosophical depth of these works. At Jowett's initiative, Francis Bacon's *Novum Organon* and Plato's *Republic* were incorporated into the Greats curriculum. More important, he contributed, perhaps more than anyone else at Oxford, to that larger intellectual movement within Victorian Hellenism that Frank Turner has analyzed so extensively, by which Greek studies became a vehicle for channeling modern progressive thought into the Victorian civic elite. For Jowett's own study and teaching of Hegel would open the way to the widely influential philosophical and civic idealism of T.H. Green among others later in the century.

The great danger posed by such studies would always be their excessively solvent, even destabilizing effects on the religious faith of Oxford men, as Jowett himself recognized from the first. "When I was an undergraduate," as he wrote an intimate friend, "almost all teaching leaned to the support of doctrines of authority." With university reform, however, had come a revolution in Oxford's teaching of metaphysics through the new reading list in Greats: Bacon, Locke, Mill's *Logic,* Plato, Aristotle, and the history of ancient philosophy. "See how impossible," Jowett declared, "this makes a return to the old doctrines of authority" (Campbell 412).

Convinced by the German critical and historicist movements that all such attempts as the Tractarians' to revive the old doctrines of clerical and theological authority ran futilely against the irresistible tide of modern thought, Jowett came to believe that "if religion is to be saved at all it must be through the laity and statesmen, &c., not through the clergy" (150). Long before his own persecution as a clergyman for heresy during the *Essays and Reviews* controversy of 1860-62, Jowett was to perceive that the center of institutional gravity at Oxford was shifting, in A. J. Engel's phrase, from clergyman to don. "One need [not] look upon one's occupation as gone" because the older, transcendental role of the clergy was being undermined by history, science, and the clergy's own failures, as Jowett told his friend: "It is in reality a higher work that opens, trying to make the laity act up to and feel their own religious principles" (Campbell 150). This higher work was Jowett's intellectual ministry to the civic elite at Oxford, his "pastoral supervision . . . of young thinkers" (203).

To guarantee that this work genuinely was "higher," Jowett and the other Oxford reformers half unconsciously turned to a source of legitimation near to hand, the very attempt of the Tractarians to resacralize Oxford as the seminary of a spiritually renewed English clergy. The Tractarians were considered disloyal religious fanatics, discredited by their series of defections to Roman Catholicism. Yet the Tractarian vision of an Oxford able to provide an England demoralized by secular materialism and commercial modernity with a class of spiritual leaders—men whose very claim to leadership lay in their communication with a transcendental realm of spiritual purpose—had nonetheless survived. It lived on in the institutional forms developed at Oxford by the Tractarians themselves: the college tutorial, the college friendship as an intense "communion of souls," and the belief in "personality" as a force in the living and bodily communication of knowledge.

This appropriation of Tractarian forms is why Jowett and Pattison in their testimony to the Royal Commission investigating Oxford in 1850 both would so vigorously defend the college system as it centered in the tutorial: because its central emphasis on "the personal influence of mind upon mind," as Pattison would say, "the mind of the fully instructed upon the young mind it seeks to form" (*Memoirs* 133), translated to the level of "the practical ideal" (Campbell 142) the moral legitimacy of Newman's tutorial cure of souls. In turn, this process of appropriation is why Dean Church would so immediately perceive how directly the Oxford liberals had become the heirs of Newman and Hurrell Froude, succeeding "where the Tractarians had failed, in becoming the masters and reformers of Oxford" (337).

The great effect of the university liberals' move to reappropriate these institutional structures and attitudes, originally molded by Tractarianism to channel an intense male homosociality toward religious ends, would be to recenter them instead upon Greek studies, a secular, indeed "pagan," body of thought now regarded within Victorian liberalism as uniquely valuable because capable of regenerating an English society threatened by uniformity and stagnation. Yet in the very intensity of these male relationships coming into being in Jowett's Oxford, as we have seen, are felt the claims of a mode of feeling for which neither the older discourse of classical republicanism nor the newer discourse of Victorian liberalism has a vocabulary.

For though Victorian liberalism has begun to supplant such categories of the older discourse as "effeminacy" which had previously set rigid limits, albeit in an incidental or unintended way, on any positive cultural response to the notion of masculine love, the newer liberal discourse remains in itself silent on such issues. Yet both in the specific program of Greek studies shaped by Jowett and the Oxford reformers and in the diversity ideal more generally diffused by Victorian Hellenism there lies a possibility undreamt of by Victorian liberals: the legitimation of love between men. In this context such late-Victorian writers as Pater, Symonds, and Wilde, urged by Victorian liberalism to save the English polity by taking Greek history and philosophy seriously, will begin to glimpse in Plato's defense of transcendental, "Uranian" love a vocabulary adequate to their own inmost hopes, and to see in "Greek love" itself the promise of a Hellenic individuality and diversity with the most positive implications for Victorian civilization.

Notes

[1] As a practical matter, the political disabilities of non-Anglican protestants had for over one hundred years been relieved through a series of toleration and indemnity acts passed by Parliament. With the sharp reaction to French revolutionary secularism and atheism in the early years of the nineteenth century, however, there came a reassertion of the Anglican rhetoric of religious hegemony. This in its turn prompted the demands of the 1820s and 1830s for wider concessions to non-Establishment religious groups. See Matthew; Best; and Clark, chapter 6.

[2] The Aristotelian ideal of rational male friendship as a spiritual intimacy involving mutual ethical formation powerfully influenced, through the mediation of Cicero's *De Amicitia,* the early church fathers and, through them, the English Tractarians. See Richards.

[3] The most thorough-going attempt to interpret Kingsley's response to Newman and Tractarianism as a species of sexual hysteria is Susan Chitty's. R. B. Martin has suggested that Kingsley's extreme reaction to Tractarian "effeminacy" arose in part because of his fears over his brother Henry's sexual indeterminacy.

[4] *Tennyson* 531, pt. I, ll. 171-72. Subsequent references are to part and line numbers of *Maud.*

[5] Cf. the second stanza of "Duke William":

> Our Soldiers so brave,
> With rage being fired,
> Had what they desired,
> With the rebels to fight;
> For they never would flinch,
> Nor give back an inch,
> Till they made them fly,
> For noble Duke William,
> For noble Duke William,
> They'll conquer or die.
>
> (Palmer 52)

The third son of George II, William Augustus, duke of Cumberland, destroyed the Highlander forces of the Jacobite pretender to the throne, Charles Stuart ("Bonnie Prince Charlie"), at Culloden on 16 April 1746, thereby ending the threat to Hanoverian rule. Cumberland had taken pains to train the English troops to withstand the extraordinary ferocity of the Highlanders' onslaught, which had been the key to their earlier victories in England. His own savage reprisals at Culloden would earn him the nickname "the Butcher."

[6] The classic account of Arnold's Hellenism is DeLaura, *Hebrew and Hellene,* which gives a particularly full and nuanced account of Arnold's debt to Humboldt and German Hellenism generally (see esp. 181-91). For Arnold's rigorous suppression of Mill's deep influence upon him, see Super's edition of Arnold, *Culture and Anarchy,* in *Prose Works.*

Works Cited

Aristotle. *The Politics.* Trans. T. A. Sinclair. Harmondsworth, Middlesex: Penguin, 1962.

[Arnold, Matthew]. *The Prose Works of Matthew Arnold.* Ed. R. H. Super. 11. vols. Ann Arbor: University of Michigan Press, 1960-77.

Bayley, C. C. *War and Society in Renaissance Florence: The "De Militia" of Leonardo Bruni.* Toronto: University of Toronto Press, 1961.

Berlin, Isaiah. "Two Concepts of Nationalism: An Interview with Isaiah Berlin." *New York Review of Books,* 21 November 1991, 19-23.

Best, G. F. A. "The Protestant Constitution and Its Supporters, 1800-1829." *Transactions of the Royal Historical Society* 8 (1958): 107-27.

Bloomfield, Samuel Thomas, trans. *The History of Thucydides.* 3 vols. London: Longman, Rees, Orme, Brown and Green, 1828.

Bowden, John Edward. *The Life and Letters of Frederick William Faber, D.D., Priest of the Oratory of St. Philip Neri, 1814-63.* London: Thomas Richardson, 1969.

Brendon, Piers. *Hurrell Froude and the Oxford Movement.* London: Paul Elek, 1974.

Brown, Horatio F. *John Addington Symonds: A Biography.* 2 vols. London: John C. Nimmo, 1895.

[Burrow, J. W.]. *Whigs and Liberals: Continuity and Change in English Political Thought.* Oxford: Clarendon, 1988.

Campbell, Lewis. *The Life and Letters of Benjamin Jowett, M.A., Master of Balliol College, Oxford.* Vol. 1. London: John Murray, 1897.

Chitty, Susan. *The Beast and the Monk: A Life of Charles Kingsley.* London: Hodder and Stoughton, 1974.

Clark, J. C. D. *English Society 1688-1832: Ideology, Social Structure, and Political Practice during the Ancien Regime.* Cambridge: Cambridge University Press, 1985.

Coleridge, Samuel Taylor. *A Lay Sermon* (1817). In *Coleridge's Writings on Politics and Society,* ed. John Morrow, 97-151. Princeton: Princeton University Press, 1991.

[Collini, Stefan.]. "Introduction." In *Collected Works of J. S. Mill,* 21:vii-lvi.

Culler, A. Dwight. *Imperial Intellect: A Study of Cardinal Newman's Educational Ideal.* New Haven: Yale University Press, 1955.

de Grazia, Sebastian. *Machiavelli in Hell.* Princeton: Princeton University Press, 1989.

[DeLaura, David J.]. *Hebrew and Hellene in Victorian England: Newman, Arnold, and Pater.* Austin: University of Texas Press, 1969.

Detienne, Marcel. "La phalange: Problèmes et controvers." In *Problèmes de la guerre en Grèce ancienne,* ed. J.-P. Vernant, 119-42. The Hague: Mouton, 1968.

Engel, A. J. *From Clergyman to Don: The Rise of the Academic Profession in Nineteenth-Century Oxford.* Oxford: Clarendon, 1983.

Faber, Geoffrey. *Jowett: A Portrait with Background.* London: Faber and Faber, 1957.

———. *Oxford Apostles: A Character Study of the Oxford Movement.* London: Faber and Faber, 1933.

Francis, Elizabeth A. "Tennyson's Political Poetry, 1852-1855." *Victorian Poetry* 14 (1976): 113-23.

Froude, Hurrell. "On State Interference in Matters Spiritual" (1833). In Parsons, *Religion in Victorian Britain,* 3:4-8.

Fyffe, Charles Alan. "Study and Opinion in Oxford." *Macmillan's Magazine* 21 (December 1869): 184-92.

Gibbon, Edward. *The Autobiography of Edward Gibbon.* Ed. Dero Saunders. New York: Meridian, 1961.

Hopkins, Gerard Manley. *The Journals and Papers.* Ed. Humphry House and Graham Storey. London: Oxford University Press, 1959.

Jowett, Benjamin, trans. *Thucydides.* 1st ed. 2 vols. Oxford: Clarendon, 1881.

Kinglake, Alexander William. *The Invasion of the Crimea: Its Origin and an Account of Its Progress Down to the Death of Lord Raglan.* 8 vols. Edinburgh: William Blackwood, 1868.

Kingsley, Charles. "Alexander Smith and Alexander Pope." *Fraser's Magazine* 48 (October 1853): 452-66.

———. "Froude's *History of England,* Vols. VII and VIII." *Macmillan's Magazine* 9 (January 1864): 211-24.

———. *The Saint's Tragedy, or True Story of Elizabeth of Hungary, Landgravine of Thuringia, Saint of the Roman Calendar.* London: John W. Parker, 1848.

———. "Thoughts on Byron and Shelley." *Fraser's Magazine* 48 (November 1853): 568-76.

———. "Why Should We Fear the Romish Priests?" *Fraser's Magazine* 37 (April 1848): 467-74.

Kingsley, Frances. *Life and Works of Charles Kingsley.* 19 vols. London: Macmillan, 1901-3.

Lattimore, Richmond, trans. *Greek Lyrics.* 2d ed. Chicago: University of Chicago Press, 1960.

[Macaulay, Thomas Babington]. *Critical, Historical and Miscellaneous Essays.* 6 vols. Boston: Dana Estes, n.d.

McGann, Jerome J. "Tennyson and the Histories of Criticism." In *The Beauty of Inflections: Literary Investigations in Historical Method and Theory,* 173-203. New York: Oxford University Press, 1988.

Machiavelli, Niccolò. *Discorsi sopra la Prima Deca di Tito Livio* in *Tutte le Opere Storiche e Letterarie di Niccolò Machiavelli,* ed. Guido Mazzoni and Mario Casella, 55-262. Florence: G. Barbera, 1929.

Martin, Robert Bernard. *The Dust of Combat: A Life of Charles Kingsley.* London: Faber and Faber, 1959.

Matthew, H. G. C. "Noetics, Tractarians, and the Reform of the University of Oxford in the Nineteenth Century." *History of Universities* 9 (1990): 195-225.

[Mill, John Stuart]. "Grote's History of Greece [II]" (1853). In *Collected Works,* 11:307-37.

———. *On Liberty.* In *Collected Works,* 18:213-310.

Mozley, Thomas. *Reminiscences, Chiefly of Oriel College and the Oxford Movement.* 2 vols. Boston: Houghton Mifflin, 1882.

Newman, John Henry. "Antony in Conflict" from *The Church of the Fathers* (1833). In *Essays and Sketches,* ed. Charles Frederick Harrold, 3:92-108. New York: Longmans, Green, 1948.

———. "Medieval Oxford" (1838). In *Historical Sketches,* 315-35.

———. "Personal Influence the Means of Propagating the Truth" (1832). In *Fifteen Sermons Preached before the University of Oxford,* 75-98. London: Longmans, Green, 1892.

———. "The Rise and Progress of Universities" (1836). In *Historical Sketches,* 1-251.

———. "Tract No. 1" (1833). In Parsons, *Religion in Victorian Britain,* 3:9-10.

Paget, Stephen. *Henry Scott Holland: Memoir and Letters.* London: Murray, 1921.

Palmer, Roy. *A Ballad History of England from 1588 to the Present Day.* London: B. T. Batsford, 1979.

Pattison, Mark. *Memoirs of an Oxford Don.* London: Cassell, 1988.

———. "Sermon V: 30 April 1865." In *Sermons,* 103-36. London: Macmillan, 1885.

Pocock, J. G. A. *The Machiavellian Moment: Florentine Political Thought and the Atlantic Republican Tradition.* Princeton: Princeton University Press, 1975.

Report of Her Majesty's Commissioners Appointed to Inquire into the State, Discipline, Studies and Revenues of the University and Colleges of Oxford. London: W. Clowes for H. M. Stationery Office, 1852.

Richards, Jeffrey. "'Passing the Love of Women': Manly Love and Victorian Society." In *Manliness and Morality: Middle-class Masculinity in Britain and America, 1800-1940,* ed. J. A. Mangan and James Walvin, 92-122. New York: St. Martin's, 1987.

Ricks, Christopher, and Edgar Shannon. "'The Charge of the Light Brigade': The Creation of a Poem." *Studies in Bibliography* 38 (1985): 1-44.

Scarry, Elaine. *The Body in Pain: The Making and Unmaking of the World.* New York: Oxford University Press, 1985.

Schlesinger, Kathleen. "Fife." In *Encyclopaedia Britannica,* 10:331. 11th ed. New York: Encyclopaedia Britannica, 1910.

Stanley, Arthur. "The Oxford School." *Edinburgh Review* 153 (April 1881): 157-72.

Tennyson, Alfred. *Tennyson: A Selected Edition.* Ed. Christopher Ricks. Berkeley: University of California Press, 1989.

Tollemache, Lionel A. *Old and Odd Memories.* London: Edward Arnold, 1908.

Tucker, Herbert F. *Tennyson and the Doom of Romanticism.* Cambridge: Harvard University Press, 1988.

Turner, Frank M. *The Greek Heritage in Victorian Britain.* New Haven: Yale University Press, 1981.

Wolffe, John. *The Protestant Crusade in Great Britain, 1829-1860.* Oxford: Clarendon, 1991.

THE LITERARY INFLUENCE

T. G. Tucker (essay date 1907)

SOURCE: "Greek Literature and English," in *The Foreign Debt of English Literature,* George Bell and Sons, 1907, pp. 5-69.

[*In the essay below, Tucker gives the first place of influence on all European literatures to classical Greek. He ascribes to Greek literature values highly cherished in nineteenth- and twentieth-century English letters: clarity, appreciation for "pure beauty," and originality.*]

Of all the literatures which have contributed to that of England, the Greek is by far the first and most important. The study of Greek literature is the indispensable introduction to the study of European literary history. Whether we review the literature of England, of Italy, of France, or of Germany, it is at Greece that we shall ultimately arrive. Take our English epic, *Paradise Lost.* It is a commonplace that it derives much inspiration from Dante's *Divine Comedy.* But, when we arrive at the *Divine Comedy,* we are assured that it would never have taken such shape but for Virgil's *Aeneid.* And, when we come to Virgil's *Aeneid,* it is a fact known to the veriest tiro that the *Aeneid* is a copy, and, in a sense, a plagiarism, of Homer's *Iliad* and *Odyssey.* The pedigree is self-evident and undeniable. Practically it is avowed at every step. Look elsewhere. Pope and Shenstone wrote "pastorals," after the fashion introduced into English by Spenser. But Spenser himself had been led to this form of composition by the Italian Sannazaro and the Latin Virgil. And, when we reach Virgil, we find that he is a liberal borrower, in matter and manner alike, sometimes even in the very phrase, from the Greek of Theocritus, Bion, and Moschus. It is the same with literary criticism. Pope's *Essay on Criticism,* like Roscommon's *Essay on Translated Verse,* is derived from Boileau's French *Art Poétique.* But Boileau is an echo of the Latin Horace and his *De Arte Poetica,* while Horace is himself a borrower from Greeks of Alexandria, and ultimately from Aristotle of Athens. And so it is throughout. Often, especially in these later days, our stars of English literature shine with a light reflected directly from Greek constellations. No less often they shine with a light transmitted through several media, but ultimately issuing from the suns of Greece.

Pre-eminent by far among the literatures to which we owe a debt stands this body of eternally great creators, who, by the clear beauty of their language, their luminous apprehension, and their simple but magnificent originality, surpass in the aggregate those whom any other nation can assemble. It is no paradox, but a simple historical fact, that the old English writers have had less influence in moulding our modern literature than have Homer and Sophocles, Plato and Demosthenes. "We are all Greeks," says Shelley, in the preface to his *Hellas.* Whether we will or no, our literature and philosophy, our canons of taste, our ideals of art, are all, in a sense, Greek.

Greek literature, unlike Latin, and unlike those of modern Europe, was mainly, if not wholly, original. What we have been able to borrow or to find readymade seems to have developed itself spontaneously in the wonderful genius of Greece. Latin literature has been called—and not without some justice—one vast plagiarism from Greek. But Greek itself is guiltless of plagiarism. Its thoughts, like its exquisite clearness and restraint of style, are almost entirely its own. With unlettered barbarians to north and west of them, with flowery, bombastic, or mystic orientals on the Asiaward side, the Greeks must be credited with a marvellous gift of their own, the instinct for sound judgement and sure taste.

But they possessed more than taste and judgement. They had inventiveness. We may reflect for a moment upon the various forms and modes of literature which we possess and practise in verse and prose. Of verse there are the epic, lyric, elegiac, satiric, dramatic, didactic, pastoral, epigrammatic, philosophic varieties. In prose there are history, oratory, philosophy, biography, criticism, fiction. To us all these forms and species, with their appropriate language, metre and tone, are taken for granted, as if they were the necessary outcome of some natural order of things. They are, no doubt, founded in nature. Nevertheless, we should remember that they must have had a beginning of their differentiation, that they must have been invented somewhere. And we discover that each of them is to be found arising in recognizable shape on the soil of ancient Greece. It is easy nowadays for us to imitate existing forms, to build with the architecture of the drama of Shakespeare and the epic of Milton, to copy the lyrical metres of Gray, Shelley, and Tennyson, to adopt the satirical machinery of Pope and Dryden. But these differentiations in mode of expression represent something deeper, some distinction evolved by the human mind between compositions of one purpose and compositions of another. It was the Greeks who first convincingly and systematically illustrated that distinction, and who found for each subject of thought its appropriate vehicle of expression. More modern times have evolved many modifications of detail in metre or rhyme, and have essayed many novelties in the way of narrative. But they have never added an entirely new form of poetry or prose to the *répertoire* of the Greeks. Tennyson does not write *In Memoriam* in the metre and language of *Paradise Lost.* Shelley's *Ode to a Skylark* does not employ the diction and rhythm of Pope's *Essay on Man.* It is recognized that the feeling and its vehicle would be incongruous. But how does this come to be recognized? A world is quite conceivable in which there might have been developed but one form of literature and one ideal of expression. In such a world the incongruity would not be felt. The early Hellenes made their own literary beginnings upon almost a clear field, and it is one of their imperishable glories that they succeeded in realizing the subtle relations between language and thought or feeling, and in expressing these latter in all the variety of extant literary forms. For heroic deeds and lofty incident they developed the epic verse; for the sweets and bitters of love, and for other passions and ardours, they built the lyric stanza; for the plaints of mourning they created the elegiac; they did this gradually, no doubt, and in the main unconsciously, but with all the more perfect result. If we inherit what Greece has created, we have no right to assume that all our happy varieties of literary form are things of course, which would somehow have come to any nation.

. . . . .

The history of Greek literature should be a study of years. Nevertheless it is not without profit to take the greater names and the more prominent types, to show their order of succession, to say something of their range and scope, to note the essentials of their style, and thence to derive some clearer idea of their influence on what we read to-day in our own English tongue.

The earliest Greek books which we now possess are Homer's *Iliad* and *Odyssey.* But these are much too polished and perfect works to have been the very first that Greeks ever composed. Indeed we know that before Homer's time there were minstrels, who sang the "glories" of heroes, very much after the manner in which the bards sang in Wales or Scotland, or the gleemen in Anglo-Saxon England. It must also be assumed that popular songs of a religious kind were in existence. Yet all these earliest efforts at literary creation have vanished; we possess no material for definite information concerning them. For us Greek literature begins with "Homer." The question as to who Homer was cannot be answered. Some critics contend that he is a mere title, and that the compositions which go by his name are patchworks, made up of a series of narratives sung by wandering bards called "rhapsodists." Homêros, they say, is but a fictitious title under which to string all these separate compositions together into one so-called epic. Others, going less far, say that there was indeed a veritable Homer, that he composed a poem on the *Wrath of Achilles,* and that this poem has been enlarged by other hands, which turned the whole into the *Iliad,* or poem on the "Siege of Troy". Even if this be true, we know nothing of the original Homer, when or where he lived. To discuss the question at any length is beyond our present province. Perhaps we may believe, with great masters of poetry like Goethe and Schiller, that a "Homer" wrote the poem of the *Iliad,* but that it has since been added to, tampered with, reconstructed. We may also believe that some one other poet wrote a corresponding portion of the *Odyssey.* These two original poets were of nearly, though not quite, the same period. They were inspired with much the same literary ideals, and were almost equal, though by no means identical, in genius. They may be supposed to have appeared in a specially fertile epoch, like the great Elizabethans, or like the Italian poets of the first Renaissance. Their artistic principles would be much the same; they would live in much the same environment; they would see the world, the gods, mankind, through much the same moral temperament. Let us grant that their work has undergone large interference and contamination. Yet it is hard to think that a motley crowd of rhapsodists could ever possess such a lofty average of genius as pervades the whole body of these inimitable poems. Both works were, beyond reasonable doubt, in complete existence before 800 B.C. Twenty-seven centuries ago the Greek genius had reached thus high a point.

The *Iliad* and the *Odyssey* are to be read in many a translation. The *Iliad* is the poem of Ilium or Troy. It deals with events during the siege of that town by the confederated Achaeans. It narrates the doings and sayings of the Grecian heroes, of Agamemnon, Achilles, Ajax, Ulysses, Diomede, Menelaus, outside Troy, and of the Trojans, King Priam, Hector or Paris within the city, where is also the traitress Helen. It narrates the counsels, quarrels, and battles of the gods, as they arise from partisanship during the siege. The poem is filled with prowess of battle, till it ends with the death of Hector, champion of Troy. The narrative is rapid and vigorous, full of valorous and exciting exploits of men interwoven with the friendly or unfriendly actions of gods. Descriptions are many, but always brief, and everywhere inimitably fresh and luminous. The whole purpose of the poem is to tell a story, and to tell it with clearness and simplicity, yet with fire and force. When it is embellished with ornaments of simile or other

Ajax defending the Greek ships against the Trojans: From Homer's Greek epic poem, The Iliad.

figure, it is because that device best brings home the picture. There is no idle lavishing of ornament for mere ornament's sake.

The *Odyssey* is the poem of Odysseus, the wandering Ulysses. He, the king of the little island of Ithaca, after being for ten years absent at the siege of Troy, starts homeward in his ship to his wife, Penelope. But on the journey he meets with adventures, strange, terrible, or happy. He is storm-tossed and delayed by the anger of offended gods. He nearly meets his death from the one-eyed cannibal monster Polyphemus; he nearly loses his crew among the Lotus-eaters; he is detained for seven years in the island of the seductive Calypso; his comrades are turned into swine by Circe the enchantress; he is wrecked between Scylla and Charybdis. He at last arrives home, only to find Penelope at the mercy of a rabble calling themselves her suitors. He slays them, and reveals himself to his wife—and so a happy ending. In this poem, as in the *Iliad,* composed nearly three thousand years ago, there is already achieved a perfection of literary art which we moderns find ourselves for ever aiming at and for ever missing. For this there is other reason than the natural genius of the Greek. The poets who wrote these two stories looked out upon the world with a frank, unclouded gaze, for which, perhaps, we are now too sophisticated. They therefore tell their tale with such simple directness that it might seem told by a grown-up child; but meanwhile with such brilliant clearness, with such firm outline, that it no less appears the work of a consummate artist. There is, it is true, no psychological probing in these books. There is no subtle moralizing, no pondering of any kind of deep question. Nowhere does there obtrude itself a desire to be clever, rhetorical, dazzling. Yet no one can read the *Iliad* without seeing those warriors face to face, as they were, in their physical strength and simplicity of character; nor can he read the *Odyssey* without feeling that he is with Ulysses on his raft, sailing through the deep, blue Mediterranean, that the salt breeze is blowing on his face, that the world is young and fresh, and that a man's part is to perform that which lies nearest to his hand.

What effect the *Iliad* and the *Odyssey* have upon the intelligent reader may be judged by their preeminence among poems of all times and all places. What an effect they have had on our literature may be judged by the number of translations, many in prose, and many better known in verse, from the hands of Chapman, Pope, Cowper, Derby, Morris, Way. It may be judged by the countless allusions to the "tale of Troy divine" which are strewn through every book of the last three millennia; by our everyday familiarity with the names of Hector and Achilles, Helen of Troy and Paris, Diomede and Ulysses, Circe and Penelope, Polyphemus and the Lotus-eaters. On reading Chapman's Homer, Keats felt like an astronomer "when a new planet swims into his ken." The same experience has been felt by all who recognize, as Keats did, "the principle of beauty in all things." But little notion of those poems can be gathered at secondhand. Of its similes we may here quote one, not because it is in any way the most beautiful, but because it has been translated by a master in the art, Tennyson. Nothing in English has ever been hit upon to give the majestic, sonorous roll of the Greek hexameter, but Tennyson has, at least, preserved the frank simplicity of his original:

> As when in heaven the stars about the moon
> Look beautiful, when all the winds are laid,
> And every height comes out, and jutting peak
> And valley, and the immeasurable heavens
> Break open to their highest, and all the stars
> Shine, and the shepherd gladdens in his heart:
> So many a fire between the ships and stream
> Of Xanthus blazed before the towers of Troy,
> A thousand on the plain; and close by each
> Sat fifty in the blaze of burning fire;
> And eating hoary grain and pulse the steeds,
> Fixed by their cars, waited the golden dawn.

Next to Homer may come, by no means in importance, but in date, the poet Hesiod. He, too, uses the hexameter line, but with a different tone and movement, and for quite another purpose. He is our first example of "didactic" verse—the verse which is intended to instruct. Hesiod, who may be dated about the year 700 B.C., composed two poems of some dimensions, the one called the *Theogony* or *Pedigree of the Gods,* the other known as the *Works and Days.* The latter is a collection of versified rules of agriculture mixed with proverbial wisdom. It is, in fact, a sort of "Farmer's Annual" of Greece combined with the proverbial wisdom of "Poor Richard." Practical farming and practical morals go together. It would almost certainly have been written in prose, but for the simple reason that prose literature had not yet been invented. All literary composition begins with verse. As a poem, there is little to be said for the *Works and Days,* except that, like all things early Greek, it is entirely unpretentious and goes straight to the point. Didactic verse has grown common since Hesiod's day, although happily it is now seldom used for agricultural purposes. Tusser's *Five Hundred Points of Good Husbandry* is one of the earliest results of the revival of Greek studies in England in the Elizabethan time, and, though it cannot count for much in literature, it is our first example of a species of work which took a more moralizing shape in Dyer's *Fleece* and many later didactics.

Of much more value is the next kind of poetry which arose among the Greeks, a kind which has been called "personal," inasmuch as it is prompted by the writer's individual feelings and emotions, and has reference to himself, his hopes, griefs, loves, and other sentiments. The epic poetry of Homer had been purely objective, dealing with incidents, things, and men outside the poet. The author makes no revelation of himself; he does not speak in the first person. But what is known as "lyric" and "elegiac" poetry is the outcome of a man's own inner experience, and is only valuable in proportion as it expresses powerfully or touchingly a real or imagined passion of the writer, which the world at large can also recognize for its own. The poetry of *Lycidas, Adonais, In Memoriam,* is "elegiac"; the poetry of songs, such as those of Herrick and Burns, is "lyric." "Elegiac" properly means "adapted to mourning," but the elegy, with its couplet rhythm varied from the hexameter, yet with a plaintive dignity all its own, was used for other feelings than those of grief. It was used for praise, exhortation, reflection, love; for anything "subjective," or springing from the mood of the writer. We need not enumerate the Greeks who at various dates wrote poetry of this personal description. After the year 700 B.C. there were many and excellent lyrists of the kind. At Lacedaemon the poet Tyrtaeus composed marching songs, which acted upon the Spartans as the *Marseillaise* and *Die Wacht am Rhein* act upon nations in modern days. Archilochus of Paros, soured by his own failings and misfortunes, wrote often in bitterness, like Burns. He is styled an "iambic" writer from a new form of composition which he employed, and he became the first great name in satire. In Lesbos, a fertile, luxurious, and cultured island, we meet with the foremost name in the poetry of passion, the famous Sappho, the first and greatest of women in literature. It is Sappho who could paint, better than poet has ever painted since, the agonizing of love. Nor was she alone. In the same island she had her school of followers, and, separately from these, the poet Alcaeus poured forth his fiery thoughts in "words that burn." But it is Sappho who, like George Sand, wrote from the "real blood of her heart and the real flame of her thought" things which have been the despair of imitator or translator. Unhappily, very little of her work is extant now, even in fragments; but what there is, is "more golden than gold." Her metres are as nobly simple as in one of Herrick's songs; her words are simple also. Yet, just as Dante could make a mighty verse out of the noun and verb, by choosing for his noun and verb the absolutely truest and most home-coming, so the simplicity of Sappho is only a deceptive covering for the most consummate art. Often as our lyrists have tried to catch something of her sacred fire, never has one quite attained to her irresistible pathos. Perhaps he who has approached nearest is Burns. Sappho is untranslatable. All absolutely best words in any language must be so. The nearest equivalent in English may be sought and found for the best word in the Greek, but in the special quality of its music or its associations it can never be the same.

The names of Pindar and Simonides are of a later date. Before them comes another, who sang to the lyre those gemlike songs of love, and joy, and wine, which the cavalier poets of the English seventeenth century made their ideal. This was Anacreon of Teos. "Anacreontics" is the name given to those polished cameo-like little poems which imitators have essayed upon Anacreon's themes. Cowley's translations into English verse are known to literature, and readers familiar with the works of Thomas Moore will remember his loose youthful version of a few true and many spurious lyrics of the Teian bard. It is to Anacreon that we may look for the prototype of those graceful trifles called *vers de société,* and of those songs of love or gaiety which Herrick, Suckling, Lovelace, and Waller have developed in such exquisite examples.

All this personal poetry was meant to be sung to the accompaniment of lyre or flute. Had it been primarily meant to be read, it might possibly, even with Greek creators, have been less simple and direct, more artificial.

There was also another class of poetry which was sung to the same accompaniment. Early Greece found many occasions for festivities, and at religious holidays, public rejoicings, and public thanksgivings, choruses sang while moving in procession or while dancing round the altars. Hymns were chanted to the gods, triumphal odes were chanted in honour of men. When literature turned to these—or when these became literature—there arose in particular two most famous poets, Simonides and Pindar, to compose such public odes, very much after the manner in which a modern laureate might compose an ode of installation or national victory, or a dirge upon a national loss. Compositions written in this spirit are seldom of the highest rank of literature. They lack the saving grace of inspiration. Pindar is strong, noble, imaginative. His odes were, no doubt, splendid compositions for chanting and musical purposes. To read them is to be conscious of a stateliness and dignity and an "eagle flight" which powerfully affect the student. But, full as they are of great imagery and diction, they are beyond doubt apt to be artificial and perplexed in structure; they are too often obscure, too often deliberately learned in allusion. To be its best, poetry must be written from the promptings of the poet's heart, and Pindar too often wrote to order, for payment, and not from inward compulsion. No exact, or very near, parallel to Pindar can be found. He has never been even tolerably well translated. This has not been for want of admirers. Gray, who imitated him in the *Progress of Poesy,* has been said by Mason (erroneously enough) to possess Pindar's fire: Cowley's tombstone calls him, without much justification, the English Pindar, and at all times down to the present writers have been led to emulate the soaring Pindaric ode. Whatever his defects, it is certain that over all modern lyric poets, even over those who could not always follow his meaning, Pindar has exercised the sway of a master and imperial spirit.

Among the kinds of poetry chiefly affected by the earlier Greeks must also be included the "gnomic" or "sententious" verse which goes under the names of Theognisand Phocylides. These writers both lived in the sixth century B.C., and both composed versified maxims or precepts of conduct and worldly wisdom. After times came to credit to those great originals any verses of this character which were current in the elegiac or the hexameter metre, and such verses played very much the same part in Greek mouths as is played by the Proverbs of Solomon or by proverbial philosophy of unknown authorship in the mouths of Englishmen. At a later date in the iambic metre the comic poet Menander introduced into his plays a large number of maxims, which gained wide vogue and which caused many more of the same species to be fathered upon him. Of the various wise saws thus current in Greece a great number were translated or adapted by Latin writers, and have so passed into the general possession of the European world.

Between the years 500 and 400 B.C. there arose in Athens that which is the special poetic glory of that city—the drama, embracing both the drama of tragedy, as wrought by Aeschylus, Sophocles, and Euripides, and the drama of comedy, as built by Aristophanes, and later, in a different form and spirit, by Menander.

The Attic drama arose on Grecian ground. At one time choruses danced round the altar of the wine-god Dionysus (or Bacchus), and chanted songs in his honour. The chorus had its leader, the Coryphaeus. In time it became the fashion for the Coryphaeus to personate the god, or some character whom story connected with him. He recited a speech, or related some legend, in which the wine-god was concerned. It naturally followed that he was next raised upon a low dais, and distinguished from the rest of the chorus. The dais later became the dramatic stage. Subsequently another member of the chorus was told off to converse with him in rough dialogue, the theme being still the history of Bacchus. So far, then, we have a chorus which dances and sings, and two actors supporting crude dramatic parts. It was from these simple beginnings that there grew to perfection in Athens, as suddenly as the Shakespearean perfection arose from the old miracle-plays and "moralities" in England, noble dramas like those of Aeschylus and Sophocles. The open sward had become a theatre, the acting art, the dialogue poetry. Drama had been raised to an art of the most absolute literary completeness. It must, however, be observed that the tragedy which grew up in this way was religious in its origin. Until the end it—theoretically at least—remained so. Its subject-matter and laws were, therefore, limited. The stage was at the same time a pulpit for moral and religious teaching. The theatre was, moreover, national. Here are some important elements of artistic difference. Those who read Shakespeare and then turn to Athenian tragedies are puzzled. They do not understand those Attic creations. They think them rather cold, with somewhat slender plot, containing few surprises. Italians and Frenchmen can understand them; the average Englishman cannot. The poetry is often admirable, but the action appears strangely simple, and for the most part over obvious. The very name "tragedy" seems sometimes misapplied. But by "tragedy" the Greeks did not necessarily mean a play which ends in death and disaster. Such an end was, indeed, usual, and hence the modern meaning of the term. But the *Eumenides* of Aeschylus ends happily, as do the *Alcestis* of Euripides and the *Philoctêtes* of Sophocles. The Greeks meant rather the working out of some great and powerful situation affording occasion for sensations of pity and fear. Here was "the luxury of grief." The spectators knew that there would be some climax in the drama; but whether it would issue in good or evil depended on the poet; they only knew that their feelings would be powerfully worked upon by great poetry greatly delivered. For the rest, they required no startling ingenuity of plot or variety of incident.

The three great dramatists in artistic sequence are Aeschylus, Sophocles, Euripides. These were all alive together, but Aeschylus was old when Euripides was young. The appearance of all these in one epoch is exactly paralleled by the cluster of superlative dramatists in the Elizabethan age or in the France of Louis XIV. Of Sophocles it has been said that he represented men as they ought to be, and of Euripides that he represented them as they were. The dictum is hardly true, and, if it were, it must be noted that, whereas to "hold the mirror up to nature" is as much the function of Greek tragedy as of English, it is no function of Greek drama to be a literal copy of literal everyday human experience. In Aeschylus all is in the grand style of an awe-inspiring simplicity. Take his *Prometheus Bound.* We have a majestic Titan figure bound to a desolate rock, there to remain in punishment for an offence against the law of Zeus. He had bestowed fire and other boons on mortal men. Therefore Zeus pinioned him on Caucasus for tens of thousands of years. In one way, and one only, could he gain his freedom—by disclosing to Zeus a certain secret of fate. But Prometheus would not repent of having exercised his benevolent freewill against the decree of Heaven. He gloried in his action; he refused to deliver up the secret. Now during the whole play the figure of Prometheus does not move: he is fixed fast. There is no action on his part, nothing but speech. Different gods, demigods, and a mortal visit him, condole with him, advise him, or threaten him. He remains firm to the end, the spectacle of an utterly resolute heart rebelling against fate.

It is not hard to recognize in English literature some of the characters to which this Prometheus has served as prototype. There is Milton's Satan, who is distinctly modelled on the Titan. Byron acknowledges that all his rebellious spirits, Cain, Manfred, and their like, are echoes of the same character. Shelley wrote a *Prometheus Unbound* for sequel. Keats's *Hyperion* shows the same influence. Swinburne's *Atalanta in Calydon* is throughout inspired by the conception of Aeschylus.

Ancient drama has much attracted the modern poet. The *Agamemnon* of Aeschylus has been translated by Browning, far more roughly—not to say grostesquely—in style than it deserves, but with the Greek spirit in no small measure retained. The same writer has translated the *Alcestis* of Euripides in the work known as *Balaustion's Adventure.*

But to the English stage Greek tragedies are not suited. Our theatre is not religious, nor national. But in France and Italy Greek plays have found a more congenial soil. Corneille and Racine in France, Alfieri in Italy, have sought to mould their dramas upon Greek lines, though, truth to tell, they much more closely suggest the rhetorical constructions of the Latins. The only deliberate attempt to compose in English directly on the Grecian model is Milton's *Samson Agonistes,* a work in which admirable poetry does not atone for a certain coldness and formality intolerable in drama, whether meant for Greece or for England. Yet inasmuch as the Italian drama was largely instrumental in developing the English from its crude and vulgar antecedents, and as Italian drama was in its turn evoked by the dramatic examples of Greece, we can even here, despite all unlikenesses, distinctly affiliate the main principles of our own stage-pieces to those of ancient Athens. We cannot, indeed, maintain that without Athens we should have had no drama; we can only assert that our greatest drama, as we have it, in its poetical dignity and its technical architecture, would hardly have been. It might have been a prose drama, and one of very different conception and ideals. But it is what it is because it took from Greece that which suited its purpose, while it left to Greece those elements which belong to so different a theatre.

It has been described how Greek tragic drama arose from the choruses singing round the altar of Dionysus. Greek comedy springs from the same source. There were two sides to a Greek festival, as there are two sides to Christmas Day. The serious part of the festivity developed serious poetry and serious action. The light, sportive, and satirical part developed humorous verse and humorous action. It is easy to see how both dramatic kinds would scene, placed in it a befitting action or situation, and called his work "a little picture." But when Virgil imitated him at Rome, the Corydons and Damoetases whom he introduces are hardly shepherds of reality. Their talk tends to be artificial and literary. Shepherds did not pipe and contend in alternate minstrelsy on the Italian farms as Greek shepherds had done, however rudely, in Cos or Sicily.

Moreover Virgil wrote with an *arrière pensée.* He was thinking of the society of his time, and more or less representing that society under the guise of obviously theatrical shepherds. In Spenser's *Shepheard's Calender* we no longer recognize any pretence at reality. The idea of merry witty shepherds piping in sylvan scenes of sunlit Sicily is natural enough; but the notion of the smock-frocked rustic of rainy Britain vying in song with another smock-frocked rustic concerning his Amaryllis or his Chloe is not a little ludicrous. Especially is this so when we know that Colin Clout, Cuddie, Hobbinol, and the other swains, are talking moral wisdom, and are nothing but Spenser's friends or contemporary celebrities with shepherds' crooks for poetic "properties."

Distinguished, however, from pastoral poetry pure and simple, as seen in Pope and Spenser, there is a more important form of creation by these Alexandrian poets, which finds its way into English literature. It is from Theocritus and his school that Milton's *Lycidas* is drawn, and it is from *Lycidas* that we get Shelley's *Adonais* and Matthew Arnold's *Thyrsis.* Here are two quite unimportant passages, the comparison of which will show at once how closely a great English poet may occasionally copy an ancient. Says Theocritus, as translated by Calverley:

> The voice of Thyrsis: Etna's Thyrsis I.
> Where were ye, Nymphs, oh where, while Daphnis pined?
> In fair Penëus or in Pindus' glens?
> For great Anapus' stream was not your haunt,
> Nor Etna's cliff, nor Acis' sacred rill.

Says Milton:

> Where where ye, Nymphs, when the remorseless deep
> Closed o'er the head of your loved Lycidas?
> For neither were ye playing on the steep,
> Where your old bards, the famous Druids, lie,
> Nor on the shaggy top of Mona high,
> Nor yet where Deva spreads her wizard stream.

Greek literature is also rich in verse "epigram" in the original sense of the word. In modern times we have come to associate with the epigram the notion of a pithy composition containing a neat and witty point, and particularly a "sting in the tail." This description seldom suits the Greek type, especially in its earlier days, but is derived rather from the custom of the epigrammatists of Rome. An "epigram" was originally a composition to be inscribed upon a monument, votive offering, or the like. That it should be brief was an obvious requirement, and it was natural that it should try to excel mere commonplace. But wit and "point" of a biting kind were alien to the first conception. A Simonides or other early poet wrote a couplet or a quatrain which might be pathetic, eulogistic, or even almost simply descriptive, and this was an "epigram" if actually intended as, or proposed as fit for, an inscription. In later times the composition of such pieces was a poetic exercise, the occasion being imaginary, and the tendency to impart point and wit naturally increased. Very many charming little cameo-poems of this kind, touching upon most of the elements of human life, are to be found in what is known as the *Greek Anthology,* some of the best being of the Graeco-Roman age and written by Romans as well as Greeks throughout the Greek world. Our own epigram, whatever may be its change of character, is derived through French and Latin channels—particularly through Martial—from the Greek invention. It is probable also that the Italian, and thence the English, sonnet owes much to the pattern set in the Greek epigram.

. . . . .

In the regions of prose we can hardly be so definite. In history, oratory, philosophy, we still return again and again to the Greeks for inspiration, but the inspiration is chiefly one of spirit, not of outward form or special thoughts.

Herodouts, who began to flourish about 450 B.C., and who writes concerning the Persian invasion of Greece, and, by way of preface, tells of Lydia, Babylon, Egypt, Scythia, is still known as the "Father of history." His undying charm is his style, the style of a delightful story-teller. Clear and direct as all the best Greek writing is, there is something so fresh, so frank, so suave, about Herodouts, that, even if he tells falsehoods knowingly—as some critics say, but as we need not believe—we cannot grow virtuously indignant with him. He is both uncritical and shrewd—shrewd where the knowledge of his times guides him, uncritical where they were ignorant. His stronger-minded contemporary Thucydides is the very pattern of an historian. His function is to tell the history of the long protracted Peloponnesian war, and he tells it inimitably. The graphic terseness of his account is only equalled by his severe impartiality. If he tells you of a battle, he describes luminously its main features, how it went, who won it, and what the consequences were. He does not attempt to minimize or explain away an Athenian defeat or crime because he is an Athenian. If a political party commits an error, he tells us so, and tells us how. It is scarcely possible to find out precisely his own political views. If he describes the terrible plague of Athens or the terrible fall before Syracuse, he describes it with moving pathos. But he does not overdo his part. The pathos is in the distinct simplicity of the picture, not worked up by labour of ambitious words. It is perhaps enough warrant of his excellence that he grew in the admiration of Macaulay with every year of Macaulay's maturing judgement.

In oratory the great name of Demosthenes stands pre-eminent. Volumes of his speeches are in our hands, political and forensic speeches equally. The word "Philippics" has become typical for invective. That Demosthenes is the prince of orators everybody knows. But why? We may imagine the crude aspirant to oratory reading a speech of Demosthenes in amazement, and asking "Where are the flashings of rhetoric? Where the dazzling flights of imagination? Where the magnificent bursts of diction?" The highest art is to conceal art, and Demosthenes would have been no perfect artist if he had allowed the novice to perceive exactly wherein his perfection lay. He is the perfect orator just because he can be graphic, cogent, pathetic, anything he will, without all those rhetorical tropes, purple patches, bouquets of flowery diction, which weaker men are driven to use. His language is like a Greek statue, instinct with a life diffused through every part, but showing no straining at effect, accentuating nothing beyond its value as a persuasive or moving force. His metaphors and similes are few; often his words are even homely; but there is a directness, a "home-coming," about his diction and his periods, a dexterity about his arrangement, a noble fervour and simplicity.

In philosophy the Greeks have been the teachers of the civilized world. Two only of their great masters need be considered here. It is said that every man is born either an Aristotelian or a Platonist. This means that there are two chief types of mind which really think, and of those one is akin to the mind of Plato, the other akin to that of Aristotle. Plato is the suggestive, but inconclusive, imaginative, transcendental philosopher. Aristotle is the matter-of-fact, logical, analytical. The style is like the men. The style of Plato is rich with poetical colour, that of Aristotle is hard and thin, prose of the prose. Between them these two cover nearly all the ground of speculative thinking, and modern thought can never emancipate itself from them. For centuries in the Middle Ages the philosophy of Aristotle was almost a religion of civilized Europe, and it is the fact that even now students of morals and politics find themselves constantly returning to Aristotle. The Stagirite, as he was called because of his birth at Stagira, lived before the days of experimental science. Yet he virtually anticipated much of modern scientific results. He was nearly an evolutionist. Plato, on the other hand, has had his votaries. He, too, was a religion in Renaissance Italy. Whether we can always follow him or not, he is a stimulating influence, and he has left his mark in many places where one would hardly look for it. We should perhaps scarcely light on Wordsworth's beautiful *Ode on the Intimations of Immortality* as an echo of Plato. Yet all its fancy concerning "a sleep and a forgetting," and the previous existence of the soul, is pure Plato. Whether Wordsworth was conscious of it or not, his mind had been pervaded by the Platonic influence. Nor was it much otherwise with Shelley. Of direct and appreciable bearing upon literature since his day, is the fact that Plato is our first model of the prose dialogue or imaginary conversation. He did not indeed absolutely invent this form of writing, but the comparatively crude work which preceded him is lost, and it is Plato who stands to Berkeley or Landor as their prototype and exemplar. Centuries later Lucian followed in his steps, though with a somewhat different purpose, combining, as he declared, the philosophical dialogue with the spirit of Attic comedy. Plato's dialogues are always serious in intention, whatever humour or lightness of touch he may display; Lucian's are but partially serious, the humour, which tends to satire, being the predominant element.

A work of Plato to which the world owes much in the way of imitation is his *Ideal Commonwealth* or *Republic,* from which are derived in succession the hints for the *Civitas Dei* or *City of God* of St. Augustine, the *Utopia* of Sir Thomas More, the *New Atlantis* of Bacon, and various minor efforts in the theoretical construction of an ideal polity.

Here we must cease to speak of Greek literature in classical Greece. The subject is inexhaustible.

Yet before we come to illustrate in some detail the effect of all this wealth of original thought and splendid style on English, we must mention two famous writers in the later or "post-classical" period of Greek literature. These introduced new forms of prose writing which have had many imitators in every European country. They are Lucian and Plutarch. Lucian wrote in Syria and in Athens during the later part of the second century of our era. He composed what we should call "articles," in the form of dialogue and essays, nearly all of them of a satirically-humorous character, but nearly all possessed of sound common sense and practical purpose. Lucian is the precursor of Swift, Voltaire, and Heine. Of Swift he is the predecessor in more ways than one. Lucian supplies us with the first instance of ironical fiction. His *True History* is composed in the same ironical vein, and with precisely the same assumption of seriousness, as Swift's *Gulliver's Travels.* It is to Lucian that Swift owes the hint for such a work, and, after all, the hint was in this case a great part of the genius. The width of Lucian's range may be recognized from the fact that both Swift and Sterne have been called the "English Lucian."

If Herodotus is the "Father of History," Plutarch (first century A.D.) is the father of biography. Strictly speaking neither is the originator of the form of literature in question; nevertheless each is to be judged rather by the influence of his example than by absolute invention of a literary species. Besides the biographies there exists much other work of Plutarch in the nature of moral essays and "articles" on historical or antiquarian subjects, and this work was liberally drawn upon by essayists after the Revival of Learning, in particular by

Montaigne and Bacon. Nevertheless his chief contribution to the development of literature was in his "Parallel Lives," a series of biographies and character-studies, in which a distinguished Greek and a distinguished Roman were studied in comparison, pair by pair. To Shakespeare the Lives were known through North's translation, and, in *Coriolanus* and the other Roman plays, they supplied not only his conception of antiquity and ancient character, but also the great bulk of the matter which he dramatized. The genesis of modern sketches of the kind represented in Macaulay's *Chatham, Lord Clive,* or *Warren Hastings,* can be distinctly traced to similar short studies in the Greek of Plutarch.

A very prolific department of literature, and one which has served as a rich source of inspiration, imitation, and allusion in all subsequent times, was that of the fable. In this domain the name of "Aesop" is supreme. Whether there was ever an historical person bearing precisely this name has been questioned. The tradition which places him in Rhodes as a slave in the middle of the sixth century B.C. cannot be implicitly trusted; but it is difficult to understand how the special name of "Aesopus" can have come to attach itself to a series of beast-stories, unless some individual who bore it, or of whom it was a sobriquet, had been distinguished for his invention, or at least for his promulgation, of such satirical narratives. It is indeed almost certain that a large number of "fables of Aesop" originally came from India and the East; yet it is in Greece that Europe first makes acquaintance with those fables which are still the best known, and which most constantly appear in the existing collections or selections. All educated or even sophisticated Greeks were supposed to know "Aesop." At a later time (in the third century A.D.) the Graeco-Roman Babrius versified such fables as were known to him, and he again was copied into Latin verse by Avianus. The Indian fables of Pilpay were not circulated in Europe till five centuries later than Babrius, nor did they ever gain such wide currency. It was primarily along the Greek channel that there was derived, if not all the matter, at least the inspiration, for the fables in French by La Fontaine, and the English fables by Gay, together with all the collections which have been printed, or which were current before the days of printing, and which have become part of the *répertoire* of childhood and a fund of reference for proverbs and for all classes of writers.

Of other kinds of writing which appear already in ancient Greece may be briefly mentioned:

(1) Character-sketches, first produced by Theophrastus (about 320 B.C.), and imitated by La Bruyère (*Characters*) in France, and in England in such works as Hall's *Characterismes of Virtues and Vices,* Overbury's *Characters or Witty Descriptions of the Properties of Sundry Persons,* and best in Earle's *Microcosmography.* (2) Essays in rhetoric, literary criticism, and *belles lettres,* such as the *Rhetoric* and *Poetics* of Aristotle, the latter of which exerted so profound an effect upon the verse, and particularly the dramatic verse, of the French, and thence upon that of the English so-called "classical" school; the essays of Dionysius of Halicarnassus (25 B.C.) upon the style of the Attic orators; and the treatise *On Sublimity* by Longinus, a writer who cannot be identified, but who wrote in the flourishing times of the Roman imperial epoch; (3) the works in grammar and dictionary-making, which range from the textual criticism and comment of great Alexandrians, like Aristophanes of Byzantium (200 B.C.), to the school grammar of Dionysius Thrax and the lexicons of the early centuries A.D.; (4) geographies and descriptive guidebooks, the former particularly represented by Strabo, about the beginning of the Christian era, and the latter by Pausanias (in the second century A.D.); (5) Miscellanies, antiquarian or literary, such as the famous *Pundits at the Dinner-Table* of Athenaeus (end of second century A.D.); (6) letters (*i.e.,* fictitious epistles), such as those of Alciphron (second century A.D.); (7) *romances,* of which the extant examples are mostly much later than the classical period, those of Longus and Heliodorus dating from the latter part of the fourth century A.D.

. . . . .

We have now cursorily surveyed the course of Greek literary history. We have shown that it comprised all the forms of literature now known to us; that in this respect at least we can claim no originality. We have incidentally alluded to some of our debts, though that part of the subject remains to be dealt with more fully. The question which now arises is—what is there distinctive about this Greek literature as a whole, to make it possess such a precious and perpetual salt and savour?

We may reply that, to begin with, the Greek writers were characteristically possessed of one prime literary virtue—lucidity, whether in their picturing of scenes or in their expression of a thought. And they expressed clearly because they saw clearly. Besides being lucid, they were restrained. For the most part they went directly to their point, and did not suffer themselves to be drawn away from the point by irrelevant attractions. They knew, as Lowell puts it, how much writing to leave in the ink-pot. There is so much "not to say." They sharank from overdoing. Floweriness, extravagance, bombast, irrelevance, these were an abomination to classical Greek taste. The Greeks proper did not fail to recognize fustian when they saw it. They were a critical, and a self-critical, people. What we see in the purity of their sculpture and architecture, we may see in their literature. A word or phrase must have a rational and artistic purpose, or it must not be there.

Again, they were eminently sane men, those Greeks. They looked out on the world with eyes like those of their Goddess of Wisdom, the imperturbable eyes of unabashed intelligence. What they saw they saw frankly: they knew facts from fancies, and recognized facts when they met them. They were mentally a healthy people, not constitutionally given to moodiness and mysticisms and impossible aspirations. They took meanwhile a wholesome delight in living, and in the boons of physical life.

This whole way of looking at things has received a name of its own. It is styled "Hellenism." The Greeks called their country "Hellas," and themselves "Hellenes." Hence this name, which means so much. Hellenic thought means direct and fresh, if not always profound, thought; Hellenic art means art of consummate simplicity, art of clear principle. Hellenic style means in literature a perfect directness and lucidity, with just so much of the figurative as will flash light upon the sense.

This is what is meant by "Classical" Hellenism. True, no scholar would dare to say that even in the classical age every Greek who has left us a book or a fragment was always as perfect as Greek principles and ideals were perfect. Homer sometimes nods. We may find palpable blemishes not a few. But we must judge a national literature as a whole; and when, as with the Greek, a literature can show so large a proportion which is flawless, when it is so obviously informed with one and the same artistic spirit, so manifestly controlled by the same canons of taste, then we may use our general terms with more confidence than we can usually feel in generalizing of whole peoples and their histories.

In later times, when Greece was no longer free, when cultured Greeks had been scattered into Asia Minor, Syria, and to Alexandria, when literature became mere reading, then Greek art and letters lost their prime virtue. Oratory declined, as poetry had done. Greek writing became more oriental, more "Asian" in its artificiality. In classical Greek the ornamentation was not compassed for its own sake. It grew spontaneously out of the subject and helped the subject. But when Greek literature became "unclassical," when it became artificial, mere imitation and make-believe, when it was not the outcome of a national spirit, but was forced in the hotbeds of literary coteries and court-favour, then ornamentation was first and foremost; poems and speeches were composed in order to bring in fine things. Rhetoric grew bombastic and poetry finical; or, as it is commonly expressed, literature became "Asiatic" instead of "Attic." This literature in general is sometimes called "Hellenistic," rather than "Hellenic"; but that term should be appropriated to other purposes. Its headquarters being at Alexandria, the title "Alexandrian" has come to be virtually a term of disparagement in literature.

When therefore we speak of the influence of Greek literature on English, we include not merely a fund of classical history and of mythology, not merely a long list of Greek words and Greek allusions, not even merely an inheritance of all the great forms of poetry and prose writing, but also that way of looking at things and that style of putting things which we call Hellenic. We mean not only so many similes, metaphors and figures of speech, but a whole scope of thinking and style.

We might, indeed, in some rough way, gauge the influence of Greece by the mere titles of English books or compositions bearing such Greek names as *Utopia, Arcadia, Comus, Pindaric Odes, Endymion, Hellas, Prometheus Unbound, Hellenics, Life and Death of Jason, The Lotus-Eaters.* We might gauge it in some measure by the allusions scattered up and down from Chaucer to Tennyson, allusions to Homer and his Agamemnon, Achilles and Hector, his Circe and all the beings of his mythology, to Greek history, to Plato and Aristotle. We might gauge it in a measure by terms like Parnassus, Clio, Helicon, Academe, and similar references to the literary haunts and divinities of Greece. We might further take the Greek words which now form part of our English vocabulary.

But the subject requires more methodical treatment, and perhaps some little retrospect. Meanwhile we may well assert with Shelley:

> But Greece and her foundations are
> Built below the tide of war,
> Based on the crystalline sea
> Of thought and its eternity;
> Her citizens, imperial spirits,
> Rule the present from the past,
> On all this world of men inherits
> Their seal is set.

As the same poet says in his preface to *Hellas,* "We are all Greeks."

. . . . .

It now remains to examine at what times, in what ways, and to what extent, our own English literature has been influenced by models so rich and virile. The points of contact have been numerous; the influence which has been felt has not always been felt in the same respects. At one time we merely borrowed some of the matter of Greek writing, some of its stories of mythology and history, some of its figures and similes, some fragments of its philosophy. At another time we have copied some of its forms of production, such as the epic form of Homer, the Pindaric Ode, the idyll of Theocritus. At another time we have borrowed its literary criticism, and either garbled and misapplied it, like Pope, or rightly assimilated it, like Matthew Arnold. It is possible also to adopt its matter, its form, its Hellenic principles of criticism, all together; and that is what so many of the best writers of to-day are, consciously or unconsciously, labouring to do.

We have, in fact, grown more and more dependent on Greece with every generation of our literature since the days of Chaucer. This may appear a paradox, but it is no more than the truth. Antecedently one might suppose that, with the progress of what is called civilization, and with the expansion of knowledge, the literature of the ancient Greeks must now have been left far behind, as a thing of remarkable interest, no doubt, but a thing which has performed its practical function, a nourishment which has been sucked dry. Yet the very contrary is the case. In verse Tennyson, Matthew Arnold, Browning, Swinburne, William Morris, in prose Newman, Froude, Ruskin, whatever may be their points of difference, or even of contrast, nevertheless agree in this, that they have all saturated themselves with Greek and the things of Greece, with its ideas, phrases, and stories, till their work is in greater or less measure dominated by what they have thence derived. A Greek scholar realizes this obvious fact at once, and with gladness. A reader to whom Greek literature has been a sealed book little thinks how many of the felicitous expressions which especially captivate him in his poets of the present age are conscious or unconscious echoes, paraphrases, or mere translations, of things written more than a score of centuries ago in pagan Athens or the Isles of Greece.

Let us take a brief preliminary survey.

To Chaucer there filtered through from Greece, by way of writers in Latin or Italian, crude notions of Greek mythology or Homeric stories. Of the style and form and historical perspective of Greek literature he had no manner of conception. To him Agamemnon and Ulysses were knights with squires; Troy was besieged as Paris might be. His debt to Greece amounts to little more than a jumble of fables at second hand.

By Spenser's day our English writers are beginning to realize how rich a store lies to their hand in the books of that Greek which men of Western Europe have once more begun to study. They learn some little of the tongue, and they borrow unsparingly its stories and its similes. But of the lesson of its style, its restrained art, they have still learned almost nothing. They are caring for little beyond the solids which it affords. The *Faerie Queene* is crammed with classical allusion, and with similitudes traceable to Homer and other Greeks; but hardly a vestige appears as yet of the Greek literary spirit of clear simplicity, self-restraint, severity of taste. The extravagance and tastelessness which so often tire and irritate the reader of the *Faerie Queene* are altogether alien from Hellenic art.

Pass onward for some generations, till we come to the days of Pope and Addison. The study of Greek is more careful and more widely spread, its history and mythology have dropped into truer perspective and proportion. Greek life, Greek thought, are somewhat better comprehended, though still far from well. Much that the Greeks have written has now become general property. Better still, criticism is alert. The principles of the Greeks have passed, in a garbled form, it is true, through Rome to France, from France to England. The English have awakened to the fact that what deserves to be said at all deserves to be said concisely and precisely. So far, so good. Perhaps we do not profoundly admire the spirit of the literature of the age of Pope and Addison. But we must perforce admire its great advance in polish of expression. As literature, it may fail from want of ideas, from thinness of its substance. In that respect it departs as far from the Greek ideal as it approaches near the Greek ideal in skill of execution. The aim of Greek literature is to express thought or feeling perfectly. But there must be a real thought or a real feeling to express. And this spontaneousness or compelling sincerity the school of Pope and Addison did not, in the main, possess. Yet it did invaluable work. It furnished a later generation, which had ideas and was not ashamed of feelings, with an improved conception of expression. The "Classical" school these writers have been called, but classical they distinctly are not, for to be classical is to express matter of sterling worth in a style for ever fresh. To utter brilliantly a nothing, an artificiality, or a commonplace, is not classical.

The Queen Anne and early Georgian school, then, so far as Greek literature is concerned, owe to it sundry healthy principles of style, not yet properly assimilated; they owe many allusions, better ordered and digested than in Spenser or Chaucer; but of its higher thoughts and deeper imaginings they exhibit little influence.

Let that century expire, and come to the generation of Wordsworth, Shelley, Keats, and Byron. In them we meet with rich ideas in plenty, and with abundance of exquisite expression. Wordsworth, Shelley, and Byron had studied Greek; Shelley read it all his life. Keats, who knew no Greek at first hand, but who had innate in him that part of the Greek spirit which, as he puts it, "loves the principle of beauty in all things," had steeped himself in Greek legend; he revelled in Greek mythology; he assimilated the Greek view of nature and at least the passion of Greek life. All the literature of this period is shot through and through with the colour of Greek myths, Greek philosophy in its widest sense, Greek ideas. It shows an advance upon the age of Pope; for now once more the matter is made of the first account, although the manner is duly cultivated to form its fitting embodiment. Expression is fashioned to great beauty in Shelley, Coleridge, Keats, and often in Wordsworth. But the matter is of the first moment. A great advance is this upon the perfectly uttered proprieties of Pope. Yet still the age of Shelley was less Greek than the following "Victorian" age. The magnificent outbursts of the "spontaneous" and "romantic" schools of the beginning of last century too often ended in extravagance of fancy and riot of imagination. The transcendental rhapsodizings of Shelley and the sensuous revellings of Keats lack the sanity and self-repression which we associate with the name of Hellas. But the aim of the last age has been to secure the perfect union of sane, clear, yet unhackneyed thought with sane, clear, yet unhackneyed phrase. This was the aim of Tennyson, as of Matthew Arnold. Even Browning aims at this ideal in his most perfect moments.

Now, if what has been said of the ages of Chaucer, Spenser, Pope, Shelley, and Tennyson respectively is true, it is anything but a paradox to assert that, generation after generation since Chaucer's day, we have been passing more and more under the domination of Greek thoughts and Greek literary principles, and that we are groping forward to a literary ideal which turns out to have been the ideal of ancient Greece.

. . . . .

The full influence of Greece, then, was not felt all at once, nor in the same way and in the same respects.

Early English literature never came into direct contact with Greek books. Our old writers knew no Greek, for it is only since what is known as the "Revival of Learning" that the borrowing, whether of thought or style, has been at first hand. Nevertheless the debt was there, though the fathers of our literature were not conscious of it. Even King Alfred drew from Greek sources, though he knew no more of Greek than of baking cakes. When there was not a man from one end of England to the other who could properly read a Greek book, the men of England were nevertheless deriving, in a mutilated form no doubt, but still deriving, philosophy and ideas from that ancient Greece which to them was shrouded in the darkness of distance and of a tongue unknown. We may endeavour to see how this came to pass.

In the first place, if our earliest writers could not read Greek, they could read Latin. If they could not read Homer, they could read Virgil; if not Sappho and Pindar, they could read Horace. The Latin literature was with them, in a considerable measure. It is true that in the Dark Ages many of the best works of Latin literature lay concealed, and that others were deliberately neglected. The taste of readers in those ages ran rather in favour of the later and inferior Latin authors. Nevertheless, Latin literature of considerable extent they did study and assimilate; and what was this Latin literature, speaking generally, but an avowed imitation or copy of Greek models? The Roman Virgil copies the Greek Homer, Hesiod, and Theocritus. The Roman Horace copies Sappho, Pindar, Archilochus, Anacreon. The Roman Plautus and Terence are practically plagiaries of the Greek Menander and his like. Latin literature is, in a very large degree, Greek literature borrowed, adapted to inferior taste, played upon like studies with variations.

When Rome became the mistress of the world, it aspired to greater glory than mere conquest can ever impart, to the glory of culture and the arts. It found these perfected in Greece, and it became the pupil and imitator of that country, just as England has at various times become the pupil of Italy or France. It would hardly be too much to say of Latin literature, as of Roman art, that most of what is vital and perennial in it comes from Greece, while its faults and shortcomings are chiefly its own. Those who possess Latin literature possess a body of Greek thought and Greek material, but lacking the sure Greek taste and the soul of spontaneity. Our English writers down to Chaucer were in this position. Even their Latin reading was unsatisfactory enough, but, so far as they practised it, they were drinking of Greek waters rendered turbid by Roman handling and adulteration.

King Alfred knew Latin enough to translate Boethius. The monks and scholars, who, till Chaucer's time, were the only writers, kept alive the reading of Latin literature. But, so far as the Greek was concerned at first hand, there was but one poorly equipped scholar here and another there in all the West of Europe. So little was it known that, even in Wyclif's day, it was necessary for that reformer in translating the New Testament to render from the Latin Vulgate, the Greek original being veritably "all Greek" to him. Chaucer, again, writes indeed of Greeks at Thebes and Troy, and refers to Aristotle and Greek authors; but his acquaintance with these is all at second hand, through Roman poets like Ovid and Statius, or even at third or fourth hand, through the literature of Frenchmen or Italians, who themselves derived from writers in Latin and not from the Greek originals.

This, then, is the first period and manner of Greek influence, an influence indirect and roundabout, exerted through the medium of Latin literature, in which the style and spirit of Greece had already been corrupted or destroyed.

The second manner of influence was still more roundabout. It came through the Saracens and Moors. When the Saracen power had reached its zenith and one caliph sat in state at Bagdad and another at Cordova, the Saracens felt what the Romans had felt, that, after all, it is culture and arts which give a nation nobility. In the eleventh and twelfth centuries in particular the Saracen kingdom in Spain flourished mightily in culture and learning. Early in the ninth century a caliph of Bagdad showed himself one of the most devoted fosterers of literature that the world has ever known. His Court was thronged with men of letters and learning; he lavished honours on them; he collected books from every source, and especially from Greece. When he dictated terms of peace to the Greek Emperor Michael he demanded as tribute a collection of Greek authors. Works of the Greeks on rhetoric and philosophy were particularly prized, translated, and commented on. But the learning of Bagdad meant also the learning of the Moors in Spain. In the eleventh and twelfth centuries the science of the Moors was sought by many western students who were not Moslems; and thus from Bagdad, round by way of Spain, there percolated to Italy, France, and England some knowledge of what classical Greece had thought and written. In particular, Averrhoes, a Saracen, translated Aristotle into Arabic; from the Arabic a Latin version was made. This version passed into general use, and the Aristotelean philosophy, which dominated, not to say tyrannized, over Europe for centuries, owes its access to Western Europe to the followers of Mohammed.

Thus far, until the Renaissance dawned in Italy, we find in Western Europe no acquaintance with Greek literature at first hand, but only so much knowledge of its contents as could be gathered from the Latin writers, who had recast it or plagiarized it, or from the Saracen writers, who had translated it in parts.

At last, however, the influence was to become direct. And first on Italy. As the Turks entered Europe, and gradually overran the empire of Greece, Greeks of learning made their way westward to Venice, Ravenna, Padua, Florence, Rome. After the year 1300, or thereabouts, during the great age of Dante, Petrarch and Boccaccio, we find writers of Italy beginning to acquire some knowledge of Greek, and some insight into the rich literary stores which that language contained. Boccaccio learned the language from a native Greek; Petrarch took lessons from the same. One Italian here, and another there, essayed translations and imitations of Greek authors. In 1453 Constantinople, the capital of the Greek empire, fell into the hands of the Turks, and Greece no longer existed. As a result, crowds of cultured Greeks streamed into Italy with books and manuscripts, prepared to teach for love or money, or from mere ardour and pride of patriotism. The Court of Cosmo de' Medici at Florence was readily opened to them, and all Italy was agog to learn whatever they could bring. The libraries of Rome and Florence were enriched with Greek manuscripts; and when, soon after, the printing press of Aldus at Venice was established, Homer or Aeschylus passed in the original into many hands, while translations of them came into many more. Greek teachers like Chalcondylas, Argyropoulos, and Lascaris have left their names to fame in Rome and Padua and Florence. The Revival of Learning had filled all Italy, and "learning" meant little but the literature of Greece; it became regular, almost inevitable, that the Italian man of letters should know Greek, and should steep himself in the writings of the Grecians. From Italy the study spread to France and England. Grocyn and Linacre at Oxford, Erasmus and Cheke at Cambridge, worked zealously to establish it against that opposition which always attends the disturbance of sluggish methods and musty privilege. The study was opposed by the "Trojans," and it was perhaps natural that these should cry out, in an ancient phrase, "Beware of the Greeks, lest they make you a heretic"; for already it was recognized that the revival of Greek learning meant the stimulation of all clear, and therefore progressive, intellectual activities.

By about the year 1550—that is to say, just in time for Spenser, Shakespeare, Bacon, and their kindred—it had become usual for the Universities and the better schools in England to teach the elements of Greek; and there were not wanting ardent students, in those pre-examination days, to prosecute the study for themselves, and to find more than ample reward in the rich intellectual resources which lay revealed before them.

We have now reached the Elizabethan age of English literature. It is in this age that there came such an outburst of splendid creation in every form as the world has seen but once or twice. Sidney, Spenser, Shakespeare, Marlowe, Bacon, Hooker, Raleigh—drama, novel, lyrics, narrative poetry, essay-writing, philosophy, history—all these made new and magnificent efforts. And why? Not merely because at this epoch was born a genius like Shakespeare's, or a lofty intellect like Bacon's. The genius must have his opportunity; the intellect must have its materials. It was because the world was electrified with a current of new thoughts and new ideas, pervading and furnishing every mind. The "revival of learning" was something more than that name alone implies. It was also a renaissance, a "new birth," both of intellect and art. The spirit of Greece had breathed life into the dry bones of the valley of the West-European mind.

The writers of the Elizabethan age flung themselves about in the gardens and orchards of Greek literature with all the impatient appetite and reckless gaiety of schoolboys on holiday. They tore at the plots of Greek epics, plays, and histories; they plucked the similes and metaphors of Greece to "stick them in their hats," so to speak; so great was their joy in the strange fresh atmosphere of this luxuriant newly-opened paradise. Their scholarly knowledge of Greek as a language was too slight, their perspective of Greek life and thought too distorted, for them to catch the artistic style and spirit while they were catching the matter and the substance. Amazingly rich as Spenser is in imagery and melody, exhaustless as Shakespeare is in ideas, boundless as he is in capacity of seeing and feeling, no one will call either Spenser or Shakespeare a flawless artist, or say that either is free from extravagance or unevenness. In short, no one will concede to them the Greek spirit, which tempers imagination with self-restraint and unfailing sanity. The wide free range of mind they have; the tactful sense of proportion and seasonableness they too often lack. The influence of Greece, beneficent and large as it is, remains yet incomplete.

We must not, however, overstate the case. No one doubts that all this stupendous outburst obtained its chief stimulus and food from Greece. Nevertheless, when speaking of these Elizabethan times and of the new Greek studies which were being fostered by the Universities and the highest schools, let us not picture to ourselves every considerable writer of that time assiduously studying Greek books in their originals. That was far from the case. Their scholarship in that way was mostly but shallow. Shakespeare, we know, learned "little Latin and less Greek." We need not claim that, after his college days, Spenser went directly to his Greek Homer, any more than that Shakespeare went directly to his Greek Plutarch. What should be understood is that the matter, though not the manner, of Greek books was now fairly abundant in those writers' hands. The Elizabethan age was the age of translations, not always accurate translations, but generally translations of spirit. Chapman's Homer and North's Plutarch are household words. And, where there existed no English translation of a Greek book, there was almost certainly one in French or in Italian. Homer, for instance, translated by Filelfo, had come within English ken even before England had begun its own direct studies in Greek. Now, though a translation can do much, there is one thing it cannot do. It cannot convey the lesson of perfect art in style, least of all can it do this when the translator allows himself liberties. And therefore the Elizabethan writers have not yet gathered from the Hellenic mind its sober aesthetic principles.

Historically considered, the ancient Greeks too often become transformed, in the respective free translations, into contemporary Italians, or Englishmen, or Frenchmen. They present themselves to the mind in an alien dress, physically and mentally. They are, in fact, anachronisms. Agamemnon and Ulysses, instead of appearing as simple Achaean chiefs, become transformed into knights in armour, gallants with rapiers, kings in purple robes and crowns. They quote philosophy, or speak of sciences and instruments they never knew.

In brief, in the Elizabethan age we have reached this—that the knowledge of Greek literature is no longer dependent on the Latin copies and plagiarisms of it, or on such driblets of philosophy as trickle through from the Saracens of Spain. It is derived, sometimes at first hand, but mostly from translations directly made in English, French, or Italian, from the Greek originals. Nor is this all. For among Englishmen who are training themselves to be the writers of the next generation there are growing up many to whom Greek itself, in all its nervous plasticity, is becoming a familiar tongue, and who will use no modern versions at the risk of distorting their taste and judgement. With this new generation will come the critical chastening of style which has hitherto been lacking.

Those who have never studied language as the classical languages are studied can scarcely hope to understand how vast is the difference between two educational results; on the one hand, of a painstaking study of that indescribable harmony of thought and word which constitutes style, and, on the other, of that superficial perusal of translations which supplies but coarse notions of the substance, notions as different from those of the scholar as the commercial plaster cast is different from the marble originals of Attic sculpture. Since the Shakespearean time our writers have become more and more scholars in Greek—witness Milton, Gray, Cowper, Shelley, among the poets—till, in our own days, it is difficult to meet with an author eminent either in prose or poetry who has not received a liberal training in the Greek language itself, and thence acquired a care of expression such as Greek models cannot fail to impress.

It may now be well to take for illustration one or two of the departments of literature—not necessarily of the first consequence—in which our debt to Greek is on the surface.

A striking form of Greek composition was the Pindaric Ode. Our English poets from Cowley to Swinburne have shown a marked fondness for this form. Cowley, Congreve, and Gray deliberately affect even the title *Pindaric Ode,* acknowledging the source of their inspiration and avowing the imitativeness of their work. The poet Mason speaks of "a Pindar's rapture in the lyre of Gray." Cowley, as has been mentioned already, is called on his tombstone the "English Pindar." Pope's *Ode on St. Cecilia's Day* is meant to be, even if it does not succeed in being, Pindaric in both shape and spirit. It is full, too, of allusion to things Greek, to the ship Argo, to the underworld, with Phlegethon and Sisyphus and Ixion, to the yellow meads of asphodel, to Orpheus and Eurydice. Dryden's *Song for St. Cecilia's Day* and his *Alexander's Feast* are imitations of Pindar and Simonides. Gray's *Progress of Poesy* is of the same stamp. When he circulated the poem in manuscript, he called it an "Ode in the Greek manner." His *Bard* belongs to the same category. Meanwhile the words which open the *Progress of Poesy*

> Awake, Aeolian lyre, awake,
> And give to rapture all thy trembling strings

profess a debt to Aeolis, the country of the lyric Sappho and Alcaeus. We must add Collins and Shelley to the list of those over whom Pindar has exercised his charm. Shelley's *Ode to Liberty,* with its panegyric stanzas on Athens, is at least as Pindaric as the avowed Pindarics of Gray or Cowley.

We have already referred to that rather artificial and not very important form of composition called the "pastoral," whether it be the "pastoral idyll" or the "pastoral elegy"—an idealizing picture of the shepherd's life, or an idealistic "shepherd's lament." We may here briefly revert to the subject.

Of this class we have in English literature such works as the *Shepheard's Calender* of Spenser, a manifest and avowed imitation of Virgil through the Italians. As, however, Virgil is but the pupil of Theocritus in this kind, it is to the Greek Theocritus that we are in the end brought back. Spenser's imitation is, indeed, anything but good. He mixes up "Fair Elisa, queen of shepherds all" with talk of Parnassus, Helicon, Pan, Cynthia and the nymphs (whom he calls "ladies of the lake"). Colin Clout, Cuddie, and Hobbinol are found side by side with Tityrus and invocations to Calliope. Moreover he justly incurs the reproach of Sir Philip Sidney by his affectation of an archaic language for his shepherds, a language which never was on land or sea. Says Sidney, "that same framing of his style to an old rusticke language I dare not allow; since neither Theocritus in Greek, Virgil in Latin, nor Sannazaro in Italian, did affect it." We have also the youthful *Pastorals* of Pope, in which the poet begins by announcing his studied imitation:

> Fair Thames, flow gently from thy sacred
> spring,
> While on thy banks Sicilian Muses sing;

that is to say, the Muses of Theocritus of Sicily. He even appends notes to show what lines he has especially copied. We meet always the familiar Greek characters, Daphnis, Strephon, Alexis, Lycidas, and Thyrsis. Like the pastorals of Spenser, they are purely and confessedly artificial; they are anachronisms, carelessly mixing modern and antique ideas and associations. When Theocritus wrote pastorals in ancient and sunny Sicily he wrote, as we have remarked, of what lay within the range of conceivable possibility. Pope relegates the pastoral to a fictitious golden age in a purely fictitious golden land.

No one nowadays is likely to set any high value upon such eclogues as Pope's *Pastorals.* Even Spenser's *Shepheard's Calender* is rather talked of than read. Sidney's *Arcadia* has had its day. But it is otherwise with a nobler species of composition which arose out of pastorals, to wit, the pastoral elegy. Theocritus and his disciples, Bion and Moschus, all compose poetic laments for a lost shepherd, either an imaginary Daphnis or a real friend lately dead. To this original conception we owe certain English poems which we could not spare. They include the *Lycidas* of Milton, on the death of his friend King, the *Adonais* of Shelley, on the death of Keats, the *Thyrsis* of Matthew Arnold, on the death of Clough. The *Daphnaida* of Spenser was apparently the first of such elegiac pastorals. Another is his *Astrophel,* "on the death of the most noble and valorous knight, Sir Philip Sidney." Dryden, too, did not disdain to write a pastoral elegy on the death of a supposed Amyntas, in which he sings his dirge in the good old style of the Sicilians. A more refined, more distant and subtle development from the same original is Tennyson's *In Memoriam.* Finally we may take leave of this rural style with brief mention of the fact that Tennyson's *Œnone* is in essence a pastoral idyll, inspired by the second of Theocritus.

We may also turn again to literary criticism. It is a significant thing that, no sooner had Sir John Cheke studied Greek and become its first regular professor at Cambridge, than he forthwith published maxims on the avoidance of bombast and pedantry in style. He had been to the fountain heads of criticism, to the Greek of Aristotle and Longinus. From that day down to the days of Matthew Arnold, in "essays in criticism" Greek principles have everywhere been theoretically worshipped, however much they may have been violated in practice. Following on the revival of Greek learning came a rage to discuss the *rationale* of the poetic art, as well as to exemplify its various forms. In the Elizabethan age Puttenham wrote on the *Art of English Poesie;* Sidney composed a *Defence of Poesie.* Later on Dryden put forth a prose treatise *Of Dramatic Poesie,* and the Earl of Roscommon an *Essay on Translated Verse.* Dryden expressly declares that true criticism began with the Greeks in the *Poetics* of Aristotle. He says:

> Such once were critics; such the happy few
> Athens and Rome in better ages knew.
> The mighty Stagirite first left the shore,
> Spread all his sails, and durst the deep
> explore;
> He steered securely, and discovered far,
> Led by the light of the Maeonian star.

Pope followed with an *Essay on Criticism,* Shelley contributed a critical *Defence of Poetry;* and since that date books, essays, articles have showered upon us, in one and all of which we are assured with increasing urgency that the true principles of literary art are the principles of Athens, the principles of Greek literature at its best.

We may now leave types of literary creation and deal with individual authors. It would require a whole book for each of the greater names, if we sought to discover how much of matter or form each owes directly or indirectly to Greece. Mr. Churton Collins has written one such book on Tennyson. Here our survey must be but very superficial, as befits an introduction to the study.

Of Spenser's *Shepheard's Calender, Daphnaida,* and *Astrophel* something has been said. It remains to observe that his *Faerie Queene* is but one mass of scenes, events, and images borrowed from sources in Italy and Greece, and that the hint for the whole design was suggested by his studies in Aristotle; for he says, "I labour to pourtraict in Arthur the image of a brave knight, perfected in the twelve moral vertues, as Aristotle hath devised." Of the Greek manner, its proportion and moderation, Spenser has unhappily learned little or nothing.

Shakespeare was, in one sense, no Grecian. Sundry of his Roman plots, *Coriolanus* and *Antony and Cleopatra* for example, he takes from North's translation of the Greek Plutarch; a certain amount of Greek mythology and history reveals itself incidentally; but he owes less to Greece and more to his own genius acting upon desultory reading, than other writers of the time or since. Dryden, indeed, in his adaptation of *Troilus and Cressida* makes him say:

Untaught, unpractised, in a barbarous age,
I found not, but created first, the stage;
And if I drained no Greek or Latin store,
'Twas that my own abundance gave me more.

But this is hardly the truth. One immensely important thing Shakespeare did owe to Greece, through scholars who were his own immediate predecessors, and that was the general shape and form of the poetic drama.

Milton was an accomplished Greek scholar. It has been already pointed out that his great epic is descended from Homer, and his *Lycidas* from Theocritus. His *Samson Agonistes* was deliberately built—though not with complete success—upon the traditional framework of Greek tragedies, and Milton himself leaves it to be judged by those who are "not unacquainted with Aeschylus, Sophocles, and Euripides." His *Ode on the Morning of the Nativity* is intended to be Pindaric. But the most palpable advance made by Milton on his predecessor Spenser is in the chastening of his style. The principles of that style Milton derived at first hand from his Hellenic models. He has learned how to use ancient material, how to adapt ancient thoughts, ancient expressions, how to sink them and imbed them in his own, not merely how to overlay or fancifully decorate his own with them. The texture of Milton's verse is shot through and through with colours borrowed from the Greek; it would often be quite possible to resolve a series of his lines into components which are imitations and quotations. But he has made them all so much a part of himself that we may often pass by his loans, as we never can those of Spenser, unconsciously.

Dryden owns himself an obedient follower of the Greeks. His ode *To the Memory of Mrs. Anne Killigrew,* like his *St. Cecilia's Day* and his *Alexander's Feast,* is Pindaric. His admiration for Pindar was indeed peculiarly ardent. He speaks of him as "the inimitable Pindar, who stretches on pinions out of sight, and is carried upward, as it were, into another world." Of his literary criticism we have spoken; there was a time when he conceived the idea of translating Homer, and he did in fact attempt versions of various writings of Greek poets.

Pope was but an indifferent Greek scholar at first hand; he did indeed freely translate and recast Homer's *Iliad* and *Odyssey* by the help of his little Greek and a translation in French, but he never entered into the spirit of Greek life or penetrated to the precise secret of Greek style. Nevertheless, he makes great pretensions to follow in the footsteps of the Greek masters. One thing he did catch—the vigour and fire of Homer; and Pope's *Iliad* is still the English Homer commonly read in these days, although Chapman had preceded him, and Cowper, Derby, and Morris have made their more or less faithful renderings since. And yet the book is far too much Pope to be Homer. Of the *Pastorals* and the *Essay on Criticism* all has been said above that need be said for our purpose. We have only to add that his burlesque heroics, the *Rape of the Lock* and the *Dunciad,* had their prototype in the heroi-comical poems of Greece, the *Battle of the Frogs and Mice* and the *Margites,* compositions which were once ascribed to Homer, and which Pope professed to have in mind.

Gray was a scholar of rare attainments in both the language and the literature of Greece. Hence, in no inconsiderable measure, his self-critical spirit. His aim, as stated by himself, is at "extreme conciseness of expression, yet pure, perspicuous and musical." As a poet he suffered from constitutional shortcomings. He is without profound imaginings or ecstatic sensibilities; but his beauties are no less undeniable, although of the sort which are mainly acquired from training. No one can fail to admire the perfect technique of his stanzas. It is doubtful, however, whether any but a Greek scholar can perceive the skill with which he has combined a mosaic of reminiscences of ancient writers into stanzas of perfect English. His *Progress of Poesy* and his *Bard* are plainly modelled on Pindar, but even his most beautiful individual expressions are sometimes but translations from the Greek. Said the Greek Phrynichus: "The purple light of love shines on her flushing cheeks." To this Gray owes his

O'er her warm cheek and rising bosom move
The bloom of young desire and purple light of
love.

Of his enthusiasm for Greece we may judge from a passage in the *Progress of Poesy:*

Woods, that wave o'er Delphi's steep,
Isles, that crown the Egaean deep,
Fields, that cool Ilissus laves,
Or where Maeander's amber waves

In lingering lab'rinths creep;
How do your tuneful echoes languish—
Mute, but to the voice of anguish?
Where each old poetic mountain
Inspiration breath'd around:
Ev'ry shade and hallowed fountain
Murmur'd deep a solemn sound:
Till the sad Nine in Greece's evil hour,
Left their Parnassus for the Latian plains.

Swift's most popular work, *Gulliver's Travels,* derives its hint from Lucian's *True History,* and all that peculiar vein of humour which runs through the *Tale of a Tub* and the *Battle of the Books,* is, consciously or unconsciously, the parallel of the characteristic irony of the same Lucian.

Of Shelley's debts to Greece one can hardly estimate the amount. Says he himself: "The poetry of ancient Greece and Rome and modern Italy and our own country has been to me like external nature, a passion and an enjoyment." During his travels in Italy "the Greek tragedies," says Mrs. Shelley, "were his most familiar companions in his wanderings, and the sublime majesty of Aeschylus filled him with wonder and delight." We find him reading Homer, Hesiod, Theocritus, Thucydides, Aeschylus, Plutarch, Plato; he even translates portions of these; he steeps himself to the lips in the literature of Greece. His own soul and genius were by nature akin to those of Plato, and his training lent to his genius clear capacity. Among those of his works which most manifestly bear the Greek impress are the lyrical drama of *Hellas*—which, he says, was suggested by the *Persae* of Aeschylus—and the drama of *Prometheus Unbound,* which is meant for a sequel to the *Prometheus Bound* of Aeschylus. Not that his drama of Prometheus is fashioned wholly like the Greek; its architecture is less simple, its character is more rhetorical, more ornamented, more metaphysical. But it owes its whole existence to the fact that Shelley lived so long in a world of Greek literature, a world very remote from that in which he moved and had his being. His *Adonais*—

I weep for Adonais—he is dead!
O weep for Adonais! though our tears
Thaw not the frost that binds so dear a head!

is an echo of Theocritus, his *Ode to Liberty* an echo of Pindar, his *Epipsychidion* an outcome of Plato. His enthusiasm for Greece may be gathered from his *Hellas:*

The world's great age begins anew,
The golden years return;
The earth doth like a snake renew
Her winter weeds outworn. . . .

A brighter Hellas rears its mountains
From waves serener far;
A new Peneus rolls its fountains
Against the morning star;
Where fairer Tempes bloom, there sleep
Young Cyclads on a sunnier deep.

Keats never learned the Greek language. But he was read, as perhaps never Englishman was read before, in Greek legend and mythology. He devoured Lemprière's *Dictionary.* His greatest poetry—his chief odes, as well as his *Hyperion* and *Endymion*—is based on subjects thence acquired. The manners and characters of Greek divinities pervade his writings. In heart and soul, in sensuous enjoyment of life, he was himself a pagan Greek. The life of the ancient world, idealized, was the world of his choice. Above all he loves the sounds uttered

In Grecian isles
By bards who died content on pleasant sward,
Leaving great verse unto a little clan.
O give me their old vigour!

"Therefore," says he,

'Tis with full happiness that I
Will trace the story of Endymion.
The very music of the name has gone
Into my being.

Had he studied Greek as language, and Greek as style, he would, we may believe, have avoided earlier his one great fault, the fault of excess, extravagance, and riot. What Keats thought of the great Greek writers whose Greek he could not read, may be gathered from his lines to Homer:

Standing aloof in giant ignorance,
Of thee I hear, and of the Cyclades,
As one who sits ashore and longs perchance
To visit dolphin-coral in deep seas:

and from those *On first looking into Chapman's Homer:*

Much have I travelled in the realms of gold,
And many goodly states and kingdoms seen;
Round many western islands have I been,
Which bards in fealty to Apollo hold.
Oft of one wide expanse had I been told,
That deep-brow'd Homer ruled as his demesne;
Yet did I never breathe its pure serene
Till I heard Chapman speak out loud and bold.
Then felt I like some watcher of the skies,
When a new planet swims into his ken;
Or like stout Cortez, when with eagle eyes
He stared at the Pacific—and all his men
Look'd at each other with a wild surmise—
Silent, upon a peak in Darien.

The name of Byron is at once associated with enthusiasm for Greece. True, it was modern Greece, but the only reason for that warm affection lay in the fervour of his admiration for the Greece of old. That "land of lost gods and godlike men" was to him a sacred land. Everyone knows his outburst touching the "isles of Greece." But not everyone perceives how profoundly the mind of Byron had been stirred by the ancient ideals and influences. Not everyone perceives that his *Manfred* is an unmistakable echo of Aeschylus' *Prometheus,* in the tone and pitch of its composition, in the firmness of the central character, in his mental suffering, in the tremendous solitude, in the supernatural of the surroundings. Yet Byron is not one whom we may quote as typifying any great direct and salutary effect of Greek upon either his style or his matter. He is too slipshod in the one and too romantic in the other. But his ardour for the land of great literature is beyond denying:

> The isles of Greece, the isles of Greece!
> Where burning Sappho loved and sung,
> Where grew the arts of war and peace,
> Where Delos rose, and Phoebus sprung!
> Eternal summer gilds them yet,
> But all, except their sun, is set.
>
> The Scian and the Teian muse,
> The lover's harp, the lover's lute,
> Have found the fame your shores refuse:
> Their place of birth alone is mute
> To sounds which echo further west
> Than your sires' "Islands of the Blest."
> And where are they? and where art thou,
> My country? On thy voiceless shore
> The heroic lay is tuneless now—
> The heroic bosom beats no more!
> And must thy lyre, so long divine,
> Degenerate into hands like mine?

During the last fifty years the study of Greek literature has been set on a new basis. A collection of ill-digested matter no longer suffices. Greek is taught more understandingly and more deeply. First comes a patient observant study of the language; afterwards, in years of maturity, are estimated the qualities of the thought and of the style; these are set in clearer lights, and turned to a direct application. Landor is the first modern in whom this sort of study reveals its effects. His Greek devotion to classical associations, to ideal beauty, his Greek aversion to the mysterious, his love for clearness and purity of outline, appear cold to many a reader. He is too pellucid, of too delicate a preciseness, they imagine. But Landor does not displease through these qualities, which are virtues. His coldness is constitutional. However that may be, his imaginary dialogues, imitated from Plato, and the poetry of his *Hellenics,* show the Greek influence in a fuller form than we have met with hitherto. Since Landor's day our literature is pervaded with Greek ideals: it aims at Greek style, and often it attains fairly to its mark. We need not deal with matter so voluminous as that of Browning, nor with a style so inconsistent. But Browning's love of Greek is matter of fame. Has he not translated the *Agamemnon* of Aeschylus, the *Alcestis* and the *Heracles* of Euripides? Nor need we deal with the poetry of Swinburne. It is enough to point out that the *Atalanta in Calydon* is in spirit intensely Greek, and that its most famous speech is a translation from Euripides.

From William Morris we have a translation of the *Odyssey;* he has written the *Life and Death of Jason* and the *Earthly Paradise,* and both of these owe almost everything—their matter and the charm of their manner—to the *Iliad* and the *Odyssey,* to Apollonius, and to the Greek tragedians.

To two of the best and purest poets of our age Greece has supplied the very breath of literary life. One is Matthew Arnold, the other is Tennyson. Matthew Arnold as critic, Matthew Arnold as poet, is equally Hellenic. He has been charged with "an air of aristocratic selectness and literary exclusiveness." The art of Pheidias is open to the same objection. What really marks the style of Matthew Arnold is his reasoned simplicity of taste, his cultivated appreciation of the delicate aroma of words and the poetical atmosphere of thought. Like Tennyson, he has a true eye for beauty, grace, and congruity of effect. He compasses the "liquid clearness of an Ionian sky." It may be that he lacks *abandon.* He may not feel with the poignancy, or soar with the boldness, of the greatest creators. But, artistically considered, he is as nearly perfect as it is given to man to be. His poetic style is, indeed, almost too perfect for the general. When he says

> Or where the *echoing* oars
> Of Argo first
> Startled the *unknown* sea.

he is using the only two adjectives which the place required, and which it truthfully admits. They are exactly the two epithets which a Greek might put. Yet, no doubt, the untutored mind asks for something more assertive, something which will cut more sharply or press more heavily into the unready imagination. Than *Mycerinus,* than *Sohrab and Rustum,* than *Philomela, Thyrsis,* or *The Strayed Reveller,* one can find nothing more absolutely Greek in point of execution, though one may know Greek passages which stir profounder emotional depths.

Tennyson's debts to classical authors have been treated by Mr. Churton Collins in a monograph. That critic is right in saying that the knowledge of a scholar is requisite to appreciate Tennyson fully, however much he may be appreciated by those who are no scholars. No man has ever been better read in previous poetry than Tennyson, and no man has known better how to assimilate what he found, or has possessed a surer tact and taste in using it. With Tennyson the Greek matter is, as with Milton, imbedded in his own, not overlaid. Greek forms of verse are moulded to his purpose. The Greek style, describing what is luminously seen in a few luminous touches, is ever conspicuous. He neither tries to disguise his borrowings, nor does he obtrude them. When he says, "for now the noonday quiet holds the hill," he is translating Callimachus; when "the charm of married brows," Theocritus; when "shadowy thoroughfares of thought," Sophocles; when "sitting well in order smite the sounding furrows," Homer. His device of making the sound answer to the sense, as in

> I heard the water lapping on the crag,
> And the long ripple washing in the reeds,

is a common device of the Greeks. In point of form his *Œnone* is modelled on Theocritus; his *Ulysses* and his *Tithonus* are framed after the soliloquies in Greek plays. His *Lotus-eaters* gets its matter from Homer, Bion, and Moschus. Everywhere we meet hints and reminiscences of Simonides, or Pindar, or Theocritus, or Anacreon. But these are all incorporated, amalgamated in a body of work which is wholly in keeping with them in taste, in tone, in diction—in short, in style.

This age of ours, to put it briefly, has been an age of stylists, of artists who work on principles derived from their education in Greek, and their love, which every scholar feels, of that glorious and undying literature.

Frederick E. Pierce (essay date 1917)

SOURCE: "The Hellenic Current in English Nineteenth-Century Poetry," in *The Journal of English and Germanic Philology,* Vol. XVI, No. 1, January, 1917, pp. 103-35.

[*In the excerpt that follows, Pierce summarizes the Victorian contribution to the nineteenth-century enthusiasm for verse influenced by Hellenism, which he finds intertwined with a taste for the "medieval."*]

The Hellenic tradition, though the child of the Romantic generation, did not collapse with its parent movement but continued on unbroken into the later nineteenth century. Certain characteristics shown in its beginning have clung to it ever since. One of these is its constant alliance with the medieval tradition. Almost every author who has written poems on ancient Greece has written others on the Middle Ages. Byron had his *Manfred,* Keats his *Eve of St. Agnes,* Tennyson his *Morte d'Arthur,* Swinburne his *Tale of Balen,* William Morris his *Ogier the Dane,* Lewis Morris his *Vision of Saints,* de Tabley his *Two Old Kings,* Landor his *Count Julian,* Matthew Arnold his *Tristram and Iseult,* and so we might go on. Hellenism and medievalism pair off against each other in volume after volume like positive and negative poles in a series of electric batteries. Another characteristic of the Greek tradition is that each poet turns to it only at intervals. No one author, not Shelley, Arnold, or Landor even, has ever surrendered himself to it as completely as Scott did to medievalism or Crabbe to harsh realism.

At the same time, while the above characteristics always hold true, the Greek current changes very perceptibly as it passes through the different waves or *Zeitgeists* of the century. Before 1830 it was mainly romantic. Between 1830 and 1860 it wavers between romanticism and the more restrained and reflective classicism, the latter finally winning a temporary triumph in the work of Landor and Arnold. The tendency away from romance is shown by contrasting Tennyson's *Œnone* and *Lotus Eaters* (1833) with the sterner and less hazily atmospheric *Ulysses* and *Tithonus* (1842).

The collapse of the Romantic generation made not even a break in the tradition we are tracing. In 1830, only three years after Hood's *Lycus, the Centaur* and directly following the Greek poems in Moore's *Legendary Ballads* appeared Tennyson's *Sea Fairies,* slight but prophetic; and in the same year were printed The Poetical Works of the Rev. George Croly written chiefty in the period between 1816 and 1823, but now first published in one collection. They contain considerable Greek verse, especially the *Gems from the Antique,* a series of short poems, each accompanied by an engraving of the carved gem on which the lines are based. W. E. Aytoun, the Scotch poet followed in 1832 with his boyish *Homer,* the story of the great epic singer and the protest of the romantic poet against the world, voiced in fifty-eight stanzas of weakly sweet *ottava rima.*

Lord Houghton (Richard Monckton Milnes) the devoted editor of Keats, in 1834 published his *Memorials of a Tour in Greece and Italy,* a series of short poems on Hellenic subjects, the dignified verse of a scholar, though not of a great master. The influence of "the Poet Keats, to whom the old Greek mind seemed instinctively familiar"[25] is obvious, especially in such lines as these:

> And downward thence to latest days
> The heritage of Beauty fell,
> And Grecian forms and Grecian lays
> Prolonged their humanizing spell.[26]

In Houghton, as in Keats, there is sympathetic harmony between classic and medieval legend. He can see in Grecian olive forests

Sylvan cathedrals, such as in old times
Gave the first life to Gothic art, and led
Imagination so sublime a way.[27]

Likewise in the opening lines of his *Modern Greece* he speaks of the medieval story of the enchanted princess as "the legend which our childhood loved."

The Preface to his *Poetical Works* of 1876 throws some light on the Hellenic current, its nature and causes:

"The Grecian poems [of 1834] have their date in that period of life which, in a cultivated Englishman, is almost universally touched and coloured by the studies and memories of the classic world; and the scenes and personages they commemorate are, as it were, the most natural subjects of his poetic thought and illustration. . . . There were, too, at that time, earnest expectations of a regenerated Greece, to which not only the visionary poet, but the sober politician must now look back with disappointment; and the agreeable associations of a glorious ideal past, with an approximate interesting future, may be said to have passed away." Incidentally Lord Houghton's article in the *Edinburgh Review* which drew public attention to the merits of *Atalanta in Calydon* connects him in later life with the Hellenic current.

We are not concerned here with translations, yet it is well to remember that in 1835 Mrs. Browning published her Aeschylus' *Prometheus Bound.* She also made other translations from the Greek, but does not belong to the succession of Attic imitators, and seems to oppose them in *The Dead Pan* where she cries to the old gods:

Get to dust as common mortals,
By a common doom and track!
Let no Schiller from the portals
Of that Hades call you back. . . .
Earth outgrows the mythic fancies
Sung beside her in her youth:
And those debonaire romances
Sound but dull beside the truth.
Phoebus' chariot-course is run!
Look up, poets, to the sun!

Thomas Noon Talfourd, author among other things of a History of Greek Poetry, produced in 1836 and 1838 his two dramas *Ion* and *The Athenian Captive;* and the growing severity of taste in classic matters may account for what Hugh Walker calls "the cold dignity of Talfourd's style."[28] Talfourd's *Ion* took some suggestions from the play of the same name by Euripides. Though now overlooked it once had wide popularity. An American edition appeared within one year after the original one, and the American editors prefixed a preface declaring that "after the production of *Ion* Sergeant Talfourd, like Lord Byron, awoke one morning and found himself famous." They also take pains to make New York readers realize the tendency of the book: "*Ion* is a splendid attempt to recall into the power of life and sympathy the long buried genius of the antique Tragedy of Fate. The plot moves and hinges upon machinery similar to that of the old Greek dramas." In Talfourd's *Ion,* Agenor speaks of the hero certain lines which seem to represent a "classic" ideal (not very well attained by the author):

So his life hath flow'd
From its mysterious urn a sacred stream,
In whose calm depth the beautiful and pure
Alone are mirror'd; which, though shapes of ill
May hover round its surface, glides in light,
And takes no shadow from them.
(I. 1)

And Ion himself (I. 1) speaks of

words which bear the spirit of great deeds
Wing'd for the future;

which might express Talfourd's unsuccessful aspiration toward the "grand style."

Thoas, the Athenian warrior captured at Corinth, when he hears the Corinthians insult his country, bursts out in praise of it which may represent the dramatist's own attitude.

'Tis not a city crown'd
With olive and enrich'd with peerless fanes
Ye would dishonour, but an opening world
Diviner than the soul of man hath yet
Been gifted to imagine—truths serene,
Made visible in beauty, that shall glow
In everlasting freshness; unapproach'd
By mortal passion; pure amidst the blood
And dust of conquests; never waxing old;
But on the stream of time, from age to age,
Casting bright images of heavenly youth
To make the world less mournful. I behold them!
And ye, frail insects of a day, would quaff
'Ruin to Athens!'
(II, 11)

And Thoas in dying says (V, 1):

Convey me to the city of my love;
Her future years of glory stream more clear
Than ever on my soul. O Athens! Athens!

The Greek poetry of Aubrey de Vere forms only a small part of his verse, but is worth mention. He seems to handle with a certain Roman Catholic reluctance "the beautiful fictions of Greek Mythology." His Masque,

The Search After Proserpine, is a pretty little patchwork of lyric and atmospheric romanticism. His *Recollections of Greece,* which he dedicated to Walter Savage Landor, are fluently mediocre and sometimes rather merry than reverent in tone; and the *Lines Written Under Delphi* arraign the ancient world for its lack of Christian virtues in a way decidedly narrow and sectarian. Yet the spell at times will grip him, as in his lines on Sophocles and Aeschylus; and the eagle calls to him on the field of Marathon: "Yes, yes—'tis Hellas, Hellas still!" His drama *Alexander the Great,* published many years later, belongs only incidentally to our subject. It deals with the post-classic period of Greek history; it has the loose, rambling structure of the most lax Elizabethans; and it is located, not in Hellas, but in the romantic Orient. The best passages of poetry in it are generally in the style of the nineteenth century romantic poets. In connection with the dramas of Talfourd and de Vere, a bare mention is ample honor for Andrew Becket's *Socrates,* "a Drama on the Model of the Ancient Greek Tragedy," which had reached an undeserved third edition by 1838. The classical drama was evidently at this time beginning to appeal to the popular taste.

In 1846 the growing tendency toward Attic dignity freed from excess of romantic atmosphere found its noblest expression in Landor's *Hellenics,*

> The bland Attic skies
> True-mirrored by an English well,[29]

as William Watson has well described them. Some poems of this collection had appeared in cruder form before; but it was now that they first really found an audience. The opening lines (of the enlarged 1847 ed.) strike the keynote of the book:

> Who will away to Athens with me? who
> Loves choral songs and maidens crown'd with flowers,
> Unenvious? mount the pinnace; hoist the sail.
> I promise ye, as many as are here,
> Ye shall not, while ye tarry with me, taste
> From unrinsed barrel the diluted wine
> Of a low vineyard or a plant ill-pruned,
> But such as anciently the Aegean isles
> Pour'd in libation at their solemn feasts:
> And the same goblets shall ye grasp, embost
> With no vile figures of loose, languid boors,
> But such as Gods have lived with and have led.

At times there is a fine reserved pleasure in flowers, sunlight, and the good things of life; more often a stoical power that in its mingling of dramatic force with statuesque language makes us think of the Laocoön. Agamemnon first meets his daughter in Hades; and Iphigenia, knowing nothing of all the adultery and murder that has happened on earth since her death, innocently asks her father for news of their family:

> Tell me then,
> Tell how my mother fares who loved me so,
> And griev'd, as 'twere for you, to see me part.
> Frown not, but pardon me for tarrying
> Amid too idle words, nor asking why
> She prais'd us both (which most?) for what we did.

Landor's *Heroic Idylls* (1863) contains lines apparently written long before, *Remonstrance and Address to Lord Byron,* saying significantly:

> Open thy latticed window wide
> For breezes from the Aegean tide;
> And from Hymettus may its bee
> Bear honey on each wing to thee.

Landor's *Hellenics,* unlike the neo-classical work of Alfieri and Racine abroad, and of Swinburne, deTabley, the two Morrises, etc., in England, ignores the lofty but somewhat threadbare themes of a too well known past, and deals in characters and stories that are new. This procedure has its drawbacks, for Landor is clumsy and obscure in the mechanical details of narrative, introducing characters without explaining their relations to others, and getting repeatedly tangled up in such an elementary matter as the reference of personal pronouns. Nevertheless his choice of subject does give a force and vitality which we often miss in other Hellenists. He was Athenian enough in his nature to know that the ancient Athenians, unlike their poetic imitators, always "desired some new thing."

Unlike most of his fellow Hellenists also,—in spite of his medieval *Count Julian*—he made no compromise with the sham medievalism of the romanticists. "It is hardly to be expected," he writes before his *Hellenics,* "that ladies and gentlemen will leave on a sudden their daily promenade, skirted by Turks and shepherds and knights and plumes and palfreys, of the finest Tunbridge manufacture, to look at these rude frescoes, delineated on an old wall high up, and sadly weak in coloring. As in duty bound, we can wait."

The later Greek poems of his *Heroic Idyls* drop the narrative form, which is always more of an incumbrance than a help to Landor, and become *Imaginary Conversations* in blank verse, often suffused with an autumnal calm of mood which reminds one of the *Œdipus at Colonus.*

Far below Landor's poetry in merit but far above it in immediate popular appeal was R. H. Horne's *Orion.* It is a narrative in blank verse, reminiscent of Keats's *Hyperion* in the gigantic nature of its characters, and of *Endymion* in occasional passages of luscious description and the mawkishness of its love affairs with goddesses, the whole often marred by a soaring grandiloquence akin to that of Bailey's *Festus*. Horne is vastly inferior to Keats as a poet, but much superior as a story-teller, and the directness and excitement of his narrative probably account partly for his ephemeral popularity, six editions of *Orion* appearing in the year of its publication (1843). The poem abounds with the most romantic incidents; and Book II opens with an echo of *Ossian:*

> Beneath a tree, whose heaped-up burthen swayed
> In the high wind, and made a rustling sound,
> As of a distant host that scale a hill,
> Autarces and Encolyon gravely sat.[30]

In 1864 Horne published *Prometheus the Fire Bringer,* a connecting link between Shelley and Mrs. Browning in the past and Robert Bridges and William Vaughn Moody in the future.

Next in importance to Landor's *Hellenics* and soon after them in time came Matthew Arnold's Greek dramas, *Empedocles on Etna* with its noble lyric choruses, and the correct but more colorless *Merope*. In connection with these dramas we must remember Arnold's remarks in his essay on *Pagan and Medieval Religious Sentiment,* which show in what direction he was trying to lead contemporary poetry: "There is a century in Greek life,—the century . . . from about the year 530 B. C. to about the year 430,—in which Poetry made, it seems to me, the noblest, the most successful effort she has ever made as the priestess of the imaginative reason, of the element by which the modern spirit, if it would live right, has chiefly to live. Of this effort . . . the four great names are Simonides, Pindar, Aeschylus, Sophocles. . . . The present has to make its own poetry, and not even Sophocles and his compeers, any more than Dante and Shakespeare, are enough for it. That I will not dispute. But no other poets so well show to the poetry of the present the way it must take; no other poets have lived so much by the imaginative reason; no other poets have made their work so well balanced; no other poets, who have so well satisfied the thinking-power, have so well satisfied the religious sense."

Charles Kingsley, who put the more familiar Greek legends in charming prose for his children, published in the same year as *Merope* his *Andromeda,* a poem about 500 lines long in dactylic hexameters. It is the old story of the saving of Andromeda by Persus. The growing influence of scholarship is seen in ultra Greek proper names, Greek accusative forms even:

> There she met Andromeden and Persea, shaped like Immortals.

The style is luxuriant, somewhat like that of Keats and Morris, yet with classic touches and phrases in the midst of its color:

> Onward they came in their joy, and around them the lamps of the sea-nymphs,
> Myriad fiery globes, swam panting and heaving; and rainbows
> Crimson and azure and emerald, were broken in star-showers, lighting
> *Far through the wine-dark depths of the crystal, the gardens of Nereus.*

Owen Meredith in 1855 published his *Clytemnestra,* a rather dull, long play dwarfed in the shadow of Aeschylus' *Agamemnon* or even of Browning's translation. Clytemnestra's interminable speeches have many reminiscences of Tennyson and *Macbeth* as well as of the Greeks. The same author's *Tales from Herodotus* (in *Chronicles and Characters*) 1868, appeared almost simultaneously with William Morris's first installment of *The Earthly Paradise.* Of the three tales, the last two are much in Morris's style, only more colorless, and the second, *Croesus and Adrastus,* handles a story adapted also by Morris.

Our previous discussion had led us to the year 1860. From that time on the growing popularity of Swinburne and William Morris, aided perhaps by advances in scholarship, produces a multitude of creditable but minor poets in our field such as no previous decade had seen. There was hardly a year from 1860 to 1900 that did not see the publication of some at least respectable verse on Greek themes. Now also Romanticism in English poetry after a temporary lapse had been revived by the Pre-Raphaelites; and once more, as early in the century, romanticism and Hellenism blend in a deep and widening stream. It is not all romantic, however. Side by side with Swinburne and Morris we have Browning at last delving deep into Greek material; and Browning shows how much the current that we are discussing adapted itself to the man, inspiring him but not reducing him to the common norm. Browning's *Balaustion's Adventure,* etc., though ultra Greek in their spelling of proper names, are in essence neither Hellenic nor romantic, but psychological, neither of the fifth century B. C. nor of the French Revolution, but of the mid-nineteenth century. It is significant that the Brownings cared less for Sophocles and Aeschylus than for Euripides, the most cosmopolitan, the least Attic of the three:

> Our Euripides the human
> With his droppings of warm tears,
> And his touches of things common
> Till they rose to higher spheres.

Here they are in sharp contrast with Landor, who preferred

No vile figures of loose, languid boors,
But such as Gods have lived with and have
 led.

F. T. Palgrave, the friend of Matthew Arnold, wrote little verse on Greek material; but he dedicated his *Lyrical Poems* (1871) to the "Immortal Memory of Free Athens"; and in the following lines from the dedicatory poem he shows what faults of romanticism the Hellenic current was trying to eradicate, what virtues of romanticism it was trying to blend with itself:

 Where are the flawless form,
The sweet propriety of measured phrase,
The words that clothe the idea, not disguise,
 Horizons pure from haze,
And calm clear vision of Hellenic eyes?

 Strength ever veiled by grace;
The mind's anatomy implied, not shown;
No gaspings for the vague, no fruitless
 fires;—
 Yet heard 'neath all, the tone
Of those far realms to which the soul aspires. . . .

 That unfantastic strain,
Void of weak fever and self-conscious cry,—
Truth bold and pure in her own nakedness,—
 What modern hand can try,
Tracing the delicate line 'twixt More and
 Less?

Along with the struggle between romanticism and classicism[31] in the Hellenic tradition, there develops in the late nineteenth century a growing tendency to interpret Greek material in a modern or realistic way. That is the final turn which Sir Lewis Morris gives to his *Epic of Hades.*

 The weary woman
Sunk deep in ease and sated with her life,
Much loved and yet unloving, pines today
As Helen.

George Barlow in his *Venus* (1881) declares

The seas of Greece were not more fair
Than this which shines in August air. . . .
'Tis *we* have changed.

Robert Buchanan wrote several poems (1863-66) which handle Greek mythological subjects in a modern, sometimes a playful vein, of which *Pan,* a blank verse poem of some length, is the best and in metre seems to imitate Tennyson's *Œnone.* His *Pan: Epilogue* quotes Mrs. Browning's "Pan, Pan is dead," and retorts:

O Pan, great Pan, thou are not dead,
 Nor dost thou haunt that weedy place . . .
But *here* 'mid living waves of fate
 We feel thee go and come! . . .
On rainy nights thy breath blows chill
 In the street-walker's dripping hair, etc.

But in the Greek tradition from 1860 to 1880 at least the dominant impulse was romantic, and found critical expression ultimately in Pater as the mid century had found voice in Arnold. Between 1875 and 1890 Walter Pater gave as lectures and published his Greek studies. In these he enforces as critical doctrine what Keats, William Morris, and others had already tacitly assumed in composition—the essential kinship of the medieval and Hellenic cultures. "Like the exaggerated diabolical figures in some of the religious plays and imageries of the Middle Age," Pentheus "is an impersonation of stupid impiety."[32] "And then, again, as in those quaintly carved and coloured imageries of the Middle Age . . . comes the full contrast, with a quite medieval simplicity and directness, between the insolence of the tyrant . . . and the outraged beauty of the youthful god."[32] "What was specially peculiar to the temper of the old Florentine painter, Giotto, to the temper of his age in general, doubtless, more than to that of ours, was the persistent and universal mood of the age in which the story of Demeter and Persephone was first created."[33] The Eleusinian Mysteries may have been a parallel to "the medieval ceremonies of Palm Sunday," etc.

In line with Morris he condemns the error which "underestimates the influence of the romantic spirit generally, in Greek poetry and art";[33] tells the academic neoclassicist that "such a conception of Greek art and poetry leaves in the central expressions of Greek culture none but negative qualities";[33] and declares "that the Romantic spirit was really at work in the minds of Greek artists."[33] He stresses the point that Claudian's *Rape of Proserpine,* which "closes the world of classical poetry,"[33] was "pre-eminently a work in colour, and excelling in a kind of painting in words"[33] (like the English Pre-Raphaelites and the French Romanticists).

How far from the conception of Greece and Greek literature expressed in Pope's *Essay on Criticism* we have moved in Pater's *Beginnings of Greek Sculpture.* "And the story of the excavations at Mycenae reads more like some well-devised chapter of fiction than a record of sober facts. Here, those sanguine, half-childish dreams of buried treasure discovered in dead men's graves, which seem to have a charm for every one, are more than fulfilled in the spectacle of those antique kings, lying in the splendour of their crowns and breastplates of embossed plate of gold; their swords, studded with golden imagery, at their sides, as in some feudal monument; their very faces covered up most strangely in golden masks."

In line with Pater, Andrew Lang in Notes to his *Helen of Troy* (1882) says: "In addition to these poetical legends about Helen, many other singular and wild traditions may be found in odd corners of Greek literature. . . . Eustathius, the Bishop of Thessalonica, had [according to Rosscher's recent book] already given the fable showing how Paris, by magic art, beguiled Helen in the form of Menelaus, just as Uther, by Merlin's aid, deceived Ygerne, the mother of Arthur."

Practically all Hellenic poetry after 1860 follows in the wake of Swinburne. He worshipped ancient Hellas as star-gazers worship the moon, fascinated by a luminary of which he saw only one side and could never see the other. He felt the old Greek love of the dark blue sea, the old Greek glory of the flesh, the old Greek love of rich, sonorous verse; but he lived in a world of lawlessness and they in a world of law; he wrote in a mood of lavish profusion, they in a mood of noble economy. He might wish to roll away the Christian centuries, and cry:

> Fire for light and hell for heaven and psalms for paeans
> Filled the clearest eyes and lips most sweet of song,
> When for chant of Greeks the wail of Galileans
> Made the whole world moan with hymns of wrath and wrong,[34]

and near the end:

> For thy kingdom is past not away. . . .
>
> We arise at thy bidding and follow,
> We cry to thee, answer, appear,
> A father of all of us, Paian, Apollo,
> Destroyer and healer, hear![34]

but Swinburne is a glorious hybrid, not such a Greek as Landor or Arnold. Yet their mantle fell on him even if he "wore it with a difference." His *Atalanta in Calydon,* (1865), the greatest Hellenic poem of the late nineteenth century—so well known that we cannot profitably discuss it here—was dedicated to Walter Savage Landor, "the highest of contemporary names." His *Erechtheus* (1876) strikes, but to finer music, the same note of praise for Athens that appears in Talfourd:

> Time nor earth nor changing sons of man . . . shall see
> So great a light alive beneath the sun
> As the aweless eye of Athens; all fame else
> Shall be to her fame as a shadow in sleep
> To this wide noon at waking . . . thine shall be
> The crown of all songs sung, of all deeds done.[35]

This drama, however, in spite of its sonorous rhythm, is somewhat harmed by excess of imitation. Athena appears at the end as with Euripides, and the metre of the dialogue varies much as that in Aeschylus' *Persians.*

Next to Swinburne in popular influence, and perhaps in poetical value, comes William Morris. He knew perfectly well what he was doing. He was drawing from the Greek stream certain elements fitted for his plans and temperament and rejecting all the rest. He seems to feel that many elements of the old Greek life and literature, admirable in themselves, could not be recalled. The old man in *News from Nowhere* says:[36] "All other moods save this [joy of life] had been exhausted: the unceasing criticism, the boundless curiosity in the ways and thoughts of man, which was the mood of the ancient Greek, to whom these things were not so much a means, as an end, was gone past recovery." Morris in the same book[37] describes the dress of his Utopians as "somewhat between that of the ancient classical costume and the simpler forms of the fourteenth century garments, though it was clearly not an imitation of either; the materials were light and gay to suit the season." This is not a bad description of his most famous poem, *The Earthly Paradise,* (1868-70), in which Greek and medieval tales alternate, and "The idle singer of an empty day" makes the stern old legends of Hellas and Scandinavia gently lyrical to suit the season in contemporary taste. The same may be said of his poetical but by no means Homeric *Life and Death of Jason.*

Yet the Hellenic current unquestionably affected Morris for good. With Keats and the German *Romantische Schule* compare the following from *News from Nowhere:*[38] "That we live amidst beauty without any fear of becoming effeminate; that we have plenty to do, and on the whole enjoy doing it. What more can we ask of life?" Then compare the same passage with Hazlitt's[39] dictum: "We have not that union in modern times of the heroic and literary character which was common among the ancients."

Sir Lewis Morris's *Epic of Hades* (1876) represents in bulk only about one-eighth of his poetry, but contains nearly all of his Hellenic verse. In mood he stands half-way between the romantic Grecianism of his greater namesake[40] and the Attic severity of Landor and deTabley. His poem is obviously modeled on Dante. Like the *Divine Comedy* it opens in "the gloom of a dark grove"; like that it is divided into three parts, Tartarus, Hades, Olympus; like Dante the poet at the end of his vision swoons in the presence of the Supreme Being; and, as in Dante, while wandering through this world of classic ghosts,

> From the confessionals I hear arise
> Rehearsals of forgotten tragedies.

As the souls in Limbo were

Only so far afflicted that we live
Desiring without hope;

so Morris's Medusa in Hades

knew no pain,
Except her painful thought.

The mild sweetness of the blank verse is Tennysonian, and many verbal echoes of Tennyson occur.[41] But Sir Lewis Morris, with all his facile sweetness, and in spite of wide popularity, is too imitative a writer to be great. He seems to feel himself that the very riches of his loved classical mythology have become shackles to him; that unlike Landor and deTabley, he has sunk into a neo-classicist.

These fair tales, which we know so beautiful,
Show only finer than our lives today
Because their voice was clearer, and they found
A sacred bard to sing them. We are pent,
Who sing today, by all the garnered wealth
Of ages of past song. We have no more
The world to choose from, who, wheree'er we turn,
Tread through old thoughts and fair. Yet must we sing.

Lord de Tabley is the follower of Landor in the stern, terse spirit of his poetry, in style more polished perhaps, certainly more lucid, and equally dignified, but with fewer single lines of condensed dramatic power. Landor says of Agamemnon:

A groan that shook him shook not his resolve;

and Landor's Iphigenia, cries in answer:

O father, grieve no more; the ships can sail!

De Tabley's Iphigenia says:

The earnest kings of Hellas carven sit,
Between the steep courts of the sanctuary,
And look the greatness of their lives in stone,
Ringed in a terrible semblance of their state,
With brooches on their chariots harnessed near:
Austere dead men, rare-hearted in their age
To push among and use the old iron days.
I am their daughter and I will not fear;
The cruel god consumes me and I go.

Occasionally, but only seldom, deTabley follows Landor in indulgent sympathy with youth and love; as in *The Nymph and the Hunter.* His usual vein is severe. His conception of love is that of Attic tragedy, not that of the romantic lyric:

Who is this stern and radiant queen of fear,
This strong god men adore, this power the nations hear?
This is that Aphrodite fully grown . . .
Pray not, for she is cruel, and thy groan
Is as sweet incense wafted to her throne . . .
'Or, queen of all delusion, come arrayed
In thy fierce beauty; come, thou long delayed,
With thy fair sliding feet and thy faint rippled hair.'[42]

DeTabley's *Philoctetes* (1866) and *Orestes* (1867) are admirable examples of modern imitations of the Greek tragedy, worthy to compare with Swinburne's *Atalanta in Calydon,* by which they have been obviously influenced, especially in the choruses. In fact, as deTabley grew older, the influence of Swinburne obviously overshadowed that of Landor. Orestes is a Greek Hamlet, with a similar terrible family problem, who cries like an echo of the royal Dane:

To act
And to act merely, cleansing from my brain
These weak irresolute fumes of thought, that hold
My hand suspended from the vital sword. . . .
Ah, to have done with thought and see my way,
Then were I man.

Both the dramas and the short poems are cold, imitative, suggestive of many books and limited experience; but they are noble and sonorous, and at times, especially in the lyric choruses, sweep us out of ourselves in a way that makes criticism an offence.

DeTabley, though greatly admired by some, has never been popular, and probably could have done better than he did had he been more encouraged. The last lines of his *Phaethon* suggest the lonely prophet of Hellenic beauty:

I think, that never more
Can one stoop down and drink: and rising up,
Flushed with a tingling inspiration, sing
Beyond himself, and in a huckster age
Catch some faint golden shadow into his page
From that great day of Hellas and Hellas gods;
Which these wise critics of the city of smoke
Sneer at as wrack and lumber of the tombs.

DeTabley, like Wordsworth in *Laodamia,* admires a noble serenity of mind:

For man is restless, but the God at rest:
And that enormous energy of man
Implies his imperfection;[43]

and the lofty atmosphere of his verse must give it a lasting value in spite of its coldness and deficiency in first-hand revelation of life.

Since 1880 the three most significant figures for our purposes—on a joint basis of bulk and merit in their Grecian poems—are perhaps Woolner, Frederick Tennyson, and the present poet laureate. In the main, their work is more scholarly and less romantic than that of their predecessors; and on the whole this is probably true of their contemporary minor figures, though with many reservations.

Thomas Woolner, a great sculptor and minor but genuine poet, published in advanced age three verse narratives of considerable length, *Pygmalion,* 1881; *Silenus,* 1884; *Tiresias,* 1886. These poems are as purely Greek in subject as Landor's *Hellenics,* filled with

> Nymphs, dryads, and wild naiades subdued,[44]

with scattered allusions to

> Stories of a mighty day when Greeks
> Were God-directed, and when men obeyed.[45]

The stiffness of sculpture mars the blank verse, yet Woolner, like Landor, has many touches of vivid description.

Frederick Tennyson in 1890 published *The Isles of Greece,* written twenty years before, and in 1891 *Daphne and Other Poems.* In many of the poems here contained, especially those of the earlier volume, Hellenic names and mythological incidents serve merely as spring-boards by means of which the poet may leap into a fairyland of atmospheric description. The verse has much negative grace, but lacks body and narrative power. The title of the 1890 volume—which deals with the story of Sappho—was probably taken from Byron's:

> The isles of Greece, the isles of Greece,
> Where burning Sappho loved and sung.

Mr. Robert Bridges, the present poet laureate, in the eighties produced three neo-classical Greek plays, well sustained, though somewhat Academic: *Prometheus the Fire-giver; The Return of Ulysses;* and *Achilles in Scyros.* All of these open with a monologue in the manner of Euripides; and the first, at least in the speeches of Prometheus to Io, has many reminiscences of Aeschylus. There are choruses in the Greek manner, but inferior in merit, we believe, to Mr. Bridges' best short poems. The same author also rendered into English the story of Eros and Psyche from the Latin of Apuleius, a theme previously handled in Lewis Morris's *Epic of Hades* and William Morris's *Earthly Paradise.* One line from his version of this poem suggests the opening of one of Mr. Bridges' finest lyrics:

> And like a ship, that crowding all her sail.

In 1905 Mr. Bridges added his *Masque* of *Demeter.*

In 1882 Andrew Lang, the well known translator of the classics, published *Helen of Troy,* a narrative poem, showing the influence of Swinburne and William Morris, but more simple and direct in its narrative than either. It includes the death of Corythos, already Englished in Landor's *Hellenics,* and the death of Paris, already given in *The Earthly Paradise.* The same author's *Hesperothen* turns mythology into allegory. His sonnet on "The surge and thunder of the Odyssey" is probably known to everybody. His attitude toward the author of *Atalanta in Calydon* is indicated by his own words in the Note to *Helen of Troy:* "Helen, as a woman, has hardly found a nobler praise, in three thousand years, than Helen, as a child, has received from Mr. Swinburne."

John A. Symonds, author among many other prose works, of *Studies of the Greek Poets* and *Sketches in Italy and Greece,* later in life wrote a number of chastened and poetical Greek studies in verse, for example, the "Poems on Greek themes" in the 1880 volume, full of music modeled on "the sweet Ionian vowels." The use of Greek material, however, was incidental rather than characteristic of his verse, however deep his love for things Hellenic.

With these men we may include the Rev. E. C. Lefroy, whose *Echoes from Theocritus* (1883) paraphrases the great Sicilian in thirty sonnets graceful and sincerely felt. Lefroy was full of the Hellenic spirit in comment and criticism as well as in verse. He said of his own ideal: "Perhaps it inclines rather to be sexless—serene beauty uncontaminated by a suspicion of fleshliness. But I know that it is Greek."[46] Unfortunately, as he resembled Keats in instinctive love for the ancient masters, so he resembled the greater poet in an untimely death.

Callirrhoe (1884) by "Michael Field" is a drama which reflects as models both Euripides and the Elizabethans; and which, if not consistently great, has many fine touches of both poetry and pathos. "The story of Callirrhoe," says the Preface, "is drawn from a classic source, but has never been raised from obscurity by ancient bard or dramatist. This fact has permitted a latitude of treatment, unstraitened by the fear of presumption." In the verse volume *Long Ago* by the same authoress (or authoresses) each lyric is suggested by a fragment of Sappho.

Ernest Myers in 1875 traveled in Greece and later translated Pindar and, in collaboration, the *Iliad.* Andrew Lang's translation of Theocritus was dedicated to him. His *Judgment of Prometheus* (1886) shows a dignified discipleship of Aeschylus and the epic poets. His *Rhodes* in passing laments the hour

When Hellas bowed, her birthright gone,
Beneath the might of Macedon;

and several short poems on Greek themes had appeared previously in *Poems* (1877).

At this point we may glance hastily over the work of certain minors and also over some more prominent figures who become minors for us from their very incidental connection with our subject. A few poems on Greek themes, sometimes of unquestionable merit, but all short, occur in the writings of Edwin Arnold, Austin Dobson, Edmund Gosse, and Charles Tennyson Turner. They remind us that almost every English poet of the late nineteenth century at some time made oblation to the Hellenic muse. Lord Tennyson, who from 1842 to 1885 published practically nothing concerning us here, printed late in the century his *Tiresias, Demeter and Persephone,* and *Death of Œnone,* the last covering ground already covered by William Morris.

Sir Edward Bulwer Lytton in the Preface to his *Lost Tales of Miletus* (1866) says of them: "I have selected from Hellenic myths those in which the ground is not preoccupied, by the great poets of antiquity in works yet extant; and which, therefore, may not be without the attraction of novelty to the general reader." The attraction of novelty is there; but the spell of poetry is not, his *Cydippe; or, The Apple* comparing but ill with William Morris's *Accontius and Cydippe.* Yet, weak as its unrhyming stanzas are, it seems a forerunner of *The Earthly Paradise.*

In the life of that arch-romanticist, William Sharp, written by his wife, we learn that Swinburne's *Atalanta in Calydon* inspired him to compose a lyrical immature drama *Ariadne in Naxos.*[47] He also speaks later of being engaged on two other classic dramas, *The Kôre of Enna*[48] and *Persephonaeia,*[49] *or The Drama of the House of Ætna.* Sharp's letters written from Greece are full of Hellenic enthusiasm.

Thomas Ashe between 1861 and 1866 published considerable Hellenic poetry, the best of it being in his drama *The Sorrows of Hypsiphyle* (1866) which, says Havelock Ellis, has "a true breath of Greek feeling."[50]

Charles Mackay's *Studies from the Antique* (1864) consist mainly of short narratives and monologues much in the style of Landor's *Hellenics,* more lucid and easy to read, but decidedly less powerful, though by no means devoid of merit. Richard Garnett published "Idylls and Epigrams, chiefly from the Greek Anthology" (1869), and *Iphigenia in Delphi* (1890). Of the former all but thirty are translations; the last is a dramatic scene, rounding out the Orestes story of Euripides' great drama. G. F. Armstrong's *Garland from Greece* (1882) deals mainly with the modern country, but sometimes with the ancient, in verse occasionally picturesque though imitative and never powerful. Two of the longer narrative poems, *Selemnos* and *The Death of Epicurus* echo William Morris and Landor respectively. Several Greek poems occur also in the work of Canon R. W. Dixon (1884-86). Ross Neil (pseud. of Isabella Harwood) in 1883 published two neo-classical plays, *Orestes* and *Pandora,* of considerable merit.

The above list naturally grows more and more tentative as it nears the present. We have doubtless omitted some who well deserve a place there, and perhaps included some with doubtful claims to a place anywhere. The latter part of our study is avowedly superficial, without any adequate knowledge in many cases of the poet's background. Nevertheless our essay as a whole may give a synthetic survey of a field not yet carefully studied. The number of poets who have habitually or incidentally versified Greek themes has steadily increased through the nineteenth century. The tradition has shown a tendency to change in style and mood with the different critical *Zeitgeists* through which it has passed, as well as with the personality of each individual author. The medieval tradition, in common apparently with others also, has done the same. Yet through all its changes the Hellenic current has had a certain modifying power, suppressing alike the horrors of Gothic romance and the equal horrors of realism in favor of beauty and serenity. From Keats to Swinburne it produced some of our greatest poetry. During the last quarter of the nineteenth century and the beginning of the twentieth its representatives have almost wholly been dignified and sincere but not entirely successful minors. Is this because poetry in general has been at ebb, or is it because that particular kind of material is wearing a little threadbare? The late Professor Moody wrote one noble poem on the subject of Prometheus; but he turned from it immediately to other fields, which he may have thought more promising. The more we can have of Greek spirit and taste, the better; but will that spirit realize itself best through the revamping of Greek legends or through the handling of more modern incidents and problems? This is not a question to be answered hastily by any one; but it is a question which our young poets and critics ought to consider.

Notes

[25] Houghton's note prefixed to *The Concentration of Athens.*

[26] *The Flowers of Helicon.*

[27] *Corfu* (written 1832).

[28] *Age of Tennyson,* p. 47.

[29] *On Landor's "Hellenics."*

[30] "Cuthullin sat by Tura's wall, by the tree of the rustling sound."

Opening of *Fingal.*

[31] That is, classicism as found in Landor, Arnold, etc.

[32] *The Bacchanals of Euripides.*

[33] *Demeter and Persephone.*

[34] *The Last Oracle.*

[35] Speech of Athena.

[36] Chap. XVIII.

[37] Chap. III.

[38] Chap. X.

[39] Waller and Glover's ed., VI, 110.

[40] A good opportunity to compare the styles of the two Morrises is given in the story of Cupid and Psyche, told by both.

[41] Compare for example the following with Tennyson's *Œnone:*

It was the time when a deep silence comes
Upon the summer earth, and all the birds
Have ceased from singing, and the world is still
As midnight, and if any live thing move—
Some fur-clad creature, or cool gliding snake—
Within the pipy overgrowth of weeds,
The ear can catch the rustle, and the trees
And earth and air are listening.

Marsyas.

Also:

A soft air breathes
Across the stream, and fills these barren fields
With the sweet odours of the earth.

Morris's *Persephone.*

A soft air fans the cloud apart; there comes
A glimpse of that dark world where I was born.

Tennyson's *Tithonus.*

While round our feet
The crocus flames like gold.

Morris's *Persephone.*

And at their feet the crocus brake like fire.

Tennyson's *Œnone.*

[41] Compare also the speeches of Athena and Hera in Morris and in Tennyson's *Œnone.*

[42] *Orestes.*

[43] *The Siren to Ulysses.*

[44] *Silenus,* p. 52.

[45] *Tiresias,* p. 24.

[46] Life and Poems, ed., by Gill, p. 49.

[47] P. 22.

[48] P. 343.

[49] P. 415. It these plays have ever been published, I am not aware of it.

[50] Poets and Poetry of the Century, Vol. 4.

Douglas Bush (essay date 1937)

SOURCE: "Early Victorian Minor Poets," in *Mythology and the Romantic Tradition in English Poetry,* Harvard University Press, 1937. Reprint by Harvard University Press, 1969, pp. 265-96.

[*In this essay, first published in 1937, Bush reviews a cast of minor early Victorian poets under the assertion that most struggled with two central conflicts: one "between Christianity and paganism" and the other between "the claims of the antique and the claims of modern realism."*]

In the years just before and after Victoria's accession English poetry was in the doldrums. Wordsworth and Southey were alive, in a sense, but of the older generation of romantics Landor alone was flourishing. Tennyson was wrapped in gloomy silence and tobacco smoke; the bud of Browning's fame was nipped by *Sordello.* Elizabeth Barrett's position, though higher than that of her future husband, was not yet consolidated by the two volumes of 1844. The great poet of the day was Sir Henry Taylor, who, said Miss Barrett, was in her opinion "scarcely a poet at all"; and every drawing-room was fragrant with the volumes of Mrs. Hemans and L. E. L. But if greatness be measured by editions, the really dominant figure was Robert Montgomery, author of *Satan* and *The Omnipresence of the Deity,* who made a Roman holiday for Macaulay. And then came Martin Tupper.

For this was a serious age, an age of middle-class literature and the middle-class conscience. If the pagan serenity of the Olympian gods was not shaken by numerous hymn-writers' yearnings for a heavenly home, or by the bray of Exeter Hall, it was disturbed by more cultivated sounds. The young men of the new generation were feeling the influence of Wordsworth, Keats, and Shelley, for the stars of Byron and Moore had waned, but now there was another kind of leaven at work. The mystical monologues of the oracle of Highgate were dying away, though their effect was still potent, when there rose like a steam of rich distilled perfumes the voice of Newman. Keats and Shelley, standing outside orthodox religion, had not been aware of a conflict between Christianity and paganism, but for a number of early Victorian writers, Mrs. Browning, Aubrey de Vere and others, the old conflict was revived, even before the advent of Rossetti and Swinburne made neo-paganism the only wear. These writers, or some of them, are united also by their sense of a conflict between the claims of the antique and the claims of modern realism. From representatives of that double strain we shall pass on to a more miscellaneous group, which includes the sturdy pagan evolutionist, Richard Henry Horne, Macaulay, whose soul is a mystery, Charles Kingsley, the muscular Christian, and "Owen Meredith," who was perhaps a better diplomat than poet.

I. ELIZABETH BARRETT BROWNING (1806-61)

Although Mrs. Browning's poetic treatment of myth has not much intrinsic importance, she is in several ways a symptomatic figure in the mythological and Hellenic tradition. All through her girlhood and later life, until marriage enlarged her activities, Greek literature, along with endless novels and modern poetry, fed the passions of a starved nature. But her Hellenic devotion was not entirely Attic.[1] She read every line of the three tragic poets, and all of Plato, and she enjoyed Greek literature for its own sake, but she enjoyed it far more when she could think of it as a vestibule to Christianity.[2] Hence for the most part Mrs. Browning's Hellenism and her faith dwelt happily together, and in a series of prefaces (which also show her evolution from eighteenth-century classicism to romantic Hellenism) the young author found evidence that the pagan Greeks, from Homer onward, had sought the divine, though darkly.[3] *Prometheus Bound* is "one of the very noblest of human imaginations," but if Aeschylus had come later he would surely have turned from Caucasus to Calvary, from the theme of hate and revenge to love and forgiveness.[4] It was in some such spirit that, during 1841, Mrs. Browning—who of course was Miss Barrett until 1846—in collaboration with Horne planned a lyrical drama on the birth and growth of the soul, *Psyche Apocalypté,* which was to end with a vision of the Cross; the extant drafts cause no regret that it was abandoned.[5] Still another attempt to blend Hellenism and Christianity was *A Drama of Exile* (1844), which shows what a Christian Aeschylus might have done with Adam and Eve; in spite of "Euripides the human," Mrs. Browning regarded Aeschylus as "the divinest of all the divine Greek souls,"[6] and, in her own wild way, she had something Aeschylean about her.

So far Christianity is in harmony with Hellenism, a half-Christianized Hellenism. But Mrs. Browning's religion, a mixture of the evangelical, the "Platonic," and the poetic, was a central fact of her nature, and the love of Greek, for all its intensity, was in comparison an external accident; if challenged, the one romantic passion was strong enough to annihilate the other. In a poem which, whatever be thought of its general quality and its rhymes, is Mrs. Browning's most serious treatment of myth, the Greek gods are brought face to face with Christian truth and put to rout. The conflict between Christ and Pan had been revived for the early nineteenth century by Schiller's *Gods of Greece,* and Mrs. Browning, having read Mr. Kenyon's paraphrase, was roused to a passionate answer, *The Dead Pan* (1844). Milton, who was Hebraic enough even in youth, had celebrated the overthrow of the pagan deities at the birth of Christ, but he had been carried out of his Christian purpose by their sonorous names and glamorous associations. Mrs. Browning has no Renaissance paganism behind her, but, along with her own fervent instincts, all the strength of early Victorian pietism. "Pan is dead," she proclaims with ruthless exultation, the vain false gods of Hellas are silent evermore. In the concluding stanzas, to which, she said, all the rest were only a prelude, she exhorts poets to remember that "God Himself is the best Poet" and "the Real is His song"; "Truest Truth" is "the fairest Beauty."[7] In letters of equal sincerity the author maintained her case against Mr. Kenyon's criticism; we do not live among dreams, and if the Christian religion is true, "the *poetry of Christianity* will one day be developed greatly and nobly."[8]

These bits of verse and prose suggest a third element in Mrs. Browning's poetic constitution which is antagonistic to myth, what may be called the modern and realistic. The poet's business is not "to rhyme the stars and walk apart" but to grapple with life. Books had always, for her, been "a substitute for living," and "nothing is more striking when at last she broke the prison bars than the fervour with which she flung herself into the life of the moment."[9] In the long meditated, intensely felt, and turbidly written *Aurora Leigh* (1857), which shocked the mammas of England, one comes upon mythological allusions which are strangely incongruous in such a setting. One may, like Oscar Wilde, see in them "the fine literary influence of a classical training,"[10] or one may think merely that such things could not help running off a bluestocking's pen. At times even these partake of Mrs. Browning's excited realism. Compare Tennyson's "Now lies the Earth all Danaë to the stars" with these lines, in the vein of Mrs. Browning's husband, on a picture of

A tiptoe Danae, overbold and hot,
Both arms a-flame to meet her wishing Jove
Half-way, and burn him faster down; the face
And breasts upturned and straining, the loose
  locks
All glowing with the anticipated gold.[11]

A little overbold and hot for pre-Swinburnian verse, and a poetess too! But more instinctive and characteristic is a denunciation of mythology and an appeal to poets to express the meanings, human and divine, of the world about them:

Never flinch,
But still, unscrupulously epic, catch
Upon the burning lava of a song
The full-veined, heaving, double-breasted
  Age.[12]

These lines remind us that Mrs. Browning's modes of thought and feeling were no more disciplined by Greek than her Christian thought and feeling were disturbed by her early reading of eighteenth-century rationalists.[13] And the whole passage, along with other evidence, explains why she never wrote a mythological narrative or idyll as almost every poet and poetaster of her time did.[14] When, long before *Aurora Leigh,* her future husband tempted her for the moment with the subject of Prometheus, she put it away from her, partly because she did not dare to follow Aeschylus, but mainly because she was on principle opposed to the antique:

> I am inclined to think that we want new *forms,* as well as thoughts. The old gods are dethroned. Why should we go back to the antique moulds, classical moulds, as they are so improperly called? If it is a necessity of Art to do so, why then those critics are right who hold that Art is exhausted, and the world too worn out for poetry. I do not, for my part, believe this: and I believe the so-called necessity of Art to be the mere feebleness of the artist. Let us all aspire rather to *Life,* and let the dead bury their dead. . . . And then Christianity is a worthy *myth,* and poetically acceptable.[15]

The enthusiastic preoccupation with Greek which effervesces in Mrs. Browning's early works and letters almost disappears after marriage has given her a new life in the great world of men and women, Italian and French politics, and the still darker mysteries of séances. Her critical remarks on Greek authors, pagan or Christian, are mostly trite in comparison with her independent and sometimes keen estimates of her contemporaries. Pagan literature had been an imaginative and romantic escape from solitude, and the lady of Shalott—or, as a Grecian might have said, the dweller in Plato's cave—was sick of shadows. Apart from *The Dead Pan,* her poems on classical subjects are happy familiar verses on the joys of reading, and even such a pleasant reminiscence as *Hector in the Garden* ends with an injunction to shun dreams and be up and doing. Once, in a springtime near the end of her life, Mrs. Browning surrendered to myth, and sang with rarely melodious felicity of Pan by the river. Her reward from posterity has been that *A Musical Instrument* (1860) is one of her best-known poems.[16] But its serious theme is that of the earlier *Vision of Poets,* "the necessary relations of genius to suffering and self-sacrifice." While at first sight Pan might seem here to have conquered Christ, it is because, for Mrs. Browning, Christ includes Pan. "All truth and all beauty and all music belong to God—He is in all things; and in speaking of all, we speak of Him."[17]

II. AUBREY DE VERE, CLOUGH, CORY, AND OTHERS

The essential problem of Christian and pagan, of modern and antique themes, is indicated in the sketch of Mrs. Browning, but it touched too many writers of the age to be dismissed without a few pages on some more or less notable names.[18] Aubrey de Vere (1814-1902) paid his chief poetical tributes to Greece in his middle twenties, and he lives not by them but by his poetry of Ireland and of religious faith; in 1851 he followed Newman to Rome. His lyrical masque, *The Search after Proserpine* (1843), appears in itself to be little more than a piece of decorative mythology, and one's opinion is not much altered by the prefatory account of the elaborate philosophic symbolism intended.[19] As a presentation of "a problem of our Humanity" the masque is only pretty tinsel compared with De Vere's poem on the Irish famine, *The Year of Sorrow*—he was himself active in relief work—and as a treatment of death and immortality it is frivolous beside the pages of his diary on the death of his father.[20] The *Proserpine* volume included *Recollections of Greece.* As a poet De Vere was too much in love with the passionless bride, divine tranquillity, but he achieved energy and salience in some sonnets, such as *Aeschylus* and the monumental *Sun God* (called *Sunrise* in 1843). The main interest, however, of these poems on Greek themes is in the conflict they reveal. De Vere felt keenly the power of Greek beauty and wisdom, while as a serious Christian he recoiled from paganism and turned more and more to the Catholic Middle Ages, not as a refuge, but because "there was a positive religious insight in the Middle Ages, which the modern world was losing."[21] In the elaborate *Lines Written Under Delphi,* he finds the Greek gods far better than the gods of modern life, "Traditions, Systems, Passion, Interest, Power," yet nothing but the worship of the God of Truth with his whole being can redeem man from devotion to the idols of passion and sense.[22] In a number of critical essays of later years, when time and increasing security of faith had mellowed his anti-pagan convictions, De Vere returned to the subject of Hellenism, and no Victorian critic treated the mythological aspects of Spenser, Landor, Wordsworth, Keats, and Shelley with his combination of insight, breadth, and scholarship.

This long but inadequate paragraph may be rounded off with a few remarks from the essay "Landor's Poetry" (1850).[23] "True poetry has ever a substratum of Religion in it," and Greek poetry owed its high character to the elements of truth in Greek religion, philosophy, and myth. But the modern world and its poetry are secular, not Christian. When Wordsworth would rather be an old pagan than a modern Englishman, he is only affirming "that Triton is better than Plutus." Considering the want of spirituality in a large proportion of modern verse, De Vere asks—and the question sums up the great contribution of the romantics to mythological poetry—where in that body of writing is to be found so close a relation, "even through type or symbol, with religious ideas," as in the portion of it based on ancient myth?

Arthur Hugh Clough (1819-61) may be mentioned here as a symptom rather than as a mythological poet. His ironic temperament, the oppressive weight of religious difficulties, and a native instinct for the modern, realistic, and satirical in poetry, these all combined to turn him aside from the conventional post-romantic path. In print he rebuked not only Alexander Smith but his friend Arnold for being led away from the realities of human life by Keatsian luxuries or by classical models.[24] But Arnold himself was a perplexed modernist who at times found a refuge in the antique world or in dreams of the warm south, and Clough too, though rarely, felt a similar impulse. He shows his capacity for enchantment in the proem to the first canto of *Amours de Voyage:*

> Come, let us go,—to a land wherein gods of the old time wandered,
> Where every breath even now changes to ether divine.[25]

In Rome, thinking (like Gibbon before him, though with less untroubled detachment) of the Catholic ritual being performed under the "Dome of Agrippa," he repeoples the niches, not with the martyrs and saints and the rest, "But with the mightier forms of an older, austerer worship," and he goes on to render the Horatian lines about Apollo of Delos and Patara.[26] The most poignantly ironical allusion, however, occurs in the fine opening of *The Shadow:*

> I dreamed a dream: I dreamt that I espied,
> Upon a stone that was not rolled aside,
> A Shadow sit upon a grave—a Shade,
> As thin, as unsubstantial, as of old
> Came, the Greek poet told,
> To lick the life-blood in the trench Ulysses made—
> As pale, as thin, and said:
> "I am the Resurrection of the Dead. . . ."

Although his few and brief mythological verses are not of much account, William Johnson Cory (1823-92) is another symbol of mingled Hellenic and modern sympathies. He lacked Clough's religious intensity, and Clough did not have Cory's patriotic fervor, which was of the kind nourished by the playing fields of Eton. But the melancholy of both was partly due to a sense of failure, to an academic consciousness of being outside the large world of actualities. Cory, the man of simpler nature, is the schoolmaster on the sidelines of life, cheering the games he cannot play, coveting the sword he cannot wield. His reading, ancient and modern, is, like Elizabeth Barrett's, a substitute for living. He is at one with Clough when he declines to pray for dryads and prefers "the presence of hungering, thirsting men."[27] In one of his two famous pieces, *Mimnermus in Church,* he craves human life and imperfect earth, not heaven and abstract perfection; Mimnermus is a mild, shy pagan, and a post-romantic one, an *enfant du siècle,*[28] as Cory called himself. His classical studies did not much alter tastes determined by his own age and by personal idiosyncrasy. "Tennyson is the sum and product of the art that began with Homer."[29] And the elegiac grace and tenderness of Cory's *Heraclitus* are partly Tennysonian. The lyric is a particular expression of the central motive of *Mimnermus,* and it is a very Victorian bit of Hellenism. One may say, with Basil Gildersleeve, "A pretty poem, Mr. Cory, but you must not call it Callimachus";[30] yet the poet probably knew what he was doing, if one may judge from his later comment on a rendering from Euripides by W. H. Mallock: "It gave me a new type of *romantic* translation, in which the modern versifier walks alongside of the classic poet, and has a colour of his own, and does not think it his duty to be concise."[31]

That a sensitive and exalted poetic nature could really be torn between Christian and Hellenic impulses one has pathetic proof in the case of Digby Mackworth Dolben (1848-67). Rugby was not the only school which nourished morbidly religious boys. Dolben's life, William Cory said, "was one gem," and Gerard Manley Hopkins knew enough of him to lament the extinction of his beautiful promise. Bridges described, though he did not print, the first section of a poem of 1864, *Vocation B.C.,* in which Dolben tried to harmonize his two loves and two worlds by showing "how a pagan might have a mystical love of God, analogous to a Christian's emotion."[32] The reconciliation of Apollo and Christ was not final. In a third part of the poem, printed as *From the Cloister,* Brother Jerome hungers for the beauties of Greece and Greek myths—when we remember Dolben's idealization of his friend Manning we understand why the tale of Hyacinth is "dearest of them all"[33]—for "sunny Athens, home of life and love,"

> Free joyous life that I may never live,
> Warm glowing love that I may never know. . . .

Weary of this squalid holiness, these hot black draperies, the incense-thickened air and the inevitable bells, he wishes that Apollo, dear bright-haired god in whom he half believes, might catch him heavenward. But this mood is overcome by thoughts of the Passion, and Brother Francis is heard singing of Jesus and eternal love. During the short time that remained to him Dolben praised Homer and Aeschylus, translated from Sappho and Catullus and Ovid, and was able to rejoice that "The world is young today." But some of his latest poems reveal the strain of living between earth and heaven, of wavering (to quote *Ash Wednesday*) between the profit and the loss. From desolating weariness, "Tired sorrow, tired bliss," he turns for quiet to a Madonna-like Persephone, "with supreme compassion pale," and envies the gods in their palaces far above the shaken trees.[34]

Before his conversion Gerard Hopkins (1844-89) gave evidence of a power which might have braced the flaccid sinews of Victorian mythological verse. The prize poem of his schooldays, *A Vision of the Mermaids* (1862), critics have mostly been content to label Keatsian, a useful but vague epithet which fits better the mythological allusions in a still earlier prize poem, *The Escorial* (1860).[35] The *Vision* is markedly and prophetically individual. Instead of the common romantic idealism and soft, idyllic prettiness of description, the young poet, with the eye of a painter, creates a sharp-edged pattern of hard, bright color and sinuous movement. Words may be strained but they are alive. If the lines

> Plum-purple was the west; but spikes of light
> Spear'd open lustrous gashes, crimson-white,

suggest an Imagist striving after novelty, they carry us on to "Kiss my hand to the dappled-with-damson west" and "Glory be to God for dappled things." It was doubtless better for English poetry that Hopkins' later visions should have been of God rather than mermaids, yet one may regret his stern asceticism.[36] Though he could praise the mythological poems of his friends Bridges and Dixon, he was opposed, on both religious and artistic grounds, to the introduction of pagan deities into modern poetry. He admitted, however, that allegorical treatment of myth might yield the most beautiful results; "the moral evil is got rid of and the pure art, morally neutral and artistically so rich, remains and can be even turned to moral uses."[37]

Thus some of these poets are linked together by their preference for the modern over the antique, and all are on the side of Christ rather than Apollo or Pan. This sketch of the problem may end, for the present, with a reference to the youthful poems of another religious devotee. At fourteen Christina Rossetti wrote an *Ariadne to Theseus*,[38] and three years later, in 1847, an inevitably Tennysonian piece, *The Lotus-Eaters.*[39] But Christina was no Hellenist (though a much finer artist than most English Hellenists, from Mrs. Browning to Swinburne), and her girlish enthusiasm for mythology was soon extinguished by her passionate and austere religious faith.[40]

III. HORNE, MACAULAY, KINGSLEY, ROBERT LYTTON

Richard Henry Horne (1803-84)

When a boy Richard Henry (later Hengist) Horne threw a snowball at John Keats as he sat in the surgeon's gig, and he survived, a quaint relic, to awaken the amused pity of Sir Edmund Gosse. His adventurous life was that of a Victorian Trelawny, though more poetical than piratical, and he carried into a pietistic age not only the humanitarian idealism of the second romantic generation but, from *Hecatompylos* (1828) to *The Last Words of Cleanthes* (1883), a half-pagan faith of his own. *Orion* (1843) was the most considerable mythological narrative since *Hyperion,* and, whatever publicity was due to its original price, it owed its many editions to more substantial causes.

One can hardly escape giving a brief outline of the poem, an outline in which allegorical continuity must compel the slighting of action and description.[41] Orion is one of a company of giants who are mostly crude, destructive, elemental beings; one, Encolyon, is a type of the obstinate reactionary, while Akinetos, the Great Unmoved, is almost sublime in his utter passivity and cynical indifference to the world outside himself. Orion has not been in spirit one of these. He is by nature a "builder-up of things, and of himself," and love of Artemis fires him with new energies, new dreams of human possibilities. But though Artemis becomes the guide of his humanitarian toil and of his spiritual progress "From tyrant senses to pure intellect," Orion is still too earth-bound and self-centered for complete happiness or attainment of his high, hard ideal. His chief lapse into the tyranny of sense is the passion he conceives for King Oenopion's daughter Merope, a beautiful creature of earth, and gratification brings vague discontent and sorrow; it brings too the loss of Merope and of his sight, for the king's soldiers remove her and put out his eyes.

Though physical passion has crippled Orion's purposeful life, it leads eventually, through blindness and distress, to wisdom and a renewal of beneficent activity. The counsels of Akinetos tempt him only for the moment to subside into apathy. Nature and Labor, represented by a shepherd and Brontes the Cyclops, direct him to Eos, goddess of the dawn. She restores his sight, and his soul, his belief in good, is reborn; " 'Tis always morning somewhere in the world." Now, with re-awakened love, Orion begins to understand the mutual support and balance of body and soul. He is still grateful to Artemis, and to Merope, but this new love unifies and inspires his head, heart, and hand; it fills him with life and happiness, yet turns his sympathies to the ills of the world. In the midst of all his "fresh designs for human weal" he is struck down by the jealous Artemis, but she, repenting, goes with Eos to entreat Zeus to restore his life. Orion's task is finished, however, and he is set in heaven as a constellation, a symbol to men of "victory over life's distress." The work of the builder lives on, a fruitful inspiration to the world, while Akinetos is turned into stone.

In the author's own words, Orion "is meant to present a type of the struggle of man with himself, *i.e.* the contest between the intellect and the senses, when powerful energies are equally balanced. *Orion* is man standing naked before Heaven and Destiny, resolved to work as a really free agent to the utmost pitch of his powers for the good of his race." That is clear enough, but no reader of the poem, or even of a bald summary, can help exclaiming, "This is a combination of *Endymion* and *Hyperion!*"[42] Orion's progress from simple realities through dreams to higher realities, from selfish love to humanitarian sympathy and action, is a large part of what all modern critics see in *Endymion.* Further, Orion is spiritualized partly through his own activity, partly through the ardors and sorrows he experiences in his love for three female beings; the three symbols are differently handled, but in the end each hero cleaves to the one who, representing human reality, represents the ideal also. The influence of *Hyperion* on the parable is less obvious, but there is a general similarity (a safer word!) in the conception of social progress and individual self-discipline; whether or not Horne understood the significance of Keats's Apollo, he had the same idea of a poet's rise to his full godlike power through the knowledge that is sorrow, the sorrow that is wisdom. The relation of art to life was not of course a problem of the romantic poets only; just before *Orion* had appeared *Sordello* and the revised *Palace of Art.* Keats's humanitarianism had been a poetic ideal, Horne's was a practical fact, though his social labors are best remembered because his report on conditions in mines and factories inspired Mrs. Browning's *Cry of the Children.*[43] Finally, *Orion* embodies something of Carlyle's gospel of work and leadership, and it anticipates Meredith's evolutionary and humanitarian ideals.[44] It anticipates also Meredith's mythological and philosophic "reading of life." Horne insisted that *Orion* was not merely a "spiritual epic," as Mrs. Browning called it, but a corporeal epic too; whereas Christian asceticism, in spite of modern physiology and psychology, had never allowed the legitimate claims of the body, he had given senses as well as intellect full scope, and set up as an ideal the harmony of the two. This is pure Meredith.

If we ask why a poem of such serious purpose does not, philosophically, come home to us, the answer applies to more and greater works than *Orion.* While Horne's faith is sincere and humane, we do not feel compelled to share a hardly won illumination kindled by intense inward conflict. The poem is not an imaginative rendering of the quality of experience, it is a theoretical pattern imposed upon experience. We are not moved as we are by such various confessional poems as *Endymion* and *Hyperion,* or *The New Sirens* and *Empedocles on Etna.* A further reason for our indifference to the author's intention is the mere amplitude of narrative and ornament, which, as in most such poems, can be enjoyed without reference to the transparent symbolism. The style of *Orion* is largely in the tradition of *Endymion,* though particular echoes of *Hyperion* are more obvious. If Horne has no lines like "Or blind Orion hungry for the morn," he avoids Keats's youthful lapses in taste, and his story is rapid and coherent. Poe, the most erratic of critics, while disliking the moral, lost his head altogether over the poetical beauties of *Orion.*[45] There is an abundance of lucid and richly colored pictures, and they have a minute realism not often found in the vaguely standardized "Greek" scenes of Victorian verse. The Nymphs have "clear elastic limbs of nut-brown hue"; Sylvans and Fauns dip their heads into a stream "Deep as the top hair of their pointed ears"; at the giants' orgy the wine

> Bubbled and leapt, and streamed in
> crimsoning foam,
> Hot as the hissing sap of the green logs.

And there are touches of another kind of realism rarer still in a philosophic and mythological "epic," namely, comedy, in connection with "the bald sage" and especially Akinetos, who is an original gem, or rather monument, of satirical and humorous imagination.

As Gosse says, Horne "was a remarkable poet for seven or eight years, and a tiresome and uninspired scribbler for the rest of his life."[46] Yet one cannot help admiring the indomitable old man who, in the remote Australian bush, could sit down after his day's work to write *Prometheus the Fire-Bringer,* and, when the manuscript was lost, could write it over again.[47] Admiration, however, stops at that point, and alarm begins when we scan the *dramatis personae* and observe a "sub-chorus of troglodytes." *Prometheus* is in fact a feeble repetition of *Orion;* Horne's faith is still in him, but what fire he had has gone out. He left behind him a work he considered his masterpiece, *Ancient Idols; or, The Fall of the Gods;* it has never reached print. But *The Last Words of Cleanthes* was a not ignoble valedictory; looking back over an austere life of fearless thought, Cleanthes returns, a tranquil Empedocles, to the elements.

Thomas Babington Macaulay (1800-59)

Scott's influence on the translating and writing of heroic ballads showed itself most obviously in the proportion of Scotsmen who took a hand in it. But the only bard who needs to be mentioned here was the very Irish

William Maginn (Thackeray's Captain Shandon), whose *Homeric Ballads* appeared in *Fraser's Magazine* in 1838.[48] Though Maginn himself was no disintegrator, his translations are a reminder that the theory of the ballad origin of the Homeric poems had become generally familiar. The year 1842 brought books from such established favorites as Sir Henry Taylor and Robert Montgomery, not to mention Tennyson's two volumes and Browning's *Dramatic Lyrics,* but Macaulay led the field. No one can count the editions of the *Lays,*[49] or—still stronger proof of vitality and popularity—the parodies they have drawn from old and young. In every generation the *Lays* have caused for one kind of reader a heightened pulse, for another a heightened eyebrow. We need not take account of Arnold's sneer (which allowed relative merit to Maginn's often slipshod work), for Arnold has been demolished by a number of critics who, not being poets, are more disposed to maintain that the house of poetry has many mansions. It should be possible to acknowledge that Macaulay did what he set out to do better than anyone else, though doubtless anyone could do it "if he had the mind." And Macaulay has had some tributes from poets. The *Lays* roused Elizabeth Barrett from her sofa; Landor more than once praised their Roman spirit; and, though Macaulay has often been blamed for corrupting the childish ear for poetry, he did not irreparably damage Swinburne or Francis Thompson or Mr. Yeats.[50]

Macaulay had begun writing ballads as a disciple of Scott, and in his early *Battle of Bosworth Field* we see not only his style in process of development but particular parallels, notably in the battle itself, with *The Battle of the Lake Regillus.*[51] But he wisely abandoned a period that Scott had made his own for the remoter antiquity in which he had spent a good part of his life. He showed instinctive tact in writing as an ancient Roman bard, reciting the great deeds of a simple heroic world, holding up to a later age the old ideals of *pietas* and patriotic valor. Macaulay's robust mind has perhaps been most tersely described, in the words of Aubrey de Vere, as having "no trace of originality, depth, breadth, elevation, subtlety, comprehensiveness, spirituality,"[52] but, without stopping to qualify the judgment, one may say that he chose themes and settings which brought out all his strength and turned his limitations into virtues of dramatic verisimilitude. Livy was his main source, and a congenial one—for Macaulay, who dreamed of being the English Thucydides, was rather the English Livy—but a man with all classical literature in his prodigious memory could not fail to draw upon a multitude of authors. And sometimes he echoed moderns as well as ancients. Such lines as

> Unwatched along Clitumnus
> Grazes the milk-white steer,

take us to Virgil, and also to Byron:

> But thou, Clitumnus . . .
> Thy grassy banks whereon the milk-white steer Grazes. . . .[53]

But the question of sources would lead us far and wide, and must be left to the editors and commentators.

Many a passage of Macaulay's prose, however garish it now seems, testifies to his vein of romance, his boyish love of heroic scenes, of historical pomp and circumstance, and he revealed something more than that in *The Last Buccaneer* and the *Epitaph on a Jacobite.* Of pathos there is not much in the *Lays,* certainly not where we might expect to find it, in *Virginia;* we forget the heroine, but not Appius gnawing his lip as the crowd close in upon him. The *Lays* do, however, possess abundant romantic feeling, quite genuine within its range. Memory and historical imagination pour out realistic, concrete details on every page. It is all so rapid and effortless that we feel a shock when, once in a while, the illusion is broken by an undramatic touch of pedantry like "Traced from the right on linen white. . . ." Macaulay is most happily and surely romantic in his handling of proper names, whether of places or persons. *The Armada,* as Chesterton says, is a good geography book gone mad, and so are the *Lays.* Macaulay had not been born in Italy, but reading and travel had made the land as rich in historical associations for him as Scotland was for Scott. Again and again the "rhymed rhetoric" of the *Lays* rises into poetry in the sonorous suggestiveness of proper names—

> Sempronius Atratinus
> Sate in the Eastern Gate.

Although by their very nature the *Lays* stand outside the main body of romantic mythological poetry, they show in their way what is true of greater works, namely, that, other things being equal, mere imitations or reproductions of the antique are usually dead, while poems informed by a modern spirit, either personal or "propagandist," are usually alive. If Macaulay's *Lays* surpassed other men's[54] the reason was not merely superiority of talent. It is not in academic effusions that brains and blood and bowels are splashed about with such Homeric joy as Macaulay displays. In an excellent essay Mr. E. E. Kellett (after recalling what Leigh Hunt told Macaulay in his begging-letter, that the *Lays* "want the aroma that breathes from the *Faerie Queene*") thus explains their unique force and fire:

> Their moving impulse was perhaps political rather than ethereal. Proud Tarquin was to him a sort of James the Second; Valerius an earlier Schomberg; Titus was the Duke of Berwick; Julius was Sarsfield, and Regillus a luckier Steinkirk: nay, the Sublician Bridge was the bridge over the Gette, which William, retreating before Luxemburg, crossed so unwillingly. Had there been no British significance

> in these old Roman stories, nay, had they not possessed a specially Whig significance, Macaulay would never have retold them with such spirit. But though his inspiration thus came as much from Constitution Hill as from Helicon, it is a high and genuine inspiration nevertheless.[55]

And we may remember the boyish cheer of Andrew Lang, who, when he came to "But Titus stabbed Valerius A span deep in the breast," scribbled in the margin, "Well done, the Jacobites!"[56]

Charles Kingsley (1819-75)

Apart from a few brief experiments, such as Hawtrey's famous rendering from Homer, English hexameters generally remind us of Dr. Johnson's dictum on women's preaching, and among whole poems in that measure *Andromeda* (1858) stands high in relative rightness and ease. Kingsley spent great pains on the mechanics of the poem, and now and then he achieved sonorous perfection—"As when an osprey aloft, dark-eyebrowed, royally crested." Yet even he did not escape the inevitable pitfalls. Though he aimed at "Homer's average of a spondee a line,"[57] *Andromeda* lacks spondaic variety, and the movement is less dactylic than anapestic.

The attractions of *Andromeda* are not merely metrical, even if it is only a poem for boys—and possibly the modern boy who reads poetry is an intellectual from the cradle. Arnold, hearing what Kingsley was about, complained, *a priori,* that he was too coarse a workman for poetry.[58] But Kingsley, if not subtle, was an outdoor man, with senses keenly alive. He loved the beauty of the myth and reveled in it more and more, making, as his habit was, dozens of pencil drawings before turning to words for "colour and chiaroscuro."[59] One need not forfeit one's adult status if one's eye and pulse respond to the description of the Nereids and Tritons (most of which was "rattled off in the last two hours, in the act of dressing and breakfasting")—

> Onward they came in their joy, and before
>   them the roll of the surges
> Sank, as the breeze sank dead, into smooth
>   green foam-flecked marble—

or the roar of wind and water, the radiant swooping figure of Perseus, the approach of the sea-monster, bulky and black as a galley, "Lazily coasting along, as the fish fled leaping before it."[60] The poem is doubtless too long, but it seldom flags, and the Homeric echoes and similes are more spontaneous at least than those of *Sohrab* and *Balder.*

While not at all a symbolist in the romantic tradition, Kingsley saw in the subject more than an excuse for heroic and sensuous objectivity. The myth was "a very deep one," and belonged to the primitive period of "human sacrifices to the dark powers of nature, which died out throughout Greece before the higher, sunnier faith in *human* gods." He wished to show Andromeda as "a barbarian" with "no notion (besides fetichism) beyond pleasure and pain, as of an animal. It is not till the thinking, sententious Greek, with his awful beauty, inspires her, that she develops into woman." Speaking of a difference in style between two parts of the poem, Kingsley said: "I felt myself on old mythic, idolatrous ground, and went slowly and artificially, feeling it unreal, and wishing to make readers feel it such. Then when I get into real *human* Greek life, I can burst out and rollick along in the joy of existence."[61] One may miss the underlying intention, but one cannot miss "the joy of existence," the genuine love for high adventure, for the brave heart and hand, that one expects from the author of *Westward Ho!* and *Hereward the Wake.* "I love these old Hellenes heartily," he said in the preface to *The Heroes,* and, in more philosophic strain, he confessed to Arnold, when thanking him for *Culture and Anarchy,* that he had been ashamed to catch himself, a clergyman, wishing he had been an old Greek rather than an Englishman.[62] However, needless to say, Kingsley is no "pagan." Next to the romances of the Christian Middle Ages, "there are no fairy tales like these old Greek ones, for beauty, and wisdom, and truth, and for making children love noble deeds, and trust in God to help them through."[63] And the conclusion of *Andromeda* reflects not only the simple Homeric world that Kingsley loved, but something of the ideals of the author of *Yeast* and *Alton Locke:*

> Chanting of order and right, and of foresight,
>   warden of nations;
> Chanting of labour and craft, and of wealth in
>   the port and the garner;
> Chanting of valour and fame, and the man
>   who can fall with the foremost,
> Fighting for children and wife, and the field
>   which his father bequeathed him.
> Sweetly and solemnly sang she, and planned
>   new lessons for mortals:
> Happy, who hearing obey her, the wise
>   unsullied Athené.

Robert Lytton (1831-91)

If the faded copies of *Lucile* on the shelves of every secondhand bookshop in the English-speaking world were ever disturbed in their eternal repose, one might say that "Owen Meredith" still lived. While *Lucile* does not concern us, two of Lytton's other works, one popular and one stillborn, help to explain what happened, on the lower levels of mythological verse, to the post-romantic tradition, and to explain also the neglect of a number of poets whom we now read. The chief thing in his first volume (1855) was the drama *Clytemnestra,* part of which he had written before he left Harrow. In his fable and structure Lytton followed the *Agamemnon,* but substituted Victorian fullness of characterization for Aeschylus' religious and philosophic vision, and for a public unable to take Greek tragedy neat he provided plenty of romantic soda-water. Clytemnestra is not so much a grand, hard murderess as one of the world's great lovers, the introspective heroine of a Victorian triangle in an exotic setting. She, who had "so much to give," found herself condemned to a loveless marriage; and she recalls the evening when she and Aegisthus lingered outside the city in the moonlight, unconscious of passing time. In this drama Lytton may be said to have won his spurs as perhaps the most notorious plagiarist of the century. Apart from Aeschylus, echoes range from *Macbeth* to Arnold's *Empedocles,* which Lytton greatly admired.[64] In the chorus describing the sacrifice of Iphigeneia, he contrives to use, and of course expand, every detail of Tennyson's picture in *A Dream of Fair Women.* This chorus makes a protracted and un-Aeschylean assault upon the feelings, a successful assault, apparently, since it drew tears from Leigh Hunt. Of the poet's taste for glossy diction, in which he was by no means alone, one specimen will be enough, a disastrous improvement on Marlowe—"Make me immortal with one costly kiss!"

Lytton's father, the novelist, was sincerely complimentary in expressing surprise at the merits of the drama.[65] That very busy man, and not injudicious critic, never ceased to urge Robert to aim at condensation and selection, and, as a means to that end, to study the Greeks, especially Homer.[66] Greek was, Robert wrote to Mrs. Browning, the only knowledge he did not regret the time spent in acquiring,[67] but its "pure cool fountains" had almost as little effect upon his style as upon hers. Keats had been his first love,[68] and his father, although since *The New Timon* he had come to admire Keats greatly, believed, like Arnold, that his influence had been unfortunate in fostering "the effeminate attention to wording and expression and efflorescent description which characterise the poetry now in vogue."[69] "The Elizabethan School has been overworked. Leave it alone."[70] Bulwer constantly urged also that Robert should try to be "popular," in the sense (the Arnoldian sense) that Homer was; but his reference on one occasion to the popular Charles Mackay, as compared with the neglected Shelley and Keats, might well lead to misunderstanding.[71] At any rate Robert produced *Lucile.* It cannot be said that Bulwer's own volume of mythological poems, *The Lost Tales of Miletus* (1866), furnished notable models of the virtues he strove to inculcate, for Robert's facile fluency and tinsel were a direct paternal inheritance.[72]

Robert inherited also his father's versatile energies—his writing was the by-product of an active diplomatic career—and he was not content with the reputation of a popular drawing-room novelist in verse. In 1868 he published an ambitious two-volume work, *Chronicles and Characters.* The first book consisted of three tales from Herodotus, of which one at least, the inevitable *Gyges and Candaules,* might seem an odd part of what attempted to be a panorama of the development of the human mind.[73] From these tales of Greece, which the always hopeful and always disappointed father described as "pretty exercises, but not the spring of a great genius into the arena," we pass to the Crucifixion in the second book. The third confronts heroic paganism, in the person of Licinius, "Rome's last Roman," with Christianity, the new gospel of love. The treatment of this theme, which was not yet threadbare, pleased both the author and his father, and it was praised by George Meredith.[74] But Robert Lytton quite lacked the power to do justice to such an impressive scheme, and even in its own day the book was a failure.

Glancing back over this chapter, and omitting such healthy extroverts as Macaulay and Kingsley, we are aware that in minor poetry at least the "paganism" of Wordsworth, Keats, and Shelley has lost most of its original force, and that the Christian hostility to Hellenism which showed itself in the Coleridges (and Wordsworth) has become a disturbing element in the Protestant Mrs. Browning and in a number of young men who took the path to Rome. Further, Keats and Shelley had instinctively treated modern and humanitarian themes through mythological symbols, but now the loss of their primitive imagination and the increasing pressure of modernism have made such attitudes and methods less possible or less instinctive. Minor poets, because they are minor, may reflect the *Zeitgeist* more clearly than great ones, and even this chapter indicates that we have left romanticism behind and are in the age of Victorian realism, pietism, and rationalism.

By 1850 Tennyson was seated firmly on his throne, Browning had an important critical following, and Arnold had published his first volume. The spasmodics (apart from that "she-spasmodic," Mrs. Browning) do not come into these pages, but we may observe that Aytoun did not forget mythology in his burlesque. We can hardly blame readers who saw no difference between the genuine article and *Firmilian:*

> Then came the voice of universal Pan,
> The dread earth-whisper, booming in mine
> ear. . . .[75]

The ruffled waters had hardly closed over the spasmodics before the literary public became aware that, to put it rather spasmodically, a fresh crew had manned the romantic craft, thrown out a good deal more ballast, and set out in a new direction. The creed of Rossetti, the master spirit, was that modern poetry had culminated in Coleridge and Keats, the poets of medieval color and enchantment, and his own early poems carried on that tradition, with a minute unearthly realism. At Oxford, William Morris and his friends looked up to Tennyson, the early romantic Tennyson; one of Morris's favorite poems was *The Hesperides.* Since Rossetti's poems were not collected until 1870, the poetic landmark for the group, though few readers as yet perceived the fact, was *The Defence of Guenevere.* Although the Morris circle was imbibing the social gospel of Carlyle (and the esthetic gospel of Ruskin), neither Morris nor Rossetti approached "life" except at Browningesque moments. As for Anglo-Catholicism, it nourished in this group, not the scruples of Dolben and Hopkins, but devotion to Gothic and ritualistic symbolism, and as much of religion as was compatible with the belief that "there is no God and the Virgin Mary is His mother." As one would expect, classic myth was not the most immediate interest. Christina Rossetti, we have seen, was the first to begin and the first to leave off. Her brother's mythological pieces came late in his career. *Atalanta in Calydon* announced the arrival of Dionysus in 1865, and *The Life and Death of Jason* appeared two years after that. Meanwhile Morris had written, though he never published, his *Scenes from the Fall of Troy.* In these poems he was reviving a tradition older than Tennyson or Keats, the tradition of the classical romances of the Middle Ages. . . .

Notes

[1] On May 1, 1832, she made a record of the number of lines of Greek she could repeat. Of the 3280 lines of Greek prose, only 90 are from "Heathen writers," and 1860 are from Gregory Nazianzen alone. The total for Greek poetry is 4420, and Aeschylus comes first with 1800, Euripides is a poor third with 350; the second is Synesius, of whose hymns she knows 1310 lines. See *Elizabeth Barrett Browning: Hitherto Unpublished Poems and Stories, with an Inedited Autobiography,* ed. H. B. Forman (Boston, 1914), II, 134-35.

[2] *Letters of Elizabeth Barrett Browning,* ed. Sir Frederic Kenyon (1897), I, 101. Hugh Boyd, who had led her to the Greek Christian writers, would apparently have confined her poetry "to the exclusive expression of Christian doctrine" (*ibid.,* I, 242, 247). Against this may be set his gift of Cyprus wine, which the pupil celebrated in verses of secular gusto.

[3] See the prefaces to *The Battle of Marathon* (1820) and the first version of *Prometheus Bound* (1833), in the *Poetical Works* (Oxford University Press, 1920).

[4] Preface to *The Seraphim* of 1838 (*Works,* pp. 78-80). Mrs. Browning's Shelleyan desire to make Prometheus into a perfect hero comes out in the discussion between her and her future husband of both the ancient drama and the one he suggested she should write. Browning, after explaining his notion of Greek realism, ends with "In your poem you shall make Prometheus our way." See *Letters of Robert Browning and Elizabeth Barrett Barrett* (1899), I, 35-40. This collection is cited henceforth as *Letters.*

[5] *Letters of Elizabeth Barrett Browning Addressed to Richard Hengist Horne,* ed. S. R. Townshend Mayer (1877), II, 61 ff.; *Hitherto Unpublished Poems,* etc., ed. Forman, II, 200 ff.; *Letters of Elizabeth Barrett Browning,* ed. Kenyon, I, 84-85.

[6] *Letters,* I, 35. She planned to write a monologue supposedly spoken by Aeschylus "just before the eagle cracked his great massy skull with a stone" (*ibid.,* I, 31). See below, ch. XI, note 12. Miss M. H. Shackford has suggested a relationship between the sufferings of Io and those of Marian Erle in *Aurora Leigh* (*E. B. Browning; R. H. Horne: Two Studies,* Wellesley, Mass., 1935, p. 15).

[7] *Works,* p. 306. Is the line "To think God's song unexcelling" (stanza xxxvii) an echo of Milton's "Sion's songs, to all true tastes excelling" in his tirade against Greek culture (*Paradise Regained,* iv. 347)?

The popular bard, Charles Mackay, wrote a *Dead Pan* (*Legends of the Isles,* 1845) on the same text, though Mrs. Browning did not feel that she had any claims against him (*Letters,* I, 393, 398). And Robert Buchanan made a poetic comment on Mrs. Browning's poem; see his *Complete Poems* (1901), I, 185.

[8] *Letters,* ed. Kenyon, I, 128-29. On the question of her rhymes, which she says were a matter of principle and not of carelessness, see *ibid.,* I, 182-83, and *Letters to Horne,* II, 113 ff.

[9] Virginia Woolf, *The Common Reader,* Second Series (1932), p. 207. For Mrs. Browning's phrase about rhyming the stars, see *Letters,* ed. Kenyon, II, 382.

[10] *Works of Oscar Wilde,* Authorized Edition (Boston [1910]), XII, 257.

[11] *Works,* pp. 411-12.

[12] *Ibid.,* pp. 449-51.

[13] Even in her paraphrases of the ancients she slipped easily into modernizing or sentimentalizing. For example, compare the passage "And if I read aright" (*Works,* p. 586) with Apuleius (*Metam.* v. 25); see Adolf Hoffmann, *Das Psyche-Märchen des Apuleius in der englischen Literatur* (Strassburg, 1908), p. 84.

[14] She perhaps approached such a thing in *The Enchantress,* which was apparently written in the early eighteen-thirties, but it was never completed or published. See *New Poems by Robert Browning and Elizabeth Barrett Browning,* ed. Kenyon (1914), pp. 78-82.

[15] *Letters,* I, 45-46.

[16] One reward at the time was an anonymous letter from a person who had hitherto regarded her "as a

great Age-teacher, all but divine," and now denounced this lyrical ebullition of her heart as immoral (*Letters,* ed. Kenyon, II, 406).

[17] *Letters,* ed. Kenyon, I, 247.

[18] One cannot take account of the small fry, since everyone learned to play variations on the contrasts between Christian and pagan ideals, but William Bell Scott and Augusta Webster may be mentioned. Contemplating the Elgin Marbles, Scott recognized the grand truths implicit in ancient fables, and, though the Cross has triumphed over all, the gods remain sublime revelations of the ideal toward which humanity must move (see my Appendix, under 1854). In *Athens* (*Blanche Lisle,* 1860, pp. 55-61), the scholarly Mrs. Webster celebrated the ancient city, but contrasted Zeus with "a greater God" and Athene with the Virgin Mary. The bulkiest contribution to the theme was Charles Kent's *Aletheia: or The Doom of Mythology* (1850), a poem of 139 pages with a mythological glossary of some 85. With picturesque and joyous exuberance the author conjures up all the figures of pagan myth, and then in the last few pages Aletheia appears to say that Pan is dead, that Truth and Love and the Christian God have banished "the Pagan devils."

[19] Landor's lack of discernment, or his native generosity, inspired a noble salute to the author in *Last Fruit off an Old Tree* (1853), p. 459; see *Poems,* ed. Wheeler, III (1935), 159, 180. For Landor's epistolary praise, see Wilfrid Ward, *Aubrey de Vere: A Memoir* (1904), p. 256, note. In connection with the symbolism, it is of some interest to find De Vere quoting Bacon's *Wisdom of the Ancients.*

[20] Ward, pp. 111 ff., 118 ff.

[21] *Ibid.,* p. 317. Cf. De Vere's two dramas, *Alexander the Great* and *Saint Thomas of Canterbury,* and his *Recollections* (1897), pp. 358 ff.

[22] *Poetical Works* (1884), I, 82-94. Cf. *Wisdom* (*ibid.,* I, 59-60).

[23] *Edinburgh Review,* XCI (1850), 408-43; *Essays Chiefly on Poetry* (1887), II, 143-88, especially 180 ff.

[24] *Prose Remains of Arthur Hugh Clough* (1888), pp. 356, 368. The review appeared in *The North American Review,* LXXVII (1853), 1 ff.

[25] *Poems* (1890), p. 269. In the next lines he feels that, wherever we turn, the world "still is the same narrow crib."

Clough's one purely mythological poem was *Actaeon,* a dubious metrical experiment (*Poems,* pp. 423-24). It was apparently first published in the *Poems and Prose Remains* (1869), II, 467-68. See also *ἐπί Λάτμῳ* (1849) and *Selene.*

[26] *Poems,* pp. 274-75; Horace, *Od.* III. iv. 58 ff.

[27] *An Invocation* (*Ionica,* 1858). Cory exemplified his remark that one's feelings lose poetic flow soon after twenty-seven or so, and he virtually said his say in this early volume.

[28] *Extracts from the Letters and Journals of William Cory,* ed. Francis Warre Cornish (Oxford, 1897), p. 458.

[29] *Ibid.,* pp. 498-99. More remarkable, from a master of Eton, is the judgment that "Greek plays are to French plays what cold boiled veal is to snipe"—and by French plays he means not Racine but Dumas and Sardou and their kind (*ibid.,* p. 458).

[30] *Selections from the Brief Mention of Basil Lanneau Gildersleeve* (Johns Hopkins University Press, 1930), p. 268 (and cf. pp. 243, 327). The poem was written in 1845.

[31] *Letters and Journals,* p. 565. See Mallock's *New Republic* (1877), II, 106-07, or his *Verses* (1893). On the lack of conciseness in Cory's lyric, see F. W. Bateson, *English Poetry and the English Language* (Clarendon Press, 1934), p. 124.

[32] *Poems of Digby Mackworth Dolben* (Oxford University Press, 1915), pp. lv ff. (and see pp. xcv ff.).

[33] Cf. the references to Hylas and Hyacinthus (*ibid.,* p. 85).

[34] Pp. 117-18, 122.

[35] The *Vision* was first printed in full in the facsimile edition of 1929, and is included in Bridges' edition of the *Poems,* re-edited by Charles Williams (Oxford University Press, 1930), pp. 130 ff.

[36] There is the sonnet *Andromeda* (1879), which was intended to be Miltonic but reminds us of Chapman's *Andromeda Liberata.*

[37] *Correspondence of Gerard Manley Hopkins and Richard Watson Dixon,* ed. C. C. Abbott (Oxford University Press, 1935), pp. 145 ff.; *Letters of Gerard Manley Hopkins to Robert Bridges,* ed. C. C. Abbott (1935), pp. 109, 216 ff.

Hopkins' discussions of Keats, in letters to Patmore of 1887-88, are not only remarkably penetrating but, in view of the whole bent of the writer's mind and life, remarkably sympathetic. See G. F. Lahey, *Gerard Manley Hopkins* (Oxford University Press, 1930), pp. 71 ff.

[38] *Poetical Works of Christina Rossetti,* ed. W. M. Rossetti (1904), p. xli. Among other unpublished poems were two concerning Sappho, of 1846 and 1848 (*ibid.,* p. xlii).

[39] It was not published in her lifetime, but is included in the *Works,* p. 111. See *ibid.,* pp. xxxvii, 467; and *New Poems by Christina Rossetti,* ed. W. M. Rossetti (1896), p. 370.

[40] See *Works,* pp. xlvii, lxix. There is one late and slightly mythological sonnet, *Venus's Looking-Glass* (pp. 387, 487).

[41] See Horne's "Brief Commentary" prefixed to the ninth edition (1872). I have used Mr. Eric Partridge's reprint of the first edition (1928). For the classical myths of Orion, see Apollodorus, *Lib.* I. iv. 3-5.

[42] Mrs. Browning defined Horne's subject as "the growth of a poet's mind" (*Athenaeum,* June 24, 1843, p. 583; see Horne's address to "the herald Poet," p. 82). That may also have been his subject in a narrower sense, for Horne had a lifelong thirst for fame. According to Mr. P. L. Carver's suggestion, Akinetos would be the immovable British public, Merope an earthly infatuation, Eos the poet's several humanitarian activities, and Artemis those studies in philosophy of which *Orion* was the intellectual product (*R.E.S.,* V [1929], 371). One may hesitate at such explicit personal symbols, though none is impossible, and such a secondary intention in Akinetos at least seems plausible. In the last sentence of her review Mrs. Browning playfully warned the public not to invite the fate of the Unmoved by neglecting the poem.

[43] The episode of the famine in Ithaca (*Orion,* pp. 15 ff.) is one admitted topical allusion, a palpable reminder of the Corn Law agitation ("Brief Commentary," p. x). In the early *Hecatompylos,* which seems to be entirely in the tradition of musings over antique ruins, Horne ends with an allusion to famine (*Athenaeum,* April 8, 1828, p. 361).

[44] Horne says that Meredith wrote to him about the poem ("Brief Commentary," p. vi, note). In 1872 Horne cites Darwinian doctrine, quite in the spirit of Meredith, as a basis for meliorist hope, not pessimism (*ibid.,* p. xvi). The Hegelian strain in Horne's work has been noticed by René Galland, *George Meredith* (Paris, 1923), p. 43, and Robert Sencourt, *Life of George Meredith* (1929), p. 23.

[45] *Works,* ed. E. C. Stedman and G. E. Woodberry (New York, 1914), VI, 323-54, especially 344 ff.

[46] "'Orion' Horne," *Selected Essays,* First Series (1928), p. 196.

[47] Dedication of *Prometheus* (Edinburgh, 1864). The drama is discussed by Miss Shackford, pp. 63-66 (see note 6 above).

[48] They were not issued in book form until 1850. Moore's *Legendary Ballads* (1830), which included mythological pieces, were only drawing-room lyrics. J. E. Bode, in publishing his *Ballads from Herodotus* (1853), took pains to say that he had conceived the idea in 1841, and had printed one ballad in *Blackwood* in April, 1842, some six months before the appearance of Macaulay's *Lays.* His inspiration came from the English and Scottish popular ballads; one does not regret his failure to defeat Arnold for the Oxford Professorship of Poetry.

[49] Their popularity has not been confined to English-speaking countries. See the article by Tommaso Tittoni cited in the bibliography.

[50] See Mrs. Browning's *Letters to Horne,* ed. Mayer, I, 166; Landor's *Works* (1846), II, 673, and *Heroic Idyls* (1863), p. 147 (*Poems,* ed. Wheeler, III, 153, 205); G. Lafourcade, *La jeunesse de Swinburne* (Paris and London, 1928), I, 95; Everard Meynell, *Life of Francis Thompson* (1926), p. 9; W. B. Yeats, *Autobiographies* (New York, 1927), p. 57.

[51] *Macaulay's Lays of Ancient Rome and other Historical Poems,* ed. G. M. Trevelyan (1928), pp. vii-viii, 176 ff.

[52] Wilfrid Ward, *Aubrey de Vere: A Memoir,* p. 75.

[53] *Georg.* ii. 146; *Childe Harold,* iv. 66 (*Works of Byron,* ed. E. H. Coleridge, II, 379). Byron's editor seems to overlook this item, but, in connection with *Childe Harold,* iv. 80 (*ibid.,* II, 391), he cites *The Prophecy of Capys,* stanza xxx.

Aubrey de Vere remarks (*Essays Chiefly on Poetry,* I, 26) that the finest passages in Scott's *Lord of the Isles* and *The Prophecy of Capys* have their original in the scene between Britomart and the priest of Isis in *The Faerie Queene* (V. vii. 20 ff.). But prophecies are common in heroic poetry, and Macaulay's famous slip about the Blatant Beast suggests that Spenser was less firmly lodged in his mind than a few hundred other authors.

[54] His nearest rival was Aytoun, whose first Scottish lay appeared in *Blackwood* in 1843. Sir Theodore Martin said that so far as Aytoun had a model it was not Macaulay but Wilhelm Müller (*Memoir of William Edmondstoune Aytoun,* 1867, p. 76). About the same time Aytoun wrote an Ovidian ballad on Lycaon, which was first printed in the *Memoir* (pp. 97-99). A couple of jocular mythological pieces were included in the Bon Gaultier *Ballads* (1845).

In his *Lays and Legends of Ancient Greece* (1857), John Stuart Blackie tried feebly to mingle sweet the classic strain with Gothic minstrelsy. See also the volume by Freeman and Cox (Appendix, under 1850).

[55] "Macaulay's Lay Figures," *Suggestions* (Cambridge University Press, 1923), p. 164. In connection with the bridge over the Gette, Mr. Kellett quotes a passage from the twentieth chapter of the *History* which recalls the situation in *Horatius* to the reader, and recalled it to the author, who refers to his old hero. See the *History* (World's Classics ed.), IV, 460.

[56] R. S. Rait *et al.*, "Andrew Lang," *Quarterly Review,* CCXVIII (1913), 300.

[57] *Charles Kingsley: His Letters and Memories of his Life. Edited by his Wife* (2d ed., 1877), I, 344.

[58] *Letters of Matthew Arnold to Arthur Hugh Clough,* ed. H. F. Lowry, p. 139. Arnold did not mention *Andromeda* in discussing hexameters in the lectures on Homer.

[59] *Charles Kingsley,* I, 339 (and 342).

[60] *Poems* (1880), p. 201. Kingsley was working at the poem in 1852 *et seq.* In Part IV of the story of Perseus in *The Heroes* (published 1855, dated 1856), the whole passage on the sea-monster is almost identical, except for its being in prose. For the personal observation that went into the simile of the osprey (*Poems,* p. 202), see *Charles Kingsley,* I, 339-40.

[61] *Charles Kingsley,* I, 338-40. For the original myth, see Ovid, *Metam.* iv. 663 ff., and Apollodorus, *Lib.* II. iv. 3.

[62] *Charles Kingsley,* II, 338.

[63] *The Heroes* (Cambridge, 1856), p. xvii.

[64] *Poetical Works of Owen Meredith* (1867), I, 24; *Personal & Literary Letters of Robert First Earl of Lytton,* ed. Lady Betty Balfour (1906), I, 49-50.

[65] *Personal & Literary Letters,* I, 54.

[66] *Ibid.,* I, 206-07, 276; *Life of Edward Bulwer First Lord Lytton By his Grandson The Earl of Lytton* (London, 1913), II, 385-86.

Since Bulwer nowadays seldom gets even disapproving attention, one may observe, quite irrelevantly, that he condemned the "false sentiment" of *Enoch Arden* (*Life,* II, 431), which both Swinburne and Arnold considered the best thing Tennyson had yet done (*Letters of Algernon Charles Swinburne,* ed. Edmund Gosse and T. J. Wise, I, 35; *Letters of Matthew Arnold,* ed. G. W. E. Russell, I, 277); Arnold did not like *Tithonus* quite so well. Further, in view of recent changes of attitude, one may quote Bulwer's complaint: "I despair of fellow-feeling with an age which says Pope is no poet and Rossetti is a great one" (*Life,* II, 431).

[67] *Personal & Literary Letters,* I, 84.

[68] *Ibid.,* I, 42.

[69] *Life,* II, 426-28.

[70] *Ibid.,* II, 385.

[71] *Personal & Literary Letters,* I, 55-56. Cf. *ibid.,* I, 146, and *Life,* II, 396 ff.

[72] For Bulwer's own comments on this work, see the *Life,* II, 362 ff. In 1844 he had published *The Poems and Ballads of Schiller,* which helped to popularize Schiller's mythological pieces; their modern idealism was quite congenial to the translator (see, for instance, Bulwer's notes on *Hero and Leander* and *The Complaint of Ceres*). Two years later he adapted *Oedipus Tyrannus* for the modern stage, but arrangements for production fell through (*Life,* II, 84-85, 90-91). The third volume (1853) of his *Poetical and Dramatic Works* included some short classical poems, and it is rather surprising, at this date, to find one, *Ganymede,* headed by a quotation from the *Mystagogus Poeticus* of Alexander Ross. Early in his hard-working career Bulwer had essayed an historical work, *Athens, Its Rise and Fall* (1836), but he wisely abandoned it after the success of Thirlwall and Grote. He turned his considerable scholarship to not very valuable account in the uncompleted historical romance, *Pausanias the Spartan* (published posthumously in 1876, but written twenty years earlier), and of course in the *Last Days of Pompeii.*

[73] The discreet but somewhat luscious rendering drew a parental admonition against being Swinburnian (*Personal & Literary Letters,* I, 206-08). "Keatsian" would have been more accurate, for the disrobing of Gyges' wife is a pallid imitation of *The Eve of St. Agnes.*

[74] See the Memorial Edition of Meredith's *Works,* XXIII (1910), 121. A similar theme had been touched in *Tannhäuser; or, The Battle of the Bards* (1861), by "Neville Temple" (*i.e.,* Julian Fane) and "Edward Trevor" (*i.e.,* Robert Lytton).

[75] See the whole passage, *Poems of William Edmondstoune Aytoun,* ed. F. Page (Oxford University Press, 1921), p. 298. The advantage of this kind of writing, as the genial author remarked, is "that you can go on slapdash, without thinking!" (Martin, *Memoir,* p. 147).

Works Cited

D. Caclamanos, "Mrs. Browning's Translations of the Odyssey." *Notes and Queries*, CLV (1928), 355 (and 391).

P. L. Carver, review of *Orion*, ed. Partridge. *R.E.S.*, V (1929), 367-71. *Poems of Digby Mackworth Dolben Edited with a Memoir by Robert Bridges.* Oxford University Press, 1915.

John Drinkwater, "William Cory." *Essays by Divers Hands: Being the Transactions of the Royal Society of Literature*, New Series, IV (1924), 1-31.

Sir Edmund Gosse, "'Orion' Horne." *Portraits and Sketches* (1913); *Selected Essays*, First Series (1928).

Orion: by R. H. Horne: With an Introduction on Horne's Life and Work, ed. Eric Partridge (1928).

Bernhard Jacobi, *Elizabeth Barrett Browning als Übersetzerin antiker Dichtungen.* Münster in Westfalen, 1908.

E. E. Kellett, "Macaulay's Lay Figures." *Suggestions* (Cambridge University Press, 1923), pp. 155-65.

William G. Kingsland, "An Unknown Poem of Mrs. Browning's" [*The Battle of Marathon*]. *Poet Lore*, III (1891), 281-84.

Federico Olivero, "On R. H. Horne's *Orion*." *M.L.N.*, XXX (1915), 33-39.

Edgar Allan Poe, "Horne's 'Orion.'" *Works*, ed. E. C. Stedman and G. E. Woodberry (New York, 1914), VI, 323-54.

John C. Rolfe, "Macaulay's *Lays of Ancient Rome*." *Classical Journal*, XXIX (1934), 567-81.

Tommaso Tittoni, "La Profezia di Capi di T. B. Macaulay." *Nuova Antologia*, CCXLVI (1926), 351-64.

George E. Woodberry, "The Poetry of Aubrey de Vere." *Makers of Literature* (New York, 1909), pp. 124-38; "Aubrey de Vere on Poetry." *Ibid.*, pp. 139-57.

FURTHER READING

Anderson, Warren D. *Matthew Arnold and the Classical Tradition.* Ann Arbor: The University of Michigan Press, 1965, 293 p.

Examines Arnold's fascination with the classical tradition, particularly his interest in the culture of ancient Greece.

Björk, Lennart. "Thomas Hardy's 'Hellenism'." In *Papers on Language and Literature Presented to Alvar Ellegard and Erik Frykman*, edited by Sven Bäckman and Gören Kjellmer, pp. 46-58. Göteborg, Sweden: Acta Universitatis Gothoburgensis, 1985.

Traces several possible sources for the Hellenism that appears in several of Hardy's novels and contends that it functions as "a criterion against which nineteenth-century life, and view of life, is measured."

Clarke, G. W., ed. *Rediscovering Hellenism: The Hellenic Inheritance and the English Imagination.* Cambridge: Cambridge University Press, 1989, 264 p.

Anthology of recent critical essays, several of which investigate aspects of Victorian Hellenism, including Richard Jenkyns on painting, James Bowen on education, and Anthony Stephens on Nietzsche.

DeLaura, David J. *Hebrew and Hellene in Victorian England: Newman, Arnold, and Pater.* Austin and London: University of Texas Press, 1969, 370 p.

Seeks primarily to demonstrate that Matthew Arnold and Walter Pater adapted "the traditional religious culture to the needs of the later nineteenth century," and also explores how each writer's approach was shaped by the importance of Hellenism in his education.

Lambropoulos, Vassilis. "Violence and the Liberal Imagination: The Representation of Hellenism in Matthew Arnold." In *The Violence of Representation: Literature and the History of Violence*, edited by Nancy Armstrong and Leonard Tennenhouse, pp. 171-93. London and New York: Routledge, 1989.

In sections four through six of this essay, Lambropoulos attempts to describe the dialectic of Hebraic and Hellenic. In investigating how Arnold defined these categories in *Culture and Anarchy*, Lambropoulos ultimately suggests that Arnold's identification of the terms with Aryan and Semitic people played into the anti-semitism that surfaced in twentieth-century Europe.

Turner, Frank M. "Antiquity in Victorian Contexts." *Browning Institute Studies: An Annual of Victorian Literary and Cultural History* 10, edited by Gerhard Joseph (1982): 1-14.

Advocates further study of Victorian Hellenism as a concrete and under-exploited route to gaining new understandings of the period; also explores specific motives for the Victorian appropriation of classical texts and images.

Nineteenth-Century Literature Criticism

Topics Volume
Cumulative Indexes

Volumes 1-68

How to Use This Index

The main references

Calvino, Italo
1923-1985.....CLC 5, 8, 11, 22, 33, 39, 73; SSC 3

list all author entries in the following Gale Literary Criticism series:

BLC = *Black Literature Criticism*
CLC = *Contemporary Literary Criticism*
CLR = *Children's Literature Review*
CMLC = *Classical and Medieval Literature Criticism*
DA = *DISCovering Authors*
DC = *Drama Criticism*
HLC = *Hispanic Literature Criticism*
LC = *Literature Criticism from 1400 to 1800*
NCLC = *Nineteenth-Century Literature Criticism*
PC = *Poetry Criticism*
SSC = *Short Story Criticism*
TCLC = *Twentieth-Century Literary Criticism*
WLC = *World Literature Criticism, 1500 to the Present*

The cross-references

See also CANR 23; CA 85-88;
obituary CA 116

list all author entries in the following Gale biographical and literary sources:

AAYA = *Authors & Artists for Young Adults*
AITN = *Authors in the News*
BEST = *Bestsellers*
BW = *Black Writers*
CA = *Contemporary Authors*
CAAS = *Contemporary Authors Autobiography Series*
CABS = *Contemporary Authors Bibliographical Series*
CANR = *Contemporary Authors New Revision Series*
CAP = *Contemporary Authors Permanent Series*
CDALB = *Concise Dictionary of American Literary Biography*
CDBLB = *Concise Dictionary of British Literary Biography*
DLB = *Dictionary of Literary Biography*
DLBD = *Dictionary of Literary Biography Documentary Series*
DLBY = *Dictionary of Literary Biography Yearbook*
HW = *Hispanic Writers*
JRDA = *Junior DISCovering Authors*
MAICYA = *Major Authors and Illustrators for Children and Young Adults*
MTCW = *Major 20th-Century Writers*
NNAL = *Native North American Literature*
SAAS = *Something about the Author Autobiography Series*
SATA = *Something about the Author*
YABC = *Yesterday's Authors of Books for Children*

Literary Criticism Series Cumulative Author Index

See also CA 85-88; CANR 45; DLB 20, 36, 100, 149
Aldiss, Brian W(ilson) 1925-**CLC 5, 14, 40; DAM NOV**
See also CA 5-8R; CAAS 2; CANR 5, 28, 64; DLB 14; MTCW; SATA 34
Alegria, Claribel 1924- ... **CLC 75; DAM MULT**
See also CA 131; CAAS 15; DLB 145; HW
Alegria, Fernando 1918- .... **CLC 57**
See also CA 9-12R; CANR 5, 32; HW
Aleichem, Sholom .... **TCLC 1, 35**
See also Rabinovitch, Sholem
Aleixandre, Vicente 1898-1984 **CLC 9, 36; DAM POET; PC 15**
See also CA 85-88; 114; CANR 26; DLB 108; HW; MTCW
Alepoudelis, Odysseus
See Elytis, Odysseus
Aleshkovsky, Joseph 1929-
See Aleshkovsky, Yuz
See also CA 121; 128
Aleshkovsky, Yuz .... **CLC 44**
See also Aleshkovsky, Joseph
Alexander, Lloyd (Chudley) 1924- .... **CLC 35**
See also AAYA 1; CA 1-4R; CANR 1, 24, 38, 55; CLR 1, 5, 48; DLB 52; JRDA; MAICYA; MTCW; SAAS 19; SATA 3, 49, 81
Alexander, Samuel 1859-1938 .... **TCLC 77**
Alexie, Sherman (Joseph, Jr.) 1966- ... **CLC 96; DAM MULT**
See also CA 138; DLB 175; NNAL
Alfau, Felipe 1902- .... **CLC 66**
See also CA 137
Alger, Horatio, Jr. 1832-1899 .... **NCLC 8**
See also DLB 42; SATA 16
Algren, Nelson 1909-1981 .... **CLC 4, 10, 33**
See also CA 13-16R; 103; CANR 20, 61; CDALB 1941-1968; DLB 9; DLBY 81, 82; MTCW
Ali, Ahmed 1910- .... **CLC 69**
See also CA 25-28R; CANR 15, 34
Alighieri, Dante
See Dante
Allan, John B.
See Westlake, Donald E(dwin)
Allan, Sidney
See Hartmann, Sadakichi
Allan, Sydney
See Hartmann, Sadakichi
Allen, Edward 1948- .... **CLC 59**
Allen, Paula Gunn 1939- . **CLC 84; DAM MULT**
See also CA 112; 143; CANR 63; DLB 175; NNAL
Allen, Roland
See Ayckbourn, Alan
Allen, Sarah A.
See Hopkins, Pauline Elizabeth
Allen, Sidney H.
See Hartmann, Sadakichi
Allen, Woody 1935- ...... **CLC 16, 52; DAM POP**
See also AAYA 10; CA 33-36R; CANR 27, 38, 63; DLB 44; MTCW
Allende, Isabel 1942-**CLC 39, 57, 97; DAM MULT, NOV; HLC; WLCS**
See also AAYA 18; CA 125; 130; CANR 51; DLB 145; HW; INT 130; MTCW
Alleyn, Ellen
See Rossetti, Christina (Georgina)
Allingham, Margery (Louise) 1904-1966**CLC 19**
See also CA 5-8R; 25-28R; CANR 4, 58; DLB 77; MTCW
Allingham, William 1824-1889 .... **NCLC 25**
See also DLB 35
Allison, Dorothy E. 1949- .... **CLC 78**
See also CA 140
Allston, Washington 1779-1843 .... **NCLC 2**
See also DLB 1
Almedingen, E. M. .... **CLC 12**
See also Almedingen, Martha Edith von
See also SATA 3
Almedingen, Martha Edith von 1898-1971
See Almedingen, E. M.
See also CA 1-4R; CANR 1
Almqvist, Carl Jonas Love 1793-1866 **NCLC 42**
Alonso, Damaso 1898-1990 .... **CLC 14**
See also CA 110; 131; 130; DLB 108; HW
Alov
See Gogol, Nikolai (Vasilyevich)
Alta 1942- .... **CLC 19**
See also CA 57-60
Alter, Robert B(ernard) 1935- .... **CLC 34**
See also CA 49-52; CANR 1, 47
Alther, Lisa 1944- .... **CLC 7, 41**
See also CA 65-68; CANR 12, 30, 51; MTCW
Althusser, L.
See Althusser, Louis
Althusser, Louis 1918-1990 .... **CLC 106**
See also CA 131; 132
Altman, Robert 1925- .... **CLC 16**
See also CA 73-76; CANR 43
Alvarez, A(lfred) 1929- .... **CLC 5, 13**
See also CA 1-4R; CANR 3, 33, 63; DLB 14, 40
Alvarez, Alejandro Rodriguez 1903-1965
See Casona, Alejandro
See also CA 131; 93-96; HW
Alvarez, Julia 1950- .... **CLC 93**
See also CA 147
Alvaro, Corrado 1896-1956 .... **TCLC 60**
Amado, Jorge 1912- ..... **CLC 13, 40, 106; DAM MULT, NOV; HLC**
See also CA 77-80; CANR 35; DLB 113; MTCW
Ambler, Eric 1909- .... **CLC 4, 6, 9**
See also CA 9-12R; CANR 7, 38; DLB 77; MTCW
Amichai, Yehuda 1924- .... **CLC 9, 22, 57**
See also CA 85-88; CANR 46, 60; MTCW
Amichai, Yehudah
See Amichai, Yehuda
Amiel, Henri Frederic 1821-1881 .... **NCLC 4**
Amis, Kingsley (William) 1922-1995**CLC 1, 2, 3, 5, 8, 13, 40, 44; DA; DAB; DAC; DAM MST, NOV**
See also AITN 2; CA 9-12R; 150; CANR 8, 28, 54; CDBLB 1945-1960; DLB 15, 27, 100, 139; DLBY 96; INT CANR-8; MTCW
Amis, Martin (Louis) 1949-**CLC 4, 9, 38, 62, 101**
See also BEST 90:3; CA 65-68; CANR 8, 27, 54; DLB 14; INT CANR-27
Ammons, A(rchie) R(andolph) 1926-**CLC 2, 3, 5, 8, 9, 25, 57, 108; DAM POET; PC 16**
See also AITN 1; CA 9-12R; CANR 6, 36, 51; DLB 5, 165; MTCW
Amo, Tauraatua i
See Adams, Henry (Brooks)
Anand, Mulk Raj 1905- **CLC 23, 93; DAM NOV**
See also CA 65-68; CANR 32, 64; MTCW
Anatol
See Schnitzler, Arthur
Anaximander c. 610B.C.-c. 546B.C. .... **CMLC 22**
Anaya, Rudolfo A(lfonso) 1937- . **CLC 23; DAM MULT, NOV; HLC**
See also AAYA 20; CA 45-48; CAAS 4; CANR 1, 32, 51; DLB 82; HW 1; MTCW
Andersen, Hans Christian 1805-1875 . **NCLC 7; DA; DAB; DAC; DAM MST, POP; SSC 6; WLC**
See also CLR 6; MAICYA; YABC 1
Anderson, C. Farley
See Mencken, H(enry) L(ouis); Nathan, George Jean
Anderson, Jessica (Margaret) Queale 1916-**CLC 37**
See also CA 9-12R; CANR 4, 62
Anderson, Jon (Victor) 1940-**CLC 9; DAM POET**
See also CA 25-28R; CANR 20
Anderson, Lindsay (Gordon) 1923-1994 **CLC 20**
See also CA 125; 128; 146
Anderson, Maxwell 1888-1959 .... **TCLC 2; DAM DRAM**
See also CA 105; 152; DLB 7
Anderson, Poul (William) 1926- .... **CLC 15**
See also AAYA 5; CA 1-4R; CAAS 2; CANR 2, 15, 34, 64; DLB 8; INT CANR-15; MTCW; SATA 90; SATA-Brief 39
Anderson, Robert (Woodruff) 1917- .... **CLC 23; DAM DRAM**
See also AITN 1; CA 21-24R; CANR 32; DLB 7
Anderson, Sherwood 1876-1941 **TCLC 1, 10, 24; DA; DAB; DAC; DAM MST, NOV; SSC 1; WLC**
See also CA 104; 121; CANR 61; CDALB 1917-1929; DLB 4, 9, 86; DLBD 1; MTCW
Andier, Pierre
See Desnos, Robert
Andouard
See Giraudoux, (Hippolyte) Jean
Andrade, Carlos Drummond de .... **CLC 18**
See also Drummond de Andrade, Carlos
Andrade, Mario de 1893-1945 .... **TCLC 43**
Andreae, Johann V(alentin) 1586-1654 .... **LC 32**
See also DLB 164
Andreas-Salome, Lou 1861-1937 .... **TCLC 56**
See also DLB 66
Andress, Lesley
See Sanders, Lawrence
Andrewes, Lancelot 1555-1626 .... **LC 5**
See also DLB 151, 172
Andrews, Cicily Fairfield
See West, Rebecca
Andrews, Elton V.
See Pohl, Frederik
Andreyev, Leonid (Nikolaevich) 1871-1919**TCLC 3**
See also CA 104
Andric, Ivo 1892-1975 .... **CLC 8**
See also CA 81-84; 57-60; CANR 43, 60; DLB 147; MTCW
Androvar
See Prado (Calvo), Pedro
Angelique, Pierre
See Bataille, Georges
Angell, Roger 1920- .... **CLC 26**
See also CA 57-60; CANR 13, 44; DLB 171
Angelou, Maya 1928- **CLC 12, 35, 64, 77; BLC; DA; DAB; DAC; DAM MST, MULT, POET, POP; WLCS**
See also AAYA 7, 20; BW 2; CA 65-68; CANR 19, 42; DLB 38; MTCW; SATA 49
Anna Comnena 1083-1153 .... **CMLC 25**
Annensky, Innokenty (Fyodorovich) 1856-1909 **TCLC 14**
See also CA 110; 155
Annunzio, Gabriele d'
See D'Annunzio, Gabriele
Anodos
See Coleridge, Mary E(lizabeth)
Anon, Charles Robert
See Pessoa, Fernando (Antonio Nogueira)
Anouilh, Jean (Marie Lucien Pierre) 1910-1987 **CLC 1, 3, 8, 13, 40, 50; DAM DRAM; DC 8**
See also CA 17-20R; 123; CANR 32; MTCW
Anthony, Florence

See Ai
Anthony, John
See Ciardi, John (Anthony)
Anthony, Peter
See Shaffer, Anthony (Joshua); Shaffer, Peter (Levin)
Anthony, Piers 1934- .... **CLC 35; DAM POP**
See also AAYA 11; CA 21-24R; CANR 28, 56; DLB 8; MTCW; SAAS 22; SATA 84
Antoine, Marc
See Proust, (Valentin-Louis-George-Eugene-) Marcel
Antoninus, Brother
See Everson, William (Oliver)
Antonioni, Michelangelo 1912- .... **CLC 20**
See also CA 73-76; CANR 45
Antschel, Paul 1920-1970
See Celan, Paul
See also CA 85-88; CANR 33, 61; MTCW
Anwar, Chairil 1922-1949 .... **TCLC 22**
See also CA 121
Apollinaire, Guillaume 1880-1918**TCLC 3, 8, 51; DAM POET; PC 7**
See also Kostrowitzki, Wilhelm Apollinaris de
See also CA 152
Appelfeld, Aharon 1932- .... **CLC 23, 47**
See also CA 112; 133
Apple, Max (Isaac) 1941- .... **CLC 9, 33**
See also CA 81-84; CANR 19, 54; DLB 130
Appleman, Philip (Dean) 1926- .... **CLC 51**
See also CA 13-16R; CAAS 18; CANR 6, 29, 56
Appleton, Lawrence
See Lovecraft, H(oward) P(hillips)
Apteryx
See Eliot, T(homas) S(tearns)
Apuleius, (Lucius Madaurensis) 125(?)-175(?) **CMLC 1**
Aquin, Hubert 1929-1977 .... **CLC 15**
See also CA 105; DLB 53
Aragon, Louis 1897-1982**CLC 3, 22; DAM NOV, POET**
See also CA 69-72; 108; CANR 28; DLB 72; MTCW
Arany, Janos 1817-1882 .... **NCLC 34**
Arbuthnot, John 1667-1735 .... **LC 1**
See also DLB 101
Archer, Herbert Winslow
See Mencken, H(enry) L(ouis)
Archer, Jeffrey (Howard) 1940- . **CLC 28; DAM POP**
See also AAYA 16; BEST 89:3; CA 77-80; CANR 22, 52; INT CANR-22
Archer, Jules 1915- .... **CLC 12**
See also CA 9-12R; CANR 6; SAAS 5; SATA 4, 85
Archer, Lee
See Ellison, Harlan (Jay)
Arden, John 1930- **CLC 6, 13, 15; DAM DRAM**
See also CA 13-16R; CAAS 4; CANR 31; DLB 13; MTCW
Arenas, Reinaldo 1943-1990**CLC 41; DAM MULT; HLC**
See also CA 124; 128; 133; DLB 145; HW
Arendt, Hannah 1906-1975 .... **CLC 66, 98**
See also CA 17-20R; 61-64; CANR 26, 60; MTCW
Aretino, Pietro 1492-1556 .... **LC 12**
Arghezi, Tudor .... **CLC 80**
See also Theodorescu, Ion N.
Arguedas, Jose Maria 1911-1969 .... **CLC 10, 18**
See also CA 89-92; DLB 113; HW
Argueta, Manlio 1936- .... **CLC 31**
See also CA 131; DLB 145; HW
Ariosto, Ludovico 1474-1533 .... **LC 6**
Aristides
See Epstein, Joseph
Aristophanes 450B.C.-385B.C. .... **CMLC 4; DA; DAB; DAC; DAM DRAM, MST; DC 2; WLCS**
See also DLB 176
Arlt, Roberto (Godofredo Christophersen) 1900-1942 .... **TCLC 29; DAM MULT; HLC**
See also CA 123; 131; HW
Armah, Ayi Kwei 1939- . **CLC 5, 33; BLC; DAM MULT, POET**
See also BW 1; CA 61-64; CANR 21, 64; DLB 117; MTCW
Armatrading, Joan 1950- .... **CLC 17**
See also CA 114
Arnette, Robert
See Silverberg, Robert
Arnim, Achim von (Ludwig Joachim von Arnim) 1781-1831 .... **NCLC 5; SSC 29**
See also DLB 90
Arnim, Bettina von 1785-1859 .... **NCLC 38**
See also DLB 90
Arnold, Matthew 1822-1888 .... **NCLC 6, 29; DA; DAB; DAC; DAM MST, POET; PC 5; WLC**
See also CDBLB 1832-1890; DLB 32, 57
Arnold, Thomas 1795-1842 .... **NCLC 18**
See also DLB 55
Arnow, Harriette (Louisa) Simpson 1908-1986 **CLC 2, 7, 18**
See also CA 9-12R; 118; CANR 14; DLB 6; MTCW; SATA 42; SATA-Obit 47
Arp, Hans
See Arp, Jean
Arp, Jean 1887-1966 .... **CLC 5**
See also CA 81-84; 25-28R; CANR 42
Arrabal
See Arrabal, Fernando
Arrabal, Fernando 1932- .... **CLC 2, 9, 18, 58**
See also CA 9-12R; CANR 15
Arrick, Fran .... **CLC 30**
See also Gaberman, Judie Angell
Artaud, Antonin (Marie Joseph) 1896-1948**TCLC 3, 36; DAM DRAM**
See also CA 104; 149
Arthur, Ruth M(abel) 1905-1979 .... **CLC 12**
See also CA 9-12R; 85-88; CANR 4; SATA 7, 26
Artsybashev, Mikhail (Petrovich) 1878-1927 **TCLC 31**
Arundel, Honor (Morfydd) 1919-1973 ... **CLC 17**
See also CA 21-22; 41-44R; CAP 2; CLR 35; SATA 4; SATA-Obit 24
Arzner, Dorothy 1897-1979 .... **CLC 98**
Asch, Sholem 1880-1957 .... **TCLC 3**
See also CA 105
Ash, Shalom
See Asch, Sholem
Ashbery, John (Lawrence) 1927-**CLC 2, 3, 4, 6, 9, 13, 15, 25, 41, 77; DAM POET**
See also CA 5-8R; CANR 9, 37; DLB 5, 165; DLBY 81; INT CANR-9; MTCW
Ashdown, Clifford
See Freeman, R(ichard) Austin
Ashe, Gordon
See Creasey, John
Ashton-Warner, Sylvia (Constance) 1908-1984 **CLC 19**
See also CA 69-72; 112; CANR 29; MTCW
Asimov, Isaac 1920-1992 **CLC 1, 3, 9, 19, 26, 76, 92; DAM POP**
See also AAYA 13; BEST 90:2; CA 1-4R; 137; CANR 2, 19, 36, 60; CLR 12; DLB 8; DLBY 92; INT CANR-19; JRDA; MAICYA; MTCW; SATA 1, 26, 74
Assis, Joaquim Maria Machado de
See Machado de Assis, Joaquim Maria
Astley, Thea (Beatrice May) 1925- .... **CLC 41**
See also CA 65-68; CANR 11, 43
Aston, James
See White, T(erence) H(anbury)
Asturias, Miguel Angel 1899-1974**CLC 3, 8, 13; DAM MULT, NOV; HLC**
See also CA 25-28; 49-52; CANR 32; CAP 2; DLB 113; HW; MTCW
Atares, Carlos Saura
See Saura (Atares), Carlos
Atheling, William
See Pound, Ezra (Weston Loomis)
Atheling, William, Jr.
See Blish, James (Benjamin)
Atherton, Gertrude (Franklin Horn) 1857-1948 **TCLC 2**
See also CA 104; 155; DLB 9, 78, 186
Atherton, Lucius
See Masters, Edgar Lee
Atkins, Jack
See Harris, Mark
Atkinson, Kate .... **CLC 99**
Attaway, William (Alexander) 1911-1986**CLC 92; BLC; DAM MULT**
See also BW 2; CA 143; DLB 76
Atticus
See Fleming, Ian (Lancaster)
Atwood, Margaret (Eleanor) 1939-**CLC 2, 3, 4, 8, 13, 15, 25, 44, 84; DA; DAB; DAC; DAM MST, NOV, POET; PC 8; SSC 2; WLC**
See also AAYA 12; BEST 89:2; CA 49-52; CANR 3, 24, 33, 59; DLB 53; INT CANR-24; MTCW; SATA 50
Aubigny, Pierre d'
See Mencken, H(enry) L(ouis)
Aubin, Penelope 1685-1731(?) .... **LC 9**
See also DLB 39
Auchincloss, Louis (Stanton) 1917- **CLC 4, 6, 9, 18, 45; DAM NOV; SSC 22**
See also CA 1-4R; CANR 6, 29, 55; DLB 2; DLBY 80; INT CANR-29; MTCW
Auden, W(ystan) H(ugh) 1907-1973**CLC 1, 2, 3, 4, 6, 9, 11, 14, 43; DA; DAB; DAC; DAM DRAM, MST, POET; PC 1; WLC**
See also AAYA 18; CA 9-12R; 45-48; CANR 5, 61; CDBLB 1914-1945; DLB 10, 20; MTCW
Audiberti, Jacques 1900-1965 .... **CLC 38; DAM DRAM**
See also CA 25-28R
Audubon, John James 1785-1851 .... **NCLC 47**
Auel, Jean M(arie) 1936-**CLC 31, 107; DAM POP**
See also AAYA 7; BEST 90:4; CA 103; CANR 21, 64; INT CANR-21; SATA 91
Auerbach, Erich 1892-1957 .... **TCLC 43**
See also CA 118; 155
Augier, Emile 1820-1889 .... **NCLC 31**
August, John
See De Voto, Bernard (Augustine)
Augustine, St. 354-430 .... **CMLC 6; DAB**
Aurelius
See Bourne, Randolph S(illiman)
Aurobindo, Sri 1872-1950 .... **TCLC 63**
Austen, Jane 1775-1817**NCLC 1, 13, 19, 33, 51; DA; DAB; DAC; DAM MST, NOV; WLC**
See also AAYA 19; CDBLB 1789-1832; DLB 116
Auster, Paul 1947- .... **CLC 47**
See also CA 69-72; CANR 23, 52
Austin, Frank
See Faust, Frederick (Schiller)
Austin, Mary (Hunter) 1868-1934 .... **TCLC 25**
See also CA 109; DLB 9, 78
Autran Dourado, Waldomiro

See also CA 143; CDBLB 1890-1914; DLB 18, 57, 174
Butler, Walter C.
See Faust, Frederick (Schiller)
Butor, Michel (Marie Francois) 1926- **CLC 1, 3, 8, 11, 15**
See also CA 9-12R; CANR 33; DLB 83; MTCW
Butts, Mary 1892(?)-1937 .... **TCLC 77**
See also CA 148
Buzo, Alexander (John) 1944- .... **CLC 61**
See also CA 97-100; CANR 17, 39
Buzzati, Dino 1906-1972 .... **CLC 36**
See also CA 160; 33-36R; DLB 177
Byars, Betsy (Cromer) 1928- .... **CLC 35**
See also AAYA 19; CA 33-36R; CANR 18, 36, 57; CLR 1, 16; DLB 52; INT CANR-18; JRDA; MAICYA; MTCW; SAAS 1; SATA 4, 46, 80
Byatt, A(ntonia) S(usan Drabble) 1936- **CLC 19, 65; DAM NOV, POP**
See also CA 13-16R; CANR 13, 33, 50; DLB 14; MTCW
Byrne, David 1952- .... **CLC 26**
See also CA 127
Byrne, John Keyes 1926-
See Leonard, Hugh
See also CA 102; INT 102
Byron, George Gordon (Noel) 1788-1824**NCLC 2, 12; DA; DAB; DAC; DAM MST, POET; PC 16; WLC**
See also CDBLB 1789-1832; DLB 96, 110
Byron, Robert 1905-1941 .... **TCLC 67**
See also CA 160
C. 3. 3.
See Wilde, Oscar (Fingal O'Flahertie Wills)
Caballero, Fernan 1796-1877 .... **NCLC 10**
Cabell, Branch
See Cabell, James Branch
Cabell, James Branch 1879-1958 .... **TCLC 6**
See also CA 105; 152; DLB 9, 78
Cable, George Washington 1844-1925 . **TCLC 4; SSC 4**
See also CA 104; 155; DLB 12, 74; DLBD 13
Cabral de Melo Neto, Joao 1920- **CLC 76; DAM MULT**
See also CA 151
Cabrera Infante, G(uillermo) 1929- . **CLC 5, 25, 45; DAM MULT; HLC**
See also CA 85-88; CANR 29; DLB 113; HW; MTCW
Cade, Toni
See Bambara, Toni Cade
Cadmus and Harmonia
See Buchan, John
Caedmon fl. 658-680 .... **CMLC 7**
See also DLB 146
Caeiro, Alberto
See Pessoa, Fernando (Antonio Nogueira)
Cage, John (Milton, Jr.) 1912- .... **CLC 41**
See also CA 13-16R; CANR 9; INT CANR-9
Cahan, Abraham 1860-1951 .... **TCLC 71**
See also CA 108; 154; DLB 9, 25, 28
Cain, G.
See Cabrera Infante, G(uillermo)
Cain, Guillermo
See Cabrera Infante, G(uillermo)
Cain, James M(allahan) 1892-1977**CLC 3, 11, 28**
See also AITN 1; CA 17-20R; 73-76; CANR 8, 34, 61; MTCW
Caine, Mark
See Raphael, Frederic (Michael)
Calasso, Roberto 1941- .... **CLC 81**
See also CA 143
Calderon de la Barca, Pedro 1600-1681 .. **LC 23; DC 3**
Caldwell, Erskine (Preston) 1903-1987**CLC 1, 8, 14, 50, 60; DAM NOV; SSC 19**
See also AITN 1; CA 1-4R; 121; CAAS 1; CANR 2, 33; DLB 9, 86; MTCW
Caldwell, (Janet Miriam) Taylor (Holland) 1900-1985 .... **CLC 2, 28, 39; DAM NOV, POP**
See also CA 5-8R; 116; CANR 5
Calhoun, John Caldwell 1782-1850 .... **NCLC 15**
See also DLB 3
Calisher, Hortense 1911- **CLC 2, 4, 8, 38; DAM NOV; SSC 15**
See also CA 1-4R; CANR 1, 22; DLB 2; INT CANR-22; MTCW
Callaghan, Morley Edward 1903-1990**CLC 3, 14, 41, 65; DAC; DAM MST**
See also CA 9-12R; 132; CANR 33; DLB 68; MTCW
Callimachus c. 305B.C.-c. 240B.C. ..... **CMLC 18**
See also DLB 176
Calvin, John 1509-1564 .... **LC 37**
Calvino, Italo 1923-1985**CLC 5, 8, 11, 22, 33, 39, 73; DAM NOV; SSC 3**
See also CA 85-88; 116; CANR 23, 61; MTCW
Cameron, Carey 1952- .... **CLC 59**
See also CA 135
Cameron, Peter 1959- .... **CLC 44**
See also CA 125; CANR 50
Campana, Dino 1885-1932 .... **TCLC 20**
See also CA 117; DLB 114
Campanella, Tommaso 1568-1639 .... **LC 32**
Campbell, John W(ood, Jr.) 1910-1971 .. **CLC 32**
See also CA 21-22; 29-32R; CANR 34; CAP 2; DLB 8; MTCW
Campbell, Joseph 1904-1987 .... **CLC 69**
See also AAYA 3; BEST 89:2; CA 1-4R; 124; CANR 3, 28, 61; MTCW
Campbell, Maria 1940- .... **CLC 85; DAC**
See also CA 102; CANR 54; NNAL
Campbell, (John) Ramsey 1946-**CLC 42; SSC 19**
See also CA 57-60; CANR 7; INT CANR-7
Campbell, (Ignatius) Roy (Dunnachie) 1901-1957 **TCLC 5**
See also CA 104; 155; DLB 20
Campbell, Thomas 1777-1844 .... **NCLC 19**
See also DLB 93; 144
Campbell, Wilfred .... **TCLC 9**
See also Campbell, William
Campbell, William 1858(?)-1918
See Campbell, Wilfred
See also CA 106; DLB 92
Campion, Jane .... **CLC 95**
See also CA 138
Campos, Alvaro de
See Pessoa, Fernando (Antonio Nogueira)
Camus, Albert 1913-1960 **CLC 1, 2, 4, 9, 11, 14, 32, 63, 69; DA; DAB; DAC; DAM DRAM, MST, NOV; DC 2; SSC 9; WLC**
See also CA 89-92; DLB 72; MTCW
Canby, Vincent 1924- .... **CLC 13**
See also CA 81-84
Cancale
See Desnos, Robert
Canetti, Elias 1905-1994 .. **CLC 3, 14, 25, 75, 86**
See also CA 21-24R; 146; CANR 23, 61; DLB 85, 124; MTCW
Canin, Ethan 1960- .... **CLC 55**
See also CA 131; 135
Cannon, Curt
See Hunter, Evan
Cape, Judith
See Page, P(atricia) K(athleen)
Capek, Karel 1890-1938 **TCLC 6, 37; DA; DAB; DAC; DAM DRAM, MST, NOV; DC 1; WLC**
See also CA 104; 140
Capote, Truman 1924-1984**CLC 1, 3, 8, 13, 19, 34, 38, 58; DA; DAB; DAC; DAM MST, NOV, POP; SSC 2; WLC**
See also CA 5-8R; 113; CANR 18, 62; CDALB 1941-1968; DLB 2; DLBY 80, 84; MTCW; SATA 91
Capra, Frank 1897-1991 .... **CLC 16**
See also CA 61-64; 135
Caputo, Philip 1941- .... **CLC 32**
See also CA 73-76; CANR 40
Caragiale, Ion Luca 1852-1912 .... **TCLC 76**
See also CA 157
Card, Orson Scott 1951- **CLC 44, 47, 50; DAM POP**
See also AAYA 11; CA 102; CANR 27, 47; INT CANR-27; MTCW; SATA 83
Cardenal, Ernesto 1925- . **CLC 31; DAM MULT, POET; HLC**
See also CA 49-52; CANR 2, 32; HW; MTCW
Cardozo, Benjamin N(athan) 1870-1938**TCLC 65**
See also CA 117
Carducci, Giosue (Alessandro Giuseppe) 1835-1907 .... **TCLC 32**
Carew, Thomas 1595(?)-1640 .... **LC 13**
See also DLB 126
Carey, Ernestine Gilbreth 1908- .... **CLC 17**
See also CA 5-8R; SATA 2
Carey, Peter 1943- .... **CLC 40, 55, 96**
See also CA 123; 127; CANR 53; INT 127; MTCW; SATA 94
Carleton, William 1794-1869 .... **NCLC 3**
See also DLB 159
Carlisle, Henry (Coffin) 1926- .... **CLC 33**
See also CA 13-16R; CANR 15
Carlsen, Chris
See Holdstock, Robert P.
Carlson, Ron(ald F.) 1947- .... **CLC 54**
See also CA 105; CANR 27
Carlyle, Thomas 1795-1881**NCLC 22; DA; DAB; DAC; DAM MST**
See also CDBLB 1789-1832; DLB 55; 144
Carman, (William) Bliss 1861-1929**TCLC 7; DAC**
See also CA 104; 152; DLB 92
Carnegie, Dale 1888-1955 .... **TCLC 53**
Carossa, Hans 1878-1956 .... **TCLC 48**
See also DLB 66
Carpenter, Don(ald Richard) 1931-1995 **CLC 41**
See also CA 45-48; 149; CANR 1
Carpentier (y Valmont), Alejo 1904-1980 **CLC 8, 11, 38; DAM MULT; HLC**
See also CA 65-68; 97-100; CANR 11; DLB 113; HW
Carr, Caleb 1955(?)- .... **CLC 86**
See also CA 147
Carr, Emily 1871-1945 .... **TCLC 32**
See also CA 159; DLB 68
Carr, John Dickson 1906-1977 .... **CLC 3**
See also Fairbairn, Roger
See also CA 49-52; 69-72; CANR 3, 33, 60; MTCW
Carr, Philippa
See Hibbert, Eleanor Alice Burford
Carr, Virginia Spencer 1929- .... **CLC 34**
See also CA 61-64; DLB 111
Carrere, Emmanuel 1957- .... **CLC 89**
Carrier, Roch 1937- ... **CLC 13, 78; DAC; DAM MST**
See also CA 130; CANR 61; DLB 53
Carroll, James P. 1943(?)- .... **CLC 38**
See also CA 81-84
Carroll, Jim 1951- .... **CLC 35**
See also AAYA 17; CA 45-48; CANR 42

See also DLB 7, 44; DLBY 81
Chayefsky, Sidney 1923-1981
See Chayefsky, Paddy
See also CA 9-12R; 104; CANR 18; DAM DRAM
Chedid, Andree 1920- .... **CLC 47**
See also CA 145
Cheever, John 1912-1982**CLC 3, 7, 8, 11, 15, 25, 64; DA; DAB; DAC; DAM MST, NOV, POP; SSC 1; WLC**
See also CA 5-8R; 106; CABS 1; CANR 5, 27; CDALB 1941-1968; DLB 2, 102; DLBY 80, 82; INT CANR-5; MTCW
Cheever, Susan 1943- .... **CLC 18, 48**
See also CA 103; CANR 27, 51; DLBY 82; INT CANR-27
Chekhonte, Antosha
See Chekhov, Anton (Pavlovich)
Chekhov, Anton (Pavlovich) 1860-1904 **TCLC 3, 10, 31, 55; DA; DAB; DAC; DAM DRAM, MST; SSC 2, 28; WLC**
See also CA 104; 124; SATA 90
Chernyshevsky, Nikolay Gavrilovich 1828-1889 **NCLC 1**
Cherry, Carolyn Janice 1942-
See Cherryh, C. J.
See also CA 65-68; CANR 10
Cherryh, C. J. .... **CLC 35**
See also Cherry, Carolyn Janice
See also DLBY 80; SATA 93
Chesnutt, Charles W(addell) 1858-1932**TCLC 5, 39; BLC; DAM MULT; SSC 7**
See also BW 1; CA 106; 125; DLB 12, 50, 78; MTCW
Chester, Alfred 1929(?)-1971 .... **CLC 49**
See also CA 33-36R; DLB 130
Chesterton, G(ilbert) K(eith) 1874-1936**TCLC 1, 6, 64; DAM NOV, POET; SSC 1**
See also CA 104; 132; CDBLB 1914-1945; DLB 10, 19, 34, 70, 98, 149, 178; MTCW; SATA 27
Chiang Pin-chin 1904-1986
See Ding Ling
See also CA 118
Ch'ien Chung-shu 1910- .... **CLC 22**
See also CA 130; MTCW
Child, L. Maria
See Child, Lydia Maria
Child, Lydia Maria 1802-1880 .... **NCLC 6**
See also DLB 1, 74; SATA 67
Child, Mrs.
See Child, Lydia Maria
Child, Philip 1898-1978 .... **CLC 19, 68**
See also CA 13-14; CAP 1; SATA 47
Childers, (Robert) Erskine 1870-1922 **TCLC 65**
See also CA 113; 153; DLB 70
Childress, Alice 1920-1994 **CLC 12, 15, 86, 96; BLC; DAM DRAM, MULT, NOV; DC 4**
See also AAYA 8; BW 2; CA 45-48; 146; CANR 3, 27, 50; CLR 14; DLB 7, 38; JRDA; MAICYA; MTCW; SATA 7, 48, 81
Chin, Frank (Chew, Jr.) 1940- .... **DC 7**
See also CA 33-36R; DAM MULT
Chislett, (Margaret) Anne 1943- .... **CLC 34**
See also CA 151
Chitty, Thomas Willes 1926- .... **CLC 11**
See also Hinde, Thomas
See also CA 5-8R
Chivers, Thomas Holley 1809-1858 .... **NCLC 49**
See also DLB 3
Chomette, Rene Lucien 1898-1981
See Clair, Rene
See also CA 103
Chopin, KateTCLC 5, 14; DA; DAB; SSC 8; WLCS**
See also Chopin, Katherine
See also CDALB 1865-1917; DLB 12, 78
Chopin, Katherine 1851-1904
See Chopin, Kate
See also CA 104; 122; DAC; DAM MST, NOV
Chretien de Troyes c. 12th cent. - ...... **CMLC 10**
Christie
See Ichikawa, Kon
Christie, Agatha (Mary Clarissa) 1890-1976**CLC 1, 6, 8, 12, 39, 48; DAB; DAC; DAM NOV**
See also AAYA 9; AITN 1, 2; CA 17-20R; 61-64; CANR 10, 37; CDBLB 1914-1945; DLB 13, 77; MTCW; SATA 36
Christie, (Ann) Philippa
See Pearce, Philippa
See also CA 5-8R; CANR 4
Christine de Pizan 1365(?)-1431(?) .... **LC 9**
Chubb, Elmer
See Masters, Edgar Lee
Chulkov, Mikhail Dmitrievich 1743-1792 .. **LC 2**
See also DLB 150
Churchill, Caryl 1938- .... **CLC 31, 55; DC 5**
See also CA 102; CANR 22, 46; DLB 13; MTCW
Churchill, Charles 1731-1764 .... **LC 3**
See also DLB 109
Chute, Carolyn 1947- .... **CLC 39**
See also CA 123
Ciardi, John (Anthony) 1916-1986 . **CLC 10, 40, 44; DAM POET**
See also CA 5-8R; 118; CAAS 2; CANR 5, 33; CLR 19; DLB 5; DLBY 86; INT CANR-5; MAICYA; MTCW; SATA 1, 65; SATA-Obit 46
Cicero, Marcus Tullius 106B.C.-43B.C. **CMLC 3**
Cimino, Michael 1943- .... **CLC 16**
See also CA 105
Cioran, E(mil) M. 1911-1995 .... **CLC 64**
See also CA 25-28R; 149
Cisneros, Sandra 1954- . **CLC 69; DAM MULT; HLC**
See also AAYA 9; CA 131; CANR 64; DLB 122, 152; HW
Cixous, Helene 1937- .... **CLC 92**
See also CA 126; CANR 55; DLB 83; MTCW
Clair, Rene .... **CLC 20**
See also Chomette, Rene Lucien
Clampitt, Amy 1920-1994 .... **CLC 32; PC 19**
See also CA 110; 146; CANR 29; DLB 105
Clancy, Thomas L., Jr. 1947-
See Clancy, Tom
See also CA 125; 131; CANR 62; INT 131; MTCW
Clancy, Tom .... **CLC 45; DAM NOV, POP**
See also Clancy, Thomas L., Jr.
See also AAYA 9; BEST 89:1, 90:1
Clare, John 1793-1864**NCLC 9; DAB; DAM POET**
See also DLB 55, 96
Clarin
See Alas (y Urena), Leopoldo (Enrique Garcia)
Clark, Al C.
See Goines, Donald
Clark, (Robert) Brian 1932- .... **CLC 29**
See also CA 41-44R
Clark, Curt
See Westlake, Donald E(dwin)
Clark, Eleanor 1913-1996 .... **CLC 5, 19**
See also CA 9-12R; 151; CANR 41; DLB 6
Clark, J. P.
See Clark, John Pepper
See also DLB 117
Clark, John Pepper 1935- **CLC 38; BLC; DAM DRAM, MULT; DC 5**
See also Clark, J. P.
See also BW 1; CA 65-68; CANR 16
Clark, M. R.
See Clark, Mavis Thorpe
Clark, Mavis Thorpe 1909- .... **CLC 12**
See also CA 57-60; CANR 8, 37; CLR 30; MAICYA; SAAS 5; SATA 8, 74
Clark, Walter Van Tilburg 1909-1971 .. **CLC 28**
See also CA 9-12R; 33-36R; CANR 63; DLB 9; SATA 8
Clarke, Arthur C(harles) 1917-**CLC 1, 4, 13, 18, 35; DAM POP; SSC 3**
See also AAYA 4; CA 1-4R; CANR 2, 28, 55; JRDA; MAICYA; MTCW; SATA 13, 70
Clarke, Austin 1896-1974**CLC 6, 9; DAM POET**
See also CA 29-32; 49-52; CAP 2; DLB 10, 20
Clarke, Austin C(hesterfield) 1934- **CLC 8, 53; BLC; DAC; DAM MULT**
See also BW 1; CA 25-28R; CAAS 16; CANR 14, 32; DLB 53, 125
Clarke, Gillian 1937- .... **CLC 61**
See also CA 106; DLB 40
Clarke, Marcus (Andrew Hislop) 1846-1881 **NCLC 19**
Clarke, Shirley 1925- .... **CLC 16**
Clash, The
See Headon, (Nicky) Topper; Jones, Mick; Simonon, Paul; Strummer, Joe
Claudel, Paul (Louis Charles Marie) 1868-1955 **TCLC 2, 10**
See also CA 104
Clavell, James (duMaresq) 1925-1994**CLC 6, 25, 87; DAM NOV, POP**
See also CA 25-28R; 146; CANR 26, 48; MTCW
Cleaver, (Leroy) Eldridge 1935- . **CLC 30; BLC; DAM MULT**
See also BW 1; CA 21-24R; CANR 16
Cleese, John (Marwood) 1939- .... **CLC 21**
See also Monty Python
See also CA 112; 116; CANR 35; MTCW
Cleishbotham, Jebediah
See Scott, Walter
Cleland, John 1710-1789 .... **LC 2**
See also DLB 39
Clemens, Samuel Langhorne 1835-1910
See Twain, Mark
See also CA 104; 135; CDALB 1865-1917; DA; DAB; DAC; DAM MST, NOV; DLB 11, 12, 23, 64, 74, 186; JRDA; MAICYA; YABC 2
Cleophil
See Congreve, William
Clerihew, E.
See Bentley, E(dmund) C(lerihew)
Clerk, N. W.
See Lewis, C(live) S(taples)
Cliff, Jimmy .... **CLC 21**
See also Chambers, James
Clifton, (Thelma) Lucille 1936-**CLC 19, 66; BLC; DAM MULT, POET; PC 17**
See also BW 2; CA 49-52; CANR 2, 24, 42; CLR 5; DLB 5, 41; MAICYA; MTCW; SATA 20, 69
Clinton, Dirk
See Silverberg, Robert
Clough, Arthur Hugh 1819-1861 .... **NCLC 27**
See also DLB 32
Clutha, Janet Paterson Frame 1924-
See Frame, Janet
See also CA 1-4R; CANR 2, 36; MTCW
Clyne, Terence
See Blatty, William Peter
Cobalt, Martin
See Mayne, William (James Carter)
Cobb, Irvin S. 1876-1944 .... **TCLC 77**
See also DLB 11, 25, 86
Cobbett, William 1763-1835 .... **NCLC 49**
See also DLB 43, 107, 158

Domecq, H(onorio) Bustos
See Bioy Casares, Adolfo; Borges, Jorge Luis

Domini, Rey
See Lorde, Audre (Geraldine)

Dominique
See Proust, (Valentin-Louis-George-Eugene-) Marcel

Don, A
See Stephen, Leslie

Donaldson, Stephen R. 1947-**CLC 46; DAM POP**
See also CA 89-92; CANR 13, 55; INT CANR-13

Donleavy, J(ames) P(atrick) 1926- . **CLC 1, 4, 6, 10, 45**
See also AITN 2; CA 9-12R; CANR 24, 49, 62; DLB 6, 173; INT CANR-24; MTCW

Donne, John 1572-1631 ... **LC 10, 24; DA; DAB; DAC; DAM MST, POET; PC 1**
See also CDBLB Before 1660; DLB 121, 151

Donnell, David 1939(?)- .... **CLC 34**

Donoghue, P. S.
See Hunt, E(verette) Howard, (Jr.)

Donoso (Yanez), Jose 1924-1996**CLC 4, 8, 11, 32, 99; DAM MULT; HLC**
See also CA 81-84; 155; CANR 32; DLB 113; HW; MTCW

Donovan, John 1928-1992 .... **CLC 35**
See also AAYA 20; CA 97-100; 137; CLR 3; MAICYA; SATA 72; SATA-Brief 29

Don Roberto
See Cunninghame Graham, R(obert) B(ontine)

Doolittle, Hilda 1886-1961**CLC 3, 8, 14, 31, 34, 73; DA; DAC; DAM MST, POET; PC 5; WLC**
See also H. D.
See also CA 97-100; CANR 35; DLB 4, 45; MTCW

Dorfman, Ariel 1942- **CLC 48, 77; DAM MULT; HLC**
See also CA 124; 130; HW; INT 130

Dorn, Edward (Merton) 1929- .... **CLC 10, 18**
See also CA 93-96; CANR 42; DLB 5; INT 93-96

Dorsan, Luc
See Simenon, Georges (Jacques Christian)

Dorsange, Jean
See Simenon, Georges (Jacques Christian)

Dos Passos, John (Roderigo) 1896-1970**CLC 1, 4, 8, 11, 15, 25, 34, 82; DA; DAB; DAC; DAM MST, NOV; WLC**
See also CA 1-4R; 29-32R; CANR 3; CDALB 1929-1941; DLB 4, 9; DLBD 1, 15; DLBY 96; MTCW

Dossage, Jean
See Simenon, Georges (Jacques Christian)

Dostoevsky, Fedor Mikhailovich 1821-1881**NCLC 2, 7, 21, 33, 43; DA; DAB; DAC; DAM MST, NOV; SSC 2; WLC**

Doughty, Charles M(ontagu) 1843-1926**TCLC 27**
See also CA 115; DLB 19, 57, 174

Douglas, Ellen .... **CLC 73**
See also Haxton, Josephine Ayres; Williamson, Ellen Douglas

Douglas, Gavin 1475(?)-1522 .... **LC 20**

Douglas, George
See Brown, George Douglas

Douglas, Keith (Castellain) 1920-1944 **TCLC 40**
See also CA 160; DLB 27

Douglas, Leonard
See Bradbury, Ray (Douglas)

Douglas, Michael
See Crichton, (John) Michael

Douglas, Norman 1868-1952 .... **TCLC 68**

Douglas, William
See Brown, George Douglas

Douglass, Frederick 1817(?)-1895 **NCLC 7, 55; BLC; DA; DAC; DAM MST, MULT; WLC**
See also CDALB 1640-1865; DLB 1, 43, 50, 79; SATA 29

Dourado, (Waldomiro Freitas) Autran 1926-**CLC 23, 60**
See also CA 25-28R; CANR 34

Dourado, Waldomiro Autran
See Dourado, (Waldomiro Freitas) Autran

Dove, Rita (Frances) 1952-... **CLC 50, 81; DAM MULT, POET; PC 6**
See also BW 2; CA 109; CAAS 19; CANR 27, 42; DLB 120

Dowell, Coleman 1925-1985 .... **CLC 60**
See also CA 25-28R; 117; CANR 10; DLB 130

Dowson, Ernest (Christopher) 1867-1900**TCLC 4**
See also CA 105; 150; DLB 19, 135

Doyle, A. Conan
See Doyle, Arthur Conan

Doyle, Arthur Conan 1859-1930 ... **TCLC 7; DA; DAB; DAC; DAM MST, NOV; SSC 12; WLC**
See also AAYA 14; CA 104; 122; CDBLB 1890-1914; DLB 18, 70, 156, 178; MTCW; SATA 24

Doyle, Conan
See Doyle, Arthur Conan

Doyle, John
See Graves, Robert (von Ranke)

Doyle, Roddy 1958(?)- .... **CLC 81**
See also AAYA 14; CA 143

Doyle, Sir A. Conan
See Doyle, Arthur Conan

Doyle, Sir Arthur Conan
See Doyle, Arthur Conan

Dr. A
See Asimov, Isaac; Silverstein, Alvin

Drabble, Margaret 1939- **CLC 2, 3, 5, 8, 10, 22, 53; DAB; DAC; DAM MST, NOV, POP**
See also CA 13-16R; CANR 18, 35, 63; CDBLB 1960 to Present; DLB 14, 155; MTCW; SATA 48

Drapier, M. B.
See Swift, Jonathan

Drayham, James
See Mencken, H(enry) L(ouis)

Drayton, Michael 1563-1631 .... **LC 8**

Dreadstone, Carl
See Campbell, (John) Ramsey

Dreiser, Theodore (Herman Albert) 1871-1945 **TCLC 10, 18, 35; DA; DAC; DAM MST, NOV; WLC**
See also CA 106; 132; CDALB 1865-1917; DLB 9, 12, 102, 137; DLBD 1; MTCW

Drexler, Rosalyn 1926- .... **CLC 2, 6**
See also CA 81-84

Dreyer, Carl Theodor 1889-1968 .... **CLC 16**
See also CA 116

Drieu la Rochelle, Pierre(-Eugene) 1893-1945 **TCLC 21**
See also CA 117; DLB 72

Drinkwater, John 1882-1937 .... **TCLC 57**
See also CA 109; 149; DLB 10, 19, 149

Drop Shot
See Cable, George Washington

Droste-Hulshoff, Annette Freiin von 1797-1848 **NCLC 3**
See also DLB 133

Drummond, Walter
See Silverberg, Robert

Drummond, William Henry 1854-1907 **TCLC 25**
See also CA 160; DLB 92

Drummond de Andrade, Carlos 1902-1987 **CLC 18**
See also Andrade, Carlos Drummond de
See also CA 132; 123

Drury, Allen (Stuart) 1918- .... **CLC 37**
See also CA 57-60; CANR 18, 52; INT CANR-18

Dryden, John 1631-1700 .... **LC 3, 21; DA; DAB; DAC; DAM DRAM, MST, POET; DC 3; WLC**
See also CDBLB 1660-1789; DLB 80, 101, 131

Duberman, Martin (Bauml) 1930- .... **CLC 8**
See also CA 1-4R; CANR 2, 63

Dubie, Norman (Evans) 1945- .... **CLC 36**
See also CA 69-72; CANR 12; DLB 120

Du Bois, W(illiam) E(dward) B(urghardt) 1868-1963 **CLC 1, 2, 13, 64, 96; BLC; DA; DAC; DAM MST, MULT, NOV; WLC**
See also BW 1; CA 85-88; CANR 34; CDALB 1865-1917; DLB 47, 50, 91; MTCW; SATA 42

Dubus, Andre 1936- ... **CLC 13, 36, 97; SSC 15**
See also CA 21-24R; CANR 17; DLB 130; INT CANR-17

Duca Minimo
See D'Annunzio, Gabriele

Ducharme, Rejean 1941- .... **CLC 74**
See also DLB 60

Duclos, Charles Pinot 1704-1772 .... **LC 1**

Dudek, Louis 1918- .... **CLC 11, 19**
See also CA 45-48; CAAS 14; CANR 1; DLB 88

Duerrenmatt, Friedrich 1921-1990 . **CLC 1, 4, 8, 11, 15, 43, 102; DAM DRAM**
See also CA 17-20R; CANR 33; DLB 69, 124; MTCW

Duffy, Bruce (?)- .... **CLC 50**

Duffy, Maureen 1933- .... **CLC 37**
See also CA 25-28R; CANR 33; DLB 14; MTCW

Dugan, Alan 1923- .... **CLC 2, 6**
See also CA 81-84; DLB 5

du Gard, Roger Martin
See Martin du Gard, Roger

Duhamel, Georges 1884-1966 .... **CLC 8**
See also CA 81-84; 25-28R; CANR 35; DLB 65; MTCW

Dujardin, Edouard (Emile Louis) 1861-1949 **TCLC 13**
See also CA 109; DLB 123

Dulles, John Foster 1888-1959 .... **TCLC 72**
See also CA 115; 149

Dumas, Alexandre (Davy de la Pailleterie) 1802-1870**NCLC 11; DA; DAB; DAC; DAM MST, NOV; WLC**
See also DLB 119; SATA 18

Dumas, Alexandre 1824-1895 ..... **NCLC 9; DC 1**
See also AAYA 22

Dumas, Claudine
See Malzberg, Barry N(athaniel)

Dumas, Henry L. 1934-1968 .... **CLC 6, 62**
See also BW 1; CA 85-88; DLB 41

du Maurier, Daphne 1907-1989 .. **CLC 6, 11, 59; DAB; DAC; DAM MST, POP; SSC 18**
See also CA 5-8R; 128; CANR 6, 55; MTCW; SATA 27; SATA-Obit 60

Dunbar, Paul Laurence 1872-1906 . **TCLC 2, 12; BLC; DA; DAC; DAM MST, MULT, POET; PC 5; SSC 8; WLC**
See also BW 1; CA 104; 124; CDALB 1865-1917; DLB 50, 54, 78; SATA 34

Dunbar, William 1460(?)-1530(?) .... **LC 20**
See also DLB 132, 146

Duncan, Dora Angela
See Duncan, Isadora

Duncan, Isadora 1877(?)-1927 .... **TCLC 68**
See also CA 118; 149

Duncan, Lois 1934- .... **CLC 26**
See also AAYA 4; CA 1-4R; CANR 2, 23, 36; CLR 29; JRDA; MAICYA; SAAS 2; SATA 1, 36, 75

Duncan, Robert (Edward) 1919-1988 **CLC 1, 2, 4, 7, 15, 41, 55; DAM POET; PC 2**
See also CA 9-12R; 124; CANR 28, 62; DLB 5, 16;

Fo, Dario 1926- .... **CLC 32; DAM DRAM**
See also CA 116; 128; MTCW
Fogarty, Jonathan Titulescu Esq.
See Farrell, James T(homas)
Folke, Will
See Bloch, Robert (Albert)
Follett, Ken(neth Martin) 1949- . **CLC 18; DAM NOV, POP**
See also AAYA 6; BEST 89:4; CA 81-84; CANR 13, 33, 54; DLB 87; DLBY 81; INT CANR-33; MTCW
Fontane, Theodor 1819-1898 .... **NCLC 26**
See also DLB 129
Foote, Horton 1916- .. **CLC 51, 91; DAM DRAM**
See also CA 73-76; CANR 34, 51; DLB 26; INT CANR-34
Foote, Shelby 1916- .. **CLC 75; DAM NOV, POP**
See also CA 5-8R; CANR 3, 45; DLB 2, 17
Forbes, Esther 1891-1967 .... **CLC 12**
See also AAYA 17; CA 13-14; 25-28R; CAP 1; CLR 27; DLB 22; JRDA; MAICYA; SATA 2
Forche, Carolyn (Louise) 1950- **CLC 25, 83, 86; DAM POET; PC 10**
See also CA 109; 117; CANR 50; DLB 5; INT 117
Ford, Elbur
See Hibbert, Eleanor Alice Burford
Ford, Ford Madox 1873-1939 **TCLC 1, 15, 39, 57; DAM NOV**
See also CA 104; 132; CDBLB 1914-1945; DLB 162; MTCW
Ford, Henry 1863-1947 .... **TCLC 73**
See also CA 115; 148
Ford, John 1586-(?) .... **DC 8**
See also CDBLB Before 1660; DAM DRAM; DLB 58
Ford, John 1895-1973 .... **CLC 16**
See also CA 45-48
Ford, Richard .... **CLC 99**
Ford, Richard 1944- .... **CLC 46**
See also CA 69-72; CANR 11, 47
Ford, Webster
See Masters, Edgar Lee
Foreman, Richard 1937- .... **CLC 50**
See also CA 65-68; CANR 32, 63
Forester, C(ecil) S(cott) 1899-1966 .... **CLC 35**
See also CA 73-76; 25-28R; SATA 13
Forez
See Mauriac, Francois (Charles)
Forman, James Douglas 1932- .... **CLC 21**
See also AAYA 17; CA 9-12R; CANR 4, 19, 42; JRDA; MAICYA; SATA 8, 70
Fornes, Maria Irene 1930- .... **CLC 39, 61**
See also CA 25-28R; CANR 28; DLB 7; HW; INT CANR-28; MTCW
Forrest, Leon (Richard) 1937-1997 .... **CLC 4**
See also BW 2; CA 89-92; 162; CAAS 7; CANR 25, 52; DLB 33
Forster, E(dward) M(organ) 1879-1970 **CLC 1, 2, 3, 4, 9, 10, 13, 15, 22, 45, 77; DA; DAB; DAC; DAM MST, NOV; SSC 27; WLC**
See also AAYA 2; CA 13-14; 25-28R; CANR 45; CAP 1; CDBLB 1914-1945; DLB 34, 98, 162, 178; DLBD 10; MTCW; SATA 57
Forster, John 1812-1876 .... **NCLC 11**
See also DLB 144, 184
Forsyth, Frederick 1938- .... **CLC 2, 5, 36; DAM NOV, POP**
See also BEST 89:4; CA 85-88; CANR 38, 62; DLB 87; MTCW
Forten, Charlotte L. .... **TCLC 16; BLC**
See also Grimke, Charlotte L(ottie) Forten
See also DLB 50
Foscolo, Ugo 1778-1827 .... **NCLC 8**
Fosse, Bob .... **CLC 20**
See also Fosse, Robert Louis
Fosse, Robert Louis 1927-1987
See Fosse, Bob
See also CA 110; 123
Foster, Stephen Collins 1826-1864 .... **NCLC 26**
Foucault, Michel 1926-1984 ...... **CLC 31, 34, 69**
See also CA 105; 113; CANR 34; MTCW
Fouque, Friedrich (Heinrich Karl) de la Motte 1777-1843 .... **NCLC 2**
See also DLB 90
Fourier, Charles 1772-1837 .... **NCLC 51**
Fournier, Henri Alban 1886-1914
See Alain-Fournier
See also CA 104
Fournier, Pierre 1916- .... **CLC 11**
See also Gascar, Pierre
See also CA 89-92; CANR 16, 40
Fowles, John 1926- **CLC 1, 2, 3, 4, 6, 9, 10, 15, 33, 87; DAB; DAC; DAM MST**
See also CA 5-8R; CANR 25; CDBLB 1960 to Present; DLB 14, 139; MTCW; SATA 22
Fox, Paula 1923- .... **CLC 2, 8**
See also AAYA 3; CA 73-76; CANR 20, 36, 62; CLR 1, 44; DLB 52; JRDA; MAICYA; MTCW; SATA 17, 60
Fox, William Price (Jr.) 1926- .... **CLC 22**
See also CA 17-20R; CAAS 19; CANR 11; DLB 2; DLBY 81
Foxe, John 1516(?)-1587 .... **LC 14**
Frame, Janet 1924- **CLC 2, 3, 6, 22, 66, 96; SSC 29**
See also Clutha, Janet Paterson Frame
France, Anatole .... **TCLC 9**
See also Thibault, Jacques Anatole Francois
See also DLB 123
Francis, Claude 19(?)- .... **CLC 50**
Francis, Dick 1920- . **CLC 2, 22, 42, 102; DAM POP**
See also AAYA 5, 21; BEST 89:3; CA 5-8R; CANR 9, 42; CDBLB 1960 to Present; DLB 87; INT CANR-9; MTCW
Francis, Robert (Churchill) 1901-1987 **CLC 15**
See also CA 1-4R; 123; CANR 1
Frank, Anne(lies Marie) 1929-1945 **TCLC 17; DA; DAB; DAC; DAM MST; WLC**
See also AAYA 12; CA 113; 133; MTCW; SATA 87; SATA-Brief 42
Frank, Elizabeth 1945- .... **CLC 39**
See also CA 121; 126; INT 126
Frankl, Viktor E(mil) 1905-1997 .... **CLC 93**
See also CA 65-68; 161
Franklin, Benjamin
See Hasek, Jaroslav (Matej Frantisek)
Franklin, Benjamin 1706-1790 **LC 25; DA; DAB; DAC; DAM MST; WLCS**
See also CDALB 1640-1865; DLB 24, 43, 73
Franklin, (Stella Maraia Sarah) Miles 1879-1954 **TCLC 7**
See also CA 104
Fraser, (Lady) Antonia (Pakenham) 1932- **CLC 32, 107**
See also CA 85-88; CANR 44; MTCW; SATA-Brief 32
Fraser, George MacDonald 1925- .... **CLC 7**
See also CA 45-48; CANR 2, 48
Fraser, Sylvia 1935- .... **CLC 64**
See also CA 45-48; CANR 1, 16, 60
Frayn, Michael 1933- ... **CLC 3, 7, 31, 47; DAM DRAM, NOV**
See also CA 5-8R; CANR 30; DLB 13, 14; MTCW
Fraze, Candida (Merrill) 1945- .... **CLC 50**
See also CA 126
Frazer, J(ames) G(eorge) 1854-1941 ... **TCLC 32**
See also CA 118
Frazer, Robert Caine
See Creasey, John
Frazer, Sir James George
See Frazer, J(ames) G(eorge)
Frazier, Ian 1951- .... **CLC 46**
See also CA 130; CANR 54
Frederic, Harold 1856-1898 .... **NCLC 10**
See also DLB 12, 23; DLBD 13
Frederick, John
See Faust, Frederick (Schiller)
Frederick the Great 1712-1786 .... **LC 14**
Fredro, Aleksander 1793-1876 .... **NCLC 8**
Freeling, Nicolas 1927- .... **CLC 38**
See also CA 49-52; CAAS 12; CANR 1, 17, 50; DLB 87
Freeman, Douglas Southall 1886-1953 **TCLC 11**
See also CA 109; DLB 17
Freeman, Judith 1946- .... **CLC 55**
See also CA 148
Freeman, Mary Eleanor Wilkins 1852-1930 **TCLC 9; SSC 1**
See also CA 106; DLB 12, 78
Freeman, R(ichard) Austin 1862-1943 **TCLC 21**
See also CA 113; DLB 70
French, Albert 1943- .... **CLC 86**
French, Marilyn 1929- ... **CLC 10, 18, 60; DAM DRAM, NOV, POP**
See also CA 69-72; CANR 3, 31; INT CANR-31; MTCW
French, Paul
See Asimov, Isaac
Freneau, Philip Morin 1752-1832 .... **NCLC 1**
See also DLB 37, 43
Freud, Sigmund 1856-1939 .... **TCLC 52**
See also CA 115; 133; MTCW
Friedan, Betty (Naomi) 1921- .... **CLC 74**
See also CA 65-68; CANR 18, 45; MTCW
Friedlander, Saul 1932- .... **CLC 90**
See also CA 117; 130
Friedman, B(ernard) H(arper) 1926- ...... **CLC 7**
See also CA 1-4R; CANR 3, 48
Friedman, Bruce Jay 1930- .... **CLC 3, 5, 56**
See also CA 9-12R; CANR 25, 52; DLB 2, 28; INT CANR-25
Friel, Brian 1929- .... **CLC 5, 42, 59; DC 8**
See also CA 21-24R; CANR 33; DLB 13; MTCW
Friis-Baastad, Babbis Ellinor 1921-1970 **CLC 12**
See also CA 17-20R; 134; SATA 7
Frisch, Max (Rudolf) 1911-1991 **CLC 3, 9, 14, 18, 32, 44; DAM DRAM, NOV**
See also CA 85-88; 134; CANR 32; DLB 69, 124; MTCW
Fromentin, Eugene (Samuel Auguste) 1820-1876 **NCLC 10**
See also DLB 123
Frost, Frederick
See Faust, Frederick (Schiller)
Frost, Robert (Lee) 1874-1963 **CLC 1, 3, 4, 9, 10, 13, 15, 26, 34, 44; DA; DAB; DAC; DAM MST, POET; PC 1; WLC**
See also AAYA 21; CA 89-92; CANR 33; CDALB 1917-1929; DLB 54; DLBD 7; MTCW; SATA 14
Froude, James Anthony 1818-1894 .... **NCLC 43**
See also DLB 18, 57, 144
Froy, Herald
See Waterhouse, Keith (Spencer)
Fry, Christopher 1907- .... **CLC 2, 10, 14; DAM DRAM**
See also CA 17-20R; CAAS 23; CANR 9, 30; DLB 13; MTCW; SATA 66

Frye, (Herman) Northrop 1912-1991 **CLC 24, 70**
See also CA 5-8R; 133; CANR 8, 37; DLB 67, 68; MTCW
Fuchs, Daniel 1909-1993 .... **CLC 8, 22**
See also CA 81-84; 142; CAAS 5; CANR 40; DLB 9, 26, 28; DLBY 93
Fuchs, Daniel 1934- .... **CLC 34**
See also CA 37-40R; CANR 14, 48
Fuentes, Carlos 1928-**CLC 3, 8, 10, 13, 22, 41, 60; DA; DAB; DAC; DAM MST, MULT, NOV; HLC; SSC 24; WLC**
See also AAYA 4; AITN 2; CA 69-72; CANR 10, 32; DLB 113; HW; MTCW
Fuentes, Gregorio Lopez y
See Lopez y Fuentes, Gregorio
Fugard, (Harold) Athol 1932-**CLC 5, 9, 14, 25, 40, 80; DAM DRAM; DC 3**
See also AAYA 17; CA 85-88; CANR 32, 54; MTCW
Fugard, Sheila 1932-............................ **CLC 48**
See also CA 125
Fuller, Charles (H., Jr.) 1939-.... **CLC 25; BLC; DAM DRAM, MULT; DC 1**
See also BW 2; CA 108; 112; DLB 38; INT 112; MTCW
Fuller, John (Leopold) 1937- .... **CLC 62**
See also CA 21-24R; CANR 9, 44; DLB 40
Fuller, Margaret .... **NCLC 5, 50**
See also Ossoli, Sarah Margaret (Fuller marchesa d')
Fuller, Roy (Broadbent) 1912-1991 ... **CLC 4, 28**
See also CA 5-8R; 135; CAAS 10; CANR 53; DLB 15, 20; SATA 87
Fulton, Alice 1952-............................... **CLC 52**
See also CA 116; CANR 57
Furphy, Joseph 1843-1912 .... **TCLC 25**
Fussell, Paul 1924- .... **CLC 74**
See also BEST 90:1; CA 17-20R; CANR 8, 21, 35; INT CANR-21; MTCW
Futabatei, Shimei 1864-1909 .... **TCLC 44**
See also CA 162; DLB 180
Futrelle, Jacques 1875-1912 .... **TCLC 19**
See also CA 113; 155
Gaboriau, Emile 1835-1873 .... **NCLC 14**
Gadda, Carlo Emilio 1893-1973 .... **CLC 11**
See also CA 89-92; DLB 177
Gaddis, William 1922-**CLC 1, 3, 6, 8, 10, 19, 43, 86**
See also CA 17-20R; CANR 21, 48; DLB 2; MTCW
Gage, Walter
See Inge, William (Motter)
Gaines, Ernest J(ames) 1933-**CLC 3, 11, 18, 86; BLC; DAM MULT**
See also AAYA 18; AITN 1; BW 2; CA 9-12R; CANR 6, 24, 42; CDALB 1968-1988; DLB 2, 33, 152; DLBY 80; MTCW; SATA 86
Gaitskill, Mary 1954- .... **CLC 69**
See also CA 128; CANR 61
Galdos, Benito Perez
See Perez Galdos, Benito
Gale, Zona 1874-1938 ..... **TCLC 7; DAM DRAM**
See also CA 105; 153; DLB 9, 78
Galeano, Eduardo (Hughes) 1940-......... **CLC 72**
See also CA 29-32R; CANR 13, 32; HW
Galiano, Juan Valera y Alcala
See Valera y Alcala-Galiano, Juan
Gallagher, Tess 1943- **CLC 18, 63; DAM POET; PC 9**
See also CA 106; DLB 120
Gallant, Mavis 1922- **CLC 7, 18, 38; DAC; DAM MST; SSC 5**
See also CA 69-72; CANR 29; DLB 53; MTCW
Gallant, Roy A(rthur) 1924- .... **CLC 17**
See also CA 5-8R; CANR 4, 29, 54; CLR 30; MAICYA; SATA 4, 68
Gallico, Paul (William) 1897-1976 .... **CLC 2**
See also AITN 1; CA 5-8R; 69-72; CANR 23; DLB 9, 171; MAICYA; SATA 13
Gallo, Max Louis 1932- .... **CLC 95**
See also CA 85-88
Gallois, Lucien
See Desnos, Robert
Gallup, Ralph
See Whitemore, Hugh (John)
Galsworthy, John 1867-1933 .. **TCLC 1, 45; DA; DAB; DAC; DAM DRAM, MST, NOV; SSC 22; WLC 2**
See also CA 104; 141; CDBLB 1890-1914; DLB 10, 34, 98, 162; DLBD 16
Galt, John 1779-1839 .... **NCLC 1**
See also DLB 99, 116, 159
Galvin, James 1951- .... **CLC 38**
See also CA 108; CANR 26
Gamboa, Federico 1864-1939 .... **TCLC 36**
Gandhi, M. K.
See Gandhi, Mohandas Karamchand
Gandhi, Mahatma
See Gandhi, Mohandas Karamchand
Gandhi, Mohandas Karamchand 1869-1948**TCLC 59; DAM MULT**
See also CA 121; 132; MTCW
Gann, Ernest Kellogg 1910-1991 .... **CLC 23**
See also AITN 1; CA 1-4R; 136; CANR 1
Garcia, Cristina 1958- .... **CLC 76**
See also CA 141
Garcia Lorca, Federico 1898-1936**TCLC 1, 7, 49; DA; DAB; DAC; DAM DRAM, MST, MULT, POET; DC 2; HLC; PC 3; WLC**
See also CA 104; 131; DLB 108; HW; MTCW
Garcia Marquez, Gabriel (Jose) 1928- **CLC 2, 3, 8, 10, 15, 27, 47, 55, 68; DA; DAB; DAC; DAM MST, MULT, NOV, POP; HLC; SSC 8; WLC**
See also AAYA 3; BEST 89:1, 90:4; CA 33-36R; CANR 10, 28, 50; DLB 113; HW; MTCW
Gard, Janice
See Latham, Jean Lee
Gard, Roger Martin du
See Martin du Gard, Roger
Gardam, Jane 1928- .... **CLC 43**
See also CA 49-52; CANR 2, 18, 33, 54; CLR 12; DLB 14, 161; MAICYA; MTCW; SAAS 9; SATA 39, 76; SATA-Brief 28
Gardner, Herb(ert) 1934- .... **CLC 44**
See also CA 149
Gardner, John (Champlin), Jr. 1933-1982**CLC 2, 3, 5, 7, 8, 10, 18, 28, 34; DAM NOV, POP; SSC 7**
See also AITN 1; CA 65-68; 107; CANR 33; DLB 2; DLBY 82; MTCW; SATA 40; SATA-Obit 31
Gardner, John (Edmund) 1926- .. **CLC 30; DAM POP**
See also CA 103; CANR 15; MTCW
Gardner, Miriam
See Bradley, Marion Zimmer
Gardner, Noel
See Kuttner, Henry
Gardons, S. S.
See Snodgrass, W(illiam) D(e Witt)
Garfield, Leon 1921-1996 .... **CLC 12**
See also AAYA 8; CA 17-20R; 152; CANR 38, 41; CLR 21; DLB 161; JRDA; MAICYA; SATA 1, 32, 76; SATA-Obit 90
Garland, (Hannibal) Hamlin 1860-1940 **TCLC 3; SSC 18**
See also CA 104; DLB 12, 71, 78
Garneau, (Hector de) Saint-Denys 1912-1943 **TCLC 13**
See also CA 111; DLB 88
Garner, Alan 1934- .. **CLC 17; DAB; DAM POP**
See also AAYA 18; CA 73-76; CANR 15, 64; CLR 20; DLB 161; MAICYA; MTCW; SATA 18, 69
Garner, Hugh 1913-1979 .... **CLC 13**
See also CA 69-72; CANR 31; DLB 68
Garnett, David 1892-1981 .... **CLC 3**
See also CA 5-8R; 103; CANR 17; DLB 34
Garos, Stephanie
See Katz, Steve
Garrett, George (Palmer) 1929- . **CLC 3, 11, 51**
See also CA 1-4R; CAAS 5; CANR 1, 42; DLB 2, 5, 130, 152; DLBY 83
Garrick, David 1717-1779 . **LC 15; DAM DRAM**
See also DLB 84
Garrigue, Jean 1914-1972 .... **CLC 2, 8**
See also CA 5-8R; 37-40R; CANR 20
Garrison, Frederick
See Sinclair, Upton (Beall)
Garth, Will
See Hamilton, Edmond; Kuttner, Henry
Garvey, Marcus (Moziah, Jr.) 1887-1940 . **TCLC 41; BLC; DAM MULT**
See also BW 1; CA 120; 124
Gary, Romain .... **CLC 25**
See also Kacew, Romain
See also DLB 83
Gascar, Pierre .... **CLC 11**
See also Fournier, Pierre
Gascoyne, David (Emery) 1916- .... **CLC 45**
See also CA 65-68; CANR 10, 28, 54; DLB 20; MTCW
Gaskell, Elizabeth Cleghorn 1810-1865**NCLC 5; DAB; DAM MST; SSC 25**
See also CDBLB 1832-1890; DLB 21, 144, 159
Gass, William H(oward) 1924-**CLC 1, 2, 8, 11, 15, 39; SSC 12**
See also CA 17-20R; CANR 30; DLB 2; MTCW
Gasset, Jose Ortega y
See Ortega y Gasset, Jose
Gates, Henry Louis, Jr. 1950- .... **CLC 65; DAM MULT**
See also BW 2; CA 109; CANR 25, 53; DLB 67
Gautier, Theophile 1811-1872**NCLC 1, 59; DAM POET; PC 18; SSC 20**
See also DLB 119
Gawsworth, John
See Bates, H(erbert) E(rnest)
Gay, Oliver
See Gogarty, Oliver St. John
Gaye, Marvin (Penze) 1939-1984 .... **CLC 26**
See also CA 112
Gebler, Carlo (Ernest) 1954- .... **CLC 39**
See also CA 119; 133
Gee, Maggie (Mary) 1948- .... **CLC 57**
See also CA 130
Gee, Maurice (Gough) 1931- .... **CLC 29**
See also CA 97-100; SATA 46
Gelbart, Larry (Simon) 1923- .... **CLC 21, 61**
See also CA 73-76; CANR 45
Gelber, Jack 1932- .... **CLC 1, 6, 14, 79**
See also CA 1-4R; CANR 2; DLB 7
Gellhorn, Martha (Ellis) 1908- .... **CLC 14, 60**
See also CA 77-80; CANR 44; DLBY 82
Genet, Jean 1910-1986**CLC 1, 2, 5, 10, 14, 44, 46; DAM DRAM**
See also CA 13-16R; CANR 18; DLB 72; DLBY 86; MTCW
Gent, Peter 1942- .... **CLC 29**

See also AITN 1; CA 89-92; DLBY 82
Gentlewoman in New England, A
See Bradstreet, Anne
Gentlewoman in Those Parts, A
See Bradstreet, Anne
George, Jean Craighead 1919- .... **CLC 35**
See also AAYA 8; CA 5-8R; CANR 25; CLR 1; DLB 52; JRDA; MAICYA; SATA 2, 68
George, Stefan (Anton) 1868-1933 .. **TCLC 2, 14**
See also CA 104
Georges, Georges Martin
See Simenon, Georges (Jacques Christian)
Gerhardi, William Alexander
See Gerhardie, William Alexander
Gerhardie, William Alexander 1895-1977**CLC 5**
See also CA 25-28R; 73-76; CANR 18; DLB 36
Gerstler, Amy 1956-............................. **CLC 70**
See also CA 146
Gertler, T. .... **CLC 34**
See also CA 116; 121; INT 121
Ghalib .... **NCLC 39**
See also Ghalib, Hsadullah Khan
Ghalib, Hsadullah Khan 1797-1869
See Ghalib
See also DAM POET
Ghelderode, Michel de 1898-1962**CLC 6, 11; DAM DRAM**
See also CA 85-88; CANR 40
Ghiselin, Brewster 1903-...................... **CLC 23**
See also CA 13-16R; CAAS 10; CANR 13
Ghose, Zulfikar 1935-.......................... **CLC 42**
See also CA 65-68
Ghosh, Amitav 1956- .... **CLC 44**
See also CA 147
Giacosa, Giuseppe 1847-1906 .... **TCLC 7**
See also CA 104
Gibb, Lee
See Waterhouse, Keith (Spencer)
Gibbon, Lewis Grassic .... **TCLC 4**
See also Mitchell, James Leslie
Gibbons, Kaye 1960-..... **CLC 50, 88; DAM POP**
See also CA 151
Gibran, Kahlil 1883-1931**TCLC 1, 9; DAM POET, POP; PC 9**
See also CA 104; 150
Gibran, Khalil
See Gibran, Kahlil
Gibson, William 1914-**CLC 23; DA; DAB; DAC; DAM DRAM, MST**
See also CA 9-12R; CANR 9, 42; DLB 7; SATA 66
Gibson, William (Ford) 1948-**CLC 39, 63; DAM POP**
See also AAYA 12; CA 126; 133; CANR 52
Gide, Andre (Paul Guillaume) 1869-1951**TCLC 5, 12, 36; DA; DAB; DAC; DAM MST, NOV; SSC 13; WLC**
See also CA 104; 124; DLB 65; MTCW
Gifford, Barry (Colby) 1946-................. **CLC 34**
See also CA 65-68; CANR 9, 30, 40
Gilbert, Frank
See De Voto, Bernard (Augustine)
Gilbert, W(illiam) S(chwenck) 1836-1911 **TCLC 3; DAM DRAM, POET**
See also CA 104; SATA 36
Gilbreth, Frank B., Jr. 1911- .... **CLC 17**
See also CA 9-12R; SATA 2
Gilchrist, Ellen 1935- . **CLC 34, 48; DAM POP; SSC 14**
See also CA 113; 116; CANR 41, 61; DLB 130; MTCW
Giles, Molly 1942-................................. **CLC 39**
See also CA 126
Gill, Patrick
See Creasey, John
Gilliam, Terry (Vance) 1940- .... **CLC 21**
See also Monty Python
See also AAYA 19; CA 108; 113; CANR 35; INT 113
Gillian, Jerry
See Gilliam, Terry (Vance)
Gilliatt, Penelope (Ann Douglass) 1932-1993**CLC 2, 10, 13, 53**
See also AITN 2; CA 13-16R; 141; CANR 49; DLB 14
Gilman, Charlotte (Anna) Perkins (Stetson) 1860-1935 .... **TCLC 9, 37; SSC 13**
See also CA 106; 150
Gilmour, David 1949- .... **CLC 35**
See also CA 138, 147
Gilpin, William 1724-1804 .... **NCLC 30**
Gilray, J. D.
See Mencken, H(enry) L(ouis)
Gilroy, Frank D(aniel) 1925- .... **CLC 2**
See also CA 81-84; CANR 32, 64; DLB 7
Gilstrap, John 1957(?)- .... **CLC 99**
See also CA 160
Ginsberg, Allen 1926-1997 **CLC 1, 2, 3, 4, 6, 13, 36, 69; DA; DAB; DAC; DAM MST, POET; PC 4; WLC 3**
See also AITN 1; CA 1-4R; 157; CANR 2, 41, 63; CDALB 1941-1968; DLB 5, 16, 169; MTCW
Ginzburg, Natalia 1916-1991 . **CLC 5, 11, 54, 70**
See also CA 85-88; 135; CANR 33; DLB 177; MTCW
Giono, Jean 1895-1970 .... **CLC 4, 11**
See also CA 45-48; 29-32R; CANR 2, 35; DLB 72; MTCW
Giovanni, Nikki 1943-**CLC 2, 4, 19, 64; BLC; DA; DAB; DAC; DAM MST, MULT, POET; PC 19; WLCS**
See also AAYA 22; AITN 1; BW 2; CA 29-32R; CAAS 6; CANR 18, 41, 60; CLR 6; DLB 5, 41; INT CANR-18; MAICYA; MTCW; SATA 24
Giovene, Andrea 1904- .... **CLC 7**
See also CA 85-88
Gippius, Zinaida (Nikolayevna) 1869-1945
See Hippius, Zinaida
See also CA 106
Giraudoux, (Hippolyte) Jean 1882-1944**TCLC 2, 7; DAM DRAM**
See also CA 104; DLB 65
Gironella, Jose Maria 1917- .... **CLC 11**
See also CA 101
Gissing, George (Robert) 1857-1903**TCLC 3, 24, 47**
See also CA 105; DLB 18, 135, 184
Giurlani, Aldo
See Palazzeschi, Aldo
Gladkov, Fyodor (Vasilyevich) 1883-1958**TCLC 27**
Glanville, Brian (Lester) 1931- .... **CLC 6**
See also CA 5-8R; CAAS 9; CANR 3; DLB 15, 139; SATA 42
Glasgow, Ellen (Anderson Gholson) 1873(?)-1945 **TCLC 2, 7**
See also CA 104; DLB 9, 12
Glaspell, Susan 1882(?)-1948 .... **TCLC 55**
See also CA 110; 154; DLB 7, 9, 78; YABC 2
Glassco, John 1909-1981 .... **CLC 9**
See also CA 13-16R; 102; CANR 15; DLB 68
Glasscock, Amnesia
See Steinbeck, John (Ernst)
Glasser, Ronald J. 1940(?)- .... **CLC 37**
Glassman, Joyce
See Johnson, Joyce
Glendinning, Victoria 1937- .... **CLC 50**
See also CA 120; 127; CANR 59; DLB 155
Glissant, Edouard 1928-**CLC 10, 68; DAM MULT**
See also CA 153
Gloag, Julian 1930- .... **CLC 40**
See also AITN 1; CA 65-68; CANR 10
Glowacki, Aleksander
See Prus, Boleslaw
Gluck, Louise (Elisabeth) 1943-**CLC 7, 22, 44, 81; DAM POET; PC 16**
See also CA 33-36R; CANR 40; DLB 5
Glyn, Elinor 1864-1943 .... **TCLC 72**
See also DLB 153
Gobineau, Joseph Arthur (Comte) de 1816-1882 **NCLC 17**
See also DLB 123
Godard, Jean-Luc 1930- .... **CLC 20**
See also CA 93-96
Godden, (Margaret) Rumer 1907- .... **CLC 53**
See also AAYA 6; CA 5-8R; CANR 4, 27, 36, 55; CLR 20; DLB 161; MAICYA; SAAS 12; SATA 3, 36
Godoy Alcayaga, Lucila 1889-1957
See Mistral, Gabriela
See also BW 2; CA 104; 131; DAM MULT; HW; MTCW
Godwin, Gail (Kathleen) 1937- **CLC 5, 8, 22, 31, 69; DAM POP**
See also CA 29-32R; CANR 15, 43; DLB 6; INT CANR-15; MTCW
Godwin, William 1756-1836 .... **NCLC 14**
See also CDBLB 1789-1832; DLB 39, 104, 142, 158, 163
Goebbels, Josef
See Goebbels, (Paul) Joseph
Goebbels, (Paul) Joseph 1897-1945 ..... **TCLC 68**
See also CA 115; 148
Goebbels, Joseph Paul
See Goebbels, (Paul) Joseph
Goethe, Johann Wolfgang von 1749-1832**NCLC 4, 22, 34; DA; DAB; DAC; DAM DRAM, MST, POET; PC 5; WLC 3**
See also DLB 94
Gogarty, Oliver St. John 1878-1957 .... **TCLC 15**
See also CA 109; 150; DLB 15, 19
Gogol, Nikolai (Vasilyevich) 1809-1852**NCLC 5, 15, 31; DA; DAB; DAC; DAM DRAM, MST; DC 1; SSC 4, 29; WLC**
Goines, Donald 1937(?)-1974**CLC 80; BLC; DAM MULT, POP**
See also AITN 1; BW 1; CA 124; 114; DLB 33
Gold, Herbert 1924- .... **CLC 4, 7, 14, 42**
See also CA 9-12R; CANR 17, 45; DLB 2; DLBY 81
Goldbarth, Albert 1948- .... **CLC 5, 38**
See also CA 53-56; CANR 6, 40; DLB 120
Goldberg, Anatol 1910-1982 .... **CLC 34**
See also CA 131; 117
Goldemberg, Isaac 1945- .... **CLC 52**
See also CA 69-72; CAAS 12; CANR 11, 32; HW
Golding, William (Gerald) 1911-1993**CLC 1, 2, 3, 8, 10, 17, 27, 58, 81; DA; DAB; DAC; DAM MST, NOV; WLC**
See also AAYA 5; CA 5-8R; 141; CANR 13, 33, 54; CDBLB 1945-1960; DLB 15, 100; MTCW
Goldman, Emma 1869-1940 .... **TCLC 13**
See also CA 110; 150
Goldman, Francisco 1954- .... **CLC 76**
See also CA 162
Goldman, William (W.) 1931- .... **CLC 1, 48**
See also CA 9-12R; CANR 29; DLB 44
Goldmann, Lucien 1913-1970 .... **CLC 24**
See also CA 25-28; CAP 2
Goldoni, Carlo 1707-1793 .... **LC 4; DAM DRAM**

See also CA 25-28R; CAAS 10; CANR 11; SATA 36
Gregor, Lee
See Pohl, Frederik
Gregory, Isabella Augusta (Persse) 1852-1932 **TCLC 1**
See also CA 104; DLB 10
Gregory, J. Dennis
See Williams, John A(lfred)
Grendon, Stephen
See Derleth, August (William)
Grenville, Kate 1950- .... **CLC 61**
See also CA 118; CANR 53
Grenville, Pelham
See Wodehouse, P(elham) G(renville)
Greve, Felix Paul (Berthold Friedrich) 1879-1948
See Grove, Frederick Philip
See also CA 104; 141; DAC; DAM MST
Grey, Zane 1872-1939 .... **TCLC 6; DAM POP**
See also CA 104; 132; DLB 9; MTCW
Grieg, (Johan) Nordahl (Brun) 1902-1943 **TCLC 10**
See also CA 107
Grieve, C(hristopher) M(urray) 1892-1978 **CLC 11, 19; DAM POET**
See also MacDiarmid, Hugh; Pteleon
See also CA 5-8R; 85-88; CANR 33; MTCW
Griffin, Gerald 1803-1840 .... **NCLC 7**
See also DLB 159
Griffin, John Howard 1920-1980 .... **CLC 68**
See also AITN 1; CA 1-4R; 101; CANR 2
Griffin, Peter 1942- .... **CLC 39**
See also CA 136
Griffith, D(avid Lewelyn) W(ark) 1875(?)-1948 **TCLC 68**
See also CA 119; 150
Griffith, Lawrence
See Griffith, D(avid Lewelyn) W(ark)
Griffiths, Trevor 1935- .... **CLC 13, 52**
See also CA 97-100; CANR 45; DLB 13
Griggs, Sutton Elbert 1872-1930(?) .... **TCLC 77**
See also CA 123; DLB 50
Grigson, Geoffrey (Edward Harvey) 1905-1985 **CLC 7, 39**
See also CA 25-28R; 118; CANR 20, 33; DLB 27; MTCW
Grillparzer, Franz 1791-1872 .... **NCLC 1**
See also DLB 133
Grimble, Reverend Charles James
See Eliot, T(homas) S(tearns)
Grimke, Charlotte L(ottie) Forten 1837(?)-1914
See Forten, Charlotte L.
See also BW 1; CA 117; 124; DAM MULT, POET
Grimm, Jacob Ludwig Karl 1785-1863 . **NCLC 3**
See also DLB 90; MAICYA; SATA 22
Grimm, Wilhelm Karl 1786-1859 .... **NCLC 3**
See also DLB 90; MAICYA; SATA 22
Grimmelshausen, Johann Jakob Christoffel von 1621-1676 .... **LC 6**
See also DLB 168
Grindel, Eugene 1895-1952
See Eluard, Paul
See also CA 104
Grisham, John 1955- .... **CLC 84; DAM POP**
See also AAYA 14; CA 138; CANR 47
Grossman, David 1954- .... **CLC 67**
See also CA 138
Grossman, Vasily (Semenovich) 1905-1964 **CLC 41**
See also CA 124; 130; MTCW
Grove, Frederick Philip .... **TCLC 4**
See also Greve, Felix Paul (Berthold Friedrich)
See also DLB 92
Grubb
See Crumb, R(obert)
Grumbach, Doris (Isaac) 1918- . **CLC 13, 22, 64**
See also CA 5-8R; CAAS 2; CANR 9, 42; INT CANR-9
Grundtvig, Nicolai Frederik Severin 1783-1872 **NCLC 1**
Grunge
See Crumb, R(obert)
Grunwald, Lisa 1959- .... **CLC 44**
See also CA 120
Guare, John 1938- **CLC 8, 14, 29, 67; DAM DRAM**
See also CA 73-76; CANR 21; DLB 7; MTCW
Gudjonsson, Halldor Kiljan 1902-
See Laxness, Halldor
See also CA 103
Guenter, Erich
See Eich, Guenter
Guest, Barbara 1920- .... **CLC 34**
See also CA 25-28R; CANR 11, 44; DLB 5
Guest, Judith (Ann) 1936- **CLC 8, 30; DAM NOV, POP**
See also AAYA 7; CA 77-80; CANR 15; INT CANR-15; MTCW
Guevara, Che .... **CLC 87; HLC**
See also Guevara (Serna), Ernesto
Guevara (Serna), Ernesto 1928-1967
See Guevara, Che
See also CA 127; 111; CANR 56; DAM MULT; HW
Guild, Nicholas M. 1944- .... **CLC 33**
See also CA 93-96
Guillemin, Jacques
See Sartre, Jean-Paul
Guillen, Jorge 1893-1984 **CLC 11; DAM MULT, POET**
See also CA 89-92; 112; DLB 108; HW
Guillen, Nicolas (Cristobal) 1902-1989 **CLC 48, 79; BLC; DAM MST, MULT, POET; HLC**
See also BW 2; CA 116; 125; 129; HW
Guillevic, (Eugene) 1907- .... **CLC 33**
See also CA 93-96
Guillois
See Desnos, Robert
Guillois, Valentin
See Desnos, Robert
Guiney, Louise Imogen 1861-1920 ...... **TCLC 41**
See also CA 160; DLB 54
Guiraldes, Ricardo (Guillermo) 1886-1927 **TCLC 39**
See also CA 131; HW; MTCW
Gumilev, Nikolai Stepanovich 1886-1921 **TCLC 60**
Gunesekera, Romesh 1954- .... **CLC 91**
See also CA 159
Gunn, Bill .... **CLC 5**
See also Gunn, William Harrison
See also DLB 38
Gunn, Thom(son William) 1929- **CLC 3, 6, 18, 32, 81; DAM POET**
See also CA 17-20R; CANR 9, 33; CDBLB 1960 to Present; DLB 27; INT CANR-33; MTCW
Gunn, William Harrison 1934(?)-1989
See Gunn, Bill
See also AITN 1; BW 1; CA 13-16R; 128; CANR 12, 25
Gunnars, Kristjana 1948- .... **CLC 69**
See also CA 113; DLB 60
Gurdjieff, G(eorgei) I(vanovich) 1877(?)-1949 **TCLC 71**
See also CA 157
Gurganus, Allan 1947- ...... **CLC 70; DAM POP**
See also BEST 90:1; CA 135
Gurney, A(lbert) R(amsdell), Jr. 1930- **CLC 32, 50, 54; DAM DRAM**
See also CA 77-80; CANR 32, 64
Gurney, Ivor (Bertie) 1890-1937 .... **TCLC 33**
Gurney, Peter
See Gurney, A(lbert) R(amsdell), Jr.
Guro, Elena 1877-1913 .... **TCLC 56**
Gustafson, James M(oody) 1925- .... **CLC 100**
See also CA 25-28R; CANR 37
Gustafson, Ralph (Barker) 1909- .... **CLC 36**
See also CA 21-24R; CANR 8, 45; DLB 88
Gut, Gom
See Simenon, Georges (Jacques Christian)
Guterson, David 1956- .... **CLC 91**
See also CA 132
Guthrie, A(lfred) B(ertram), Jr. 1901-1991 **CLC 23**
See also CA 57-60; 134; CANR 24; DLB 6; SATA 62; SATA-Obit 67
Guthrie, Isobel
See Grieve, C(hristopher) M(urray)
Guthrie, Woodrow Wilson 1912-1967
See Guthrie, Woody
See also CA 113; 93-96
Guthrie, Woody .... **CLC 35**
See also Guthrie, Woodrow Wilson
Guy, Rosa (Cuthbert) 1928- .... **CLC 26**
See also AAYA 4; BW 2; CA 17-20R; CANR 14, 34; CLR 13; DLB 33; JRDA; MAICYA; SATA 14, 62
Gwendolyn
See Bennett, (Enoch) Arnold
H. D. .... **CLC 3, 8, 14, 31, 34, 73; PC 5**
See also Doolittle, Hilda
H. de V.
See Buchan, John
Haavikko, Paavo Juhani 1931- .... **CLC 18, 34**
See also CA 106
Habbema, Koos
See Heijermans, Herman
Habermas, Juergen 1929- .... **CLC 104**
See also CA 109
Habermas, Jurgen
See Habermas, Juergen
Hacker, Marilyn 1942- **CLC 5, 9, 23, 72, 91; DAM POET**
See also CA 77-80; DLB 120
Haggard, H(enry) Rider 1856-1925 ..... **TCLC 11**
See also CA 108; 148; DLB 70, 156, 174, 178; SATA 16
Hagiosy, L.
See Larbaud, Valery (Nicolas)
Hagiwara Sakutaro 1886-1942 **TCLC 60; PC 18**
Haig, Fenil
See Ford, Ford Madox
Haig-Brown, Roderick (Langmere) 1908-1976 **CLC 21**
See also CA 5-8R; 69-72; CANR 4, 38; CLR 31; DLB 88; MAICYA; SATA 12
Hailey, Arthur 1920- .. **CLC 5; DAM NOV, POP**
See also AITN 2; BEST 90:3; CA 1-4R; CANR 2, 36; DLB 88; DLBY 82; MTCW
Hailey, Elizabeth Forsythe 1938- .... **CLC 40**
See also CA 93-96; CAAS 1; CANR 15, 48; INT CANR-15
Haines, John (Meade) 1924- .... **CLC 58**
See also CA 17-20R; CANR 13, 34; DLB 5
Hakluyt, Richard 1552-1616 .... **LC 31**
Haldeman, Joe (William) 1943- .... **CLC 61**
See also CA 53-56; CAAS 25; CANR 6; DLB 8; INT CANR-6
Haley, Alex(ander Murray Palmer) 1921-1992 **CLC 8, 12, 76; BLC; DA; DAB; DAC; DAM MST, MULT, POP**

See Creasey, John
Hope, Christopher (David Tully) 1944- . **CLC 52**
See also CA 106; CANR 47; SATA 62
Hopkins, Gerard Manley 1844-1889 . **NCLC 17; DA; DAB; DAC; DAM MST, POET; PC 15; WLC**
See also CDBLB 1890-1914; DLB 35, 57
Hopkins, John (Richard) 1931- .... **CLC 4**
See also CA 85-88
Hopkins, Pauline Elizabeth 1859-1930**TCLC 28; BLC; DAM MULT**
See also BW 2; CA 141; DLB 50
Hopkinson, Francis 1737-1791 .... **LC 25**
See also DLB 31
Hopley-Woolrich, Cornell George 1903-1968
See Woolrich, Cornell
See also CA 13-14; CANR 58; CAP 1
Horatio
See Proust, (Valentin-Louis-George-Eugene-) Marcel
Horgan, Paul (George Vincent O'Shaughnessy) 1903-1995 .... **CLC 9, 53; DAM NOV**
See also CA 13-16R; 147; CANR 9, 35; DLB 102; DLBY 85; INT CANR-9; MTCW; SATA 13; SATA-Obit 84
Horn, Peter
See Kuttner, Henry
Hornem, Horace Esq.
See Byron, George Gordon (Noel)
Horney, Karen (Clementine Theodore Danielsen) 1885-1952 .... **TCLC 71**
See also CA 114
Hornung, E(rnest) W(illiam) 1866-1921**TCLC 59**
See also CA 108; 160; DLB 70
Horovitz, Israel (Arthur) 1939- . **CLC 56; DAM DRAM**
See also CA 33-36R; CANR 46, 59; DLB 7
Horvath, Odon von
See Horvath, Oedoen von
See also DLB 85, 124
Horvath, Oedoen von 1901-1938 .... **TCLC 45**
See also Horvath, Odon von
See also CA 118
Horwitz, Julius 1920-1986 .... **CLC 14**
See also CA 9-12R; 119; CANR 12
Hospital, Janette Turner 1942- .... **CLC 42**
See also CA 108; CANR 48
Hostos, E. M. de
See Hostos (y Bonilla), Eugenio Maria de
Hostos, Eugenio M. de
See Hostos (y Bonilla), Eugenio Maria de
Hostos, Eugenio Maria
See Hostos (y Bonilla), Eugenio Maria de
Hostos (y Bonilla), Eugenio Maria de 1839-1903 **TCLC 24**
See also CA 123; 131; HW
Houdini
See Lovecraft, H(oward) P(hillips)
Hougan, Carolyn 1943- .... **CLC 34**
See also CA 139
Household, Geoffrey (Edward West) 1900-1988 **CLC 11**
See also CA 77-80; 126; CANR 58; DLB 87; SATA 14; SATA-Obit 59
Housman, A(lfred) E(dward) 1859-1936 **TCLC 1, 10; DA; DAB; DAC; DAM MST, POET; PC 2; WLCS**
See also CA 104; 125; DLB 19; MTCW
Housman, Laurence 1865-1959 .... **TCLC 7**
See also CA 106; 155; DLB 10; SATA 25
Howard, Elizabeth Jane 1923- .... **CLC 7, 29**
See also CA 5-8R; CANR 8, 62
Howard, Maureen 1930- .... **CLC 5, 14, 46**
See also CA 53-56; CANR 31; DLBY 83; INT CANR-31; MTCW
Howard, Richard 1929- .... **CLC 7, 10, 47**
See also AITN 1; CA 85-88; CANR 25; DLB 5; INT CANR-25
Howard, Robert E(rvin) 1906-1936 .... **TCLC 8**
See also CA 105; 157
Howard, Warren F.
See Pohl, Frederik
Howe, Fanny 1940- .... **CLC 47**
See also CA 117; CAAS 27; SATA-Brief 52
Howe, Irving 1920-1993 .... **CLC 85**
See also CA 9-12R; 141; CANR 21, 50; DLB 67; MTCW
Howe, Julia Ward 1819-1910 .... **TCLC 21**
See also CA 117; DLB 1
Howe, Susan 1937- .... **CLC 72**
See also CA 160; DLB 120
Howe, Tina 1937- .... **CLC 48**
See also CA 109
Howell, James 1594(?)-1666 .... **LC 13**
See also DLB 151
Howells, W. D.
See Howells, William Dean
Howells, William D.
See Howells, William Dean
Howells, William Dean 1837-1920**TCLC 7, 17, 41**
See also CA 104; 134; CDALB 1865-1917; DLB 12, 64, 74, 79
Howes, Barbara 1914-1996 .... **CLC 15**
See also CA 9-12R; 151; CAAS 3; CANR 53; SATA 5
Hrabal, Bohumil 1914-1997 .... **CLC 13, 67**
See also CA 106; 156; CAAS 12; CANR 57
Hsun, Lu
See Lu Hsun
Hubbard, L(afayette) Ron(ald) 1911-1986**CLC 43; DAM POP**
See also CA 77-80; 118; CANR 52
Huch, Ricarda (Octavia) 1864-1947 ..... **TCLC 13**
See also CA 111; DLB 66
Huddle, David 1942- .... **CLC 49**
See also CA 57-60; CAAS 20; DLB 130
Hudson, Jeffrey
See Crichton, (John) Michael
Hudson, W(illiam) H(enry) 1841-1922 **TCLC 29**
See also CA 115; DLB 98, 153, 174; SATA 35
Hueffer, Ford Madox
See Ford, Ford Madox
Hughart, Barry 1934- .... **CLC 39**
See also CA 137
Hughes, Colin
See Creasey, John
Hughes, David (John) 1930- .... **CLC 48**
See also CA 116; 129; DLB 14
Hughes, Edward James
See Hughes, Ted
See also DAM MST, POET
Hughes, (James) Langston 1902-1967 **CLC 1, 5, 10, 15, 35, 44, 108; BLC; DA; DAB; DAC; DAM DRAM, MST, MULT, POET; DC 3; PC 1; SSC 6; WLC**
See also AAYA 12; BW 1; CA 1-4R; 25-28R; CANR 1, 34; CDALB 1929-1941; CLR 17; DLB 4, 7, 48, 51, 86; JRDA; MAICYA; MTCW; SATA 4, 33
Hughes, Richard (Arthur Warren) 1900-1976 **CLC 1, 11; DAM NOV**
See also CA 5-8R; 65-68; CANR 4; DLB 15, 161; MTCW; SATA 8; SATA-Obit 25
Hughes, Ted 1930- .... **CLC 2, 4, 9, 14, 37; DAB; DAC; PC 7**
See also Hughes, Edward James
See also CA 1-4R; CANR 1, 33; CLR 3; DLB 40, 161; MAICYA; MTCW; SATA 49; SATA-Brief 27
Hugo, Richard F(ranklin) 1923-1982 **CLC 6, 18, 32; DAM POET**
See also CA 49-52; 108; CANR 3; DLB 5
Hugo, Victor (Marie) 1802-1885**NCLC 3, 10, 21; DA; DAB; DAC; DAM DRAM, MST, NOV, POET; PC 17; WLC**
See also DLB 119; SATA 47
Huidobro, Vicente
See Huidobro Fernandez, Vicente Garcia
Huidobro Fernandez, Vicente Garcia 1893-1948 **TCLC 31**
See also CA 131; HW
Hulme, Keri 1947- .... **CLC 39**
See also CA 125; INT 125
Hulme, T(homas) E(rnest) 1883-1917 .. **TCLC 21**
See also CA 117; DLB 19
Hume, David 1711-1776 .... **LC 7**
See also DLB 104
Humphrey, William 1924-1997 .... **CLC 45**
See also CA 77-80; 160; DLB 6
Humphreys, Emyr Owen 1919- .... **CLC 47**
See also CA 5-8R; CANR 3, 24; DLB 15
Humphreys, Josephine 1945- .... **CLC 34, 57**
See also CA 121; 127; INT 127
Huneker, James Gibbons 1857-1921 ... **TCLC 65**
See also DLB 71
Hungerford, Pixie
See Brinsmead, H(esba) F(ay)
Hunt, E(verette) Howard, (Jr.) 1918- .... **CLC 3**
See also AITN 1; CA 45-48; CANR 2, 47
Hunt, Kyle
See Creasey, John
Hunt, (James Henry) Leigh 1784-1859 **NCLC 1; DAM POET**
Hunt, Marsha 1946- .... **CLC 70**
See also BW 2; CA 143
Hunt, Violet 1866-1942 .... **TCLC 53**
See also DLB 162
Hunter, E. Waldo
See Sturgeon, Theodore (Hamilton)
Hunter, Evan 1926- .... **CLC 11, 31; DAM POP**
See also CA 5-8R; CANR 5, 38, 62; DLBY 82; INT CANR-5; MTCW; SATA 25
Hunter, Kristin (Eggleston) 1931- .... **CLC 35**
See also AITN 1; BW 1; CA 13-16R; CANR 13; CLR 3; DLB 33; INT CANR-13; MAICYA; SAAS 10; SATA 12
Hunter, Mollie 1922- .... **CLC 21**
See also McIlwraith, Maureen Mollie Hunter
See also AAYA 13; CANR 37; CLR 25; DLB 161; JRDA; MAICYA; SAAS 7; SATA 54
Hunter, Robert (?)-1734 .... **LC 7**
Hurston, Zora Neale 1903-1960 . **CLC 7, 30, 61; BLC; DA; DAC; DAM MST, MULT, NOV; SSC 4; WLCS**
See also AAYA 15; BW 1; CA 85-88; CANR 61; DLB 51, 86; MTCW
Huston, John (Marcellus) 1906-1987 .... **CLC 20**
See also CA 73-76; 123; CANR 34; DLB 26
Hustvedt, Siri 1955- .... **CLC 76**
See also CA 137
Hutten, Ulrich von 1488-1523 .... **LC 16**
See also DLB 179
Huxley, Aldous (Leonard) 1894-1963**CLC 1, 3, 4, 5, 8, 11, 18, 35, 79; DA; DAB; DAC; DAM MST, NOV; WLC**
See also AAYA 11; CA 85-88; CANR 44; CDBLB 1914-1945; DLB 36, 100, 162; MTCW; SATA 63
Huxley, T. H. 1825-1895 .... **NCLC 67**

Author Index

Lizardi, Jose Joaquin Fernandez de 1776-1827 **NCLC 30**
Llewellyn, Richard
See Llewellyn Lloyd, Richard Dafydd Vivian
See also DLB 15
Llewellyn Lloyd, Richard Dafydd Vivian 1906-1983 **CLC 7, 80**
See also Llewellyn, Richard
See also CA 53-56; 111; CANR 7; SATA 11; SATA-Obit 37
Llosa, (Jorge) Mario (Pedro) Vargas
See Vargas Llosa, (Jorge) Mario (Pedro)
Lloyd Webber, Andrew 1948-
See Webber, Andrew Lloyd
See also AAYA 1; CA 116; 149; DAM DRAM; SATA 56
Llull, Ramon c. 1235-c. 1316 .... **CMLC 12**
Locke, Alain (Le Roy) 1886-1954 .... **TCLC 43**
See also BW 1; CA 106; 124; DLB 51
Locke, John 1632-1704 .... **LC 7, 35**
See also DLB 101
Locke-Elliott, Sumner
See Elliott, Sumner Locke
Lockhart, John Gibson 1794-1854 .... **NCLC 6**
See also DLB 110, 116, 144
Lodge, David (John) 1935- .. **CLC 36; DAM POP**
See also BEST 90:1; CA 17-20R; CANR 19, 53; DLB 14; INT CANR-19; MTCW
Lodge, Thomas 1558-1625 .... **LC 41**
See also DLB 172
Lodge, Thomas 1558-1625 .... **LC 41**
Loennbohm, Armas Eino Leopold 1878-1926
See Leino, Eino
See also CA 123
Loewinsohn, Ron(ald William) 1937- ... **CLC 52**
See also CA 25-28R
Logan, Jake
See Smith, Martin Cruz
Logan, John (Burton) 1923-1987 .... **CLC 5**
See also CA 77-80; 124; CANR 45; DLB 5
Lo Kuan-chung 1330(?)-1400(?) .... **LC 12**
Lombard, Nap
See Johnson, Pamela Hansford
London, Jack ..... **TCLC 9, 15, 39; SSC 4; WLC**
See also London, John Griffith
See also AAYA 13; AITN 2; CDALB 1865-1917; DLB 8, 12, 78; SATA 18
London, John Griffith 1876-1916
See London, Jack
See also CA 110; 119; DA; DAB; DAC; DAM MST, NOV; JRDA; MAICYA; MTCW
Long, Emmett
See Leonard, Elmore (John, Jr.)
Longbaugh, Harry
See Goldman, William (W.)
Longfellow, Henry Wadsworth 1807-1882 **NCLC 2, 45; DA; DAB; DAC; DAM MST, POET; WLCS**
See also CDALB 1640-1865; DLB 1, 59; SATA 19
Longley, Michael 1939- .... **CLC 29**
See also CA 102; DLB 40
Longus fl. c. 2nd cent. - .... **CMLC 7**
Longway, A. Hugh
See Lang, Andrew
Lonnrot, Elias 1802-1884 .... **NCLC 53**
Lopate, Phillip 1943- .... **CLC 29**
See also CA 97-100; DLBY 80; INT 97-100
Lopez Portillo (y Pacheco), Jose 1920- . **CLC 46**
See also CA 129; HW
Lopez y Fuentes, Gregorio 1897(?)-1966 **CLC 32**
See also CA 131; HW
Lorca, Federico Garcia
See Garcia Lorca, Federico
Lord, Bette Bao 1938- .... **CLC 23**
See also BEST 90:3; CA 107; CANR 41; INT 107; SATA 58
Lord Auch
See Bataille, Georges
Lord Byron
See Byron, George Gordon (Noel)
Lorde, Audre (Geraldine) 1934-1992 **CLC 18, 71; BLC; DAM MULT, POET; PC 12**
See also BW 1; CA 25-28R; 142; CANR 16, 26, 46; DLB 41; MTCW
Lord Houghton
See Milnes, Richard Monckton
Lord Jeffrey
See Jeffrey, Francis
Lorenzini, Carlo 1826-1890
See Collodi, Carlo
See also MAICYA; SATA 29
Lorenzo, Heberto Padilla
See Padilla (Lorenzo), Heberto
Loris
See Hofmannsthal, Hugo von
Loti, Pierre .... **TCLC 11**
See also Viaud, (Louis Marie) Julien
See also DLB 123
Louie, David Wong 1954- .... **CLC 70**
See also CA 139
Louis, Father M.
See Merton, Thomas
Lovecraft, H(oward) P(hillips) 1890-1937 **TCLC 4, 22; DAM POP; SSC 3**
See also AAYA 14; CA 104; 133; MTCW
Lovelace, Earl 1935- .... **CLC 51**
See also BW 2; CA 77-80; CANR 41; DLB 125; MTCW
Lovelace, Richard 1618-1657 .... **LC 24**
See also DLB 131
Lowell, Amy 1874-1925 **TCLC 1, 8; DAM POET; PC 13**
See also CA 104; 151; DLB 54, 140
Lowell, James Russell 1819-1891 .... **NCLC 2**
See also CDALB 1640-1865; DLB 1, 11, 64, 79
Lowell, Robert (Traill Spence, Jr.) 1917-1977 **CLC 1, 2, 3, 4, 5, 8, 9, 11, 15, 37; DA; DAB; DAC; DAM MST, NOV; PC 3; WLC**
See also CA 9-12R; 73-76; CABS 2; CANR 26, 60; DLB 5, 169; MTCW
Lowndes, Marie Adelaide (Belloc) 1868-1947 **TCLC 12**
See also CA 107; DLB 70
Lowry, (Clarence) Malcolm 1909-1957 **TCLC 6, 40**
See also CA 105; 131; CANR 62; CDBLB 1945-1960; DLB 15; MTCW
Lowry, Mina Gertrude 1882-1966
See Loy, Mina
See also CA 113
Loxsmith, John
See Brunner, John (Kilian Houston)
Loy, Mina .... **CLC 28; DAM POET; PC 16**
See also Lowry, Mina Gertrude
See also DLB 4, 54
Loyson-Bridet
See Schwob, (Mayer Andre) Marcel
Lucas, Craig 1951- .... **CLC 64**
See also CA 137
Lucas, E(dward) V(errall) 1868-1938 .. **TCLC 73**
See also DLB 98, 149, 153; SATA 20
Lucas, George 1944- .... **CLC 16**
See also AAYA 1; CA 77-80; CANR 30; SATA 56
Lucas, Hans
See Godard, Jean-Luc
Lucas, Victoria
See Plath, Sylvia
Ludlam, Charles 1943-1987 .... **CLC 46, 50**
See also CA 85-88; 122
Ludlum, Robert 1927- . **CLC 22, 43; DAM NOV, POP**
See also AAYA 10; BEST 89:1, 90:3; CA 33-36R; CANR 25, 41; DLBY 82; MTCW
Ludwig, Ken .... **CLC 60**
Ludwig, Otto 1813-1865 .... **NCLC 4**
See also DLB 129
Lugones, Leopoldo 1874-1938 .... **TCLC 15**
See also CA 116; 131; HW
Lu Hsun 1881-1936 .... **TCLC 3; SSC 20**
See also Shu-Jen, Chou
Lukacs, George .... **CLC 24**
See also Lukacs, Gyorgy (Szegeny von)
Lukacs, Gyorgy (Szegeny von) 1885-1971
See Lukacs, George
See also CA 101; 29-32R; CANR 62
Luke, Peter (Ambrose Cyprian) 1919-1995 **CLC 38**
See also CA 81-84; 147; DLB 13
Lunar, Dennis
See Mungo, Raymond
Lurie, Alison 1926- .... **CLC 4, 5, 18, 39**
See also CA 1-4R; CANR 2, 17, 50; DLB 2; MTCW; SATA 46
Lustig, Arnost 1926- .... **CLC 56**
See also AAYA 3; CA 69-72; CANR 47; SATA 56
Luther, Martin 1483-1546 .... **LC 9, 37**
See also DLB 179
Luxemburg, Rosa 1870(?)-1919 .... **TCLC 63**
See also CA 118
Luzi, Mario 1914- .... **CLC 13**
See also CA 61-64; CANR 9; DLB 128
Lyly, John 1554(?)-1606 **LC 41; DAM DRAM; DC 7**
See also DLB 62, 167
L'Ymagier
See Gourmont, Remy (-Marie-Charles) de
Lynch, B. Suarez
See Bioy Casares, Adolfo; Borges, Jorge Luis
Lynch, David (K.) 1946- .... **CLC 66**
See also CA 124; 129
Lynch, James
See Andreyev, Leonid (Nikolaevich)
Lynch Davis, B.
See Bioy Casares, Adolfo; Borges, Jorge Luis
Lyndsay, Sir David 1490-1555 .... **LC 20**
Lynn, Kenneth S(chuyler) 1923- .... **CLC 50**
See also CA 1-4R; CANR 3, 27
Lynx
See West, Rebecca
Lyons, Marcus
See Blish, James (Benjamin)
Lyre, Pinchbeck
See Sassoon, Siegfried (Lorraine)
Lytle, Andrew (Nelson) 1902-1995 .... **CLC 22**
See also CA 9-12R; 150; DLB 6; DLBY 95
Lyttelton, George 1709-1773 .... **LC 10**
Maas, Peter 1929- .... **CLC 29**
See also CA 93-96; INT 93-96
Macaulay, Rose 1881-1958 .... **TCLC 7, 44**
See also CA 104; DLB 36
Macaulay, Thomas Babington 1800-1859 **NCLC 42**
See also CDBLB 1832-1890; DLB 32, 55
MacBeth, George (Mann) 1932-1992 **CLC 2, 5, 9**
See also CA 25-28R; 136; CANR 61; DLB 40; MTCW; SATA 4; SATA-Obit 70
MacCaig, Norman (Alexander) 1910- .. **CLC 36; DAB; DAM POET**
See also CA 9-12R; CANR 3, 34; DLB 27
MacCarthy, (Sir Charles Otto) Desmond 1877-1952 **TCLC 36**

Mann, Emily 1952- .... **DC 7**
See also CA 130; CANR 55
Mann, (Luiz) Heinrich 1871-1950 .... **TCLC 9**
See also CA 106; DLB 66
Mann, (Paul) Thomas 1875-1955 **TCLC 2, 8, 14, 21, 35, 44, 60; DA; DAB; DAC; DAM MST, NOV; SSC 5; WLC**
See also CA 104; 128; DLB 66; MTCW
Mannheim, Karl 1893-1947 .... **TCLC 65**
Manning, David
See Faust, Frederick (Schiller)
Manning, Frederic 1887(?)-1935 .... **TCLC 25**
See also CA 124
Manning, Olivia 1915-1980 .... **CLC 5, 19**
See also CA 5-8R; 101; CANR 29; MTCW
Mano, D. Keith 1942- .... **CLC 2, 10**
See also CA 25-28R; CAAS 6; CANR 26, 57; DLB 6
Mansfield, Katherine TCLC 2, 8, 39; DAB; SSC 9, 23; WLC
See also Beauchamp, Kathleen Mansfield
See also DLB 162
Manso, Peter 1940- .... **CLC 39**
See also CA 29-32R; CANR 44
Mantecon, Juan Jimenez
See Jimenez (Mantecon), Juan Ramon
Manton, Peter
See Creasey, John
Man Without a Spleen, A
See Chekhov, Anton (Pavlovich)
Manzoni, Alessandro 1785-1873 .... **NCLC 29**
Mapu, Abraham (ben Jekutiel) 1808-1867 **NCLC 18**
Mara, Sally
See Queneau, Raymond
Marat, Jean Paul 1743-1793 .... **LC 10**
Marcel, Gabriel Honore 1889-1973 .... **CLC 15**
See also CA 102; 45-48; MTCW
Marchbanks, Samuel
See Davies, (William) Robertson
Marchi, Giacomo
See Bassani, Giorgio
Margulies, Donald .... **CLC 76**
Marie de France c. 12th cent. - .... **CMLC 8**
Marie de l'Incarnation 1599-1672 .... **LC 10**
Marier, Captain Victor
See Griffith, D(avid Lewelyn) W(ark)
Mariner, Scott
See Pohl, Frederik
Marinetti, Filippo Tommaso 1876-1944 **TCLC 10**
See also CA 107; DLB 114
Marivaux, Pierre Carlet de Chamblain de 1688-1763 .... **LC 4; DC 7**
Markandaya, Kamala .... **CLC 8, 38**
See also Taylor, Kamala (Purnaiya)
Markfield, Wallace 1926- .... **CLC 8**
See also CA 69-72; CAAS 3; DLB 2, 28
Markham, Edwin 1852-1940 .... **TCLC 47**
See also CA 160; DLB 54
Markham, Robert
See Amis, Kingsley (William)
Marks, J
See Highwater, Jamake (Mamake)
Marks-Highwater, J
See Highwater, Jamake (Mamake)
Markson, David M(errill) 1927- .... **CLC 67**
See also CA 49-52; CANR 1
Marley, Bob .... **CLC 17**
See also Marley, Robert Nesta
Marley, Robert Nesta 1945-1981
See Marley, Bob
See also CA 107; 103
Marlowe, Christopher 1564-1593 .... **LC 22; DA; DAB; DAC; DAM DRAM, MST; DC 1; WLC**
See also CDBLB Before 1660; DLB 62
Marlowe, Stephen 1928-
See Queen, Ellery
See also CA 13-16R; CANR 6, 55
Marmontel, Jean-Francois 1723-1799 .... **LC 2**
Marquand, John P(hillips) 1893-1960 **CLC 2, 10**
See also CA 85-88; DLB 9, 102
Marques, Rene 1919-1979 **CLC 96; DAM MULT; HLC**
See also CA 97-100; 85-88; DLB 113; HW
Marquez, Gabriel (Jose) Garcia
See Garcia Marquez, Gabriel (Jose)
Marquis, Don(ald Robert Perry) 1878-1937 **TCLC 7**
See also CA 104; DLB 11, 25
Marric, J. J.
See Creasey, John
Marryat, Frederick 1792-1848 .... **NCLC 3**
See also DLB 21, 163
Marsden, James
See Creasey, John
Marsh, (Edith) Ngaio 1899-1982 **CLC 7, 53; DAM POP**
See also CA 9-12R; CANR 6, 58; DLB 77; MTCW
Marshall, Garry 1934- .... **CLC 17**
See also AAYA 3; CA 111; SATA 60
Marshall, Paule 1929- . **CLC 27, 72; BLC; DAM MULT; SSC 3**
See also BW 2; CA 77-80; CANR 25; DLB 157; MTCW
Marsten, Richard
See Hunter, Evan
Marston, John 1576-1634 .. **LC 33; DAM DRAM**
See also DLB 58, 172
Martha, Henry
See Harris, Mark
Marti, Jose 1853-1895 .. **NCLC 63; DAM MULT; HLC**
Martial c. 40-c. 104 .... **PC 10**
Martin, Ken
See Hubbard, L(afayette) Ron(ald)
Martin, Richard
See Creasey, John
Martin, Steve 1945- .... **CLC 30**
See also CA 97-100; CANR 30; MTCW
Martin, Valerie 1948- .... **CLC 89**
See also BEST 90:2; CA 85-88; CANR 49
Martin, Violet Florence 1862-1915 ..... **TCLC 51**
Martin, Webber
See Silverberg, Robert
Martindale, Patrick Victor
See White, Patrick (Victor Martindale)
Martin du Gard, Roger 1881-1958 ...... **TCLC 24**
See also CA 118; DLB 65
Martineau, Harriet 1802-1876 .... **NCLC 26**
See also DLB 21, 55, 159, 163, 166; YABC 2
Martines, Julia
See O'Faolain, Julia
Martinez, Enrique Gonzalez
See Gonzalez Martinez, Enrique
Martinez, Jacinto Benavente y
See Benavente (y Martinez), Jacinto
Martinez Ruiz, Jose 1873-1967
See Azorin; Ruiz, Jose Martinez
See also CA 93-96; HW
Martinez Sierra, Gregorio 1881-1947 .. **TCLC 6**
See also CA 115
Martinez Sierra, Maria (de la O'LeJarraga) 1874-1974 .... **TCLC 6**
See also CA 115
Martinsen, Martin
See Follett, Ken(neth Martin)
Martinson, Harry (Edmund) 1904-1978 . **CLC 14**
See also CA 77-80; CANR 34
Marut, Ret
See Traven, B.
Marut, Robert
See Traven, B.
Marvell, Andrew 1621-1678 **LC 4; DA; DAB; DAC; DAM MST, POET; PC 10; WLC**
See also CDBLB 1660-1789; DLB 131
Marx, Karl (Heinrich) 1818-1883 .... **NCLC 17**
See also DLB 129
Masaoka Shiki .... **TCLC 18**
See also Masaoka Tsunenori
Masaoka Tsunenori 1867-1902
See Masaoka Shiki
See also CA 117
Masefield, John (Edward) 1878-1967 **CLC 11, 47; DAM POET**
See also CA 19-20; 25-28R; CANR 33; CAP 2; CDBLB 1890-1914; DLB 10, 19, 153, 160; MTCW; SATA 19
Maso, Carole 19(?)- .... **CLC 44**
Mason, Bobbie Ann 1940- **CLC 28, 43, 82; SSC 4**
See also AAYA 5; CA 53-56; CANR 11, 31, 58; DLB 173; DLBY 87; INT CANR-31; MTCW
Mason, Ernst
See Pohl, Frederik
Mason, Lee W.
See Malzberg, Barry N(athaniel)
Mason, Nick 1945- .... **CLC 35**
Mason, Tally
See Derleth, August (William)
Mass, William
See Gibson, William
Masters, Edgar Lee 1868-1950 **TCLC 2, 25; DA; DAC; DAM MST, POET; PC 1; WLCS**
See also CA 104; 133; CDALB 1865-1917; DLB 54; MTCW
Masters, Hilary 1928- .... **CLC 48**
See also CA 25-28R; CANR 13, 47
Mastrosimone, William 19(?)- .... **CLC 36**
Mathe, Albert
See Camus, Albert
Mather, Cotton 1663-1728 .... **LC 38**
See also CDALB 1640-1865; DLB 24, 30, 140
Mather, Increase 1639-1723 .... **LC 38**
See also DLB 24
Matheson, Richard Burton 1926- .... **CLC 37**
See also CA 97-100; DLB 8, 44; INT 97-100
Mathews, Harry 1930- .... **CLC 6, 52**
See also CA 21-24R; CAAS 6; CANR 18, 40
Mathews, John Joseph 1894-1979 **CLC 84; DAM MULT**
See also CA 19-20; 142; CANR 45; CAP 2; DLB 175; NNAL
Mathias, Roland (Glyn) 1915- .... **CLC 45**
See also CA 97-100; CANR 19, 41; DLB 27
Matsuo Basho 1644-1694 .... **PC 3**
See also DAM POET
Mattheson, Rodney
See Creasey, John
Matthews, Greg 1949- .... **CLC 45**
See also CA 135
Matthews, William (Procter, III) 1942-1997 **CLC 40**
See also CA 29-32R; 162; CAAS 18; CANR 12, 57; DLB 5
Matthias, John (Edward) 1941- .... **CLC 9**
See also CA 33-36R; CANR 56
Matthiessen, Peter 1927- . **CLC 5, 7, 11, 32, 64; DAM NOV**
See also AAYA 6; BEST 90:4; CA 9-12R; CANR 21, 50; DLB 6, 173; MTCW; SATA 27

Maturin, Charles Robert 1780(?)-1824 **NCLC 6**
See also DLB 178
Matute (Ausejo), Ana Maria 1925- .... **CLC 11**
See also CA 89-92; MTCW
Maugham, W. S.
See Maugham, W(illiam) Somerset
Maugham, W(illiam) Somerset 1874-1965**CLC 1, 11, 15, 67, 93; DA; DAB; DAC; DAM DRAM, MST, NOV; SSC 8; WLC**
See also CA 5-8R; 25-28R; CANR 40; CDBLB 1914-1945; DLB 10, 36, 77, 100, 162; MTCW; SATA 54
Maugham, William Somerset
See Maugham, W(illiam) Somerset
Maupassant, (Henri Rene Albert) Guy de 1850-1893 .. **NCLC 1, 42; DA; DAB; DAC; DAM MST; SSC 1; WLC**
See also DLB 123
Maupin, Armistead 1944- ... **CLC 95; DAM POP**
See also CA 125; 130; CANR 58; INT 130
Maurhut, Richard
See Traven, B.
Mauriac, Claude 1914-1996 .... **CLC 9**
See also CA 89-92; 152; DLB 83
Mauriac, Francois (Charles) 1885-1970**CLC 4, 9, 56; SSC 24**
See also CA 25-28; CAP 2; DLB 65; MTCW
Mavor, Osborne Henry 1888-1951
See Bridie, James
See also CA 104
Maxwell, William (Keepers, Jr.) 1908- . **CLC 19**
See also CA 93-96; CANR 54; DLBY 80; INT 93-96
May, Elaine 1932- .... **CLC 16**
See also CA 124; 142; DLB 44
Mayakovski, Vladimir (Vladimirovich) 1893-1930 **TCLC 4, 18**
See also CA 104; 158
Mayhew, Henry 1812-1887 .... **NCLC 31**
See also DLB 18, 55
Mayle, Peter 1939(?)- .... **CLC 89**
See also CA 139; CANR 64
Maynard, Joyce 1953- .... **CLC 23**
See also CA 111; 129; CANR 64
Mayne, William (James Carter) 1928- . **CLC 12**
See also AAYA 20; CA 9-12R; CANR 37; CLR 25; JRDA; MAICYA; SAAS 11; SATA 6, 68
Mayo, Jim
See L'Amour, Louis (Dearborn)
Maysles, Albert 1926- .... **CLC 16**
See also CA 29-32R
Maysles, David 1932- .... **CLC 16**
Mazer, Norma Fox 1931- .... **CLC 26**
See also AAYA 5; CA 69-72; CANR 12, 32; CLR 23; JRDA; MAICYA; SAAS 1; SATA 24, 67
Mazzini, Guiseppe 1805-1872 .... **NCLC 34**
McAuley, James Phillip 1917-1976 .... **CLC 45**
See also CA 97-100
McBain, Ed
See Hunter, Evan
McBrien, William Augustine 1930- ..... **CLC 44**
See also CA 107
McCaffrey, Anne (Inez) 1926- .... **CLC 17; DAM NOV, POP**
See also AAYA 6; AITN 2; BEST 89:2; CA 25-28R; CANR 15, 35, 55; CLR 49; DLB 8; JRDA; MAICYA; MTCW; SAAS 11; SATA 8, 70
McCall, Nathan 1955(?)- .... **CLC 86**
See also CA 146
McCann, Arthur
See Campbell, John W(ood, Jr.)
McCann, Edson
See Pohl, Frederik
McCarthy, Charles, Jr. 1933-
See McCarthy, Cormac
See also CANR 42; DAM POP
McCarthy, Cormac 1933- .... **CLC 4, 57, 59, 101**
See also McCarthy, Charles, Jr.
See also DLB 6, 143
McCarthy, Mary (Therese) 1912-1989**CLC 1, 3, 5, 14, 24, 39, 59; SSC 24**
See also CA 5-8R; 129; CANR 16, 50, 64; DLB 2; DLBY 81; INT CANR-16; MTCW
McCartney, (James) Paul 1942- ...... **CLC 12, 35**
See also CA 146
McCauley, Stephen (D.) 1955- .... **CLC 50**
See also CA 141
McClure, Michael (Thomas) 1932- ... **CLC 6, 10**
See also CA 21-24R; CANR 17, 46; DLB 16
McCorkle, Jill (Collins) 1958- .... **CLC 51**
See also CA 121; DLBY 87
McCourt, James 1941- .... **CLC 5**
See also CA 57-60
McCoy, Horace (Stanley) 1897-1955 ... **TCLC 28**
See also CA 108; 155; DLB 9
McCrae, John 1872-1918 .... **TCLC 12**
See also CA 109; DLB 92
McCreigh, James
See Pohl, Frederik
McCullers, (Lula) Carson (Smith) 1917-1967 **CLC 1, 4, 10, 12, 48, 100; DA; DAB; DAC; DAM MST, NOV; SSC 9, 24; WLC**
See also AAYA 21; CA 5-8R; 25-28R; CABS 1, 3; CANR 18; CDALB 1941-1968; DLB 2, 7, 173; MTCW; SATA 27
McCulloch, John Tyler
See Burroughs, Edgar Rice
McCullough, Colleen 1938(?)-**CLC 27, 107; DAM NOV, POP**
See also CA 81-84; CANR 17, 46; MTCW
McDermott, Alice 1953- .... **CLC 90**
See also CA 109; CANR 40
McElroy, Joseph 1930- .... **CLC 5, 47**
See also CA 17-20R
McEwan, Ian (Russell) 1948- **CLC 13, 66; DAM NOV**
See also BEST 90:4; CA 61-64; CANR 14, 41; DLB 14; MTCW
McFadden, David 1940- .... **CLC 48**
See also CA 104; DLB 60; INT 104
McFarland, Dennis 1950- .... **CLC 65**
McGahern, John 1934- ... **CLC 5, 9, 48; SSC 17**
See also CA 17-20R; CANR 29; DLB 14; MTCW
McGinley, Patrick (Anthony) 1937- ..... **CLC 41**
See also CA 120; 127; CANR 56; INT 127
McGinley, Phyllis 1905-1978 .... **CLC 14**
See also CA 9-12R; 77-80; CANR 19; DLB 11, 48; SATA 2, 44; SATA-Obit 24
McGinniss, Joe 1942- .... **CLC 32**
See also AITN 2; BEST 89:2; CA 25-28R; CANR 26; INT CANR-26
McGivern, Maureen Daly
See Daly, Maureen
McGrath, Patrick 1950- .... **CLC 55**
See also CA 136
McGrath, Thomas (Matthew) 1916-1990**CLC 28, 59; DAM POET**
See also CA 9-12R; 132; CANR 6, 33; MTCW; SATA 41; SATA-Obit 66
McGuane, Thomas (Francis III) 1939- **CLC 3, 7, 18, 45**
See also AITN 2; CA 49-52; CANR 5, 24, 49; DLB 2; DLBY 80; INT CANR-24; MTCW
McGuckian, Medbh 1950- **CLC 48; DAM POET**
See also CA 143; DLB 40
McHale, Tom 1942(?)-1982 .... **CLC 3, 5**
See also AITN 1; CA 77-80; 106
McIlvanney, William 1936- .... **CLC 42**
See also CA 25-28R; CANR 61; DLB 14
McIlwraith, Maureen Mollie Hunter
See Hunter, Mollie
See also SATA 2
McInerney, Jay 1955- .... **CLC 34; DAM POP**
See also AAYA 18; CA 116; 123; CANR 45; INT 123
McIntyre, Vonda N(eel) 1948- .... **CLC 18**
See also CA 81-84; CANR 17, 34; MTCW
McKay, Claude ... TCLC 7, 41; BLC; DAB; PC 2
See also McKay, Festus Claudius
See also DLB 4, 45, 51, 117
McKay, Festus Claudius 1889-1948
See McKay, Claude
See also BW 1; CA 104; 124; DA; DAC; DAM MST, MULT, NOV, POET; MTCW; WLC
McKuen, Rod 1933- .... **CLC 1, 3**
See also AITN 1; CA 41-44R; CANR 40
McLoughlin, R. B.
See Mencken, H(enry) L(ouis)
McLuhan, (Herbert) Marshall 1911-1980**CLC 37, 83**
See also CA 9-12R; 102; CANR 12, 34, 61; DLB 88; INT CANR-12; MTCW
McMillan, Terry (L.) 1951- .. **CLC 50, 61; DAM MULT, NOV, POP**
See also AAYA 21; BW 2; CA 140; CANR 60
McMurtry, Larry (Jeff) 1936-**CLC 2, 3, 7, 11, 27, 44; DAM NOV, POP**
See also AAYA 15; AITN 2; BEST 89:2; CA 5-8R; CANR 19, 43, 64; CDALB 1968-1988; DLB 2, 143; DLBY 80, 87; MTCW
McNally, T. M. 1961- .... **CLC 82**
McNally, Terrence 1939-**CLC 4, 7, 41, 91; DAM DRAM**
See also CA 45-48; CANR 2, 56; DLB 7
McNamer, Deirdre 1950- .... **CLC 70**
McNeile, Herman Cyril 1888-1937
See Sapper
See also DLB 77
McNickle, (William) D'Arcy 1904-1977**CLC 89; DAM MULT**
See also CA 9-12R; 85-88; CANR 5, 45; DLB 175; NNAL; SATA-Obit 22
McPhee, John (Angus) 1931- .... **CLC 36**
See also BEST 90:1; CA 65-68; CANR 20, 46, 64; MTCW
McPherson, James Alan 1943- .... **CLC 19, 77**
See also BW 1; CA 25-28R; CAAS 17; CANR 24; DLB 38; MTCW
McPherson, William (Alexander) 1933-**CLC 34**
See also CA 69-72; CANR 28; INT CANR-28
Mead, Margaret 1901-1978 .... **CLC 37**
See also AITN 1; CA 1-4R; 81-84; CANR 4; MTCW; SATA-Obit 20
Meaker, Marijane (Agnes) 1927-
See Kerr, M. E.
See also CA 107; CANR 37, 63; INT 107; JRDA; MAICYA; MTCW; SATA 20, 61
Medoff, Mark (Howard) 1940- **CLC 6, 23; DAM DRAM**
See also AITN 1; CA 53-56; CANR 5; DLB 7; INT CANR-5
Medvedev, P. N.
See Bakhtin, Mikhail Mikhailovich
Meged, Aharon
See Megged, Aharon
Meged, Aron
See Megged, Aharon
Megged, Aharon 1920- .... **CLC 9**
See also CA 49-52; CAAS 13; CANR 1

Mehta, Ved (Parkash) 1934- .... **CLC 37**
See also CA 1-4R; CANR 2, 23; MTCW
Melanter
See Blackmore, R(ichard) D(oddridge)
Melikow, Loris
See Hofmannsthal, Hugo von
Melmoth, Sebastian
See Wilde, Oscar (Fingal O'Flahertie Wills)
Meltzer, Milton 1915- .... **CLC 26**
See also AAYA 8; CA 13-16R; CANR 38; CLR 13; DLB 61; JRDA; MAICYA; SAAS 1; SATA 1, 50, 80
Melville, Herman 1819-1891**NCLC 3, 12, 29, 45, 49; DA; DAB; DAC; DAM MST, NOV; SSC 1, 17; WLC**
See also CDALB 1640-1865; DLB 3, 74; SATA 59
Menander c. 342B.C.-c. 292B.C. **CMLC 9; DAM DRAM; DC 3**
See also DLB 176
Mencken, H(enry) L(ouis) 1880-1956 . **TCLC 13**
See also CA 105; 125; CDALB 1917-1929; DLB 11, 29, 63, 137; MTCW
Mendelsohn, Jane 1965(?)- .... **CLC 99**
See also CA 154
Mercer, David 1928-1980 .. **CLC 5; DAM DRAM**
See also CA 9-12R; 102; CANR 23; DLB 13; MTCW
Merchant, Paul
See Ellison, Harlan (Jay)
Meredith, George 1828-1909**TCLC 17, 43; DAM POET**
See also CA 117; 153; CDBLB 1832-1890; DLB 18, 35, 57, 159
Meredith, William (Morris) 1919-**CLC 4, 13, 22, 55; DAM POET**
See also CA 9-12R; CAAS 14; CANR 6, 40; DLB 5
Merezhkovsky, Dmitry Sergeyevich 1865-1941 **TCLC 29**
Merimee, Prosper 1803-1870**NCLC 6, 65; SSC 7**
See also DLB 119
Merkin, Daphne 1954- .... **CLC 44**
See also CA 123
Merlin, Arthur
See Blish, James (Benjamin)
Merrill, James (Ingram) 1926-1995**CLC 2, 3, 6, 8, 13, 18, 34, 91; DAM POET**
See also CA 13-16R; 147; CANR 10, 49, 63; DLB 5, 165; DLBY 85; INT CANR-10; MTCW
Merriman, Alex
See Silverberg, Robert
Merritt, E. B.
See Waddington, Miriam
Merton, Thomas 1915-1968**CLC 1, 3, 11, 34, 83; PC 10**
See also CA 5-8R; 25-28R; CANR 22, 53; DLB 48; DLBY 81; MTCW
Merwin, W(illiam) S(tanley) 1927-**CLC 1, 2, 3, 5, 8, 13, 18, 45, 88; DAM POET**
See also CA 13-16R; CANR 15, 51; DLB 5, 169; INT CANR-15; MTCW
Metcalf, John 1938- .... **CLC 37**
See also CA 113; DLB 60
Metcalf, Suzanne
See Baum, L(yman) Frank
Mew, Charlotte (Mary) 1870-1928 .... **TCLC 8**
See also CA 105; DLB 19, 135
Mewshaw, Michael 1943- .... **CLC 9**
See also CA 53-56; CANR 7, 47; DLBY 80
Meyer, June
See Jordan, June
Meyer, Lynn
See Slavitt, David R(ytman)
Meyer-Meyrink, Gustav 1868-1932
See Meyrink, Gustav
See also CA 117
Meyers, Jeffrey 1939- .... **CLC 39**
See also CA 73-76; CANR 54; DLB 111
Meynell, Alice (Christina Gertrude Thompson) 1847-1922 .... **TCLC 6**
See also CA 104; DLB 19, 98
Meyrink, Gustav .... **TCLC 21**
See also Meyer-Meyrink, Gustav
See also DLB 81
Michaels, Leonard 1933- .... **CLC 6, 25; SSC 16**
See also CA 61-64; CANR 21, 62; DLB 130; MTCW
Michaux, Henri 1899-1984 .... **CLC 8, 19**
See also CA 85-88; 114
Micheaux, Oscar 1884-1951 .... **TCLC 76**
See also DLB 50
Michelangelo 1475-1564 .... **LC 12**
Michelet, Jules 1798-1874 .... **NCLC 31**
Michener, James A(lbert) 1907(?)-1997**CLC 1, 5, 11, 29, 60; DAM NOV, POP**
See also AITN 1; BEST 90:1; CA 5-8R; 161; CANR 21, 45; DLB 6; MTCW
Mickiewicz, Adam 1798-1855 .... **NCLC 3**
Middleton, Christopher 1926- .... **CLC 13**
See also CA 13-16R; CANR 29, 54; DLB 40
Middleton, Richard (Barham) 1882-1911**TCLC 56**
See also DLB 156
Middleton, Stanley 1919- .... **CLC 7, 38**
See also CA 25-28R; CAAS 23; CANR 21, 46; DLB 14
Middleton, Thomas 1580-1627 .... **LC 33; DAM DRAM, MST; DC 5**
See also DLB 58
Migueis, Jose Rodrigues 1901- .... **CLC 10**
Mikszath, Kalman 1847-1910 .... **TCLC 31**
Miles, Jack .... **CLC 100**
Miles, Josephine (Louise) 1911-1985 . **CLC 1, 2, 14, 34, 39; DAM POET**
See also CA 1-4R; 116; CANR 2, 55; DLB 48
Militant
See Sandburg, Carl (August)
Mill, John Stuart 1806-1873 .... **NCLC 11, 58**
See also CDBLB 1832-1890; DLB 55
Millar, Kenneth 1915-1983 . **CLC 14; DAM POP**
See also Macdonald, Ross
See also CA 9-12R; 110; CANR 16, 63; DLB 2; DLBD 6; DLBY 83; MTCW
Millay, E. Vincent
See Millay, Edna St. Vincent
Millay, Edna St. Vincent 1892-1950 **TCLC 4, 49; DA; DAB; DAC; DAM MST, POET; PC 6; WLCS**
See also CA 104; 130; CDALB 1917-1929; DLB 45; MTCW
Miller, Arthur 1915-**CLC 1, 2, 6, 10, 15, 26, 47, 78; DA; DAB; DAC; DAM DRAM, MST; DC 1; WLC**
See also AAYA 15; AITN 1; CA 1-4R; CABS 3; CANR 2, 30, 54; CDALB 1941-1968; DLB 7; MTCW
Miller, Henry (Valentine) 1891-1980**CLC 1, 2, 4, 9, 14, 43, 84; DA; DAB; DAC; DAM MST, NOV; WLC**
See also CA 9-12R; 97-100; CANR 33, 64; CDALB 1929-1941; DLB 4, 9; DLBY 80; MTCW
Miller, Jason 1939(?)- .... **CLC 2**
See also AITN 1; CA 73-76; DLB 7
Miller, Sue 1943- .... **CLC 44; DAM POP**
See also BEST 90:3; CA 139; CANR 59; DLB 143
Miller, Walter M(ichael, Jr.) 1923- .. **CLC 4, 30**
See also CA 85-88; DLB 8
Millett, Kate 1934- .... **CLC 67**
See also AITN 1; CA 73-76; CANR 32, 53; MTCW
Millhauser, Steven (Lewis) 1943- ... **CLC 21, 54**
See also CA 110; 111; CANR 63; DLB 2; INT 111
Millin, Sarah Gertrude 1889-1968 .... **CLC 49**
See also CA 102; 93-96
Milne, A(lan) A(lexander) 1882-1956 ... **TCLC 6; DAB; DAC; DAM MST**
See also CA 104; 133; CLR 1, 26; DLB 10, 77, 100, 160; MAICYA; MTCW; YABC 1
Milner, Ron(ald) 1938- ..... **CLC 56; BLC; DAM MULT**
See also AITN 1; BW 1; CA 73-76; CANR 24; DLB 38; MTCW
Milnes, Richard Monckton 1809-1885 **NCLC 61**
See also DLB 32, 184
Milosz, Czeslaw 1911-**CLC 5, 11, 22, 31, 56, 82; DAM MST, POET; PC 8; WLCS**
See also CA 81-84; CANR 23, 51; MTCW
Milton, John 1608-1674 . **LC 9; DA; DAB; DAC; DAM MST, POET; PC 19; WLC**
See also CDBLB 1660-1789; DLB 131, 151
Min, Anchee 1957- .... **CLC 86**
See also CA 146
Minehaha, Cornelius
See Wedekind, (Benjamin) Frank(lin)
Miner, Valerie 1947- .... **CLC 40**
See also CA 97-100; CANR 59
Minimo, Duca
See D'Annunzio, Gabriele
Minot, Susan 1956- .... **CLC 44**
See also CA 134
Minus, Ed 1938- .... **CLC 39**
Miranda, Javier
See Bioy Casares, Adolfo
Mirbeau, Octave 1848-1917 .... **TCLC 55**
See also DLB 123
Miro (Ferrer), Gabriel (Francisco Victor) 1879-1930 .... **TCLC 5**
See also CA 104
Mishima, Yukio 1925-1970**CLC 2, 4, 6, 9, 27; DC 1; SSC 4**
See also Hiraoka, Kimitake
See also DLB 182
Mistral, Frederic 1830-1914 .... **TCLC 51**
See also CA 122
Mistral, Gabriela .... **TCLC 2; HLC**
See also Godoy Alcayaga, Lucila
Mistry, Rohinton 1952- .... **CLC 71; DAC**
See also CA 141
Mitchell, Clyde
See Ellison, Harlan (Jay); Silverberg, Robert
Mitchell, James Leslie 1901-1935
See Gibbon, Lewis Grassic
See also CA 104; DLB 15
Mitchell, Joni 1943- .... **CLC 12**
See also CA 112
Mitchell, Joseph (Quincy) 1908-1996 ... **CLC 98**
See also CA 77-80; 152; DLBY 96
Mitchell, Margaret (Munnerlyn) 1900-1949 **TCLC 11; DAM NOV, POP**
See also CA 109; 125; CANR 55; DLB 9; MTCW
Mitchell, Peggy
See Mitchell, Margaret (Munnerlyn)
Mitchell, S(ilas) Weir 1829-1914 .... **TCLC 36**
Mitchell, W(illiam) O(rmond) 1914- ... **CLC 25; DAC; DAM MST**
See also CA 77-80; CANR 15, 43; DLB 88
Mitford, Mary Russell 1787-1855 .... **NCLC 4**
See also DLB 110, 116
Mitford, Nancy 1904-1973 .... **CLC 44**
See also CA 9-12R

CANR-24; MTCW
Phillips, Richard
See Dick, Philip K(indred)
Phillips, Robert (Schaeffer) 1938- .... **CLC 28**
See also CA 17-20R; CAAS 13; CANR 8; DLB 105
Phillips, Ward
See Lovecraft, H(oward) P(hillips)
Piccolo, Lucio 1901-1969 .... **CLC 13**
See also CA 97-100; DLB 114
Pickthall, Marjorie L(owry) C(hristie) 1883-1922 **TCLC 21**
See also CA 107; DLB 92
Pico della Mirandola, Giovanni 1463-1494 **LC 15**
Piercy, Marge 1936-.... **CLC 3, 6, 14, 18, 27, 62**
See also CA 21-24R; CAAS 1; CANR 13, 43; DLB 120; MTCW
Piers, Robert
See Anthony, Piers
Pieyre de Mandiargues, Andre 1909-1991
See Mandiargues, Andre Pieyre de
See also CA 103; 136; CANR 22
Pilnyak, Boris .... **TCLC 23**
See also Vogau, Boris Andreyevich
Pincherle, Alberto 1907-1990 **CLC 11, 18; DAM NOV**
See also Moravia, Alberto
See also CA 25-28R; 132; CANR 33, 63; MTCW
Pinckney, Darryl 1953-......................... **CLC 76**
See also BW 2; CA 143
Pindar 518B.C.-446B.C. .... **CMLC 12; PC 19**
See also DLB 176
Pineda, Cecile 1942- .... **CLC 39**
See also CA 118
Pinero, Arthur Wing 1855-1934 **TCLC 32; DAM DRAM**
See also CA 110; 153; DLB 10
Pinero, Miguel (Antonio Gomez) 1946-1988 **CLC 4, 55**
See also CA 61-64; 125; CANR 29; HW
Pinget, Robert 1919-1997 .... **CLC 7, 13, 37**
See also CA 85-88; 160; DLB 83
Pink Floyd
See Barrett, (Roger) Syd; Gilmour, David; Mason, Nick; Waters, Roger; Wright, Rick
Pinkney, Edward 1802-1828 .... **NCLC 31**
Pinkwater, Daniel Manus 1941- .... **CLC 35**
See also Pinkwater, Manus
See also AAYA 1; CA 29-32R; CANR 12, 38; CLR 4; JRDA; MAICYA; SAAS 3; SATA 46, 76
Pinkwater, Manus
See Pinkwater, Daniel Manus
See also SATA 8
Pinsky, Robert 1940- . **CLC 9, 19, 38, 94; DAM POET**
See also CA 29-32R; CAAS 4; CANR 58; DLBY 82
Pinta, Harold
See Pinter, Harold
Pinter, Harold 1930-**CLC 1, 3, 6, 9, 11, 15, 27, 58, 73; DA; DAB; DAC; DAM DRAM, MST; WLC**
See also CA 5-8R; CANR 33; CDBLB 1960 to Present; DLB 13; MTCW
Piozzi, Hester Lynch (Thrale) 1741-1821 **NCLC 57**
See also DLB 104, 142
Pirandello, Luigi 1867-1936 ... **TCLC 4, 29; DA; DAB; DAC; DAM DRAM, MST; DC 5; SSC 22; WLC**
See also CA 104; 153
Pirsig, Robert M(aynard) 1928- ... **CLC 4, 6, 73; DAM POP**
See also CA 53-56; CANR 42; MTCW; SATA 39
Pisarev, Dmitry Ivanovich 1840-1868 . **NCLC 25**
Pix, Mary (Griffith) 1666-1709 .... **LC 8**
See also DLB 80
Pixerecourt, Guilbert de 1773-1844 ... **NCLC 39**
Plaatje, Sol(omon) T(shekisho) 1876-1932 **TCLC 73**
See also BW 2; CA 141
Plaidy, Jean
See Hibbert, Eleanor Alice Burford
Planche, James Robinson 1796-1880 . **NCLC 42**
Plant, Robert 1948- .... **CLC 12**
Plante, David (Robert) 1940-**CLC 7, 23, 38; DAM NOV**
See also CA 37-40R; CANR 12, 36, 58; DLBY 83; INT CANR-12; MTCW
Plath, Sylvia 1932-1963 **CLC 1, 2, 3, 5, 9, 11, 14, 17, 50, 51, 62; DA; DAB; DAC; DAM MST, POET; PC 1; WLC**
See also AAYA 13; CA 19-20; CANR 34; CAP 2; CDALB 1941-1968; DLB 5, 6, 152; MTCW; SATA 96
Plato 428(?)B.C.-348(?)B.C. **CMLC 8; DA; DAB; DAC; DAM MST; WLCS**
See also DLB 176
Platonov, Andrei .... **TCLC 14**
See also Klimentov, Andrei Platonovich
Platt, Kin 1911- .... **CLC 26**
See also AAYA 11; CA 17-20R; CANR 11; JRDA; SAAS 17; SATA 21, 86
Plautus c. 251B.C.-184B.C. ...... **CMLC 24; DC 6**
Plick et Plock
See Simenon, Georges (Jacques Christian)
Plimpton, George (Ames) 1927- .... **CLC 36**
See also AITN 1; CA 21-24R; CANR 32; MTCW; SATA 10
Pliny the Elder c. 23-79 .... **CMLC 23**
Plomer, William Charles Franklin 1903-1973 **CLC 4, 8**
See also CA 21-22; CANR 34; CAP 2; DLB 20, 162; MTCW; SATA 24
Plowman, Piers
See Kavanagh, Patrick (Joseph)
Plum, J.
See Wodehouse, P(elham) G(renville)
Plumly, Stanley (Ross) 1939- .... **CLC 33**
See also CA 108; 110; DLB 5; INT 110
Plumpe, Friedrich Wilhelm 1888-1931 **TCLC 53**
See also CA 112
Po Chu-i 772-846 .... **CMLC 24**
Poe, Edgar Allan 1809-1849 **NCLC 1, 16, 55; DA; DAB; DAC; DAM MST, POET; PC 1; SSC 1, 22; WLC**
See also AAYA 14; CDALB 1640-1865; DLB 3, 59, 73, 74; SATA 23
Poet of Titchfield Street, The
See Pound, Ezra (Weston Loomis)
Pohl, Frederik 1919- .... **CLC 18; SSC 25**
See also AAYA 24; CA 61-64; CAAS 1; CANR 11, 37; DLB 8; INT CANR-11; MTCW; SATA 24
Poirier, Louis 1910-
See Gracq, Julien
See also CA 122; 126
Poitier, Sidney 1927- .... **CLC 26**
See also BW 1; CA 117
Polanski, Roman 1933- .... **CLC 16**
See also CA 77-80
Poliakoff, Stephen 1952- .... **CLC 38**
See also CA 106; DLB 13
Police, The
See Copeland, Stewart (Armstrong); Summers, Andrew James; Sumner, Gordon Matthew
Polidori, John William 1795-1821 ..... **NCLC 51**
See also DLB 116
Pollitt, Katha 1949- .... **CLC 28**
See also CA 120; 122; MTCW
Pollock, (Mary) Sharon 1936- ... **CLC 50; DAC; DAM DRAM, MST**
See also CA 141; DLB 60
Polo, Marco 1254-1324 .... **CMLC 15**
Polonsky, Abraham (Lincoln) 1910- ..... **CLC 92**
See also CA 104; DLB 26; INT 104
Polybius c. 200B.C.-c. 118B.C. .... **CMLC 17**
See also DLB 176
Pomerance, Bernard 1940-**CLC 13; DAM DRAM**
See also CA 101; CANR 49
Ponge, Francis (Jean Gaston Alfred) 1899-1988 **CLC 6, 18; DAM POET**
See also CA 85-88; 126; CANR 40
Pontoppidan, Henrik 1857-1943 .... **TCLC 29**
Poole, Josephine .... **CLC 17**
See also Helyar, Jane Penelope Josephine
See also SAAS 2; SATA 5
Popa, Vasko 1922-1991 .... **CLC 19**
See also CA 112; 148; DLB 181
Pope, Alexander 1688-1744 **LC 3; DA; DAB; DAC; DAM MST, POET; WLC**
See also CDBLB 1660-1789; DLB 95, 101
Porter, Connie (Rose) 1959(?)- .... **CLC 70**
See also BW 2; CA 142; SATA 81
Porter, Gene(va Grace) Stratton 1863(?)-1924 **TCLC 21**
See also CA 112
Porter, Katherine Anne 1890-1980 . **CLC 1, 3, 7, 10, 13, 15, 27, 101; DA; DAB; DAC; DAM MST, NOV; SSC 4**
See also AITN 2; CA 1-4R; 101; CANR 1; DLB 4, 9, 102; DLBD 12; DLBY 80; MTCW; SATA 39; SATA-Obit 23
Porter, Peter (Neville Frederick) 1929- **CLC 5, 13, 33**
See also CA 85-88; DLB 40
Porter, William Sydney 1862-1910
See Henry, O.
See also CA 104; 131; CDALB 1865-1917; DA; DAB; DAC; DAM MST; DLB 12, 78, 79; MTCW; YABC 2
Portillo (y Pacheco), Jose Lopez
See Lopez Portillo (y Pacheco), Jose
Post, Melville Davisson 1869-1930 ...... **TCLC 39**
See also CA 110
Potok, Chaim 1929-**CLC 2, 7, 14, 26; DAM NOV**
See also AAYA 15; AITN 1, 2; CA 17-20R; CANR 19, 35, 64; DLB 28, 152; INT CANR-19; MTCW; SATA 33
Potter, (Helen) Beatrix 1866-1943
See Webb, (Martha) Beatrice (Potter)
See also MAICYA
Potter, Dennis (Christopher George) 1935-1994 **CLC 58, 86**
See also CA 107; 145; CANR 33, 61; MTCW
Pound, Ezra (Weston Loomis) 1885-1972 **CLC 1, 2, 3, 4, 5, 7, 10, 13, 18, 34, 48, 50; DA; DAB; DAC; DAM MST, POET; PC 4; WLC**
See also CA 5-8R; 37-40R; CANR 40; CDALB 1917-1929; DLB 4, 45, 63; DLBD 15; MTCW
Povod, Reinaldo 1959-1994 .... **CLC 44**
See also CA 136; 146
Powell, Adam Clayton, Jr. 1908-1972 ... **CLC 89; BLC; DAM MULT**
See also BW 1; CA 102; 33-36R
Powell, Anthony (Dymoke) 1905- **CLC 1, 3, 7, 9, 10, 31**
See also CA 1-4R; CANR 1, 32, 62; CDBLB 1945-1960; DLB 15; MTCW

See Lovecraft, H(oward) P(hillips)
Raleigh, Sir Walter 1554(?)-1618 ...... **LC 31, 39**
See also CDBLB Before 1660; DLB 172
Rallentando, H. P.
See Sayers, Dorothy L(eigh)
Ramal, Walter
See de la Mare, Walter (John)
Ramon, Juan
See Jimenez (Mantecon), Juan Ramon
Ramos, Graciliano 1892-1953 .... **TCLC 32**
Rampersad, Arnold 1941- .... **CLC 44**
See also BW 2; CA 127; 133; DLB 111; INT 133
Rampling, Anne
See Rice, Anne
Ramsay, Allan 1684(?)-1758 .... **LC 29**
See also DLB 95
Ramuz, Charles-Ferdinand 1878-1947 **TCLC 33**
Rand, Ayn 1905-1982**CLC 3, 30, 44, 79; DA; DAC; DAM MST, NOV, POP; WLC**
See also AAYA 10; CA 13-16R; 105; CANR 27; MTCW
Randall, Dudley (Felker) 1914- ... **CLC 1; BLC; DAM MULT**
See also BW 1; CA 25-28R; CANR 23; DLB 41
Randall, Robert
See Silverberg, Robert
Ranger, Ken
See Creasey, John
Ransom, John Crowe 1888-1974 **CLC 2, 4, 5, 11, 24; DAM POET**
See also CA 5-8R; 49-52; CANR 6, 34; DLB 45, 63; MTCW
Rao, Raja 1909- .... **CLC 25, 56; DAM NOV**
See also CA 73-76; CANR 51; MTCW
Raphael, Frederic (Michael) 1931- ... **CLC 2, 14**
See also CA 1-4R; CANR 1; DLB 14
Ratcliffe, James P.
See Mencken, H(enry) L(ouis)
Rathbone, Julian 1935- .... **CLC 41**
See also CA 101; CANR 34
Rattigan, Terence (Mervyn) 1911-1977 .. **CLC 7; DAM DRAM**
See also CA 85-88; 73-76; CDBLB 1945-1960; DLB 13; MTCW
Ratushinskaya, Irina 1954- .... **CLC 54**
See also CA 129
Raven, Simon (Arthur Noel) 1927- .... **CLC 14**
See also CA 81-84
Rawley, Callman 1903-
See Rakosi, Carl
See also CA 21-24R; CANR 12, 32
Rawlings, Marjorie Kinnan 1896-1953 . **TCLC 4**
See also AAYA 20; CA 104; 137; DLB 9, 22, 102; JRDA; MAICYA; YABC 1
Ray, Satyajit 1921-1992**CLC 16, 76; DAM MULT**
See also CA 114; 137
Read, Herbert Edward 1893-1968 .... **CLC 4**
See also CA 85-88; 25-28R; DLB 20, 149
Read, Piers Paul 1941- .... **CLC 4, 10, 25**
See also CA 21-24R; CANR 38; DLB 14; SATA 21
Reade, Charles 1814-1884 .... **NCLC 2**
See also DLB 21
Reade, Hamish
See Gray, Simon (James Holliday)
Reading, Peter 1946- .... **CLC 47**
See also CA 103; CANR 46; DLB 40
Reaney, James 1926- **CLC 13; DAC; DAM MST**
See also CA 41-44R; CAAS 15; CANR 42; DLB 68; SATA 43
Rebreanu, Liviu 1885-1944 .... **TCLC 28**
Rechy, John (Francisco) 1934- **CLC 1, 7, 14, 18, 107; DAM MULT; HLC**
See also CA 5-8R; CAAS 4; CANR 6, 32, 64; DLB 122; DLBY 82; HW; INT CANR-6
Redcam, Tom 1870-1933 .... **TCLC 25**
Reddin, Keith .... **CLC 67**
Redgrove, Peter (William) 1932- ...... **CLC 6, 41**
See also CA 1-4R; CANR 3, 39; DLB 40
Redmon, Anne .... **CLC 22**
See also Nightingale, Anne Redmon
See also DLBY 86
Reed, Eliot
See Ambler, Eric
Reed, Ishmael 1938- . **CLC 2, 3, 5, 6, 13, 32, 60; BLC; DAM MULT**
See also BW 2; CA 21-24R; CANR 25, 48; DLB 2, 5, 33, 169; DLBD 8; MTCW
Reed, John (Silas) 1887-1920 .... **TCLC 9**
See also CA 106
Reed, Lou .... **CLC 21**
See also Firbank, Louis
Reeve, Clara 1729-1807 .... **NCLC 19**
See also DLB 39
Reich, Wilhelm 1897-1957 .... **TCLC 57**
Reid, Christopher (John) 1949- .... **CLC 33**
See also CA 140; DLB 40
Reid, Desmond
See Moorcock, Michael (John)
Reid Banks, Lynne 1929-
See Banks, Lynne Reid
See also CA 1-4R; CANR 6, 22, 38; CLR 24; JRDA; MAICYA; SATA 22, 75
Reilly, William K.
See Creasey, John
Reiner, Max
See Caldwell, (Janet Miriam) Taylor (Holland)
Reis, Ricardo
See Pessoa, Fernando (Antonio Nogueira)
Remarque, Erich Maria 1898-1970 **CLC 21; DA; DAB; DAC; DAM MST, NOV**
See also CA 77-80; 29-32R; DLB 56; MTCW
Remizov, A.
See Remizov, Aleksei (Mikhailovich)
Remizov, A. M.
See Remizov, Aleksei (Mikhailovich)
Remizov, Aleksei (Mikhailovich) 1877-1957 **TCLC 27**
See also CA 125; 133
Renan, Joseph Ernest 1823-1892 .... **NCLC 26**
Renard, Jules 1864-1910 .... **TCLC 17**
See also CA 117
Renault, Mary .... **CLC 3, 11, 17**
See also Challans, Mary
See also DLBY 83
Rendell, Ruth (Barbara) 1930-**CLC 28, 48; DAM POP**
See also Vine, Barbara
See also CA 109; CANR 32, 52; DLB 87; INT CANR-32; MTCW
Renoir, Jean 1894-1979 .... **CLC 20**
See also CA 129; 85-88
Resnais, Alain 1922- .... **CLC 16**
Reverdy, Pierre 1889-1960 .... **CLC 53**
See also CA 97-100; 89-92
Rexroth, Kenneth 1905-1982 **CLC 1, 2, 6, 11, 22, 49; DAM POET; PC 20**
See also CA 5-8R; 107; CANR 14, 34, 63; CDALB 1941-1968; DLB 16, 48, 165; DLBY 82; INT CANR-14; MTCW
Reyes, Alfonso 1889-1959 .... **TCLC 33**
See also CA 131; HW
Reyes y Basoalto, Ricardo Eliecer Neftali
See Neruda, Pablo
Reymont, Wladyslaw (Stanislaw) 1868(?)-1925 **TCLC 5**
See also CA 104
Reynolds, Jonathan 1942- .... **CLC 6, 38**
See also CA 65-68; CANR 28
Reynolds, Joshua 1723-1792 .... **LC 15**
See also DLB 104
Reynolds, Michael Shane 1937- .... **CLC 44**
See also CA 65-68; CANR 9
Reznikoff, Charles 1894-1976 .... **CLC 9**
See also CA 33-36; 61-64; CAP 2; DLB 28, 45
Rezzori (d'Arezzo), Gregor von 1914- .. **CLC 25**
See also CA 122; 136
Rhine, Richard
See Silverstein, Alvin
Rhodes, Eugene Manlove 1869-1934 ... **TCLC 53**
R'hoone
See Balzac, Honore de
Rhys, Jean 1890(?)-1979**CLC 2, 4, 6, 14, 19, 51; DAM NOV; SSC 21**
See also CA 25-28R; 85-88; CANR 35, 62; CDBLB 1945-1960; DLB 36, 117, 162; MTCW
Ribeiro, Darcy 1922-1997 .... **CLC 34**
See also CA 33-36R; 156
Ribeiro, Joao Ubaldo (Osorio Pimentel) 1941- **CLC 10, 67**
See also CA 81-84
Ribman, Ronald (Burt) 1932- .... **CLC 7**
See also CA 21-24R; CANR 46
Ricci, Nino 1959- .... **CLC 70**
See also CA 137
Rice, Anne 1941- .... **CLC 41; DAM POP**
See also AAYA 9; BEST 89:2; CA 65-68; CANR 12, 36, 53
Rice, Elmer (Leopold) 1892-1967**CLC 7, 49; DAM DRAM**
See also CA 21-22; 25-28R; CAP 2; DLB 4, 7; MTCW
Rice, Tim(othy Miles Bindon) 1944- ..... **CLC 21**
See also CA 103; CANR 46
Rich, Adrienne (Cecile) 1929-**CLC 3, 6, 7, 11, 18, 36, 73, 76; DAM POET; PC 5**
See also CA 9-12R; CANR 20, 53; DLB 5, 67; MTCW
Rich, Barbara
See Graves, Robert (von Ranke)
Rich, Robert
See Trumbo, Dalton
Richard, Keith .... **CLC 17**
See also Richards, Keith
Richards, David Adams 1950- ..... **CLC 59; DAC**
See also CA 93-96; CANR 60; DLB 53
Richards, I(vor) A(rmstrong) 1893-1979**CLC 14, 24**
See also CA 41-44R; 89-92; CANR 34; DLB 27
Richards, Keith 1943-
See Richard, Keith
See also CA 107
Richardson, Anne
See Roiphe, Anne (Richardson)
Richardson, Dorothy Miller 1873-1957 **TCLC 3**
See also CA 104; DLB 36
Richardson, Ethel Florence (Lindesay) 1870-1946
See Richardson, Henry Handel
See also CA 105
Richardson, Henry Handel .... **TCLC 4**
See also Richardson, Ethel Florence (Lindesay)
Richardson, John 1796-1852 .... **NCLC 55; DAC**
See also DLB 99
Richardson, Samuel 1689-1761 **LC 1; DA; DAB; DAC; DAM MST, NOV; WLC**
See also CDBLB 1660-1789; DLB 39
Richler, Mordecai 1931- **CLC 3, 5, 9, 13, 18, 46, 70; DAC; DAM MST, NOV**
See also AITN 1; CA 65-68; CANR 31, 62; CLR

17; DLB 53; MAICYA; MTCW; SATA 44; SATA-Brief 27

Richter, Conrad (Michael) 1890-1968 ... **CLC 30**
See also AAYA 21; CA 5-8R; 25-28R; CANR 23; DLB 9; MTCW; SATA 3

Ricostranza, Tom
See Ellis, Trey

Riddell, J. H. 1832-1906 .... **TCLC 40**

Riding, Laura .... **CLC 3, 7**
See also Jackson, Laura (Riding)

Riefenstahl, Berta Helene Amalia 1902-
See Riefenstahl, Leni
See also CA 108

Riefenstahl, Leni .... **CLC 16**
See also Riefenstahl, Berta Helene Amalia

Riffe, Ernest
See Bergman, (Ernst) Ingmar

Riggs, (Rolla) Lynn 1899-1954 . **TCLC 56; DAM MULT**
See also CA 144; DLB 175; NNAL

Riley, James Whitcomb 1849-1916 .... **TCLC 51; DAM POET**
See also CA 118; 137; MAICYA; SATA 17

Riley, Tex
See Creasey, John

Rilke, Rainer Maria 1875-1926 . **TCLC 1, 6, 19; DAM POET; PC 2**
See also CA 104; 132; CANR 62; DLB 81; MTCW

Rimbaud, (Jean Nicolas) Arthur 1854-1891 **NCLC 4, 35; DA; DAB; DAC; DAM MST, POET; PC 3; WLC**

Rinehart, Mary Roberts 1876-1958 ..... **TCLC 52**
See also CA 108

Ringmaster, The
See Mencken, H(enry) L(ouis)

Ringwood, Gwen(dolyn Margaret) Pharis 1910-1984 **CLC 48**
See also CA 148; 112; DLB 88

Rio, Michel 19(?)- .... **CLC 43**

Ritsos, Giannes
See Ritsos, Yannis

Ritsos, Yannis 1909-1990 .... **CLC 6, 13, 31**
See also CA 77-80; 133; CANR 39, 61; MTCW

Ritter, Erika 1948(?)- .... **CLC 52**

Rivera, Jose Eustasio 1889-1928 .... **TCLC 35**
See also CA 162; HW

Rivers, Conrad Kent 1933-1968 .... **CLC 1**
See also BW 1; CA 85-88; DLB 41

Rivers, Elfrida
See Bradley, Marion Zimmer

Riverside, John
See Heinlein, Robert A(nson)

Rizal, Jose 1861-1896 .... **NCLC 27**

Roa Bastos, Augusto (Antonio) 1917- . **CLC 45; DAM MULT; HLC**
See also CA 131; DLB 113; HW

Robbe-Grillet, Alain 1922- **CLC 1, 2, 4, 6, 8, 10, 14, 43**
See also CA 9-12R; CANR 33; DLB 83; MTCW

Robbins, Harold 1916-1997 .. **CLC 5; DAM NOV**
See also CA 73-76; 162; CANR 26, 54; MTCW

Robbins, Thomas Eugene 1936-
See Robbins, Tom
See also CA 81-84; CANR 29, 59; DAM NOV, POP; MTCW

Robbins, Tom .... **CLC 9, 32, 64**
See also Robbins, Thomas Eugene
See also BEST 90:3; DLBY 80

Robbins, Trina 1938- .... **CLC 21**
See also CA 128

Roberts, Charles G(eorge) D(ouglas) 1860-1943 **TCLC 8**
See also CA 105; CLR 33; DLB 92; SATA 88; SATA-Brief 29

Roberts, Elizabeth Madox 1886-1941 ... **TCLC 68**
See also CA 111; DLB 9, 54, 102; SATA 33; SATA-Brief 27

Roberts, Kate 1891-1985 .... **CLC 15**
See also CA 107; 116

Roberts, Keith (John Kingston) 1935- .. **CLC 14**
See also CA 25-28R; CANR 46

Roberts, Kenneth (Lewis) 1885-1957 .. **TCLC 23**
See also CA 109; DLB 9

Roberts, Michele (B.) 1949- .... **CLC 48**
See also CA 115; CANR 58

Robertson, Ellis
See Ellison, Harlan (Jay); Silverberg, Robert

Robertson, Thomas William 1829-1871 **NCLC 35; DAM DRAM**

Robeson, Kenneth
See Dent, Lester

Robinson, Edwin Arlington 1869-1935 . **TCLC 5; DA; DAC; DAM MST, POET; PC 1**
See also CA 104; 133; CDALB 1865-1917; DLB 54; MTCW

Robinson, Henry Crabb 1775-1867 .... **NCLC 15**
See also DLB 107

Robinson, Jill 1936- .... **CLC 10**
See also CA 102; INT 102

Robinson, Kim Stanley 1952- .... **CLC 34**
See also CA 126

Robinson, Lloyd
See Silverberg, Robert

Robinson, Marilynne 1944- .... **CLC 25**
See also CA 116

Robinson, Smokey .... **CLC 21**
See also Robinson, William, Jr.

Robinson, William, Jr. 1940-
See Robinson, Smokey
See also CA 116

Robison, Mary 1949- .... **CLC 42, 98**
See also CA 113; 116; DLB 130; INT 116

Rod, Edouard 1857-1910 .... **TCLC 52**

Roddenberry, Eugene Wesley 1921-1991
See Roddenberry, Gene
See also CA 110; 135; CANR 37; SATA 45; SATA-Obit 69

Roddenberry, Gene .... **CLC 17**
See also Roddenberry, Eugene Wesley
See also AAYA 5; SATA-Obit 69

Rodgers, Mary 1931- .... **CLC 12**
See also CA 49-52; CANR 8, 55; CLR 20; INT CANR-8; JRDA; MAICYA; SATA 8

Rodgers, W(illiam) R(obert) 1909-1969 .. **CLC 7**
See also CA 85-88; DLB 20

Rodman, Eric
See Silverberg, Robert

Rodman, Howard 1920(?)-1985 .... **CLC 65**
See also CA 118

Rodman, Maia
See Wojciechowska, Maia (Teresa)

Rodriguez, Claudio 1934- .... **CLC 10**
See also DLB 134

Roelvaag, O(le) E(dvart) 1876-1931 ..... **TCLC 17**
See also CA 117; DLB 9

Roethke, Theodore (Huebner) 1908-1963 **CLC 1, 3, 8, 11, 19, 46, 101; DAM POET; PC 15**
See also CA 81-84; CABS 2; CDALB 1941-1968; DLB 5; MTCW

Rogers, Thomas Hunton 1927- .... **CLC 57**
See also CA 89-92; INT 89-92

Rogers, Will(iam Penn Adair) 1879-1935 **TCLC 8, 71; DAM MULT**
See also CA 105; 144; DLB 11; NNAL

Rogin, Gilbert 1929- .... **CLC 18**
See also CA 65-68; CANR 15

Rohan, Koda .... **TCLC 22**
See also Koda Shigeyuki

Rohlfs, Anna Katharine Green
See Green, Anna Katharine

Rohmer, Eric .... **CLC 16**
See also Scherer, Jean-Marie Maurice

Rohmer, Sax .... **TCLC 28**
See also Ward, Arthur Henry Sarsfield
See also DLB 70

Roiphe, Anne (Richardson) 1935- .... **CLC 3, 9**
See also CA 89-92; CANR 45; DLBY 80; INT 89-92

Rojas, Fernando de 1465-1541 .... **LC 23**

Rolfe, Frederick (William Serafino Austin Lewis Mary) 1860-1913 .... **TCLC 12**
See also CA 107; DLB 34, 156

Rolland, Romain 1866-1944 .... **TCLC 23**
See also CA 118; DLB 65

Rolle, Richard c. 1300-c. 1349 .... **CMLC 21**
See also DLB 146

Rolvaag, O(le) E(dvart)
See Roelvaag, O(le) E(dvart)

Romain Arnaud, Saint
See Aragon, Louis

Romains, Jules 1885-1972 .... **CLC 7**
See also CA 85-88; CANR 34; DLB 65; MTCW

Romero, Jose Ruben 1890-1952 .... **TCLC 14**
See also CA 114; 131; HW

Ronsard, Pierre de 1524-1585 .... **LC 6; PC 11**

Rooke, Leon 1934- .... **CLC 25, 34; DAM POP**
See also CA 25-28R; CANR 23, 53

Roosevelt, Theodore 1858-1919 .... **TCLC 69**
See also CA 115; DLB 47

Roper, William 1498-1578 .... **LC 10**

Roquelaure, A. N.
See Rice, Anne

Rosa, Joao Guimaraes 1908-1967 .... **CLC 23**
See also CA 89-92; DLB 113

Rose, Wendy 1948- **CLC 85; DAM MULT; PC 13**
See also CA 53-56; CANR 5, 51; DLB 175; NNAL; SATA 12

Rosen, R. D.
See Rosen, Richard (Dean)

Rosen, Richard (Dean) 1949- .... **CLC 39**
See also CA 77-80; CANR 62; INT CANR-30

Rosenberg, Isaac 1890-1918 .... **TCLC 12**
See also CA 107; DLB 20

Rosenblatt, Joe .... **CLC 15**
See also Rosenblatt, Joseph

Rosenblatt, Joseph 1933-
See Rosenblatt, Joe
See also CA 89-92; INT 89-92

Rosenfeld, Samuel
See Tzara, Tristan

Rosenstock, Sami
See Tzara, Tristan

Rosenstock, Samuel
See Tzara, Tristan

Rosenthal, M(acha) L(ouis) 1917-1996 .. **CLC 28**
See also CA 1-4R; 152; CAAS 6; CANR 4, 51; DLB 5; SATA 59

Ross, Barnaby
See Dannay, Frederic

Ross, Bernard L.
See Follett, Ken(neth Martin)

Ross, J. H.
See Lawrence, T(homas) E(dward)

Ross, Martin
See Martin, Violet Florence
See also DLB 135

Ross, (James) Sinclair 1908- .... **CLC 13; DAC; DAM MST; SSC 24**
See also CA 73-76; DLB 88

See also CA 153; HW
Sanchez, Luis Rafael 1936- .... **CLC 23**
See also CA 128; DLB 145; HW
Sanchez, Sonia 1934-**CLC 5; BLC; DAM MULT; PC 9**
See also BW 2; CA 33-36R; CANR 24, 49; CLR 18; DLB 41; DLBD 8; MAICYA; MTCW; SATA 22
Sand, George 1804-1876 ... **NCLC 2, 42, 57; DA; DAB; DAC; DAM MST, NOV; WLC**
See also DLB 119
Sandburg, Carl (August) 1878-1967**CLC 1, 4, 10, 15, 35; DA; DAB; DAC; DAM MST, POET; PC 2; WLC**
See also AAYA 24; CA 5-8R; 25-28R; CANR 35; CDALB 1865-1917; DLB 17, 54; MAICYA; MTCW; SATA 8
Sandburg, Charles
See Sandburg, Carl (August)
Sandburg, Charles A.
See Sandburg, Carl (August)
Sanders, (James) Ed(ward) 1939-.......... **CLC 53**
See also CA 13-16R; CAAS 21; CANR 13, 44; DLB 16
Sanders, Lawrence 1920-1998**CLC 41; DAM POP**
See also BEST 89:4; CA 81-84; CANR 33, 62; MTCW
Sanders, Noah
See Blount, Roy (Alton), Jr.
Sanders, Winston P.
See Anderson, Poul (William)
Sandoz, Mari(e Susette) 1896-1966 .... **CLC 28**
See also CA 1-4R; 25-28R; CANR 17, 64; DLB 9; MTCW; SATA 5
Saner, Reg(inald Anthony) 1931-............ **CLC 9**
See also CA 65-68
Sannazaro, Jacopo 1456(?)-1530 .... **LC 8**
Sansom, William 1912-1976**CLC 2, 6; DAM NOV; SSC 21**
See also CA 5-8R; 65-68; CANR 42; DLB 139; MTCW
Santayana, George 1863-1952 .... **TCLC 40**
See also CA 115; DLB 54, 71; DLBD 13
Santiago, Danny .... **CLC 33**
See also James, Daniel (Lewis)
See also DLB 122
Santmyer, Helen Hoover 1895-1986 ...... **CLC 33**
See also CA 1-4R; 118; CANR 15, 33; DLBY 84; MTCW
Santoka, Taneda 1882-1940 .... **TCLC 72**
Santos, Bienvenido N(uqui) 1911-1996 . **CLC 22; DAM MULT**
See also CA 101; 151; CANR 19, 46
Sapper .... **TCLC 44**
See also McNeile, Herman Cyril
Sapphire 1950- .... **CLC 99**
Sappho fl. 6th cent. B.C.- **CMLC 3; DAM POET; PC 5**
See also DLB 176
Sarduy, Severo 1937-1993 .... **CLC 6, 97**
See also CA 89-92; 142; CANR 58; DLB 113; HW
Sargeson, Frank 1903-1982 .... **CLC 31**
See also CA 25-28R; 106; CANR 38
Sarmiento, Felix Ruben Garcia
See Dario, Ruben
Saroyan, William 1908-1981**CLC 1, 8, 10, 29, 34, 56; DA; DAB; DAC; DAM DRAM, MST, NOV; SSC 21; WLC**
See also CA 5-8R; 103; CANR 30; DLB 7, 9, 86; DLBY 81; MTCW; SATA 23; SATA-Obit 24
Sarraute, Nathalie 1900-**CLC 1, 2, 4, 8, 10, 31, 80**
See also CA 9-12R; CANR 23; DLB 83; MTCW
Sarton, (Eleanor) May 1912-1995 **CLC 4, 14, 49, 91; DAM POET**
See also CA 1-4R; 149; CANR 1, 34, 55; DLB 48; DLBY 81; INT CANR-34; MTCW; SATA 36; SATA-Obit 86
Sartre, Jean-Paul 1905-1980 . **CLC 1, 4, 7, 9, 13, 18, 24, 44, 50, 52; DA; DAB; DAC; DAM DRAM, MST, NOV; DC 3; WLC**
See also CA 9-12R; 97-100; CANR 21; DLB 72; MTCW
Sassoon, Siegfried (Lorraine) 1886-1967 .. **CLC 36; DAB; DAM MST, NOV, POET; PC 12**
See also CA 104; 25-28R; CANR 36; DLB 20; MTCW
Satterfield, Charles
See Pohl, Frederik
Saul, John (W. III) 1942- ... **CLC 46; DAM NOV, POP**
See also AAYA 10; BEST 90:4; CA 81-84; CANR 16, 40
Saunders, Caleb
See Heinlein, Robert A(nson)
Saura (Atares), Carlos 1932- .... **CLC 20**
See also CA 114; 131; HW
Sauser-Hall, Frederic 1887-1961 .... **CLC 18**
See also Cendrars, Blaise
See also CA 102; 93-96; CANR 36, 62; MTCW
Saussure, Ferdinand de 1857-1913 ..... **TCLC 49**
Savage, Catharine
See Brosman, Catharine Savage
Savage, Thomas 1915-........................... **CLC 40**
See also CA 126; 132; CAAS 15; INT 132
Savan, Glenn 19(?)- .... **CLC 50**
Sayers, Dorothy L(eigh) 1893-1957 **TCLC 2, 15; DAM POP**
See also CA 104; 119; CANR 60; CDBLB 1914-1945; DLB 10, 36, 77, 100; MTCW
Sayers, Valerie 1952- .... **CLC 50**
See also CA 134; CANR 61
Sayles, John (Thomas) 1950- ...... **CLC 7, 10, 14**
See also CA 57-60; CANR 41; DLB 44
Scammell, Michael 1935-...................... **CLC 34**
See also CA 156
Scannell, Vernon 1922-......................... **CLC 49**
See also CA 5-8R; CANR 8, 24, 57; DLB 27; SATA 59
Scarlett, Susan
See Streatfeild, (Mary) Noel
Schaeffer, Susan Fromberg 1941-**CLC 6, 11, 22**
See also CA 49-52; CANR 18; DLB 28; MTCW; SATA 22
Schary, Jill
See Robinson, Jill
Schell, Jonathan 1943- .... **CLC 35**
See also CA 73-76; CANR 12
Schelling, Friedrich Wilhelm Joseph von 1775-1854 .... **NCLC 30**
See also DLB 90
Schendel, Arthur van 1874-1946 .... **TCLC 56**
Scherer, Jean-Marie Maurice 1920-
See Rohmer, Eric
See also CA 110
Schevill, James (Erwin) 1920- .... **CLC 7**
See also CA 5-8R; CAAS 12
Schiller, Friedrich 1759-1805 .. **NCLC 39; DAM DRAM**
See also DLB 94
Schisgal, Murray (Joseph) 1926- .... **CLC 6**
See also CA 21-24R; CANR 48
Schlee, Ann 1934- .... **CLC 35**
See also CA 101; CANR 29; SATA 44; SATA-Brief 36
Schlegel, August Wilhelm von 1767-1845**NCLC 15**
See also DLB 94
Schlegel, Friedrich 1772-1829 .... **NCLC 45**
See also DLB 90
Schlegel, Johann Elias (von) 1719(?)-1749 **LC 5**
Schlesinger, Arthur M(eier), Jr. 1917- **CLC 84**
See also AITN 1; CA 1-4R; CANR 1, 28, 58; DLB 17; INT CANR-28; MTCW; SATA 61
Schmidt, Arno (Otto) 1914-1979 .... **CLC 56**
See also CA 128; 109; DLB 69
Schmitz, Aron Hector 1861-1928
See Svevo, Italo
See also CA 104; 122; MTCW
Schnackenberg, Gjertrud 1953-........... **CLC 40**
See also CA 116; DLB 120
Schneider, Leonard Alfred 1925-1966
See Bruce, Lenny
See also CA 89-92
Schnitzler, Arthur 1862-1931 **TCLC 4; SSC 15**
See also CA 104; DLB 81, 118
Schoenberg, Arnold 1874-1951 .... **TCLC 75**
See also CA 109
Schonberg, Arnold
See Schoenberg, Arnold
Schopenhauer, Arthur 1788-1860 ...... **NCLC 51**
See also DLB 90
Schor, Sandra (M.) 1932(?)-1990 .... **CLC 65**
See also CA 132
Schorer, Mark 1908-1977 .... **CLC 9**
See also CA 5-8R; 73-76; CANR 7; DLB 103
Schrader, Paul (Joseph) 1946- .... **CLC 26**
See also CA 37-40R; CANR 41; DLB 44
Schreiner, Olive (Emilie Albertina) 1855-1920 **TCLC 9**
See also CA 105; 154; DLB 18, 156
Schulberg, Budd (Wilson) 1914- ...... **CLC 7, 48**
See also CA 25-28R; CANR 19; DLB 6, 26, 28; DLBY 81
Schulz, Bruno 1892-1942 . **TCLC 5, 51; SSC 13**
See also CA 115; 123
Schulz, Charles M(onroe) 1922- .... **CLC 12**
See also CA 9-12R; CANR 6; INT CANR-6; SATA 10
Schumacher, E(rnst) F(riedrich) 1911-1977**CLC 80**
See also CA 81-84; 73-76; CANR 34
Schuyler, James Marcus 1923-1991 **CLC 5, 23; DAM POET**
See also CA 101; 134; DLB 5, 169; INT 101
Schwartz, Delmore (David) 1913-1966 **CLC 2, 4, 10, 45, 87; PC 8**
See also CA 17-18; 25-28R; CANR 35; CAP 2; DLB 28, 48; MTCW
Schwartz, Ernst
See Ozu, Yasujiro
Schwartz, John Burnham 1965- .... **CLC 59**
See also CA 132
Schwartz, Lynne Sharon 1939- .... **CLC 31**
See also CA 103; CANR 44
Schwartz, Muriel A.
See Eliot, T(homas) S(tearns)
Schwarz-Bart, Andre 1928- .... **CLC 2, 4**
See also CA 89-92
Schwarz-Bart, Simone 1938-.................. **CLC 7**
See also BW 2; CA 97-100
Schwob, (Mayer Andre) Marcel 1867-1905**TCLC 20**
See also CA 117; DLB 123
Sciascia, Leonardo 1921-1989 .... **CLC 8, 9, 41**
See also CA 85-88; 130; CANR 35; DLB 177; MTCW
Scoppettone, Sandra 1936- .... **CLC 26**
See also AAYA 11; CA 5-8R; CANR 41; SATA 9, 92

See also CA 128
Skram, Amalie (Bertha) 1847-1905 .... **TCLC 25**
Skvorecky, Josef (Vaclav) 1924-**CLC 15, 39, 69; DAC; DAM NOV**
See also CA 61-64; CAAS 1; CANR 10, 34, 63; MTCW
Slade, Bernard .... **CLC 11, 46**
See also Newbound, Bernard Slade
See also CAAS 9; DLB 53
Slaughter, Carolyn 1946-...................... **CLC 56**
See also CA 85-88
Slaughter, Frank G(ill) 1908-............... **CLC 29**
See also AITN 2; CA 5-8R; CANR 5; INT CANR-5
Slavitt, David R(ytman) 1935- .... **CLC 5, 14**
See also CA 21-24R; CAAS 3; CANR 41; DLB 5, 6
Slesinger, Tess 1905-1945 .... **TCLC 10**
See also CA 107; DLB 102
Slessor, Kenneth 1901-1971 .... **CLC 14**
See also CA 102; 89-92
Slowacki, Juliusz 1809-1849 .... **NCLC 15**
Smart, Christopher 1722-1771 **LC 3; DAM POET; PC 13**
See also DLB 109
Smart, Elizabeth 1913-1986 .... **CLC 54**
See also CA 81-84; 118; DLB 88
Smiley, Jane (Graves) 1949- **CLC 53, 76; DAM POP**
See also CA 104; CANR 30, 50; INT CANR-30
Smith, A(rthur) J(ames) M(arshall) 1902-1980 **CLC 15; DAC**
See also CA 1-4R; 102; CANR 4; DLB 88
Smith, Adam 1723-1790 .... **LC 36**
See also DLB 104
Smith, Alexander 1829-1867 .... **NCLC 59**
See also DLB 32, 55
Smith, Anna Deavere 1950- .... **CLC 86**
See also CA 133
Smith, Betty (Wehner) 1896-1972 .... **CLC 19**
See also CA 5-8R; 33-36R; DLBY 82; SATA 6
Smith, Charlotte (Turner) 1749-1806 **NCLC 23**
See also DLB 39, 109
Smith, Clark Ashton 1893-1961 .... **CLC 43**
See also CA 143
Smith, Dave .... **CLC 22, 42**
See also Smith, David (Jeddie)
See also CAAS 7; DLB 5
Smith, David (Jeddie) 1942-
See Smith, Dave
See also CA 49-52; CANR 1, 59; DAM POET
Smith, Florence Margaret 1902-1971
See Smith, Stevie
See also CA 17-18; 29-32R; CANR 35; CAP 2; DAM POET; MTCW
Smith, Iain Crichton 1928-.................. **CLC 64**
See also CA 21-24R; DLB 40, 139
Smith, John 1580(?)-1631 .... **LC 9**
Smith, Johnston
See Crane, Stephen (Townley)
Smith, Joseph, Jr. 1805-1844 .... **NCLC 53**
Smith, Lee 1944- .... **CLC 25, 73**
See also CA 114; 119; CANR 46; DLB 143; DLBY 83; INT 119
Smith, Martin
See Smith, Martin Cruz
Smith, Martin Cruz 1942-**CLC 25; DAM MULT, POP**
See also BEST 89:4; CA 85-88; CANR 6, 23, 43; INT CANR-23; NNAL
Smith, Mary-Ann Tirone 1944- .... **CLC 39**
See also CA 118; 136
Smith, Patti 1946- .... **CLC 12**
See also CA 93-96; CANR 63
Smith, Pauline (Urmson) 1882-1959 ... **TCLC 25**
Smith, Rosamond
See Oates, Joyce Carol
Smith, Sheila Kaye
See Kaye-Smith, Sheila
Smith, Stevie .... **CLC 3, 8, 25, 44; PC 12**
See also Smith, Florence Margaret
See also DLB 20
Smith, Wilbur (Addison) 1933- .... **CLC 33**
See also CA 13-16R; CANR 7, 46; MTCW
Smith, William Jay 1918- .... **CLC 6**
See also CA 5-8R; CANR 44; DLB 5; MAICYA; SAAS 22; SATA 2, 68
Smith, Woodrow Wilson
See Kuttner, Henry
Smolenskin, Peretz 1842-1885 .... **NCLC 30**
Smollett, Tobias (George) 1721-1771 .... **LC 2**
See also CDBLB 1660-1789; DLB 39, 104
Snodgrass, W(illiam) D(e Witt) 1926-**CLC 2, 6, 10, 18, 68; DAM POET**
See also CA 1-4R; CANR 6, 36; DLB 5; MTCW
Snow, C(harles) P(ercy) 1905-1980**CLC 1, 4, 6, 9, 13, 19; DAM NOV**
See also CA 5-8R; 101; CANR 28; CDBLB 1945-1960; DLB 15, 77; MTCW
Snow, Frances Compton
See Adams, Henry (Brooks)
Snyder, Gary (Sherman) 1930-**CLC 1, 2, 5, 9, 32; DAM POET; PC 21**
See also CA 17-20R; CANR 30, 60; DLB 5, 16, 165
Snyder, Zilpha Keatley 1927-................ **CLC 17**
See also AAYA 15; CA 9-12R; CANR 38; CLR 31; JRDA; MAICYA; SAAS 2; SATA 1, 28, 75
Soares, Bernardo
See Pessoa, Fernando (Antonio Nogueira)
Sobh, A.
See Shamlu, Ahmad
Sobol, Joshua .... **CLC 60**
Soderberg, Hjalmar 1869-1941 .... **TCLC 39**
Sodergran, Edith (Irene)
See Soedergran, Edith (Irene)
Soedergran, Edith (Irene) 1892-1923 .. **TCLC 31**
Softly, Edgar
See Lovecraft, H(oward) P(hillips)
Softly, Edward
See Lovecraft, H(oward) P(hillips)
Sokolov, Raymond 1941- .... **CLC 7**
See also CA 85-88
Solo, Jay
See Ellison, Harlan (Jay)
Sologub, Fyodor .... **TCLC 9**
See also Teternikov, Fyodor Kuzmich
Solomons, Ikey Esquir
See Thackeray, William Makepeace
Solomos, Dionysios 1798-1857 .... **NCLC 15**
Solwoska, Mara
See French, Marilyn
Solzhenitsyn, Aleksandr I(sayevich) 1918- **CLC 1, 2, 4, 7, 9, 10, 18, 26, 34, 78; DA; DAB; DAC; DAM MST, NOV; WLC**
See also AITN 1; CA 69-72; CANR 40; MTCW
Somers, Jane
See Lessing, Doris (May)
Somerville, Edith 1858-1949 .... **TCLC 51**
See also DLB 135
Somerville & Ross
See Martin, Violet Florence; Somerville, Edith
Sommer, Scott 1951- .... **CLC 25**
See also CA 106
Sondheim, Stephen (Joshua) 1930- **CLC 30, 39; DAM DRAM**
See also AAYA 11; CA 103; CANR 47
Song, Cathy 1955- .... **PC 21**
See also CA 154; DLB 169
Sontag, Susan 1933- **CLC 1, 2, 10, 13, 31, 105; DAM POP**
See also CA 17-20R; CANR 25, 51; DLB 2, 67; MTCW
Sophocles 496(?)B.C.-406(?)B.C. . **CMLC 2; DA; DAB; DAC; DAM DRAM, MST; DC 1; WLCS**
See also DLB 176
Sordello 1189-1269 .... **CMLC 15**
Sorel, Julia
See Drexler, Rosalyn
Sorrentino, Gilbert 1929- . **CLC 3, 7, 14, 22, 40**
See also CA 77-80; CANR 14, 33; DLB 5, 173; DLBY 80; INT CANR-14
Soto, Gary 1952-**CLC 32, 80; DAM MULT; HLC**
See also AAYA 10; CA 119; 125; CANR 50; CLR 38; DLB 82; HW; INT 125; JRDA; SATA 80
Soupault, Philippe 1897-1990 .... **CLC 68**
See also CA 116; 147; 131
Souster, (Holmes) Raymond 1921- ... **CLC 5, 14; DAC; DAM POET**
See also CA 13-16R; CAAS 14; CANR 13, 29, 53; DLB 88; SATA 63
Southern, Terry 1924(?)-1995 .... **CLC 7**
See also CA 1-4R; 150; CANR 1, 55; DLB 2
Southey, Robert 1774-1843 .... **NCLC 8**
See also DLB 93, 107, 142; SATA 54
Southworth, Emma Dorothy Eliza Nevitte 1819-1899 .... **NCLC 26**
Souza, Ernest
See Scott, Evelyn
Soyinka, Wole 1934-**CLC 3, 5, 14, 36, 44; BLC; DA; DAB; DAC; DAM DRAM, MST, MULT; DC 2; WLC**
See also BW 2; CA 13-16R; CANR 27, 39; DLB 125; MTCW
Spackman, W(illiam) M(ode) 1905-1990 **CLC 46**
See also CA 81-84; 132
Spacks, Barry (Bernard) 1931- .... **CLC 14**
See also CA 154; CANR 33; DLB 105
Spanidou, Irini 1946- .... **CLC 44**
Spark, Muriel (Sarah) 1918- **CLC 2, 3, 5, 8, 13, 18, 40, 94; DAB; DAC; DAM MST, NOV; SSC 10**
See also CA 5-8R; CANR 12, 36; CDBLB 1945-1960; DLB 15, 139; INT CANR-12; MTCW
Spaulding, Douglas
See Bradbury, Ray (Douglas)
Spaulding, Leonard
See Bradbury, Ray (Douglas)
Spence, J. A. D.
See Eliot, T(homas) S(tearns)
Spencer, Elizabeth 1921- .... **CLC 22**
See also CA 13-16R; CANR 32; DLB 6; MTCW; SATA 14
Spencer, Leonard G.
See Silverberg, Robert
Spencer, Scott 1945- .... **CLC 30**
See also CA 113; CANR 51; DLBY 86
Spender, Stephen (Harold) 1909-1995**CLC 1, 2, 5, 10, 41, 91; DAM POET**
See also CA 9-12R; 149; CANR 31, 54; CDBLB 1945-1960; DLB 20; MTCW
Spengler, Oswald (Arnold Gottfried) 1880-1936 **TCLC 25**
See also CA 118
Spenser, Edmund 1552(?)-1599 ... **LC 5, 39; DA; DAB; DAC; DAM MST, POET; PC 8; WLC**
See also CDBLB Before 1660; DLB 167
Spicer, Jack 1925-1965 .... **CLC 8, 18, 72; DAM POET**

Storey, David (Malcolm) 1933- ... **CLC 2, 4, 5, 8; DAM DRAM**
See also CA 81-84; CANR 36; DLB 13, 14; MTCW
Storm, Hyemeyohsts 1935- **CLC 3; DAM MULT**
See also CA 81-84; CANR 45; NNAL
Storm, (Hans) Theodor (Woldsen) 1817-1888 **NCLC 1; SSC 27**
Storni, Alfonsina 1892-1938 **TCLC 5; DAM MULT; HLC**
See also CA 104; 131; HW
Stoughton, William 1631-1701 .... **LC 38**
See also DLB 24
Stout, Rex (Todhunter) 1886-1975 .... **CLC 3**
See also AITN 2; CA 61-64
Stow, (Julian) Randolph 1935- .... **CLC 23, 48**
See also CA 13-16R; CANR 33; MTCW
Stowe, Harriet (Elizabeth) Beecher 1811-1896 **NCLC 3, 50; DA; DAB; DAC; DAM MST, NOV; WLC**
See also CDALB 1865-1917; DLB 1, 12, 42, 74; JRDA; MAICYA; YABC 1
Strachey, (Giles) Lytton 1880-1932 ..... **TCLC 12**
See also CA 110; DLB 149; DLBD 10
Strand, Mark 1934- ... **CLC 6, 18, 41, 71; DAM POET**
See also CA 21-24R; CANR 40; DLB 5; SATA 41
Straub, Peter (Francis) 1943- **CLC 28, 107; DAM POP**
See also BEST 89:1; CA 85-88; CANR 28; DLBY 84; MTCW
Strauss, Botho 1944- .... **CLC 22**
See also CA 157; DLB 124
Streatfeild, (Mary) Noel 1895(?)-1986 .. **CLC 21**
See also CA 81-84; 120; CANR 31; CLR 17; DLB 160; MAICYA; SATA 20; SATA-Obit 48
Stribling, T(homas) S(igismund) 1881-1965 **CLC 23**
See also CA 107; DLB 9
Strindberg, (Johan) August 1849-1912 **TCLC 1, 8, 21, 47; DA; DAB; DAC; DAM DRAM, MST; WLC**
See also CA 104; 135
Stringer, Arthur 1874-1950 .... **TCLC 37**
See also CA 161; DLB 92
Stringer, David
See Roberts, Keith (John Kingston)
Stroheim, Erich von 1885-1957 .... **TCLC 71**
Strugatskii, Arkadii (Natanovich) 1925-1991 **CLC 27**
See also CA 106; 135
Strugatskii, Boris (Natanovich) 1933- . **CLC 27**
See also CA 106
Strummer, Joe 1953(?)- .... **CLC 30**
Stuart, Don A.
See Campbell, John W(ood, Jr.)
Stuart, Ian
See MacLean, Alistair (Stuart)
Stuart, Jesse (Hilton) 1906-1984 **CLC 1, 8, 11, 14, 34**
See also CA 5-8R; 112; CANR 31; DLB 9, 48, 102; DLBY 84; SATA 2; SATA-Obit 36
Sturgeon, Theodore (Hamilton) 1918-1985 **CLC 22, 39**
See also Queen, Ellery
See also CA 81-84; 116; CANR 32; DLB 8; DLBY 85; MTCW
Sturges, Preston 1898-1959 .... **TCLC 48**
See also CA 114; 149; DLB 26
Styron, William 1925- . **CLC 1, 3, 5, 11, 15, 60; DAM NOV, POP; SSC 25**
See also BEST 90:4; CA 5-8R; CANR 6, 33; CDALB 1968-1988; DLB 2, 143; DLBY 80; INT CANR-6; MTCW
Suarez Lynch, B.
See Bioy Casares, Adolfo; Borges, Jorge Luis
Su Chien 1884-1918
See Su Man-shu
See also CA 123
Suckow, Ruth 1892-1960 .... **SSC 18**
See also CA 113; DLB 9, 102
Sudermann, Hermann 1857-1928 .... **TCLC 15**
See also CA 107; DLB 118
Sue, Eugene 1804-1857 .... **NCLC 1**
See also DLB 119
Sueskind, Patrick 1949- .... **CLC 44**
See also Suskind, Patrick
Sukenick, Ronald 1932- .... **CLC 3, 4, 6, 48**
See also CA 25-28R; CAAS 8; CANR 32; DLB 173; DLBY 81
Suknaski, Andrew 1942- .... **CLC 19**
See also CA 101; DLB 53
Sullivan, Vernon
See Vian, Boris
Sully Prudhomme 1839-1907 .... **TCLC 31**
Su Man-shu .... **TCLC 24**
See also Su Chien
Summerforest, Ivy B.
See Kirkup, James
Summers, Andrew James 1942- .... **CLC 26**
Summers, Andy
See Summers, Andrew James
Summers, Hollis (Spurgeon, Jr.) 1916- **CLC 10**
See also CA 5-8R; CANR 3; DLB 6
Summers, (Alphonsus Joseph-Mary Augustus) Montague 1880-1948 .... **TCLC 16**
See also CA 118
Sumner, Gordon Matthew 1951- .... **CLC 26**
Surtees, Robert Smith 1803-1864 ...... **NCLC 14**
See also DLB 21
Susann, Jacqueline 1921-1974 .... **CLC 3**
See also AITN 1; CA 65-68; 53-56; MTCW
Su Shih 1036-1101 .... **CMLC 15**
Suskind, Patrick
See Sueskind, Patrick
See also CA 145
Sutcliff, Rosemary 1920-1992 .... **CLC 26; DAB; DAC; DAM MST, POP**
See also AAYA 10; CA 5-8R; 139; CANR 37; CLR 1, 37; JRDA; MAICYA; SATA 6, 44, 78; SATA-Obit 73
Sutro, Alfred 1863-1933 .... **TCLC 6**
See also CA 105; DLB 10
Sutton, Henry
See Slavitt, David R(ytman)
Svevo, Italo 1861-1928 ...... **TCLC 2, 35; SSC 25**
See also Schmitz, Aron Hector
Swados, Elizabeth (A.) 1951- .... **CLC 12**
See also CA 97-100; CANR 49; INT 97-100
Swados, Harvey 1920-1972 .... **CLC 5**
See also CA 5-8R; 37-40R; CANR 6; DLB 2
Swan, Gladys 1934- .... **CLC 69**
See also CA 101; CANR 17, 39
Swarthout, Glendon (Fred) 1918-1992 ... **CLC 35**
See also CA 1-4R; 139; CANR 1, 47; SATA 26
Sweet, Sarah C.
See Jewett, (Theodora) Sarah Orne
Swenson, May 1919-1989 **CLC 4, 14, 61, 106; DA; DAB; DAC; DAM MST, POET; PC 14**
See also CA 5-8R; 130; CANR 36, 61; DLB 5; MTCW; SATA 15
Swift, Augustus
See Lovecraft, H(oward) P(hillips)
Swift, Graham (Colin) 1949- .... **CLC 41, 88**
See also CA 117; 122; CANR 46
Swift, Jonathan 1667-1745 **LC 1; DA; DAB; DAC; DAM MST, NOV, POET; PC 9; WLC**
See also CDBLB 1660-1789; DLB 39, 95, 101; SATA 19
Swinburne, Algernon Charles 1837-1909 **TCLC 8, 36; DA; DAB; DAC; DAM MST, POET; WLC**
See also CA 105; 140; CDBLB 1832-1890; DLB 35, 57
Swinfen, Ann .... **CLC 34**
Swinnerton, Frank Arthur 1884-1982 .. **CLC 31**
See also CA 108; DLB 34
Swithen, John
See King, Stephen (Edwin)
Sylvia
See Ashton-Warner, Sylvia (Constance)
Symmes, Robert Edward
See Duncan, Robert (Edward)
Symonds, John Addington 1840-1893 **NCLC 34**
See also DLB 57, 144
Symons, Arthur 1865-1945 .... **TCLC 11**
See also CA 107; DLB 19, 57, 149
Symons, Julian (Gustave) 1912-1994 **CLC 2, 14, 32**
See also CA 49-52; 147; CAAS 3; CANR 3, 33, 59; DLB 87, 155; DLBY 92; MTCW
Synge, (Edmund) J(ohn) M(illington) 1871-1909 **TCLC 6, 37; DAM DRAM; DC 2**
See also CA 104; 141; CDBLB 1890-1914; DLB 10, 19
Syruc, J.
See Milosz, Czeslaw
Szirtes, George 1948- .... **CLC 46**
See also CA 109; CANR 27, 61
Szymborska, Wislawa 1923- .... **CLC 99**
See also CA 154; DLBY 96
T. O., Nik
See Annensky, Innokenty (Fyodorovich)
Tabori, George 1914- .... **CLC 19**
See also CA 49-52; CANR 4
Tagore, Rabindranath 1861-1941 ... **TCLC 3, 53; DAM DRAM, POET; PC 8**
See also CA 104; 120; MTCW
Taine, Hippolyte Adolphe 1828-1893 .. **NCLC 15**
Talese, Gay 1932- .... **CLC 37**
See also AITN 1; CA 1-4R; CANR 9, 58; INT CANR-9; MTCW
Tallent, Elizabeth (Ann) 1954- .... **CLC 45**
See also CA 117; DLB 130
Tally, Ted 1952- .... **CLC 42**
See also CA 120; 124; INT 124
Tamayo y Baus, Manuel 1829-1898 ...... **NCLC 1**
Tammsaare, A(nton) H(ansen) 1878-1940 **TCLC 27**
Tam'si, Tchicaya U
See Tchicaya, Gerald Felix
Tan, Amy (Ruth) 1952- .... **CLC 59; DAM MULT, NOV, POP**
See also AAYA 9; BEST 89:3; CA 136; CANR 54; DLB 173; SATA 75
Tandem, Felix
See Spitteler, Carl (Friedrich Georg)
Tanizaki, Jun'ichiro 1886-1965 . **CLC 8, 14, 28; SSC 21**
See also CA 93-96; 25-28R; DLB 180
Tanner, William
See Amis, Kingsley (William)
Tao Lao
See Storni, Alfonsina
Tarassoff, Lev
See Troyat, Henri
Tarbell, Ida M(inerva) 1857-1944 .... **TCLC 40**
See also CA 122; DLB 47
Tarkington, (Newton) Booth 1869-1946 **TCLC 9**

Author Index

Author Index

Young, Collier
See Bloch, Robert (Albert)
Young, Edward 1683-1765 .... **LC 3, 40**
See also DLB 95
Young, Marguerite (Vivian) 1909-1995 . **CLC 82**
See also CA 13-16; 150; CAP 1
Young, Neil 1945- .... **CLC 17**
See also CA 110
Young Bear, Ray A. 1950- **CLC 94; DAM MULT**
See also CA 146; DLB 175; NNAL
Yourcenar, Marguerite 1903-1987**CLC 19, 38, 50, 87; DAM NOV**
See also CA 69-72; CANR 23, 60; DLB 72; DLBY 88; MTCW
Yurick, Sol 1925- .... **CLC 6**
See also CA 13-16R; CANR 25
Zabolotskii, Nikolai Alekseevich 1903-1958 **TCLC 52**
See also CA 116
Zamiatin, Yevgenii
See Zamyatin, Evgeny Ivanovich
Zamora, Bernice (B. Ortiz) 1938-**CLC 89; DAM MULT; HLC**
See also CA 151; DLB 82; HW
Zamyatin, Evgeny Ivanovich 1884-1937**TCLC 8, 37**
See also CA 105
Zangwill, Israel 1864-1926 .... **TCLC 16**
See also CA 109; DLB 10, 135
Zappa, Francis Vincent, Jr. 1940-1993
See Zappa, Frank
See also CA 108; 143; CANR 57
Zappa, Frank .... **CLC 17**
See also Zappa, Francis Vincent, Jr.
Zaturenska, Marya 1902-1982 .... **CLC 6, 11**
See also CA 13-16R; 105; CANR 22
Zeami 1363-1443 .... **DC 7**
Zelazny, Roger (Joseph) 1937-1995 ...... **CLC 21**
See also AAYA 7; CA 21-24R; 148; CANR 26, 60; DLB 8; MTCW; SATA 57; SATA-Brief 39
Zhdanov, Andrei A(lexandrovich) 1896-1948 **TCLC 18**
See also CA 117
Zhukovsky, Vasily 1783-1852 .... **NCLC 35**
Ziegenhagen, Eric .... **CLC 55**
Zimmer, Jill Schary
See Robinson, Jill
Zimmerman, Robert
See Dylan, Bob
Zindel, Paul 1936- **CLC 6, 26; DA; DAB; DAC; DAM DRAM, MST, NOV; DC 5**
See also AAYA 2; CA 73-76; CANR 31; CLR 3, 45; DLB 7, 52; JRDA; MAICYA; MTCW; SATA 16, 58
Zinov'Ev, A. A.
See Zinoviev, Alexander (Aleksandrovich)
Zinoviev, Alexander (Aleksandrovich) 1922-**CLC 19**
See also CA 116; 133; CAAS 10
Zoilus
See Lovecraft, H(oward) P(hillips)
Zola, Emile (Edouard Charles Antoine) 1840-1902 **TCLC 1, 6, 21, 41; DA; DAB; DAC; DAM MST, NOV; WLC**
See also CA 104; 138; DLB 123
Zoline, Pamela 1941- .... **CLC 62**
See also CA 161
Zorrilla y Moral, Jose 1817-1893 .... **NCLC 6**
Zoshchenko, Mikhail (Mikhailovich) 1895-1958 **TCLC 15; SSC 15**
See also CA 115; 160
Zuckmayer, Carl 1896-1977 .... **CLC 18**
See also CA 69-72; DLB 56, 124
Zuk, Georges
See Skelton, Robin
Zukofsky, Louis 1904-1978**CLC 1, 2, 4, 7, 11, 18; DAM POET; PC 11**
See also CA 9-12R; 77-80; CANR 39; DLB 5, 165; MTCW
Zweig, Paul 1935-1984 .... **CLC 34, 42**
See also CA 85-88; 113
Zweig, Stefan 1881-1942 .... **TCLC 17**
See also CA 112; DLB 81, 118
Zwingli, Huldreich 1484-1531 .... **LC 37**
See also DLB 179

Literary Criticism Series Cumulative Topic Index

This index lists all topic entries in Gale's *Classical and Medieval Literature Criticism, Contemporary Literary Criticism, Literature Criticism from 1400 to 1800, Nineteenth-Century Literature Criticism,* and *Twentieth-Century Literary Criticism.*

Topic Index

Topic Index

NCLC Cumulative Nationality Index

ISBN 0-7876-1908-6